THE 1965

WORLD BOOK

REVIEWING EVENTS OF 1964

YEAR BOOK

An Annual Supplement to
THE WORLD BOOK ENCYCLOPEDIA

FIELD ENTERPRISES EDUCATIONAL CORPORATION, PUBLISHERS

Merchandise Mart Plaza, Chicago, Illinois 60654

CHICAGO · LONDON · ROME · TORONTO · SYDNEY

EDITORIAL STAFF

PREFACE

AS EACH YEAR approaches its close, the members of THE YEAR BOOK
Board of Editors take themselves off to some remote place and consider the events which they believe will one day mark this time in history.
Such a meeting was held in Bermuda after the November elections. Professor
Lawrence Cremin flew in from California, where he was devoting a sabbatical
year to one of education's "think tanks." "Scotty" Reston and Alistair Cooke
came hot off the campaign trail. John Glenn, on his first airplane flight since
his accident, came in from Houston. Paul-Henri Spaak arrived from Brussels,
slipping quietly in to avoid the occasion for diplomatic protocol. And from
their various other walks, the board assembled.

In shirtsleeves and sportswear, seated comfortably in the lounge of one of
Bermuda's small guesthouses, overlooking the pink coral beach, the board re-
lived the events of the year. Each member, in turn, reviewed his own field,
striving to put a chaotic year "in focus"—a focus that grew sharper as his
colleagues interjected their own views, seen from their differing perspectives.
As the two-day meeting moved along, one theme, of profound significance
for the people of our time, recurred again and again. Professor Cremin hit upon
it first. And this was natural, because the theme was "education." As he has
written in the *Focus* section of THE YEAR BOOK, education faces a crisis that is
almost beyond our comprehension.

But this theme did not die with the comments of our education specialist.
John Glenn kept it alive when he launched into the subject of our space endeavor, the technological standards it demands, and the trained engineers and
scientists it requires. Scotty Reston looked back over the work of the 88th
Congress and concluded that it had achieved historic accomplishments in three
areas: civil rights, tax policy—and education. Sylvia Porter, that delightful
bundle of energy and statistics, reeled off the problems of the economy. Most
basic of these, she said, was the need to train our people to work in this automated age. "Without an iota of doubt,"she said, "the most basic requirement
of a continued sound economy is education—*Education, Education, Education!*"

Our friend from Europe, Paul-Henri Spaak—this great and humble man—
sat quietly through this part of the meeting, nodding an occasional agreement
and now and then asking a question. His masterful review of world affairs
had laid bare the critical issues confronting the world's statesmen. Yet at times
Mr. Spaak sat more as an observer than as a participant. He asked more questions than he answered. And his answers were careful, cautious, often hedged
with alternatives. The humility of true wisdom shone through his words.

En route to the airport after the meeting, it was time to say good-by until
next year. On behalf of the staff, we expressed to the Foreign Minister our
indebtedness to him, and our appreciation of his making time in his crowded
schedule for the meeting.

"The debt is mine," he replied. "It is important that we Europeans know
what America is thinking about. I cannot imagine a better place to learn this."
A deferential customs agent waved Mr. Spaak quickly through to the loading
gate. We walked at his side toward the plane, picking up the conversation.
"And what, if I may ask, Mr. Spaak, have you concluded that the American
people are thinking about?" His massive face brightened, and, with a touch of
whimsy, he replied: "*Education, Education, Education!*" Then Mr. Spaak added,
"And they are right."

With that he boarded his jetliner headed for Washington, where, with the
President, he was to make final plans for the joint American-Belgian rescue
mission in the Congo.   R.M.F.

TABLE OF CONTENTS

A Chronology of the Most Important Events of 1964 Will Be Found on Pages 8 to 12. A Preview of 1965 Will Be Found on Pages 629 and 630.

1 THE YEAR IN FOCUS . . . . page 13

The members of THE YEAR BOOK Board of Editors focus their attention on significant developments of the year.

2 YEAR BOOK SPECIAL REPORTS . . page 61

Six special articles and the exclusive YEAR BOOK Trans-Vision® bring special treatment to subjects chosen for their current importance and lasting interest.

3
4
5
6

CONTRIBUTORS

Anderson, Joseph P., M.S.S.A., Ph.B.; Exec. Director, National Association of Social Workers.
Social Organizations

Bedingfield, Robert E.; Assistant to the Financial-Business Editor, *The New York Times.* Industry Articles

Bhote, Keki R., B.E., M.S.; Author; Lecturer. INDIA; PAKISTAN

Bradley, Van Allen, B.J.; Literary Editor, *Chicago Daily News.* LITERATURE

Bryan, Leslie A., Ph.D., LL.B.; Dir., Institute of Aviation, University of Illinois. AVIATION

Buck, Pearl S., A.B.; Nobel Prize in Literature; Pulitzer Prize; Author, *The Good Earth.* Special Report

Burnet, Alastair, B.A.; Political Editor, *Independent Television News,* London. British Commonwealth Articles

Byerly, Florence, B.S.; Home Fashion Coordinator, Famous-Barr Co.
INTERIOR DECORATION

Cain, Charles C., III, A.B.; Automotive Editor, Associated Press.
AUTOMOBILE; RUBBER

Carruth, Hayden, A.B., M.A.; Poet.
LITERATURE (Poetry)

Colegrove, Kenneth, Ph.D., Litt.D.; Professor Emeritus, Northwestern University. CIVIL LIBERTIES

Conley, Clare, B.A.; Managing Editor, *Field & Stream.*
HUNTING AND FISHING

Cook, Robert C.; President, Population Reference Bureau. POPULATION

Csida, June Bundy; Radio-TV Editor, *Music Business Magazine.*
RADIO; TELEVISION

Dammann, Harle; Foreign Correspondent, *Chicago's American.*
Eastern Europe Articles

Dammann, Tom, B.A.; Foreign Correspondent, *Chicago's American.*
Eastern Europe Articles

Darby, Edwin W., B.S.J.; Financial Editor, *Chicago Sun-Times.*
Business Articles

Dewald, William G., Ph.D.; Associate Professor of Economics, Ohio State University. Finance Articles

Drury, Allen, B.A.; Pulitzer Prize for Fiction; Author, *Advise and Consent, A Shade of Difference.* Special Report

Dumouchel, J. Robert; Director of Community Relations, Land Clearance for Redevelopment Authority of Kansas City, Mo. HOUSING

Dunaway, James O., B.S.; Eastern Editor, *Track and Field News.*
Sports Articles

Edom, Clifton C., B.J.; Director of Photojournalism, University of Missouri. PHOTOGRAPHY (Supplement)

Farr, David M. L., M.A. D. Phil.; Dean of Arts, Carleton University, Ottawa. CANADA

Feather, Leonard G.; Author, *Encyclopedia of Jazz.* Music Articles

Feinberg, Harold, B.A., M.A., Ph.D.; Associate Professor, University of Illinois School of Medicine.
BIOCHEMISTRY; BIOLOGY

Fenner, Frank E., B.S., FPSA, ARPS; WORLD BOOK ENCYCLOPEDIA Photographs Editor. PHOTOGRAPHY

Freeman, Leslie G., Jr., Ph.D.; Assistant Professor, Department of Anthropology, Tulane University.
ANTHROPOLOGY; ARCHAEOLOGY

Freudenheim, Milt, A.B.; United Nations Correspondent, *Chicago Daily News.* UNITED NATIONS

Friesen, Ernest C., A.B., LL.B.; Dean, National College of State Trial Judges, University of Colorado.
Law Articles

Gassner, John, M.A.; Sterling Professor of Playwriting and Dramatic Literature, Yale University.
THEATER

Goy, Robert W., B.S., Ph.D.; Assoc. Scientist, Oregon Regional Primate Research Center. PSYCHOLOGY

Grevatt, Ren, B.A., M.B.A.; Editor, *Music Business Magazine.*
RECORDINGS FOR CHILDREN

Griffin, Alice, M.A., Ph.D.; Associate Professor of English, Hunter College.
THEATER, AMATEUR

Gronouski, John A., M.A., Ph.D.; Postmaster General. POST OFFICE

Hall, Clyde C., A.B.; Writer-Editor.
COMMUNICATIONS

Harper, Frank B., A.B., B.J.; Agricultural and resources conservation writer. Agricultural Articles

Hartshorn, Jack; Business Editor, *The London Economist.*
EUROPE (Close-Up)

Havighurst, Robert J., Ph.D.; Prof. of Education, University of Chicago; Author, *Older People.* OLD AGE

Hechinger, Fred M., B.A., LL.D.; Education Editor, *The New York Times.*
EDUCATION

Holmes, Jay E., B.A.; Deputy Director, Special Operations, Manned Space Flight, NASA. (Views expressed are not necessarily those of NASA) SPACE TRAVEL

Hood, Robert E., B.A.; Executive Editor, *Boys' Life.* Special Report

Hooper, Marjorie S., B.A.; Braille and Large Type Editor, American Printing House for the Blind. BLINDNESS

Hussey, Hugh H., M.D.; Director of Scientific Activities, American Medical Association. Medical Articles

Isaacs, Stanley P., B.A.; Sports Columnist, *Newsday.* Sports Articles

Jessup, M.E., A.B.; News Editor, *Civil Engineering.*
Engineering Articles

Johnson, Robert I., A.B.; Director, Adler Planetarium and Astronomical Museum. ASTRONOMY

Jones, Virgil Carrington, B.A.(J); Author, *The Civil War at Sea.*
CIVIL WAR CENTENNIAL

Joseph, Lou, B.A.; Asst. Director, Bureau of Public Information, American Dental Association. DENTISTRY

Junge, Charlotte, B.A., M.A., Ph.D.; Professor of Education, Wayne State University; co-author, *Growth in Arithmetic.* Mathematics Articles

Kertzer, Morris N., M.A., D.H.L.; Rabbi, Larchmont Temple, New York. JEWS AND JUDAISM

Knight, Arthur, B.A.; Assoc. Prof., University of Southern California Department of Cinema.
MOTION PICTURES

Koczy, F. F., Ph.D.; Professor, Institute of Marine Sciences, University of Miami. OCEAN

Lach, Alma, Diplome de Cordon Bleu; Food Editor, *Chicago Sun-Times.*
FOOD

Leakey, L. S. B., M.A., Ph.D., D.Sc., LL.D., Fellow of the British Academy; Honorary Director of the Coryndon Centre of Pre-History and Palaeonthology, Nairobi, Kenya; Author, *Olduvai Gorge.*
Special Report

Lenormand, Sergei; Asst. Director of Public Relations, Illinois Institute of Technology Research Institute. Science Articles

Lewis, Ralph H., A.B., M.A.; Chief, Museum Branch, National Park Service. MUSEUM

Lief, Donald W., A.B.; Managing Editor, *Nation's Cities*. City Articles

Lisagor, Peter, A.B.; Chief, Washington Bureau, *Chicago Daily News*. Political Party Articles

Logan, Rayford W., A.B., A.M., Ph.D.; Professor, Department of History, Howard University. NEGRO

Lohman, Joseph D., B.A., M.A.; Dean, School of Criminology, University of California. CRIME; PRISON

Maki, John M., B.A., M.A., Ph.D.; Professor of Japanese Politics, University of Washington. JAPAN; KOREA

Manchester, P. W.; Managing Editor, *Dance News*; New York Dance Critic, *Christian Science Monitor*. DANCING

Marsh, Robert C., A.M., Ed.D.; Music Critic, *Chicago Sun-Times*. MUSIC

Marty, Martin E., B.D., S.T.M., Ph.D.; Associate Editor, *The Christian Century*. PROTESTANT

Mattick, Hans W., B.A., M.A.; Director, Chicago Youth Development Project. JUVENILE DELINQUENCY

Mauldin, William H.; Editorial Cartoonist, *Chicago Sun-Times*; Pulitzer Prize, 1944 and 1958. Cartoons

Maxon, John, M.A., Ph.D.; Director of Fine Arts, The Art Institute of Chicago. PAINTING AND SCULPTURE

McCaul, Eugene B.; Director, Statistical Department, American Transit Association. TRANSIT

McGaffin, William, A.B., B.Sc.; Washington Correspondent, *Chicago Daily News*. U.S. Government Articles

Mencher, Melvin, B.A.; Asst. Professor, Graduate School of Journalism, Columbia University. PUBLISHING

Miller, Richard A., A.B., B.Arch.; Architect, Helge Westermann, Richard Miller, and Associates. ARCHITECTURE

Morse, Walter F., A.B.; Assistant News Editor, *Chicago Sun-Times*. Biographies

Morton, Elizabeth H., B.A.; Executive Director, Canadian Library Association. CANADIAN LITERATURE

Mullen, Frances A., Ph.D.; Assistant Supt. of Schools, Chicago Board of Education. CHILD WELFARE

Neal, Jean Krueger, B.A.; Fashion Editor, *Chicago Sun-Times*. FASHION

Newman, A. L., A.B., M.A.; Deputy Director of Information, U.S. Department of the Interior. Conservation Articles

O'Leary, Theodore M., A.B.; Special Correspondent, *Sports Illustrated* Magazine. PET; Hobby Articles

Pannwitt, Fred J., B.A., M.S.; Editorial Writer, *Chicago Daily News*. Europe Articles

Patterson, William D., A.B.; Associate Publisher, *The Saturday Review*. HOTEL TRAVEL

Perkins, R. Marlin; Director, St. Louis Zoo. ZOOS AND AQUARIUMS

Pickford, James H., B.S., M.S.; Assistant Director, American Society of Planning Officials. CITY PLANNING

Prastein, S. Matthew, A.B., M.S.; Head, Physics Department, Illinois Wesleyan University. PHYSICS

Pyle, Howard; President, National Safety Council. SAFETY

Ravenholt, Albert; Special Foreign Correspondent, *Chicago Daily News*. Asia Articles; Special Report

Reinsberg, Mark, M.A., Ph.B.; Staff Associate, The Transportation Center at Northwestern University. Transportation Articles

Richardson, Eugene S., Jr., A.B., M.S., Ph.D.; Curator, Fossil Invertebrates, Chicago Natural History Museum. TRANS-VISION

Rogers, Warren; Chief Washington Correspondent, Hearst Newspapers. Military Articles

Rosenblum, Victor G., A.B., LL.B., Ph.D.; Professor of Political Science, Northwestern University. SUPREME COURT (Close-Up)

Rue, Eloise, M.A., B.A. in L.S.; Associate Professor of Library Science, University of Wisconsin, Milwaukee. LITERATURE FOR CHILDREN

Russell, I. Willis, A.B., M.A., Ph.D.; Professor of English, University of Alabama. WORDS AND PHRASES, NEW

Scammon, Richard M., M.A.; Director, U.S. Bureau of the Census. CENSUS

Schmemann, The Rev. Alexander, S.T.D.; Dean, St. Vladimir's Seminary. EASTERN ORTHODOX

Shearer, Warren W., Ph.D.; Chairman, Department of Economics, Wabash College. Business Articles

Sheen, Fulton J., Ph.D., D.D., LL.D.; National Director, Society for the Propagation of the Faith, New York City. ROMAN CATHOLIC

Shelton, William, B.A.; Editorial Director-News, World Book Encyclopedia Science Service. ASTRONAUTS

Skilling, H. Gordon, B.A., M.A., Ph.D.; Professor of Political Science, University of Toronto. COMMUNISM; RUSSIA

Smothers, Frank; Director of Publications, The Council of State Governments. STATE GOVERNMENT

Spencer, William, A.B., A.M., Ph.D.; Educational Consultant, U.S. Office of Education. Africa and Middle East Articles

Stalker, John N., B.A., M.A., Ph.D.; Professor of History, University of Hawaii. Asia Articles

Stern, James L., B.S., Ph.D.; Professor of Economics, the University of Wisconsin. AUTOMATION; LABOR

Thomas, Benjamin E., M.A., Ph.D.; Professor of Geography, University of California. Africa Articles

Thompson, Carol L., A.B., M.A.; Editor, *Current History* magazine. U.S. Government Articles

Uphaus, Robert A., B.S., M.S., Ph.D.; Chemist, Argonne National Laboratory. CHEMISTRY

Warren, Harris Gaylord, B.S., A.M., Ph.D.; Professor and Chairman, Department of History, Miami University. PRESIDENT (Close-Up)

Webster, Mary C., B.A.; Editor, *Noticias* Magazine. Latin America Articles

White, Ruth M., B.S. in Ed., B.S. in L.S., A.M.; Headquarters Librarian, American Library Association. LIBRARY

Wright, Donald E., B.A., M.A.; Chief, Bureau of Library Services, Conn. State Department of Education. AMERICAN LIBRARY ASSOCIATION

JANUARY

4-6—**Paul VI Visits Holy Land,** first Roman Catholic pope to make pilgrimage to birthplace of Christianity.

5-6—**Communists Reclose East Berlin Wall,** ending West Berliners year-end holiday visits to relatives.

7—**Bahamas Inaugurate Internal Self-Government,** with Sir Roland Symonette as prime minister.

88th Congress of U.S. Opens its second session in Washington, D.C.

8—**President Johnson Delivers State-of-the-Union Message** to Congress. War on poverty and civil rights among major issues.

9-12—**Panama Canal Zone Riots** set off by flag incidents, 23 persons killed.

12—**Revolt in Zanzibar.** Sultan and prime minister flee from island country.

19—**Dahomey Elects New President,** Sourou Migan Apithy, Democratic party candidate.

21—**Relay II Launched** at Cape Kennedy, the second communications satellite.

22—**Smithsonian Institution Museum of History and Technology Dedicated** by President Johnson in Washington, D.C.

23—**South Dakota Ratifies Poll Tax Ban,** giving required 38 states approval for resolution to become U.S. Constitution Amendment 24.

17—**U.S. Cuts Cuban Water Pipes at Guantanamo.** Reply to Castro's charge that naval base was stealing water.

Supreme Court Rules on Congressional Districts: 6-to-3 decision rules U.S. Constitution requires districts within each state be substantially equal in population.

19—**George Papandreou Returns as Premier of Greece.** His Center Union party won 174 of 300 seats in Chamber of Deputies Feb. 16.

23—**U.S. and British Military Bases Must Go,** Libya says, when leases expire in 1970's.

25—**Cassius Marcellus Clay New World Heavyweight Champion.** Defeats Sonny Liston.

26—**Tax-Reduction Bill Signed** by President Johnson. Provides income tax reductions for individuals and corporations.

27—**Cosmos XXV Launched into Space** by Russia.

28—**New U.S. Information Agency Director.** Carl T. Rowan succeeds Edward R. Murrow.

29—**A-11 Jet Fighter Plane Revealed** by President Johnson. Secretly developed craft flies some 2,000 mph, and at altitude of 70,000 feet.

MARCH

4—**United Nations Peace Force for Cyprus** approved by Security Council.

6—**King Paul of Greece Dies.** Crown Prince Constantine proclaimed King of the Hellenes.

1964·CHRONOLOGY

25—**Echo II Launched into Orbit** at Vandenberg Air Force Base, California.

27—**France Recognizes Communist China.** Two countries announce plans to establish diplomatic relations for first time.

29-Feb. 9—**IX Winter Olympic Games** in Innsbruck, Austria. Russians win 11 gold medals.

30—**Ranger VI Launched into Space** at Cape Kennedy, on 66-hour trip to moon.

Elektrons I and II Launched into Space by Russia, country's first twin launching.

Coup d'État in South Vietnam topples military junta that deposed Ngo Dinh Diem regime in late 1963.

FEBRUARY

2—**Ranger VI Hits Moon,** but fails to send back photographs to earth.

4—**U.S. Constitution Amendment 24 Proclaimed,** signed by President Johnson. Bans poll tax as right-to-vote prerequisite in federal elections.

6—**Cuba Cuts Off Water to Guantanamo Naval Base,** except for one hour a day.

8—**South Vietnam Names Chief of State,** Maj. Gen. Duong Van Minh, but new premier, Maj. Gen. Nguyen Khanh, holds real power.

10—**Nationalist China Severs Relations with France** after President De Gaulle grants diplomatic recognition to Communist China.

10—**Third Son Born to Queen Elizabeth II.** Displaces Princess Anne as third in line of succession to British throne.

11—**Venezuela Inaugurates President.** Raul Leoni succeeds Rómula Betancourt, country's first constitutionally elected president to serve full 5-year term of office.

14—**Jack L. Ruby Condemned to Death** in electric chair for murder of Lee Harvey Oswald, alleged assassin of President John F. Kennedy.

16—**President Johnson's War on Poverty Program Goes to Congress.** Requests an Office of Economic Opportunity to direct program.

16-19—**President of France in Mexico.** Charles de Gaulle in first good-will visit to Latin America.

18—**Earth Satellite Launched** by Russia.

19—**First Road Tunnel in Alps Opens.** Great Saint Bernard Tunnel links Cantine d'en Haut, Switzerland, and St. Rhémy, Italy.

Pierre Salinger Quits White House for California senatorial race. President Johnson names George E. Reedy Press Secretary.

21—**Russia and Yemen Sign 5-Year Friendship Treaty,** and accords for economic and technical cooperation.

27—**Alaska Earthquake Most Violent in North America** in years kills at least 66 persons.

United Nations Troops in Cyprus. Canadians relieve British, there since December, 1963.

Cosmos XXVII Launched into Space by Russia.

28-31—King Saud Stripped of Powers. Half brother Crown Prince Faisal controls Saudi Arabia.

APRIL

1—**President João Goulart Deposed** by military revolt in Brazil.

2—**New Chancellor in Austria.** Josef Klaus replaces Alfons Gorbach, who resigned.
Zond I Launched by Russia.

3—**U.S. and Panama to Resume Diplomatic Relations,** broken by Panama in January.

4—**President Makarios Repudiates Cyprus Treaty of Alliance,** which permitted Turkey and Greece to base troops on island.
Cosmos XXVIII Launched into Space by Russia.

5—**General of the Army Douglas MacArthur Dies** after month' illness.

9—**U.S.S.** *Daniel Webster* **Joins Fleet** at Groton, Conn., navy's 18th Polaris submarine.
Explorer IX Re-Enters Atmosphere and Burns. Launched Feb. 16, 1961.

11—**New President in Brazil.** Congress elects Humberto de Alencar Castelo Branco to replace deposed João Goulart.

12—**Polyot II Launched** by Russia.

15—**Chesapeake Bay Bridge-Tunnel Opens** between Cape Charles and Norfolk, Va.

16—**Casey Stengel Dedicates Shea Stadium,** new home of Mets in New York City.

12—**Brazil Severs Diplomatic Relations with Cuba,** charging Castro interferes in Brazil's internal affairs.

14—**Aswan High Dam Celebration,** while Russian Premier Khrushchev visits United Arab Republic, marks end of project's first stage.

17—**Thailand Opens Bhumibol Dam,** $100,000,000 facility north of Bangkok.

18—**Cosmos XXX Launched into Space** by Russia.

21—**World's First Nuclear-Powered Lighthouse Opens** at Baltimore, Md., in Chesapeake Bay. Can operate for 10 years unattended.

23—**George C. Marshall Research Library Dedicated** by President Johnson at Virginia Military Institute, alma mater of originator of European Recovery Program, or Marshall Plan.

24—**Peruvians Riot at Soccer Game,** kill 318 spectators in Lima.

26—**Moselle Canal Opens in Europe.** Developed by France, West Germany, and Luxembourg.

27—**Jawaharlal Nehru Dies** in New Delhi, Prime Minister of India since independence (1947).

30—**A. J. Foyt Wins Indianapolis Speedway Race.** Two drivers fatally burned.

31—**Bolivia Elects President.** Victor Pas Estenssoro wins a third term.
Major League Baseball Records: longest game (7 hrs. 22 min.) and longest double header (10 hrs. 23 min.) double victory for San Francisco Giants over Mets in New York City.

1964 JANUARY 1964						
SUN.	MON.	TUE.	WED.	THU.	FRI.	SAT.
			1	2	3	4
5	6	7	8	9	10	11
12	13	14	15	16	17	18
19	20	21	22	23	24	25
26	27	28	29	30	31	

1964 FEBRUARY 1964						
SUN.	MON.	TUE.	WED.	THU.	FRI.	SAT.
						1
2	3	4	5	6	7	8
9	10	11	12	13	14	15
16	17	18	19	20	21	22
23	24	25	26	27	28	29

1964 MARCH 1964						
SUN.	MON.	TUE.	WED.	THU.	FRI.	SAT.
1	2	3	4	5	6	7
8	9	10	11	12	13	14
15	16	17	18	19	20	21
22	23	24	25	26	27	28
29	30	31				

22—**New York World's Fair Opens.** President Johnson dedicates Federal Pavilion. Civil righters stage demonstrations in area.
National Railroad Strike Averted. Companies and unions settle work rules dispute.

23—**Shakespeare Quadricentennial Opens** at Stratford-on-Avon, where famous English playwright was born Apr. 23, 1564.
New President in Bulgaria. Georgi Traikov succeeds deceased Dimiter Ganev.

25—**Cosmos XXIX Launched into Space** by Russia.

26—**United Republic of Tanganyika and Zanzibar Created.** Reduces newly independent African countries to 32, and United Nations membership to 112.

29—**Netherlands Princess Irene Weds Spanish Prince** Carlos Hugo of Bourbon-Parma in Rome, after renouncing rights (second in succession) to Dutch throne. Her family not at ceremonies.

MAY

2—**Northern Dancer Wins Kentucky Derby** at Louisville in record time of 2 min.

5—**Israel Opens Arab-Opposed Irrigation System.** Tests of pipeline from Sea of Galilee (replenished by Jordan River) to Negev precedes full operation of system.

10—**Panama Elects President.** Marco Aurelio Robles begins 4-year term October 1.

JUNE

1—**United States and Russia Sign Consular Convention,** opening way for such offices in cities outside Washington, D.C., and Moscow.

4—**United Nations to Investigate Cambodia and South Vietnam.** Security Council votes for a committee to check on border violations.

6—**Cosmos XXXI Launched into Orbit** by Russia.

8—**Transatlantic Nuclear Navigation Opens.** N.S. *Savannah* leaves New York on European tour 145 years after first *Savannah* inaugurated steam navigation in Atlantic.

9—**New Prime Minister in India.** Lal Bahadur Shastri succeeds the late Jawaharlal Nehru.

10—**Cosmos XXXII Launched into Orbit** by Russia.

12—**Sweden Sentences Spy to Life at Hard Labor.** Stig Wennerstrom admitted being a Soviet spy from 1948 until his arrest in June, 1963.
East Germany and Russia Sign 20-Year Friendship Treaty, which recognizes West Berlin as an "independent political entity."

14—**Formosa Dedicates Shimen Dam,** $80,000,000 multipurpose facility southeast of Taipei.

15—**Supreme Court Rules on Reapportionment,** saying both houses of state legislatures "must be apportioned on population basis."

19—**Transpacific Submarine Cable Opens** between Japan and Hawaii. Carries nearly 130 telephone channels.

21—**Three Civil Rights Workers Disappear** in Philadelphia (Miss.) area.
23—**Cosmos XXXIII Launched into Space** by Russia.
25—**Picturephone Service Inaugurated** between
Washington, D.C., New York City, and
Chicago.
29—**Castro's Sister Defects.** Juanita Castro Ruz tells
story on television in Mexico City.
30—**United Nations Troops Leave Congo** after 4
years of peace efforts in African country.

JULY

1—**West Germany Elects President** Heinrich Luebke
to second 5-year term.
Cosmos XXXIV Launched into Space by Russia.
2—**Civil Rights Act of 1964 Signed** by President
Johnson on the same day controversial bill is
passed by Congress.
**Brooklyn Bridge Designated a National Historical
Monument** in New York City.
5—**Mexico Elects New President.** Gustavo Díaz
Ordaz begins 6-year term December 1.
6—**Nyasaland Wins Independence.** Takes name of
Malawi, and remains in British Common-
wealth.
New Chairman of Joint Chiefs of Staff. Gen.
Earle G. Wheeler replaces Gen. Maxwell D.
Taylor, who was appointed U.S. Ambassador
to South Vietnam.

17-21—**African Unity Organization Conference** chooses
Addis Ababa, Ethiopia, as its permanent
headquarters, and Guinea's Diallo Telli
Boubacar as its first Secretary-General.
18-23—**New York City Race Riots** follow killing of
Negro boy, shot by off-duty policeman.
22—**Brazil Extends President's Term.** Humberto de
Alencar Castelo Branco to serve until Mar.
15, 1967.
24-26—**Riots in Jersey City.** New Jersey State Police
and National Guard help restore order.
26—**OAS Acts Against Cuba.** Organization of
American States signs resolution asking member states to end economic and diplomatic
relations with Castro regime.
27—**National Baseball Hall of Fame Admits New
Members:** Red Faber, Luke Appling, Heinie
Manush, Burleigh Grimes, and the late Miller
Huggins, Tim Keefe, and John M. Ward.
28—**Ranger VII Launched on Flight to Moon** at Cape
Kennedy.
30—**Cosmos XXXVI Launched into Space** by Russia.
31—**Ranger VII Hits Moon.** Takes and televises to
earth 4,316 close-up photographs of moon
during last minutes of flight.

AUGUST

2—**North Vietnam Fires on U.S. Destroyer** *Maddox*
in Gulf of Tonkin. President Johnson issues

1964	APRIL	1964

SUN.	MON.	TUE.	WED.	THU.	FRI.	SAT.
			1	2	3	4
5	6	7	8	9	10	11
12	13	14	15	16	17	18
19	20	21	22	23	24	25
26	27	28	29	30		

1964	MAY	1964

SUN.	MON.	TUE.	WED.	THU.	FRI.	SAT.
					1	2
3	4	5	6	7	8	9
10	11	12	13	14	15	16
17	18	19	20	21	22	23
24 31	25	26	27	28	29	30

1964	JUNE	1964

SUN.	MON.	TUE.	WED.	THU.	FRI.	SAT.
	1	2	3	4	5	6
7	8	9	10	11	12	13
14	15	16	17	18	19	20
21	22	23	24	25	26	27
28	29	30				

New Premier in Jordan. Bahjat Abdul Khadr
Talhouni is named to succeed Sharif Husain
bin Nasir.
9—**New Orleans Cotton Exchange Closes** after 93
years (February, 1871).
9-10—**Moise Tshombe Premier of Congo.** Former secessionist Katanga (province) president forms
coalition government to end rebellions.
11—**Elektrons III and IV Launched by One Rocket**
into separate orbits by Russia.
13-18—**Republican Party National Convention** in San
Francisco nominates U.S. Senator from Ari-
zona Barry M. Goldwater and U.S. Representative from New York William E. Miller as
presidential and vice-presidential candidates.
14—**Iraq Nationalizes Banks, Insurance Companies,**
and 30 industrial and commercial concerns.
15—**Anastas I. Mikoyan Elected President of Russia**
by Supreme Soviet succeeding Leonid I.
Brezhnev, now to devote full time to duties as
member of Communist party Secretariat.
Cosmos XXXV Launched into Orbit by Russia.
17—**New World Land Speed Record of 403.1 MPH
Set** by Donald Campbell in jet-propelled automobile at Lake Eyrie Salt Flats, Australia.
Three Sentry Satellites Launched by one rocket
at Cape Kennedy, designed to detect clan-
destine high-altitude nuclear explosions.
U.S.S. *Ulysses S. Grant* **Joins Fleet** at Groton,
Conn., navy's 22d Polaris submarine.

order for navy to strike back in the future,
when attacked in international waters.
4—**Civil Rightists' Graves Found** near Philadelphia, Miss. The three men disappeared June 21.
5—**U.S. Bombs North Vietnam Bases** after second
unprovoked attack in Gulf of Tonkin.
7-9—**Turkey Attacks Northwestern Cyprus** on behalf
of Turkish Cypriots.
10—**Pope Paul VI Issues First Encyclical of His Reign.**
Calls "godlessness the most serious problem of
our time."
11—**Chile Ends Relations with Cuba** in accordance
with OAS resolution of July 26.
12—**Lumpa Cult Leader Surrenders** in Northern
Rhodesia. Some 500 persons killed since
July 24.
13—**Arab Common Market Established** by United
Arab Republic, Iraq, Jordan, Kuwait, and
Syria.
14—**Cosmos XXXVII Launched** by Russia.
Federal Employees Salary Act Signed by President Johnson. Raises pay of Vice-President,
Cabinet, Congress, Supreme Court, and
others.
16—**Maj. Gen. Nguyen Khanh President of South
Vietnam** under country's new constitution.
18—**New President in Lebanon.** Charles Helou
begins 6-year term September 23.
Cosmos XXXVIII, XXXIX, and XL Launched into
orbit by single rocket, Russia announces.

20—**Roosevelt Campobello International Park Dedicated** in New Brunswick, Canada.
Anti-Poverty Act Signed by President Johnson.

21—**Bolivia Severs Relations with Cuba** in compliance with OAS resolution of July 26.

22—**Cosmos XLI, XLII, and XLIII Launched** into Space by Russia.

25—**Ionosphere Explorer A Launched into Orbit** at Point Arguello, California.

25-29—**President Khanh Resigns in South Vietnam,** and new constitution withdrawn. Buddhist and student demonstrations followed by violence between Buddhists and Catholics.

28—**Nimbus I Launched** at Vandenberg Air Force Base. Takes clear nighttime pictures.

28-30—**North Philadelphia Rioters Smash and Loot Shops.** Some 240 persons injured.

SEPTEMBER

3—**Wilderness Act Signed** by President Johnson for permanent National Wilderness Preservation system of some 9,000,000 acres.
Robert F. Kennedy Resigns as U.S. Attorney General to enter the U.S. senatorial race in the State of New York.

4—**OGO I Launched into Space** at Cape Kennedy, Orbiting Geophysical Observation satellite.
Chile Elects President. Eduardo Frei Montalva begins his 6-year term November 3.

17—**Russia Casts Its 102d Veto in United Nations.** Defeats Security Council resolution to condemn Indonesian attacks on Malaysia.
U.S. Has 2 Weapons to Destroy Hostile Satellites, President Johnson says. One developed by army, and other by air force.

18—**Royal Wedding in Athens.** King Constantine XIII of Greece and Princess Anne-Marie of Denmark take vows in Greek Orthodox Cathedral.

20-21—**Malta Proclaims Independence.** Mediterranean island remains in British Commonwealth.

21—**French President on Second Latin-American Visit.** Charles de Gaulle begins tour in Caracas, Venezuela.

22—**Senate Confirms Sargent Shriver as Director of Office of Economic Opportunity.** Head of anti-poverty program remains as Peace Corps director.

24—**Warren Report on President Kennedy's Assassination** presented to President Johnson by Chief Justice Earl Warren and commission.
Cosmos XLVI Launched into Space by Russia.

26—**High National Council in South Vietnam Established** by Premier Nguyen Khanh, includes rival groups, and political leaders.

30—**Nazi Officer Gets 15 Years at Hard Labor** in West Germany. Former Elite Guard Maj. Gen. Karl F. Wolf was found guilty of contributing to murder of Jews in World War II.

1964	JULY					1964
SUN.	MON.	TUE.	WED.	THU.	FRI.	SAT.
			1	2	3	4
5	6	7	8	9	10	11
12	13	14	15	16	17	18
19	20	21	22	23	24	25
26	27	28	29	30	31	

1964	AUGUST					1964
SUN.	MON.	TUE.	WED.	THU.	FRI.	SAT.
						1
2	3	4	5	6	7	8
9	10	11	12	13	14	15
16	17	18	19	20	21	22
23 30	24 31	25	26	27	28	29

1964	SEPTEMBER					1964
SUN.	MON.	TUE.	WED.	THU.	FRI.	SAT.
		1	2	3	4	5
6	7	8	9	10	11	12
13	14	15	16	17	18	19
20	21	22	23	24	25	26
27	28	29	30			

7—**Great Britain and Russia Sign $84,000,000 Contract** for Siberia fiber plant. In the negotiations, Russia obtains 15-year credit of $67,000,000.

8—**National Football Hall of Fame Inducts New Members:** Clarke Hinkle, Ed Healey, August Michalske, Arthur J. Rooney, James G. Conzelman, Roy Lyman, and George Trafton.
Uruguay Severs Diplomatic Ties with Cuba. Mexico now remains as the only Latin-American country maintaining relations with Castro regime.

9—**New York World's Fair Hall of Science Dedicated** as permanent science center.

10—**Ten-Nation Commission for Congo Established** by Organization of African Unity.

12—**Canyonlands National Park Created** in Utah. Legislation signed by President Johnson.

13—**Cosmos XLV Is Launched into Space** by the Soviet Union.

14—**Vatican Council Third Session Opens** in Rome.

15—**Vatican and Hungary Sign Religious Accord.** Diplomatic relations broken in 1945.

15-21—**U.S. Retains America's Cup.** *Constellation* outsails Britain's *Sovereign* in 4 yacht races off Newport, R.I.

16—**Columbia River Treaty Implemented** by U.S. and Canada. President Johnson and Prime Minister Lester B. Pearson hold ceremonies at International Peace Arch in Washington.

OCTOBER

1—**New East-West Berlin Pass Agreement in Force** for West Berliners to visit relatives in East Berlin, to end in June, 1965.

2-5—**Fifty-Seven East Germans Flee to West Berlin** through secret tunnel. Largest such escape since Communist built wall in 1961.

3—**Explorer XXI Launched into Space** at Cape Kennedy, Florida.
88th Congress of U.S. Ends second session, longest (in number of days for both houses) since 81st first session (1949–1950).

4—**Autostrada del Sol Opens in Italy,** 4-lane Highway of the Sun links Milan and Naples.

5—**World Land Speed Record of 434.02 MPH Set.** Art Arfons surpasses 413.20 mph mark by Tom Green on October 2, both on Bonneville Salt Flats, Utah.

5-11—**Nonaligned Nations Conference** in Cairo shut out Congo Premier Moise Tshombe. United Arab Republic President Nasser detains him in palatial villa.

5-13—**Queen Elizabeth II Visits Canada.** Royal tour is marred by French Canadian separatists' resentment of her visit.

6—**Cosmos XLVII Launched into Orbit** by Russia.

7-15—**St. Louis Cardinals Win World Series,** beat New York Yankees 4 games out of 7.

9—**Explorer XXII Launched** in California.

10-24—**XVIII Olympiad, First in Asia,** held in Tokyo, Japan.

12-13—**Russia Orbits First Multipassenger Spaceship.** *Voskhod* (*Sunrise*) circles earth 16 times and lands near Kustanai. Commander Col. Vladimir M. Komarov, space medicine specialist Boris B. Yegorov, and scientist-spacecraft designer Konstantin P. Feoktistov are first to make space trip in ordinary clothes.

13—**Congolese Welcome Home Premier Moise Tshombe** after his defeat at Nonaligned Nations Conference in Cairo, United Arab Republic.

14—**Cosmos XLVIII Launched into Space** by Russia.

15-16—**Khrushchev Falls From Power in Russia.** Leonid I. Brezhnev named Communist party first secretary, and Aleksei N. Kosygin, premier. **Labour Party Wins British Elections,** ending 13-year Conservative rule. Harold Wilson takes helm as prime minister.

16—**Communist China Explodes Its First Atom Bomb** at remote site in Taklamakan Desert, Sinkiang province. **French President De Gaulle Ends Latin-American Tour** in Brazil. Returns to Paris.

17—**Spain and Portugal Dedicate Hydroelectric Power Plant** at Aldeadavila, Spain, and dam at Bemposta, Portugal, joint projects.

18—**Pope Paul VI Proclaims Sainthood for 22 African Martyrs.** Ugandans died for their faith under persecution (1885–1887).

NOVEMBER

2—**Faisal Proclaimed King of Saudi Arabia.** Replaces dethroned half brother Saud.

3—**Lyndon B. Johnson Elected President** in landslide victory.

3-5—**Revolt in Bolivia.** President Victor Paz Estenssoro flees to Peru. René Barrientos Ortuño emerges as new president.

4—**South Vietnam Installs Civilian Government** with Phan Khac Suu as chief of state, and Tran Van Huong as premier.

5—**Mariner III Launched into Space** at Cape Kennedy, but fails to function properly.

6—**Explorer XXIII Launched** at Wallops Island.

9—**New Premier in Japan.** Eisaku Sato succeeds retiring Hayato Ikeda.

12—**Grand Duchess Charlotte Ends 45-Year Rule** in Luxembourg. Crown Prince succeeds to throne as Grand Duke Jean.

21—**Two Explorer Satellites Launched into Space** by single rocket at Vandenberg Air Force Base. **Vatican Council Third Session Ends** in Rome.

24—**Congo Rebels Kill White Hostages** in Stanleyville, including American Paul E. Carlson.

28—**Mariner IV Launched on Way to Mars** at Cape Kennedy. **Congo Rescue Ended by United States and Belgium** on fifth day of operation.

30—**Zond II Launched into Space** by Russia.

1964 OCTOBER 1964								1964 NOVEMBER 1964								1964 DECEMBER 1964					
SUN.	MON.	TUE.	WED.	THU.	FRI.	SAT.		SUN.	MON.	TUE.	WED.	THU.	FRI.	SAT.		SUN.	MON.	TUE.	WED.	THU.	FRI.	SAT.
				1	2	3		1	2	3	4	5	6	7				1	2	3	4	5
4	5	6	7	8	9	10		8	9	10	11	12	13	14		6	7	8	9	10	11	12
11	12	13	14	15	16	17		15	16	17	18	19	20	21		13	14	15	16	17	18	19
18	19	20	21	22	23	24		22	23	24	25	26	27	28		20	21	22	23	24	25	26
25	26	27	28	29	30	31		29	30							27	28	29	30	31		

New York World's Fair Closes first session. More than 27,000,000 persons visit the fair.

19—**Ionosphere Spacecraft Launched** at Wallops Island, Virginia, and lands in ocean.

20—**Herbert Clark Hoover Dies at Age of 90.** Thirty-day mourning period proclaimed for 31st President of the United States (1929–1933).

22—**Five Kiloton Atomic Explosion in Mississippi.** Underground blast in Tatum Salt Dome part of U.S. detection system development.

24—**Cosmos XLIX Launched into Space** by Russia. **Northern Rhodesia Proclaims Independence as Republic of Zambia** after 73 years of rule under the British.

26—**British Labour Government Puts Surcharge** on some imports and tax incentive on exports because of country's balance-of-payments deficit.

27—**World Land Speed Record of 536.71 MPH Set** by Art Arfons, surpasses 526.26 mph mark of Craig Breedlove on October 15.

28—**Cosmos L (50) Launched into Space** by Russia.

29—**Bolivia Ends Diplomatic Relations with Czechoslovakia,** charging Czechs supplied weapons for recent rioting. **Tanzania New Name of Tanganyika and Zanzibar,** the united republic announces.

31—**Sudan Installs Civilian Government** with Sirel-Khatim el-Khalifa as premier, after 11 days of rioting.

DECEMBER

1—**United Nations General Assembly Opens.** Alex Quaison-Sackey of Ghana elected president. **Mexico Inaugurates President** Gustavo Díaz Ordas for 6-year term.

2—**UN Admits New Nations.** Malawi, Malta, and Zambia, former British territories. **Juan D. Perón Flies to Brazil,** but not permitted to stay or go on to Uruguay.

2-5—**Pope Paul VI in India.** Attends International Eucharistic Congress in Bombay.

10—**Cosmos LI (51) Launched into Space** by Russia.

12—**Spain Warns Juan D. Perón** to give up politics or leave country in a month. **Kenya Proclaimed a Republic.** Former dominion remains in British Commonwealth.

14—**New Prime Minister in British Guiana.** Forbes Burnham replaces defeated Cheddi B. Jagan.

16—**Secretary of Commerce Luther H. Hodges Resigns.** John T. Connor named to post.

21—**Russia Casts 103d Veto in UN.** Defeats resolution on Israeli-Syrian conflict. **Explorer XXVI Launched** at Cape Kennedy.

24—**U.S. Officers Quarters Bombed in Saigon,** South Vietnam. Two Americans killed.

28—**Italy Elects New President.** Giuseppe Saragat replaces ailing Antonio Segni.

29—**Bolivia Returns to Organization of American States,** after two-year absence.

CONTENTS OF SECTION ONE

THE YEAR BOOK Board of Editors analyzes the significant developments of 1964 and considers their impact upon contemporary affairs. The Related Articles list following each report directs the reader to THE YEAR BOOK's additional coverage of related subjects.

THE YEAR IN FOCUS

PAUL-HENRI SPAAK

THERE WAS NO RETURN to the Cold War during 1964, but neither was there any substantial progress toward settlement of the great international problems.

Until the latter part of the year, one might simply have said that the Union of Soviet Socialist Republics was pursuing the same line of policy it had previously. Under the leadership of Nikita S. Khrushchev, the USSR showed proof of discretion and a rather conciliatory spirit in Europe and in Asia, as well as in Africa and Latin America. Its interventions in Southeast Asia, in the Congo (Léopoldville), in Cyprus, and in Cuba—the crises spots in world politics— had been reduced to a minimum. The impression even prevailed that in certain parts of the world the USSR was attempting to disengage itself.

Mr. Khrushchev's exit raised a whole series of new questions. It seems to me that at this time, even though this judgment must be cautious and may have to be revised, the official explanation for Mr. Khrushchev's downfall given by the new leaders of the Soviet Union can in general be accepted as accurate.

Beyond doubt, Khrushchev's personality must have made the strict application of a system of shared authority more and more difficult. On many occasions, he may, and probably must have, ruffled, and perhaps alarmed, his colleagues.

It is also a fact that not all his undertakings were successful. From our point of view, we have to be thankful to him for the way in which he applied the policy of peaceful coexistence. But from the communist point of view, in the cases of Cuba, Germany, and agriculture, to mention only a few, he was not successful. Under a democratic system, failures even less important than these would have been enough to make a political leader lose his prestige.

The conflict with China, however, probably dominates all the other grievances. It has always seemed inexplicable to me that Khrushchev decided to make peaceful coexistence not only a principle of international policy, but also a point of communist doctrine. In this case, he chose the wrong ground. In my opinion, the manner in which he conducted his struggle against Peking was dangerous to himself, and finally it turned out to be fatal.

The near future will tell whether his successors will be able to correct the course that was previously followed. They will be able

There Were No Signs of a Major Conflict Between the Great Powers, but Many Difficult Problems Remained to be Solved Throughout the World.

FOCUS ON THE WORLD

Philippe Halsman for THE YEAR BOOK

to do so if the struggle between Moscow and Peking is essentially ideological. But they will not succeed if, as there is every reason to believe, we are faced with a nationalistic conflict between the two great communist powers of the world.

IN THE UNITED STATES, it seems to me that the death of President John F. Kennedy at the end of 1963, and the presidential election of 1964 forced that country to avoid taking extreme stands or embarking upon any bold initiatives.

The year was one of transition, dominated by events in Southeast Asia. In that part of the world, the United States was involved in an extremely arduous undertaking. Its policy there was in principle not different from that undertaken and carried to a successful conclusion in Europe to save that continent from the communist threat. That policy began about 15 years ago through the Marshall Plan and the Atlantic Pact.

However, the circumstances and prospects for success in Southeast Asia seem very different. In Europe, the U.S. found relatively strong and stable governments and a population whose standard of living and traditions prevented it from being seduced by communism. In Asia, these two elements do not seem to exist.

The type of warfare the U.S. supported in Southeast Asia was particularly dangerous. Communist guerrillas operated against a regular army, and it was almost impossible to destroy the military bases from which their attacks were being launched.

The fact must be underlined that U.S. policy in Southeast Asia is not well understood in Europe. The trend in favor of the recognition of Communist China grows steadily stronger. The idea that only a political solution is possible is making great prog-

15

"The whole European policy of the past 20 years has been questioned by De Gaulle."

ress, even though the proponents of this idea, particularly President Charles de Gaulle, after having stated the principle, seemed incapable of defining its practical application.

In the coming months, Southeast Asia will certainly be one of the most dangerous areas in the world, and the recognition of Red China and its admission to the United Nations one of the most disputed topics.

IN EUROPE, French policy continued on its course. The actions of General de Gaulle represented a growing threat to the North Atlantic Treaty Organization (NATO). His destructive offensive now has spread to the European Economic Community (EEC, or Common Market).

In brief, De Gaulle contended that Europe must move away from the United States in order to affirm its independence. The recognition of Communist China by France in February, 1964, was a very clear indication of this tendency.

The proclamation by France of a Southeast Asia policy opposed to that of the United States was another manifestation of this independence.

The very recent stand taken on NATO's proposed multilateral force (MLF) is even more revealing. After having proclaimed that the multilateral force does not interest him, it seemed that De Gaulle called upon West Germany to refuse to participate in it.

He addressed Germany in the same way that he addressed Great Britain after the conclusion of the Nassau agreements. In effect, he said to Germany: "If you enter into an alliance with the U.S. to solve your nuclear problems, you are proving that you are not European. As a result, the Franco-German treaty will lose its value, and there can no longer be any question of making progress in the creation of European political union."

All this had to be noted with a certain anxiety. The whole European policy of the last 20 years has been questioned by De Gaulle. Step by step, he was undoing France's NATO and Common Market ties.

What will De Gaulle do with his regained freedom?

It is difficult to say and dangerous to forecast, but it does not seem impossible that France's next move will be a rapprochement with the Soviet Union. In this respect, the last Franco-Russian commercial treaty offers a valuable indication of this. And the recent exchange of diplomatic niceties is one of the elements upon which such a judgment might be made.

THE COMMON MARKET was threatened by the same crisis that beset NATO.

The success of the European Economic Community in the industrial field remained very great. Trade within the Community was expanding at an appreciably faster pace than the average in world trade. Difficulties, however, arose in connection with agricultural problems, and in this field France also played a role.

The French position relating to the exports of agricultural products was fundamentally sound. It is indeed impossible to imagine a Common Market in which the progress of industrial policy would not be

"... the immediate future of Europe was fraught with difficulties and confusion."

paralleled by that in the agricultural field.

Germany seemed to have understood the danger. It is now abandoning its policy of maintaining high prices for its agricultural products. Germany put forward a number of proposals which, in principle, were acceptable to French views.

This undoubtedly represented great progress. But it must be stated that if an end had come to the time of political immobility, then a new period had just dawned. It will be a period of difficulties. Altogether, we find ourselves still far distant from the solution of the problem. Yet, solutions are vital, since the consequences of a failure would be very grave and would inevitably encompass a much larger geographical area than the Common Market.

A failure would also endanger the successful outcome of the Kennedy Round, the great tariff negotiation which was initiated in Geneva, and which aims at a lowering of all tariffs. A failure of the Kennedy Round would seriously complicate relations between the U.S. and Europe.

Lastly, a failure in the agricultural field would end all endeavors toward establishing new political links between the countries of the Common Market.

IN THE UNITED KINGDOM, policy was profoundly influenced by the elections of October. The Conservative party, defeated by Labour, inevitably found itself waiting on the sidelines.

The question now was to what extent the Labour victory might bring about a change in British policy. It seems to me that the following points have to be noted.

(1) I believe there will be more effective cooperation with the United Nations, although this cooperation will not always be easy, notably in regard to the colonial questions which still remain to be settled.

(2) There will be reduced cooperation with the six countries of the European Economic Community, for the double reason that the British government has given up the idea of entering the Common Market, and that it shows little interest for European political union.

(3) There will be great difficulty in taking a stand on certain NATO problems such as the multilateral nuclear force.

(4) There will be real difficulties in the economic field. The first steps taken by the Labour government made this quite clear. They also showed that for an industrial nation such as Great Britain, it is almost impossible to find a solution to its problems in isolation.

In conclusion, it seemed that the immediate future of Europe was fraught with difficulties and confusion.

MIDDLE EASTERN PROBLEMS remained unchanged in 1964. No improvement of the relations between Israel and the Arab countries was in sight.

IN AFRICA, the difficulties in Portuguese Angola and in the Republic of South Africa also remained unchanged. In Angola, however, a degree of improvement in the military position of the Portuguese could be noted. It is difficult to say whether this was a temporary or definitive turn for the better. Personally, I am inclined to think that it is only temporary.

Attention still focused on the Congo. The

"They imprisoned a great number...whom they beat and threatened with...death."

FOCUS SPAAK

take-over of the government by Moise Tshombe surprised many people and created serious concern in a large number of African countries.

It is very difficult to explain how the star of Tshombe, who was in exile in Madrid, could rise to the point that his return to the Congo and his take-over of the government became possible. It is not correct to see in these events the influence of the United States or Belgium. This was specifically a Congolese event. Tshombe's popularity can probably be attributed to the fact that he stood up to the United Nations. For this reason, he gave the impression of being a strong man. He was also a rather dangerous man. He might draw those who helped him into a line of policy that would be rejected by the great majority of African nations.

By year's end, the Congo was in the grip of a real civil war. Although it is quite evident that Peking maintained relations with a number of leaders of the rebellion, it was not simply a communist plot. Rather it was a revolt against authorities who had proved corrupt on more than one occasion, and against the excesses of an army that lacked discipline. It was also a struggle among individuals for power and all the great advantages that power entails in that unfortunate African country.

The events in Stanleyville in November cast a new light on the situation.

Belgium and the United States found themselves forced to intervene to save the lives of all foreigners, primarily whites, who were held by the rebels. The latter, defying all international and human laws, held innocent men, women, and children as hostages. They imprisoned a great number of them whom they beat and threatened with torture and death. The Belgian-U.S. operation did not succeed in saving all the hostages, but it, nevertheless, made possible the evacuation of several hundred people.

The operation provoked criticism only in those countries that place their political and ideological passions above everything else. On the other hand, the intervention received the sympathy of the great majority of governments that remained sensitive to humanitarian acts.

The question might be asked whether the intervention of the Organization of African Unity could bring back peace to the Congo. This was sincerely to be wished but also very doubtful. Future prospects, therefore, were rather dim at year's end.

THE UNITED NATIONS session which opened in December was marred by the possibility of the enforcement of Article 19 of the charter, which would take away the vote in the General Assembly from countries that are in arrears in their UN contributions, in particular the USSR and the other communist countries. The legal position of the United States seemed fully justified. But from the practical and political viewpoint, it seemed like a big order to deprive the communist countries of their right to vote in the General Assembly, while the USSR retained all its rights and privileges in the Security Council, including its veto power.

THE INTERNATIONAL situation at

"The new American administration will certainly have to reappraise its policy..."

the end of the year did not manifest any sign of a grave conflict between the major powers, but it was not as good as it was at the end of 1963. There are many difficulties in Asia, Africa, and Europe, and the solution to these problems unfortunately does not seem to be easy for the people of the world to find.

The new American administration will certainly have to reappraise its policy throughout the world. Clear-sighted and bold action on the part of the United States is to be hoped for.

Related Articles

For a complete report on the year 1964, see articles on the various nations in Section Three. In the same section, see also the following:

THE FIGHTING between progressive and conservative forces in the United States is never finished. The thrust of one provides the tug of the other. Stagnation eventually provokes movement and progress. Revolution produces counterrevolution. Discrimination against one group generates opposition from others. Thus, in democratic theory, balance and moderation are achieved.

This perpetual conflict between the forces that favor change and the forces that resist change is the heart of American politics. When it has reached the flash point of decision on such great issues as the fight for independence, the Bill of Rights, the Civil War over the Union of the states, or human rights versus property rights, it has produced the landmark years in the history of America.

It may be too much to say that 1964 was such a year. Yet these ancient contending forces of the progressives and the conservatives met then in a sharper conflict of principle than at any other time in a generation. The national scene was dominated by the election of President Lyndon B. Johnson of Texas over his Republican opponent, Senator Barry Goldwater of Arizona, but this was more than a competition between men and parties. It was a dispute over the proper relationships between the individual and the state; between the several states and the central government; between the nation and its allies and its adversaries.

It was, in essence, a revolt of a faction of conservatives, not only against the Democratic party and the Republican progressives, but against the main trend of domestic and foreign policy of a whole generation. Thus, the decision of the people was a judgment on the history of the post-World War II era, and it was highly significant for several specific reasons.

Philippe Halsman for THE YEAR BOOK

JAMES B. RESTON FOCUS

FIRST, it tested in real terms a theory that had been put forward for over a generation by the most conservative leaders in the nation. This theory was that the progressive elements in both the Republican and Democratic parties, based primarily in the large urban areas of the Northeast, had imposed a form of centralized, progressive welfare state government on the nation against the wishes of the majority of the people.

This was the reason, according to this theory, why the Republican party was fighting a losing battle with the Democratic party. The conservatives pointed to the record. The Republicans had controlled the White House for only eight of the last 32 years. During this period, the Republican party had not nominated "genuine conservatives." but had put up progressives who favored most of the domestic and foreign policies of the Democrats.

Using this argument, and with a well-organized campaign in the Republican state party caucuses, conventions, and primary elections, the conservatives succeeded in nominating Senator Goldwater, who was the principal spokesman for the most conservative wing of the party.

Regardless of the outcome, there was a certain historical justification in Goldwater's nomination. He represented the faction of his party which had shouldered the burden of opposition to the Democrats in Congress during the 20-year rule of the New Deal and the Fair Deal from 1932 to 1952. He was undoubtedly the sentimental favorite of the men and women whom the Republicans had permitted or chosen to run the county, state, and national organizations of the party. And he worked for the nomination while many of the progressive Republican leaders stood apart from the battle.

Nevertheless, though he conducted a vigorous campaign, he was defeated by the largest popular margin in the history of the presidency, carrying only six states, all in the South and Southwest.

SECOND, on the home front, the U.S. election of 1964 was a test as to whether Americans wanted the federal government in Washington to continue an active interventionist role in the social and economic life of the country, or whether they wanted to slow down or reverse that policy and give a larger role to the states. This dispute centered, not on the ends of policy, but on the means. Both sides favored racial equality and full employment for all the people of the country. But they differed on how to achieve equality for the American Negro, and they differed on tax policy.

Senator Goldwater advocated leaving the question of the Negro's civil rights to the judgment of the states. President Johnson, though raised in the Southwest, favored

In the Election of 1964, Progressives and Conservatives Contended with Each Other More Sharply Than in a Generation.

ON THE NATION

federal action to assure the Negro's civil rights against the opposition of the South.

Senator Goldwater more nearly supported the traditional tax policies of the past, arguing the merits of a balanced budget during times of prosperity. President Johnson advocated a major innovation in theory and practice. His argument was that despite the current prosperity, the economic growth of the nation could not be sustained under an annually balanced budget but that the federal government had to stimulate the economy by maintaining a high level of government spending and cut taxes substantially even at the risk of an appreciable budget deficit.

Only in this way, he contended, could poverty and unemployment be reduced. It could not be done by the normal procedure of taxing the rich for the benefit of the poor. It could be done only by expanding the activity of the whole economy, and increasing the prosperity of rich and poor alike.

Again, the decision of the representatives of the people went with Johnson. During the year, the U.S. Congress passed the most progressive civil rights bill in a hundred years, approved a tax cut which may yet amount to more than $13,000,000,000 and an $800,000,000 "anti-poverty bill" in the full knowledge that this would produce a very large deficit in the federal budget. Senator Goldwater voted against all three bills.

Third, in the field of foreign policy, the election of 1964 dealt with a fundamental question: Should the United States take more active measures of military opposition to the communist powers, or continue the policy of "containing" their aggressions while trying to reach limited accommodations with them? Senator Goldwater advocated a more aggressive policy of military opposition. He contended that no honorable accommodations with the communists were likely, and that a policy of trying to compromise with them would lead not to peace but to war.

This view was opposed not only by President Johnson, but by all the nations of the Western alliance. They did not argue that major accommodations with the communists were likely. They did assert, however, that a more aggressive military policy toward the communists would split and weaken the alliance, tighten the control of the Soviet Union over its people at home and its allies in Eastern Europe, encourage Moscow to try to end its conflicts with Peking, and maybe even lead to war with China over South Vietnam under conditions highly favorable to the Chinese.

The judgment of most observers was that Senator Goldwater lost more votes on this issue than any other. While the people were obviously frustrated by the endless uncertainties and disappointments of the Cold War, the Senator's foreign policy proposals seemed to many to involve greater risks of actual war. Especially since the advent of atomic weapons, this has seldom been a popular prospect in the American mind.

IT DOES NOT FOLLOW from this that the American people in 1964 were very enthusiastic about the trend toward a planned economy and an even larger and more powerful federal government, or about

FOCUS RESTON

"... in the field of foreign policy, the election of 1964 dealt with a fundamental question."

"planned budget deficits," or "reaching accommodations with the communists." Nor does it follow that they were enthusiastic about equality of voting, desegregation in the schools, public accommodations, and housing—especially housing next door—for the American Negroes.

There was, on the contrary, a great deal of evidence that they deplored many of these trends in American life. Actually, Senator Goldwater held out to them the kind of America many of those voting against him would have preferred. He appealed to their nostalgic longing for a simpler life, based on "individualism," personal responsibility, the community, the state, and the church. But apparently they did not believe that this simpler life was either practical or attainable in the modern world.

There were, of course, other reasons for Goldwater's defeat. President Johnson had been in the White House for less than a year after the assassination of President Kennedy. He benefited from the American sense of fair play, of giving-the-new-man-a-chance, which had elected Theodore Roosevelt, Calvin Coolidge, and Harry S. Truman after they reached the White House as Vice-President after the death of the President. Also, he had made a remarkable record in getting his legislative program through the Congress. Nevertheless, it was probably the realities of life, rather than sentiment for Goldwater's "Lost Arcadia" or President Johnson's newness in office, that determined the outcome.

THE WORLD in 1964 was moving fast into new and complex problems. The population of America had increased by almost 50,000,000 since the death of Franklin D. Roosevelt, by over 10,000,000 since the last presidential election of 1960. People were moving away from the land and the small towns, where local government was comparatively simple, into the vast urban and suburban complexes, where the problems of life and government were much more complicated. Once prosperous communities, and even states, were stagnating through the competition of more efficient or cheaper products which were being produced elsewhere. As young people moved away from home to find employment, the family was no longer providing the customary shelter and security for the old.

This same torrent of change was affecting the rest of the world. Europe was no longer dependent economically on America, and was therefore not so inclined to follow its policies. In fact, the nations of Europe were increasingly following independent policies, and taking their own line toward the Soviet Union and China.

Therefore, in a changing world, the American people voted for those who seemed more flexible and willing to change, rather than for those who seemed to be resisting change, even though the people may have preferred no change at all.

In doing so, they followed several well-established patterns in American political life. Unlike Europeans, American voters have always favored the pragmatic, rather than the ideological, approach to practical political problems. They are more concerned about the future than the past. They tend to go along with the party in power if they are reasonably prosperous and safe. And while approving of change, they don't

"... Goldwater held out ... the kind of America many voting against him would have preferred."

like radical changes unless they are faced with economic depression or war.

SENATOR GOLDWATER made an ideological appeal to the people. He urged them to reject what he regarded as the "socialistic" economic and social policies of the present and return to the more individualistic policies of the past. He approached the communist problem in terms of religious warfare. And he insisted that his brand of conservatism was the true Republican doctrine from which the Republican progressives had departed. It has been a mark of American political life, however, that politics is not a moral crusade, but a practical give-and-take affair designed to reach agreement between the largest possible group of voters within each party and the nation.

In what he called "this extensive republic," James Madison pointed out early in the history of the Union that faction was inevitable in so diverse a nation of "fallible, heterogeneous, heterodox, opinionated, quarrelsome men." Therefore, he concluded, since faction was unavoidable, the art of politics was the art of compromise.

This is precisely the principle President Johnson followed in the campaign. He avoided ideological discussion. He appealed to all classes, all parties, and all regions, to help deal in practical ways with the difficult practical problems of the day. In the process, he not only held most of the quarreling factions of his own party together, but succeeded in gaining the support of many

Republican voters in the nation as well.

The actual vote totals were staggering. President Johnson received slightly more than 43 million votes to Senator Goldwater's 27 million. The President thus gained 61 per cent of the popular vote, the largest percentage in history.

In six states with 173 electoral votes, President Johnson's plurality exceeded 1,000,000 votes, and in crucial New York he won by 2,669,597 votes.

In Maine and Vermont, two states that had stayed with the Republicans in the Roosevelt landslide of 1936, the Democrats won 68.8 per cent and 66.3 per cent of the vote respectively.

Goldwater's defeat was so overwhelming that it weakened his party and his brand of conservatism. The Democrats not only retained control of the White House, but increased their majority in the Senate to 68 to 32, and in the House of Representatives to 295 to 140. At the start of 1965, the Republicans had only 17 governors in the state houses, to 33 for the Democrats.

Many Republican progressive candidates were dragged under by the tide of Democratic votes. Running for the Senate from Ohio, Robert Taft, Jr., pulled over 400,000 more votes than Senator Goldwater but lost to Senator Stephen M. Young. The Republican candidate for governor in Illinois, Charles Percy, ran more than 300,000 votes ahead of Senator Goldwater but lost to incumbent Otto J. Kerner. Senator Kenneth Keating lost his seat in New York to Robert F. Kennedy, even though he topped Goldwater's vote total by more than 700,000.

This does not justify most of the gloomy forecasts about the "death of the Republican

FOCUS RESTON

"...politics is not a moral crusade, but a practical give-and-take affair..."

party" nor even the post-election speculation about a "realignment" of the political parties in America. The Republican party is not merely a single political organization. It is 50 state organizations and countless more county and municipal organizations. They will go on nominating and electing officials, and most of them are not very interested in trying to win elections after 1964 by appealing only to conservative voters.

What the 1964 election accomplished, among other things, was to reaffirm the view that no party can win a national election by appealing to one or two factions, or one or two regions in the nation. It must put together a coalition of voters on the basis of a compromise program all will support.

Thus, the year 1964 did not establish any new trends of policy, but merely rejected the Goldwater proposal that present trends be modified or reversed.

Usually, it has been the progressive elements in American political life who have wanted to make moderate or even radical changes in contemporary policy. This time it was the Goldwater conservatives. Though 27,000,000 people voted Republican, 43,-000,000 refused to go along.

Related Articles

For a complete report on the year 1964 in national affairs, see Section Two, CONGRESS MAKES A DECISION. See also the following articles in Section Three:

"...no party can win a national election by appealing to one or two factions..."

SYLVIA PORTER

THE TOWERING ACHIEVEMENT of the United States economy in 1964 was a powerful, across-the-board, noninflationary upsurge to all-time peaks—for the fourth year in a row. Prosperity of this magnitude for four consecutive years has no precedent in peacetime anywhere.

The towering challenge facing the United States economy will be duplicating this achievement. This will demand extraordinary knowledge, economic statesmanship of the highest order by all segments of our society, and a hefty dose of luck.

The average life of all U.S. business upturns during the past 110 years has been 30 months. January, 1965, marked the 47th month of this advance. And as 1965 began, there was no doubt that the expansion was still very much alive.

Meanwhile, prices at every level remained extraordinarily stable. In all of 1964, consumer prices rose only a bit more than 1 per cent. Over the whole period of 1961 to 1965, the cost of living climbed only about 5 per cent, and wholesale prices barely budged. This is a price record no other major country in the world can match.

Wage increases generally continued moderate, with the one glaring exception of the auto wage hikes in the fall. Consumers spent freely, but they put away all-time high amounts of savings. Businessmen hiked their spending on new plants and equipment by a strong but not speculative 14 to 15 per cent, and they also showed caution in stocking their shelves with goods.

The result of this moderation has been an impressive gain in the real buying power of the average family. With his after-tax personal income up 22.5 per cent since the start of 1961, and his cost of living up roughly 5 per cent, the average U.S. worker is way ahead of the financial game.

What's more, in 1964 we made the first significant breakthrough in our seven-year fight on the unemployment rate. True, the overall jobless rate stayed above 5 per cent, but this primarily reflected steep unemployment among our untrained teen-agers and unskilled older workers. A fundamental point about 1964 is that joblessness among adult men sank to the "tolerable" unemployment rate of 4 per cent. Joblessness among adult married men—the family breadwinners—sank well below the "tolerable" unemployment rate. This breakthrough occurred even though our labor force jumped markedly in 1964. It occurred even though automation and other labor-cost saving devices have been wiping out existing jobs in a great many

The American Economic Challenge Is to Manage Our Policies in Such a Way as to Prolong the Strong, Non-inflationary Upsurge With Which We Are Now Favored.

FOCUS ON THE ECONOMY

industries throughout the entire nation.

The United States achievement was acknowledged throughout the world in very practical ways. Although the United States continued to spend far more abroad than it earned and the 1964 deficit in our balance of payments remained at a dangerous level, the U.S. dollar made an enormous comeback in the world's money markets. There was no run on the dollar in 1964 and no threat of one. A key reason was our creditors' recognition of the fact that we were holding our economy in a sustained growth while at the same time keeping price and wage increases under control.

No one can reasonably call an accelerating economic expansion in the fourth year of prosperity an accident. How did we manage to accomplish it?

THE BASIC EXPLANATION for our achievement, I think, is that, in 1964, our politicians finally "grew up" into mid-20th century fiscal policy thinking. As a result, there was nothing less than a revolution in economic thought at the highest policy-making levels of our government.

In the past, our politicians have always considered it imperative to hail an annually balanced budget as economic purity, to condemn a budget deficit as fiscal sin, and to shrink from tax reduction in the face of budget deficits as unspeakably reckless. But in 1964, the federal budget deficit was accepted as actually desirable because this meant the federal government was pouring funds into the economic stream, and this money would help lift us to levels of full employment and full use of our great industrial capacity.

In early 1964, despite a long string of yearly multibillion-dollar budget deficits, President Lyndon B. Johnson fought for, and

"The President's gamble turned out to be a triumph for economic planning."

Congress passed, a tax reduction bill which will amount to more than $13,000,000,000 when fully effective this year.

THE TAX CUT was of critical importance. Beginning in March, it added some $800,000,000 a month to take-home pay. It cut corporation tax rates. It provided a variety of special new tax breaks for individuals and businessmen. Consumers responded by sharply boosting their spending and saving, and by speeding repayment of their debts. Businessmen responded to the new tax reductions by substantially increasing their spending on plant and equipment.

At the same time, President Johnson openly wooed businessmen by emphasizing his understanding of the role adequate profits play in a prosperous economy. He also restrained federal government spending. The President took a calculated risk with the U.S. economy when he called for curbs on the growth of federal spending and for tax cuts. His gamble was that individuals and corporations would rise to the challenge and take over more of the job of sustaining the nation's prosperity.

The President's gamble turned out to be a triumph for economic planning. In 1964, private consumers and businessmen, and not the federal government, fueled the upturn. The switch in emphasis from ballooning public expenditures to tax reduction to speed our economic growth was an enormously important development.

Businessmen showed unusual economic statesmanship in their pricing practices. 1964's overall price pattern was one of remarkable stability. This stability was crucial in stimulating spending by U.S. families and in helping American businessmen to broaden their penetration of overseas markets.

Labor leaders showed unusual restraint in their wage demands, too. Until the auto wage settlement, 1964's wage pattern was among the most moderate of the whole post-World War II period. This comparative stability was crucial in fattening corporation profits and in maintaining corporation profit margins.

Because wage and price increases were modest, the Federal Reserve System also was able to pursue, for the fourth straight year, a monetary policy of relatively easy credit. Until 1964's final weeks, acceptable borrowers could get all the cash they wanted at fairly inexpensive interest rates. Among the most extraordinary aspects of the 1961–1965 expansion was the degree to which our central banks kept credit ample and pivotal borrowing costs comparatively steady.

Weren't there any major problems? Of course—and the problems clearly were intensifying and widening as 1964 wore on. To specify just five giant ones:

• UNEMPLOYMENT among our untrained teen-agers and older unskilled workers is unacceptably high. After 1964's experience, it is abundantly obvious that even a booming economy will not absorb workers who do not have the needed education or skills.

In 1964, we improved existing programs and launched new ones in a many pronged attack on these problems. We are drastically

"...there is an awful gap between what we are doing and what we must do."

revising our school curricula to make education more versatile. We have begun to upgrade the caliber of vocational education. We have started to provide far more pre-school and post-school training programs to improve our guidance services.

We are finally trying to develop reliable data on job vacancies so we can know how many jobs are seeking workers, and in what occupations and regions there are job opportunities. Through the Economic Opportunity Act of 1964, we have made a national commitment to fight poverty by means of education. (See Section One, LAWRENCE A. CREMIN ON EDUCATION.)

Still, on every front, there is an awful gap between what we are doing and what we must do. The first essential to the solution of unemployment is a sustained economic advance powerful enough to keep creating new jobs for our swelling labor force. The second essential is educating and training our workers so they can take on the jobs our economy creates.

● THE DEFICIT in our balance of payments remains threateningly large. Despite some progress in narrowing the gap between what we spend and earn abroad, the red ink in our international financial accounts amounted to substantially more than $2,000,000,000 in 1964.

Our exports of goods have soared 60 per cent in the past five years, and are billions of dollars above our imports. This trade surplus has been of vital help in reducing our deficit. We have taken a variety of technical steps to stem the outflow of dollars and gold from our shores, and we have also cut back hard on spending of U.S. government dollars abroad. Nevertheless, what we have done has not been sufficient to restore balance in our international financial accounts.

● OUR TRADE RELATIONS with the European Common Market, with Britain, and with the Soviet Union were in a highly delicate state when 1965 began.

It is imperative that we expand our trade with the world in order to earn enough dollars to lessen the deficit in our balance of payments, to preserve the position of the U.S. dollar as the pivotal currency of the world, and to create jobs for American workers. But in early 1963, France's President Charles de Gaulle shattered our grand hopes for a quickly developing Atlantic Alliance and a vast free trade area by vetoing Britain's entry into the European Common Market. While De Gaulle hasn't destroyed the future, he certainly has delayed and probably shifted the shape of the Atlantic Community.

The Common Market's long-sustained boom was showing some signs of running out of steam in 1964, telegraphing the probability that its exporters will become tougher competition for us. A substantial lowering of trade barriers under our Trade Expansion Act of 1962 has been befuddled by bickering. When 1965 opened, the Kennedy Round of tariff reductions—the biggest negotiation on world trade there has ever been—was getting nowhere fast in Geneva, and it was questionable where it would ultimately get and when.

As for U.S. trade with the East, there is widespread and mounting approval among American businessmen for expanding commerce with the Soviet Bloc. But there are difficult problems involved.

"...there were nagging doubts about the ...momentum of 1965's economic rise."

FOCUS PORTER

• WARNINGS of a renewed wage-price upswing were emerging as 1964 wore on. Should the warnings become reality, both our domestic prosperity and our foreign trade would be endangered.

The Federal Reserve System then would move deliberately to discourage borrowing by making loans more difficult as well as more expensive to get. This weapon of tight money can be extremely powerful; in the past (notably 1959) it has been a key factor in switching upturn into recession.

No one could be sure whether the fat wage settlement won by the auto workers would establish a new wage pattern and put a squeeze on profit margins. The likelihood of a hefty steel wage contract plus steel price increases was raising a danger signal. Prices of sensitive commodities and key metals were starting to climb in late 1964.

• FINALLY, at year's end, there were nagging doubts about the speed, extent, and momentum of 1965's economic rise.

It's a cinch that 1965's economy will top 1964's record prosperity. Consumer spending is certain to rise by billions in 1965, and consumers account for two-thirds of all spending. Federal, state, and local spending is sure to go up—although the rise at the federal level will be curbed. Business spending also is still heading up. With all three types of spending climbing, the overall economic trend for 1965 is obvious.

But as the President worked on the new federal budget in December, the assumption of his closest advisers was that our economy might level off in the second half of 1965 because increases in the three forms of spending would be slowing down. At a time when record numbers will be crowding into our labor force, we cannot afford even an economic "hiccup."

CAN WE DUPLICATE in 1965 and in the years following our magnificent record of the past four years?

As a realistic student of economics, I wouldn't bet that we can. I doubt that we have yet developed the extraordinary knowledge, and even more extraordinary ability to use both anti-recession and anti-inflation weapons at the right time and to the right degrees. But there are at least seven basic policies we might follow to help us sustain the prosperity of our private enterprise economy for a long time ahead.

(1) Additional tax cuts in 1965 and after to spur our economy by stimulating more consumer and business spending. We have proved that tax cuts work. We can both prevent and fight recessions with them. This is our first line of offense and defense.

(2) New stimulants to encourage businessmen to continue investing rising billions of dollars in new plants, modern equipment, research, and development. This type of investment is essential if business is to cut its production costs, increase the output-per-hour of workers, and thus make our products more attractive in the world's markets.

(3) Vastly expanded drives to raise the level of education of our young and older unskilled workers, plus programs to increase spending by our elderly retired citizens. The widely publicized anti-poverty law is at this

stage a poverty-stricken operation, but it has focused the nation's attention as never before on the paradox of poverty and pools of joblessness during unprecedented prosperity.

(4) Restraint on price and wage increases. It is in this area of price-wage policies that our business and labor leaders either will or will not demonstrate the necessary degree of economic statesmanship.

(5) Government spending programs geared to meet the demands of a rising population and to qualify us as a "Great Society." It is sensible to put percentage ceilings on federal spending in order to give top priority to tax cuts to prop our prosperity. But it is nonsense to put dollar ceilings on this spending. Our needs and wants inevitably must grow with our population.

(6) Pioneering laws to permit distribution of some of the U.S. Treasury's climbing tax intake through increased annual grants to the states. These grants would help our states and local communities finance programs traditionally under their responsibility. Many are in desperate financial straits now.

(7) A breakthrough on expanded world trade with the Soviet Bloc and with Europe. Every $1,000,000,000 rise in our exports creates 100,000 new jobs within the U.S.

This is only a partial blueprint, and, even with many other policies added, we still may not be able to duplicate the remarkable achievement of 1961–1965.

Perhaps, then, our biggest promise for 1965 and beyond lies in the fact that the economic-financial policymaking has reached a new high level of maturity. We have grown up into the knowledge that our central challenge is to sustain a strong, non-inflationary economic upturn. That knowledge alone will spur us to use and refine the pro-prosperity, anti-recession weapons we have and to try to develop better ones.

Related Articles

For a complete report on the 1964 year in economics, see the following articles in Section Three:

THE UNIVERSE seems to have unending surprises in store for the men who stare at the heavens. Every time a new astronomical instrument is developed, a new world of wonder opens up. Now it is the radio telescope that is leading the way.

Where an ordinary telescope gathers and concentrates the tiny waves of visible light, a radio telescope gathers and concentrates the much longer radio waves. As far as ordinary light is concerned, astronomers have always been aware that certain heavenly objects are particularly strong sources. They are the bright first-magnitude stars. Beginning in the early 1940's, astronomers became aware that there were bright "radio stars," too; heavenly regions that sent out unusually strong beams of radio waves.

The radio stars were not ordinary stars, and were very difficult to pinpoint because the long radio waves present a fuzzier picture of the heavens than the much shorter light waves. By 1951, however, one of the brightest radio stars was pinned down, not to a single star, but to an odd-looking galaxy (a system of hundreds of billions of stars) about 200,000,000 light-years away. (Our nearest neighbor among the stars is only four light-years away.) Astronomers took a closer look at this odd galaxy and found it was not a galaxy at all, but two galaxies in the process of collision.

This led to great excitement, for it showed that radio telescopes could define objects more clearly at great distances than ordinary light telescopes. It showed also that radio waves could be made to reveal heavenly catastrophes that had previously gone unnoticed by astronomers.

Were there more bright and very distant radio stars? Yes, indeed, quite a number. In fact, as more of them were discovered, astronomers began to be disturbed. Surely,

Philippe Halsman for THE YEAR BOOK

ISAAC ASIMOV FOCUS

ISAAC ASIMOV FOCUS

32

they couldn't all be colliding galaxies. Galaxies were too thinly spread through space for collisions to be that common.

Yet, if colliding galaxies were eliminated, what else could produce a flood of radio waves so great that they were detectable over hundreds of millions of light-years? The English astronomer Fred Hoyle suggested that supernovas were the answer. (These are stars which explode, burning a billion-year supply of nuclear fuel in a few months). Supernovas can indeed produce radio waves. One of the brightest radio sources in the sky is the Crab Nebula, which is a patch of turbulent gas representing all that is left of a supernova that flared up more than 900 years ago. The Crab Nebula is, however, only 5,000 light-years away. The radio waves from a supernova could never be strong enough for detection over hundreds of millions of light-years.

HOYLE, HOWEVER, said that not one supernova was involved, but many; perhaps even millions. In the crowded center of some galaxy, one supernova might flare, and its radiation might cause another star nearby to explode. Together the two might set off additional stars, one after the other, like tumbling dominoes. The mighty blast of radio waves would register throughout the universe.

Astronomers have been looking for such a situation. In 1961, a radio star was made out to be a galaxy in the Big Dipper, one that was known as M 82. It is 10,000,000 light-years away, and a large explosion might exist there.

The 200-inch telescope at Mount Palomar was used to photograph M 82 with special filters that let through only the light produced by hydrogen. (Hydrogen gas makes up most of the thin material spread out between the stars, and a huge explosion would send it flying outward in great streams.)

In late 1963, the startling results were announced. Jets of hydrogen up to 1,000 light-years long were bursting out of the center of M 82. The total quantity of hydrogen involved was equal in mass to at least 5,000,000 average stars. From the rate at which the jets were traveling and the distance they had covered, the explosion was calculated as having been in progress for 1,500,000 years. Since the light had taken 10,000,000 years to reach us, those millions of stars exploded 11,500,000 years ago.

Galaxy M 82 is the first "exploding galaxy" to be discovered. No doubt there are others. Theories aside from Hoyle's have been advanced to account for this.

Radio waves pinpointed still stranger objects. In 1960, some radio stars were found to be ordinary stars—at least they

Astronomy, Oldest of the Sciences, Has Taken on Fresh Life With Discoveries by its Newest Tool, the Radio Telescope.

ON SCIENCE

seemed, in appearance, to be faint stars belonging to our own Milky Way Galaxy. But why should they produce such strong radio waves?

Astronomers began to look more closely at those stars and by 1963, they were stupefied, but convinced. Those stars were receding from us at rates approaching half the speed of light. This means those stars are not part of the Milky Way at all. They are, rather, the most distant objects known, for one of them may perhaps be as much as 7,000,000,000 light-years away.

For objects that distant to appear as bright as those stars seem to be, as much light as that of 100 ordinary galaxies must be radiated. Yet measurements made it seem that these stars could not be more than 10 light-years across whereas an ordinary galaxy might have a diameter of 50,000 light-years.

In short, these objects that resembled stars in appearance couldn't be ordinary stars. They were therefore called "quasi-stellar objects" ("star-resembling objects") or "quasars" for short.

Where do they get the energy to pump out so much radiation? Fred Hoyle suggests that it is not an explosion this time but an implosion. A million stars or more suddenly fall together, converting vast quantities of gravitational energy into radiation. Astronomers are by no means in general agreement on this point, however.

Are there any other kinds of new catastrophes in the heavens? Astronomers are

FOCUS ASIMOV

looking for the weirdest of all, starting with hints from waves much shorter than light. Rockets sent up beyond our atmosphere in April, 1963, were equipped with special devices to detect X rays coming from the heavens. Here on the surface of the earth, any X rays that might be bombarding us would not be detected because they are absorbed by the atmosphere. In space, however, X rays were detected.

X rays seemed, in fact, to be arriving with particular intensity from two specific points in the heavens. The brighter of these "X-ray stars" came from a spot in the constellation Scorpius, and in that spot no actual star, or anything else, could be seen. The second X-ray star, only $\frac{1}{8}$ as strong, is in the Crab Nebula.

Should the Crab Nebula be sending out X rays? Puzzled astronomers had to admit they didn't think so. X rays would be emitted by stars with surface temperatures of 1,000,000° C. or so, but no such superhot stars have ever been known. Our own sun has a surface temperature of only 6,000° C.

WHEN A STAR EXPLODES as the Crab Nebula once did, what is left collapses into a shrunken sphere of smashed atoms. This is called a "white dwarf" because it is white-hot, and because it is much smaller than ordinary stars. The subatomic particles making up ordinary atoms take up a great deal of room so that an atom is mostly empty space. When the atom is smashed and the subatomic particles are crowded together, the star shrinks down until it is not much bigger than a planet.

Even the subatomic particles in a white dwarf still leave a great deal of space be-

"...these objects that resembled stars in appearance couldn't be ordinary stars."

tween them. What if a supernova explosion were so catastrophic that the star shrank down further? If, for some reason, its subatomic particles were converted to neutrons, these neutrons, being electrically uncharged, would not repel each other. They could be squeezed together until they touched.

If a star like the sun collapsed into a "neutron star", it would end as a tiny sphere not more than eight miles in diameter, but still containing all the mass it always had. One cubic inch of such a star would weigh 35,000,000 tons! Furthermore the surface of such a neutron star would have a temperature of 10,000,000° C. and would release a powerful flood of X rays. A neutron star would be an X-ray star as well.

A neutron star would be far too small to see even if it were only a few light-years away, but there was a possible way of checking the matter. Every once in a while, the moon crosses in front of the Crab Nebula, blocking its X rays. If the X rays are blocked all at once, then they must arise from a very small source and, quite possibly, from a neutron star. If, however, the X rays fade off gradually, then the source must be spread out in space, and the Crab Nebula could not contain a neutron star.

In July, 1964, the moon passed in front of the Crab Nebula, and a rocket was sent up to record the results. The X rays, it turned out, faded out gradually! The Crab Nebula did not contain a neutron star! But, if so, what else could serve as the X-ray source? Astronomers haven't figured that one out yet.

And what about the X-ray star in Scorpio, eight times as strong as the Crab Nebula? That might yet be a neutron star.

Clearly, the universe is filled with catastrophic events we've only begun to understand. The universe is a harsher place than it had seemed to be.

For further information about the quasars and about the nature of the universe, see Section Two, THE UNFOLDING UNIVERSE.

Astronomers in 1964 were getting a clearer look at places closer to home, too.

SOVIET SCIENTISTS, at the end of 1963, sent a radar beam (composed of the same sort of short radio waves that reach us from radio-stars) to Jupiter and then detected the returning echoes. Radar contact with other worlds began in 1946 when American scientists touched the moon. Since then, radar contact has been made with Venus, Mars, Mercury, and the Sun, but Jupiter represents the new long-distance record. As such echoes are analyzed, we may, for the first time, get a notion of what goes on below Jupiter's upper atmosphere, which is all we see through an ordinary telescope.

New studies of the light reaching us from the planet Venus have produced definite proof that water vapor exists there. Venus' clouds are therefore like ours, but whereas Earth has oceans under its clouds, Venus doesn't. It is too hot on Venus for water to remain liquid. (Oddly enough, astronomers discovered also in 1964 that certain cool giant stars possess water vapor in their atmospheres. Such "water stars" are still another new object in our 1964 heavens.)

Finally, even our closest neighbor, the moon, gets the benefit of a new look. Despite the fact that it is but a quarter of a million miles away, there is much that remains to be discovered about our satellite.

"...the universe is filled with catastrophic events we've only begun to understand."

Beginning in October, 1963, for instance, observers have been noting red spots here and there on the moon as if one crater or another is producing a feeble volcanic-like eruption. Astronomers had thought the moon had cooled to the point where its landscape could no longer be tumbled about by quakes or volcanic-like eruptions. It looks, now, as though the report of the moon's death had been slightly exaggerated.

The moon's real headline news of the year, however, came with the photographs taken by the moon-probe, Ranger VII. This rocket made impact with the moon on July 31, 1964, and before it struck, it took a series of photographs that are by far the best ever taken of the moon. Tiny craters show up, as well as something that looks like a boulder.

Most astronomers studying these photographs concluded that the surface of the moon is not covered with the thick layer of dust that some had suspected might be present. The surface might be crunchy, perhaps, like crusted snow, but it could be walked on without trouble. Nor did the surface show any signs of large cracks or fissures, and that was good news, too. It looked very much as though that part of the moon's surface at which Ranger VII had been aimed might indeed be safe for future lunar explorers.

It has been difficult for any of the other sciences to compete in excitement with what has been astronomy's year of glamour, but they made a valiant try.

CHEMISTS ARE BEGINNING to feel at home with the protein molecule. Those complex molecules, made up of thousands of atoms, can be broken down into about 20 different types of smaller units (each made up of a dozen or so atoms) called amino acids. Chemists can now work out the exact order of these amino acids along the length of the protein molecule.

For instance, every oxygen-breathing species contains a protein called "cytochrome c" made up of about 105 amino acids. During 1964, chemists of Abbott Laboratories in Chicago were among those who worked out the amino acid pattern of the cytochrome c molecule in a number of species and found differences from species to species. The greater the separation of the species in the evolutionary scheme, the greater the number of differences.

Thus the cytochrome c of man differed from that of the rhesus monkey in only one amino acid in the entire chain. Between the cytochrome c of man and of a tuna fish, there were 21 differences, and between the cytochrome c of man and of a yeast cell, there were 48 differences.

As the intimate detail of the structure of more and more different proteins in more and more different species is worked out, science may well have at its fingertips a map of the evolutionary tree more detailed and accurate than any they have ever before dared dream of.

The scientific event of 1964 with the most exciting (and chilling) significance for mankind himself was the feat of seven physicians at the Western Reserve University School of Medicine in Cleveland. In June of 1964, it was announced that they were successful,

FOCUS ASIMOV

"...science may well have at its fingertips a map of the evolutionary tree..."

no less than 35 times during 1963 and 1964, in keeping an isolated brain of a rhesus monkey alive, by maintaining an artificial circulation through its blood vessels.

In one particular case, the brain was kept alive for 18 hours. A study by an electroencephalograph, (an instrument that measures the brain waves) showed that it was functioning much as it did in the intact animal, and might even be conscious.

Such an isolated brain could be very useful. Substances could be added to the fluid entering the blood vessels and tested for in the fluid emerging. In this way, a great deal could be found out about the chemistry of the brain.

Will there come a time when the brain of a young man about to die of an accident, or of a sickness not affecting his mind, might be withdrawn and kept alive for years? Could mankind continue to get the use of the brain of a genius long years after it might otherwise be dead? Could the life of an isolated brain be bearable under such conditions to a human being?

It will be long years before men will have to consider such questions, but the day will surely come.

Related Articles

For a complete report on the 1964 year in science and in technology, see Section Two, THE UNFOLDING UNIVERSE; and the following articles in Section Three.

"Could mankind continue to get the use of the brain... after it might otherwise be dead?"

LAWRENCE A. CREMIN

THROUGHOUT their history, U.S. public schools have been locally supported and locally controlled. The word "education" appears nowhere in the United States Constitution. While the federal government has always been interested in education, its influence has traditionally been weak.

Since 1945, however, there has been a steady rise in federal concern. Congress, acting under its responsibility to provide for the common defense and general welfare, has appropriated increasing sums for educational purposes. The year 1964 saw a surge in this concern, as education became the chief instrument in a nationwide attack on the causes of poverty.

President Lyndon B. Johnson once referred to the 88th Congress as "the education Congress," and with good reason. During the sessions that lasted from January, 1963, to October, 1964, the 88th probably passed more new and significant educational legislation than any other Congress in history. One program, authorized by the Vocational Education Act of 1963 and by a series of amendments to the Manpower Development and Training Act of 1962, greatly expanded and liberalized federal participation in state and local job training programs (see the 1964 YEAR BOOK, pp. 39–40). Another program, authorized by the Health Professions Educational Assistance Act of 1963, and the Nurse Training Act of 1964, made available federal grants to schools of medicine, dentistry, and nursing, and to the students who attend them.

STILL ANOTHER PROGRAM, authorized by the Higher Education Facilities Act of 1963, provided grants and loans to construct college and university classrooms, libraries, and laboratories, and committed the federal government to developing first-rate graduate centers across the country.

By far the most significant educational measures of the 88th Congress were the revised National Defense Education Act (NDEA) of 1964 and the Economic Opportunity Act of 1964. The original National Defense Education Act, passed in 1958 during the furor following the flight of the Russian Sputnik I, had been conceived as a "crash program" to upgrade teaching in the natural sciences, mathematics, and foreign languages, and to enlarge guidance and counseling services in the secondary schools. Congress had twice extended the act, but on both occasions had retained its specialized character. Now, the revision of 1964 substantially broadened its scope, adding English, reading, history, and geography to the list of aided subjects, and including elementary as well as secondary school guidance.

As others have pointed out, the new NDEA program came close to being a substitute for general federal school aid.

The Year Saw a Dramatic Rise of Educational Programs That Were Designed to Attack the Causes of Poverty.

FOCUS ON EDUCATION

It was the Economic Opportunity Act that provided the most significant innovations in the federal program. Recognizing that ignorance is often at the heart of unemployment, Congress turned to education as its chief device for breaking the vicious circle in which poverty breeds poverty.

AMONG THE MANY programs established under the act were: (1) a Job Corps for unemployed young people between 16 and 21; (2) a program to assist local communities in developing sustained attacks on "the special educational problems of the poor" (for example, the establishment of preschool day-care centers for three-year-olds); (3) a program to help states and localities meet the special educational needs of migrant farmworkers and their children; and (4) a domestic Peace Corps, to be known as VISTA (Volunteers in Service to America), that would recruit and train volunteers to serve in the anti-poverty effort. The total appropriation under the act was close to $1,000,000,000, of which some $750,000,000 would eventually go to educational activities.

Even a hasty glance at these several programs would indicate that Washington was very much in the education business in 1964. Yet the fact is that these programs accounted for only a fraction of the total federal effort.

A study presented by Congresswoman Edith Green of Oregon revealed that the federal government was spending some $2,200,000,000 a year on education and research, of which about half was going directly to the schools and colleges. This money was being disbursed by more than a dozen different government departments and agencies. The largest program was run by the Department of Defense.

In October, based on a recommendation from Mrs. Green, President Johnson created

"...was the long-debated question of...federal aid to education a false one?"

FOCUS CREMIN

an Interagency Council on Education. It was made up of representatives from the various departments and offices conducting educational programs, and was headed by Commissioner of Education Francis Keppel.

More importantly, perhaps, Mrs. Green concluded that the long-debated question of whether there should be federal aid to education was a false one. The real question was whether the $2,200,000,000 already allocated to education was being spent sensibly, economically, and in the public interest. Undoubtedly, there would still be sharp controversies over how much money would be given to education, and where it would go. And in particular, there would be battles over whether or not to aid denominational elementary and secondary schools. But by 1964 it was abundantly clear that certain *national* policies were emerging in education. While the 50 state legislatures and the 30,000 local school boards of the country would continue to oversee the schools, they were destined, more than ever, to work with the federal government.

NO SEGMENT of American education was changing more rapidly in 1964 than the colleges and universities. Even the most conservative analysts warned that enrollments would rise from 4,800,000 to 7,000,000 by 1970. No one really knew where the additional buildings and professors would come from. A report of the Educational Facilities Laboratories noted that at 1964 rates of construction, the nation would lack over 1,000,000 seats by 1970, and shortages of professors would dictate substantial changes in instructional techniques.

Already, teaching machines, electronic language laboratories, televised lectures, automated libraries, and computerized registration procedures were appearing in institutions across the country. "Nothing is certain about the shape of college facilities," the Educational Facilities report continued, "except the probability that what happens in them today will not be happening in them in the same way a decade from now."

One response to soaring enrollments was a flurry of state efforts to expand public higher education. Of these, California's was clearly the most impressive. Based on a "master plan", California was building what was commonly referred to as a "three-tier" system of public higher education.

The first tier consisted of 71 two-year junior colleges, widely available in localities throughout the state and open to all high school graduates who wished to attend. The second tier consisted of 18 four-year state colleges (most of which offered fifth-year Master of Arts programs), open to those in the upper third of their high school graduating classes. The third tier consisted of nine great university centers, eight of them with highly selective undergraduate colleges as well as advanced graduate and professional schools (the ninth was the San Francisco Medical Center).

By 1964, California was spending in excess of $600,000,000 a year on its public higher education system, and the full-time enrollment stood at around 300,000 students. The projected figures for 1975 were $1,000,000,000 and 600,000 full-time students.

"...the colleges and universities had become deeply involved in the...welfare of the nation."

Other states were moving in similar directions. The American Association of Junior Colleges estimated that local two-year colleges would double their enrollments in a decade, and that to keep pace with the expansion, new community colleges would have to be opened or projected at the rate of one every two weeks. In addition, scores of former teachers colleges and agricultural colleges were being converted into general four-year institutions, offering both liberal and technical courses.

Some of these, in turn, were rapidly adding graduate and professional faculties, thereby becoming universities.

IF ENROLLMENT PRESSURES were dictating major changes, even more fundamental changes were growing out of scientific and technological advances. Like it or not, the colleges and universities had become deeply involved in the political and economic welfare of the nation. They were creating much of the new knowledge basic to industrial progress and military preparedness, and they were training the skilled personnel required to apply that knowledge. In a vast range of fields, from weaponry to medical care, from urban renewal to space exploration, the simple fact was that higher education held the key to America's future.

Congress, of course, was well aware of this, and seemed willing to appropriate hundreds of millions of dollars annually to support specialized programs of teaching and research. Yet, the very presence of this money was exercising a transforming influence on the institutions themselves. President Clark Kerr of the University of California made this transformation the subject of his widely discussed Godkin Lectures at Harvard, published under the title, *The Uses of the University*. Kerr reported a host of tensions which had been generated by massive federal assistance.

The university's control over its own destiny had been substantially reduced, as professors tended to shift their loyalties from academic departments to the Washington bureaus that granted funds. A few top universities had received the lion's share of the aid, increasing even further the qualitative gap between themselves and the next-ranking institutions. The sciences and engineering had expanded very rapidly, but often at the expense of the humanities. And graduate research programs had attracted the best professors, often to the detriment of teaching in general, and undergraduate teaching in particular.

Despite these problems, Kerr ended on an optimistic note. Federal assistance to the universities, he concluded, had helped greatly in meeting certain national needs, and it had helped the universities themselves. Both were stronger as a result.

Kerr's optimism was far from universal, and his concerns were widely echoed during 1964. In Washington, there was sharpening criticism of the concentration of federal assistance in certain academic subjects, in certain universities, and in certain regions of the country. In response, the National Science Foundation announced a multi-million-dollar Science Development Program, designed to foster new "centers of excellence" in science and technology comparable to the leading universities and institutes on both the East and West coasts.

And in August, Congressman William S.

"...there were indications of concerted attacks on academic imbalance and overspecialization."

FOCUS CREMIN

Moorhead of Pennsylvania proposed the establishment of a National Humanities Foundation that would undertake for the arts and letters what the National Science Foundation had done for the sciences and engineering. No action was taken on Moorhead's bill, but shortly after the November elections, he announced that he would sponsor similar legislation in the 89th Congress.

In the universities themselves, there were indications of concerted attacks on academic imbalance and overspecialization. Columbia, Harvard, and the University of Chicago, which had pioneered the idea of "general education" 25 years earlier, were attempting to breathe new life into their general education courses. New institutions were experimenting with clusters of small colleges, each with its own particular traditions and emphases. At the graduate level, there were renewed efforts to cut across rigid disciplinary boundaries. A host of new programs were coming into being, ranging from psycholinguistics to space studies. Indeed, the sum total of all this ferment seemed to be a reform movement in higher education that might ultimately parallel in scope and intensity the reform of the elementary and secondary schools that had been going on for more than a decade.

AT THE OTHER END of the educational system, there were new stirrings in nursery school education, as psychologists began to re-emphasize the crucial role of early learning in later school performance.

Educators had long been aware of the fact that middle-class children learned certain skills and attitudes at home that later contributed substantially to their success in school. Books, newspapers, pictures, music, conversation, words, ideas—the very stuff of education—were part and parcel of the middle-class child's world from the day he was born. Slum children, on the other hand, had few such experiences. Not surprisingly, they entered the first grade lacking certain concepts and interests that were already thoroughly familiar to their middle-class age-mates. They learned less rapidly what teachers thought they ought to be learning, and they proved more difficult to teach. Experiencing failure, they became less and less interested in learning, and fell behind in their work.

Perhaps the most promising approach to curing such educational deprivations came in the work of Dr. Martin Deutsch at the Institute of Developmental Studies of New York Medical College. Abandoning the idea of any fixed mental capacity in human beings, Deutsch argued that what often appeared as "native" intelligence at the age of six, especially on IQ tests, was largely the result of the child's having learned how to learn. Therefore, he set out to train teachers to give slum youngsters certain basic experiences in learning that they were not getting at home: opportunities to talk and listen; opportunities to ask and answer questions; opportunities to converse with adults; opportunities to play with books and toys of every sort and variety.

The results were impressive. Deutsch revealed in a March, 1964, interview that a group of four-year-olds in his experimental

"...cities...were setting up prekindergarten projects in slum neighborhoods."

classes had actually raised their IQ's at the rate of a point a month, while a "control" group that had stayed at home was dropping at roughly the same rate.

Based largely on such findings, a growing number of cities, including Baltimore, Boston, Chicago, New Haven, New York, and Richmond, were setting up special prekindergarten projects in slum neighborhoods aimed at providing "enrichment programs" for three- and four-year-olds. By October, Superintendent Calvin Gross of New York City was referring to such projects as "the hottest thing that ever came down the pike"; doubtless they would figure prominently in the national anti-poverty program.

OTHER 1964 PROGRAMS were trying to compensate for educational deprivations all along the line. Thus, Rutgers, Princeton, and Yale set up special summer sessions to give selected high school youngsters intensive training in English, science, and mathematics. Dartmouth established an eight-week course for some 50 young people who were scheduled to enter prestige pre-

paratory schools in the fall. Similarly, the National Association of Independent Schools arranged for more than 200 students to attend summer enrichment programs at Milton Academy, Belmont School, and Shady Hill School in the Boston area. All these programs sought to ease the transition from poor-quality high schools to more prestigious schools and colleges.

Beyond the specific knowledge these programs provided, they left an unquenchable thirst for further education. Their value was best summed up, perhaps, by 14-year-old Rosemary Gibbs, the daughter of a Pennsylvania shipyard worker, who was interviewed shortly after spending the summer of 1964 at Swarthmore College. "When I came here," Rosemary said, "I might have felt 'shamed or that something was wrong with me if I couldn't say what I learned. But I don't feel like that now. I mean, it's because I know how to think about things now. Yeah, that's it. I learned how to learn."

There were few more important things that Swarthmore could have taught Rosemary, or that Rosemary could have mastered.

Related Articles

For a complete report on the 1964 year in education, see the following articles in Section Three.

AMERICAN LIBRARY ASSOCIATION	CONGRESS OF THE UNITED STATES	LIBRARY LITERATURE	PROTESTANT ROMAN
BLINDNESS	EDUCATION	LITERATURE FOR CHILDREN	CATHOLIC
CANADIAN LIBRARY ASSOCIATION	EDUCATIONAL FOUNDATIONS	NEGRO	STATE GOVERNMENT
CANADIAN LITERATURE	HANDICAPPED, THE	PARENTS AND TEACHERS,	TELEVISION
CHILD GUIDANCE	JOB CORPS	NATIONAL	VISTA
CHILD WELFARE	JUVENILE DELINQUENCY	CONGRESS OF	VOCATIONAL EDUCATION
CIVIL LIBERTIES			

FOR THE FIRST TIME since 1960, the U.S. went through the year in 1964 without launching a man into space. The American space effort, however, was not standing still. The year was a time for consolidating, improving, building, and testing. It was a time for upgrading the accuracy and reliability of our rockets and payloads. It was, in short, a time of getting ready—getting ready for the exhilarating pace that will mark Phase II of our manned exploration of space. Evidence of this will become abundantly clear in 1965.

Phase I ended with Project Mercury, which proved that man could survive and effectively function—at least for limited periods—in the weightless world beyond our atmosphere. Phase II—the complex Gemini and Apollo programs—is designed to send two or more astronauts into space for up to two weeks, and to perfect the technique of joining two spacecraft while in orbit. It is also designed to enable astronauts to navigate the 239,000 miles to the moon, to explore the lunar surface, and to bring back their newly acquired knowledge. Once Phase II is under way, Americans can expect to see two or more astronauts launched into space every few months.

There are several ways we go about getting information from the new area about which we know so little. These methods have preceded the manned efforts and will continue to complement and supplement the flow of information as time goes on. The manned efforts to date have, in fact, been predominantly those of just working out the "transportation problem" of the man and the machine, of perfecting methods and techniques that will enable the greater explorations and observations to begin.

One of the chief goals of the space program is to gain new information concerning

JOHN H. GLENN, JR. FOCUS

those areas above the surface of the earth, and primarily beyond the earth's atmosphere. The National Aeronautics and Space Administration (NASA) has adopted several methods to get this information. In addition to manned flights, they include space probes, orbiting laboratories, and working satellites.

1964 might well be remembered as a good year for really useful, practical working satellites. It is hard to realize that we have come to this stage in the scant six years since the launching of Explorer I on Jan. 31, 1958. In that same period, the accuracy of our big booster rockets and the reliability of our satellites gave us a number of practical examples of how the frontier of space is already being made to serve mankind.

The effective and promising Telstar satellite is a case in point. During the year, this cooperative, government-business project successfully handled transoceanic communications of many kinds, including a TV broadcast of the remarks of the heads of government of Britain, Ireland and West Germany. I had the pleasure of taking part in one of the first broadcasts. The potential impressed me that day and still does.

Also in 1964, the National Aeronautics and Space Administration's Relay satellites not only carried British election results to the U.S., but transmitted the outcome of our November elections to Europe.

THE SYNCOM III satellite, launched August 19, opened a new transpacific communications link with a 15-minute TV broadcast from Japan. Syncom III's orbital speed so precisely matched that of the earth that it drifted less than a mile and a half per day from its apparent fixed position in space.

Another satellite project which became a functioning system to provide highly accurate position data to ships and aircraft all over the world, was Transit, known as the Navy Navigation Satellite. And the weather satellites, Tiros and Nimbus, photographed the spawning of hurricanes and continued to furnish meteorologists with valuable world-wide weather data.

I have had a very personal interest in the Tiros satellites. The Tiros pictures and weather information were one of the prime sources used to brief me on world-wide weather conditions prior to the flight of *Friendship 7* in February, 1962. It was most impressive to view the Tiros pictures and then see approximately the same weather patterns from the vantage point of space high above all weather formations. The major difference was in perspective. Tiros circled the earth at altitudes of over 1,000 miles, while my altitude did not exceed 163.

All these working satellites are not just experimental. They demonstrate that we are now able to take the knowledge we have

Though America Sent No Men into Space, There Were Important Technical Advances That Would Lead to Great Future Triumphs.

ON SPACE

about space and put it to constructive use. The success of communications satellites means that it is not unrealistic to think that in the foreseeable future we will be able to drop a coin in a slot and call someone in India, just as today we can dial Aunt Florence in Cambridge, Ohio. And it is quite certain that TV relay satellites will soon enable us to see events as they happen all over the world.

SATELLITES are not the only things working for us. Space probes have already preceded man to the moon and the planets. Such probes greatly increase our knowledge. The 4,316 close-up photographs of the moon provided in July, 1964, by the cameras aboard Ranger VII furnished detailed data never before available to astronomers.

Equally promising was the November launch of the Mariner IV Mars probe scheduled to pass close to the red planet in the summer of 1965. If, after a 325,000,000-mile journey, Mariner IV's delicate instruments tell us as much about Mars as Mariner II told us regarding Venus, we will be making another huge deposit in the bank of man's knowledge about the universe. Hopefully, with its primary mission accomplished, Mariner IV will then join its predecessors in orbiting the sun.

It will have company, for Orbiting Solar Observatory (OSO) is already in solar orbit and has sent back valuable information. And the Orbiting Geophysical Observatory (OGO), continues in earth orbit.

FOCUS GLENN

These sources of information give us fundamental building blocks to proceed with the most important step of all: sending man to the areas beyond our world where he can use his unique and indispensable ability to perceive what is new, analyze its value and relate it to his future. That is exploration . . . discovery of the new and unexpected. It will probably prove at least as valuable in space as it has previously, in earthbound explorations.

The unforeseen benefits of such exploration are already being demonstrated in a small way. I recently saw a listing of nearly 200 examples of how new knowledge generated in the space program is being put to use in the direct production of commercial items that would not otherwise be possible. These are just the first few "fallouts" that were not planned at the beginning of the space program but will become increasingly important in the future.

1964 was also the year in which major policy decisions were put into effect that will launch United States military pilots into space, not on specific military missions, but on assessment flights to determine military applications that may someday be necessary. When Secretary of Defense Robert S. McNamara canceled the Dyna-Soar program, he announced simultaneously that the Air Force would be given responsibility for developing a Manned Orbital Laboratory. The MOL, which is about the size of a small house trailer (25 feet by 10), is scheduled for launching with military pilots aboard in late 1967 or early 1968. As 1964 ended, however, the extent and direction of military participation was undefined and still under discussion.

"These sources . . . give us . . . building blocks to proceed with the most important steps of all . . ."

We hope it will never be necessary to use space for military purposes, but it is a very regrettable fact that in the past wherever man has learned to travel, he has also learned to fight. To prepare and be ready for whatever may occur in space is just common sense.

Part of our concern with the military uses of space results from the secret emphasis the Soviet Union has consistently given to this area.

During 1964, the Soviets continued their series of launches of the unmanned Cosmos satellites. In fact, in August they announced they had launched three satellites at once from a single rocket. Although Russia insists these satellites have a purely scientific purpose, a number of U.S. defense experts believe they are also used as reconnaissance satellites to spy on U.S. defense installations.

In October, the Russians launched three men at once from their Kazakhstan rocket site in a large satellite they named *Sunrise*. An interesting fact was that the three passengers did not wear cumbersome space suits while in orbit. Instead, they functioned in a "shirt-sleeve environment" inside a pressurized cabin. We have always chosen to wear the familiar silver space suit as a backup protection against loss of cabin pressure, even though the space suit has never been needed. Whether the Russians have developed any new techniques in this area, or have just foregone the added safety of wearing the suit, is not known.

In late November, the Russians also launched an unmanned spacecraft, Zond II, toward Mars. Thus two deep space probes—one U.S., one Russian—proceeded simultaneously on their way to Mars.

The continued parallel exploration of space by the world's two strongest nations inevitably revived several controversial subjects: the "race" aspect between the U.S. and Russia, and whether or not space exploration should be a cooperative venture.

Americans I talk to or correspond with seem most interested in the "race" aspect. But it's important to remember that America is not running just a drag race. The big and overriding purpose of our national thrust into space is research and exploration.

What we stand to gain is not so much victory at a given finish line as continuous, constructive knowledge about the origin and nature of our universe. We very well may learn within the next few years more about the earth and its place in the universe than since recorded history began.

SHOULD WE SHARE such a profound adventure with others? And should we cooperate with the Soviet Union?

I think we have already answered these questions. Since the beginning of the space program, we have made available to everyone scientific data obtained from both manned and unmanned flights. To be secretive in an endeavor can sometimes mean either shame at the effort or an ulterior motive, and we have had neither in our space efforts. We have shared our information with the world in the belief that the potential benefits from space exploration are so huge that all mankind should be a party to the effort.

The U.S., in fact, is involved in working agreements with 65 nations which are engaged either in tracking operations or that furnish scientists to make observations.

"We may very well learn ... more about the earth ... than since recorded history began."

If Russia ever follows our lead in sharing information with the world, then perhaps we may look forward to cooperative Russian-American efforts that will reduce unnecessary duplication.

If cooperation ever comes, however, it will not resolve all obstacles in the conquest of space. But it should avoid some costly duplication of effort, and it should result in faster world-wide dissemination of significant new knowledge.

Russia and the U.S., and all the other nations of the world which are participating, or plan to participate, in the exploration of space, need both to reduce costs and to spread knowledge. Space is the most difficult frontier man has ever tried to penetrate and—like the sea—exacts a high price for careless performance, shoddy workmanship or inferior equipment. To a degree perhaps, the old slogan seen on many hanger or ready-room walls might apply, "Flying in itself is not inherently dangerous, but it is mercilessly unforgiving of human error."

Whether man continues to flit in and out of the fringes of space or proceeds to the challenging depths beyond, depends primarily on the reliability of man-made devices. This all-important reliability, which in the year just concluded represented such a superb technical accomplishment, must be —in the explorations to come—repeated and perfected to limits as yet undreamed of.

As recently as 1958, the U.S. had only five successes and eight failures in attempting to achieve earth orbits. By 1961, we had progressed to 35 successes as compared to 12 failures. In 1963, we were capable of sustaining over 25 straight successes in placing objects in orbit. As of July, 1964, the U.S. had orbited 212 payloads, compared to 70 for Russia. The total Russian orbital space tonnage, however, approximately triples our loads.

WE LEARNED in Project Mercury what exacting performance the Space Age places upon us. For instance, the initial orbiting speed was approximately 17,555 mph., but the exact conditions that are required for a satisfactory orbit are extremely precise. During Project Mercury, we knew that every 1.4 foot-per-second error in speed at booster cutoff time would create approximately a one mile variation in apogee (the highest point of orbit) on the far side of the earth. At that time, the spacecraft was accelerating at a rate of 240 feet per second.

It was necessary to calculate and correct for every possible known time factor to the finest microsecond and to include such items as time for radar signals to return from the spacecraft, transmission times on telephone lines to the computers a thousand miles away, time spent in the computers, and transmission time back to the Cape and to the spacecraft. It was also necessary to take into account time delays in the spacecraft and booster for relays, valves, and mechanical equipment to operate, a figure for the last boost of thrust from the engines as they "tail-off" after shutdown, and another figure for the thrust of the small, posigrade rockets that give the spacecraft a gentle separation push away from the booster.

To do all this and still come out with an

FOCUS GLENN

"Space... exacts a high price for... shoddy workmanship or inferior equipment."

actual speed within a couple of feet per second, while accelerating at 240 feet per second, 350 miles downrange from the Cape, is an accuracy hard to comprehend.

That is launch.

For return to earth, every second of error in the firing of the retrorockets means a five-mile difference in where the spacecraft touches down on earth. It's not hard to see why space pilots should be free of sniffles and sneezes, for if we calculate a sneeze as taking two seconds from beginning to end, a good sneeze at the wrong time could alter your touchdown point by 10 miles. You can't afford any 10-mile sneezes.

Such fine tolerances and highly precise calculations by both man and machine will be vastly increased in the Gemini and Apollo projects and subsequent programs.

THE PRECISION and accuracy required pinpoint the difficulty in adhering to a strict schedule. The overriding issue in all our manned space efforts is the safety of the crew. In any operation as inherently dangerous as this, we don't take chances if tests show an area to be doubtful. Instead, we redesign and retest. To me, one of the amazing parts of the manned space program has been not that some schedules have slipped, but that target dates have been hit as closely as they have.

During 1964, we not only increased our precision and accuracy, but also learned— with the launch of 37,700 orbital pounds, or approximately 20,000 payload pounds, by the new Saturn I rocket—to put the needed muscle in our long range space program. This is the greatest single load boosted into space yet, either here or in Russia.

So the year in space ended on yet another threshold with paths beyond that defied prediction. But a toll was exacted with a major tragedy—the loss of Captain Theodore Freeman. Ted became the first training astronaut to lose his life, and it is ironic that Ted's loss occurred not in proving the fine points of space exploration to which he was so dedicated, but in an aircraft accident on a routine training flight. Had he lived, I am sure he would have marveled with the rest of us at the steadily unfolding explorations in space.

For we are only at the beginning.

In the past, we have been limited to what we could do on earth. We could only look up at the sky and wonder. We are fortunate that our lifetime happens to fall at a period in history when we can do much more than simply wonder.

Related Articles

For a complete report on the 1964 year in space see Section Two, THE UNFOLDING UNIVERSE. See also the following articles in Section Three:

"... the year in space ended... with paths beyond that defied description."

IN THE 1920's, the generation now in its 60's stood indicted by its elders. It was accused of violating the moral code, destroying family life, defying the Noble Experiment with a hip flask, and leading the civilized world into decadence and damnation to the wailing of the saxophone and the shameless gyrations of the Charleston. Noel Coward, whose immense popularity was due to his ability to set the fashions he was deploring, wrote a kind of litany for his generation:

Dance, dance, dance, little lady,
Life is fleeting
To the rhythm beating
In your mind.
Dance, dance, dance, little lady,
So obsessed
With second best, no rest
You'll ever find.
Time and time and trouble
Will never, never wait.
Let the cauldron bubble,
Justify your fate —so
Dance, dance, dance, little lady
Dance, dance, dance, little lady
Leave tomorrow behind.

These people, now in their mid-60's or beyond, have, I suppose, produced their quota of drug addicts and pleasure hounds. But a large number of them, it seems to me, wrote remarkable books, painted memorable pictures, and composed most of our charming songs. Others turned into able statesmen, fine architects, law-abiding citizens, devoted parents, and only recently provoked the surprised admiration of their grandchildren by teaching them how to do the Charleston.

The irresistible inference is to say that old people always bemoan the morals and manners of the young and are always wrong. The fact that is often overlooked is that sometimes the old people have been right. An old Roman codger, lamenting in the fourth century A.D. that the empire was going to rack and ruin, was absolutely correct. A Greek doctor who, in the first century A.D. feared that his trade was in serious decline, was never pessimistic enough to guess that for a thousand years or more medicine would flounder in a dark age of quackery and superstition before it again enlisted the scientific insight of Hippocrates. An English theatergoer, though complaining, in 1630 or thereabouts, that the best trage-

Are We Sliding Into a Period of Moral Anarchy? In at Least Some of the Arts, Society Seems Incapable of Establishing Standards Adequate to its Own Protection.

50

FOCUS ON THE ARTS

dies had all been written in his youth, would hardly have guessed that no decent tragedies at all would appear in English for another 250 years.

Our national obsession with the doctrine that progress is inevitable disguises from us the truth that civilizations, too, have their ups and downs. Because we can "hang" glass buildings on a steel frame does not necessarily make us the superiors of John Nash, Andrea Palladio, or Louis Sullivan. The fact that we have seen in our time—from about 1910 on—the birth and glory of the great age of bacteriology is no guarantee that it is going to go on.

THESE GLOOMY REMINDERS are meant to preface a personal suspicion that we may now be sliding down a slope into a period of moral anarchy. I know it is un-fashionable, i.e., square, to say this. But in one or two branches of the arts at least, we have come to a moral dead end, in the sense that society no longer seems able to set up sensible laws for its own protection.

I am thinking about censorship and ob-scenity. In one of the 1964 state primaries, a candidate for a judgeship warned his con-stituents that, since the courts had allowed the publication of D. H. Lawrence's *Lady Chatterley's Lover*, they had "opened the flood-gates to every sort of obscenity."

Because this man spouted moral cliches, and was also a father of ten, he was gen-erally regarded as a figure of fun. He lost. But I think what he said was right. The D. H. Lawrence, Henry Miller and *Fanny Hill* decisions were essentially the same in Great Britain and the United States. After them, the line between what is plausible literature and what is outright pornography has become so hard to draw that the courts have, for all practical intents and purposes,

"...only a few years after four-letter words required dots...you can print almost anything."

FOCUS COOKE

given up. Today, only a few years after four-letter words required dots between the first letters and the last, you can print almost anything.

Many a drugstore and most newsstands now display novels and girlie magazines that patently have no other intention than the blatant exploitation of pornography for profit. There is even a publishing house that goes beyond the commercial aim of any of the most notorious Paris presses in providing at least one thoroughly dirty book for every season of the year.

The old statute, devised sometime in the 1880's, spelled out the test by which the courts of the English-speaking world managed, until Lawrence and Miller, to separate a sincere literary intention from the flagrant manufacture of obscenity and pornography. It defined obscenity as "tending to corrupt the average citizen according to the standards of his time and place." It was satisfactory enough so long as judges and serious readers shared the same assumptions about what constituted "the standards of his time and place." Evidently now they do not. At any rate, the classic definition is now seen to be a very wayward guide in a revolutionary time.

The definition was first seriously challenged even in the moment when it was pretending to be successfully applied. That was in the famous ruling of Judge Woolsey which allowed James Joyce's *Ulysses* into the United States in 1931. The judge's memorable reason for thinking that Joyce was conforming to "the standards of his time and place" was to say that the lewd fantasies of one Dubliner during an 18-hour reverie were passable because "the milieu was Celtic, and the season was spring." This charming and highly sophisticated decision was upheld by the superior courts. But it seems to me (to coin a phrase) to have opened the floodgates. For it ignores, or disdains, the fact that the average Irish reader, like anyone else, could still be corrupted in the spring!

THIS IS NOT THE PLACE to say that books like *The One Hundred Dollar Misunderstanding* or *Candy* or *The Naked Lunch* are not literature. But it is the place to ask why they should be considered as such, and it is a good time for this generation to redefine "obscenity" and "pornography." It is a good time to ask if the courts have any right to protect the citizenry on moral grounds, to say how, where, and when private life ends, and public order begins.

It is possible that to some teen-age readers this all may sound very stuffy. But it has been the stuff of vital debate since Moses. Plato, Bacon, Voltaire, Milton, Gladstone, Jefferson, Karl Marx, Justice Holmes, and Norman Mailer, no less than Judge Woolsey and the man who lost in the state primary, have all wrestled with it as a question essential for any working society to answer. Even George Bernard Shaw, in his most rebellious days, warned young revolutionaries that it is a very dangerous thing to tear down one convention before you set up another to replace it.

Even when they ignore music, architecture, and ballet, these annual Focus reports

"...even knowledgeable collectors are as prone to fads as the rest of us..."

of mine always seem to take in painting. This may be because in recent years painting has been riffling through new fashions at a terrific rate. This could mean that painting in our day is immensely vital or quite rootless. Or it could mean that for the first time in the history of painting, the United States has taken the lead from Europe.

Anyway, the year 1964 seemed to toll the bell on the long popularity of abstract art. A fairly well-known abstractionist saw a painting that had sold only three or four years ago for $5,000 go for a mere $150. This does not prove that abstract art has been exposed or debunked. It does prove that even knowledgeable collectors are as prone to fads as the rest of us, and that the true judgment of a good painting is a will-o'-the-wisp that eludes almost everybody living at the time the painting is done.

THE PRE-RAPHAELITES, despised or ignored for the last three generations at least, are now back in Christie's in London and Parke Bernet's in New York. And Cecil Beaton alone, by his set designs for the film of *My Fair Lady*, revived a taste for William Morris wallpaper; of all things, among the rich and chic.

There is certainly a transatlantic rejection of abstract art as striking as the uncritical embrace of it a few years ago. Young painters therefore are being called on once more to show that they can draw.

From what is going on in New York, London, and Paris (also, I am told, in Prague) they appear to be responding in one of two ways. They react with furious petulance against the charge that they can't draw and proceed to draw, as exactly and

boringly as a photograph, all the objects that always have been thought to be, in their actual likeness, the essence of nonart: the shining can of tomatoes, a bathing suit advertisement, or a Shell Oil sign. This was the first reaction against abstractionism and has produced the movement which is known as Pop art.

The other response, perhaps only slightly less petulant, is to say, "Very well, then, we will not try to draw well. We will be cute and uninstructed." This has produced a modern variation on what we used to call Primitives: scrawny or dumpy two-dimensional figures against childlike landscapes. No perspective, no chiaroscuro. The French call this school *Les Naïfs*; in a word, the Granddaughter Moses school.

The very latest thing (a fad so late that by the time this report appears it may have faded) is Op, or optical, art. This carries the protest against the academicians still further. It implies that in our day, the day of the laser with its dramatic amplification of microwaves of light, painting has a duty to create or exploit optical illusions.

The U.S. Science Pavilion at the Seattle Fair had a whole street whose deceptive objects might well have inspired Op art. A sidewalk, whose adjoining buildings were tilted beyond a right angle, produced pains in the thighs and, sometimes, nausea from the feeling that you were walking uphill and down at the same time. The sidewalk, in fact, was completely flat. Two balloons, swinging back and forth like pendulums, were seen at close range to be stationary and in the same plane. They were simply inflating and deflating in turn. The Op artists, working mostly on flat surfaces (sometimes

"The Beatles seemed to have discovered...
the first universal form of folk song."

FOCUS COOKE

using collage and the rear projection of light), compose wavy lines of black and white, combinations and juxtapositions of color so abrupt that they deceive the optical sense. This movement is sufficiently serious, or, pretentious if you prefer, to have warranted showings at the Louvre in Paris, the Tate in London and the Museum of Modern Art in New York.

IN MUSIC—and I am thinking not only of "popular" music—the outstanding phenomenon of 1964 was the world-wide mania for the Beatles. It enjoyed the same intensity in Los Angeles as in Stockholm, in Berlin as in Sydney. The Beatles seemed to have discovered nothing less than the first universal form of folk song. Certainly, nothing else that had gone before—madrigals, the blues, gypsy songs, flamenco, Scottish ballads, or Japanese laments—had ever appealed to such a diverse audience of human beings.

Classical musical critics tended to dismiss the whole thing as a symptom of mass infantilism having little to do with music. But the august critic of the *London Times* noted that the Beatles' compositions were musically much more sophisticated than the tunes of Tin Pan Alley.

Harmonically, you would have had to go back to the improvised counterpoint of medieval choirs to find as complex a form totally accepted by a mass audience. The lyrics were something else again. In their joyful insistence on fidelity, wholesomeness, and the desire to be understood ("I hope you'll understand" was almost a signature line), there seemed to be a healthy, childlike reaction against the negativism, the casual violence, and the distortion or suppression of emotion that is all around us in fiction, painting, and avant-garde movies.

This is probably a very large claim indeed. It is written, however, after considerable talk with teen-age Beatles fans. At least the Beatles are a puzzling phenomenon, and they are worth more than the passing tribute of a sneer or a scream.

Both in America and Europe, the theater gave us several interesting variations on familiar talents. The Brechtian and post-Brecht schools of playwrights were still the far-out mode in London and Paris and New York and East and West Berlin. But to me, the most striking element of theatrical entertainment in the United States and Britain was the vogue for social and political satire, mostly by witty and embittered Negroes or by witty and irreverent Englishmen.

In the climate of McCarthyism, we used to lament that there was no political satire in the United States. Now it searches every closet for skeletons, and they rattle through every revue and nightclub in London, New York, and San Francisco. It began as a new broom, but now threatens to whisk away the baby with the refuse. Mort Sahl's first target was the Republicans. Jonathan Miller and Peter Cook, Peter Sellers, Dick Gregory, Lenny Bruce, and the casts of "That Was The Week That Was" have been winging and wounding all politicians of all countries, the integrationist as well as the segregationist, Parliament and Congress, marriage and adultery, liberalism, conservatism, communism, socialism, saints and

"There must surely be a limit to liberty in society, or soon there will be no society..."

sexpots, the Africans and the Europeans, Christ on the Cross and invalids.

The best satire, for example, that of Voltaire, Pope, Restoration Comedy, the plays of Sheridan and Bernard Shaw, has always flourished in stable societies. This is on the principle, I suppose, that the follies and vices of men can best be castigated against a reliable background of all good men and true. Today, the good men and true are equally the victims.

IT IS ALL VERY ROUSING, sometimes extremely funny, but I had better end where I began. There must surely be a limit to liberty in society, or soon there will be no society at all. I am troubled at the thought that the range of these clever, and originally salutary, young satirists is excessive. Starting out as a healthy rage against the pretensions and abuses of authority, it could encourage in its audiences an amused distrust for any system or authority at all.

I may be, and I hope I am, all wrong about this. But I should like to pass on to our readers the suggestion that the price of wholesale satire may come dangerously high. It may produce a superficial and general contempt for the institutions that give us the freedom to laugh at them. Winston Churchill, remarking that it was a privilege to have Shaw ridiculing the war while it was on, belaboring democracy and lauding communism, did not fail to add that "under a communist government, he would be its first victim."

Related Articles

For a complete report on the 1964 year in the arts, see the following articles in Section Three:

MOST PHILOSOPHERS AGREE that if God had intended man to run, He would have given him four legs. Many centuries ago, however, some Greeks conceived the notion that foot-racing could be fun, this being before Aristotle pointed out the advantages of just sitting and thinking.

Their idea has never lost its popularity. Every fourth year, if no major war intervenes, the young of all nations gather in a designated place to run, leap, fling hardware about, and engage in other competitions crowding the calendar of the Olympic Games. It is always the biggest and most colorful sports show on earth.

For the first time since man learned to stand on his hind legs, the United States in 1964 had a runner considered capable of winning at 10,000 meters (about six and a quarter miles). We have never excelled at distance running because if an American kid wants to travel more than a city block, he asks Dad for the car.

Except for the 1904 games in St. Louis, which were not truly international in character, the only time an American won a gold medal at more than 3,000 meters was in 1908 in London when Italy's Dorando Pietri, leading the marathon after more than 26 miles, collapsed and was dragged across the finish line by excited countrymen. Dorando was disqualified, moving Johnny Hayes of the United States up from second place, and in Tin Pan Alley a young composer dashed off a song, "Dorando, He'sa Gooda for Not'," and signed it Irving Berlin.

In 1964, though, an undersized 18-year-old named Gerry Lindgren of Spokane, Wash., ran so well in the American tryouts that optimists ranked him among the world's best. Then a few days before the carnival opened in Tokyo, Lindgren was training on the grounds of a Shinto shrine,

Philippe Halsman for THE YEAR BOOK

RED SMITH FOCUS

stepped in a sacred gopher hole and sprained an ankle. Up like the smoke from the Olympic flame went America's hopes for a historic breakthrough.

NOW IT WAS getting on toward 5 P.M. on October 14, the first day of track and field competition. The misty sky was darkening over Meiji Stadium. Rain puddles stood on the brick-red track, and weary runners were staggering all over the course when a rangy lieutenant of the United States Marines came weaving through the traffic.

Billy Mills, a staunch Sioux brave out of South Dakota by way of Coffeyville, Kans., had been knocked halfway across the track and almost sent sprawling in a jam on the turn into the backstretch. Yet he recovered and creamed the finest distance runners in creation, the way his ancestors gave it to George Armstrong Custer at Little Big Horn.

Flabbergasted newspapermen sought out Ron Clarke of Australia, who was leading before Mills turned on the heat.

"In your planning for the race," they asked, "did you ever worry about Mills?"

"Worry about him?" Clarke said. "I never heard of him."

Neither had some members of the American press. Mills confessed that when sportswriters were swarming through Olympic Village seeking interviews, not one said hello to him. Now 26, he'd been running since he took up roadwork as a kid boxer in Pine Ridge, S.Dak., and until this day he had never found a major race at any distance which he could win.

The following evening, with torches lighting the finish line of the Toda Rowing Course and parachute flares and a big, yellow tourist bureau moon overhead, the Vespers Rowing Club of Philadelphia clobbered the "unbeatable" Ratzeburg crew of Germany, 1960 champions, restoring American supremacy in the featured eight-oared race. Three days after that, Bob Schul, a skinny farmer from West Milton, Ohio, closed with a fine burst to win the 5,000-meter run, and the United States had an unprecedented double in the distance events.

This was the pattern—surprise piled on surprise with the American kids dominating the major competitions; swimming and men's track and field, as few nations ever have. The Yanks led the world in gold medals, though Russia picked up enough seconds and thirds to shade our delegates in total hardware accumulated.

Highlighted by the Glorious Spectacle of the Olympic Games, 1964 Was a Year Filled with Surprises in Sports; a Year in Which the Bizarre and Unexpected Were Normal.

ON SPORTS

Probably the American boys and girls in swimsuits made up the finest single team ever entered in international competition, and it was generally agreed that the Japanese topped all predecessors at organizing and staging the Orient's first Olympics. Two examples of the Japanese touch:

The Toda Rowing Course is a 2,000-meter ditch dug especially for the games, with a rather steep, concrete bank on one side. On the Saturday night before the games, there were complaints that backwash from waves bouncing off this wall handicapped the boats on that side. On Sunday, the embankment wore a mile and a quarter of burlap carpeting.

In Meiji Stadium, white tapes divided the 400-meter track into eight lanes. Several days before the opening, a doll in a kimono was observed carrying a paint bucket and a brush suitable for inscribing the Lord's Prayer on the head of a pin. She would take a short step, scrunch down, make a dab with the brush, take another step, scrunch down again. Investigation disclosed that she was painting the heads of nails which had been set a few inches apart all around the track to hold the tapes in place.

THE OLYMPICS held many surprises, and that figured. That was the pattern of all sports in 1964, a year when the unexpected was normal, and the bizarre commonplace.

It was a year that saw the heavyweight champion of the world relinquish his title sitting in his corner, saw the invincible New York Yankees forced to fight for their lives in a desperate pennant drive, saw a National League race so close that on the season's last day, four teams could have tied for the championship, saw the manager of the World Series winners quit his job to replace the man whose team had lost in seven games, saw the hugely profitable Yankees sold outright to television, saw the kings of professional football toppled unceremoniously, and saw resurgent Notre Dame come back after 10 lean years and go barreling along unbeaten at the top of the college football heap until the last quarter of the season's tenth and final game.

THE FIRST STRAW in the wind was an announcement that ringside seats for a heavyweight championship in Miami Beach could be had for $250 each. The price did not seem more ridiculous than the match, which paired Cassius Clay, a noisy composer of rhymes, with Sonny Liston, an ogre who couldn't even read poetry, let alone write it.

Both fighters wanted to quit, and one succeeded. At one point, Clay appeared to have been blinded by a medication which had gotten into his eyes. He screamed he couldn't continue, but his handlers plucked him off the stool and shoved him out toward midring where he astonished everybody by outboxing the champion.

Bewildered and demoralized, Liston surrendered between rounds, complaining of an injury to his left arm. A team of eight doctors discovered damage to the biceps. The new champion espoused the Black Muslim cause and changed his name to Muhammad Ali.

The old one went home to Denver and—

FOCUS SMITH

"...the Japanese topped all predecessors at ...staging the Orient's first Olympics."

perhaps having lost faith in his fists—got picked up for illegal possession of a firearm.

A rematch was scheduled for November in Boston, but just before that, Clay was operated on for a hernia that had attacked him while he watched television. Presumably he strained something by squirming when Matt Dillon was slow on the draw.

HOPING YOGI BERRA's great popularity would offset the extraordinary appeal of the Mets, the Yankees made Berra manager for 1964. But the world's worst baseball team still outdrew the world's best by half a million. What's more, after the Yankees won the American League pennant in a fierce fight but lost the World Series, Yogi got fired and joined the Mets.

Meanwhile, Gussie Busch, the beer baron whose St. Louis Cardinals had not won a pennant since 1946, fired his general manager, Bing Devine, and made up his mind to fire Johnny Keane, the field manager.

Before he could get around to telling Keane where to go, the Cardinals caught fire and won the pennant in a race so close that on the season's last day St. Louis, Cincinnati, Philadelphia, and San Francisco were within range of a first-place tie. After the Cardinals had whipped the Yankees in the World Series, Keane shrugged off Busch's offers and joined the defeated Yankees as Berra's successor. To Busch's further discomfiture, Bing Devine, the man he had fired as general manager, was chosen executive-of-the-year by acclamation.

The Yankees, who bent a suppliant knee and hired the man who had engineered their second straight World Series defeat, were not quite the same Yankees the fans used to regard with an affection ordinarily reserved for United States Steel. They had cast off their image of cool, pin-striped efficiency and, with their sale to the Columbia Broadcasting System, had become part of an entertainment package that also includes the "Beverly Hillbillies," "*My Fair Lady*," and "What's My Line?"

MOST BASEBALL FANS and two owners of American League clubs were aghast when Del Webb and Dan Topping sold the Yankees to the network for $14,000,000. Fans are seldom so naive as to be unaware that baseball is more business than sport. Still they were dashed to see the game treated as big business in league with even bigger business.

The deal was made in secrecy and approved in haste, over the loud protests of Arthur Allyn, of the Chicago White Sox, and Charles Finley, of Kansas City. They feared the connection with television might make baseball vulnerable to antitrust action. Eight clubs, however, cast their votes in favor of the sale, and a few weeks later all 20 teams took a step that could be even riskier. They followed the lead of professional football and adopted a draft of free agents—that is, high school, college, and sandlot players who were without any professional affiliation.

For years, authorities in Washington have looked askance at baseball's "reserve clause," which gives a ballplayer's employer absolute control of the boy's professional future from the moment he signs his first contract. There has been no federal legislation against this slave trade because of court decisions exempting baseball from antitrust laws.

"...the world's worst baseball team still outdrew the world's best by half a million."

Now the boy is to be deprived of the only free choice he had; the selection of his original employer. There has always been an open market on free agents, with as many as 20 teams competing for a boy's services and some offering bonuses up to and beyond $100,000. From now on, when a boy has been selected by, say, the Baltimore Orioles, no other club may approach him. His bargaining position is lost, his hopes for a big bonus shattered. He must sign with Baltimore, or open oysters for a living.

This reckless measure was adopted by the owners for the owners' financial benefit, to put a stop to extravagant payments. It will save money, and possibly cost baseball its privileged status.

WHILE ALL THIS WAS BREWING, college and professional fans were butting heads in football. Pro fans were startled when the National League's defending regional champions, the Chicago Bears and New York Giants, were mauled; and the Green Bay Packers, considered the best in the world, lost five games.

That surprise was small, however, compared to the sensation Notre Dame created by racing undefeated through its first nine games under Ara Parseghian, a new coach and the first nonalumnus to inherit the mantle of Knute Rockne. Seldom ranked among the national leaders during the last decade, Notre Dame topped all the polls from its sixth game to the tenth, when undistinguished Southern California came on in the final quarter to score the upset of the year, 20 to 17.

Southern Cal's victory gave Pacific Coast football prestige a mighty lift. The following week, the conference fathers showed their appreciation by choosing Oregon State, instead of USC, to play in the Rose Bowl. The year drew to a close with the whole of Southern California threatening to secede and re-enlist under the banner of Spain.

Related Articles

"This reckless measure was adopted by the owners for the owners' financial benefit."

CONTENTS OF SECTION TWO

THE UNFOLDING UNIVERSE

DISCOVERY OF MYSTERIOUS SOURCES OF ENERGY TRILLIONS OF TIMES GREATER THAN OUR SUN PROMISES MAN A NEW UNDERSTANDING OF HIS UNFOLDING UNIVERSE

BY MARK M. PERLBERG

Astronomer Maarten Schmidt closed the door to his living quarters on Palomar Mountain on a chill, late afternoon in January, 1964, and walked along a snow-covered path toward the great observatory dome that shelters the largest optical telescope in the world. The dome glinted coldly in the fading light. The sun was dropping into a line of clouds that had settled over the blunt peaks in the distance, and Dr. Schmidt

Illustration on pages 62-63
by Mervin Corning
for THE YEAR BOOK

was on his way to begin a historic night's work at the observatory.

Knocking the snow from his boots, he went into the building, greeted the night assistant, and walked into the darkroom. He selected several photographic plates, and then returned to the cold and darkening dome. It was cold because the dome's shutters, weighing 100,000 pounds each, and forming a vast doorway to the cosmos, had been rolled back by electric motors so the inside temperature would match that of the mountain air outside. This would prevent warping of the giant 200-inch mirror in the Hale telescope. A warped mirror would distort star images.

The men were dwarfed by the enormous instrument that had been designed to advance the study of cosmology, the branch of astronomy by which man endeavors to learn the physical laws to which the universe at large adheres. Held in its vast horseshoe bearing, the telescope was a crisscross of shadowy girders six stories high.

Moving in the dusky chamber, Dr. Schmidt entered an elevator that carried him up the side of the dome, as the telescope, with an almost imperceptible hum of motors, was swung to meet him. He stepped from the car into the observer's cage, settled himself in a metal seat where he would spend the night, and loaded a camera attached to the prime focus. With specially sensitive film, exposed over several hours, the camera could "see" and record objects more than 4,000,000 times fainter than any visible to the unaided eye. Consulting a chart, Dr. Schmidt located the region he wanted to photograph burning amid the silvery star fields in the constellation Auriga, the Charioteer. Then he telephoned his readiness to the night assistant seated at the control console below, his face faintly lighted by the glow of illumined dials. The assistant pushed a series of buttons, and the telescope, 1,000,000 pounds of glass and steel, turned almost soundlessly toward the points of early evening stars.

A STARTLING DISCOVERY

Two weeks after Dr. Schmidt came down from the mountain and completed measuring and comparing his latest plate with others he had taken since 1962, he announced that he had identified the fastest-moving, most distant body yet observed in the universe. It was one of some two-dozen quasi-stellar radio sources, a type of astronomical body unknown before 1960, and the most unusual ever discovered in the history of astronomy.

The quasi-stellars are inconclusively named because of the fact that scientists are not yet sure what they are. Dr. Schmidt's quasi-star, or quasar, designated only as 3C 147, was rushing toward the edge of the observable universe at the unbelievable speed of perhaps 76,000 miles a second. It was believed to have been observed at a distance of perhaps 7,000,000,000 light-years. Since a light-year, the distance light travels in a year at the rate of about 186,000 miles a second, is 6,000,000,000,000 miles, the astonishing 3C 147 was photographed at some 42,000,000,000,-000,000,000,000 miles out in space. Astronomers calculated that quasars, to be photographable at such distances, must be giving off 100 times as much energy as the 100,000,000,000 stars in our Milky Way.

Because of their unparalleled brilliance, their distance and velocity, quasars may well serve as beacons by which scientists will determine the

Mt. Palomar Observatory houses the largest optical telescope in the world, the 200-inch Hale instrument, partly visible through the dome's open shutters.

Mt. Wilson and
Palomar Observatories

size, extent, and depth of the universe. So reported Dr. Ira Bowen, long-time director of Mount Wilson and Mount Palomar observatories, after Maarten Schmidt's discovery. But first, astronomers must solve the puzzle of the quasars themselves. This means that they must determine how the quasars emit such fantastic amounts of energy. The solution will not come easily; it may involve recasting of some of the most basic laws of physics.

The discovery of the quasars by the radio telescope has added great excitement to the yeasting field of cosmology, which, surprisingly enough, was elevated to the status of a full-fledged science only in the past 40 years. Before that, except for certain exceptional practitioners, cosmology lay in the realm of speculative philosophy. Only 40 years ago, for example, most astronomers believed the Milky Way made up the entire universe.

Cosmology came of age, in fact, with the development of the great optical telescopes at Mount Wilson and Mount Palomar; the improvement of mathematical tools by men such as Albert Einstein, the prince of theoretical cosmologists; and the perfecting after World War II of the radio telescope, which can pierce through clouds of interstellar dust and gas that are opaque to optical telescopes. Before the decade is out, many cosmologists hope to determine which of three principal theories of the structure and evolution of the universe is the correct one if, of course, the nature of the quasar does not render all three theories obsolete.

What follows is the story of the development of cosmology, of how brilliantly inquisitive men and women, struggling to puzzle out the shape and extent of the universe, learned to map the Milky Way itself, and then set out to determine what, if anything, lay beyond our local system of stars. In the process, they answered or are still attempting to answer such tantalizing questions as these: Has the universe always been present? If not, what is its age? How deep is the universe? Is it crowded with astronomical objects, or is it mostly empty? What are its chief building blocks? Where are *we* located in the physical scheme of things? How much of the universe can we see?

TWO GREAT AIMS

The man who founded observational cosmology was Sir William Herschel, who emigrated to England from Hanover, Germany, in 1757, when he was 19. One of the greatest observational astronomers of all time, Herschel had a master passion: to discover the construction of the heavens. This involved essentially two great aims: to determine the size, shape, and extent of the universe, and to settle the question of whether the Milky Way filled all of space, or was simply one of an unknown number of separate "island universes."

The theory of a multitude of vast stellar systems, or island universes, had been announced on the basis of pure speculation by two men before Herschel. One was Thomas Wright, an English instrument maker. The other was the great German philosopher Immanuel Kant. Wright published his theory in 1750, five years before Kant. Both men based their speculations on a number of luminous objects called nebulae because of their misty appearance to the naked eye. Both assumed that the nebulae would resolve into myriads of stars like the Milky Way if telescopes suffi-

WILLIAM HERSCHEL
Portraits by Michael Lowenbein
for THE YEAR BOOK

65

ciently powerful could be constructed for viewing the deeps of space.

Like his father before him, the young Herschel was a musician. He left Hanover to escape the devastation and suffering of the Seven Years' War. In England, he made rapid progress in his profession, until, in 1766, he was appointed organist of the Octagon Chapel at Bath. There, he composed and conducted, and tutored up to 35 pupils a week.

Sometime after his arrival in England, Herschel read a treatise on the works of Isaac Newton, discoverer of the law of gravity. He became intensely interested in astronomy, and, in the spring of 1774, after some 200 attempts, succeeded in constructing a fine astronomical telescope. Seven years later, Herschel announced a discovery that shot him to fame. He had discovered a new planet—the first since prehistoric times. The new planet was given the name "Uranus." Its discovery so impressed King George III that he appointed the busy amateur to the post of Astronomer Royal and awarded him a pension for life.

The discovery of Uranus doubled the extent of the solar system, for it was determined that the planet was twice as far from the sun as was Saturn, previously the most distant planet known.

Herschel was to make two other cardinal discoveries in cosmology in his lifetime. One was that the sun is in motion and is drifting with other nearby stars in the general direction of the constellation Hercules; the other, that double stars, or binaries, circle around each other in predictable orbits, much as the planets circle the sun. The first discovery, announced in 1802, put an end to Copernicus' idea of the sun as a stationary center of the solar system. But if this seemed to open the door to a universe of cosmic chaos, whose only constants seemed to be motion and change, the second did the opposite. It proved that Newton's law of gravitation, which described how the planets move through the heavens, was valid out to the far more distant stars.

MAPPING THE HEAVENS

In attempting to measure the shape and extent of the stellar system, Herschel carried out five "sweeps" of the heavens, each one taking several years. He recorded the positions of the stars, and tried to measure their distances. Because he found the greatest number clustering in vast clouds in the direction of the constellation Sagittarius, the Archer, he reasoned that this must be the center of the Milky Way. He noted that the stars were thickest in the plane of the Galaxy, as the Milky Way is sometimes called, and that there were comparatively few near the poles of the system (see paintings on page 69). Hence, he concluded that the Milky Way, if viewed edge-on, would resemble a disk with the sun near the center.

To determine the Galaxy's dimensions, he assumed that all its stars were of equal brightness, although we now know that they differ in luminosity by as much as a billion times. Then using the inverse square law,

Mt. Wilson and Palomar Observatories

The Great Andromeda Galaxy photographed through the screen of stars of the Milky Way. The two adjacent patches of light are satellite galaxies. Because of its distance, the Andromeda spiral was seen by Herschel and others only as a cloudy blur. It is 2,200,000 light-years away.

which says that the brightness of a source of light diminishes in intensity according to its distance from the observer, he concluded that the diameter of the Milky Way was five times greater than its maximum thickness.

On the question of separate island universes, Herschel veered now one way, now the other. By 1802, he had cataloged 2,500 star clusters and nebulae, and for a time he believed that some of the nebulae were external galaxies. But as he discovered more and more nebulae, of a bewildering variety, and found vaster and vaster star fields in the Milky Way, and because he lacked an adequate distance scale to measure to the nebulae, he came to believe that they all were parts of the great skein of stars that spangles earth's sky at night.

In the 100 years after the death of Sir William Herschel in 1822, astronomy advanced in many areas. The spectroscope and the camera enabled astronomers to learn the chemical makeup of stars, their temperatures, and their relative motions in the line of sight; and, indirectly, their sizes, masses, and densities. These devices also enabled the pioneers of astrophysics to construct a theory describing the internal structure of the stars and to classify them according to type. The surface of the moon was mapped, the orbits of the planets neatly worked out, and an eighth planet, Neptune, was discovered in 1846. In America, great observatories, using instruments Herschel would have envied, were preparing to open up entire new chapters in cosmology.

But man's picture of the extent and content of the universe had changed little from the days of Herschel, or from about the time of George Washington through the days of World War I. This can be clearly seen in the prodigious labors of the next great observational cosmologist, a methodical Hollander named Jacobus Cornelius Kapteyn.

AN UNTIRING MAN

Using Herschel's star count method, but in a manner greatly refined by advances in astronomy, Kapteyn and a co-worker painstakingly measured the positions of about 400,000 stars in the Southern Hemisphere recorded on photographic plates. Unlike Herschel, Kapteyn made some allowance for differences in the true brightness of stars, and like Herschel, and all of the astronomers of his own time, he assumed that the space between them was transparent. He then estimated their distances by using the inverse square law. The picture of the Milky Way that emerged when this untiring man completed his labors in about 1920 was not essentially different from Herschel's model of the universe.

Kapteyn found the Milky Way to be a lens-shaped aggregation of stars 55,000 light-years in diameter and about 11,000 light-years thick. Like Herschel, he believed that the sun occupied a nearly central position, and that the Galaxy contained all of the objects in the sky. This, then, was the picture of the universe held by most astronomers and by the public at large through the mid-1920's.

But even while Kapteyn was completing his labors, a young American woman at work in Harvard College Observatory was providing astronomers with the first reliable yardstick for measuring distances in the universe. With her work as background, an American astronomer named

Herschel's Milky Way, left, was about 6,100 light-years across. *Kapteyn estimated the Milky Way*, center, at 55,000 light-years. *Shapley first believed the Galaxy*, right, was some 300,000 light-years in diameter.

Paintings of the Milky Way, based on modern scientific evidence, show how it might appear if we could survey the galaxy from a point far outside it in space. White arrows in renderings, below, show the relative position of the solar system. In the edge-on view, note the dark dust line, opaque to optical telescopes, along the central plane. The great object is now known to be 100,000 light-years in diameter.

Illustrations by Antonio Petrocelli for THE YEAR BOOK

NORTH GALACTIC POLE

SOUTH GALACTIC POLE

CENTRAL PLANE

Harlow Shapley went out to Mount Wilson, and there evolved the first reasonably accurate map of the Milky Way.

At Harvard, Miss Henrietta Leavitt had been studying photographs of two enormous groups of stars that lie like swarms of silvery bees in the sky south of the equator. They are called the Large and Small Magellanic Clouds, in honor of the Portuguese explorer who had written an elaborate description of them. Within the clouds, she had noted a number of stars that were behaving in a decidedly curious manner—their brightness rapidly increasing and then slowly dying down again in regular fashion. These peculiar stars, later named Cepheid variables because of their similarity to a pulsating star in the constellation Cepheus, went through their cycle as regularly as clocks—some in days, others in weeks and months.

After carefully studying the Cepheids, Miss Leavitt had an inspired notion. Could there be a relationship between the cycles of the Cepheid variables and their true brightness? She found that the brighter these stars became, the longer they took to complete their cycles. Miss Leavitt published her period-luminosity tables, showing this relationship, in 1912. The net effect of her discovery was that one could determine the true brightness of a Cepheid variable (such as the North Star) simply by clocking it to see how long it took to go through its cycle. Thus, the principle for eventually establishing an accurate distance scale finally had been made ready for the world's astronomers.

SHARPENING A FORMULA

Harlow Shapley, then a young Ph.D. from Princeton, began to work with Miss Leavitt's discovery, realizing that her yardstick could be used to measure distances in the universe more precisely. Shapley used the difference between the star's *true* brightness and its *apparent* brightness to produce a scale of distance.

Dr. Shapley spent a few years sharpening Miss Leavitt's formula, then applied it to the Milky Way. He found Cepheid variables in the great clusters in the direction of Sagittarius, above and below the plane of the Milky Way. Like Herschel, he pronounced this region as the center of the Galaxy. However, by using the new Cepheid scale to measure distances, he concluded that the Milky Way was some 30,000 light-years thick and more than five times the diameter of the Kapteyn universe—some 300,000 light-years in extent (see page 69). He also found that the sun was not in the center of the Galaxy at all. It was blazing away some 50,000 light-years distant from the center in one of the Galaxy's spiral arms. Thus mankind's passion to be in the center of something celestial received another heavy blow.

Most of the scientists of the period believed that Shapley's map of the Milky Way was a picture sketched by an extremist. They favored Kapteyn's model, and a controversy blew up noisily on the extent of the Milky Way. To give both camps a chance to air their views, the National Academy of Sciences held "The Great Debate on the Scale of the Universe" in Washington, D.C., in 1920. Shapley argued for his model of the universe, and Heber D. Curtis of Lick Observatory upheld the Kapteyn model.

In the next 25 years, an accurate picture of the Milky Way was rounded

HARLOW SHAPLEY

Two of the three main types of galaxies are NGC 147, above, and the Large Magellanic Cloud, right. The former is an elliptical galaxy; the latter is termed irregular. The spiral is the third major form (see page 66). NGC 147 is one of the companion galaxies of Andromeda. The Cloud, about 170,000 light-years distant, is a companion galaxy of our own Milky Way.

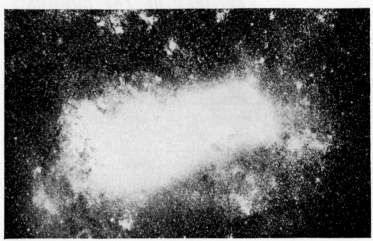

out. In 1930, R. J. Trumpler of Lick Observatory scaled down the great object by two-thirds by proving that the existence of interstellar dust and gas had interfered with Shapley's measurements. Earlier, in 1926, B. Lindblad of Stockholm Observatory provided evidence that the Milky Way—all 100,000,000,000 stars of it—was rotating. He did so by discovering that stars toward the center of the Galaxy were moving more rapidly and in a different direction than those farther out. Lindblad and, later, Jan Oort put the center of the Galaxy and the place of the sun in the same relative position as did Shapley, and this finally carried the day for Harlow Shapley's view of our sun's position in the Milky Way.

Today, the Milky Way is seen as a vast pinwheel, spinning in the unimaginable deeps of space. According to modern measurements, the Milky Way is about 100,000 light-years from end to end, and some 15,000 light-years thick at its center. Our sun is located about 30,000 light-years from the center. Discoveries in the past 15 years have proved that the center of the Milky Way is populated with cool, old stars, and radio telescopes show that the Galaxy is ejecting enormous volumes of hydrogen, while new stars are being born out of gas clouds in its whirling spiral arms.

Though the astronomers had finally accomplished the prodigious feat of mapping the Milky Way, the perplexing question remained as to what lay beyond. In the great Shapley-Curtis debate of 1920, Shapley had argued that the distant nebulae were a part of the Milky Way Galaxy. Curtis supported the theory of island universes. This question now resolved itself into finding the distances to the nebulae. If they proved to be far greater than the length and breadth of the Milky Way, then clearly the nebulae had to be outside our own Galaxy. The problem was immense because we glimpse everything in the universe through our own ocean of stars. It is difficult to know if a distant object is a drop in our starry ocean or lies in the space beyond. But a solution to the problem and a revolution in the way mankind looked at the universe was at hand. This began with the completion in 1918 of the 100-inch Hooker telescope at Mount Wilson.

EXPLORER OF THE COSMOS

The next year, there came to Mount Wilson a tweedy, pipe-smoking Rhodes Scholar named Edwin P. Hubble. Hubble, who was to turn out to be a sort of Christopher Columbus of the cosmos, was one of the first to use the new 100-inch. He trained the telescope on a nebula in the constellation Andromeda—and to man's eternal enlightenment, the milky blur partly resolved into a vast and beautiful spiral dense with stars (see photograph on page 66). Some of the stars were Cepheid variables and, because of the work already done with the distance scale, Hubble was able to estimate the distance to the spiral. It worked out to be in the neighborhood of 900,000 light-years—nine times the now established length of the Milky Way.

With this momentous discovery, announced in 1923, the debate on the nature of the nebulae came to an end. Shapley, who was partly vindicated on his concept of the Milky Way, lost out to Curtis' concept of island universes. The era of modern cosmology was born. For the Great Nebula in Andromeda, as the extraordinary object had long been called, proved not to be a nebula at all, but a galaxy similar in size and shape to the Milky Way itself. Subsequent revisions of the distance scale have shown that the Great Andromeda Galaxy, or M 31 as it is also known, is about 2,200,000 light-years away, or more than twice as far from the sun as Hubble thought it to be.

For several years, Hubble surveyed and classified the nebulae, and succeeded in proving more and more of them to be external galaxies. It was discovered that Andromeda, with the two smaller stellar systems that wheel in space near it, and the Large and Small Magellanic Clouds, were all galaxies thousands of light-years across and tens of thousands of light-years distant. Together with the Milky Way, they form a part of a cluster of about 20 galaxies now known to astronomers as the Local Group.

Since Hubble's death in 1953, it has been estimated that 75 per cent of the galaxies in the observable universe are spiral, 20 per cent elliptical, and 5 per cent irregular. Their shape is a clue to their age. Highly irregular forms, such as the Magellanic Clouds, are rich with hot, blue stars

EDWIN HUBBLE

and are the youngsters among these building blocks of the universe. The middle-aged specimens are the spirals similar to Andromeda.

How many galaxies are in the presently observable universe? Our enterprising cosmologists have estimated that the universe is populated by some tens of billions of these enormous bodies, each probably thousands of light-years in diameter, and separated from its neighbors by much greater reaches of space.

With the settling once and for all of the question of island universes, one would think that Edwin Hubble had added more than his share to mankind's store of knowledge. But in 1929, he announced the most startling news of all: the galaxies—those huge aggregations of stars, gas, and dust—were all rushing away from each other at barely imaginable speeds. In short, the universe was expanding.

How was Hubble able to determine that the galaxies were flying apart from each other? By special application of the spectroscope to astronomy. Earlier, in 1912, a lone pioneer by the name of V. M. Slipher, using the spectrograph at Lowell Observatory in Flagstaff, Ariz., made historic observations of the velocities of a handful of spiral galaxies by determining the degree of the shift in the lines of their spectra. But it remained for Hubble and his colleague, Milton Humason, working with the 100-inch telescope, to prove that all types of galaxies showed a phenomenon known as the Doppler Effect.

The Doppler Effect is one of the pillars of modern cosmology. It can be compared to the familiar fact that the pitch of a train whistle rises when the train is approaching and drops as the train goes away from an observer. This happens because more sound waves per second reach the observer as the train approaches. When the train has passed, fewer sound waves reach the observer in the same time interval, causing the pitch of the whistle to drop.

A similar effect occurs when light is given off by a body moving rapidly toward or away from an observer, as is the case with many stars. A spectroscope attached to a telescope breaks up the starlight into the hues of the spectrum, or rainbow. Each such band of color is crossed with a char-

Great masses of dust and gas between the stars, such as the nebula M 16 in the constellation Serpens, long interfered with the measurement of distance in deep space.

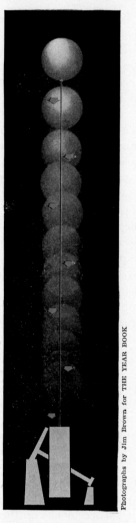
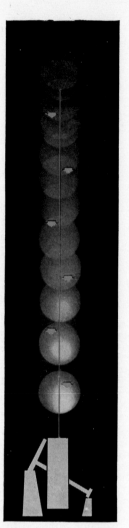

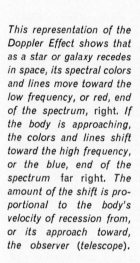

This representation of the Doppler Effect shows that as a star or galaxy recedes in space, its spectral colors and lines move toward the low frequency, or red, end of the spectrum, right. If the body is approaching, the colors and lines shift toward the high frequency, or the blue, end of the spectrum far right. The amount of the shift is proportional to the body's velocity of recession from, or its approach toward, the observer (telescope).

acteristic pattern of dark lines. If a hot, gaseous body, such as a star, is rapidly receding from earth, all its spectral colors and lines shift toward the red end of the spectrum. If the star is approaching, the colors and lines shift toward the blue end of the spectrum. The velocity of the recession or approach of the body is proportional to the degree of the shift of its spectral lines from their normal position.

By applying this relationship to the galaxies, Hubble and Humason found, for example, that the galaxy M 81 is dashing toward the edge of the observable universe at about 50 miles per second.

The result of all this labor was the discovery that the more distant galaxies appear to be receding from us faster than the nearby ones, and that this rate is proportional to their distance. This is known as Hubble's Law. It states that for every 1,000,000 light-years out in space, a galaxy recedes at an additional speed of 20 miles per second. The question now became: Where are the galaxies rushing off to? It was equal to the riddle of the Sphinx. But a young man named Albert Einstein, working on theoretical aspects of cosmology since about 1900, had arrived at some of the answers. By 1915, he had constructed a framework against which all subsequent thinking on the subject had to be related.

In 1905, while working as an examiner for the Swiss Patent Office, Einstein published a brief paper that eventually changed the way cosmologists viewed the universe. In it, he formulated what later came to be known as the Theory of Special Relativity. He was then 26 years old.

EINSTEIN'S QUEST

Einstein based much of his work on the results of a celebrated experiment performed by two American physicists, Albert Michelson and Edward Morley, concerning the velocity of light. Building on their work and that of others, Einstein evolved the equations stating that a body gains in mass as it approaches the speed of light, and that it shortens or compresses in the direction of its motion. Hence, if a body were to reach the speed of light, it would become infinitely massive as well as infinitely small—a logical impossibility. Thus, Einstein concluded that the speed of a body can never quite equal the speed of light.

Behind Einstein's quest for the solution of such seemingly impenetrable problems was doubtless his desire to find order in the universe. He once stated in another connection, "I cannot believe that God plays dice with the universe." It was certainly this objective that led him between 1915 and 1917 to formulate his theory of gravitation called General Relativity, which was an extension of Special Relativity.

According to Einstein's mathematics, a body (galaxy) could rush out forever at a speed constantly approaching that of light without ever attaining it, as an inch can be divided into smaller units without end. Further, it showed that the galaxies could continue in outward flight for an indefinite period; hence, the universe might be expanding forever.

Interestingly enough, Albert Einstein was so upset by his conclusions that he tampered with his own equations to keep the galaxies static. After all, nothing had been observed in nature to indicate that the universe might be expanding. Then along came Hubble—approximately 12 years later—with observational proof that the galaxies were in fact rushing apart. Applying Hubble's Law (if it does apply at very great distances in space), the expansion would have begun about 15,000,000,000 years ago.

Relativity deals with the largest and the smallest building blocks in the universe—the world of the atom and of the galaxies—because it is concerned with ultimate velocities and notions of mass, time, and space. The subatomic world has supplied nuclear physicists with proof of Einstein's notion that a body increases in mass as it approaches the speed of light. Special Relativity also provided the famous equation $E = mc^2$, which says that the amount of energy in any body (E) is equal to the mass (m) of the body multiplied by the velocity of light (c) squared. This is the equation that enabled scientists to determine the way in which stars generate their energy, which is the same reaction, but on a much larger scale, that occurs in a hydrogen bomb explosion. This knowledge enabled cosmologists to estimate the ages of the stars, and, hence, the probable lifetime of galaxies.

One of Einstein's starting points was his effort to determine why Newton's law of gravitation failed to account accurately for a very slight

ALBERT EINSTEIN

75

advance in the orbit of the planet closest to the sun, namely Mercury.

In his attempt to clear up this problem, and thereby arrive at as accurate a description of the natural world as possible, Einstein had an inspiration. He thought: Let us suppose that space is not simply nothingness, but an entity capable of being affected by massive objects within it, such as stars and galaxies. Further, let us suppose these massive bodies would act upon space in their general neighborhood, causing space to curve in a spherical fashion around them. Mercury would then follow the curvature the sun makes in space; starlight approaching the sun or any other vast object would be bent in the sun's neighborhood. Thus space could be conceived of as being dimpled with curvatures around massive celestial bodies. Further, the great mass of all bodies in the universe would cause the edge of space to curve.

Using the concepts of General Relativity, scientists now had a means of mapping the universe.

Three principal theories of the structure and destiny of the universe, each based on relativity, have thus far stood the test of time. They are called the Big Bang Theory, the Steady State Theory, and the Oscillating Universe. Within the decade, cosmologists hope that they will be able to choose between them.

THE BIG BANG THEORY

The Big Bang Theory was proposed in 1927 by a Belgian priest and mathematician, Abbé Georges Lemaître. The chief authors of the Steady

These 90-foot radio telescopes at Owens Valley, Calif., first located the source of enormous radio energy that was later identified as the quasar 3C 147 by astronomer Maarten Schmidt, working with Mount Palomar's 200-inch optical telescope (see pages 78–79).

State Theory, proposed in 1948, are the English cosmologists, Fred Hoyle, Thomas Gold, and Hermann Bondi.

Lemaître supposed that all the matter in the universe was condensed long ago into one enormous, superdense, superheated ball of pure energy. Physicists have since calculated that Lemaître's "primeval atom," because of its great density, would have reached only from the sun to the orbit of Mars. Almost immediately, the great ball of energy, because of its unstable nature, would have exploded with the biggest bang of all time, changing into vast clouds of matter that later condensed to form the outward rushing galaxies.

Unlike the Steady State Theory, the Big Bang Theory envisions a beginning and an end to the universe. It supposed that the density of the universe will lessen as the galaxies fly outward forever, although they would eventually fade, turning dark and cold in space.

Variants of the Big Bang Theory have been proposed, each one depending greatly on the density of matter in the universe. If the density is greater than is presently supposed, then the gravitational attraction of the galaxies would cause them to slow down and eventually draw together until they all collided again in another primeval atom. Then a second big bang would occur, and the whole process would start all over. The Oscillating Universe states that (if the density of matter is somewhat greater than a supposed critical point) the galaxies will eventually approach each other, but will bound outward again before they collide.

Just how crowded is the universe according to the present estimates? Despite the vast number of galaxies, it is empty indeed. Scientists have calculated that if all the galaxies that populate space (the estimate of average density of matter in the universe is 2 over 1 followed by 29 or 30 zeros per cubic inch) were turned into powder in some celestial grinding machine, and if the powder were sprinkled through the cosmos, it would form an invisible cloud with a density of about one hydrogen atom for every one to 10 cubic yards.

THE STEADY STATE THEORISTS

All relativistic theories of the universe are based on the axiom that the laws of physics, as we know them, hold true for any portion of the universe. Another assumption is that any large portion of the universe will be found to be much like any other. To the latter axiom, the Steady State theorists have added the notion that any portion of the universe would be found to be similar to any other *at all times*, in the past as well as the future. Hence, in their world model, the universe has no beginning and no end. It was always present, as their term implies, in a steady state.

But the Steady State theorists are faced with the fact that the galaxies are flying apart, which means that the density of the universe is thinning out steadily. To be consistent with their idea that the universe is the same in all its regions at all times, past, present, and future, the Steady State theorists require that galaxies be born to maintain a constant density. Thus, they propose that matter is continuously created out of nothing.

Critics of the Steady State Theory, ask, "How can matter be created from nothing?" Proponents reply that it would take a tiny amount of

Photograph on pages 78-79
Mt. Wilson and
Palomar Observatories

Arrow marks the quasar 3C 147, the
fastest-moving and most distant body yet
identified in the universe. The two objects
that appear to be close by 3C 147 are actually
Milky Way stars billions of light years nearer
to us than the amazing quasar.

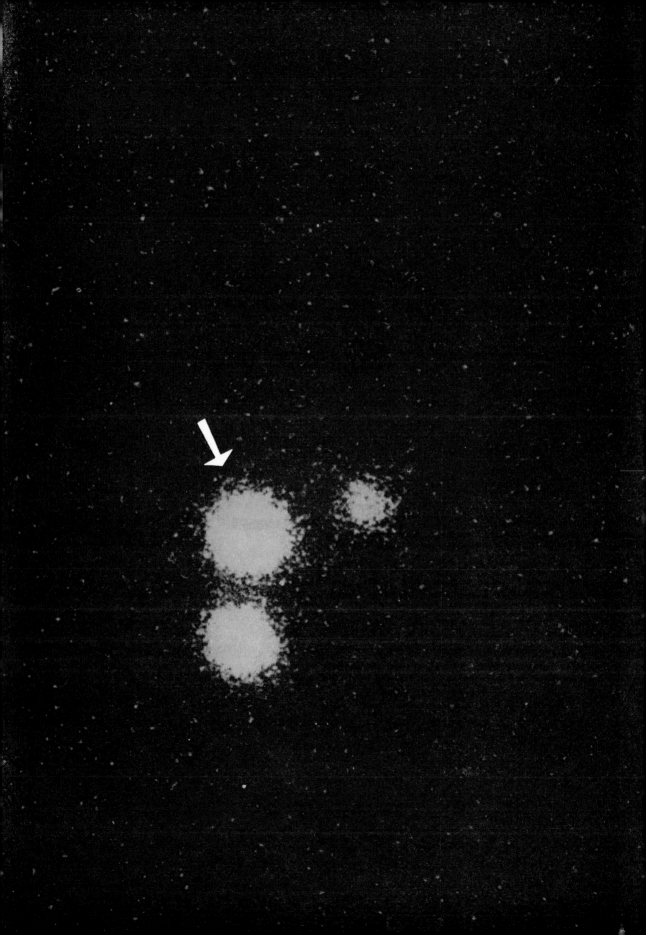

matter, too tiny to be detected by present means of measuring—about one atom of hydrogen in a volume of space the size of a living room once every few million years. "Besides," they retort, "where do you Big Bang people get your primeval atom?"

STRANGE RADIO SOURCES

Determining which of the theories is correct is keeping cosmologists busy trying to sharpen their density figure, and trying to discover if galaxies—at the present limit of observation—are a mixture of both young, and old, which would uphold the Steady State Theory. Such, essentially, was the state of cosmology until June of 1960, when Rudolph Minkowski of Mount Palomar discovered the then most distant radio source.

Minkowski's object, 3C 295, was first discovered by the radio telescope as a source of an enormous amount of radio energy. He locked the 200-inch onto the position given by the radio astronomers and worked hard to obtain a spectrogram. This has also been the procedure with the handful of quasars studied thus far: pinpointing by the radio telescope and then a search to photograph the object with the 200-inch telescope.

To the astonishment of astronomers around the world, Minkowski found an unprecedented amount of red shift—an amount that indicated that 3C 295 was somehow receding at a velocity of 67,000 miles per second, and was perhaps 5,000,000,000 light-years out in space. This made 3C 295 the most distant object ever found until Maarten Schmidt's identification of the quasar 3C 147 in January of 1964.

The importance of the quasars cannot be overestimated. Because of their brilliance, they have more than tripled the range of the 200-inch telescope, long believed to have been 2,000,000,000 light-years. More important is the fact that no known energy generation process explains their incredible output. So vital was the question of the quasars that the world's leading cosmologists met in Dallas in December, 1963, in an effort to arrive at some conclusions about their puzzling behavior.

A few cosmologists believed them to be the product of galaxies in collision. One thought they might be the result of some kind of chain reaction of exploding stars. Others theorized that their energy might be the result of the catastrophic collapse of a star with a mass perhaps 1,000,000,000 times that of the sun. Unfortunately for the latter theory, no such massive star has yet been discovered. Indeed, to explain the fantastic quasars, the laws of relativity themselves might have to be amended. Should this turn out to be the case, astronomy would be faced with a major revolution.

The progress of cosmology has been one of man's richest intellectual adventures. It is an adventure that embodies a deeply spiritual quest which cannot but make men humble and proud at once—humble because of the unimaginably vast scale of the universe; proud because of the very scope of the questions asked, and the knowledge already garnered.

See also Section One, Focus On Science; Section Three, Astronomy; and the 1964 Year Book, Section Two, *Our Target in the Sky*.

This article was prepared in consultation with Robert I. Johnson, director of the Adler Planetarium and Astronomical Museum, Chicago, Ill.

OUT OF THE SEA
THE LIFE STORY OF A CONTINENT

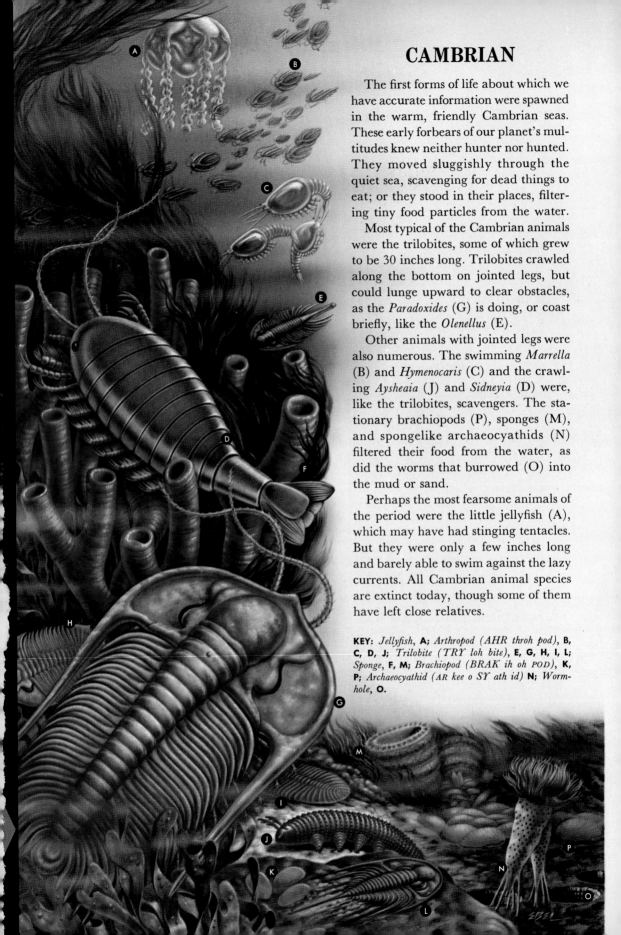

CAMBRIAN

The first forms of life about which we have accurate information were spawned in the warm, friendly Cambrian seas. These early forbears of our planet's multitudes knew neither hunter nor hunted. They moved sluggishly through the quiet sea, scavenging for dead things to eat; or they stood in their places, filtering tiny food particles from the water.

Most typical of the Cambrian animals were the trilobites, some of which grew to be 30 inches long. Trilobites crawled along the bottom on jointed legs, but could lunge upward to clear obstacles, as the *Paradoxides* (G) is doing, or coast briefly, like the *Olenellus* (E).

Other animals with jointed legs were also numerous. The swimming *Marrella* (B) and *Hymenocaris* (C) and the crawling *Aysheaia* (J) and *Sidneyia* (D) were, like the trilobites, scavengers. The stationary brachiopods (P), sponges (M), and spongelike archaeocyathids (N) filtered their food from the water, as did the worms that burrowed (O) into the mud or sand.

Perhaps the most fearsome animals of the period were the little jellyfish (A), which may have had stinging tentacles. But they were only a few inches long and barely able to swim against the lazy currents. All Cambrian animal species are extinct today, though some of them have left close relatives.

KEY: *Jellyfish*, **A**; *Arthropod (AHR throh pod)*, **B, C, D, J**; *Trilobite (TRY loh bite)* **E, G, H, I, L**; *Sponge*, **F, M**; *Brachiopod (BRAK ih oh POD)*, **K, P**; *Archaeocyathid (AR kee o SY ath id)* **N**; *Wormhole*, **O**.

THE GEOLOGIC TIME SCALE

The earth's crust is so old, so much has happened to it, and so much of the record is forever lost, that we cannot trace its history year by year. Nor, if we could do so, would anyone have the time either to write the story or to read it. We can, however, trace its history in broad strokes through the record left in its scarred and shifting rocks. Ever since its formation, the earth's rocky crust has risen and fallen in response to local stresses. Volcanoes, earthquakes, streams, and even the seas themselves have shaped and reshaped the earth's surface.

For a long time before the periods pictured in this Trans-Vision® , mountains rose and were worn away, though no living thing was there to see the changes. The marks of this early but complex history are found in the exposed hard core of the continent, known as the Pre-Cambrian, or Canadian, Shield. The shield covers much of central Canada. But a similar hard core is found at the heart of every continent. Overlapping the edges of the shield are younger rocks, formed beneath the waters of vanished seas. They lie layer on layer, to a thickness of thousands of feet.

When men first tried to date the rocks, they noted that some were hard and crushed, violently folded, and therefore probably very old. These they called "Primary" rocks. Lying upon them were sandstones, limestones, and shales, not so hard, much less folded, and thus clearly younger. These they called "Secondary." On top of these, in turn, were soft rocks, not folded at all, which they called "Tertiary." Further study showed, however, that a better guide to the earth's history is found in the fossils imbedded in the rocks.

Geologists then began to divide the history of the earth into periods, based upon what the fossils told. Each of the periods lasted for millions of years. Though the seas moved back and forth across the continents a number of times during each period, the land stood high at the end of each, the seas withdrew, and the record shows a natural break.

The names for these geological periods are taken from areas where the rocks show a clear historical record. Thus the name "Cambrian" comes from the Roman name for Wales, and the word "Devonian" comes from Devonshire, England, where that period was first identified in the local sandstone. Only two of the periods bear names taken from North America—one from the Mississippi Valley, the other from Pennsylvania.

Some rocks containing radioactive minerals as well as fossils can be dated with great precision. Since radioactive materials break down at a known rate, geochemists can measure the amount of the original mineral that still remains in the rock against the amount of the decay product, and thus learn how many millions of years old the rock is. That is how the years of the time scale on this page were determined.

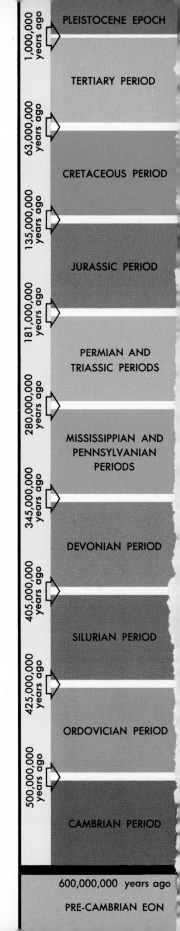

1,000,000 years ago	PLEISTOCENE EPOCH
	TERTIARY PERIOD
63,000,000 years ago	
	CRETACEOUS PERIOD
135,000,000 years ago	
	JURASSIC PERIOD
181,000,000 years ago	
	PERMIAN AND TRIASSIC PERIODS
280,000,000 years ago	
	MISSISSIPPIAN AND PENNSYLVANIAN PERIODS
345,000,000 years ago	
	DEVONIAN PERIOD
405,000,000 years ago	
	SILURIAN PERIOD
425,000,000 years ago	
	ORDOVICIAN PERIOD
500,000,000 years ago	
	CAMBRIAN PERIOD

600,000,000 years ago

PRE-CAMBRIAN EON

Robert Amft for THE YEAR BOOK

The life story of a continent is, necessarily, an autobiography. A continent tells its own story in the shape of its land and in the fossils of its past. Like living things, a continent is never entirely at rest. Its land masses emerge from the surrounding sea and then sink back, only to rise again. Over the ages, climate varies repeatedly: from hot to cold, from wet to dry, and back again.

Movements of the earth, such as earthquakes, we can observe directly. Other changes we can deduce from rocks. Shells of marine animals embedded in rocks thousands of feet up in the mountains tell of ancient uplifts of the earth's crust. Fossil coral reefs in the middle of the continent bear witness to vanished seas. Beds of coal and the fossils associated with them recall enormous swamps. In the following pages, we shall trace some of the variations of the ever-changing North American continent during the last 600,000,000 years.

During this great span of time, life itself became ever more widespread and complex. Beginning with simple plants and small animals that were confined to the seas, life everywhere adapted and readapted to the changes in its environment. Such has been the course of life on earth. After more than half a billion years, man, the most complex and adaptive of all living beings, took his place in the order of things.

Copyright ©1965 by Field Enterprises Educational Corporation.

All Rights Reserved.

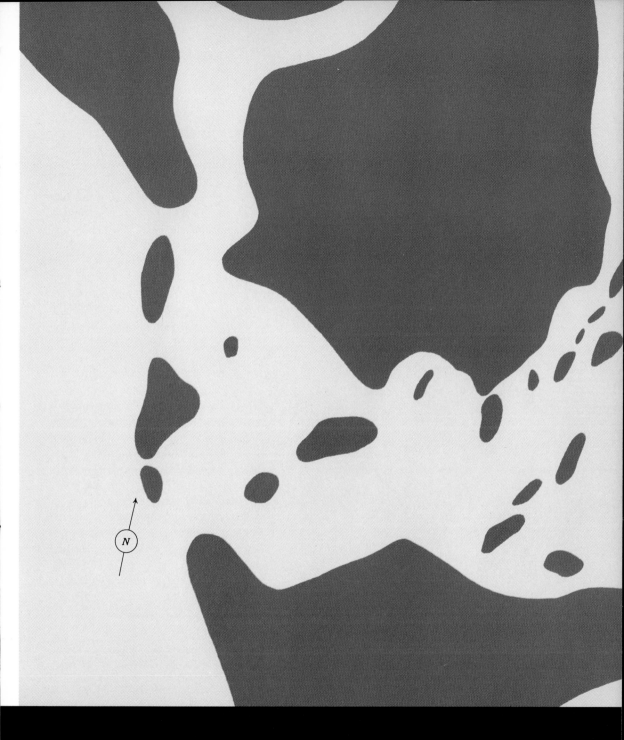

The upper part of this map shows a land mass including much of the Canadian Shield. This shield forms the core of North America and contains the oldest rocks found on the continent. During each geologic period, the seas swept across the edges of the shield. In these seas were deposited the fossil-bearing rocks which are the clues to the changing shape of the continent. The land areas of this map, and the ones that follow, indicate those parts of the continent that remained above water throughout the respective periods. It should be remembered that during the millions of years depicted here, the sea shifted its boundaries many times. As the Cambrian period began, the sea first flooded long, narrow troughs on the west and east coasts. Eventually it covered more than 30 per cent of the continent. Use the transparent overlay to compare the Cambrian land mass with present-day North America.

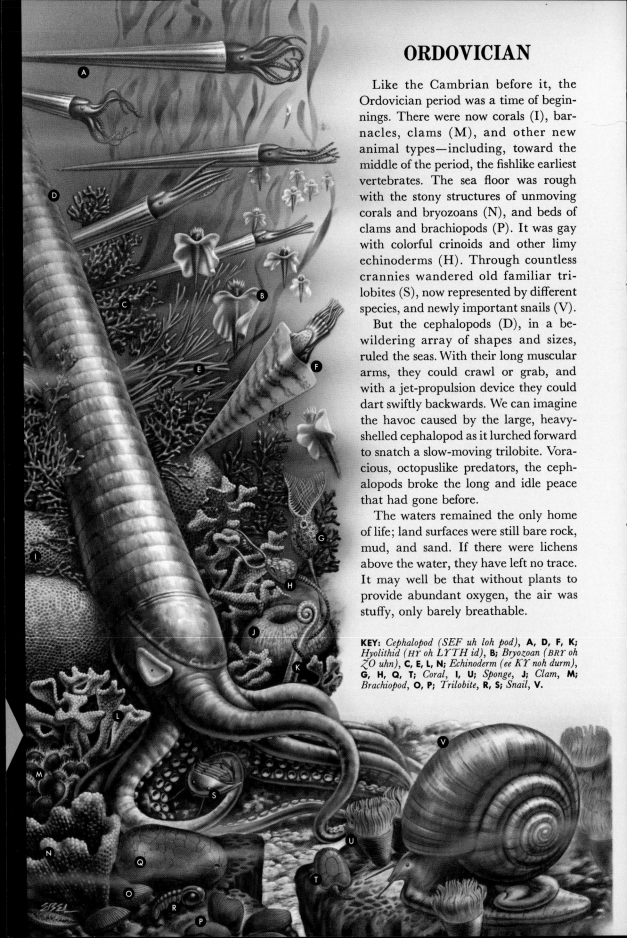

ORDOVICIAN

Like the Cambrian before it, the Ordovician period was a time of beginnings. There were now corals (I), barnacles, clams (M), and other new animal types—including, toward the middle of the period, the fishlike earliest vertebrates. The sea floor was rough with the stony structures of unmoving corals and bryozoans (N), and beds of clams and brachiopods (P). It was gay with colorful crinoids and other limy echinoderms (H). Through countless crannies wandered old familiar trilobites (S), now represented by different species, and newly important snails (V).

But the cephalopods (D), in a bewildering array of shapes and sizes, ruled the seas. With their long muscular arms, they could crawl or grab, and with a jet-propulsion device they could dart swiftly backwards. We can imagine the havoc caused by the large, heavy-shelled cephalopod as it lurched forward to snatch a slow-moving trilobite. Voracious, octopuslike predators, the cephalopods broke the long and idle peace that had gone before.

The waters remained the only home of life; land surfaces were still bare rock, mud, and sand. If there were lichens above the water, they have left no trace. It may well be that without plants to provide abundant oxygen, the air was stuffy, only barely breathable.

KEY: *Cephalopod* (*SEF uh loh pod*), **A, D, F, K;** *Hyolithid* (*HY oh LYTH id*), **B;** *Bryozoan* (*BRY oh ZO uhn*), **C, E, L, N;** *Echinoderm* (*ee KY noh durm*), **G, H, Q, T;** *Coral,* **I, U;** *Sponge,* **J;** *Clam,* **M;** *Brachiopod,* **O, P;** *Trilobite,* **R, S;** *Snail,* **V.**

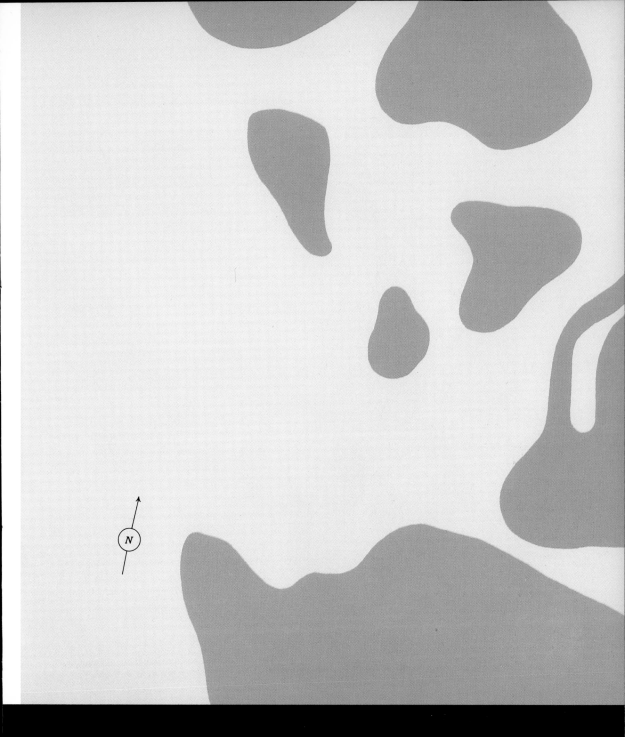

This is the time of the greatest submergence of our continent. North America, as the Ordovician period began, was a vast and featureless plain of unknown outline. Great patches of gray mud marked the position of the vanished Cambrian seas, only recently drained off. Now, new downwarpings of the earth's crust again brought shifting shallow seas onto the continent. By the end of the period, they had covered much of its present area. The existence of a land mass, known as Llanoria, in the Caribbean area is suggested by sedimentary rocks in Texas deposited by the erosion of a southern source. East of the old shield arose a new land mass, Atlantica. As it grew to mountainous height, streams carried mud and sand and gravel down its slopes to the Appalachian trough at its base. Volcanoes erupted from Newfoundland to Pennsylvania, and ash fell from Minnesota to Alabama.

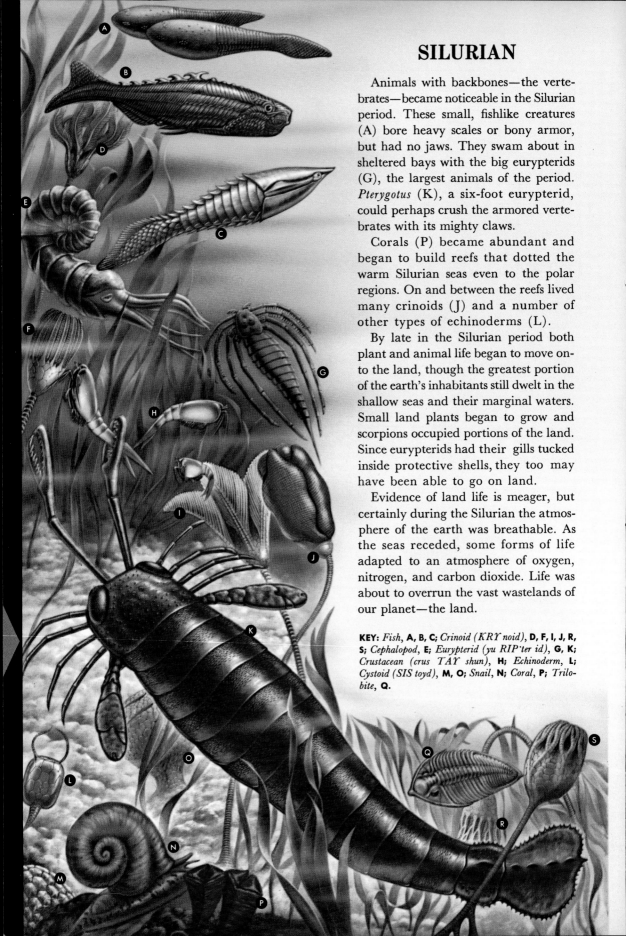

SILURIAN

Animals with backbones—the vertebrates—became noticeable in the Silurian period. These small, fishlike creatures (A) bore heavy scales or bony armor, but had no jaws. They swam about in sheltered bays with the big eurypterids (G), the largest animals of the period. *Pterygotus* (K), a six-foot eurypterid, could perhaps crush the armored vertebrates with its mighty claws.

Corals (P) became abundant and began to build reefs that dotted the warm Silurian seas even to the polar regions. On and between the reefs lived many crinoids (J) and a number of other types of echinoderms (L).

By late in the Silurian period both plant and animal life began to move onto the land, though the greatest portion of the earth's inhabitants still dwelt in the shallow seas and their marginal waters. Small land plants began to grow and scorpions occupied portions of the land. Since eurypterids had their gills tucked inside protective shells, they too may have been able to go on land.

Evidence of land life is meager, but certainly during the Silurian the atmosphere of the earth was breathable. As the seas receded, some forms of life adapted to an atmosphere of oxygen, nitrogen, and carbon dioxide. Life was about to overrun the vast wastelands of our planet—the land.

KEY: *Fish,* **A, B, C;** *Crinoid (KRY noid),* **D, F, I, J, R, S;** *Cephalopod,* **E;** *Eurypterid (yu RIP'ter id),* **G, K;** *Crustacean (crus TAY shun),* **H;** *Echinoderm,* **L;** *Cystoid (SIS toyd),* **M, O;** *Snail,* **N;** *Coral,* **P;** *Trilobite,* **Q.**

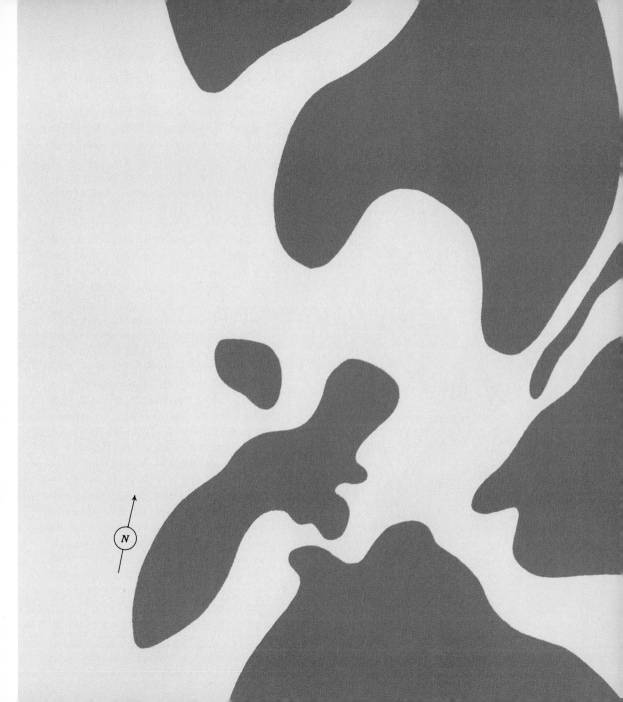

DEVONIAN

The first flourishing of both plant and animal life on land came in the Devonian period. During the span of this period, land plants developed from little ones only a yard tall (E) to great scale trees (A) and tree ferns (B) more than 40 feet tall. The spreading fronds of these ferns, some as much as nine feet long, created patches of forest in whose friendly, damp shelter small amphibians lurked. These were the first vertebrates to live on land. They caught and ate the earliest insects, which lived in swampy places and made the first short flights.

Amphibians, such as the late Devonian *Ichthyostega* (K), were the ancestors of all land-dwelling vertebrates of the years to come. They were themselves descendants of lobe-finned fishes, such as *Eusthenopteron* (L). Some of these fishes were able to breathe air and to hobble across the muddy flats from one stream or pond to another. Through the course of generations, they developed true lungs and their fins evolved into legs.

Far from land, corals (W) in enormous variety peppered the sea floors, some forming massive reefs and others solitary clumps of limestone. The largest of these corals, *Siphonophrentis* (T), was about two feet tall. Some of the trilobites, such as *Terataspis* (P), developed spiny shells, a useful protection from the cephalopods (V). Others grew large, one reaching a length of 29 inches.

KEY: *Plant,* **A, B, C, D, E, F, G, H, I, J;** *Amphibian,* **K;** *Lobe-finned Fish,* **L;** *Armored Fish,* **M, N;** *Coral,* **O, R, S, T, U, W, X, Y, Z;** *Trilobite,* **P, Q;** *Cephalopod,* **V.**

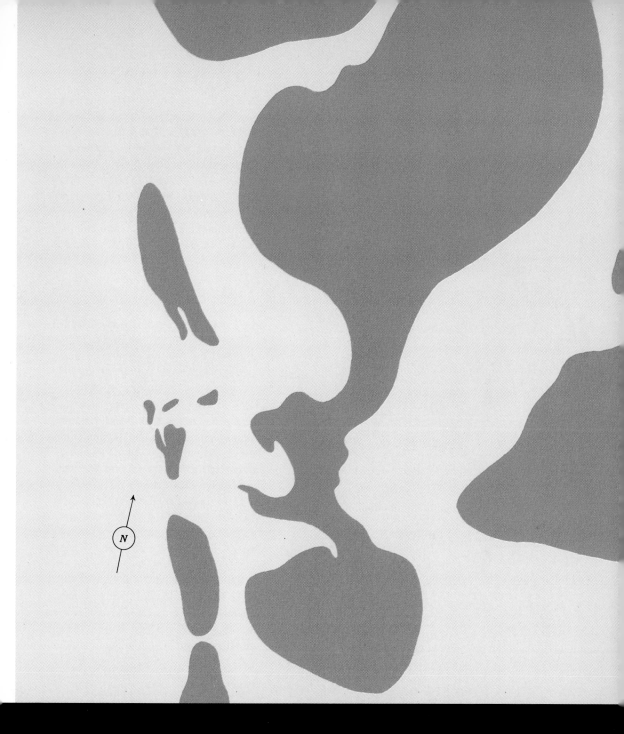

Two early Devonian seas advanced across low-lying country, one northeastward into Wyoming and Montana, the other in the Appalachian trough. Later, these narrow seaways expanded, the western one extending from Canada to Mexico and the Pacific, the other widening to include the Mississippi Valley. About the middle of the period, a mountain chain began to rise on the fringe of Atlantica. Deep beneath the rising mountains, crustal

rocks melted, some coming to the surface in volcanic eruptions, the rest solidifying as the granite now to be seen in New Brunswick, Nova Scotia, and New England. From newly built mountains, late Devonian deltas fanned out across New York, the Gaspé Peninsula, East Greenland and the Mackenzie delta country. The sediments carried from Atlantica into the Appalachian trough were equal in volume to the present Sierra Nevada range

MISSISSIPPIAN-PENNSYLVANIAN

Never before or since has the world known such forests. At their climax, in the Pennsylvanian period, they flourished in warm, swampy lowlands on all continents, including even Antarctica. Scale trees (A) and seal trees (G) grew rapidly to heights of 100 feet or more. Their trunks were covered with scars formed as their lower leaves died and dropped to the ground. Tree ferns (B) and giant horsetails (E) competed with the other plants for light.

In the shady depths of the forests, small plants (F) and mosses grew among the decaying trunks and leaves. It was the ideal home for amphibians (H), insects, and the first small reptiles. Cockroaches (I), as much as four inches long, crawled boldly about. Giant dragonflies (C) whirred through the forests on wings a foot long. It was the age of insects as well as the age of swamp forests.

So rapidly did trees grow, shed their leaves, and topple over, that the forest floors were continually covered with thick mattresses of plant material. Repeatedly, the inland sea advanced across the forests, burying this plant material under beds of mud and sand. In time, the vegetable debris was squeezed and wrung out to become coal.

The Mississippian and Pennsylvanian periods together are called the Carboniferous period, a word which means "coal-bearing."

KEY: *Scale Tree*, **A**; *Tree Fern*, **B**; *Dragonfly*, **C**; *Horsetail*, **D**, **E**; *Sphenophyllum (SFE no FILL um)* **F**; *Seal Tree*, **G**; *Amphibian*, **H**; *Cockroach*, **I**.

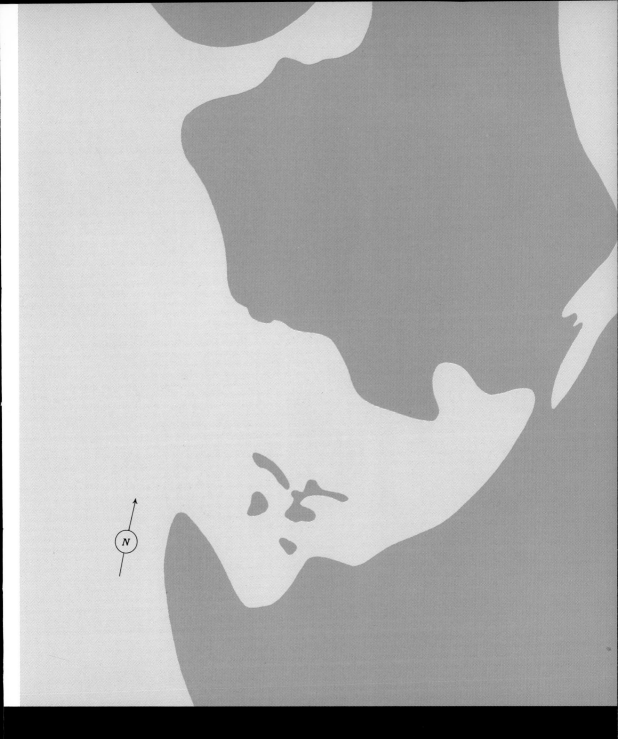

A Mississippian sea covered the western part of the continent and spread widely across the continental interior. The shield was low, and in the west the water was clear and limy. The limestone that now stands in cliffs in the Grand Canyon, the Yellowstone country, and the Mississippi Valley was formed at this time. Mountains in Atlantica and Llanoria contributed mud and sand to the eastern part of the sea. The mountains continued to rise, and by Pennsyl- vanian time were sending so much sediment across Pennsylvania and the Midwest that the sea was repeatedly choked full, and extensive swamps took its place. Deposits in those swamps now form great coal reserves. Mountainous islands arose in Colorado late in Mississippian time, and, somewhat later, other mountain chains near the Texas-Oklahoma border. The eroded stumps of these ranges now form the Wichita and Arbuckle Mountains.

PERMIAN-TRIASSIC

The age of reptiles now began. Large and strange ones inhabited the land in the Permian period. In the Triassic, appeared the dinosaurs, and some inconspicuous furry animals, the first mammals.

Dimetrodon (G), a Permian reptile, grew a sail on its back that may have been useful in catching heat from the sun. Both *Dimetrodon* and the Triassic *Cynognathus* (F), the "dog-jawed" reptile, had teeth in several sizes, as had the later mammals. Other reptiles, the pterosaurs, developed wings. And though the largest dinosaurs were to come later, the Triassic *Plateosaurus* (B) grew to be about 20 feet long.

In the sea, trilobites, horn corals, and other forms familiar from the past, quietly faded away. Permian amphibians grew to enormous size. One of these, *Eryops* (I), reached eight feet in length. Phytosaurs (D), resembling crocodiles, lived in Triassic ponds, as did the first turtles. These were reptiles that had returned to the watery home of their ancestors, the amphibians. Other Triassic reptiles, the ichthyosaurs, became so well adapted to the sea that their legs became finlike. Swimming plesiosaurs, with snakelike neck and tails, developed flippers.

The periods through the Permian are together called the Paleozoic era, "the time of ancient life." With the Triassic period, we enter the Mesozoic era, "the time of middle life."

KEY: *Cycad*, **A, C, E**; *Dinosaur*, **B**; *Reptile*, **D, F, G**; *Horsetail*, **H**; *Amphibian*, **I**.

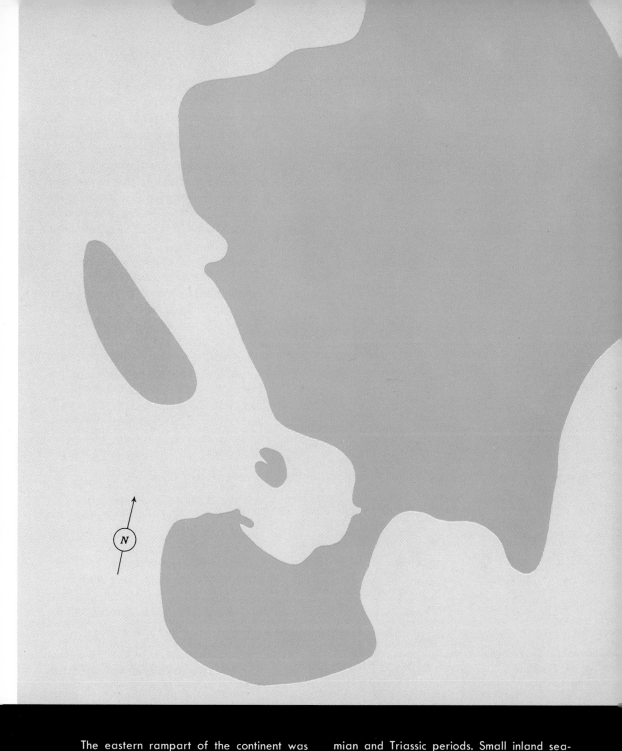

The eastern rampart of the continent was never again invaded by the sea. Sediments nine miles thick had accumulated in the Appalachian trough, where they had been deposited during millions of years by streams rising in Atlantica. Now the internal pressures of the earth squeezed this great mass of rock into long wrinkles, whose roots today are the Appalachian Mountains. Volcanoes from Alaska to Mexico spouted ash and lava during the Per-

mian and Triassic periods. Small inland seaways and arid lowlands occupied the West. A Permian marine basin in Texas and New Mexico was hemmed in by dry, hot country. As the water evaporated, salt deposits formed. Permian salt beds extend from Kansas to New Mexico. During the Triassic, rift valleys formed from Nova Scotia to the Carolinas as lava oozed from volcanic vents. Part of this lava composes the Palisades of the Hudson River

JURASSIC

The Jurassic period was the heyday of reptiles, great animals that overshadowed the tiny mammals and the earliest birds. Dinosaurs, some of them the largest land animals of all time, roamed the world. Marine reptiles, the ichthyosaurs, turtles, and plesiosaurs, cruised in the open seas, as did fishes similar to those we know today. Woods and forests contained cycads (F), ginkgoes, tree ferns (A), and conifers.

Archaeopteryx (E), or "ancient wing," was the earliest known bird, little changed from its reptile ancestors. Unlike later birds, it had clawed forefeet; a long, fleshy tail; and teeth. It was probably attacked by *Ornitholestes* (D), the "bird botherer," a small dinosaur. A curiously armored dinosaur, the 30-foot *Stegosaurus* (C), or "covered reptile," had only about two ounces of brain. It was a vegetarian. Another vegetarian was the 65-foot *Apatosaurus* (B). Dinosaurs of this type, known as brontosaurs, or "thunder reptiles," were so heavy that they spent most of their time in water to buoy up their weight.

The descendants of the reptiles, the birds and mammals, were warm-blooded. Their feathers and hair evolved from reptile scales. While the birds gradually lost their teeth, the mammals developed teeth of many shapes and milk glands. Throughout the Jurassic, the mammals remained tiny animals no bigger than rats.

KEY: *Tree Fern,* **A**; *Dinosaur,* **B, C, D**; *Bird,* **E**; *Cycad,* **F**.

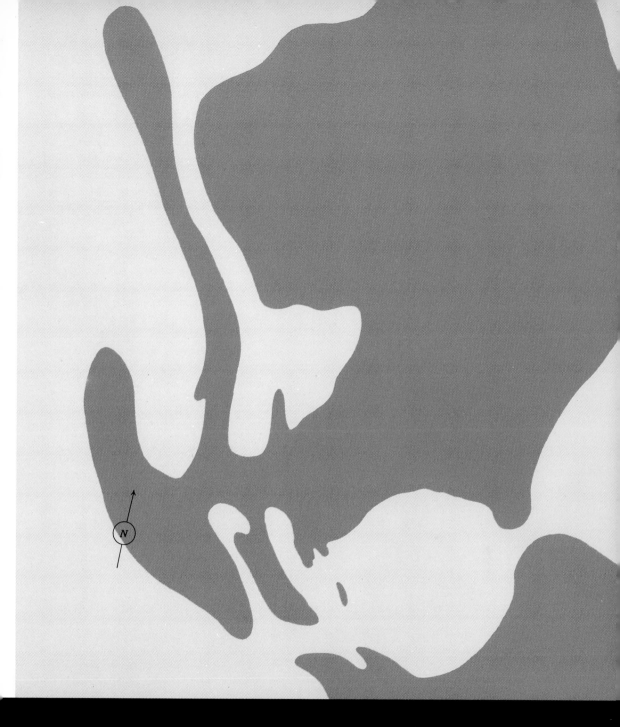

N

A sag in the earth's crust, stretching from the Arctic down into the western states, allowed a narrow sea to advance southward in Jurassic times. The sea was bordered on the west by a long, thin strip of mountains. These interrupted the moisture-bearing winds from the west and cast a rain shadow that turned the area from Idaho to New Mexico into a howling desert of big sand dunes. Some of these Jurassic sands can be seen today in the sandstone cliffs of Zion National Park. By late Jurassic time, the sea had gradually retreated, leaving a low plain on which dinosaurs roamed. In the East, the Appalachian region was high and probably rugged. On the Gulf Coast, under a small overlap of the sea, oil-bearing sediments were deposited, and thick beds of salt formed as coastal lagoons dried up. The Jurassic period closed with the uplift of many western mountain ranges, all subsequently to be worn away.

CRETACEOUS

The Cretaceous period marked the climax of the age of reptiles, and by its close all dinosaurs, pterosaurs, and great swimming reptiles had become extinct.

Tyrannosaurus (B), the "tyrant reptile," was a 50-foot carnivorous dinosaur that could kill any other animal of its time. It stalked on powerful hind legs, balancing its heavy body with a long, bulky tail. An easy prey for *Tyrannosaurus* was *Hadrosaurus* (C), a plant-eating dinosaur which had only one defense against the savage carnivore. It was able to escape into the water where it could swim or stay almost entirely submerged. Another plant-eating dinosaur, *Styracosaurus* (D), was fortunate in having a spiny frill of heavy bone to protect its neck and shoulders from an attack by *Tyrannosaurus*. In the air, the largest of the pterosaurs, or flying reptiles, *Pteranodon* (A), soared on wings that spanned 26 feet.

A few plants had developed a new kind of seed encased in a protective and nourishing coating. These were the flowering plants, or angiosperms, of which the *Magnolia* (E) is an ancient example.

New things were stirring. Birds were now plentiful, some of them large and specialized. And though mammals remained small and timid, in the next period they would predominate. The end of the Cretaceous not only brought the downfall of the dinosaur, but ended the "time of the middle life."

KEY: *Pterosaur (TAIR oh sore)* **A;** *Dinosaur,* **B, C, D;** *Flowering Plant,* **E.**

For the last time, extensive seas lay upon the heartland of North America. They filled a trough that cut the continent in two. The shield was low and stable. Erosion reduced the Appalachian Mountains to a plain. But from western Canada to Mexico, a long chain of mountains and volcanoes towered above the western shore of the 1,000-mile wide inland sea. As streams dug into them and carried them off as mud, sand, and gravel, they were continually raised and renewed. In time, a million cubic miles of rock were transferred to the East. As the period closed, these thick sediments were squeezed and uplifted, forming the Rocky Mountains. This was the greatest mountain building episode since Pre-Cambrian times. Deep within the earth's crust, granite and ores were formed as rocks melted. The period also marked the formation of important petroleum, coal, and chalk deposits.

TERTIARY

The Cenozoic era, the "time of modern life," was next. No sooner had the great reptiles vanished than mammals came forth from hiding. They were still small, shy, and stupid. Some, like the moles and shrews, remained so. Other mammal families gradually developed larger bodies and larger brains. At the same time, a new family of plants came into being—the grasses. They became the primary diet of such mammals as horses, which had been leaf-eaters.

The early terrier-sized horses scampered about on four-toed front feet and three-toed hind feet. During the Tertiary period, their descendants gradually grew larger and developed teeth shaped for munching on the tough grasses. By the middle of the period, horses had three toes on all feet and were about as big as ponies (F). They needed great speed, for they were often the prey of flesh-eaters (G), which were also growing larger.

Other plant-eating mammals included long-necked camels (C), primitive elephants (A), and distant relatives of the pigs, known as entelodonts (D), some of which stood six feet tall. One plant-eater, the giant rhinoceroslike uintathere (E), stood five feet tall and ate only tree leaves.

Some birds also grew to great size. *Diatryma* (H), a vicious flesh-eater from Wyoming, was seven feet tall and unable to fly.

KEY: *Pre-elephant,* **A**; *Sycamore,* **B**; *Pre-camel,* **C**; *Entelodont (en TELL o dont),* **D**; *Uintathere (yu IN ta THEER),* **E**; *Pre-horse,* **F**; *Carnivore,* **G**; *Bird,* **H**.

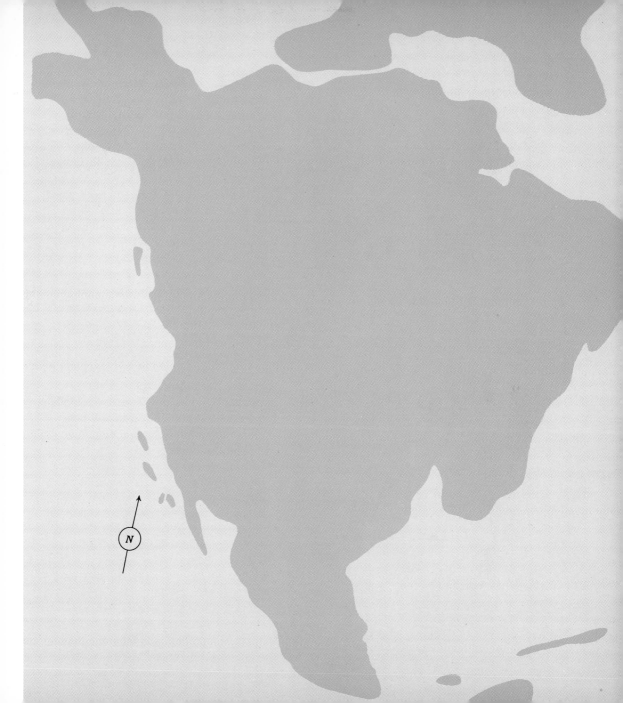

PLEISTOCENE

The many changes of climate in the Pleistocene epoch brought a series of calamitous ice ages separated by long periods of warmth. The rapid changes made for wide variation in the types of animals and plants that inhabited the continent. During cold times, musk-ox and other northern animals crowded as far south as Arkansas and Texas. Fir and spruce trees grew in Florida and beech-maple forests, typical of the North, grew in Louisiana. During the periods of warmth, ground sloths, horses, and antelopes from the temperate climates wandered north to Alaska, and paw-paw trees grew in Ontario. The Pleistocene vertebrates many times were forced to migrate by the rugged climatic changes, and nearly three quarters of those in North America failed to survive. Elephants, tapirs, camels, ground sloths, saber-tooth cats (C), and rhinoceroses vanished from this continent.

When ice sheets covered Canada, land connected Asia to Alaska, and woolly mammoths (A), bears, and other animals moved freely back and forth. Following this same route, man, late in the epoch, first set foot in North America. At that time, North America still had mastodons, giant bison, ground sloths, a few camels, and three species of horses, now all extinct. Man, the hunter (B), guided by intelligence beyond the powers of other mammals, and using tools, weapons, and fire, may have sped their extinction. Now it was the Age of Man.

KEY: *Mammoth,* **A;** *Man,* **B;** *Saber-tooth Cat,* **C.**

On this bedrock map of North America, the colors are keyed to the ones on the time scale on page 3. The pattern shows where rocks formed in each period would be found if we should strip off the cover of soil and cities and the deposits of streams and ice sheets. By the study of maps such as this, and the rocks themselves, geologists have been able to piece together the story outlined on the preceding pages. The color that isn't on the time scale represents rocks that are still unstudied. The ancient Pre-Cambrian, or Canadian, Shield, central bastion of North America, is the largest unit of the pattern. Smaller patches of the same tint show where the deepest rocks have been brought to the surface in times of mountain building. Surrounding the exposed shield are the younger sedimentary rocks, formed in the transient seas of former periods. Each tint shows a different period.

A LOOK AHEAD

Like a rippling awning seen in slow motion, the crust of North America moves and bends. We have followed its changing shape through 600,000,000 years of ceaseless activity. Can we believe that its form is now fixed for all time to come? No. We cannot ignore the rising mountains of the western seaboard, pressing themselves upon our minds with the great earth shocks of 1906 in California and 1964 in Alaska, plus countless lesser quakes. We cannot overlook the enormous burden of mud and sand carried seaward by every stream, nor the ceaseless gnawing of the ocean waves upon our shores. The surest lesson of the geologic past is its boding for the future: destruction of the old, creation of the new.

Never in the geologic record has North America stood so large and so high as it does today. Man, coming upon the scene as the continent attained its present contour, has made himself at home on most of its varied surface. Where he doesn't live, he visits. His cities pave the coasts and valleys, speckle the plains, and lap against the very mountains. Almost all of North America is home and comfort to the human race.

We live at the close of the glacial times. The chill of the fourth great ice advance has not yet left the land. In western mountains, remnants of Pleistocene glaciers still glisten in the warming sun, and central Greenland still lies encased in its armor of Pleistocene ice. But weather records of the last few decades show that the climate is rapidly growing warmer. No one can say whether this is a minor fluctuation of the climate or a signal of the end of the Pleistocene. Professor Carl O. Dunbar, in his book, *Historical Geology*, has summed up our present situation:

"Meanwhile the sword of Damocles hangs over us. If the ice sheets should again spread to the limits they occupied a few thousands of years ago, mass migrations would occur on a scale without precedent in the history of mankind, for the densely populated centers of Europe and the United States, to say nothing of all Canada, would slowly become uninhabitable. And, if, on the contrary, the climate should return to its geologic norm and the last of the ice sheets should disappear, the meltwater would raise sea level by 70 to 100 feet, slowly submerging all the great seaport cities of the world. In any event, the changes will come too slowly to concern any one now living, but they may profoundly shape the destiny of civilization within the next few thousands of years."

PRODUCED BY the editors of The World Book Year Book. *TEXT BY* Eugene S. Richardson, Jr., Curator of Fossil Invertebrates, Chicago Natural History Museum. *ART WORK BY* Arnold R. Chalfant, Alex Ebel, and Lowell Stumpf. *CRITICAL REVIEWERS:* Robert H. Denison, Curator of Fossil Fishes, Chicago Natural History Museum; Erling Dorf, Professor of Geology, Princeton University; Malcolm McKenna, Assistant Curator of Vertebrate Paleontology, American Museum of Natural History; Norman D. Newell, Curator of Fossil Invertebrates, American Museum of Natural History; and Rainer Zangerl, Chief Curator of Geology, Chicago Natural History Museum.

Printed in U.S.A. by the Trans-Vision® Division, Milprint Incorporated.

THE CHAPTER OF MAN UNFOLDS

Recent discoveries have caused anthropologists to reexamine long held theories about man's early development. On the following pages, the man who has made perhaps the most important of these discoveries, Dr. Louis Seymour Bazett Leakey, reviews these finds and gives his own views of their significance. Dr. Leakey has been carefully uncovering the rich history of early man in Africa for nearly 40 years. Born there in 1903, the son of early missionaries, he returned after studies at Cambridge University to explore the prehistory of East Africa. His unearthing of the 2,000,000-year-old fossils of *Homo habilis,* which he recounts here, has touched off a new round of theory and controversy (see Section Three, ANTHROPOLOGY). Some persons will question Dr. Leakey's interpretation of these finds, either on scientific or on religious grounds. The editors of THE YEAR BOOK present his article as a means of keeping its readers abreast of these fascinating developments in the world of science.

MAN'S BEGINNINGS

By L. S. B. Leakey

A World–Famous Anthropologist
Relates the Latest Findings in One of
the Fascinating Mysteries of Science

TANGANYIKA'S HIGH PLATEAU COUNTRY stretches west-ward from the foot of snow-capped Kilimanjaro across nearly 200 miles of the finest wildlife reserves in the world. Members of motorized safaris crisscross this great plateau to observe zebras, gazelles, buffaloes, and lions that still roam this remote African wilderness. In winter, the safaris are cloaked with dust. The plateau, called the Serengeti Plain, is yellowed with parching grass, and its water holes are mostly dry. But when summer comes, the rains turn the plain into a green carpet of undulating grassland and scattered thorn scrub. Water lies everywhere, running along the ground in many-fingered channels. Lakes fill to overflowing, and rivulets pour into the deep natural gash that slices across the southeast corner of the plateau. This gash is the Olduvai Gorge, where man—after almost 2,000,000 years—is coming face to face with his own beginnings.

The layers of Olduvai's steep walls have given up fossils that have forced science to discard previously accepted theories of the origin of man. Early man, these fossils tell us, made tools, hunted, and lived on the shores of a prehistoric Serengeti lake. He lived twice as many years ago as science had thought possible. And he was not a clumsy, apelike creature, but a person who, though smaller, somewhat resembled man of today. My wife, Mary, and I were the fortunate ones to whom Olduvai gave up its secret. After careful study we, with our colleagues, Phillip V. Tobias and John R. Napier, named him *Homo habilis*, which means "the man with ability."

THE DISCOVERY of *Homo habilis* culminates a dramatic five-year period in anthropology. During this time, scientists have ripped the existing textbooks to shreds. They have radically altered the once-simple picture of man's family tree and have created a grand, new plot for the greatest mystery story on earth: the origin of man.

To understand the true importance of this latest find, we need to look at earlier theories of the development of man held in the years after World War II. It was then popular to regard human development as having taken place through four successive stages. These were:

Stage 1—an apelike stage represented by fossil apes and gibbons found in many parts of the world. One group of these were to evolve into Stage 2, the other into modern apes.

Stage 2—a "near-man" stage represented by several fossil skulls and parts of skulls found in southern Africa by Raymond Dart, Robert Broom, and John Robinson.

Stage 3—a Java Man stage represented by a number of skulls found in Java and near Peking.

Stage 4—a modern stage represented by all living men, as well as Neanderthal Man.

This four-stage oversimplification is still to be found in most physical anthropology books. Few dared express contrary ideas, and, when they did, they were challenged to produce proof. This, of course, was impossible without further fossil discoveries. Some have now come out of Olduvai.

For more than 30 years, Mary and I had been drawn inexorably to the 300-foot-deep Olduvai Gorge. We patiently explored its steep walls, chipped into its stone face, and sifted its trash. Now and then, we fell upon a tiny, white spot in the rock and meticulously worked it free with

YEAR BOOK maps

The Olduvai Gorge forms part of the Great Rift Valley of Eastern Africa. It stretches for 25 miles across a wild plateau area that is called the Serengeti Plain. Once the area was a part of a lake.

Tanganyika's 300-foot-deep Olduvai Gorge is the place
where Dr. Leakey has discovered the fossils of many
prehistoric creatures, some he believes to be early man.

Dr. Leakey, right, and his wife, Mary, continue
their hunt for fossils on the site where they
found the bones of Homo habilis.

AFRICA

AREA
OF MAP

TANGANYIKA

OLDUVAI GORGE

SITE OF
FOSSIL
REMAINS

MT.
LOOLMALASIN
11,969'

MT.
LEMAGRUT
10,276'

Munge

NGORONGORO
CRATER

MT. OLDEANI
10,460'

Ngorongoro

Lake
Eyasi

Karatu

to Arusha

Miles 0 5 10

The ape Oreopithecus, which is now extinct, lived 10 to 16 million years ago. Its brain was comparable to that of a modern ape.

delicate camel's-hair brushes and dental picks. Through this tedious process, we attempted to learn whether Olduvai had given us just another bit of rubble, or a fossil clue to its long-guarded secret.

Olduvai's promise had been suspected since the early 1900's, when a German expedition uncovered some interesting fossil specimens there. These gave evidence that life roamed this part of the Serengeti Plain when Olduvai formed the edge of a great lake whose waters deposited silt and sand as they rose and fell. In time, many animal species were buried under the lake deposits and fossilized. Then, about 100,000 years ago, violent earthquakes reshaped the land. A resulting chasm, deepened and widened by erosion, was to become Olduvai Gorge.

Olduvai is a veritable museum of prehistoric life. But it has its drawbacks, too. Unwelcome animals stray into the gorge, forcing us to keep dogs with us at all times for protection. In our early years of digging, we had to limit our work season because of the lack of good water during the dry spell and of good roads in the rainy period. Four out of every five working hours were spent patiently and tediously searching for those likely bits of imbedded bone. Even so, each time we went to Olduvai we found enough interesting fossils to justify our return. Gradually, we improved the physical facilities of our camp. Today, assisted by the National Geographic Society Research Committee, we maintain a staff of one or two European assistants and about 40 Africans the year around. With their help, we have found evidence of large numbers of different types of extinct animals, and we have discovered the bones of several fossil men and pre-men.

Undoubtedly, one of the most exciting finds at Olduvai came on July 17, 1959. It was one that bore directly on the four-stage theory of man's evolution. I had remained in camp that day, bedridden with fever. Mary had gone to a promising site we first investigated in 1931 to search its slopes again. There she sighted a bit of skull. Even upon casual examination she knew that it most certainly resembled a piece of human bone. Excitedly, she searched higher up the slope, finally locating two dark, almost iridescent teeth just protruding from the hillside. Mary raced back to camp, and for the next few weeks we were both painstakingly digging out and collecting the almost 400 fragments that together formed the skull of a creature we named *Zinjanthropus*.

THE LONG FACE of *Zinjanthropus*, the brow ridges rising above the level of its backward-sloping forehead—these and other telltale signs established our find as that of a "near-man." But what made the find most remarkable was the fact that this "near-man" was surrounded by many primitive, stone tools and the bones of animals. These bones had been broken open to expose the marrow, a sure indication that someone, or something, had used these animals for food. This was the first time a "near-man" had been found amid such surroundings, although Wilfred Le Gros Clark and other scientists had already shown that the representatives of the "near-man" stage were more like human beings in skull structure than like apes. Here, we concluded, was a "near-man" who seemingly had the manlike capability of making tools with his own hands.

Thus, this discovery logically strengthened the four-stage theory.

After all, would not "near-man," coming between the stages of ape and Java Man, be perhaps starting to make tools? It seemed plausible, and, with a deep sense of elation, we accepted our find in this way. Little did we dream that a scant four years later we would look back on this day from the perspective of another even more revealing find and realize the error of our deduction. By misinterpreting the place of *Zinjanthropus*, we unwittingly were etching deeper the erroneous four-stage theory of man's evolution.

Since the discovery of *Zinjanthropus*, a great deal of other evidence has been found, both at Olduvai and elsewhere, and some of the early discoveries have for the first time been adequately studied. This has resulted in a complete re-evaluation of the stages of man's development. In my opinion, these discoveries have firmly established that man's birthplace was indeed in Africa, the continent Darwin aptly referred to as "the cradle of mankind." They have proved that man's family tree is nowhere nearly as simple as the four-stage theory suggests.

FIRST OF ALL, Stage 1, which was thought to have included two branches—one leading to the family of man and the other to modern apes—turned out to be far more complex. The first clue to this fact grew out of a controversy over an important fossil swamp ape named *Oreopithecus*. A nearly complete *Oreopithecus* skeleton had been found by Johannes Huertzler and his colleagues early in 1958 in the lignite coal beds of northern Italy. The creature was alive 10,000,000 to 16,000,000 years ago. *Oreopithecus* resembled the family of man in respect to some of its teeth, skull, and parts of its skeleton, but in other features it was closer to the apes. It had a stout body, stood about four feet high, and its face was short, unlike that of either the apes or any of the "near-men." The controversy centered on whether this creature should be treated within the stock of the family of man or the family of apes. So long as only two families were recognized, *Oreopithecus* had to be placed in one or the other. Actually, it belongs to neither, a conclusion that has now been generally accepted. It represents an additional family within Stage 1.

The apelike Proconsul lived 25,000,000 years ago, above, and Kenyapithecus, below, lived 14,000,000 years ago. Both were primates which existed long before man.

Once this was accepted for *Oreopithecus*, a similar conclusion was applied to the riddle of the gibbons. For many years, it had been widely agreed that gibbons, both living and fossil forms, were different from the other great apes. Studies of the chromosomes, blood, and general biochemistry of these mammals showed clearly that they were a distinct group. If scientists could accept three families within Stage 1, why not four?

Thus, many anthropologists today accept four distinct families of apes and apelike men within Stage 1. These are: (1) the apes, or to give them their scientific name, Pongidae; (2) the gibbons, or Hylobatidae; (3) the branch containing *Oreopithecus*, or Oreopithecidae; and (4) the branch leading to man, or Hominidae. All four branches may have come from a common source, probably more than 40,000,000 years ago.

The earliest fossil that seems to fit on the branch of man is a skull of a family of apelike creatures collectively named *Proconsul*. They lived at least 25,000,000 years ago. I discovered some fragments of a *Proconsul* jaw in 1931 on Rusinga Island in Lake Victoria. Then in October, 1948, working on the same island, Mary located a tooth that led to a nearly complete

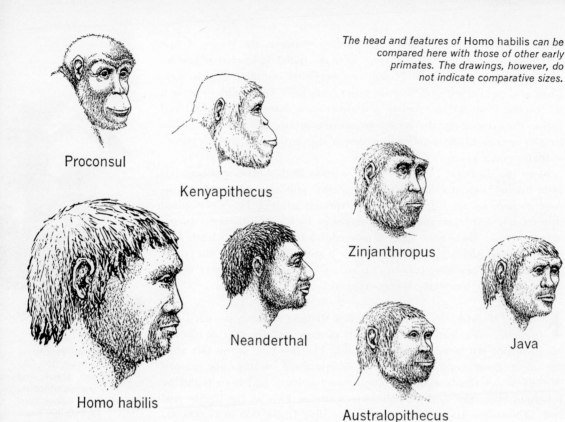

Proconsul

Kenyapithecus

Zinjanthropus

Neanderthal

Java

Homo habilis

Australopithecus

The head and features of Homo habilis can be compared here with those of other early primates. The drawings, however, do not indicate comparative sizes.

Margaret Estey for THE YEAR BOOK

Sketches of *Homo habilis* accompanying this article are the first attempts to reconstruct the creature Dr. Leakey believes to be the most primitive man. They were drawn by Margaret L. Estey, distinguished science illustrator, on the basis of the best available information. While approving the use of these sketches, Dr. Leakey points out that existing evidence of *Homo habilis* is not yet sufficient to establish detailed anatomical features. "We know *Homo habilis* was small in stature and slender in build," Dr. Leakey explains, "with rather massive shoulders, indicated by the collarbone, and strong fingers. We know his brain was a lot smaller than that of present-day man, probably only about half that of a European male today, i.e., relatively small, even for a body size of $4\frac{1}{2}$ feet. We suspect, from the jaw of *Homo habilis*, that his face was rather short, and do not yet know for certain what his forehead was like."

Proconsul skull. This we painstakingly removed from the surrounding rock, and Mary carried it, wrapped in a padded box, to London. This *Proconsul* skull of the species *africanus* was smaller than that of a chimpanzee, and it had a forehead and region above the eyes more like man than any ape.

Since most anthropologists expected soon to find a common ancestor of both man and the fossil apes, it was only logical that Le Gros Clark and I should treat some of the *Proconsuls* as the possible, or even probable, common ancestor. But other finds contemporary with *Proconsul*, made in the past five years, have upset this idea. Fossil apes, both large and small, have been found side by side with the remains of this creature. *Proconsul*, then, was living at the same time as the fossil apes, and so could not have been their ancestor. But because of this discovery, *Proconsul* became, more

Dr. Leakey Charts Man's Links to the Past

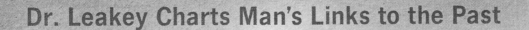

COMMON POOL

HOMINIDAE   HYLOBATIDAE   PONGIDAE   OREOPITHECIDAE
(gibbons)   (other apes)   (extinction)

*The line that leads to
modern man, as
suggested by Dr.
Leakey, is here charted
with a representative
skull for each major
stage of development.*

PROCONSUL

KENYAPITHECUS

ZINJANTHROPUS
(near-man)

(extinction)

HOMO HABILIS

(possibly)

(probably)

PITHECANTHROPUS
(Java Man)

NEANDERTHAL MAN

HOMO SAPIENS
(modern man)

(extinction)

**Time
in
Years**

25,000,000

14,000,000

5,000,000
4,000,000
2,000,000
1,750,000

1,000,000

500,000

70,000

Raymond Perlman
for THE YEAR BOOK

clearly than ever before, the probable "pool" from which man eventually developed. A common ancestor for both the apes and *Proconsul* will perhaps someday be found in the deposits and rock strata of a period at least 10,000,000 years earlier.

Another major discovery of the last five years was that of *Kenyapithecus wickeri*, a primate that may well have developed from the *Proconsul* stock. This 14,000,000-year-old fossil creature came from Fort Ternan in Kenya, and the first fragment of its jaw was found by my African assistant, Heslon Mukiri. The overlying rocks were carefully dated by University of California scientists using the potassium-argon process, a method somewhat like the radiocarbon dating process in determining age. *Kenyapithecus* is represented, so far, only by fragmentary material that consists of two pieces of the upper jaw with teeth, an isolated upper central incisor, and a lower second molar, all apparently belonging to a single individual. Since the material was so fragmentary, I did not, in my preliminary account of this discovery, consider the evidence sufficient to justify placing *Kenyapithecus* in the family of man, but suggested that this might prove to be the case in time.

Other scientists have been bolder, and several have published papers treating *Kenyapithecus*, from East Africa, and an equally old fossil, *Ramapithecus*, from the Siwalik hills in India, as the two earliest known true members of the family of man. (The latter apelike fossil, the first example of which was found by G. E. Lewis in 1935, is also represented by a second upper jaw specimen in the possession of the Indian Geological Survey.) Elwyn Simons of Yale has even gone so far as to suggest that *Kenyapithecus* and *Ramapithecus* are one and the same genus and merely Asian and African representatives of the same stock.

NOW WE HAVE SEEN that what was once thought to be Stage 1, the apelike stage, was in reality a series of steps, with many of the ape and gibbon fossils forming separate branches, not a part of man's family at all. The steps of man's family seem to rise from *Proconsul* to *Kenyapithecus* and *Ramapithecus*. Since Stage 1 has been so radically altered by the studies of the last five years, we can expect the same of Stage 2. And this is indeed exactly what has happened.

Stage 2 was thought to be the "near-man" stage, and to have included *Zinjanthropus*, the "near-man" we discovered surrounded by tools. Scientists call the near-men "Australopithecines." *Zinjanthropus* was similar to the others in physical appearance, but it differed from them in certain respects and was geologically older.

Zinjanthropus is particularly important because its discovery established the existence, 1,750,000 years ago, of "near-men," associated with tools of a well-developed Stone Age culture. The date has been carefully determined by the potassium-argon process, and is 1,000,000 years earlier than most anthropologists had expected toolmakers to have lived.

During 1964, we discovered a new lower jaw of the *Zinjanthropus* type northeast of Olduvai and to the west of Lake Natron. This lower jaw, dug out of a strata of more recent date, is of considerable importance since it indicates that the *Zinjanthropus* type of "near-man" continued to exist for a very long time.

Zinjanthropus lived 1,750,000 years ago, and it was once thought that the stone tools found with his bones were his handiwork. But Dr. Leakey now suggests that they were made by Homo habilis *and found only accidentally with Zinjanthropus.*

Does the association of fossil and tools mean that the "near-man" *Zinjanthropus* made and used the cutting tools of stone? We do not know. But it is a possibility, for it has been found that even some apes use tools. A study of chimpanzees, for example, in their natural Tanganyikan habitat, shows that they regularly make and use simple tools. The study was made by Miss Jane Goodall from 1962 to 1964. Their tools were not stone tools, but broken reeds, twigs, creepers, and sticks that could be used to fish for termites from their underground chambers. Simple as such tools may be, they are tools, and this suggests that *Zinjanthropus*, though not a true man, also could have made and used a variety of tools, since he was certainly closer to man physically than is a chimpanzee.

But there is one other possibility—the tools could have been made by a man living at the same time as *Zinjanthropus* and abandoned at the *Zinjanthropus* site. This suggestion would have seemed impossible before our amazing discovery of a true member of the genus *Homo*, that is a true man, in geological deposits of the same age as *Zinjanthropus* and even in deposits of an earlier date. The man we found was, of course, *Homo habilis*, which we are now ready to discuss.

Shortly after the initial discovery of *Zinjanthropus*, we made other new discoveries at Olduvai. These consisted of parts of a skull, a lower jaw, and a hand of a juvenile, as well as parts, including a foot, probably of an elderly female. At the time, the evidence was too fragmentary to make any claim about their relationship to man. I did note, however, that the child's skull was different in shape and had a larger brain capacity than

117

did the adult *Zinjanthropus* male, while its teeth, especially the premolars and the canines, were opposite in structure to those of any "near-man."

In the closing months of 1963, we discovered parts of still other individuals of the same physical type at Olduvai. After careful study of the fragments, my colleagues and I published the startling news that a previously unsuspected species of the genus *Homo* (the genus to which we all belong) had been found. It is our belief that he represents the earliest member of the branch that directly developed into modern man.

Homo habilis is characterized by some features that must be briefly mentioned. In particular, the shape of the occipital bone, or back of the head, is much more like that of present-day man than that of the "near-men" or even the Java Man types. Second, the greatest width of the brain case is located higher on the walls of the skull than it is in the other two types, a position it has in present-day man. Third, the contour of the internal arch of the lower jaw has a remarkably human appearance. And the teeth are unusual in that the premolars resemble those of certain present-day populations, and not those of the "near-men."

A NUMBER OF IMPORTANT FACTS arise out of the discovery of *Homo habilis*. In the first place, it is now established that two distinct manlike creatures, *Homo habilis* and the "near-man" *Zinjanthropus*, existed side by side over a very long period of time. The oldest known remains of *Homo habilis* are considerably older than the earliest known remains of *Zinjanthropus*, while the type as a whole straddles a period of perhaps a million years. Though both groups lived at the same time, they mainly occupied entirely different ecological niches, making use of different food sources, and seldom, if ever, seriously competing with each other.

A second fact arising from the discovery is that it shows us a form of very early true man who, although small-brained and rather large-toothed, was infinitely more like man of today in a number of important characteristics than like the later Java Man. This fact cuts away all the arguments for regarding the Java Man type as one of the stages leading to man of today, and suggests that the Java Man type should now be thought of as a side branch to the genus *Homo*, who left no descendants to the present day.

The third important point is that in *Homo habilis* we see the retention of a pattern of lower molars that is truly primitive and in many respects characteristic of the very ancient *Proconsul*. In particular, the first molar is the shortest, and the third molar is the longest, as was the case in *Proconsul* but is not the case with modern man. Today the normal situation is for the third molar to be the shortest and the second, or sometimes even the first molar, to be the longest.

By studying his teeth, we can tell a great deal also about the diet of *Homo habilis*. The *Homo habilis* molars in a young adult show hardly any signs of wear, and nowhere is the enamel removed to expose the dentine. In contrast, the molars of *Zinjanthropus*, who probably died at roughly the same age as the *Homo habilis* female, are very worn indeed. This difference in wear is probably due to a difference in diet.

When we look at the teeth of primitive types of present-day men, we find that differences in diet cause similar differences in tooth wear. The

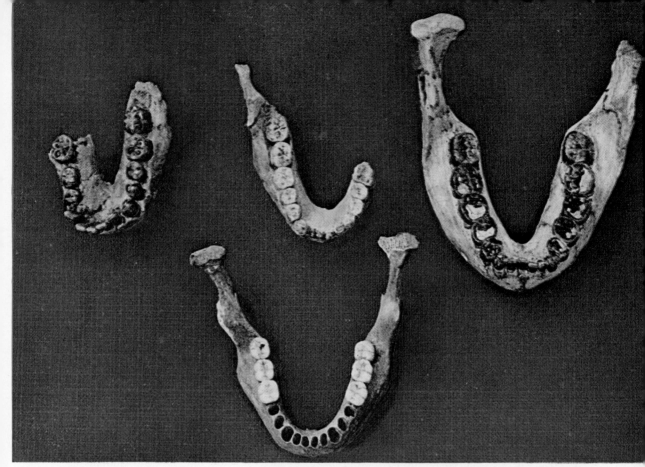

A comparison of jawbones shows that the two from Homo habilis, upper left, *are quite distinct from* Zinjanthropus, upper right, *and the jawbone of modern man in lower position.*

Homo habilis *skull piece on cast of* Zinjanthropus *skull shows a near match in brain case size.*

Composite skull from two finds of Zinjanthropus *shows that he had a long face and a low brow.*

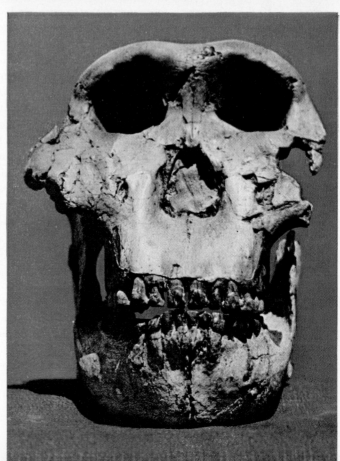

teeth become greatly worn at an early age among those tribes whose diet consists mainly of coarse vegetable foods, which they frequently eat raw because they have no cooking vessels, and which they seldom wash free of soil because water is scarce. Examples can be found both in southern Australia and among some of the bushmen of the Kalahari. On the other hand, tribes such as the Masai and Wanderobo of East Africa, who live almost entirely on a diet of meat, milk, honey, and a few soft fruits, have teeth that show little wear on their surfaces, even at middle age.

In other words, the difference in the wear on the crowns of the teeth shows that *Zinjanthropus* was probably mainly an eater of coarse vegetable foods, while *Homo habilis* was probably mainly a flesh-eater.

Even before early man learned to make good hunting weapons, he learned to produce tools that enabled him to cut skin and flesh from dead animals. This was something he could not do with his teeth and finger-nails, for these are wholly unsuited to tearing through the hide of large animals or for cutting away large joints of meat. Since *Homo habilis* exhibits little-worn teeth while *Zinjanthropus* has heavily worn ones, there is strong reason to suppose that it was *Homo habilis* who was the principal maker and user of the stonecutting tools that were found near the first skull of *Zinjanthropus*. The tools must have been used by a meat-eater to kill and cut up animals for food.

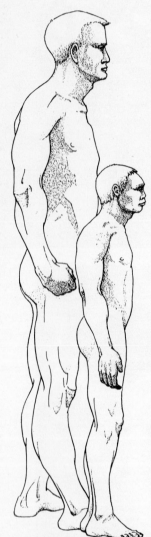

Full-grown Homo habilis *was much smaller than modern European man, as in drawing above.*

I T HAS BEEN MY PRACTICE for more than 35 years to fashion stone tools similar to the ones made by early man. I think that this is the only way Stone Age techniques can be fully appreciated, or even properly understood. I have, in fact, actually cut up dead animals as large as zebras with the stone tools I made. On one recent occasion, to the great surprise of onlookers, I skinned and disjointed a ram in less than 20 minutes with one of my stone choppers.

Returning to the physical features of *Homo habilis*, it is interesting to note that in addition to having a skull, teeth, and lower jaw that resembled those of modern man, he also had a foot structure very close to our own. His hand, however, was rather primitive and perhaps more muscular. This should not be surprising, since the hand would not begin to evolve to more manlike proportions until the foot had become completely capable of supporting the body for moving about in an upright position.

To explain, most primates use their hands and arms for support—monkeys hold onto tree branches to keep from falling, and many apes walk part of the time on their knuckles as well as on their feet. But as long as hands and arms are needed for support, hands cannot develop into good tool holders and manipulators. Thus erect posture is known to precede specialized hand development and erect posture can be sustained only on well-developed feet.

The discovery of *Homo habilis* has virtually wiped out the second stage of the old four-stage theory. The "near-men" now appear to form a side branch, rather than a direct part of man's lineage. For even the earliest "near-man," *Zinjanthropus*, has been found only in deposits of a later date than the first *Homo habilis*.

One last thing should be said of the "near-men" and the effect of the discovery of *Homo habilis* on them. In brain size, they were within only the 400 to 600 cubic centimeter range of the apes, but their bodies resembled ours in a large number of characteristics. *Zinjanthropus*, however, appeared more manlike than the others with respect to some features of the skull. Therefore, it was suggested at the time of the *Zinjanthropus* discovery, that this creature might represent a common ancestor for both man himself and the South African "near-men." The discovery of a true member of the genus *Homo* that includes man, living at an earlier time, has of course made this view untenable.

A recent discovery by the French paleontologist, Yves Coppens, near Lake Chad in Equatorial West Africa, may well represent another example of *Homo habilis*, although it was not so described when it was found. In his preliminary reports, Coppens described this specimen as an Australopithecine, or "near-man," although it differs greatly in appearance, and almost certainly represents something quite distinct. If it does not prove to be *Homo habilis*, it may represent yet another type of apelike creature of the Lower Pleistocene epoch.

I have suggested that, in addition to the side branch of *Zinjanthropus* and the main branch of *Homo habilis*, there may have been a third branch which led to certain African forms and to Peking and Java types in the Far East. If this is so, then the so-called third stage of our four-stage theory is eliminated in the same way as was the second. The evidence for this suggestion comes from the discovery of important fossil remains at Ternifine, Algeria, by Professor Camille Arambourg of Paris. Though he discovered them a number of years ago, it was only in 1964 that he published a full description of the material. He found them in geological deposits that were formed at a much later date than those of either *Homo habilis* or *Zinjanthropus*.

PROFESSOR ARAMBOURG has named his new fossils *Atlanthropus*, and has suggested that this new genus is closely allied to the Java and Peking types of men from the Far East. His specimens were found in direct association with large quantities of fossil animal remains and many stone tools made by the early men of a hand-ax culture known to anthropologists as Acheulean.

The *Atlanthropus* fossil material does not include any whole or even nearly complete skull, but there are three reasonably well-preserved lower jaws, as well as a number of teeth and some skull fragments. The resemblance between the Java fossils and the Ternifine remains is mainly in the jaws and teeth. But there is really too little evidence to make the categorical statement that they are the same type of creature.

Arambourg uses the supposed close relationship between his finds and those of the Far East to support the theory that modern man passed through a Java-Peking stage of development. He further supports his view with a discovery I made at Olduvai in 1962. This find was a piece of large, manlike skull with heavy brow ridges and other overall resemblances to the Peking and Java skull type. Arambourg believes that the Ternifine fossils, together with the skull from Olduvai, and the famous Mauer jaw (estimated to be about 360,000 years old) from Heidelberg, Germany, represent a western form of the Java-type man. He would regard the whole group as ancestral to modern man, a view that must now, as we have already demonstrated, be completely revised in the light of *Homo habilis*.

These fossils from Ternifine and elsewhere do, however, open another field of possibility in respect to the story of human development.

Peking Man and Java Man were present in the Far East approximately 500,000 years ago. It is certain that they did not suddenly appear there from nowhere. If it is true that man originated on the African continent, and all available evidence suggests this, then the ancestors of the Java-Peking Man must have left Africa at least 1,000,000 years ago. (I say 1,000,000 years because it probably took as much as 500,000 years for them to reach Asia. Migrations, especially those by human beings, do not normally proceed directly, or at any regular speed.) It is therefore not impossible that in Africa there may have been a stock that was the common ancestor for both the Peking and Java men, and for the Ternifine types. Only further evidence can show whether this view is correct.

In this connection, however, it is necessary to point out that two skulls of much more recent date could easily represent the final end products of the African branch of such a stock. These are the Rhodesian and Saldanha skulls, often referred to as "African Neanderthals." The Rhodesian skull is estimated to be about 25,000 years old, and the Saldanha skull to be about 40,000 years old. At the same time, the 75,000-year-old fossil skulls from Solo in Java could represent the end products of the Far Eastern branch of this stock. It is also possible that we will one day find evidence of a genuine European branch of this stock, with Neanderthal Man as its end product. As Professor Arambourg has suggested, the Mauer jaw is such a European example, but evidence for this is tenuous.

The author uses dental picks and paintbrushes to remove an important fossil specimen from the surrounding rock.

SINCE WE HAVE REFERRED to the well-known Neanderthals, I should point out that recently there has been a considerable change in the scientific ideas concerning this type of man. Today, most physical anthropologists treat the Neanderthal, who lived between 75,000 and 40,000 years ago, as no more than an overspecialized subspecie of *Homo sapiens*, or present-day man. Now, with the discovery of *Homo habilis*, it seems reasonably certain that man, as we know him today, never passed through any greatly overspecialized stage of development such as found in Neanderthal or Java Man.

We are now at the end of this report on five years of anthropological discoveries and study. The old four-stage theory lies in shreds on the museum floor. Stage 1 has become a series of steps. Stages 2 and 3 have turned out to be just side branches, and *Homo habilis* has taken their place. Only the last stage, that of modern man, remains somewhat intact, though here, too, certain representatives, such as the European and African Neanderthals, should most likely be moved to the Java Man side branch.

Space does not permit a discussion of all our other finds, which in one way or another relate to fossil man. Important ones, such as Chellean Man, have been widely reported elsewhere. I have, however, included each of those that relate to the story of man's development from *Proconsul* to *Homo habilis*. What we shall find in the next few years at Olduvai, no one can say. But as we discover the past and understand it, we also gain clues to the future of man.

See also Section Three, ANTHROPOLOGY.

AWAKENING THE LAND

BY PEARL S. BUCK

This field of mine lies sleeping after the winter. I see it through the window of my workroom. It is only one small part of the stretch of land I call my own, and yet it has a larger meaning for me. Everywhere else upon this good earth, others like me are looking at their land, planning how to use it, how to make it yield the most and the best at harvest time. I know, as I face my land here in the United States, that others like me, who are lovers and owners of land, are considering the same problem, asking the same questions, dreaming the same dreams.

This is true whether they be American farmers in the great stretches of the West, the owners of thousands of acres in vast underpopulated countries, or the peasants of India on their individual acre or two. It is true whether they use

A Nobel Prize Winning Author Tells of The Challenge Man Faces in Developing the Good Earth

Toiling Greek farmer breaks new ground in never-ceasing struggle to wrest a living from the soil. Trees planted on hillside have helped halt erosion of precious topsoil.

machines and run their farms as modern industries or plow with wooden, handmade tools drawn by an ox. We all share a common goal: How can we awaken the earth's sleeping land to its fullest production?

We have a deep sense of responsibility, we landowners and landworkers. The earth is our treasure, but not only ours. In a sense, we use it for the benefit of the entire human race. From our land and labor, all must be fed. If we can persuade and compel the land to produce its utmost, then all can eat. But if we allow some land to lie asleep, or only half awake, many human beings must go hungry or even die of malnutrition. It is a grave responsibility. Hungry children never develop into healthy, creative human beings. Starving men create riots and revolutions. The dead do not speak. Thus the full use of the land is essential not only for peace and prosperity, but also for life itself.

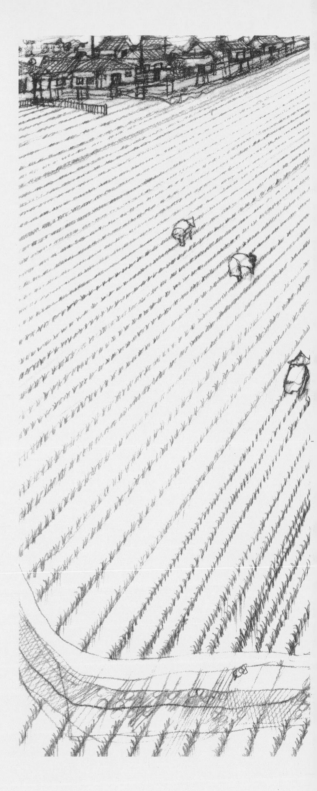

Can the hunger pangs of an ever-increasing world population be satisfied? We peoples of the earth have under cultivation only about 1.5 acres of land for every man, woman, and child alive. And yet we are told by some experts that mankind as a whole cannot be fed and clothed adequately on less than 2.5 acres per person—using, as a yardstick, our present quantity of available land farmed by our present methods. With the world's population increasing enormously, the problem grows acute. What shall we do? Is it inevitable that some of us starve, or that many of us go half-starved all our lives? Let us remember that peace and prosperity come only from well-fed peoples. The Chinese have an old proverb: "When the price of rice goes higher than a common man can pay, Heaven ordains a new ruler." That is to say, when food is too scarce, people revolt.

The responsibility of landowner and landworker alike for the use of the land is great indeed. Are they meeting this responsibility? Differently, it must be stated, in different

Lush rice paddies near Taichung, Formosa, are being
weeded by farmhands whose use of better seed varieties
and such modern techniques as chemical fertilizers and
pesticides results in two and sometimes three crops a year.

countries. Farmers in Japan, for example, produce three times as much rice per acre as do farmers in the rest of Asia. They harvest seven times as much per acre as compared to farmers in India. The farmers of Holland obtain food for all their people on about two-thirds of an acre per person. Some experts maintain that if the world tilled its potentially arable land as efficiently as do the Dutch farmers, we could feed 28,000,000,000 people, or about nine times the number of people who now inhabit the earth.

The knowledge that the land can be awakened and put to work to feed all peoples is bringing new hope everywhere. For centuries, most of the earth's people have thought that hunger was inevitable. Now, from the snowy wastes of Siberia to the tropical savannas of Brazil, all are beginning to realize that we already have the means of feeding our increasing numbers.

What is the process? What are the steps between knowing and doing? How shall we awaken the sleeping land?

First, we must reclaim the acreage that has lost its fertility either through erosion, overgrazing, flooding, and deforestation, or simply through bad farming practices. This can be done, primarily, by scientific management of soil and water. Water is the magic force, water drawn skyward by natural evaporation from the seas, thence to fall upon the land and nourish it with rain and snow. Water is life's necessity. Until now, too much of the precious liquid has been wasted in flood and run-off. Now, hope for a better life inspires people to save and store their water and, by controlling its release, to awaken the sleeping land.

In Egypt, the giant Aswan High Dam, three miles long and a half mile thick, will increase the nation's arable land by one-third. It will reclaim 1,000,000 acres of desert and enable another 700,000 acres to produce two and perhaps three crops a year. In the Kharga Depression, new wells have turned desert sands into green fields of alfalfa and orchards of apricots and other fruits.

In Iran, the stored waters of the great dam on the Sefid River, 150 miles north of Tehran, the capital, will help to end the catastrophic droughts in Quilan province. India's largest dam, the Bhakra-Nangal project, stands completed.

In Sudan, crops planted on 1,000,000 acres of newly revitalized land are flourishing under the irrigative waters of the Gezeira project. In southern Africa, the recently harnessed water of the Zambezi River is now awakening millions of acres of land to production. Both in Africa and

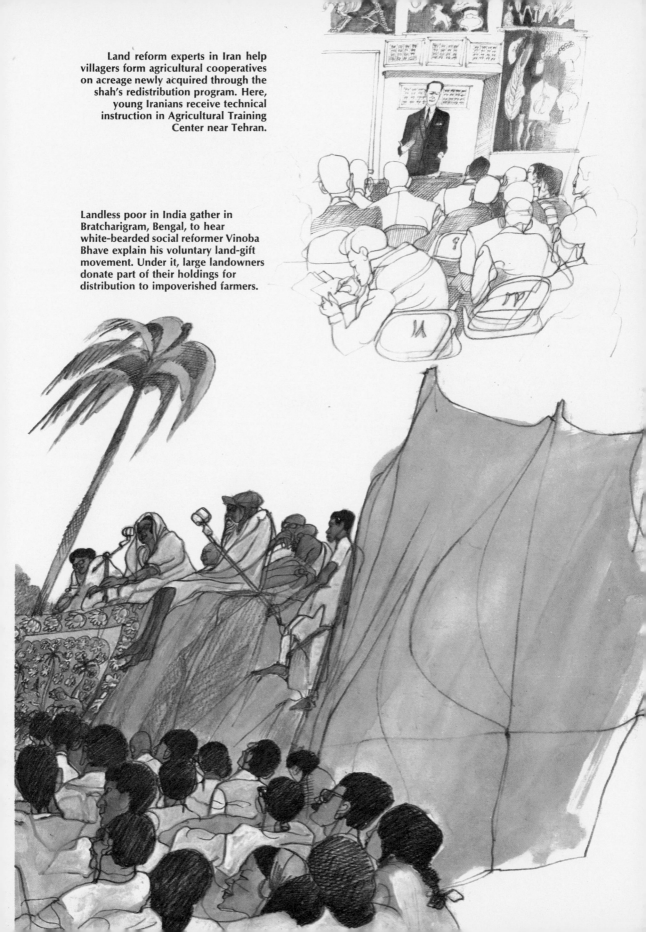

Land reform experts in Iran help villagers form agricultural cooperatives on acreage newly acquired through the shah's redistribution program. Here, young Iranians receive technical instruction in Agricultural Training Center near Tehran.

Landless poor in India gather in Bratcharigram, Bengal, to hear white-bearded social reformer Vinoba Bhave explain his voluntary land-gift movement. Under it, large landowners donate part of their holdings for distribution to impoverished farmers.

Ancient wells of a small oasis near Cairo, Egypt,
supply barely enough moisture to keep melon patch alive.
Primitive irrigation methods are one of the chief reasons
why some nations are unable to win from the soil all
the food it is capable of producing.

In the bountiful hills of Kiryat Anavim, an Israeli kibbutz,
right, presents a modern-day agricultural miracle. The
once-barren slopes have been made to bloom primarily
through an extensive irrigation system by which water is
pumped through pipelines, foreground, from far away.

in South America, the water in newly built reservoirs will perform the same miracle upon now dry and useless land.

Yet water alone is not enough to revitalize tired soil, or soil that has been ruined by erosion. In some areas essential minerals have been exhausted by long use, or wasted by run-off. The land has turned acrid or retired into desert. Such land must be restored and revived. Shifting sands must be held and fixed by the roots of growing plants. What plants can grow in such acidity? In West Africa, the Food and Agricultural Organization (FAO) of the United Nations (UN) is sponsoring research to discover just such plants. In the barren dunes of the Gaza Strip, mimosa seedlings are being grown under a UN desert reclamation project. Erosion, too, must be halted. How? In Greece, some 17,000,000 tree seedlings have been planted on hills and mountainsides to stay the further erosion of precious topsoil. These are but two examples of what can be done with unproductive land.

All this is still not enough. The awakening land cannot produce fully without good seed. New and hardier strains of wheat, introduced into Argentina, Australia, and Austria, have tripled crop yields since the end of World War II. Greece increased its grain production from an average of 1,500,000 tons a year in 1952 to 2,500,000 tons in the 1959-1960 season. In Mexico, the increase rose from 4,000,000 to 7,400,000 tons in the same period. Thus did the land respond to good seed; seed of high-yielding, disease-resistant varieties. For however willing the land may be, however fertile we can make it, it can give bumper harvests only when the seed with which it is planted is good.

Knowing this, FAO, through its World Seed Campaign, is providing and promoting the use of high quality seeds in

Iranian villager signs loan application at government
center in Marmasin as others await their turn. Easy credit
at low interest rates enables farmers to purchase
supplies needed to increase their harvests.

Farm machine pool near Marmasin, in Iran, provides tractors and mechanized plows for use of farmers in the area. They are fast replacing primitive farming tools.

more than 60 countries. New hybrid varieties of corn, to use only one example, have produced harvests of about 64 bushels an acre, whereas a generation ago a harvest of about 24 bushels was considered remarkable.

Yet seed and soil must work together. When soil is thin and poor, it must be enriched by fertilizers, and by efficient management through rotation of crops. In Formosa, India, and Pakistan, legumes and grasses are used to add humus and nitrogen to the soil. In Cambodia and much of Africa, the introduction of compost piles and animal manure has shown remarkable results in increasingly bountiful harvests.

Even good seed and good soil are not enough, however, to guarantee good harvests. Insects may gorge while people starve. Diseases may destroy before men can reap. About one-fifth of the world's food-crop planting is thus lost or seriously damaged each year. In 1959, as an example, world production of cereal grains was 3,293,750,000 bushels. One-tenth of this was destroyed in storage, an amount which, at the rate of 800 grams per person per day, would have fed 300,000,000 people for a whole year.

Can anything be done to avoid such wasted human efforts to produce food? Something is being done. Science is bringing controls. In Libya, the extermination of fruit flies has helped citrus fruit farmers double their crops. In the Middle East and in East Africa, a new chemical, Dieldrin, is fast wiping out the swarms of locusts that consume so much of the crops there. And even in the United States, modern methods of grain storage and rodent control are helping reduce the loss of some $200,000,000 in food heretofore consumed annually by weevils and rodents.

White-walled Marmasin village was once one of dozens owned by a single landlord. Now, under Iranian law, such large holdings are illegal. Former large landowners are limited to one village.

There remain yet other necessities before the land awakens to full life. Man can cultivate only as much as his tools allow. A man with a primitive wooden plow drawn by an ox or a water buffalo can produce barely enough to feed a handful of people. However, that same man on the same land, equipped with modern tools, can do far better. By using modern methods and equipment, the average farmer in the United States, for example, produces enough to feed himself and 27 other persons. In West Germany in 1962, modern agricultural techniques helped the farmers produce twice as much as they did in 1952.

Many lands are adopting modern methods. Metal hoes are now used instead of wooden digging sticks. Steel points are put on wooden plowshares. Scythes, animal-drawn carts, and threshing machines are replacing primitive sickles, spades, stone hammers, and threshing sledges. In Libya's Cyrenaica province, gasoline-powered cultivators were introduced in 1958. In that same season, 6,000 new acres of forage and cereal crops were seeded—an amount of land which otherwise would have lain unused were it not for the new equipment. By 1963, such acreage had been tripled; the yields were superior in quantity and quality.

Governments are now beginning to realize the importance of man's quest for food. Farmers are being given greater incentives to produce. Reliable markets, with good prices and improved facilities for transport, storage, and handling, are being developed. Channels of supply for fertilizers, pesticides, and improved seeds are being expanded. Institutions concerned with farm credit are being built up. Advisory and research programs have been set up to help the farm family organize its life more efficiently. In India, a rural community development program, begun in 1952, now reaches 370,000 of the nation's estimated 500,000 villages. In 10 years, some 350,000 village-level workers were trained and placed in productive service.

All this is still not enough to assure full harvests. A landlord can still absorb all the increase of a harvest and so discourage a tenant farmer from his efforts to improve. It is sometimes necessary, therefore, to reform the system of land ownership. Egypt adopted one method when the government expropriated 750,000 acres of land and parceled it out among 100,000 landless farmers. The shah of Iran adopted another method by giving all his personal property to a foundation for sale and redistribution among landless farmers. In Latin America, land reform is of first importance.

Floating market in Bangkok, Thailand, is colorful but slow means of transporting produce to market. Government-built roads are replacing these congested klongs, or canals, as a means of mass-transporting food to the cities.

Traffic clutter in Tehran
marketplace vividly contrasts old
and new modes of
transportation. A modern truck
vies for road space with camels,
donkeys, and pushcarts.

Venezuela has already redistributed thousands of acres. Peru, Chile, and Brazil have land redistribution programs under way. In summation, then, the sleeping land must be awakened to its fullest life if all mankind is to be amply fed. To accomplish this goal, all methods must be used in combination. The lack of any one may make the others useless, and then the land still sleeps, and man still starves. Can such a combination be brought about? One affirmative answer can be found in Israel. There, by sheer necessity, the people of the country have made the desert bloom and bear rich fruit. There, by a combination of effort, skill, and science the barren, sandy acres of the once-arid Negev are now growing three-fourths of Israel's food requirements, and 32 per cent of its exports. Since 1949, the nation's agricultural output has been increasing by about 16 per cent a year.

But perhaps one of the best examples lies in Formosa, where sweeping land reform, accomplished in a peaceful, democratic spirit, has not only helped to abolish farm tenancy, but also to improve the livelihood of the farmers and increase agricultural output. Thanks to land reform, as Albert Ravenholt points out in the following article, Formosa has become the agricultural showcase of Asia. As you read this article, remember that, while wars threaten and nations are in upheaval, the work of awakening the sleeping land goes on. This work is the strongest force for peace in our world, the most rational source for man's hope in the future.

Mechanical giants, such as this cotton picker, are one of the reasons a farmer in the United States produces enough to feed himself and 27 other persons.

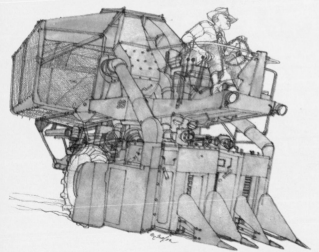

Illustrated by Franklin McMahon

AWAKENING THE LAND

By ALBERT RAVENHOLT

How Land Reform in Formosa Is Creating a Better Life

LEE CHUN-SHENG, a 67-year-old Formosan farmer, can neither read nor write. But Elder Brother Lee, as he is known, is a happy man. He confidently tends his crops and rears his family in Nantou County on Formosa's gardenlike west-central plain. He owns $3\frac{1}{4}$ acres of land, which he tills with the aid of his four sons.

His younger brother, Lee Chun-ho, who is 58, is even more prosperous. Younger Brother Lee owns only $2\frac{1}{2}$ acres, which he works with two of his three sons, but he earns additional income by buying pigs from other farmers, fattening them, and trucking them to market. His new, two-story, concrete home dominates the old courtyard where the crops are dried. Ducks and geese wander about, and healthy grandchildren play together. An electric fan helps cool the house; a radio brings music and news into the home.

All across the Formosan countryside today there are signs of a vigorous prosperity comparable to that which the Lees

Elder Brother Lee, once a victim of a harsh tenant system, works rice paddy he owns under land reform.

enjoy. Modern brick houses are replacing the traditional thatched huts. Almost every farmhouse has electricity. Radios and sewing machines, once virtually unheard of, are commonplace. Many farmhouses now have electrical appliances such as rice cookers; some even have refrigerators. Mechanized farm equipment and up-to-date food processing plants are increasingly evident.

So rosy was the economic outlook in Formosa that the United States government in 1964 announced that it would end its economic aid to the island in 1965. After 15 years—and 1,400,000,000 U.S. dollars—the island economy was ready to stand on its own feet.

A System of Virtual Slavery

TO GRASP THE TRUE SIGNIFICANCE of this transformation, one needs to look back. For over 4,000 years, the people of Asia have been chiefly farmers. They have always looked to the land for life, but the earth has been more cruel than kind. Peasants, charged with feeding more than half the human race, farmed with sticks and shovels. They grubbed at worn-out soil. They suffered under drouth and pestilence. And, to top it all, they were shackled in virtual slavery by a tenant-landlord system that wrung from them most of what they did produce.

The story of the Lee family of Formosa—coming as it does at a time of exploding population and emerging nations—has a profound significance for the world. The Lees have been swept ahead by social and economic changes that may be applied to many other parts of the world. These changes—loosely described as "land reform"—constitute a remarkable chapter in modern history.

The Lee story really begins back in 1948 in Washington, D.C., where the U.S. Congress passed the historic "China-Aid Act." Intended mainly to bolster the Chinese Nationalists against the communist threat, the act nonetheless specified that for every nine U.S. dollars spent on Chinese military strength, at least one dollar must go to improve the economy of hard-pressed rural areas. To administer this program, a Joint Commission on Rural Reconstruction (JCRR) was set up. It was staffed by three Chinese commissioners and two American commissioners.

But before the JCRR could make a significant impact upon Chinese agricultural life, communist armies overran the mainland, and President Chiang Kai-shek and his Chinese Nationalist government withdrew to Formosa. So it was Formosa, not the mainland, that was to become the scene of this dramatic story.

"We saw that we had two major tasks," said Chiang Monlin, the late chairman of the JCRR. "First, we had to

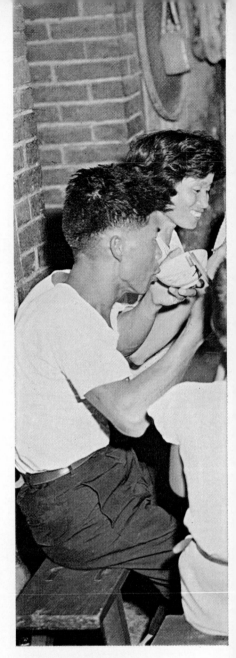

Evening meal of the Lee family is characteristically simple, but nutritious and abundant. By using better seeds and chemical fertilizers introduced under the land reform program, the Lees and many other Formosan farmers produce two, and often three, high-quality crops each year from the same patch of land.

break the economic and social obstacles that had blocked any chance for the peasant to get ahead. Then, we needed to introduce better farming methods that would assure greater, more dependable harvests."

The shift of scene from the mainland to Formosa brought both advantages and disadvantages. More than 2,500,000 mainland Chinese suddenly were superimposed on the economy of an estimated 7,300,000 Formosans. The Formosans, although largely of Chinese ancestry, had problems of their own. As far back as 1683, when Formosa became a prefecture of China, the Formosans had been victimized by

137

officials appointed from faraway Peking. Special taxes exacted by these imperial mandarins eliminated many small landowners, forcing them to work for others. Hence, there emerged on Formosa a large landlord class which took a portion of every harvest. For 200 years, tenant farmers worked the land of others, keeping little for themselves.

Formosa Is Ceded to Japan

IN 1895, FORMOSA WAS CEDED to Japan as part of the booty of the Chinese-Japanese War. Japan began at once to develop the island as an agricultural granary to supply its own industrial empire. The Japanese built new irrigation canals, stepped-up fertilizer production, and developed better seed varieties. They built new processing plants, railroads, and seaports. Production of tea, rice, bananas, and pineapples increased. Mineral production boomed. But the lot of the Formosan peasant changed little. Elder Brother Lee remembers those days well.

"We were farming with our father and Middle Brother," he said. "Together, we worked 10 acres, but we paid seven-twelfths of all we produced to the landlord. We had barely enough left to live on, but we had no choice. We did not own the land, and pressure for land got greater and greater."

Perhaps life for the Lees under the Japanese would have been better had not the population of Formosa grown as it did. In 50 years of Japanese rule, the number of Formosans increased from 2,000,000 to 7,300,000—over three and a half times! Credit for this population growth must go largely to modern public health programs, medical facilities, and doctors trained by the Japanese. It was a great achievement, but it intensified an already critical over-population problem in Formosa because the total of cultivated land remained fixed at about 2,153,000 acres.

"We could only have moved to the sea or the mountains," a county official says in describing their dilemma. As the population grew, ever more tenants competed to farm the same land. Landowners pushed rents higher, sometimes up to 70 per cent of the main crops. They also bought out smaller farmers when bad weather or family misfortune forced the latter to sell. Toward the close of the Japanese period, 68 per cent of the farm families on Formosa lived under a system of tenure.

Formosa was restored to China in August, 1945. Paradoxically, this at first made life even more difficult for farmers suffering from disrupted shipping, bombed-out railroads, and lack of fertilizers. Japanese administrators and technicians were sent home. They were replaced by Chinese officials, who now saw a chance to enrich themselves after lean years in the wartime capital of Chungking. Formosans

Market day for townspeople of Tsao Tun mingles business, pleasure, and tradition. Traveling salesmen for a patent medicine company (center foreground above) stage an outdoor show for prosperous farmers. Village deities are honored by farmers' wives (right), with joss sticks and food offerings during religious festival known as Pai Pai, a big event in Formosa's rural life.

Farmers in shorts display their dried jute in courtyard of Farmers Association, a cooperative venture set up with government help to aid in marketing.

had at first welcomed the mainland Chinese as liberators, but disillusionment turned to anger, and by February, 1947, it sparked an uprising that was suppressed with bloodshed.

Economically hard-pressed, tenant farmers became even more clearly "second class citizens." They hesitated to speak out in their dealings with landowners who often were the only available moneylenders. Formosa was developing bitter rural discontent similar to that which had given rise to communism in mainland China.

By 1949, Chinese Nationalist leaders, having learned a bitter lesson from their earlier reverses on the mainland, were ready to try new ideas. To revive production, and at the same time ease mounting social unrest, the provincial government led by then Governor and now Vice-President Chen Cheng put into effect the program of land reform originally planned for the mainland. The Joint Commission on Rural Reconstruction was revitalized, and a radical yet simple three-stage program was set up. As a first step, rents were to be reduced. Second, public land was to be sold to tenant farmers. Third, limits were to be set on how much land landlords could hold, and the surplus—to be purchased by the government—was to be subsequently resold to the tenant farmers.

The first step was taken in 1949. All farm rents were

chopped to a maximum of 37.5 per cent of the annual main crop. (A photograph of the period shows a tenant farmer with his "37.5 per cent bride"—the girl he had been waiting for and now could afford to bring home with the extra cash retained from the crop.) Tenant farmers were guaranteed security by providing them with written leases for a minimum of six years. No family could be ousted from the fields it tilled without cause.

With JCRR assistance, more than 4,000 local officials and young people, including students, were recruited for intense educational "short courses." They then fanned out into the countryside to spread the word. Public meetings were held to explain the program. Posters, pamphlets, and mass media such as radio and newspapers were used to mobilize public enthusiasm before opponents of land reform could organize resistance. The volunteers supervised the writing of new land leases, especially those involving illiterate farmers. Since only a few Nationalist government officials owned land on Formosa, there was little political objection to the action at the top.

Going After the Tenants

CRUCIAL TO THE SUCCESS of the program were locally elected land commissions. These commissions, on which tenants and farm laborers held the majority of seats, arbitrated disputes between landowners and tenants and among tenant farmers themselves. Because the commissions were composed of neighbors who knew each others' affairs intimately, they were able to act quickly and with a minimum of political involvement. The few problems they could not solve were referred to the courts. Some charged that this first step in land reform was high-handed. But Dr. Tang Hui-sun, chief of JCRR's Land Division, had a simple, compelling answer. "When you are fighting a civil war, who do you want on your side? The few who are landlords, or the many who are discontented tenants?"

Dramatic results followed. By the end of 1949, more than 370,000 leases had been signed and registered with village officials. Tenant farmers, who now knew they would be on the same land the next year, built pigpens and dug compost pits. Some planted fruit trees and green manure crops that could be plowed under to enrich the soil. Other developments were almost as revealing. Prior to reform, there had been considerable speculation in farmland. Now, however, with returns from farmland stabilized, families with wealth looked for alternative sources of income. This encouraged a more modern business attitude in the towns.

In 1951, the government initiated the second part of its program. Government-owned land was put up for sale to the tenant farmers. This land, involving almost one-fifth of all the farmland on Formosa, had been acquired by the government in 1945 as former enemy property. Only a part of it was held back for sugar plantation management. The price per acre was fixed at two-and-one-half times the value of the annual main crops. It could be paid for in semiannual installments spread over a 10-year period. Within two years, 121,953 farming families had bought 155,610 acres of government land. Income from these land sales in turn produced a much needed source of government revenue.

Quiet dignity and an aura of modest pride are mingled in the wrinkled faces of Elder Brother Lee and his wife, shown seated in the courtyard of their home.

Meanwhile, provincial officials and JCRR specialists had launched a massive survey of available land and its potentials. All privately owned agricultural land was registered. This land in turn was classified as to productivity. By April, 1952, the task force assigned to the job had compiled and organized all the data on 6,600,000 "Land-Record and Landownership Cards." It was a large undertaking but well worth the effort, for the painstakingly gathered information became the basis of land reform legislation which was drafted the following month.

The Provincial Assembly, where Formosa's landowners were well represented, was offered an opportunity to comment. Then the draft was submitted to the Legislative Yuan of the Chinese Nationalist government. On Jan. 20, 1953, the Yuan, after great deliberation, passed three related laws. One provided for the transfer of government enterprises to private ownership; a second authorized the provincial government to issue land bonds in kind—redeemable in crops—and the third was the "Land-to-the-Tiller" Act.

In the Land-to-the-Tiller Act, the Nationalist government gave scrupulously fair consideration to the rights of landlords who had obtained their holdings legally under the prevailing land system. Every landlord was entitled to keep approximately 7.5 acres of irrigated land, or 15 acres of dry land. This he could continue leasing to tenants on terms provided earlier by law. All land in excess of these amounts was bought by the government.

Success of land reform on Formosa has given rise to a new middle class of which the Lee family is typical. To satisfy the needs of this new social group, former landlords have turned to manufacturing such commodities as electric refrigerators, one of which is being examined by Younger Brother Lee (right). He plans eventually to buy one for his home.

Water buffalo, (right), are still principal means of hauling produce to market. But just as rubber-tired wheels have replaced wooden ones, so, too, are many farmers replacing oxen with trucks.

Under the program, the landowners received 30 per cent of the purchase price in shares of stock in government-owned corporations which, under the act now became private enterprises. The remaining 70 per cent due the landowners was paid in commodity bonds representing stipulated quantities of rice or sweet potatoes and bearing 4 per cent annual interest. The bonds were redeemable in cash or kind to guard against currency inflation. They were payable semi-annually over a 10-year period. Tenant farmers were then offered this land at the same price paid by the government and on the same terms—4 per cent interest in 20 installments spread over 10 years. Under the new act, 194,823 farmers bought 354,612 acres of land. By the end of 1953, more than three-fourths of all the agricultural land on Formosa was being cultivated directly by owners. The remaining one-fourth either continued to be rented—thus providing a "ladder" for new farmers to get started toward eventual ownership of their own land—or it was used for government

enterprises such as the Taiwan Sugar Corporation, schools, experimental stations, or similar projects.

To understand what all this meant to the average farmer, let us turn again to the Lees. At the close of World War II, three Lee brothers were still working the original 10 acres their father had rented. When local political pressures compelled them to give up this land, they pooled their meager resources and bought $1\frac{1}{4}$ acres of land. Next, they managed to rent an additional two acres of privately owned land. In a third, separate plot, they also leased $2\frac{1}{4}$ acres of government land. This was the extent of their holdings when the Land-to-the-Tiller Act was passed.

"Since we were really cultivating these fields ourselves," Elder Brother Lee explains, "we had the first right to buy them under the act. When the land reform program was completed, we owned approximately six acres. These we divided into three equal parts. But later, when our Middle Brother decided to give up farming and go into business, he sold his shares to us. As for me," Elder Brother goes on, "I was allowed 10 years under the law to pay for my new fields. But I paid for them in six. We made good money raising pigs for several years, and I thought the safest thing was to pay for my land."

New Business Ventures

NOT ALL FORMOSAN LANDLORDS were happy to part with their fields. For generations, land had been the most trusted investment, both as a status symbol and as a prized possession to be passed on to the children. But now, with rentals from land either stabilized or non-existent, families with wealth to invest had to look elsewhere for alternatives. Many former landlords embarked on new ventures. Some joined with the new entrepreneurs who were remaking the faces of Formosa's cities. A Taipei stock exchange soon appeared, trading shares in the corporations now controlled by former landlords. Within a decade, Formosa was manufacturing most of its textiles, though it continues to import raw cotton, especially from the United States. New glass plants, plastics factories, brick kilns, metal fabricating shops, and electrical manufacturing firms sprang up and absorbed capital and talents in often highly profitable pursuits. Thus, a new class of citizen—the businessman—was born on Formosa.

Simultaneously, the old-type tenant farmer had disappeared. Farmers were now secure on their lands and were fortified with new incentives. Still, only one-half of the goal had been achieved. The new landowners now needed a knowledge of more scientific farming methods. A most crucial need, too, was credit and marketing. In a society where

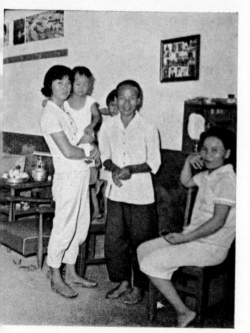

Neatly furnished Lee family living room, complete with electric fan, (below), exemplifies transition of many Formosan farmers from peasant to middle-class status.

143

interest on private loans often exceeded 40 per cent annually, the farmer still risked becoming a victim of the moneylender. To avoid this, the JCRR began reorganizing the Farmers Associations. These had originally been established by the Japanese and acted as rural banks as well as suppliers of seed, fertilizer, and mill rice. Most, however, were financially unstable. Also, they were controlled by city merchants. Ordinary farmers had little authority in their management. Now, however, they were redesigned into genuine cooperatives. Only families that earned more than half of their income from farming were allowed to vote. Association managers and their staffs were given thorough training. Proper accounting procedures were introduced. Experts from provincial government headquarters audited each cooperative's books every six months. In addition, JCRR grants and loans helped pay for new rice hulling machines, peanut and soybean seed granaries, fertilizer and rice warehouses, and orange-packing plants.

In more personal terms, the Lees again serve as examples of what has taken place. Both brothers are among the 7,503 members of the Tsao Tun Township Farmers Association which is located in a bustling, brown-plastered building on the edge of town. Its 15 directors and comptrollers are elected every three years. But every November, about 90 per cent of the members assemble for two days to talk over association business. They also approve the budget for the coming year's operations.

Formosa's First Mass Market

THE ASSOCIATION'S ACTIVITIES are many. It serves, for example, as a bank. "I have on deposit cash equal to 105 U.S. dollars," says Elder Brother Lee. It earns him interest at the rate of $4\frac{1}{2}$ per cent annually if he leaves it for one month, and twice this rate of return when left for six months. As a member, he is entitled to borrow at a somewhat higher rate of interest from total deposits in the association. These deposits are equal to about $825,000.

Behind the association's main headquarters is a warehouse. There the Lee brothers and other members of the cooperative trade rice for fertilizer. There, too, they sell their jute and buy farm equipment, such as Elder Brother Lee's new paddy-field marker which enables him to transplant rice seedlings in straight rows.

The warehouse also has a merchandise department where farmers can buy pesticides, bicycles, or even electric rice cookers, the latter priced at $12. Lately, the department has been selling on installment half a dozen small electric refrigerators a month which cost the equivalent of $274. "They still cost more than I can afford," says Younger

Farm life on Formosa, as elsewhere, is a cooperative venture involving the entire family. Among the Lees, for whom mixed farming is a profitable innovation made possible by land reform, pig-raising is a business in which all share—from the womenfolk, who help feed the hungry piglets, (top) to the menfolk (right), whose brawn is needed to weigh in the fatted sows for marketing.

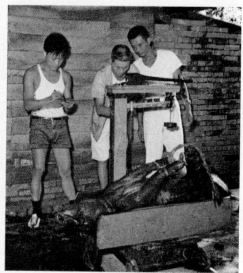

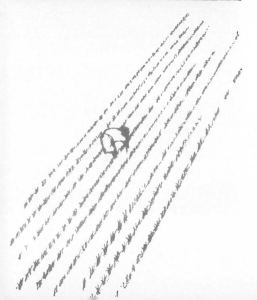

Brother Lee, "even though the women at home would like one." But already farm families are providing Formosa's first mass market for consumer durables, sometimes manufactured by their former landlords.

Profits earned by the Tsao Tun Township Farmers Association annually have totaled the equivalent of $26,000. Thirty per cent of this went into a sinking fund. The cooperative is building a new $70,000 headquarters. An 11-man cooperative extension staff includes three veterinarians who vaccinate pigs and water buffalo, and a manager of the livestock breeding farm that specializes in artificial insemination of sows. Two 4-H Club directors guide 850 boys and girls belonging to 49 clubs. Among the club members is Younger Brother Lee's bright and eager 20-year-old third son. "I work in the daytime reading irrigation water meters," he says. "On weekends and in the mornings and evenings I am out in the field helping my brother to see if we can set a rice production record." He would like to try for a college education when another brother returns from army service.

New ideas move through this network into the bosom of the family. A home economics supervisor from the Farmers Association visits with housewives, showing them how to save costly fuel by rebuilding the open Chinese kitchen stove, preserve vegetables, and cook more nutritious, yet simple meals. Four extension specialists explore fields in the township daily for opportunities to give technical help. In the evening, they meet with adult farmers in village "agricultural discussion groups."

A Source of Pride

FORMOSA'S FARMERS take a great deal of pride in their production records. Over the past decade, island output of rice has increased 40 per cent to above 2,100,000 tons, leaving a surplus for export. Sweet potato production has increased 50 per cent, and the harvest of peanuts even more. Pineapple production tripled, and the area growing citrus fruit has increased nearly threefold. New crops now being canned and exported, such as mushrooms, earn Formosan farmers $7,000,000 annually. A growing Chinese taste for milk has aroused interest in dairy farming, especially among 4-H Club members who have returned from visits to America. Modern milk pasteurization plants have begun bottling milk from black-and-white Holsteins that graze on the dikes between the tiny fields and on new pastures planted on the hillsides. Unlike most of the burdened lands of South and Southeast Asia, rural Formosa has reached that dynamic stage where it can now digest new forms of technology.

The results of these new ideas can be seen in the fields of Elder Brother Lee. His first crop yielded a return of $2\frac{1}{3}$ tons of paddy rice per acre, and the second crop was almost as much. A winter crop of sweet potatoes and beans, however, was killed by unusual frost. Jute, first interplanted with rice, was stripped and sold for cash. Cucumbers and other vegetables were grown for family use and as feed for pigs and poultry. "Even though I don't write it down, I have a pretty good idea of what we make," Elder Brother Lee admits. He calculates that the annual crops yielded a gross cash return equal to $1,160. Chemical fertilizer, which island farmers use intensively, was the largest single expense. It cost Lee $149. Other major operating costs were for taxes —which are high, he thinks—insecticides, and irrigation fees. These totaled $174. Labor is the biggest factor in growing rice. If paid for, it would have cost Lee the equivalent of $286, even at the prevailing rural wage of one U.S. dollar per day. But since he has grown sons, the family can till the paddy fields, transplant rice seedlings, weed, and harvest largely with their own manpower, or, if the occasion demands, by exchanging work with their neighbors.

A High Living Standard

LIKE FARMERS IN MANY OTHER LANDS, the Lee brothers calculate their income as much by their standard of living as in cash. Food for the family is chiefly homegrown, and the Lees eat well. Daily caloric intake on Formosa rivals Japan's, the highest in Asia. Meat, especially pork and fowl, or fish appear on the table almost daily. Clothing is simple, yet ample, and becoming more colorful as women buy the new prints. Rubber raincoats are replacing the traditional straw capes among farmers. By choice, the Lees still go barefoot in the paddy fields, but they own rubber boots. The old rural fear of illness has relaxed. "We trust and use the modern drugs and doctors," they say, referring to the health stations and centers which have been established on the island with help from JCRR and the provincial government.

Education has a new importance. All seven sons of the two Lee brothers completed primary school and two attended middle school, although the cost still bars the children of some farmers. Since they can read and write and manage figures, the sons help their fathers in business calculations. They study the rural magazine *Harvest*, published fortnightly in Taipei, and glean ideas on crops and animal care from extension pamphlets. Unlike the cities, rural Formosa has little juvenile delinquency. Young people are productively and satisfyingly involved in many of the affairs of the community.

Rural success story is a reality to Elder Brother Lee, tenant farmer turned landowner. His fertile fields lie behind him. A life-giving irrigation canal laps at his feet as he trudges homeward.

Photographs by K. C. Tan

Elder Brother Lee measures his lot in life by contrasting it with that of his father. Farming is still hard work from sunrise to dusk, but the rewards are vastly greater. "Someday, I may lighten the work a bit," he says, "by buying one of those new little tractors to replace the water buffalo. But not yet." Mechanization will become more practical as the provincial government, with JCRR assistance, helps farmers trade land and rebuild dikes so they can consolidate fragmented holdings and simplify cultivation. Lee and his neighbors feel they could make more money out of poultry and pigs if there were a large packing plant in Tsao Tun Town to stabilize prices and manage marketing.

Good farming and cautious use of his income since land reform have made Elder Brother Lee a man of solid financial means. At today's prices, his fields are worth $9,750, or almost $3,000 per acre, based on Formosan dollars which have an official exchange rate of 40 for one U.S. dollar. Another measure of the prosperity that has come to Formosa is the annual average income of its farming families. Between 1952 and 1964, it has more than doubled. To help make this possible, the JCRR has spent some $7,100,000 in grant aid and roughly the equivalent of $127,800,000 in counterpart funds—Chinese currency generated by the sale of U.S. farm surpluses like cotton on Formosa and partly used for loans that financed irrigation construction.

A New Way of Life

FORMOSA HAS BECOME Asia's agricultural "showcase," a kind of pilot plant where ancient civilization and Western techniques have combined to provide a new way of rural life. Formosan agricultural specialists, invited to many Asian, African, and Latin-American countries under technical cooperation arrangements, now are demonstrating modern rice growing methods in Liberia, Libya, and the Ivory Coast. Nations in many parts of the world send their own agricultural experts to Formosa to see an agricultural miracle in operation. Many take home with them ideas on land reform and crop production to put into use in their own countries.

Although political institutions on Formosa leave much to be desired, rural communities have achieved social and economic democracy. For the Lee family and its neighbors, the hard old days are a fading memory. The better life, to which land reform was crucial, holds out a promise to emerging peoples in many parts of the world.

See also Section Three, ASIA; CHINA; FORMOSA; INDIA. For related Special Reports, see also *Dos Gringas Americanas;* THE 1962 YEAR BOOK, *The South Goes to Town;* THE 1963 YEAR BOOK, *Breakthrough in the Breadbasket.*

BY
ROBERT
HOOD

THE VILLAGE OF CUNDAY (*coon-DIE*) is only a few hours drive southwest of Bogotá, the capital of Colombia, but it seemed a world away to the two young American girls as their jeep jounced along the dusty road that coiled through lush mountains like a snake about to swallow its tail. With each coil, their driver, Chuck Brady, Regional

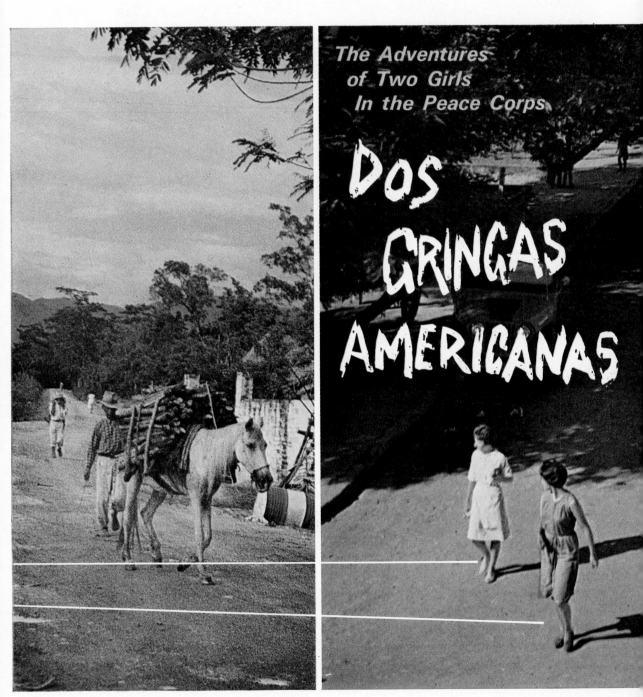

The Adventures
of Two Girls
In the Peace Corps

DOS
GRINGAS
AMERICANAS

Dos Gringas Americanas take time out for an early morning chat
with a villager as passengers wait to board two highway
buses in the village square.

Peace Corps Director at Bogotá, sounded the horn to warn approaching
traffic. At a high point, they could see for miles across the peaceful valley
below. Far down the winding road, a puff of dust pinpointed a moving
vehicle. A half mile away grazed a solitary cow, a tiny embossment on
the vast expanse of tropical greenness.

Then the final drop, zigzagging down, down the mountainside, past a
wrinkled peasant leading a burro laden with wood, and into Cunday.
After a stop at the home of a group of local teachers, the jeep turned into
the village square, peopled with passengers from an unloading bus and
with idle country folk sipping soft drinks. Then, with a jolt, it pulled up
at the headquarters of a detachment of the Colombian army. A sentry,
the sun glinting from his helmet, snapped to present arms as a dapper
officer strode out of the headquarters and greeted the driver.

"Buenos días, Chuck," he said, "how nice to see you again." The wiry,
young Peace Corps man returned the colonel's smile.

"Good morning, Colonel Galvis," said Brady. "Permit me to introduce
our two Peace Corps volunteers."

The girls brushed dust from their skirts, patted their hair into place, and
stepped down from the jeep.

"Miss Karen Gardner," Brady said, bowing slightly toward the tall
dark-haired girl on his right. "And this is Miss Susan Holtz." He spoke

150

A world away, the tropical village of Cunday nestles
in the mountains some 70 winding miles from Bogotá,
the bustling capital of Colombia.

with a slight air of formality, a gesture that matched the colonel's air of
Latin courtliness.

"What a pleasure," responded Colonel Galvis. "Welcome to Cunday.
We have been awaiting your arrival. We've heard so much about you."
The girls chattered back to Colonel Luis Galvis Moreno in graceful
Spanish. Trained as health educators, they would soon become a vital
part of the life of this hot, remote village in the foothills of the Andes.

**A Gracious
Welcome
to Cunday**

IN A DINING ROOM not far from the village square, an orderly
served a light lunch while the colonel told the girls that they needn't worry
about moving into their own house until they had had time to adjust to
their new environment. "Please, I have put *my* house at your disposal for
your first few days here," he said. "No. I insist. As we like to say in
Colombia, 'My house is your house.' "

After lunch, with the scorching sun past its zenith, Chuck Brady drove
off, Colonel Galvis moved into his temporary quarters in the army compound, and the girls began to unpack. They would spend two weeks here
and two in the village hospital before finding their own quarters.

Thus did Karen Gardner, 22, from Costa Mesa, Calif., and soft-spoken
Susan Holtz, 23, of Escondido, Calif., begin their tour of duty.

For the next day or so, the girls got their belongings together, talked

151

about their assignment, and went for walks in the village. During these walks, they waved and nodded hello, and were greeted shyly by many a *campesino*, the dirt-poor Colombian farmer, who often stared after them with a kind of awe and wonderment. Why did you young *gringas Americanas* come to Cunday, they seemed to be asking.

The girls had only to look about them to know why they were needed in Cunday, and why Peace Corps volunteers are needed throughout Colombia, for Cunday is a microcosm of the problems confronting Colombia, and for that matter, of depressed nations everywhere.

Behind the Pleasant Façade

CUNDAY IS A VILLAGE of 4,000 souls. It is grouped around a town square, or plaza, like most Latin-American villages. Small shops front the square, as does the church, the village administration building, the jail, and the hotel. The latter, with accommodations for 12 guests, has screenless windows, seatless toilets, and a small bar. On almost any pleasant afternoon, men from the countryside gather near the hotel, playing guitars, or perhaps a 12-stringed instrument called the *tiple*, and drinking beer or *aguardiente*. And, on any afternoon, sounds from the hotel and the shops mingle with the slow clop-clop of a heavily loaded burro, the chatter of passengers boarding a bus, the shouts of children.

The picture appears pastoral, peaceful, but the reality of life in Cunday is quite the opposite. A glimpse behind the outward appearance reveals poverty, chronic malnutrition, a tragically high infant mortality rate, illiteracy, despair, and the threat of violence.

About 80 per cent of the people of Cunday are poor, and perhaps 30 per cent of this number live on a bare subsistence level. The homes of those in

Children of Cunday frown and smile shyly to clicking shutters after insisting on being photographed by the *gringo* visitor. Under present conditions, their life expectancy is 39 years.

the latter group usually consist of two rooms with thatched roofs and dirt floors. They lack inside toilets, electric lights, or beds. The family sleeps on the floor on blankets or gunny sacks.

The father seldom has a job. The mother (who bears an average of six children) strains to squeeze out a living, often by washing clothes for others, and baking and selling little cakes.

There is no industry in the town. During the coffee harvest in the spring, most of the men work on plantations. A few own small plots of land in the country, but because of outmoded farming methods, their plots are comparatively unproductive. Above the poorest of the poor are laborers, who earn about $250 a year working on the roads and houses. Then come the skilled workers, the carpenters, and the equipment operators.

Above these "blue-collar" workers is the almost nonexistent middle class —the class that generally gives stability to a nation. In Cunday, it consists of a few shop owners, the local government officials, a handful of teachers, the priest, army officers, and a young doctor who spends a portion of his week in the town. And of course, in a class by themselves, are the children of the poor.

The average child of Cunday is lucky to live long enough to reach the first grade. He is often ridden with disease. The most common are hookworm, ringworm, tapeworm, malaria, rickets, and amebic dysentery. As Karen and Sue were soon to learn, there have been cases in Cunday in which 80 to 90 parasites (worms), some of them a foot long, were removed from the body of a single child. Hence, it is saddening, if not surprising, to find that the life expectancy of the Cundayuno is roughly that of the nation as a whole: 39 years.

Way at the top of this economic pyramid are *los ricos* (the rich), the handful who own the all-important coffee plantations and cattle ranches.

The Problems of the Country

THIS SKETCH OF ONE VILLAGE can serve as an index to the conditions of life in Colombia, and for most of the people of Latin America. Colombia has a population of approximately 15,600,000, and a land area larger than that of Texas and California combined. Its population density is light, 35 persons to a square mile, but the land does not grow enough to feed the people. Only about 4 per cent of the country is cultivated. Also, Colombia needs to diversify its economy, which is too closely tied to the growing of coffee.

The second largest in the world, the coffee crop accounts for 70 per cent of Colombia's export earnings. The resources that would make diversification possible are there—rich soils and pasturelands, great stands of timber, and huge mineral deposits—but adequate development is lacking. Furthermore, the nation must improve its agriculture, particularly the cotton, banana, sugar and tobacco crops, and modernize its timber and cement industries. At present, per capita income is about as low as it can get, amounting to only $260 a year.

Colombia also lags in the sphere of education. It is estimated that half the population is illiterate, and that 25 to 35 per cent attend school for only one year. Most of the secondary schools are privately owned. Hence, about 5 per cent of Colombian families can afford the tuition. Only 2 per cent of Colombia's young people are enrolled in universities.

153

Nevertheless, Colombia is determined to do something about its deep-rooted and widespread problems. In 1958, after a devastating civil war, it created *Acción Communal* (Community Action), a division of the government designed to help change the basic social and political patterns of village life. Later, Colombia became one of the first countries to invite a U.S. Peace Corps group. Acción Communal trained 50 young Colombians (all high school graduates) to work with the first group of 61 volunteers, which arrived in September, 1961. As with many Peace Corps projects, the administering agency for the program is CARE, the private U.S. relief organization. Although the volunteers reported to CARE and to the Peace Corps representative in Bogotá, Dr. Christopher Sheldon, they were directly responsible to Acción Communal. Karen Gardner and Susan Holtz arrived in Colombia in October, 1963, among a group requested by the Ministry of Health to help improve health education and medical facilities in rural areas. Currently, with 600 volunteers, Colombia has the largest Peace Corps contingent of any nation.

Helping
People
Help
Themselves

PEACE CORPS VOLUNTEERS Karen and Sue were familiar in outline with the problems of Cunday. Equally important, they were thoroughly schooled and personally believed in the methods and goals of the Peace Corps as practiced in Colombia and in 45 other underdeveloped nations. Briefly stated, the Corps tries to help people help themselves. In practice, this means working to instill by example, by patient cooperation, and by actual accomplishment, the notion that change really *is* possible, that one *can* help oneself. The hard-pressed campesino may sometimes dream of bettering his lot, but it is a dream that has been shattered for centuries by a life mired in poverty and neglect. Initiative? To the average Colombian, it is only a word in the dictionary.

Karen and Sue knew that to gain the confidence of the Cundayunos they needed the support of the leaders of the town. Since the most influential leader in rural areas is the resident priest (the nation is 90 per cent Roman Catholic), the girls called on Father Xavier Ignacio Vásquez shortly after their arrival in town.

The threesome sipped coffee at Father Vásquez's wooden desk. "My people are simple," the priest began. "They are poor. They are illiterate. Too many of them are ill. They do not understand the need for sanitation; that drinking unboiled water, for example, might be harmful to them; that a mother, after changing her baby, should not handle food without washing her hands. They need to learn on many levels. And the young, our boys and girls, need new and wholesome forms of recreation. Anything you can do for the people will be of value."

The three talked on. Father Vásquez was interested in the girls' background. He learned that Susan Holtz received a B.A. degree in Spanish from the University of California in Santa Barbara, and that Karen held the same degree from Willamette University in Salem, Ore. Karen had long been interested in Latin America and spent her junior year of college in Mexico. During her high school days, she worked with a church youth group and spent Easter vacations among migrant farmworkers. Sue spent her last two college Easter vacations at the First Methodist Church in Tijuana, Mexico, helping to build a new church. On summer weekends,

Under a tropical sun, volunteers work on the community athletic field, the girls' first big project.

Day's work done, Karen Gardner, *right,* relaxes, strumming songs of her new-found friends. Sue Holtz, *below,* teaches English in one of the evening classes attended by adult Cundayunos.

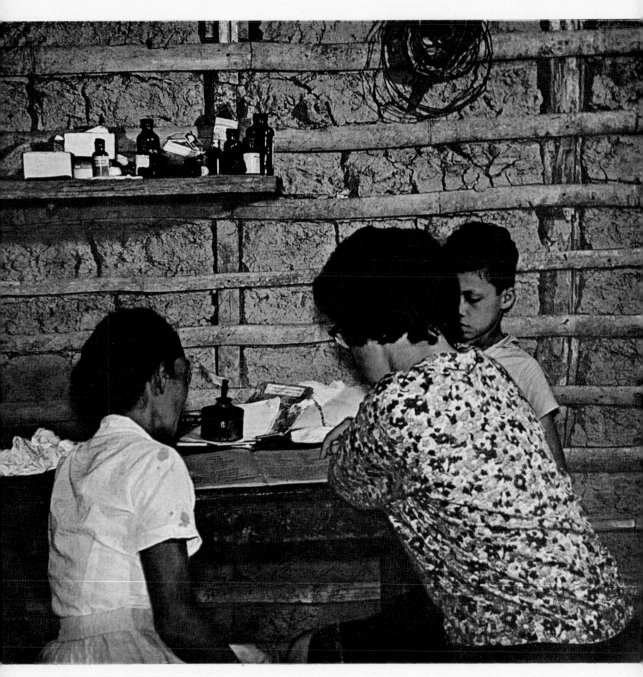

By the light of a flickering lamp in a typical Cunday home,
Karen shows a mother how to teach reading
to some of her less-educated neighbors.

between terms, she worked on *Project Amigos*, which provided food and
clothing, and literacy and sewing classes to the poor of Tijuana.

At the end of the interview, the first of many, Father Vásquez assured
the girls that they could count on him to support their efforts in Cunday.

The mayor of Cunday, Don Leonel Rubio Lerma, warmly greeted the girls at the administration building in his shirtsleeves, and led them into his office. A tall, wiry man, he was well aware of the difficulties facing his country. Well he might be—they nearly cost him his life, for he had been shot and left for dead during Colombia's civil war.

"Miss Holtz, Miss Gardner," Don Leonel began. "One cannot understand Colombia unless one knows and feels something of the horrors of the *Violencia*. It was a terrible time for us—like your Civil War."

The Violencia began in the capital in 1948 with the murder of Liberal party leader Jorge Gaitán. The crime started a four-day blood bath that devastated Bogotá and began five years of civil war between adherents of Conservative and Liberal party leaders. Families fought one another. Villages were pillaged and leveled. Many fled to the countryside and joined marauding bandit chiefs. The Violencia lasted until 1953, and cost the lives of an estimated 200,000 people. At its end, Lieutenant General Gustavo Rojas Pinilla was in power. He stamped out much of the lawlessness, but did so by means of a repressive military dictatorship. This, too, was overthrown by a popular revolution in 1957.

A coalition government was ratified by referendum in 1958, with Alberto Lleras Camargo as president of the republic. He was succeeded in 1962 by the Conservative, Guillermo Léon Valencia. Under the coalition, scheduled to continue until 1974, the office of the presidency will alternate every four years, with the Liberals serving one term, and the Conservatives the next. All elective and appointive offices—national, provincial, and local—will be allocated in a similar manner between the two parties.

"The war," Mayor Rubio reminded the girls, "was a national disaster. There are still bandits in the hills. In fact, I would appreciate it if you did not go into the countryside without asking Colonel Galvis for an escort of soldiers."

As the priest had done, the mayor promised to support the efforts of the Peace Corps in Cunday. "You can rely on the local administration, señoritas," he said. "We are deeply grateful that you dedicated young women are here."

A Dedicated Doctor

SOMEWHAT LATER, Sue and Karen returned to the hospital they had visited on their first day in Cunday, and where they lived for a time before they found their own five-room house. The building, with accommodations for about 40 patients, is on a hill on the outskirts of town. It left much to be desired as a medical facility. It lacked a laboratory and had no registered nurses. Still, the girls found the doctor there a hopeful sign for the Colombia of the future.

Dr. Juan Osorio, 29, worked for the hospital two days a week without fee under the auspices of INCORA, the Colombian Institute for Agricultural Reform. He delivered babies, performed minor surgery, and carried on a general practice. The rest of the week he practiced in the province of Toluma. In Cunday, he had the cooperation of the army doctor in charge of the hospital. He was a graduate of the University of Buenos Aires, where he hoped to return to study skin pathology.

A handsome, olive-skinned man of medium height, he had a quiet but passionate concern for his countrymen. "They are superstitious," he told the volunteers. "If a child has worms, the *campesino* puts a ring of garlic around his neck. To cure pimples, they smear a cut orange on their faces. Many believe that if you take a bath on Good Friday, you will die."

In answer to Sue's question as to what they could do to help him, the doctor noted that the girls might start sanitation classes. He also suggested that they take an inoculation census to determine which if any Cundayunos had been inoculated, and for which diseases. Like the priest, he spoke of the need for recreational facilities for the young, adding that prostitution and illegitimacy were serious problems in the town.

Getting to Know the Villagers

IN MEETINGS SUCH AS THOSE with the priest, the mayor, and the doctor, Peace Corps volunteers Sue and Karen introduced themselves to the leading townsmen of Cunday and began to understand the problems facing the village and the ways in which they might be useful. Now it was time to go out and meet the villagers directly. The girls decided to do this by making a house-to-house tour, covering as many homes as they could.

"Hello," they would say, "my name is Susan Holtz, and this is Karen Gardner. We're from the Peace Corps, and we would like to do whatever we can to help you." During these first visits, most of the villagers were shy. Some were skeptical. Nevertheless, after about two months, the girls were accepted in the town.

Then the Cundayunos began to come to them with their problems. Sometimes they were unsolvable, occasionally tragically so. Once, Karen was called to the home of a campesino to attend a child. She carried the 8-year-old girl to the hospital in her arms, but—alas—the little girl died soon after of anemia. She was the third child of that family to die, and, at the time of her death, two other children in that family were seriously ill, their stomachs swollen by hunger and disease. The event did not leave Karen or Sue unmarked.

Gradually, the girls established a series of programs based primarily on what the villagers asked for, and on what the volunteers considered most important for them. They formed mothers' clubs, one group led by Sue, the other by Karen. Their aim was to teach the rudiments of sanitation. The two groups, each consisting of about a dozen women, met once a week in one of the homes. Sue and Karen, working separately, talked of the necessity of boiling water, of washing one's hands at appropriate times, of refusing to allow the children to use their back yards as latrines. They labored to get the women to put shoes on their children because certain kinds of parasitic worms, such as hookworm, can enter the body through the skin when soil is contaminated.

Several of the villagers wanted to learn to read and write their own language. Hence, the girls began informal literacy classes. Their method was to train "block leaders" to read and write. They, in turn, were assigned to teach their neighbors what they had learned. The girls met with the block leader once a week. When the first group completed its work, Sue and Karen arranged a little celebration in honor of the graduates. It was a candlelight ceremony, signifying the light of knowledge, and it was as meaningful as it was touching. "Candlelight ceremonies are something they don't have here," Sue said, "and it was impressive. We made up little certificates and gave them out to everyone."

The girls had other projects, too. They were working with the local

Street scenes in Cunday offer studies in color
and the slow pace of tropical life. In front
of homes, *left,* and in the street, *below,*
time waits for the exchange of news and greetings.

Schoolgirls stop their recess play to giggle and stare at the *gringo* they spotted taking their picture with a telephoto lens. Even though they are dressed for school, some are shoeless.

authorities to keep pigs and other farm animals penned so that they would not foul the streets and eat up vegetable gardens. One of the girls' most cherished goals was a plan to get the babies off the dirt floors and into cradles, a sanitary precaution that was totally foreign to most of the mothers of the town.

Sue and Karen hit on the notion of having the cradles built of *cana brava* (bamboo). Colonel Galvis lent them his aid. He sent soldiers from his battalion into the countryside to cut down the bamboo. Then the girls enlisted teen-agers to build the cradles and raffle them off. They even printed simple instructions to show the townspeople how to build the cradles themselves. The teen-agers spent the money earned in the raffles to buy sports equipment for the athletic field the villagers were constructing at the suggestion of *dos gringas Americanas*.

The athletic field was by far the largest single project attempted by the girls in their first year in Cunday. It met almost immediate approval with everyone because all of the townspeople sensed the need for one. Of course, two young women could not build a large athletic field by themselves. But they could and did organize and spark the forces that were available to get the work done. Mayor Rubio okayed the use of the land. It was a piece of property behind one of the town's three schools, one of them a one-story brick building built by the Alliance for Progress funds. INCORA lent a bulldozer for three days to level off the four connecting lots, two for use as volleyball courts and two for basketball courts. INCORA also donated two backboards for the basketball courts, and the Colombian Coffee Federation donated two others. And soldiers and civilians, including children, went to work with picks and shovels.

It was a big project. The bulldozers started work in January. Then, in April, with the backing of Father Vásquez and the mayor, Karen and Sue

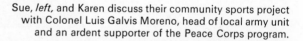

Sue, *left,* and Karen discuss their community sports project with Colonel Luis Galvis Moreno, head of local army unit and an ardent supporter of the Peace Corps program.

organized a bazaar and gala fiesta to raise money for the field. About 5,000 *pesos* ($500)—a good deal of money for a little town—was collected. The money was obtained in several ways. Two donated calves were raffled off. Two thousand tickets at two pesos each were sold, along with beer and aguardiente. Streets were roped off, and the automobile drivers "taxed" before they could pass. Serenades were sung. Little paper decorations were pinned on people, and the persons thus honored paid a small sum of money.

The girls were often present during the construction, and this example spurred the work on. Smiles and greetings were exchanged all around, as the men gathered about Sue or Karen on the field. Since no educated Colombian woman ventures out in the dazzling afternoon sun, especially to

Schoolchildren often call on Sue, *left,* and Karen. Their smiling faces reflect the affection the children hold for *Dos Gringas Americanas* and the Peace Corps they serve.

chat with workmen, such appearances were regarded as unusual and, in their way, inspiring.

Thus the girls' days in the village of Cunday were busy ones. They began at about 6:30 A.M. and ended well after dark. And throughout the long day, Sue and Karen sought to better the lives of the villagers, by teaching them directly and by setting a good example in their own living habits. They tried to communicate their pleasure in learning to the youngsters who constantly crowded into their home, making privacy and solitude difficult to obtain. They planted a vegetable garden behind their house in the hope of encouraging the villagers to grow and eat nutritious food. It was a rugged job. They terraced the plot, dug drainage ditches, and laid on topsoil. As in the case of their appearances at the athletic field, this also astonished and won the approval of most Cundayunos, for educated Colombian women avoid manual labor of any kind.

For their part, the villagers have showered *las gringas* with gifts of fruits and vegetables and many other tangible items they cannot afford to give, as well as their personal friendship.

Last Easter, for example, a family with whom Sue had become particularly close (she is the *comadre* [comother] of one of the children) wanted to share their Easter celebrations with her on their little farm in the country. Colonel Galvis begged her not to go, or to permit him to send soldiers along because of the *banditos* in the hills. The presence of soldiers would spoil such a celebration, Sue said, and she went on a trip that she will probably always remember.

It was a three-hour journey. The mother rode on horseback, carrying the new baby. Sue also rode a horse, while the rest of the family walked. When they reached the farm in the hills, they baked bread and bananas

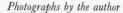
Photographs by the author

in a brick oven, fished with nets in a river, and spent part of the night cleaning their catch by moonlight and candlelight.

"It was something special," says Sue, "that Saturday night before Easter. Another family and some friends joined us. People were playing guitars and singing, and we danced until the sun came up."

Karen and Sue, who at this writing are still working in Cunday, are giving a great deal of themselves to help the people of Cunday learn to help themselves. Are they succeeding?

Father Vásquez said, "They have performed many services which were long needed." And Mayor Rubio: "The work of these girls is very important. Their gift with our language, their sympathy and understanding, and their concern with the problems of the village make them indispensable." Says Colonel Galvis: "Karen and Sue give direction and set goals for major programs. They have brought a new spirit to Cunday."

See also Section Three, COLOMBIA; LATIN AMERICA; PEACE CORPS.

163

A YEAR BOOK SPECIAL REPORT

CONGRESS MAKES A DECISION

Allen Drury, Pulitzer prize-winning author of the best-selling book *Advise and Consent*, takes an understanding look at the workings of Congress as it grapples with one of the most controversial issues of our times. This vivid, inside account of the passage of the Civil Rights Act of 1964 provides a classic example of how one of the great institutions of our democracy goes about its work.

Illustrations by Parviz Sadighian

THE CONFRONTATION

The story of the Civil Rights Act of 1964 is one of the great political dramas of our republic, a legislative achievement of classic proportion. It is a complex and many-sided story. In part, it is the story of two Presidents, John F. Kennedy and Lyndon B. Johnson, who first tentatively and uncertainly approached the issue of civil rights, but then embraced the cause as their own and devoted to it all their influence and power.

It is the story of two veteran Republicans, Senate Minority Leader Everett McKinley Dirksen of Illinois and Representative William M. McCulloch of Ohio, and Senate Democratic Whip Hubert H. Humphrey of Minnesota, who worked patiently to compromise party differences and produce a law they hoped would correct the major source of social unrest in the United States. It is the story of Senator Richard B. Russell of Georgia and his fellow Southerners, fighting desperately, as was their right, to turn back a tide of history they could temporarily delay, but in no way thwart. And it is the story of Negro leaders, some fully responsible and some completely irresponsible, who organized a fury of protests that helped to produce the national climate in which the bill could be passed.

It is the story, finally, of a majority of the American people, confused and upset, not entirely sure of the wisdom of all the bill's provisions, but sensing that the time had come to render justice in an area where justice had too long, in too many areas, both North and South, been neglected.

Out of all these factors, some human and emotional, some political and calculated, some springing out of the immediate crisis and some reaching back into the dim reaches of American history and the American conscience, Congress arrived at its decision on the Civil Rights Act of 1964. It was a decision whose consequences no man can now accurately foresee, but one which probably had to be made in 1964, in this way, in just this fragile yet imperative hope that it would indeed be the answer for a tense and troubled land.

As with any piece of legislation that reaches the floor in the House and Senate, the civil rights bill had its roots in events long before 1964.

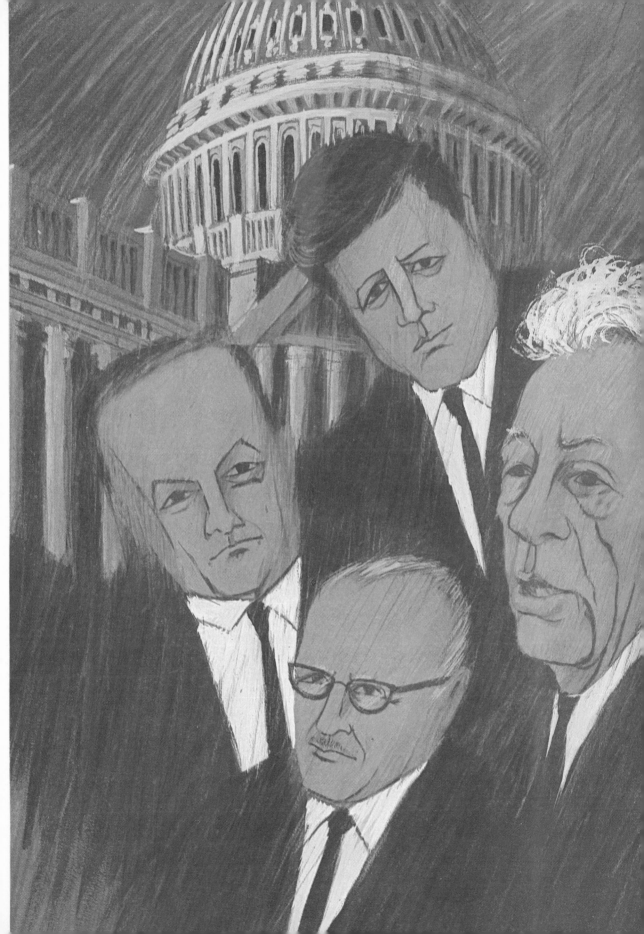

In 1957 and 1960, Congress had passed two mild civil rights bills that were designed mainly to ease restrictions on voting. This had been done with the help of the then Senate Majority Leader, Lyndon B. Johnson of Texas. (Johnson opposed certain further measures in 1960 which he was to support wholeheartedly in 1964, an inconsistency which alienated Representative McCulloch to the point where he was tempted to withhold his support of the 1964 bill.) It was not until 1963 that everything began to come together and move toward the climax that was to be reached on July 2, 1964. On that day, President Lyndon B. Johnson, using 72 pens to write his 14-letter signature, signed the bill into law at the White House.

To understand the events of 1964, it is necessary to go back to 1963 and set in perspective the situation that existed at the start of that fateful year. It was the year of the so-called "Negro revolution," and of the shattering drama of presidential assassination.

The year 1963 began with a rising tide of complaint against President Kennedy. Though committed to civil rights by the Democratic platform of 1960 and by his own campaign speeches, he seemed curiously hesitant to use his executive power in an area so full of potential disaster. The criticism came from Republicans. It came from Democrats. It came from Negro leaders. In March of 1961, John F. Kennedy had ordered an end to racial discrimination in hiring for federal jobs. He had, when events made it inescapable, ordered troops to the University of Mississippi to enforce integration. But aside from these actions and occasional statements, he had done little. It appeared to many that he might be following the pattern of his predecessor, Dwight D. Eisenhower, in holding the executive branch aloof from the civil rights battle.

On March 1, 1963, following a long series of urgings from such men as Senator Humphrey and Representative McCulloch, President Kennedy sent his first message to Congress on the subject. It dealt with proposals to intervene in certain cases of voting discrimination, with legislation to extend the life of the Civil Rights Commission, and with authorization for federal assistance to schools and communities that were working to end racial discrimination.

The message was received with lukewarm enthusiasm by civil rights groups. Republicans in Congress, jealous of their historic record as the party that ended slavery in the Civil War, greeted it with the introduction of close to a hundred other civil rights measures. These were generally much stronger than the Kennedy proposals in the fields of voting, educa-

The Tide
Of Complaint
Was Rising

tion, housing, employment, and the general administration of justice in civil rights abuses. There, for a while, the matter rested.

Washington, both in the White House and on Capitol Hill, evidently felt that it was doing enough with these paper gestures. The Negro community did not agree.

In May, bitter riots occurred in Birmingham, Ala. The violent clashes between police and Negroes had a deeply searing effect upon America's image abroad and America's conscience at home. The President, propelled finally into direct action, ordered out federal troops for use if necessary. The crisis eased a little, but it was now clear that the tide of discontent would not subside.

On June 11, President Kennedy was forced once more into direct participation by the onrush of events. He federalized the Alabama National Guard to make Governor George C. Wallace stand aside from the door of the University of Alabama and permit the enrollment of two Negro students. In a somber address to the nation, the President then promised new legislation, including a ban on discrimination in places of public accommodation. He also pleaded with his countrymen to help solve the racial crisis in their own homes and in their own hearts.

A day later, Medgar W. Evers, Mississippi Negro leader, lay dead at the hands of an unidentified murderer, and Mr. Kennedy was meeting with former President Dwight D. Eisenhower in an attempt to enlist his support for the forthcoming administration proposals. General Eisenhower came away from the meeting to tell a group of Republican Congressmen in a private talk that "a bundle of laws" wouldn't solve anything. On the same day, Senator Russell met with 18 fellow Southerners, 17 Democrats, and Republican Senator John G. Tower of Texas, to pledge that he would lead the fight against the civil rights bills "with every means and resource at my command."

The stage was set, and the lines for and against civil rights action were beginning to form. At the White House, President Kennedy, now fully committed, held meetings with pro-civil rights Democrats and Republicans in Congress. He conferred with former President Harry S. Truman (who did not give him much encouragement), and he talked to some 300 union leaders in further attempts to ensure the broadest possible backing for his forthcoming proposals. The first act of the drama of the Civil Rights Act of 1964 was about to begin.

*Governor
George Wallace
Stands Aside*

THE
CURTAIN RISES

It opened in the House of Representatives, the result of a carefully considered decision on the part of the administration. "We decided that we would start in the House," according to Burke Marshall, Assistant Attorney General in charge of civil rights, "because of the progress of the tax-cut bill. The House had finished with it. Its decks were clear. The Senate was still considering the tax bill. The President did not want the Senate to become involved in a fight over civil rights until that bill had become law."

Representative McCulloch, looking back, takes a somewhat harsher view:

"The President was more interested in passing a tax bill to benefit some segments of the economy than in passing a civil rights bill for all of us." And one of the main architects of the Senate version of the civil rights bill, Senate Republican Whip Thomas H. Kuchel of California, remembers that "it was common knowledge in Congress that President Kennedy didn't want a civil rights bill. He deemed the tax cut more important to the economy. He was afraid that if he pushed civil rights too aggressively he would antagonize the powerful Southern chairmen of major committees who might be able to stop the tax bill as a means of getting revenge."

Wherever the truth lies, the decision was made. The first priority of business for the administration was to enlist the support of Congressman McCulloch, ranking Republican on the House Judiciary Committee which would write the bill.

"It was obvious to us," recalls Nicholas Katzenbach, then Deputy Attorney General, who later moved into the top post, "that the Republicans in both houses had to be fully committed if the bill was to succeed. There had to be bipartisan backing first, because of the proposed fundamental changes in social practice that would require the broadest possible support from all parts of the national community. Secondly, we needed broad support in order to stop a filibuster in the Senate."

There was also another reason, grounded in the practical realities of the two-party system. Neither party could afford to take exclusive blame for the bill

A Plea To The Country

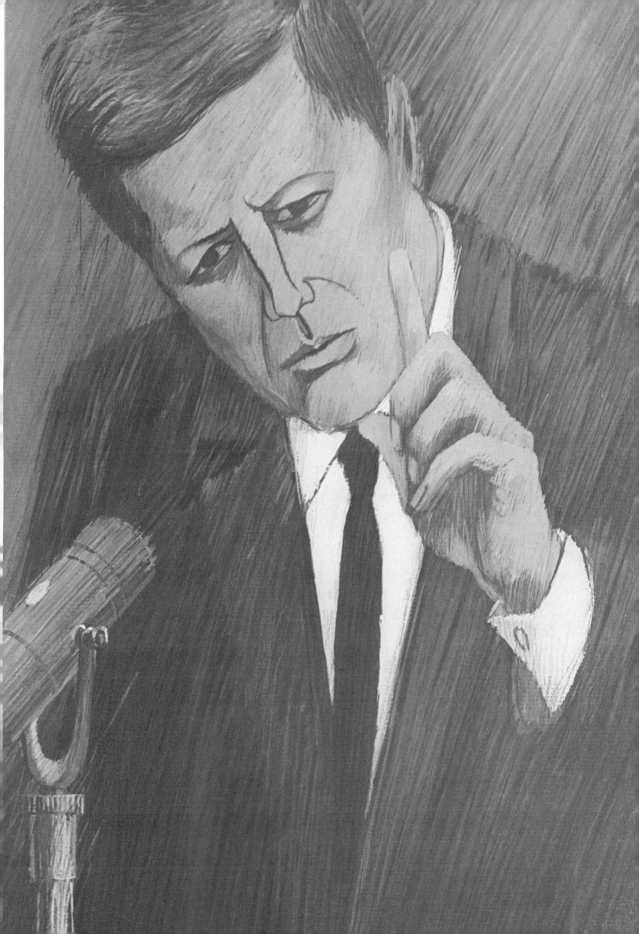

should something go wrong with its application, and neither party could allow the other to take exclusive credit should it work well. The Negro protest, cutting across the country and across political boundaries, made bipartisanship both necessary and inevitable.

Marshall was assigned the job of enlisting McCulloch's help, and flew immediately to the Congressman's home in Ohio for a series of private conferences. Marshall soon gained McCulloch's support. "I had decided a couple of years previously," McCulloch recalls, "that the time had come for implementing the Constitution for all citizens."

With McCulloch's backing assured, the administration's bill, carrying out the principal recommendations in the President's message, was introduced in the House by the chairman of the Judiciary Committee, Representative Emanuel Celler, Democrat, of New York. Hearings were promptly opened with testimony by the Attorney General, Robert F. Kennedy, and proceeded smoothly to their conclusion. During this period, the President held numerous conferences with key Democrats and Republicans in the House. The Department of Justice "team," led by his brother Robert, Katzenbach, and Marshall, did the same. Many Southerners were consulted, too. While most did not agree with the administration position, a good many were privately relieved that the issue was going to be settled finally by the Congress, thus freeing them of the necessity for further futile battles to stop the tide of events.

This attitude served to increase the mood of general friendliness that prevailed throughout most of the debate in both chambers—a mood which contributed materially to the extraordinary feat of peaceable democratic legislating that the Civil Rights Act of 1964 turned out to be.

Southern Leaders Plan Their Strategy
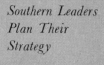

In the Senate, the administration still hoped to have the tax cut passed before the 1963 session ended—a hope that did not materialize until 1964—and therefore the strategy was to have the civil rights bill considered in committee until the tax bill might be out of the way.

Thus the legislation was introduced in the Senate in three forms. There was an omnibus bill, containing all the administration's proposals, introduced by Senate Majority Leader Mike Mansfield of Montana. There was a bill containing most of the administration's proposals but deleting the public accommodations section, introduced jointly by Senators Mansfield and Dirksen. There was also a bill containing the public accommodations clause only, introduced by Chairman Warren G. Magnuson, Democrat of Washington, of the Senate Commerce Committee. The Commerce Committee promptly began work on the Magnuson bill. The Senate Judiciary

Committee, chaired by Senator James O. Eastland, Democrat of Mississippi, took up the Mansfield-Dirksen measures.

The President, his brother the Attorney General, and the Department of Justice team met repeatedly with members of both the Senate and the House. Their policy of patient and careful persuasion did not, however, have quite the effect in the Senate it appeared to be having in the House. "We had only two possibilities," says Senator Russell, leader of the Southern forces. "We could let them pass the bill, or we could fight it. There was no chance of compromise."

Senator Dirksen, Justice officials, and some other Senators maintain that they were always receptive to Southern ideas. The Southerners disagreed. As they saw it then, and still see it, they faced a solid phalanx determined to pass a bill that they honestly believed would do serious damage both to their own region and to the Constitution.

The Massive March On Washington

The initial drive of the Southerners occurred in the committee hearings. The Judiciary Committee hearings, according to one tart-tongued Northerner, "were apparently designed to give Senator Sam Ervin of North Carolina a chance to argue with Bobby Kennedy." The senior Senator from North Carolina did indeed argue with the Attorney General for nine straight days of hearings. After that, the bill was sent to a subcommittee where further arguments went on. It was beginning to be obvious that the chances were dim for Senate passage of a bill in 1963.

Administration efforts were lent an extra edge of determination by the continuing impatience of the Negro community. On June 22, Dr. Martin Luther King; Roy Wilkins, executive secretary of the National Association for the Advancement of Colored People (NAACP); and James Farmer, national director of the Congress of Racial Equality (CORE), met with the President at the White House and urged faster action. And on July 2, Negro leaders met in New York City to plan a mass march on Washington, D.C., for August 28.

The President, meanwhile, held a series of meetings with influential groups throughout the nation, including church leaders, 93 woman's organizations, and business leaders. On July 12, he sent letters to thousands of school boards across the country, appealing to them for help in solving the civil rights problem. Also urging passage of the bill were non-Negro groups such as the American Federation of Labor and Congress of Industrial Organizations (AFL-CIO); Protestant, Catholic, and Jewish groups; many national publications; and numerous educators. But the central battleground still remained the Congress.

A RUNAWAY
HOUSE

In the House, where the bill was in the hands of a Judiciary Subcommittee for drafting, matters appeared to be moving steadily toward a satisfactory conclusion for the administration. Then, in October, the picture abruptly changed. A majority of the subcommittee, honest in the conviction that the administration bill was not strong enough, suddenly brought out a bill giving the federal government much more drastic powers to move directly into civil rights disputes without waiting for state action. A major political problem was presented with dismaying impact to the President and his advisers. They were aware a bill that strong would not be approved by the House, and that, if the full Judiciary Committee sent it to the House for debate, it would simply be amended to death and returned to committee. This would mean that there would be no bill at all. The administration switched course and began a desperate, and ultimately successful, attempt to kill the bill brought out by the subcommittee.

Again, the attempt could not have succeeded without the help of Republican leaders in the House. Lawrence "Larry" F. O'Brien, President Kennedy's legislative liaison man, tried and failed to convince subcommittee members of the practical situation facing the administration in Congress. He also spent five hours one Sunday afternoon trying to convince Negro leaders. They urged the administration to ride roughshod over congressional moderates and try to pass an extreme bill.

Instead, Mr. Kennedy and his advisers turned once more for help to Representative McCulloch and to such other powerful Republicans as House Minority Leader Charles A. Halleck of Indiana, and Representative Clarence F. Brown of Ohio, high-ranking member of the House Rules Committee. Hasty and repeated conferences were held. The President himself participated in several of them. The problem was made more complicated by the fact that Southern members of the subcommittee, acting on Senator Russell's advice, were supporting the subcommittee bill on the theory that it was so extreme it would be killed when it reached the floor of the House.

Bobby Takes The Heat

For the public record, the Attorney General returned to the Capitol and, in Marshall's words, "took the heat and said what had to be said"—that the subcommittee bill was unacceptable because it would give the federal government too great a power to intervene in civil rights disputes, and that this in turn would bring its defeat in the House. As a result of his testimony, and a number of conferences held by administration spokesmen, sentiment began to swing away from the subcommittee bill and toward the more moderate administration position.

A long Sunday afternoon talk between Representative McCulloch and Representative John V. Lindsay of New York, leader of the Republican liberals on the subcommittee, led ultimately to a compromise. One administration adviser later termed it "a gentlemen's agreement without fringe benefits." Impressed by McCulloch's arguments that it was now or never for civil rights legislation, Lindsay in turn enlisted the support of fellow Republicans and liberal Democrats on the subcommittee. The Republicans demanded, and got, an administration promise that the President himself would inform recalcitrant Democrats of the final compromise terms, and that neither he nor any other Democrat would claim partisan credit for the compromise. With assurances of good faith all around, administration aides and the Republicans sat down in a closely guarded room in the Congressional Hotel and went to work.

The result was a 56-page draft that retained basic administration proposals with just enough of the liberals' ideas to secure a favorable vote from the full Judiciary Committee. These included a Fair Employment Commission that could bring suit in federal court to ensure nondiscrimination in hiring but could not—as the subcommittee had wished—decide such issues on its own. The compromise bill also gave the Attorney General the right to intervene in civil rights cases, but only if he joined in a suit already filed by someone else, or if the case involved a segregated state or city facility. The measure also excluded some public accommodations such as barbershops, shoeshine parlors, and smaller boarding houses. And the voting-rights section, which the subcommittee had wanted to have cover state elections as well as federal, was narrowed down to federal only.

With this draft before them, the President and Representative Halleck met at the White House and agreed that the administration and the Republican leadership would join to oppose the subcommittee bill, support the compromise, and fight against any amendments submitted on the House floor.

The next day, the full Judiciary Committee defeated the subcommittee

*A Compromise
Is Fashioned*

bill 19–15; voted 20–14 to take up the compromise bill; and then voted 23–11 to approve the compromise. The President and the Attorney General praised Halleck and McCulloch. McCulloch praised Celler. Celler praised McCulloch. And the Leadership Conference on Civil Rights, an informal group of civil rights leaders, issued a statement declaring that it "deplored" the defeat of the subcommittee bill and considered the moderate compromise "inadequate to the needs of 1963."

The civil rights bill was now ready for House passage, but two things intervened: the death of President Kennedy and the Southern-dominated House Rules Committee. The President's assassination caused an inevitable slowdown in many of the processes of government. This was particularly true on Capitol Hill where members adopted an attitude of watchful waiting toward the actions of the new President, Lyndon B. Johnson. This in turn permitted the powerful Rules Committee, which decides when bills are to be debated in the House, to hold back the civil rights bill. Its chairman, Representative Howard W. Smith, Democrat of Virginia, promised to hold hearings on the bill "reasonably soon" after Congress reconvened in January of 1964. Despite repeated requests from President Johnson, he would not budge from that position.

But as 1964 opened, the new President put both the civil rights and tax bills at the top of his legislative priority list. Responding to his vigorous personal leadership, Congress first passed the tax bill. Then on January 30, the House Rules Committee voted 11–4 to send the civil rights bill to the floor of that body.

Next day, the House debate began, its outcome a foregone conclusion. The Northern Democratic-Republican coalition stood firm against attempts to amend the bill. If the new administration had ever had any intention of bargaining away such features as the Fair Employment Commission to gain support in the Senate—something House leaders in both parties were afraid of—McCulloch and his Republican colleagues made sure it would not be done.

"We've worked too long and too hard for this bill to stand for any White House deals made just for the sake of preserving Democratic unity in next fall's election," McCulloch said tartly. Ten days later the House endorsed his position by approving the bill just as it stood, with an overwhelming vote of 290–130.

On virtually a take-it-or-leave-it basis, the bill was now on its way to the Senate. The second and most fateful phase of the drama of the Civil Rights Act of 1964 was about to begin.

Halleck Sides With The Administration

STRATEGY IN
THE SENATE

"If the day ever comes," the baggy-eyed, tousle-haired, syrup-voiced gentleman in the rumpled suit told his Senate colleagues on Feb. 17, 1964, "when, under pressure, or as a result of picketing or other devices, I shall be pushed from the rock where I must stand to render an independent judgment, my justification in public life will have come to an end."

And that, obviously, was something that Senator Everett McKinley Dirksen was not about to have happen. Both by his own estimate, and by that of his colleagues and of the White House, the Senate Minority Leader was the key to a successful civil rights bill.

"We had to have Dirk," the Democrats' top strategist, Senator Humphrey, remarked later.

"He was the key," said Larry O'Brien at the White House.

A determined campaign was accordingly undertaken to secure Dirksen's support, and, with it, that of a sufficient number of Republican Senators to ensure the limitation of debate. This was necessary if the Senate was ever to reach a final vote.

The Senate Majority Leader, Mike Mansfield, early decided to give Senator Humphrey complete charge of the floor fight and devote his own time to placating and reconciling heated opinions on both sides of the political aisle. Together, he and Senator Humphrey, aided occasionally by administration spokesmen, sought with careful casualness to bring Senator Dirksen around to support of the House-approved bill.

"Senator Dirksen," O'Brien explained later, "had been given a rough time by impatient Negro leaders in Illinois. He had always supported their cause, but in the last couple of years they had begun to criticize him and picket him and issue hostile statements that he wasn't doing enough. When he ran for re-election last time, Negroes, who had always supported him, didn't turn out to help him. He was suspicious and resentful. So for some time, we just didn't mention civil rights to him, except very casually in passing. We had to give his resentment time to die down."

Almost equal in importance to the strategy of

All Viewed Dirksen As A Key Man

winning over Senator Dirksen were the other strategies, of organization, of publicity, of legislative maneuvering, devised by the voluble, vigorous, supremely astute Senator Humphrey. So too were the strategies of Senator Russell and his Southern colleagues. They were to delay passage of the bill for four months, and provoke the first use of cloture (limitation of debate) on a civil rights bill in the history of the Senate.

On Feb. 26, 1964, the issue was joined. The Senate voted 54–27 to bypass its Southern-dominated Judiciary Committee and place the House bill directly on the calendar of bills awaiting Senate action, without further hearings. There followed two weeks of parliamentary maneuvering as pro-civil rights members sought to bring about an immediate debate, and Southerners sought to delay one. Then, on March 16, Senator Mansfield made the necessary motion to place the bill formally before the Senate for action. The motion was debatable, and the fight was on.

"We knew from the outset," Senator Russell says, "that the odds against the South were all but impossible. Some 60 members were already signed, sealed and delivered to support the leaders on cloture, when the debate began. Every decent human being is in favor of civil rights. I'd like to have bigger, better, and finer civil rights for all citizens everywhere. But my colleagues and I did not feel we could honestly support this bill, whose primary impact would be upon the South and whose ultimate result would be a definite weakening of constitutional liberties for all Americans. I found right away there was no hope of compromise. It was either fight or surrender, so we fought. It will be a long time again before 19 men can wage as intensive a struggle as we waged, over so long a time."

Because of this attitude, the administration and most pro-civil rights Senators knew that cloture was imperative for Senate passage.

"We hoped nobody would start hollering about it right off," then Deputy Attorney General Katzenbach recalls, "but we knew it was the only possibility of getting civil rights legislation. We were also leery of making any early charges of 'filibuster.' We just wanted to let time pass, let the debate run on, let other legislation get logjammed behind the bill, and gradually let the Senate become impatient for a decision."

This strategy was in major part devised by Senator Humphrey, who has said, "I had to make up my mind on my mental approach to it. I recall literally talking to myself, conditioning myself to the long ordeal that lay ahead. I thought through what I wanted to do, and how I would act. I made up my mind that this fight, which I knew would be a very hard and

Mansfield Opened
The Fight

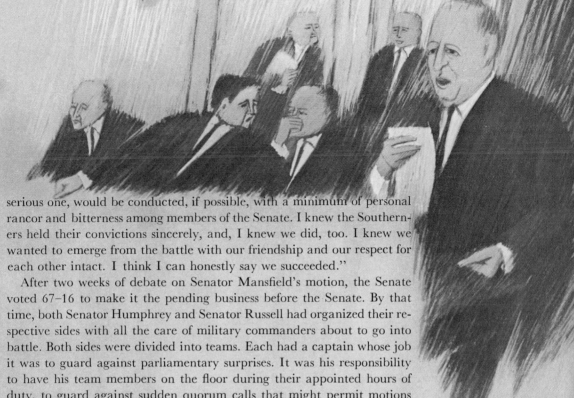

serious one, would be conducted, if possible, with a minimum of personal rancor and bitterness among members of the Senate. I knew the Southerners held their convictions sincerely, and, I knew we did, too. I knew we wanted to emerge from the battle with our friendship and our respect for each other intact. I think I can honestly say we succeeded.''

After two weeks of debate on Senator Mansfield's motion, the Senate voted 67–16 to make it the pending business before the Senate. By that time, both Senator Humphrey and Senator Russell had organized their respective sides with all the care of military commanders about to go into battle. Both sides were divided into teams. Each had a captain whose job it was to guard against parliamentary surprises. It was his responsibility to have his team members on the floor during their appointed hours of duty, to guard against sudden quorum calls that might permit motions that could either set aside the bill or unexpectedly speed its passage. In addition, Senator Humphrey established a research center staffed with aides from the Department of Justice and the Senate Commerce Committee. He also decided to issue a daily civil rights newsletter reviewing the previous day's debate and other developments in the field.

Senator Russell
Organizes
His Team

Senator Russell and his 18 Southern colleagues, arguing the unpopular side of the issue, were less well-financed. They were unable to call upon the administration for help, and were unable to command the support of vast segments of the press and other powerful lobbying groups. Nonetheless, by forming three teams and spelling each other every two days, they, too, manned the floor on an around-the-clock basis.

Looking back now, it is possible that the filibuster could have been broken. As some civil rights leaders demanded, Senator Mansfield and Senator Humphrey could have held the Senate in session without a break until the Southerners literally dropped from exhaustion. But this would really have caused bitterness, and would never have been forgiven. More was involved in the debate than the civil rights bill. Also important was the preservation of the Senate as a place where men could continue to be friends—and so continue to legislate together on other matters of national importance long after the civil rights bill became law.

Of the 67 votes (two-thirds of the Senate) necessary for cloture, pro-civil rights forces felt that they could count on 61, about 16 Republicans and perhaps 45 Democrats. Possibly they might get more Democrats, but they could not be certain. This meant that at least another six or seven Republicans would have to vote for limiting debate. Senator Dirksen, the man who could do the persuading, remained an enigma.

TIME FOR DECISION

Limitation of debate is, in the eyes of a majority of the Senate, a genuinely serious step. Smaller states have often found in unlimited debate a protective shield against domination by larger states, and both liberals and conservatives have, upon occasion, found it a potent weapon for their causes. Therefore those who sought to limit it now needed support of the most distinguished and influential kind. For a while, Senator Dirksen, possibly enjoying their discomfiture, kept them guessing.

"I remember saying many times," Senator Humphrey relates, " 'Well, Dirk, when do you think we ought to meet and talk things over?' And he'd say, 'Well, give us a couple more days. It isn't time yet.' And this went on week after week. And finally we were able to get him to call together a meeting."

"Hubert Humphrey suggested that he and I get together and talk it over," Senator Dirksen recalls, "and I made a countersuggestion: that we get the leadership on both sides of the aisle together, and also get the Justice Department crowd, Bobby (Kennedy), Katzenbach, Marshall, and so on. I had already given a lot of thought to rewriting Title II (public accommodations) to take out some of the stump speeches the House had put into the bill, and also to bring it closer to state control, instead of federal.

"They agreed, and we held the first of five meetings in my office here in the Capitol. We'd meet from about 10 A.M. to 1 P.M. and then go to lunch, and then to the floor. After lunch, our staffs and the Justice people would get together and tinker with the language we'd suggested. Next morning, we in turn would go over their suggestions and either accept or amend, and then send some more ideas to them. Finally, we had about 70 amendments relating to different parts of the bill.

"Along with this, I called several Republican Conference meetings (composed of the entire Senate Republican membership) to explain the proposed changes to them and get their ideas. It was all terribly tedious work, but at last, after about a month, we had what looked like a final draft ready to submit to the Senate."

Humphrey Takes The Offensive

The Dirksen amendments were basically just minor changes in language. Senator Kenneth B. Keating of New York, an active participant in all the Dirksen conferences, summed it up best after the battle was over:

"There was a psychological problem which the Dirksen amendments satisfied. In order to pick up the extra Republicans needed for cloture, there had to be what appeared to be substantial changes. Actually the changes were not very extensive nor of any great significance. They just gave the states a little more authority in the opening stages of civil rights disputes. But they did provide doubtful Senators with a reason to justify voting for cloture."

Later, Senator Dirksen himself remarked privately with some satisfaction that he had "applied a little of the old oil-can technique" to his balky colleagues when he proposed his amendments. The principal one gave the states a 90-day period of grace in which to prosecute public accommodation cases before the federal government moved in. But because of it, and other minor amendments which he drafted, sufficient votes were won for cloture, and the way was thus open to pass the bill.

The way was not opened, however, without much shrewd strategy on the part of other Senators as well. Here, Senator Humphrey did the major and most effective work. Early in March, he held a series of meetings with church organizations, business groups, labor officials, and Negro leaders. Through them, he arranged for civil rights rallies in many states, with the clergy taking the lead. Senator Russell, in fact, credits the clergy with the largest share of influence in swinging public sentiment behind the bill.

In addition, Senator Humphrey made up his mind not to let the Southerners, as he put it, "occupy the press." To forestall what he regarded as undue publicity for the Southern argument, he and his colleagues "took the offensive and got a good press."

"We encouraged our people to be on radio and television," he says. "I wrote each friendly senator suggesting that he go on these media as often as possible to state our case. I encouraged reprinting our key material in the Congressional Record so that it could be sent out to the country under our franking privilege. We were active, at no time passive, and at all times challenging the opposition.

"We engaged in a predetermined program to arouse the public, to create a sense of wrath and indignation in the public and also in the Senate," Senator Humphrey recalls. "We knew we must keep the public stirred up and genuinely interested in passing the legislation."

As for "using the old oil-can technique," there remains some question as to who used it upon whom. Senator Dirksen thought he used it on his

The Justice Department Team Helps Find A Solution

Republican colleagues, but there is also evidence that Senator Humphrey used it on Senator Dirksen.

"I knew if I pushed myself forward any more than I did," Senator Humphrey remembers, "that the bill would fail. Dirksen had to be out front. Dirksen is a leader, a great dramatist and a fine legislator. He had the right to be out front. I gave him every opportunity to be there."

Senator Humphrey was also anxious that Senate Majority Leader Mansfield should become more deeply committed. "I knew," Senator Humphrey says, "that Mike had to get a little angry to become really involved. This came about when Dick Russell refused to let the Senate proceed to vote on the jury trial amendments."

There are varying interpretations of this episode, which came about halfway in the debate, but most Senators consider it to have been a definite turning point. Senator Mansfield thought he had Senator Russell's agreement to permit a vote on several amendments providing for jury trials in civil rights violations. He so announced to the Senate. Senator Russell then declared that it had been a misunderstanding, and he certainly would not permit a vote. Senator Mansfield was angered, and so were many other Senators who had not yet become fully committed to the civil rights cause.

Senator Kuchel, the Republican whip, remembers that a meeting was held in the Republican cloakroom right after Senator Russell made his statement. "At that moment many of us became convinced that the Southerners were completely intractable. Had they been a little more flexible, they might have been able to get some concessions."

Senator Humphrey said later that he was "rather surprised at the Southerners' tactics in not permitting us to vote on amendments from time to time. If they had done so, they could have claimed before the country that the legislative process was working, and that they were not stalling the Senate's work. Instead, they kept obstructing."

To this Senator Russell repeats simply, "It was fight or surrender. So we fought."

Even so, thanks to Senator Humphrey's efforts and Senator Russell's own innate decency and the great personal respect and friendship for him in both parties, the debate went forward, aside from this one episode, without notable bitterness or personal animosity. But it was, as most participants now believe, a fateful episode for the Southern cause.

As the Senate came closer and closer to the day when most members

The Decision
Hardens

185

now felt that cloture must be attempted if the bill was to pass, a threat to Senator Dirksen's leadership began to develop within his own Republican ranks. This came from Senator Bourke B. Hickenlooper of Iowa, senior to Senator Dirksen in point of Senate service and long jealous of Dirksen's selection as Senate Minority Leader. Senator Humphrey, who had a friend in the Republican inner councils "reporting to me regularly," warned Senator Dirksen that Senator Hickenlooper was becoming increasingly disgruntled and, if not appeased, would refuse to vote for cloture, and would also take several Republican votes with him.

Senator Dirksen at first told Senator Humphrey not to worry, that he had 26 certain Republican votes. Senator Humphrey told Senator Dirksen that Senator Hickenlooper was picking up votes, "that we were in trouble." Aware of the embarrassment the Hickenlooper group was causing the leaders, the Southerners began to press for immediate roll calls on various parts of the bill.

"We refused and held the floor for about a week. This gave us more time to nail down the cloture votes of the Hickenlooper group," Senator Humphrey remembers. "I recall Senator Russell complaining quite bitterly that we would not cooperate with him in voting on amendments now, when we had wanted to earlier. I remember saying to him. 'Well, Dick, you haven't any votes to give us for cloture, and these fellows do.' That was the sum and substance of it."

After several days of negotiation, the leaders worked out what became known in the Senate as "the Hickenlooper Unanimous Consent Package." It was an agreement that three major amendments—the jury trial, Fair Employment Commission, and public accommodations sections of the bill—would be voted upon by the Senate on Tuesday, June 9. If those amendments could be voted upon separately at that time, Senator Hickenlooper and his friends agreed, they would give their votes for cloture.

The amendments were voted upon. Only one, guaranteeing jury trials in criminal contempt proceedings under all provisions of the act save those governing voting in elections, was adopted. But Senator Hickenlooper and his friends, true to their word, prepared to cast their votes to limit debate.

At 7:30 that night Senator Humphrey called President Johnson—who had for the most part remained out of the legislative battle—and told him that the votes for cloture were secure. Next day, an hour before the cloture vote, Senator Humphrey passed a note to Senator Philip A. Hart, Democrat of Michigan, predicting that the civil rights forces would have 69 votes, two more than necessary for cloture. When the roll was called in a tensely quiet Senate chamber, they had 71. For only the sixth time in history, and for the first time in a civil rights debate, the Senate had voluntarily abandoned its jealously guarded privilege of unlimited debate.

Even so, under the terms of the cloture rule, each of the 100 Senators still had the right to a full hour of debate on the bill and its amendments before the final vote. But many waived this privilege. After several futile Southern attempts to amend the bill, a motion was made on June 17 to drop the House bill and vote on the so-called "Dirksen-Mansfield substitute" hammered out in so many conferences and negotiations during the long weeks of debate.

The vote was 76–18 in favor of this. "I have never known such a feeling of relief as I did when that vote came," Senator Mansfield was to remember later. Final Senate approval of the bill became a matter of hours.

At 7:49 P.M. on June 19, after 83 days of debate and some of the most patient and dedicated legislating in Congress' long history, the Senate approved the bill, 73–27, and returned it to the House for its compliance.

There occurred several more days of lull as Southerners in the House made futile, final attempts to stop the legislation. Then on June 30, the House Rules Committee voted 10–5 over last-ditch Southern protests to send the Senate bill to the floor of the House for action.

On July 2, the House approved it 289–126.

Three hours later, using 72 pens, President Lyndon B. Johnson signed the Civil Rights Act of 1964 into law, and the great battle was over.

Thus Congress made its decision: a decision reached, as democratic decisions always are reached, on a confused and often conflicting basis of opposing pressures, opposing opinions, opposing ambitions and ideals and needs and desires, out of which, by some miracle, comes the forward progress of the United States. On few issues in the nation's history have there been such tense emotions and such embittered feelings. Yet on few issues, remarkably enough, has there been such basically decent and good-hearted legislating by the Congress. While riots and violence flared in many places over the country, on Capitol Hill the nation's business went forward in an atmosphere of mutual understanding and respect.

This did not prevent men from opposing one another to the limits of their abilities. But it did prevent them from becoming enraged with one another and thereby losing sight of the best interests of the country.

"The nearer it came time to vote," says Congressman McCulloch for the House, "the more assured I became that I didn't need to needle, cajole, persuade or arm-twist my colleagues. They felt as I did, that the time had come to pass this legislation."

"I used some of the old oil-can technique," repeats Senator Dirksen, but he believes basically that "it was history that did it. It was an idea whose time had come. We just helped it along."

And for the White House, Larry O'Brien remembers it this way:

"There was very little talk of political patronage or deals. This one was clean. Sometimes you have to offer a dam here, or a defense project there, to get a bill through. This is a tough game, and sometimes we do make deals. But not in this case. This bill went through because men were convinced that it was time for it to go through. It was a good feeling."

"There are four stages in the life of a law," says one of the most influential Senate backers of the bill, Republican George D. Aiken of Vermont. "First comes enactment. Then interpretation. Then application. And then, most important of all, the willingness of the people to accept."

Congress' decision on the Civil Rights Act of 1964 was only Step One. But it provided an example of the democratic process in action which may be helpful to the rest of the country as it undertakes Steps Two, Three, and Four.

For a summary of the provisions of the Civil Rights Act of 1964, see Section Three, CIVIL LIBERTIES. See also, CONGRESS; DEMOCRATIC PARTY; PRESIDENT OF THE UNITED STATES; REPUBLICAN PARTY.

"Man is part of nature, and his war against nature is inevitably a war against himself." Rachel Carson

CALL TO
THE WILDERNESS

A Family's Hike Into the Northern Cascades

BY ROBERT A. IRWIN

T HE SUNSET'S COPPERY REDS and pinks had
shaded into darkness, and night, at last, had come to
Washington's Northern Cascades. As we huddled around
our campfire, only a pale shimmer of light filtered through
the fringy spruce spires that flanked the creek. The rushing water picked up and was suffused by the glow of
starshine and the faint moonlight that was reflected off the
surrounding peaks. The sweet incense of aspen smoke
from our fire, and the droning, almost hypnotic, roar of

the rapids, added to the mystical quality of this, our last night at our primitive camp on Grizzly Creek.

We—my wife, three school-age daughters, and I—had set up camp on a high bank overlooking the creek. We had back-packed all our gear and food into this wild, high valley. It was already late in July, yet no one else had entered this beautiful and remote wilderness since the melting of the winter's snow. The trails showed us only the tracks of bear, deer, and elk. Not a sign of a human bootprint.

As we were sipping our hot tea around the fire, we let the experiences of the day's expedition up the North Fork of Bridge Creek sink in and become part of us. My daughters were chuckling over how I had thrown myself down in exhaustion on springy clumps of bear grass after we had reached the top of a series of grueling switchbacks on the hot, dusty trail. Everyone else flopped down, too. It was utter, delicious relaxation—all of us oblivious to the bees, the flies, and the dust of the trail.

Just then in the narrow corridor of sky above our campfire, we noticed that one of the stars around the Big Dipper seemed to have shaken loose and was moving across the sky to the northeast. It was too bright and too high for a jet. It was Echo II, the man-made moon. It was ironic, at this most primitive and isolated of all our campsites, that the only active evidence of humanity should be this intrusion of an unmanned, highly sophisticated product of electronic and aeronautical wizardry. It was ironic, too, that the intrusion was in the new wilderness of space, a province of exploration undreamed of in our pioneer past.

THE TEA WAS FINISHED. The rest of the family was bedded down. As I doused the fire for the night, the embers and blackened stones of our crude fireplace hissed above the roar of Grizzly Creek. The moon had cleared the wall of mountains to the southeast, its rays stabbing into a misty colonnade of alpine fir. A pair of deer exchanged soft, whistling signals somewhere in the shadows. I turned in, but, seemingly a moment later, awoke. A cold, paralyzing terror gripped me. Grizzly Creek was rumbling ominously. Was a wall of water racing downstream to engulf us?

As fear seized one corner of my mind, cold calculations raced through another. Perhaps a natural ice-and-snow dam on some high, glacial lake had given way. A landslide? Or an earthquake? If it was a natural catastrophe, we were trapped. Higher land was too far away. If it was just a sudden rush of flood water, we were safe—10 feet or so above creek level. "Don't alarm the family," I told myself. "Just sit tight and wait it out."

A few moments more of heart-pounding listening. The rumble grew no louder. My tenseness drained away, and I sheepishly realized the creek had two throats—a tenor one in the swirling current below us and a *basso profondo* amid the falls and rapids upstream. It all had been a hallucination, but one with a fundamental lesson. It was a chastening reminder that we, as members of *Homo sapiens*, were in the wilderness on the same terms as any other species. We enjoyed no special privileges. We were not exempt from the age-old forces of nature.

What had impelled us, a typical, comfort-loving, suburban family, to immerse ourselves in the wilds of the Northern Cascades? We had had to drive 2,100 miles across prairie, plain, and mountain; abandon our station

After hiking all day from road's end, we caught sight of Glacier Peak, showpiece of the Northern Cascades.

wagon to ride on *The Lady of the Lake* ferry to the end of 51-mile-long Lake Chelan; and be transported 23 more miles by truck from the hamlet of Stehekin at the head of the lake to the end of a rough, gravel road. Finally, we had to pack supplies on our backs and tramp over forest and mountain trails for a week at a time. Why all this effort?

First of all, we wanted to take a close-up look at a sample of the type of undeveloped, untrammeled, primeval land that was about to come under the protection of the Wilderness Act. After eight years of deliberations, the Congress, on Aug. 20, 1964, finally enacted this landmark conservation legislation. It was the most far-reaching action to preserve the U.S. wilderness since the National Park Service Act of 1916.

By 1960, only 28,204,390 acres remained as undeveloped and wild out of the 1,938,029,440 acres of primeval land that awaited the first settlers

Photographs
by
Ethel M. Irwin

of what the Alaskans call the "lower 48 states." In that year of 1960, the Outdoor Recreation Resources Review Commission (ORRRC)—authorized by Congress in 1958—began a monumental study. Its purpose was to assay the recreational needs of the American people up to the year 2000, inventory the available land and water resources, and recommend policies and programs. The ORRRC, in its study, limited its concept of wilderness to roadless tracts of 100,000 acres or larger. Under the Wilderness Act, however, tracts as small as 5,000 acres may classify as wilderness. Thus more than 61,000,000 acres in all 50 states and U.S. possessions could be included in the National Wilderness Preservation System. (See *The Wilderness Act—and its Wilderness Preservation System* [below] for

THE WILDERNESS ACT —— AND ITS

A U.S. CONSERVATION LANDMARK
Public Law 88-577, Approved Sept. 3, 1964

HAWAII

ALASKA

PURPOSE. *The Wilderness Act:*
• For the first time, has declared it to be national policy "to secure for the American people of present and future generations the benefits of an enduring resource of wilderness."
• Establishes a National Wilderness Preservation System of federally owned land.
• Provides that all wilderness areas shall continue under the jurisdiction of their present administrators, who are now bound by statute—not by mere departmental regulations.

STANDARDS. *The Act:*
• Defines wilderness and thereby provides criteria for areas that are incorporated into the system. They must be areas (1) "where the earth and its community of life are untrammeled by man, where man himself is a visitor who does not remain," (2) of undeveloped federal land "without permanent improvements or human habitation," (3) largely unaffected by the forces

of civilization, (4) providing "outstanding opportunities for solitude," and (5) of 5,000 acres or large enough to make preservation practicable.
• Prohibits commercial enterprises, roads, structures, motorized transport or equipment, and the landing of aircraft within wilderness areas—with certain exceptions.

TIMETABLE. *The Act:*
• Immediately incorporates into the system 9,121,000 acres of National Forest lands in 18 Wilderness Areas, 35 Wild Areas, and the Boundary Waters Canoe Area in Minnesota.
• Sets up an orderly procedure for administrative review of certain federal lands during the 10 years ending Sept. 3, 1974. By that time, the Secretary of Agriculture, after due notice and public hearings, must make his recommendations to the President as to the suitability or nonsuitability for preservation as wilderness of the more than 5,477,000 acres of Primitive

the act's major provisions, and for maps of the system's areas.)

In addition to wanting to see what the American taxpayers—through their duly elected Congress—were getting, we also felt a deep, personal desire to experience the beauty and solitude of a bit of primeval, uncluttered North America. And, I suppose like many parents, we wanted our children to experience the land as it was when the earliest explorers or fur trappers entered it. We wanted them to hear the howl of coyotes, feel the icy water of glacial pools, smell the duff of deep hemlock forests.

These riches of wilderness have always distinguished the New World from the Old, where the primeval forest is no more. For Americans, in particular, wilderness travel offers a renewal of roots that tap their recent

WILDERNESS PRESERVATION SYSTEM

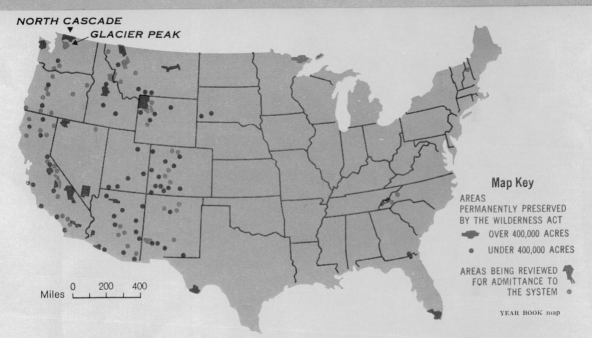

Map Key

AREAS PERMANENTLY PRESERVED BY THE WILDERNESS ACT

🖛 OVER 400,000 ACRES

• UNDER 400,000 ACRES

AREAS BEING REVIEWED FOR ADMITTANCE TO THE SYSTEM

YEAR BOOK map

Areas of National Forests in 10 states. Likewise, the Secretary of the Interior must submit his recommendations on the nearly 46,600,000 acres of parks, monuments, wildlife refuges, and game ranges in 20 states, (see maps above).

SPECIAL PROVISIONS. *The Act:*

• Does not establish any new agency or call for any new jobs or appropriations for the 54 National Forest wilderness areas established under the act.

• Recognizes (1) any established use of parks, monuments, forests, refuges, or ranges and (2) pre-existing private rights and practices, such as grazing, use of motorboats and aircraft, or access to property.

• Permits mineral prospecting in the 54 areas if "carried on in a manner compatible with the preservation of the wilderness environment."

• Allows mining development in the 54 areas under the U.S. mining laws and all laws pertaining to mineral leasing until Dec. 31, 1983.

• Provides that *patents* (titles to mining claims) granted after Sept. 3, 1964, would convey title only to the mineral deposits, unless prior existing rights required otherwise. Timber cutting would be allowed under certain conditions only if necessary to mining operations.

• Permits the President to authorize any water or power project in the 54 areas if it "will better serve the interests of the United States and the people thereof than will its denial."

With sturdy staves to brace ourselves against the water's force, Nancy and I waded across Rainbow Creek.

historical past. It provides a challenge, a test of old skills that were essential to survival before the frontier disappeared. On the importance of keeping these old arts alive, U.S. forester and conservationist Aldo Leopold observed: "You either know it in your bones, or you are very, very old." When we heard our call to the wilderness, we knew it in our bones! We wanted to go into it by ourselves—on our own and under our own power. But we knew we would have to do so on nature's own terms.

The summer before, we had hiked into the Northern Cascades with a group of more than 50 persons, and had used pack horses. Before that, we had car-camped for several summers in remote areas, mostly in the West. Now we were ready to go in alone.

The Northern Cascade Range has withstood the incursions of man and remains one of the nation's last vast, scenic mountain wildernesses. And vast it is. Not a road or railroad track penetrates its rocky bastions from Stevens Pass northward for 100 miles to Allison Pass in British Columbia.

We learned how impenetrable this country could be, even on foot, that day of my hallucination of disaster at Grizzly Creek. We had set out for a "Sunday stroll" along the North Fork of Bridge Creek, a round trip of no more than seven miles. It was all day and into the evening before we got back to camp. And this without knapsacks. I had cached them about seven feet off the ground in a thicket of small western fir. This was to get them out of the way of any bear, pack rat, or other varmint that might have come snooping around camp in our absence.

THAT JOB DONE, we were off—almost. We had underestimated the creek. We first had to ford Grizzly Creek's turbulent waters, which came up to the hips of my youngest daughter, 10-year-old Nancy. Use of a long, stout pole made the crossing safer for her—as well as for her sisters, Susan, 15, and Barbara, 18. My wife, Ethel, and I also lent a shaky hand. As we dried numbed feet and laced up our boots, we started to fret about lost time. Then we stopped and reminded ourselves that we were there to enjoy and absorb the beauty around us, and not to worry about any schedule—except nature's. We had only to watch our time to make it back to camp before nightfall.

At that moment, a chunky, gray water ouzel, or dipper, flew past us and up beyond our campsite on the opposite bank. We had been amused by its antics the evening before. It would let out a peeping whistle as it flew low, skimming above the rushing water. When it lit upon a boulder, it would do a little dipping dance, and then duck down under water to take a walk on the bottom of the torrent to catch insects that were swept along below the surface of the swift-moving stream.

A full half hour had passed by the time the last boot was laced and we were on our way again. The trail led along an evergreen ridge, dipped down across a couple of boulder-strewn washes, then climbed into an open, parklike forest. A sudden whir of wings broke the stillness. A white-tailed ptarmigan flew out of the lower branches of a ponderosa pine. This sturdy member of the grouse family has adapted efficiently to its alpine environment: snowy white plumage in the winter, a brown and black mixture in the summer.

Not much farther up the trail, we encountered a much less wary and

195

normal bird, a cousin of the ptarmigan. It was a fool hen, or Franklin's grouse. The hen made an apologetic clucking noise, fluttered off the trail onto a mossy log, and proceeded to observe us curiously and without any sign of fear. Nearby, its brood of three chicks wandered about aimlessly. These trusting birds would long have been extinct if it were not for their camouflage—a mottled brown plumage almost impossible to spot.

Fresh tracks of bears reminded us further that we were intruders in the wilderness. Long-toed prints in the red clay of the trail, fresh droppings, and a clawed, rotted log where a bear had grubbed for ants—all these prompted us to bang our metal cups, and to sing and talk loudly. Such noisemaking warns a bear of intruders and prevents what could be a perilous confrontation, especially if it should be with a sow and its cubs.

The trail, which had been winding through a conifer forest high on the slopes above Bridge Creek, plunged through a series of alder and willow thickets. Only our feet—not our eyes—could tell us which way the overgrown trail went. Our slow, noisy progress through one bushy tangle flushed an elk. We caught sight of its dark, tawny flanks as it thrashed through the brush. Across a wide, level snowfield, past alpine spruces, we came upon a maze of boulder-strewn, dry watercourses. The trail lost itself in the jumble of rocky washes leading up the slope to our right. As we stood there trying to sort out a possible trail, a pair of raucous Clark's nutcrackers croaked at us derisively. I chose the widest and smoothest-looking wash, and we began to climb. About half a mile farther and 400 feet higher, we stopped. We had not found a trace of the trail. As we scanned the country below us, Barbara asked, "Isn't that it down there by the creek?" It was.

It was 3 P.M. when we reached a dancing brook in a willow-lined ravine. The spot at last for lunch. We dipped our cups into the water and proceeded to devour our hard sausage, Swiss cheese, and Swedish *knäckebröd* (hardtack) lubricated with butter or jam from plastic tubes. In wilderness travel, one must keep weight at a minimum. In the Northern Cascades there is no need to load oneself down with water—either in canteens or in foods. That is one of the joys of these mountains. Any lake, any stream offers pure, clear, ice-cold refreshment.

As we finished our meal, we speculated on what lay ahead. We hoped that the jungle was behind us. At any rate, we gave ourselves another half hour to reach the end of the trail and all its promised glories. We also complimented ourselves on our wisdom that morning in deciding not to break camp at Grizzly Creek. Slogging through the underbrush with knapsacks would have been an ordeal because, in our normal mode of travel, Nancy lugged a load of a little over 20 pounds. On the trail, her two sisters carried 25 to 30 pounds; her mother, as much as 35. My load averaged 45 pounds. Even without the burden of knapsacks, we would need at least three hours to get back to camp.

IN OUR SELF-ALLOTTED HALF HOUR, we came to the end of the visible trail. Beyond a large, granite tabletop, a snowfield stretched away 400 yards to the base of a turbulent falls. Its angry waters foamed through a gap in the wall of snow and ice that covered a high ledge, plunged 60 feet, and gnawed at the sides of the snowbank below.

A visiting deer in velvet warily approached our camp for a handout of salt.

Snow-clogged trails and passes bedeviled us throughout our Cascades adventure. Frequently we had to revise our planned routes, backtracking or taking long, difficult detours. The heavy snowpack made it a particularly dangerous year for high-country travel. Snowslides and a fall down a steep snowfield had taken three lives in one weekend in Washington's Cascades. But the snow had its compensations. The snowbank beside us provided the base for a refreshing dessert: a cupful of clean winter snow with lemonade mix stirred in.

We lounged on the top of the granite slab, absorbing the warmth of the afternoon sun and savoring our "glacier sherbet." A clump of purple penstemon bloomed bravely, just out of reach of the snow below. Honeybees struggled down into the long, tube-like blossoms to collect nectar. Frantic undulations inside the purple trumpet showed the bee's progress as it backed out to buzz into the next fragrant tube. A piercing whistle from across the creek put an end to this drowsy amusement. A hoary marmot had spied us and alerted his brethren. There he was, perched on a boulder, his blunt, gray nose pointed our way. This strangely assembled, shaggy member of the rodent tribe is roughly the size of a dachshund. Its rump and bushy tail are a rusty brown, the rest of its body a tawny gray and black.

Beyond the marmot, the scree of fragmented, black rock sloped up steeply. The gravel and the dark ledges above were laced with rivulets from the snowfields and the massive, bulging snouts of Goode Glacier. The dark, icy peak of Goode Mountain reared above it as a sentinel on the south. Above the falls' snow-bridged brink, 9,080-foot-high Mount Logan stood guard, vast glaciers grinding down on both its flanks. The

We took a cupful of snow, stirred in lemonade mix, leaned back on the rock, and lazily savored our "glacier sherbet."

blue-black shadows on the glaciers and the scree above were creeping nearer. It was time for us to be heading back to camp.

Reluctantly, we abandoned our smooth, warm slab. The trail led us back into the same boulder field where earlier we had gone astray. We learned why when we turned around in the field. There was no sign of where the trail entered the brush. Only after we had looked closely could we see where we had just trampled an occasional fern or bit of sedge. Aided by downhill grades, we reached Grizzly Creek shortly after 6 P.M.

During "Operation Boots Off" to ford the creek again, we realized we all were hot, tired, and dusty. The sun was still shining warmly on our camp and on a small sheltered pool of water upstream. Why not take a quick dip and get cleaned up? A volley of squeals pierced the creek's roar, as the girls eased themselves into nature's chilly bathtub.

A satisfying meal of onion soup, boneless pork chops, diced potatoes, carrot flakes, lemon pudding, coffee, and cocoa capped our day. Of course, our menu of lightweight, tasty, freeze-dry and dehydrated foods leaned heavily on modern civilization. But its tastiness and adequateness also owed something to my wife's skill over our crude campfires.

The sun dropped behind the magnificent backdrop of Mount Logan. The mists gathered among the spires of spruces along the creek. We hunched closer to the fire. The ouzel was on patrol again. The meal over, we stirred about to clean up the

Leaner, tougher—and wiser—after our stay in the high alpine solitudes, we hiked back down to Lake Chelan and civilization.

Glacier lilies

Western pasqueflower

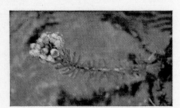
Turk's-cap lily

Tall painted cup

Pink heather

White marsh marigold

dishes and get camp ready for night. It was after that that we unwound, sipping our tea around the dying embers of the campfire.

It had been almost a week since we watched the rear of Ray Courtney's dusty van disappear down the narrow forest road back toward the mountain hamlet of Stehekin. It had been raining then. We were on our own, and each of us knew it. Some days later, Barbara admitted, "You know, Dad, when Ray let us out and drove off, I had some doubts about the whole thing. We'd have to do everything ourselves, including carrying all our stuff on our backs. Well, we're doing it, aren't we!"

Lanky, Lincolnesque Ray, one of Stehekin's two packers, had cautioned us about the snow. A few days before our arrival, he had flown over some of the high country with Sim Beeson, the U.S. Forest Service fire protection chief from Chelan. They had found snow covering all the high lakes and meadows around Glacier Peak. We, therefore, deferred our plans to revisit that area until the end of our Cascade pilgrimage. We would go into the Cascade Pass area first—or so we thought. Our first two days in the wilderness came to nothing short of backtracking frustration. Shoulder-high snow thwarted our attempts to camp beside two high alpine lakes. On the third day, however, we were magnificently repaid for our efforts. We succeeded in making our way into the mysterious inner reaches of Horseshoe Basin.

It was a late July walk into early March. The tall, weedy corn lily measured the retrogression of the seasons. As we advanced into the snow-covered basin over a distance of not more than 400 yards, the corn lilies gradually shrank. Finally, where the snow was thin or had just melted off the wet, silty soil, tender, pale green shoots the size of a man's thumb were thrusting through. All plant life seemed to be in an impatient rush to grow and mature before fresh snow would fall and engulf it. Ferns showed the same pell-mell urge to thrive—delicate, fiddle-headed fronds beside the snowbanks and great, spreading stalks not far down the trail.

The basin itself was ringed on three sides by a high, horseshoe-shaped ledge. I counted at least 20 large cataracts or waterfalls spilling over the rim. They sprang from the glaciers and snowfields spreading down from Boston Peak and Sahale Mountain. As we absorbed the overwhelming magnitude of this panorama of ice, snow, water, and rock, spring kept rushing in. A breeze stirred a nearby willow, a slab of snow fell softly into a stream, and the unburdened branch, already bearing its blossoms of pussy willows, arched gracefully into the sunlight.

AFTER OUR FIRST WEEK in the back country, we had learned something about humility: that human plans do not always accord with nature's and that when they do conflict, nature prevails. As Henry Thoreau observed more than 100 years ago at Walden Pond, "We need to witness our own limits transgressed, and some life pasturing freely where we never wander." In the wilderness, we, too, learned to adjust our ways to nature's. We learned how to stop and observe natural, living things —the delicate, yellow glacier lily blooming in the middle of a snowbank, or a *pika* (rock rabbit) peering at us quizzically beside a high trail.

Nancy made friends with a golden mantled ground squirrel as it tucked away food for its seven or eight months of hibernation.

And when we met Ray Courtney again down at the forest camp alongside the Stehekin River Road at Bridge Creek, we learned a few things about the wild, unspoiled valley of the Stehekin, a modern-day version of Walden on a grand scale. Ray has lived in the valley all of his 44 years. His father had settled along the river as a homesteader in 1916. Now Ray and his vivacious, dark-haired wife, Esther, are rearing six boys, aged 3 to 11, in a simple log cabin near the old place. Four sons attend a one-room, log-cabin school. All of the Courtneys, as well as the rest of the 45 year-round residents of Stehekin, are in love with their valley. When I later visited the Courtney home, Esther looked up from one of Ray's tarps she was mending and recalled one time the previous winter when it had snowed all day and through the night:

"Ray and I strapped on our skis and glided over the quiet snow down to the village. It was all so beautiful and peaceful. The snow was so deep, we could go right over fences and boulders."

Simple pleasures; honest values; plain, homespun virtues; and an intelligent harmony with nature—all these are nurtured in this rare corner of pioneer America. Yet they all are under a threat, a threat that is both a blessing and a curse to today's world—a highway.

As Ray and I rested in the shade of a stately, shaggy-barked Alaskan cedar beside the dusty Stehekin road, he told me of the valley's fear:

"There's talk of running a road down here from the new cross-state highway, when they get that job done. It would run along Bridge Creek to join this road right about where we are sitting now. It would spoil this whole valley. We'd become another resort town like Chelan. Practically everyone in the valley is against it. And," he added in his slow, thoughtful way, "we've got to expect *some* kind of change, but not that road!"

Harold Zahniser, the late executive director of the Wilderness Society and "father of the Wilderness Act," pointed to this same inexorable factor of change in testifying for the bill in 1962: "All our land is destined to be put to some human use. The pressures of civilization are such that none of the land of the United States can be expected to escape . . . (and) endure as wilderness accidentally." Pressures triggered by the population explosion and growing affluence have built up against wild and scenic areas from coast to coast:

• Real estate development with the draining of adjacent swampland has imperiled plant and animal life in the Florida Everglades.

• Demand for dams, for both water and power, threaten to inundate vast scenic stretches of the Grand Canyon.

• In California, it is superhighways versus 2,000-year-old redwood groves.

• In the Allagash River wilderness of Maine, the conservationists are pitted against the enlightened but tenacious owners of nearly 1,000,000 acres of rugged, lake-studded timberland over future management of the area.

So far the pressures on the Stehekin Valley and the rest of the Northern Cascades have been weak. Its beauty has escaped despoliation largely by accident. It is too out-of-the-way, its slopes too steep, its veins of minerals too thin. Over the years, however, roads began to creep up the narrow valleys, and logging invaded some scenic areas. Conservationists in the Northwest became concerned and in 1957 formed the North Cascades Conservation Council. Supported by other outdoor and conservation groups, it has proposed a North Cascades National Park. It would include the 458,505-acre Glacier Peak Wilderness Area plus 849,681 acres of adjacent forest land, including the Stehekin Valley. Only the Glacier Peak area is protected now by the Wilderness Act. Should a national park be established, other roadless sections in it could be eligible for protection. The economic future of this entire area has been placed in the hands of a team of officials from the U.S. Department of Agriculture and the U.S. Department of the Interior. This North Cascades Study Team is preparing a report to the President, who, in turn, can ask Congress to act.

NATIONAL PARK STATUS for some or all of the Northern Cascades, however, would be no cure-all. It would create the problem of handling an ever-growing number of visitors and controlling their impact on the wilderness. Some of this impact we saw firsthand when we spent a week of knapsacking in the roadless back country of Glacier National Park, in northwestern Montana. In our 62-mile North Circle hike, we met several families out enjoying the wilderness, some with preschool children. The heavy traffic we saw on the trails diminished the feeling of solitude, as did the awareness that civilization—a road, chalet, or motel—was just over the ridge. And worst of all, were the convenient but ugly prefabricated steel shelter cabins. What a contrast with our camps at Grizzly Creek or Rainbow Lake in the Northern Cascades!

None of us will forget that last day in the Cascades. As we sailed back down Lake Chelan on *The Lady of the Lake*, we thought back on our experiences of the past two weeks. We looked back on the time when we had sat in awe in Horseshoe Basin watching the secret rites of spring. And when we had heard a sudden, dry-leaf, rattling noise along the hot trail up Rainbow Creek and caught sight of a diamondback rattler slithering away from us over the sharp rocks. Even that rattlesnake had its beauty and helped to teach us its and our respective places in nature. And the time

We'll never forget our camp at Grizzly Creek. We hated to leave that sunny bank after our last breakfast there.

when we had climbed through billowing mists toward Cascade Pass into a hushed grove of massive cedars and spruce, their roots still covered with a shoulder-high mantle of snow.

At that moment, from the deck of the lake boat, we could see the thickening clouds swirling down from the peaks flanking Railroad Creek. They were drawing their gray curtain across our Cascades adventure. A year earlier almost to the day—we were on the same boat going back into the world of supermarkets and superhighways. We had vowed then that we would return by ourselves. We would revisit the high country at the head of Railroad Creek and beyond: Lyman Lake, Cloudy Pass, Miners Ridge, and above all, Glacier Peak. That spectacular, glacier-draped mountain lies so deep within the wilderness that its lonely 10,528-foot summit cannot be seen from any major road. We would camp beside a jewel of a tarn, Canyon Lake, that we had spied from a high, craggy knife-edge. High snow and, now, mountain storms had dashed those plans.

No, we had not been able to keep that part of our vow. We had, however, succeeded in immersing ourselves in some of the mysteries and marvels of a tossed ocean of jagged peaks. We had entered an enchanting and forbidding land of glaciers, rushing water, towering trees, high alpine crags, and meadows. We had gone into the wild, free haunts of the golden eagle, bear, ptarmigan, elk, and mountain lion.

We all agreed that our camp along Grizzly Creek had been the high point. Barbara called it "my idea of a real primitive camp. It was fun and challenging to be all on our own." Nancy agreed. "Yes, our Grizzly Creek camp was keen," she said. Aside from enjoying the sheer beauty of the mountain landscape, Susan liked the freedom of the wilderness. "It makes me sick to think that for a whole year I'll have to live fenced-in. Out here we could go where we wanted when we wanted and do what we wanted."

My wife looked out of the rain-spattered window of the boat, which was crowded with one-day excursionists. "It was a vacation as it should be— alone with my family," she said. "No intruding cars, people, radios, television. Sometimes at night, when we were all in our sleeping bags, I couldn't help but think what a wonderfully beautiful country ours must have been before it was all tamed and harnessed."

We all learned something about ourselves. There was no room for bickering. We were part of a natural world that made no special rules for human beings. We had survived its challenges. We had enjoyed its beauties and its solitudes. We came out of the wilderness a little proud of ourselves—and a little chastened.

As all of us lounged dry, warm, and comfortable below decks on *The Lady of the Lake*, we knew we were leaner, tougher, more confident, more aware of our place in the scheme of things. In a word, we were wiser than on that rainy afternoon two weeks earlier when we watched Ray Courtney's truck disappear in the mists of the road back to Stehekin.

At the same time, we knew well that we were not done with the Northern Cascades—that wild, faraway range with its immensities and infinite variety of moods, aspects, challenges, and wondrous beauties. We "knew it in our bones" that we would come back again, that we would always be listening for our call to the wilderness.

See also Section Three, OUTDOOR RECREATION; PARKS; WILDLIFE.

CONTENTS OF SECTION THREE

YEAR BOOK contributors report on the major developments of 1964 in their respective fields.

THE YEAR ON FILE, 1964

Articles in this section are arranged alphabetically by subject matter. Titles refer directly to articles in THE WORLD BOOK ENCYCLOPEDIA.

ADEN. See SOUTH ARABIA, FEDERATION OF.

ADVERTISING quickened its tempo during prosperous 1964. Total volume of advertising in the United States jumped more than 6 per cent to a record high estimated at more than $13,900,000,000.

Advertisers invested about $1,800,000,000 in television, an increase of 9 per cent. The magazine industry marked up an 8 per cent gain with $1,100,-000,000 in advertising revenues. Newspapers also finished a strong year, taking in more than $810,-000,000 from national advertisers, for an increase of 6 per cent. Radio stations were able to show a 2 per cent gain with a $290,000,000 cut of the advertising pie. Statistics showed good gains for other forms of advertising such as direct mail, but outdoor advertising was able only to hold its own.

Part of the gain in revenues was accounted for by higher charges rather than greater use. Climbing costs were of major concern to both the advertising agencies and to their clients.

Costs also were a factor in the disappearance of big-name, single-sponsor TV shows such as the "DuPont Show of the Week." Magazines benefited. At least some TV advertising money was being switched to magazines.

In the United States, a "czar" was named to administer the cigarette industry's advertising code, which was adopted by the nine major tobacco companies in April, 1964. Robert B. Meyner, former governor of New Jersey, was given power to impose fines as high as $100,000 on violators.   EDWIN W. DARBY

See also PUBLISHING; RADIO; TELEVISION.

AFGHANISTAN took a bold political step in 1964. On September 19, the 452-member grand assembly approved a new constitution under which, for the first time, freedom of speech and of the press were guaranteed and political parties allowed to form. It barred close relatives of the king from politics and key government posts, and it clearly defined the succession to the throne.

The new constitution was endorsed on October 2 by King Mohammed Zahir Shah, who had been one of the driving forces behind its modern concepts. Following the king's endorsement, parliament was dissolved. A transitional government was to rule by royal decree until Oct. 14, 1965, at which time a new parliament would convene following elections.

Great Britain granted Afghanistan about $2,300,-000 in credits to modernize its sugar industry and build a cottonseed-oil-extracting plant. Soviet Union engineers completed the Salang Tunnel in the Hindu-Kush mountain range, linking north and south Afghanistan by road.

Population: 15,200,000. **Government:** King Mohammed Zahir Shah; Prime Minister Mohammed Yousof. **Foreign Trade:** exports, $115,000,000; imports, $59,000,000. **Principal Exports:** caracul, carpets, dried fruits and nuts.   WILLIAM SPENCER

See also MIDDLE EAST.

AFRICA

AFRICA remained a continent in political ferment in 1964. Malawi, the former British protectorate of Nyasaland, became independent on July 6. Northern Rhodesia, another former British possession, became the independent state of Zambia on October 24. Both had been members of the defunct Federation of Rhodesia and Nyasaland. Tanganyika and Zanzibar merged on April 26 as the Republic of Tanganyika and Zanzibar. In October, they adopted the name of Tanzania. Britain gave Basutoland and Gambia increased responsibility for internal self-rule;

PLACARD-WIELDING CROWD attending election rally in Lagos, Nigeria, typifies the enthusiasm with which the African nations have taken to Western-style politics.

Associated Press

Student Driver

independence was planned for both countries in 1965. See BASUTOLAND; GAMBIA; MALAWI; TANZANIA; ZAMBIA.

Congo (Léopoldville) again attracted world-wide attention during the year when rebel forces in control of the eastern part of the country captured and held as hostages all the whites in the area. Belgium and the United States were forced to intervene on humanitarian grounds. A military force of Belgian paratroopers, transported in U.S. planes, succeeded in rescuing scores of whites from the rebels, but other white prisoners, including Dr. Paul Carlson, an American medical missionary, were massacred. See BELGIUM; CARLSON, PAUL EARLE; CONGO (LÉOPOLDVILLE).

Pan-Africanism. The prospects for pan-African union looked brighter than ever in 1964. The Organization of African Unity (OAU) completed the first 18 months of its existence with an impressive record of unity on issues vital to Africa's development and future.

In February, an OAU meeting of 34 foreign ministers was convened in Lagos, Nigeria. Agreements were reached on a number of far-ranging questions. Africa was declared a nuclear weapons-free zone. A newly formed Commission of African Jurists was incorporated as an OAU body. A resolution was adopted urging increased African membership in the United Nations (UN) Security Council. The ministers also urged Great Britain

to prevent a unilateral declaration of independence in Rhodesia by the minority white settler regime there. They also called for a ban by African states on all aircraft and ships trading with the Republic of South Africa.

Later, the organization's African Liberation Committee of Nine formed itself into a "committee of action" to accelerate freedom for the Portuguese Overseas Territories of Angola, Mozambique, and Portuguese Guinea, as well as the British High Commissioner territories of Basutoland and Bechuanaland Protectorate (see ANGOLA; MOZAMBIQUE). Transit camps were to be established to help refugees from countries still awaiting liberation, and a mission was sent to the Republic of South Africa in what turned out to be a futile attempt to form the country's African nationalist political parties into a united front.

Tshombe Incident. The heads of state of the OAU assembled in Cairo in July for their second annual meeting, at which Diallo Telli Boubacar was elected first permanent secretary-general. Several African nations threatened to boycott the meeting should the delegation from Congo (Léopoldville) include Premier Moise Tshombe. As a result, neither Congolese President Joseph Kasavubu nor Tshombe attended the conference. However, at a meeting of the nonaligned nations in Cairo late in the year an attempt by Tshombe to attend resulted in his being held by Egyptian authorities for several days. His detention set off a violent reaction in Congo, where the Kasavubu government retaliated by sealing off the UAR and Algerian embassies in Léopoldville. Tshombe was permitted to leave the UAR only after the Congolese restrictions against the two embassies had been lifted.

International Relations. African countries cooperated repeatedly on intercontinental matters. Nine African countries attended an April ministerial meeting in preparation for a Second Afro-Asian Conference set for March, 1965. The intercontinental meeting was to be held in an African state to be determined by the OAU.

A Union of Nonindependent African States was formed to hasten independence and help end rivalry between various liberation movements on the continent. The union cooperated with the OAU liberation committee. In June, delegates representing trade union organizations in some 30 African countries met in Bamako, Mali, to attend the second conference of the All-African Trades Union Federation. The group planned to establish a Pan-African Trade Union which would have its headquarters in Accra, Ghana. Union strikes, boycotts, and demonstrations were advocated in countries still struggling for independence.

The merging of Tanganyika and Zanzibar into a single state brought a fourth African region into discussions on a proposed federation of Kenya, Tanganyika, and Uganda. Although Kenya and

Tanganyika appeared to be near agreement in May on all aspects of the federation problem, Uganda believed that political federation was not feasible and that attempts to strengthen the East African Common Services Organization should be worked out instead.

In West Africa, the heads of state of Guinea, Ivory Coast, Liberia, and Sierra Leone studied the formation of an African Free Trade Zone. A ministerial working commission was appointed to draft proposals which would in turn be submitted to the four heads of state at a subsequent meeting set for April, 1965, in Monrovia, Liberia. Gambia and Senegal continued to explore the possibility of a "Senegambian" association upon the achievement of Gambian independence in 1965 (see SENEGAL).

Revolts and Mutinies. Problems of internal security plagued a number of Africa's new nations. In Ghana, an unsuccessful attempt to assassinate President Kwame Nkrumah resulted in a sweeping reorganization of the police force and an increase of the president's powers over the judiciary system. Plots against the presidents in Congo (Brazzaville) and in Togo also were discovered and suppressed by government forces (see CONGO [BRAZZAVILLE]; GHANA; TOGO).

In May, the government of Gabon was overthrown in a swift and bloodless military coup during which President Léon Mba was taken prisoner. French troops were rushed in, however, under the terms of a Gabonese-French security and assistance agreement, and within 24 hours they had routed the rebels and restored President Mba to his position. See GABON.

Dahomey and Rwanda both experienced uprisings that had to be put down by military force. The rioting in Dahomey was touched off by Bariba supporters of former President Hubert Maga who

TROUBLE SPOTS IN AFRICA

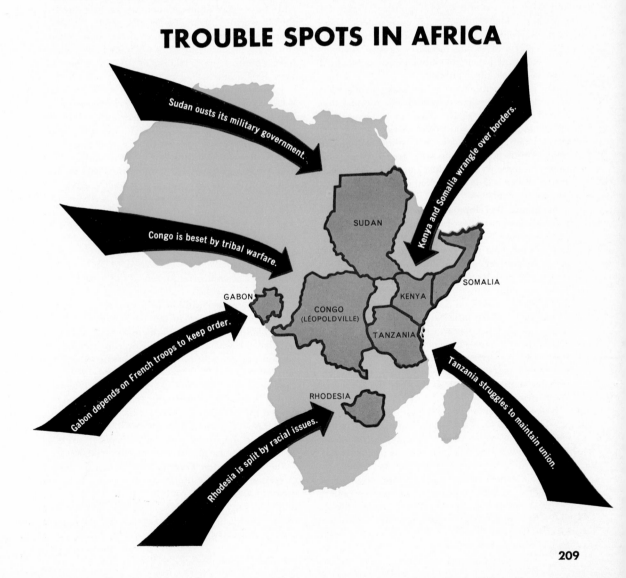

had been ousted late in 1963. Government troops re-established order and arrested 190 rampaging Bariba tribesmen, including their leader, Chabi Mama. In Rwanda, the disorders were inspired by a terrorist organization known as Inyenzi. When the terrorist attacks continued despite efforts of the police and civilian self-defense units, Rwanda called on the United Nations to investigate. See DAHOMEY; RWANDA.

A wave of military rebellions swept East Africa. In Zanzibar, where the unrest began, the government was overthrown. In Kenya, Tanganyika, and Uganda, however, African leaders were able to suppress military mutinies with the help of British troops whose presence they had requested. See GREAT BRITAIN.

South Africa. The African nations continued to press the UN for measures that would prevent the Republic of South Africa from punishing those Africans who opposed its strict segregation policies and who decried the lack of political rights for nonwhites. The South African government, however, objected to UN interference in its internal affairs and took strong measures against Africans who committed acts of sabotage or advocated violence against the republic.

The government, however, did make a concession to world opinion when it announced in April that it had decided to shelve plans to implement its apartheid policies in South-West Africa, a trust territory it administers under UN authorization. To retain jurisdiction over the area, South Africa continued to argue its case at the Court of International Justice at The Hague in The Netherlands. See SOUTH AFRICA, REPUBLIC OF.

Economic Development. Notable development projects were pushed further along in 1964 in many parts of Africa. New oil refineries went into production in both East and West Africa. Kenya opened a new oil refinery at Mombasa, the first in East Africa. Senegal opened the first refinery in French-speaking West Africa. The Malagasy Republic laid plans for a new oil refinery at Tamatave.

The Ivory Coast, in its largest investment agreement since independence, arranged for the Krupp Consortium of West Germany to build a $25,000,-000 paper plant east of Abidjan. The new seven-year development plan of Guinea included a petroleum refinery as well as the first steelworks in West Africa.

Nigeria also obtained two large loans from the World Bank to help finance its Niger River hydroelectric project and a power plant in the Mid-West Region. Sierra Leone, which opened its first bauxite mine in 1964, launched a program to develop a national rubber industry. In an effort to increase its ability to resist outside economic pressure, South Africa began an intensive search for oil. It also accelerated a huge program for harnessing the Orange River for power. BENJAMIN E. THOMAS

AGRICULTURE in the United States continued to reap the harvest of improvements whose seeds were sown in 1961. President Lyndon B. Johnson and his 3,500,000 fellow farm operators could look back on a year of relative stability, one that was counted upon to carry through 1965. Net farm income and production held close to 1963's record highs. Per capita farm income reached a new high, as did farm exports.

The prosperous U.S. population consumed about 1 per cent more food per person than in 1963; more than $1,500,000,000 worth of agricultural products were sent abroad through the Food for Peace program; and the farm work force had lost another 224,000 hands over a 12-month period ending in October, when it totaled 5,126,000.

New Wheat and Cotton price-support programs were provided in the Agricultural Act of 1964. The voluntary plan for wheat producers was enacted at the President's personal behest. Wheat farmers had rejected a compulsory two-price system in a nationwide 1963 referendum. Without action by Congress, the old wheat program would have continued. Price supports, however, would have dropped to 50 per cent of parity, or about $1.25 per bushel. This would have threatened a $600,000,000 loss in income on their 1964 crop.

Under the new program, enacted April 11, 1964, a farmer who voluntarily agreed to reduced plantings could sell his crop on the market or put it under a price support of $1.30 a bushel. In addition, he would have received domestic and export marketing certificates with cash values of 70 cents and 25 cents a bushel, respectively, when his planted acreage was determined, or an average price of $1.77. About 45 per cent of his crop qualified for the 70-cent certificate, another 45 per cent for the 25-cent certificate. Also, he would be paid a subsidy for diverting cropland from wheat-growing to conservation uses. For the 1965 program, price supports were cut to $1.25, but certificates were raised to 75 cents and 30 cents. The cash price for wheat in December was about $1.65 a bushel.

Wheat Growers with 76 per cent of the national allotment participated in the 1964 program, which helped hold down wheat production. Feed grain output likewise was held in check by conservation diversion payments to farmers. The estimated 2,190,-000,000-bushel U.S. wheat supply for the 1964-1965 marketing year was the smallest since 1957-1958.

The U.S. Department of Agriculture (USDA) figured the 1964 wheat program had restored about $450,000,000 of the threatened $600,000,000 loss to growers on their 1964 crop. In addition, it put storage savings to the government at $108,000,000.

The 1964 Cotton Program was designed to give growers more flexibility, to cut down the yearly increase in surplus carry-over, and to help U.S. textile mills buy cotton at prices comparable to the lower export prices foreign buyers had been paying for U.S.-grown cotton. The law provided, among other

Record of the Year's Major Crops

Crop	Unit	World Production (000,000 omitted) 1964††	1963	Crop	Unit	U.S. Production (000,000 omitted) 1964††	1963
Corn	Bushels	7,755	8,055	Corn	Bushels	3,541	4,082
Wheat	Bushels	9,170	8,335	Wheat	Bushels	1,286	1,138
Oats	Bushels	2,970	3,200	Sorghum (grain)	Bushels	483	583
Barley	Bushels	4,210	4,070	Soybeans	Bushels	702	701
Rice (rough)*	Tons	164.1	162.6	Cotton	Bales	15.4	15.3
Tobacco	Pounds	9,727	9,520	Oats	Bushels	893	981
Cotton	Bales	51.6	50.1	Barley	Bushels	388	400
Sugar	Tons	65.7	59.3	Rice	Cwt.	72	70
Coffee	Bags†	52.7	68.0	Tobacco	Pounds	2,206	2,337

*Excluding Communist Asia   †132.276-pound bags
††Estimate

Source: U.S. Department of Agriculture
††Estimate

things, for price-support loans averaging 30 cents a pound for cotton grown under regular allotments, and for "equalization" payments to such nongrowers as buyers and millers (see TEXTILE).

Production. Farmers sowed 2,000,000 fewer acres than in 1963, when 309,000,000 acres were planted. But they harvested 1,000,000 acres more than 1963's 293,000,000 acres, for the second-highest production and yields on record. The all-crops production index of 109 per cent of the 1957-1959 average failed to match the 1963 record of 112, and the per-acre composite yield index of 113 for 28 major crops also lagged behind the 1963 high of 116. Drought in some major producing areas caused the slight declines.

Corn yields dropped to 60.6 bushels per acre from a record of 67.3 bushels in 1963, and grain sorghums from 43.3 to 40.9 bushels. But wheat yields increased by 1.1 bushels to 26.2 bushels per acre, and cotton from the record of 516 pounds of lint per acre in 1963 to a new high of 528 pounds. Per-acre yields of soybeans and oats were lower, but those of barley and rice were higher.

For totals of major U.S. and world crops, see tables. For other farm production, see DAIRYING; LIVESTOCK; POULTRY.

Farmers' Net Income for the fourth straight year hovered near the $12,500,000,000 mark. Gross farm income in 1964 climbed to $41,900,000,000, from $41,700,000,000 in 1963. But expenses also rose, from $29,200,000,000 to $29,500,000,000, bringing estimated 1964 net income to $12,400,000.

Exports of farm products totaling a record $6,100,-000,000 against $4,500,000,000 in imports in the fiscal year ended June 30, 1964, gave the United States its largest recorded favorable agricultural trade balance in half a century.

Rural Areas Development, authorized in 1962, had by Nov. 1, 1964, organized 2,132 local committees that had planned or started 16,783 projects for developing industries, recreation facilities, and other community improvements. Of these, 8,089 were completed, 226 of them financed in part by Area Redevelopment Administration loans.

The Food Stamp program, begun as a test by President John F. Kennedy in 1961, was expanded and extended nationwide by act of Congress on August 31. Under the plan, needy persons use the stamps, issued by the government, as money to purchase food from stores. Participants buy the food stamps with the money they normally spend on food, getting about $10 worth of stamps for each $6 of cash outlay. The discount varies according to the needs of the recipient.   FRANK B. HARPER

See also CHEMICAL INDUSTRY; FARM EQUIPMENT; FUTURE FARMERS OF AMERICA; INSECT; LIVESTOCK SHOW; SOIL CONSERVATION.

AILES, STEPHEN (1912-   ), Under Secretary of the Army for the past three years, was advanced to Secretary of the Army in January, 1964. He replaced Cyrus R. Vance, now Deputy Secretary of Defense (see NATIONAL DEFENSE).

Color blindness prevented Ailes from serving in the armed forces during World War II. He joined the staff of the Office of Price Administration (1942), and was assistant general counsel (1945-1946). He also was counsel to the United States Economic Mission to Greece (1947). Ailes joined the Steptoe & Johnson law firm, and practiced in Washington, D.C., between 1946 and 1961.

Stephen Ailes was born in Romney, W.Va. He received his A.B. degree at Princeton University (1933), and his law degree at the West Virginia University (1936), where he was an assistant professor of law (1937-1940). Ailes practiced in Martinsburg, W.Va. (1936-1937, 1940-1942).

AIR FORCE, U.S. See NATIONAL DEFENSE.

AIR POLLUTION. See POLLUTION.

AIR RACES. See AVIATION.

AIRLINE. See AVIATION.

AIRPLANE. See ARMED FORCES OF THE WORLD; AVIATION; NATIONAL DEFENSE.

ALBANIA was the only European communist country to applaud the overthrow of Russian Premier Nikita S. Khrushchev. The Albanians continued to call for a total reversal of the Soviet Union's policy despite the fact that Communist Chinese Premier Chou En-lai, who had visited Albania early in 1964, was in Moscow in November ostensibly to patch up differences. See COMMUNISM; RUSSIA.

The latest available statistical data indicated Albania had completely recovered from the effects of its 1961 economic rupture with the Soviet Union. Communist Chinese financial and technical assistance had enabled the Albanians to complete 25 factories. Foreign trade, too, had increased with Algeria, China, East Germany, Finland, Ghana, Italy, Poland, Romania, and the United Arab Republic.

In other areas, Albania sought to break its isolation from the West. On July 28, Albania and Italy upgraded their diplomatic missions to embassy status.

Population: 1,850,000. **Government:** Communist Party First Secretary Enver Hoxha; Premier Mehmet Shehu. **Foreign Trade:** exports, $49,000,000; imports, $72,000,000. **Principal Exports:** foodstuffs, minerals. TOM AND HARLE DAMMANN

See also EUROPE.

ALBERTA. See CANADA.

ALGERIA. The power struggle between President Ahmed Ben Bella and his political opponents dominated developments in Algeria. The president had certain key assets. They included the solid backing of the army and the majority of members of the national assembly, plus the apathy of the Algerian public after eight years of war.

President Ben Bella moved steadily to whittle down the opposition. Ferhat Abbas, one of the founders of the nationalist movement, was barred from the ruling National Liberation Front (FLN) party and placed under house arrest, as was Abderrahmane Fares, a former president of the FLN executive council. In June, Mohammed Khider, the party's secretary, fled to Switzerland. Colonel Mohammed Chaabani, a Khider supporter who had led resistance forces, also broke with Ben Bella.

The most serious opposition to the regime came in the Kabyle Mountains, where Hocine Aït Ahmed had set up the Socialist Forces Front (FFS). In October, however, soon after FFS forces had attacked the president's villa, Aït Ahmed was captured and imprisoned. His arrest left only one opposition leader, Colonel Si Sadok, at large in Algeria. Khider and Mohammed Boudiaf, another of the original leaders of the rebellion against France, continued to oppose the government from abroad.

Population: 11,200,000. **Government:** President Ahmed Ben Bella. **Foreign Trade:** exports, $675,000,000; imports, $1,024,000,000. **Principal Exports:** citrus fruits, iron ore, wine. WILLIAM SPENCER

See also AFRICA; MIDDLE EAST.

AMERICAN LEGION. See VETERANS.

AMERICAN LIBRARY ASSOCIATION (ALA).

U.S. Commissioner of Education Francis Keppel keynoted the 83rd annual conference of the ALA held in St. Louis, Mo., from June 28 to July 4. He called for "dynamic, well-stocked, well-staffed libraries" to meet the problems of an expanding industrial society.

Preconference meetings featured discussions on data processing, bibliotherapy, library buildings, rare books, curriculum design, and educational media. Professional concern centered on social problems and on the role of technology in libraries.

The Adult Services Division of ALA began a study of methods and materials for public library service to functionally illiterate adults in 1964. This research was made possible by a portion of the J. Morris Jones-World Book Encyclopedia-ALA Goals Award. It was announced that this award will also finance two workshops: (1) on how libraries can work with legislators in the best interest of libraries; and (2) on ALA action for assistance to libraries and librarians under attack from would-be censors.

Knapp Progress. A new motion picture, ". . . And Something More," was introduced at the conference. The film depicted quality school libraries. It was prepared by the Knapp School Libraries Project.

The Knapp Foundation, which supports the project, made grants in 1964 to: the Casis School in Austin, Tex.; Allisonville School of the Metropolitan School District of Washington Township, Indiana; and Mount Royal School, Baltimore, Md.

At the Fair. In cooperation with the American Documentation Institute and the Special Libraries Association, ALA sponsored an exhibit, "Library/USA", at the New York World's Fair. The exhibit embodied a demonstration of library services, including a reference book collection; a children's center with a collection of children's books; tape recorded book reviews that could be dialed by phone; and a duplicate of the books selected for the White House Library.

New Review. A major new book review journal, *Choice*, was established by the Association of College and Research Libraries with a grant from the Council on Library Resources, Inc. The publication, planned for college libraries, features book reviews by college and university specialists.

New Officers. Edwin Castagna, director of the Enoch Pratt Free Library in Baltimore, was installed as president of ALA. Robert Vosper, librarian of the University of California Research Library (Los Angeles), was installed as vice-president and president-elect.

Awards in 1964 included:
The **J. Morris Jones-World Book Encyclopedia-ALA Goals Award** of $25,000 as reported above.
E. P. Dutton-John Macrae Award of $1,000 for advancement of library service to children and young people, to Priscilla L. Moulton, coordinator, Elementary School Libraries, Swampscott (Mass.) Public Schools.
Grolier Society Award of $500, to Mrs. Inger Boye, children's librarian, Highland Park, Ill., in recog-

nition of her outstanding contribution to the reading needs of young people.

Lippincott Award of $1,000, for distinguished service to librarianship, to Robert Bingham Downs, dean of library administration, University of Illinois.

Melcher Scholarship of $1,000, for study in children's librarianship, to Mrs. Dallas D. Shaffer, bookmobile senior clerk, St. Louis Public Library.

Melvil Dewey Medal for creative professional achievement to John W. Cronin, director of the processing department, Library of Congress.   DONALD E. WRIGHT

See also CANADIAN LIBRARY ASSOCIATION; CANADIAN LITERATURE; EDUCATION; LIBRARY; LITERATURE; LITERATURE FOR CHILDREN; SENDAK, MAURICE.

ANGOLA continued to seek its independence from Portugal. Under the leadership of Holden Roberto, the revolutionary government-in-exile of Angola carried on the fight from headquarters in Congo (Léopoldville).

Roberto, in his drive to lead Angola to self-government, had at first taken a strong neutralist stand, refusing help from either the East or the West. Early in 1964, however, he announced he would accept aid from Communist China and other communist countries. These nations, he said, could provide the arms and money necessary for an early victory. In April, further evidence of this policy shift came when Roberto's party, the National Front for the Liberation of Angola (FLNA), announced it would permit the communist-oriented wing of the Popular Movement for the Liberation of Angola (MPLA) to join it.

Portugal continued to maintain an estimated 50,000 troops in Angola despite Portuguese claims that the nationalist rebellion had been stamped out.

Population: 4,832,000. **Government:** Governor-General Venancio Augusto Deslandes. **Foreign Trade:** exports, $148,000,000; imports, $136,000,000. **Principal Exports:** coffee, sugar.   BENJAMIN E. THOMAS

See also AFRICA; PORTUGAL.

ANIMAL. See DAIRYING; LIVESTOCK; LIVESTOCK SHOW; PET; WILDLIFE; ZOOLOGY; ZOOS AND AQUARIUMS.

ANTARCTICA. See EXPLORATION.

ANTHROPOLOGY. The discovery of a new fossil man by Dr. L. S. B. Leakey in East Africa excited anthropologists throughout the world (see Section Two, MAN'S BEGINNINGS). Dr. Leakey, who named his discovery *Homo habilis*, expressed the belief that its skull resembles modern man's so closely that anthropologists could well regard the fossil Neanderthal man, Java man, and Peking man as overspecialized offshoots from the generally accepted family tree of man.

Although all anthropologists were agreed on the importance of *Homo habilis*, not all accepted the position that the Neanderthals, Java men, or Peking men should be removed from the list of man's ancestors. Some, in fact, argued that Neanderthals were really only a subspecies of *Homo sapiens* (modern man). Others pointed out that in the past it had

been thought that a near-man, such as some *Australopithecus*, must have been ancestral to any *Homo*, and now Leakey's *Homo habilis* could be said to be the very *Australopithecus* that would take that place on man's family tree.

Wadi Halfa Skulls. Another interesting group of human fossils, 38 in all, were discovered in the Wadi Halfa region of Sudan. Many features in the skeletons and the surrounding tools indicated that these were *Homo sapiens*, though the skulls appeared more primitive than those of most other *Homo sapiens*, except perhaps some of the Neanderthals. They had massive "brow ridges," rounded chins, and robust lower jaws. When a study of these skeletons has been completed, a great deal more may become known about the forces of change that operated on prehistoric populations.

Blood Types. Studies yielded more information on the behavior and physical nature of the great apes and other primates. One study of the blood group called the ABO complex, which occurs in apes as well as in man, showed that most chimpanzees have type A blood, while a few have type O. Orang-utans, gibbons, and baboons, on the other hand, have types A, B, and AB, but not O. Such studies are useful in determining the effects of forces such as natural selection on these animals, and serve to indicate the closeness of relationship in the various groups.

Chimpanzee Behavior. The study of wild chimpanzees in East Africa, made by Jane Goodall of Cambridge University, England, was expected to call for a revision of opinions about the unique abilities of man. Man has long been defined as "the toolmaker," but Miss Goodall found that chimps also make and use simple tools. One was a sponge of chewed leaves used to soak up drinking water from otherwise inaccessible places.   LESLIE G. FREEMAN, JR.

ARABIA. See SAUDI ARABIA.

ARBUTHNOT, MAY HILL (1884-   ), popular lecturer and recipient of the Regina medal in 1964, was honored by the Catholic Library Association for her lifelong dedication to children and books. The former kindergarten teacher has taught and supervised kindergarten and teacher-training classes. Her *Children and Books* (1947) is a college textbook.

While Western Reserve University education associate professor (1927-1949), Mrs. Arbuthnot also was children's book review editor for *Childhood Education* (10 years) and edited a similar section for *Elementary English* magazine. *Time for Poetry, Time for Fairy Tales* (1952), and *Time for True Tales* (1953) appear in *The Arbuthnot Anthology* (1953).

May Hill was born in Mason City, Iowa. She taught summers (1914-1922), received her B.Ph. degree (1922) at the University of Chicago, and took her M.A. degree at Columbia University (1924). May Hill was director of the Cleveland (Ohio) Kindergarten-Primary Training School (1922-1927).

See also LITERATURE FOR CHILDREN (Awards).

213

ARCHAEOLOGY

ARCHAEOLOGY. The earliest undisturbed European site of prehistoric stone tools and extinct animals was found during the year by Professor Laszlo Vertes in Hungary. Named Verteszöllös, the find extended man's knowledge of early European cultures several thousand years. Until 1964, Torralba, Spain, had been the earliest known site.

Stone flake tools of the Clactonian culture were present at Verteszöllös, but no bifacial hand axes as at Torralba. While no one has yet explained the reason for this difference, it is likely that the answer will be found in future comparisons of materials from both sites.

Primitive Art. In the Akkele Guzai region of Ethiopia, Professor Paolo Graziosi found and described more than 20 sites containing rock paintings. Some resembled primitive Spanish Levantine art, with naturalistic cattle and stylized men in orange and red. Other, later paintings resembled some of the Bushmen drawings from South Africa.

The cave at Lascaux, France, containing man's most famous treasures of prehistoric art, was closed to the public, probably never to be reopened. Extensive murals on the walls of the cave, believed to be at least 15,000 years old, were being slowly covered by a green mold. The mold apparently resulted from lighting in the cave and an imbalance in the cave's atmosphere caused by the breathing of thousands of visitors. Plans were to make the fascinating, prehistoric art accessible to the public through photographs and television.

Civilization's Start. Professor James Mellaart of the University of Istanbul, Turkey, presented evidence that makes civilization more ancient than had previously been thought. He gathered his evidence in excavations of the earliest known city in the world,

Çatal Hüyük, in Turkey. The city was flourishing at least 7,000 years ago. It included information on the religious and social life of the Çatal Hüyük city dwellers and new data on the origins of ceramics. Archaeologists had long wondered if the earliest pots they found at sites all over the world were not clay copies of earlier stone bowls.

But in his careful excavations at Çatal Hüyük, Mellaart noted that the use of stone bowls was minor. He found, however, a number of wooden bowls. This was unusual—since materials of wood are rarely if ever found in excavations because of their rapid decay. Other vessels were made of bone. Though Çatal Hüyük has revolutionized knowledge on the development of cities, excavations at the site have only begun. Tests show that there are still 30 feet of unexplored strata.

Writing. Excavations at Warka in southern Iraq have produced clay tablets with cuneiform inscriptions from a period dating to 4,000 B.C. These are the earliest known written signs. LESLIE G. FREEMAN, JR.

ARCHITECTURE

ARCHITECTURE. Ever since Sir Joseph Paxton built his great glass and iron Crystal Palace for the London Exhibition of 1851, some of the most significant architecture of the modern era has come out of specific, one-time events. The year 1964 was no exception, for if the New York World's Fair was largely an architectural bust, a group of buildings designed by the brilliant young Japanese architect, Kenzo Tange, for the Olympics in Tokyo caught the attention of the architectural world. In his main

SAIL-LIKE ROOF over swim-pools, designed for the Olympics by Japanese architect Kenzo Tange, is suspended from masts 415 feet apart.

Japan Information Service

building, Tange arranged boomerang-shaped walls with entrances in the gaps at each end. Overhead he hung a suspension roof like a great, wind-blown sail.

Best of the Fair. Although outdone by the dramatic Olympics buildings as well as by the modest and gay collection of structures built for the 1964 Swiss National Exhibition along the lake shore in Lausanne, the frenetic New York fairgrounds did contain a few buildings of interest. In addition to the International Business Machines' 50-ton egg in a steel forest, architecturally successful buildings were the coolly elegant Spanish Pavilion, the succession of display platforms in a large pond housing New Jersey's Tercentenary Exhibit, and the collection of barn-red and white, clapboard-sided buildings grouping the New England exhibits around a common.

New York Pavilion. The only building at the World's Fair in the grand tradition of Paxton's great structure was Philip Johnson's New York State Pavilion. Johnson ringed a great central court with circular concrete columns from which the multicolored plastic roof was hung. Around the circumference, he placed an auditorium decorated with pop art murals and a cluster of three concrete observation towers, which had glass-enclosed elevators outside the structures. The circular concrete columns and towers were notable for another reason: the slip-form method by which single steel forms were jacked up to mold the concrete as it was poured, stage by stage.

Exposed Steel. In terms of material technology, however, 1964 may be marked as the year when steel came back outside. Using a steel that developed its own protective coating and needed no paint, Deere & Company, the farm machinery manufacturer, completed its new administrative headquarters in Moline, Ill. The building was one of the last designed by the late Eero Saarinen. More akin to Paxton's Crystal Palace than other contemporary-appearing structures, Saarinen's masterpiece looked like an intricate steel truss bridging a ravine.

Boat-Shaped Tower. The year saw the completion of the first urban renewal project to fully seize advantage of urban renewals' potential for rejuvenating the downtown area. At Hartford, Conn., one of the smoothest-working teams of local citizens and local government officials completed the four-block-long Constitution Plaza. Although Harrison & Abramovitz's sleek boat-shaped tower was the symbol of Constitution Plaza, its important achievement was a well-conceived, delightfully detailed pedestrian plaza several levels above the old streets that connected the various parts of the project.

Award. The American Institute of Architects (AIA), sticking to a tradition of its own, awarded its 1964 gold medal to Italian engineer Pier Luigi Nervi, best known, perhaps, for his buildings housing the 1960 Rome Olympics. With this award, the AIA virtually completed its homage to the great foreigners, with the possible exception of the young Tange or Denmark's old Arne Jacobson.　RICHARD A. MILLER

ARGENTINA remained tense as political conflicts and labor problems posed a test for President Arturo Umberto Illia's policy of national conciliation. Political leadership was weak. It was further shaken in December by an attempted return from exile of ousted dictator Juan D. Perón. Pro-Perón demonstrators were of considerable embarrassment to the government during an earlier state visit by French President Charles de Gaulle. See FRANCE.

State controls and governmental interference mushroomed in all sectors of the economy, plaguing both industry and agriculture. Under a newly enacted supply law, the government assumed almost unlimited power over virtually every phase of private enterprise. The General Labor Confederation staged various strikes, demonstrations, and temporary plant take-overs in its bid for higher wages, stricter price controls, and the complete freedom of activities for various extremist parties. The administration, with an eye on the March, 1965, congressional elections, took little direct action so as not to "upset" labor. Instead, it enacted a law for national adjustable minimum wages.

The budget deficit for the fiscal year that ended October 31 totaled over 150,000,000,000 pesos, with expenditures up more than 50 per cent over the previous year. Sharp increases in the money supply and paper money in circulation, plus heavy government borrowing from the Central Bank, gave the economy the initial push it so badly needed. But the price paid for resumed growth was high—inflation was rampant, and the overvalued peso was wobbly.

Impressive production increases of from 30 to 60 per cent were reported in some industrial sectors. However, these were in comparison with exceptionally low 1963 figures, and many plants still worked far below capacity. Good weather also helped agriculture, the droughts of the previous two years giving way to rains and, subsequently, bumper crops. High world prices for beef increased foreign exchange earnings, even though the volume of meat exports was sharply down because of excessive regulations on cattle raising and marketing.

Population: 22,000,000. **Government:** President Arturo Umberto Illia. **Foreign Trade:** exports, $1,428,000,000; imports, $910,000,000. **Principal Exports:** meat, wheat, wool.　MARY C. WEBSTER
See also LATIN AMERICA.

ARMED FORCES OF THE WORLD. The West maintained a 4-to-1 nuclear superiority over the communists in 1964, and was at least even in conventional fighting ability. Both sides possessed "overkill"—more than enough nuclear weapons to obliterate the other.

In this grim stand-off, the West was far ahead, due to the numbers, diversity, and deployment of U.S. nuclear weapons. The balance in conventional power was also maintained by U.S. emphasis on mobility and flexibility of ground forces.

Chinese Bomb. Communist China's success in exploding a nuclear device in October did not alter the military balance of power (see CHINA). Most experts agreed it would be some years before they could develop a nuclear weapon.

Missiles. The United States had four times as many intercontinental ballistic missiles (ICBM) as the Soviet Union. The 853 U.S. ICBM's, almost all in hardened and dispersed silos underground, included 650 Minuteman, 108 Titan, and 95 Atlas. The Soviet Union had about 200, a few in hardened silos. The United States, while tapering off ICBM production, was replacing Minuteman I with Minuteman II, considered eight times as effective.

Soviet medium and intermediate missiles totaled about 800, some mobile, and some fixed and zeroed in on European targets. As a counterpoise, the United States was operating 18 nuclear-powered Polaris submarines bearing 288 missiles.

Air Power. The West was ahead in numbers and quality of strategic bombers. The U.S. Air Force had 1,100, of which 540 maintained a constant 15-minute alert and a few others flew 'round-the-clock on airborne alert. Additionally, the U.S. Navy had more than 100 fighter-bombers assigned strategic targets. The Soviets, in contrast, could send 270 bombers round-trip against the U.S. mainland, with about another 1,300 medium and light jet bombers capable of making it only one way.

Manpower. The North Atlantic Treaty Organization (NATO) and its communist rival, the Warsaw Pact, each had about 4,500,000 men under arms. NATO deployed $26\frac{1}{3}$ divisions in Europe, including 12 West German, five U.S., three British, two French,

ASIA

COMPARATIVE MILITARY MANPOWER

	United States	Russia	Communist China
Army	972,500	2,000,000	2,600,000
Navy	859,000*	400,000	60,000
Air Force	853,500	900,000	175,000
Totals	2,685,000	3,300,000	2,835,000

*Includes 190,000 marines

two Belgian, and two Dutch, plus one Canadian brigade. The Warsaw Pact boasted 212 divisions, but fewer than half were combat-ready.

The 212 communist divisions included 62 from eastern Europe and 150 from the Soviet Union. The Russians kept 20 divisions in East Germany, two in Poland, four in Hungary, and 40 in western Russia. Fourteen other front-line Soviet divisions were deployed in the Far East, and an additional 70, most of them divisions in name only, were in reserve.

Communist China maintained a fighting force of some 2,835,000 men. Its army totaled about 2,600,-000, but was short of modern equipment. Obsolescence plagued its air force of some 2,500 planes, including 2,000 jet fighters.　　　　WARREN ROGERS

See also NATIONAL DEFENSE.

ARMY, U.S. See NATIONAL DEFENSE.

ART. See PAINTING AND SCULPTURE.

ASIA was shaken politically as well as physically by an atomic explosion triggered by Communist China in October. It was a technological achievement that deeply impressed the Asiatic nations being courted by China. But for those whose inner stability was already threatened by the Chinese colossus, it was an ominous portent of a step-up in pressure that was sure to come. See ATOMIC ENERGY; CHINA, PEOPLE'S REPUBLIC OF; DISARMAMENT.

Despite its nuclear triumph, China reaped no immediate military advantage. It continued to rely for the most part on subversion to gain its ends in Asia. The Communist Chinese continued to exploit the war in

GRIM HARVEST. Under protective gun of armored personnel carrier, a South Vietnamese farmer resumes his labors in rice paddy ravaged by bitter fighting.

PICTURES OF THE YEAR/Jim Howard, United Press Int.

United Press Int.

ALLIED DETERMINATION to oppose communist aggression in Asia was reaffirmed at annual meeting of Southeast Asia Treaty Organization in Manila. Here, Philippine President Diosdado Macapagal welcomes U.S. Secretary of State Dean Rusk.

South Vietnam where rivalry among various political, military, and religious groups repeatedly bogged down all-out efforts of the South Vietnamese government to achieve political stability and a military victory (see VIETNAM).

In Burma, the Revolutionary Council government of General Ne Win saw a resurgence of guerrilla warfare as the pro-communist Red Flag and White Flag rebels unified their forces (see BURMA).

Indonesia, meanwhile, remained determined to break up the Federation of Malaysia which it viewed as an attempt to perpetuate British colonialism in Asia. Indonesian guerrilla forces were active throughout Malaysia though their depredations were kept to a minimum by Australian, British, and New Zealand troops in the area (see INDONESIA; MALAYSIA).

In Laos, pro-communist sympathizers in the government repeatedly threatened to bring down the shaky coalition that had been arranged under international auspices (see LAOS). Pakistan remained preoccupied with its dispute with India involving Kashmir; India itself kept an anxious watch over its borders where Communist Chinese troops remained entrenched (see INDIA; PAKISTAN). Thailand, too, was restive under Communist Chinese pressures along its borders (see THAILAND).

Hunger and Economic Woes were equally as serious as political problems in most of Asia where, according to a report published by the United Nations Economic Commission for Asia and the Far East (UNECAFE), the population was growing faster than food production (see POPULATION, WORLD).

The UNECAFE report, which covered 22 countries, left out only mainland China, Mongolia, North Korea, and North Vietnam. It revealed that food production—increasing by half a per cent annually against a 2.4 per cent rise in population—was down in India and Pakistan, two of the region's most populous areas, and in Afghanistan, Nepal, and South Korea. Food production in Indonesia, whose population was over 100,000,000, held level, requiring substantial imports.

Trade deficits for that part of Asia included in the survey had trebled in the last decade, a trend UNECAFE reported as likely to continue. Balance of payments and foreign reserves problems were widespread. Capital inflow into the area has leveled off since 1960, when it had reached a peak, and there was little hope that it would rise under prevailing conditions.

Inflation struck hard in at least three countries—Indonesia, Korea, and Laos. Industry made giant strides in Japan, and also expanded in Australia, Formosa, India, and Malaysia. But industrial benefits to the area as a whole were negligible. Most of the new production was absorbed by the larger population at home. When there were exportable surpluses, prices often were not competitive internationally.

There was one bright spot. The long-range Mekong River Project for Southeastern Asia continued to progress despite recurring crises in Cambodia, Laos, South Vietnam, and Thailand—the four countries involved. The development, which was launched in 1957, is a UN-sponsored venture whose goal is to harness the Mekong's mainstream and tributaries with dams, power stations, and irrigation canals. Its cost was expected to reach $2,000,000,000.

Colombo Plan Aid. The developed countries of the world continued their efforts to spur economic growth in Asia. In November, the Colombo Plan, which had been founded in 1950, was extended for a five-year period that would end in 1971. The move followed a meeting of the plan's consultative committee in London at which all 22 member nations, excepting Cambodia, were represented. Aid contributed by the Colombo Plan to various Asiatic countries during the year was about $2,165,000,000. Since the plan's inception, aid to the "have not" nations has totaled approximately $14,000,000,000.

The largest part of it has come from the United States, but considerable contributions have also been made by Australia, Canada, Great Britain, Japan, and New Zealand.

SEATO Strategy. Defense plans for the area were also of international concern. In April, the tenth annual council meeting of the eight-nation Southeast Asia Treaty Organization (SEATO) was held in Manila, in the Philippine islands. One of the key issues discussed by the delegates representing Australia, France, Great Britain, New Zealand, Pakistan, the Philippines, and the United States was a proposal made by French President Charles de Gaulle earlier in the year. De Gaulle, whose nation had officially recognized the Communist Chinese

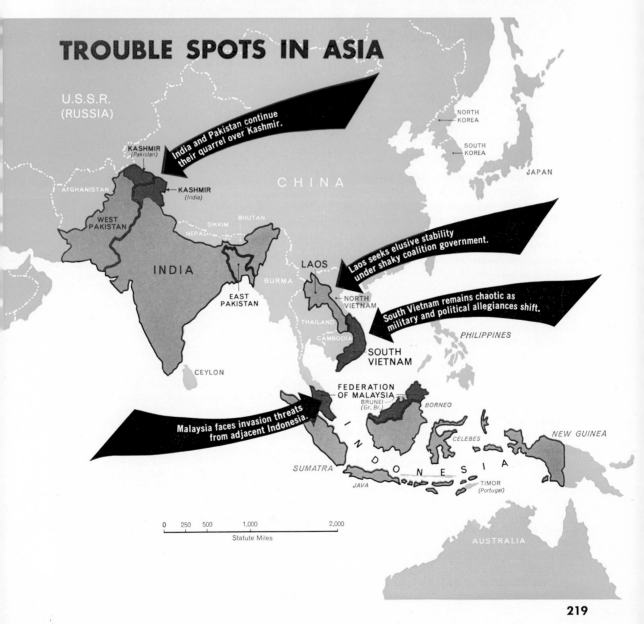

TROUBLE SPOTS IN ASIA

India and Pakistan continue their quarrel over Kashmir.

Laos seeks elusive stability under shaky coalition government.

South Vietnam remains chaotic as military and political allegiances shift.

Malaysia faces invasion threats from adjacent Indonesia.

"Before you start dealing, Charlie—where are your chips?"

regime in Peking, had urged that the troubled Indo-chinese peninsula be neutralized through an agreement reached with the Asian communists.

The French delegate to the SEATO conference, however, was unable to win support for the De Gaulle proposal.

ANZUS Treaty. In July, representatives of the three ANZUS security-pact nations held a two-day conference in Washington, D.C., to discuss Asian security problems. The conferees were led by U.S. Secretary of State Dean Rusk, Prime Minister Keith J. Holyoake of New Zealand, and Australia's Minister for External Affairs Paul M. C. Hasluck. All three nations indicated a continuing determination to contain communism in the Southeast Asia area.

Communist Maneuvers. The Communist Chinese continued to parry the West's thrusts in Asia. In June, a second Asian Economic Seminar was held in Pyongyang, the capital of North Korea. The communist-organized meeting was attended by delegates from most of the Asian countries.

Overtones of the ideological dispute between the Soviet Union and Communist China were introduced when Nan Han-chen, head of the Chinese delegation, warned the underdeveloped countries that they would become subject to Soviet domination if they accepted aid from Moscow. It was part of Communist China's continuing campaign to undermine the attraction of Soviet economic programs in the area. See COMMUNISM; RUSSIA.   PAUL C. TULLIER

ASTRONAUTS. The 14 new astronauts selected in October, 1963, reported to the newly completed Manned Spacecraft Center near Houston, Tex., early in 1964, and received their assignments of specialties. Like the 16 selected before them, they practiced survival training in the Panamanian jungle where they learned to live on tropical tree snails, birds, snakes, lizards and, wild tropical plants. They also endured 150°F. surface temperatures in the Nevada desert with nothing to aid them but their survival kits and parachutes.

Moon Walking. In anticipation of a moon landing, the men took intensive courses in geology and made a series of field trips to study rock formations. Astronaut R. Walter Cunningham experimented with walking and climbing in a heavy space suit on a rocky lava and pumice bed in central Oregon. The formation was believed to resemble lunar terrain. Cunningham had difficulty moving and recommended changes in the design of the pressurized moon suit.

Gemini Pilots. In April, 1964, the National Aeronautics and Space Administration (NASA) announced the names of the men who would pilot the first two Gemini missions. They were Major Virgil "Gus" Grissom of Mitchell, Ind. (command), and Lieutenant Commander John W. Young of San Francisco. Their backup crew was Commander Walter M. "Wally" Schirra, Jr. (command), of Hackensack, N.J., and Major Thomas P. Stafford of Weatherford, Okla. The flight was expected to take place in the first quarter of 1965, and was scheduled for three orbits.

In July, NASA announced the pilots selected for the proposed four-day follow-on mission, also expected in the first quarter of 1965. They were Captain James A. McDivitt (command) of Chicago and Captain Edward H. White II of San Antonio, Tex. Designated as backup crew were Major Frank Borman (command) of Gary, Ind., and Lieutenant Commander James A. Lovell, Jr., of Cleveland.

"Scienauts." In October, the space agency announced that from 10 to 20 "scientist-astronauts" would be selected in 1965. In designating qualifications, NASA did not exclude women. The criteria: the astronaut must be a U.S. citizen, born on or after Aug. 1, 1930, be no taller than six feet, and hold a doctor's degree in medicine, engineering, or the natural sciences, or have the equivalent in experience.

John H. Glenn, Jr., the first American to orbit the earth, resigned from NASA on January 16 to enter the U.S. Senate race from his native state of Ohio. But on February 26, he was injured when he struck his head in a fall in the bathroom of his apartment in Columbus, damaging his inner ear. Glenn withdrew from the race, and entered an air force hospital. His retirement from the U.S. Marine Corps was held up pending his recovery. In October, John Glenn was promoted to full colonel by President

ASTRONAUTS train in Nevada desert. Captain Theodore C. Freeman, left, was later killed returning from a routine flight. His companion is R. Walter Cunningham.

Lyndon B. Johnson, and the Royal Crown Cola Corporation announced that he had been elected to its board. On Jan. 4, 1965, he retired from the corps. Glenn was expected to continue to work with NASA as a part-time consultant.

Commander Alan B. Shepard, Jr., also suffered prolonged inner ear infection that temporarily grounded him. In addition, he underwent surgery to remove a benign growth on his thyroid gland. Lieutenant Commander M. Scott Carpenter was injured in a motorbike accident in Bermuda.

An Astronaut Dies. On October 31, Air Force Captain Theodore C. Freeman of Haverford, Pa., one of the third group of astronauts, was killed returning from a routine training flight. His T-38 supersonic jet trainer crashed as he was preparing to land at a military field near the Manned Spacecraft Center. Captain Freeman was the first astronaut to die since the U.S. space program began. He was buried with full military honors in Arlington National Cemetery.

An Astronaut Marries. America's only bachelor astronaut, Captain Clifton Curtis "C.C." Williams, Jr., of Mobile, Ala., married a North Carolina beauty queen, the former Jane Elizabeth Lansche, on July 1.   WILLIAM SHELTON

See also SPACE TRAVEL; Section One, JOHN H. GLENN, JR., ON SPACE.

ASTRONOMY, in the midst of astounding quasi-stellar discoveries, celebrated the 400th anniversary of the birth of Galileo Galilei (1564-1642), the first man to study the sky with a telescope. Many scientific organizations throughout the world conducted symposiums and other special programs on his contributions to scientific knowledge.

The quasi-stellar objects, or quasars, first reported in December, 1963, were extensively studied. They are unlike any previously known celestial bodies, and the red shifts in their spectra indicate that they are apparently moving away from the Milky Way at extremely high velocities. They have also been found to be the most luminous objects in the universe, and to be powerful sources of radio energy. Though these objects appear to be stars on photographic plates, they have luminosities far exceeding even the brightest galaxies (see Section Two, THE UNFOLDING UNIVERSE).

Moon. Close-up photographs were made of the moon on July 31, when the Ranger VII spacecraft transmitted television views to scientists in California before it crashed into the lunar surface. These photographs showed details approximately a thousand times clearer than any made by photographs through earthbound telescopes. Craters as small as three feet across were visible. See EUROPE (picture); PHOTOGRAPHY; SPACE TRAVEL.

221

YEARS OF THE QUIET SUN

ALL THROUGH 1964 rockets roared upward, balloons drifted high above the earth, and satellites probed deep into space. It was the beginning of a two-year, 69-nation effort to increase man's understanding of the workings of the sun. Called the International Years of the Quiet Sun (IQSY), and nicknamed "Ick-See," the program was a sequel and a complement to the International Geophysical Year (IGY), 1957 to 1958.

As the name IQSY implied, the undertaking had been designed to take the greatest possible advantage of the period in which the sun was relatively quiet—more or less free from solar flare eruptions and sunspots. One of the main objectives was to compare the data gathered during this period of minimum solar activity with that gathered during the IGY period, a period of maximum solar activity.

As everyone knows, the activity of the sun influences life and its environment on earth. But the relationship between the sun's activity and the resulting effects on earth are still not fully understood. Through the earlier IGY program, a picture of the broad outlines of this relationship emerged. When the present studies are completed, the picture should be clearer.

A number of specific scientific interests were involved in IQSY. These were meteorology; geomagnetism; studies of auroras, airglow, and the ionosphere; solar physics; and aeronomy. Emphasis was being placed on investigations of the atmosphere beyond an altitude of 12 miles.

THE METEOROLOGICAL program was designed to study the large-scale characteristics of the upper atmosphere, with particular emphasis on the relationship between solar activity and the composition, motion, and temperature of the upper atmosphere. The incidence and nature of clouds, the circulation of upper air, and the distribution of ozone and water vapor were also recorded.

Of special interest were geomagnetic influences and earth currents because of their extreme sensitivity to certain solar influences. Data were being obtained with magnetometers, which measure magnetic fields, placed among other instruments aboard rockets, satellites, aircraft, and ships.

Also under observation were the auroras, or Northern and Southern Lights, which result from the interaction of charged particles in the earth's upper atmosphere. During IQSY, direct measurements of these phenomena were being made with instruments carried by balloons, rockets, and satellites that were being sent aloft in narrow zones near the North and South poles.

The closely related study of the properties of airglow (a continual emission of atmospheric light) as it relates to solar activity was expected to yield important information about the composition of the upper atmosphere. Rocket-borne instruments were providing the data for this study.

Several programs of continuous observations of the ionosphere were being conducted through a worldwide network of stations. They were using radar for sounding the ionosphere to great heights and for obtaining information about electron and ion temperatures in that layer of the earth's atmosphere.

SOLAR physicists were turning their attention also to low-energy, rather than to high-energy, cosmic rays. During IGY, such low-energy rays were generally shielded from the earth by solar forces in periods of maximum solar activity. To make this study, the scientists used widely dispersed equipment that included new neutron monitors and meson telescopes.

The discipline of aeronomy, which deals with both the physics and chemistry of the atmosphere, overlapped all other investigations in the IQSY program. Relevant observations included temperature and density studies of the atmosphere, studies of the atmospheric response to inputs of solar energy, and studies of ionization in the atmosphere and its chemical composition.

The level of scientific interest directed toward the sun during IGY shattered all records since Galileo first observed the presence of sunspots in 1612. Although the magnitude of the IQSY program considerably exceeded that of IGY, the program was proceeding quietly and as yet almost unnoticed outside of scientific circles. Nevertheless, the ultimate impact of the project was expected to be of great importance. SERGEI LENORMAND

A YEAR BOOK CLOSEUP

Several times since the late 1950's, the appearance of bright, reddish areas on the moon have been reported. On Nov. 1, 1963, at the Pic du Midi Observatory in France, such temporary reddenings near the crater Kepler were observed twice within two hours. The French observers concluded that these were caused by solar flares which propelled energetic material to the moon. Others thought the red spots could have originated from below the lunar surface. They were also observed near the crater Aristarchus by U.S. astronomers, and in the crater Alphonsus by Russian astronomers.

Venus. On February 21, the spectrum of the planet Venus was observed from a balloon at an altitude of 87,500 feet, and it was established that the planet has water vapor in the upper levels of its atmosphere. The total amount of water in the planet's atmosphere cannot be estimated because the chemical composition and density of the Venusian atmosphere are not accurately known. It has now been suggested that the clouds surrounding the planet are not composed of dust, as previously thought, but of water vapor. See BALLOON.

The world's largest radio-radar telescope at Arecibo, Puerto Rico, confirmed earlier observations that Venus rotates in an opposite direction to the other planets in the solar system (with the exception of Uranus). Measurements revealed that the planet makes one rotation every 248 to 258 days.

Dense Galaxies. For several years the 200-inch telescope at Mount Palomar has been used in an attempt to discover the densest of the galaxies, those that are almost indistinguishable from stars on photographic plates. It has now been found that such small, compact galaxies occur in pairs and in multiple systems. Observations indicate that they contain material moving with velocities as great as a few thousand miles per second, or that they are in a state of explosive expansion. The true brightness of the compact galaxies ranges from 100,000,000 to 10,000,000,000 times that of the sun, and their masses are from 10,000,000,000 to 1,000,000,000,000 solar masses. ROBERT I. JOHNSON

See also Section Two, ISAAC ASIMOV ON SCIENCE.

ATOMIC ENERGY. The detonation of its first atomic bomb by China on October 16 sent a shock wave around the world. It produced political repercussions in Russia, led to an upgrading of the U.S. estimate of China's scientific capability, and added a fifth member to the atomic club. See CHINA.

The bomb, a fission device built of enriched uranium, was basically the same in yield and design as the atomic bomb the United States dropped on Hiroshima, Japan, in 1945. But its explosive trigger was apparently much more advanced than that used in the Hiroshima device. Few persons outside China, however, applauded this achievement of a nation that refused to sign the October, 1963, ban on nuclear testing in the atmosphere. See DISARMAMENT.

Nuclear Power. U Thant, United Nations (UN) Secretary-General, told delegates to the UN Third International Conference on Peaceful Uses of Atomic Energy, at Geneva, that only nuclear power could fill the energy needs of the world in future years. The 10-day meeting, held at Geneva, Switzerland, in September, was attended by about 3,500 scientists and industrial observers from 71 nations. The meeting opened with a warning that the world's coal and oil reserves will be exhausted within 30 years.

Dr. Glenn T. Seaborg, chairman of the U.S. Atomic Energy Commission (AEC) and a delegate to the conference, predicted that more than half the world's electric power will be generated by nuclear power plants by the end of the 20th century. At the same time, he warned that the objective of harnessing the energy of the H-bomb may never be achieved. See ELECTRIC POWER.

Reactor Development. At the conference, scientists of Atomics International described lilliputian atomic power plants that convert heat by fissioning uranium directly into electricity. These tiny reactors will soon be powering American satellites, and are also planned for power plants on the moon. Called SNAP 10A, the 500-watt thermoelectric system weighs only 950 pounds, and includes a thermoelectric converter made of an alloy of silicon and germanium, a zirconium-hydride moderator, and 215 pounds of enriched uranium.

The Soviet Union published a detailed description of a mobile atomic reactor plant mounted on a self-propelled tracked vehicle for use in Siberia, the Arctic, and other remote areas. According to *Pravda*, the 1,500-kilowatt unit was the only one of its type.

The first fast nuclear reactor in Scandinavia, known as FR-O, went into operation early in the year. The reactor, an experimental zero-energy breeder reactor, is similar to the Advanced Epithermal Test Reactor developed by Atomics International. It also is similar to the British Vera reactor at Aldermaston in that it consists of two halves, one of which is movable and on rails. It is located at Studsvik, Sweden.

Desalting Plants. Two separate reports to the Joint Congressional Committee on Atomic Energy, released in March, described how atomic energy can serve the dual purpose of providing power and fresh water. One of these, by presidential science adviser Donald F. Hornig, described a nuclear reactor capable of generating enough heat to convert enormous quantities of steam into purified water and also to produce millions of kilowatts of electricity. Meanwhile, four different reactors were being designed at the AEC's Oak Ridge Laboratory to desalinate sea water. One of these is designated for Key West, Fla., an area the International Atomic Energy Agency (IAEA) recommended for a nuclear desalting plant. The IAEA also suggested that energy and fresh-water needs can be met with dual-purpose reactors in desert regions. See WATER AND FLOOD CONTROL. SERGEI LENORMAND

AUSTRALIA

AUSTRALIA enjoyed a soaring economy for the second successive year. Means of controlling this growth became the chief problem of Prime Minister Sir Robert Gordon Menzies and his Liberal-Country party coalition. The Gross National Product (GNP) rose 9 per cent in 1963-1964. The wool clip was at a record high, and wheat, too, commanded top prices. Cuba's troubles ensured good prices for the Australian sugar crop (see CUBA). But with a mere 1 per cent of the working population unemployed, the authorities feared a labor shortage and wage inflation. Treasurer Harold E. Holt, in his budget presented in August, tried to moderate internal spending, jacking up the income tax by 5 per cent and imposing higher sales taxes.

Business confidence was reinforced by the success of the burgeoning oil industry. Supplies were beginning to flow in commercial quantities. More oil strikes were reported in the latter half of the year.

The continued fighting between Indonesia and Malaysia, where Australian forces were committed, added to the nation's defense worries. In November, Australia reinstated the selective service system it had dropped in 1959. See INDONESIA; MALAYSIA.

Population: 11,325,000. **Government:** Governor-General Viscount De L'Isle; Prime Minister Robert Gordon Menzies. **Foreign Trade:** exports, $3,182,-000,000; imports, $3,246,000,000. **Principal Exports:** meat, wheat, wool.   ALASTAIR BURNET

AUSTRIA continued to steer a profitably neutral course. Politically, it was still divided almost evenly between the People's party and the Socialists, thus necessitating a coalition government in which each was equally represented.

In April, Alfons Gorbach was replaced as chancellor by Josef Klaus, chairman of the People's party. Klaus, to reinvigorate his party, replaced the ministers of agriculture, defense, education, and finance with younger men. The Socialists, too, endeavored to revitalize their forces. Party chairman Bruno Pitterman, who was also vice-chancellor and minister of nationalized industry, traveled widely to increase contacts with the East and the West. In October, another Socialist, Foreign Minister Bruno Kreisky, visited Hungary, where he signed an agreement settling the problem of prewar Austrian properties in Hungary. See HUNGARY.

Austria's application for some type of relationship with the European Economic Community was still pending. Foreign trade increased and, although the gap between imports and exports widened unfavorably, it was filled by increased tourist receipts of almost $500,000,000.

Population: 7,225,000. **Government:** President Adolf Schaerf; Chancellor Josef Klaus. **Foreign Trade:** exports, $1,422,000,000; imports, $1,841,000,000. **Principal Exports:** iron and steel, lumber, machinery, petroleum.   TOM AND HARLE DAMMANN

See also EUROPE.

AUTOMATION surged ahead in 1964 with more efficient labor-saving machines and processes. It affected transport, office, mine, and factory. A new continuous coal-mining machine that doubled its productivity to 75 tons of coal per man-day was shown at a trade fair. In the auto industry, Chrysler began using computers instead of industrial engineers to "balance the line," or calculate how much work each man on an assembly line should do to keep the amount of waiting time at a minimum. At the new Kansas City (Mo.) plant of the Western Electric Company, employees punched in at automatic data processing "badge reading stations" instead of using timecards. The electronic engine room of the S.S. *Mormacvega*, launched in March, 1964, allowed the reduction of the usual 20-man crew to only 11 men.

Productivity and Jobs. New industrial processes and use of new materials also brought about fundamental technological changes during the year. The oxygen furnace, to cite one example, made better steel in one-fifth the time taken by the old open-hearth method (see IRON AND STEEL). Developments such as these, multiplied a hundredfold, combined with the low growth rate of the U.S. economy between 1957 and 1962, helped explain much of the unemployment problem.

The Department of Labor, in a 1964 study covering those years, found that in no major industry where productivity expanded more than 2.5 per cent did demand for additional output rise enough to prevent some layoffs. Conditions improved, however, during 1964. With the aid of the tax cut, the economic growth rate increased slightly and provided more new jobs in 1964—1,500,000 against about 1,000,000 in each of the previous two years (see LABOR).

Analysis of the Jobless. Continued high unemployment caused management, union, and government officials to examine carefully who was unemployed, where he was located, and what had happened to his job. In June, the Department of Labor reported on five plant shut-downs that were to some degree brought on by technological change. Its study disclosed that only about 2,000 of the 3,000 displaced employees found new jobs.

Another study showed that the introduction of electronic data processing (EDP) in a large insurance company office resulted in a net loss of jobs. The number of new people hired for "entry jobs" and routine clerical tasks dropped noticeably. In the meantime, no letup in the pace of new EDP installations was forecast.

At the urging of the President's Labor-Management Advisory Committee and others, Congress established a National Commission on Technology, Automation, and Economic Progress in August. It was to undertake studies in 1965 and submit its recommendations by Jan. 1, 1966.   JAMES L. STERN

See also COMPUTER; EDUCATION; INDUSTRY; LIBRARY; SHIP; VOCATIONAL EDUCATION.

AUTOMOBILE

THE U.S. auto industry was hampered by strikes and parts short-ages in 1964 but finished the calendar year with near-record pro-duction and sales figures. According to final, unofficial tabulations by *Automotiue News*, 7,746,000 passenger cars rolled off the lines. That made it the second best calendar year in U.S. automotive history, second only to the 7,941,538 cars built and 7,920,186 sold in 1955. In 1963, the fig-ures were 7,644,377 and 7,637,728, respectively.

At the start of the year, practically every automotive executive confi-dently predicted U.S. assembly plants would build and sell a new record

Don Stebbing for THE YEAR BOOK

THE BIG, LUXURY-CAR LOOK of the Ambassador 990, above, sets the pace for the American Motors line. Four-door model increased 10 inches in overall length. Pontiac's prestige Grand Prix, left, sports a modified fastback, with its sloping roof and flat deck.

Don Stebbing for THE YEAR BOOK

LONG, FLAT, AND FINLESS Dodge Custom 880, above, emphasizes the no-nonsense sleekness of the 1965 Chrysler Corporation iine. And Ford, too, carries out the squared-off, boxy look in the hexagon-shaped taii lamps of its Galaxie, right.

of 8,000,000 cars. The industry's negotiations with the AFL-CIO United Auto Workers (UAW) on new three-year contracts running until September, 1967, threw some major roadblocks in the path to that goal. See OLD AGE.

General Motors (GM) was hit September 25 by a nationwide strike. Ten days later, terms on a national settlement were reached. But unsettled local issues kept GM plants shut down until October 27. Similar local strikes later plagued Ford. It was not until November 23 that the industry's main labor troubles ended. On that date the national Ford-UAW contract was signed. Chrysler, the first of the Big Three—GM, Ford, and Chrysler —to come to terms with the UAW, escaped with practically no labor trouble for the year. The GM settlement came after President Lyndon B. Johnson had said that a continuation of the strike would not be in the national interest. American Motors Corporation (AMC), the fourth largest U.S. auto maker, was hampered by some local plant strikes but escaped a company-wide shutdown. It worked out an agreement with the UAW on modifications and continuation of the profit-sharing plan adopted in 1961 by AMC and the UAW. See LABOR.

Loss of Production from the strikes cost GM and Ford over 400,000 units. But when labor peace was restored, both companies used overtime operations generously to recoup as much as possible of the lost production before year's end. The industry's December factory assemblies exceeded 870,000 cars, a new high for any month on record.

Amid the labor turmoil, Chrysler was able to push ahead strongly, continuing its spectacular comeback of 1963. For the full calendar year, it expanded its share of total assemblies of passenger cars from 13.6 per cent in the 1963 period to 16.0 per cent. Ford gained from 25.6 to 27.7; GM dropped to 51.1 from 53.4; and AMC fell to 5.1 from 6.3 per cent in 1963.

In the Showrooms, a late November-December selling push by U.S. dealers was aimed at sending retail sales to a new calendar year high of 7,550,000 cars. The record of 7,408,000 domestically made cars sold in the U.S. market had been set in 1955.

While domestic car makers had their troubles, imports fared well. U.S. dealers in foreign cars predicted sales of over 480,000, well ahead of the 386,000 they sold in 1963, but not up to record 1959 when they sold 614,000 imports. Combined domestic and import car retail sales were expected to top out at about 8,030,000 cars—a new high.

The 1965 Line in general was described as "the year of the stylist." In the minds of the motoring public, engineering changes were subordinated to changes in the overall appearance of the cars. Engines got a bit more power. But car warranties were basically unchanged.

U.S. auto makers offered buyers a choice of 343 new models. GM cars presented softer, curving

lines and a racy look; Ford featured sharp, crisp shapes; Chrysler and American Motors added a bit more sweep and roundness to their cars' sharp contours. Most models grew in length.

If any new model deserved a "car of the year" title, it was Ford's Mustang. From the day of its off-season introduction on April 17, until year's end, Ford had turned out 303,275 of the sporty models. Plymouth, too, was well pleased with the reception of its racy Barracuda.

Overseas Activity. Chrysler Corporation, which already controlled Simca in France, bought a $35,000,000 minority interest in Rootes Motors, Ltd., of England in June. Chrysler said it would not increase its 30 per cent stake in the British firm. General Motors and Ford also continued their overseas expansion.

All of the Free World's auto factories were busy. Their 1964 production, U.S. included, was estimated at 16,200,000 cars. Thus, for the second year in a row, foreign production exceeded that of the U.S. auto makers.

A "Poor Man's Rolls" was offered the motoring public during the summer, the result of a bit of

FLAMES *from Dave McDonald's car engulfed others during the Indianapolis 500 on May 30. The race continued, though McDonald and another driver were killed.*

British industrial teamwork. Rolls-Royce, Ltd., supplied the aluminum, six-cylinder engine, and British Motor Corporation built the body of the new car, the Vanden Plas Princess R. Its selling price was a shade under $5,600, against $15,400 for a Rolls Silver Cloud III. The Princess R was about the size of a Mercedes-Benz, with a top speed of 112 miles an hour.   CHARLES C. CAIN III

AUTOMOBILE RACING. In the closest competition of Grand Prix history, Ferrari driver John Surtees of England captured the world driving championship by a one-point margin in 1964. Surtees won the title by finishing second in the season's final race, the Mexican Grand Prix. He moved into second place only one lap from the finish, passing defending champion Jim Clark of Scotland who had led for 63 of the race's 65 laps. In the final standings, Surtees had 40 points to 39 for 1962 champion Graham Hill, while Clark had 32.

After several years of eclipse, Ferrari cars also won the Grand Prix manufacturers' championship, and took the first three places in the grueling Le Mans 24-hour endurance test.

A. J. Foyt of Houston, Tex., for the fourth time in five years, was the leading driver in U.S. Auto Club (USAC) competition, winning a record-breaking total of 10 USAC races. Included in Foyt's victory string was the Indianapolis 500.

In stock car racing, Richard Petty of Randleman, N.C., drove a Plymouth to take the 1964 National Association for Stock Car Racing (NASCAR) title.

The world land speed record was broken five times in three weeks on the Bonneville Salt Flats in Utah. Art Arfons of Akron, Ohio, ended the year in possession of the record by hitting 536.71 mph in his homemade "Green Monster" on October 27. Arfons, a self-taught engineer, built his 21-foot four-wheeler, powered by a surplus air force jet engine. He eclipsed the mark of 526 mph set just a few days earlier by Craig Breedlove of Los Angeles.

Attendance at U.S. auto racing events also reached new highs in 1964, with more than 200,000 spectators at the Indianapolis 500.   JAMES O. DUNAWAY

227

AVIATION

AVIATION jetted to new heights of prosperity in 1964, the 50th anniversary of scheduled air transportation. The airlines of the United States nearly doubled their profits for the year, from slightly over $76,-000,000 in 1963 to an estimated $130,000,000. Expanded jet fleets, low promotional fares, the boom in travel, operating economies—all contributed. This prosperity reached overseas as well. The April cut of 20 per cent in transatlantic fares, after three months, brought a 40.5 per cent increase in passenger traffic and a 15 percentage point rise in the average passenger load to 62.3 per cent of capacity on transatlantic flights, according to the International Air Transport Association (IATA).

Stereophonic music, first-run movies, and television were used to lure more passengers aboard. In-flight entertainment pioneered by Trans World Airlines on overseas flights in 1961, became routine in 1964. American Airlines and Continental Airlines added these features. Some other air carriers were planning to follow suit.

Air freight, subsidized to some extent by income from passenger operations, increased its ton-mileage in the year about 10 per cent, with total revenues exceeding $250,000,000. The introduction of the Boeing 707-320C, a convertible passenger-cargo version of the Boeing 707, aided in the expansion of long-range cargo traffic.

"Third-level" air carriers formed an association for mutual betterment. These carriers enjoy certain advantages. They fly small planes, which can use downtown airports and are exempt from rate and route regulations. They connect neighboring large cities or small cities that are not served by other air carriers.

Airports. On September 25, the Federal Aviation Agency (FAA) announced its $1,200,000,000, five-year plan for airport development. It recommended the construction of 727 new airports and the improvement of 2,537 existing landing facilities. FAA estimated the total cost of the new construction at $268,900,000 and improvements at $960,500,000. Of the 727 new airports, heliports, and seaplane bases, 579 were recommended for general aviation (nonairline) use exclusively. This National Airport Plan serves as a guide to Congress for grants of federal aid for airports. The FAA reported that as of Jan. 1, 1964, the number of U.S. airports had risen to 8,788. The year's increase of 726 was more than twice that of the preceding year.

LaGuardia Airport, New York City, completed the major portion of its $119,000,000 renovation plan. It dedicated its $36,000,000 passenger terminal on April 16 and began its first regular jet aircraft movements on June 1. Nearby Newark (N.J.) Airport late in the year revealed plans for a $150,-000,000 modernization program. Construction began on three of four new terminal buildings.

AVIATION PIONEER. The 2,000-mph XB-70A bomber takes off in a series of tests designed to study the problems of a supersonic airliner.

Delays of Airliners. A joint study by the Air Transport Association (ATA) and the FAA found that delays most often resulted from on-the-ground conditions at airports. Inadequate runways, taxiways, ramp space, and gate positions were the main causes of the surface congestion. Air traffic control problems and bad weather conditions were the next most frequent causes of delays.

The shortage of pilots was indeed critical, the FAA Aviation Human Resources Study Board reported. The world-wide pilot pinch had been the chief topic of the IATA meeting in Montreal early in the summer. The study board estimated that the number of professional pilots needed by all U.S. commercial aviation for replacement and expansion would be about 3,650 in 1965, 4,350 in 1970, 5,700 in 1975, and 6,300 in 1980. Comparatively few young persons were learning to fly.

Air Traffic Control made two significant strides during the year. Area Position Control (APC) separation service was completed November 12 with the opening of the Great Falls (Mont.) Air Route Traffic Control Center. With all 22 such centers in operation, all of the airspace between 24,000 and 60,000 feet over continental United States came under positive control.

Also, a simplified airways route structure was implemented by the FAA on September 17 when the existing three-layer system was replaced by a two-layer system for all states except Alaska and Hawaii. In the lower layer, airways run between 1,000 feet and 18,000 feet above the surface.

Air safety continued to be emphasized by the FAA. Among the projects that yielded helpful results was one that used surplus airliners to simulate accidents. Instrument landing experiments continued. On December 8, a United Air Lines Caravelle with 44 persons aboard made a series of completely automatic landings at Dulles International Airport.

New Aircraft. The most imaginative aircraft proposed during the year was the Lockheed rocket plane. According to the company, it might be carrying 10 passengers and a crew of two between the earth and an orbiting space station by 1975. Prospective round-trip fare was estimated at $11,700.

Progress on building a supersonic transport (SST) continued, but with a little less enthusiasm. The French-British combine building the *Concorde* admitted that the development costs would be at least $800,000,000—75 per cent more than originally planned. Great Britain's new Labour government late in the year showed coolness toward the project. See GREAT BRITAIN.

The United States, too, began to voice reservations about building a supersonic transport. In July, FAA Administrator Najeeb E. Halaby conceded that sonic boom was a "more serious" problem for the SST than had been supposed. The FAA in tests at Oklahoma City had found that some pressure waves were magnified before reaching the ground, creating

forces as much as 50 per cent above expectations. Nonetheless, the U.S. still planned to build an SST.

In the everyday, subsonic field, two new jetliners went into service early in the year. Boeing's compact, three-engine 727 made its first commercial passenger flight—under the Eastern Air Lines flag—from Miami, Fla., to Washington, D.C., on Feb. 1, 1964. Boeing, in midsummer, announced that it would produce a cargo version; the 727C would go into service in 1966. Great Britain's VC-10, probably the last of the big long-range subsonics, completed its maiden flight from London to Lagos, Nigeria, on April 29. According to *The Economist* of London, it was a weak challenger to the Boeing 707 because of its 10 to 15 per cent higher operating costs.

New "baby jets" were introduced in 1964 to tap the growing executive aircraft market. Two U.S. planes, the Lear Jet and the Jet Commander, were facing competition from the British Hawker-Siddeley DH-125, the French Dassault Mystère 20 Fan Jet Falcon, and the German HFB 320 Hansa.

Noteworthy Flights. Mary Ann Noah and copilot Mary Aikins won the 18th Annual All-Women's Transcontinental Air Race (Powder Puff Derby) over the 2,573-mile route from Fresno, Calif., to Atlantic City, N.J., July 4 to 9.

Geraldine L. Mock became the first woman to fly solo around the world. She left Columbus, Ohio, on March 19, and returned on April 18. Her trip covered 23,206.37 miles and was made in a Cessna 180.

Mrs. Joan Merriam Smith, in a Piper Apache, flew 27,750 miles on her 57-day flight around the world, starting March 17, 1964.

Aviation Trophy and Award winners in 1964:

Air Force Association Awards to General Curtis E. LeMay, USAF, for his military leadership; Mark S. Watson for aerospace writing; and Major Sidney J. Kubesch, USAF, for his 1963 Tokyo-London flight.

Barbour Air Safety Award to Philip Donely, NASA, for his studies of safe, rough-air flight techniques.

Frank G. Brewer Trophy to Marilyn Link for service to Air Youth in aerospace education.

Robert J. Collier Trophy to Clarence L. Johnson, Lockheed Aircraft Corporation, for the development of the A-11 aircraft.

Fédération Aéronautique Internationale Gold Medal to Jacqueline Auriol of France, who set the world closed-course speed record for women (1,266 mph).

Daniel Guggenheim Medal to Robert H. Goddard, posthumously, for "exceptional achievements in the flight sciences."

Harmon International Aviation Trophies to Astronaut L. Gordon Cooper, Jr.; Mrs. Betty Miller for her solo flight from Oakland, Calif., to Sydney, Australia, April 30 to May 12, 1963; and Lieutenant Colonel Fitzhugh L. Fulton, Jr., USAF, who established two world altitude records in a B-58 on Sept. 14, 1962.

Lawrence Sperry Award to Daniel M. Tellep, Lockheed Missiles and Space Corporation, for his studies of heat transfer in aerospace programs.

Wright Brothers Memorial Trophy to Harry F. Guggenheim for public service to aviation.   LESLIE A. BRYAN

See also ARMED FORCES OF THE WORLD; BALLOONS; DISASTERS; ENGINE AND ENERGY; INVENTION; NATIONAL DEFENSE; SPACE TRAVEL; TRAVEL.

AWARDS AND PRIZES presented in 1964 included the following:

General Awards

Academy of American Poets Awards, for distinguished poetic achievement, to Elizabeth Bishop, who also received the academy's 1964 fellowship; and Eric Daniel Feldman.

American Academy of Arts and Letters and National Institute of Arts and Letters Awards. *Award of Merit Medal* to author John O'Hara. *Gold Medals* to playwright Lillian Hellman and artist Ben Shahn. *Marjorie Peabody Waite Award,* for "continuing integrity in her work, to writer Dawn Powell. *Russell Loines Award for Poetry* to John Berryman. *Rosenthal Foundation Awards* to Ivan Gold for his volume of stories *Nickel Miseries;* and to Gregory Gillespie as a younger painter of "great distinction who has not yet won recognition." *Brunner Memorial Prize in Architecture* to Harry Weese. *Awards in Literature* to Lionel Abel, Dorothy Baker, Norman Fruchter, Thom Gunn, David Ignatow, Eric Hoffer, and Kenneth Rexroth. *Awards in Art* to Thomas Browne Cornell, Edward J. Hill, Reuben Kramer, Michael Maxur, Bernard Perlin, Sarai Sherman, and Charles Wells. *Awards in Music* to Leslie Bassett, Gordon Binkerd, Hall Overton, and Julia Perry. *Traveling Fellowship in Literature* to writer Edward Hoagland.

American Academy of Arts and Sciences Emerson-Thoreau Medal to Mark Van Doren, poet, critic, fiction writer, and biographer.

Anisfield-Wolf Awards by the *Saturday Review,* for books that deal most creditably with race-relation problems, to Nathan Glazer and Daniel Patrick Moynihan for *Beyond the Melting Pot;* Harold R. Isaacs for *The New World of Negro Americans;* and Bernhard E. Olson for *Faith and Prejudice.*

Aspen Institute for Humanistic Studies Awards, presented for the first time in 1964. *Aspen Award for Services to the Humanities* to the eminent British composer Benjamin Britten. *Trustees Award for Distinguished Citizenship* to Mrs. Walter Paepcke of Chicago for her contribution to the development of Aspen.

Brandeis University Awards. *Creative Arts Award* to author Vladimir Nabokov. *Special Notable Achievement Award* to inventor and architect R. Buckminster Fuller. *Lifetime Achievement Medals* to composer Carl Ruggls, sculptor David Smith, and theatrical producer Cheryl Crawford. *Promising Young Artist Awards* to composer Donald Martino, sculptor Peter Agostini, author Richard Tates, and playwright Jack Richardson.

Columbia University Awards. *Alice M. Ditson Conductor's Award* to Emerson Buckley, director of the Fort Lauderdale (Fla.) Symphony Orchestra. *Frederic Bancroft Prizes,* for studies in American history, diplomacy, and international relations, to William E. Leuchtenburg for *Franklin D. Roosevelt and the New Deal, 1938-1940;* Paul Seabury for *Power, Freedom and Diplomacy;* and John L. Thomas for *The Liberator: William Lloyd Garrison.*

Denmark's Sonning Prize to Dominique Georges Henri Pire, Belgian Roman Catholic priest and Nobel peace prize laureate of 1958, for his humanitarian work with European and Asian refugees.

Freedoms Foundation Awards. *George Washington Medal,* foundation's highest award, to astronaut John H. Glenn, Jr., for "personifying the American way of life by sincere patriotic words and deeds in our country's hours of challenge." *Special Award* to Gen. Lauris Norstad, U.S. Air Force, retired, who served as Supreme Commander of North Atlantic Treaty Organization forces in Europe (1956-1963).

National Book Awards. *Fiction Award* to John Updike for *The Centaur. Arts and Letters Award* to Aileen Ward for *John Keats: The Making of a Poet. Science, Philosophy and Religion Award* to Christopher Tunnard and Boris Pushkarev for *Man-Made America: Chaos or Control? History and Biography Award* to William H. McNeill for *The Rise of the West. Poetry Award* to John Crowe Ramson for his *Selected Poems.*

Poetry Society of America Lowell Mason Palmer Award to Arkansas poet Edsel Ford for *The Night of the Fox.*

Presidential Medal of Freedom, the nation's highest civilian honor, was presented to 30 distinguished persons "who contribute significantly to the quality of American life" by President Johnson at White House ceremonies on September 14.

Medals and citations of "special distinction for service in the government" were presented to former U.S. Secretary of State (1949-1953) Dean Acheson; Democratic U.S. Representative from Georgia (from Nov. 3, 1914 to 1964) Carl Vinson; and former television commentator Edward R. Murrow, who was U.S. Information Agency director (1961-1964).

The other recipients were: Detlev W. Bronk, neurophysiologist and president of the National Academy of Sciences (1950-1962); Aaron Copland, composer; Walt Disney, artist and animated cartoon films pioneer; James Frank Dobie, Texas author (see DEATHS OF NOTABLE PERSONS); Lena F. Edwards, physician and humanitarian; T. S. Eliot, U.S.-born British author and Nobel laureate (1948) (See POETRY); John W. Gardner, president of the Carnegie Foundation for the Advancement of Teaching; Theodore M. Hesburgh, Roman Catholic priest and president of the University of Notre Dame; Clarence L. Johnson, designer of the U-2 reconnaissance and the A-11 interceptor planes; Frederick Russell Kappel, engineer and the chairman of the board of the American Telephone and Telegraph Company; Helen Adams Keller, internationally famous blind lecturer and author; Willem de Kooning, artist; John L. Lewis, president of the United Mine Workers of America (1920-1960); Walter Lippmann, journalist and author; Alfred Lunt and Lynn Fontanne, the American theater's distinguished husband and wife team; Ralph Emerson McGill, publisher and former editor of *The Atlanta (Ga.) Constitution;* Samuel Eliot Morison, noted historian; Lewis Mumford, author, social philosopher, and architecture and city planning authority; Reinhold Niebuhr, theologian and Protestant leader; Leontyne Price, concert and opera singer; A. Philip Randolph, president of the Brotherhood of Sleeping Car Porters and civil rights leader; Carl Sandburg, poet and biographer; John Steinbeck, author, playwright, and Nobel literature laureate (1962); Helen B. Taussig, president-elect of the American Heart Association, with the late Alfred Blalock (see DEATHS OF NOTABLE PERSONS) developed the blue baby surgery; Thomas J. Watson, Jr., president of the International Business Machines Corporation; and Paul Dudley White, noted heart diseases authority.

Ramón Magsaysay Foundation Awards. *Public Service Award* to Augustine Nguyen Lac Hoa, Chinese Roman Catholic priest-soldier; *International Understanding Award* to Mrs. Welthy Honsinger Fisher, Rome, N.Y., who founded the Literacy House in Lucknow, India; *Journalism and Literature Award* to Kayser Sung, Chinese-born British writer, and Richard Garrett Wilcon, British writer; *Community Leadership Award* to Pablo Tapia, Filipino banker; *Government Service Award* to Yukiharu Miki, Japanese.

Royal Swedish Academy Gold Medal to Arvid Paulson, Swedish actor, director, scholar, and master of the Swedish and English languages, for translating into English some 40 dramas by August Strindberg.

Society of American Historians Francis Parkman Prize, for an American history book that best combines sound scholarship and literary excellence, to William E. Leuchtenburg for *Franklin D. Roosevelt and the New Deal.*

231

AWARDS AND PRIZES

United Nations Fridtjof Nansen Medal, for services to refugees, to: Dame May Curwen, founder of the British Council for Aid to Refugees, and to François Preziosi of the United Nations High Commissioner for Refugees office and Jean Plicque of the International Labor Organization, both Frenchmen, who were killed in August, 1964, while assisting refugees in Congo (Léopoldville).

Yale University Prizes. *Yale Series of Younger Poets Award* to Jean Valentine for her manuscript of poems, to be published in early 1965. *Outstanding Secondary School Teachers Awards* to: Mrs. Margaret J. Hawkes, Hyde Park High School botany and biology teacher, Chicago; Alice B. Rogers, Messick High School English, Latin, and French teacher, Memphis, Tenn.; Frederick S. Allis, Jr., Phillips Academy history teacher and director of financial aid, Andover, Mass.; and James Wichterman, Senior High School philosophy and history teacher, Mercer Island, Wash.

Science and Industry

Albert and Mary Lasker Foundation Awards. *Medical Journalism Awards: Newspaper Award* to Bill Burrus of the Dallas (Tex.) *Times Herald* for a series on mental illness. *Magazine Award* to Gilbert Cant, *Time* magazine medicine editor, for an article on surgery. *Special Citation* to Lois Mattox Miller and James Monahan for their article in *Reader's Digest* on health hazards of smoking. *Television Award* to Paul Cunningham for his series on mental retardation on the National Broadcasting Company's *Today* show. *Medical Research Awards: Clinical Research Award* to Nathan S. Kline, Rockland (N.Y.) State Hospital director of research, for work on antidepressant drugs, which has advanced mental illness treatment. *Basic Medical Research Award* to Renato Dulbecco, Salk Institute of Biological Studies (San Diego, Calif.) resident fellow, for research on bacterial viruses leading to a research method on virus infection of normal cells; and Harry Rubin, University of California (Berkeley) virology professor, for his research on viruses that produce cancer.

American Chemical Society Awards. *Priestley Medal* to William J. Sparks, Esso Research and Engineering Company scientific adviser, who invented Butyl rubber (with Robert M. Thomas of Esso) and directed the development of its manufacturing process. *William H. Nichols Medal* to Herbert E. Carter, University of Illinois chemistry and chemical engineering department head, for his discovery of several antibiotics and research on the chemistry of streptomycin. *Outstanding Young Chemist Award* to Marshal Fixman, University of Oregon Institute of Theoretical Science director, for explaining mathematically the behavior of synthetic molecules.

American Heart Association Research Achievement Award to Rebecca C. Lancefield, Rockefeller Institute professor and the first woman to receive this award, for research on the natural history of streptococcal infections, rheumatic fever, and acute nephritis.

American Institute of Architects Gold Medal to Pier Luigi Nervi, Italian designer of concrete buildings and other structures for the past 40 years.

American Institute of Physics Karl Taylor Compton Medal to Henry A. Barton, first director of the American Institute of Physics.

American Public Health Association Awards. *William T. Sedgwick Memorial Medal* to Leona Baumgartner, assistant administrator of the Agency for International Development. While New York health commissioner (1954-1962), she developed a health code, and added units in basic research, radiological health, and social science to the city's health department. *Samuel Bronfman Foundation Prizes* to: Robert H. Felix, dean of Saint Louis University School of Medicine, for his work while director of the National Institute of Mental Health (1949-1964); Malcolm H. Merrill, California Department of Public Health director, for developing new protective standards for air, water, and food purity in the state; and George E. Moore, director of Roswell Park Memorial Institute, Buffalo, N.Y., for his leadership in developing one of the world's leading cancer research institutions.

Case Institute of Technology Albert A. Michelson Award to Haldan Keffer Hartline, Rockefeller Institute biophysics professor, for his research on sense organs, and especially for discoveries in the physics and biology of visual perception.

Columbia University Awards. *Charles Frederick Chandler Medal* to Henry Taube, Stanford University chemistry professor, for research on how electrons are transferred between molecules in solution. *Vetlesen Prize* to Penitti Eelis Eskola, University of Helsinki (Finland) geology and mineralogy professor emeritus, who originated the concept that a homogeneous belt of rock called *eklogit* runs under the earth's crust; and Arthur Holmes, former University of Edinburgh professor, who developed the use of isotope geology in measuring the age of the earth.

Dickinson College Joseph Priestley Memorial Award to Isidor Isaac Rabi, Columbia University Higgins Professor of Physics and Nobel laureate (1944), known for his studies of molecular beams and magnetic properties of atomic nuclei.

Franklin Institute Awards. *Franklin Medal* to Gregory Breit, Yale University Donner Professor of Physics and nuclear physics pioneer, for his theoretical analyses of the results of scattering experiments.

National Academy of Sciences Awards. *Public Affairs Medal* to Detlev W. Bronk, neurophysiologist and academy president (1950-1962), for his contributions to science as a whole. *Cyrus B. Comstock Award* to Chien-shiung Wu, Columbia University physics professor and the first woman recipient of this award, provided the first experimental confirmation of the violation of the law of "parity conservation," or right-left symmetry, in the nucleus. *James Craig Watson Medal* to Willem J. Luyten, University of Minnesota astronomer, known for his extensive studies of the dying stars.

National Medal of Science, presented by President Johnson, to: Luis Walter Alvarez, University of California (Berkeley) physics professor, known for his work in experimental high energy physics; Vannevar Bush, electrical engineer whose inventions range from vacuum tubes to calculating machines; John Robinson Pierce, executive director of the Bell Telephone Laboratories Research Communications Principles and Communications Systems Divisions, for his many contributions to communications; Cornelius Bernardus van Niel, Stanford University professor emeritus, for fundamental research on the biochemistry of microorganisms and the basic mechanisms of photosynthesis, and for excellence as a teacher; and Norbert Wiener (see DEATHS OF NOTABLE PERSONS).

Research Corporation Awards to: Paul J. Cohen, Stanford University associate professor of mathematics, for two theorems: the continuum hypothesis and the axiom of choice; Heisuke Hironaka, Brandeis University associate mathematics professor, for his work in algebraic geometry, which solved the problem of how to resolve singularities (unusual specific solutions) of algebraic curves and surfaces.

Royal Canadian Geographical Society Massey Medal to Yves Oscar Fortier. See FORTIER, YVES OSCAR.

See also NOBEL PRIZES; PULITZER PRIZES; and Awards sections of articles such as ATOMIC ENERGY, AVIATION, and LITERATURE FOR CHILDREN.

BAHAMAS attained internal self-rule on January 7 when Governor Sir Robert de Stapeldon Stapeldon handed over the government to Sir Roland Symonette, the island's first prime minister. Under the new constitution, Great Britain retained responsibility for Bahama's foreign relations and defense. A new governor and commander in chief, Sir Ralph Grey, arrived in April.

The island's tourist boom continued with new investments flowing into hotels, casinos, yacht marinas, and golf courses. Development centered in the free port area of Grand Bahama Island. It was assisted by a tax holiday until 1990 and a moratorium on customs and excise taxes until 2054.

Population: 118,000. **Government:** Governor Sir Ralph Grey; Prime Minister Sir Roland Symonette. **Foreign Trade:** exports, $9,000,000; imports $69,000,000. **Principal Exports:** apparel, hardware, provisions. ALASTAIR BURNET

BAKER, ROBERT "BOBBY" G. (1928-   ), was the object of a congressional investigation into "influence peddling" and the center of a scandal, known as the "Bobby Baker case." A shrewd, alert, and personable man, Baker virtually grew up in the Senate. He came there from his home in Pickens, S.C., as a Senate page at the age of 14.

Baker made a good impression on the Senators, and in his spare time earned a law degree. He enjoyed the patronage of both the late Senator Robert S. Kerr, Democrat of Oklahoma and President Lyndon B. Johnson, who, when Democratic leader, named Baker secretary to the Senate majority. His wife was an employee of a Senate committee.

Baker's outside activities came to light in September, 1963, when a suit was filed in the U.S. District Court against him, two associates, and the Serv-U Corporation of which Baker was a principal stockholder. The suit charged that Baker had been instrumental in the transfer of a vending contract from another company to Serv-U Corp. One of his two associates, Fred Black, Jr., was subsequently convicted of income tax evasion.

Baker resigned his Senate post on October 7, 1963, following charges that he had used his position to pyramid a $19,600 salary into a fortune of about $2,000,000. Questions were raised as to whether his activities conflicted with his duties as a Senate employee, and also about the possible involvement of various Senators in his business dealings. The furor led to an inquiry by the Senate Rules Committee, which limited its scrutiny to Senate employees, not Senators.

The Baker episode also became a part of the election campaign as both the Republican presidential and vice-presidential candidates raised it as evidence of Democratic "corruption" in Washington. At the end of the year, the Senate Rules Committee was continuing its investigation.

BALLET. See DANCING.

Wide World

HANGING ON tightly, 12-year-old Danny Nowell rose 3,000 feet, April 13, before the pilot became aware of his plight and landed.

BALLOONS soared to new heights in both scientific studies and recreation. During the year, Tracy Barnes of Wayzata, Minn., broke seven world records. On May 10, he ascended more than 37,000 feet in his homemade class 3-A balloon. This broke the 23,286-foot class 3-A record set by Russia's Boris Nevernov in 1940. In this flight, Barnes also broke five records held by Don Picard of Sioux Falls, S.D., and one held by I. J. Burzinski of Poland. His balloon reached its record altitude 55 minutes after take-off.

The National Scientific Balloon Flight Station at Palestine, Tex., also known as the National Center for Atmospheric Research (NCAR), launched nearly 75 balloons in 1964, varying in capacity from 25,000 to 10,000,000 cubic feet.

A University of Minnesota physics team sponsored a noteworthy series of launches as part of the International Years of the Quiet Sun (see ASTRONOMY [CLOSE-UP]). It sent balloons aloft at Point Barrow, Alaska, to be carried by continuously revolving air currents around the North Pole. The purpose was to study cosmic rays and the earth's magnetic fields. At Holloman Air Force Base in New Mexico, a Northwestern University team succeeded in getting telescopic pictures of Venus with a balloon that rose 87,500 feet early in April.   SERGEI LENORMAND

BANDA, HASTINGS KAMUZU (1905-), whose middle name means "little root," is the prime minister of Malawi (formerly Nyasaland), one of Africa's newest independent nations. See MALAWI.

The prime minister was born in a village in the Central Province of Nyasaland. His parents were poor, uneducated Chewas. In his desire to acquire an education, he ran away from home, heading first for Johannesburg, South Africa, and later, the United States. In 1931, he received his B.A. degree from the University of Chicago and, in 1937, an M.D. from Meharry Medical College in Nashville, Tenn. He practiced medicine in England until the 1950's, when he returned to his homeland.

Banda had maintained close relations through the years with tribal leaders in Nyasaland. As the chief spokesman for the extremists in the Nyasaland African National Congress, he became a symbol of the nation's struggle for freedom.   WALTER F. MORSE

BANKS AND BANKING. In the closing weeks of 1964, the U.S. banking community adjusted to the Federal Reserve Board (FRB) increase in its discount rate from $3\frac{1}{2}$ per cent to 4 per cent (see MONEY). There was uneasiness that commercial banks would follow suit and raise their basic rates on business loans. Three banks did raise their prime rate from $4\frac{1}{2}$ to $4\frac{3}{4}$ per cent. But the largest of them, the First National Bank of Boston, on December 3, bowed to presidential urging and rescinded its earlier increase. Only then was it apparent that major banks would hold the line on the prime rate.

All through the year demand for credit grew, putting pressure on the banks to find money to lend. That pressure led banks to some interesting new ways to attract funds. A Long Island (N.Y.) bank sold "participations" in their consumer installment loans in $10,000 units with a $4\frac{1}{2}$ per cent return. Others sold bonds or tapped the money market by issuing unsecured notes. In September the First of Boston

pioneered this device, which the Federal Reserve Board ruled a lawful way to avoid interest rate and reserve regulations.

One relatively recent way, negotiable certificates of deposit, however, brought difficulties to some banks in 1964. First, with a 4 per cent rate-of-interest ceiling, the certificates became less attractive to investors as other interest rates firmed. In addition, the certificates played a part in some dramatic bank failures. Desperate for funds, some banks allowed agents to sell certificates at less than face value and thus, in effect, raise the interest rate above the 4 per cent ceiling. When several of those banks failed, the Federal Deposit Insurance Corporation (FDIC) sued to bar insurance claims on deposits receiving more than the ceiling rate.

And the Federal Home Loan Bank Board (FHLBB) ruled that savings and loan associations (SLA's) could not count certificates as part of their legal reserves if they had received a "consideration" or fee from

U.S. Personal Savings (in billions of dollars)		
Type	1964	1963
Commercial Banks	122.1	108.1
Savings and Loan Assns.	98.9	87.9
Mutual Savings Banks	47.9	43.7
U.S. Savings, other bonds	68.2	66.4
Postal Savings	.4	.5
Annual rate of savings	31.0	27.0

Note: Figures at end of September each year.
Sources: *Federal Reserve Bulletin*; U.S. Department of Commerce

an agent or anyone but the issuing bank. Because some banks and SLA's failed as the result of manipulations that occurred soon after transfers of ownership, Congress authorized the federal agencies to screen new owners of financial institutions.

Feuding and Infighting among federal regulatory agencies continued in 1964 despite some efforts at reconciliation. Comptroller of the Currency James J. Saxon sought to free national banks from restrictions on the rates of interest they pay, the types and size of their investments, and the location and number of their offices. With rare exceptions, FDIC and FRB spokesmen opposed his views.

New Banks chartered by the comptroller in the first half of 1964 rose to 100, almost twice the number that opened with state charters.

More than 1,700 new bank buildings were constructed in 1964. The First National Bank of Chicago bought the adjacent 46-story Morrison Hotel and began a world's record wrecking job to clear the site for a new office skyscraper (see CHICAGO).

The Department of Justice won a significant victory in 1964 in its effort to apply antitrust standards to federally regulated enterprises. The Supreme Court upset the 1961 merger of two Lexington (Ky.) banks despite its prior approval by the then comptroller, Ray Gidney, and a federal court. The department, FRB, and FDIC each had advised Gidney the merger would hurt competition. WILLIAM G. DEWALD

BROKEN BAT got a single for Yankees' Phil Linz in the third inning of the final World Series game, October 15. The Cardinals' pitcher was Bob Gibson.

BASEBALL. John Joseph Keane started the 1964 season among the least heralded of the 20 big league managers. He ended it as the central figure in some of the most astounding developments in the history of baseball.

Keane managed the St. Louis Cardinals to the National League pennant in a topsy-turvy finish that went down to the very last day of the season. He then led the Cardinals to a World Series victory over the New York Yankees. He resigned as Cardinal manager the day following the end of the series because, he said, of the lack of faith the owner had shown in him during the season. Four days later, Keane was named to manage the Yankees. Keane replaced Yogi Berra, who was fired because Yankee officials felt Berra had not maintained proper team discipline. In mid-November, the New York Mets hired Berra to coach under his old Yankee boss, Casey Stengel.

This was the second year in a row the Yankees had lost the series. The Los Angeles Dodgers defeated them in four straight games in 1963, and now the Cardinals won the first, fourth, fifth, and seventh games. The Cardinals' pitcher, Bob Gibson, who lost the second game but took the fifth and the seventh, set a series record of 31 strikeouts.

The National League. The collapse of the Philadelphia Phillies set off late excitement. The Phillies led the league most of the season, and were ahead $6\frac{1}{2}$ games, with two weeks remaining. Then they lost 10 straight games. The Cardinals and the Reds went into the final day tied for first place, a game ahead of the Phillies, who still hoped for a three-way tie. Then the Cardinals won the pennant by beating the New York Mets, 11-5, while the Reds lost to the Phillies, 10-0. The Phillies and the Reds finished in a tie for second place.

Jim Bunning of the Phillies became the first National League pitcher in this century to pitch a perfect game—27 batters, no hits, no runs, no errors. The game was played on Father's Day against the Mets.

The American League. Despite more huffing and puffing than they had been accustomed to, the Yankees won their record-tying fifth straight pennant with a strong drive over the final six weeks. After reaching a low point in which they lost six straight games, the Yankees put on steam to reach first place by September 17, a feat that included a league-high winning streak of 11 games. The Yankee comeback could be traced to the pitching of rookie Mel Stottlemyre, and to the flamboyant relief pitcher, Pedro Ramos, who won one game and saved seven after coming to New York from Cleveland, too late to be eligible for the World Series.

Front Office. The Yankees were sold to the Columbia Broadcasting System, which purchased an 80 per cent interest in the team for $11,200,000. Before the season started, the American League rejected attempts by Charles O. Finley to move his Athletics

FINAL STANDINGS IN MAJOR LEAGUE BASEBALL

AMERICAN LEAGUE

	W.	L.	Pc.	GB.
New York..............	99	63	.611	—
Chicago...............	98	64	.605	1
Baltimore.............	97	65	.599	2
Detroit................	85	77	.525	14
Los Angeles...........	82	80	.506	17
Cleveland.............	79	83	.488	20
Minnesota.............	79	83	.488	20
Boston................	72	90	.444	27
Washington...........	62	100	.383	37
Kansas City...........	57	105	.352	42

Leading Batters

Batting Average—Tony Oliva, Minnesota......	.323
Home Runs—Harmon Killebrew, Minnesota.....	49
Runs Batted In—Brooks Robinson, Baltimore....	118
Hits—Tony Oliva, Minnesota.................	217
Runs—Tony Oliva, Minnesota.................	109

Leading Pitchers

Games Won—Chance, L.A.; Gary Peters, Chi...	20
Win Average—Whitey Ford, New York (17-6)..	.739
Earned Run Average—Dean Chance, L.A.......	1.65
Strikeouts—Al Downing, New York...........	217

NATIONAL LEAGUE

	W.	L.	Pc.	GB.
St. Louis...............	93	69	.574	—
Cincinnati.............	92	70	.568	1
Philadelphia...........	92	70	.568	1
San Francisco..........	90	72	.556	3
Milwaukee.............	88	74	.543	5
Los Angeles...........	80	82	.494	13
Pittsburgh.............	80	82	.494	13
Chicago...............	76	86	.469	17
Houston...............	66	96	.407	27
New York..............	53	109	.327	40

Leading Batters

Batting Average—Roberto Clemente, Pittsburgh.	.339
Home Runs—Willie Mays, San Francisco.......	47
Runs Batted In—Ken Boyer, St. Louis..........	119
Hits—Roberto Clemente, Pitts.; Curt Flood, St. L.	211
Runs—Richie Allen, Philadelphia.............	125

Leading Pitchers

Games Won—Larry Jackson, Chicago........	24
Win Average—Sandy Koufax, L.A. (19-5).....	.792
Earned Run Average—Sandy Koufax, L.A......	1.74
Strikeouts—Bob Veale, Pittsburgh	250

franchise from Kansas City to Louisville. At the end of the season, the Braves voted to move to Atlanta from Milwaukee in 1966 following an earlier move from Boston to Milwaukee in 1953. The management of the Indians voted to remain in Cleveland despite financial losses and talk of moving to Seattle.

There were eight managerial changes. Johnny Keane's switch to New York resulted in the elevation of coach Red Schoendienst to the post of Cardinal manager. Other coaches who moved into manager's jobs were: Herman Franks for Alvin Dark at San Francisco; Billy Herman for Johnny Pesky at Boston; and Dick Sisler for cancer-stricken Fred Hutchinson at Cincinnati. Hutchinson died in November. Harry Walker replaced Danny Murtaugh at Pittsburgh; Luman Harris replaced Harry Craft at Houston; and Mel McGaha replaced Ed Lopat at Kansas City.

In December, league owners restored absolute power over both leagues to the commissioner, Ford Frick. The National League also separately adopted an amendment to its constitution providing that the "controlling interest in any club may not be transferred without approval of three-fourths of all members of the league in a regular meeting." Prompted by the Yankee sale, the purpose of the rule was to prevent "sneak purchases" of any of its clubs.

Minor Leagues. Minnesota won the National Collegiate Athletic Association (NCAA) title, and West Liberty State College of West Virginia won the National Association of Intercollegiate Athletics (NAIA) crown. Staten Island, N.Y., won the Little League championship on a 4-0 no-hitter pitched by 12-year-old Danny Yaccarino, who struck out eight Monterrey (Mexico) players. The Babe Ruth crown went to El Segundo, Calif.

Award Winners in the major leagues were:

National League Most Valuable Player—Ken Boyer of the St. Louis Cardinals.

American League Most Valuable Player—Brooks Robinson of the Baltimore Orioles.

Cy Young Award, to the "pitcher of the year"—Dean Chance of the Los Angeles Angels.

National League Rookie of the Year—Richie Allen of the Philadelphia Phillies.

American League Rookie of the Year—Tony Oliva of the Minnesota Twins.

National League Manager of the Year—Johnny Keane of the St. Louis Cardinals (Associated Press); Gene Mauch of the Philadelphia Phillies (United Press International).

American League Manager of the Year—Hank Bauer of the Baltimore Orioles. STANLEY ISAACS

BASKETBALL. The University of California at Los Angeles (UCLA) went through the season undefeated, a feat previously accomplished only by San Francisco in 1956 and by North Carolina in 1957. UCLA climaxed its success with 98-83 triumph over Eastern champion Duke University in the National Collegiate Athletic Association (NCAA) tournament final. John Wooden of UCLA was voted coach of the year. His All-American guard, Walt Hazzard, won the player-of-the-year honors and was designated the outstanding player in the NCAA finals at Kansas City, Mo.

Bradley won the National Invitation Tournament (NIT) with an 86-54 victory over New Mexico at Madison Square Garden. Evansville captured its third NCAA small-college title in eight years by defeating Akron, 72-59. Rockhurst (Mo.) College won the National Association of Intercollegiate Athletics (NAIA) title by beating the defending champion Pan American College of Edinburg, Tex., 66-56.

Howard "Butch" Komives of Bowling Green won the national scoring title with an average of 36.7 points per game, edging out the defending champion, Nick Werkman of Seton Hall. Detroit was the country's highest scoring team with a 96.1 average. The best defensive team was San Jose State, which limited the opposition players to an average of 54.5 points per game.

Among the conference champions were Princeton (Ivy League), Kentucky (Southeast), Texas A&M (Southwest), Ohio and Michigan (Big Ten), and Kansas State (Big Eight).

AAU Champions. The Goodyear Wingfoots of Akron, Ohio, stopped the Phillips 66 Oilers of Bartlesville, Okla., in their bid for a third straight Amateur Athletic Union (AAU) title. The final game at Denver, Colo., ended in an 86-78 victory for the Akron players.

Nashville Business College and Wayland (Tex.) Baptist College met in the women's AAU finals for the third straight year, with Nashville again winning, by a 58-46 score.

Professional. The Boston Celtics showed no signs of relinquishing their hold on professional basketball honors. In relatively easy fashion, they won an unprecedented sixth straight National Basketball Association championship, probably the longest unbroken championship string in professional sports history. After topping the Eastern Division standings

---

1964 College All-American Team
(Source: NCAA consensus All-American)

Players	School
Walt Hazzard	UCLA
Bill Bradley	Princeton
Gary Bradds	Ohio State
Cotton Nash	Kentucky
Dave Stallworth	Wichita

---

for the eighth straight season, the Celtics swept through the play-offs by eliminating Cincinnati in five games and whipping San Francisco, the survivor in the Western Division, in the same number of games.

Oscar Robertson of the Cincinnati Royals was voted the league's most valuable player. San Francisco's Wilt Chamberlain led the league in scoring for the third straight year with an average of 36.9 points per game. Boston's Bill Russell, the most valuable player in the three previous seasons, led in rebounds, and Robertson in assists and free-throw percentage. Jerry Lucas of Cincinnati was voted rookie-of-the-year.

Boston owner Walter Brown, one of the league's most popular figures, died at age 59. He had not only headed the Celtics, but also was one of the founders of the National Basketball Association and the head of Bruins in the National Hockey League. Red Auerbach, Celtic coach, assumed the duties of general manager.   STANLEY ISAACS

BASOV, NIKOLAI GENNADIEVICH (1922-), is one of two Russian radio physicists who, with American Charles H. Townes, was awarded the Nobel physics prize in 1964. They were cited for their "fundamental work in the field of quantum electronics, which led to the construction of oscillators and amplifiers based on the maser-laser principle." Basov, Aleksandr M. Prokhorov, and Townes did their original research in the 1950's.

The two Russians also are credited with having developed a quantum optical generator. Basov has been deputy scientific director of the Soviet Academy of Sciences Lebedev Physics Institute since 1958. He is a graduate of the Moscow Engineering and Physics Institute (1950).

Nikolai Basov has been a member of the Communist party since 1958, and was elected a corresponding member of the Soviet Academy of Sciences in 1962. He has twice attended scientific conferences in the United States (1959, 1962).

See also NOBEL PRIZES; PROKHOROV, ALEKSANDR M.; TOWNES, CHARLES H.

BASUTOLAND, a British-ruled area in South Africa, moved closer to independence. At a conference held in London from April 20 to May 15, an 11-man Basutoland delegation pressed the British government for a new constitution and an earlier date for independence than had been formerly planned. As a result, it was agreed that full independence would follow, within one year, a parliamentary election scheduled for December, 1964.

In August, Basutoland was upgraded from a territory to a colony. The post of resident commissioner was raised to that of governor.

Population: 685,000. **Government:** Paramount Chief Motlotlehi Moshoeshoe II; Governor A. F. Giles. **Foreign Trade:** exports, $707,148; imports, $1,508,579. **Principal Exports:** maize, mohair, peas and beans, wool.   BENJAMIN E. THOMAS

See also AFRICA.

BATE, WALTER JACKSON (1918-   ), Harvard University English department chairman, was awarded the Pulitzer prize in 1964 for his biography, *John Keats*, and the Phi Beta Kappa Christian Gauss award. Various critics have judged it the most definitive and perceptive biography yet written on the English poet. Bate also wrote *Negative Capability: The Intuitive Approach to Keats* (1939) and *The Stylistic Development of Keats* (1945).

Phi Beta Kappa gave Bate its Gauss award (1956) for *The Achievement of Samuel Johnson*. Bate also edited the Yale edition of *The Works of Samuel Johnson*.

Walter Bate was born in Mankato, Minn. He is Harvard educated (A.B. cum laude, 1939; M.A., 1940; and Ph.D., 1942), has taught at the university since 1946, and is now Abbott Lawrence Lowell Professor of the Humanities. See PULITZER PRIZES.

BELGIAN CONGO. See CONGO (LÉOPOLDVILLE).

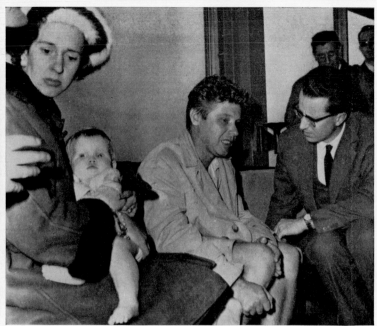

Wide World   Wide World

GRIM-FACED Belgian Foreign
Minister Paul-Henri Spaak
reads about actions in Congo.

ROYAL SYMPATHY of King Baudouin 1, right, is given a grieving
refugee from Congo whose wife was slain by rebels. Queen
Fabiola holds refugee's motherless daughter.

BELGIUM found itself inescapably involved with events in its former African colony, Congo (Léopold-ville). In November, it joined forces with the United States to rescue hundreds of whites held hostage by Congolese rebels in Stanleyville. The decision to drop 600 Belgian paratroopers was, according to Belgian Foreign Minister Paul-Henri Spaak, "the gravest . . . of my career . . . even more difficult than the decision to go to war in 1940." See Congo (Léopoldville); Section One, Paul-Henri Spaak on The World.

On June 25, Belgium's doctors and the government signed an agreement covering a new health service plan, thus ending a three-month-old dispute that had caused an 18-day medical strike in April. The country's doctors and dentists charged that the government's health plan would have abolished professional secrecy and lowered standards.

Belgium's economy continued to expand. Exports had more than doubled in 10 years, full employment prevailed, and foreign workers were being brought in from as far away as Turkey to fill jobs. Although there was some concern about inflation, wages were rising faster than prices. In three years, prices had risen 6.3 per cent, while wages were up 22 per cent. Belgium contributed to programs for developing nations, assisting particularly in Congo, where Belgian investments continued high.

Construction began on an auto and railway tunnel under the Schelde River at Antwerp. The tunnel,

scheduled for completion in four years, is to be 158 feet wide, with three lanes for automobiles, one for motorcycles, and three for railway lines.

Population: 9,325,000. **Government:** King Baudouin I; Prime Minister Théodore Lefèvre. **Foreign Trade** (including Luxembourg): exports, $5,610,000,-000; imports, $6,009,000,000. **Principal Exports:** iron and steel, machinery, textiles.   Fred J. Pannwitt

See also Europe.

BERMUDA welcomed a new governor on May 14 when Sir Roland Robinson, former member of the British Parliament, succeeded Major General Sir Julian Gascoigne.

The islands' preoccupation with the tourist trade was interrupted for a time in 1964 by a dispute between the Right Reverend John Armstrong, Bishop of Bermuda, and his residentiary canon, the Reverend W. J. Manning. Their quarrel, which involved control of the diocese, led to the formation of a church committee that seemed designed to act as a brake on Bishop Armstrong for the remainder of his tenure.

In September, the U.S. satellites Echo I and II indicated that Bermuda was 220 feet farther north and 105 feet farther west than had been thought.

Population: 60,000. **Government:** Governor Sir Roland Robinson. **Foreign Trade:** exports, $26,000,-000; imports, $68,000,000. **Principal Exports:** alcoholic beverages, clothing, food.   Alastair Burnet

BHUTAN, a tiny Himalayan kingdom that lies between India and Tibet, seethed with political unrest. On April 5 its premier, Jigme P. Dorji, was assassinated in Phuntsoling, a Bhutanese town near the West Bengal-Bhutan border. The assassination was reportedly the result of a feud instigated by officers who opposed the premier's plans to reform the army. Forty-one persons, including the army's deputy commander, Bahadur Namgyal, were arrested on orders of the maharajah, Jigme Wangchuk, Dorji's brother-in-law and absolute monarch of the kingdom. Namgyal was subsequently executed.

In November, the maharajah foiled what was apparently an armed attempt to depose him. A number of army officers were arrested. Several of Bhutan's senior officials fled the country, fearing they would be charged with treason.

Population: 750,000. **Government:** Maharajah Jigme Dorji Wangchuk; Premier Lhendup Dorji. **Foreign Trade:** No statistics available. JOHN N. STALKER

BIBLIOGRAPHY. See CANADIAN LITERATURE; LITERATURE; LITERATURE FOR CHILDREN.

BIOCHEMISTRY. Man came closer to a full understanding of the forces that guide the development of all living creatures in 1964. What was once a great mystery now had been isolated in the genetic material of cells—deoxyribonucleic acid (DNA) and ribonucleic acid (RNA). These two complex molecules had been found to be interrelated and to act upon each other in the production of protein. The action has been shown to follow these steps: DNA influences the formation of RNA, and RNA, in turn, converts amino acids into proteins.

The series of steps could not have been deciphered if scientists had not been able to produce some of the complex molecules in their laboratories. In 1961, Dr. Marshall W. Nirenberg and Dr. J. Henrich Matthaei, working at the National Institutes of Health, produced the first synthetic RNA and had shown that these man-made molecules could be substituted for natural RNA in directing the synthesis of artificial protein.

Since DNA molecules and RNA molecules are composed of less complex units linked into long chains, much attention has been directed toward how the chains are put together. To the researchers, it is apparent that the arrangement of the less complex units, known as nucleotides, determines the particular arrangement of amino acids in the protein. The generally accepted theory holds that the nucleotide arrangement occurs in triplets, and each triplet acts as a template to direct the formation and arrangement of other subunits into RNA, in the case of DNA; and into protein molecules, in the case of RNA.

Breaking the Code. The triplet arrangement is called the genetic code. Much of it has yet to be solved, but findings indicate that it has two important features. First, the code appears to be uni-

versal, since, in different organisms the same nucleotide combinations produce the same amino acid combinations. Second, the code appears to be "degenerate," *i.e.,* two different nucleotide triplets may designate the same amino acid. Biochemists see this as a distinct advantage since any damage to the genetic material that might harm or eliminate a given triplet will not cause a loss of the capacity of the DNA or RNA molecule to utilize a given amino acid.

Two new approaches to the problem of solving the entire genetic code were advanced during the year. These were developed by Dr. Nirenberg and Dr. H. Gobind Khorona of the University of Wisconsin. One involves the isolation of single triplets from a whole strand of DNA and then a matching of these units to single amino acids so that they can be studied chemically. The other involves the creation of short chains of DNA through a process of joining three or four triplets of known sequence. These then produce short chains of synthetic RNA, which in turn make synthetic proteins that can be analyzed and decoded.

Unfolded Enzymes. Chemical changes in living cells take place through the action of many enzymes. The ability of these complex protein substances to effect changes was found to depend on their normal folded shape. Biochemists, using a chemical agent to unfold them, found that the enzymes could no longer do their work. Removal of the chemical agent responsible for the unfolding resulted in a spontaneous recovery of their working ability.

Cell Regulation. Several simple but efficient means have been found within one-celled organisms for regulating the interaction of enzymes with the other substances of the cell. The discovery of these processes is important since they are somewhat like those that regulate the cells in higher organisms, such as man.

One means of regulation, known for some time, is the process of depression of enzyme activity. It is this process that explains most interactions of enzymes with foreign substances, such as drugs. This process involves the substitution of a structurally similar substance for the normal substance so that there can be no interaction of the enzyme with the normal substance.

Another means of regulation, discovered in 1964, influences a series of enzymes working in concert. The product of one enzyme reaction provides the substrate for the next enzyme, and so on, to the final product. It has been observed that the final product may inhibit the entire sequence if the structure of the final product does not resemble the initial substance. Apparently, the final product interacts with the first enzyme in the series and produces a change in conformation of that enzyme.

Still another regulatory mechanism also has been recognized. In the process of cell division, each new cell receives a copy of the total genetic information retained in the parent cell. However, not all cells from the parent are alike in their capacity to carry out reactions. For example, brain cells and liver cells, though apparently containing the same coded information, are obviously quite different in function. Scientists have now shown that segments of the genetic material are rendered inactive as a result of being masked by simple substances. The insertion of hormones into the cell disrupts the masking process, and the cell will then exhibit previously repressed activity.

Cytochrome-C. Recent work in many laboratories has disclosed a fundamental chemical unity in all living things that utilize oxygen in the production of useful energy. The substance is the enzyme cytochrome-c. Studies have determined the actual sequence and position of every amino acid (104 to 108 amino acids are combined to make up this particular protein) in cytochromes extracted from organisms ranging in the evolutionary scale from yeasts to humans. It was found that cytochrome-c in man and the rhesus monkey differs by only one amino acid; those of mammals and birds differ by 10 to 15; that of fish by 18 to 21; and that of yeast by 43 to 49 amino acids. From the data, it was possible to estimate that during the slow course of biological evolution it took an average of about 22,000,000 years for a new amino acid difference to appear in the cytochromes, as a given species evolved into a higher species. HAROLD FEINBERG

See also BIOLOGY; BOTANY; CHEMISTRY; MEDICINE.

BIOLOGY. Biologists took another look at a famous meteorite in an attempt to determine whether life exists elsewhere in space—a question that has long intrigued scientists as well as science fiction writers.

New evidence that some think supports such a possibility was obtained from a century-old meteorite that fell near Orguel, France, in 1864. At that time, the meteorite was found to contain significant amounts of organic material resembling peat or low-grade coal, but careful studies seemed to indicate that the matter was nonorganic in origin. In 1952, a classical experiment by Stanley L. Miller and Nobel prize winner (1934) Harold C. Urey demonstrated that heat and electrical fields can influence inorganic elements to form complex organic molecules similar to those derived from living creatures. The meteor's long passage through space, followed by entry into the earth's atmosphere, could have approximated these conditions. See 1964 YEAR BOOK, Section One, ISAAC ASIMOV ON SCIENCE.

In 1964, a team of six researchers, led by Bartholomew Nagy of Fordham University, found that some of the material from the meteorite had the ability to rotate polarized light passing through it, a clear indication of a biological origin. However, other experts stated that this organic matter must have entered the meteorite from the earth's atmosphere rather than from any extraterrestrial source. At the University of Chicago a team of scientists led by Dr.

Edward Anders, investigating another piece from the same meteorite, uncovered a century-old hoax. They found a plant seed imbedded in the fragment which evidently was placed there long ago by some person, for it was clearly of terrestrial origin.

Cell Particles. The ability of animals, plants, and their cells to adapt to environmental changes has long been studied. Now it has also been found that particles within the cell, such as chloroplasts (from plants) and mitochondria (from animals), have adaptive capabilities. During the life span of a single cell there may be many generations of such subcellular particles. The recent findings suggest that fission (splitting in two) of the particles gives rise to their successive generations. Changes in the particles, brought about by adaptation, result in mutations that are continued through the successive generations of the particles.

DNA Repair. Radiation, though a useful diagnostic and therapeutic tool, often results in cell damage. However, the stability of the genetic material of a cell, deoxyribonucleic acid (DNA), following radiation, suggests the existence of a means to repair and preserve its structure. In one study, radiation was applied to certain strains of bacteria to produce an abnormal link between the adjacent parts of the DNA. This created a distortion in one strand of the DNA's two-stranded helix structure. Repair appeared to take place through enzyme action that removed the abnormally linked strand so that it could be replaced according to the pattern of the nearby undamaged strand of DNA.

Cell Photography. The first photographs of a living cell taken by means of its own light were shown by Dr. George Reynolds of Princeton University. He used a new image intensifier, one that can amplify light as much as 1,500,000 times, to take a picture of a tiny phosphorescent sea creature. The cell was thus investigated without the disturbing effects of external lighting. HAROLD FEINBERG

See also BIOCHEMISTRY; BOTANY; INSECT; ZOOLOGY.

BIRTHS. See VITAL STATISTICS.

BLINDNESS. The Royal National Commonwealth Society of London estimated the blind population of the world at 14,000,000 in 1964 and predicted that it would rise to 16,000,000 by 1975. The society found that one of the principal causes of blindness in countries outside the United States and Western Europe is malnutrition in pregnant women, and in children up to the age of 3. Hence, it pointed out that a large portion of blindness is preventable.

The integration of blind children in public schools for the sighted, where the blind children work with styluses on metal slates or with braillewriters, gained momentum as the international trend. In the United States, nearly 60 per cent of the blind children attended public schools in 1964.

Education and Rehabilitation. During the year, new, integrated public school facilities, some including teacher-training programs, were begun around the world in Peru, the Philippines, Portugal, Saudi Arabia, and Thailand.

The year showed a sharp increase in recognition of the need for providing comprehensive rehabilitation and industrial training services for newly blind adults. Programs in this area were newly underway in Costa Rica, India, Japan, Pakistan, Panama, and Tunisia. To serve as a demonstration project for the blind in the Arab world, a poultry raising section was added to the recently opened agricultural and rural training center in Syria. New rural training facilities were begun in Malaysia and Sierra Leone.

Braille Codes were standardized in the United States to facilitate the transcription of textbooks in mathematics, science, and other areas. A standard notation system of braille in Spanish was also adopted in 1964. This is expected to facilitate production of Spanish-language braille materials.

Conferences. International conferences of significance included the Third Quinquennial World Assembly of the World Council for the Welfare of the Blind, which met in August in New York City; the International Research Conference on Mobility for the Blind (guide dogs and cane techniques), which met at The Hague, The Netherlands, in August; and the World Braille Council Conference in Spanish-Portuguese Braille Problems, which met in Montevideo, Uruguay, in April. MARJORIE S. HOOPER

See also HANDICAPPED, THE.

BLOCH, KONRAD EMIL (1912-   ), Harvard University Higgins Professor of Biochemistry, was one of two scientists awarded the Nobel medicine prize in 1964. He and Feodor Lynen were cited for "their discoveries concerning the mechanism and regulation of cholesterol and fatty acid metabolism." How cholesterol is produced and the sequence of 36 steps in the animal cell's manufacture of the fatty substance are major results of their individual research.

Although Bloch had a chemical engineering degree (1934), he took his Ph.D. degree in biochemistry (1938) at Columbia University. He went to the University of Chicago as a research associate (1944), and advanced to professor of biochemistry (1950-1954). Bloch has been at Harvard since 1954.

Konrad Bloch was born in Neisse, Germany (now in Poland). He was graduated from Technische Hochschule in Munich, and came to the United States in 1936. Bloch was naturalized in 1944.

See also LYNEN, FEODOR; NOBEL PRIZES (Science).

BOATS AND BOATING enjoyed another tremendous year of growth, both as a sport and as an industry. Boat shows sprang up everywhere—even at harness race tracks—and wherever they were held, throngs of boat-lovers attended to browse and to buy. At New York City's National Motor Boat Show, bellwether of the industry, sales topped $40,000,000, beating the previous high by more than $4,000,000.

Fiberglass continued to gain in popularity as a hull material, especially for smaller boats.

In Europe, boating grew at an even faster pace than it did in the United States. Attendance at the 10-day Paris boat show was up 60 per cent, and the total number of outboard motors in use on the continent was estimated at 500,000. In Great Britain, where pleasure boats had increased from 15,000 to 250,000 in 10 years, the Admiralty announced a loan program to help local governments and private firms build more moorings.

Illinois became the first state to open a waterway especially for pleasure boating and touring. The new Illinois Water Trail runs for 325 miles along the Illinois River from Alton, on the Mississippi, to Chicago. It follows the historic route of Joliet, LaSalle, and Marquette.

Water Safety. An old problem, water pollution by boat sewage, became acute as a result of the growing number of pleasure craft. Many states and municipalities passed laws calling for marine toilets to be sealed while boats were in their waterways. The National Park Service was considering a similar rule.

The U.S. Coast Guard reported an increase in negligent and reckless pleasure boating, and announced that it had to assign fully 20 per cent of its officers to accident prevention during the height of the season. A coast guard advisory panel of boating administrators recommended the adoption of a compulsory passenger capacity-plate law for pleasure boats. The purpose would be to help reduce capsizing accidents, now often caused by overloading.

A Safe Boating Week and other safe-boating activities were sponsored by the United States Power Squadrons (USPS) and the Coast Guard Auxiliary, both composed mainly of boat-owning volunteers. More than 75,000 boaters attended safety courses conducted by the USPS.

Motorboat Racing. Unlimited hydroplane racing flourished, partly as a result of a 1963 tax ruling that allows companies to deduct boat operating costs as business expenses. Some of the fast new boats were *Tahoe Miss*, *Miss Exide*, *Miss Eagle Electric*, *Miss Budweiser*, and *Miss Smirnoff*. But the national championship winner was again Ron Musson of Seattle, who drove the old reliable *Miss Bardahl*. Along the way, Musson and *Miss Bardahl* also won a second straight Gold Cup at Detroit.

Harold Abbott of Miami won the Miami-Nassau race in a 31-foot Bertram runabout. He covered the course of 160 miles in 4 hours 54 minutes 50 seconds. Bertram boats also took second and third place, and won the 245-mile Long Island Marathon race.

The Miami-New York speed record was lowered for the third year in a row. Charles F. Johnson, a 67-year-old Florida boat company president, broke his own record for the event by nearly 15 hours. He made the trip in 31 hours 32 minutes. Kenny Baker of California set a new standing-quarter-mile drag record, 100.55 mph. JAMES O. DUNAWAY

BOLIVIA. President Victor Paz Estenssoro fled the country in early November following a military revolt headed by General Alfred Obando Candia. His ouster had stemmed in part from his decision to arbitrarily change the constitution and run for a third four-year term. This move had been bitterly opposed by a number of factions, including members of his own Nationalist Revolutionary Movement.

Following the ouster, General Obando assumed full control of the government. Bowing to popular demonstrations, he agreed, however, to share the presidency with General René Barrientos Ortuño. Within hours of the swearing-in ceremonies, Barrientos replaced Obando and took over as chief of state. He promised to retain Paz's social reforms and to schedule new elections.

Population: 3,675,000. **Government:** President René Barrientos Ortuño. **Foreign Trade:** exports, $80,000,000; imports, $104,000,000. **Principal Exports:** lead, silver, tin.   MARY C. WEBSTER

See also LATIN AMERICA.

BOOKS. See CANADIAN LITERATURE; LITERATURE; LITERATURE FOR CHILDREN.

BOSTON. About 25 per cent of the city was in the throes of redevelopment in 1964. The largest project, Government Center, was rising on the demolished slum, Scollay Square. Work was in progress on the center's 26-story, $18,000,000 John F. Kennedy federal office building, and on the $20,000,000 city hall. In Back Bay, the 52-story Prudential Tower was topped out, and Prudential Center's 29-story hotel neared completion.

Redevelopment of 159 acres of the downtown shopping district was in the planning stage, as was the scheme to renovate 100 acres of Boston's historic waterfront. In residential areas of the city, rehabilitation rather than wholesale demolition of residences was being stressed by development czar Edward J. Logue. Plans called for the rehabilitation of about 6,500 units and construction of another 1,500 in Washington Park, a Negro district.

Backed by $225,000,000 in state bonds, the Massachusetts Bay Transportation Authority began operations in July. It will oversee development of a comprehensive transit system.   DONALD W. LIEF

BOTANY. Seasonal flowers can be made to bloom continuously all year long by increasing their supply of light and chemicals, horticulturist Henry M. Cathey revealed at the Food and Home Fair of the U.S. Department of Agriculture held in Washington, D.C., in the spring. In his paper, he outlined recent discoveries about light requirements of plants and the part played by a pigment called *phytochrome* (a protein substance found in all plants) in regulating the growth of flowers. By adding light and new chemicals, such as B-9, phosfon, and Cycocel, azaleas, rhododendrons, and other spring flowers could be made to bloom throughout the year.

Evergreen Chill. Dr. Richard P. Pharis and Dr. Henry Hellmers of the California Institute of Technology reported that subfreezing temperatures damaged the photosynthesis mechanism in evergreen trees. They explained that cold weather temporarily slowed down the plant's ability to use sunlight in converting carbon dioxide and water into carbohydrates. Over a period of about five days, the photosynthetic process dropped to 50 or 60 per cent of the efficiency of the prefreezing level.

Salt-Water Cultivation. Dr. Hugo Boyko, ecological adviser in the ministry of agriculture of Israel, reported that plants irrigated with seawater in Israel had easily survived a nine-month drought that had killed the same species irrigated with fresh water. He further reported that 180 species of plants had been successfully irrigated with seawater.

Atrazine Study. Agronomists R. D. Schirman and K. P. Buchholtz at the University of Wisconsin reported finding the process by which atrazine kills quack grass. The chemical was found to block the mechanism used by the plants to build carbohydrates with energy from the sun. It did not, however, affect the processes by which the plant used its food reserves. The result was that large amounts of carbohydrates in quack grass roots were quickly depleted, and the roots died.   SERGEI LENORMAND

See also GARDEN AND LAWN.

BOWLING. Billy Hardwick of San Mateo, Calif., and LaVerne Carter of St. Louis, Mo., were voted "Bowlers of the Year" by the Bowling Writers' Association of America.

Hardwick was the only double champion at the $330,262 American Bowling Congress (ABC) tournament in Oakland, Calif., a competition of 65 days among more than 20,000 bowlers. He won both the classic singles and all-events title. The St. Louis Falstaffs won the team competition and Bob Strampe and Hal Jolley of Detroit captured the doubles crown.

Mrs. LaVerne Carter, wife of top bowler Don Carter, won the women's title for the first time in the $100,000 Bowling Proprietor's Association of America (BPAA) All-Star tournament at Dallas, Tex. Strampe won the men's title, his first national title in five years of professional competition. Dick Weber, defending champion, finished fourth. Strampe also won the $7,500 first prize of the Professional Bowlers Association (PBA) title at Garden City, N.Y.

World's Invitational. The $52,000 World's Invitational Bowling Championship, held in Chicago in November, was won by Jim St. John of Santa Clara, Calif., the defending champion. St. John had a margin of 17.07 Petersen Classic points over Strampe. Dave Soutar was third. Marion Ladewig took the women's title for her fifth Invitational victory.

Bob Thiel, a public utility employee of Hobart, Ind., beat out 15,872 bowlers with a score of 1,684 to win the $30,000 first prize in Chicago's seven-month-long Petersen Classic.   STANLEY ISAACS

Wide World

EXCITED Cassius Clay is restrained as he struggles toward the center of the ring shouting threats at his defeated opponent, titleholder Sonny Liston.

BOXING. Heavyweight champion Sonny Liston, though an 8-to-1 favorite, lost his title to Cassius Clay in February, when he failed to answer the bell for the seventh round in a title bout at Miami Beach, Fla.

During the bout Liston suffered a torn tendon in his left arm. He gave up after Clay took command in the sixth round. Clay himself had come dangerously close to losing earlier, when it appeared he might not come out for the fifth because his eyes were temporarily blinded from a caustic that had been applied to stop Liston's bleeding.

After the fight, the flamboyant new champion revealed that he was a member of the controversial Black Muslim sect and insisted that he be called by his "nonslave" name of Muhammad Ali. To most boxing enthusiasts, however, the champion remained Cassius Clay.

The Liston-Clay contract called for a rematch, in violation of the rules of the World Boxing Association (WBA). After the rematch was signed for Boston, November 16, the WBA stripped Clay of his title and called for a tournament of ranking contenders. The Liston-Clay fight was nevertheless looked upon as a fight for the championship since boxing tradition decrees that titles are usually won and lost in the ring. Three nights before the scheduled fight, however, the champion suffered a hernia and had to be rushed to the hospital for an operation, thus postponing the fight. It was estimated that $400,000 was lost on the promotion. See CLAY, CASSIUS.

Boxing Investigation. The Liston-Clay developments produced hearings in Washington before a Senate subcommittee that was appointed to draft legislation to regulate boxing.

Though the members of the committee reaped publicity by revealing questionable arrangements in the Liston-Clay contract and reputed underworld entanglements by Liston, they brought no bill to the floor of Congress.

The New Champions. Two other championships changed hands. Sugar Ramos lost the featherweight title, on a technical knockout, to 21-year-old Vincente Saldivar at Mexico City in October. Pone Kingpetch of Thailand won the flyweight crown for an unprecedented third time with a split decision over Japan's Hiroyuki Ebihara. The 15-round match took place in 90-degree Bangkok heat in February. STANLEY ISAACS

WORLD CHAMPION BOXERS

Division	Champion	City or Country	Year Won
Heavyweight	Cassius Clay	Miami	1964
Light-Heavyweight	Willie Pastrano	Miami	1963
Middleweight	Joey Giardello	Cherry Hills, N. J.	1963
Welterweight	Emile Griffith	New York	1962
Lightweight	Carlos Ortiz	New York	1962
Featherweight	Vincente Saldivar	Mexico City	1964
Bantamweight	Eder Joffre	Brazil	1960
Flyweight	Pone Kingpetch	Thailand	1964

BOY SCOUTS OF AMERICA

BOY SCOUTS OF AMERICA welcomed President Lyndon B. Johnson as their honorary president during ceremonies at the White House in February that marked the 54th anniversary of the organization. It was a return to Scouting for the President, who had served as a leader in his native Texas and helped organize a Scout troop among congressional page boys in 1936. As honorary president, he received an official membership card, a leather-bound copy of the 20,000,000th *Boy Scout Handbook*, and a copy of the annual "Report to the Nation," which summarized Scout activities for the preceding year.

President Johnson was honored along with Lady Baden-Powell, widow of the British founder of the Boy Scouts, at the Sixth National Scout Jamboree, held July 17 to 23 at Valley Forge, Pa. More than 52,000 boys and adult leaders, representing all 50 states and 41 countries, attended.

At the New York World's Fair, Scouts from all parts of the country served in a "Scout Service Corps," as aides to handicapped and aged persons.

Silver Buffalo awards for distinguished service to boyhood were presented to President Johnson, A. Frank Bray, Albert L. Cole, Ralph W. McCreary, Robert Moses, E. Laurence Palmer, Thomas F. Patton, Gilbert R. Pirrung, and Howard Tellepsen.

Thomas A. Watson, Jr., president of International Business Machines Corporation, was elected president of the National Council of the Boy Scouts of America at the annual meeting held in May at Cleveland, Ohio.   JOSEPH P. ANDERSON

BOYS' CLUBS OF AMERICA

BOYS' CLUBS OF AMERICA delegates to the 58th annual convention in Washington, D.C., in May, learned of the completion of plans to establish the Herbert Hoover Foundation.

The initial purpose of the foundation, announced by the former President in 1963, will be to enlist community support in a membership campaign entitled "One Thousand Boys' Clubs for One Million Deserving Boys." In 1964, 635 clubs served about 625,000 boys in 410 communities.

Convention reports on program activities showed that clubs in all sections of the country were giving emphasis to the effects of smoking on health, school drop-outs, and to intergroup relations, or problems that arise in clubs serving boys of different ethnic, religious, social, and racial backgrounds.

Michael Rapinchuk, 16, of Phoenix, Ariz., was named the 1964 "Boy of the Year," and was honored by President Lyndon B. Johnson as the nation's leading example of "Juvenile Decency." He received a $1,000 scholarship from the Reader's Digest Foundation. This award is a part of a total of $3,200 awarded annually by the foundation to encourage interest in higher education.

Richard M. Nixon, former Vice-President of the United States, was elected chairman of the board of the Boys' Clubs to succeed the late President Herbert Hoover.   JOSEPH P. ANDERSON

BRAZIL

BRAZIL changed chiefs of state three times within a 16-day period during 1964. On March 31, the army revolted against the regime of President João Goulart, replacing him on April 2 with Dr. Pascoal Ranieri Mazzilli, who was sworn in as interim president. On April 15, he was succeeded by General Humberto de Alencar Castelo Branco, army chief of staff. Castelo Branco had been elected at a joint session of congress under a new "institutional" act promulgated April 9 by the military command. Under it, the government was also empowered to suspend for 10 years the political rights of any individual charged with either communism or corruption. Subsequently, the political rights of some 400 persons were canceled, including three former Brazilian presidents, various congressmen, and scores of labor leaders and military officers. The act also provided that any bills sent to congress by the president must be considered within 30 days by each house; otherwise they would be considered as ratified.

The New Regime took drastic measures to remedy the nation's ills, which, earlier in 1964, had brought it to the brink of political, social, and economic disaster. The domestic budget deficit threatened to top $1,300,000,000. Living costs had been soaring at an annual rate of from 120 to 144 per cent. Extreme leftists were organizing the illiterate peasants in the destitute northeast. Politicians were attacking foreign business, and men openly sympathetic to communism had taken over key posts in the government and in the labor movement.

To create order and stability, the new president called on the nation's top economists and monetary experts. The cabinet came up with a number of agrarian, fiscal, and tax reform programs. It abolished petroleum and wheat import subsidies in a move to reduce the 1964 budget deficit. Thousands of superfluous civil servants were discharged, and all ministries were ordered to cut expenditures drastically. The anti-foreign investment profit remittance law promulgated by Goulart was amended to attract much needed foreign capital. Arrangements also were made with various foreign creditors to refinance or consolidate Brazil's foreign debts, estimated at between $3,445,000,000 and $4,500,000,000. The new cabinet also made plans to reduce the inflation rate.

Waning Popularity. Despite an initial exuberance, the popularity of the new regime began to wane when business, labor, large landholders, and other interests realized what sacrifices they would have to make to put the nation on its feet. The new government, however, was respected. Meanwhile, recurrent food shortages were frustrating reminders of the time it would take to effect improvements.

Population: 81,000,000. **Government:** President Humberto de Alencar Castelo Branco. **Foreign Trade:** exports, $1,247,000,000; imports, $1,315,000,000. **Principal Exports:** chemicals and pharmaceuticals, coffee, cotton, iron ore.   MARY C. WEBSTER

See also LATIN AMERICA.

A NEW YORK HARBOR SALUTE *marked the opening of the Verrazano-Narrows Bridge on November 21. Luxury liner United States and lesser craft sailed by.*

BREZHNEV, LEONID ILYICH (1906-   ), one of the Soviet Union's "rising new class of technicians," became the new First Secretary of the Soviet Communist party in October. He had long been a protégé of the man he replaced, Nikita S. Khrushchev.

Brezhnev was born Dec. 16, 1906, at Kamenskoye, now Dneprodzerzhinsk, the son of a steelworker. He, too, was employed as a youth in the steel industry, but turned early to Communist party work, being admitted to full party membership in 1931. He advanced steadily, and by 1952 he had become a member of the ruling Presidium. By 1956, he had entered the powerful Secretariat of the Presidium's Central Committee, and in May, 1960, he was elected president of the Soviet Union. Since then, he has visited many countries.

Brezhnev, in addition to being an able administrator, appears to have built personal political organizations in the areas he has served and to hold some control over the police. He is a ruggedly handsome man. Western diplomats have found him friendly, though reserved, and a man of keen intelligence. He is the first top Russian communist whose only contact with the 1917 Revolution consists of childhood memories.   WALTER F. MORSE

See also COMMUNISM; RUSSIA.

BRIDGE AND TUNNEL. Traffic began to roll across the "bridge of superlatives"—the Verrazano-Narrows Bridge—on November 21. With a center span of 4,260 feet vaulting across New York Harbor to link Brooklyn and Staten Island, the $325,000,000 structure boasted the longest suspension span in the world—60 feet longer than the previous record holder, the Golden Gate Bridge.

Europe's longest suspension bridge, across the Firth of Forth, near Edinburgh, Scotland, opened to traffic September 4. It replaced a ferry service that had been under royal charter since 1164. With a 3,300-foot center suspension span, the four-lane vehicular structure is the world's fifth longest.

When the Gladesville Bridge over the Parramatta River in Sydney, Australia, opened in September it became the world's longest concrete arch span. It measured 1,900 feet between abutments, with a main span of 1,000 feet. It was started in 1959.

In the spring, work started on a companion suspension span to the Delaware Memorial Bridge between New Castle, Del., and Pennsville, N.J. When completed in June, 1967, the $76,000,000 twin facility will carry four lanes of traffic each way over the Delaware River. Farther down the coast, the Chesapeake Bay Bridge-Tunnel opened on schedule on April 15, connecting Norfolk with Virginia's Eastern Shore. See 1964 YEAR BOOK, BRIDGE AND TUNNEL.

Europe's first automobile tunnel through the Alps, the 3.4-mile Great Saint Bernard Tunnel, was opened officially on March 19. The $35,200,000 bore connected St.-Rhémy, Italy, with Cantine d'en Haut, Switzerland. A second Alpine motor tunnel, the world's longest, was to be completed by early 1965. The $7\frac{1}{4}$-mile Mont Blanc Tunnel cut driving time between Paris and Milan by several hours.

On February 6, Great Britain and France announced a joint decision to build a railroad tunnel under the English Channel—an idea dating from Napoleon's time. The proposed 32-mile tunnel, through which automobiles will be carried on flatcars, would connect Folkestone, west of Dover, with Sangatte, north of Boulogne.   M. E. JESSUP

BRIDGE, CONTRACT. Italy maintained its international supremacy in contract bridge by winning the World Bridge Olympiad at New York City in May. While it was the seventh world championship for the Italians in eight years, it was the first Italian victory in the Olympiad, which is played in place of the regular matches every four years. Members of the winning team were Pietro Forquet, Benito Garozzo, Walter Avarelli, Giorgio Belladonna, Massimo D'Alelio, and Camillo Pabis-Ticci. Great Britain won the women's championship, with the U.S. team finishing second.

At the spring tournament of the American Contract Bridge League (ACBL) at Portland, Ore., the Harold S. Vanderbilt Cup was won by a team that included Howard Schenken and Peter Leventritt, both of New York City; Donald Krauss, Lewis Mathe, and Edward Kantar, all of Los Angeles; and Robert Hamman of Van Nuys, Calif. The Open Pair championship went to Oswald Jacoby of Dallas, Tex., and Barry Crane of Van Nuys, Calif.

A Canadian team won the Spingold trophy for the first time at the ACBL summer tournament in Toronto. All the members of the winning team, Eric Murray, Sammy Kehela, Bruce Elliot, and Percy Sheardown, were from Toronto. Theodore M. O'Leary

BRITISH COLUMBIA. See Canada.

BRITISH COMMONWEALTH OF NATIONS. See Great Britain; and articles on various countries of the Commonwealth.

BRITISH GUIANA toppled Cheddi B. Jagan from the premiership in elections held on December 7. Jagan's People's Progressive party (PPP) captured 109,332 votes, representing 45.81 per cent of the total cast. Under a new proportional representation plan, this gave the PPP 24 seats in the 53-seat legislature. The People's National Congress party headed by Forbes Burnham tallied 96,557 votes, or 40.5 per cent and 22 seats. In third place was the United Force party of Peter D'Aguiar, with 29,612 votes—or 12.4 per cent—and 7 seats. Despite Jagan's refusal to resign, Burnham was sworn in as prime minister by Sir Richard Luyt, British governor, who acted under a mandate from Queen Elizabeth II.

Jagan's powers had been eroded by political and racial strife in which the nation's East Indian and Negro communities had repeatedly clashed during the year. The violence was an outgrowth of a sugar workers' strike that had started in February and, until its settlement on July 27, had caused 160 deaths. The rioting had been so fierce that Governor Luyt had assumed emergency powers on June 13.

Population: 637,000. **Government:** Governor Sir Richard Luyt; Premier Forbes Burnham. **Foreign Trade:** exports, $85,260,538; imports, $86,796,926. **Principal Exports:** rice, rum, sugar. Alastair Burnet

See also Latin America.

BRITISH WEST INDIES See Jamaica; Trinidad and Tobago.

BROSIO, MANLIO (1897-   ), who was Italy's ambassador to Washington, D.C., from 1955 to 1961, took office on August 1 as secretary-general of the North Atlantic Treaty Organization (NATO). He had been unanimously elected to succeed Dirk U. Stikker of The Netherlands.

During World War I, Brosio was an Alpine artillery officer. He entered politics in 1918. An early opponent of fascism, he was banned from political activity when Benito Mussolini came to power. He returned to the private practice of law, but remained a leader in the underground democratic opposition. Following Mussolini's overthrow, in 1944 Brosio was named secretary-general of the reborn Liberal party.

Brosio was born in Turin on July 10, 1897, and was graduated in law from the University of Turin in 1920. He and his wife Clotilde were married in 1936. They have no children. Walter F. Morse

BUDGET. See Congress of the United States; Taxation.

BUILDING AND CONSTRUCTION completed in 1964 reached an estimated record value of $65,898,-000,000, an increase of 5.6 per cent from 1963. *Engineering News-Record* (ENR) predicted a 3 per cent gain in heavy construction contracts for 1965.

Building costs continued to climb. The ENR 20-city index rose an average of 1.3 per cent during the third quarter of 1964. Average hourly pay rates outpaced wages in other industries, rising 3.7 per cent during the nine-month period.

Early in the year, the Port of New York Authority announced plans to erect the world's tallest buildings—twin, 110-story office towers for its proposed World Trade Center in downtown Manhattan. The start on the 1,350-foot-high structures was set for early 1965.

The largest building in terms of enclosed volume of space got underway early in 1964 at Merritt Island, near Cape Kennedy, Florida. The huge building—524 feet high with a floor plan of 674 feet by 513 feet—will be used for assembling rockets for the U.S. space program. Doors will open to a height of 456 feet to allow for removal of rockets. M. E. Jessup

See also Architecture; Bridge and Tunnel; Dam; Housing; Roads and Highways; Water and Flood Control; Waterways.

BULGARIA remained ideologically closer to Russia than any other East European nation. Within hours of Soviet Premier Nikita S. Khrushchev's downfall, it had congratulated the new Kremlin leadership notwithstanding its own leaders' debt to Khrushchev. See Communism; Russia.

Georgi Traikov, a noncommunist party protégé of the deposed Soviet leader and chief of the Bulgarian National Agrarian Union, was elected titular head of state. He succeeded Dimiter Ganev, who died on April 20.

Despite Bulgaria's closeness to Russia, the nation took a firm step toward normalizing its relations with Greece. On June 28, Bulgaria agreed to pay $22,000,000 in settlement of Greek World War II reparation claims of $45,000,000. Agreements also were signed to re-establish transportation services between the two countries.

Population: 8,175,000. **Government:** Communist Party First Secretary Todor Zhivkov; President Georgi Traikov. **Foreign Trade:** exports, $838,000,-000; imports, $915,000,000. **Principal Exports:** clothing, metal ores, tobacco. TOM AND HARLE DAMMANN

See also EUROPE.

BURMA remained under the militant rule of General Ne Win. His determination to eliminate the guerrilla bands and bandits met with considerable success. However, while the right-wing tribes in Karen province signed a truce with the Burma Revolutionary Council, left-wing communist bands in central Burma continued the fighting. The effectiveness of the communist bands was sharply reduced, however, by steady military pressures.

Ne Win continued to lead Burma into socialism. Practically all businesses were nationalized. This, along with the previous nationalization of large, foreign-owned companies and banks, made the government solely responsible for practically all business in the country. Thousands of business men left Burma as the campaign for socialism intensified.

Population: 24,350,000. **Government:** Revolutionary Council Chairman Ne Win. **Foreign Trade:** exports, $312,000,000; imports, $194,000,000. **Principal Exports:** lumber, oilseed, rice. JOHN N. STALKER

See also ASIA.

BURNINGHAM, JOHN (1938?-   ), promising young English artist, was awarded the Kate Greenaway medal in 1964 by the British Library Association. He wrote and illustrated *Borka: The Adventures of a Goose with No Feathers*, his first book. The large, simple illustrations, in dark and bright hues, reflect the changing moods of little Borka. His second book is *Trubloff: The Mouse Who Wanted to Play* (1964).

The artist's *A.B.C.* book also came out in 1964. Burningham illustrated the late Ian Fleming's only book for children, *Chitty-Chitty-Bang-Bang: The Magical Car*, which came out in late 1964 (see DEATHS OF NOTABLE PERSONS). John Burningham studied at the Central School of Art, where he received the school's diploma and the National Diploma of Design. He lived in Israel for a while, doing set designs, models, and puppets for a film company.

See also LITERATURE FOR CHILDREN (Awards).

BURTON, HESTER (1913-   ), English author, was awarded the Carnegie medal in 1964 by the British Library Association. *Time of Trial* is a skillfully written novel about England in 1801. It grew out of material the author came upon when doing research for *Castors Away!*

The author is a former teacher, having read English at St. Anne's College. She was educated at Headington School and St. Anne's, both at Oxford. Her husband is an Oxford University don. They have three girls. Mrs. Burton edited *Coleridge and the Wordsworths* and *Tennyson* for the Oxford Sheldonian English Series, and was an assistant editor of the *Oxford Junior Encyclopedia.*

Hester Burton was born and grew up in Beccles, Suffolk, the daughter of a local doctor.

See also LITERATURE FOR CHILDREN (Awards).

BURUNDI. Premier Pierre Ngendandumwe was forced to resign in March, after less than a year in office. His resignation coincided with a cabinet shakeup, which was made, reportedly, because several members either were unable or unwilling to promote peaceful coexistence between the nation's two main tribal groups, the Batusi and the Bahutu. Albin Nyamoya was named to head a new government.

In April, Burundi signed an agreement with France providing for technical training of Burundi radio personnel. A week later, several members of the national assembly arrived in Peking, China, for a series of official visits.

Population: 2,725,000. **Government:** Mwami (King) Mwambutsa IV; Premier Albin Nyamoya. **Foreign Trade:** no figures available. **Principal Export:** coffee. BENJAMIN E. THOMAS

See also AFRICA.

BUS. The nation's intercity bus industry rode out 1964 in profitable style, especially in the East, where the New York World's Fair stimulated heavy charter-bus patronage. The industry's 27,000 buses, operated by 1,450 carriers, made nearly 466,000,000 trips totaling 1,321,000,000 bus-miles in 1964. It all added up to 22,500,000,000 passenger-miles—a 3 per cent rise over 1963 and a 10-year peak.

Operating revenues of the 161 major Class I carriers (12,000 buses) were estimated at $586,600,000 in 1964. Expected net earnings were $49,300,000, or 4 per cent above 1963. Projected gross revenue for all other bus firms totaled $130,000,000.

The Greyhound Corporation began building buses for its own use and for sale to other carriers through a wholly owned subsidiary, Motor Coach Industries, Pembina, N.Dak. Greyhound sought further diversification through a request to the Interstate Commerce Commission (ICC) for permission to purchase up to 60 per cent of REA (Railway Express Agency) stock, a move opposed by the major companies of the trucking industry.

Despite well-advertised financial difficulties, 1,183 municipally and privately owned urban bus lines added over 3,000 new buses in 1964, to bring their fleet total to over 50,000 vehicles. Local bus patronage —4,752,000,000 fares and $985,500,000 operating revenue in 1963—improved by a fraction of 1 per cent in 1964. MARK REINSBERG

See also TRANSIT; TRAVEL.

BUSINESS

THE TREND OF THE U. S. ECONOMY

INDUSTRIAL PRODUCTION

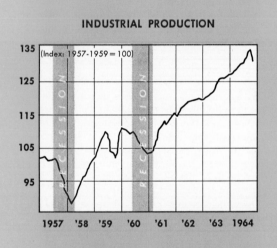

(Index: 1957-1959 = 100)

135
125
115
105
95

1957 '58 '59 '60 '61 '62 '63 1964

CAPITAL INVESTMENT
(For new plant and equipment) *EST.*

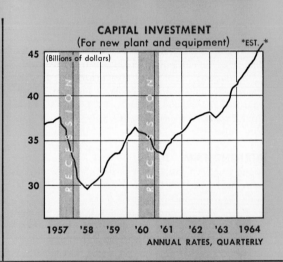

(Billions of dollars)

45
40
35
30

1957 '58 '59 '60 '61 '62 '63 1964

ANNUAL RATES, QUARTERLY

CORPORATE PROFITS

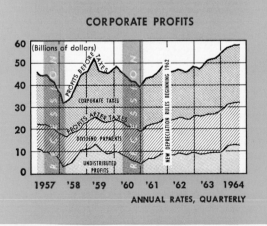

(Billions of dollars)

60
50
40
30
20
10
0

PROFITS BEFORE TAXES
CORPORATE TAXES
PROFITS AFTER TAXES
DIVIDEND PAYMENTS
UNDISTRIBUTED PROFITS
NEW DEPRECIATION RULES BEGINNING 1962

1957 '58 '59 '60 '61 '62 '63 1964

ANNUAL RATES, QUARTERLY

PERSONAL INCOME

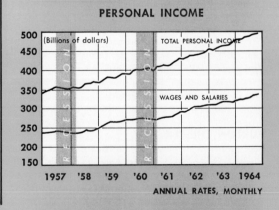

(Billions of dollars)

500
450
400
350
300
250
200
150

TOTAL PERSONAL INCOME
WAGES AND SALARIES

1957 '58 '59 '60 '61 '62 '63 1964

ANNUAL RATES, MONTHLY

SPURRED BY A multibillion-dollar tax cut, a 12 per cent increase in expenditures for new plant and equipment, and a third straight boom year in automobile sales and production, the U.S. economy surged to a $625,000,000,000 output of goods and services, or Gross National Product (GNP). This represented a 7 per cent rise over the $584,000,000,000 of 1963 and more than a 5 per cent growth when price increases were taken into account. In December the boom passed into its 46th month. This longest period of expansion since World War II topped the previous record 45-month upswing during the Korean War.

For the second year in a row, the economy outperformed the prediction of the professional economists. The President's Council of Economic Advisers had forecast a GNP of $623,000,000,000 if the tax cut went into effect in February and a drop of $2,000,000,000 for every month it was delayed. The cut became effective in March, but the economy actually exceeded the most optimistic predictions.

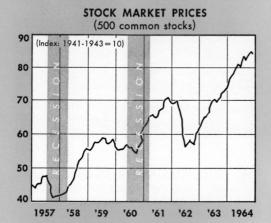

SIX KEY INDICATORS

STOCK MARKET PRICES
(500 common stocks)

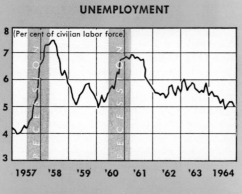

UNEMPLOYMENT

All Charts, Except Stock Market, Are Adjusted for Seasonal Variations

Thanks to the reduction in personal income taxes, U.S. consumers saw their per capita incomes (after taxes) rise to more than $2,330, a gain of almost 5 per cent over 1963—by far the largest increase both percentage-wise and in absolute dollars in 10 years. Adding to the general cheer was a drop in the level of unemployment from 5.6 per cent early in the year to about 5 per cent at year-end (see LABOR).

Stock prices followed the economy upward. The Dow Jones average of 30 industrials closed 1963 at 762.95, soared to an all-time closing high of 891.71 on November 18, and closed the year at 874.13, about 15 per cent higher than at the beginning of the year (see STOCKS AND BONDS). Rising corporate profits by the end of the third quarter had reached $32,000,000,000 after taxes, and dividend payments, more than $20,000,000,000. These increases of $5,000,000,000 and $2,000,000,000, respectively, in the 12 months helped kindle investor enthusiasm.

Industrial Production, as measured by the Federal Reserve Board index, rose to a record high of 134 (1957-1959 = 100) in September, fell slightly in October due to an almost complete shutdown of General Motors auto production, and then rebounded to close the year at 137. A 31-day strike against General Motors and scattered strikes in Ford plants dashed the industry's hopes to produce 8,000,000 cars, breaking the 1955 record of more than 7,900,000. Final production was only slightly better than the 7,644,000 cars of 1963. It was a third straight good year for the industry, however. See AUTOMOBILE.

Output of steel, however, did top the 1955 record. The mills poured nearly 127,000,000 ingot tons. See IRON AND STEEL.

Prices Held remarkably stable despite industry's rush to produce. As measured by the U.S. Bureau of Labor Statistics, consumer prices continued their slow, gradual climb. The index inched slightly above 108 (1957-1959 = 100), less than a point higher than in December, 1963. Wholesale prices rose even less.

The remarkable stability of U.S. prices was brought

THE PULSE OF BUSINESS

Important Indicators	Bottom of 1961 Recession (Feb.,1961, or 1st quarter)	1963 (October, or 3d quarter)	Latest (Oct.,1964, or 3d quarter)
Total output (gross national product, billions, annual rate)..	$500.4	$587.2	$628.4
Output of industry (1957=100)	102.1	126.1	131.7
Autos, other hard goods.....	94.3	126.0	130.4
Clothing, other soft goods....	110.8	127.7	134.2
Civilian employment (millions)..	66.7	69.8	71.1
Unemployment (millions).......	5.0	3.9	3.2
Personal income (billions, annual rate)...............	$404.2	$472.7	$498.6
Farm net income (billions, annual rate)...............	$ 12.5	$ 12.9	$ 12.6
Retail trade (billions monthly)....	$ 17.8	$ 21.5	$ 22.7
New construction (billions annual rate)...............	$ 54.6	$ 64.9	$ 65.4
Housing starts, private (millions, annual rate)........	1.2	1.8	1.4
Business inventories (billions)..	$ 93.4	$103.7	$107.1
Factories' new orders (billions monthly)...........	$ 29.1	$ 35.3	$ 37.7
Unfilled orders, hard goods (billions, end of month).......	$ 42.8	$ 47.2	$ 53.1
Factory workweek (avg. hrs.)...	39.3	40.7	40.7
Corporation profits (billions, annual rate, before taxes).....	$ 38.5	$ 51.3	$ 58.0
Spending for plant and equipment (billions, annual rate, December).............	$ 33.8	$ 40.0	$ 46.1
Exports of goods (billions monthly)..................	$ 1.7	$ 1.9	$ 2.1
Imports of goods (billions monthly)..................	$ 1.1	$ 1.4	$ 1.5
Cost of living (1957–1959 = 100)..................	103.9	107.2	108.5

Note: Figures are seasonally adjusted, except for unfilled orders and cost of living. Table is based on U.S. official figures.

THE PRICE OF COMMODITIES

	1963 (Dec. 9)	1964 (Dec. 11)
FOODS		
Flour, hard winter NY cwt..........	$6.72	$6.64
Coffee, Santos 4s NY lb.............	.37	.46
Cocoa, Accra NY lb.................	.26	.24
Sugar, Refined NY lb...............	.1285	.0975
Broilers, 3 lb. & under lb...........	.14¼	.14⅜
Hogs, Chicago top cwt..............	15.65	16.75
Steers, choice cwt..................	23.50	25.00
GRAINS AND FEEDS		
Wheat, No. 2 ord. hard KC bu.......	2.17½	1.64¼
Corn, No. 2 yel. Chicago bu........	1.23½	1.27½
Oats, No. 1 wh. heavy, Chgo. bu.....	.73½	.73½
Rye, No. 2 Minneapolis bu.........	1.44¼	1.20⅝
Soybeans, No. 1 yel. Chicago bu.....	2.70½	2.93¾
Flaxseed, Minneapolis bu..........	3.05	3.17
Linseed Meal, Minneapolis ton......	61.50	59.50
Cottonseed Meal, Memphis ton......	69.50	61.00
FATS AND OILS		
Cottonseed Oil, crd. Miss. Vly. lb.....	.09¼	.12⅛
Corn Oil, crude Chicago lb..........	.10	.14¼
Peanut Oil, crd. Southeast lb........	.10½	.15
Coconut Oil, crd. Pac. Cst. lb........	.12½	.13¾
Copra, Pacific Coast ton...........	177.50	185.00
Lard, Chicago lb..................	.08⅝	.10⅞
Linseed Oil, raw NY lb.............	.1388	.1498
TEXTILES AND FIBERS		
Cotton, one in. mid Memphis lb......	.3300	.3025
Print Cloth, 80x80 39 in. NY yd.....	.19	.20¼
Burlap, 10 oz. 40 in. NY yd........	.1165	.1285
Wool, fine staple terr. Bstn. lb......	1.40	1.35
Rayon, satin acetate NY yd........	.26½	.28½
METALS		
Steel Scrap, 1 hvy. melt Pgh. ton...	25.00	40.00
Copper, Conn. Valley lb............	.31	.34
Lead, NY lb.......................	.12½	.16
Zinc, East St. Louis lb..............	.13	.14½
Tin, NY lb........................	1.28⅜	1.59½
Aluminum, ingot, NY lb............	.23	.24½
Quicksilver, NY 76 lb. flask........	220.00	490.00
Silver, NY oz.....................	1.293	1.293
MISCELLANEOUS		
Rubber, smoked sheets NY lb........	.24⅞	.27
Hides, light native cows Chgo. lb.....	.12½	.14
Gasoline, 91 Oct. Mid-cont. gal......	.11¼	.12
Fuel Oil, No. 2 Mid-cont. gal........	.09	.08¾

Source: *The Wall Street Journal*

out graphically in *The Economist* of London in August when it compared the percentage increases in the cost of living among various Western nations:

1952 to 1963		June, 1963, to June, 1964	
Spain	80	Finland	11.2
Finland	54	Britain	3.6
Britain	38	Spain	3.1
West Germany	20	West Germany	2.7
United States	16	Canada	1.9
Canada	14	United States	1.3

The predictions of U.S. inflation, made quite freely while the tax cut was under discussion, had not been borne out at year's end. A part of the answer lay in the fact that business, spurred by the act, had spent more than $44,000,000,000 on new plant and equipment, $5,000,000,000 more than in 1963. Such expenditures served to prevent inflation by increasing the productive capacity of the economy (supply) to meet the rising demand of consumers for goods and services. Expenditures for new plant were expected to climb in 1965, but not at the 12.5 per cent rate of increase attained in 1964. See INDUSTRY.

Consumer Optimism about the future rose higher than at any time since 1956, the Survey Research Center of the University of Michigan found. In September, its index of consumer sentiment reached 100.2 (autumn, 1956=100); it was 98.3 in January, 1963. Planned spending—especially among those with annual incomes of $7,500 and more—gave every indication of continuing to boost the economy well into 1965.

Retail sales during the rest of the year confirmed this optimism. Merchants, after adding up their Christmas business, reported a 6 per cent rise in volume for all of 1964. See RETAILING.

How Long the Boom? was the question being asked as 1964 ended. It was prompted by two developments late in the year:

First, the new automobile industry contracts called for annual wage and fringe benefit increases of approximately 4.9 per cent, well above the Johnson administration's guideline level of 3.2 per cent. There was fear this settlement might set a pattern that would place other less prosperous industries in a cost-price "squeeze" on profits. Another fear was of spreading inflation. Neither the "squeeze" nor the inflation materialized in 1964.

Second, an uncertainty over interest rates was touched off by the Bank of England's increase in its bank rate from 5 per cent to 7 per cent on November 23. In the United States, the Federal Reserve Board immediately raised the discount rate from $3\frac{1}{2}$ per cent to 4 per cent, and short-term rates firmed. By year's end, U.S. banks by and large had not increased their *prime* (basic business-loan) rates. If interest rate increases should spread in 1965, however, their impact on the economy would be twofold. It would become increasingly costly for (1) business firms to borrow funds for expansion and (2) consumers to get financing for major purchases.

Total consumer debt rose almost 10 per cent in the 12 months since September, 1963. Installment debt spurted 11 per cent to $57,446,000,000, of which over $24,000,000,000 went for automobiles. If there were to be any significant cutback in consumer willingness to assume debt, the rapid pace of economic expansion could scarcely be expected to continue into the new year.

Looking forward to 1965, President Lyndon B. Johnson had, however, already suggested a substantial reduction in excise taxes. If the economy were to show signs of slowing down, action by a new Congress—one more to his persuasion—might be expected to be fairly swift. In addition, the lawmakers and the nation had already seen the effectiveness of the income tax cut of 1964 in catapulting the economy to lofty new peaks.   WARREN W. SHEARER

For other related articles, see Section One, SYLVIA PORTER ON THE ECONOMY, and its Reading and Study Guide.

CABINET. Robert F. Kennedy resigned from his post as Attorney General in President Lyndon B. Johnson's Cabinet on September 3, after accepting a nomination to run for Senator from the state of New York. The vacancy was temporarily filled by the Acting Attorney General Nicholas deB. Katzenbach. In December, the President appointed John T. Connor to succeed Luther H. Hodges, who resigned, as Secretary of Commerce. See CONNOR, JOHN T.

Members of the 1964 Cabinet, in order of succession to the presidency, are: *Secretary of State*, Dean Rusk; *Secretary of the Treasury*, C. Douglas Dillon; *Secretary of Defense*, Robert S. McNamara; *Attorney General* (Acting), Nicholas deB. Katzenbach; *Postmaster General*, John A. Gronouski, Jr.; *Secretary of the Interior*, Stewart L. Udall; *Secretary of Agriculture*, Orville L. Freeman; *Secretary of Commerce*, Luther H. Hodges; *Secretary of Labor*, W. Willard Wirtz; and *Secretary of Health, Education, and Welfare*, Anthony J. Celebrezze.

CALDECOTT MEDAL. See LITERATURE FOR CHILDREN; SENDAK, MAURICE.

CAMBODIA. Prince Norodom Sihanouk and his tiny country were embroiled in a border dispute with South Vietnam. Their quarrel also involved the United States. The Vietnamese had become angered by repeated guerrilla thrusts from bases in Cambodia. They had tangible evidence, too, that arms flowing from Communist China into Cambodia were being used against them. On October 20, Vietnamese troops pursued the guerrillas across the ill-defined Cambodian border.

Cambodia protested the invasions to the United Nations Security Council. It also, in effect, broke diplomatic relations with Great Britain and the United States. On November 17, however, Prince Sihanouk agreed to a meeting between U.S. and Cambodian delegates to discuss means of ending the deterioration of relations between the two countries.

Population: 6,100,000. **Government:** Chief of State and Premier Prince Norodom Sihanouk. **Foreign Trade:** exports, $48,000,000; imports, $88,000,000. **Principal Exports:** maize, rice, rubber. JOHN N. STALKER

See also ASIA.

CAMEROON held national legislative elections based on universal suffrage for the first time in 1964. It was also the first such election held since East and West Cameroon became a federation in October, 1961. Both areas, however, had maintained their separate political parties.

Election returns gave 40 of the federal assembly's 50 seats to the Union Camerounaise, a part of East Cameroon. The remaining 10 seats were filled by the Kamerun National Democratic party of West Cameroon. Later, both parties signified their desire to eventually form a single national party.

Population: 4,800,000. **Government:** President Ahmadou Ahidjo; Premier Charles Assali. **Foreign Trade:** exports, $103,000,000; imports, $102,000,000. **Principal Exports:** bananas, cocoa, coffee, cotton, palm oil, timber.   BENJAMIN E. THOMAS

See also AFRICA.

CAMP FIRE GIRLS received a grant of $62,385 from the U.S. Department of Health, Education, and Welfare for a three-year research and demonstration project in the field of youth services. The grant will be used to extend the organization's Metropolitan Critical Areas Project, begun in 1963 in several West Coast communities to determine how youth agencies can reach more children in congested communities.

The research projects will be carried on by teams made up of a social group worker, a social scientist, and a skilled trainer. They will be conducted in Boston, Detroit, and Washington, D.C. Additional special studies will be made in Bakersfield, Calif.; Baltimore; Chicago; Dallas; Eugene, Ore.; Indianapolis and South Bend, Ind.; Minneapolis, Minn.; and Syracuse, N.Y. The studies are expected to indicate the type of programs needed to further the social development of girls in low-income areas, and determine the best use of adult volunteers for enriching these programs.   JOSEPH P. ANDERSON

CANADA

ON THE VERGE of celebrating its first 100 years of union, Canada faced the sore problem of maintaining that unity in 1964. The quickening pace of Quebec's "quiet revolution" introduced new strains into the Canadian community. It was a culmination of years of French-Canadian nationalism. Under Premier Jean Lesage, Quebec was undergoing a sweeping transformation in all walks of life: in education, toward state control and a broader curriculum; in economic affairs, toward more industrialization. Everywhere in Quebec efforts were being made to strengthen the participation of French Canadians in the management of the province's economy. This goal was expressed in the phrase: *maîtres chez nous* (masters in our own house).

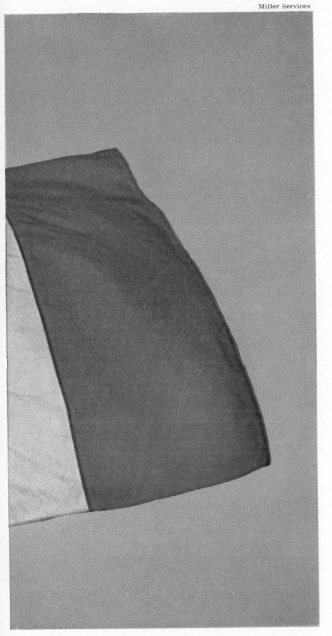

Inevitably, the Lesage program required a readjustment of Quebec's fiscal and constitutional relationship with the federal government in Ottawa. The Compact of Canadian Confederation under the British North America Act of 1867 guaranteed the French-Canadian culture equal status with the British. The people of Quebec were demanding that the rest of Canada respect that charter provision.

Outside Quebec, in matters of language, education, and economic opportunity, French Canadians often felt themselves to be "second-class citizens." As a group, they were determined that this discrimination must cease. The more extreme French-Canadian nationalists advocated Quebec's secession. A handful sought this goal through terrorism. Thus, with Quebec in a ferment, Canada moved toward the centenary of Confederation in 1967, realizing that the very basis of its existence as a transcontinental nation was being questioned as never before. But Canadians found comfort in the words of Prime Minister Lester B. Pearson:

"I have no doubt about our ability to meet the test. Confederation has been tested before; it will survive to be tested many times again."

Federal-Provincial Relations. Pearson's minority Liberal government, elected in April, 1963, tried to satisfy Quebec's claims and at the same time uphold broad national purposes. It turned to "cooperative federalism," a system of joint federal-provincial arrangements in areas of common concern. A national contributory pension plan was projected under this heading. In other fields, where the provinces were allowed to carry out independent policies, Ottawa agreed to turn over to the provinces a share of federal tax revenues equal to the amount they would have received had they participated in a joint plan.

Three important federal-provincial conferences were held between November, 1963, and November, 1964. At the first meeting, in Ottawa in November, 1963, the federal government turned over an additional $87,000,000 to the provinces in the form of transfer payments. The complicated formula deter-

NEW NATIONAL FLAG, with a few minor changes in the maple leaf design, was flying over Canada's public buildings in 1965.

mining equalization payments to assist the poorer provinces was revised at this conference.

The second meeting was held in Quebec City in early April. The provinces accepted Prime Minister Pearson's proposal for a "review in depth" of the federal and provincial tax structures. The federal government in September extended family allowance payments to children aged 16 and 17 who were attending high school or university. An interest-free loan plan to university students also went into effect for the new university year that began in September. Quebec considered that this plan trespassed upon the provincial responsibility for education.

The Third Meeting—of attorneys general in Ottawa in October—settled the controversial question of how to amend Canada's written constitution, embodied in the North America Act. This act, a statute of the British Parliament, could be amended only by that legislature on request from Canada.

Under the plan, the Canadian Parliament took over complete amending power. The plan required the unanimous concurrence of all 10 provinces to amend sections dealing with education and the basic rights of language and the role of the Crown in Canadian government. On most other matters, amendment was to be made by the Parliament of Canada, supported by the legislatures of at least two-thirds of the provinces, provided they represented a minimum of 50 per cent of Canada's population. It was also decided that the federal government and the provinces could delegate certain powers to each other.

Federal Politics. A closely divided House of Commons meant that 1964 was a year of bitter political rivalry in Ottawa. The Liberal party continued to hold 129 seats, retaining in by-elections four seats that had fallen vacant since the 1963 election. The Conservatives attracted two Quebec members from the Social Credit party in April, but lost an Ontario seat in a by-election in November, leaving them with 96 seats. The Social Credit movement formally divided into a Quebec wing under Réal Caouette (Ralliement des Créditistes) with 13 seats and a group from western Canada under the former national leader, Robert N. Thompson, with nine seats. The New Democratic party (socialist) under former Saskatchewan Premier T. C. Douglas, which took the Ontario seat from the Conservatives in November, increased its standing to 18 seats.

Cabinet Changes. The Liberal administration lost a veteran member early in 1964 when Minister of Justice Lionel Chevrier resigned to become High Commissioner for Canada in London, the first French-speaking person to fill that post. He was succeeded by Guy Favreau, a lawyer and former civil servant. John W. Pickersgill took over as Minister of Transport.

The Flag Dispute. Prime Minister Pearson, seeking to strengthen national unity by the adoption of a distinctive Canadian flag, proposed a new design in April. For years, the British red ensign with the shield

from the Canadian coat of arms on the field had been flown unofficially. Pearson recommended a new flag: three red maple leaves on a white background between two vertical blue borders.

The Conservatives demanded a national plebiscite on the issue, which went to Parliament. For 22 summer days the Commons was embroiled in an exhausting flag debate, which was ended only by referring the choice of a design to an all-party committee. In late October, the committee, by a 10-to-4 majority, recommended a single red maple leaf on a white field, with a vertical red bar on each side. Parliament, after 33 days of more debate, invoked cloture for the first time in eight years and approved the design on December 15. Senate approval followed shortly. Only royal assent was required to make the new design the official flag of Canada. And as the year opened, royal approval was announced in London and Ottawa.

New Legislation. Pearson's ambitious program of legislation made slow headway because of the difficulties over the flag. Old age pensions were increased, and a new federal labor code, providing a minimum wage of $1.25 an hour and a 40-hour week, was proposed. A 12-mile protected fishing zone off the coasts of Canada was proclaimed, and changes were made in financial aid to farmers. In November, Parliament established four-member commissions in each province to define federal electoral districts after each decennial census. The important Canada Pension Plan had not come to a vote when Parliament ended its longest session in history—214 days—on December 18.

Royal Visit. Queen Elizabeth II and Prince Philip paid an eight-day visit to Canada early in October to join in ceremonies marking the centenary of the first Confederation conferences. In Charlottetown, Prince Edward Island, the Queen opened a new memorial auditorium and library. In Quebec City, after a two-day sail on the royal yacht *Britannia*, the Queen encountered mild demonstrations by hostile separatists. No incidents occurred, however, and the Queen ended her short Canadian tour with two days in Ottawa, where she received an enthusiastic welcome.

Canadian-U.S. Relations attracted less notice on the Dominion's political scene than in 1963. There was quiet achievement in reaching final agreement on the Columbia River power project, which will double the water-storage capacity of the Northwest. British Columbia agreed to build three dams on the Columbia and its tributary, the Kootenay. The United States agreed to build the Libby Dam in Montana and to pay British Columbia $274,000,000 for the downstream power benefits that the United States would realize from the new dams over a 30-year period. Also, it would pay British Columbia another $69,600,000 later for flood control benefits.

During the summer the Canadian Parliament approved the revised treaty, which came into force on

WITH BACKS TURNED ON QUEEN, *youthful separatists show their resentment of Queen Elizabeth's visit to Canada as she rides past on Quebec City street.*

September 16. A check for $253,929,534 (U.S.) from a group of U.S. utilities was turned over to Canada. Work began immediately on one of the largest and most significant projects in the history of Canadian-U.S. cooperation. See WATER AND FLOOD CONTROL.

Peace on the Lakes. The industrial dispute among seamen on the Great Lakes only simmered during 1964. The Canadian government continued its trusteeship over five maritime unions, designed to eliminate the corruption and lawlessness that had characterized union activity on the lakes.

The president of the Seafarers' International Union of Canada (SIU), Hal Banks, was found guilty of conspiring to assault a rival union official and sentenced to five years in prison. Released on $25,000 bail, he fled to the United States. Early in the year, Banks had been removed from his post as president of the SIU by the government trustees. Later, he lost his position as one of the vice-presidents of the international union.

Foreign Affairs. Canada took up another peacekeeping responsibility in 1964—Cyprus. At the request of the United Nations (UN), Canada supplied 1,150 men of the famed French-Canadian regiment —the Royal 22nd, or *Van Doos* (Vingt-deuxième). See CYPRUS.

Stand-By Force for UN. The government called a 23-nation conference in November to consider how a stand-by international force could be maintained for UN assignments. Prime Minister Pearson had inspired the emergency force used after the Suez dispute in 1956. See UNITED NATIONS.

Foreign Visits. The Prime Minister visited France early in 1964 to discuss a wide range of economic and cultural topics. Dr. Ludwig Erhard, the German federal chancellor, visited Canada in June; and Sir Alec Douglas-Home, British Prime Minister, arrived for a short visit in February.

Canada raised her grant to the Colombo Plan for Southeast Asia development and set aside $50,000,-000 for low-interest loans to Latin America.

Defense. Early in 1964, Prime Minister Pearson reviewed Canada's North Atlantic Treaty Organization (NATO) obligations. He disclosed that a Canadian air base in France would have to be abandoned because of France's refusal to allow the storage of nuclear arms on its soil.

In February, the United States and Canada agreed on a plan for the custody and control of nuclear weapons used by the Royal Canadian Air Force (RCAF) squadrons in Europe.

Military Unification. Minister of National Defense Paul Hellyer gained approval for a plan to integrate the command of the army, navy, and air force. The old advisory Chiefs of Staff Committee was discontinued, and a new post, the Chief of Defense Staff, was established. Air Chief Marshal Frank R. Miller was appointed, and became the first service chief of the combined forces in Canada's history.

Hellyer also mounted an economy drive. He ordered the laying-up of 14 destroyers and minesweepers and eliminating over 23,000 men from the militia and reserves. Many small militia units would disappear.

The Budget, 1964. Minister of Finance Walter L. Gordon announced his second federal budget on March 16. Expenditures were estimated at $7,125,-000,000, with revenues at $6,705,000,000. Defense costs were lower, but health and welfare charges continued to grow. In August, Gordon reported the final deficit for the fiscal year, as $619,197,480 and revised his estimate of the 1964-1965 deficit upward, from $440,000,000 to $455,000,000.

The Minister of Finance continued to study methods to encourage a larger Canadian control of business and industry. In September, he introduced a bill limiting the participation of non-Canadians in Canadian banks, and life insurance, trust, and loan companies. The measure also made it easier for insurance companies to invest in common stocks of Canadian corporations, which had depended mainly on the New York market for new financing.

The Domestic Economy maintained the growth it had shown since 1961. The Gross National Product (GNP) for 1964 was estimated at $46,000,000,000, an increase of about 7 per cent over the 1963 level. By the end of September, the value of production had exceeded the March estimates. Slightly higher prices accounted for some of the rise in value.

The labor force grew by about 3 per cent in 1964 and the rate of unemployment (seasonally adjusted) remained at 5 per cent, the lowest annual rate since 1957. Exports were extremely strong in 1964, reflecting heavy sales abroad for such typical Canadian commodities as chemicals, lumber, newsprint, nickel, paper, petroleum, and wheat. The value of exports in the first eight months racked up a 23 per cent gain over the same 1963 period. Total exports of goods and services were running at an annual rate of $10,500,000,000 for 1964.

Capital spending—for homes, plants, machinery, and equipment—climbed smartly in 1964, for an estimated 19 per cent increase for the year as a whole. The government's encouragement to residential building during the winter months helped to "even out" the pace of construction over the year.

St. Lawrence Seaway traffic continued to grow in 1964, reaching a volume of about 38,500,000 tons, an increase of 8,500,000 tons over the traffic flow in 1963. Canadian flag vessels accounted for nearly one-half of the 1,561 ships that had entered the Seaway in the year up to August 31. See WATERWAYS.

Legislation to divide the Northwest Territories into two districts was held over by Parliament to allow for further study of the rapidly changing situation in Canada's North.

The Provinces

Alberta helped Canada's oil industry celebrate its golden anniversary in 1964 with the discovery of a vast reserve of heavy viscous crude oil 120 miles northwest of Edmonton. Larger than all the light oil reserves now known in Alberta, the deposit was distinct from the famous Athabasca tar sands, still largely unexploited.

British Columbia. The provincial government planned to establish a commercial bank, the Bank of British Columbia, under a federal charter. Premier William A. C. Bennett early in the year said the province expected to put up some of the capital required. There was talk of using some of the $274,-000,000 advance Columbia River power payment from the United States for the bank. Bennett arranged to lend $100,000,000 of that payment to the province of Quebec. In December, the Senate killed the bill to incorporate the bank.

Manitoba's five-year-old Crop Insurance Fund wound up the year with an estimated surplus of $57,000. It had been $856,261 in the red at the start of 1964. The fund insured 1,000,000 acres for a cov-

Premiers of Canadian Provinces

Province	Premier	Political Party
Alberta	Ernest C. Manning	Social Credit
British Columbia	William A. C. Bennett	Social Credit
Manitoba	Dufferin Roblin	Conservative
New Brunswick	Louis J. Robichaud	Liberal
Newfoundland	Joseph R. Smallwood	Liberal
Nova Scotia	Robert L. Stanfield	Conservative
Ontario	John P. Robarts	Conservative
Prince Edward Is.	Walter R. Shaw	Conservative
Quebec	Jean Lesage	Liberal
Saskatchewan	Ross Thatcher	Liberal

erage of $14,657,000 in 1964. What was thought to be Canada's first collectively owned cooperative housing project was launched in September. The $2,500,000 project will house 200 Winnipeg families in the $3,200-to-$6,000 income bracket.

New Brunswick. Premier Louis J. Robichaud suggested that Canada's four Atlantic provinces consider uniting into a single province. Its total population would amount to almost 2,000,000. While the premiers of Newfoundland and Prince Edward Island were cool to the idea, Premier Robert L. Stanfield of Nova Scotia offered to cooperate with New Brunswick in a joint legislative study of the proposal.

Lord Beaverbrook, the English press lord who grew up in New Brunswick, left $12,600,000 to the Beaverbrook Canadian Foundation for educational and charitable work in his native province.

Newfoundland. The prospect of using power from Grand Falls on Labrador's Hamilton River to run the subways of New York moved closer to reality in 1964. Earlier, Quebec had raised some legal hurdles against the plan to run lines across that province. An engineering report found that it would be feasible to transmit the power by undersea cable. Thus, the power could by-pass Quebec by using a coastal route through the Maritime Provinces and New England.

Nova Scotia. Halifax studied a bold new redevelopment plan in midsummer. The $35,000,000, 19-acre Cornwallis Center will include three 22-story apartment towers, a 450-room hotel, and a shopping and recreation complex. The province's new Lord's Day Act went into effect on June 1, permitting some businesses to open on Sundays.

Ontario. A record Ontario budget was introduced in February. Revenues were expected to total $1,200,000,000 for the fiscal year ending March 31, 1965. Education costs amounted to 35 per cent of the province's planned expenditure total of $1,300,-000,000. A new Department of University Affairs was set up to spend more than $100,000,000 granted to the universities of the province in 1964-1965.

One of the most spectacular mineral discoveries in Canadian history occurred in the Timmins area in the spring when the Texas Gulf Sulphur Company announced the finding of a deposit of 25,000,000 tons of copper, zinc, and silver ore. In June, it revised the estimated size of the ore body to 55,000,000 tons (see MINES AND MINING). A flurry of prospecting activity was set off and there were days of wild speculation on the Toronto Stock Exchange.

Prince Edward Island celebrated the centenary of the first Confederation conference, held at Charlottetown, by completion of the Fathers of Confederation Memorial Building. The handsome structure, located on a square in the heart of Charlottetown, contains an auditorium and concert hall, together with a library and art gallery. Before its formal opening by Queen Elizabeth II in October, it had been used for meetings by a number of national organizations.

Quebec. A bill to create the first department of education in Quebec's history passed the legislature early in 1964. In the place of a council of education relying on religious committees, the bill provided for a more centralized organization under state direction. Paul Gérin-Lajoie, a young member of the cabinet of Premier Jean Lesage, became the province's first Minister of Education.

Terrorist organizations, representing a tiny minority group among Quebec separatists, were active during the early part of 1964. Several raids against federal military depots netted some small arms.

Work proceeded on preparing the St. Lawrence River site for the Montreal World's Fair, Expo '67. Capital and operating costs for the fair were estimated at $167,000,000. A new 620-room hotel was planned for Montreal in time for the opening of the fair in April, 1967.

Saskatchewan. The only socialist government in Canada tumbled from power after 20 years in office in Saskatchewan in April. Under a 47-year-old businessman, Ross Thatcher, the Liberals won 33 seats in the legislature and the New Democratic party (socialist), 25. The popular vote for each party was almost the same. A single Conservative was also elected, the first in 34 years. Premier Thatcher assembled a young cabinet and began preparations, in his words: "to take the government out of business and put more business in government."

Population: 19,445,000. **Government:** Prime Minister Lester B. Pearson. **Foreign Trade:** exports, (C) $10,564,000,000; imports, (C) $10,912,000,000. **Principal Exports:** nonferrous metals, paper and pulp, wheat.   DAVID M. L. FARR

CANADIAN LIBRARY ASSOCIATION (CLA) held its 19th annual conference in Halifax, Nova Scotia, in June. The conference's principal topic was "Libraries and Canadian Dualism."

The Book of the Year for Children medals were presented to Roderick Haig-Brown for *The Whale People*, and to Cécile Chabot for *Férie*. The titles were selected by the Canadian Association of Children's Librarians as outstanding works in the English and French languages.

The Canadian Library Trustees' Association presented its Merit Award to two trustees for outstanding contributions to the progress of libraries in Canada. They were Theresa Falkner of the Toronto Public Library and Maxwell R. Van Loon of the Ottawa Public Library.

The association also forwarded a brief to the Royal Commission on Bilingualism and Biculturalism. It urged the establishment of intercultural programs in Canadian libraries to better acquaint the nation with its two predominant cultures, French and English, as well as with the other cultures of Canada.

Young Canada's Book Week was celebrated November 15 to 22 under the patronage of Dr. John B. Macdonald, president of the University of British Columbia. Canadian Library Week was celebrated April 4 to 11 under the patronage of Prime Minister Lester B. Pearson. He said: "In sharing and fostering the love of books, our librarians, like many Canadians, surely feel that this love springs from somewhere close to the soul of freedom." ELIZABETH H. MORTON

CANADIAN LITERATURE. History books were prominent among the distinguished volumes published in Canada in 1964. *The Road to Confederation*, the story of Canada's emerging nationhood, was written in a splendid prose style by Donald Creighton. *Mr. Prime Minister, 1867-1964*, by Bruce Hutchison, was a dramatic study of 14 prime ministers. Two outstanding volumes in the Canadian Centenary series appeared. They were *Canada Under Louis XIV, 1663-1701*, by W. J. Eccles; and *The Critical Years, the Union of British North America, 1857-1873*, by W. L. Morton.

In Fiction, two titles were of paramount interest: *The Deserter*, by Douglas LePan; and *The Stone Angel*, by Margaret Laurence.

In Poetry, *Within the Zodiac*, by Phyllis Gottlieb, introduced the work of a new poet. *The Laughing Rooster*, by Irving Layton, and *Near False Creek Mouth*, by Earle Birney, continued the reputations of the two established poets.

The Governor-General's Literary Awards for 1964 went to: J. M. S. Careless for *Brown of the Globe* (English nonfiction); Hugh Garner for *Hugh Garner's Best Stories* (English fiction); Gustave Lanctot, *Histoire du Canada* (French nonfiction); and Gatien LaPointe, *Ode au Saint-Laurent* (French poetry). No awards were made for poetry in English or for fiction in French.   ELIZABETH H. MORTON

CARLSON, PAUL EARLE (1928-1964), a quiet, self-effacing medical missionary of the Evangelical Covenant Church of America, was murdered in Stanleyville, Congo, on November 24 by Congolese rebels. Dr. Carlson had been held by them on charges of spying. See CONGO (LÉOPOLDVILLE); BELGIUM.

Carlson was the son of a Swedish-immigrant machinist. Born in Culver City, Calif., he was reared in a deeply religious atmosphere. On his 18th birthday he enlisted as a seaman in the U.S. Navy. After a two-year hitch, he enrolled under the GI Bill as a student at North Park College in Chicago where he met Lois Lindblom, whom he later married.

A six-month visit to Congo in 1961 ultimately changed, and ended, his life. Deeply moved by the suffering he had seen there, Carlson gave up a growing private practice in Torrance, Calif., late in 1963 to serve on a tiny salary in Wasalo, a remote part of Congo. There, he worked an 18-hour day, the only doctor available to a population estimated at 100,000. Foreseeing the rebel uprising that was coming, Dr. Carlson took his wife and their children, Wayne, 9, and Lynnette, 7, to safety in Bangui, Central African Republic. He returned to care for his patients, staying at his post until his capture by rebels in mid-September. WALTER F. MORSE

CARNEGIE MEDAL. See BURTON, HESTER; LITERATURE FOR CHILDREN (Awards).

CASTELO BRANCO, HUMBERTO DE ALENCAR (1900-   ), a retired army general, was sworn in as president of Brazil on April 15. He was elected by congress to complete the remaining portion of ousted President João Goulart's term. On July 22, congress extended Castelo Branco's term until March 15, 1967. See BRAZIL.

The new president was born in the state of Ceará, in northeastern Brazil. He entered military service in his early manhood. A graduate of the United States Army Command and General Staff School at Fort Leavenworth, Kans., he served during World War II with Brazilian forces in Italy.

Because he is a widower, his daughter, Mrs. Dona Antonieta Castelo Branco Dinis, serves as his official hostess. His son Paulo is a Brazilian navy commander. WALTER F. MORSE

CATHOLIC. See ROMAN CATHOLIC.

CELEBRATIONS and anniversaries observed in 1964 included the following:

Year-Long Celebrations

British Royal Marines Tercentenary. England's first unit of soldiers for service at sea was organized in 1664 by the Lord High Admiral, the Duke of York (later James II).

City of New York Tercentenary is to continue through 1965, commemorating 1664, the year the British took New Amsterdam from the Dutch and renamed it New York for the Duke of York.

Civil War Centennial. See CIVIL WAR CENTENNIAL.

Columbia University School of Engineering and Applied Science Centennial began on March 7, and continues into June, 1965. The first school of its kind in the Western Hemisphere opened on Nov. 15, 1864.

Galileo Galilei Quadricentennial. The famous Italian, commemorated as the father of modern experimental science, was born in Pisa on Feb. 15, 1564. His greatest contributions were, perhaps, in the fields of astronomy and physics. Galileo died at Arcetri, near Florence, Italy, on Jan 2, 1642. See ASTRONOMY.

Merton College Septcentenary. One of Oxford University's oldest colleges was founded in 1264 by Walter de Merton, chancellor of England's Henry III.

Michelangelo Quadricentenary commemorated the death of the famous Italian Renaissance artist on Feb. 18, 1564. He was born Michelangelo Buonarroti in Caprese, Tuscany, in 1475. See FAIRS AND EXHIBITIONS (color pictures).

Montana Territorial Centennial commemorated the establishment of Montana Territory in 1864, the year that gold was discovered in the Last Chance Gulch. Seventy-five years ago, on Nov. 8, 1889, the territory was admitted to the Union as its 41st state.

Nevada Centennial Year commemorated the admission to the Union of Nevada Territory as the 36th state on Oct. 31, 1864.

New Jersey Tercentenary commemorated 1664, the year England took over Dutch domains in North America. Charles II gave them to his brother, the Duke of York. John Lord Berkeley and Sir George Carteret were made coproprietors of all the land between the Delaware and Hudson Rivers, which was named New Jersey for England's Jersey Island, birthplace of Carteret.

Richard Strauss Centennial was a major theme of music festivals in 1964. The composer won world fame for such operas as Der Rosenkavalier (see MUSIC). Strauss was born in Munich June 11, 1864.

Saint Louis Bicentennial. See SAINT LOUIS, Mo.

Shakespeare Quadricentennial. See LITERATURE; THEATER.

War of 1812 Sesquicentennial. The Treaty of Ghent, negotiated in Ghent, Belgium, and signed on Dec. 24, 1814, ended the futile three-year conflict between the United States and Great Britain. Americans remember Aug. 24, 1814, the day the British occupied Washington, D.C., and burned the White House, the Capitol, and other government buildings. The British bombardment of Fort McHenry (in Baltimore harbor), September 13-14, inspired Francis Scott Key to write "The Star-Spangled Banner."

World War I 50th Anniversary. The assassination of Archduke Francis Ferdinand, crown prince of Austria-Hungary, on June 28, 1914, was the start of World War I. Gavrilo Princip shot the Archduke and his wife, who were visiting in Sarajevo, Bosnia (then a province of Austria-Hungary).

World War II 25th Anniversary. On Sept. 1, 1939, Germany invaded Poland. Great Britain and France declared war on Germany on September 3, and, on September 17, Russia marched into Poland from the east. On November 30, Russia invaded Finland.

Shorter Celebrations

Feb. 13—ASCAP Golden Anniversary. The American Society of Composers, Authors and Publishers, a performing arts organization, was founded on Feb. 13, 1914. Victor Herbert, "the prince of operetta," was one of its nine founding members.

Feb. 28-June 8—Swarthmore College Centennial. The coeducational, nonsectarian institution near Philadelphia, Pa., was founded by the Society of Friends (Quakers) in 1864. Swarthmore was named for Swarthmoor Hall, the home in Lancashire, England, of the Quakers' founder George Fox.

May 24-31—Anzio 20th Anniversary official observance commemorated the World War II battle in Italy (Jan. 22-May 25, 1944). The American-British victory over entrenched German forces was followed by the fall of Cassino (May 27) and the advance on Rome, the first Axis capital to capitulate (June 4).

May 31—Notre Dame de Paris Octocentenary was celebrated a year late, because of the death in 1963 of Pope John XXIII. Construction of the famous French cathedral began in 1163, and partly completed by 1245. There, Henry VI of England was crowned King of France in 1431. In 1804, Napoleon I was crowned Emperor of France.

June 6—D-Day 20th Anniversary commemorated the World War II invasion of the Normandy coast of France. On June 6, 1944, troops from England swarmed across the English Channel, secured five beachheads, and began the advance toward Germany.

June 19-21—New Harmony Sesquicentennial. This Indiana farm town in Posey County was founded in 1814 as the Village of Harmonie by George Rapp, leader of a religious group called Rappites. His experiment in harmonious communal living ended in 1825. Robert Owen, a Welsh-born industrialist from Scotland, bought Harmonie and renamed it New Harmony.

July 2—Northern Pacific Railroad Centennial. On July 2, 1864, President Lincoln signed a land-grant bill for the building of a railroad between the Lake Superior region and Puget Sound, Washington Territory. After many setbacks, the Northern Pacific held its "Last Spike" ceremony at Gold Creek, Montana Territory, on Sept. 8, 1883.

July 26-Aug. 1—Lincoln Park Centennial Week. Chicago's north side park was founded in 1864 as Lake Park. On June 5, 1865, it was renamed in memory of martyred President Lincoln.

Aug. 15—Allied Landings in Southern France began on Aug. 15, 1944, by American and French troops on the Mediterranean Coast between Toulon and Nice. A cemetery and chapel at Draguignan commemorates 1,154 Americans killed in the campaign.

Aug. 22—International Red Cross Centennial commemorated the signing in Geneva, Switzerland, by 12 European countries of the first international Red Cross Convention on the "amelioration of the conditions of the wounded and sick in the armed forces in the field."

Oct. 20—U.S. Invasion of the Philippines began 20 years ago, with an amphibious assault on the central island of Leyte. Later, General MacArthur waded ashore proclaiming, "People of the Philippines, I have returned," fulfilling his promise made to them in March, 1942. See DEATHS OF NOTABLE PERSONS (Close-Up).

Oct. 29-30—The Hartford Courant Bicentennial. The oldest newspaper in continuous publication in the United States dates back to 1764, when it first appeared as The Connecticut Courant.

Nov. 8—President Abraham Lincoln Re-Election Centennial. One hundred years ago on this day, President Lincoln won election for a second term. He defeated his Democratic opponent, Union Army General George B. McClellan, by an electoral vote of 212 to 21, and a popular majority of some 400,000 votes.

Dec. 6—Lutherans of New York Tercentenary was commemorated at St. Matthew Lutheran Church. In 1664, the first British governor of New York, Richard Nicolls, granted the city's Lutherans a charter of permission to "freely and publicly Exercise Divine worship according to their Consciences." Martin Luther's followers had to worship in secret when the Dutch ruled Nieuw Amsterdam, renamed New York by the British in 1664.

CENSORSHIP. See CIVIL LIBERTIES.

CENSUS. U.S. population growth in 1964 dropped to its slowest pace for any year since 1946-1947, when the postwar bumper baby crop put the rate near 2 per cent. On July 1, 1964, the estimated population of 192,072,000, including members of the armed forces overseas, had increased 1.4 per cent in 12 months. For calendar 1964, the indicated growth rate was also about 1.4 per cent—from 190,809,000 on Jan. 1, 1964, to about 193,500,000 on Jan. 1, 1965.

Taking a close look at its figures, the Bureau of the Census projected a total U.S. population well in excess of 200,000,000 by 1969. In its midyear review, it also found:

• The nonwhite population had increased by 10.3 per cent since the 1960 census, compared with the white population increase of 6.2 per cent.

• Nonwhites comprised 11.8 per cent of the total population, up from 11.4 per cent in 1960.

• There were about 97 men for every 100 women in 1964, against a ratio of nearly 98 to 100 in 1960.

• Children under 5 years of age numbered 20,658,000 in 1964—fewer than in any year since 1961, when there were 20,660,000. At the other end of the age scale, persons 65 and older had increased by 1,301,000 since 1960, and now numbered 17,861,000.

• California officially became first in population, a rank held by New York since 1810. California residents were estimated at 18,084,000 as of July 1, 1964, compared with 17,915,000 in New York.

• Nevada was far outrunning all other states in rate of growth, with a 1960-1964 gain of 43.1 per cent. Its nearest rival was Arizona, with a rate of 21.4 per cent.

Special Censuses taken since the nationwide count on April 1, 1960, totaled more than 300 by June 30, 1964. They were conducted in places ranging in size from the entire Louisville (Ky.) metropolitan area, to newly incorporated Perrytown, Ark., with a June 4, 1964, population of 71.

Usually, special censuses are requested and paid for by local governments, but not the Louisville count. Census Bureau officials chose Louisville to test new techniques—particularly a do-it-yourself census by mail—under consideration for the nationwide count in 1970. In two weeks, 88 per cent of the 220,000 forms mailed to the residents of Jefferson County, Kentucky, and Floyd and Clark counties in Indiana had been filled out and returned. Census takers then visited or telephoned those who had failed to respond or who had omitted some answers.

Other Censuses—of business, manufactures, mineral industries, commercial fisheries, and transportation—were conducted during the year, largely by mail. They covered 1963 activities. A census of agriculture followed the 1964 harvest season, with census takers visiting every farm; first reports were due in 1965.   RICHARD M. SCAMMON

See also POPULATION, WORLD; VITAL STATISTICS.

CENTRAL AMERICA. See LATIN AMERICA; and the articles on the individual countries.

CEYLON was beset by mounting economic distress. Throughout the year, the government was confronted with a series of crippling strikes. The government nevertheless pushed ahead with its nationalization program.

In May, Mrs. Sirimavo Bandaranaike formed a coalition government with the Trotskyites who demanded and got a program that included curbing the press, and tightening controls on trade. In December, the program was defeated 74-73 in parliament. Parliament was dissolved and new elections were scheduled for March, 1965.

Population: 10,950,000. **Government:** Governor-General William Gopallawa; Prime Minister Sirimavo Bandaranaike. **Foreign Trade:** exports, $411,000,000; imports, $412,000,000. **Principal Exports:** coconut oil, rubber, tea.   JOHN N. STALKER

See also ASIA.

CHAD bickered with France, its former ruler, in 1964. The national assembly passed a resolution calling for the withdrawal of all French troops, the evacuation of the French base at Fort-Lamy, and the Africanization of the civil service. A few French citizens, mostly businessmen, were expelled. President François Tombalbaye, recognizing the continuing need for French protection, signed an agreement, however, permitting Chaadiens to receive technical training in France.

The assembly changed Chad's political structure during the year. It gave the political bureau of the Partie Progressiste Chaadien the responsibility of directing all government activity and of choosing all candidates for elective offices.

Population: 2,800,000. **Government:** President François Tombalbaye. **Foreign Trade:** exports, $17,000,000; imports, $29,000,000. **Principal Exports:** cotton, hides, meat, skins.   WILLIAM SPENCER

See also AFRICA.

CHEMICAL INDUSTRY prices firmed as sales climbed throughout 1964 in the constantly and swiftly increasing market for chemicals of all kinds. The industry had shaken itself out of the overcapacity and sagging-price doldrums, which got a mild start at the end of 1960 and bottomed out in mid-1963.

Sales reached about $39,000,000,000 in 1964, 10 per cent higher than the $35,500,000,000 of 1963. With a firmer price structure, profits were expected to climb to $3,000,000,000.

Sulfur, the basic raw material for the most widely used of all chemicals, *sulfuric acid*, was in heavy demand. In April, Texas Gulf Sulphur Company hiked the price of sulfur $2 a ton. Other producers did likewise.

High-density polyethylene, polypropylene, and the acrylates—which the consumer buys as rigid, transparent, or translucent articles—failed to share the general price-firming.   ROBERT E. BEDINGFIELD

See also CHEMISTRY; PLASTICS; POLLUTION.

CHEMISTRY. A new element was added to the periodic chart with the announcement of the production of element 104 by Soviet scientists. The chemical element, as yet unnamed, was produced by the bombardment of plutonium atoms with high velocity neon ions in the accelerator at Dubna, Soviet Union. The nuclei of the atoms combined to form one large nucleus. But all such heavy nuclei are inherently unstable and must emit radiation until they attain a more stable arrangement. The half-life of element 104 was reported to be only about three-tenths of a second.

Space Saliva Test. An unusual application of chemistry to a major problem in long, manned space flights became a possibility when it was found that chemical analysis of saliva accurately reflects the state of body chemistry. The finding, by scientists at Beckman Instruments in Scotland, was considered important because a continuous check of many physiological variables is essential during long flights in outer space. The technique, involving the collection of saliva and its subsequent chemical analysis, is said to have advantages over the use of urine or blood samples.

Food from Microbes. The chemistry of fermentation received heightened attention. In 1964, experiments produced protein-rich products through the fermentation of petroleum. In Europe, the British Petroleum Company is operating a plant producing 50 tons of dry cellular material a day. Such material has high nutritional value as livestock feed. In Japan, however, research emphasis included fermentation processes aimed at the production of materials suitable for human consumption. In the future, such densely populated regions as Japan may be dependent on fermentation to produce a large percentage of their food needs. In addition to food, the wide variety of fermentation reactions available today make possible the production of a vast number of substances, such as amino acids, antibiotics, enzymes, and vitamins. Several million pounds are produced commercially each year, all by fermentation.

Seawater Studies. Research during 1964 aimed at perfection of various methods of producing fresh water from the sea. One process, announced by the Aerojet-General Corporation in California, utilizes a "reverse osmosis" process. In ordinary osmosis, pure water separated from a salt solution by a film or membrane will pass through the membrane into the solution because it has a higher osmotic pressure. In reverse osmosis, pressure is exerted on the solution side, and this pressure exceeds the osmotic pressure of the water. Water then passes from the salt solution through the membrane to increase the quantity of pure water. A more concentrated salt solution results on the other side of the membrane. Such a process requires much less expenditure of energy than the methods that utilize freezing or distillation.   ROBERT A. UPHAUS

See also BIOCHEMISTRY.

CHESS. For the first time in 16 years, the United States failed to qualify a player for the world title competition. The process of selecting a challenger for the world champion, Tigran Petrosian of Russia, included, as a first step, the Interzonal Chess Tournament at Amsterdam in May and June. The qualifiers from this tournament were Bent Larsen of Denmark; Vassilly Smyslov, Boris Spassky, and Mikhail Tal, all of Russia; Boris Ivkov of Yugoslavia; and Lajos Portisch of Hungary. Portisch had earlier defeated Samuel Reshevsky of the United States in a play-off match.

The qualifiers, along with two seeded players, Mikhail Botvinnik and Paul Keres, both of Russia, were to compete in the Candidates chess tournament at a date and site yet to be selected. The winner will then challenge Petrosian. Bobby Fischer, the U.S. champion, refused to play in the Interzonal because the rules changes he had demanded did not go far enough to satisfy him.

Fischer, however, played spectacularly in winning the U.S. chess championship at New York City in January. In taking his sixth U.S. title, Fischer scored a clean sweep by winning all 11 of his games. Larry Evans of New York City was runner-up, and Sonja Graf of Los Angeles won the Women's title. Pal Benko of New York City won the U.S. Open chess championship at Boston in August. Sharing the Women's Open title were Mrs. Catherine Slater of New York City and Cecilia Rock of Boston. Russia won the World Students' championship at Kraków, Poland, in August.   THEODORE M. O'LEARY

CHICAGO began operation of the world's largest water filtration plant in October, 1964. Filtered water was thus available for the first time to some 2,800,000 residents north of 39th Street and in the suburbs. Previously, these Chicagoans drank unfiltered Lake Michigan water treated only with chlorine. The plant took 13 years to build, and cost $105,000,000.

The tallest building on the city's skyline, the 648-foot, glass and steel Civic Center was topped out, and a block-long, 30-story federal building was dedicated in October. On Michigan Avenue, the $25,000,000 35-story Equitable Life Assurance Building was also topped out. In the Loop, the Morrison Hotel, an old landmark, awaited demolition with two other buildings to make room for a bank. The 46-story hotel will be the tallest building in the nation ever razed for new construction.

On the transit scene, the 17.5-mile Southwest Expressway opened, while for the fourth straight year, O'Hare International Airport was the world's busiest. It handled some 18,500,000 passengers in 1964.

On the cultural scene, restoration began on the famed Chicago Auditorium designed by Louis Sullivan and Dankmar Adler. Dead at 70 in New York City was Ben Hecht, co-author of the play *The Front Page*, and chronicler of Chicago's earlier years (see DEATHS OF NOTABLE PERSONS).   DONALD W. LIEF

CHILD WELFARE. The Economic Opportunity Act of 1964 (the Anti-Poverty Bill), which became law on August 20, was a milestone in child welfare. A major provision was the Job Corps, which included plans, during its first year, for enrolling 40,000 volunteers—young men and women between the ages of 16 and 21—who have not completed high school and have not found satisfactory employment. The corps' educational program is designed to develop their basic skills in reading, arithmetic, science, technology, and citizenship. Also, the volunteers' employable skills are to be developed through work experience and vocational training. See EDUCATION; JOB CORPS; SOCIAL WELFARE (Close-Up).

Aid to Migrant Children. Another section of the act provides aid for the children of migrant farmworkers. Typically, their needs have not been effectively met by existing school, health, and welfare facilities in the communities through which they pass. The new act authorized $15,000,000 as an initial appropriation to aid the states in establishing and operating new and better services for this group.

Conference Follow-Up. A Joint Conference on Children and Youth was held April 4 to 8 in Washington, D.C., designed to follow up the 1960 White House Conference on Children and Youth. Representatives came from 400 national voluntary agencies, 39 federal agencies and departments that make up the Interdepartmental Committee on Children and Youth, and the Children's Commissions of the various states. Youth delegates also attended.

New Grants; Fresh Needs. In announcing child welfare training grants totaling $1,750,000 in May, Katherine E. Oettinger, chief of the Children's Bureau of the U.S. Department of Health, Education, and Welfare, noted that only about half of the nation's counties have child welfare workers. By law, these federal grants are conditional on state plans designed to ensure that by 1975 all political subdivisions of each state will have public child welfare services. This is estimated to require 20,000 additional workers.

Child Guidance. To help children develop their full potential and to lessen the development of emotional and social problems, professionals in the field were depending more and more on group work with parents. Effective pamphlets and books for parents and professionals planning to organize child guidance groups were published in 1964 by the Child Study Association, the Gesell Institute, and the Family Service Association of America.

Mentally Ill Child. Mounting concern for the mentally ill child emerged in 1964. The National Association for Mental Health published a useful *Directory of Resources for Mentally Ill Children in the United States.* An important publication was *No Language But a Cry*, by Mrs. Bert Kruger Smith of the Hogg Foundation of the University of Texas. The book put into layman's language an effective description of the kinds of children classified as mentally ill, and the kinds of services gradually becoming available to them.

Heredity vs. Environment. The importance of a stimulating environment for mental development of infants and children was dramatically emphasized in the first reports of a follow-up of children studied 21 years ago by the Iowa Child Welfare Research Institute. The original studies aroused much controversy because they demonstrated that children of mentally retarded mothers, placed as infants in adoptive homes, or in situations where much mothering and stimulation was available, developed normally and showed average or better intellectual ability. On the other hand, similar infants placed in an institution where staff shortages prevented individual attention developed as mentally handicapped children.

"An Interim Brief," issued in March by the National Institute of Mental Health-Iowa Follow-Up Studies, indicated that these environmentally caused differences have now been found to persist into adulthood, and into the children and grandchildren of the original babies. This follow-up study may well be considered the most important child guidance research of the decade.   FRANCES A. MULLEN

See also MENTAL HEALTH; SOCIAL WELFARE (Close-Up).

CHILDREN'S BOOKS. See LITERATURE FOR CHILDREN.

CHILDREN'S THEATER. See THEATER, AMATEUR.

CHILE inaugurated Eduardo Frei Montalva as its president on November 3. In defeating Socialist-Communist Salvador Allende, Frei became the first Christian Democrat ever to be elected a chief of state in Latin America.

He promised a list of economic reforms, including welfare and public works programs and the distribution of land to 100,000 landless farmers within five years. As for the politically sensitive copper question, Frei planned "Chileanization" rather than nationalization. The government, he insisted, was to be a partner in the industry rather than its owner. The new president hoped to double industrial production in a few years. See FREI MONTALVA, EDUARDO.

Frei inherited a formidable number of problems. They included inadequate farm and industrial production, inflation, and a sinking peso. Gold and foreign exchange reserves were low and foreign debts totaled more than $2,300,000,000. Prior to his inauguration, Frei had sent missions to Europe and the United States to discuss ways to ease debt repayments. The missions also explored the possibility of new aid for the nation's economic and social development plans.

Population: 7,950,000. **Government:** President Eduardo Frei Montalva. **Foreign Trade:** exports, $587,000,000; imports, $594,000,000. **Principal Exports:** copper, iron ore, saltpeter.   MARY C. WEBSTER

See also LATIN AMERICA.

CHINA

THE PEOPLE'S REPUBLIC of China became the world's fifth atomic power when it exploded a nuclear device in October. It was only the day before that Soviet Premier Nikita S. Khrushchev fell from power, and, with his downfall, Chinese Communist Party Chairman Mao Tse-tung emerged as senior leader of the Marxist-Leninist communist world. These two developments symbolized China's growing international stature. Having challenged the Soviet Union for the allegiance of both the smaller communist countries and parties, Peking set about building its own world bloc in Africa, Asia, and Latin America. It even sought to outmaneuver Moscow in Eastern Europe. See COMMUNISM; RUSSIA.

An Atomic Power. The explosion of a nuclear bomb was announced on October 16. China's entry into the "nuclear club" did not yield any immediate military advantage, largely because the nation lacked either aircraft or intercontinental missiles needed to deliver nuclear bombs. But the event did have important political repercussions. With greater authority than ever before, the Chinese could claim that their participation was essential to any settlement of world issues. See DISARMAMENT; UNITED NATIONS.

An Enemy Eliminated. More consequential, perhaps, than China's technological triumph was the ousting of Soviet Premier Nikita S. Khrushchev from power. Ever since competition between China and the Soviet Union had erupted in the late 1950's, the communist leaders in Peking had argued that their interparty differences with the Soviet Union were with misguided comrades in Moscow and not with the majority of the Soviet party members. Khrushchev in particular was singled out as the focus of their wrath. His fall from power on October 15, just as he was preparing to summon the world's communist leaders to a conference in Moscow, was seemingly a victory for the Chinese Communists.

Some doubts remained, however, as to the extent of the victory. In November, Premier Chou En-lai attended the anniversary celebrations of the Bolshevik Revolution in Moscow. As a result, both the Chinese and the Soviet Union moderated the public aspects of their ideological dispute. But many experts believed that their differences were too basic to permit genuine settlement. Nor did the visit diminish to any appreciable extent the increasingly nationalistic

Eastfoto

OMINOUS CLOUD *churning over China on Oct. 16, 1964, marks triggering of first atom bomb by Communist Chinese.*

competition between the two communist countries.

Contest for Converts. Peking's aggressive challenge to Moscow was felt most acutely within the smaller communist countries. In Mongolia, where the government leaned toward the Soviet Union, the Chinese lost ground. But North Korea aligned itself with China and so did North Vietnam. The Communist party in Indonesia came more fully under Peking's sway. Japanese communists likewise sided with the Chinese. In Europe, however, Chinese influence remained largely restricted to Albania.

China's cultivation of friends and influence was pursued with comparable vigor through expanding government ties and more open diplomacy. Late in February, Premier Chou En-lai completed a seven-week swing through Africa. He later visited Pakistan and Ceylon. Other Chinese diplomats were busy throughout the year paying visits to many of the Asiatic countries. See ASIA.

Domestic Qualms. The Communist Chinese, however, while displaying such power and purpose abroad, were less confident at home. Agriculture remained the base of China's economy, and while it was beginning to show improvement, China nevertheless continued to depend on imports to help feed its multitudes. To spur production, the government stepped up the distribution of chemical fertilizers, improved seed varieties, and technical services.

The government also initiated large irrigation and drainage works projects as well as soil surveys. An erosion control program was showing results, particularly in northwest China and Manchuria, where shelter belts of trees, planted by millions of peasants and urban folk who had been mobilized in "shock brigades" five and four years before, were beginning to hold in place the light *loess* topsoil along the upper reaches of the Yellow River.

The nation stepped up its attempt to modernize agriculture by establishing state farms. They were designed to serve as large-scale models of what could be accomplished with innovations and mechanization. During the year, there were approximately 2,000 such farms covering roughly 10,000,000 acres.

Although the communist leaders and the official press emphasized such examples of progress, the great majority of China's 600,000,000 peasants still farmed largely with the methods they have employed for centuries. Party leaders continued to permit the peasant farmers to cultivate private garden plots. Such plots, however, were limited to a total of 7 per cent of the cultivated land in a commune. Many a farmer was allotted only 2,000 square feet. Despite these limitations, their yields offered dramatic evidence of what the Chinese farmers could accomplish when given incentives. Vegetables, fruits, pigs, ducks, and chickens were being raised in ever-increasing abundance in 1964.

Peasants were permitted to sell produce not consumed at home in various types of "free markets" and "rural fairs." While the communists were suspicious of such "capitalist" influences, they hesitated to curb farmer incentives too drastically for fear of again facing critical shortages.

Heavy Industry, which was recovering from the setbacks and mismanagement it had suffered during the "Great Leap Forward," made headway in its new role as a backstop to agriculture. Six large chemical fertilizer plants were either being built or enlarged in northeast and central China, partly with European-made equipment. The Loyang Tractor Plant, the largest in China, was expanded to provide equipment that would help increase mechanized plowing. Water pumps were being manufactured in ever-greater numbers.

While steel production may have been only two-thirds of the 18,000,000 tons claimed in 1960, quality improved as the Chinese introduced foreign technology to turn out more specialized products. New emphasis was placed on the production of machine tools and other capital goods, including electric power generating equipment and transformer stations. China reported itself self-sufficient in petroleum output as production expanded in remote Chinghai, Kansu, and Sinkiang.

Light Industry, so long relegated to a secondary role, received new priorities. Food processing, cigarette and leather manufacture, and sugar refining were expanded, both for domestic consumption and for export. Pharmaceuticals, paper, and glass showed improvement in quality. Chemicals became important for production of plastics and synthetic fibers.

In order to ease the textile industry's dependence upon raw cotton and other agricultural supplies, China purchased complete vinyon and polyethylene plants from Japan and Great Britain. However, textile output was still short of China's requirements.

Ideological Concern. Communist party leaders showed uneasiness over the ideological state of the society they were trying to remold. Although "socialist education" was required in every factory and village, the nation's leaders were still far short of their avowed goal of making everyone "Red and Expert." To counter this condition, the party decreed that all means by which public attitudes might be influenced should be "cleansed." This meant tighter propaganda control over everything from opera to motion pictures and literature.

Enormous attention was given, too, to inducing all literate Chinese to study the "thought of Mao Tse-tung." Peasants and others who had not yet become literate were expected to master the essentials in group discussions. Particular emphasis was upon Communist Party Chairman Mao Tse-tung's interpretation of Marxism-Leninism.

Population Control again won official sanction as the nation's leaders realized the dimensions of the population dilemma confronting China. With the population increasing by some 2.5 per cent annually, the communists hoped to limit the size of families.

The officially endorsed ideal was a family that limited its offspring to two children.

Population: 740,000,000. **Government:** Communist Party Chairman Mao Tse-tung; Chairman of the Republic Liu Shao-chi; Premier Chou En-lai. **Foreign Trade:** exports, $1,280,000,000; imports, $1,145,-000,000. **Principal Exports:** coal, metal ores and concentrates, soya beans, tea, textiles. ALBERT RAVENHOLT

CITY.

The Supreme Court of the United States, in a landmark decision on June 15, ruled that the states must apportion their legislatures on a basis of equal population of legislative districts. Some observers termed the decision "the most important in a century," because it will end the long-standing rural domination of state government by shifting political power from rural to populous urban areas. See STATE GOVERNMENT; SUPREME COURT OF THE UNITED STATES.

Legislation. Paralleling the high court decision, the Congress of the United States took two significant steps that will bring aid to cities. The Urban Mass Transportation Act, passed in June, set up a three-year aid program totaling $375,000,000 for commuter, bus, train, and subway systems. The wide-ranging Economic Opportunity Act set in motion the War on Poverty. See SOCIAL WELFARE (Close-Up); TRANSIT. Congress also extended the urban renewal program—despite a number of critical books, articles, and congressional hearings—but failed to pass all parts of the omnibus housing bill recommended by President Lyndon B. Johnson. Other congressional actions that will result in aid to cities were appropriation bills for highway construction, and juvenile delinquency control.

Social Unrest. In both Northern and Southern cities, smoldering Negro resentment erupted in violence aimed at securing civil rights and economic opportunity. First, Jacksonville, in March, then St. Augustine, in June, were Florida battlegrounds. In July and August, New York's Harlem and Brooklyn were scenes of massive mob violence. Jersey City, N.J.; Philadelphia, Pa.; and Rochester, N.Y., also faced the unfamiliar sights and sounds of major disorder. See CIVIL LIBERTIES; PROTESTANT; Section Two, CONGRESS MAKES A DECISION.

Supercities, resulting from continued migration to urban areas, were seen by the World Health Organization (WHO) as one of the most pressing problems facing mankind. WHO, a United Nations (UN) agency, reported that rural migration to urban areas "may reach catastrophic dimensions" in 20 years.

Today's greatest supercity, stretching from north of Boston to south of Washington, D.C., was extended southward in April with the opening of the 17.6-mile bridge-tunnel across Chesapeake Bay. It linked Norfolk, Va., and its neighbors to the vast sprawl of the Atlantic seaboard "megalopolis" home of some 37,000,000 Americans.

The Central Business District in the United States fought back against dire predictions of decline.

Hartford, Conn., opened its $40,000,000, 12-acre Constitution Plaza. Standing where one of New England's worst slum areas had been, it includes eight large office buildings, parking for some 1,800 cars, and landscaped walks and plazas.

New York City planned mighty twin skyscrapers that will be taller than the Empire State Building. They will house a World Trade Center downtown, and will be surrounded by a cluster of smaller satellite buildings. The complex will cost $350,000,000. Other notable high-rise buildings were underway in Boston, Chicago, Dallas, Kansas City, New Orleans, Phoenix, and San Francisco. Cleveland also opened its new $15,000,000 convention hall, the largest such city-owned facility.

CITY PLANNING.

Pressure to increase the number of apartment buildings in suburbia met with widespread opposition in 1964 from single-family dwellers. Nevertheless, the experts expected multiple-family construction to maintain its high percentage of total housing starts in the suburbs for the next few years. This was chiefly because apartment developers could buy land cheaper there than in urban areas, enabling them to offer lower rentals and to reach an ever-greater market.

Concerned Commuters. The belief that suburbanites cared little about what happened to their central city appeared to be disproved by a survey conducted in the New York metropolitan area. The Regional Plan Association queried more than 5,600 civic, business, and labor leaders in a three-state, 22 county area, asking them to assist in planning the region by answering a lengthy questionnaire.

GRAND PLAN for restyling Pennsylvania Avenue, in Washington, D.C., would make the street end in a National Square near the Treasury.
Louis Checkman

Ninety-three per cent felt that their local community was more than a little affected by what happened in other parts of the metropolitan area. They overwhelmingly endorsed improving public transportation and favored increased state and federal financial aid to improve cities. They also backed the idea of a metropolitan, county, or state zoning agency with real but limited powers over the local municipality, and the acquisition of more land for the development of parks.

A National Goal. In spite of heavy congressional cutbacks, the National Planning Association (NPA), a businessmen's study group, urged that urban renewal be given major consideration in the allocation of our national economic resources. The association estimated that total requirements for new facilities for mass transit and urban renewal, excluding investments in private industrial plants, should average $100-to $110,000,000,000 per year over the next 20 years. While an increase in expenditures of $75-to $80,000,000,000 would normally occur, merely through increases in population in urban areas in the next 20 years, an additional $25-to $30,000,000,000 will be needed.

The funds would be raised from private sources at a ratio of private to public investment of $2\frac{1}{2}$ to 1. The NPA said that while a shift in the resources of the U.S. economy would be substantial, it "would not present an insuperable task." JAMES H. PICKFORD

CIVIL DEFENSE proved that it could react with speed and efficiency in the face of natural disaster. It met the test of new duties imposed by the Congress of the United States in 1963, to utilize its units to cope with disasters.

Civil defense served victims of the Alaskan earthquake, which struck on Good Friday, March 27. The civil defense setup for the entire state consisted of a staff of six members. But within 10 minutes, Douglas Clure, who had resigned a month earlier as director of civil defense in Anchorage, and others trained in civil defense were taking over in Anchorage, Kodiak, Seward, and Valdez. Backed by U.S. Army units, they cared for the dead and injured, fought fires, restored power, fed the homeless, and, above all, maintained communications via a radio network. See GEOLOGY.

Nevertheless, from its halcyon days as a vital agency during the 1961 Berlin Crisis, civil defense became just another of the duties of the Secretary of the Army in 1964. Steuart L. Pittman resigned in March as assistant secretary of defense for civil defense and the post was abolished. William P. Durkee, deputy assistant secretary of defense under Pittman, became director of civil defense under the Secretary of the Army.

President Lyndon B. Johnson requested $358,000,-000 for civil defense. Congress appropriated $105,-200,000 for research, shelter survey and marking, operation, and maintenance. WARREN ROGERS

CIVIL LIBERTIES. Overshadowing all other events anywhere in the field of civil liberties in 1964 was the action of the Congress of the United States in passing the Civil Rights Act, designed to protect the constitutional rights of Negro citizens. This legislation, although controversial, was in keeping with the American tradition of equality under law for all citizens and of respect for the dignity of mankind. Before taking up this subject in detail, let us look at civil liberties across the world.

In Africa, several new constitutions contained elaborate provisions regarding civil liberties. In the United Arab Republic (UAR), President Gamal Abdel Nasser proclaimed, in March, a provisional constitution, which included guarantees of freedom of religion, speech, and press; free education of all citizens; and the right of labor to organize. The guarantee of free speech and press, however, was limited by the proviso reading: "within the limits of the law," which meant that restrictions on free speech and press were in the hands of the president and the national assembly rather than within the jurisdiction of the courts.

Malawi (formerly Nyasaland), the 37th African state to gain independence, was recognized by Great Britain on July 8, with a constitution containing guarantees of religious liberty and freedom of speech and press. Likewise, the independence of the Republic of Zambia (formerly Northern Rhodesia), the 38th African state, was recognized by Great Britain on October 24, with a constitution containing safeguards for the rights of individuals. But it remained to be seen how effective these paper provisions would prove.

The inadequacy of some constitutional guarantees was proved by events in Ghana. Its constitution provided for full democratic liberty. Nevertheless, under President Kwame Nkrumah, persecution of opponents of the governing political party began early. Finally, on Jan. 27, 1964, an election by the voters gave Nkrumah power to turn Ghana into a one-party state, and also power to dismiss the judges of the supreme and high courts. According to a governmental announcement, 99.9 per cent of the voters were in favor of this grant of authority. But, prior to the election, the citizens were repeatedly warned by the government-controlled press and radio that anyone failing to vote, or who voted "no," would be punished as "counter-revolutionaries." To ensure compliance, ballots were marked with the voters' serial numbers.

In the Soviet Union, the new "collective leadership" relaxed a few of the restrictions on Soviet citizens after the deposition of First Secretary Nikita S. Khrushchev. It was not certain that these new liberties would be permanent. At any rate, the new dictatorship allowed, among other things, peasants to keep gardens for their own food supply, and also to sell their produce in the market. On the other hand, the trend toward anti-Semitism was continued

CIVIL RIGHTS ACT is signed by President Lyndon B. Johnson as the men who aided its passage look on. From left, near the President, is Senator Everett M. Dirksen, the then Senator Hubert H. Humphrey, and Representative Charles A. Halleck.

when the official newspaper *Izvestia* published an attack on the Jews. See COMMUNISM; RUSSIA.

The United Nations. On February 4, 1964, U Thant, Secretary-General of the United Nations (UN), made a remarkable address before the Algerian national assembly. He declared that racial discrimination was a "most dangerous form of sickness," that it should be treated with "restraint and care." Otherwise there would be a disastrous "vicious circle" of hate and violence. The UN continued its concern with *apartheid* (separation of races) in the Republic of South Africa. On June 9, the Security Council condemned trials of violators of apartheid in South Africa. The consequences of the "vicious circle" of hate of which Thant warned, was seen in November, when Congolese rebels murdered nearly a hundred white persons held as hostages. See CONGO (LÉOPOLDVILLE).

The Roman Catholic Church took important action against discrimination, when the bishops in the third session of Vatican Council II adopted, and sent to Pope Paul VI a declaration that all humanity, and not simply the Jews, was responsible for the crucifixion of Christ. A proposed declaration on religious liberty, however, was postponed to the fourth session of the Vatican Council. See JEWS AND JUDAISM; ROMAN CATHOLIC.

In the United States, the Department of Justice continued its program of protecting the voting rights of Negroes under federal laws which had been passed in 1957 and 1960. Title I (Voting Rights) of the Civil Rights Act of 1964 strengthened these acts by barring unequal application of registration procedures. Progress was also made in desegregation of public schools under federal court orders. The Supreme Court of the United States, for example, ordered the reopening of public schools in Prince Edward County, Virginia, after the schools had been closed to avoid integration.

The Department of Justice used the Federal Bureau of Investigation (FBI) to apprehend persons who committed crimes against Negroes and civil rights workers. FBI agents, after weeks of investigation, found the bodies of three civil rights workers who had been murdered in Mississippi. On December 4, the FBI arrested 21 white men in connection with the crime. On December 10, in an unprecedented move, a local U.S. commissioner dismissed 19 of the

HIGHLIGHTS OF THE CIVIL RIGHTS ACT OF 1964

Title I (Voting Rights)

Bars unequal application of voting registration requirements; states that applicants will not be rejected for minor errors; that literacy tests be administered in writing and copies of the results be furnished upon request; presumes a person is literate if he has completed the sixth grade in a public or private school accredited by any state.

Title II (Public Accommodations)

Outlaws discrimination in most hotels and motels, in restaurants, gasoline stations, and places of amusement, if the discrimination is supported by state law or actions, or if it involves interstate commerce; exempts rooming houses with not more than five rooms for rent and with the owner living on the premises (the "Mrs. Murphy clause"); also exempts private clubs, unless some of the facilities of the club are available to customers of a business that falls under the act, such as a restaurant.

Title III (Public Facilities)

Allows the Attorney General, upon receiving written complaint, to bring suit against any segregated facility operated by a state or a municipality, such as a park, swimming pool, or library.

Title IV (Public Education)

Authorizes the Attorney General to bring school desegregation suits on written complaints; allows the U.S. Office of Education to give technical and financial assistance to public schools to help set up training institutes to ease desegregation problems; re-quires the office to report to Congress within two years on school desegregation progress on all levels.

Title VI (Federally Assisted Programs)

Bars discrimination under any program receiving federal aid; permits the government to cut off funds, with qualifications, to federally assisted programs where discrimination persists; makes such action subject to judicial review.

Title VII (Employment)

Forbids discrimination by employers or unions with 100 or more employees or members (this total to be reduced over five years to 25); provides for an Equal Employment Opportunity Commission (EEOC) to investigate complaints; decrees that the EEOC will not begin its activities for a year.

Title IX (Intervention)

Authorizes the Attorney General to intervene in cases brought under Amendment 14 of the U.S. Constitution where he finds the case of "general public importance."

Title X (Community Relations Service)

Provides for a Community Relations Service to mediate community disputes before they need to be brought into court.

Title XI (Miscellaneous)

Ensures trial by jury in cases of criminal contempt brought under any portion of the act except Title I; limits contempt sentences to six months in prison and a $1,000 fine.

---

men. The government served notice, however, that it would continue to prosecute the case.

Again, the FBI, after diligent search, apprehended and arrested four Ku Klux Klansmen in Georgia, charged with the sniper murder of Lemuel Penn, a Negro educator from Washington, D.C. The state of Georgia cooperated and indicted three of the men. A white jury, however, failed to convict them. In these cases, the efforts of the federal government were handicapped by the fact that criminal jurisdiction was in the hands of local authorities.

The Civil Rights Act of 1964. An entirely new authority was conferred upon the President of the United States and the Department of Justice by the Civil Rights Act, which Congress passed on July 2, 1964. This power was given in Title II.

Under the new law, any Negro who is denied service in a segregated place may file a suit in a federal court. In such a case, the judge may name an attorney for the complainant and authorize the suit without cost to the complainant. If the judge believes that there is a chance of obtaining voluntary compliance, he may refer the case to the Community Relations Service, which was created by the law. If the service cannot settle the Negro's grievance, the suit goes to court. The first official act of the President under the new law was to appoint LeRoy Collins, former governor of Florida, as director of the service. See COLLINS, (THOMAS) LEROY.

In each case, the Community Relations Service has 120 days to try to settle the grievance by persuasion. If its attempt fails, the Negro's suit goes to court, and the judge may issue an injunction or restraining order directing the accused restaurant owner or innkeeper to refrain from barring Negroes. If the accused defies the court order, he may be arrested and jailed for 45 days, until he agrees to obey the court, or be fined for each day that he refuses. All of this can be done by the judge alone, without a jury. Afterward, if a criminal contempt of court is filed against the accused, a jury trial is permitted.

The Civil Rights Act was passed with bipartisan support. In the Senate, 46 Democrats and 27 Republicans voted for the bill, while 21 Democrats and 6 Republicans voted against it. After the enactment of the measure, both major parties declared for loyal enforcement of the Civil Rights Act. In signing the bill, President Johnson said: "We must not approach the observance and enforcement of this law in a vengeful spirit. Its purpose is not to punish. Its purpose is not to divide, but to end divisions—divisions which have lasted too long."

In December, the Supreme Court of the United States upheld the controversial Title II of the act. It also quashed sit-in proceedings that occurred in the types of places named in the act.

Mass Demonstrations and picketing preceded enactment of the act, and contributed toward an atmosphere of tension that flared into mob violence in the South and in several cities in the North during the so-called "long, hot summer" of 1964. Riots occurred in New York City's Harlem; in Rochester, N.Y.; Jersey City, N.J.; and in Philadelphia, Pa.

An FBI investigation, ordered by President Johnson, reported on September 26 that there was "no systematic planning or organization" behind the riots, that they were basically "senseless attacks on all constituted authority."

As the elections neared, it became clear that if the riots continued, their effect would rebound against the civil rights cause. Hence, rights leaders pleaded with the Negroes to cease rioting, and to halt their demonstrations until after the elections. They were successful in their pleas.

Police Brutality. But still lingering after the riots were charges of police brutality against Negroes occasioned by the attempt to prevent demonstrations prohibited by local law in Southern states, and to curb mob violence in Northern states. On numerous occasions, the police used dogs, fire hose, and tear gas, and wielded billy clubs when demonstrators refused to obey orders to disperse. To preserve order, such tactics were employed not only against Negro demonstrators, but also against white violators.

In particular, Negro leaders condemned the New York Police Department for not punishing a policeman for shooting on July 16 a Negro youth who attacked him with a knife during a fracas on the street. New York's Mayor Robert Wagner resisted attempts to weaken the authority of the police department by the appointment of a civilian board to review charges of police brutality.

"One Man, One Vote." In recent years, legislatures and courts have tended to treat political rights, such as voting, as civil rights. In June, the Supreme Court of the United States handed down a decision stating that the election districts of both houses of the state legislatures must be "substantially equal" in population. In all, the decision directly affects 15 states with cases before the Court (see SUPREME COURT [Close-Up]). But the order was applicable to all of the 50 states of the Union. The 6-to-3 opinion was based on the principle of "one man, one vote." In the words of Chief Justice Warren: "Legislators represent people, not trees or acres." Unequal election districts, according to this opinion, deprived citizens in heavily populated districts of their due weight in government. KENNETH COLEGROVE

See also COURTS AND LAWS; NEGRO; PROTESTANT; STATE GOVERNMENT; SUPREME COURT OF THE UNITED STATES; Section Two, CONGRESS MAKES A DECISION.

CIVIL WAR CENTENNIAL. A symposium on Lincoln's Gettysburg Address was held in Washington, D.C., on January 13, in the midst of one of the worst blizzards in years. It was one of the few functions not canceled that evening. Papers were read (they were later published in book form by the University of Illinois Press) by author John Dos Passos, Pulitzer prize poet Robert Lowell, U.S. Senator Paul Douglas of Illinois, and theologian Reinhold Niebuhr. Those in attendance reported that the program was one of the most enlightening of the centennial.

In February, the Southern Company, an affiliate of power companies, granted $20,000 to assist in the publication of the papers of Confederate President Jefferson Davis. And in March, a program was held in Washington to mark General Ulysses S. Grant's assumption of command of the Union armies.

Centennial Stamps. In May, the U.S. Post Office issued the fourth of five stamps marking the centennial. The 5-cent commemorative showed three artillerymen firing their cannon against a background of shattered trees. It marked the Battle of the Wilderness, one of the bloodiest of the war.

The lone Civil War action in New England was recalled in August by the Vermont Civil War Centennial Commission and the chamber of commerce of St. Albans, Vt. The action occurred in October, 1864, when Confederate raiders attacked St. Albans and escaped to Canada.

War Medal. In 1866, the West Virginia state legislature authorized a medal for each man from the state who served in the Union armies. A total of 26,099 medals was struck. Recently, 6,500 unclaimed medals were found in a warehouse. In the fall of 1964, West Virginia was seeking to give the unclaimed medals to the nearest living relatives of the men it had thus honored. V. C. JONES

CLAY, CASSIUS MARCELLUS, JR. (1942-   ), won the heavyweight boxing crown of the world on February 25. He defeated Sonny Liston, who failed to come out for his corner for the seventh round of a 15-round match in Miami Beach, Fla. A return bout scheduled with Liston for November 16 was postponed when Clay underwent emergency surgery. See BOXING; Section One, RED SMITH ON SPORTS.

The new champion was born in Louisville, Ky., on Jan. 18, 1942. His father was a sign painter. Clay turned professional in 1960 after graduating from Central High School. During his schooling, he had built a successful career as an amateur by winning the Olympic and Amateur Athletic Union heavyweight titles, the Golden Gloves heavyweight championship, and the light-heavyweight championship of the 1960 Olympic Games held in Rome.

On August 14, he married Sonji Roi, a former model. In applying for the license, Clay signed himself as Muhammad Ali, the name he uses as a member of the Black Muslims. WALTER F. MORSE

CLOTHING. See FASHION; TEXTILE.

COAL producers kept the fires of industry well stoked in 1964. Bituminous output, estimated at 474,000,000 tons, topped 1963's revised total of 458,000,000 tons by $3\frac{1}{2}$ per cent. Exports held at about 49,000,000 tons. Mine prices, at a little less than $4.50 a ton, failed to increase noticeably from the 1963 level, despite greater demand.

Generally, coal producers seemed satisfied with the price movement—or the lack of it—to assure a continued rise in demand from the electric utilities, which consistently took 50 per cent or more of soft coal's production throughout 1964.

A milestone was passed in September when the minemouth plant of the Tennessee Valley Authority (TVA) at Owensboro, Ky., completed a year of operation. TVA was getting its coal at $2.95 a ton, and reported that savings in fuel costs far outweighed power transmission losses.

As the year ended, coal operators were hopeful that the Cabinet-level committee headed by Secretary of Defense Robert S. McNamara would act to hold down imports of residual fuel oil, and at the same time push to remove foreign trade barriers against U.S. coal exports.   ROBERT E. BEDINGFIELD

See also ELECTRIC POWER; GAS; PETROLEUM.

COAST GUARD. See NATIONAL DEFENSE.

COIN COLLECTING. See HOBBIES.

COLLINS, JAMES FRANCIS (1905-   ), was called from a brief retirement as an army general to become president of the American Red Cross on April 1. Prior to his retirement, he had been army commander in chief in the Pacific since 1961.

Collins had spent his life in military service, beginning as a second lieutenant after graduation, in 1927, from the U.S. Military Academy of West Point. He reached the rank of full general in 1959.

Collins was born in New York City on Sept. 2, 1905. He and his wife, the former Marian McLaughlin, have one daughter. She is married to an army captain.   WALTER F. MORSE

COLLINS, (THOMAS) LEROY (1909-   ), president of the National Association of Broadcasters, was appointed director of the Community Relations Service by President Lyndon B. Johnson, after he signed the Civil Rights Act of 1964 on July 2. The new law provided for the establishment of the agency in the Department of Commerce to help the nation adjust to the Civil Rights Act (see CIVIL LIBERTIES).

The former Florida governor (1955-1961) grew up in a segregated society, and understands well the problems of his native South. He is convinced that the South must now find a solution to these problems.

LeRoy Collins was born in Tallahassee, Fla. He practiced law there, after getting his degree at Cumberland (Tenn.) University (1931). As a state representative (1934-1940), a senator (1940-1945), and later as governor, he had a major role in Florida's economic and industrial growth.

COLOMBIA made good economic progress on various fronts but without achieving any real momentum. Higher coffee exports at better prices, plus tight control on imports, narrowed the January-to-June trade deficit to $15,500,000 against $85,000,000 in the same period in 1963. There were several minuses, however. Living costs zoomed, unemployment remained high, and there was monetary instability. Political apathy was high. Some 70 per cent of the electorate abstained from voting in the congressional and municipal elections held in March.

The government continued its efforts to end a painful internal problem. In May, a $30,000,000 military and civilian program was launched in Marquetalia, an area long known for its banditry and poverty. While the army began the job of clearing the interior of outlaws, other troops were put to work on such improvements as roads, schools, and wells. See Section Two, DOS GRINGAS AMERICANAS.

Population: 15,600,000. **Government:** President Guillermo Léon Valencia. **Foreign Trade:** exports, $536,000,000; imports, $583,000,000. **Principal Exports:** coffee, cotton, petroleum.   MARY C. WEBSTER

See also LATIN AMERICA.

COMMON MARKET. See EUROPE.

COMMUNICATIONS. World space—in the air, on land, under the sea—was more heavily loaded with words and pictures in 1964 than ever before in history. During the year, the nations of the world joined hands to keep people-to-people dialogue moving freely over modern turnpikes of international communication. Increasing numbers of communication channels were opened within, to, and from the United States to meet the growing demand for more electronic highways to step up the pace of the nation's economy through faster transmission of packaged data.

• In July, representatives of 14 nations met in Washington, D.C., and agreed to work together to establish and maintain a global communications system using satellites as relay stations.

• New cables were strung under the oceans, linking more nations—evidence enough that the cable would not soon be crowded out by its more dramatic cousin, the man-made satellite.

• Transmission of data grew faster than either private-line, regular telephone, or telegraph services. The American Telephone and Telegraph Company (AT&T) introduced its "Telpak," a wideband, bulk communications service permitting flexible use by big customers of computer-based, facsimile, and other types of data—a revolutionary device for conducting business.

A Syncom Feat. In retrospect, the Federal Communications Commission (FCC) said that the "outstanding telecommunications event of all time has been the extension of international communication into outer space by means of satellite relay." U.S. citizens could well believe it as they proudly watched

AT&T

FIRST LADY MAKES FIRST CALL over the Bell System's Picturephone on June 24 as she talks from Washington, D.C., to Dr. Elizabeth A. Wood in New York City.

telecasts of their athletes in the Olympic Games at Tokyo in October. Olympic contests were converted to TV pictures by streams of microwaves accelerated by an incredibly marvelous satellite, Syncom III.

This feat was accomplished under the direction of the Communications Satellite Corporation (Comsat), assisted by the technological genius of the National Aeronautics and Space Administration (NASA) and the Hughes Aircraft Corporation. Comsat was authorized by Congress in 1962.

Undersea Cables. However dramatic the new satellite system, the big load of international communications continued to be pulled by the undersea work-horses of a world-wide cable system. In June, President Lyndon B. Johnson opened a new submarine telephone cable to Japan when he put in a telephone call from Washington, D.C., to the then Prime Minister Hayato Ikeda in Tokyo.

Meanwhile, the fourth transatlantic submarine telephone system (TAT-4) was promised for completion by mid-1965 as cable was stretched between New Jersey and France. A second U.S. mainland-to-Hawaii cable was opened in midsummer, and the first cable to link the Philippines with terminal stations on Guam was to be opened by year's end.

Domestic Communications developed more sophisticated ways to serve its clientele. The Bell System, essentially through AT&T, served more customers—about 70,000,000 telephones, against 68,600,000 in 1963—than any other U.S. business.

Frederick R. Kappel, AT&T's board chairman, hoped this expansion also would go far to make up for the estimated $100,000,000 loss in revenue from U.S.-ordered rate cuts. On November 25, the FCC issued new rate reductions ranging to as much as 42 per cent on interstate, long-distance, station-to-station calls, to take effect Feb. 1 and April 1, 1965.

New communications symbols were coming into common usage: WATS (wide area telephone service, which provided unlimited long-distance service for a flat monthly charge), Bellboy (pocket receiver that signals you "with a pleasant tone" wherever you are when a phone call comes into your office), ESS (electronic switching system—a device that, among other things, can call a third party into your two-party conversation without help from an operator).

And in 1964, for the first time, you could see the fellow on the other end of the line. Commercial Picturephone Service went into operation in June. The first call was made by Mrs. Lyndon B. Johnson, from the White House, to Dr. Elizabeth A. Wood, a Bell Telephone Laboratories scientist, in New York City. Late in the year, Western Union Telegraph Company opened its 7,500-mile, transcontinental microwave system. The $80,000,000 network can accommodate all types of record and voice communications.   CLYDE C. HALL

See also ELECTRONICS; RADIO; Section ONE, ISAAC ASIMOV ON SCIENCE; SPACE TRAVEL; TELEVISION.

COMMUNISM

COMMUNISM abruptly changed leadership in 1964 when Nikita S. Khrushchev was removed as First Secretary of the Communist Party of the Soviet Union. He was also deposed as premier of the Union of Soviet Socialist Republics (USSR). See RUSSIA.

Until Khrushchev's ouster in October, all signs seemingly pointed to an irreparable division between communism's two giants, Russia and China, and to the disintegration of international communism. Khrushchev's successor as party leader, Leonid I. Brezhnev, immediately gave evidence, however, of a desire not only to postpone the split but to mend it, if possible. The changeover seemed to be a victory for the Chinese, who had made Khrushchev the target of their attacks. His downfall justified a visit to Moscow by Premier Chou En-lai in November, where he held private talks with the new Soviet leaders. See BREZHNEV, LEONID I.; KOSYGIN, ALEKSEI N.

Time, Inc. © 1964

This remarkable turn of events followed months of controversy between Moscow and Peking and disarray in the communist camp. In April and May, after a period of relative silence on the part of the USSR and abortive efforts at mediation by the Romanian Communist party, the controversy burst out anew in fiery polemics and in letters exchanged between the two parties.

The immediate issue was whether a world communist conference should be called to attempt to resolve the disagreement, and, if so, when it should take place. Khrushchev was confident he had the support of a majority of the Communist parties. He insisted on a preliminary meeting of 26 of them in Moscow on December 15 to prepare for a world gathering in 1965. The Chinese were aware of their minority position. They warned that the meeting would cause an open split.

The procedural question was but an added source of friction in the profound controversy over fundamental principles of policy and strategy. The Soviet Union had continued to express its belief in peaceful coexistence and in the possibility of limited agreements with the United States, such as the 1963 nuclear test-ban treaty. China, however, had emphasized the continuing danger of American imperialism. It considered ultimate revolution as the only real guarantee of peace and security. The Russians preferred to rely on economic competition between the capitalist and communist worlds.

Growing Nationalism. The dispute spilled over into internal affairs. Moscow attacked the Chinese for the "cult of the personality" of Mao, and for their lack of party democracy. Peking condemned Khrushchev as the "betrayer of Marxism-Leninism." It accused him of seeking to restore capitalism in the Soviet Union. In September, boundary and territorial claims were injected into the quarrel. While

UNHEALED BREACH. While Premier Chou En-lai, left, demonstrates his disinterest, his Soviet colleagues applaud a speech by Premier Aleksei Kosygin reaffirming a policy of peaceful coexistence.

Mao Tse-tung censured Soviet aggrandizement in Europe and Asia, Khrushchev in turn charged the Chinese with expansionist ambitions in Asia. It was clear that behind the veil of ideological polemics and personal denunciations, profound questions of national interest were involved.

A Divided Camp. As the struggle intensified, the communist camp as a whole became more bitterly divided, not only on the issues under debate, but also on the procedures for settling them. Apart from the Albanian communists, China had won its support mainly in Asia. But it also had sympathizers throughout the world. The Communist party of the Soviet Union had its firmest base in Europe.

Dissension in the Ranks. Many were disturbed, however, by Khrushchev's tactics, especially his insistence on the December conference. There also were serious misgivings on the part of some pro-Soviet parties about the desirability of a new international communist organization hinted at by Khrushchev. Although China's views were distasteful to most European communists, its espousal of the equality and independence of individual parties had considerable appeal. The Romanians, for example, issued a statement in April favoring the independence of each Communist party and state.

Khrushchev's Removal, ironically enough, produced fresh conflicts. The suddenness and arbitrariness of his ouster shocked most of the pro-Soviet parties. At the same time, it awakened fears of a renewed Soviet interference in their affairs, the abandonment of peaceful coexistence, and even a return to Stalinism.

The ouster of Khrushchev, coupled with the deaths of such veteran communist leaders as Finland's Otto V. Kuusinen, France's Maurice Thorez, and Italy's Palmieri Togliatti, put China's Mao Tse-tung in a position of almost unrivaled seniority in the communist world. At the same time, the changeover in the Soviet Union brought to the forefront men not personally associated with either the 1917 Bolshevik Revolution or with the international communist movement. They were *apparatchiki* (party functionaries) and bureaucrats who were more concerned with the Soviet Union's economic development and the defense of its national interests than with revolution abroad.

Brezhnev, in a speech on November 7, made an obvious bid for intraparty reconciliation, and stressed the urgent need for world communist unity on the basis of equality. At the same time, however, he proclaimed his faith in peaceful coexistence and the need for improving the lot of the Soviet consumer. He reiterated, too, other points that had been condemned by the Chinese in earlier debates.

Thus, the ousting of Khrushchev and the renewal of contacts between Peking and Moscow might have reduced the intensity of the controversy. But it was not very likely they would bring about an early solution. H. GORDON SKILLING

COMPUTERS entered a new field when Bell Telephone Laboratories at Murray Hill, N.J., made a 17-minute animated cartoon by using a computer linked to a cathode-ray tube and a movie camera. The picture was formed on a grid of spots on the face of the cathode-ray tube, much as a picture appears on a television tube, and then photographed by the camera. A programmer indicated the length and placement of all lines that the computer was to draw. The film took four hours of computer time and 2,000 hours of film processing, but its total cost was comparable to that of conventional animated cartoons.

Early in the year, RCA Communications, Inc., demonstrated the world's first computerized telegraph system, said to be the most versatile message system ever developed. In September, the first two units of an electronic "editor" that could compose, read, or edit material stored in a computer's data files was being field-tested for the U.S. Air Force by its developer, the Raytheon Company.

By far the most significant scientific application was the direct linkage of a powerful computer with an atom-smashing cyclotron at the University of Chicago. The computer, MANIAC III, permits a scientist to monitor nuclear bombardments in a cyclotron instantaneously.

One technological advance that may have important significance was the construction of artificial nerve cells, called electrochemical neurons, in the laboratories of Space-General Corporation at Los Angeles. According to the company, this "may result in a revolutionary type of computer capable of functioning like the human brain." Scientists used iron and silver wires to make a neuron with the property of inhibition. Tests indicated that a wide range of behavior could be produced. SERGEI LENORMAND

See also AUTOMATION; ELECTRONICS.

COMSAT (Communications Satellite Corporation). See COMMUNICATIONS; STOCKS AND BONDS.

CONGO (BRAZZAVILLE) suppressed an attempted counter-revolutionary coup in February. The attempt had been made by supporters of former President Fulbert Youlou, who had been imprisoned in August of the preceding year. Strong measures were taken to eliminate subversive groups in the nation. In June, President Alphonse Massemba-Débat announced that the Movement National de la Révolution, a new political party, would be consolidated with all political and trade union forces. Later, it officially became Congo's sole party.

In March, the government endorsed a new provisional four-year plan for economic and social development that will cost an estimated $200,000,000.

Population: 855,000. **Government:** President Alphonse Massemba-Débat; Premier Pascal Lissouba. **Foreign Trade:** exports, $20,000,000; imports, $79,000,000. **Principal Exports:** lumber, oilseeds, petroleum. BENJAMIN E. THOMAS

See also AFRICA.

Yves-Guy Berges

SUDDEN DEATH. Two Congolese rebels, wearing headgear prescribed by sorcerers, pause after mowing down a police officer whose corpse lies just beyond them.

CONGO (LÉOPOLDVILLE) began the year in bloodshed and ended it in an orgy of mass murder. Hundreds of white and black residents were slain indiscriminately during the year-long fighting in which internal rebel groups savagely resisted the efforts of a weak central Congolese government to subdue them. Terrorism erupted early in the year when a 2,000-man force led by Pierre Mulele went on a rampage in Kwilu, a province in western Congo. Several missionaries were killed; dozens of villages and bridges were burned. Although the Congolese government troops were able eventually to quell the disturbances there, they were unsuccessful in controlling armed bands roaming throughout Kivu central province where the rebels sought to seize administrative control of the larger towns.

By the middle of the year, the situation had become so threatening that President Joseph Kasavubu declared Kivu to be in a state of emergency. Simultaneously, Premier Cyrille Adoula appealed to the United Nations (UN) requesting that a 600-troop Nigerian contingent of the UN's military force be sent to the area. However, with the June 30 deadline for the withdrawal of UN troops looming less than a month away, UN Secretary-General U Thant turned down the request, suggesting instead that Adoula negotiate a bilateral agreement with Nigeria for assistance in Congo's highly explosive state.

On June 23, violence had broken out in Stanleyville, Congo's third largest city, bringing on its heels the imposition of a city-wide 6 P.M.-to-6 A.M. curfew. In less than a week, rebel forces had seized Albertville, an important town in eastern Congo, and set up a revolutionary regime. Rebellion and chaos continued to spread northward and westward virtually without opposition.

Such was the internal situation in the Congo on June 30, when the rearguard of the once 20,000-man strong UN peace-keeping force left the country after a four-year sojourn. Just three hours later, Congolese President Joseph Kasavubu revealed that Premier Cyrille Adoula and his government had resigned. The following day, Kasavubu called on Moise Tshombe to help him form a new government. Tshombe,

275

United Press Int.

MISSIONARY MARTYR, Dr. Paul Carlson, left, is greeted here by Congolese children to whom he devoted his practice. He was slain a few weeks later by rebels.

the former president of Katanga province whose secessionist activities had been largely responsible for the chaotic conditions in Congo, had returned from self-exile on June 26.

On July 10, Tshombe was sworn in as premier. He faced the twofold task of putting an end to the wave of rebellion sweeping the country and of simultaneously meeting a nine-month target date set for the holding of national elections. Tshombe immediately set out on a nationwide tour, calling for an end to the bloodshed, and at the same time calling on the rebellious faction to cooperate with the central government in the interests of national unity. But Tshombe's tour theme, "Give me three months, and I will give you a new Congo," was not enough to quench the fires of revolt. In mid-August, he appealed to Ethiopia, Liberia, the Malagasy Republic, Nigeria, and Senegal for military assistance. Early in September, he asked that the Organization of African Unity (OAU) be convened in extraordinary session to discuss the rebellion in his country, which he maintained was being supported by neighboring Congo (Brazzaville) and Burundi.

Meanwhile, an attempt was made to strengthen the central government. A 120-man commission, which had been appointed by the president to revise the constitution, subsequently recommended a new one under which a strong presidential form of government would replace the existing parliamentary system. Under the new document, too, motions of confidence and censure would be outlawed, leaving conviction of treason, violation of the constitution, and corruption as the only reasons for which a president and his ministers could be ousted. The work of the constitutional commission won national approval in a referendum that began June 27 and ended July 10.

Hostages Held. Rebellion continued to flare throughout the nation, particularly in Stanleyville where a rebel regime headed by Christophe Gbenye had announced the establishment of a Congolese People's Republic on September 7. Earlier, the Stanleyville rebels had begun rounding up all of the city's white men, women, and children to be held as hostages against any air raids by the Congolese government. On October 28, the rebels disclosed that Dr. Paul Earle Carlson, a 36-year-old medical missionary, had been arrested and brought to rebel headquarters on charges of "spying" (see CARLSON, PAUL EARLE).

By November 7, the number of white hostages in rebel hands included 60 Americans, 800 Belgians, and 500 other foreigners. Whenever their fortunes ebbed, the rebels threatened to execute Dr. Carlson, who had been sentenced to death by a military tribunal. They turned a deaf ear to pleas for the safety of the hostages that were repeatedly made by the United States and Belgium. On November 24, a rescue mission consisting of 600 Belgian paratroopers flown in U.S. planes landed near Stanleyville. Minutes before the paratroop drop, however, Dr. Carlson and at least 18 men, women, and children were executed by the rebel soldiers. By November 28, when the airlift ended, about 1,700 foreigners had been evacuated. Some 900 others, however, remained, and at year's end their fate was uncertain.

On the economic front, noteworthy developments took place. The financial dispute that had existed between Congo and Belgium since Congolese independence in 1960 was finally settled. It provided for payment of the Congolese preindependence debt and a schedule of indemnification payments to Belgian victims of internal disturbances in Congo since 1960. The agreement also committed Belgium to a $3,600,000 program for the development of cotton plantations in Congo. See BELGIUM.

Earlier, in April, the government announced it had achieved its first balanced budget in four years of independence. Finance Minister Emmanuel Bamba indicated that the country's revenues for fiscal 1964-1965 would match the budgeted expenditures of about $229,000,000.

Population: 15,200,000. **Government:** President Joseph Kasavubu; Premier Moise Tshombe. **Foreign Trade:** exports, $117,000,000; imports $130,000,000. **Principal Exports:** coffee, copper, crude rubber, palm oil. BENJAMIN E. THOMAS

See also AFRICA.

United Press Int.

JUBILANT PREMIER Moise Tshombe, above, is borne aloft by admiring supporters after his return from exile to head the Congolese central government. Weary hostages held by Congolese rebels reach safety in Léopoldville, bottom left, but victims in Stanleyville, bottom right, remain where they were massacred. The body clad in white trousers, center, is that of U.S. medical missionary Paul Carlson.

Wide World

Wide World

CONGRESS OF
THE UNITED STATES

THE SECOND SESSION of the 88th Congress of the United States "enacted more major legislation, met more national needs, disposed of more national issues, than any other session in this century or the last." This was the grateful tribute President Lyndon B. Johnson paid to the U.S. lawmakers in a "Salute to Congress" party on the White House lawn in August. And by the time the session adjourned on October 3, the list of enacted bills had grown to a total of 409, from 257 in the first session. Among the major measures passed in the second session, and their dates of enactment, were: the tax cut of $11,500,000,000 a year, February 26; wheat and cotton price supports, April 11; Civil Rights Act, July 2; urban mass transit aid, July 9; $947,500,000 war on poverty, August 20; $1,100,000,000 Housing Act of 1964, September 2; wilderness preservation system, September 3; and the Land and Water Conservation Act, September 3.

Wide World

The State of the Union message, President Johnson's first, asked Congress on Jan. 8, 1964, to do "more for civil rights than the last hundred sessions combined," to declare "all-out war on human poverty and unemployment," to reform "our tangled transportation and transit policies." All this and more could be done without an increase in spending, the President said.

The second session appropriated $105,962,918,996; the total administration request had been for $110,097,358,556. In its two sessions, the 88th Congress authorized spending in excess of $200,000,000,000—more than any other Congress, in peace or in war.

Tax Reduction was the first major achievement of the second session. The statute aimed at an eventual annual income tax reduction of $11,500,000,000—about $9,100,000,000 for individuals, and $2,400,000,000 for corporations. President Johnson called it "the single most important step that we have taken to strengthen our economy since World War II." With the boom, some economists were projecting even larger tax savings. See BUSINESS; TAXATION; Section One, SYLVIA PORTER ON THE ECONOMY.

Civil Rights. Only after a historic Senate cloture vote had choked off a 73-day Southern filibuster on June 10, was a compromise bill finally accepted by both houses of Congress. It was signed into law on the evening of July 2. For a detailed account of how the most far-reaching civil rights legislation since Reconstruction days became law, see Section Two, CONGRESS MAKES A DECISION; for its provisions and later developments, see CIVIL LIBERTIES; NEGRO.

War on Poverty. In August, Congress authorized a $947,500,000 offensive in President Johnson's wide-ranging war against poverty. It provided for aiding rural families, setting up a domestic peace corps, and stimulating community campaigns against poverty. Also, in providing for retraining and edu-

END OF A HISTORIC CONGRESS. House page boys toss papers into the air to celebrate the 88th Congress's adjournment on October 3.

Wide World

MONUMENTAL $86,400,000 Rayburn House Office Building was rushed toward completion to accommodate incoming members of the 89th Congress.

cating young people and setting up a part-time job program for college students, the anti-poverty legislation followed up the 88th Congress's earlier steps to bolster U.S. education. See EDUCATION; JOB CORPS; SOCIAL WELFARE (Close-Up); VISTA; Section One, LAWRENCE A. CREMIN ON EDUCATION.

Congress also authorized the expansion of the pilot food-stamp plan into a nationwide program. In October, Congress appropriated $861,550,000 to finance the anti-poverty program. In Congress's scramble to adjourn, however, the authorization of $1,060,200,000 in special aid to the poverty-stricken, Appalachian region failed to pass the House.

Urban Mass Transit. Late in June, Congress completed action on a bill providing $375,000,000 in federal grants over a three-year period to help metropolitan areas improve commuter bus, subway, and train services (see TRANSIT). In another bill, it appropriated $2,400,000,000 for road construction over two years, beginning July 1, 1965.

In August, Congress approved $558,000,000 in salary increases for some 1,700,000 civilian federal employees. Senators, Representatives, and most federal judges received annual increases of $7,500.

Conservation Congress was one of the titles the productive second session earned. It passed landmark legislation providing for parks and outdoor recreation. It voted:

• A Federal Land and Water Conservation Fund to finance and develop state and federal park and recreation areas (see OUTDOOR RECREATION).

• A 4,300-acre National Seashore park at Fire Island, off Long Island, New York, and the nation's first new mainland National Park in 17 years— Canyonlands in southeastern Utah (see PARKS).

• A National Wilderness Preservation System that brought immediate statutory protection to 9,100,000 acres of undeveloped National Forest lands (see Section Two, CALL TO THE WILDERNESS).

Foreign Affairs. During the Tonkin Gulf naval crisis in Vietnam in August, Congress adopted a joint resolution giving the President prior sanction to take measures to repel aggression against U.S. forces. Congress also approved "all necessary steps" of the President to help defend any Southeast Asia Treaty Organization (SEATO) power. In May, the House reversed an earlier stand and approved a $312,000,000 contribution to the International Development Association, a World Bank affiliate.

After long, futile maneuvering to tack a reapportionment rider onto the foreign aid bill, Congress finally passed a $3,250,000,000 appropriation—the smallest amount of foreign aid in five years. See STATE GOVERNMENT; SUPREME COURT (Close-Up).

In Economic Legislation, Congress voted to:

• Tighten regulation of the securities industry and tax U.S. citizens' purchases of foreign securities (see STOCKS AND BONDS).

• Require banks to notify federal agencies of changes in control or management (see BANKS and BANKING).

• Reduce meat import levels 15 per cent below the 1963 record level (see LIVESTOCK).

• Change cotton and wheat price supports, including a subsidy to allow textile mills to buy U.S. cotton at the world price (see AGRICULTURE; TEXTILE).

• End the 18-year government monopoly on fissionable materials and put private nuclear power on its own after June, 1973 (see ATOMIC ENERGY).

• Strengthen control over sales of pesticides (see CHEMICAL INDUSTRY).

Other Legislation included:

• A National Council of Arts.

• A $287,600,000 program of federal aid for nurses training over a period of five years.

• $135,000,000 in federal aid to improve the nation's library services (see LIBRARY).

• Provision of free legal counsel for needy defendants being tried in federal courts on charges of felony

MEMBERS OF THE UNITED STATES SENATE

The Senate of the 89th Congress consists of 68 Democrats and 32 Republicans, compared with the 67 Democrats and 33 Republicans for the 88th Congress. Senators shown starting their terms in 1965 were elected for the first time in the Nov. 3, 1964, elections. Those shown ending their current terms in 1971 were re-elected to the Senate in the same balloting. The second date in each listing shows when the term of a previously elected Senator expires.

State	Birthday	Birthplace	Term
ALABAMA			
Lister Hill, D.	Dec. 29, '94	Montgomery, Ala.	1938-69
John J. Sparkman, D.	Dec. 20, '99	near Hartselle, Ala.	1946-67
ALASKA			
E. L. "Bob" Bartlett, D.	Apr. 20, '04	Seattle, Wash.	1959-67
Ernest Gruening, D.	Feb. 6, '87	New York City, N.Y.	1959-69
ARIZONA			
Carl T. Hayden, D.	Oct. 2, '77	Hayden's Ferry (now Tempe), Ariz.	1927-69
Paul J. Fannin, R.	Jan. 29, '07	Ashland, Ky.	1965-71
ARKANSAS			
John L. McClellan, D.	Feb. 25, '96	Sheridan, Ark.	1943-67
J. William Fulbright, D.	Apr. 9, '05	Sumner, Mo.	1945-69
CALIFORNIA			
Thomas H. Kuchel, R.	Aug. 15, '10	Anaheim, Calif.	1953-69
George L. Murphy, R.	July 4, '02	New Haven, Conn.	1965-71
COLORADO			
Gordon L. Allott, R.	Jan. 2, '07	Pueblo, Colo.	1955-67
Peter H. Dominick, R.	July 7, '15	Stamford, Conn.	1963-69
CONNECTICUT			
Thomas J. Dodd, D.	May 15, '07	Norwich, Conn.	1959-71
Abraham A. Ribicoff, D.	Apr. 9, '10	New Britain, Conn.	1963-69
DELAWARE			
John J. Williams, R.	May 17, '04	near Frankford, Del.	1947-71
J. Caleb Boggs, R.	May 15, '09	Kent County, Del.	1961-67
FLORIDA			
Spessard L. Holland, D.	July 10, '92	Bartow, Fla.	1946-71
George A. Smathers, D.	Nov. 14, '13	Atlantic City, N.J.	1951-69
GEORGIA			
Richard B. Russell, D.	Nov. 2, '97	Winder, Ga.	1933-67
Herman E. Talmadge, D.	Aug. 9, '13	near McRae, Ga.	1957-69
HAWAII			
Hiram L. Fong, R.	Oct. 1, '07	Honolulu, Hawaii	1959-71
Daniel Ken Inouye, D.	Sept. 7, '24	Honolulu, Hawaii	1963-69
IDAHO			
Frank Church, D.	July 25, '24	Boise, Idaho	1957-69
Leonard B. Jordan, R.	May 15, '99	Mount Pleasant, Utah	1962-67
ILLINOIS			
Paul H. Douglas, D.	May 26, '92	Salem, Mass.	1949-67
Everett M. Dirksen, R.	Jan. 4, '96	Pekin, Ill.	1951-69
INDIANA			
R. Vance Hartke, D.	May 31, '19	Stendal, Ind.	1959-71
Birch E. Bayh, D.	Jan. 22, '28	Terre Haute, Ind.	1963-69
IOWA			
Bourke B. Hickenlooper, R.	July 21, '96	Blockton, Ia.	1945-69
Jack R. Miller, R.	June 6, '16	Chicago, Ill.	1961-67
KANSAS			
Frank Carlson, R.	Jan. 23, '93	Concordia, Kans.	1950-69
James B. Pearson, R.	May 7, '20	Nashville, Tenn.	1962-67
KENTUCKY			
John Sherman Cooper, R.	Aug. 23, '01	Somerset, Ky.	1956-67
Thruston B. Morton, R.	Aug. 19, '07	Louisville, Ky.	1957-67
LOUISIANA			
Allen J. Ellender, Sr., D.	Sept. 24, '90	Montegut, La.	1937-67
Russell B. Long, D.	Nov. 3, '18	Shreveport, La.	1948-69
MAINE			
Margaret Chase Smith, R.	Dec. 14, '97	Skowhegan, Me.	1949-67
Edmund S. Muskie, D.	Mar. 28, '14	Rumford, Me.	1959-71
MARYLAND			
Daniel B. Brewster, D.	Nov. 23, '23	Baltimore County, Md.	1963-69
Joseph D. Tydings, D.	May 4, '28	Asheville, N.C.	1965-71
MASSACHUSETTS			
Leverett Saltonstall, R.	Sept. 1, '92	Chestnut Hill, Mass.	1945-67
Edward M. Kennedy, D.	Feb. 22, '32	Brookline, Mass.	1962-71
MICHIGAN			
Patrick V. McNamara, D.	Oct. 4, '94	North Weymouth, Mass.	1955-67
Philip A. Hart, D.	Dec. 10, '12	Bryn Mawr, Pa.	1959-71
MINNESOTA			
Eugene J. McCarthy, D.	Mar. 29, '16	Watkins, Minn.	1959-71
Walter F. Mondale, D.	Jan. 5, '28	Ceylon, Minn.	1964-67
MISSISSIPPI			
James O. Eastland, D.	Nov. 28, '04	Doddsville, Miss.	1943-67
John Cornelius Stennis, D.	Aug. 3, '01	Kemper County, Miss.	1947-71
MISSOURI			
Stuart Symington, D.	June 26, '01	Amherst, Mass.	1953-71
Edward V. Long, D.	July 18, '08	Lincoln County, Mo.	1960-69
MONTANA			
Mike J. Mansfield, D.	Mar. 16, '03	New York City, N.Y.	1953-71
Lee Metcalf, D.	Jan. 28, '11	Stevensville, Mont.	1961-67
NEBRASKA			
Roman Lee Hruska, R.	Aug. 16, '04	David City, Nebr.	1954-71
Carl T. Curtis, R.	Mar. 15, '05	near Minden, Nebr.	1955-67
NEVADA			
Alan Bible, D.	Nov. 20, '09	Lovelock, Nev.	1954-69
Howard W. Cannon, D.	Jan. 26, '12	St. George, Utah	1959-71
NEW HAMPSHIRE			
Norris Cotton, R.	May 11, '00	Warren, N.H.	1954-59
Thomas J. McIntyre, D.	Feb. 20, '15	Laconia, N.H.	1962-67
NEW JERSEY			
Clifford P. Case, R.	Apr. 16, '04	Franklin Park, N.J.	1955-67
Harrison A. Williams, Jr., D.	Dec. 10, '19	Plainfield, N.J.	1959-71
NEW MEXICO			
Clinton P. Anderson, D.	Oct. 23, '95	Centerville, S.Dak.	1949-67
Joseph M. Montoya, D.	Sept. 24, '15	Penablanca, N.Mex.	1965-71
NEW YORK			
Jacob K. Javits, R.	May 18, '04	New York City, N.Y.	1957-69
Robert F. Kennedy, D.	Nov. 20, '25	Boston, Mass.	1965-71
NORTH CAROLINA			
Sam J. Ervin, Jr., D.	Sept. 27, '96	Morganton, N.C.	1954-69
B. Everett Jordan, D.	Sept. 8, '96	Ramseur, N.C.	1958-67
NORTH DAKOTA			
Milton R. Young, R.	Dec. 6, '97	Berlin, N.Dak.	1945-69
Quentin N. Burdick, D.	June 19, '08	Munich, N. Dak.	1960-71
OHIO			
Frank J. Lausche, D.	Nov. 14, '95	Cleveland, Ohio	1957-69
Stephen M. Young, D.	May 4, '89	near Norwalk, Ohio	1959-71
OKLAHOMA			
A. S. Mike Monroney, D.	Mar. 2, '02	Oklahoma City, Okla.	1951-69
Fred R. Harris, D.	Nov. 13, '30	Walters, Okla.	1965-71
OREGON			
Wayne L. Morse, D.	Oct. 20, '00	near Madison, Wis.	1945-69
Maurine Brown Neuberger, D.	Jan. 9, '07	Cloverdale, Ore.	1960-67
PENNSYLVANIA			
Joseph S. Clark, Jr., D.	Oct. 21, '01	Philadelphia, Pa.	1957-69
Hugh D. Scott, Jr., R.	Nov. 11, '00	Fredericksburg, Va.	1959-71
RHODE ISLAND			
John O. Pastore, D.	Mar. 17, '07	Providence, R.I.	1950-71
Claiborne de Borda Pell, D.	Nov. 22, '18	New York City, N.Y.	1961-67
SOUTH CAROLINA			
Olin D. Johnston, D.	Nov. 18, '96	Honea Path, S.C.	1945-69
Strom Thurmond, R.	Dec. 5, '02	Edgefield, S.C.	1956-67
SOUTH DAKOTA			
Karl E. Mundt, R.	June 3, '00	Humboldt, S.Dak.	1948-67
George S. McGovern, D.	July 19, '22	Avon, S.Dak.	1963-69
TENNESSEE			
Albert A. Gore, D.	Dec. 26, '07	Granville, Tenn.	1953-71
Ross Bass, D.	Mar. 17, '18	near Pulaski, Tenn.	1965-67
TEXAS			
Ralph W. Yarborough, D.	June 8, '03	Chandler, Tex.	1957-71
John G. Tower, R.	Sept. 29, '25	Houston, Tex.	1961-67
UTAH			
Wallace F. Bennett, R.	Nov. 13, '98	Salt Lake City, Utah	1951-69
Frank E. Moss, D.	Sept. 23, '11	Holladay, Utah	1959-71
VERMONT			
George D. Aiken, R.	Aug. 20, '92	Dummerston, Vt.	1941-59
Winston L. Prouty, R.	Sept. 1, '06	Newport, Vt.	1959-71
VIRGINIA			
Harry Flood Byrd, D.	June 10, '87	Martinsburg, W.Va.	1933-71
A. Willis Robertson, D.	May 27, '87	Martinsburg, W.Va.	1946-67
WASHINGTON			
Warren G. Magnuson, D.	Apr. 12, '05	Moorhead, Minn.	1944-69
Henry M. Jackson, D.	May 31, '12	Everett, Wash.	1953-71
WEST VIRGINIA			
Jennings Randolph, D.	Mar. 8, '02	Salem, W.Va.	1958-67
Robert C. Byrd, D.	Jan. 15, '18	N. Wilkesboro, N.C.	1959-71
WISCONSIN			
William Proxmire, D.	Nov. 11, '15	Lake Forest, Ill.	1957-71
Gaylord A. Nelson, D.	June 4, '16	Clear Lake, Wis.	1963-69
WYOMING			
Gale W. McGee, D.	Mar. 17, '15	Lincoln, Nebr.	1959-71
Milward L. Simpson, R.	Nov. 12, '97	Jackson, Wyo.	1962-67

MEMBERS OF THE UNITED STATES HOUSE

The House of the 89th Congress consists of 295 Democrats and 140 Republicans, compared with 259 Democrats and 176 Republicans for the 88th Congress. Table shows congressional districts, winner and party affiliation. Asterisk denotes those who served in the 88th Congress. AL denotes "At Large."

ALABAMA
1. Jack Edwards, R.
2. William L. Dickinson, R.
3. George Andrews, D.*
4. Glenn Andrews, R.
5. Armistead I. Selden, Jr., D.*
6. John Buchanan, R.
7. James D. Martin, R.
8. Robert E. Jones, Jr., D.*

ALASKA
(AL) Ralph J. Rivers, D.*

ARIZONA
1. John J. Rhodes, R.*
2. Morris K. Udall, D.*
3. George F. Senner, Jr., D.*

ARKANSAS
1. E. C. Gathings, D.*
2. Wilbur D. Mills, D.*
3. James W. Trimble, D.*
4. Oren Harris, D.*

CALIFORNIA
1. Don H. Clausen, R.*
2. Harold T. Johnson, D.*
3. John E. Moss, D.*
4. Robert L. Leggett, D.*
5. Phillip Burton, D.*
6. William S. Mailliard, R.*
7. Jeffery Cohelan, D.*
8. George P. Miller, D.*
9. Don Edwards, D.*
10. Charles S. Gubser, R.*
11. J. Arthur Younger, R.*
12. Burt L. Talcott, R.*
13. Charles M. Teague, R.*
14. John F. Baldwin, Jr., R.*
15. John J. McFall, D.*
16. B. F. Sisk, D.*
17. Cecil R. King, D.*
18. Harlan Hagen, D.*
19. Chet Holifield, D.*
20. H. Allen Smith, R.*
21. Augustus F. Hawkins, D.*
22. James C. Corman, D.*
23. Del Clawson, R.*
24. Glenard P. Lipscomb, R.*
25. Ronald Brooks Cameron, D.*
26. James Roosevelt, D.*
27. Ed Reinecke, R.
28. Alphonzo Bell, R.*
29. George E. Brown, Jr., D.*
30. Edward R. Roybal, D.*
31. Charles H. Wilson, D.*
32. Craig Hosmer, R.*
33. Ken W. Dyal, D.
34. Richard T. Hanna, D.*
35. James B. Utt, R.*
36. Bob Wilson, R.*
37. Lionel Van Deerlin, D.*
38. John V. Tunney, D.

COLORADO
1. Byron G. Rogers, D.*
2. Roy H. McVicker, D.
3. Frank E. Evans, D.
4. Wayne N. Aspinall, D.*

CONNECTICUT
1. Emilio Q. Daddario, D.*
2. William L. St. Onge, D.*
3. Robert N. Giaimo, D.*
4. Donald J. Irwin, D.
5. John S. Monagan, D.*
6. Bernard F. Grabowski, D.*

DELAWARE
(AL) Harris B. McDowell, Jr., D.*

FLORIDA
1. Robert L. F. Sikes, D.*
2. Charles E. Bennett, D.*
3. Claude Pepper, D.*
4. Dante B. Fascell, D.*
5. A. Sydney Herlong, Jr., D.*
6. Paul G. Rogers, D.*
7. James A. Haley, D.*
8. D. R. (Billy) Matthews, D.*
9. Don Fuqua, D.*
10. Sam Gibbons, D.*
11. Edward J. Gurney, R.*
12. William C. Cramer, R.*

GEORGIA
1. G. Elliott Hagan, D.*
2. Maston O'Neal, D.
3. Howard H. Callaway, R.
4. James A. Mackay, D.
5. Charles L. Weltner, D.*
6. John J. Flynt, Jr., D.*
7. John W. Davis, D.*
8. J. Russell Tuten, D.*
9. Phil M. Landrum, D.*
10. Robert G. Stephens, Jr., D.*

HAWAII
(AL) Spark M. Matsunaga, D.*
(AL) Patsy T. Mink, D.

IDAHO
1. Compton I. White, D.*
2. George Hansen, R.

ILLINOIS
1. William L. Dawson, D.*.
2. Barratt O'Hara, D.*
3. William T. Murphy, D.*
4. Edward J. Derwinski, R.*
5. John C. Kluczynski, D.*
6. Daniel J. Ronan, D.
7. Frank Annunzio, D.
8. Dan Rostenkowski, D.*
9. Sidney R. Yates, D.
10. Harold R. Collier, R.*
11. Roman C. Pucinski, D.*
12. Robert McClory, R.*
13. Donald Rumsfeld, R.*
14. John N. Erlenborn, R.
15. Charlotte T. Reid, R.*
16. John B. Anderson, R.*
17. Leslie C. Arends, R.*
18. Robert H. Michel, R.*
19. Gale Schisler, D.
20. Paul Findley, R.*
21. Kenneth J. Gray, D.*
22. William L. Springer, R.*
23. George E. Shipley, D.*
24. Melvin Price, D.*

INDIANA
1. Ray J. Madden, D.*
2. Charles A. Halleck, R.*
3. John Brademas, D.*
4. E. Ross Adair, R.*
5. J. Edward Roush, D.*
6. Richard L. Roudebush, R.*
7. William G. Bray, R.*
8. William E. Denton, D.*
9. Lee H. Hamilton, D.
10. Ralph Harvey, R.*
11. Andrew Jacobs, Jr., D.

IOWA
1. John R. Schmidhauser, D.
2. John C. Culver, D.
3. H. R. Gross, R.*
4. Bert Bandstra, D.
5. Neal Smith, D.*
6. Stanley L. Greigg, D.
7. John R. Hansen, D.

KANSAS
1. Robert Dole, R.*

2. Chester L. Mize, R.
3. Robert F. Ellsworth, R.*
4. Garner E. Shriver, R.*
5. Joe Skubitz, R.*

KENTUCKY
1. Frank A. Stubblefield, D.*
2. William H. Natcher, D.*
3. Charles P. Farnsley, D.
4. Frank Chelf, D.*
5. Tim Lee Carter, R.
6. John C. Watts, D.*
7. Carl D. Perkins, D.*

LOUISIANA
1. F. Edward Hébert, D.*
2. Hale Boggs, D.*
3. Edwin E. Willis, D.*
4. Joe D. Waggonner, Jr., D.*
5. Otto E. Passman, D.*
6. James H. Morrison, D.*
7. T. A. Thompson, D.*
8. Speedy O. Long, D.

MAINE
1. Stanley R. Tupper, R.*
2. William D. Hathaway, D.

MARYLAND
1. Rogers C. B. Morton, R.*
2. Clarence D. Long, D.*
3. Edward A. Garmatz, D.*
4. George H. Fallon, D.*
5. Hervey G. Machen, D.
6. Charles McC. Mathias, Jr., R.*
7. Samuel N. Friedel, D.*
(AL) Carlton R. Sickles, D.*

MASSACHUSETTS
1. Silvio O. Conte, R.*
2. Edward P. Boland, D.*
3. Philip J. Philbin, D.*
4. Harold D. Donohue, D.*
5. F. Bradford Morse, R.*
6. William H. Bates, R.*
7. Torbert H. Macdonald, D.*
8. Thomas P. O'Neill, Jr., D.*
9. John W. McCormack, D.*
10. Joseph W. Martin, Jr., R.*
11. James A. Burke, D.*
12. Hastings Keith, R.*

MICHIGAN
1. John Conyers, Jr., D.
2. Weston E. Vivian, D.
3. Paul H. Todd, Jr., D.
4. Edward Hutchinson, R.*
5. Gerald R. Ford, R.*
6. Charles E. Chamberlain, R.*
7. John C. Mackie, D.
8. James Harvey, R.*
9. Robert P. Griffin, R.*
10. Elford A. Cederberg, R.*
11. Raymond F. Clevenger, D.
12. James G. O'Hara, D.*
13. Charles C. Diggs, Jr., D.*
14. Lucien N. Nedzi, D.*
15. William D. Ford, D.
16. John D. Dingell, D.*
17. Martha W. Griffiths, D.*
18. William S. Broomfield, R.*
19. Billie S. Farnum, D.

MINNESOTA
1. Albert H. Quie, R.*
2. Ancher Nelsen, R.*
3. Clark MacGregor, R.*
4. Joseph E. Karth, D.*
5. Donald M. Fraser, D.*
6. Alec G. Olson, D.*
7. Odin Langen, R.*
8. John A. Blatnik, D.*

MISSISSIPPI
1. Thomas G. Abernethy, D.*
2. Jamie L. Whitten, D.*
3. John Bell Williams, D.*
4. Prentiss Walker, R.
5. William M. Colmer, D.*

MISSOURI
1. Frank M. Karsten, D.*
2. Thomas B. Curtis, R.*
3. Leonor K. (Mrs. John B.) Sullivan, D.*
4. Wm. J. Randall, D.*
5. Richard Bolling, D.*
6. W. R. Hull, Jr., D.*
7. Durward G. Hall, R.*
8. Richard H. Ichord, D.*
9. William L. Hungate, D.*
10. Paul C. Jones, D.*

MONTANA
1. Arnold Olsen, D.*
2. James F. Battin, R.*

NEBRASKA
1. Clair Callan, D.
2. Glenn Cunningham, R.*
3. Dave Martin, R.*

NEVADA
(AL) Walter S. Baring, D.*

NEW HAMPSHIRE
1. J. Oliva Huot, D.
2. James C. Cleveland, R.*

NEW JERSEY
1. William T. Cahill, R.*
2. Thomas C. McGrath, Jr., D.
3. James J. Howard, D.
4. Frank Thompson, Jr., D.*
5. Peter H. B. Frelinghuysen, R.*
6. Florence P. Dwyer, R.*
7. William B. Widnall, R.*
8. Charles S. Joelson, D.*
9. Henry Helstoski, D.
10. Peter W. Rodino, Jr., D.*
11. Joseph G. Minish, D.*
12. Paul J. Krebs, D.
13. Cornelius E. Gallagher, D.*
14. Dominick V. Daniels, D.*
15. Edward J. Patten, D.*

NEW MEXICO
(AL) E. S. Johnny Walker, D.
(AL) Thomas G. Morris, D.*

NEW YORK
1. Otis G. Pike, D.*
2. James R. Grover, Jr., R.*
3. Lester L. Wolff, D.
4. John W. Wydler, R.*
5. Herbert Tenzer, D.
6. Seymour Halpern, R.*
7. Joseph P. Addabbo, D.*
8. Benjamin S. Rosenthal, D.*
9. James J. Delaney, D.*
10. Emanuel Celler, D.*
11. Eugene J. Keogh, D.*
12. Edna F. Kelly, D.*
13. Abraham J. Multer, D.*
14. John J. Rooney, D.*
15. Hugh L. Carey, D.*
16. John M. Murphy, D.*
17. John V. Lindsay, R.*
18. Adam C. Powell, D.*
19. Leonard Farbstein, D.*
20. William F. Ryan, D.*
21. James H. Scheuer, D.
22. Jacob H. Gilbert, D.*
23. Jonathan B. Bingham, D.
24. Paul A. Fino, R.*
25. Richard L. Ottinger, D.

26. Ogden R. Reid, R.*
27. John G. Dow, D.
28. Joseph Y. Resnick, D.
29. Leo W. O'Brien, D.*
30. Carleton J. King, R.*
31. Robert C. McEwen, R.
32. Alexander Pirnie, R.*
33. Howard W. Robison, R.*
34. James M. Hanley, D.
35. Samuel S. Stratton, D.*
36. Frank J. Horton, R.*
37. Barber B. Conable, Jr., R.
38. Charles E. Goodell, R.*
39. Richard D. McCarthy, D.
40. Henry P. Smith III, R.
41. Thaddeus J. Dulski, D.*

NORTH CAROLINA
1. Herbert C. Bonner, D.*
2. L. H. Fountain, D.*
3. David N. Henderson, D.*
4. Harold D. Cooley, D.*
5. Ralph J. Scott, D.
6. Horace R. Kornegay, D.*
7. Alton Lennon, D.*
8. Charles Raper Jonas, R.*
9. James T. Broyhill, R.*
10. Basil L. Whitener, D.*
11. Roy A. Taylor, D.*

NORTH DAKOTA
1. Mark Andrews, R.
2. Rolland Redlin, D.

OHIO
1. John J. Gilligan, D.
2. Donald D. Clancy, R.*
3. Rodney M. Love, D.
4. William M. McCulloch, R.*
5. Delbert L. Latta, R.*
6. William H. Harsha, R.*
7. Clarence J. Brown, R.*
8. Jackson E. Betts, R.*
9. Thomas L. Ashley, D.*
10. Walter H. Moeller, D.
11. J. William Stanton, R.
12. Samuel L. Devine, R.*
13. Charles A. Mosher, R.*
14. William H. Ayres, R.*
15. Robert T. Secrest, D.*
16. Frank T. Bow, R.*

17. John M. Ashbrook, R.*
18. Wayne L. Hays, D.*
19. Michael J. Kirwan, D.*
20. Michael A. Feighan, D.*
21. Charles A. Vanik, D.*
22. Frances P. Bolton, R.*
23. William E. Minshall, R.*
(AL) Robert E. Sweeney, D.

OKLAHOMA
1. Page Belcher, R.*
2. Ed Edmondson, D.*
3. Carl Albert, D.*
4. Tom Steed, D.*
5. John Jarman, D.*
6. Jed Johnson, Jr., D.

OREGON
1. Wendell Wyatt, R.*
2. Al Ullman, D.*
3. Edith Green, D.*
4. Robert B. Duncan, D.*

PENNSYLVANIA
1. William A. Barrett, D.*
2. Robert N. C. Nix, D.*
3. James A. Byrne, D.*
4. Herman Toll, D.*
5. William J. Green, III, D.*
6. George M. Rhodes, D.*
7. G. Robert Watkins, R.
8. Willard S. Curtin, R.*
9. Paul B. Dague, R.*
10. Joseph M. McDade, R.*
11. Daniel J. Flood, D.*
12. J. Irving Whalley, R.*
13. Richard S. Schweiker, R.*
14. William S. Moorhead, R.*
15. Fred B. Rooney, D.*
16. John C. Kunkel, R.*
17. Herman T. Schneebeli, R.*
18. Robert J. Corbett, R.*
19. N. Neiman Craley, Jr., D.
20. Elmer J. Holland, D.*
21. John H. Dent, D.*
22. John P. Saylor, R.*
23. Albert W. Johnson, R.*
24. Joseph P. Vigorito, D.
25. Frank M. Clark, D.*
26. Thomas E. Morgan, D.*
27. James G. Fulton, R.*

RHODE ISLAND
1. Fernand J. St. Germain, D.*
2. John E. Fogarty, D.*

SOUTH CAROLINA
1. L. Mendel Rivers, D.*
2. Albert W. Watson, D.*
3. W. J. Bryan Dorn, D.*
4. Robert T. Ashmore, D.*
5. Tom S. Gettys, D.*
6. John L. McMillan, D.*

SOUTH DAKOTA
1. Ben Reifel, R.*
2. E. Y. Berry, R.*

TENNESSEE
1. James H. (Jimmy) Quillen, R.*
2. John J. Duncan, R.
3. W. E. (Bill) Brock, R.*
4. Joe L. Evins, D.*
5. Richard Fulton, D.*
6. William R. Anderson, D.
7. Tom Murray, D.*
8. Robert A. Everett, D.*
9. George W. Grider, D.

TEXAS
1. Wright Patman, D.*
2. Jack Brooks, D.*
3. Lindley Beckworth, D.*
4. Ray Roberts, D.*
5. Earl Cabell, D.
6. Olin E. Teague, D.*
7. John Dowdy, D.*
8. Albert Thomas, D.*
9. Clark W. Thompson, D.*
10. J. J. Pickle, D.*
11. W. R. Poage, D.*
12. Jim Wright, D.*
13. Graham Purcell, D.*
14. John Young, D.*
15. Eligio de la Garza, D.
16. Richard White, D.
17. Omar Burleson, D.*
18. Walter Rogers, D.*
19. George Mahon, D.*
20. Henry B. Gonzalez, D.*
21. O. C. Fisher, D.*
22. Bob Casey, D.*
(AL) Joe R. Pool, D.*

UTAH
1. Laurence J. Burton, R.*
2. David S. King, D.

VERMONT
(AL) Robert T. Stafford, R.*

VIRGINIA
1. Thomas N. Downing, D.*
2. Porter Hardy, Jr., D.*
3. David E. Satterfield III, D.
4. Watkins M. Abbitt, D.*
5. William M. Tuck, D.*
6. Richard H. Poff, R.*
7. John O. Marsh, Jr., D.*
8. Howard W. Smith, D.*
9. W. Pat Jennings, D.*
10. Joel T. Broyhill, R.*

WASHINGTON
1. Thomas M. Pelly, R.*
2. Lloyd Meeds, D.
3. Julia Butler Hansen, D.*
4. Catherine May, R.*
5. Thomas S. Foley, D.
6. Floyd V. Hicks, D.
7. Brock Adams, D.

WEST VIRGINIA
1. Arch A. Moore, Jr., R.*
2. Harley O. Staggers, D.*
3. John M. Slack, Jr., D.*
4. Ken Hechler, D.*
5. James Kee, D.

WISCONSIN
1. Lynn E. Stalbaum, D.
2. Robert W. Kastenmeier, D.*
3. Vernon W. Thomson, R.*
4. Clement J. Zablocki, D.*
5. Henry S. Reuss, D.*
6. John A. Race, D.
7. Melvin R. Laird, R.*
8. John W. Byrnes, R.*
9. Glenn R. Davis, R.
10. Alvin E. O'Konski, R.*

WYOMING
(AL) Teno Roncalio, D.

PUERTO RICO
Resident Commissioner
Santiago Polanco-Abreu, D.

---

or misdemeanor (see COURTS AND LAWS; CRIME).
• Increased benefits for veterans and their pensioned widows (see VETERANS).

Unfinished Business. In addition to aid to Appalachia, other major legislative casualties included: health and hospital insurance for the aged under Social Security (Medicare); increased Social Security benefits; rail-and-water transportation reforms; liberalization of immigration laws; "truth in lending" and "truth in packaging" laws; and revision of presidential succession.

Senate Inquiries. During 1964, the Senate Rules Committee intermittently inquired into the affairs of Robert G. "Bobby" Baker, former secretary to the Democratic majority in the Senate. On a yearly salary of $19,600, Baker reportedly amassed a fortune of $2,000,000. In July, the committee found Baker "guilty of many gross improprieties" but not of breaking the law. Republican charges of "whitewash" ensued. After a 75-to-13 Senate vote, the committee reopened the inquiry October 1. It recessed for the elections and reconvened on December 1. See BAKER, ROBERT "BOBBY" G.

On September 30, a majority report of the Senate Permanent Subcommittee on Investigations criticized the U.S. Department of Agriculture for its "slipshod" methods but exonerated it of any wrongdoings in connection with the cotton-allotment transactions of Billie Sol Estes. The committee's Republican minority issued an angry dissent.

Leaders. The second session of the 88th Congress kept its first-session chiefs in their posts:

In the Senate, Carl Hayden of Arizona, president *pro tempore;* Mike Mansfield of Montana, majority leader; Hubert H. Humphrey of Minnesota, majority whip; Everett M. Dirksen of Illinois, minority leader; and Thomas H. Kuchel of California, Republican whip.

In the House, John McCormack of Massachusetts, Speaker; T. Hale Boggs of Louisiana, Democratic whip; and Charles A. Halleck of Indiana, minority leader. Leslie C. Arends of Illinois was appointed Republican whip.　　　　CAROL L. THOMPSON

See also CITY; DEMOCRATIC PARTY; ELECTIONS; HOUSING; REPUBLICAN PARTY; Section One, JAMES B. RESTON ON THE NATION.

283

CONNOR, JOHN T. (1914-   ), leading drug company executive, on December 16 was named to succeed Luther H. Hodges as Secretary of Commerce. Connor resigned as president of Merck & Company, Inc., to assume the post in mid-January, 1965. He was vice-chairman and founder of the National Independent Committee for Johnson-Humphrey during the 1964 election campaign.

Connor grew up in Syracuse, N.Y., and graduated *magna cum laude* from Syracuse University. He then attended Harvard Law School where he was one of a group of promising students surrounding the future Supreme Court Justice Felix Frankfurter.

His first experience in Washington came in 1942 when he went to work as a lawyer for the Lend-Lease Administration, and shortly thereafter for the Office of Scientific Research and Development. In 1944, he went on active duty with the Marine Corps. He joined Merck & Co. in 1947 as general attorney.

See also CABINET; PRESIDENT OF THE UNITED STATES.

CONSERVATION. See Section Two, CALL TO THE WILDERNESS; FORESTRY AND FOREST PRODUCTS; PARKS; SOIL CONSERVATION; WATER AND FLOOD CONTROL; WILDLIFE.

CONSTANTINE XIII (1940-   ) became king of Greece on March 6, succeeding his father King Paul I, who died in Athens at the age of 63. The early months of Constantine's reign were overshadowed by the civil war between Greek and Turkish Cypriots on Cyprus. See CYPRUS; GREECE.

King Constantine was born on June 2, 1940, during the Italian invasion of Greece. He was only nine months old when his family fled with him, first to Crete, then to Cairo, and finally to South Africa.

From the age of 10, he was regularly included in meetings with government ministers on orders of King Paul. It was, the king said, part of the process of training the boy to be "a constitutional monarch who may reign but never govern."

On September 18, Constantine was married to Princess Anne-Marie of Denmark.   WALTER F. MORSE

CONTRACT BRIDGE. See BRIDGE, CONTRACT.

COSTA RICA. The Irazu volcano continued to cast a disastrous pall over the nation. In August, it was estimated that property and production losses resulting from the volcanic eruptions, which had been spewing ashes almost continuously since March, 1963, had reached $160,000,000. One quarter of the loss was in coffee, the republic's chief export. The 1964-1965 coffee crop was nearly 30 per cent less than the preceding year's crop.

The United States granted Costa Rica a $1,000,000 loan for disaster relief. It also sent corn to help feed cattle in the stricken farm areas as well as a Seabee construction team and earth-moving equipment.

Despite its problems, the republic announced plans for an industrial and free trade zone. It would consist of three areas: Limón on the Caribbean, Puntarenas on the Pacific, and El Coco airport, which is near San José.

Population: 1,425,000. **Government:** President Francisco José Orlich Bolmarcich. **Foreign Trade:** exports, $134,000,000; imports, $116,000,000. **Principal Exports:** bananas, cacao, coffee.   MARY C. WEBSTER

See also LATIN AMERICA.

COURTS AND LAWS. Events arising out of the assassination of President John F. Kennedy were of deep significance in the law. The Warren Commission, after nearly a year of careful investigation, issued its detailed report on the facts surrounding the assassination and came to definite conclusions (see WARREN COMMISSION; THE WARREN REPORT). It recommended that ". . . representatives of the bar, law enforcement associations, and the news media should work together to establish ethical standards concerning the collection and presentation of information to the public so that there will be no interference with pending criminal investigations."

Ruby Case Evaluated. The trial of Jack Ruby for the murder of Lee Harvey Oswald dominated the news of the courts for several months. The news handling of the case served to bring about a re-evaluation of the press coverage of crimes and criminal trials (see PUBLISHING; RUBY, JACK).

The American Bar Association (ABA) investigated charges that two of its Canons of Judicial Ethics had been violated. Neither canon, however, has been specifically adopted in Texas. Canon 20 prohibits a lawyer from making any comments for publication that may interfere with a fair trial. Canon 35 forbids the taking of photographs in the courtroom, and undignified broadcasting or televising of court proceedings. The ABA, under Chief Judge J. Edward Lumbard, U.S. Court of Appeals, Second Circuit, launched an extensive research project to draw up a new code of minimum standards for criminal justice.

And in August, Attorney General Robert F. Kennedy appointed James Vorenberg, Harvard Law School professor, to head a watchdog Office of Criminal Justice in the Department of Justice.

New U.S. Legislation affecting law enforcement and the courts included:

• The far-reaching Civil Rights Act of 1964 (see CIVIL LIBERTIES).

• Pay raises of $7,500 per year for federal judges and $4,500 a year for Supreme Court justices.

• The Criminal Justice Act, which authorized federal courts to compensate attorneys for representing indigent defendants.

The National Conference of State Trial Judges broke precedent among the common law countries in opening a National College for new trial judges. Ninety-two new judges from 47 states spent the month of July at the University of Colorado School of Law in Boulder working with experienced judges on some of the problems they will face on the bench.

State Court Decisions in several instances carried nationwide significance in indicating the possible direction of the development of the law. California ruled unconstitutional its statute that held adult children responsible for supporting parents committed to mental institutions. In both the District of Columbia and New Jersey, under certain circumstances, court-ordered blood transfusions to religious objectors were upheld.

Permanent residence in Alaska no longer was necessary to the granting of a divorce, that state's Supreme Court ruled. California held an auto dealer, with the manufacturer, liable for injuries resulting from defective brakes.

The law lost a venerable champion in 1964 with the death of 93-year-old Roscoe Pound, dean emeritus of the Harvard Law School (see DEATHS OF NOTABLE PERSONS). ERNEST C. FRIESEN, JR.

See also CITY; CONGRESS OF THE UNITED STATES; Section Two, CONGRESS MAKES A DECISION; STATE GOVERNMENT; SUPREME COURT.

CRIME. A federal court ruling, handed down in 1964, could result in the release of thousands of prisoners who could not be tried again because witnesses and evidence would no longer be available, some observers believed. They based this opinion on the fact that the U.S. Court of Appeals of the Second Circuit held on March 26, 1964, that the 1963 decision of the Supreme Court of the United States, *Gideon vs. Wainright*, was "retroactive without limit." That high court decision was considered a legal landmark because it established the principle that free legal services must be provided for defendants too poor to retain counsel. See 1963 YEAR BOOK, CIVIL LIBERTIES.

Narcotics Cache. Federal narcotics agents and Canadian police uncovered a cache of heroin on February 21 totaling 134 pounds. Part of the cache had been hidden in Montreal and part in New York City. It was reported to be valued at more than $50,000,000 on the illegal drug market. The Mexican ambassador to Bolivia, Salvador Pardo-Bolland, and two other men were arrested. Pardo-Bolland was fired by Mexico. The men were tried in New York. Pardo-Bolland received an 18-year sentence and a $40,000 fine. His accomplices also were sentenced and fined.

Embezzler. Five years' imprisonment was ordered in San Francisco on March 19 for Dolly Dee, manager of the Chinatown branch of the Bank of America for 34 years, following her plea of guilty to bank embezzlement of some $340,000. Her explanation for three decades of theft: the money was used to cover up poor investments made by her father, who was a bank official some 45 years earlier.

Mass Murder. Forty-four persons were killed near Danville, Calif., on May 7, when a twin-engine commercial plane crashed into a hillside. Investigation indicated that the pilot and the copilot had been shot to death in midair. While all the facts may

Wide World

HEADY EXPERIENCE with vandals broke up Copenhagen's famed Little Mermaid, but a new head soon restored her composure.

never be learned, it appeared that the disaster was caused by a young man who took out a $60,000 flight insurance policy before boarding the plane. He was reported to have lost heavily in gambling in casinos in Reno, Nev.

Star of India. One of the great jewel thefts in modern history took place on October 29, when a cat burglar entered a fourth-floor window in the American Museum of Natural History in New York City and stole the fabulous 563.35-carat Star of India, the world's largest star sapphire; the 100-carat De Long Star Ruby, the finest and largest (100.32 carats) gem of its kind in the world; and other valuable jewels. A museum official said the market value of the jewels was $380,000. Three young men from Florida, who described themselves as "surfers," were arrested for the crime. One of them, Allan Dale Kuhn, 25, helped police early in 1965 to recover the Star of India; the Midnight Star, also a sapphire; five emeralds; and two aquamarines. But the other gems in the famous collection were still missing.

Major Crime in the United States increased 15 per cent in the first six months of 1964 over the same period in the preceding year, according to Federal Bureau of Investigation (FBI) reports. Suburban areas showed the greatest percentage increase: 23. Rural crime rates were up 9 per cent; cities over 25,000 had increases of 14 per cent. JOSEPH D. LOHMAN

See also JUVENILE DELINQUENCY.

CUBA

CUBA was offered the cheerless prospect of more hard work and a leaner larder by Premier Fidel Castro in September. The island's economy had suffered gravely from a drop in world sugar prices. Production failures in agriculture had brought widespread complaints about the inability of the rationing system to fulfill family food quotas. The nation was also aware that various communist countries were becoming increasingly tired of carrying Cuba.

The island, of necessity, cut back its industrial investment and turned to expanding its sugar output. It bought 2,000 trucks and 500 sugar cane harvesting machines from Russia to handle the anticipated sugar crop in 1965. Russia also provided a $1,700,000 dry dock for a new fishing port in Havana.

Buying Curtailed. In August, Cuban purchasing agents were told to stop all buying negotiations. The move was precipitated by the nation's chaotic finances and a sharp decline in world sugar prices. The National Bank of Cuba apparently had no idea what commitments had been made, what the terms of purchase agreements were, nor when payments were due. The moratorium on buying enabled the bank to review its records while trying to unsnarl the situation and determine its actual outstanding commitments.

With its economy shaky and the communist countries eager to lessen Cuban dependence on them, various Cuban officials hinted during the year that Havana might like to improve its relations with the United States. It thus hoped, perhaps, to gain back a well-paying sugar customer. The United States, however, ignored the hint.

Sanctions Adopted. On July 26, the Organization of American States (OAS) formally signed resolutions calling for sanctions against Cuba. The resolutions, which also branded Cuba as an aggressor against Venezuela, called for the strengthening of hemispheric defenses against Cuban subversion. The sanctions prescribed a break in diplomatic ties and the suspension of trade and maritime transport. Only food and medical supplies were exempted from the ban.

The carrying out of the sanctions was left to the discretion of the individual governments. Only Mexico eventually refused to break all ties, arguing that the OAS resolution was illegal and that it was desirable for humanitarian and political reasons to maintain ties.

On June 29, Juanita Castro Ruz, sister of Premier Castro, became a self-exile in Mexico City. She charged Castro with betraying Cuba to Russian imperialism and with directing subversive infiltration throughout Latin America.

Population: 7,000,000. **Government:** President Osvaldo Dorticós Torrado; Premier Fidel Castro. **Foreign Trade:** exports, $798,000,000; imports, $932,000,000. **Principal Exports:** fruit, sugar, tobacco. MARY C. WEBSTER

See also LATIN AMERICA.

286

CYPRUS

A bitter civil war, in which its Greek and Turkish communities were the chief opponents, split Cyprus in 1964. For a time, the disorders threatened to bring war between Greece and Turkey, each of which was determined to support its respective communities on the island. Only intervention by the United Nations (UN) prevented hostilities from spreading into an international conflict. See UNITED NATIONS.

The trouble began on January 1 when Archbishop Makarios, president of Cyprus, decided to abrogate the nation's treaties with Great Britain, Greece, and Turkey. These treaties, which guaranteed the island's constitution as well as its territorial integrity, had been signed in 1960 when the island received its independence from Great Britain. Subsequently,

TERROR AFOOT. A Turkish Cypriot, his Sten gun on the ready, lunges down a street in Limassol during bitter fighting on wartorn island of Cyprus. Greek Cypriot bullets killed 50 Turks before British troops could restore order.

Donald McCullin, *The Observer*

CYPRUS

the two ethnic groups clashed repeatedly over constitutional amendments proposed by Makarios. The Greek Cypriots felt that the special rights guaranteed the Turkish community in the original constitution had a divisive effect on the country. The Turkish Cypriots, fearful of their minority status, resented the proposed changes.

The outbreak of factional fighting that followed the Makarios decision to abrogate the treaties in January ended a tenuous cease-fire negotiated a month earlier. To quell the disorders, Great Britain reinforced the garrison it maintained in Cyprus under the treaty with about 2,000 troops. It then arranged for an international conference to explore solutions to the constitutional quarrel.

Peace Efforts. The conference opened in London on January 14. In addition to representatives of Great Britain, Greece, and Turkey, it also was attended by Greek and Turkish Cypriot leaders. A walkout by Turkey was avoided on January 29 when the United States gave its assurances that U.S. forces would join a proposed peace-keeping command on the island to be drawn from the North Atlantic Treaty Organization (NATO) countries. This plan, however, was rejected by Archbishop Makarios, who, as head of a sovereign state, insisted on a UN, rather than a NATO command. On February 7, his viewpoint received diplomatic backing from the Soviet Union. The Greek Cypriot irregulars were now emboldened to either attack or set up blockades around Turkish Cypriot settlements. On February 13, even as U.S. President Lyndon B. Johnson and British Prime Minister Sir Alec Douglas-Home were discussing Cyprus in Washington, D.C., Greek Cypriot forces struck in the port of Limassol, and killed 50 Turks.

UN Difficulties. Two days later, Sir Alec turned the crisis over to the UN Security Council. British troops, now raised to a force of 7,000, still remained the only peace-keeping force separating the warring factions. It was a responsibility the British now felt should be shared internationally. On March 4, after considerable debate in the UN Security Council, UN Secretary-General U Thant was authorized to raise a peace-keeping force and to appoint a UN mediator. The United States agreed to contribute $2,000,000 toward the upkeep of this force, and Great Britain promised another $1,000,000.

Meanwhile, as the fighting intensified, Turkey threatened to invade the island. It backed its threat with naval maneuvers off the Turkish coast opposite Cyprus. To counteract the Turkish threat, Greece alerted its own forces. These belligerent moves brought swift international response. By March 15, U Thant had mustered a total of 3,000 men from Canada, Finland, Ireland, and Sweden. By March 27, the UN command had become fully operational. The British troops allocated to it had also put on the UN "blue helmet." Yet it was now clear that the Greek and Turkish forces on the island were resolved

on a trial of arms, and the cautious instructions given to the UN's forces made them helpless to intervene whenever the bullets began to fly.

UN Mediator Sakari S. Tuomioja, a Finnish diplomat, began discussions in Geneva, Switzerland, in July. Under a proposal put forward by former U.S. Secretary of State Dean Acheson, who was attending the conference as an observer, Cyprus was to be united with Greece. In return, Greece would cede the Dodecanese island of Kastellorizo to Turkey, which would also be allowed to maintain a military base in Cyprus. Turkish Cypriots would retain two enclaves, while those who left the island would be compensated. This solution, however, was unacceptable to either the Turks or to Archbishop Makarios. Fierce fighting continued on the island.

The most serious clashes took place in the Kyrenia area in the north and in and around Paphos on the southeast coast. In the Paphos fighting, six Greek Cypriots and a Turkish Cypriot were killed. The Turks seized nearly 300 Greek hostages. Only swift intervention by British troops helped restore an uneasy peace.

Late in April, armed Greek Cypriots launched a major attack against St. Hilarion Castle, the last major Turkish Cypriot stronghold in northeastern Cyprus. Despite the ferocity of their attack, the Greek Cypriots failed to dislodge the Turks. Six Turkish Cypriots and three Greek Cypriots died during the fighting.

Turkey Intervenes. By early August, the military plight of the Turkish Cypriots was desperate. Their villages were cut off and blockaded. The Greeks were acquiring heavy arms from abroad. A Greek offensive against Turkish villages on the coast of northwest Cyprus now threatened to cut off their last sea link for supplies and reinforcements from Turkey. The Turkish government, responding to appeals for help, ordered air strikes against Greek Cypriot positions and the Greek ships supplying them with arms. These measures saved the Turkish Cypriots from annihilation, but they also provoked Archbishop Makarios into appealing to the Soviet Union and the United Arab Republic for military aid.

At the UN Security Council's urging, a cease-fire was agreed upon, but it remained a tenuous one. Nor were prospects for peace greatly enhanced by the return of General George Grivas, a former terrorist leader who took over the Greek Cypriot forces on August 13. By year's end, both the Greek government and Grivas seemed to be working for *enosis* (the union of the island with Greece). Turkey wanted the island partitioned or made into a federal state. Archbishop Makarios, however, was still holding out for full independence.

Population: 600,000. **Government:** President Archbishop Makarios. **Foreign Trade:** exports, $55,000,000; imports, $86,000,000. **Principal Exports:** copper, fruits, iron pyrites.   ALASTAIR BURNET
See also EUROPE.

DAIRYING

CZECHOSLOVAKIA. The national assembly re-elected President Antonín Novotný to a second seven-year term on November 12. His re-election came less than a month after Russia's ouster of its premier, Nikita S. Khrushchev (see Russia). Novotný remained as leader of the Czechoslovakian Communist party. Earlier, Novotný's position was jeopardized by an economic slump, by demands for intraparty reform, and by intellectual ferment. Aid to Africa and Cuba was blamed for contributing to the nation's lowering standard of living. See Cuba.

Following the June 14 parliamentary elections, the government announced shorter working hours and an economic reform program. Pensioners, housewives, and invalids could work in specific one-man enterprises; and family houses could, under certain circumstances, be privately bought. The intellectual ferment exposed at a conference of the Slovak Writers Union in April, 1963, produced continued critical writing in the press, satire in the theater, and general liberalization in the arts.

Novotný supported Khrushchev's stand against Communist China, and immediately after Khrushchev's fall, his regime announced its intention to expedite reform and expand contacts with the West. Novotný further demonstrated his independence by refusing to attend a Russian-called summit meeting with Chinese Premier Chou En-lai in November. See Communism.

Czechoslovakia was the only communist nation participating in the so-called Kennedy Round tariff agreement talks in Geneva, Switzerland.

Population: 14,100,000. **Government:** President Antonín Novotný; Premier Josef Lenart. **Foreign Trade:** exports, $2,462,000,000; imports, $2,160,000,000. **Principal Exports:** fuels, hops, machinery, textiles, wheat.   Tom and Harle Dammann

See also Europe.

DAHOMEY. Former Vice-President Sourou Migan Apithy was elected president in nationwide balloting held January 19, 1964. The Dahomean Democratic party's 42 candidates were elected to the national assembly. Apithy's government replaced a provisional regime that had been in power since the ouster of President Hubert Maga in October, 1963.

In mid-March, Dahomean troops quelled an insurrection by Bariba tribesmen in the northern Parakou region. The government arrested 192 persons and Bariba leader Chabi Mama, an ardent follower of Maga.

Efforts to settle the Dahomey-Niger dispute, which had caused a deterioration in relations between the two countries, were suspended without any appreciable results in late June.

Population: 2,150,000. **Government:** President Sourou Migan Apithy. **Foreign Trade:** exports $14,000,000; imports, $25,000,000. **Principal Exports:** coffee, palm oil, peanuts.   Benjamin E. Thomas

See also Africa.

DAIRYING proved relatively stable in 1964. Cash receipts of U.S. dairy farmers reached a record of nearly $5,000,000,000. Milk production rose nearly 1,000,000,000 pounds over 1963, to an estimated 125,700,000,000 pounds. But commercial marketings were expected to climb by about 1,500,000,000 pounds, because fewer farmers kept cows for home use. Numbers of milk cows continued a nearly 20-year slide to an estimated 16,063,000, or about 3 per cent below 1963's total. Production per cow, however, increased nearly 4 per cent, to about 7,800 pounds. The average yearly gain per cow during the 1954-1963 period had been 3.1 per cent.

The record cash income from milk and cream—up from the 1963 total of $4,800,000,000 and the previous record of $4,900,000,000 in 1949—resulted from higher prices and sales. Prices averaged about $4.14 per 100 pounds of milk, or 4 cents above 1963, continuing a three-year uptrend. Underpinning this price were: (1) the $3.15 support price for manufactured milk, or 75 per cent of parity, for the marketing year ending April, 1965, and (2) milk-marketing orders regulating pricing in 77 markets.

Government Buying of butter, cheese, and nonfat dry milk, for price supports and subsidized commercial exports, absorbed about 8,000,000,000 pounds of 1964's milk production, up 250,000,000 pounds from 1963. Civilian use of milk rose to an estimated 118,500,000,000 pounds, reflecting slightly higher donations of government-purchased dairy products to welfare and school lunch programs. Government surpluses dropped to 4,460,000,000 pounds in milk equivalent on Sept. 1, 1964, from 10,166,000,000 pounds a year earlier.

U.S. Dairy Exports rose in 1964 because of the relatively low world stocks of dairy products and the steadily rising overseas demand. From February through October, 1964, the U.S. export sales price of butter climbed more than 10 cents a pound, and the price of nonfat dry milk to foreign purchasers rose from about 7 cents a pound in January, 1964, to almost the domestic price of about 15 cents a pound at year's end.

And, largely because of the U.S. Payment-in-Kind Program, exports of nonfat dry milk increased from about 403,000,000 pounds in 1963 to 660,000,000 in 1964. During the same period, U.S. exports of butter climbed from 67,000,000 pounds to about 110,000,000 pounds.

Pesticide Indemnity payments went to the relatively small number of farmers whose milk was kept off the market because it contained residues of federally approved pesticides. They were announced by the Secretary of Agriculture on October 27 for the period Jan. 1, 1964, to Jan. 31, 1965. The payments, authorized under the Economic Opportunity (War on Poverty) Act of 1964, were based on the farmer's normal prices and the quantity marketed.   Frank B. Harper

See also Agriculture.

289

Wide World

A GIANT HARNESS of 7,000,000 horsepower rises to tame Quebec's Manicouagan River. First power from the dam is expected in 1968.

DAM. In May, Egypt completed the first stage of its Aswan High Dam with the diversion of the main channel of the Nile River around two cofferdams above and below the damsite. In the first phase of construction, 15,565,200 cubic yards of granite rock, dirt, and sand were excavated; a 3,772-foot-long diversion canal was dug; and the foundation for the 12-turbine hydroelectric power station was laid.

Ghana's Aksombo Dam also marked a milestone in May. With the curtailment of flow in the dam's 30-foot diameter diversion tunnel, the Volta River's waters started to back up. By the end of the year, the major work on the dam itself had been completed. Two to four years, depending on rainfall, will be

required to fill the 3,275-square-mile reservoir, Lake Volta. It will form the world's fourth largest man-made body of water.

Also in May, the first electric power was generated at the Bhumibol Dam on the Ping River in Thailand. The key feature of the $100,000,000 multipurpose project was a 505-foot-high concrete arch dam, the highest ever built in Southeast Asia. The dam impounds nearly 10,000,000 acre-feet of water. In June, Formosa dedicated its $80,000,000 multipurpose Shihmen Dam.

Canada's ratification of the Columbia River Basin treaty in September cleared the way for construction of four dams on the Upper Columbia River (see CANADA; WATER AND FLOOD CONTROL).

Glen Canyon Dam, completed in 1963 on the Colorado River in Arizona, received the 1964 Outstanding Civil Engineering Achievement Award, sponsored by the American Society of Civil Engineers. A dry spring delayed output of the project's first electric power until autumn, to give its reservoir, Lake Powell, time to refill.

Detailed information on nearly 10,000 large dams was made available in the four-volume *World Register of Dams*, completed in 1964 by the International Commission on Large Dams, 345 East 47th Street, New York City, N.Y. 10017.

Texas and Louisiana began construction of their joint $60,000,000 Toledo Bend Dam on the Sabine River in May. Closure of the 9,500-foot-long, rolled earth-fill dam was scheduled for July, 1966. Financing was arranged by the two states on a 50-50 basis, without federal aid.   M. E. JESSUP

See also ELECTRIC POWER.

DANCING. The largest program of grants ever awarded the ballet in the United States ran into a barrage of criticism throughout 1964. The grants, totaling $7,756,750, had been awarded by the Ford Foundation late in 1963 to strengthen U.S. professional ballet.

The criticism was based on the fact that the major contribution went to the New York City Ballet and its school, the School of American Ballet, and that the rest of the money was given to companies directly or indirectly connected with the prestigious New York City ballet company.

The Boston Ballet and the Pennsylvania Ballet received Ford money to enable them to operate as professional companies, that is, to pay the dancers for the few performances that each gives in any one year. The Houston Ballet and the Utah Ballet in Salt Lake City were also recipients of the grants, although the Houston company did not perform in 1964.

New Theater. To the New York City Ballet fell the privilege of opening the New York State Theater in April. The building was the newest in the Lincoln Center complex (see NEW YORK CITY). The company's spring season ran through May 17, and it held a second season in the fall and winter.

Michaelangelo Durazzo

A DANCE SENSATION in the West since he defected from Russia in 1961, Rudolf Nureyev directs his own version of Swan Lake, which co-starred Margot Fonteyn.

New Company. The Rebekah Harkness Foundation, which for two years had sponsored the Robert Joffrey Ballet, decided to withdraw its support early in the year, leaving Joffrey temporarily without a company. However, the Joffrey company in November received a Ford Foundation grant of $155,000 so that it could be reactivated. In the meantime, the Rebekah Harkness Foundation combined efforts with the William Hale Harkness Foundation to organize a new company, The Harkness Ballet, which made its debut at a White House performance in October as part of the official entertainment during the visit of Philippine President Diosdado Macapagal. George Skibine, a naturalized American citizen of Franco-Russian parentage, became the artistic director.

Modern Dance. Donald McKayle staged an evening-long modern dance work, *Reflections in the Park*, at Hunter College in March. Two other great modern dance events took place during the American Dance Festival held at Connecticut College in New London in August. One was the première of *A Choreographic Offering*, José Limón's hour-long tribute to the memory of choreographer Doris Humphrey.

The other was Martha Graham's personal revival of three of her great early works, *Frontier*, *El Penitente*, and *Primitive Mysteries*. They were performed as a memorial for Louis Horst, composer of the music for all three. Horst died in January (see DEATHS OF NOTABLE PERSONS). The 32nd Jacob's Pillow Dance

Festival, held in Lee, Mass., featured the U.S. debut of the Royal Winnipeg Ballet, one of the finest small troupes in the world.

U.S. Dance Abroad. American Ballet Theatre, which toured the United States, also went to South America and Mexico for three months on a U.S. Department of State Cultural Presentations Program.

The modern dance companies of Merce Cunningham, Paul Taylor, and Alvin Ailey all participated in European tours.

Visiting Companies included the second U.S. tour of the Leningrad Kirov Ballet, Antonio and his Ballets de Madrid, Mazowsze of Poland, National Ballet of Canada, Russia's Raduga, the Sahm-Chun Li and Arirang troupes from Korea, the Bayanihan dancers of the Philippines, and the Chilean Ballet.

U.S. Festivals. The Ninth Annual Southeastern Regional Ballet Festival was held in Nashville, Tenn., in April; and the Second Southwestern Regional Ballet Festival was held in Houston, Tex.

An important development in dance occurred in November when the New York State Council on the Arts provided funds to make possible two performances in the New York State Theater of a repertory modern dance company, the American Dance Theater, directed by José Limón. It was hoped that this might lead to the establishment of a company that would be able to perform the great works of modern dance, rarely seen because of lack of performing opportunities.   P. W. MANCHESTER

291

DEATHS OF NOTABLE PERSONS

THE YEAR 1964 saw the passing of not only notable persons, but some of the truly great men and women of our time. Among them were Pierre Monteux in music; Dame Edith Louise Sitwell and Sean O'Casey in literature; the sage of science, John B. S. Haldane, and the mathematical wizard, Norbert Wiener.

General of the Army Douglas MacArthur was among the greatest military leaders of his time. Elder statesman and former President of the United States Herbert Clark Hoover was known internationally for his humanitarian work, and as an adviser to several Presidents who succeeded him. Another renowned international statesman was Jawaharlal Nehru of India (see India [Close-Up]).

Pictorial Parade

The persons listed below were Americans unless otherwise indicated. An asterisk (*) means that the person has a biography in THE WORLD BOOK ENCYCLOPEDIA.

*Aguinaldo, Emilio (1869-Feb. 6), Filipino patriot, fought against Spain (1896, 1898) and then the Americans. Captured in March, 1901, he pledged his loyalty to the United States, retired from public life, and wrote his memoirs, A Second Look at America (1957).

Alexander, Franz (1891-Mar. 8), Hungarian-born director of the Chicago Institute of Psychoanalysis (1925-1956), pioneered in psychosomatic medicine.

Allen, Gracie (1906-Aug. 27), with George Burns formed the great husband-and-wife comedy team of stage, screen, radio, and television (1923-1958).

*Archipenko, Alexander (1887-Feb. 25), Ukrainian-born artist and pioneer in cubist-abstract sculpture, used convex and concave surfaces and often combined plastic, metal, cement, and other materials in a single work.

*Astor, Dowager Lady (Viscountess) Nancy Witcher Langhorne (1879-May 2), was the first woman to serve in the British House of Commons (1919-1945). The Virginia belle and Waldorf Astor, later Lord (Viscount, 1919) Astor, were married in 1906.

Atkinson, J. Robert (1888?-Feb. 1), blinded at 25, founded (1919) and was managing director (1919-1957) of the Braille Institute of America, Los Angeles.

Augustus, Ellsworth Hunt (1897-May 16), industrialist, had been president of the National Council of the Boy Scouts of America since 1959.

Baker, Howard H. (1902-Jan. 7), had been Republican U.S. Representative from Tennessee since January, 1951.

Barkley, Jane Rucker Hadley (1911-Sept. 6), widow of Democratic U.S. Senator from Kentucky (1927-1949, 1955-1956) and Vice-President of the United States (1949-1953) Alben W. Barkley. She wrote I Married the Veep (1958).

Basso, Hamilton (1904-May 13), author of A View from Pompey's Head (1954), also wrote Cinnamon Seed (1934), In Their Own Image (1935), Courthouse Square (1936), and other novels about his native South.

Baxter, Sir (Arthur) Beverley (1891-Apr. 26), Canadian-born House of Commons (Conservative) member (since 1935), and Lord Beaverbrook (William Maxwell Aitken) were the "Bax and Max" of London's Fleet Street (1920's). Sir Beverley (knighted, 1954) was editor and also a director of various Beaverbrook newspapers.

FUNERAL CORTEGE of Greek King Paul I moves through Athenian crowd. Symbolic royal crown of office surmounts the flag-draped coffin.

293

Karsh, Ottawa

LORD BEAVERBROOK, head of a newspaper empire and former British cabinet member, died at 85.

Wide World

THEODORE C. FREEMAN, one of the U. S. astronauts, died in a jet landing at Houston. He was 33.

Wide World

LEO SZILARD, a nuclear physicist who had helped develop the atomic bomb, died at age 66.

*Beaverbrook, Lord (Sir William Maxwell Aitken) (1879-June 9), a Canadian financier before going to London (1907), began his newspaper empire with *The London Daily Express* (acquired, 1916). A Conservative House of Commons (1910-1916) and House of Lords (since 1917) member, held Cabinet posts in World Wars I and II.

Behan, Brendan (Francis) (1923-Mar. 20), Irish author and revolutionist, won fame with *Borstal Boy* (autobiography, 1958). His plays include *The Quare Fellow* (1956, filmed, 1962), *The Hostage* (1958), and *Richard's Cork Leg* (not yet staged). He wrote poetry in Gaelic, and *Brendan Behan's Island: An Irish Sketch-book*, (1962), *Hold Your Hour and Have Another* (1963) and *The Scarperer* (1964).

Bell, Clive (1881-Sept. 17), British writer on art and literature, championed such painters as Cezanne, Picasso, Van Gogh, and Gauguin in England. His writings include *Landmarks in Nineteenth Century Painting* (1927); *An Account of French Painting* (1931); and *Old Friends* (1956), his memoirs.

Bendix, William (1906-Dec. 14), remembered as Chester Riley in *The Life of Riley* (film, radio, and television), played in *Two Years Before the Mast* and other films, and also in Broadway plays.

Bennett, John B. (1904-Aug. 9), Republican U.S. Representative from Michigan since 1947, also served (1943-1945).

Blalock, Alfred (1899-Sept. 15), Johns Hopkins Hospital surgeon in chief (1941-1964), with Helen B. Taussig (see AWARDS AND PRIZES: General Awards [Presidential Medal of Freedom]) performed (1944) the first "blue baby" operation and opened a new field of surgery.

Blatz, William E. (1895-Nov. 1), University of Toronto child psychology professor, supervised the famous Dionne quintuplets during their early childhood, of which he wrote in *The Five Sisters*.

*Blitzstein, Marc (1905-Jan. 22), piano prodigy, composed *The Cradle Will Rock* (1937-1938), *Regina* (1949), and *Reuben, Reuben* (1951-1953) operas; music for stage plays; and adapted the *Threepenny Opera* (1952) from the German work.

Bombardier, Armand (1908?-Feb. 18), Canadian manufacturer of vehicles to go anywhere (Skidoo, Muskeg tractor), invented the Snowmobile (1937).

Brendel, El (1898-Apr. 9), famed for his Swedish accent ("yumpin' yiminy"), was a vaudeville, stage, and motion-picture comedian.

Brown, Nacio Herb (1896-Sept. 28), motion-picture composer, wrote the music for "The Wedding of the Painted Doll," "Singing in the Rain," "You Are My Lucky Star," "Pagan Love Song," "You're an Old Smoothie," and many other songs.

Brown, Russ (1892-Oct. 19), singer and character actor, sang in *Firefly*, and was Finian in *Finian's Rainbow* and Van Buren in *Damn Yankees*.

Burke, Johnny (1908-Feb. 25), wrote the lyrics for "The Beat of My Heart," "Annie Doesn't Live Here Any More," "Pennies from Heaven," "Swinging on a Star," and many other popular songs.

*Burton, Harold Hitz (1888-Oct. 28), an Associate Justice of the Supreme Court of the United States (1945-1958), was a Republican U.S. Senator from Ohio (1941-1945).

Cannon, Clarence (1879-May 12), whose books on House procedure are standard references, had been U.S. Representative from Missouri since 1923.

*Cantor, Eddie (1892-Oct. 10), song-and-dance man in all entertainment media for some 50 years, in his early days starred in such stage productions as *Make It Snappy* (1922), *Kid Boots* (1923-1926), and *Whoopee* (1928-1930).

*Carson, Rachel (1907-Apr. 14), biologist, won distinguished awards as author of *Under the Sea* (1941), *The Sea Around Us* (1951), *The Edge of the Sea* (1956), and *Silent Spring* (1962).

Chiarlo, Carlo Cardinal (1881-Jan. 21), for years a Vatican diplomat, was elevated to the Sacred College of Cardinals in 1958.

Collins, "Ted" Joseph Martin (1900?-May 27), Kate Smith's manager, producer, and announcer, discovered the singer (1929) and selected her theme song "When the Moon Comes Over the Mountain."

Compton, Francis (1885-Sept. 17), son of the noted English theater family, often played suave butler as well as other roles.

Crampton, C. Ward (1877-Oct. 20), geriatrician and author of physical fitness books, devised the Crampton test to determine if a patient might suffer fatal shock in surgery.

Creech-Jones, Arthur (1891-Oct. 23), House of

PIERRE MONTEUX, French-born orchestra conductor, died at the age of 89 after a long illness.

KEN HUBBS, second baseman for the Chicago Cubs baseball team, died at age 22 in a plane crash.

HARPO MARX, nonspeaking member of the Marx Brothers comedy team, died at the age of 70.

Commons Labour party member (1935-1950, 1954-1964), was Colonial Secretary (1946-1951), when Ceylon, India, and Pakistan won independence and several other nations left the British Commonwealth.

Crosby, Percy L. (1891-Dec. 8), creator of the comic strip *Skippy* (film of 1931 made Jackie Cooper a star), wrote such books as *Skippy and Other Humor* (1929), *A Cartoonist's Philosophy* (1931), and *Always Belittlin'* (1938). He also was internationally known for his paintings, water colors, and other art work.

Daniels, Josephus, Jr. (1894-Feb. 15), The News and Observer Publishing Company board chairman since 1956, began his career with the North Carolina newspaper organization in 1918.

*****Davis, Stuart** (1894-June 24), who often included signs, store fronts, and billboards in his abstract paintings, did murals for Radio City Music Hall, Rockefeller Center, and radio station WNYC in New York City.

De Francisci, Anthony (1887-Oct. 20), Italian-born artist, did portrait sculpture and the Ann Daly Morrison Memorial in Boise, Idaho, and other monuments. He designed medals, decorations, and the World War II veterans' discharge emblem (termed the "ruptured duck" by GIs).

Defrère, Désiré (1888-Aug. 31), Belgian-born New York Metropolitan Opera stage director since 1935 and baritone (1935-1938), first sang in Europe, then with the Chicago company (1911-1934).

De Paolis, Alessio (1893-Mar. 9), Metropolitan Opera star since 1938, played nearly 200 roles during a career that began in his native Italy.

*****Dobie, James Frank** (1888-Sept. 18), humorist and chronicler of Texas history and folklore, wrote *Coronado's Children*, *Apache Gold*, *The Longhorns*, *The Mustangs*, and other books. See AWARDS AND PRIZES (General Awards: Presidential Medal of Freedom).

Dochez, A. Raymond (1882-June 30), Columbia University professor of medicine (1925-1949), isolated (1924) a scarlet fever serum (antitoxin).

*****Domagk, Gerhard Johannes Paul** (1895-Apr. 24), German chemical therapy researcher, was awarded the Nobel medicine prize in 1939 (but could not accept then because of Hitler) for developing the first sulfa drug *prontosil* for streptococcic and other infections.

Dumke, Ralph (1900?-Jan. 4), with the late Ed East, did the *Sisters of the Skillet* radio program (1920's-1930's) and later played in musical comedies, such films as *All the King's Men* and *The President's Lady*, and television shows.

Elliott, Alonzo (1891-June 24), composer and co-lyricist (with Stoddard King) of "There's a Long, Long Trail"; wrote the music for "There's a Wee Cottage on a Hillside" and other songs.

Engle, Clair (1911-July 30), Democratic U.S. Senator from California since 1959, served in the House of Representatives (1943-1959).

Euler-Chelpin, Hans von (1873-Nov. 8?), German chemist, with the late Sir Arthur Harden of England, was awarded the Nobel chemistry prize (1929) for their research on sugar fermentation and enzymes.

Field, Stanley (1875-Oct. 28), English-born president of the Chicago Natural History Museum (founded as Field Museum of Natural History in 1893 by his uncle, Marshall Field I) since 1909, also was associated with Marshall Field & Company for 70 years.

Fitzgerald, Josephine Mary Hannon (1866?-Aug. 8), maternal grandmother of the late President John F. Kennedy, was the widow of John F. Fitzgerald, Boston mayor (1906, 1907, 1910-1914) and Democratic U.S. Representative from Massachusetts (1895-1901).

Fleming, Ian (1908-Aug. 12), English creator of the British Secret Service agent James Bond, wrote *Doctor No*, *From Russia With Love*, *Goldfinger* (all filmed), and other books.

Fox, Fontaine Talbot, Jr. (1884?-Aug. 9), was creator of the *Toonerville Trolley* cartoons (1920-1955).

*****Franck, James** (1882-May 21), German-born scientist, and Gustav Hertz received the Nobel physics prize (1925) for proving (1914) that electrons occupy certain levels in atoms.

Frank, Harry "Pat" Hart (1907-Oct. 12), known for his *Mr. Adam* (1946), also wrote *Alas, Babylon; How to Survive the H-Bomb and Why;* and other books.

Goodyear, Anson Conger (1877-Apr. 23), industrialist, was a founder and first president of New York's Museum of Modern Art (1929-1939).

Gosfield, Maurice (1913?-Oct. 19), stage, radio, and screen actor, played Private Doberman on the *Sergeant Ernie Bilko* television show (1955-1959).

Greenawalt, John E. (1868?-Mar. 11), invented the

Fred Ward, Black Star

Wide World

Erich Hartmann, Magnum

CLARENCE CANNON, for 40 years a U.S. Representative from Missouri, died at age 85.

BRENDAN BEHAN, controversial Irish playwright, died in a Dublin hospital. He was 41 years old.

RACHEL CARSON, biologist and author of the controversial book Silent Spring, died at 56.

Greenawalt downdraft process for sintering of iron ore and other raw minerals. His other work included the electrolytic recovery of zinc.

Gruenberg, Louis (1884-June 9), Russian-born composer of *Green Mansions*, *Jack and the Bean Stalk*, and *Emperor Jones* (operas), also composed symphonic and piano compositions and songs.

Hagedorn, Hermann (1882-July 27), author of *The Boys' Life of Theodore Roosevelt* (1918), *The Roosevelt Family of Sagamore Hill* (1954), and other Roosevelt books, also wrote other biographies and poetry.

Haldane, John B. S. (1892-Dec. 1), great British scientist who often used himself as a laboratory rabbit, was the first to map the human chromosome and to measure the mutation rate of a human gene. His many books include *The Causes of Evolution* (1933) and *The Biochemistry of Genetics* (1953).

Hardwicke, Sir Cedric Webster (1893-Aug. 6), English actor knighted (1934) for his Shavian roles, played the father in *The Barretts of Wimpole Street*, the doctor in *The Late Christopher Bean*, and numerous other stage as well as motion-picture roles.

Hayes, Carlton J. H. (1882-Sept. 3), a Columbia University student and teacher (1900-1950) and author of many volumes on Europe and the Atlantic Community, wrote about his years as U.S. Ambassador to Spain (1942-1945) in *Wartime Mission in Spain*.

*****Hecht, Ben** (1894-Apr. 18), newspaperman and author of novels and other works, with the late Charles MacArthur, wrote such plays as *The Front Page* (1928) and *Ladies and Gentlemen* (1939). He wrote scenarios for the films *Wuthering Heights*, *Notorious*, and *Spellbound*.

Herold, J. Christopher (1919-Dec. 10), Czech-born author of *Mistress to an Age: A Life of Madame de Staël* (won National Book nonfiction award, 1958), wrote *Joan, Maid of France* (1952), *The Mind of Napoleon* (1955), and other volumes on European history.

Hess, Victor F. (1883-Dec. 17) Austrian-born scientist, received the Nobel physics prize (1936, shared with Carl D. Anderson) for discovery of cosmic rays.

Horst, Louis, (1884-Jan. 24), modern dance pioneer, was musical director for Ruth St. Denis and Ted Shawn (1916-1926) and then Martha Graham. He founded (1934) *The Dance Observer* magazine.

Howard, John Tasker (1890-Nov. 20), composer of piano, string, and orchestral works and music for religious anthems, was known as a lecturer and writer. His many books include *Stephen Foster: America's Troubadour* (a definitive biography), *Our American Music* (1929, a standard reference work), and *The World's Great Operas* (1948).

Howard, Roy Wilson (1883-Nov. 20), Scripps-Howard Newspapers executive committee chairman and developer of the United Press International, had held many major posts in the organization since joining it in 1905.

Irvine, William (1906-Oct. 7), Stanford University Victorian Literature professor whose *Apes, Angels and Victorians* (1955) won wide acclaim, also wrote *The Universe of G. B. S.* and other biographies.

Janssens, Jean Baptiste (1889-Oct. 5), a Belgian scholar, had been Superior General of the Society of Jesus since 1946, the Roman Catholic religious order of men known as the Jesuits.

Joy, Nicholas (1889-Mar. 16), English character actor who played in such Broadway plays as *Rain*, *A Journey by Night*, *The Philadelphia Story*, and *The Iceman Cometh*, appeared in many other stage productions and in many films.

Kilbride, Percy (1888?-Dec. 11), Pa Kettle of the *Ma* (played by Marjorie Main) *and Pa Kettle* films, created the garrulous caretaker role in *George Washington Slept Here* (his first Hollywood role, 1942). He made his Broadway debut (1928) in *Those We Love*, and played some 800 roles (stage and screen).

Kunc, Bozidar (1904?-Apr. 1), Yugoslav composer and pianist and brother of the Metropolitan Opera soprano Zinka Milanov, wrote songs, nine symphonies, two piano sonatas, and other compositions.

Ladd, Alan Walbridge (1913-Jan. 29), screen star whose first big success was as the killer in *This Gun for Hire* (1941), played in 150 pictures. Perhaps his greatest performance was as the star of *Shane*.

Larsen, Henry Asbjorn (1899-Oct. 28), Norwegian-born retired Royal Canadian Mounted Police superintendent, was commander of the *St. Roch* patrol schooner, the first vessel to navigate the Northwest Passage from west to east (1940-1942), also to make two-way voyage (completed east-west, 1944), and the first to circumnavigate North America (from Vancouver to Halifax, returning via Panama Canal).

The General Who Was An Emperor

THE DEATH of General of the Army Douglas MacArthur, on April 5, was mourned by many nations, but most notably by Japan, the nation that less than two decades before had lain prostrate before the conqueror. It was perhaps the greatest of tributes, for this American general had led the outcast empire back into the family of nations.

Former Premier Yoshida summed up the national feeling when he said, "I cannot forget the great achievement of the general in rebuilding our nation out of the ashes of defeat."

This general, who had led the Allied victory over Japan in World War II and who had commanded the United Nations forces in the Korean War, was, seemingly, born to lead. He was keen, proud, and powerful, and he had a gift for putting words into striking and stirring phrases. His military career spanned 52 years and three great wars, and though he was known as the general who never deigned to dodge a bullet, his ultimate message to his own countrymen appeared to be one of peace.

On his 75th birthday, the famous fighter called on his country to proclaim its readiness to abolish war, and pointed out that modern warfare had become suicide.

MACARTHUR formally ended his military career following his return from Korea in the spring of 1951. He had been relieved of his command by President Truman, who believed that his strategy in the Korean War could trigger World War III. His homecoming was momentous. He addressed a joint meeting of Congress in defense of his policies and then closed with these memorable words:

"And like the old soldier of a military ballad, I now close my military career and just fade away, an old soldier who tried to do his duty as God gave him the light to see that duty. Good-by."

THEREAFTER, the general largely dropped from public view. He served as a board chairman, but increasingly withdrew to the privacy of his New York apartment. In 1962, he was honored by both houses of Congress. And he addressed the graduating class of the U.S. Mili-

United Press Int.

Douglas MacArthur (1880-1964)

tary Academy at West Point, N.Y., giving the young men this guidepost:
"Duty, honor, country."

And then he ended with this moving word picture:

"The shadows are lengthening for me. The twilight is here. My days of old have vanished—tone and tints. They have gone glimmering through the dreams of things that were. Their memory is one of wondrous beauty, watered by tears and coaxed and caressed by the smiles of yesterday.

"I listened then, but with thirsty ear, for the witching melody of faint bugles blowing reveille, of far drums beating the long roll.

"In my dreams I hear again the crash of guns, the rattle of musketry, the strange, mournful mutter of the battlefield . . ."

MacArthur's body now rests in the green marble crypt in the MacArthur Memorial in Norfolk, Va. He will be remembered as one of the great military men of our time. FOSTER STOCKWELL

DEATHS OF NOTABLE PERSONS

Wide World

GRACIE ALLEN, comedienne of radio and television for 34 years, died in Hollywood at age 58.

Wide World

IAN FLEMING, author and creator of secret service agent hero James Bond, died at age 56.

United Press Int.

PALMIRO TOGLIATTI, leader of the Italian Communist party, died in Yalta after a stroke at age 71.

Lebrun, Rico (1900-May 9), Italian-born expressionist painter known for his murals about the good and evil in man, did a *Crucifixion* series (1947-1950) and the *Genesis* (1961) at Pomona (Calif.) College. His illustrations for Dante's *Divine Comedy* and his drawings are considered among his best work.

Lesnevich, Gus (1911?-Feb. 28), world light-heavyweight boxing champion, fought Tami Mauriello for the title (abandoned by Billy Conn) and won it on Aug. 26, 1941, defended it four times, and lost it to Freddie Mills in 1948.

Lewis, Meade Lux (1905-June 7), self-taught jazz pianist and boogie-woogie pioneer, composed "Honky Tonk Train Blues" (1929), "Yancey Special," "Boogie Woogie Prayer," and other such compositions, and appeared in *New Orleans* (film).

Lorre, Peter (1904-Mar. 23), Hungarian-born film actor noted for his sinister bad man roles after playing the pathological killer in the German-produced *M* picture (1931), came to Hollywood in 1934. He played in such pictures as *The Maltese Falcon, Casablanca, Crime and Punishment*, and the *Mr. Moto* series.

Maas, Melvin J. (1898-Apr. 13), chairman of the President's Committee on Employment of the Handicapped since 1954 and of the Committee for the Handicapped (People-to-People program) since 1956, was blinded (1951) after being wounded on Okinawa (1945). The Marine Corps veteran was Republican U.S. Representative from Minnesota (1927-1933, 1935-1945).

Madeleva, Sister Mary (1887-July 25), when president of St. Mary's College (South Bend, Ind., 1934-1961), founded the Graduate School of Sacred Theology (1944), the first of its kind for women. Her many books include *Chaucer's Nuns and Other Essays, Conversations with Cassandra*, and books of poetry.

Malotte, Albert Hay (1895?-Nov. 16), who set to music the first popular version of "The Lord's Prayer," wrote stage and screen-play scores, music for Disney shorts such as the Silly Symphonies, and "The Song of the Open Road" and other songs.

Mannes, Leopold Damrosch (1899-Aug. 11), concert pianist and president of Mannes College of Music, with Leopold Godowsky, invented and developed the Kodachrome color process for photography (1936).

*****Marx, Harpo (Arthur)** (1893-Sept. 28), the non-speaking member of the famous Marx Brothers, was a skilled harpist and pantomimist.

McKenna, Richard Milton (1913?-Nov. 1), who won fame and fortune with *The Sand Pebbles* (novel, 1962), also graduated from the University of North Carolina with honors, after 22 years in the U.S. Navy.

McLean, Sir Robert (1884-Apr. 9), former Vickers-Super Marine Aviation Company chairman, named Britain's *Spitfire*, famous World War II fighter plane.

McNeill, Sir James (1892-July 24), naval architect and engineer, was mainly responsible for designing the famous British Cunard liners *Queen Mary* and *Queen Elizabeth*.

McPhee, Colin (1901-Jan. 7), Canadian authority on Balinese music and author of *A House in Bali*, composed *Tabuh-Tabuhan, Balinese Ceremonial Music, Sea Shanty Suite*, and other compositions.

Mitchell, James P. (1902-Oct. 19), labor-relations expert, was U.S. Secretary of Labor (1953-1961).

*****Monteux, Pierre** (1875-July 1), French-born symphonic and operatic conductor, was one of the great musical figures of the century. His major conducting positions were with the Boston (1919-1924), Paris (1930-1938), San Francisco (1934-1952), and London (since 1961) symphony orchestras; the Amsterdam Concertgebouw Orchestra (1924-1934); and the New York Metropolitan Opera (1917-1919, 1954-1956).

Morrison, deLesseps S. (1912-May 22), mayor of New Orleans (1946-1961), was U.S. Ambassador to the Organization of American States (1961-1963).

Moser, Frank (1886?-Sept. 30), former newspaper cartoonist, with Paul Terry, created and produced the *Terrytoons* animated cartoon films.

Mott, Frank Luther (1886-Oct. 23), University of Missouri School of Journalism dean (1942-1951) whose multivolume *A History of American Magazines* won the Pulitzer (1939) and Bancroft (1958) history prizes, also wrote the definitive journalism textbook *American Journalism, 1690-1950*.

Nelson, Nels (1875-Mar. 5), Danish-born American Museum of Natural History prehistoric archaeology curator (1928-1943), was one of the first to use stratigraphic dating in his profession.

Nomura, Kichisaburó (1877-May 8), Japanese Ambassador to the U.S. at the time of Japan's attack on

298

DAME EDITH SITWELL, British poet and writer, died in a London hospital. She was 77 years old.

SIR CEDRIC HARDWICKE, veteran English actor, died in New York of a lung ailment at age 71.

SERGEANT ALVIN YORK, Tennessee hero of World War I, died at 76 after a long illness.

United Press Int. Wide World Wide World

Pearl Harbor, maintained that he did not know of the attack until he met with Secretary of State Cordell Hull that day (Dec. 7, 1941) to end peace negotiations in Washington, D.C.

Norblad, Walter (1908-Sept. 20), had been Republican U.S. Representative from Oregon since 1946.

Nussbaum, Arthur (1877-Nov. 22), German-born authority on international law, wrote such classics as *Principles of Private International Law* (1943) and *A Concise History of the Law of Nations* (1947).

O'Brien, Thomas J. (1878-Apr. 14), had been Democratic U.S. Representative from Illinois since 1933, except when Cook County sheriff (1939-1942).

***O'Casey, Sean** (1880-Sept. 18), who fought the English for Irish independence, lived in London after trouble with his countrymen. His best-known plays include *Juno and the Paycock* (1924), *The Plough and the Stars* (1926), and *The Silver Tassie* (1928). His six-volume autobiography is *Mirror in My House*.

Ogdon, Ina Duley (1872?-May 18), wrote the words of "Brighten the Corner Where You Are," "You Must Carry Your Cross With a Smile," and numerous other hymns, anthems, and cantatas, and also poems, stories, and magazine articles.

***Paul I** (1901-Mar. 6) had been King of the Hellenes since Apr. 1, 1947. See GREECE.

Pearson, Hesketh (1887-Apr. 9), British biographer of such notables as Benjamin Disraeli, Sir Walter Scott, and Sir Arthur Conan Doyle, also wrote *G.B.S.: A Full-Length Portrait* (1942), among the best books on George Bernard Shaw. *Think It Over* (1938), his autobiography, is as clever and entertaining as his other books.

***Peattie, Donald Culross** (1898-Nov. 16), naturalist and *Reader's Digest* roving editor since 1943, won fame with *An Almanac for Moderns* (1935). His other books include *Singing in the Wilderness* (1935), *A Child's Story of the World* (1937), and *The Road of a Naturalist* (1941).

Petrunkevitch, Alexander (1875-Mar. 9), Russian-born world authority on spiders and other arachnids, classified arachnid families, had many newly discovered spider species named for him, invented various laboratory techniques, and wrote *Catalogue of American Spiders* (1911, a standard encyclopedia).

***Porter, Cole** (1893-Oct. 15), composer and lyricist who wrote mostly for stage and screen musicals, had

his first big success with *Fifty Million Frenchmen* (1929). *Mexican Hayride; Kiss Me, Kate;* and *Can-Can* came later. "Begin the Beguine" and "What Is This Thing Called Love?" are among his many songs.

***Pound, Roscoe** (1870-July 1), Harvard University Law School dean (1916-1936) who advocated sociological jurisprudence, wrote *The Spirit of the Common Law* (1921), *Law and Morals* (1924), *Social Control Through Law* (1942), and many other volumes.

Pratt, Edwin J. (1883-Apr. 26), Canadian poet who won acclaim for *The Roosevelt and the Antinoe* (1930), wrote such story poems of the sea as *The Witches Brew* (1926) and *The Titanic* (1935), and *Brébeuf and His Brethren* (1940).

Raglan, Lord FitzRoy Richard Somerset (1885-Sept. 14), British soldier, anthropologist, and author of such books as *How Came Civilization* and *Death and Rebirth*, completed the first Lotuko-English dictionary while in the Sudan.

Robus, Hugo (1885-Jan. 14), whose creed was rhythm in sculpture, did many female figures. *Dawn, Walking Figure, Three Caryatids,* and *Woman Combing Her Hair* are among his major works.

Roques, Clement Emile Cardinal (1880-Sept. 4), Archbishop of Rennes (France) since 1940, was elevated to the Sacred College of Cardinals in 1946.

Rowan, Richard Wilmer (1894-Aug. 13), author of such books as *Spy and Counter-Spy* (1928), *Secret Agents Against America* (1939), and *Stalin's Secret Service* (1952), wrote with such authority and detail that the Japanese used his books in their espionage-training program before World War II.

Rummel, Joseph Francis (1876-Nov. 19), German-born Roman Catholic Archbishop of New Orleans and racial segregation opponent, excommunicated three of his prominent parishioners who opposed his order (1962) for integrated schools in his archdiocese.

Sawyer, Charles B. (1894-Mar. 24), a beryllium industry pioneer, developed modern uses for beryllium in nuclear physics and space rockets.

Schildkraut, Joseph (1895-Jan. 21), Hungarian-born actor remembered as the father in *The Diary of Anne Frank* (stage and screen), won wide critical acclaim during his 50-year career. He received the Motion Picture Academy best supporting actor award as Capt. Dreyfus in *The Life of Emile Zola* in 1937.

299

Herbert Hoover
(1874-1964)

The Man Who Served Mankind

HERBERT CLARK HOOVER gave 50 years of a long life in unselfish service to mankind. As a mining engineer and business promoter he enjoyed spectacular success; as 31st President of the United States he suffered bewildering frustration. The Great Depression had struck the United States seven months after he took office in 1929.

Unknown to the public before World War I, Hoover enjoyed a meteoric rise to fame as director of wartime relief in Belgium. As head of the Food Administration under President Woodrow Wilson, he stimulated production and distribution of food. In an even greater task after the armistice, Hoover directed postwar relief. His experience made him a valued adviser to Wilson in the treaty negotiations.

Hoover's fame had grown so that he was urged by members of both political parties to enter the 1920 presidential race. He refused, but joined President Warren G. Harding's Cabinet, where he was called "Secretary of Commerce and undersecretary of everything else."

AS Secretary of Commerce, Hoover's achievements were many and enduring. Among them he:
• Brought order to the infant airtransport and radio industries.
• Sent commercial agents abroad to improve markets for U.S. goods.
• Promoted development of inland waterways.
• Encouraged, through trade associations, producers to standardize products, to eliminate waste, and to improve quality.

In his eight years as Cabinet member and four years as President, Hoover proved himself a strong champion of conservation. He encouraged reclamation projects, the conservation of water and other natural resources, and the creation of wildlife refuges. An ardent fisherman, he was an enemy of stream pollution and unregulated commercial fishing. He supported the establishment of many national parks and monuments. Beyond question, he was the greatest Secretary of Commerce in our history.

DURING his presidency, an unending series of economic crises confronted Hoover. His farm program was a costly failure, and the 1930 Smoot-Hawley tariff law seriously hampered foreign trade.

Hoover refused to use federal resources to provide direct relief for the unemployed. This policy, combined with a rapidly worsening economic situation, ended his popularity. As a last resort, he advocated a series of bold economic moves. Thus, for the first time in U.S. history, the federal government was called upon to intervene to end a depression.

In his foreign policy, Hoover enjoyed modest success. He was a world leader for disarmament and cooperated with the League of Nations. He refused to recognize Russia. When Japan became aggressive in the Far East, Hoover refused to support measures that might risk war.

HOOVER, moderately liberal in his economic views, believed that the individual should have the maximum opportunity to achieve according to his abilities; but in the process he must recognize the rights of others. Hoover never ceased to emphasize that individualism and self-interest must be blended with "a sense of service." These ideals were among the guidelines he followed in his long career as a public servant.

His own career provided a splendid example. Government, he believed, should aid, protect, police, and promote social welfare, but it must not compete with private enterprise in the production and distribution of goods and services. People must "stand up to the emery wheel of competition."

Hoover left the White House in 1933 a discredited, embittered man. Much of his remaining life was given to defending his policies and to opposing measures that would, he feared, weaken individualism and initiative.

But his was a loyal opposition. He served Presidents Harry S. Truman and Dwight D. Eisenhower as a trusted adviser on foreign problems and governmental reorganization. Slowly Herbert Hoover won back the esteem of his countrymen, and when, on Oct. 20, 1964, he died in the 91st year of his life, much of the world joined a sorrowing nation in mourning the truly Great Humanitarian.

HARRIS G. WARREN

Wide World   Wide World   CBS

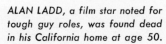

ALAN LADD, a film star noted for tough guy roles, was found dead in his California home at age 50.

LADY ASTOR, the first woman to sit in the British House of Commons, died in London at 85.

COLE PORTER, composer of many "hit" songs, died in a Santa Monica hospital at the age of 71.

Shilkret, Jack (1897?-June 16), orchestra conductor, pianist, and radio and recording artist, composed such successes as "April Showers Bring May Flowers" and "Lazy Summer Moon."

Sillanpää, Frans Eemil (1888-June 3), Finnish author of *Meek Heritage* (1919) and *The Maid Silja* (1931), was awarded the Nobel literature prize (1939) "for his exquisite art in painting the peasant life and nature of his country."

*****Sitwell, Dame Edith Louise** (1887-Dec. 9), great poetess and English lady of letters, often recited her poetry in rather bizarre and dramatic settings. She had a great affinity for Queen Elizabeth I, whom she somewhat resembled in appearance and dress. Dame Sitwell's books include *Collected Poems* (1930, 1954, 1957) and other poetry volumes, *The Pleasures of Poetry* (1930-1932), *Trio: Dissertations on Some Aspects of National Genius* (with brothers Sir Osbert and Sacheverell, 1937), and *The Atlantic Book of English and American Poetry* (anthology, 1958).

Stept, Sam H. (1897-Dec. 3), wrote "That's My Weakness Now" (1928) and the World War II song "Don't Sit Under the Apple Tree." He did musical scores for screen and stage plays, and wrote (with others) such songs as "Please Don't Talk About Me When I'm Gone" and "I Came to Talk for Joe."

Stott, Earl C. (1908-Sept. 4), founder and president of Polymer Corporation, pioneered in extruding nylon stock shapes, and introduced centrifugal casting and sintering techniques in plastics and low-cost casting of massive nylon shapes.

*****Szilard, Leo** (1898-May 30), Hungarian-born physicist and one of the great scientists who created the atomic bomb, with the late Enrico Fermi created the first nuclear chain reaction (1942) at the University of Chicago. He later turned to biophysics, and in 1964 left Chicago to join the Salk Institute for Biological Studies, La Jolla, Calif.

*****Teagarden, "Jack" Weldon J.** (1905-Jan. 15), was a great jazz trombonist, singer, and recording artist.

Toch, Ernst (1887-Oct. 1), Hungarian-born composer awarded the Pulitzer music prize (1956) for his *Symphony No. 3*, composed string quartets, some operas, and much chamber music. He had a successful career in Europe before coming to the United States in the 1930's.

Uhlmann, Erich Myron (1901-Sept. 14), German-born radiologist and Michael Reese Hospital (Chicago) tumor clinic director since 1938, is credited with development of the linear accelerator for electron treatment of cancer.

White, Terence Hanbury (1906-Jan. 17), British scholar and author of *The Sword in the Stone*, *The Ill-Made Knight*, *The Candle in the Wind*, and other King Arthur books, wrote *The Once and Future King*, basis of the musical *Camelot* (1960).

*****Wiener, Norbert** (1894-Mar. 18), scientist and mathematician known as the father of automation, was a developer of high-speed computers. He created the term *cybernetics*, and wrote *Cybernetics: Or Control and Communication in the Animal and Machine* (1948).

Willcox, Walter F. (1861-Oct. 30), Cornell University economics and statistics professor (on staff, 1891-1931), then served as a Bureau of the Census statistician. He promoted legislation which limits the U.S. House of Representatives to 435 members (1929), and advocated reducing its number to 300 by eliminating one seat a year for 135 years.

Williams, Oscar (1900?-Oct. 10), author of *Golden Darkness* (1921), *Hibernalia* (1938), *The Man Coming Toward You* (1940), and other poetry books, and edited the *Little Treasury* series of poetry books.

Williamson, John Finley (1888?-May 28), noted choral conductor and founder (1929) of the Westminster Choir College, Princeton, N.J., retired as its president in 1958.

Wright, Lawrence (1888-May 16), English music publisher and author of the ever-popular "Among My Souvenirs," also wrote "Are We Downhearted?" (World War I song); "That Old-Fashioned Mother of Mine" (lyricist, Worton David); and "Babette."

Wynyard, Diana (1906-May 13), English actress, played Jane Marryot in *Cavalcade* (1933), Grand Duchess in *Rasputin and the Empress*, and appeared in many other films. *Marching Song*, *The Bad Seed*, *Camino Real*, and *The Sea Gull* were stage successes.

*****York, Alvin C.** (1887-Sept. 2), the World War I Congressional Medal of Honor infantryman from Tennessee and subject of the film *Sergeant York*, was a corporal when he killed some 20 Germans and forced 132 others to surrender on Oct. 8, 1918, in the Meuse-Argonne offensive.

DEMOCRATIC PARTY

THE 1964 ELECTION left the Democratic party stronger than at any time since Franklin D. Roosevelt's landslide triumph of 1936. President Lyndon B. Johnson, who succeeded the assassinated John F. Kennedy on Nov. 22, 1963, ran for a full four-year term in his own right against the Republican candidate, Barry M. Goldwater of Arizona. He carried all but six states, amassing an electoral vote margin of 486 to 52.

It was ironic, however, that five states of the Deep South—Alabama, Georgia, Louisiana, Mississippi, and South Carolina—bolted from the first Southerner to occupy the White House since the other Johnson, Andrew, of Tennessee, in April, 1865. The Southern reverses were offset by Democratic gains in perennial Republican sections of New England and the Middle West. Vermont voted for a Democratic presidential candidate for the first time.

The party's fortunes in Congress were improved by overwhelming margins. Democrats gained 38 seats in the House of Representatives, giving them a majority of 155 seats, the greatest since 1936. In the Senate, a net two-seat gain gave them a 68-to-32 edge, the largest since 1940.

In the state legislatures, the Democrats staged some surprising advances. They captured both branches in Indiana, Iowa, Maine, Michigan, New York, and Utah. Since many states face redistricting, the Democrats were in a position to make changes advantageous to their future—as have the Republicans in the legislatures they dominated. In contests for governorships, the party lost control of three governors' mansions and took over two, still giving the Democrats a lopsided 33-to-17 gubernatorial edge. See ELECTIONS; GOVERNORS OF THE STATES; STATE GOVERNMENT.

The Wide Appeal of the party in 1964, according to political scientists and analysts, lay in the fact that to most voters it represented the broad center of American political life. The Republicans, on the other hand, advocated uncompromising conservative positions. They challenged such basic, established policies as Social Security, membership in the United Nations, and the attempt to contain yet coexist with the communist world. They also attacked the steady growth of the federal bureaucracy and its influence in the national life. Democratic campaign themes stressed peace, prosperity, and preparedness. Clearly, most people felt a sense of well-being and were satisfied with the way Lyndon Johnson had assumed the presidency under conditions of national tragedy and shock, and with the way he had performed his duties. See GOLDWATER, BARRY M.; REPUBLICAN PARTY; Section One, JAMES B. RESTON ON THE NATION.

As the party in power, the Democrats suffered few financial embarrassments during the campaign. Wherever he traveled, Mr. Johnson made a point of

PICTURES OF THE YEAR/Bob Gomel, *Life* © 1964 Time Inc.

A BLISTERING ATTACK on the Republicans was delivered by the Democrats' fiery keynoter, Senator John O. Pastore of Rhode Island.

RUNNING MATES BECOME SADDLE MATES as President Lyndon B. Johnson, left, and Senator Hubert H. Humphrey relax at the Johnson ranch after their victory.

visiting the so-called "President's Club," which consisted of substantial contributors in the large cities. Donations also came, of course, from thousands of other less affluent contributors.

Party Leadership unquestionably centered in the person of President Johnson. For the campaign he retained John M. Bailey as chairman of the Democratic National Committee. The cigar-chewing Connecticut strategist had been appointed in 1961 by President John F. Kennedy. Bailey was assisted by two other Kennedy aides, Lawrence F. O'Brien, special assistant in charge of congressional relations, and P. Kenneth O'Donnell, who had served both Presidents as appointments secretary.

The election brought to the fore other potential leaders, including two Kennedy brothers. Former Attorney General Robert F. Kennedy, who established residence in New York in a controversial move to run for the U.S. Senate, succeeded in unseating Senator Kenneth B. Keating in a tough race. Senator Edward M. "Ted" Kennedy, of Massachusetts, who ran for a full six-year term for the seat once occupied by his late brother, handily won re-election by a large margin, although hospitalized during the entire campaign with a broken back suffered in a crash of a light plane.

However, the man in the best position to assume the mantle of party leadership for the future was Vice-President-Elect Hubert H. Humphrey, the Senator from Minnesota chosen by Johnson to be

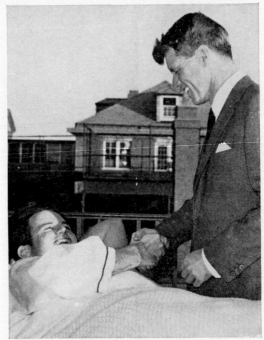

KENNEDY SENATE TEAM. Hospitalized Edward "Ted" M. and Robert F. shake after their respective victories in the Massachusetts and New York elections.

his running mate. His image as a man who stood too far on the liberal left to win popular support was substantially dissipated in the campaign. See HUMPHREY, HUBERT H.; KENNEDY, ROBERT F.

The Party Convention saw a break with tradition when President Johnson went before the Democrats at Atlantic City, N.J., to announce his choice of Humphrey and to place him in nomination. Earlier in the year, the President had eliminated Robert Kennedy from the list of possible vice-presidential choices. Southern opposition to Humphrey, who had been in the forefront of the civil rights battle since 1948, was considerably blunted by the Senator's successful mediation in a convention dispute over the seating of the Mississippi delegation. A Negro-led group calling itself the Mississippi Freedom Democratic party had challenged the all-white delegation, claiming Negroes had been excluded deliberately.

A highlight of the convention was the tribute to John F. Kennedy. His brother, Robert, mounted the rostrum to speak a few words but had to wait for nearly 20 minutes while the assembled delegates applauded, cheered, wept, and acclaimed with roars their testimonial to the memory of the late President.

Lyndon Baines Johnson had placed his vivid brand on the party, but the Kennedy name and influence, through the two senatorial brothers, was expected to remain strong in party councils.   PETER LISAGOR

See also JOHNSON, LYNDON B; KENNEDY, JOHN F.; PRESIDENT OF THE UNITED STATES.

"I just happened to be passing by . . . "

DENMARK expanded its contacts and trade with the U.S.S.R. and the communist nations in 1964. In February, Prime Minister Jens Otto Krag visited Russia, where he settled Danish property claims in territories taken over by the Soviets in World War II. Later, Premier Nikita S. Khrushchev visited Denmark and agreed to a trade expansion program between the two countries. Denmark also concluded trade pacts with Bulgaria, Hungary, and Yugoslavia.

Denmark, Norway, and Sweden began work on plans for a 3,800-man Scandinavian peace force to be placed at the service of the United Nations. Denmark also participated in the Nordic Council which, in February, rejected proposals that Scandinavia be declared a nonnuclear zone.

The Social Democratic party, headed by Krag, retained its 76 seats in parliament in the September elections. The premier's coalition partners, the Radical Liberals, lost one seat to the opposition Conservatives. As a result, the coalition no longer had its one-vote majority, and Krag resigned. Krag returned as prime minister, however, at the head of a minority government with an all-Social Democratic cabinet.

Population: 4,750,000. **Government:** King Frederik IX; Prime Minister Jens Otto Krag. **Foreign Trade:** exports, $1,992,000,000; imports, $2,746,000,000. **Principal Exports:** butter and cheese, machinery, meat.   FRED J. PANNWITT

See also EUROPE.

DENTISTRY became increasingly interested in techniques for transplanting teeth, which may someday lead to the establishment of tooth banks for the storage of replacement teeth. Dr. James Hayward, oral surgeon at the University of Michigan School of Dentistry, reported that the best results had been achieved in the transplanting of a patient's own wisdom teeth (third molars) to the first molar position. Wisdom teeth transplanted in this way have continued to live and function for many years. He emphasized that successful transplants depend on the re-establishment of the tooth's blood vessels and vital nerves in the new position.

The difficulty of performing successful transplants is due to the body's rejection of grafts transplanted from one person to another. Within the patient's own mouth, however, transplants have been relatively successful. Dr. Milton Siskin of the University of Tennessee College of Dentistry reported three successful transplants from one individual to another. The teeth used were healthy, but had been removed because of gum disease or for replacement by dentures. After the teeth were cleaned and the pulp (nerve) removed, they were stored in a refrigerator. Dr. Siskin noted that the removal of the pulp does not greatly affect a fully developed tooth, although there may be a slight color change and the tooth becomes slightly more brittle.

Oral Cancer. The dental profession joined other national health groups in warning the public about the hazards of smoking. The American Dental Association (ADA) House of Delegates adopted a resolution calling on all its members "to undertake an educational effort to inform their patients of the health hazards of the use of tobacco and, especially with young people, to warn against acquiring the habit of cigarette smoking."

Another possible connection between certain types of oral cancer and smoking was reported by the chief dental officer of the U.S. Army, who told members at the ADA's 105th annual session that the effect of smoking should be considered in diagnosis and treatment of oral cancer. Meanwhile, the ADA urged continued expansion of the new oral smear technique by which it is possible to detect oral cancer in the early stage.

Electric Toothbrushes. For the first time, two brands of electric toothbrushes received ADA recognition as "effective cleansing devices." But the ADA stressed that advertising claims must be limited to the cleansing value of the toothbrushes and exclude any therapeutic claims.

Dental Health Measures. The ADA reported that more than 1,000,000 high school and college football players were wearing mouth protectors, and that soon all football players would be expected to wear these protective devices because of their "proven effectiveness in reducing dental injuries."

With the fluoridation of New York City's water supply expected to begin in the spring of 1965, U.S. Public Health Service figures indicated that more than 62,000,000 persons will be receiving the benefits of this program.   LOU JOSEPH

DETROIT. After a 134-day press blackout, the *Detroit News* and the *Detroit Free Press* resumed publication on November 25. The blackout was caused by the longest effective strike against major metropolitan dailies in the United States. See PUBLISHING.

During the strike, city voters, despite strong opposition from most key state and local officials, passed a controversial ordinance giving property owners almost unlimited control of the use and sale of their property. A court test of the law was expected. Also passed was an amendment to the city charter which made it possible for Detroit's transit line to receive U.S. government aid.

Detroit's booming urban renewal program expanded to include spectacular new projects in 1964. Plans proceeded on a 302-acre housing and development project to be built near Wayne State University, which will purchase the first 100 acres for its own use. Land was cleared for Elmwood Park, a giant 460-acre, $200,000,000 housing project. Also, portions of the 236-acre Detroit Medical Center went into construction. This 10-year project will provide a $100,000,000 medical center.

In the planning stage was International Village, a cultural and commercial center to be erected on Detroit's now demolished skid row.   DONALD W. LIEF

DÍAZ ORDAZ, GUSTAVO (1911-   ), took office as the 58th president of Mexico on December 1. He succeeded Adolfo López Matéos, a friend of long standing. See MEXICO.

The Party of Revolutionary Institutions nominated Díaz Ordaz on Nov. 17, 1963, and he campaigned throughout the nation. He was strongly opposed by the communists. His principal opponent, however, was a right-winger, José Gonzales Torres of the National Action party. Díaz Ordaz won about 90 per cent of some 10,000,000 votes cast.

The new president was born in the state of Puebla. His father was a government accountant and his mother a teacher. He worked his way through the University of Puebla as an office boy in the agency where his father worked. He was graduated from law school in 1937. After a few years as a court clerk and later as a district attorney, he was named a judge. Díaz Ordaz rose from state to national prominence in 1943 when elected to the chamber of deputies. In 1946 he won a seat in the senate. He is a hard worker and known for serious-mindedness. Golf is one of his principal relaxations. He is slightly built and has a deeply lined face. President Díaz Ordaz and his wife have a daughter and two sons.   WALTER F. MORSE

DICTIONARY. See WORDS AND PHRASES, NEW; Section Five, DICTIONARY SUPPLEMENT.

DIPLOMAT. United States ambassadors and ministers in December, 1964, included the following:

Country	U.S. Ambassador
Afghanistan	John M. Steeves
Algeria	William J. Porter
Argentina	Edwin M. Martin
Australia	Vacant
Austria	James W. Riddleberger
Belgium	Douglas MacArthur II
Bolivia	Douglas Henderson
Brazil	Lincoln Gordon
Bulgaria	*Vacant
Burma	Henry A. Byroade
Burundi	Donald A. Dumont
Cambodia	Randolph A. Kidder
Cameroon	Leland G. Burrows
Canada	W. Walton Butterworth
Central African Rep.	Claude G. Ross
Ceylon	Cecil B. Lyon
Chad	Brewster H. Morris
Chile	Ralph A. Dungan
Colombia	Covey T. Oliver
Congo (Brazzaville)	Henry L. T. Koren
Congo (Léopoldville)	G. McMurtrie Godley
Costa Rica	Raymond J. Telles
Cyprus	Fraser Wilkins
Czechoslovakia	Outerbridge Horsey
Dahomey	Clinton Everett Knox
Denmark	Katharine Elkus White
Dominican Republic	W. Tapley Bennett, Jr.
Ecuador	Maurice M. Bernbaum
El Salvador	Murat W. Williams
Ethiopia	Edward M. Korry
Finland	Tyler Thompson
Formosa	Jerauld Wright
France	Charles E. Bohlen
Gabon	Charles F. Darlington
Germany, West	George C. McGhee
Ghana	William P. Mahoney, Jr.

Country	U.S. Ambassador
Great Britain	David K. E. Bruce
Greece	Henry R. Labouisse
Guatemala	John O. Bell
Guinea	James I. Loeb
Haiti	Benson E. L. Timmons III
Honduras	Charles R. Burrows
Iceland	James K. Penfield
India	Chester A. Bowles
Indonesia	Howard P. Jones
Iran	Julius C. Holmes
Iraq	Vacant
Ireland	Vacant
Israel	Walworth Barbour
Italy	G. F. Reinhardt
Ivory Coast	James W. Wine
Jamaica	William C. Doherty
Japan	Edwin O. Reischauer
Jordan	Robert G. Barnes
Kenya	William Attwood
Korea, South	Winthrop G. Brown
Kuwait	Howard Rex Cottam
Laos	William H. Sullivan
Lebanon	Armin H. Meyer
Liberia	Charles Edward Rhetts
Libya	E. Allan Lightner, Jr.
Luxembourg	William R. Rivkin
Malagasy Republic	C. Vaughan Ferguson, Jr.
Malawi	Sam P. Gilstrap
Malaysia	James D. Bell
Mauritania	Philip M. Kaiser
Mexico	Fulton Freeman
Morocco	Vacant
Nepal	Henry E. Stebbins
Netherlands, The	John S. Rice
New Zealand	Herbert B. Powell
Nicaragua	Aaron S. Brown
Niger	Robert Joseph Ryan
Nigeria	Elbert G. Mathews
Norway	Margaret Joy Tibbetts
Pakistan	Walter P. McConaughy
Panama	Jack H. Vaughn
Paraguay	William P. Snow
Peru	J. Wesley Jones
Philippines	William McC. Blair, Jr.
Poland	John M. Cabot
Portugal	George W. Anderson, Jr.
Romania	*William A. Crawford
Russia	Foy D. Kohler
Rwanda	Charles D. Withers
Saudi Arabia	Parker T. Hart
Senegal	Mercer Cook
Somalia	Horace G. Torbert, Jr.
South Africa, Rep. of	Joseph C. Satterthwaite
Spain	Robert F. Woodward
Sudan	William M. Rountree
Sweden	J. Graham Parsons
Switzerland	W. True Davis, Jr.
Syria	Ridgway B. Knight
Tanzania	William K. Leonhart
Thailand	Graham A. Martin
Togo	William Witman II
Trinidad-Tobago	Robert G. Miner
Tunisia	Francis H. Russell
Turkey	Raymond A. Hare
Uganda	Olcott H. Deming
United Arab Republic	Lucius D. Battle
Upper Volta, Rep. of	Thomas S. Estes
Uruguay	Wymberley De Renne Coerr
Venezuela	C. Allan Stewart
Vietnam, South	Maxwell D. Taylor
Yemen	*Parker T. Hart
Yugoslavia	C. Burke Elbrick

*Indicates minister

DISARMAMENT. A mushroomlike cloud funneling ominously from a nuclear explosion inside Communist China on October 16 hovered like a question mark over the year's efforts toward disarmament. It was a bitter blow to the 18-nation disarmament committee that had convened in Geneva, Switzerland, on January 21 in a fallout-free atmosphere of hope.

The preceding year had witnessed the signing of the partial nuclear test-ban treaty, the "hot line" agreement, and the United Nations (UN) resolution against the use of nuclear weapons in outer space. The Soviet Union had announced on Dec. 16, 1963, that it planned to reduce its military expenditures by 4.5 per cent of its total budget. U.S. Secretary of Defense Robert S. McNamara followed with an announcement on December 30 that the U.S. planned a military budget cut of $1,000,000,000. Later, President Lyndon B. Johnson raised this sum by an additional $100,000,000 in his budget message.

The President, in his State of the Union message on Jan. 8, 1964, announced that a cut of 25 per cent would be made in the production of enriched uranium. The Atomic Energy Commission (AEC), he said, would close four of its 14 reactors producing plutonium for weapons. He asked the Soviets to follow suit. Subsequently, as conferees representing 17 nations gathered in Geneva's *Palais des Nations* in a spirit of hope, President Johnson sent a list of five potential agreements to the conferees. They included: (1) prohibition of the threat or use of force, directly or indirectly, to change the boundaries or demarcation line of any nation, or to interfere in the adminis-

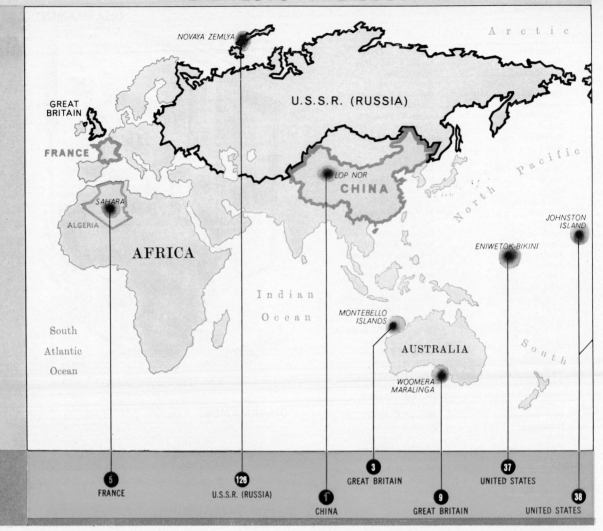

tration of, or access to, such territory; (2) a verified freeze of the number and characteristics of nuclear vehicles; (3) a verified agreement on the cessation of the production of fissionable materials; (4) creation of a system of observation posts to further reduce the danger of war by accident, miscalculation, or surprise attack; and (5) agreement to halt the spread of nuclear weapons.

Semyon K. Tsarapkin, the Soviet delegate, reiterated previous Russian proposals which included: (1) the reduction of military budgets; (2) a nonaggression pact between the North Atlantic Treaty Organization (NATO) and the Warsaw Pact countries; (3) the retention of some nuclear delivery vehicles until the end of Stage III, when all such vehicles would be destroyed; and (4) the establishment of observation posts, accompanied by a reduction of foreign troops in Germany and a commitment not to disseminate nuclear weapons to either East or West Germany. On January 28, Tsarapkin restated his

government's program, adding to it a proposal to destroy not merely the U.S. B-47 and its Soviet counterpart, the Badger, as the U.S. had previously recommended, but all bombers.

On April 20, President Johnson announced a further cut of 15 per cent in the production of enriched uranium over a period of four years, thus raising the total reduction to 40 per cent. Simultaneously, Russia disclosed that it had halted the construction of two reactors, that it would reduce substantially the production of U-235, and that it planned to devote more fissionable materials to peaceful uses. Next day, the then British Prime Minister Sir Alec Douglas-Home told Parliament that Great Britain's production of military plutonium was being gradually terminated.

Discussions in Geneva centered on measures for the destruction of bombers, the reduction of military budgets, and for halting the spread of nuclear weapons. But it was this latter subject that became

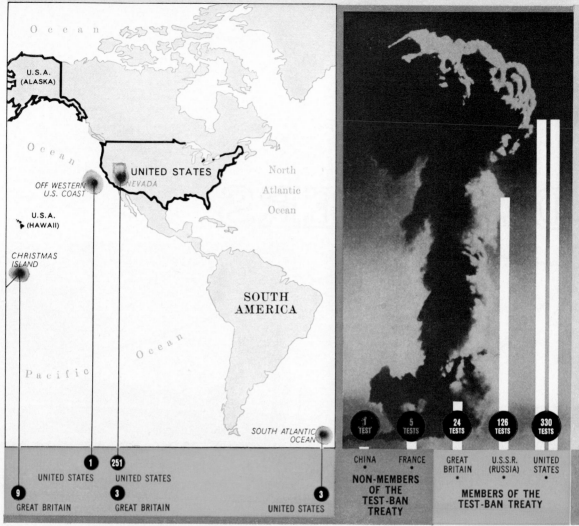

UNITED STATES · NEVADA

1 UNITED STATES

251 UNITED STATES

9 GREAT BRITAIN

3 GREAT BRITAIN

3 UNITED STATES

-1 TEST	5 TESTS	24 TESTS	126 TESTS	330 TESTS
CHINA ·	FRANCE ·	GREAT BRITAIN ·	U.S.S.R. (RUSSIA) ·	UNITED STATES ·
NON-MEMBERS OF THE TEST-BAN TREATY		MEMBERS OF THE TEST-BAN TREATY		

YEAR BOOK Map

the focal topic, with the proposed NATO multilateral force (MLF) proving the major stumbling block. The Soviet Union contended that MLF would open the door to acquisition of nuclear weapons by the NATO countries, especially West Germany. It was an argument calculated to play on the almost universal European fear of Germany. The United States countered that MLF would help to halt the spread of nuclear weapons because it would lock the West Germans into a nuclear force over which they would have no control; and that through participation, Germany's nuclear ambitions would be dissipated. Russia insisted that any agreement was contingent on the abandonment of MLF. See NORTH ATLANTIC TREATY ORGANIZATION (NATO).

The conference recessed on September 17. It was to reconvene in 1965, after the United Nations (UN) General Assembly had considered the negotiations. The inconclusiveness of the 1964 sessions undoubtedly resulted from uncertainties inherent in the British and American elections and from Russian Premier Nikita S. Khrushchev's difficulties with China and other communist powers. See COMMUNISM; RUSSIA.

One day after Khrushchev was ousted from the premiership, the Communist Chinese exploded their bomb. Although long forecast, alarm spread around the globe. On October 20, Chinese Premier Chou En-lai sent a message to all the world's leaders calling for a meeting to negotiate complete nuclear disarmament, reiterating the message he had sent immediately after the signing of the nuclear test-ban treaty in Moscow on Aug. 5, 1963. The only U.S. response was to suggest that Communist China sign the treaty. Late in 1964, Russia announced it would cut defense spending by $550,000,000. Later, the United States announced that it would reduce its national defense budget below the $50,000,000,000 mark by 1966.   TOM AND HARLE DAMMANN

See also ATOMIC ENERGY; CHINA, PEOPLE'S REPUBLIC OF.

DISASTERS

THE LAND, SEA, AND AIR continued to be scenes of disasters caused by human error and frenzy. The sports arena tragedy in Lima, Peru, was among the most shocking of 1964. It took 318 lives. Perhaps the most difficult to understand in this age of radar and technology was the sudden cutting in two of the tanker *Stolt Dagali* on Thanksgiving Day.

The number of lives lost in single aircraft disasters seemed to be on the rise with the increase of passenger capacity on the great jet airliners. Fires continued to claim many lives, often entire families, in single- and multiple-unit dwellings. Careless smoking practices, children playing with matches, and faulty heating units were among the major causes. Bus and truck accidents showed an increase in many countries due in part to greater world usage of motorized transportation.

The worst natural disasters continued to be those caused by hurricane-force winds and floods. These occurred most often in Asia, particularly India and Pakistan, and in the Pacific area of the world.

Major disasters around the world included the following:

Aircraft Crashes

Jan. 9—Zárate, Argentina. An Argentine airlines DC-3 caught fire in flight and crashed, killing 28 of 31 persons aboard.

Feb. 25—Northwest of New Orleans, La. An Eastern Air Lines DC-8 crashed in Lake Pontchartrain, and killed 58 persons aboard.

Feb. 29—Austrian Alps. A British Eagle International Airlines Britannia turbojet hit Mount Glungezer, and burned; 83 persons were killed.

Mar. 1—Tahoe City, Calif. A Paradise Airlines Constellation crashed near Lake Tahoe, killing 85 persons.

Mar. 8—Colombia. A Taxader Airlines DC-3 crashed between Madrid and Subacoche, killing 30 persons.

Mar. 28—Near Somma Vesuviana, Italy. An Alitalia Airlines plane crashed on Mount Vesuvius, killing 45 persons.

Apr. 17—Persian Gulf. A Middle East Airlines Caravelle crashed during a sandstorm; all 49 persons aboard were killed.

May 7—Near Dublin, Calif. A Pacific Airlines F-27 crashed, killing all 44 persons aboard. A passenger had shot the pilot and copilot.

May 8—Santa Rosa, Peru. An Argentine Military Transport Service DC-4 crashed into a coastal sand dune, killing 46 persons.

May 11—Clark Air Force Base, Philippines. A U.S. Military Air Transport Service Stratolifter C-135 crashed and burned. Most of the 78 persons killed were Air Force and Navy enlisted men.

June 20—Fengyüan, Formosa. A Chinese Civil Air Transport Line plane crashed, killing 53 persons.

July 9—Near Newport, Tenn. A United Air Lines Viscount crashed in the Great Smoky Mountains. All 39 persons aboard were killed.

Sept. 4—Near Nova Friburgo, Brazil. A Viação Aerea São Paulo Air Transport Viscount turboprop crashed on Nova Caledonia Mountain, killing 39 persons.

Oct. 2—Southeast of Granada, Spain. A Union des Transports Africains DC-6 crashed into a Sierra Nevada peak, killing all 80 persons aboard.

Steve McCutcheon

STREETS BUCKLED in Anchorage, Alaska, when the most violent North American earthquake since 1899 occurred on March 27.

DISASTERS

TRAGIC PROTEST. Soccer riot at the Lima, Peru, stadium, killed 318 persons. Rioting began when a fan disputed the referee's decision in a match between Argentina and Peru.

Nov. 15—Southwest of Las Vegas, Nev. A Bonanza Air Lines turboprop F-27 crashed on a mountain during a snowstorm, killing 29 persons.

Nov. 20—Near Angelholm, Sweden. A Linjeflyg Airlines plane struck an electric power line, and crashed; 31 persons were killed.

Nov. 23—Fiumicino Airport, Rome, Italy. A Trans World Airlines Boeing 707 skidded into a power roller and exploded, killing 48 persons.

Bus and Truck Accidents

Feb. 14—Near Resende, Brazil. Thirty-six persons drowned when a bus fell into a river.

Feb. 15—Near Rawalpindi, West Pakistan. A truck, taking children to a festival, skidded and fell into the Jhelum River; 40 children drowned.

Feb. 16—Near Sargodha, West Pakistan. A truck fell into a lake, drowning 26 children.

Apr. 6—Near Sebinkarahisar, Turkey. A bus plunged into the Alucura River; 35 persons drowned.

June 14—Near Rize, Turkey. A truck ran off a mountain road into a lake; 23 children drowned.

June 16—Louisiana. A Continental Trailways bus fell off the Lake Pontchartrain causeway into the water; 6 passengers drowned. Two gravel barges rammed into the bridge pilings, and 4 sections of the roadway fell into Lake Pontchartrain just as the bus came along.

July 11—Near Bergerac, Southwestern France. A truck ran into the railing of a canal bridge on which a crowd gathered to watch the Tour de France bicycle racers. The truck plunged into the canal and swept some 30 persons into the water with it; 10 of the 30 drowned.

July 27—Near Vittel, Eastern France. A bus fell off a railroad bridge; 19 persons were killed in the plunge.

Aug. 16—Near Bourg-St. Maurice, France. A bus plunged into a ravine, killing 17 young campers.

Aug. 29—Near Zempala, Mexico. Failing brakes plunged a bus into a ravine, killing 20 persons.

Sept. 20—Near Pasto, Colombia. Bad brakes caused a bus to plunge 500 feet down a cliff; 25 persons were killed.

Earthquakes

Jan. 18—Southern Formosa. The island's worst earthquake in 23 years killed about 100 persons.

Mar. 27—South Central Alaska was rocked by the strongest earthquake recorded in North America since 1899. The heaviest damages were in Anchorage. At least 66 persons were killed. See CIVIL DEFENSE; GEOLOGY.

June 16—Northern Japan. An earthquake hit Niigata, Yamagata, and Akita prefectures, claiming about 30 lives. The worst damage was in Niigata city, Japan's largest petroleum- and natural gas-producing center. Exploding oil tanks set off fires, adding to the quake's destruction.

July 5—Guerrero, Mexico. An earthquake in this Pacific Coast state shattered cities and mountain villages, killing about 40 persons.

Oct. 6—Northwestern Turkey. A series of earthquakes killed at least 30 persons.

Explosions and Fires

Jan. 22—Near Miami, Fla. A dynamite explosion at a rock quarry killed 3 men.

Jan. 31—Melbourne, Australia. Fire destroyed a suburban day nursery, killing 7 infants.

May 8—Manila, Philippines. Explosions and fire in a 6-story building killed about 30 persons.

May 26—Near Liège, Belgium. At least 19 persons perished in a fire at Wegimont Castle, now a state-owned vacation home for elderly persons.

July 8—Aurangabad, India. A fireworks factory explosion killed 20 persons.

July 15—Tokyo, Japan. Drums of oil, paint, and chemicals exploded, setting off harbor warehouse fires; 19 firemen were killed.

Aug. 24—Atlatlahuca, Central Mexico. A fireworks and gas explosion killed 45 persons.

Dec. 18—Fountaintown, Ind. Fire engulfed the McGraw Convalescent Home, a 60-year-old, two-story building, and killed 20 elderly patients.

Floods

Jan. 20—Minas Gerais, Brazil. Floods in the Jequitinhonha River Valley killed at least 60 persons.

Mar. 8-17—Ohio River Valley. Floods in Pennsylvania, Ohio, West Virginia, Kentucky, and Indiana killed 15 persons.

Mar. 27-29—Crescent City, Calif. A tidal wave, set off by the Alaskan earthquake, killed 12 to 15 persons.

June 8-10—Northern Montana. Heavy rains and melting snow brought floods, which broke dams and killed at least 30 persons.

July 17-19—Japan. Torrential rains, floods, and landslides killed more than 100 persons. Shimane prefecture was the hardest-hit area.

Aug. 15—South Korea. Heavy rains for the past week killed about 70 persons.

Sept. 13—Central South Korea. A rainstorm, flood, and landslides killed about 420 persons.

Sept. 29—Macherla, India. An irrigation reservoir broke following a three-day rain. About 1,000 persons died as water surged through the town.

Dec. 14—South Vietnam. Week-end floods in Khanhhoa and Ninhthuan provinces killed 500 persons.

Dec. 22-27—Pacific Northwest. Rain and melting snow brought floods to northern California, Oregon, Washington, Idaho, and Nevada. More than 40 lives were lost during the disaster.

Hurricanes, Cyclones, and Typhoons

Apr. 10-12—Eastern Pakistan. A cyclone killed about 2,000 persons in the Jessore district.

June 30—Northern Philippines. Typhoon *Winnie* killed at least 16 persons.

Aug. 22-24—Caribbean Sea. Hurricane *Cleo* killed 14 persons on Guadeloupe Island, and 124 in southern Haiti.

Aug. 25—Kyushu, Japan. Typhoon *Kathy* killed 13 persons on this island.

Sept. 5—South China Sea. Typhoon *Ruby* killed 30 or more persons in Hong Kong and Portuguese Macao. Refugees from mainland China reported 700 were killed in Kwangtung province.

Sept. 8—Florida. Hurricane *Dora* lashed 100 miles of the state's coast. Two navy fliers were killed as they took off from the Sanford Naval Air Station.

Sept. 25—Japan. Typhoon *Wilda* swept the west coast, killing more than 30 persons.

Oct. 13—Hong Kong was battered by typhoon *Dot*, which claimed at least 22 lives.

Oct. 13-14—Cuba and Florida. Hurricane *Isbell* killed 4 persons in Cuba, and 1 in Florida.

Nov. 20—Philippines. Typhoon *Louise* swept across 13 southern provinces, killing 200 to 300 persons.

Dec. 23—India and Ceylon. A cyclone and gigantic tidal wave swept Dhanushkodi islet in the Gulf of Mannar and northeastern Ceylon, taking more than 2,000 lives.

Mine Disasters

Feb. 9—Keelung, Formosa. An explosion in the Shui Kang coal mine killed 17 men.

May 25—Prestea, Southwest Ghana. A fire in a gold mine killed 12 miners.

June 12—Northern Afghanistan. An explosion in a mine killed 74 men.

July 27—Near Champagnole, France. Fourteen men were trapped by a cave-in in a limestone mine; 9 were rescued 8 days later, but the others were not located.

Dec. 20—Goyllarisquizga, Peru. A gas and dust explosion in a coal mine killed 57 men.

Shipwrecks

Feb. 11—Off South Wales, Australia. The Australian destroyer *Voyager* sank after colliding with the aircraft carrier *Melbourne;* 82 of the *Voyager's* crew were lost.

Feb. 19—Atlantic Ocean, 1,000 miles east of New York. The British merchant freighter *Ambassador,* wrecked by gale winds and mountainous seas, sank, taking 14 lives.

May 10—East Pakistan. A boat sank crossing the River Padma, taking the lives of 50 persons.

May 18—Off West Coast of Mexico. Forty-five persons were rescued from the burning *Sandanger,* a Norwegian passenger-freighter; 10 were missing.

June 30—Gulf of Mexico. A drilling barge exploded, burned, and sank, taking the lives of 20 men.

July 4—Off Cape Finisterre, Spain. The Spanish tanker *Bonifaz* collided with the French tanker *Fabiola.* Both caught fire, but the *Bonifaz* sank; 21 of its crew were lost.

July 23—Bône, Algeria. Explosions aboard the Egyptian munitions ship *Star of Alexandria* sank the freighter, damaged the harbor, and killed more than 100 persons.

Sept. 29—Off Coromandel Coast, India. About 450 fisherman in 75 boats were missing after a heavy gale.

Oct. 25—Sulu Archipelago, Philippines. A motor launch capsized, drowning 40 persons.

Nov. 26—Off New Jersey Coast. The Israeli luxury liner *Shalom* collided with the Norwegian tanker *Stolt Dagali* in a heavy fog. The tanker broke in two, and its stern section sank, drowning 19 of its crewmen.

Tornadoes

Mar. 4—Southern United States. Tornadoes in Alabama, Arkansas, Kentucky, Missouri, and Tennessee killed 6 persons.

Apr. 3—Wichita Falls, Tex. A tornado in the northwestern suburbs killed 7 persons.

Apr. 11—Middle Western United States. Tornadoes in parts of Iowa, Kansas, Missouri, and Nebraska, and a dust storm in Oklahoma killed 6 persons.

May 8—Southeastern Michigan. A tornado killed 10 persons. Worst hit area was Chesterfield Township.

Oct. 3—Larose, La. A tornado, spawned by hurricane *Hilda,* killed 19 persons.

Train Wrecks

Jan. 4—Jajinci, Yugoslavia. A commuter train ran into a standing passenger train, and hurled some of the commuter's old wooden coaches into the air; 66 persons were killed.

Feb. 1—Altamirano, Argentina. An express train ran head-on into a standing freight train. Their engines exploded, showering the coaches with burning diesel fuel; about 70 persons perished.

July 26—Custoias, Portugal. A train derailment killed 94 persons.

Oct. 16—Mirigama, Ceylon. A train was derailed, and coaches telescoped, killing 28 persons.

Nov. 1—Near Langhagen, East Germany. An express train ran head-on into the engine of a freight train, killing 39 persons.

Nov. 30—Saigon, South Vietnam. A big diesel locomotive, unattended, suddenly smashed into the city's main railway station; 17 persons were killed.

Dec. 20—Tacotalpa, Mexico. A fast-moving freight train ran into a passenger train, making a 10-minute stop at this mountain village, and killed 41 persons.

Other Disasters

Jan. 15—Paris, France. A 12-story, low-cost apartment building, under construction, collapsed and killed at least 15 workers.

Apr. 4—Madurai, Southern India. A two-story school building collapsed, killing 38 students and 2 teachers.

Apr. 24—Salvador, Brazil. A landslide in the suburban village of Lobato killed about 40 persons.

May 24—Lima, Peru. A Peru-Argentine soccer game ended in riot and panic, when the Uruguayan referee called a foul on Peru; 318 spectators were killed, many of them trampled to death in a sudden rush to the stadium exits before the steel gates were opened.

July 7—Near Chamonix, France. A snow slide on the Mont Blanc peak of Aiguille Verte killed 14 climbers. Among them was former world ski champion and Alpine guide Charles Bozon.

Aug. 23—Venezuela. A Caroni River Falls bridge collapsed, killing at least 30 sightseers.

Oct. 2—Cairo, United Arab Republic. A five-story apartment house collapsed, killing at least 24 persons.

Oct. 10—Wanli, Formosa. A landslide killed 22 persons.

Oct. 13—Anatolia, Turkey. Three landslides, caused by heavy rains, killed 13 persons.

Nov. 6—Piracicaba, Brazil. A nearly completed 15-story building collapsed, killing about 50 persons.

Nov. 29—Jalapa Enríquez, Mexico. A crowd of some 3,000 persons, rushing to leave a stadium, trampled to death about 20 persons.

DOMINICAN REPUBLIC

DOMINICAN REPUBLIC remained under the rule of the civilian triumvirate that had replaced the ousted president, Juan D. Bosch, in 1963. The government weathered various political and social crises as well as dissension among its own members to emerge stronger by the end of the year.

In October, a crisis in the armed forces was settled by the transfer of several high-ranking officers on the orders of President Daniel Reid Cabral Huberto. Most Dominicans had thought such an action would be impossible without precipitating a military coup. In September, a new law was promulgated setting Sept. 1, 1965, as the date for presidential, congressional, and municipal elections. The law also specified that campaigning would not be permitted before June, 1965.

Despite strong opposition, the government imposed taxes on alcoholic beverages, cigarettes, and gasoline. It introduced new import taxes, and imposed controls on foreign exchange. Social security deductions of employers also were raised to check increasing costs and prices and to bring in needed revenue that would help meet growing expenses and foreign trade debts.

Population: 3,500,000. **Government:** Civilian junta. **Foreign Trade:** exports, $205,000,000; imports, $208,000,000. **Principal Exports:** bananas, coffee, sugar. MARY C. WEBSTER

See also LATIN AMERICA.

DRUG. Despite continued criticism from government, scientists, and even the medical profession, the drug industry counted up total 1964 sales of about $3,700,000,000, or some 7 per cent above 1963. The biggest gains were in exports. For several years, sales abroad have grown about one and a half times faster than those at home. The industry's net profits were expected to climb in the range of 8 to 10 per cent for the year.

Federal Regulations for enforcing the advertising provisions of the 1962 Kefauver-Harris Act were announced in November. The U.S. Food and Drug Administration (FDA) was to keep a sharp eye on the advertising in the medical journals to ensure a fair balance "between the information of effectiveness and side effects."

In May, the FDA set up procedures, under the 1962 law, for manufacturers to prove the effectiveness of almost all drugs marketed since 1938 and still being sold. The industry had about five months to file its reports on the 2,000 or so products. But 41 drugmakers filed federal suit in July. They contended that the FDA had no right to require data on drugs placed on the market before 1963.

Challenges and Charges. The American Medical Association (AMA) and the FDA warned against potentially fatal side effects of two common drugs, *aminopyrine* and *dipyrone*, in November. During the year, the FDA seized several types of cold pills on charges of false claims. Antiwrinkle lotions also were seized for not being registered as drugs. The AMA later came to the defense of the creams, reporting that they did not harm the skin or cause demonstrable, long-lasting changes in skin tissue. Later, some of the lotions were put back on the market.

Industry Battle. The AMA also entered into the *tetracycline* fray in November by urging doctors to prescribe it by brand name rather than by its chemical, or generic, name. In August, the nation's largest drug wholesaler, McKesson & Robbins, Inc., had begun to market the antibiotic under its generic name, tetracycline, at $6 per 100 capsules, wholesale. The pharmaceutical manufacturers were selling it under their own brand names at about $17.50 per 100 capsules. Manufacturers reacted by cutting off supplies of the drug to McKesson. Out of a welter of legal suits and cross-suits, a federal court ordered the manufacturers to resume sales to McKesson.

The doctor who writes "tetracycline" lets the druggist fill the prescription with *any* tetracycline, including the low-priced McKesson's. If he writes a brand name, in most states the pharmacist must, by law, supply that brand. With total retail sales of tetracycline reaching $175,000,000 a year, the doctors' practice could make a big difference—in price to the patient and in profits to the pharmaceutical maker. ROBERT E. BEDINGFIELD

See also HEALTH; MEDICINE; MENTAL HEALTH.

EARTHQUAKES. See CIVIL DEFENSE; DISASTERS; GEOLOGY.

EASTERN ORTHODOX. The Patriarch of Constantinople (Istanbul) Athenagoras I, the first among the equal within the episcopate of the Eastern Orthodox Churches, met Pope Paul VI in the Holy Land in January. This was the first encounter of the Bishop of Rome with a primate of the Greek church since the ill-fated Council of Florence (1438-1439).

As a result of the meeting, which raised a storm of protest in some Orthodox circles, a special commission of Roman Catholic and Eastern Orthodox theologians will be created to study the doctrinal issues between the two churches.

For the first time since the beginning of the Vatican Council II, three official observers were appointed by Patriarch Athenagoras to attend the third session of the council. At the first two sessions, the Orthodox Churches were represented by official observers of the patriarchate of Moscow and a few theologians, who were guests of the Roman Catholic Secretariat for Promoting Christian Unity.

Russian Orthodox. In September, Alexis, the Patriarch of Moscow and head of the Russian Orthodox Church, paid an official visit to the head of the Anglican Church, Dr. Arthur Michael Ramsey, Archbishop of Canterbury.

The representative of the Moscow patriarchate in Western Europe, Archbishop Anthony Bloom, resigned and was replaced by Archbishop Pitirim, former dean of the Theological Academy in Moscow and a Soviet citizen. Archbishop Anthony, a White Russian émigré, had presided at a January meeting held in London to protest religious persecutions in the Soviet Union.

In the United States, the Standing Conference of Canonical Orthodox Bishops met in April to appoint a special committee of theologians to study the further unification of the 12 Orthodox jurisdictions in America.   ALEXANDER SCHMEMANN

ECUADOR continued under the rule of the four-man military junta which, on July 11, celebrated its first year in office. The reformist zeal with which the junta had taken charge was reflected in the nation's generally healthy economic situation.

During the year, import regulations were eased to soften the impact of a prolonged drought. In July, a new agrarian reform law was enacted under which 1,000,000 landless farmers were expected to benefit.

In 1964, for the first time in their operations, the World Bank, the International Development Association, the Agency for International Development, and the Inter-American Development Bank combined forces to provide a single loan. They granted Ecuador $39,000,000 to help finance a five-year road building program to cost $62,200,000.

Population: 4,950,000. **Government:** Military junta. **Foreign Trade:** exports, $158,000,000; imports, $123,000,000. **Principal Exports:** bananas, cocoa beans, coffee.   MARY C. WEBSTER

See also LATIN AMERICA.

PICTURES OF THE YEAR/Evelyn Straus, *New York Daily News*

ANGRY FACES reflect opposition to the busing of students to and from schools to achieve racial balance in New York City.

EDUCATION was marked by a significant increase in federal participation in school financing, important new developments on the civil rights front, and the recognition that education must shoulder the lion's share of the battle against poverty in the United States.

Federal appropriations to the United States Office of Education were approximately $1,000,000,000—they will rise to $1,500,000,000 in 1965—but even this was only a fraction of the total national contribution to education. Perhaps most significant, the Congress of the United States recognized for the first time that the national defense posture required a much broader educational booster than could be expected from the mere underpinning of science and mathematics.

Defense Education Act. The 88th Congress was called the "Education Congress" by President Lyndon B. Johnson. Building on its previous achievements, Congress in 1964 voted significant broadening of the National Defense Education Act (NDEA) of 1958. All the act's previous provisions for retraining teachers and the purchase of equipment and teaching materials (including laboratories) had been confined to science, mathematics, and foreign languages. But, with the 1964 congressional action, the same benefits were accorded history, geography, civics, English, remedial reading, and special education for

Wide World

STUDENT STRIFE. University of California students, at Berkeley, face a police line, as they protest university ruling concerning campus speechmaking.

disadvantaged children. Furthermore, librarians were to receive the same support as teachers.

In the past, recipients of NDEA loans who taught in public schools after graduation, could claim forgiveness of 10 per cent of the loan for each year of teaching (up to a maximum of 50 per cent). This privilege has now been extended to all teachers in public, private, and parochial schools, as well as in higher education.

Anti-Poverty Action. At least as important as the direct legislative steps for aid to education was the fact that about 60 per cent of the total effort and appropriations for community action under the Economic Opportunity Act will require educational action (see Social Welfare). During its first year, the measure's community action programs will provide some $240,000,000 to support such programs as preschool training for children, summer studies, and afterschool and weekend tutoring centers, to aid children in slum areas.

The work-training part of the program will offer $112,500,000 to help youths (16 to 21 years of age)

from slum areas to work and acquire good work habits while going to school part time or full time. A work-study program will offer some $56,000,000 for salaries for needy college students who will spend up to 15 hours a week serving in hospitals, social agencies, or in the community action program itself. A network of Job Corps residential centers and camps will not only provide basic education for thousands of youths, but will also become training centers from which teachers may go forth to staff schools in distressed rural and urban areas. The sites of 42 camps, the first of an expected 100, were announced during 1964. See Job Corps; VISTA.

Dr. Conant Continued. Following up the publication of his controversial book, *The Education of American Teachers*, Dr. James B. Conant, former president of Harvard University, announced in 1964 that he would help a number of colleges and universities translate his recommendations into action. In New York, aided by the state education department, five institutions—Brooklyn, Vassar, and Fredonia State colleges, and Cornell and Colgate universities—volunteered to attempt institution-wide responsibility for their own teacher training. Under this plan, the certification of a teacher would no longer be the responsibility of accrediting bodies which tend to represent education departments, but by all the relevant university departments.

At the same time, Dr. Conant published the next volume in his reform series, *Shaping Educational Policy.* He urged drastic housecleaning and subsequent strengthening of all state education authorities, including the elimination of political elections of chief state school officers. Following such reforms, he urged the establishment of an interstate commission for the shaping of a nationwide (rather than a rigidly national) educational policy.

School Enrollment. When the 1964-1965 academic year opened, 52,700,000 students were enrolled in all institutions, public and private, from kindergarten through university, according to estimates by the U.S. Office of Education and the National Catholic Welfare Conference.

The Elementary Grades, from kindergarten through grade eight, accounted for about 35,200,000 pupils, compared with 35,000,000 the year before. About 29,700,000 were in public schools and some 4,600,000 in Roman Catholic parochial schools.

In the High Schools (grades 9 through 12), the total was estimated at 12,600,000, compared with 12,200,000 the previous year. Public high schools accounted for 11,200,000, with Roman Catholic parochial schools adding another 1,068,424. Also, there were about 1,400,000 enrolled in all other private schools.

On the College Scene, the U.S. Office of Education reported 4,950,000 enrolled for full-time credit in 2,172 institutions, an increase of 6.7 per cent over the previous academic year. This included a junior college enrollment of about 700,000.

Classroom Shortage. President Johnson said in November that 400,000 additional classrooms would be needed in the next five years. This would total at least 50,000 more classrooms than are being provided at the current pace of construction.

Major Issues. In the North, the issue of *defacto* segregated schools remained the major issue. This was climaxed in New York City by two massive one-day civil rights school boycotts, and one two-day boycott by primarily white parents' groups against certain integration measures. But the conflict also led to important new experiments, including the pairing of schools. Also underway were crash saturation programs that included compensatory education for deprived three-year-old youngsters of unschooled, nonverbal parents in ghetto areas.

The Berkeley campus of the mammoth University of California was rent with strife at year-end. The immediate cause was typical of the issues that gripped students in colleges and universities in civil-rights conscious 1964: whether the university had a right to discipline students for political activity off campus that might result in illegal activity. Cancellation by the university of the right to solicit for political causes on campus resulted in the arrest of some 800 sit-ins on December 3. Some observers thought that behind the turmoil they detected a still deeper issue facing education today: the protest of the students against the anonymity of the giant "multiversity."

Aid Ideology. The Educational Policies Commission and the National Education Association (NEA) which, in the past, had supported only across-the-board federal aid, to be distributed to local schools on a state-wide basis, reversed their stand and approved of such categorical aid as the National Defense Education Act. This step was taken in recognition of the fact that the church-state controversy is likely to block general aid for some time to come.

Teachers. The rivalry between the NEA (more than 903,000 members) and the AFL-CIO-affiliated American Federation of Teachers (AFT) continued. The AFT made further gains in big cities and, to capitalize on its capture of New York City, named Charles Cogen, former New York local president, to the presidency of the Chicago-based AFT. In New York City, the AFT asked for a scale of salaries ranging from $6,000 to $14,000.

Vocational Education

The annual federal appropriation to vocational education was boosted to $60,000,000 in 1964 by a provision of the milestone bill passed in Congress late in 1963. This sum will rise to an ultimate high of $225,000,000 in 1967, and in every year thereafter.

In 1964, the stress of new vocational aid programs and corresponding federal support was needed for training in a variety of new industries, including the electronics and computer fields. But even more important was the recognition that, as many blue-collar areas of employment were shrinking, white-collar office and service jobs in the service industries were expanding.

Equally important was the expanding scope of institutions. In addition to the traditional vocational schools, the two-year community colleges were taking over an important part of up-to-date vocational training.

The Larger Picture. An important factor in making vocational education a new partnership of local and national interest was the availability of federal funds on a 50-50 matching basis, with half of the contribution coming from the states. Even more significant, vocational aid was being considered as part of a greater enterprise. This became especially clear with the passage of the Economic Opportunity Act of 1964, which would set up new links between school, training, and employment.   FRED HECHINGER

See also AMERICAN LIBRARY ASSOCIATION (ALA); LIBRARY; Section ONE, LAWRENCE A. CREMIN ON EDUCATION.

EDUCATIONAL FOUNDATIONS

EDUCATIONAL FOUNDATIONS. Major educational foundations reporting on their activities in 1964 included the following:

Alfred P. Sloan Foundation, Inc., New York City, reported assets of $299,428,278 as of Sept. 30, 1964. Grants of nearly $1,400,000 were made to 94 scientists in United States and Canadian universities for basic research in the physical sciences. The foundation now supports 440 scholarships in some 45 universities.

Carnegie Corporation of New York reported grants exceeding $10,600,000 for educational purposes in 1962-1963. Research experiments and training programs in education and public and international affairs in the United States received $9,827,589 in grants. Educational institutions and individuals in British Commonwealth countries, principally in Africa, were given $811,000. New grants announced included $100,000 for the nation's first survey of Japanese immigrants to the United States before 1924.

The Commonwealth Fund, New York City, reported assets of $86,423,355 as of June 30, 1964. Appropriations totaled $4,833,432. Medical education and community health received $3,341,432; fellowships and awards in the field of health, $574,000; and the Division of International Fellowships, $600,000.

Field Foundation, Inc. New York City, reported assets of $39,082,813 as of Sept. 30, 1964. Grants to child welfare, interracial relations, and social service totaled $2,142,382. The Bank Street College of Education received $300,000 for an educational poverty project in New York City's slum area.

Ford Foundation, New York City, reported assets of $2,725,586,958 as of Sept. 30, 1963, and an income of $140,311,913. Grants approved included $62,332,289 for education in the United States; $5,601,108 for the humanities and the arts; $14,-221,913 for public affairs; $5,882,200 for population projects; $16,017,141 for international training and research; $17,615,700 for science and engineering; $15,841,957 for economic development and administration; $10,032,578 for international affairs; and $37,303,994 for overseas development.

John A. Hartford Foundation, Inc., New York City, reported assets of $181,213,698 as of Dec. 31, 1963. Income totaled $15,086,819. Grants for programs in medical research, treatment of illnesses, and education came to $14,810,767.

John and Mary R. Markle Foundation, New York City, reported assets of $31,211,876 as of June 30, 1964. Income totaled $1,486,267, and appropriations, $1,779,845. Scholars in Academic Medicine received $750,000, and medical education program, $440,000.

John Simon Guggenheim Memorial Foundation made fellowship awards of $1,882,000 to 312 scholars, scientists, and artists to further their studies.

Rockefeller Foundation, New York City, began its second half century in 1963, and defined major areas in which it would now work: the world-wide conquest of hunger, solutions of population problems, the strengthening of emerging universities in the developing countries and in the United States, the improvement of educational opportunities for disadvantaged minorities, and the development of cultural opportunities for all. Appropriations in these respective areas were: $8,094,248 to the agricultural sciences; $6,928,840 to the medical and natural sciences; $11,-904,772 to the humanities and social sciences; more than $4,300,000 to prepare disadvantaged Negro and other students for college and for special scholarships for them; and some $600,000 for drama and mus.c training projects and the development of performing arts centers.

EGYPT. See United Arab Republic (UAR).

EIRE. See IRELAND.

318

ELECTIONS

CROSS THE NATION, on Nov. 3, 1964, the American people gave Lyndon Baines Johnson an overwhelming mandate for his "Great Society." President Johnson and his running mate, Senator Hubert H. Humphrey of Minnesota, carried 44 states and the District of Columbia. The landslide swept the Democratic party into firmer control of Congress and into power in many of the states.

The 1964 election was a record breaker. President Johnson, according to official returns compiled by *Congressional Quarterly*, won 61.0 per cent of the total popular vote, the largest percentage in U.S. history. The previous record was the 60.8 per cent for Franklin D. Roosevelt in 1936.

POLITICAL PANDEMONIUM BREAKS OUT on the convention floor at Atlantic City after Democrats acclaim Lyndon B. Johnson as their 1964 standardbearer.

John Dominis, *Life* © 1964 Time Inc.

Gene Pesek, *Chicago Sun-Times*

Wide World

TWO LOOKS, one sad and the other glad, portray the 1968 presidential hopes of two Republican governorship contenders. Illinois' Charles H. Percy, left, grimly watches tally of defeat. Michigan's George Romney gives his wife, Lenore, a victory hug.

Winning 43,121,085 of the record 70,640,289 votes cast, Lyndon Johnson also rolled up a record plurality of 15,975,924 votes.

For the first time in its history, the rock-ribbed Republican state of Vermont voted for a Democratic presidential candidate. Johnson won 66.3 per cent of its vote. The Democrats also won in the usually "safe" Republican states of Maine, Nebraska, Indiana, Colorado, and Kansas. Even in the Democratic South, where the administration's civil rights stand sent many voters into the Republican camp, the President won 51.7 per cent of the popular vote and held the electoral votes of six of the 11 states.

It was a shattering defeat for the type of Republican conservatism that was espoused by Barry M. Goldwater. The Senator from Arizona and his running mate, vice-presidential candidate William E. Miller, tried to offer the voters "a choice, not an echo." Voters chose the Republicans in only five Southern states and, by a narrow margin, in Goldwater's home state of Arizona. Goldwater carried, besides Arizona, the states of Alabama (where the President's name was not even on the ballot), Georgia, Louisiana, Mississippi, and South Carolina. Except for Georgia, those states also broke with the Democratic party in 1948, when they voted for J. Strom Thurmond's States' Rights Democratic party.

The Electoral College, which met on December 14, cast 486 electoral votes for Lyndon Johnson and Hubert Humphrey, and 52 for Barry Goldwater and William Miller. The Electoral College victory was the second largest in history, topped only by Roosevelt's 523-to-8 triumph in 1936.

Goldwater began his disastrous campaign by declining to compromise with the moderate and liberal wings of his party, which he had so badly outmaneuvered in the preconvention electioneering. He declared in his acceptance speech at San Francisco that ". . . extremism in the defense of liberty is no vice . . . and moderation in the pursuit of justice is no virtue." Against the background of charges that the Arizonan was being supported by radicals and extremists in society, the speech merely rubbed salt into the party wounds.

As the campaign progressed, Goldwater and Miller attacked the increasing role of the federal government. Goldwater denied that poverty was a pressing concern. He argued that civil rights protection for Negroes was a state responsibility, and he blamed the administration for corruption and for contributing to a low moral tone in the nation. In the field of foreign relations, he accused the Democrats of being "soft on communism."

The Democratic Strategy. Their confidence buoyed by the opinion polls and the country's amazing fourth year of prosperity, Democratic candidates Johnson and Humphrey played a quiet, defensive game. They mostly ignored the charges of the Goldwater-Miller camp. In their jet-borne campaign swings across thousands of miles of U.S. countryside, the two Democrats asked for an overwhelming mandate at the polls and warned against overconfidence.

President Johnson credited his administration with continuing prosperity and avoiding a major war. He pointed proudly to the Civil Rights Act of 1964, tax reductions, and the steps that were taken toward nuclear arms reduction.

Congressional Elections. When the 88th Congress adjourned, the Democrats held 66 Senate seats to the Republicans' 34. In the 1964 election, 35 Senate seats—26 Democratic and 9 Republican—were contested. The Democrats gained two more seats, winning 28 of the senatorial contests. Thus, when the Senate of the 89th Congress convened, the Democrats held 68 seats, the Republicans, 32. See CONGRESS OF THE UNITED STATES (tables).

In three Senate races, the Democratic tide swept out Republican incumbents. In *New York*, former Attorney General Robert F. Kennedy, the late President's brother, took a seat from incumbent Republican Kenneth B. Keating, a moderate who refused to support the Goldwater ticket. In *New Mexico*, Goldwater Republican incumbent Edwin L. Mechem was unseated by Representative Joseph M. Montoya. In *Maryland*, Joseph Davies Tydings was the third Democrat to replace a Republican Senator. He won his father's old seat from incumbent J. Glenn Beall. In another show of Democratic strength *Ohio*'s Senator Stephen M. Young held off challenger Robert A. Taft, Jr., who was trying to follow in his father's footsteps into national Republican prominence.

Ticket splitting saved the day for the Republicans in *California*. There, despite the Johnson landslide, Republican actor George Murphy bested Democratic incumbent Senator Pierre Salinger. Ticket splitting also helped *Pennsylvania's* moderate Republican Senator Hugh D. Scott, Jr., defeat Genevieve Blatt in an extremely close race.

In the House of Representatives of the 88th Congress, there were 257 Democrats and 178 Republicans, including the five vacancies. All 435 seats were contested in November. When the 89th convened, the Democrats held the largest majority since 1936, with 295 seats to the Republicans 140. The net Democratic gain was 38. And the Republican-conservative Democrat coalition, which so often opposed liberal legislation in the 88th Congress, would be weakened in the 89th.

Governorship Races were the only election category where Republicans scored a net gain. In the 25 state contests the Democrats won 17 and the Republicans eight, a gain of one. Republicans turned out Democrats in Massachusetts, Washington, and Wisconsin. Democrats defeated Republicans in Arizona and Utah. See GOVERNORS OF THE STATES.

Two races were watched for their bearing on the future leadership of the Republican party. The second-term victory of Michigan Republican George M. Romney put him in strong contention for the Republican presidential nomination in 1968. Another frequently mentioned Republican presidential possibility, Illinois' Charles H. Percy, however, lost to Democratic incumbent Governor Otto J. Kerner. Romney had avoided endorsement of the Goldwater ticket, which Percy had backed without much ardor.

The Legislatures. In six states, the Democratic landslide swept Republicans out of both houses of the legislature. Riding the crest of the Johnson wave, Democrats won in all 62 counties of New York, gaining control of both houses of the New York legislature for the first time since 1934. In Indiana, also, the Democrats wrested control of the legislature from the Republicans for the first time since 1936.

Exactly a month after some of the most cumbersome balloting in the nation, Illinois voters learned that all 118 Democratic legislative candidates and only 59 of the 118 Republicans had been elected. Because a reapportionment formula could not be found in time, the state representatives had to be elected at-large. With 236 names on a bath towel-sized ballot, it was a slow job for voters and a nightmare for tally clerks. With the Johnson landslide, straight-ticket votes gave the Democrats their unprecedented 2-to-1 majority in the lower house.   CAROL THOMPSON

See also DEMOCRATIC PARTY; GOLDWATER, BARRY M.; HUMPHREY, HUBERT H.; JOHNSON, LYNDON B.; MILLER, WILLIAM E.; REPUBLICAN PARTY; Section One, JAMES B. RESTON ON THE NATION; STATE GOVERNMENT.

"That's progress, old boy."

ELECTRIC POWER rode the crest of the business boom as the industry strove to meet the energy demands of the industrialized nations' mushrooming populations and rising incomes. In the United States, total utility and industrial power production rose about 7.2 per cent in 1964, reaching 1,080,000,-000,000 kilowatt-hours (kwh). In Canada, the year's gain was 6.8 per cent, to about 130,000,000,000 kwh in 1964. By the end of 1964, the U.S. electric-power industry had expanded its total capacity to 221,-900,000 kw, a rise of 5.7 per cent for the year. And 60,800,000 kw more were to be added during the five years 1964 through 1968. But more than capacity was needed.

The delivery of peak loads of electric power at widely separated points at varying hours was taxing capacity. The industry made notable progress in the year toward the answer—an eventual nationwide power grid. A Federal Power Commission (FPC) study issued in December urged such a grid for the nation's 3,600 power systems. It saw a saving in costs to consumers of 27 per cent by 1980, or an average power cost of 1.2 cents per kwh versus the present 1.7 cents, if such a plan were carried out.

In September, a $700,000,000, 11-state *intertie* (an interconnecting network of transmission lines and generating plants) was approved by Congress. Four long-distance, extra-high-voltage lines will interlink public and private power between the Pacific Northwest and California and the Southwest. Plans for expansion of at least five other vast interties or power pools were announced later in the fall.

Gross operating revenues of investor-owned electric utilities in the United States in 1964 were estimated at $12,190,000,000, a rise of 5.3 per cent above the $11,580,000,000 in 1963. Capital outlays for new construction climbed nearly 9 per cent in 1964 to $3,600,000,000.   Robert E. Bedingfield

See also Atomic Energy; Coal; Dam; Engine and Energy; Water and Flood Control.

ELECTRICAL EQUIPMENT makers, particularly the utility suppliers, faced a brightening future in 1964. They had gone through several lean years after having slashed prices heavily in the 1950's to get utilities to buy generators and other heavy equipment. Then efforts to firm up prices resulted in price-fixing convictions and some 2,000 triple-damage suits, many of which were finally settled in 1964. Such payments were ruled tax-deductible as business expenses, the Internal Revenue Service ruled in July. General Electric reported it had made settlements totaling $173,000,000 covering 95 per cent of its suit-challenged sales.

With those difficulties past, the heavy equipment makers have begun to profit from two developments in the electric utility industry: (1) the mushrooming demand for electricity and thus the need for more generating facilities, and (2) the move toward *interties* (interconnections to exchange power between utility systems or pools). This led to a surge in demand for heavier equipment to generate and transmit extra-high voltages over long distances.

Appliance and electronic equipment sales increased in 1964, sparked by a rise of about 50 per cent in sales of color television receivers to more than 1,250,000 sets. Development of the space-saving rectangular tube was expected to help increase sales of color television sets.   Robert E. Bedingfield

See also Communications; Radio; Television.

ELECTRONICS recorded striking technological advances in wireless power, including the test flight of an aircraft powered solely by radio energy. The experimental flight in November, conducted by Raytheon Company at Burlington, Mass., involved the energizing of a small helicopter with a beam of 2,450-megacycle microwaves, which had an initial power of three kilowatts. The power transmission was developed from a discovery that small silicone diodes can pick microwave energy out of the air and turn it into direct current with reasonable efficiency.

Earlier in the year, scientists at the same company sent several hundred watts of electricity through the air over a distance of 25 feet. Although only 25 per cent efficient, the wireless transmission was considered a major step toward a goal scientists have sought for 65 years.

Light-Beam Transmitter. At the Langley Research Center of the National Aeronautics and Space Administration (NASA) in Hampton, Va., a new system was developed for voice communication on a beam of light. The only power needed was a set of two batteries, one for the light source and another for the receiving amplifier.

The system has such potential uses as air-to-sea rescue work, in blasting operations, and in combat situations. The system is also said to be adaptable to infrared and ultraviolet light.

Lasers. A host of practical applications for lasers were developed in 1964. Among them were:
• A "laser eraser" capable of vaporizing typewriter ink without marking the paper, developed by Dr. Arthur L. Schawlow of Stanford University in California.
• A laser beam capable of destroying dental cavities, discovered at the Children's Hospital Research Foundation in Cincinnati by four doctors—Leon and Bernard Goldman, Peter Hornby, and Robert Meyer.

Early in the year, two strains of cancer in mice were destroyed by a laser developed at the Redstone Arsenal in Huntsville, Ala., by Dr. John Peter Minton of the National Cancer Institute.

Radio Corporation of America engineers disclosed that they had used a laser to drill microscopic holes, one ten-thousandth of an inch in diameter, in tungsten wire.   Sergei Lenormand

See also Automation; Computers; Electrical Equipment.

EL SALVADOR. Opposition leaders congratulated President Julio Adalberto Rivera on the elections held in March. It was the consensus that for the first time since 1931 nationwide voting took place without interference from the military. The president's Party of National Conciliation maintained its majority in the legislative assembly.

Renewed political and economic confidence was felt by the republic's business community. Coffee producers estimated that the 1964-1965 crop would yield about 1,800,000 bags as compared to 1,650,000 for the previous season. A regional network of cold storage warehouses was under construction throughout the country to improve the marketing of various foodstuffs.

Population: 2,825,000. **Government:** President Julio Adalberto Rivera. **Foreign Trade:** exports, $256,000,000; imports, $191,000,000. **Principal Exports:** coffee, cotton, seafoods.   MARY C. WEBSTER

See also LATIN AMERICA.

EMPLOYMENT. See AUTOMATION; BUSINESS; EDUCATION; JOB CORPS; LABOR; Section One, JAMES B. RESTON ON THE NATION; SYLVIA PORTER ON THE ECONOMY; SOCIAL WELFARE; VISTA.

ENGINE AND ENERGY. Rapid developments in the field of magnetohydrodynamic (MHD) generators may increase the efficiency of conventional fossil fuel furnaces to more than that of nuclear power plants, the Central Electricity Generating Board in Great Britain revealed in studies published in 1964. The studies upset previous estimates that nuclear power would rapidly outstrip fossil fuel efficiency in the coming years. In an MHD generator, current is produced by a stream of electrically conductive gas, moving through the lines of force in a magnetic field, somewhat in the manner of a conventional generator in which a moving copper wire cuts the lines of magnetic force.

In July, 400 scientists from 26 countries gathered in Paris to exchange information on the latest experimental developments in the field of MHD technology. At the meeting, Westinghouse engineers described the first "closed-loop" system to have both a MHD generator and an MHD motor, thus producing electricity without moving parts of any kind.

Submarine Engine. At the American Chemical Society in Philadelphia, Pa., the design of a new hydrogen generator was described by W. H. Heffner of the M. W. Kellogg Co., New York City. When developed, it may result in nonatomic submarines that can stay under water for months at a time. In the proposed generator, wood alcohol and steam would be changed into hydrogen, carbon monoxide, and carbon dioxide. These gases would then enter a coil of palladium and silver that would allow only the hydrogen to pass through its walls to feed fuel cells and generate electric power. The waste gases would be burned with oxygen to produce the heat needed to operate the generator.

Solar Power. In January, a new solar engine was patented by Dr. Farrington Daniels, professor emeritus at the University of Wisconsin, and Dr. Theodor Finkelstein of the Battelle Memorial Institute in Columbus, Ohio, where a small model of the device is in operation. The new engine's unique feature is a transparent plate of quartz which absorbs the sun's radiant energy directly, rather than indirectly and less efficiently through a metal surface as in other types of solar machines.   SERGEI LENORMAND

ENGLAND. See GREAT BRITAIN.

ENTOMOLOGY. See INSECT.

ESPIONAGE. Rome's bustling Fiumicino Airport was the scene of the year's most bizarre spy story. On the night of Nov. 17, 1964, United Arab Airlines Flight 784 prepared to take off for Cairo. Suddenly, a minibus from the embassy of the United Arab Republic (UAR) darted up to the jetliner. Two Egyptian diplomats began putting a wardrobe trunk labeled "Diplomatic Mail 33" aboard the plane. Italian customs officials were routinely clearing it, when they heard someone whimpering in Italian inside the trunk, "Help! Assassins!"

The Egyptians fled, with Italian police in hot pursuit. After a wild chase, a police car forced them to halt on the road to Rome. The police opened the

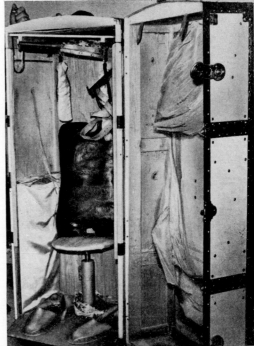

Wide World

"DIPLOMATIC MAIL #33," was the label on this bizarre device with which Egyptian functionaries tried to smuggle a man by jetliner out of Italy.

trunk. Inside, they found one Mordecai Luk, 28, an Israeli who reportedly defected to Egypt in 1961. He was bound, gagged, drugged, and strapped to a chair that looked like something out of a medieval torture chamber. A steel device held his head. Built-in boots imprisoned his feet. Marks inside the trunk indicated it had been similarly used before.

Luk told police he spoke 10 languages, including Arabic and Hebrew, and that he had been paid by the United Arab Republic (UAR) to "supply them with information sooner or later." He had a "cover" job as a tourist interpreter in Naples. The Italian government completed his travels by deporting him to Israel, where it was said that he was a deserter from the Israeli army. Italy ousted his abductors. But nagging questions remained: Was Luk really an Israeli double-agent, unmasked by the Egyptians? And, for whom else had the strange, white "trunk" been used in the past?

America's U-2 spy planes kept photo-reconnaissance watch over Cuba, Laos, Eastern Europe, Communist China, and other trouble spots. But the high-flying U-2 was almost old hat. Lockheed, which built the U-2, came out with a faster, higher-flying replacement (see AVIATION). Communist China reported shooting down a pilotless robot U-2. Meanwhile, the U.S. Samos satellite maintained photo-reconnaissance over the Soviet Union. At the same time the Soviets boasted they had the same kind of space-spy capability.

Apparently tipped by a Soviet defector, U.S. experts found 40 *bugs* (hidden microphones) in the walls of the U.S. embassy building in Moscow. It was presumed they were put there in 1952, when Soviet workmen refurbished the building.   WARREN ROGERS

ETHIOPIA signed a truce with its neighbor, Somalia, in March, calling for an end to their six-month border dispute. Partly as a result of its relations with Somalia, which remained strained, Ethiopia signed a defense pact with Kenya in June. Kenya, like Ethiopia, had also been embroiled with Somalia over border warfare (see KENYA; SOMALIA).

Addis Ababa, Ethiopia's capital, was named permanent headquarters for the Organization of African Unity (OAU). In August, Ethiopia rejected a request by Congolese Premier Moise Tshombe for military aid, saying all such aid should be given through the OAU.

The World Bank gave Ethiopia a $23,500,000 loan in 1964 to help finance a hydroelectric power development program. Japanese textile firms invested $1,500,000 in Ethiopia's state-owned cotton factory.

Population: 21,500,000. **Government:** Emperor Haile Selassie I; Premier Akilou Abde Wold. **Foreign Trade:** exports, $100,000,000; imports, $99,000,000. **Principal Exports:** coffee, fruits, hides and skins, and vegetables.   WILLIAM SPENCER

See also AFRICA.

EUROPE

EUROPE FLOUNDERED in indecision and a maze of cross purposes in 1964. In both Western and Eastern Europe, old allegiances and dependencies were fading, and no clear guide to the pattern that might replace them had yet emerged.

Western Europe, sidetracked since early 1963 on its road to economic and political unity, struggled to find a middle course between the nationalism of Charles de Gaulle and the aspirations of those who sought to build an integrated community in cooperation with the United States (see FRANCE). The North Atlantic Treaty Organization (NATO) showed signs of serious strain, particularly in the quarrel over creating a multilateral force (MLF) with nuclear weapons (see NORTH ATLANTIC TREATY ORGANIZATION [NATO]). The European Economic Community (EEC, or Common Market) made a historic breakthrough in December to a unified policy on agricultural prices, but found its economic progress slowed throughout the year by political bickering.

Trade patterns were complicated by the continuing split between the Common Market and its rival group of West European nations, the European Free Trade Association (EFTA). The deputy secretary-general of EFTA, Knut Hammarskjöld, speaking in Detroit, Mich., on December 9, summarized the situation in Western Europe by saying it "is more fluid today than it has been since the Hundred Years' War, which ended five centuries ago. . . . So many aspects of Western Europe's life, so many facets of the sovereignties of its constituent countries, are in the melting pot. The mixture is boiling and changing shape almost day by day. The search for a crystallization of the mixture into new and larger units still continues."

Eastern Europe, too, was in the crucible of change, both economically and politically in 1964 as it moved farther away from the unity that had been imposed upon it by the Soviet Union in the years following World War II. The so-called satellite nations exhibited a new spirit of independence in their relations with Moscow. The fall of Soviet Premier Nikita S. Khrushchev from power appeared to hasten the movement away from political solidarity and

National Aeronautics and Space Administration

WAY OUT VIEW of Western Europe was recorded by Nimbus I, a weather satellite. Great Britain lies in the center; below it is the coastline of France.

toward national experimentation (see RUSSIA). Some of the communist states leaped ahead of the Soviet Union in introducing economic reforms based on what was admitted to be a "profit motive." Observers in the West spoke wryly of "creeping capitalism" in Eastern Europe. But, whatever it was, it formed part of an incomplete picture that included a further relaxation of tensions and the mutual recognition in both the East and the West that shifting conditions had produced a similarity of problems.

Unity and ways to achieve it continued to dominate the discussions of Western Europe, but progress was scant. The economic base on which political unity had been predicated grew at a slower pace in 1964 than in previous years. Inflation threatened, and measures adopted to ward off that threat succeeded mainly in slowing the "boom" that Western Europe had enjoyed for years.

Inflation Woes, to a greater or lesser degree, plagued all of the countries of the Common Market—Belgium, France, Italy, Luxembourg, The Netherlands, and West Germany. Similar troubles beset the members of the EFTA—Austria, Denmark, Great Britain, Norway, Portugal, Sweden, and Switzerland. A general, though uneven, rise in prices and wages meant that goods produced in Europe lost much of the price advantage they had formerly held over products from the higher-priced, higher-waged United States. The Common Market as a whole ran up a trade deficit. Only West Germany enjoyed a surplus. See INTERNATIONAL TRADE.

The governments imposed monetary controls and clamped down on consumer spending by restricting credit and increasing taxes. The rate of expansion sagged along with the receding pressures on budgets and currencies. Although the Common Market was well ahead of the original schedule established in the Treaty of Rome for internal tariff reductions, and was well on its way to becoming a true customs union by the new target date of Jan. 1, 1967, some of the steam had gone out of the drive. Political disagreements and national aspirations had caused a loss of momentum and direction.

Political Dissension. Much of the disagreement among Europe's nations centered around the policies of President Charles de Gaulle of France. Alone of the Common Market nations, France looked to the creation of an independent Europe that could act in the foreseeable future as a balancing force between the United States and the Soviet Union—a "third force" in defense as well as in political and economic development. West Germany, Italy, and the Benelux nations (Belgium, The Netherlands, and Luxembourg) continued to strive for a solution that would bring Great Britain and the Scandinavian countries into closer association with the Common Market and also with the United States. West Germany's insistence on close ties with the United States led to growing coolness between the government of Chancellor Ludwig Erhard and that of De Gaulle (see

Wide World

FRENCH PRESIDENT Charles de Gaulle gives West Germany's Chancellor Ludwig Erhard a seemingly uncheerful earful during meeting in Bonn.

GERMANY). France threatened to repudiate the Franco-German treaty of 1963 if West Germany joined with the United States in a NATO multilateral nuclear force as West Germany wanted to do. France also brought stern pressures on West Germany to reduce farm prices in the Common Market effort to establish uniform agricultural policies. De Gaulle even went so far as to hint that France would withdraw from the Common Market if his terms were not met by December 15.

Farm Price Negotiations. Less than 24 hours before that deadline arrived, negotiators in Brussels reached agreement on a community-wide price policy and set a schedule of grain prices to become effective no later than July 1, 1967. West Germany retreated from its demand for high prices to protect the relatively inefficient West German farms. France agreed to raise its prices slightly. Italy was allowed to keep its feed-corn price lower than that of other Common Market members for five years after the agreement becomes effective. The single price policy put the Common Market in a position to negotiate as a unit on agricultural as well as industrial products in the continuing conferences on tariff reduction held under the auspices of the General Agreement on Tariffs and Trade (GATT).

Kennedy Round. The 58 members of GATT opened their discussions in Geneva in May. The world-wide tariff-cutting effort was referred to as the

NOBODY KNEW, on Wednesday, June 10, 1964, whether there was any natural gas under the North Sea. But if there is, that Wednesday may become a key date in the history of Europe. For it was on that date that the Geneva Convention on the Continental Shelf came into force. Only then did the enormous gamble of exploring the bed of the North Sea for gas or oil—which had already begun—acquire any rightful status in law.

Commercially usable reserves of natural gas have still to be discovered under the North Sea bed. And though geological indications are promising, no gas or oil worth developing may be found. But an eager band of prospectors, including most of the world's major oil companies, are ready to stake $300,000,000 or more on finding out.

Two facts make this prodigious gamble worth while. First, the North Sea is in the middle of what could be the most profitable market in the world for low-cost fuel. Second, one of the largest gas fields in the world has already been discovered on the edge of it.

NORTHWESTERN Europe is one of the heavily industrialized areas on earth. Its huge appetite for energy is growing rapidly. By 1975, countries around the North Sea may be using the equivalent of nearly 1,000,000,000 tons of coal a year. Yet the coal on which they built their industry is in economic decline.

European coal costs are relatively high; technically, production can hardly be increased; and government protection or subsidy is needed even to maintain present output against the competition of cheaper imported energy. The North Sea countries already depend on imported oil, mainly from the Middle East, for over 40 per cent of their energy supplies. Their oil dependence upon a politically unstable area is certain to grow.

Only abundant, new, low-cost energy in northwestern Europe itself could provide real insurance for the continuing economic growth of these countries. On Aug. 14, 1959, these North Sea countries were given their first real hope of this insurance. On that date, drillers of Slochteren No. 1 well, in the Groningen province of The Netherlands, tapped enormous riches of natural gas.

$300,000,000 GAMBLE
ON A NORTH SEA BUBBLE

SLOCHTEREN, with reserves estimated at more than a trillion cubic meters, was the second largest gas field ever discovered—second only to the Hugoton field in the Texas Panhandle. And this new field was rich with possibility. Similar gas-laden strata might extend out under the North Sea itself.

Within months, companies were planning to explore offshore. Aerial magnetometer and seismic surveys began in 1962. But beyond territorial waters, these explorers had no real rights—until the June, 1964, ratification of the Geneva Convention. Each of the seven coastal countries around the North Sea gained legal right to explore and exploit the resources of the seabed out to "median lines." All seven nations thus became empowered to grant exploration licenses.

THE FIRST offshore wells were drilled (off Germany and Holland) early in 1964. On Sept. 17, 1964, Great Britain granted exploration and production licenses to 22 groups. The drilling off English shores will get underway in earnest by mid-1965.

The first real start was made in December on the Dogger Bank, about 170 miles east of Newcastle. *Mr. Cap*, a mobile barge complete with heliport, was towed out to the site in the center of the North Sea. *Mr. Cap's* owner, American Overseas Petroleum, Ltd., an affiliate of Texaco and Standard Oil of California, planned to continue drilling throughout the winter. Its rivals in the gamble were watching this wildcat test closely for clues to the North Sea's hidden wealth.

Already, from Slochteren and other European gas fields, it is expected that natural gas may provide 6 to 10 per cent of Western Europe's energy by 1975. If gas reserves rivaling Slochteren's magnitude were to be found under the North Sea, that percentage could climb as high as 12 to 15 per cent by 1980. Along with its own supplies of coal, and a rising capacity for nuclear electricity, Europe could begin to moderate its dependence on oil from the Middle East, and secure a surer base for economic growth. JACK HARTSHORN

"Kennedy Round" because its origin lay in the U.S. Trade Expansion Act passed in 1962 at the urging of the late President John F. Kennedy.

The nations involved passed a first hurdle by filing lists of "exceptions" to meet a November deadline. These were lists of commodities on which the interested country or group of countries refused to negotiate toward the 50 per cent cut which was the conference goal. Some nations filed a long list, others withheld relatively few commodities from tariff reduction. The Common Market exceptions list accounted for 20 per cent of the total trade of its member countries.

The EFTA filed no unified schedule, but five of its members asked no exceptions at all. The EFTA came close to living up to its name in the final accounting, which showed only 3 per cent of EFTA trade exempted from the Kennedy Round negotiations. Bargaining on the thousands of items in world trade that were not exempted was so complex, however, that the Kennedy Round was still in the preliminary stages as the year ended.

European Defense plans were a continuing source of friction. France forged ahead with its independent nuclear deterrent and withdrew more of its support from NATO. West Germany pressed for a greater share in nuclear policy through the proposed MLF—a fleet of surface vessels manned by nationals of several NATO nations and equipped with nuclear Polaris missiles. Great Britain joined the United States in deploring the spread of nuclear weapons and sought ways of merging its own nuclear deterrent with that of France and the United States.

The narrow victory of the Labour party in the British elections in October left Britain's position on defense, as on other matters, somewhat clouded. The financial crisis that followed the election also created frictions within the EFTA. The government of Prime Minister Harold Wilson imposed a 15 per cent surcharge on tariffs of industrial imports to help overcome a serious deficit in Britain's balance of payments. The other members of EFTA protested this barrier to their trade with Britain.

Despite all the frictions, however, Western Europe and the United States acted quickly and in concert when the British pound sterling came under speculative attack late in November. Japan and Canada also joined in the 11-nation rescue mission that put together a $3,000,000,000 fund to bolster the pound at the official rate of $2.80. See GREAT BRITAIN.

Marxism Questioned. In Eastern Europe, rigid controls failed again to bring production and trade up to expectations, and the economic philosophy of Marxism was called into question at the same time that political relations within the Soviet bloc were in turmoil. Although there were some improvements over the agricultural disasters of the previous years, collective farming did not produce the quantity, quality, and variety of food that the people of the communist countries desired.

Industry, too, fell short of its goals. Public complaints arose, not only about shortages and high prices, but about shoddy goods that were unusable or unsalable at any price. Czechoslovakia, one of the most highly industrialized of the East European countries, took the lead in experimenting with decentralized planning and, on closer look, appeared to be borrowing techniques from capitalism.

Factory managers in a limited number of cases were instructed to gear their production to the sales outlets they served. Instead of producing to a quota set from above, they were to be responsive to the demand from the consumers. Hand in hand with this shift toward the basic economic law of supply and demand came a plan to run the factories on what was conceded to be a "profit motive." The managers were held responsible for earning fair margins on goods sold, and incentives in the form of higher wages and bonus payments were instituted for workers. Although it was a long way from a free market economy in the Western sense, the Czechoslovakian experiment went beyond the economic ideas for decentralization that were beginning to appear in the Soviet Union, and edged closer to Western practices.

International Trade between Western Europe and the Soviet bloc increased in 1964 from the record $3,000,000,000 figure of the previous year. Although the ban on strategic goods remained in effect, Western nations seeking new markets broke through another barrier—the gentleman's agreement against granting long-term credits to communist countries. In June, the British government agreed to guarantee a 12-year credit of $10,000,000 to Czechoslovakia for a fertilizer plant. Italy and France followed with approval of trade deals in which the former five-year limit on credit was breached. The Iron Curtain was crossed and recrossed by trade groups from both East and West in search of expanded markets. Romania, which also exhibited a strong trend toward political independence from Moscow, increased its trade with the West to more than a third of its total trade figure. See CZECHOSLOVAKIA; ROMANIA.

Politically, Eastern Europe suffered profound shock with the sudden change of leadership in the Soviet Union. The news that Khrushchev had been replaced by the dual leadership of Leonid I. Brezhnev and Aleksei N. Kosygin brought public expressions of dismay in several nations that had accepted in silence previous changes in Moscow. (see BREZHNEV, LEONID I; KOSYGIN, ALEKSEI N.). Party leaders journeyed to the Soviet capital seeking explanations. Brezhnev and Kosygin met Poland's communist leader, Wladyslaw Gomulka, in a hideaway at the Polish border to reassure him. Subsequent declarations of support for the new Soviet regime were linked to words and actions that testified to a degree of independence in the "satellites" not seen in many years. See COMMUNISM; and the various European country articles.   FRED J. PANNWITT

MOUNTAIN RANGE in Antarctica, 4,000 to 6,000 feet high, was discovered by the crew of a U.S. Navy plane on February 10. The range is in an uncharted area.

EXPLORATION. A museum of exploration, the new Explorer's Hall of the National Geographic Society, was opened to the public in January following a formal dedication by President Lyndon B. Johnson. Located in Washington, D.C., the colorful panorama of displays included the original gondola of the Explorer II stratospheric balloon, and "breath-taking" photos of last year's conquest of Mount Everest.

Mountain Climbing. Although less spectacular, more climbing feats were achieved in 1964 than in the previous year. In May, a Chinese Communist team was reported to have reached the summit of the 26,291-foot Shisha Pangma on the Nepal-Tibet border. That same month, a member of a West German ski expedition reached the top of Cho Oyu, a 26,750-foot Himalayan mountain. And at the end of May, another West German team scaled the 23,800-foot Himalayan Talung peak. Then in October, a Japanese team member reached the top of the 23,450-foot glacial dome in the western Nepal Annapurna Massif. A month later, in Africa, the sheer east face of Mawenzi, a 16,800-foot twin peak to Mount Kilimanjaro, was conquered by two British climbers.

Deep-Sea Diving. In 1964, however, men plunged farther into the depths of the sea than they climbed upward on the face of the earth. In May, three men in the French bathyscaph *Archimede* reached the deepest known spot in the Atlantic Ocean, the bottom of the 27,510-foot Puerto Rico Trench, where pressures ran to 12,000 pounds per square inch. Surprisingly, they found a great abundance of life. Even more startling was the discovery of 100-mile-wide terracing on both the north and south walls of the trench. The joint Franco-American scientific expedition began in April and ended in August.

In September, the USNS *Eltanin* docked in New Zealand, after two months in stormy antarctic seas. Operated by a civilian crew of the United States Military Sea Transport Service, the ship is the only research vessel continuously on duty in that region. Its cruise through polar waters was the tenth since the *Eltanin* left the United States in mid-1962. Highlights in the ship's expeditions were the discovery of a submarine mountain 10,500 feet in height and the drilling of the longest core yet taken of the antarctic seabed. The core, studied to reconstruct the geological history of the area, is 86.4 feet long.

Antarctica. U.S. Navy explorers, under the leadership of Rear Admiral James R. Reedy, discovered a new mountain range and the world's longest glacier in the Antarctic. The discovery was made during a 10-hour flight in a C-130 Hercules, equipped with snow skis, on February 10. The uncharted mountains, ranging in height from 4,000 to 6,000 feet, are an extension of the Shackleton range some 100 miles west of Queen Maud Land. The crew dropped a U.S. flag and the expedition pennant into the mountains.

The international program of antarctic study during the Years of the Quiet Sun included the longest trek across the continent since Sir Vivian Fuchs led a British expedition on a 2,160-mile trip in 1958. In this case, it was an all-Soviet party that traveled 1,700 miles from Queen Maud Land to the Soviet base of Molodeshnaya. In December, an international team, including about 150 American scientists, set forth on the first leg of a four-year expedition into what is the last unexplored region of Antarctica.   SERGEI LENORMAND

See also ASTRONOMY (Close-Up); OCEAN.

EXPLOSION. See DISASTERS.

FAIRS AND
EXHIBITIONS

R AVES, mutterings, and bitter charges—along with 27,000,000 visitors—attended New York City's dazzling extravaganza in Flushing Meadow from the day it opened, April 22, until it closed, Oct. 18, 1964.

The New York World's Fair impresario, Robert Moses, was disappointed at the turnout. He had expected 40,000,000 to push through the gates. As a result, profit estimates for the two years of the fair had to be trimmed from $53,000,000 to $30,000,000. The Lake Amusement Area, where the public had to pay admission fees, was particularly hard-hit. Several attractions folded. See NEW YORK CITY.

Pictorial Parade

The expectation of profit was one of the two major points of controversy that arose even before the fair opened. The other was its lack of official recognition by the International Bureau of Expositions. Since a sanctioned World's Fair had been held in Seattle in 1962, the United States was not eligible to hold another for 10 years.

The Brighter Side. Despite setbacks—as well as labor disputes, racial demonstrations, complaints of long waiting lines, and high prices in restaurants—the public in general was enthusiastic about what it saw. Most of the big industrial exhibitors were well satisfied with the returns on their investments in terms of publicity and good will.

More than 300 companies, 66 nations, and several religious groups were represented. Spain, Vatican City (with its *Pietà* by Michelangelo), the United States, and the state of New York proved to be the most popular of the governmental exhibitors. The most successful industrial attractions were those of Bell Telephone, Ford, General Electric, General Motors, International Business Machines, Johnson's Wax, and Pepsi-Cola. The fair was to reopen for its second year on April 21, 1965. See AMERICAN LIBRARY ASSOCIATION; ARCHITECTURE; INTERIOR DECORATION.

Another Major Fair whose success could be assessed as mixed was the Swiss National Exposition. Held at Lausanne on the shores of Lake Geneva, it received wide acclaim for its creative presentation of the "Swiss Way of Life." But its attendance, 11,500,000, fell at least 2,000,000 short of expectations.

Fair enthusiasts will not have to wait long to attend another major exposition. Montreal is already engaged in construction for its Expo '67, known officially as the Canadian Universal and International Exposition (see CANADA). It has been sanctioned by the world bureau, thus guaranteeing participation by at least 50 nations when it opens in April, 1967. The United States is planning to spend $13,500,000 to build a pavilion there.

Over on the west coast of Canada, Vancouver, British Columbia, was also planning a fair for 1967, this one an industrial show in honor of its centennial.

THE MOST POPULAR ATTRACTION of the New York World's Fair, Michelangelo's Pietà, *was viewed by up to 100,000 persons a day.*

Harry Amdur, Pix from Publix

*THE NEW YORK WORLD'S FAIR AT NIGHT vibrates with light, color, and soaring
lines of the industrial exhibits—the fair's most popular attractions.
In foreground, is petal-leaf dome of Johnson's Wax exhibit building.*

C. A. Peterson, Pix from Publix

*FLAG-LINED PROMENADE leads to the Unisphere,
the focal point of the New York World's Fair
and its theme, "Peace Through Understanding."*

In 1968, San Antonio, Tex., will celebrate its
250th anniversary with a "Fair of the Americas."
Its director is Edwin Dingwall, who directed the
1962 fair in Seattle. Bonds already have been issued
to cover some of the $85,000,000 in projected ex-
penses.   ROBERT E. BEDINGFIELD

FAISAL, ABDEL AZIZ AL SAUD AL FAISAL

(1904-   ), took over the throne of Saudi Arabia on
November 2. He succeeded ·his ailing half brother
Saud, who was dethroned by the cabinet, the con-
sultative council, and high religious authorities. See
SAUDI ARABIA.

The new king is the second son of the late King
Abdel Aziz Ibn Saud, who founded the kingdom.
Faisal, as his father's favorite, had played a key role
in state affairs even in his youth. As one of his father's
most trusted diplomats, he had been sent on numerous missions abroad.

In 1958, Faisal took over as premier at the request
of the family, a post he held until 1960 when he resigned in protest against his brother Saud's extrava-
gance. He reassumed the post in 1962.

King Faisal lives a monogamous life with his wife,
Iffat. They are the parents of seven sons, all of whom
have received part of their education in the United
States.   WALTER F. MORSE

FALLOUT. See ATOMIC ENERGY; CIVIL DEFENSE.

FARM EQUIPMENT manufacturers brought in another fine crop of sales and profits figures in 1964, and Wall Street began to talk about their business as a growth industry. The reason: the unlimited potential overseas. This was traced to Europe's big strides toward mechanization, and the first small steps—a light tractor in place of a human back—in Africa, India, and other underdeveloped areas. From 10 to 14 per cent of sales of three of the U.S. industry's leading firms were going overseas. Total Free World volume was estimated at $5,500,000,000.

Figures from the world's Big Three manufacturers reflected the industry's growth. Deere & Company, International Harvester, and Massey-Ferguson farm equipment sales totaled about $900,000,000 in 1954. By 1964, *Forbes* magazine estimated they had risen to well over $2,000,000,000, for a compounded annual growth rate of 8.3 per cent. It also estimated that their profits had climbed even faster, from about $40,000,000 to $130,000,000—a compounded gain of 12.5 per cent per year over the same period.

In the United States alone, farmers bought $894,800,000 worth of machinery and equipment and $648,800,000 in tractors from the industry in the 12 months ended June 30, 1964. Purchases were up impressively from their respective 1963 totals of $837,100,000 and $579,200,000.   Edwin W. Darby

FASHION was hit by a shock wave of nudity that extended around the globe and caused world-wide controversy in 1964. First came the deeply plunging necklines introduced in Paris spring collections. Then came the American versions, attributed to the Academy Award motion picture, *Tom Jones*. The wave reached its crest with the creation of a topless bathing suit by designer Rudi Gernreich.

Dress manufacturers quickly jumped on the bandwagon, creating sheer-topped evening dresses with only the filmiest layer of flesh-colored net used for a bodice. The effect on U.S. fashion was to make deep *décolletage* the look for the dress-up evenings in the fall-winter season.

Indiscreet Creation. Certainly, Gernreich fired the shot heard 'round the fashion world. A respected and award-winning couturier, his topless swimsuit was created, he said, to illustrate a fashion trend that he believed would materialize "in five or 10 years." When photographs of the suit appeared (back view) in a national magazine, the furor was on. The suit was modeled privately for buyers representing some of the best-known names in American retailing. Much to Gernreich's amazement, they insisted on ordering topless swimsuits for immediate sale to their customers.

News of the suit brought prompt bans on such nonapparel from public officials and private clubs alike. These actions made for continuing publicity. In Chicago, a young woman was arrested for appearing in one on a public beach. In Paris, Mme. Charles de Gaulle made it known that she would boycott any

United Press Int.

PINCHED. Model Toni Lee Shelly, 19, was arrested for appearing at a Chicago beach in a topless swimsuit. The charge: improper attire.

store that sold the indiscreet creation. Throughout the summer, comments concerning the controversial design were published around the globe.

Fragile Look. "Feminine" was perhaps the most overworked word in 1964's fashion vernacular. It referred to swinging, knee-high skirts, fitted bodices, ruffles, pleats, a lace revival, and the return of the hair bow as the coiffure accessory for women of all ages. Paris couturière Gabrielle "Coco" Chanel was responsible for this hair bow revival.

The cosmetics industry reflected the fragile, feminine look that had come to fashion. Pale lipsticks and nail polish replaced vivid shades for the sought-after "natural look." Hair was no longer curly, but merely waved to follow the contour of the head. Eyebrow-brushing bangs became the trademark of the young, along with hair bows worn front, rear, and off-center. Girls with hair too curly besieged hairdressers known for their "straightening" techniques—a chemical method that often cost them $40 a session.

"Yé Yé" and Discothèque. Significant Parisian trends were side-buttoning dresses and coats, first introduced by Cristobal Balenciaga. The trim mili-

Don Stebbing for THE YEAR BOOK

TEXTURED STOCKINGS were a fresh development in legwear in 1964. They were seen everywhere, in a variety of colors and patterns.

tary-looking coat, in crisp hard-surfaced fabrics, was also inspired by Balenciaga and became the most important new-look coat in fall-winter collections.

Fashion headlines were made when Paris fall collections included pants designs by several respected members of the couture. "Coco" Chanel's status slacks were styled with wide legs and a flat sailor-type panel across the stomach; André Courrèges designed pants suits with thigh-length jackets for daytime city wear; Jacques Heim and the House of Dior showed harem pants for at-home entertaining.

Paris contributed two new terms to fashion's dictionary for 1964. In the United States, "discothèque dressing" referred to the appropriate kind of dress for dancing in impossibly crowded night clubs which featured discothèque music (a jukebox accompanied by live musicians). In Paris, "yé yé" girls (a French slang expression) wore knee-high, full-skirted, often ruffled dresses especially designed for this young crowd by Louis Feraud and Mlle. Arlette of Paris.

Textured Stockings. Paris and New York made legs a focal point of fall-winter fashions by dressing them in textured stockings that sometimes matched— often contrasted—with costume colors. Winter also saw the revival of fuller skirts, smaller coiffed heads under close-fitting helmet hats, the return of the big ball-gown, and a multitude of tiered and tunic coats and dresses.

Men's Wear. The accent was on youthful appearance. Suit colors were lighter and brighter. Suit coats and sports jackets were shorter, with wider lapels. Trousers were often uncuffed. A wider stripe ap-

peared on shirts, and stripes were popular in sweaters. The influence and popularity of the sports car made for shorter overcoats.

Children's Wear. Synthetic fibers and fabrics continued to dominate the children's wear field. Plastic shoe materials were introduced by manufacturers, and a fabric that looks and feels like leather was used in coats and jackets for children.

Awards. Most important fashion awards of the year went to Geoffrey Beene and Jacques Tiffeau, who received Coty American Fashion Critics Hall of Fame Awards, and Anne Fogarty, who collected the annual Cotton Award. All of the award winners are New Yorkers. JEAN KRUEGER NEAL

FEDERAL BUREAU OF INVESTIGATION (FBI). See CIVIL LIBERTIES; CRIME; JUVENILE DELINQUENCY.

FINLAND ended nine months under a caretaker government when a new, four-party coalition led by Premier Johannes Virolainen took office in September. Despite their surface unity, however, deep division remained among the parties over means of bolstering the lagging economy and checking inflation. The Virolainen government withdrew tax proposals that had been put forward by the previous cabinet as a means of balancing the budget. All parties agreed that neutrality should remain the basis of Finland's foreign policy. But resentment lingered over Russian pressures to keep all "anti-Russian" parties and persons out of the Finnish government.

Finland played a major role in the United Nations (UN) peace force in Cyprus in 1964. It sent troops and lent the mediatory services of its ambassador to Sweden, Sakari Severi Tuomioja. See CYPRUS.

Finland and the Soviet Union signed a five-year agreement in August providing for a 20 per cent increase in trade between the two countries. The USSR was to sell Finland electrical equipment.

Population: 4,600,000. **Government:** President Urho K. Kekkonen; Premier Johannes Virolainen. **Foreign Trade:** exports, $1,302,000,000; imports, $592,000,000. **Principal Exports:** lumber, machinery, pulp and paper. FRED J. PANNWITT

See also EUROPE.

FIRE. See DISASTERS; FORESTRY; SAFETY.

FISHERY. Despite U.S. efforts to improve their competitive position, the nation's commercial fishermen continued to haul in fewer fish in 1964. The United States still ranked fifth in volume of catch—behind Peru, Japan, China, and the Soviet Union. Increased catches of salmon, tuna, and haddock failed to offset sharply reduced landings of menhaden and ocean perch.

The total U.S. fish catch of about 4,700,000,000 pounds fell about 50,000,000 pounds short of the 1963 volume. Its value, however, held close to the 1963 level of $378,000,000 because of good prices for salmon, tuna, and shrimp. Imports rose to about 60 per cent of U.S. consumption.

To help U.S. fishermen, Congress authorized:
• A five-year, $50,000,000 program for modernizing and rebuilding the fishing fleet, permitting the federal government to pay for one-half the cost of advanced-design fishing vessels.
• $28,000,000 in aid to states over a five-year period to promote development of commercial fisheries.
• Aid of about $2,600,000 to states suffering from a commercial fishery disaster, such as the earthquake and tidal wave that destroyed much of the Alaskan fishing fleet and facilities in March.
• Stiff penalties for foreign trawler fleets that poach in U.S. continental shelf waters.

On September 28, the U.S. Bureau of Commercial Fisheries dedicated its $600,000 seafood-irradiation plant in Gloucester, Mass. Penetrating rays from radioactive cobalt-60 kill 99 per cent of the bacteria, keeping the food fresh "for at least three weeks under proper refrigeration," according to John D. Kaylor, project supervisor.   A. L. NEWMAN

FISHING. See HUNTING AND FISHING.

FLOOD. See DISASTERS; WATER AND FLOOD CONTROL.

FLOWER. See GARDEN AND LAWN.

FOOD. The food industry in 1964 concentrated on developing tastier products that were easy to prepare and attractive to the eye. The new margarines on the market emphasized quality rather than price. Dairy replacement products, such as coffee whiteners and vegetable whips, challenged cream and whipped cream in much the same way margarine had earlier competed with butter.

General Foods marketed a dessert mix which could be used without cooking as the basis for any dessert from cheese cake to marbled molds. Another development was brown sugar that did not lump and poured like salt. Melted chocolate in plastic bags served as a replacement for bars of chocolate and powdered cocoa in baking. Iced-tea mixes, with their own sugar and lemon included, became summertime favorites.

The U.S. Department of Agriculture reported in October that the American homemaker in 1964 spent just 19 cents of her after-tax dollar for food. This was a sharp reduction from the 26 cents she paid in 1949.

With excellent food available at low prices, the overweight problem became even greater for the average American. Nutritionists recommended a lower daily consumption of calories—both in food and in alcoholic drinks (see HEALTH).

President Lyndon B. Johnson appointed Esther Peterson as special assistant on consumer affairs in the Department of Labor, as part of his "War on Poverty" program. She was instructed to scrutinize the food industry closely because food represents a large portion of the low-income budget.   ALMA LACH

See also AGRICULTURE; PACKAGING; SOCIAL WELFARE (Close-Up); Section Two, AWAKENING THE LAND.

FOOTBALL. Notre Dame came within 95 seconds of achieving its first perfect record since 1949 when Southern California struck for a touchdown in the most dramatic upset game of the season. The 20 to 17 loss dropped Notre Dame from first place ratings. Alabama, undefeated champion of the Southeastern Conference, then became the popular choice, ahead of Arkansas, undefeated winner of the Southwest Conference title. Alabama's mythical crown lost its luster in the Orange bowl, where Texas defeated her. Princeton, the Ivy League champion, was the only other major school with an undefeated, untied record.

Arkansas administered the only defeat to Texas, a one-point margin. A one-point loss was also the

1964 Conference Champions

Conference	School
Big Ten	Michigan
Southeastern	Alabama
Southwest	Arkansas
Big Six	Montana State
Big Eight	Nebraska
Atlantic Coast	North Carolina State
Ivy League	Princeton
Middle Atlantic	Gettysburg
Southern	West Virginia
Missouri Valley	Cincinnati
Yankee	Massachusetts
Pacific Athletic	Oregon State, Southern California (tie)

only blot on the record of Michigan, winner of the Big Ten title and Rose Bowl victor. Southern California and Oregon State tied for Pacific Coast honors, and Oregon State was awarded the Rose Bowl nomination despite Southern California's victory over Notre Dame.

The biggest upset was a crushing 27 to 0 defeat handed Ohio State by Penn State, which went on to be voted the best team in the East.

Top Players. John Huarte, who sat on the Notre Dame bench most of his sophomore and junior years, was made first-string quarterback by new coach Ara Parseghian, and went on to win the Heisman Trophy, awarded to the outstanding football player. Top backs were Joe Namath of Alabama, Gale Sayers of Kansas, Craig Morton of California, Bob Timberlake of Michigan, Archie Roberts of Columbia, Cosmo Iacavazzi of Princeton, Brian Piccolo of Wake For-

The Bowl Games

Bowl	Winner	Loser
Rose	Michigan 34	Oregon 7
Orange	Texas 21	Alabama 17
Cotton	Arkansas 10	Nebraska 7
Sugar	Louisiana State 13	Syracuse 10
Gator	Florida State 36	Oklahoma 19
Liberty	Utah 32	West Virginia 6
Bluebonnet	Tulsa 14	Mississippi 7

est, and Jerry Rhome of Tulsa, who broke 14 national records for passing. Outstanding linemen were Glenn Ressler of Penn State, Dick Butkus of Illinois, Jack Snow of Notre Dame, Larry Kramer of Nebraska, and Steve DeLong of Tennessee.

United Press Int.

HERO OF THE DAY, Coach Ara Parseghian of Notre Dame, was carried triumphantly from the field after his team beat tough Michigan State, 34 to 7, on November 14.

Rule Change. The liberalization of the substitution rule in 1964 brought a return to the use of offensive and defensive platoons, as in the years following World War II up to 1952. A 5.02 per cent increase in attendance over 1963 was represented by the all-time high of 23,354,477 spectators at college football games. The cost of fielding a football team, however, forced the University of Detroit to drop the sport.

Elected to the Football Hall of Fame were Red Blaik, Charley Carroll, Ray Evans, Bob Herwig, Pooley Hubert, Bill Mallory, Kyle Rote, and Earl Sprackling, along with two players from the pre-1900 period, Langdon Lea of Princeton and Charley Rinehart of Lafayette.

Standings in National Football League

Eastern Conference

	W.	L.	T.	Pc.
Cleveland	10	3	1	.769
St. Louis	9	3	2	.750
Philadelphia	6	8	0	.429
Washington	6	8	0	.429
Dallas	5	8	1	.385
Pittsburgh	5	9	0	.357
New York	2	10	2	.167

Western Conference

Baltimore	12	2	0	.857
Green Bay	8	5	1	.615
Minnesota	8	5	1	.615
Detroit	7	5	2	.583
Los Angeles	5	7	2	.417
Chicago	5	9	0	.357
San Francisco	4	10	0	.286

Standings in American Football League

Eastern Division

Buffalo	11	2	0	.846
Boston	10	2	1	.833
New York	5	7	1	.417
Houston	3	10	0	.231

Western Division

San Diego	8	4	1	.667
Kansas City	6	7	0	.462
Oakland	4	7	2	.364
Denver	2	10	1	.167

Professional. The Cleveland Browns won the National Football League (NFL) championship with a surprising 27 to 0 victory over the Baltimore Colts. In the American Football League (AFL) championship game, the Buffalo Bills brought the city of Buffalo its first major sports championship with a 20 to 7 victory over the San Diego Chargers.

As significant as the action on the field was the continuing war between the leagues. The 45-year-old NFL continued to be the dominant organization, but the 4-year-old AFL scored a major victory that probably ensured its permanent existence. The AFL sold its television rights to the National Broadcasting Company for fees that can total $34,000,000 over five years, a pact that in effect represents a subsidy of the league.

Canadian Football. The British Columbia Lions avenged a 1963 loss with a 34 to 24 victory over the Hamilton Tiger-Cats to earn Canadian football's Grey Cup. STANLEY ISAACS

FORESTRY AND FOREST PRODUCTS. Despite an unusually dry summer, forest fires in 1964 were held below the 10-year average annual burn of 6,000,000 acres. The number of fires also declined. The improvement was attributed in part to the increase in cooperative forest fire control procedures. These brought organized protection to 95 per cent of the 453,000,000 acres of state and private timber and rangelands. The unprotected gap is being narrowed at the rate of 3,000,000 acres a year.

New Methods. A big factor in the reduction of fires was the use of new techniques, such as the development of new chemical retardants. These chemicals, nontoxic to plant life, permit season-long fireproofing in high-hazard areas.

Airborne infrared scanning equipment, which could locate fires through dense smoke, proved successful in the destructive Santa Barbara (Calif.) brush fire in late September. It was able to locate spot fires thrown out from the main fire and hot spots that threatened breakouts. The new equipment gave out information in minutes instead of hours.

Despite the new methods and the mobilization of more than 2,000 fire fighters, the California blaze charred some 90,000 acres, jumped man-made firebreaks, and destroyed almost 100 homes.

Lumber Production in the year climbed to about 35,600,000,000 board feet. U.S. consumption rose to 40,500,000,000, from 38,900,000,000 board feet in 1963. Imports totaled 5,500,000,000, up about 300,000,000 board feet from 1963. Exports steadied at around 975,000,000 board feet.

The timber cut from National Forests continued its climb in 1964 to an estimated record high of 10,900,000,000 board feet, about 900,000,000 above the 1963 cut. Likewise, on Indian reservations, timber cuts and sales rose to an all-time high of 741,000,000 board feet. New federal legislation contributed to the year's increase of about 200,000,000 board feet.   A. L. NEWMAN

FORMOSA, or TAIWAN, remained a showcase of what ingenuity, hard work, and the judicious use of foreign aid could do. The Gross National Product was increasing by roughly 12 per cent annually. Exports were booming, and the government held rich reserves of foreign exchange, earning a surplus of $146,000,000 in 1964. The nation's standard of living rivaled Japan's as the highest in Asia. See Section Two, AWAKENING THE LAND.

In February, Formosa severed diplomatic relations with France. It acted after the French government recognized Communist China. The Chinese Nationalists continued coastal raids on Communist China during the year, but only sporadically.

On May 28, the United States announced it would end its economic aid to Formosa in June, 1965. Altogether, since 1949, the U.S. had provided Formosa with $3,600,000,000 in assistance, including $2,200,000,000 in military aid, $1,200,000,000 in economic aid, and $205,000,000 in agricultural products. The U.S., however, would continue to help train and modernize Formosa's 500,000-man military force.

Population: 12,250,000. **Government:** President Chiang Kai-shek; Vice-President Chen Cheng; Premier C. K. Yen. **Foreign Trade:** exports, $504,000,000; imports, $358,000,000. **Principal Exports:** cement, fruits, sugar, tea, textiles.   ALBERT RAVENHOLT

See also ASIA.

FOUNDATIONS. See EDUCATIONAL FOUNDATIONS.

FORTIER, YVES OSCAR (1914-   ), chief of the Canadian Geological Survey's Economic Geology Division, received the Royal Canadian Geographical Society Massey medal in 1964. He was cited for exploration and study of the Northwest Territories and the Arctic Archipelago.

The pioneer work of Fortier dates back to 1943, when he joined the Geological Survey of Canada. He found that mountain systems once covered the Queen Elizabeth Islands, a major structural framework he named the *Innuitian Region*. Bituminous carbonate rock on Victoria Island convinced him of the Arctic's oil potentials, and led to drilling operations on Bathurst, Cornwallis, and Melville islands.

Yves Fortier was born in Quebec City, where he later attended Laval University. He studied at Queen's University, and did graduate work at McGill University and at California's Stanford University. He has a Ph.D. degree.

FOUR-H CLUBS. Half a century of "learn by doing" achievement was observed by 2,190,000 boys and girls in 94,800 4-H clubs as they set a new course for 1964—"learning for living." Since 1914, more than 22,830,000 youths have worn the 4-H emblem. In 1964, more than 3,500,000 young people were members of 4-H or 4-H-type clubs that have been formed in 76 other countries since 1949.

The 1963 majority of nonfarm rural, suburban, and city youths continued to grow in 1964; Chicago alone had more than 5,000 4-H'ers. Farm projects still ranked high in importance, however.

Six representative club members made the 1964 "Report to the Nation" to national leaders and the public in Washington, D.C.; New York City; and elsewhere in April. They were: Linda Curtiss, 18, Williamstown, Vt.; Claudia Truax, 19, Plainfield, Ind.; Roger Hamlin, 17, Corvallis, Ore.; Ann Williams, 18, Angleton, Tex.; Allen Leman, 19, Eureka, Ill.; and Ronald Keys, Council Grove, Kans.

At the 43rd National 4-H Club Congress in Chicago, November 29 through December 3, 215 of the 1,500 delegates were awarded national scholarships totaling $123,000. The highest honors, the Presidential Awards went to: David Quisenberry, Okeene, Okla.; Ina Huffman, Fincastle, Va.; Mary R. Denton, Blackwell, Okla.; Robert Thompson, Ogdensburg, N.Y.; Joe Boylan, Clifton, Colo.; and Marjorie Hutchinson, Lincoln, Nebr. FRANK B. HARPER

FRANCE

FRANCE CONTINUED TO PLAY a dominant political and diplomatic role in West European and world affairs. The efforts of President Charles de Gaulle to reshape the economic and political patterns of Europe, and indeed the world, kept him in the spotlight as the most controversial Western leader of the decade. His untiring promotion of policies designed to further French national interests led to a widening gulf between France and the United States, a cooling of relations with West Germany, and a near-crisis in the European Economic Community (EEC, or Common Market), and the North Atlantic Treaty Organization (NATO). The keystone of French foreign policy remained an independent Europe. Although its outline was only vaguely defined by De Gaulle, it was clearly intended to be a "third force" between the two world superpowers, the United States and the Soviet Union. It was equally clear that this third force was to be led by France. It was a concept opposed to a greater or lesser degree by all of France's allies, who preferred a close working arrangement with the United States. France made no new converts to De Gaulle's plan for a loose confederation of European states, but it succeeded in stalling plans, for another year, for a closely integrated Western Europe in which economic union would pave the way for political unification.

Alliances in Question. A French threat to withdraw from the Common Market unless an agreement on agricultural policy was reached by December 15 provoked an atmosphere of near-crisis. Germany's decision to lower its grain prices, however, cleared the atmosphere. France also hinted strongly that it might withdraw from NATO if West Germany and the United States carried out their proposal to join in a multilateral nuclear force (MLF) within NATO. Due largely to French opposition, the plan for a fleet of surface vessels, manned by personnel of NATO nations and carrying nuclear-type Polaris missiles, was held in abeyance.

De Gaulle, meanwhile, withdrew French naval officers from NATO commands in the Mediterranean and the English Channel, a move that made the French navy wholly independent and further weakened NATO. See NORTH ATLANTIC TREATY ORGANIZATION (NATO).

Independence and nationalism also marked France's foreign policy outside Europe. De Gaulle broke ranks with most of the West by recognizing Communist China in January, thus forcing Nationalist China to break relations with France. The United States protested the move, as did West Germany. The West German government, which had not been advised in advance of the move, contended it was contrary to the Franco-German treaty of 1963. France, nevertheless, exchanged ambassadors with

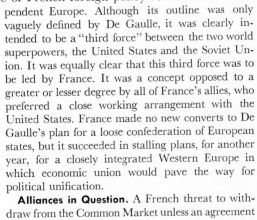

United Press Int.

EAST MET WEST at a cocktail party when French President Charles de Gaulle welcomed new Communist Chinese ambassador, far right, to Paris.

FRANCE

Communist China in accordance with the agreement on recognition. After several months, however, France had little to show for its move.

Proposals on Asia. During the year, De Gaulle intermittently urged that Southeast Asia be neutralized. This added to the growing estrangement between the United States and France, and made U.S. involvement in South Vietnam an increasingly delicate subject between the two nations. In one of his infrequent press conferences in July, De Gaulle offered a plan whereby the United States, the Soviet Union, Communist China, and France would all agree to stay out of the Indochina peninsula (formerly French Indochina). As an additional inducement to end the fighting there, he proposed massive economic and technical aid to North and South Vietnam, Cambodia, and Laos once fighting ended.

Fading Empire. The dissolution of the once vast French empire neared completion when the last French troops left Algeria in June. Their withdrawal came nearly a year earlier than was required by the treaty through which Algeria had gained its independence in 1962.

France also moved to dismantle its nuclear test base in the Sahara, and planned for future testing in the Pacific Ocean area. In contrast, however, France quickly intervened in a former colony when a revolt unseated President Léon Mba in Gabon in February. French troops restored Mba to power (see GABON).

Politics and Health. De Gaulle's health and age became a factor in French policy, both foreign and domestic. The general underwent surgery in April, shortly after returning from a state visit to Mexico. Premier Georges Pompidou took the helm in his absence, and doubts were widespread that De Gaulle could resume his active guidance of the nation after so serious an illness. However, three weeks after the operation he was back in his office. In June, he toured northern France to demonstrate his recovery. In September and October, he made a 10-nation tour of Latin America (see LATIN AMERICA).

De Gaulle celebrated his 74th birthday amid the growing conviction that he intended to try for a second seven-year term as president of France in 1965. One candidate had already announced running against him—Mayor Gaston Deferre of Marseille.

The French Communist party, still the largest single party in France despite its reduction to an estimated 250,000 card carriers, lost its leader of 30 years with the death of Maurice Thorez in July. In October, the French Communists published a resolution declaring their independence and that of all other Communist parties in the world movement. This declaration, coming a few days before the downfall of Soviet Premier Nikita S. Khrushchev, was believed to have had some bearing on that event. See COMMUNISM; RUSSIA.

Domestic Economy. The inflation that had threatened the French economy appeared to be under control in 1964. The Gross National Product (GNP)

340

stood at $72,000,000,000, compared to $31,000,000,000 20 years earlier.

Much of the economic gain had come through cooperation with France's neighbors in the Common Market and such international enterprises as the coal and steel communities. Yet French policy under De Gaulle was becoming more nationalistic, and the nation more isolated in Europe and in the world.

Population: 49,000,000. **Government:** President Charles de Gaulle; Premier Georges Pompidou. **Foreign Trade:** exports, $9,096,000,000; imports, $10,667,000,000. **Principal Exports:** iron and steel, machinery, transportation equipment.   FRED J. PANNWITT

See also EUROPE.

FREI MONTALVA, EDUARDO RODRÍGUEZ

(1911-   ), was elected the 28th president of Chile on September 4. He was inaugurated for a six-year term on November 3, succeeding Jorge Alessandri Rodríguez. See CHILE.

Frei Montalva attended public schools in Lontue, a working-class suburb of Santiago. He later took a degree in law at the Catholic University in Santiago. He has been active in politics since 1935. Prior to his election to the presidency, he served as a senator. He and his wife, Maria, a schoolteacher, have seven children.   WALTER F. MORSE

FUTURE FARMERS OF AMERICA (FFA) sowed seeds for future growth in suburban areas in 1964. The FFA took advantage of the 1963 Vocational Agriculture Act's broadened provisions for training urban high school students in landscaping, greenhouse operation, and other farm-related skills. Consolidated schools also offered more orientation courses to help students find agribusiness vocations in food processing, manufacturing, and other fields. Thus, these factors in 1964 helped to set another FFA membership record—401,468, up 5,656 from 1963, in 8,260 chapters.

Don Carlton Tyler, 21, of Conneautville, Pa., was named 1964 Star Farmer of America and awarded $1,000 at the FFA's annual convention in Kansas City, Mo., in mid-October. Tyler, also North Atlantic regional winner, had attained a $36,000 net worth by 1964. He achieved this by assuming responsibility, at 12, for running the 225-acre family farm when his father was injured.

Three other regional Star Farmers were selected, each receiving $500. They were: Merlin Hamilton, 20, Queen Creek, Ariz. (Pacific); Lyle F. Nielson, 21, Creighton, Nebr. (Central); and George H. Culverhouse, 21, Fort Pierce, Fla. (Southern).

Kenneth H. Kennedy, 20, Cadiz, Ky., was elected national FFA president for 1964-1965, with four regional vice-presidents: Ivan Ray Hunt, 20, Litchfield Park, Ariz. (Pacific); Larry Prewitt, 19, Thayer, Mo. (Central); Robert Page, 20, Hoboken, Ga. (Southern); and Joe Perrige, 19, Weare, N.H. (North Atlantic).   FRANK B. HARPER

FUTURE HOMEMAKERS OF AMERICA (FHA)

circulated a questionnaire on problems of concern to teen-age girls after its 1964 national convention in Chicago, July 13 to 16. The answers will help shape a new, four-year National Program of Work to be adopted by the FHA in 1965. The main concerns the girls listed were: (1) developing individuality; (2) physical and mental health; (3) careers and purposeful responsibility; (4) morals and developing personal codes of ethics; (5) good family relations; (6) citizenship awareness; (7) understanding others; (8) youth as consumers; and (9) better use of leisure time. The FHA program gave special attention to such problems as school drop-outs and early marriages.

Phyllis Christiansen, Aitken, Minn., was elected president for 1964-1965. New national vice-presidents were: Jenny Talton, Smithfield, N.C. (national projects); Judy Mohrmann, Buzzards Bay, Mass. (public relations); and Patricia Bowman, Monticello, Ind. (recreation). Andrea Bowden, Lonaconing, Md., was elected treasurer; Joann Garrett, Wheatland, Wyo., historian; Shirley Ross, Durant, Okla., secretary; and Janet Zwight, Entiat, Wash., reporter. New regional vice-presidents were Pamela Russell, Chowchilla, Calif. (Pacific); Frances Geisser, Stockton, Mo. (Central); Cynthia Ramay, Akron, Ala. (Southern); and Hazel Upton, Gainesville, N.Y. (North Atlantic).   FRANK B. HARPER

GABON.

At dawn on February 18, President Léon Mba was overthrown in a bloodless coup organized by four Gabonese lieutenants. A spokesman for the revolutionary committee said Mba was removed to prevent violent demonstrations by discontented groups during parliamentary elections scheduled for February 23. Widespread discontent had followed Mba's decision on January 21 to dissolve the existing assembly and to hold new elections. The opposition suspected Mba of trying eventually to establish a one-party system under his own leadership.

Within 24 hours, French troops were airlifted in from Chad and Congo (Brazzaville) to restore order and the Mba government. President Mba, who had been captured by the rebels, was rescued and returned to the capital under French military escort to resume his official functions. Mba postponed the parliamentary elections until April 12, at which time his party captured 31 of the 47 seats in the new national assembly.

Following a report by a commission investigating the revolt, approximately 300 persons were arrested. Included among them was Jean-Hilaire Aubame, premier of the short-lived provisional government. He was sentenced to 10 years in prison to be followed by banishment.

Population: 475,000. **Government:** President and Premier Léon Mba. **Foreign Trade:** exports $55,000,-000; imports $36,000,000. **Principal Exports:** iron ore, petroleum, plywood, timber.   BENJAMIN E. THOMAS

See also AFRICA; FRANCE

GAMBIA was promised its independence by Great Britain following an eight-day conference that opened in London on July 22. Freedom day was set for Feb. 18, 1965. The conference, however, ruled against holding new elections before independence.

Meanwhile, ministerial delegations from Gambia and Senegal met in Dakar to discuss a United Nations (UN) study of the economic and political systems of the two countries and the feasibility of a "Senegambian" association when Gambia became independent. The UN report recommended either integration, federation, or a friendship treaty as three possible bases for a post-independence association between Gambia and Senegal.

Population: 320,000. **Government:** Prime Minister David Jawara. **Foreign Trade:** no statistics available. **Principal Export:** peanuts.   BENJAMIN E. THOMAS

See also AFRICA

GAMES, MODELS, AND TOYS.

It was the year of the monsters as grotesque, fantastic, and somewhat sinister figures showed up on toy counters and became an immediate hit. Made of plastic, they included old stand-bys such as Frankenstein's monster and Dracula, and also strange new characters called "Weird-Ohs," "Rat and Bat Finks," "Drag Hags," and "Surfink" (a monster on a surfboard). They were used in games, in jigsaw puzzles, and even in liquid bath soap containers tagged to "Scare You Clean."

Predictably, the trend brought complaints from parents, but toy companies found support for their monsters in the opinions of psychiatrists such as Dr. Alfred Bronner of Passaic, N.J. "The monsters," the doctor said, "are a safe outlet and lead to the externalization of inner aggressive and antisocial drives."

Dolls, however, returned to the more conventional. The high-fashion, sophisticated doll, typified by "Barbie," waned in popularity, and, as Christmas approached, was being supplanted by "Skipper," billed as "Barbie's little sister." Skipper was a more innocent preteen-ager, totally lacking in the curves that characterized her older sister.

Miniature, electrically powered racing cars continued to cut deeply into the popularity of the electric train. Now a more than $100,000,000 industry, toy manufacturers were producing more than 250 ready-made body shells and endless chassis variations, as well as all sorts of tracks and accessories to give realism to racing. Fans developed their own publications and international associations. They even held a 100-lap Grand Prix at Wilkes-Barre, Pa., in July, with a full-size sports car as first prize.

Skates and Yo-Yos. Children all over the country were learning to perform on skate boards. These resembled small surfboards with rollers attached to each end. Riders controlled the progress of the boards by shifting their weight.

The international yo-yo contest, held at Disneyland in June, found Patrick Maley, 14, of Huntington Park, Calif., the winner of the yo-yo return-top contest, and Pete Span, 15, of Phoenix, Ariz., the winner of the spin-top contest. Each won a $5,000 college scholarship from Donald F. Duncan, Inc.

Model Making. Bill Wisniewski of Lakewood, Calif., won the individual speed championship at the radio-controlled model airplane match, held at Budapest, Hungary, in July and August. The United States also won the speed and stunt team championships, while Russia took the team speed race. On September 18, Maynard L. Hill, metallurgist at Silver Spring, Md., set a new world record for model plane endurance, 8 hours 52 minutes, beating the old record held by Russia's A. Malenkov. Hill is also the holder of the world's model plane altitude record, 13,320 feet, which was also previously held by Malenkov. Hill's model had a wingspan of less than eight feet.

At the National Model Airplane championships at Dallas, Tex., in July, Phillip Bussell of Dallas won both the grand and open titles. Dubby Jett of Seagoville, Tex., took the senior championship, and Wayne Meriwether of Kansas City, Kans., captured the junior championship. The Fort Worth JAC's won the club championship, and the team championship went to the U.S. Air Force.

Other Awards in 1964 included:

Craftsman's Guild Winners. In the annual Fisher Body Craftsman's model car building contest, university scholarships went to: *Senior Division*—Tom Semple, Medford, Ore., $5,000; Michael B. Antonick, Mt. Vernon, Ohio, $4,000; Richard L. Beck, Louisville, Ky., $3,000; and Michael S. Reese, Houston, Tex., $2,000. *Junior Division*—Richard R. John, Arlington, Va., $5,000; John D'Mura, Flagstaff, Ariz., $4,000; Melvin Gable, Ypsilanti, Mich., $3,000; and Walter Peeler, Reelsville, Ind., $2,000.   THEODORE M. O'LEARY

GARDEN AND LAWN. Flower lovers from Park Avenue to the Pecos could well look upon 1964 as a rewarding year. There were, for example, the increasing numbers of apartment dwellers who were substituting elaborate indoor gardens of flowers, shrubs, and even trees for grandma's pots of ferns and geraniums. U.S. Department of Agriculture (USDA) plant researchers reported methods to induce off-season blooming of certain kinds of azaleas and other spring-flowering indoor plants. Under the process, chemical treatment stimulates new buds. After a chilling period to break dormancy, the plants are returned to growing conditions to bloom again. Because of the closely controlled temperature, light, and other factors, this is not yet a do-it-yourself project for home gardeners.

A limited number of plants of a hardy, new, dark red chrysanthemum variety especially adapted to the southern Great Plains was made available to nurserymen for propagation in 1964. It was developed by the USDA at Cheyenne, Wyo. The variety, "Red Chief," produces double flowers $3\frac{1}{4}$ inches across.

New Flower Varieties galore were brought out by commercial nurserymen to delight 1965 gardeners. To name a few: the "Derby" begonia, a new color

combination; scarlet "Beauty Queen" dwarf aster; "American Marigold" chrysanthemum; scarlet-and-white dwarf "Starfire" petunia; a "Sugar Pink" petunia; and the well-named "Fragrance" hybrid rose, ranging from red to cerise.

All-America Rose Selections for 1965 marked a special milestone, the 25th anniversary of these awards. "Camelot," a grandiflora, and "Mister Lincoln," a hybrid tea, joined the list of beauties that have found their way into rose lovers' gardens and hearts. Camelot is luminous coral pink, of "shimmering iridescence," with unusually large buds opening into double-petaled blooms 5 inches across. Mister Lincoln is an intensely fragrant everblooming rose, whose double blossoms, in dark, glossy foliage, are up to 6 inches in diameter.

Five All-America selections of other flowers for 1965 were: "Connecticut Yankee" delphinium, "Red Monarch" dianthus barbatus hybridus, "Apple Blossom" petunia grandiflora single, "Floral Carpet Rose" hybrid snapdragon, and "Yellow Zenith" zinnia.

The Pesticide Dilemma remained far from resolved in 1964. Two years after the late Rachel Carson's bombshell of a book, *Silent Spring*, scientists and administrators were able to report some progress in developing ways to fight pests and minimize the hazards of wholesale pesticide use. See DEATHS OF NOTABLE PERSONS (picture).

There were several avenues of attack. Research by teams of specially trained entomologists, wildlife specialists, and chemists was stepped up. Special eduational programs for homemakers and gardeners were conducted. New regulations were ordered.

Measures being considered for future pest control include: Use of mass-produced disease-causing organisms to destroy plant pests; insect sterilization control and controlled baiting (already used successfully against screwworms and fire ants, respectively); breeding more disease-resistant plants; using cropping systems that suppress disease-causing soil organisms; finding nonlasting insecticides toxic only to specific insects; and using *systemics* (insecticides that are absorbed *inside* the plant when applied to the surrounding soil or injected into the roots).

Windsor Bluegrass. A million pounds of seed of this first bluegrass ever patented (1962 U.S. Patent No. 2364) became available in 1964. It all goes back to a single plant Victor A. Renner, research director for O. M. Scott and Sons, selected from a tiny patch he found in his back yard in 1949. The dense turf grass is claimed to be drought and disease resistant, tolerant to pesticides—and to require as little as half the mowing other turf grasses need.

Awards and Meetings. The National Council of State Garden Clubs awarded its Gold Seal to David Burpee at its 35th annual convention in New York City, May 17 to 21. He was recognized as a "world gardener" and for his contribution to the "Seeds for Peace" program.

In Washington, D.C., a new building at the National Arboretum was dedicated April 27 by Secretary of Agriculture Orville L. Freeman. It includes, in addition to offices and laboratories, a herbarium to house 1,750,000 plant specimens. The American Rose Society held its 65th annual meeting, and the National Rose Show, at Phoenix, Ariz., October 22 to 24.   FRANK B. HARPER

See also AGRICULTURE; BOTANY; CHEMICAL INDUSTRY; INSECT; POLLUTION; WILDLIFE.

GAS was igniting an "energy revolution" in Western Europe in 1964. A Morgan Guaranty Bank survey pointed to huge discoveries of natural gas in The Netherlands and to the probability of further extensive fields under most of the North Sea. Up to 1964, gas had taken care of only about 3.5 per cent of Western Europe's total energy needs, in contrast to a figure of 34 per cent for the United States' total requirements. See EUROPE (Close-Up).

In addition to the gas starting to come from the trillion-cubic meter reserves of The Netherlands field, a new source was tapped. In October, a specially insulated tanker, the *Methane Princess*, docked at Canvey Island, near London, with the first load of liquid natural gas from Algeria's new Hassi r'Mel field. Britain and France had contracted to import 50,000,000,000 cubic feet of the liquefied methane annually over the next 20 years.

In the United States, natural gas sales continued to grow, but much slower than in the 1950's. Dollar sales of gas utilities topped $7,000,000,000 for the first time, but this less-than-6 per cent increase was only half of 1955's 12 per cent gain.

Despite stepped-up competition, particularly from electricity, 72 per cent of the new homes built in 1964 were heated by gas. Two other potential markets opened up noticeably in the year: (1) gas air conditioning, and (2) the *total energy package* (a gas-fueled turbine that generates electric power to operate lighting, heating, and cooling systems).

Price Regulation by the Federal Power Commission (FPC) was still being protested by the industry. But, with the election of a liberal, consumer-minded Congress, the most that realistic gas producers could hope for was a change from the FPC's cost-to-produce pricing yardstick to one based on the value of the gas sold to the user.

In September, in the first ruling by an FPC examiner on an area-rate case—that of the Permian Basin, in West Texas and New Mexico—a two-price system was recommended. Ceiling prices of gas from gas wells would be higher than for by-product gas from oil wells. This, the examiner said, would spur exploration for gas wells. The full commission still must act, and, most likely, years of litigation in the courts lie ahead.   EDWIN W. DARBY

See also ELECTRIC POWER; PETROLEUM.

GASOLINE. See PETROLEUM.

GEOLOGY. The greatest earthquake ever recorded on the North American continent occurred in Alaska on March 27. It lifted more than 25,000 square miles of the earth's surface from three to eight feet, and pushed one end of uninhabited Montague Island 33 feet upward, exposing a strip of sea floor some 1,350 feet wide. Conversely, a 35,000-square-mile region around Kodiak and Anchorage sank two to six feet. Buildings and pavement in Anchorage fell 30 feet in a few seconds. See CIVIL DEFENSE.

The quake sent shock waves around the world. In far-off Iran, the ground surface rose and fell a third of an inch. Streets in Houston, Tex., rose nearly five inches, Georgia well water moved up and down 10 to 20 feet, and a showboat was torn from its moorings in Vicksburg, Miss. Six months later the earth was still quivering in Alaska, where more than 9,200 after-shock quakes had been recorded, most of them too slight to be noticed by the inhabitants.

Mohole. After many delays, the ambitious project to drill a hole through the earth's crust was finally grinding away at a site 10 miles southeast of Uvalde, Tex. This 5,000-foot test hole was being drilled to check out equipment and techniques for later use in the main six-mile hole that will be drilled through the bed of the ocean. The site of the present drilling is underlaid by a massive formation of basalt, which is 12 times harder than the better grades of concrete. It is hoped that samples and measurements in the Mohole project will furnish fundamental new information about the origin and age of the earth.

Inside the Earth. The earth's inner core—an area about 1,600 miles in diameter—is surrounded by a ring of dense rock, according to Dr. K. E. Bullen of the University of Sydney, Australia. He based his theory on studies of the seismic wave patterns generated by earthquakes. The dense rock, he estimated, is 300 miles thick. Surrounding it is a 1,000-mile layer of molten rock, surmounted by the solid mantle, some 1,800 miles thick.

Another study of the inner workings of the earth was published in the spring by Dr. M. H. P. Bott of the University of Durham, England. He found that vast circular movements of radioactive heat deep within the earth are forcing the continents to drift slowly apart. He showed that the upper region of these huge convection currents lies about 40 to 80 miles below the earth's surface.

International Mantle Study. On May 14, an eight-nation scientific committee (including representatives from the United States and Russia) began an international project to study the upper mantle of the earth. The purpose of the project was to gain more knowledge about the origin of rocks and minerals and thus to forecast the location of mineral deposits needed by expanding economies. Professor Vladimir V. Belousev of Russia was named chairman of the committee.   SERGEI LENORMAND

See also ASTRONOMY (Close-Up); Section Two, OUT OF THE SEA (Trans-Vision®).

343

GERMANY

THE TWO SEGMENTS of divided Germany sparred over trade and population movements. They made no progress, however, toward the unification that remained the goal of every German, East or West. The prosperity of the Federal Republic of (West) Germany contrasted sharply with the economic difficulties of the German Democratic Republic (East Germany). Despite the cracks that appeared in international alliances on both sides of the Iron Curtain, West Germany remained firmly committed to Western democracy, while East Germany looked to the communist bloc and to the Soviet Union for direction. See COMMUNISM.

For the third year, the communist-built wall in Berlin was the focus of East-West aspirations and divisions. An agreement signed September 24 opened the wall to visitors from the West on October 1 and again on four other specified dates in 1964 and 1965.

Although the August 13 anniversary of the wall's erection passed without incident, violence flared a month later when an East Berliner was shot by East German guards as he tried to escape to the West. A U.S. military policeman went to his rescue, while West German guards held the East Germans at bay with tear gas and gunfire. It was the first time a U.S. soldier had crossed the wall for rescue purposes.

Amnesty "Deal." In October, East Germany announced an amnesty freeing 10,000 political prisoners. It also offered elderly persons, no longer able to work, a chance to visit or join relatives in the West. But these concessions, like the agreement opening the wall, were not without their price. While West Germany rejected demands for greater trade credits, it shipped food and consumer goods valued at millions of dollars into East Germany in return for the release of political prisoners. It was reported, without official confirmation, that the "ransom" of 800 prisoners came to $10,000 each.

Two serious incidents occurred in the air during the year. Soviet fighters shot down an unarmed T-39 jet training plane of the U.S. Air Force when it strayed over East Germany on January 28. Soviet fighters also shot down a U.S. Air Force RB-66 reconnaissance bomber on a training flight on March 10 when it, too, accidentally crossed the border. The United States thereafter banned training flights within 70 miles of the border.

French Pressures. Strains developed in West Germany's foreign relations as the United States and France moved farther apart. Chancellor Ludwig Erhard resisted pressures from French President Charles de Gaulle and complained that De Gaulle sought to force West Germany to choose between France and the United States. The Franco-German relationship built while Konrad Adenauer was chancellor cooled as Erhard backed proposals De Gaulle opposed—notably the U.S. plan for a multilateral

EAST BERLIN-BOUND visitors from West Germany line up at checkpoint during brief relaxation of border-crossing restrictions.

Pix, from Publix

SLUGGISH ECONOMY of East Berlin begins to produce a smattering of consumer goods, as this view of the communist-controlled city indicates.

nuclear force (MLF) within the North Atlantic Treaty Organization (NATO). A French threat to withdraw from the European Economic Community (Common Market) over grain prices, primarily directed at West Germany, was also a source of friction. See EUROPE; FRANCE; NORTH ATLANTIC TREATY ORGANIZATION (NATO).

Domestic Problems. The farm price dispute also added to Chancellor Erhard's growing difficulties. Not only the farmers, but other groups as well, began to display dissatisfaction with Erhard's leadership. His Christian Democratic Union showed strength in the April provincial election in Baden-Württemberg, but the October municipal and county elections in three southern states revealed a swing toward the opposition Social Democrats, who gained about 5 per cent at the expense of Erhard's party.

Erhard's problems were complicated by Adenauer, the 88-year-old former chancellor, who continued to deal directly with De Gaulle. Adenauer went to Paris on November 9 for private talks with De Gaulle. A "Gaullist" faction developed within the Christian Democrats, led by Adenauer and the former German defense minister, Franz Josef Strauss. The Social Democrats, headed by Mayor Willy Brandt of West Berlin, spoke with rising optimism about their chances in the general elections to be held in 1965. The president of West Germany, Heinrich Luebke, 69, was re-elected to a new five-year term on July 1.

The domestic economy continued strong. So much foreign capital flowed into West Germany to escape inflation threats elsewhere that the government imposed taxes on the yield of German bonds held by foreigners. West Germany also had a surplus in international trade, and took measures to reduce it.

East German Difficulties. The situation was far different in East Germany. Prices of basic materials and freight were up 25 to 30 per cent. Despite a 20-year "friendship and cooperation" pact with the Soviet Union, signed in Moscow on June 12, the U.S.S.R. and other members of the communist bloc failed to meet East Germany's needs, and it looked westward for trade and credit.

Willi Stoph, 50, was elected prime minister of East Germany on September 24, replacing Otto Grotewohl, who died in East Berlin after a long illness. Walter Ulbricht remained as head of the Communist party and effective head of the government.

Germany (East). Population: 17,270,000. **Government:** Communist Party First Secretary Walter Ulbricht; Prime Minister Willi Stoph. **Foreign Trade:** exports, $2,673,000,000; imports, $2,287,000,000. **Principal Exports:** coal, motor vehicles, potash.

Germany (West). Population: 58,680,000. **Government:** President Heinrich Luebke; Chancellor Ludwig Erhard. **Foreign Trade:** exports, $16,209,000,000; imports, $14,166,000,000. **Principal Exports:** chemicals, machinery.   FRED J. PANNWITT

GHANA became a one-party state at midnight on February 1 under a constitutional amendment adopted by national referendum late in January. At that time, the voters also approved a new national flag and the establishment of a three-man presidential commission to replace President Kwame Nkrumah in the event of his death, resignation, or absence from Ghana. The voters also approved an amendment empowering the president to dismiss supreme and high court judges.

On January 2, Nkrumah escaped unscathed from another attempt on his life. It was the fifth such try since 1956. The would-be assassin was arrested and sentenced to death. Within a week, the government had launched a widespread police purge in which the commissioner and nine other high ranking police officers were dismissed.

Opposition leader Joseph B. Danquah was arrested as a suspect and imprisoned under the Preventive Detention Act which empowered Nkrumah to detain persons evading arrest up to five years. On May 1, a new preventive detention bill was passed increasing the five-year limit to 10 years. It also gave President Nkrumah the right to restrict individuals' movements in the country.

In June, the government announced plans to offer paramilitary training to the 7,500 members of the Ghana's Workers Brigade. The group had been organized seven years ago to give unemployed urban youths work on useful social and economic projects.

Population: 7,600,000. **Government:** President Kwame Nkrumah. **Foreign Trade:** exports, $291,000,000; imports, $333,000,000. **Principal Exports:** diamonds, gold, timber.   BENJAMIN E. THOMAS

See also AFRICA.

GIRL SCOUTS of the United States of America launched a two-year Urban Special Areas project designed to set up specialized services for selected local Girl Scout councils in communities with a high incidence of poverty, unemployment, school dropouts, and racial conflict.

Senior Girl Scouts held their first Campus Conference from July 23 to August 3 at Cazenovia (N.Y.) College. Over 200 girls, 15 to 17 years old, from 43 states participated. The conference theme, "A Quest for Quality," was based on findings outlined in the "Report of the President's Commission on the Status of Women, 1963."

A new service, "training by television," was made available to local Girl Scout councils by the national organization for distribution to local television stations or for use at meetings and training sessions.

International activity continued to be a highlight of Girl Scouting in 1964. More than 300 girls and adults from 45 countries took part in the Girl Scout international exchange program. Thirty-two girls, representing all sections of the United States, were selected for a special "Traveling Troop" tour of Europe.   JOSEPH P. ANDERSON

GIRLS CLUBS OF AMERICA (GCA), INC., extended special birthday greetings to its oldest club —the Waterbury (Conn.) Girls Club—on the 100th anniversary of its founding. A special Waterbury Day program highlighted the 19th annual conference of the GCA in New York City in April. The Waterbury club began on a small scale in February, 1864, as the Waterbury Industrial School for Girls. It now serves 1,100 members. The club was also honored during the year by the city of Waterbury for its work in establishing the national organization and for its assistance to GCA programs in other communities.

Lynn Diane Hadar, 16, of Bridgeport, Conn., was named "1964 Girl of the Year," for outstanding accomplishments in homemaking skills and club activities. The Career Key scholarship award of $750 went to Lillian N. Riley, 17, of Wilmington, Del.

The winners of other national contests were: "Senior Homemaker of the Year" to Barbara Kessler, 16, of Franklin, Ind.; "Junior Homemaker of the Year" to Kathleen Petty, 12, of Newport News, Va.; Lucile M. Wright Citizenship Award to Gay Brummitt, 16, of Bowling Green, Ky.; and first prize in the GCA Poster Contest to Alice Millar, 12, of Boston. Mrs. Horace Gooch of Worcester, Mass., was elected president of GCA, succeeding Mrs. David K. Spofford of Pittsfield, Mass.   JOSEPH P. ANDERSON

GOLDMAN, ERIC F. (1915-), Princeton University Rollins Professor of History, is President Lyndon B. Johnson's consultant on ideas. His task is to supply the President with a continuous flow of new ideas on both the domestic and foreign fronts. He selected a 20-man group for each field to help him make wide contact and get the best possible thinking.

Although Goldman has a White House office, he continues as a Princeton professor and works on his projected four-volume United States history. He is still moderator on the National Broadcasting Company television program *The Open Mind*, which won the New York Academy of Television Arts and Sciences Emmy award in 1962. Dr. Goldman's *Modern America* is one of Princeton's heaviest enrolled courses. Several senior classes have voted him the university's "best lecturer." His *Rendezvous with Destiny: A History of Modern American Reform* was awarded the Columbia University Frederic Bancroft prize (1953). He has written other history books, contributed to *The New Republic*, *Saturday Review*, and other magazines, and writes reviews for *The New York Times* and *New York Herald Tribune* book sections.

Eric Goldman was born in Washington, D.C., and later lived in Baltimore, Md. He worked most of the time while getting an education. Johns Hopkins University granted him an M.A. degree in history (1935) without benefit of an A.B. degree. He stayed on as an instructor, and took his Ph.D. degree in 1938. He was a *Time* magazine staff member for several years before going to Princeton in 1942.

GOLDWATER, BARRY M. (1909-   ), ran unsuccessfully for President of the United States on the Republican ticket in 1964. He was defeated on November 3 by President Lyndon B. Johnson.

Goldwater was born in Phoenix, Ariz., on Jan. 1, 1909, three years before Arizona became a state. His grandfather, an adventuresome Polish immigrant known as "Big Mike" Goldwater, went to Arizona during the gold rush of 1862. A few years later, Big Mike and his brother, Joe, bought a general store in the mining camp of La Paz, across the Colorado from California. Out of this modest start came the prosperous Goldwater department stores of Arizona. Barry's father, Baron Goldwater, made a great success of the store that was opened later in Phoenix. His uncle, Morris, ran another Goldwater store in Prescott, and dabbled in politics.

Conservative Beginnings. Barry was closer to his Uncle Morris than to his father. He used to spend summer vacations in his uncle's store in Prescott listening to him criticize big federal government and high taxes. It was Morris who planted the seed of Barry's later conservative philosophy.

The son of a Jewish father and a Protestant mother, Barry was reared in the Episcopal faith of his mother. His father died of a heart attack in 1929. He was 64. His mother, 89, is still living.

Barry, a high-spirited boy full of pranks, had a keen interest in practically everything except schoolbooks. At 13, he became a ham radio operator—a hobby he returned to in manhood.

He was elected president of his freshman class during the year (1928-1929) he spent at the University of Arizona in Tucson. He played football, joined Sigma Chi, and drove a flashy roadster. After his father died, he left the university. He has since described that step as the worst mistake he ever made. He then went to work in the Goldwater store as a junior clerk. In 1937, at the age of 28, he was elected president of Goldwater's.

Earlier, on Sept. 22, 1934, he had married Margaret "Peggy" Johnson, a wealthy Indiana beauty. She had met him while visiting in Phoenix. They have four children and four grandchildren.

World War II. Goldwater, an infantry lieutenant in the Army Reserve, reported for duty in August, 1941. Two years later he became a pilot in the Air Transport Command, leaving the service in 1945 as a lieutenant colonel.

He entered politics more or less by accident. In 1949, when one of the seven reform-slate nominees for the Phoenix city council had to drop out at the last minute, Goldwater agreed to fill in. All seven were elected, and Goldwater was chosen vice-mayor of the council.

In 1952, barnstorming in his private plane, he captured the U.S. Senate seat held by Democrat Ernest W. McFarland, and found himself launched on a meteoric political career.   WILLIAM McGAFFIN

See also ELECTIONS; REPUBLICAN PARTY.

GOLF. Ken Venturi made the year's greatest comeback, Tony Lema moved to the forefront of ranking golfers, Arnold Palmer won another Masters tournament, and Jack Nicklaus ended the season with the most money.

The 33-year-old Venturi, who had not won a tournament in three years, survived a near physical collapse in 100-degree heat on Washington's Congressional Country Club course to win the United States Open. He shot a four-round total of 278. His comeback highlighted the year in sports, and as a result he was awarded the annual Sportsman of the Year award by *Sports Illustrated*.

Lema had the hottest golf clubs in the land when he won three tournaments in four weeks: taking the Thunderbird at Rye, N.Y.; the Buick Open at Grand Blanc, Mich.; and then coming back from a 20th-place finish in the U.S. Open to win the Cleveland Open. Lema also captured the British Open, and won the World Series of Golf over Venturi, Palmer, and Bobby Nichols.

Palmer swept up an unprecedented fourth Masters title, and he won the Piccadilly Match Play title in Wentworth, England. The Professional Golfers Association (PGA) title was won by Bobby Nichols. Nicklaus led the PGA list of money winners with earnings of $113,284.50, topping Palmer by $81.31. Nicklaus took four of the 24 PGA tournaments but was shut out in the U.S. Open, the Masters, and the PGA tournaments.

The Canada Cup was won by the United States for the fifth straight year. Nicklaus was first and Palmer second in the individual standing.

Amateur Golf. Bill Campbell, insurance broker from Huntington, W.Va., won the National Amateur title at Cleveland. Houston University took its seventh National Collegiate Athletic Association (NCAA) title in nine years, and the NCAA individual title went to Terry Small of San Jose State. Gordon Clark of Great Britain won the British Amateur crown. Britain also captured the biennial United States Golf Association World Amateur team championship for the Eisenhower Trophy. Canada was second in the 33-nation field in Rome.

Women's Play. Mickey Wright won an unprecedented fourth U.S. Women's Open title. She then went on to take 10 PGA tournaments. Barbara McIntyre of Colorado Springs captured her second Women's Amateur title, and Carol Sorenson, 21, of Janesville, Wis., became the fifth American since 1893 to win the British Women's Amateur crown. At the Prairie Dunes Country Club in Hutchinson, Kans., she defeated JoAnne Gunderson, who had taken the championship three times.

The United States defeated Great Britain for the third straight time in the Curtis Cup matches at Porthcawl, Wales. France won the 25-nation competition for the Women's World Amateur team championship, defeating the United States by one stroke at Paris.   STANLEY ISAACS

GOVERNORS OF THE STATES holding office in 1965 are listed below, with their political affiliations and their years in office. Twenty-five states elected governors on Nov. 3, 1964. There are now 33 Democratic and 17 Republican governors. The Democrats in 1964 won two previously held Republican governorships—in Arizona and in Utah. But the Republicans captured three governors' mansions from the Democrats. The governor of Washington, Albert D. Rosellini, was beaten, as was Wisconsin's Democratic Governor John W. Reynolds. In Massachusetts, Democrat Francis X. Bellotti, who had upset Governor Endicott Peabody in the primary, was upset himself by former Governor John A. Volpe. But Volpe faced a strongly Democratic legislature. Rhode Island re-elected a Republican governor for the first time in 34 years. North Dakota elected its governor to a four-year term for the first time. In order to avoid gubernatorial races during presidential election years, Florida limited Governor Haydon Burns' current term to only two years. As a result, he may run in 1966 for a full four-year term, though under Florida law a governor cannot succeed himself.

GOVERNORS OF THE 50 STATES

State	Governor	Born	Birthplace	Terms
Alabama	George C. Wallace, D.	Aug. 25, 1919	Clio, Ala.	1963–1967
Alaska	William A. Egan, D.	Oct. 8, 1914	Valdez, Alaska	1959–1967
Arizona	Samuel P. Goddard, Jr., D.	Aug. 8, 1919	Clayton, Mo.	1965–1967
Arkansas	Orval E. Faubus, D.	Jan. 7, 1910	near Combs, Ark.	1955–1967
California	Edmund G. Brown, D.	Apr. 21, 1905	San Francisco, Calif.	1959–1967
Colorado	John A. Love, R.	Nov. 29, 1916	Gibson City, Ill.	1963–1967
Connecticut	John N. Dempsey, D.	Jan. 3, 1915	Cahir, Ireland	1961–1967
Delaware	Charles L. Terry, Jr., D.	Sept. 17, 1900	Camden, Del.	1965–1969
Florida	Haydon Burns, D.	Mar. 17, 1913	Chicago, Ill.	1965–1967
Georgia	Carl E. Sanders, D.	May 15, 1925	Augusta, Ga.	1963–1967
Hawaii	John A. Burns, D.	Mar. 30, 1909	Ft. Assiniboine, Mont.	1963–1967
Idaho	Robert E. Smylie, R.	Oct. 31, 1914	Marcus, Iowa	1955–1967
Illinois	Otto J. Kerner, Jr., D.	Aug. 15, 1908	Chicago, Ill.	1961–1969
Indiana	Roger D. Branigin, D.	July 26, 1902	Franklin, Ind.	1965–1969
Iowa	Harold E. Hughes, D.	Feb. 10, 1922	Ida Grove, Iowa	1963–1967
Kansas	William H. Avery, R.	Aug. 11, 1911	Wakefield, Kans.	1965–1967
Kentucky	Edward T. Breathitt, D.	Nov. 26, 1924	Hopkinsville, Ky.	1963–1967
Louisiana	John J. McKeithen, D.	May 28, 1918	Grayson, La.	1964–1968
Maine	John H. Reed, R.	Jan. 5, 1921	Ft. Fairfield, Me.	1960–1967
Maryland	J. Millard Tawes, D.	Apr. 8, 1894	Crisfield, Md.	1959–1967
Massachusetts	John A. Volpe, R.	Dec. 8, 1908	Wakefield, Mass.	*1965–1967
Michigan	George W. Romney, R.	July 8, 1907	Chihuahua, Mexico	1963–1967
Minnesota	Karl F. Rolvaag, D.	July 18, 1913	Northfield, Minn.	1963–1967
Mississippi	Paul B. Johnson, Jr., D.	Jan. 23, 1916	Hattiesburg, Miss.	1964–1968
Missouri	Warren E. Hearnes, D.	July 24, 1923	Moline, Ill.	1965–1969
Montana	Tim M. Babcock, R.	Aug. 27, 1919	Little Fork, Minn.	1962–1969
Nebraska	Frank B. Morrison, D.	May 20, 1905	Golden, Colo.	1961–1967
Nevada	Grant Sawyer, D.	Dec. 14, 1918	Twin Falls, Idaho	1959–1967
New Hampshire	John W. King, D.	Oct. 10, 1918	Manchester, N.H.	1963–1967
New Jersey	Richard J. Hughes, D.	Aug. 10, 1909	Florence, N.J.	1962–1966
New Mexico	Jack M. Campbell, D.	Sept. 10, 1916	Hutchinson, Kans.	1963–1967
New York	Nelson A. Rockefeller, R.	July 8, 1908	Bar Harbor, Me.	1959–1967
North Carolina	Daniel K. Moore, D.	Apr. 2, 1906	Asheville, N.C.	1965–1969
North Dakota	William L. Guy, D.	Sept. 30, 1919	Devils Lake, N.Dak.	1961–1969
Ohio	James A. Rhodes, R.	Sept. 13, 1909	Jackson County, Ohio	1963–1967
Oklahoma	Henry Bellmon, R.	Sept. 3, 1921	Tonkawa, Okla.	1963–1967
Oregon	Mark O. Hatfield, R.	July 12, 1922	Dallas, Ore.	1959–1967
Pennsylvania	William W. Scranton, R.	July 19, 1917	Madison, Conn.	1963–1967
Rhode Island	John H. Chafee, R.	Oct. 22, 1922	Providence, R.I.	1963–1967
South Carolina	Donald S. Russell, D.	Feb. 22, 1906	Lafayette Springs, Miss.	1963–1967
South Dakota	Nils Boe, R.	Sept. 10, 1913	Baltic, S.Dak.	1965–1967
Tennessee	Frank G. Clement, D.	June 2, 1920	Dickson, Tenn.	†1963–1967
Texas	John B. Connally, Jr., D.	Feb. 28, 1917	near Floresville, Tex.	1963–1967
Utah	Calvin L. Rampton, D.	Nov. 6, 1913	Bountiful, Utah	1965–1969
Vermont	Philip H. Hoff, D.	June 29, 1924	Greenfield, Mass.	1963–1967
Virginia	Albertis S. Harrison, Jr., D.	Jan. 11, 1907	near Alberta, Va.	1962–1966
Washington	Daniel J. Evans, R.	Oct. 16, 1925	Seattle, Wash.	1965–1969
West Virginia	Hulett C. Smith, D.	Oct. 21, 1918	Beckley, W.Va.	1965–1969
Wisconsin	Warren P. Knowles, R.	Aug. 19, 1908	River Falls, Wis.	1965–1967
Wyoming	Clifford P. Hansen, R.	Oct. 16, 1912	Zenith, Wyo.	1963–1967

*Served previous term (1961–1963).
†Served previous term (1955–1959).

G REAT BRITAIN elected a Labour government for the first time in 13 years. On October 15, Labour leader (James) Harold Wilson, a 48-year-old economist, became the youngest prime minister of Great Britain in the 20th century, even though his party's majority in the 630-seat House of Commons was a paper-thin five seats over the Conservative and Liberal parties combined.

Despite this parliamentary weakness, Wilson put on a bold front by announcing a radical legislative program and by launching a shakeup in various government departments. He was determined to avoid the experience of the last, brief Labour government headed by Clement Attlee in 1950-1951, which had held a scant majority of six and which had fallen after being riddled by internal disputes. (Wilson himself had resigned from it in sympathy with the late Aneurin Bevan.) Despite Wilson's bold ploy in October, the opposition Conservative party believed he would have to call another general election within six to 18 months.

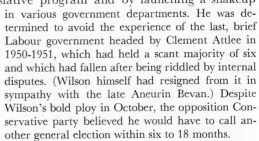

Deputy Labour leader George Brown was given a major new post as first secretary of state and minister for economic affairs. The exact division of responsibility between Brown and newly appointed Chancellor of the Exchequer (Leonard) James Callaghan, the party's third in command, remained ill-defined. To serve as foreign secretary, Wilson chose Patrick Gordon-Walker, a former Oxford tutor with right-wing sympathies, even though Gordon-Walker had lost his parliamentary seat at Smethwick in the October election.

Wilson also created two cabinet posts. Frank Cousins, a nuclear disarmament proponent, a spokesman for the left, and a trade union leader, was named head of a new ministry of technology. James Griffiths, 74, was named secretary of state for Wales, the second new post.

Election Cliffhanger. Because of glaring Conservative party weaknesses revealed in parliamentary by-elections, local elections, and the public opinion polls, Conservative Prime Minister Sir Alec Douglas-Home had been forced to delay the general election to the extreme limit of his party's five-year term. Sir Alec campaigned on two themes: the growing prosperity of the ordinary family under Conservative rule and (the issue he personally stressed) the retention of British national control over nuclear weapons. Labour, on the other hand, favored abandonment of national control in exchange for some type of joint U.S.-British control of atomic arms. In addition, Labour promised social reform and better governmental relations with the trade unions.

The election results showed that out of 27,650,213 votes cast the Conservatives had lost by about 1,750,000. It was the closest finish in British history.

BILLOWING SMOKE fails to dim the happy gleam in the eye of Labour party leader Harold Wilson, Britain's new prime minister.

351

MOODY BROOD. Leather-jacketed "Rockers," a juvenile gang, congregate glumly outside a British court after battle with rival "Mods" resulted in scores of arrests.

The swing to Labour as a whole was about 3.2 per cent over 1959, although there were wide regional variations. But if a mere 84 Labour voters in three particular constituencies had stayed away from the polls, Wilson's party would have been in a minority. Sadly, it was the first general election since 1900 in which Sir Winston Churchill did not take part.

Economic Emergency. The new government's first task was to tackle a balance-of-payments crisis that was expected to produce a deficit of $2,985,000,-000 by the end of the year. Exports, after some good months early in the year, became sluggish; outgoing funds for overseas investment were exceptionally large, and imports soared dangerously, especially in manufactured goods.

The new government promptly slapped a 15 per cent surcharge on all imports except food and raw materials, a move that aroused protests, especially from Britain's partners in the European Free Trade Association (EFTA). Stand-by credits were negotiated with the International Monetary Fund (IMF) and central bankers. Minor new incentives were offered to British exporters. Though the Labour government declared these measures to be temporary, and blamed the outgoing Conservatives for conditions, their critics feared that a socialist Britain might be withdrawing behind protective trade barriers. The pound needed massive IMF supports to stave off devaluation.

Labour's Program. Other government policies announced on November 3 in the traditional speech

to Parliament by Queen Elizabeth II promised bitter political infighting. The most contentious one was a plan to renationalize the steel industry, which had been briefly in public ownership under the Attlee government. Labour also proposed that all building land be nationalized under a Crown Land Commission, a measure that was intended to check land costs throughout the nation, but especially in crowded southeast England. Rent controls were to return. Medical prescription charges under the National Health Service would be abolished.

A Labour government promise to raise old-age pensions was kept, but when the increases were announced in the chancellor of the exchequer's budget on November 11, they were accompanied by provisions for extra taxation. The new budget, which was considered a deflationary one, also raised the "standard" income tax rate from $38\frac{3}{4}$ to $41\frac{1}{4}$ per cent. Gasoline and motor oil taxes rose seven cents a gallon. The government also hoped to secure agreements on price and wage restraint from companies and labor unions.

Rhodesian Headache. Both the outgoing Conservative and the incoming Labour governments adamantly turned aside Rhodesia's claims for full independence. Britain had granted independence to Malawi (formerly Nyasaland) on July 6, and Zambia (formerly Northern Rhodesia) on October 24. There was unanimous agreement, however, that independence could not be given to the remaining, white-dominated segment of the defunct three-member

Pix from Publix

TOUSLED-HAIRED Prince Charles, left, heir to the British throne, gets taste of seaman's life aboard yacht skippered by his father, the Duke of Edinburgh.

federation in Rhodesia until its electoral laws were changed to give the African majority its due. At one point the Rhodesian government threatened to declare itself independent. See RHODESIA.

Commonwealth Wars. British forces found themselves engaged in a series of shooting wars and skirmishes around the Commonwealth. The major engagements, which threatened to strain the regular army's manpower capacity, were in Cyprus, the Federation of Malaysia, and the Federation of South Arabia. The fight to protect independent Malaysia against Indonesian guerrillas was the most serious of the campaigns. Yet British opinion was most visibly aroused by a report in May that the heads of two British soldiers killed in South Arabia had been cut off and displayed on posts in the Yemeni town of Ta'izz. Though this was denied by the Yemeni republican government (which Britain did not recognize), the headless bodies of two British soldiers were later recovered from the desert. See CYPRUS; MALAYSIA; SOUTH ARABIA, FEDERATION OF; YEMEN.

After the left-wing revolution in Zanzibar on January 12, British forces were called in by the governments of Kenya, Tanganyika, and Uganda to put down mutinies in their own territories by disaffected African troops. Mobility and speed stamped out the revolts with no serious British casualties. See KENYA; TANZANIA; UGANDA.

Alliance Issues. On February 12, Sir Alec Douglas-Home arrived in Washington, D.C., to discuss Britain's right to trade with Cuba (see CUBA).

While U.S. President Lyndon B. Johnson and the prime minister agreed to disagree on this, they promised each other full support in South Vietnam and Malaysia. No progress could be made, however, on the U.S. plan for a North Atlantic Treaty Organization (NATO) multilateral nuclear force (MLF). See NORTH ATLANTIC TREATY ORGANIZATION (NATO).

Missile Scandal. While the British taxpayer dug into his pocket for missile projects that frequently fell by the way, political tempers were raised even more by the discovery, on July 28, that the highly successful Bloodhound guided weapons system had provided Ferranti, Ltd., its manufacturer, with what was officially described as an excessive profit. An inquiry revealed that the contractor had made an 82 per cent profit on the deal largely by misleading the ministry of aviation over labor costs. After Labour party demands for the resignation of the minister, Julian Amery, and for stricter accounting in Whitehall, Ferranti, Ltd., reluctantly agreed to repay $12,000,000 to the government.

In rows involving civil aviation, Amery resisted a demand by the state-owned British Overseas Airways Corporation (BOAC) to cancel an order for 30 British-made VC-10 airliners. BOAC feared that the VC-10's would be less economical to fly than Boeing 707's. Soaring estimates for the projected Anglo-French supersonic airliner, the *Concorde*, led the new Labour minister, Roy Jenkins, to order a go-slow pending a final decision on the commercial practicality of supersonic travel (See AVIATION).

353

Wide World

SCUFFLE embroils Kenya's Prime Minister Jomo Kenyatta, in fancy hat, with an attacker during Commonwealth conference in London.

Education Targets. Belatedly, Britain moved to catch up with other advanced countries on the educational front. On January 27, the government ruled that the school-leaving age should be raised to 16 in the 1970 school year. Surveys and studies had indicated that only 40 per cent of Britain's children would voluntarily remain at school. Despite a rapid expansion of teacher-training programs, educational reformers faced an estimated shortage of 55,000 teachers in 1970.

Juvenile Violence. Police authorities in various coastal resorts clamped down severely during the year on disturbances set off by rival adolescent groups known as "Mods" and "Rockers." The Mods were smart and even effeminate in their dress. They were intellectually alert and middle-class-aspiring. The Rockers were a leather-jacketed, motor-bicycling, working-class-conservative group. This mass misbehavior, new on such a scale in Britain, seemed prompted both by boredom and by a mobility that temporarily banished the home environment and discipline. Clashes between the two groups on the Easter, Whitsun, and August bank holiday weekends were shocking in their fury. Together with a rising incidence of crime and venereal disease among the nation's youth, the clashes revealed an unexpected social problem in the nation's prospering society which local youth service authorities seemed ill-equipped to handle.

Channel Tunnel. It was announced on February 6 that Britain and France had decided to go ahead with the building of a railroad tunnel under the Strait of Dover. See BRIDGE AND TUNNEL.

Royal Arrivals. In the biggest flurry of royal births for over a century, the following was the order of arrivals: February 29, to Princess Alexandra and Angus Ogilvy, a son, James; March 10, to Queen Elizabeth II and Prince Philip, Duke of Edinburgh, a son, Prince Edward Antony Richard Louis (their fourth child and third in succession after Prince Charles and Prince Andrew); April 28, to the Duke and Duchess of Kent, a daughter, Lady Helen Windsor; and May 1, to Princess Margaret and the Earl of Snowden, a daughter, Lady Sarah Armstrong-Jones.

Population: 54,600,000. **Government:** Queen Elizabeth II; Prime Minister (James) Harold Wilson. **Foreign Trade:** exports, $12,656,000,000; imports, $15,641,000,000. **Principal Exports:** machinery, motor vehicles, textiles. ALASTAIR BURNET

See also EUROPE; MUSIC, POPULAR; and articles on Commonwealth countries.

GREECE came perilously close to war with Turkey in 1964. Each nation was determined to support the rights of its respective nationals on Cyprus, where Greek and Turkish Cypriots were locked in a bitter civil war (see CYPRUS). An outbreak of open hostilities was avoided, however, largely through the conciliatory efforts of Great Britain, the United Nations, and the United States. See UNITED NATIONS.

The war in Cyprus came at a most inopportune time for 76-year-old Greek Premier George Papandreou, whose Center Union party had won a clearcut victory in general elections held in February. The new government had campaigned on promises of domestic reforms such as tax cuts, pay raises, improvement in education, and rural development. The promised reforms were delayed, however, by the overriding problem of Cyprus.

Threats of war also scared off foreign investors as well as the profitable tourist trade. Three of every 20 foreign visitors who were expected to tour the country between January and June had changed their minds, according to official statistics published in Athens late in the year.

Income from tourism between January and April rose to $20,420,000, a 2.7 per cent rise over the same period in 1963. But the threat of war reduced tourism drastically in the last half of 1964. Year-end figures indicated that total tourist income would be slightly below the preceding year.

Greece took steps during the year to improve relations with its Balkan neighbors. On June 29, Greece and Bulgaria agreed to end their 20-year quarrel involving Greek war reparations claims totaling $45,000,000 (see BULGARIA). On September 29, the foreign ministers of both countries, meeting in Sofia, agreed to drop all their respective territorial claims as well. A day later, Greek and Yugoslav diplomats met in Athens to discuss the possible reinstatement of a frontier traffic agreement that had been suspended by Greece in March, 1962. The Greek foreign office already had opened negotiations with Romania for a settlement of their differences over the nationalization of Greek properties.

The nation was plunged into mourning on March 6 by the death of King Paul I. He was succeeded by his 23-year-old son who ascended the throne as King Constantine XIII. Members of Europe's royal families who journeyed to Athens for the king's funeral returned to the capital in September for a happier occasion—the marriage of King Constantine to Princess Anne-Marie of Denmark (see CONSTANTINE XIII; DENMARK).

Population: 8,500,000. **Government:** King Constantine XIII; Premier George Papandreou. **Foreign Trade:** exports, $296,000,000; imports, $844,000,000. **Principal Exports:** cotton, currants, olives and olive oil, fruits, tobacco.   FRED J. PANNWITT

GUATEMALA enjoyed growing prosperity at home and increased respect abroad. Most of the credit for the upswing went to the interim government of Colonel Enrique Peralta Azurdia.

Gold and U.S. dollar reserves climbed to their highest mark in years. The administration started liquidating an untidy backlog of unpaid government bills. The nation chalked up a $1,500,000 budget surplus in the fiscal year ended June 30, thus ending seven consecutive years of deficits. This improvement was due to the austerity program, the creation of new basic taxes, and record exports.

Population: 4,250,000. **Government:** Chief of State Colonel Enrique Peralta Azurdia. **Foreign Trade:** exports, $153,000,000; imports, $164,000,000. **Principal Exports:** bananas, coffee.   MARY C. WEBSTER

See also LATIN AMERICA.

GUINEA announced early in 1964 that retail trade, which was under government supervision, would be returned to private ownership. The government's regional transport system was to be dissolved and operations turned over to cooperatives formed by private carriers. A seven-year economic development program was also adopted to increase industrialization. Among other things, the plan called for the construction of a petroleum refinery and the first steelworks in West Africa.

During the year, Guinea signed radio and television broadcasting cooperation agreements with Communist China and Hungary. It also signed economic and trade agreements with the United Arab Republic (UAR).

Population: 3,500,000. **Government:** President Sékou Touré. **Foreign Trade:** exports, $50,000,000; imports, $55,000,000. **Principal Exports:** bananas, bauxite, iron ore, palm oil products. BENJAMIN E. THOMAS

See also AFRICA.

United Press Int.

PERSPIRING GUARDS surround Haiti's iron-fisted François Duvalier as he accepts lifetime presidency voted him by the legislative assembly.

HAITI. The national assembly voted to retain the nation's president for life on June 21. It also proclaimed a new constitution that had been ratified in a national referendum by a vote of 2,800,000 to 3,234. Under its provisions, President François Duvalier will rule for life, with absolute powers. The country's flag was changed from red and blue to red and black, the black symbolizing the republic's ties with Africa.

The economy of the poverty-stricken nation was in ruins. Business was stagnant due to government extortions. The countryside, still unrecovered from the havoc wrought in October, 1963, by Hurricane Flora, was further devastated by Hurricane Cleo in August, 1964. In midyear, it was reported that Haiti had only $700,000 in bank reserves versus a foreign debt of $43,500,000. Duvalier trimmed expenditures to $1,800,000 a month, of which $1,400,000 was to pay all government employees. Trade earnings dropped sharply; the tourist industry disappeared.

Rebel bands roamed the mountains, plaguing the Duvalier regime. In September, an undisclosed number of fighter-bomber planes were smuggled out of the United States into Haiti by what were described as American "adventurer pilots." The Haitian government hoped to use them against the guerrillas.

Population: 4,600,000. **Government:** President François Duvalier. **Foreign Trade:** exports, $42,000,000; imports, $45,000,000. **Principal Exports:** coffee, sisal, sugar.   MARY C. WEBSTER

See also LATIN AMERICA.

HANDICAPPED, THE. Rehabilitation of persons with physical and mental disabilities reached a new peak during the year ended June 30, 1964. The total number helped to obtain gainful employment was 119,708, a 9 per cent increase over 1963. Pennsylvania again led all states, with 11,581 persons returned to the labor force. New York was second with 8,103. Georgia moved up to third place with 6,803, followed closely by North Carolina with 6,737.

Appointments. President Lyndon B. Johnson appointed Harold Russell chairman of the President's Committee on Employment of the Handicapped to succeed Major General Melvin J. Maas, USMC, Ret., who died. Russell, who lost his hands during World War II, starred in the movie *The Best Years of Our Lives* for which he won an Oscar as best supporting player. See RUSSELL, HAROLD.

A new women's committee of the President's Committee was organized to promote the development of special services for disabled women. Mrs. Lyndon B. Johnson was named honorary chairman.

Mechanical Aids. A device that may eliminate the need for Braille was developed by Professor John G. Linvill of Stanford University. The instrument uses photoelectric cells to scan a printed page and activate reeds that vibrate against the fingertips of the reader, thus giving him an outline of each letter. For those with impaired hearing, Bell Telephone System developed special telephone receivers that allow two persons to see and read each other's lips as they talk, a small diaphragm through which a caller can feel Morse Code impulses, and special telephone attachments on which deaf persons can write and receive messages instantaneously.

Awards in 1964 included:
The Distinguished Service Award of the President's Committee on Employment of the Handicapped to Gallaudet College, the only college for the deaf in the world, on the occasion of its 100th anniversary.
Handicapped American of the Year for 1963 to Jerry J. Walsh, 41, founder of Courage, Inc., which placed more than 500 disabled persons in jobs.
Employer of the Year for 1963 to W. Blackie, President, Caterpillar Tractor Company, Peoria, Ill.
Physician of the Year for 1963 to Dr. John S. Young, Denver, Colo.
American Congress of Physical Medicine and Rehabilitation Gold Key to Mary J. Switzer, commissioner of Vocational Rehabilitation Administration, U.S. Department of Health, Education, and Welfare.
National Essay Contest, sponsored by the President's Committee, $1,000 first prize to Donald Joseph LaVoy, Reno, Nevada. JOSEPH P. ANDERSON

See also BLINDNESS; HEALTH; MEDICINE; MENTAL HEALTH; OLD AGE; SOCIAL WELFARE.

HARNESS RACING. Three outstanding standardbred horses—Bret Hanover, Ayres, and Speedy Scot—captured most of the major honors in 1964.

Two-year-old pacer Bret Hanover was awarded horse-of-the-year honors. He won all of his 24 starts. Ayres became the third horse to win the triple crown for trotters. The three-year-old, owned by Mrs. Charlotte N. Sheppard and driven by Johnny Simpson, won the Yonkers Futurity; harness racing's traditional prize, the Hambletonian at DuQuoin, Ill.; and the Kentucky Futurity at Lexington, Ky., in two heats. Ayres won 13 of 15 starts.

Speedy Scot, the triple crown trotter of 1963, continued in high-stepping fashion as a four-year-old. Driven by Ralph Baldwin, he won 12 of his 14 starts. He also became the first winner of the Roosevelt Founders Plate, awarded for completing a three-year grand slam of the Westbury Futurity for two-year-olds, the Dexter Cup for three-year-olds, and the Realization for four-year-olds.

Vicar Hanover won the Little Brown Jug at Delaware, Ohio, and Race Time, a stablemate of Speedy Scot, won the Messenger Stakes at Roosevelt Raceway as well as the Cane Futurity at Yonkers Raceway. STANLEY ISAACS

HEALTH authorities continued to study the effects of smoking following a report issued by the Surgeon General's Advisory Committee on January 11. This committee said that it had found a statistical relationship between smoking, especially cigarette smoking, and several respiratory diseases, including

New Calorie Table

The typical American should eat less, according to the Food and Nutrition board of the National Academy of Sciences. A revised edition of the board's "Recommended Dietary Allowances" was issued in May. It showed the following daily calorie allowances recommended to hold weight steady.

MEN

Desired Weight	25 Years	45 Years	65 Years
110	2,300	2,050	1,750
121	2,450	2,200	1,850
132	2,600	2,350	1,950
143	2,750	2,500	2,100
154	2,900	2,600	2,200
165	3,050	2,750	2,300
176	3,200	2,900	2,450
187	3,350	3,050	2,550

WOMEN

88	1,600	1,450	1,200
99	1,750	1,600	1,300
110	1,900	1,700	1,450
121	2,000	1,800	1,550
128	2,100	1,900	1,600
132	2,150	1,950	1,650
143	2,300	2,050	1,750
154	2,400	2,200	1,850

lung cancer. Among the other cigarette studies in progress were one by the Education and Research Foundation of the American Medical Association (AMA) and one sponsored by six major tobacco firms, who made a five-year grant of $10,000,000 for the study. See 1964 YEAR BOOK, SMOKING.

Reports that large numbers of fish and shrimp were killed in the lower Mississippi River, apparently by

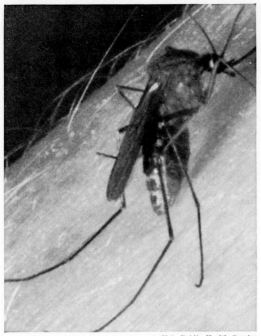

U.S. Public Health Service

DEADLY FEMALE culex mosquito was the cause of a sleeping sickness epidemic in Houston and other parts of Texas during the summer and fall.

pesticides, caused controversy over whether the chemicals, as used at present, constitute a public health problem. Pesticide contamination of air, water, and food has been cited by some persons as possibly hazardous to man, as well as to domestic and wild animals. Others deny any large-scale hazard, and point out that pesticides are necessary to maintain a high level of food production and to help man control a number of diseases. See POLLUTION.

Houston Epidemic. An epidemic of viral encephalitis, popularly called sleeping sickness, struck Houston and surrounding areas of Texas in midsummer, with more than 700 suspected cases reported by October 1. Health authorities undertook a campaign to eliminate the culex mosquito, which transmits the encephalitis virus from animals to man.

Heart and Diet. The American Heart Association stirred up sharp controversy by recommending that people reduce the amount of fat they eat and begin "reasonable substitution" of vegetable oils and "polyunsaturated" fats for animal fats. It was the first time the association, or any other major medical group, had suggested such dietary changes for the general public, although they had previously made such recommendations for people considered prone to heart attacks. Representatives of the dairy industry criticized the action.   HUGH H. HUSSEY

See also DENTISTRY; HOSPITAL; HOUSTON; MEDICINE; MENTAL HEALTH.

HELOU, CHARLES (1912-   ), diplomat, lawyer, and editor, was elected president of Lebanon by a 92-to-7 vote of the chamber of deputies on August 18. He became the nation's fourth president since it became independent of France in 1943. He took the oath of office on September 23, succeeding Fouad Chehab, another political moderate. Both men were acceptable as centrists to the opposing Moslem and Christian factions (see LEBANON). Helou is the son of a druggist who belonged to the Maronite Christian faith. After graduating from the University of Saint Joseph, he became editor of a new French-language daily newspaper, *Le Jour.* In 1958, he served as Lebanese representative to the Vatican. Before his election to the presidency he held the post of minister of education.   WALTER F. MORSE

HIGHWAY. See ROADS AND HIGHWAYS.

HOBBIES. Stimulated by the issuance of the Kennedy half dollar, interest in coin collecting verged on mania in the United States. In stamps, the late President also was the strongest single influence, as many countries in the world issued postage stamps honoring his memory. First-day sales of the U.S. Kennedy commemorative at the Boston post office on May 29 reached 2,003,096, breaking all postal cancellation records for a first day. The previous high had been 1,656,346, for the New York World's Fair commemorative, issued April 22.

Coins. The Treasury Department acted drastically to combat a coin shortage partly brought about by hoarding on the part of collectors and dealers. The number of coin collectors in the United States was estimated at nearly 10,000,000, four times the number active a decade ago. To discourage hoarding of 1964 coins for speculative purposes, Congress froze the 1964 date on all new coins for the duration of the coin shortage emergency. In addition, the Treasury Department boosted production of the Kennedy half dollar from the original 1964 goal of 90,000,000 to more than 200,000,000.

The Treasury Department also halted the issuance of proof coins (coins specially minted from highly polished dies). So great was the demand for proof sets that in June dealers were selling them for as high as $12. They originally sold at the mint for $2.10 and included one each of all coins through the 50-cent piece to give them a face value of 91 cents. As early as January 11, the mint cut off all proof orders and cut in half all 100-set orders already received. Orders were again taken briefly early in March on a two-set-per-person basis but the final cutoff came March 10.

The tremendous interest in coin collecting was dramatized in March when hundreds of persons, many carrying gunny sacks and pulling coaster wagons, lined up outside the Treasury Department in Washington, D.C., to purchase silver dollars in the hope of finding rare coins in their grab bags. In four days, they reduced the Treasury's supply of silver dollars from 13,000,000 to 3,000,000, whereupon

MEMORIES OF A TRAGEDY. *Countries the world over issued stamps in honor of the late President John F. Kennedy. The seven stamps, above, are representative designs.*

Treasury Secretary Douglas Dillon called a halt. Later in the year, legislation was enacted calling for the minting of 45,000,000 silver dollars. See MONEY.

Stamps. Next to President Kennedy, the man whose memory was most frequently honored on stamps in 1964 was William Shakespeare, born 400 years ago. On his birthday, April 23, Great Britain set a precedent by issuing five Shakespeare stamps, the first time any person other than the monarch had appeared on British postage stamps. Many other countries, including the United States, issued Shakespeare commemoratives. See LITERATURE (Close-Up).

The United States, too, set a precedent with its first four-in-one stamp issue—four red and green Christmas stamps, each different, but issued in sheets of 100, containing blocks of 25 each of the four stamps. Also unprecedented was the first U.S. abstract art stamp, the work of the late Stuart Davis.

Probably the most unusual stamps of the year were issued by Sierra Leone. The seven regular issues and the seven for air post were all in cutout forms of a miniature map of the African nation. This was unusual, but what made the Sierra Leone stamps unique was the use of a self-sticking glue on the back.

KENNEDY COMMEMORATIVE, *selected by Mrs. John F. Kennedy from 100 stamp designs, was the subject of much discussion, pro and con.*

One of the celebrated 1918 U.S. 24-cent inverted airmail stamps was auctioned at New York in November for $15,500, the highest price ever paid for a U.S. stamp. Raymond Weill of New Orleans bought it. In October, Ezra Cole of Nyack, N.Y., paid $10,500 for a similar stamp on behalf of Herbert Klee of Highland Park, Ill.

Autographs and Books. Collectors in other fields also were active during the year. An Oxford (England) book dealer, B. H. Blackwell, Ltd., paid $1,540 at a London auction for a collection of every American President's signature from Washington to Kennedy. Two copies of "As We Remember Joe," a limited-edition collection of essays memorializing the late President Kennedy's brother, Joseph P. Kennedy, Jr., killed in World War II, brought $2,600 and $2,400 at autograph and book auctions held in New York City. THEODORE M. O'LEARY

HODGKIN, DOROTHY CROWFOOT (1910-), Wolfson Research Professor of the Royal Society and a fellow at Somerville College, Oxford, is the first Englishwoman to receive a Nobel prize. Professor Hodgkin was cited for determining the structure of biochemical compounds, notably penicillin and vitamin B_{12}. The latter is now used in treating pernicious anemia.

Professor Hodgkin's prize-winning work was done at Somerville College, where she graduated (1932) and has taught since 1935. She did work on pepsin crystals at Cambridge University, and was granted a Ph.D. degree in 1937.

When notified of her Nobel prize, Mrs. Hodgkin was in Accra, Ghana, visiting her husband, Thomas. He is director of the University of Ghana Institute of African Studies. Their eldest son, Luke, teaches in Algeria at the University of Algiers. Daughter Elizabeth teaches at a girl's school in Zambia, and son Tobias, now 18, is in India, with a voluntary Peace Corps-type service. Mrs. Hodgkin's birthplace is given as Cairo, Egypt.

See also NOBEL PRIZES.

HOFSTADTER, RICHARD

HOFSTADTER, RICHARD (1916-   ), Columbia University DeWitt Clinton Professor of American History, received the Pulitzer nonfiction prize for *Anti-Intellectualism in American Life*. The nonfiction prize was created in 1964, because the Hofstadter book did not rightly belong in any of the existing categories. He received the history prize in 1956 for *The Age of Reform: From Bryan to F.D.R. The Structure of American History* is a 1964 book.

Professor Hofstadter's other volumes include *Social Darwinism in American Thought* (1944), *The American Political Tradition and the Men Who Made It* (1948), and *Great Issues in American History* (1958).

Richard Hofstadter was born in Buffalo, N.Y. He was graduated from the University of Buffalo (1937), and took his M.A. (1938) and Ph.D. (1942) degrees at Columbia University. Hofstadter was a University of Maryland assistant professor (1942-1946) before going to Columbia.

See also PULITZER PRIZES.

HOME ECONOMICS. See FASHION; FOOD; FUTURE HOMEMAKERS OF AMERICA; INTERIOR DECORATION.

HOME FURNISHINGS. See INTERIOR DECORATION.

HONDURAS was plagued by an invasion of beetles that threatened its pine forests and coffee farms. In October, it was forced to call on various countries for aid in eradicating the pests. Experts feared that the entire pine belt stretching across Central America might be destroyed.

During the year, the nation's economic council concentrated on a five-year development plan starting in 1965. Top priority was to be given to port rehabilitation and expansion at Puerto Cortés. Also programmed was the rerouting and paving of the Northern Highway at an estimated cost of $20,000,000. A new $7,500,000 International Monetary Fund stand-by arrangement was granted in August.

Population: 2,100,000. **Government:** Chief of State and Head of Military Junta Colonel Osvaldo Lopez Arellano. **Foreign Trade:** exports, $83,000,000; imports, $95,000,000. **Principal Exports:** bananas, coffee, lumber.   MARY C. WEBSTER

See also LATIN AMERICA.

HORSE RACING. After a slow beginning in which he lost his first two races, the great horse Kelso came on late in the year to win five big races and earn horse-of-the-year honors for an unprecedented fifth straight time. The seven-year-old gelding replaced Round Table as the all-time money winner, accumulating $1,893,362 for owner Mrs. Richard C. duPont. Kelso also captured the only race that had eluded him—the Washington, D.C., International. In the race, he beat Gun Bow, after finishing second for three successive years.

Northern Dancer, owned by Canadian E. P. Taylor, earned the three-year-old championship by winning the Kentucky Derby and the Preakness. He failed to win the triple crown when he came in third

in the Belmont Stakes—won by Quadrangle. Northern Dancer went on to win the Queen's Plate, Canada's foremost race, and then was retired to stud in July after suffering an injury to a tendon. He had a record of seven victories in nine starts in both of his years of campaigning and was never out of the money in 18 races.

The Wheatley Stables swept honors among two-year-old thoroughbreds with Bold Lad voted the top two-year-old colt and Queen Empress the top two-year-old filly. Bold Lad won eight times in 10

MAJOR U.S. RACES OF 1964

Race	Winner	Value to Winner
Arlington Classic	Tosmah	$ 69,000
Arlington-Washington Futurity	Sadair	134,925
Belmont Futurity	Bold Lad	85,566
Belmont Stakes	Quadrangle	110,850
Brooklyn Handicap	Gun Bow	71,500
Champagne Stakes	Bold Lad	116,825
Delaware Handicap	Old Hat	79,254
Flamingo Stakes	Northern Dancer	89,830
Garden State Stakes	Sadair	181,020
Gardenia Stakes	Queen Empress	112,854
Gulfstream Handicap	Gun Bow	76,600
Hawthorne Gold Cup	Going Abroad	77,100
Hollywood Gold Cup	Colorado King	102,100
Kentucky Derby	Northern Dancer	114,300
Metropolitan Handicap	Olden Times	75,010
Monmouth Handicap	Mongo	69,875
Preakness	Northern Dancer	124,200
Santa Anita Derby	Hill Rise	87,400
Santa Anita Handicap	Mr. Consistency	102,100
Suburban Handicap	Iron Peg	71,500
United Nations Handicap	Western Warrior	75,000
Washington (D.C.) International	Kelso	90,000
Widener Handicap	Mongo	85,020
Woodward Stakes	Gun Bow	70,330

MAJOR FOREIGN RACES OF 1964

Race	Winner	Value to Winner
Epsom Derby	Santa Claus	$201,787
Grand National Steeplechase	Team Spirit	56,784
Grand Prix de Paris	White Label	153,220
Irish Derby	Santa Claus	149,730
Prix de l'Arc de Triomphe	Prince Royal	223,000

races, beating Sadair, his foremost rival, in their only two meetings. After Bold Lad was retired for the season, Sadair went on to win $498,217, the most money earned by a two-year-old.

Tosmah was voted the best three-year-old filly and Bon Nouvel was awarded top honors in the steeplechase class.

Jockey Willie Shoemaker moved into second place in all-time victories as he passed the 5,000 mark. He trailed the still active Johnny Longden by more than 900 victories. Shoemaker also became the all-time money-winning jockey, with 15-year earnings well above the 30-year earnings of retired Eddie Arcaro. Walter Blum rode the most winners for the second successive year.   STANLEY ISAACS

HOSPITAL costs showed the greatest rise over a period of 29 years, according to the American Medical Association's (AMA) Commission on the Cost of Medical Care. Its study showed that between 1935 and 1963 prices for medical services rose 136 per cent, while prices for all other goods and services rose only 123 per cent. The most rapid and extended rise occurred in hospital daily service charges, almost four times, or 480 per cent. Physicians' fees increased 112 per cent.

The AMA study also showed that the average length of hospital stay fell from about 11 days in 1946 to about eight days in 1961. Average patient charges for a hospital stay rose from $82 in 1946 to $259 in 1961, an increase of 215 per cent.

On March 2, the Supreme Court of the United States left standing a decision by a lower court that any hospital built with federal aid may not segregate its patients or its staffs, a decision that was expected to have a long-range effect on an estimated 2,000 hospital and medical facilities throughout the South particularly.   HUGH H. HUSSEY

HOTEL attrition gained momentum in 1964, even though the year was generally profitable for the accommodations industry. Sale and demolition of older properties were the natural aftermath of the nationwide burst of construction. In New York City, such well-known hostelries as the Savoy, Park Lane, and New Weston, all first-class or deluxe hotels, were marked for replacement by office buildings. Even the boom from the New York World's Fair could not halt the trend. The fair gave the city's hotels a gain of 20 per cent, or $100,000,000 in income, and a 76 per cent occupancy average.

The Waldorf-Astoria, gleaming from a multimillion-dollar refurbishment, remained queen of the city, despite such glossy new competitors as the New York Hilton, the Regency, and the Americana. The venerable Plaza launched a $9,000,000 modernization program to maintain its traditional status as the arbiter of elegance.

In the rest of the country's 74,000 hotels and motels, occupancy ratios rose or fell spottily from the 1963 average of 62.8 per cent. Gross income rose slightly from $4,371,000,000 in 1963 to $4,500,000,000 for 1964 because of more rooms—a total of 2,500,000 —to rent. Washington, D.C., hotel rentals were up 11 per cent; San Francisco, 4 per cent; Philadelphia, 3 per cent; and New Orleans, 6 per cent. Boston rentals fell 4 per cent; Baltimore, 8 per cent; and Chicago, 1 per cent.

Elegance was the keynote of 1964's new hotels such as the Century Plaza going up in Los Angeles, the refurbished Warwick in Houston, and the Kahala Hilton in Honolulu. At the same time, the nation's 29,000 hotels began to emulate the 45,000 motels by offering such lures as easier parking, simplified checking in, and swimming pools. Motels similarly became more like hotels, offering more service, facilities such as restaurants and bars, and entertainment and recreation.

The major U.S. hotel chains continued to expand abroad. Intercontinental Hotel Corporation, subsidiary of Pan American Airways, opened hotels in Vienna; Geneva; Jerusalem; Amman, Jordan; and Karachi, Pakistan. Intercontinental now operates 31 hotels overseas, compared to 26 for Hilton, and 13 for Sheraton.   WILLIAM D. PATTERSON

HOUSING. The year became a landmark for housing legislation when, on September 2, President Lyndon B. Johnson signed the Housing Act of 1964. Of special interest was the unprecedented bipartisan support for the law, which made possible continued federal assistance in public housing and urban renewal programs. The U.S. House of Representatives, by a vote of 309 to 70, and the Senate, without even a roll-call vote, approved the expenditure of $971,800,000 for new public housing, urban renewal, and community development projects. This appropriation will allow public housing and urban renewal programs to continue through Oct. 1, 1965. Hence, new legislation was expected during 1965.

Timely Action. By the time Congress had acted on the measure, both the Public Housing Administration (PHA) and the Urban Renewal Administration had run completely out of funds. PHA had applications pending for some 45,000 units of public housing. Construction of approximately 37,500 new units was authorized by the new law.

Housing Law Changes. Amendments to existing housing legislation approved in 1964 were expected to have far-reaching effects on local housing and renewal activities. The amendments include the following new provisions: (1) cities can now carry out housing code enforcement programs as "urban renewal projects" with federal financial assistance; (2) direct loans for housing rehabilitation may be granted up to $10,000 for residences, and up to $50,000 for businesses, at 3 per cent interest or lower, for up to 20-year periods; and (3) the Federal Housing Administration is authorized to increase the limits on home mortgages it insures from $25,000 to $30,000 for one-family homes, with proportionate increases authorized for multifamily structures.

Housing Starts, seemingly on an endless climb since 1960 because of heavy apartment construction activity, leveled off during 1964, apparently because of local and regional oversupply. Nonfarm residential construction, at about 1,500,000, pumped some $21,275,000,000 into the economy, just slightly less than in 1963.

Housing vacancy rates, holding at 7.7 per cent of the total supply over the last few years, did not climb during 1964. Hence, there was no reason to expect any serious downturn in residential construction in the near future.   J. ROBERT DUMOUCHEL

See also BUILDING AND CONSTRUCTION; CITY; CITY PLANNING; OLD AGE.

Wide World

FAMILY PORTRAIT. *Before his vice-presidential nomination, Senator Hubert H. Humphrey and his wife, Muriel, gathered with family: from left, son Robert, son-in-law C. Bruce Solomonson and wife Nancy, Hubert III and wife Nancy Lee, and son Douglas.*

HOUSTON. Thousands of residents conducted a house-to-house drive against mosquito breeding places in August, as a result of a rare epidemic of encephalitis that struck the city. It was suspected to have caused 32 deaths, and hundreds of persons had to be hospitalized. See HEALTH.

The emergency measures to eliminate mosquitoes, which carry the deadly virus, were followed in November by voters' approval of a new mosquito abatement ordinance.

At year's end, the world's largest air-conditioned, clear-span stadium was virtually complete. The $31,600,000 Harris County Dome Stadium will seat up to 45,000 for baseball and 50,000 for football.

Now fully operational, the Manned Spacecraft Center of the National Aeronautics and Space Administration (NASA) proved a strong magnet for new employment in research and development. Three private firms began construction of adjacent facilities emphasizing space-age technology.

Houston's growth continued to require large public expenditures. In June, voters approved bond issues amounting to $87,000,000 for facilities, such as streets, sewage disposal, freeways, and expansion of water mains, all needed to meet the needs of a growing metropolis.   DONALD W. LIEF

HUMPHREY, HUBERT HORATIO (1911-   ), a vigorous and well-rounded Democratic liberal with a reputation as a skilled politician, was elected Vice-President in 1964. He had been U.S. Senator from Minnesota since 1949, and with ability and determination had risen rapidly in that body. In his first two terms he sponsored a phenomenal total of 1,044 bills and joint resolutions. His proposals have led to such major legislative actions as the Peace Corps, the National Defense Education Act, and the U.S. Arms Control and Disarmament Agency.

Humphrey was born on May 27, 1911, in Wallace, S.Dak., the son of a druggist. Financial difficulties arising from the depression forced him to drop out of the University of Michigan in 1929 and return home to help his father in the drugstore. In 1933, he earned a degree at the Denver College of Pharmacy. He returned to the University of Michigan in 1937, graduated *magna cum laude* in 1939, and took a master's degree the next year. His wife, the former Muriel Buck, whom he married in 1936, helped to support him through school. They now have four children and two grandchildren.

Humphrey taught school for a time, and in 1943, ran for mayor of Minneapolis. He was defeated, but ran for the office two years later, and won. As mayor,

361

Wide World

VIGOROUS CAMPAIGNER Hubert H. Humphrey invades the "enemy territory" of Georgia, one of the six states he and the President lost.

Humphrey set in motion a vigorous crackdown on gambling and rackets. He also reorganized the city's housing and social welfare programs. His term in office was also a period for building the Democratic-Farmer-Labor alliance, the basis for his political strength in the state. In 1947 he was re-elected mayor, and in 1948 was elected U.S. Senator.

It was in 1948, as a delegate to the Democratic National Convention, when he made a speech calling for strengthening of the civil rights plank, that he first came to national attention. In this action he was opposed by powerful party leaders. He successfully overcame them, and a more vigorous plank was accepted.

In the Senate, Humphrey became a most persuasive cloakroom negotiator. He worked as one of the majority leader's most trusted lieutenants, and when Lyndon B. Johnson left the Senate in 1961, Humphrey was named majority whip to work closely with the new majority leader, Mike Mansfield.

Unlike some liberals, Humphrey does not question the motives of those who oppose him. He well knows that on the next issue he may need their votes. Perhaps the best example of his negotiating and legislative skill was shown during the debate prior to the passage of the 1964 Civil Rights Bill. He worked tirelessly to weld Democrats and Republicans alike behind the legislation. See Section Two, CONGRESS MAKES A DECISION.   FOSTER STOCKWELL

362

HUNGARY. The official celebration of Christmas in 1963, for the first time under communist rule, was a portent of the cautious liberalization that continued in 1964. During the year, the nation saw such significant developments as: (1) the travel of nearly 200,000 Hungarians to Western Europe; (2) the easing of property restrictions on people who had fled the country between April, 1945, and March, 1963; and (3) the signing of an agreement with the Vatican, giving the Roman Catholic Church more liberty and independence.

Hungary enjoyed the most prosperous economy and the highest standard of living of any communist country in Eastern Europe. Because there were signs that the economy might be faltering, however, the government stepped up its efforts to stimulate industry and speed development of collectivized farms.

Nikita S. Khrushchev visited for a week in April. He again castigated Communist China and declared that "goulash"—schools, housing, and ballet—was more important than revolution. He was echoed by Communist party chief János Kádár who, despite his rise to power atop Soviet tanks in 1946, had gained some approval by proving that what had been lost at the barricades could be won by more cautious means. After Khrushchev's fall, Kádár praised him and demanded explanations. See COMMUNISM; RUSSIA.

Population: 10,135,000. **Government:** Communist Party First Secretary and Premier János Kádár; President István Dobi. **Foreign Trade:** exports, $1,206,-000,000; imports, $1,306,000,000. **Principal Exports:** bauxite, machinery, textiles.   TOM AND HARLE DAMMANN

See also EUROPE.

HUNTING AND FISHING. The biggest news about 1964 fishing was its spurt in popularity. The number of persons who took up the sport as a recreation continued to grow much faster than the U.S. population. With ever-mounting fishing pressure on streams, lakes, and oceans, the future became a conservationist's nightmare and a tackle manufacturer's dream come true. In the latest year with complete tabulations, 1963, the Sports Fishing Institute reported that 19,800,000 persons had spent $57,800,000 just for fishing licenses, stamps, and tags.

But the question remained: How many fishermen can the waters of the United States support? According to predictions by the Outdoor Recreation Resources Review Commission, there will be 63,000,000 U.S. anglers by the year 2000. Two obvious ways to meet the need for more fishing waters were (1) to improve those on hand and (2) to find new ones.

Anglers began to show increasing concern about pollution of streams and lakes. The most outstanding 1964 case was the winter die-off of several million fish in the lower Mississippi River. See POLLUTION.

New fishing areas came into greater use during the year. Outstanding was the Tree River, which flows into the Arctic Ocean's Coronation Gulf, about 1,000 miles north of Edmonton, Alberta. There, late in 1963, most recent year tabulated, the only new world record of that year was taken—a 27-pound, 4-ounce arctic char caught by William Murphy. The previous 24-pound record char also came from the same river, which was first fished in 1960.

Hunting, like fishing, continued to gain devotees —245,000 in one year. The U.S. Bureau of Sport Fisheries and Wildlife, reporting in 1964 on the year 1962, said that almost 14,000,000 hunters— about an 80 per cent gain from 1940—had bought licenses, permits, and tags worth more than $68,000,-000. It estimated that another 2,800,000 persons hunted legally without licenses.

An old-American "big game" bird—the wild turkey—was being hunted more widely than ever across the United States. Figures showed that 82,306 were bagged in 1963, for an increase of 21 per cent. In 1964, 26 states held turkey seasons, up from 18 states in 1960. More states joined the list each year as planted populations established themselves and grew to huntable numbers.

Still the most hunted big-game animal in the United States was the deer, with 1,933,158 of all kinds taken in 1963. Mourning doves and cottontails, the meat and potatoes of American hunting, were taken in untallied millions.   CLARE CONLEY

See also OUTDOOR RECREATION; WATER AND FLOOD CONTROL; WILDLIFE.

IACOCCA, LEE A. (LIDO ANTHONY) (1924-), added to his considerable eminence in the U.S. automotive industry by developing the Mustang, a Ford Motor Company moderately priced, four-passenger cross between a sports car and a sedan. The car was introduced in the spring, and enjoyed a phenomenal success. By the end of 1964, more than 300,000 had come off Ford assembly lines.

Iacocca was named general manager of the Ford division on Nov. 9, 1960. Almost at once, he ordered a study of the division's ultimate goals. Out of weeks of meetings and study, Iacocca concluded that Ford had to appeal to the "young at heart"—and the theme for the Mustang was born.

After taking two engineering degrees, a B.S. from Lehigh University and an M.E. from Princeton, Iacocca joined Ford in 1946, completing its 18-month training course at Dearborn, Mich., in nine months. Assigned to be an automatic-transmission engineer in Edgewater, N.J., he asked instead to be put in sales. Turned down, he departed and got a job in sales at the Ford assembly plant at Chester, Pa.

Thereafter his rise was rapid, spurred on by a remarkable ability to increase sales. He worked in the truck marketing division and advanced to manager of the vehicle marketing division, from which Henry Ford II named him to head the Ford division.

Iacocca was born in Allentown, Pa., on Oct. 15, 1924. Both his parents were born in Italy. He and his wife, the former Mary McCleary, have one daughter, 5-year-old Katharyn.   WALTER F. MORSE

ICE HOCKEY. The champion Toronto Maple Leafs fell to third place in the regular season of National Hockey League play, but then went on to win their third straight Stanley Cup championship. In the Stanley Cup play-offs, the Maple Leafs edged out Montreal, four games to three. The regular season of play found Montreal the winner, followed by Chicago, Toronto, and Detroit.

Other Results. Russia reigned as champion of amateur hockey with its victory in the Winter Olympics at Innsbruck, Austria. Sweden was second, and Czechoslovakia, third. The University of Michigan defeated Denver to win its first National Collegiate Athletic Association (NCAA) title in eight years. The Cleveland Barons, third in American Hockey League play, swept nine play-off games to win the Calder Cup.

Awards in the National Hockey League:
Calder Trophy (top rookie), Jacques Laperriere, Montreal.
Hart Trophy (most valuable player), Jean Beliveau, Montreal, also winner in 1956.
Lady Byng Trophy (sportsmanship), Ken Wharram, Chicago.
Norris Trophy (best defenseman), Pierre Pilote, Chicago, for second straight year.
Vezina Trophy (leading goalie) Charlie Hodge, Montreal.
Ross Trophy (leading scorer), Stan Mikita, Chicago.
                                    STANLEY ISAACS
See also OLYMPIC GAMES.

ICE SKATING continued to be dominated by Europeans, though young Americans made steady progress. In figure skating, the leaders were Manfred Schnelldorfer, 21, of West Germany, and Sjoukje Dijkstra, 22, of Holland. Schnelldorfer won the men's world title as well as the Olympic championship. Miss Dijkstra added an Olympic gold medal to the silver one she won in 1960 at Squaw Valley. She also captured her third straight world championship. She later became a professional skater.

The outstanding American skater was Scott Allen of Smoke Rise, N.J., who, at 14, became the youngest skater ever to win the American men's title. He went on to take third place in the Olympics and fourth in the world competition. Peggy Fleming of Pasadena, Calif., 15, won the U.S. women's crown; and Judianne and Jerry Fotheringill of Tacoma, Wash., again won the U.S. pairs championship.

Speed Skating. Olympic 5,000-meter winner Knut Johannesen of Norway captured the world overall championship in speed skating at Helsinki, Finland, with victories in the 5,000- and 10,000-meter races. Terry McDermott won the Olympic 500-meter gold medal, the only important trophy the U.S. men's team brought home.

Russia's Lydia Skoblikova, winner of an unprecedented four Olympic gold medals, repeated her 1963 sweep by again winning all four world championship races. The top U.S. woman at the world meet was Janice Smith, 18, of Rochester, N.Y., who finished in 12th place.   JAMES O. DUNAWAY

ICELAND

ICELAND was swept by a wave of protest over the rising cost of living. Icelanders, who had won 15 per cent wage increases through strikes late in 1963 and early 1964, indignantly watched most of their gains disappear as prices continued upward.

A widespread demand that the wage-price spiral be halted was welcomed by the Conservative-led, two-party government of Prime Minister Bjarni Benediktsson which found its economic stabilization program in jeopardy. In May, the government indicated it might be willing to legislate a guarantee of the purchasing power of wages by linking them to prices in an escalator arrangement.

Population: 190,000. **Government:** President Ásgeir Ásgeirsson; Prime Minister Bjarni Benediktsson. **Foreign Trade:** exports, $107,000,000; imports, $168,000,000. **Principal Exports:** fish and fish products, hides and skins.   FRED J. PANNWITT

IMMIGRATION AND EMIGRATION. As a place to settle, the United States was in somewhat less demand in 1964. But for an increasing number of foreigners it was a popular place to visit. The immigrant quota system remained in effect, since the 88th Congress failed to enact the reform proposals that had been recommended by President John F. Kennedy in July, 1963. And in 1964, the proposed legislation became a lively campaign issue.

During the fiscal year ended June 30, 1964, 292,248 aliens were admitted to the United States, 4.6 per cent fewer than in fiscal 1963. The number of quota immigrants, 102,844, was almost as great as the previous year's 103,036. But the nonquota immigrants, 189,404, dropped 7 per cent. In this same period, 112,234 persons became U.S. citizens.

Among the new arrivals, 123,064 were from Europe; 112,973 from North America (principally Canada, Cuba, and Mexico); 31,102 from South America; 20,885 from Asia; 2,887 from Africa; and 1,325 from Oceania (principally Australia and New Zealand). Twelve came from miscellaneous other countries.

Incoming visiting aliens totaled 1,744,808, a 16 per cent increase over fiscal 1963. In this category, 1,105,268 came on vacation, and 144,680 on business. Another 44,952 came as students, and 33,371 on cultural exchange programs. See TRAVEL.

The United States deported 8,746 aliens. The principal causes were: entering the country illegally (4,580), violating conditions of nonimmigrant status (2,473), lacking proper documents (688), and being criminals (417) or narcotics violators (146).

The U.S. Immigration and Naturalization Service reported that 1,430,736 aliens and 2,709,196 U.S. citizens departed the United States by sea and air during fiscal 1964. It did not indicate, however, how many of these were emigrating and how many were simply on vacations.   WILLIAM McGAFFIN

INCOME. See AGRICULTURE; BUSINESS.

INCOME TAX. See TAXATION.

INDIA

O F ALL ITS 18 YEARS since independence, India marked 1964 as its most difficult. The loss of its towering father figure, Jawaharlal Nehru, climaxed the events of a year that saw a crippling food crisis, frustrations in economic development, a deluge of refugees from East Pakistan, mounting nervousness over Kashmir, and political tremors in the wake of the Chinese nuclear explosion. But 1964 also saw a resolute India courageously tackling these monumental problems.

When Nehru died in office on May 27, there were dire predictions that India's cultural diversities would produce either a chaotic Balkaniza-

FIERY FAREWELL. Hissing flames begin consuming the funeral pyre of India's late Prime Minister Jawaharlal Nehru at riverside cremation rites in New Delhi.

United Press Int.

The Light is Out . . . A Glow Remains

A YEAR BOOK CLOSEUP

JAWAHARLAL NEHRU (1889-1964)

"THE LIGHT has gone out of our lives and there is darkness everywhere . . ." The words were Nehru's; the time—Gandhi's assassination. But India felt the poignancy of these words even more excruciatingly when Jawaharlal Nehru—prime minister, foreign policy architect, economic czar, and chief social reformer—died in government harness on May 27, 1964.

For 17 years, he was the voice and soul of India, inspiring the colonial world to independence, frustrating the West with nonalignment, blocking the communists in their global designs, and striving valiantly for world peace.

Until independence, Nehru had lived under the shadow of Mahatma Gandhi. But Pandit (learned man) Nehru was a philosopher in his own right. Whereas Gandhi was spiritual, Nehru was secularly intellectual; whereas Gandhi was insular, Nehru was internationalist; whereas Gandhi distrusted industrialization and big government, Nehru saw in them the key to India's prosperity. Yet, with his dedication to nonviolence, Jawaharlal Nehru remained a dedicated and devoted disciple of Mahatma Gandhi until the end of his life.

BUT 17 YEARS of decision making can produce flaws—even in a Jawahar (jewel). Nehru's mystic preoccupation with foreign affairs and capital-devouring projects, like steel, while his countrymen went hungry; his brooding socialism that throttled India's economic momentum; his near schizophrenia in preaching nonviolence but spending 50 per cent of India's budget on defense; in lecturing on peace, but making a power grab for Goa; in professing nonalignment, but seeking military assistance from the West—all were popular targets for quips and comments by columnists and cartoonists.

Yet Nehru's domestic achievements showed his amazing vision. He hammered away at social justice, almost to the point of reverse discrimination. He launched India's five-year plans—now a blueprint for orderly economic growth in many underdeveloped countries. And, in a nation where religion, lingualism, and provincialism still dominate nationalism, Nehru was the dynamic cement that repeatedly prevented the fledgling nation from flying completely apart.

But his greatest gift to India, and indirectly to Asia, was his passion for democracy in the face of authoritarian temptations as a short cut to progress. The effectiveness of a democracy is measured by actual adherence to the constitution and by the smoothness of leadership succession. Nehru's life testified to the former; his death proved the latter, when the baton went to Lal Bahadur Shastri (see SHASTRI, LAL BAHADUR). In the stormy, unsettling seas of the Afro-Asian world it is this Indian stability that stands out as a Rock of Gibraltar.

Abroad, Nehru put India on the world map. A militarily impotent country with not even a compensating economic strength, India was heard and respected because of Nehru's political magnetism. African and Asian leaders regarded him as the bellwether of the colonial world, leading them to freedom. He opposed racial discrimination in all forms, everywhere, and brought dignity to the colored people of the world.

HE gave the West its most uncomfortable moments as the high priest of nonalignment. The West criticized his underrating of the communist menace and his double standard in speaking softly to the communists while berating the West with a big stick.

Nehru countered that his nation had fought too hard for independence to lose it now for a mess of communist pottage or Western subservience. India could not contribute military strength to any alliance. But its tradition of tolerance and history of nonviolence equipped it to provide a useful meeting ground before all countries chose sides and blew up the world.

HE WORKED diligently for world peace—as a mediator, in the halls of the United Nations, in Korea, in Congo (Léopoldville), and in Indochina. And although the Chinese invasion of India in 1962 made a shambles of his nonalignment theory, he lived to see the beginnings of a détente between the United States and the Soviet Union. In the words of President Johnson: "He has given expression to man's yearnings for peace. This was the issue of our age . . . There could be no more fitting memorial to him than a world without war." KEKI R. BHOTE

tion or a dictatorship. An ugly split in the ruling Congress party did, indeed, threaten to develop when conservative Morarji Desai, former finance minister, attempted a bid for power with rightist and leftist support. But a mainstream sentiment for unity and continuity prevailed, and moderate, self-effacing Lal Bahadur Shastri, former home minister, was elected prime minister on June 1. India thus passed, with flying colors, the acid test of a democracy, the smoothness of transition from one leader to the next.

It had long been conceded that it would be difficult for any successor to follow in Nehru's giant footsteps. The initial public reaction to Shastri was one of pity. The Communist party attacked him as "incoherent" and his administration as "chaotic." Shastri also found it difficult to tighten up the cumbersome administrative apparatus. But Shastri's strength —as a conciliator and unifier—seemed to fit India's greatest need. His ability to get antagonists "to reason together" for the public good worked to his advantage. By year's end, slowly but surely, communist ridicule was giving way to fear, public pity to respect.

Shastri, while committed to the basic Nehru policies of democratic socialism at home and nonalignment in foreign affairs, encouraged a greater role for free enterprise in industry and a closer, though undeclared, identification with the West. Unlike Nehru, who sometimes had antagonized the West with his homilies on world problems, Shastri concentrated on solving India's internal problems.

Food Crisis. The most pressing of domestic problems was the crisis in food. Agricultural production rose a meager 2.4 per cent. Inadequate concentration on agriculture in previous five-year plans, and subversion of land reform by unscrupulous landlords, in granting only oral tenancies, took their toll. Land reform itself had not been a howling success, with technology, marketing, and financing incomprehensible to the average Indian farmer. Agricultural distribution was even worse, bogged down as it was by poor planning, an overworked transport system, hoarding, profiteering, and interstate jealousies.

Poor planning and inefficient distribution caused a 45 per cent jump in wheat costs, with the wholesale price index soaring 14 per cent—the largest single increase since independence. The scarcity led to mass riots, looting of food stores, and general lawlessness. The communists staged a three-day, nationwide demonstration. Belatedly, the government stepped in with price ceilings, fair price shops, and a crackdown on hoarding. In the turbulent province of Kerala, rationing had to be introduced, and special food trains were rushed in.

India turned to the United States for help, and the response was generous and immediate. A $398,-000,000 loan agreement for food and edible oil was signed, including 4,000,000 tons of wheat, which

United Press Int.

WHITE-CAPPED Lal Bahadur Shastri was his nation's choice to succeed the late Jawaharlal Nehru as prime minister of India.

has been reaching India at the rate of 20,000 tons a day. For the long range, the government planned massive increases in fertilizers, intensive irrigation, and easier rural credit. There was recognition now that unless a minimum 5 per cent growth rate in agriculture could be attained, India's industrial progress might be washed away.

General Lawlessness. Religious riots in Pakistan brought a deluge of 295,000 Hindu refugees into India, triggering massacres of 1,300 Moslems before order could be restored. Corruption in state governments toppled the chief ministers of Orissa and Punjab and brought on "President's rule" in Kerala. For their sinister role in capitalizing on all this unrest, over 600 pro-Chinese Communist leaders were arrested. See PAKISTAN.

Fourth Five-Year Plan. Yet another setback was the disappointing performance of the third five-year plan which would end in 1966. National income rose only 4.3 per cent in fiscal 1963-1964, and industrial output 6.9 per cent against a targeted 11 per cent. The public sector in industry had been handicapped by government red tape, corruption, and civil service administrators with little knowledge of industry. The private sector, generally, had been short-sighted in its desire for quick amortization, large profits, and government protection against competition. Only exports showed an encouraging upward trend of 10 per cent.

Recognizing its uphill task, the government, under T. T. Krishnamachari, India's pragmatic finance minister, came closer to an acceptance of classical market economics than at any time during the Nehru era. Milder taxation policies, easing of throttling import licenses, concessions to attract foreign investment, and insistence on respectable profit from public sector industries were reassuring evidence to the world business community.

Kashmir Issue. Hopes for a solution to the Kashmir problem brightened momentarily when Nehru, in a magnanimous gesture to cut the Gordian knot, released Sheik Abdullah, the popular Kashmiri leader. Abdullah, who had been jailed for 10 years by the New Delhi government for advocating self-determination in Kashmir, proposed a 10-year United Nations trusteeship for Kashmir, to be followed by a plebiscite, or, alternately, a condominium with India and Pakistan sharing sovereignty. But, after separate meetings with Nehru and President Ayub Khan of Pakistan, nothing came of the proposals, and Kashmir returned to its deadening status quo. See PAKISTAN.

Population: 479,000,000. **Government:** President Sarvepalli Radhakrishnan; Prime Minister Lal Bahadur Shastri. **Foreign Trade:** exports, $1,791,000,000; imports, $2,285,000,000. **Principal Exports:** jute, tea, textiles. KEKI R. BHOTE

See also ASIA.

INDIAN, AMERICAN. President Lyndon B. Johnson in January enlisted the American Indians in his war on poverty. He told representatives of the National Congress of American Indians that the Indians had suffered the most from poverty. He pledged that his administration would help to wipe it out. See SOCIAL WELFARE (Close-Up).

In July, Secretary of the Interior Stewart L. Udall called on the Bureau of Indian Affairs (BIA) to develop a comprehensive 10-year plan to "raise the standard of living on Indian reservations." At a conference of the Council on Indian Affairs in May, U.S. Commissioner of Indian Affairs Philleo Nash attributed much of the poverty among Indians to "the continuous spin-off of the highest achieving individuals" from the reservations, leaving behind those least able to cope with their problems.

Public Housing Administration loans became available to reservation Indians for the first time in 1964. As a result, 3,200 housing units won approval in 17 states. New business and industry projects on reservations were advanced more than $6,700,000 from the BIA's revolving loan fund. This stimulated further tribal investments of $25,000,000 and private investments of $100,000,000.

Congress approved a $15,000,000 damage and rehabilitation fund to help New York's Seneca Indians adjust to the flooding of their lands along the Allegheny River. Another tribe, the Seminole, stood to receive as much as $40,000,000 in damages from the U.S. government. The award, which may not come for years, will be based on the 1823-1832 fair market value of their Florida land. A. L. NEWMAN

INDONESIA continued its bitter opposition to the Federation of Malaysia. Yet the serious problems within the country were often obscured by the inflammatory statements issued to the world at large by President Sukarno, much of whose "crush Malaysia" campaign seemed designed to divert attention from domestic issues. See MALAYSIA, FEDERATION OF.

The year began in violence, with the seizure by communist unions of plantations owned by British and Dutch oil companies. Although the government intervened, it later nationalized the companies. There were large-scale rice shortages and starvation in many areas. Further, Indonesian credits and foreign reserves with which to buy foodstuffs abroad were exhausted by March. Inflation was rampant.

Civil Discontent, too, was rampant within the island nation. Communist mobs often were in evidence destroying property and creating disorder. The most overt of such actions occurred in Celebes, where rebel rightists conducted a spirited battle

"Don't clap yet—maybe the show's just started."

against the central government. The government suffered a severe setback with the defection of a full battalion that had been sent to crush the rebels.

Despite troubles at home, Sukarno continued what was termed as his hard line on Malaysia. Repeated conferences between President Diosdado Macapagal of the Philippines and Malaysia's prime minister, Tunku Abdul Rahman, came to nothing. Mediative efforts by the United States also failed. Sukarno continued to demand a "crush Malaysia" policy, boasting that a million Indonesian volunteers could do the job. Yet the action in a military sense was at best sporadic. Occasional paratroop drops on Malaya proper were quickly snuffed out by constabulary forces. Indonesian moves in Sarawak and Sabah were countered quickly by British and Australian troops. Great Britain and Australia made it abundantly clear that they intended to stand behind Malaysia. Sukarno then retaliated by recognizing North Vietnam.

Late in the year, after Malaysia was given a seat in the United Nations Security Council, Sukarno vowed he would withdraw from the United Nations. See UNITED NATIONS.

Population: 103,100,000. **Government:** President Sukarno. **Foreign Trade:** exports, $697,000,000; imports, $514,000,000. **Principal Exports:** palm oil, petroleum products, rubber.   JOHN N. STALKER

See also ASIA.

INDONESIAN PARATROOPER, captured by British during airdrop over Malaysia, stares stolidly at bodies of his fellow guerrillas.

Wide World

INDUSTRY underwent a massive campaign of expansion in 1964, spurred by a $1,700,000,000 reduction in corporate income tax and other liberalizations of the tax laws. One sensitive index of that expansion was the amount of money companies spent on the machines used to make machines. Net new orders for such machine tools totaled approximately $1,350,000,000, about 45 per cent more than the $931,200,000 spent in 1963.

The advance was so sustained that not a single month in 1964 fell below the 1963 monthly average of $77,600,000. That average jumped to $112,500,000 in 1964. This strong demand for machine tools was such that the United States became an especially ripe market for foreign producers. Japan in particular made small, but significant, gains in her U.S. sales.

On a wider scale, U.S. industry poured unprecedented funds into the economy to expand plant capacity and improve efficiency. To meet the rush of orders, some companies had to reopen antiquated facilities. In September, U.S. Steel Corporation started up a 1917 plate mill in Gary, Ind., that had been tagged for the scrap heap. Kaiser Aluminum later reopened a smelter it had closed in 1958.

New Plant and Equipment total spending swept past all earlier estimates for 1964, to $44,650,000,000 —up $5,000,000,000 from 1963. The 1962 to 1963 gain had been only $2,000,000,000 and the rise from 1961 to 1962, $3,000,000,000.

Here's what major segments of industry spent on expansion and their percentage gains from 1963:

Industry	Billions	Per Cent
Durable goods	$9.35	19.0
Nondurable goods	9.16	16.8
Mining	1.17	12.5
Railroads	1.46	32.7
Transportation	2.30	19.8
Public Utilities	6.15	8.8

The steel industry alone invested $1,800,000,000 in new equipment in 1964.

Technological Improvements, particularly automation, accounted for a substantial amount of the capital spending. The oil and gas industry, for example, was more than one-third computerized by the end of the year. Wider use of computers for phasing and regulating production, storage, and pipelining of oil and gas was being implemented. Even the assembly line was beginning to be taken over by robots, particularly where fine precision work and close tolerances were necessary. See AUTOMATION; COMPUTER.

Other new methods, techniques, and materials played prominent parts in improving productivity in almost every industry. *For steel,* it was the growth of the oxygen-injection process and perfection of continuous casting techniques (see IRON AND STEEL).

In soft coal, use of continuous mining equipment expanded. Late in the year, Peabody Coal Company put the world's largest power shovel to work night and day at its Illinois strip mine. Its single operator was able to move 140 cubic yards of earth in one bite.

INDUSTRY

For air transport, the wider use of jets, along with improvements in all-weather landing methods gave the airlines one of their best years (see AVIATION).

In machine tools, electrochemical "cutters" performed frictionless, cold machining. An electrolytic solution flowing over the work surface dissolved the unwanted metal.

New Materials were jostling the old (plastics versus steel, wood, and glass), or combining with them (vinyl-coated steel), or battling with each other (nylon versus Vectra or Delrin against Celcon). Substitutes for some basic materials could be found, but not enough to lessen the demand for the nonferrous metals. Prices of antimony, copper, lead, tin, and other metals climbed in 1964, some to unprecedented heights. See METAL INDUSTRY; PLASTICS.

Strong Sales Gains matched the expansion of production facilities in almost every segment of industry. Personal spending by consumers on the flood of goods from U.S. mills and factories rose about 8 per cent in the year. This was the record, in billions of dollars, seasonally adjusted yearly rate:

Type of Goods	All '63	1st Qtr. '64	4th Qtr. '64
Durable	$ 52.1	$ 55.9	$ 60.0
Nondurable	167.5	172.9	180.0

Among key industries reporting hefty increases in estimated output for the year were:
- *Steel:* A 16.5 per cent spurt to a historic high of 127,000,000 ingot-tons.
- *Automotive:* A 2.2 per cent rise to a total of 9,307,443 cars, trucks, and buses assembled.
- *Construction:* A 5.6 per cent gain in value of all new construction put in place, to $65,900,000,000.
- *Electric power:* A 6.8 per cent step-up in output, to 1,076,000,000,000 kilowatt-hours.
- *Petroleum:* An increase of about 2 per cent in production of crude oil and natural gas liquids, to a total of 3,200,000,000 barrels.

Sales Chain Reactions among the thousands of U.S. suppliers of goods and services were analyzed and charted by federal economists and released late in the year. The Department of Commerce's Office of Business Economics broke down the economy into 86 major segments, plotting the *input* (purchases) and *output* (sales) of each group by source and destination, respectively. Using 1958 data, the study showed the number of dollars per $1,000 each group sold to every other, as well as to *end users* (consumers, governments, users abroad, inventories).

The input-output tables enabled a producer of limestone, say, to anticipate his production needs that an upsurge in automobile buying might trigger. More steel would be needed, and, in turn, more of his limestone to feed the steel mills. Some ripples in the industrial ocean would affect only a few industries. Others, such as a cut in defense spending, would affect many. The charts showed which ones and to what degree.   ROBERT E. BEDINGFIELD

See also Section One, SYLVIA PORTER ON THE ECONOMY; and its Related Articles.

INSECT control was stressed by President Lyndon B. Johnson when he asked Congress, in July, for $29,000,000 to conduct research in safer pest-control methods. The highly poisonous, but widely used, chemical pesticides were found to have caused death to large numbers of fish in the Mississippi River, and concern over their continued use was widespread. See POLLUTION.

In a resolution adopted at the 12th International Congress of Entomology in London, scientists warned that indiscriminate methods of insect control would lead to outbreaks of pests throughout the world. The remedy, they said, lies with integrated pest control which would combine chemical, biological, and cultural techniques. It was especially emphasized that insecticides should be fitted into nature's scheme and "not merely imposed on it."

Trapping Insects. One novel approach to the control of insects was developed by Martin Jacobson and Morton Beroza, researchers for the U.S. Department of Agriculture.

Instead of employing odiferous repellents or indiscriminate poisons, the technique involved the use of chemicals that simulate the scents of the opposite sex, food, or natural habitat to attract insects into lethal traps.

The developers also pointed out that such attractants for pest control are less costly and more efficient, and at the same time the problem of the contamination of the environment by toxic materials is vastly reduced.

Computer Pests. The similarity of a mosquito to a programmed computer was described by Dr. R. H. Wright of the British Columbia Research Council in Canada. His investigations indicated that a mosquito is guided to its target by a series of reactions to chemical stimuli not involving memory or sense of direction. Once airborne, the mosquito's behavior is very much like that of a robot.

Dr. Wright found that repellents work, not because the smell is offensive, but because the chemicals disrupt the attack program, much as a radio beam upsets a bomber's autopilot.

Professors Lawrence L. Ogborn and Daniel Shankland of Purdue University believe the cockroach is a possible source of information for developing more reliable computers. Using micro-miniature components and tiny electrodes attached to the insects' reflex systems, the scientists were able to monitor electrical activity and pick up frequency and phase changes in the signals carried by the insects' nerves.

From this work they learned that fibers, called stretch receptors, send out a code that is picked up and translated by ganglia, or nerve centers, and then relayed back via nerves as orders to activate muscles. They also learned that stretch receptors seem capable of measuring displacement and velocity, thereby serving as natural transducers.   SERGEI LENORMAND

See also HEALTH; HOUSTON.

INSURANCE companies played an increasingly important role in the nation's daily economic life in 1964. One example: life insurance in force at the end of the year totaled nearly eight times the amount of the entire U.S. federal budget. Figures released by the Life Insurance Association of America show the strength of U.S. life companies. At the end of 1964 their assets totaled $149,700,000,000. The net increase of $8,600,000,000 over 1963 was the largest for any single year. In billions of dollars, their investments broke down roughly as follows:

Federal, state, and local bonds	12
Corporate bonds	68
Common and preferred stocks	8
Land and building mortgages	54
Policy loans and other assets	8

With prosperity and increasing population, the amount of life insurance in force with legal reserve companies continued to climb. At the close of 1963, Americans were insured for a total of more than $731,000,000,000, an increase of 140 per cent in just 10 years. In 1964, sales of life insurance to the public increased 14 per cent. This brought a 9 per cent net increase in the amount of life insurance in force, pushing the total to just a little under $800,000,000,000.

Life Insurance Benefits collected by U.S. families during the year came to nearly $10,000,000,000. Of this amount, life companies paid about $1,000,000,000 in annuity benefits. A large portion of these annuity payments went to retired workers under group company pension plans, the fastest-growing segment of the annuity field.

On June 1, the Prudential Insurance Company of America lost its appeal to the Supreme Court of the United States on its plan to sell individual variable annuities without regulation by the federal Securities and Exchange Commission (SEC). Prudential planned to go ahead, however, with its group annuities subject to SEC controls.

Fire and Casualty insurance companies turned in slightly better results in 1964 than they did in 1963. But they were still having their troubles with a profits squeeze caused by high payouts in relation to rates charged for insurance.

A record number of windstorms in the Midwest, Florida, and Louisiana didn't help. Estimated losses from Hurricane Cleo alone amounted to $65,000,000. See DISASTERS; WEATHER.

During the year, the industry sought some increases in rates and changes in some policy terms to protect itself against undue losses. In New York, for example, higher auto physical damage rates went into effect in August. Boosts ranged from 4.3 to 25 per cent. New car-insurance rates also were scheduled to go into effect the first of 1965 in at least 39 states. And terms of homeowner, multiperil policies, a fast-growing end of the insurance business, were being modified with a much wider use of exclusion and deductible clauses.   EDWIN W. DARBY

See also SOCIAL SECURITY; VETERANS.

INTERIOR DECORATION. In an exhibit called "The House of Good Taste" at the New York World's Fair, the public had an opportunity to view homes and interiors that, for once, were not futuristic, but which typified the "good life" as it is being lived in the 1960's.

Actually, the exhibit was made up of three homes, each completely furnished and landscaped, showing three variations of contemporary-style living.

The First House was traditional Early American in style. The front was adapted from early Cape Cod homes with small-paned windows and shutters. But the rear had large sliding glass doors in the current style. Kitchen, baths, and laundry were the height of modern efficiency. Furnishings, not restricted to a single period, included styles adapted from 18th-century England, Queen Anne, and Chippendale, and some 19th-century Hitchcock adaptations.

The Second House illustrated the growing trend toward the self-contained home with solid-walled exteriors around an inner courtyard, or atrium. This arrangement assures privacy and many believe it is becoming a necessity in crowded residential areas that lack lawn and garden space.

The house featured a central room with a skylight. Beneath the circular skylight were large bushes in pots, a slender tree, and garden-style furniture, which suggested outdoor living. Yet this atrium area was usable the year round. All the other rooms surrounded this pleasant view. Furniture was contemporary, softened with plants and the use of large, modern paintings.

The Third House of Good Taste combined four distinct units, each with a separate peaked roof, all grouped around an outdoor swimming pool. It also had a large skylight in the living room. Decoration was contemporary and featured strong color.

The fair's Pavilion of American Interiors was a three-story oval building containing model rooms with displays by manufacturers. Emphasis was on educational displays, not startling innovations.

Home Furnishings Industry. Financially, 1964 was an excellent year for the home furnishings industry. Orders and sales of furniture were at an all-time high. Hence factories emphasized production, not style changes.   FLORENCE BYERLY

INTERNATIONAL TRADE. Throughout most of 1964, the outlook for international trade expansion hung on another ultimatum from President Charles de Gaulle of France. He had given the European Economic Community (EEC, or Common Market) until December 15 to arrive at a common, lower price on grain. If it did not, France would leave the EEC. Early on the morning of the deadline date, the Common Market nations—Belgium, France, Italy, Luxembourg, The Netherlands, and West Germany —reached agreement. Uniform grain prices were to go into effect on July 1, 1967. De Gaulle called it a step that "opens all sorts of possibilities in the way of European construction." Two weeks later, the EEC cut industrial tariffs 10 per cent, effective Jan. 1, 1965. See EUROPE; FRANCE.

But in Britain, a block to freer flow of international trade was erected. Rising imports and stagnating exports had caused the largest deficit in the balance of payments in British history. It forced the new Labour government of Harold Wilson to impose a 15 per cent surtax over and above tariffs on all goods but food and raw materials. Wilson also offered tax incentives to spur exports.

Britain's associates in the European Free Trade Association (EFTA) complained bitterly. Late in November, Britain promised it would begin to remove the surtax "in a matter of months." The moves also had been taken to protect the pound sterling, which had fallen close to $2.78, the minimum permissible level under the rules of the International Monetary Fund. See GREAT BRITAIN; MONEY.

The Kennedy Round of tariff-cutting negotiations scheduled to take place at Geneva, Switzerland, early in 1965 received a considerable lift from the Common Market grain pact. Seventeen nations of the General Agreement on Tariffs and Trade (GATT) on November 16 had submitted their lists of items to be exempted from the sweeping reductions of

proving the U.S. balance of trade over 1963. The merchandise export surplus increased to almost $5,000,000,000 for the first three quarters of 1964 from $3,600,000,000 in the same 1963 period. Patterns of U.S. trade deviated a little from 1963. Mexico and India moved up to fifth and sixth on the best customer list; and West Germany climbed from fifth to third on the principal supplier tally.

Industrial Europe's imports rose somewhat faster than its exports, but other transactions kept the reserve position strong, with the exception of Italy. Japan's reserve position worsened slightly, caused—as was Britain's—by rapidly mounting imports in the first six months of the year.

Apart from the problems besetting the British, 1964 was a year of normal growth and development of international trade, more of a marking time for the Kennedy round. If those tariff negotiations succeed, the world will continue on the path of generally lower trade barriers—a path it has followed since 1934. If the GATT negotiations fail, rising protectionist pressures in France and the United States may be expected to become the guideposts to a less specialized trading world. Similarly, if British problems are not resolved, the maintenance of its tariff surcharges may provoke retaliation from its trading partners.   WARREN W. SHEARER

See also articles on individual nations for yearly merchandise exports and imports.

U.S. FOREIGN TRADE
(Average monthly volume in millions of dollars)

Best Customers	1964	1963	1962
(Exports)	(9 Mo.)		
Canada	$376.9	$343.2	$319.4
Japan	153.6	141.5	117.9
Britain	114.9	96.8	89.6
West Germany	104.1	92.0	90.0
Mexico	85.8	68.7	67.1
Principal Suppliers			
(Imports)	(9 Mo.)		
Canada	$347.8	$319.1	$305.0
Japan	144.1	124.8	113.2
West Germany	93.2	83.6	80.1
Britain	92.9	89.9	83.8
Venezuela	79.6	78.1	81.3

up to 50 per cent in tariffs that will be negotiated. With EEC's agriculture issue resolved, other hurdles still remained in the GATT negotiations: the lists of exceptions, nontariff barriers to trade such as quotas and other import regulations, wide tariff disparities, and policies for undeveloped nations.

Year's Trade Rises. If there were doubts about the future, there were few on the overall course of international trade during 1964. Total volume was up approximately 10 per cent over 1963 levels, but its gains were unevenly distributed. U.S. exports rose above $25,000,000,000 for the first time in history. Britain's exports showed practically no gain, however, while those of industrialized Western Europe rose about the same as the U.S. rate. Gains for Canada, Japan, and the less developed countries of Africa were above average.

U.S. imports rose slower than exports, thus im-

INVENTION was still an active and prolific field— one hundred years after government officials considered closing the patent office because they thought just about everything imaginable had been invented. Inventors were gaining patents for devices that ranged from airplanes to fish lures.

One invention expected to have a major impact on the entire field of scientific research was a new system of photography that makes sharp, clear pictures without a lens and offers hope of providing the first photographs of minute organisms and even atoms.

The inventors, Dr. Emmett N. Leith and Juris Upatnieks of the Institute of Science Technology at the University of Michigan, believe the technique has the theoretical possibility of enlarging 100,000 times pictures taken with X-ray cameras and electron microscopes. The system converts the phase differences in light waves into intensity differences, much like a radio receiver captures electromagnetic waves and converts them into usable sound signals.

This is done by shining a reference beam of light into the camera at the same time the reflected light from the subject reaches the film. The result is a phenomenon called interference, which changes the phase differences into differences in the brightness of the light. The negative appears to be only a smudge, but the smudge can be then converted into a recognizable image by shining the same monochromatic light back through the negative to project a clear image of the subject onto a screen.

Changing Glass. A glass that darkens on exposure to light and clears again as the light fades was invented by Dr. S. Donald Stookey and Dr. William H. Armistead, of the Corning Glass Works. It was claimed to be the first photochromic material to retain indefinitely the ability to darken quickly and clear again.

Snake Poison. A poison that kills cold-blooded creatures but not warm-blooded animals, won a patent for James R. Jenni of Oklahoma City, Okla. In one test the toxicant was sprayed on a snake-infested area in Texas. Three days later 248 snakes were found dead. SERGEI LENORMAND

IRAN entered the second phase of its 10-year-old land reform program in 1964. Hassan Ali Mansur, who was named premier by Shah Mohammed Riza Pahlevi when Asadollah Alam resigned in March, won parliamentary approval for the new reform bill in May. See Section Two, AWAKENING THE LAND.

In November, new lower limits were set on land ownership. Individual farmers were permitted to own only 75 acres in fertile areas, but a maximum of 300 acres in such arid areas as Baluchistan. Dispossessed landlords would be given immediate cash compensation. This replaced a previous policy under which landlords were repaid over a 15-year period. Operators of mechanized farmland tilled by hired labor and machines were allowed to keep 1,250 acres.

Population: 22,800,000. **Government:** Shah Mohammed Riza Pahlevi; Premier Hassan Ali Mansur. **Foreign Trade:** exports, $1,120,000,000; imports, $581,000,000. **Principal Exports:** carpets, cotton, petroleum, wool. WILLIAM SPENCER

See also MIDDLE EAST.

IRAQ negotiated a cease-fire with the rebellious Kurds in February. There was general relief at the signing of a truce in the unpopular, costly struggle. Unfortunately, the ending of hostilities brought the government no closer to solving the Kurdish problem. The desires of Kurdish leader Mullah Mustafa al-Barzani for Kurdish autonomy within a decentralized Iraqi state clashed with President Abdul Salam Muhammad Arif's plan to unite Iraq with the United Arab Republic (UAR).

Iraq moved hesitantly toward an "Arab socialism" modeled after that of UAR President Gamal Abdel Nasser. It formed a new National Oil Company to exploit 99 per cent of Iraq's land, leaving the 1 per cent concession area (750 square miles) still held by the Iraqi Petroleum Corporation (IPC). In July, banks, insurance companies, and about 30 industrial firms were nationalized.

Population: 7,100,000. **Government:** President Abdul Salam Muhammad Arif; Premier Taher Yahya. **Foreign Trade:** exports, $886,000,000; imports, $321,000,000. **Principal Exports:** barley, dates, petroleum. WILLIAM SPENCER

See also MIDDLE EAST.

IRELAND suffered an economic jolt when Great Britain's newly elected Labour government slapped a 15 per cent surcharge on manufactured imports in October. Prime Minister Seán F. Lemass protested personally in London. Ireland's new dependence on industrial exports, especially to Britain, was emphasized in the nation's new seven-year plan which set the annual growth rate for industry at 7 per cent as compared to only 2.7 per cent for agriculture.

In the February elections, the Fianna Fáil party of Prime Minister Lemass not only held onto the vital seat in County Cork but also won a seat from Labour in County Kildare. These two victories assured the Lemass government of a full five-year term that would not end until 1966.

Population: 2,855,000. **Government:** President Éamon de Valéra; Prime Minister Seán F. Lemass. **Foreign Trade:** exports: $594,000,000; imports, $1,014,000,000. **Principal Exports:** alcoholic beverages, cattle, meat. ALASTAIR BURNET

IRON AND STEEL. The steel industry fittingly celebrated its 100th birthday with sharply rising output and profits in 1964. U.S. production was estimated at a record 127,000,000 tons, compared with 109,000,000 in 1963 and the previous record of 117,000,000 in 1955. It was on Sept. 14, 1864, that the first commercial *heat* (batch) of steel was poured by a Bessemer-type process in Wyandotte, Mich.

High production in the capital goods, construction, appliance, and automobile industries, along with the trend toward larger cars, boomed the output of steel. Toward the end of 1964, inventory accumulation as a hedge against a possible strike in 1965 and a steel price increase added to steel demand. Such heavy hedge buying in the first half—without an early labor settlement—could mean sagging sales and output in the second half, despite an expected rise in actual steel consumption of about 2 per cent.

Accumulation of inventories at the end of 1964 was some 3,000,000 tons of finished products above normal requirements. Consumption in the year shot up 7.5 per cent from 1963 and stood 7 per cent above the previous record in 1955.

Profits and Prices. Earnings for most companies in 1964 were up sharply from those for 1963. Yet industry spokesmen cited the relatively low rates of return on investment. From midsummer into fall, there were calls for price increases.

Late in October, President Lyndon B. Johnson said he was watching the price situation closely and that he was opposed to any price boost. The cost of a generous settlement with the United Steelworkers of America could have a bearing on steel prices.

Steel Imports and inroads of other metals into steel's markets, however, have exerted a downward pressure on prices. Imports, which had risen 33 per cent in 1963, slowed down to a 10 per cent gain in 1964, leveling off at about 6,000,000 tons. Booming business in Europe and Japan, where steel producers are hard-pressed to supply their customers at home, brought some increases in import prices. Also a factor in taking some of the luster off imported steel was the success of American steel mills in reducing costs through massive modernization programs.

New Processes of steelmaking accounted for the bulk of the industry's $1,800,000,000-a-year capital outlays in 1963 and 1964. Most of these funds were going into three new steel processes:

• *The oxygen furnace*, which blasts pure oxygen through molten iron and scrap to refine the mixture into steel. It makes better steel cheaper and five times faster than an open hearth.

• *Continuous casting*, which permits the pouring of molten steel directly from the furnace into a variety of shapes instead of into ingots only.

• *Vacuum degassing*, using a vacuum vessel to suck impurities—mostly hydrogen—out of molten steel, produces more uniform steel.

New Sources of raw material to feed the steel furnaces were assured in 1964. In September, Standard Oil Company (Indiana) reported a find of about a billion tons of low-grade iron ore in Alaska. Two months later, the voters of Minnesota approved a tax amendment encouraging the development of the vast deposits of *taconite* (low-grade iron ore) in Minnesota.   ROBERT E. BEDINGFIELD

ISRAEL and Syria strafed one another's boundaries with jet-fighter fire in November. Each claimed that border violations committed by the other had precipitated the air strikes. At Syria's urgings, the matter was placed before the United Nations (see SYRIA; UNITED NATIONS).

Despite this outbreak of hostilities, Israel experienced relatively little difficulty with its other Arab neighbors, although its controversial plan to divert water from the River Jordan to irrigate the Negev desert had augured otherwise.

Israel extended the reparations agreement it had signed with West Germany in 1963. During the 1964-1965 fiscal year it will receive $250,000,000 in West German goods. Israel also signed a three-year agreement with the European Economic Community reducing tariffs on Israeli goods up to 40 per cent.

On December 15, Prime Minister Levi Eshkol and his government resigned. The immediate issue was Eshkol's opposition to a plan sponsored by David Ben-Gurion for a judicial inquiry into the 10-year-old "Lavon affair" involving former Defense Minister Pinhas Lavon in an alleged "security mishap." Eshkol formed a new government which was approved on December 22. It later voted against holding the investigation.

Population: 2,530,000. **Government:** President Schneor Zalman Shazar; Prime Minister Levi Eshkol. **Foreign Trade:** exports, $365,000,000; imports, $816,000,000. **Principal Exports:** diamonds, fruits and vegetables, textiles.   WILLIAM SPENCER

See also JEWS AND JUDAISM; MIDDLE EAST.

ITALY

ITALY struggled to achieve economic and political stability in 1964, but with only limited success. The inflationary trend of the preceding year had been halted, but a recession had followed. Although the precarious center-left coalition government weathered a month-long cabinet crisis, it emerged no stronger than before.

The government of Premier Aldo Moro resigned on June 26, after a parliamentary defeat over its program to increase state aid to private (*i.e.*, Roman Catholic) schools. Moro, however, remained as caretaker premier, and in July he resumed office. Pietro Nenni, leader of the left-wing Socialists, again became vice-premier. Other parties in coalition with Moro's Christian Democrats were the Democratic Socialists and the Republicans. The defection of the Republicans on the school aid issue had toppled the cabinet in June.

On August 7, President Antonio Segni was incapacitated by a stroke. His duties were taken over by Cesare Merzagora, the president of the senate. Provincial elections held in November showed a further decline in Christian Democratic strength and a small gain for the Communist party.

Early in December, President Segni resigned. He was succeeded on December 28 by Foreign Minister Giuseppe Saragat, a compromise candidate who won on the 21st ballot cast by the presidential electors. Saragat, a pro-Western, moderate Socialist, was the first of his party to be elected president of Italy.

Economic Doldrums. The Italian economy lagged behind the upward trend enjoyed by most of Western Europe. Credit restrictions, higher taxes, and other austerity measures were enacted to forestall inflation and overcome an unfavorable balance of trade. In the spring, with the Italian stock market dropping and the lira in trouble in world markets, Italy obtained a $1,200,000,000 emergency loan from the International Monetary Fund, the World Bank, and the United States.

Businessmen blamed the recession on the "opening to the left" which had brought the left-wing Socialists into the government and led to the nationalization of electrical power and rapid rises in wages. These, in turn, caused a loss of business confidence and overspending on consumer goods. The communists, on the other hand, accused the government

HAIL TO THE CHIEF. *Newly elected president of Italy, Giuseppe Saragat, smiles broadly as Premier Aldo Moro, left, salutes his election with a courtly bow.*

of favoring big business in its efforts to counteract the slump. Exports were on the rise, however, and some economists believed that economic recovery was close at hand.

On May 10, two northeastern provinces, Friuli and Venezia Giulia, elected a 61-member regional parliament, thus creating Italy's fifth semi-autonomous region under the constitution's decentralization plan. Meanwhile, Italy's dispute with Austria over the Trentino-Alto Adige (South Tyrol) region remained unresolved.

Population: 50,650,000. **Government:** President Giuseppe Saragat; Premier Aldo Moro. **Foreign Trade:** exports, $5,818,000,000; imports, $7,676,-000,000. **Principal Exports:** machinery, motor vehicles, textiles.   FRED J. PANNWITT

See also EUROPE.

IVORY COAST. President Félix Houphouet-Boigny reshuffled his government on September 10, reducing his cabinet from 17 to 11. In addition, he unseated several members of the State Security Court, including the court's former president, Jean-Baptiste Mockey, who had been under house arrest following the discovery in 1963 of a plot to assassinate the president. Houphouet-Boigny subsequently called a meeting in Abidjan of civic and political leaders to urge loyalty, unity, work, and peace in Ivory Coast. He also met with the heads of four other African states in an effort to establish measures for their mutual security.

Population: 3,550,000. **Government:** President Félix Houphouet-Boigny. **Foreign Trade:** exports, $181,000,000; imports, $146,000,000. **Principal Exports:** bananas, cocoa, coffee, timber. BENJAMIN E. THOMAS

See also AFRICA.

JAMAICA pushed ahead with its industrial development program with the opening of a new $16,800,-000 oil refinery, plans for a steel mill, and a port extension program to be financed through the Commonwealth Development Corporation. On October 5, after a visit by a Communist Chinese economic mission, Prime Minister Sir William Alexander Bustamente declared himself ready to explore trade links with Peking.

Independence was not an easy state. To underline Jamaica's social and economic struggle, a government survey published on October 6 revealed that 31 per cent of the population was still unable to read.

On March 22, the United States relinquished its last defense bases on the island. The bases had been acquired under the World War II arrangement with Great Britain.

Population: 1,675,000. **Government:** Governor-General Sir Clifford A. Campbell; Prime Minister Sir William Alexander Bustamente. **Foreign Trade:** exports, $286,000,000; imports, $274,000,000. **Principal Exports:** bauxite, sugar.   ALASTAIR BURNET

See also GREAT BRITAIN.

JAPAN

JAPAN PLAYED HOST to the Olympic Games in October. It was the first time the competitions ever had been held in Asia. The Japanese, taking great pride in their unprecedented role, expended considerable money, effort, and time to make the games a success. Many of the preparations were of permanent value—freeways, new subways, improved rail facilities, new hotels, and new athletic installations. See OLYMPIC GAMES.

IMPERIAL SPLENDOR and traditional costumes mark wedding of Prince Yoshi, son of Japan's Emperor Hirohito, to Hanako Tsugaru, shown here in their wedding portrait.

United Press Int.

Wide World

TUG-OF-WAR. A helmeted policeman is manhandled by ultra-leftist Japanese students protesting arrival of U.S. nuclear-powered submarine in Japanese waters.

Politics. Japan changed its national leadership during the year. Prime Minister Hayato Ikeda, who had been re-elected head of the Liberal Democratic party by a narrow margin in July, resigned because of illness. He was succeeded by Eisaku Sato, who had run second to Ikeda (see Sato, Eisaku).

The new prime minister soon was faced with a minor repetition of anti-U.S. riots. In August, Japan informed the United States that it would not object to visits by U.S. nuclear-powered submarines provided they were not armed with Polaris-type nuclear missiles. The decision had been reached after nearly 20 months of negotiations and reflected strong Japanese sentiment against nuclear armament of any kind. In November, however, a visit by the U.S. nuclear-powered submarine *Seadragon* touched off new riots.

Earlier in the year, a mentally unbalanced youth attacked U.S. Ambassador Edwin O. Reischauer, inflicting a stab wound that required four months of convalescence. There was, however, no political significance to the attack.

Economics and Trade. In July, the government announced that the Gross National Product (GNP) for the 1963 calendar year totaled $59,936,390,000. It represented an increase of 13.6 per cent over 1962 and amounted to a real increase of 8.3 per cent. The 1963 gross national income was slightly less than $49,000,000,000, or about $509 per capita. It compared to $451 for 1962. Consumer goods' prices continued to rise, but this was matched by an increase in real wages. The expanding economy still faced a labor shortage, however. At the end of the school year in March, there were approximately four times as many job openings as there were graduates from junior and senior high schools.

On April 28, Japan became the 21st member of the Organization for Economic Cooperation and Development (OECD). In September, the nation was host to the 19th annual meeting of the International Monetary Fund and the World Bank. About 1,400 representatives from 102 countries attended.

Liberalization of import restrictions resulted in an all-time six-month (January to June) record total of $952,000,000 in imports from the United States. This was 20 per cent above the 1963 figure. Informal trade with Communist China was expected to amount to about $300,000,000 (exports and imports) for the year, more than double the 1963 figure, but only about 2 per cent of Japan's total trade.

Other Developments. The city of Niigata was hit by a disastrous earthquake on June 16. Property damage was high, but loss of life was low. Prince Yoshi, second son of Emperor Hirohito, married Hanako Tsugaru, a commoner, in a traditional ceremony in the Imperial Palace on September 30.

Population: 97,300,000. **Government:** Emperor Hirohito; Prime Minister Eisaku Sato. **Foreign Trade:** exports, $6,295,000,000; imports, $8,248,000,000. **Principal Exports:** light goods, machinery, transportation equipment, textiles, steel. John M. Maki

See also Asia.

JAZZ. See Music, Jazz.

JEWS AND JUDAISM. Jewish religious leaders in the United States played important roles in the principal domestic issue of 1964: the civil rights crisis. In June, 17 rabbis joined in the picketing of a motel in St. Augustine, Fla., and several others aided the voter-registration drive for Negroes in Mississippi. See CIVIL LIBERTIES.

The Jewish population of the United States in 1964 had reached a plateau at about 5,599,000 persons, or about 2.97 per cent of the total U.S. population. This was a drop from 3.7 per cent in the 1950's. Studies indicated that Jewish families were among the smallest in the nation. Nevertheless, religious and charitable activities continued to expand.

Jewish-Catholic Relations. The activities that caught the imagination of the world's 13,121,000 Jews in 1964 revolved principally around Judaism's relationship with the Roman Catholic Church. Much controversy was created early in the year with the opening in New York City of the play, *The Deputy*. It was written by a young German Protestant, Rolf Hochhuth, who condemned the late Pope Pius XII for his silence during the Nazi persecutions (see THEATER). New York's Francis Cardinal Spellman denounced the play as a distortion of the truth.

U.S. Jewish-Catholic relations were not disturbed by the play, however. This was evident in Rome, where U.S. churchmen joined with those of Germany and Great Britain to push through the third session of Vatican Council II a statement declaring that the Jews were not responsible for the death of Jesus, since the crucifixion represented the collective guilt of all mankind.

Action on the matter had been postponed since 1963, principally because of the insistence of bishops in Arab countries. However, in November, the bishops overwhelmingly adopted a strongly worded statement. The text read, in part: "What happened to Christ in His passion cannot be attributed to the whole (Jewish) people. Besides, the church held and holds that Christ underwent His passion and death freely because of the sins of all men and out of infinite love." The statement, if and when promulgated by Pope Paul VI, was expected to serve as a mandate for the removal from Catholic liturgical and educational texts all references to the Jews as a deicide people and, hence, to greatly lessen overt causes of anti-Semitism.

In January, Pope Paul visited Israel. He was warmly greeted by Israeli President Schneor Zalman Shazar. Though the Vatican does not recognize Israel, Pope Paul's visit seemed to indicate an informal kind of recognition.

Jews in the Soviet Union enjoyed no such rapprochement. Despite official denials, it was apparent that some synagogues had been closed and that training of rabbis had come to a halt. Jewish communities viewed these developments with an increasing sense of urgency.   MORRIS N. KERTZER

See also ISRAEL; ROMAN CATHOLIC.

JOB CORPS. As 1964 closed, about 1,000,000 American youths, ages 16 to 21, were out of work. They were the high school drop-outs without the education and needed skills to get a job. They lived in city and rural slums. To give them a chance to help themselves, the Office of Economic Opportunity, the new government bureau created to coordinate the anti-poverty program, authorized its first Job Corps camps in 1964.

Youths who volunteered to serve in the Job Corps were to be given $30 a month for pocket money plus room, board, and clothing. When they leave the corps, they will receive $50 a month for the 12 or so months they will have spent in the corps.

In the rural areas, the youths will work under the supervision of the Forest Service, the National Park Service, and the Bureaus of Indian Affairs, Land Management, Reclamation, Fisheries, and Wildlife. They will perform needed conservation work and, at the same time, get a basic education in reading, writing, speaking, and arithmetic. Special vocational training will include basic surveying and typing.

In the city areas, Job Corps camps will be set up on unused military and other government facilities. The youths who live in the camps will learn how to become office machine operators, sales clerks, hospital orderlies, waiters, cooks, auto repairmen, meat cutters, and machine tool operators.

The Job Corps enrollment goal was 40,000 in the first year, and 100,000 in the second. Dr. Otis A. Singletary, 43, chancellor of the University of North Carolina at Greensboro, was named director of the Job Corps.   WILLIAM McGAFFIN

See also CHILD WELFARE; EDUCATION; OFFICE OF ECONOMIC OPPORTUNITY; SINGLETARY, OTIS A.; SOCIAL WELFARE (Close-Up); VISTA.

JOHNSON, HAROLD KEITH (1912-   ), deputy chief of staff for military operations, succeeded Earle G. Wheeler as army chief of staff in July, 1964. Johnson also was advanced in rank to a full general. He came to the Pentagon early in 1963, after serving (1960-1963) as commandant of the Command and General Staff College at Fort Leavenworth, Kans.

General Johnson's early military service was in the Philippines. He was captured by the Japanese in 1942, survived the Bataan death march, and was freed by the American forces at Inchon, Korea, in September, 1945. Johnson returned to Korea in the summer of 1950, and saw heavy fighting there throughout that conflict. He was chief of staff of the 7th Army (1957-1959), and chief of staff of the North Atlantic Treaty Organization Central Army Group (1959-1960) in Europe.

Harold Johnson, who likes to speak of himself as "just a country boy," was born in Bowesmont, N. Dak., and later lived in Kansas. He was graduated from the U.S. Military Academy in 1933.

See also NATIONAL DEFENSE.

JOHNSON, LYNDON B.

JOHNSON, LYNDON BAINES (1908–   ), threw himself into the most difficult job in the world in 1964 with an energy and competence that reassured the American people, still shaken by the assassination of President John F. Kennedy. His and his party's tremendous landslide victory at the polls in November he termed "a mandate for unity."

He brought a new atmosphere to the White House, entertaining informally on the White House lawn, greeting tourists and showing them around the White House, driving his own car, cajoling Congressmen in person and by telephone to win them to his program in Congress.

PICTURES OF THE YEAR/Ted Rozumalski, *The Houston Chronicle*

The vigorous, 6-foot, 3-inch Texan would rise before 7 A.M. and work far into the night, pausing only to watch the 11 P.M. newscasts. Meals often became working conferences with legislators or other officials. He read 13 daily newspapers and a few weekly news magazines. He enjoyed telephoning, hunting, horseback riding, entertaining newsmen, and greeting crowds.

The President's folksy manner was matched by a sense of thrift. In January, he noted that the White House electric bill totaled several thousand dollars a month and asked aides to turn off lights in the Executive Mansion whenever possible.

Americans soon discovered that their new President was proud of his wife and teen-age daughters, and of his Texas ranch, the LBJ. There, on 438 acres of pasture, which Mrs. Johnson called "this little spread," the family raised white-faced Hereford cattle. The President often visited the ranch for vacations or brief conferences. He spent Christmas of 1963 and the early days of 1964 entertaining West German Chancellor Ludwig Erhard, calling on relatives and friends, and talking to Cabinet members about his proposed budget cuts. After the election, he relaxed there in a victory celebration with Vice-President-Elect Hubert H. Humphrey (see HUMPHREY, HUBERT H.).

Press Criticism of the President was touched off in April after reports of his driving his own car near the LBJ ranch at 85 miles an hour, forcing an oncoming car off the road. The danger to the life of the President in such an incident worried the public.

Throughout 1964, Lyndon Johnson was sensitive to such criticism. Usually, he called press conferences informally and with little notice. But in April, he held his first live television conference in the setting used by the late President John F. Kennedy. Late that same month, he entertained 61 business executives and their wives at a White House dinner. In June, he similarly entertained 61 labor leaders.

Children's Hour. In May also, the President invited newsmen to bring their families to a news conference on the White House lawn. The 1,200 visiting

HE'S THEIR CANDIDATE, TOO. Admiring daughters Lynda, left, and Luci, far right, share platform with President and Mrs. Johnson.

PICTURES OF THE YEAR /Bill Allen, Wide World

WARM SUPPORT AND A FIRM HANDCLASP from an admiring Mrs. Johnson go to the President after his historic signing of the Civil Rights Act on July 2.

reporters and their wives and children were served 4,000 cookies and 150 gallons of pink punch. After a fast rundown on affairs of state—from the war in Vietnam to the size of corporate profits—the President and youngsters milled about in a half-hour bedlam of mashed cookies, squirming dogs, trampled grass, and lost toddlers.

As the American people began to realize, the 36th President of the United States was a dynamic, colorful, and sometimes controversial figure. The avid huntsman enjoyed showing off his 7-month-old beagle hounds, Him and Her. In April, and again in May, he pulled the beagles' ears to make them yelp for newsmen. Enraged pet lovers raised a storm of protest. But the President maintained that Him and Her liked the attention. In November, Her died, not from ear pulling, but from swallowing a stone.

Family and Politics. The campaign of 1964 revealed the President as a thoroughly political personality. He enjoyed political and "nonpolitical" tours, and proved to be a tireless handshaker who enjoyed and sought out crowds.

His vivacious wife, Lady Bird (née Claudia Alta Taylor), campaigned also, although she did not seek publicity. In October, she whistle-stopped 1,700 miles through her native South on the "Lady Bird Special." In 47 speeches in four days, she appealed for Southern support for the Democratic party. Earlier in the year, she had toured the Appalachian states with the President. And in August, on a "nonpolitical" tour of the Northwest, she was adopted as a

member of Montana's Crow Indian tribe and re-named "Pretty Walking Bird."

Throughout the year, Mrs. Johnson, with the help of her elder daughter, Lynda Bird, 20, entertained at many White House receptions for visiting dignitaries. In January, the President's wife took Washington newswomen on a precedent-breaking tour of the family's rooms in the White House. That same month, she gave the first of a series of luncheons for prominent American women, and also entertained 100 guests at a luncheon for Queen Frederika of Greece.

Lynda Bird, as well as her 17-year-old sister, Luci Baines, also took part in the Johnsons' innumerable trips and public appearances. Early in 1964, Lynda transferred from the University of Texas to George Washington University in Washington, D.C. Her friend, Warrie Smith, came with her and moved into the White House to keep Lynda company. In April, Lynda's engagement to Navy Lieutenant Bernard Rosenbach was ended by mutual consent.

In February, Lynda's younger sister announced that she spelled her name "Luci" instead of "Lucy." In April, Luci reigned as Queen of the Shenandoah Apple Blossom Festival in Virginia.

On November 17, the Johnsons celebrated their 30th wedding anniversary. When they were asked about the hour of their wedding, the President ventured, "In the evening, about 10 o'clock, wasn't it?" Mrs. Johnson smiled and quietly corrected the President, "No, about 7."

Family Wealth became an election issue. Some of the Johnson family fortune was built by Mrs. Johnson. She had bought television-radio station KTBC in Austin, Tex., in 1942, with inherited funds, and worked it into a million-dollar concern. In August, President Johnson made public an audit of the total Johnson family holdings. They were valued at about $3,500,000, based on the original purchase prices.

Troubles of two Johnson associates played roles in the political campaign. The "Bobby" Baker case, with its charges of payoffs and influence peddling, gave ammunition to the Republicans (see BAKER, ROBERT "BOBBY" G.; CONGRESS OF THE UNITED STATES). And in the closing days of the campaign, presidential aide and close Johnson friend Walter Jenkins was arrested in a Washington YMCA for "disorderly conduct." It was discovered that he had also been arrested on a similar charge in 1959. President Johnson termed this event a "personal tragedy" and said he had no knowledge of either arrest until the story appeared in the press. No evidence of a security lapse was uncovered, but clearance procedures were questioned.

Honors and Degrees were bestowed on President Johnson in profusion in 1964. He made the awarding of his honorary degree at the University of Michigan in May the occasion for his first vision of the "Great Society." In an appeal to the nation's youth, he urged them to meet "the challenge of the next half-century" and use America's resources "to enrich and elevate our national life and to advance the quality of American civilization."

Later that same month, the University of Texas granted both the President and Mrs. Johnson the third and fourth honorary degrees it had ever awarded. In August, the President received an honorary degree (his 25th) from Syracuse University, where he spoke at the dedication of the Samuel I. Newhouse Communications Center.

Election night found the President with his family and close friends in a Texas hotel waiting for the election results. Later, at the LBJ Ranch, he enjoyed a mammoth barbecue celebration with Vice-President-Elect and Mrs. Humphrey.   CAROL THOMPSON

See also DEMOCRATIC PARTY; PRESIDENT OF THE UNITED STATES.

JORDAN mended its diplomatic fences with the United Arab Republic (UAR) in 1964 following an Arab summit conference in Cairo which was attended by King Hussein I. Jordan also recognized the republican regime in Yemen as legitimate, the king having conceded that ex-Imam Badr's chances of regaining power were practically nonexistent.

Jordan also expanded its contacts with the communist countries as it exchanged ambassadors with Czechoslovakia, Hungary, and Poland. This brought the total to six recognized since the establishment of relations with the Soviet Union in mid-1963. See UNITED ARAB REPUBLIC; YEMEN.

King Hussein steered a neutral course among Arab leaders at home and abroad. On his visit to the United States he declared that the Arabs wished to live in peace with Israel. At home, he supported the idea of creating a "Palestine Army," but only on condition that the troops would be recruited from all the Arab states on an equal basis.

Jordan changed governments in July when Premier Sharif Nasir resigned because of illness. He was succeeded by Bahjat Abdul Khadr Talhouni, who had served briefly as premier in August, 1960.

Population: 1,875,000. **Government:** King Hussein I; Premier Bahjat Abdul Khadr Talhouni. **Foreign Trade:** exports, $32,000,000; imports, $196,-000,000. **Principal Exports:** fertilizers, tomatoes, watermelons.   WILLIAM SPENCER

See also MIDDLE EAST.

JUNIOR ACHIEVEMENT (JA) made further changes in policies and procedures dealing with membership qualifications and recruitment at its 21st National Junior Achievers Conference held August 23 to 28 on the campus of Indiana University at Bloomington. The conference was attended by 1,250 delegates, representing 4,876 JA companies throughout the United States and Canada.

Under the revised policies, membership is open only to high school students in the three upper grades, regardless of age, as well as to some non-students. The latter must be between the ages of 16 and 19, and must be approved by the appropriate school principal. Previously, some college students had been members of JA companies. The changes became effective July 1.

Mike Arthur, 18, of Detroit, Mich., was installed as National Junior Achievement president, and Heather Harden, 17, of Omaha, Nebr., was named "Miss JA of 1964."

The "JA Company of the Year" award went to SEROCO of Columbus, Ga.; second place to JALOK of Rockford, Ill.; and third place to JAMATCO of Minneapolis, Minn. GRENORCO of St. Paul, Minn., won the award presented by the New York Stock Exchange for the best JA Company Report to Stockholders.   JOSEPH P. ANDERSON

JUVENILE DELINQUENCY. Boys' clubs, settlements, and youth centers became more complexly related to their communities in 1964. Instead of merely serving the youths that came to them, more and more of the private agencies reached into the community to work with youths and adults who would not ordinarily use the services of such organizations. Such experimental programs included the Chicago Youth Development Project of the Chicago Boys' Clubs. It was working with 44 street gangs, 15 block clubs, and 20 other local civic groups, as well as the juvenile police, school, and employment resources in a massive community effort to combat juvenile delinquency.

383

Legislation. On the national level, the federal government extended the Juvenile Delinquency and Youth Offenses Control Act of 1961 through June 30, 1966. It authorized $10,000,000, and provided for special studies of compulsory school attendance, child labor laws, and an antidelinquency demonstration project that was already underway in the Washington (D.C.) area.

But the legislative weapon that promised to do most in the long run to help curb delinquency was the passage of the antipoverty bill, which embodied a wide range of provisions and programs that related to the problem. See EDUCATION; JOB CORPS; SOCIAL WELFARE (Close-Up); VISTA.

Statistics. The FBI, reporting in July, 1964, for 1963, noted an 11 per cent increase in the arrest of persons under 18 years of age over the previous year. Persons under 18 comprised 17 per cent of all criminal arrests. The range was from 15 per cent in rural areas to 25 per cent of criminal arrests in suburban counties. Almost half of the juvenile cases were handled by the police departments, with referral to the juvenile courts.   HANS W. MATTICK

KAUNDA, KENNETH (? –), was sworn in as president of newly independent Zambia on October 25. Zambia, a former British protectorate, had been part of the Federation of Rhodesia and Nyasaland until its dissolution. See ZAMBIA.

Kaunda, like many of the new African leaders, began life in humble tribal surroundings. As a boy, he helped his widowed mother earn their livelihood by digging drains and gathering firewood. His first schooling was at the Church of Scotland's mission in Lubwa. Later, he was selected for teacher training and subsequently took over as headmaster of the school in Lubwa.

In his early 20's, he became interested in politics. Serving first as a propagandist for the African National Congress, he eventually became secretary of the organization.

Twice arrested because of his political zeal, and twice released after intervals in prison, Kaunda subsequently helped form a new political party, the United National Independence Party (UNIP) of which he was head at the time of his inauguration to the presidency.

KENNEDY, JOHN FITZGERALD (1917-1963). It was the closing session of the 1964 Democratic National Convention. A slender figure with an unruly shock of brown hair mounted the speaker's platform. Immediately, wave upon wave of applause engulfed him. It was the delegates' tribute to the man who, save for an assassin's bullets, would have been leading them and dominating their convention—John Fitzgerald Kennedy. His brother stood there composed yet obviously moved, waiting a full 16 minutes for the roaring ovation to subside. Then in a few simple words, Robert Kennedy introduced the 20-minute filmed memorial to his brother's brief term in the presidency, "A Thousand Days." See KENNEDY, ROBERT FRANCIS.

The President's widow, Jacqueline, had begun the year by thanking the 800,000 persons who had sent their expressions of sympathy. This she did in a telecast on January 14 from her brother-in-law Robert's office in the Justice Department. It was the first time she had spoken publicly since the President's assassination on Nov. 22, 1963.

Later in the year, she appeared as a witness to assist the Warren Commission in its exhaustive investigation of the assassination of her husband. The seven-member commission, headed by Chief Justice Earl Warren, presented a 296,000-word report to President Lyndon B. Johnson on September 24. Its unanimous conclusion was that Lee Harvey Oswald had acted alone in the murder of the President. See WARREN COMMISSION; WARREN REPORT (appendix).

Mrs. Kennedy sold her home in the Georgetown section of Washington, and moved to an apartment in New York to escape the intrusion into her privacy.

Mrs. Josephine M. H. Fitzgerald, the late President's maternal grandmother, died in Boston on August 8 at the age of 98.

Aid to the Retarded. The Kennedy family continued its fight to aid the mentally retarded. International awards for achievement in this field were presented by President Johnson at the second annual awards dinner of the Joseph P. Kennedy, Jr., Foundation in New York City, February 5. President Johnson promised to carry on the battle begun by President Kennedy against "mental retardation and mental illness and poverty and every other foe of the land he loved." Canadian Prime Minister Lester B. Pearson turned over to the foundation $70,000 raised by Canadians. He announced that a Canadian John F. Kennedy Memorial Fund for Mental Retardation had been established and that special research projects were being planned for each of Canada's 10 provinces.

The Kennedy family was represented at the dinner by Mrs. Rose F. Kennedy, mother of the late President, and her son, Robert.

Awards totaling more than $200,000 were given by the Kennedy Foundation to Dr. Robert P. L. Lafon, neuropsychiatry professor of the University of Montpellier, France; Dr. Lionel S. Penrose, geneticist at University College, London; Dr. Grover Francis Powers, Yale University Medical School professor emeritus of pediatrics; Senator Lister Hill, Alabama Democrat; Representative John E. Fogarty, Democrat of Rhode Island; and Bert T. Combs, former Democratic governor of Kentucky.

Memorials. John F. Kennedy was honored in many parts of the world. At home, the Congress of the United States authorized $15,500,000 to assist in the construction of the John F. Kennedy Center for the Performing Arts in Washington, D.C. Private contributions came within $2,000,000 of matching

United Press Int.

TWO CAPITAL MEMORIALS to President John F. Kennedy. The simple, expansive design for a tomb, above, on the site of the late President's grave in Arlington National Cemetery, was approved by his widow in November. Ground was broken on December 2 for the John F. Kennedy Center for the Performing Arts, below, which will rise on the east bank of the Potomac River.

National Cultural Center

the government's 50 per cent at the time of ground-breaking ceremonies on December 2. See MUSIC.

The John Fitzgerald Kennedy Memorial Library was to be built on Harvard University land in Boston. In addition to housing President Kennedy's own papers, it would contain a great variety of memorabilia of the Kennedy era. In December, Robert Kennedy named architect I. M. Pei as the library's designer, and announced that an institute for advanced political studies would be established at the library. The $10,000,000 fund goal was reached, but fund-raising would go on to provide an endowment for the institute. In other memorials, at home and abroad, the martyred President's name was given to airports, expressways, squares, schools, and bridges. Special coins and stamps were issued (see HOBBIES).

In Arlington National Cemetery, where "an eternal flame" flickered over his grave, an estimated 8,000,000 Americans and foreigners went to pay their respects during 1964. Plans for a permanent monument of simple, low-lying design were approved in November. The flame will remain as its central symbol. The cost of the tomb and its approaches was estimated at $2,000,000. The Kennedy family's share of the projected cost would be between $200,000 and $400,000.

These were the memorials in brick, stone, and mortar. Would the kind of memorial given to John Kennedy by the Democrats at Atlantic City endure? Would he, in office less than three years, go down in history as one of the great American Presidents? His biographer, historian James MacGregor Burns, thinks he will. In an interview in *U.S. News & World Report*, the historian declared that "both Kennedy's image as a person, as a President, and his impact as formulator of policy will be with us for a long time. . . . I would say he made himself, as President, unforgettable."   WILLIAM McGAFFIN

KENNEDY, ROBERT FRANCIS (1925-   ), who,

resigned as Attorney General of the United States in September, was elected United States Senator from New York on Nov. 3. In his victory, he had overcome the issue of his "carpetbag" candidacy. Kennedy, a younger brother of the late President John F. Kennedy, had been living in Virginia and voting in Massachusetts. He campaigned tirelessly and defeated the moderate anti-Goldwater Republican, Senator Kenneth B. Keating, 3,823,749 votes to 3,104,056. The magic of the Kennedy name, the backing of New York Mayor Robert F. Wagner, and the heavy, 2,669,597 plurality for Lyndon B. Johnson—all helped take votes from Keating.

Robert Kennedy had served as Attorney General since 1961, when he became the first person in the history of the United States to be named to the Cabinet by a President-brother. On July 30, President Johnson announced that he had removed all Cabinet members—Kennedy, of course, included—from consideration for Vice-President.

In January, Kennedy visited the Far East as a special representative of President Johnson and negotiated a truce between Malaysia and Indonesia (see MALAYSIA). Back in Washington, he sat down with Senate Democratic and Republican leaders to smooth the way for passage of the 1964 civil rights bill (see Section Two, CONGRESS MAKES A DECISION).

Kennedy is a graduate of Harvard and the University of Virginia Law School. He and his wife, Ethel, have nine children.   WALTER F. MORSE

See also KENNEDY, JOHN FITZGERALD.

KENYA was confronted with an army mutiny in

January, less than one month after gaining its freedom from Great Britain. The uprising, in protest against low pay and the continued presence of British officers, followed similar ones in Tanganyika and Uganda. At the request of Prime Minister Jomo Kenyatta, Britain sent 700 troops to put down the revolt. In April, leaders of the mutiny were tried by court-martial. Sixteen were given prison terms.

On December 12, Kenya formally became a republic. Though the nation remained a member of the Commonwealth, Prime Minister Kenyatta duly changed his title to president, replacing Queen Elizabeth II as head of state.

Marauding Somali tribesmen in Kenya's Northern Frontier District continued their demands that the area be annexed by Somalia, causing Prime Minister Kenyatta to declare a state of emergency in the North-Eastern Region. See ETHIOPIA; SOMALIA.

During the year, Kenya put into full operation the first oil refinery in East Africa. It was located near Mombasa. Aid agreements were signed with Communist China, Denmark, Great Britain, Japan, the Soviet Union, the United States, and the United Nations to further economic development.

Population: 9,200,000. **Government:** President Jomo Kenyatta. **Foreign Trade:** exports, $124,000,-000; imports, $195,000,000. **Principal Exports:** coffee, hides and skins, sisal, tea.   BENJAMIN E. THOMAS

See also AFRICA.

KING, MARTIN LUTHER, JR. (1929-   ), who,

by practicing nonviolence, helped to give dignity and discipline to the U.S. civil rights movement, was the youngest person ever to receive the Nobel peace prize and the third Negro to win the honor. Zulu chieftain Albert John Luthuli received the prize in 1960 for his nonviolent struggle against racial segregation in South Africa. American Ralph J. Bunche, the United Nations under secretary for political affairs, was the 1950 laureate.

The Reverend Doctor King initiated a bus boycott in Montgomery, Ala., on Dec. 5, 1955. He was arrested and his home bombed, but the boycott did not end until Dec. 21, 1956, after the Supreme Court of the United States ruled unconstitutional Alabama's law on segregated seating of bus passengers. Dr. King has led many and varied types of protests, and has gone to jail more than a dozen times since then. He has continued to preach nonviolence.

Dr. King's moral leadership was never more evident, perhaps, than at the historic civil rights march on Washington, D.C., in 1963. Many national leaders appeared there on August 28, but it was Dr. King's speech in late afternoon that alternately drew tumultuous roars and cast moments of hushed silence over the great crowd. He said, "We must not allow our creative protests to degenerate into physical violence. Again and again, we must rise to the majestic heights of meeting physical force with soul force."

When accepting the peace prize in Norway, Dr. King said, "Today I come to Oslo as a trustee, inspired and with renewed dedication to humanity. . . . I accept this prize on behalf of all men who love peace and brotherhood. I say I come as a trustee, for in the depths of my heart I am aware that this prize is much more than an honor to me personally." Speaking in London's St. Paul's Cathedral on December 6, he made such declarations as: "We must not . . . substitute injustice of one type for that of another." Dr. King spoke for 45 minutes on "The Three Dimensions of a Complete Life." His was the first evensong sermon ever delivered in historic St. Paul's by a non-Anglican.

Martin Luther King is the son of a Baptist minister. He was born and lives in Atlanta, Ga., where he founded the Southern Christian Leadership Conference. The National Association for the Advancement of Colored People awarded him its Spingarn medal in 1957. He has degrees from Morehouse College (A.B., 1948), Crozer Theological Seminary (B.D., 1951), and Boston University (Ph.D., 1955). While at Boston University, he met the singer, Coretta Scott. They were married in 1953, and now have four children. MARY JANE BAILEY

See also CIVIL LIBERTIES; NEGRO; NOBEL PRIZES.

KIWANIS INTERNATIONAL. See SERVICE CLUBS.

KLAUS, JOSEF (1910-   ), chairman of the Conservative Peoples party, was sworn in on April 2 as chancellor of Austria. He had been named by the Austrian parliament to succeed Alfons Gorbach, who was forced out of office by the Conservatives on a charge that he had not been firm enough in his dealings with the Socialists. See AUSTRIA.

The new chancellor attended the University of Marburg an der Lahn in Germany, and holds a doctor of jurisprudence degree from the University of Vienna. He was captured by Allied forces in World War II. On his release in 1945, he returned to the practice of law. From 1949 to 1961, he served as governor of the province of Salzburg. He was named federal minister of finance late in 1961, a position he occupied at the time of his appointment to the chancellorship. He and his wife, the former Erna Seywald, have two daughters and three sons. WALTER F. MORSE

KOREA experienced continuing political difficulties that were exemplified by a series of student riots in March and again in June. Although the riots resembled those of mid-1960, in which President Syngman Rhee had been ousted, they did not result in the collapse of the government. They were a reaction to the difficult external and internal problems confronting the country.

Early in 1964, negotiations were held in Tokyo for the establishment of normal diplomatic relations between Korea and Japan. Korea, however, had been a Japanese colony from 1910 to 1945, and, lingering resentment over the harshness of Japanese colonial rule made Korea reluctant to enter into formal relations with Japan.

Rioting in March was touched off by students who feared that the Korean representatives in Tokyo were not protecting their country's interests. The negotiations ended and were not resumed until early December. In August, the Korean government suspended all credit imports from Japan until normal relations could be resumed.

Economic Problems. The country continued to face pressing economic problems, including unemployment, rising commodity prices, labor unrest, and depressed conditions for the farmers. The student riots in June were caused in part by dissatisfaction with the government's failure to improve economic conditions.

Political Issues. President Chung Hee Park, who had been elected in October, 1963, remained in power despite the riots. Because of them, however, Colonel Kim Chong Pil, the second most powerful man in the government, was forced to resign.

President Park imposed a 56-day period of martial law following the June outbreaks. He also attempted to force the passage of two laws by the legislature, one imposing press control and the other forbidding student demonstrations. Neither was passed. On the other hand, President Park suspended almost 600 government officials for alleged corruption, against which the demonstrations and rioting in June also had been directed.

North Korea apparently aligned itself with Communist China in the Moscow-Peking split over communist policy (see COMMUNISM). There were no significant military developments along the 38th parallel truce line, nor were there any indications of progress toward the eventual unification of North and South Korea.

North Korea: Population: 12,000,000. **Government:** Chairman Choe Yong Kun; Prime Minister Kim Il-sung. **Foreign Trade:** figures not available, but about 97 per cent with communist countries.

South Korea: Population: 28,500,000. **Government:** President Chung Hee Park. **Foreign Trade:** exports, $86,400,000 (est.); imports, $450,000,000 (est.). **Principal Exports:** food products, light manufactured goods, minerals. JOHN M. MAKI

See also ASIA; JAPAN.

KOSYGIN, ALEKSEI NIKOLAEVICH (1904-   ), an economic expert, succeeded Nikita S. Khrushchev as premier of the Soviet Union in October. Kosygin had been first deputy premier of the nation since May, 1960. See COMMUNISM; RUSSIA.

Kosygin, who was born Feb. 20, 1904, in St. Petersburg (now Leningrad), was educated in Soviet state schools. He became a Communist party member as a youth, but as late as 1938 Aleksei Kosygin still was an obscure official.

In 1939, he was put in charge of Soviet textile production. It was the turning point in his career. He became a full member of the Politburo in 1948 and, as finance minister of the Soviet Union, headed the consumer goods industry.

In 1952 and 1953, Kosygin was excluded from the Politburo. He was readmitted, however, in 1957, by which time the organization had been renamed the Presidium. He was raised to the rank of deputy premier in December, 1953, and became first deputy premier of the Soviet Union in 1960.

Kosygin is a hollow-eyed, serious-looking man, who has indicated great interest in Western affairs. The new Soviet premier speaks a little English and is fluent in German.   WALTER F. MORSE

KUWAIT played the role of an oil-rich banker in the Middle East during 1964. It gave Jordan financial assistance to help build a series of electric power stations and a tourist hotel in Jerusalem.

The United Arab Republic (UAR) received financial support from Kuwait for its planned improvements to the Suez Canal. In April, however, Sheik Abdullah as-Salim as-Sabah ruled that all future loans to Arab nations would be made through the Kuwait Fund for Arab Economic Development instead of directly by the state.

The government negotiated new agreements with various foreign oil companies operating in its territory. It required them to pay taxes within the fiscal year in which they had been incurred. Another decree to control foreign business activities in booming Kuwait prohibited any foreign companies from carrying on commercial operations there except through a Kuwaiti agent.

During the year, Kuwait set up an international fund to support a newly organized Palestine Liberation Organization (PLO). The PLO was set up by various Arab leaders during a conference in Cairo early in the year. It was to lead "the Arab struggle for the recovery of Palestine" from Israel. Funds would be derived from taxes levied on theaters and on the salaries of Palestinian refugees working in Kuwait.

Population: 350,000. **Government:** Sheik Abdullah as-Salim as-Sabah; Prime Minister Sabah as-Salim as-Sabah. **Foreign Trade:** exports, $1,130,000,000; imports, $285,000,000. **Principal Exports:** petroleum, skins, wool.   WILLIAM SPENCER

See also MIDDLE EAST.

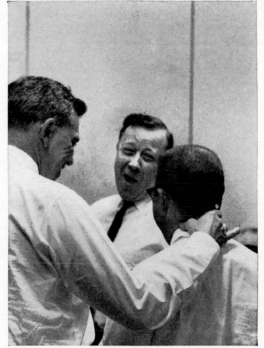

Joe Clark, *Life* © Time Inc., 1964

HAPPY BARGAINER Walter Reuther, auto union chief, center, jokes with aides after coming to generous contract terms with Chrysler.

LABOR problems, rooted in the events of 1963 and previous years, still were demanding solutions in 1964. Although most disputes were settled without strikes and gains were made in employment, a basic atmosphere of unrest persisted.

The $4\frac{1}{2}$-year-old work-rules dispute between the railroads and the five unions representing operating personnel was finally settled in April, only after the personal intervention of President Lyndon B. Johnson. Some concessions were made by each side during the final, frantic two weeks of negotiations and mediation. Most of the similar disputes about job protection between the railroads and six shopcraft unions representing nonoperating personnel were settled near the end of the year on the basis of presidential emergency board recommendations. See RAILROAD.

Job security, too, kept the shipping industry in rough water. A year-long study of dock employment practices by the U.S. Department of Labor formed the basis of the difficult mediation efforts in the longshoremen's disputes on the East and Gulf coasts. After a one-day strike and a court-ordered 80-day "cooling-off" period, agreement was reached in December. Yet at the year's end, some locals bolted and struck rather than accept the recommendations about crew sizes and job guarantees made by the study groups and mediators.

Time lost due to strikes remained relatively low

until the fourth quarter's widespread walkouts over local plant problems in the auto industry. Short strikes at Ford plants and the 31-day strike at General Motors raised the number of man-days lost through strikes above the low levels of the preceding four years. Extended strikes or national emergency injunctions were rare, however.

Wages, Prices, and Jobs. Wage increases of about 2 to 4 per cent and supplementary benefits such as additional paid holidays, an extra week of vacation, and increased pension and insurance benefits were typical of agreements negotiated in the auto, apparel, chemical, communication, construction, meat packing, trucking, and other industries. The average wage increase was slightly over 9 cents an hour, about 3.2 per cent of average hourly earnings. This amount conformed to the government's "guideposts" for noninflationary wage and price movements. Productivity in the nonagricultural private economy increased by 3.2 per cent in 1960-1963. See Business.

The average weekly wage of production workers in manufacturing averaged over $102 in 1964, the first year that this figure passed the $100 mark. Prices remained relatively constant. See Business.

Although total employment was up by 1,500,000, unemployment fell by only about 500,000 because of the increased number of young people entering the labor force. The unemployment rate fell from 5.5 per cent in December, 1963, to 4.9 per cent at the end of 1964—a figure still significantly higher than the 4 per cent government target.

Bargaining Innovations. The auto settlements created significant new patterns in job security. The United Auto Workers (UAW) did not press for the traditional objective of shorter hours per day, but for fewer years on the job over a worker's lifetime. The key feature was the early-retirement supplement enabling a worker with 30 years' service to retire at age 60 with a pension of 70 per cent of his earnings up to a maximum of $400 per month. Also, regular pension benefits were increased substantially and were made available without reduction to people retiring at age 62, and with a reduction to long-service workers retiring as early as age 55.

Another substitute for shorter hours was an extra week off with pay—to be used as sick leave, personal leave, or vacation—along with two more paid holidays, bringing the total to nine per year. The whole economic package was valued at 55 cents an hour.

Union Leadership battles broke out in 1964. The American Federation of State, County and Municipal Workers elected its first new president in its 28 years as a union. Jerry Wurf replaced the union's founder, incumbent Arnold Zander. James B. Carey, president of the International Union of Electrical Workers (IUE), deposed his second in command but, in turn, only narrowly won re-election in his first real battle to keep his job. Carl Megel, the president of the American Federation of Teachers (AFT), stepped down, only to have his personal choice of successor defeated by Charles Cogen, the leader of the New York City teachers' union in its successful fight for a collective bargaining agreement. Dissatisfaction with top union leadership took a different form with the International Brotherhood of Pulp, Sulphite and Paper Mill Workers when the locals on the West Coast seceded and founded an independent union.

Union Growth in 1964, as in past times of economic recovery, brought on some of the unions' internal ferment. U.S. union membership in 1961 had declined about 1,200,000 from the 1956 peak of 17,500,000. Since then the trend has been reversed, membership increasing by 300,000 between 1961 and 1962. Subsequent unofficial estimates suggest that this rate of increase continued through 1963 and 1964. Rising employment in unionized sectors of the economy and intensified union activity among government workers were the chief factors.

Other Developments. Title VII of the Civil Rights Act of 1964 banned discrimination in employment because of race, color, religion, national origin, or sex, effective in 1965 (see Civil Liberties). National concern about poverty and unemployment was reflected in the passage of the Economic Opportunity Act of 1964. It included a three-part youth program: (1) a Job Corps to provide young people with education, training, and work experience at a center away from home; (2) work training for unemployed youths living at home; and (3) a work-study program to provide financial aid to college students (see Job Corps; Social Welfare (Close-Up); VISTA). James L. Stern

See also Automation; Industry; Old Age; and articles on various industries.

LAOS remained a troubled country split between its rightist and leftist factions. The rightists were under the leadership of Prince Phoumi Nosavan. Prince Souphanouvong was the leader of the leftist Pathet Lao guerrillas. Caught in a vise between the two was Prince Souvanna Phouma, the premier of Laos's shaky coalition, neutralist government.

Throughout 1964, the two warring factions concentrated on either widening their own political powers or increasing the geographical areas under their control. By year's end, the Pathet Lao guerrillas controlled about three-fourths of the country. The rightists retained their hold on the principal cities of Vientiane and Luang Prabang, and a thin strip of land along the Thai border. Although Premier Souvanna Phouma tried to maintain what might be termed a legitimately neutral military force, it continued to dwindle.

Population: 2,000,000. **Government:** King Savang Vathana; Premier Prince Souvanna Phouma. **Foreign Trade:** exports, $1,000,000; imports, $24,000,000. **Principal Exports:** coffee, minerals, wood and wood products. John N. Stalker

See also Asia.

LATIN
AMERICA

LATIN AMERICA accorded a tumultuous welcome to French President Charles de Gaulle during his September tour. His earlier trip to Mexico, in March, was the first time a European head of state had paid a state visit to any Latin-American country.

The later De Gaulle visit, which began September 21 and ended October 16, touched 10 countries. The purpose was to reintroduce French influence and trade in an area where France was overshadowed by the United States, and equaled or surpassed by Germany, Great Britain, and Japan. De Gaulle offered the Latin-American republics increased technical cooperation while holding out hope that France was prepared to support their drive for better trade relations with the European Economic Community (EEC, or Common Market). See FRANCE.

Latin America benefited greatly during the year from an upturn in international commodity prices on most of its major exports—coffee, cotton, meat, and tin. Total export earnings were expected to be as much as 10 per cent above the estimated 1963 total of $11,000,000,000. Another healthy sign was the flow of foreign investments into the area, reversing a trend in which foreign capital had stayed away.

Political Developments presented a mixed picture. The presidents of Bolivia and Brazil were ousted by military revolts. Brazil and Chile barely avoided being ruled by far-leftists and communists. In Haiti, François Duvalier was proclaimed president for life. Military regimes in Ecuador and Guatemala, ruling intelligently, were able to achieve some economic progress.

In Paraguay, the 10-year rule of strongman Alfredo Stroessner enabled that republic to achieve a further degree of monetary stability and slow down inflation. In Venezuela, a democratically elected president fulfilled his term and handed over power to a similarly chosen successor for the first time.

Chile, Mexico, and Panama voted in and inaugurated new presidents in orderly fashion, even though the Panamanian campaign was bitter. In Puerto Rico, Governor Luis Muñoz Marín declined to run for a fifth term. He was succeeded by a close political associate, Robert Sanchez Vilella.

U.S.-Panamanian relations were badly jarred in January when mobs, trying to storm the Canal Zone, fought with U.S. troops. But relations improved with the passage of time. See PANAMA.

In July, the Organization of American States (OAS) formally signed resolutions calling for diplomatic and economic sanctions against Cuba. The resolutions also called for a strengthening of the hemisphere against Cuban subversion. In the OAS, only Mexico continued to recognize the Cuban regime of Fidel Castro.

SWIRLING RAINBOW of fluttering paper thickens the air as French President Charles De Gaulle makes a dramatic entrance into Mexico City.

391

Wide World

HANDS UP. Delegates to a conference of the Organization of American States vote, by a show of hands, to impose sanctions against communist Cuba.

New Group. On September 24, the Atlantic Community Development Group for Latin America (ADELA), a multination private investment company, was formally established at a meeting in Luxembourg. Some $17,000,000 of its authorized $40,000,000 capital was subscribed to by over 50 major companies and banks in Canada, Europe, Japan, and the United States.

ADELA hoped to "foment" investment of between $150,000,000 and $200,000,000 by going into partnership with local private capital. It also envisaged substantial financial support from the Inter-American Development Bank. Earlier, in June, ADELA launched its first financial venture when it joined with the International Finance Corporation to help underwrite a steel forgings plant in Colombia.

On March 16, the seven-member Inter-American Committee for the Alliance for Progress (CIAP) was inaugurated, headed by Carlos Sanz de Santamaria, Colombia's former minister of finance.

On the occasion, U.S. President Lyndon B. Johnson asserted "public funds are not enough; we must work together to insure the maximum use of private capital and foreign. . . . Progress cannot be created by international organizations; it cannot be imposed by foreign countries; it cannot be purchased with large amounts of money or large amounts of good will. . . . There is no magic formula to avoid the complex and sometimes painful and difficult task of basic social reform and economic advance. . . . Although help can come from without, success must come only from within."

Goals Set. The CIAP began a series of country-by-country analyses to determine external financing needed during 1965 and 1966 to supplement internal efforts by the republics. It termed agriculture, the activities of private enterprise in Latin America, and delays in the approval of external financing for development projects as the weakest points in the Alliance's program.

The organization estimated that $28,000,000,000 in investments or loans from abroad would be needed during the period that began in 1962 and would end in 1971 if the Alliance's objectives were to be met. This would mean an annual inflow of capital of $2,800,000,000 against the $1,500,000,000 figure set in 1962. Alliance officials warned, too, that new formulas would be needed to reconcile Latin America's foreign debt problems with new assistance, if the area's development was to proceed successfully.

. The region's external debt exceeded $10,000,-000,000 with nearly half of it due for repayment within the next five years. Total U.S. loan commitments toward the Alliance in the first half of 1964 reached an estimated $450,000,000 compared to $400,000,000 for all of 1963.

Progress Report. Alliance goals during the year ending in June, 1965, called for 104,000 new homes, 13,000 more classrooms, distribution of 4,400,000 schoolbooks, 90,000 new agricultural loans, more than 1,000 additional water systems, and food for almost 2,000,000 people. From 1961, when the program began, through June, 1964, the Alliance had helped provide 222,600 new homes, 23,400 new classrooms, 6,800,000 schoolbooks, 207,000 agricultural loans, and 1,056 water systems. The Alliance also provided daily meals for more than 20,000,000 needy people.

As of October 29, the Inter-American Development Bank (IADB) had sold six bond issues since it began operations in 1960. Of the $272,600,000 issued, $225,000,000 were sold in the United States and $47,600,000 in Europe. In August, the IADB topped the $1,000,000,000 mark in authorized development loans to Latin America. In April, it granted its first export credits under its new $30,-000,000 program to finance exports of capital goods. The United States offered to contribute to the IADB about $750,000,000, over the next three years, to help expand the bank's financial facilities.

LAFTA and CACM. In October, the nine-member Latin American Free Trade Association (LAFTA) reached a turning point, when its delegates sat down to the hard, complex task of lowering duties on manufactured items. Earlier meetings on bilateral tariff cuts within the group had met the annual target of 8 per cent average reductions. Most of these,

however, involved easy-to-make cuts, largely on primary products. Now, the program was meeting opposition from vested interests in each of the member countries.

Though tariff reductions on some 2,000 items had helped increase trade among the members, these cuts still covered only about 7 per cent of their total trade. Officials of some countries believed bold new steps—such as across-the-board tariff cuts—might be necessary if LAFTA was to reach its goal of free trade by 1972.

While LAFTA negotiations were painfully slow, the Central American Common Market nations (CACM) signed a protocol increasing to 98 per cent the proportion of all imports now subject to the unified Central American tariff. Later, the governments also settled the most difficult problem facing the market: tariffs on imported cloth. Within five years, they agreed, all such cloth would be subject to identical tariffs in the five member republics. Meanwhile, a Central-American Monetary Council was established in San Salvador to work for the eventual unification of the currencies of the five nations concerned.

Economic Activities. Latin America's first workers' bank opened in Lima, Peru, on July 4, to deal mainly in savings and housing loans. It received a $3,000,000 loan from the U.S. AFL-CIO to help it capitalize.

Colombia made plans with Venezuela and with Ecuador for integrated socio-economic development plans along their respective common frontiers. These programs will be the first binational efforts of their kind ever attempted in Latin America.

In November, 15 Latin-American nations agreed to set up a permanent commission to seek to establish a zone free of nuclear weapons in the Western Hemisphere. It would be headquartered in Mexico.

Legislative representatives from fourteen Latin-American countries met in Lima, Peru, on December 9 to approve tentatively the statutes of a permanent Latin-American parliament that would meet annually to coordinate legislation and consider other measures to achieve closer cooperation.

It marked the first time a meeting of Latin-American legislators had been called for the purpose of achieving political, economic, and cultural union. Six of the 20 Latin-American republics were not represented. They were Bolivia, Cuba, the Dominican Republic, Ecuador, Haiti, and Honduras.

The Caribbean Council, meeting in Curaçao in December, adopted a resolution calling on the governments of France, Great Britain, The Netherlands, and the United States to terminate the agreement establishing the Caribbean Organization, the council's parent body.   MARY C. WEBSTER

See also Section Two, DOS GRINGAS AMERICANAS; and the various articles on Latin-American countries.
LAW. See COURTS AND LAWS; CIVIL LIBERTIES; CRIME; Section Two, CONGRESS MAKES A DECISION; SOCIAL SECURITY; SUPREME COURT.

LEBANON paid a unique honor to its outgoing president, General Fouad Chehab. On May 26, shortly after the newly elected 99-member chamber of deputies had convened, a group of 44 deputies urged Chehab to accept a second term in office.

Chehab, who was limited to one six-year term by law, refused to approve the move, nor would he recommend a successor. In August, the chamber met to elect a new president. A crisis developed, reflecting only too accurately the fragmented, multi-party nature of Lebanese politics. It was settled by the unanimous election of Charles Helou, a political moderate and a minister of education in the care-taker cabinet.

Lebanon and Tunisia signed a judicial treaty providing for the mutual extradition of criminals. Late in the year, the government reported that its "Green Project"—a land reclamation and reforestation program that had been approved in 1963—had ended its first year of operations representing an investment of $280,000,000. Meanwhile, Lebanon's first central bank began operations.

Population: 1,925,000. **Government:** President Charles Helou; Premier Rachid Karamí. **Foreign Trade:** exports, $59,000,000; imports, $358,000,000. **Principal Exports:** fruits and vegetables, tobacco, wool.   WILLIAM SPENCER

See also MIDDLE EAST.

LEONI, RAUL (1905-   ), was installed on March 11 for a five-year term as president of Venezuela. He succeeded Rómulo Betancourt, marking the first time that one democratically elected president had been succeeded by another in Venezuela. See VENEZUELA.

Leoni is a founder of the Democratic Action party. His opposition to totalitarian regimes began at the age of 16 when he was jailed for criticizing the dictatorship of Juan Vicente Gómez. Leoni had been exiled three times since 1928. He lived in various Latin-American countries and in the United States.

Leoni was born in Upata, a small town, on April 26, 1905. He is of Corsican descent. He attended the Central University of Caracas for five years, preparing for a career in law. He married a fellow Upatan, Carmen América Fernández Alcalá, at Washington, D.C., in 1940. They have five children. None was born in Venezuela.   WALTER F. MORSE

LIBERIA celebrated the 117th year of its independence in 1964. In observing the occasion, President William V. S. Tubman announced that adult citizens and foreign residents would be assessed $10 annually over a three-year period during which the government hoped to raise about $60,000,000 for its educational programs.

The president also established four new counties as part of a "unification" policy designed to end the long-standing differences between the remote, undeveloped rural provinces and the more advanced coastal counties.

Liberia was granted a $3,250,000 loan by the World Bank early in the year for highway maintenance and the construction of new routes to farm and rubber production areas.

Late in November, the Liberian government signed a 10-year cultural and friendship agreement with Ethiopia. It provided for the exchange of teachers, students, films, radio programs, books, concerts, plays, and sports delegations between the two African countries.

Population: 1,375,000. **Government:** President William V. S. Tubman. **Foreign Trade:** exports, $83,000,000; imports, $69,000,000. **Principal Exports:** diamonds, iron, rubber.   BENJAMIN E. THOMAS

See also AFRICA.

LIBRARY. Public, school, and college libraries will receive financial and consultant help as a result of major laws passed in 1964 by the 88th Congress of the United States.

A bill amending the Library Services Acts became law on February 11. Congress appropriated $55,000,000 for the fiscal year ending June 30, 1965, for public library services and construction. It also enlarged the rural phases of the program to include libraries in the urban areas.

The National Defense Education Act, broadened in 1964, authorized funds for school library books in a wider variety of subjects, and for school librarian institutes. Under the Economic Opportunity (War on Poverty) Act, libraries became eligible for aid in programs designed to help economically deprived persons. See EDUCATION; SOCIAL WELFARE (Close-Up).

Automation. With the tremendous increase in the number and variety of publications in mind, the Library of Congress, largest research library in the nation, made two studies of its services and procedures to learn how automation might be applied. The studies showed that certain routine tasks could be profitably automated to better meet the needs of researchers.

The National Library of Medicine used perhaps the fastest computer-driven phototypesetter in the United States to compose the *Index Medicus*. Called the new Graphic Arts Composing Equipment (GRACE), it operated at 300 characters per second, or no less than 3,600 words per minute.

Routine jobs were automated in numerous libraries, but no one had yet worked out a system that approximated the work of a good reference librarian in methodically selecting and producing the particular piece of information needed by a particular researcher.

Specialized Libraries. The original goal of $10,-000,000 for the John F. Kennedy Memorial Library was met in December. The library will be built on the banks of the Charles River, at Harvard University. In Chicago, the Newberry Library, a major research library specializing in history and literature,

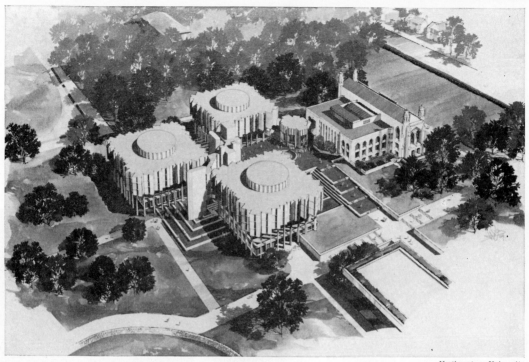

*RESEARCH PAVILIONS of Northwestern
University will triple library facilities.
Project will be on reclaimed lake land.*

made headlines when it purchased the famed Louis
H. Silver collection of rare books and manuscripts
for $2,750,000. Included in the purchase were 19
Shakespeare quartos and four folios, a first edition
of Spenser's *The Faerie Queene*, and manuscripts of
Cellini and Michelangelo.

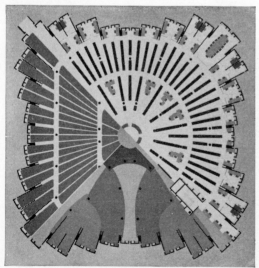

*FLOOR PLAN of pavilion, above (with ceil-
ing plans superimposed), shows interiors
for wide amount of book and reader space.*

International Scene. The International Federation of Library Associations (IFLA) held its largest
annual meeting in Rome from September 14 to 18.
More than 350 delegates from 95 member associations met to discuss the IFLA's obligations to all
libraries in all countries.   RUTH M. WHITE

See also AMERICAN LIBRARY ASSOCIATION (ALA);
CANADIAN LIBRARY ASSOCIATION; EDUCATION; LITER-
ATURE; LITERATURE FOR CHILDREN.

LIBYA notified the United States and Great Britain
that it would not renew the treaties governing their
bases on Libyan soil when they expire in 1973. Both
the U.S. and British governments agreed in principle
to give up their installations.

In March, King Idris I abandoned his proposed
abdication in response to appeals by Premier
Mahmud Muntasser and to public demonstrations
of loyalty to the king.

In August, it was announced that Libya had
become the world's eighth largest producer of oil.

Population: 1,300,000. **Government:** King Idris I;
Premier Mahmud Muntasser. **Foreign Trade:** ex-
ports, $608,000,000; imports, $276,000,000. **Principal
Exports:** olive oil, peanuts, petroleum. WILLIAM SPENCER
See also AFRICA.

LIFE INSURANCE. See INSURANCE.

LIONS INTERNATIONAL. See SERVICE CLUBS.

LITERATURE

THE BEST SELLER LIST has many uses in the world of publishing and selling books, including, some cynics say, the promotion of lagging titles by overzealous dealers, from whose reports of sales the lists are compiled. Certainly, as all except the most unsophisticated of novel readers know, such lists can rarely be depended upon as a true index to the best books. They serve instead to reflect what the public is buying.

In most years, public taste being what it is, the lighter novels—"entertainments" as Graham Greene has called them—dominate. But there is also strong competition for a high place on the best-seller list whenever a really important and deserving novel appears.

Fiction of 1964

Minnesota Theatre Company

In 1964, however, the mere absence of such competition from heavyweight contenders served as clear evidence of the state of fiction. In midyear, the leading seller was a spy adventure tale, John Le Carre's *The Spy Who Came in From the Cold*, a book of no serious literary pretensions, while such leftovers from 1963 as Mary McCarthy's *The Group* and Morris L. West's *The Shoes of the Fisherman* were still being ranked well up on the lists. By fall, the late Ian Fleming's newest James Bond thriller, *You Only Live Twice*, had joined Le Carre's novel in the lively competition, and only two novels of serious import—Saul Bellow's *Herzog* and Louis Auchincloss' *The Rector of Justin*—appeared to have entered the competition for public favor.

The Best Fiction. The novel of the year was unquestionably *Herzog*. It had been long awaited by reviewers and critics familiar with Saul Bellow's career as a novelist, and many of them called it his best performance. It told the story of a middle-aged scholar, caught in the breakup of a second marriage, who was seeking to get his bearings and to justify his place in the world. Technically, it was an intricate performance, and thus offered difficulties to the casual reader, but on the whole it was a book of power and distinction. It exhibited Bellow's vivid prose style at its best.

Louis Auchincloss, another veteran fiction writer whose work has reflected a concern for style, provided competition for the year's honors with his novel *The Rector of Justin*. This was a quiet story about the headmaster of a school for boys near Boston. Auchincloss made of it an absorbing study of character.

Vladimir Nabokov, a master of precise and evocative prose, was represented with an early work, *The Defense*. Translated from Russian, it chronicled the rise and fall of an eccentric chess master.

One of the surprises of the fall publishing season was Frederick Manfred's well-reviewed *Scarlet Plume*,

STILL MASTER in the house of world literature was a Renaissance poet-playwright named William Shakespeare. His 400th birthday was celebrated in April. The Tyrone Guthrie Theatre commemorated the event with a rousing Henry V.

LITERATURE

a novel of the wandering Sioux of the Great Plains, which shocked many readers by the violence and sexuality of certain of its scenes, but which, nevertheless, was a moving portrait of a lost land and a lost people. It seemed to many critics to be a major achievement in the career of Manfred, and a fulfillment of the promise he showed in earlier novels written under his real name, Feike Feikema.

John Cheever added to the New England family story begun with the highly polished *The Wapshot Chronicle* by publishing a sequel, *The Wapshot Scandal*, about a new generation of St. Botolphians. It was followed late in the fall with the publication of a group of his mordant, neatly handled short stories, *The Brigadier and the Golf Widow*.

Shirley Ann Grau, another established writer who is equally at home in the short story or the novel, turned to racial conflict for the theme of a novel of contemporary Louisiana, *The Keepers of the House*. It was a dramatic tale, told with skill and sensitivity, and it reinforced Miss Grau's claim to high rank among women novelists. Two other well-known novelists who published new work were Gore Vidal and Robert Lewis Taylor. Vidal's *Julian* was his first novel in 10 years. It was a study of the Roman emperor, known as The Apostate, after his turn from Christianity to paganism. Taylor's *Two Roads to Guadalupe* was an excellent tale in picaresque fashion drawn from little known phases of the Mexican War. He is a Pulitzer prize novelist.

Few first novels of distinction appeared during the year, but one that arrested the attention was *The Martyred*, by Richard E. Kim, a young Korean who studied creative writing at the fiction workshop directed by Paul Engle at the University of Iowa. It was a well-written story about the martyrdom of 12 Christian ministers captured by the communists and why two other captives escaped death.

The Novel from Abroad that attracted the most attention from American readers was Sir Charles P. Snow's *Corridors of Power*, a story of British politics. It drew its theme from a consideration of decision making in the highest echelons. It was less impressive than some of the other Snow novels in the *Strangers and Brothers* series, but was nonetheless of special interest in view of the year's elections in Britain. Another well-known series of British novels, Anthony Powell's *The Music of Time* series, was advanced with the publication of *A Dance to the Music of Time: Second Movement* and *The Valley of Bones*. The latter novel, written with Powell's customary gift for the creation of comic character, was the first part of a projected trilogy dealing with World War II and the beginning of a sequence planned as the second half of *The Music of Time* series.

Veteran English novelist and short story writer, Elizabeth Bowen, brought out *The Little Girls*. It was a haunting tale of a pixie-ish woman in her 60's who compulsively seeks out old school chums. And William Golding, author of the powerful *Lord of*

the Flies of a few years back, published an allegorical tale, *The Spire*. Set in 13th century England, the novel told of the building of a 400-foot spire on what was probably Salisbury Cathedral. It was a difficult but arresting tale of good and evil.

Two short story collections of unusual interest came from abroad. One was Alan Sillitoe's *The Ragman's Daughter and Other Stories*, an amusing series showing Sillitoe's mastery of the short form, and a translation by Gabriella Azrael of the Soviet author Yuri Kazakov's *Going to Town and Other Stories*, an impressive collection by a writer previously unpublished in this country.

Nonfiction

Biography, autobiography, and memoirs dominated the nonfiction field, and the top honors, by general agreement, went to Jean-Paul Sartre's *The Words*. In this small masterpiece of self-examination, the French existentialist philosopher and novelist (who turned down the Nobel prize for literature) looked back upon the transformation of the boy Jean-Paul, into Sartre the man. See SATRE, JEAN-PAUL.

One of the best of the year's literary biographies was Christopher Hassall's *Rupert Brooke: A Biography*, a brilliant portrait of the English poet who was once lionized in both Britain and the United States. In his autobiographical *Vive Moi!*, Sean O'Faolain, the Irish novelist and short story writer, wrote entertainingly of his life and work, including his sojourn in America and his decision to return to the "auld sod." Evelyn Waugh, the English novelist, published a section of his autobiography in *A Little Learning*, which engagingly recalled a happy childhood. Leonard Woolf, husband of Virginia Woolf, one of the major writers of the century, published the third volume of his own story, *Beginning Again: An Autobiography of the Years 1911-1918*. It told of his marriage to Virginia, of her breakdowns, and her suicide in 1941.

The late Ernest Hemingway's Parisian memories were published in *A Moveable Feast*, which provided a revealing background for all interested in his development as a writer. The 400th anniversary of Shakespeare's birth brought forth several biographies, the most notable of which was A. L. Rowse's *William Shakespeare: A Biography*. See THEATER (Close-Up).

One of the year's most widely heralded autobiographies was General Douglas MacArthur's *Reminiscences*, and while it was an important book for the record, it proved disappointing to many critics and readers because of its flamboyant and unclouded vision of its heroic subject's own deeds, right or wrong (see MACARTHUR, DOUGLAS). Another disappointment among the autobiographies was Charles Chaplin's *My Autobiography*, also important for the record but determinedly concerned with the commercial aspect of being Chaplin and less than frank about many matters, including wiving and his left-wing associations.

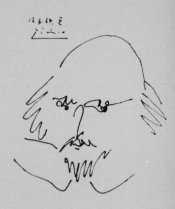

HEADS OF STATE, prime ministers, and many millions of plain people paid homage in 1964 to the man who, more than any other in literature, held the mirror up to human nature. The man was, of course, William Shakespeare. The 400th anniversary of his birth was commemorated on April 23.

The celebrations took many forms and were held throughout the year. In Tokyo, Kabuki actors gave the Japanese première of *Richard III*. To do so they had to unlearn their centuries-old Kabuki style of acting. They performed to packed houses. In the Soviet Union, a well-known director produced a black-and-white, wide-screen version of *Hamlet* in a translation by Boris Pasternak.

A replica of the Danish castle at Elsinore was built for the production on the coast of Estonia. In Denmark, Canadian actor Christopher Plummer made a film version of *Hamlet* for TV in a real Danish (Kronberg) castle. In France, Pablo Picasso, in a tribute from one genius to another, tossed off an interesting drawing of Shakespeare (see margin). Scenes from the plays were performed at the White House, and the Washington Opera Society gave the U.S. première of *Beatrice and Benedick*, an opera by Hector Berlioz based on *Much Ado About Nothing*.

TO HELP MARK the year, the Marlowe Society of London (it was also Christopher Marlowe's 400th anniversary year) completed its monumental recording cycle, begun in 1957, of all of Shakespeare's works (uninterrupted listening time: more than five days). A number of books appeared. One claimed to tell all about the poet-playwright's love life; another was a scholarly biography that caused much controversy because, among other things, it claimed to answer the riddles of the sonnets (including the identity of the person to whom they were dedicated and the period when they were written).

In Britain and the United States, colleges and universities performed the plays. In England, it seemed everyone wanted to get into the act. Some 60 towns and villages decked themselves out in Elizabethan dress. "Try not to miss them," the British Travel Association advertised, "you won't get another chance until 2064."

"Shakespeare's Year," cried the travel posters, "Jet B.O.A.C. To Britain." The British Arts Council listed some 342 events, and, in London, a Sunday newspaper began a column called "Bard Briefing" to keep its readers up to date.

IN ENGLAND, critics agreed that the performance of the year was Sir Laurence Olivier's *Othello*, a role he had shied away from in the past, because of its difficulties. And at Stratford-on-Avon, the town where the poet was born, the Royal Shakespeare Company performed seven of the history plays depicting 100 years of English history from Richard II to Richard III. It was the first such a cycle ever attempted.

In North America, the most memorable single performance may have been Morris Carnovsky's noble and agonized *King Lear*. Other headline performances included a Broadway *Hamlet* with Richard Burton, a stripped down but eloquent *Lear*, and *The Comedy of Errors*, provided by the Royal Shakespeare Company on tour in New York, Philadelphia, and Washington, D.C. The American Shakespeare Festival celebrated its 10th anniversary at Stratford, Conn., with *Richard III*, *Hamlet*, and *Much Ado About Nothing*. The Tyrone Guthrie Theatre in Minneapolis opened with *Henry V*, and the celebrated Stratford, Ontario, Festival of Canada performed *Richard II* and *King Lear*.

BUT naturally enough, the festivities fanned out from Stratford-on-Avon, 80 miles from London. On the day before the anniversary, Eugene R. Black, former head of the World Bank, opened a new Shakespeare Center. On the anniversary day itself, the flags of 115 nations flew above the town. Prince Philip opened a large Shakespeare Exhibition Building; the Earl of Avon, Anthony Eden, read a tribute from the queen. Ambassadors of more than 100 nations walked in a procession to Holy Trinity Church to lay flowers on the grave of Shakespeare, who was buried beneath the chancel floor. Behind the ambassadors came a line of people, marching four abreast, that stretched a mile and a half. They had come, in this most gala of literary celebrations, to do likewise.   MARK M. PERLBERG

All the World A Stage for Bard in 1964

Pablo Picasso's private life came in for some revealing exposition at the hands of Francoise Gilot, a former mistress, whose *Life with Picasso*, written with Carlton Lake, appeared destined to become a standard source work on the Spanish painter's life and art.

Louis Fischer, a veteran observer of the Russian scene, produced perhaps the best biography of Lenin yet written in *The Life of Lenin*. Ernest Samuels completed his notable three-volume study of one of New England's immortals in *Henry Adams: The Major Phase*. Ralph Ellison, perhaps the nation's leading Negro novelist, published *Shadows and Act*, a collection of essays. It was generally well reviewed.

Letters and Journals provided some of the year's more notable books. In the political field, David E. Lilienthal, a veteran government administrator, told of his work with the Tennessee Valley Authority and the Atomic Energy Commission in *The Journals of David E. Lilienthal*. The editorial group in charge of the Adams papers published Volumes I and II of *Diary of Charles Francis Adams*, a series covering the years 1825 to 1829. In the literary field, there was major interest in several works. They included Julian Green's *Diary 1928-1957*, which recorded not only this American-born novelist's experiences in France but his relationships with such French contemporaries as Camus and Gide; *The Letters of Alexander Pushkin*, a rich three-volume collection of the great Russian poet's correspondence; and *Isaac Babel: The Lonely Years, 1925-1939*, which told the story of that writer's life under the suffocating hand of the Stalinists in Russia.

One of the year's most diverting autobiographical books was H. E. F. Donohue's tape recorded *Conversations with Nelson Algren*, in which the Chicago novelist and wit discussed his literary life uninhibitedly and at the same time had some sharp words about various contemporaries.

Perhaps the most unusual book of the year was *Markings*, by the late Secretary-General of the United Nations, Dag Hammarskjöld. It was a highly contemplative journal, probably not intended for publication, and it contained short, moving poems and meditations on life and death.

History. Among the year's books on World War II, one of the most interesting was Ladislas Farago's *Patton: Ordeal and Triumph*, a thick biographical study which pursued the late General George S. Patton, Jr.'s controversial argument that he might have ended the war in the summer of 1944 had it not been for Generals Montgomery and Eisenhower.

Two books dealt ably and interestingly with Russia's role in World War II. One was Soviet Field Marshal V. I. Chuikov's *The Battle for Stalingrad*, a vivid account of that important engagement, which proved to be the downfall of Hitler. The other was Alexander Werth's *Russia at War*, which provided the best account in English of how the Russian people themselves fared during the conflict.

The books that dealt with John F. Kennedy were for the most part pictorial, the best being *The Kennedy Years*, a well-edited selection of photographs covering all the late President's public life, accompanied by a text selected from the pages of *The New York Times*. The Official Warren Commission Report on the assassination of President Kennedy became one of the year's most widely read documents, following a publishing effort that broke speed records upon its official release. See WARREN COMMISSION; WARREN REPORT (appendix).

Two pictorial books which also had excellent texts, were among the best productions in the field of history. One of these was *The Horizon History of Christianity*, written by the editors of *Horizon* magazine and Roland H. Bainton, a Protestant scholar, with scrupulous objectivity and accompanied by an excellent selection of pictures covering the 2,000 years of Christianity. The other was *The American Heritage Book of World War I*, written by S. L. A. Marshall and well illustrated in the manner of other books in the American Heritage series.

Some neglected areas of American history were ably treated in two books. Gene Smith's *When the Cheering Stopped* investigated the last year and a half of the ailing President Woodrow Wilson's administration, using material that had not been available until the death of Wilson's widow in 1961. Aside from its value as a historical record, Smith's book raised important questions about the problem of a disabled President. Ralph K. Andrist's *The Long Death*, subtitled "The Last Days of the American Plains Indian," told the story of how the white man in his westward progress destroyed the agrarian basis of Plains Indian life. Written with sensitivity and a sense of justice, it was one of the more impressive books of Western history to appear in recent years.

Among the books dealing with older periods, one of the year's best was C. V. Wedgwood's *A Coffin for King Charles*, in which that accomplished woman historian told the dramatic story of the execution of Charles I.

VAN ALLEN BRADLEY

POETRY

Few poets in the English-speaking world could fail to mark their own overshadowing in 1964 by the spectral eminence of their master, William Shakespeare, whose 400th birthday was celebrated in special publications, convocations, seminars, and other solemn revels. If here and there working poets gathered to hoist a tankard in honor of the "Gentleman of Stratford," their festivities foundered in the magnitudes of "official" ceremony. They could only return to their desks, humbled and bemused.

The Year's New Books, however, included several that seemed not unworthy. The last poems of Theodore Roethke, who died in 1963, were collected in *The Far Field*. They were extremely well reviewed both at home and abroad. John Berryman's *77 Dream Songs* was acclaimed enthusiastically, and in

Richard Eberhart's *The Quarry*, many critics detected a renewal of his earlier lyric power. Robert Lowell's *For the Union Dead* was praised extravagantly in the public press, though some austerer journals voiced reservations. Other books by well-known poets included Denise Levertov's *O Taste and See*, J. V. Cunningham's *To What Strangers, What Welcome*, and Winfield Townley Scott's *Change of Weather*. Among books of interest by newer poets was *The Window*, by Vern Rutsala.

Nabokov's Pushkin. Meanwhile, the year's chief controversy centered on a translation: Vladimir Nabokov's rendering of Pushkin's Russian classic *Eugene Onegin*. It appeared in four volumes, complete with the author's extensive notes, exegeses, observations, and waspish commentaries on other translators. Nabokov's supporters praised the work for its erudition, thoroughness, and poetic felicity. Others condemned it, calling the felicity only a verbal surface, the scholarship only pedantry, the whole work only a mirror of Nabokov's vexatious personality. In the rumpus, two other excellent translations of the same text, also published in 1964, were passed over almost unnoticed. They were by Walter Arndt and Eugene M. Kayden.

Negro Poets. The civil rights movement, pervading the nation's life, influenced poetry, too. In addition to many individual poems on themes of racial justice (and two important anthologies that appeared in 1963, one edited by Arna Bontemps, the other by Langston Hughes), critics offered new estimates of former generations of Negro writers. These included James Weldon Johnson, Paul Laurence Dunbar, Countee Cullen, and especially Jean Toomer, the Harlem poet of the 1930's, often compared with Hart Crane. Of the Africans, the poet-president of Senegal, Léopold Sedar Senghor, had been virtually the only poet known to Americans a year earlier. Now such names as John Pepper Clark and Christopher Okigbo of Nigeria, and Alioune Diop of Senegal became familiar. Younger American Negro poets commanded wide attention. This was especially true of Gwendolyn Brooks, Pulitzer prize winner of 1950, and Le Roi Jones, a fiery poet from Manhattan.

Little Magazines: Two announcements concerning little magazines had special interest: the inauguration of the *Alaska Review* at Anchorage, that state's first little magazine; and the planned revival at Baton Rouge, La., in 1965 of *The Little Review*, one of the best magazines of the 1930's.

A Master Dies. Perhaps the single most influential figure in contemporary poetry, T. S. Eliot, died at his home in London at 76, on Jan. 4, 1965. In his best-known work, *The Waste Land* (1922), the St. Louis-born poet gave voice and form to the disillusion that followed World War I.   HAYDEN CARRUTH

See also AWARDS AND PRIZES.

LITERATURE, CANADIAN. See CANADIAN LIBRARY ASSOCIATION; CANADIAN LITERATURE.

LITERATURE FOR CHILDREN. Anniversary celebrations in 1964 were represented in some of the year's outstanding publications. The William Shakespeare Quadricentennial, observed throughout the English-speaking world, was the occasion for the publication of several worthwhile books for older children about England's bard and the Elizabethan age in which he lived (see LITERATURE; THEATER). There continued to be volumes for young people on the Civil War in the fourth year of its centennial, and on World War II, now nearly 20 years in the past. The election year was reflected in books on the United States presidency and the nation's history and heritage. See CIVIL WAR CENTENNIAL.

There were stories and histories from other times and around the world as well as biographies of persons who made history. Science was made interesting and attractive to many ages.

The Horn Book Magazine celebrated its 40th anniversary. *Margin for Surprise: About Books, Children and Librarians* was written by the magazine's present editor, Ruth Hill Viguers. She followed in the footsteps of Bertha E. Mahony and Elinor Whitney who, in 1924, initiated this important selection aid devoted entirely to young people's books. Anne Carroll Moore and Frances Clarke Sayers are among those who helped promote real literature for children by reviewing books for *Horn Book*, and also by assisting children and young people in the choice of good reading material in libraries.

A companion volume for *Margin for Surprise* is *A Storyteller's Choice* for parents, teachers, and librarians. Eileen Colwell, a children's librarian and storyteller in London, made this selection, with notes on how to tell the stories.

Outstanding Books published in 1964 included the following:

Shakespeare

Shakespeare and His World, by Ivor Brown, pictures details of Elizabethan London, which is good background material for understanding the plays.

How Shakespeare Spent the Day, another Ivor Brown book, presents facts about a genius and businessman in setting of Elizabethan life.

Shakespeare's England by *Horizon* magazine editors. Elizabethan London set the right stage for a young man of dramatic ability.

Shakespeare's Theatre, by the English author-artist C. Walter Hodges, traces the development of the drama from early times to the Globe Theatre.

The Enchanted Island: Stories from Shakespeare by Ian Serraillier. Illus. by Peter Farmer. Eleven tales chosen for children 10 to 12 stress action.

Five Plays from Shakespeare ed. by Katherine Miller. Illus. by Lynd Ward. Skillfully cut, with musical arrangements by Norman Cazden and production notes, the three comedies and two tragedies may be acted by those of junior high age.

American History and Way of Life

Pilgrim Neighbors: More True Pilgrim Stories by Elvajean Hall. Customs of Indians and settlers from 1621 to 1691 are well researched and interesting.

Through These Arches, the Story of Independence Hall by Katherine Milhous. The reader sees Penn and the

FROM THE HAPPY OWLS. *Illustrations and text by Celestino Piatti. Two little owls are wisely contented in a quarrelsome world. Publisher: Atheneum.*

ILLUSTRATORS' ART

The illustrations in this article are a selection from the 10 best-illustrated children's books of 1964, according to a jury chosen by The New York Times Book Review.

Indians, the tavern, the State House, and celebrations through the years as Philadelphia grew.

Presidents of the United States, by Cornel Adams Lengyel, contains many photographs.

The Sports of Our Presidents, by John Durant, begins with Washington and ends with Johnson, and should tempt reluctant readers.

Washington, D.C., by Irene Smith, is a *Cities of the World* volume for young people. It is factual, well-illustrated, and useful as a guide.

Forts in America, by Harold L. Peterson, represents 400 years of American military history.

Wild and Woolly by Earl Schenck Miers. From such sources as diaries, songs, and old newspapers, we learn of Lewis and Clark, the Donner party, the Whitmans, Frémont, Custer, the Forty-Niners, and the trappers—all the people, in fact, who helped make the American West.

Walt Whitman's America, ed. and illus. by James Daugherty, contains selections from *Leaves of Grass* and other works. It is a book that children may share with parents.

Across Five Aprils by Irene Hunt. The Civil War as seen by Jethro, the author's grandfather. He managed his invalid father's farm, while the older boys were off fighting.

The Greatest Cattle Drive, by Paul I. Wellman, is an account of the 1866 drive from Texas to Montana.

The First Book Edition of John F. Kennedy's Inaugural Address is an attractive documentary for all ages.

World War II

A Castle for the Kopcheks by James Stagg. A refugee story in the first person of 15-year-old Sondra is an E. Nesbit Memorial prize book.

Yugoslav Mystery by Arthur Catherall. A boy, his father, and his grandfather outwit their pursuers in a suspense story that lasts just 36 hours.

Air War Against Hitler's Germany, by the editors of *American Heritage* and Stephen W. Sears, tells how the Allies drove the Luftwaffe from the skies.

The Long Escape by Irving Werstein. Nurse Raymond had 50 child patients at the Château in Heyst on the Belgian coast when war came. How they were evacuated to England is a true story.

The Battle of El Alamein: Decision in the Desert, by Correlli Barnett, is a detailed account of troop movements and commands by a military historian.

History and Historical Tales

Seven Famous Trials in History by Robin McKown. Socrates, Joan of Arc, Galileo, Peter Zenger, Robert Emmett, the Dreyfus Affair, and the Nuremberg Trial.

Pathways to Freedom by Edwin D. Hoffman. Nine events dramatically told point up our fundamental freedoms without flag-waving or preaching.

Trial by Jury: A Complete Guide to the Jury System by Samuel W. McCart. Detailed, yet short and easily understood by older boys and girls.

From Spinning Wheel to Spacecraft: The Story of the Industrial Revolution by Harry Edward Neal. How social and political events followed new inventions.

The Lion in the Gateway by Mary Renault. Battles of the ancient Greeks and Persians, such as the stand at Thermopylae, can rival any adventure story when an author of this stature writes for young people.

The Namesake by author-artist C. Walter Hodges. A story of courage in the 9th century is told by a lame boy, Alfred the Dane-Leg, namesake of Alfred the Great, King of the West Saxons in England.

The Burning of Njal retold by Henry Treece. Bloody battles are dramatized in terse action-filled prose, in this tragic Icelandic saga of 11th century Vikings.

1066 by Franklin Hamilton. Diagrams of Anglo-Saxon and Norman royal lineages as well as politics of the times lead up to the Battle of Hastings.

The Queen's Blessing by Madeleine Pollard. In 11th century Scotland, Merca and her brother are saved by Queen Margaret, wife of King Malcolm, whose army overran their lands and killed their parents.

Marco Polo's Adventures in China, by *Horizon* magazine editors and Milton Rugoff, has maps and illustrations from colored scrolls.

Simon's Way by Margery Evernden. From France to Norway in the 13th century, Simon, befriended by Helgi the Birchleg, sought his father.

The Star and the Flame by Rosemary Weir. A boy at the time of the plague and the great fire in London.

Galleys and Galleons, by Walter Buehr, pictures a way of life on ships dependent on slavery.

Real People

Portraits of Nobel Laureates in Medicine and Physiology by Sarah R. Riedman. Science students will find interest in Nobel and the winners.

Give Me Freedom by May McNeer. Illus. by Lynd Ward. Biographies of seven persons concerned with the rights of men, women, and children, and temperance and the abolition of slavery.

They Showed the Way: Forty American Negro Leaders, by Charlemae Hill Rollins, is about fellow Americans from many walks of life.

Paul Revere, the Man Behind the Legend by Margaret Green. Good dialogue helps one love the man and understand events in our early history.

Thomas Jefferson: The Making of a President by John Dos Passos. A rich picture of his early life.

A Dawn in the Trees: Thomas Jefferson, the Years 1776 to 1789 by Leonard Wibberley. His talents, devotion to family, and relationship to contemporaries are portrayed with good dialogue.

Dawn from the West: The Story of Genevieve Caulfield by Margaret Rau. A blind American woman works for peace in Southeast Asia.

Andrew Carnegie by Clara Ingram Judson. Characteristic of her other writing is the depiction of the man who built the steel industry and gave his wealth for the education of Americans, the support of public libraries, and the world peace movement.

Edith Wharton, 1862–1937, by Olivia Coolidge. New York society, European travel, and interesting people all influenced her writing.

FROM THE CHARGE OF THE LIGHT BRIGADE. *Paintings by Alice and Martin Provensen illustrate the famous poem. Publisher: Golden Press.*

LITERATURE FOR CHILDREN

His Majesty's chief vizier, in fact, has come to tell me.

I am to have the great honor and the great pleasure of taking an extraordinary trip.

FROM THE GIRAFFE OF KING CHARLES X. *Text and pictures by Miche Wynants.*
This is the story of the first giraffe to visit Europe. Publisher: McGraw-Hill.

Lucretia Mott: Gentle Warrior by Dorothy Sterling. An author who treats human history with understanding has written of a 19th century advocate of civil rights for women and for Negroes.

Triumphant Adventure: The Story of Franklin D. Roosevelt, by Frances Cavanah, is a warm story of the man, his family, and personal life.

Science

When Animals Are Babies, by Elizabeth and Charles Schwartz, was designed especially for the young by artist-scientists.

The Story of Ants by Dorothy E. Shuttlesworth. Illus. by Su Zan Noguchi Swain. Detailed pictures aid in the recognition of anatomy and habits of various species. An attractive book for all ages.

Butterfly Time by Alice E. Goudey. Illus. by Adrienne Adams. Stages of development are explained, and species illustrated by a versatile artist.

Green Is for Growing by Winifred and Cecil Lubell. Algae, fungi, moss, ferns, flowers, grass, and weeds are described in rhythmic lines and pictures.

Peek the Piper by Vitali V. Bianki, trans. by S. K. Lederer, and illus. by Paul Galdone. A field mouse Robinson Crusoe learns self-preservation, and is finally tamed by two children.

Listen, Rabbit by Aileen Lucia Fisher. Illus. by Symeon Shimin. The story of a boy and a cottontail he lovingly watches in hope of making friends is told in lilting verse and sensitive drawings.

The Courtship of Animals, by Millicent E. Selsam and illus. by John Kaufmann, gives scientific details of the rituals of fish, birds, mammals, and insects.

The Captive Sea: Life Behind the Scenes of the Great Modern Oceanariums by Craig Phillips. The entire family will enjoy these sea creatures.

The Wind. Written and illus. by Jeanne Bendick. Discusses folklore such as the Greek King of the Winds as well as the importance of air to climate, weather, and seasons.

Thaddeus Lowe: Uncle Sam's First Airman, by Lydel Sims, tells of Lowe's balloon activities during the Civil War.

Picture Books

The Beach Before Breakfast by Maxine W. Kumin. Illus. by Leonard Weisgard. A man and a boy silently watch birds and shore creatures as dawn comes.

The Lion and the Rat, a fable by Jean de La Fontaine. Illus. by Brian Wildsmith. A gold lion walks through a forest of dark trees filled with jewel-toned birds. He saves the rat, who is the only one able to save him from the net.

May I Bring a Friend? by Beatrice Schenk de Regniers. Illus. by Beni Montresor. Dramatic nonsense and playful pictures of zoo animals at the palace.

Little Toot on the Thames by Hardie Gramatky. Beloved, personified tugboat has an exciting international adventure, and is escorted home by the *Queen Elizabeth. Little Toot* made his debut in New York harbor just 25 years ago.

The Tomato Patch by William Wondriska. A timely fable about how two unusual kingdoms, which looked exactly alike, changed from armor-making to agricultural pursuits.

Pavo and the Princess by author-artist Evaline Ness. Unhappy Phoebe torments her pet peacock. Both are too proud to cry, but this is the tale of how they learned.

Benjie by John M. Lexau. Illus. by Don Bolognese. In searching for Granny's earring, Benjie lost his shyness and made friends with those who helped.

A Baby Sister for Frances by Russell Hoban. Illus. by Lillian Hoban. The little badger feels very unwanted because baby Gloria needs attention.

Ride the Gold Wind by Anico Surany. Illus. by Leonard Everett Fisher. Paco, an Indian boy who herds llamas, wants to be a fisherman like his father.

Whistle for Willie by Ezra Jack Keats. The young hero of *The Snowy Day* learns to call his dog.

Preep, the Little Pigeon of Trafalgar Square, by Milton Shulman and illus. by Dale Maxey, pictures a gay London.

Tico and the Golden Wings by Leo Lionni. "Each is different because of his own memories." Flawless pictures enhance the story of a little bird giving his gold feathers to help others.

Exactly Alike by Evaline Ness. The tale of Elizabeth and her four freckle-faced brothers, who looked almost exactly alike.

The Life of a Queen by Colette Portal. An ant colony is somewhat humanized in lovely colored illustrations, but adheres to life cycle of ants.

The Wave. Adopted from Lafcadio Hearn's *Gleanings in Buddha-Fields* by Margaret Hodges. The illustrations are by Blair Lent.

Poetry

Fee Fi Fo Fum: A Picture Book of Nursery Rhymes by Raymond Briggs. This gay English edition of Mother Goose is excellent fun for four-year-old children to dramatize.

The Hungry Goat by Alan Mills. Illus. by Abner Graboff. Colorful, humorous nonsense for the entire family to read, to look at, or to sing.

Drums and Trumpets: Poetry for the Youngest selected by Leonard Clark. Illus. by Heather Copley. For adults to read while children listen. Spenser and Coleridge as well as Rossetti and De La Mare are introduced to the reader.

Cricket Songs. Japanese haiku translation by Harry Behn, has pictures selected from Sesshu and other Japanese masters. A haiku is a poem written in three lines of *five*, *seven*, then *five* syllables about something natural, and has no rhyme.

The Moment of Wonder: A Collection of Chinese and Japanese Poetry, ed. by Richard Lewis, has paintings by Chinese and Japanese masters.

Roofs of Gold: Poems to Read Aloud comp. by Padraic Colum. Birds, animals, seasons, man and time, and the heartbreak and romance of history.

A Taste of Chaucer: Selections from the Canterbury Tales. Ed. by Anne Malcolmson. Illus. by Enrico Arno. The brief biography of Chaucer, with excerpts in old and modern English, is a book parents and young people will enjoy together.

Middle Grade Stories

Carolina's Courage by Elizabeth Yates. A small pioneer trades dolls with the Indian chief's daughter, and the entire party is given safe-conduct.

The Salty Skinners by Adele and Cateau De Leeuw. A navy man stresses safety in skin and scuba diving as he teaches the Atlantic coast community.

Daddles: The Story of a Plain Hound-Dog, by Ruth Sawyer, concerns two children and two summers in Maine, and a dog they borrow from a neighbor.

The Mouse Palace by Frances Carpenter. Illus. by Adrienne Adams. When the son of the king of Siam makes a mistake and lets the mice out, the king forgives him.

My Bird Is Romeo by Thomas Fall. Emily matures as her sparrow hawk grows. She teaches him to hunt, then gives him freedom.

Olle and the Wild Geese by Mary Lewis. Olle learns to train wild decoys for his uncle, but finds some hunters disregarding legal limits.

A Far Voice Calling by Margaret Weeks Adair. A pet sea lion helps bring understanding to a Finnish fisherman and his son.

FROM THE BAT-POET. *Pictures by Maurice Sendak; story by Randall Jarrell. A young bat sees the world differently from his friends. Publisher: Macmillan.*

FROM RAIN MAKES APPLESAUCE. *Intricate and fanciful paintings by Marvin Bileck illustrate whimsical sayings by Julian Scheer. Publisher: Holiday House.*

Stories for Boys

The Grizzly by Annabel and Edgar Johnson. David learns to overcome fear and makes his father proud of him when a grizzly attacks.

There Is a Tide by Elspeth Bragdon. An unhappy boarding school boy goes with his father to the Maine coast, where they learn to know each other.

Fisherman's Choice by Elsa Pedersen. A farmer's teen-age son takes a man-size job on a boat to help purchase an Alaskan homestead.

Terror by Satellite by Hugh Walters. Two teen-age ham radio operators succeed in saving the world from a power-mad scientist.

The Pushcart War by Jean Merrill. A war between pushcarts and trucks in New York in 1976 is a tale to be savored as a humorous satire on city traffic.

Stories for Girls

The Nickel-Plated Beauty by Patricia Beatty. Earning $25 for mother's Christmas stove in Washington Territory was not easy for children in 1886.

The Far-Off Land by Rebecca Caudill. Sixteen-year-old Ketty, brought up by Moravians, keeps her sense of values throughout the harsh pioneer journey to Tennessee.

Kirsti by Helen Markley Miller. A pioneer Finnish girl finally convinces her father that the American boy will be a worthy husband.

Laughter in Our House by Bianca Bradbury. Two young people learn to understand their mother, and help her recover from a mental breakdown.

Sea Courage by Dorothy Pitkin. The summer Vicky becomes 16, she grows up, and discovers new friends and finds a vocation.

A Love, or a Season. Mary Stolz's story of young love is a superior book for teens and parents.

Folk Tale and Fantasy

The Mitten by Alvin Tresselt. Illus. by Yaroslava. A Ukrainian folk tale, adapted from E. Rachev's version, is the story of a lost mitten and how all the animals try to crowd into it.

Oniroku and the Carpenter, retold by Tadashi Matsui, illus. by Suekichi Akaba, and trans. from the Japanese by Masako Matsuno. An ogre builds a bridge, and the carpenter must guess his name.

Turkish Fairy Tales, collected by Selma Ekrem, are sparkling tales of peasant girls and princes appearing in disguise.

The Hound of Ulster, retold by Rosemary Sutcliff, is for older boys and girls who love Irish heroes.

Gaelic Ghosts by Sorche Nic Leodhas. Woodcuts by Nonny Hogrogian. Scottish tales, both humorous and scary.

An Enemy at Green Knowe by Lucy M. Boston. Witchcraft comes to the old English estate made famous by this Carnegie medal author. One reads breathlessly even though sure that Mrs. Oldknow and her friends will triumph.

Linnets and Valerians by Elizabeth Goudge. A fantasy with real people and animals, a charming book for those who enjoyed the beloved English author's *Little White Horse.*

The Magic Stone by Penelope Farmer. Friendship develops when two girls, 13 and 14, find the stone whose magic depends upon their cooperation.

Three Princes of Serendip by Elizabeth Jamison Hodges. Drawings by Joan Berg. Three princes seek what their father commanded in a poetic fantasy from Ceylon, known as Serendip.

The Book of Three by Lloyd Alexander. The author, after reading Welsh mythology, creates the Land of Prydain, where the forces for good and evil struggle.

Other Lands

Israel Reborn, by Oden Meeker, is a well told, illustrated history of Jewish people pioneering in an old land.

The Tuareg: Nomads and Warriors of the Sahara by Sonia Bleeker. Another book in the African tribes series tells how oil and water wells are changing desert economy.

Meeting with a Stranger by Duane Bradley. Illus. by E. Harper Johnson. Teffera of Ethiopia learns new ways of sheep care from an American.

Taiwo and Her Twin, by Letta Schatz, tells of the importance of a new school to a small Nigerian girl.

The Takula Tree. Elizabeth P. Fleming tells an exciting story of a missionary's son and an African boy who are caught up in racial violence.

The White Bungalow, by Aimée Sommerfelt and trans. by Evelyn Ramsden, is a sequel to the award-winning *Road to Agra*. Lalu decides to help at home, and not accept the medical scholarship.

Made in Thailand. Margaret Ayer, a long-time resident and artist, relates arts and crafts to the people and the land.

Lotte's Locket, by Virginia Sorensen, is the story of a Danish girl who finds it difficult to accept an American stepfather.

Far Out the Long Canal by Meindert DeJong. The only American winner of the Hans Christian Andersen award tells about a Dutch boy of Wierum and his fears as he learns to skate.

Awards in 1964

Newbery Medal, for the most distinguished contribution to American literature for children in 1963, to Emily Cheney Neville for *It's Like This, Cat.* See NEVILLE, EMILY CHENEY.

Runners-up: Sterling North, author of *Rascal, A Memoir of a Better Era;* and Ester Wier, author of *The Loner.*

Caldecott Medal, for the most distinguished American picture book in 1963, to Maurice Sendak for *Where the Wild Things Are.* See SENDAK, MAURICE.

Runners-up: Leo Lionni for *Swimmy;* Evaline Ness for *All in the Morning Early,* by Sorche Nic Leodhas; and Philip Reed, compiler and illustrator of *Mother Goose and Nursery Rhymes.*

The New York Herald Tribune Awards were presented at the newspaper's 28th Spring Festival of Children's Books.

Picture Books: The Coconut Thieves, adapted by Catharine Fournier, and illustrated by Janina Domanska. *Honorable Mention* to: Denise and Alain Trez for *Sophie;* Juliet Kepes, author and illustrator of *Lady Bird, Quickly;* Jan Garten and Muriel Batherman for *The Alphabet Tale;* and Charles Francis Potter and William Wiesner for *More Tongue Tanglers and a Rigmarole.*

For Children 8 to 12: Joan M. Phipson, author of *The Family Conspiracy,* illustrated by Margaret Horder. *Honorable Mention* to: Pauline Clarke for *The Return of the Twelves,* illustrated by Bernarda Bryson; Emma Smith for *Out of Hand,* illustrated by Antony Maitland; Robert Burch for *Skinny,* illustrated by Don Sibley; and Lorenzo Allen for *Fifer for the Union,* illustrated by Brian Wildsmith.

For Older Boys and Girls: Marion Downer for *The Story of Design. Honorable Mention* to: Maia Wojciechowska, author of *Shadow of a Bull,* illustrated by Alvin Smith; Eilís Dillon for *The Coriander,* illustrated by Vic Donahue; Elisabeth Kyle for *Girl with a Pen: Charlotte Brontë;* and Hester Burton, author of *Time of Trial,* illustrated by Victor G. Ambrus.

Canadian Library Association Book of the Year for Children Awards. See CANADIAN LIBRARY ASSOCIATION (Awards).

Carnegie Medal by the British Library Association, for an outstanding book for children, to Hester Burton for *Time of Trial.* See BURTON, HESTER.

The Child Study Association of America Children's Book Awards. *Fiction Award* to Mildred Lee for *The Rock and the Willow. Nonfiction Award* to Betty Schechter for *The Peaceable Revolution.*

Hans Christian Andersen Prize, awarded every two years by the International Board on Books for Young People, to René Guillot of France for *The Fantastic Brother, Riders of the Wind,* and his other books.

Jewish Book Council of America Isaac Siegel Memorial Juvenile Award to Sulamith Ish-Kishor for *A Boy of Old Prague.*

Kate Greenaway Medal by the British Library Association, for the most distinguished illustrated book for children, to John Burningham, author and illustrator of *Borka: The Adventures of a Goose with No Feathers.* See BURNINGHAM, JOHN.

Regina Medal by the Catholic Library Association, for a lifetime dedication to the highest standards of literature for children, to May Hill Arbuthnot. See ARBUTHNOT, MAY HILL.

Thomas Alva Edison Foundation National Mass Media Awards: *For the Best Children's Book on Natural Science* to: S. Carl Hirsch for *The Globe for the Space Age. For the Best Science Book for Youth* to Judith Groch for *You and Your Brain. For Special Excellence in Contributing to the Character Development of Children* to Betty Schechter for *The Peaceable Revolution. For Special Excellence in Portraying America's Past* to Richard B. Morris and James Woodress, editors of *Voices from America's Past.*   ELOISE RUE

LIVESTOCK. Cattle boats were running again, outbound from the United States, for the first time in decades. From January through August, beef and veal exports soared 79 per cent while imports fell 20 per cent from the 1963 period. Live cattle imports were the lowest in eight years.

A world beef shortage had developed in 1964, a sharp contrast to the world market glut in 1963. Droughts in 1962-1963 had caused herd reductions in Western Europe and Argentina. Also in 1964, the United States reached agreements with Australia, Ireland, Mexico, and New Zealand to limit meat sales to the United States. And Congress authorized the Secretary of Agriculture to set an overall import quota on fresh beef and lamb.

At Home, both beef production and demand were rising. With the boom continuing, Americans were buying more beef—100 pounds per person versus 95 pounds in 1963. At the same time, the calf crop was increasing 2 per cent from 1963's 41,744,000 head, and cattle slaughter rose 11 per cent to 31,200,000 head. As a result, prices firmed late in the year. Choice steers at Chicago reached $25.75 per hundredweight in December, up from the 1964 low of $20.52 in May and about $23.50 in December, 1963.

Futures trading in live cattle was opened by the Chicago Mercantile Exchange on November 30. The new operation was designed to protect cattlemen against unfavorable price changes during the time required to feed and bring their cattle to market.

The 1964 Pig Crop declined 7 per cent, to 88,367,000 head; slaughter dropped 2 per cent; pork consumption dipped about $1\frac{1}{2}$ pounds per person; and pork exports rose 30 per cent in the year. Competition from plentiful beef held hog prices to the 1963 level of $14.90 per hundredweight.

Lamb production slipped again in 1964, to 18,000,000 head from 19,690,000 in 1963. Lamb slaughter dropped 7 per cent, and consumption per person fell about $\frac{1}{2}$ pound. Prices, however, rose to the highest level in several years.

Bovine Tuberculosis Eradication was reported by the U.S. Department of Agriculture to be 99.9 per cent complete in 1964, after a 47-year battle. Dairy herds in 426 counties were entirely free, and those in 2,725 counties showed an incidence of less than 0.5 per cent.   FRANK B. HARPER

LIVESTOCK SHOW. Fifteen-year-old Janet Perring's Angus steer Charger was named 1964 grand champion at the 65th International Live Stock Exposition in Chicago November 27 to December 5 and promptly became the first winner ever selected for showing abroad. The Le Roy (Ill.) girl's $17,500 animal was bought by the Central National Bank of Chicago, which gave Charger to the U.S. Department of Agriculture for exhibition at a fair in West Berlin Jan. 28 to Feb. 6, 1965, to promote U.S. beef. Another "first" for the International was the showing of the Charolais breed and selection of its grand champion bull, Perfecto Sam, exhibited by Charles Litton and his son, Jerry, of Chillicothe, Mo.

A nameless, crossbred pig won the grand championship over the champions of seven breeds. The 215-pound barrow was shown by Euel Liner of Lubbock, Tex., who named it Buster on winning the title. His white Duroc-Hampshire-Yorkshire mixture brought him $17.50 a pound. A record price of $11.20 a pound was paid for the grand champion market lamb, a 105-pound Southdown exhibited by Michigan State University, East Lansing.

Canada's Royal Agricultural Winter Fair, held in Toronto November 13-21, chose a nameless Aberdeen-Angus as its grand champion steer. Shown by Meadow Lane Farm, North Salem, N.Y., it was sold for $11 a pound to Dominion Stores, Ltd.

At the 66th American Royal Live Stock and Horse Show in Kansas City, Mo., October 16-24, the grand champion steer, a 1,015-pound Angus, was shown by James Mailander of Wiota, Iowa. It brought $5.86 a pound, down from the $7.10 paid in 1963.

A 2-year-old Hereford bull, Dominican Cruiser 8, won in both the Chicago and the Kansas City shows. He was entered by Still House Hollow Farm, Hume, Va.; Blakeley Farm, Charles Town, W.Va.; and Brookshore Hereford Farm, Natrona Heights, Pa.

American Royal's grand champion winners included a 210-pound, $6\frac{1}{2}$-month-old Hampshire barrow exhibited by Richard Millican, a high school lad from Jones, Okla.; and a 90-pound fat lamb, Southdown, which was entered by Oklahoma State University.   FRANK B. HARPER

LOS ANGELES accounted for nearly one-fourth of the nation's new housing starts in 1964, with much of the new building taking shape in planned communities on the region's perimeter. The area's 853,000 factory workers challenged metropolitan Chicago as the nation's second largest industrial work force, and the region continued to gobble up a large amount of undeveloped land daily. With all these forces that make for sprawling growth in full tide, the downtown area, nevertheless, waxed strong, as it fought to resist the forces of dispersion.

The Central City opened the first of a three-building cultural hub, in December, when the Pavilion was inaugurated with appropriate fanfare (see MUSIC). The 3,250-seat concert and opera hall was designed by Welton Becket and Associates.

Far less in scale, but of great importance downtown, was the $150,000 spent on refurbishing the once bleak Pershing Square. With far better lighting, and minus its litter, the square was a landmark once again instead of a blemish.

A 32-story office tower in Occidental Center was completed in 1964, and the office building for the city's Department of Water and Power added 15 stories and 880,000 square feet of office space. Still growing was the Federal Office Building near Civic Center, as was California Mart's $60,000,000 complex of towers and a 16-story hotel.

Long plagued by auto congestion, residents hoped that the new Southern California Rapid Transit District (SCRTD) could solve the transportation crisis. Established by state law, the SCRTD supplanted the Metropolitan Transit Authority in November. It represented the area's 76 cities more directly, had the power of eminent domain, and could incur bonded indebtedness.

Outside of downtown, the nation's largest privately financed urban development project, Century City, continued to rise.   DONALD W. LIEF

LUXEMBOURG marked the end of a 45-year reign when Grand Duchess Charlotte voluntarily abdicated the throne on November 12 in favor of her son, Crown Prince Jean. Charlotte had been chosen grand duchess by a plebiscite in 1919. The new ruler had been gradually sharing the royal duties as "lieutenant" for his mother since 1961.

Luxembourg continued to share in the prosperity of Western Europe. It also worked closely with its partners in the European Economic Community (EEC, or Common Market) and the North Atlantic Treaty Organization (NATO). Steel production reached record levels during the year and full employment prevailed.

Population: 330,000. **Government:** Grand Duke Jean; Premier Pierre Werner. **Foreign Trade** (combined with Belgium): exports, $5,610,000,000; imports, $6,009,000,000. **Principal Exports:** iron and steel, machinery, textiles.   FRED J. PANNWITT

See also EUROPE.

LYNEN, FEODOR (1911-   ), West German bio-chemist, shared the Nobel medicine prize in 1964 with Konrad E. Bloch, an American. The two were cited for basic research on the fatty substance choles-terol. Dr. Lynen's research has been on the en-zymatic steps of the fatty acid cycle.

As long ago as 1951, Dr. Lynen discovered that activated acetic acid is identical chemically with acetyl-coenzyme A. A more recent discovery con-cerns the action of the vitamin biotin in the me-tabolism of fats.

Feodor Lynen was born in Munich, and was educated at the University of Munich. He joined the university's faculty as a lecturer in 1947. Five years later, he was given a professorship. Dr. Lynen is now head of Munich's biochemistry department and director of the Max Planck Institute for Cell Chemistry, also in Munich. His wife is the daughter of Heinrich Wieland, who was the winner of the Nobel chemistry prize in 1927 for research on gall acids and related substances.

See also BLOCH, KONRAD E.; NOBEL PRIZES (Science).

MAGAZINE. See PUBLISHING.

MALAGASY REPUBLIC remained one of the most stable of African governments. During the year, it took several new steps toward economic develop-ment. A newly created oil company, owned jointly by the government and several international oil companies, made plans to build an oil refinery at Tamatave. The refinery was to begin operations in July, 1966.

In July, President Philibert Tsiranana visited Washington, D.C., where he obtained a pledge of U.S. aid for his nation's five-year development program. Formosa (Nationalist China), meanwhile, agreed to help expand the nation's fishing industry. An agreement was also reached with Zanzibar fixing market quotas on cloves. The two countries together produce nearly 98 per cent of the cloves appearing on the world market.

Population: 5,950,000. **Government:** President Philibert Tsiranana. **Foreign Trade:** exports, $94,000,000; imports, $122,000,000. **Principal Ex-ports:** cloves, coffee, rice, sugar.   BENJAMIN E. THOMAS
See also AFRICA.

MALAWI, in a flag-raising ceremony held at mid-night, July 5-6, became an independent state. As a former member of the Federation of Rhodesia and Nyasaland, it had been known as Nyasaland. Prime Minister Hastings Kamuzu Banda, in his independ-ence day address, reaffirmed Malawi's foreign policy of neutralism. See also BANDA, HASTINGS KAMUZU; RHODESIA; ZAMBIA.

In October, barely three months after achieving independence, dissension among Prime Minister Ban-da and his top leaders caused a cabinet crisis. Three ministers were dismissed; two others resigned. Points

of controversy included: (1) the degree of authority to be accorded cabinet officers; (2) a proposal to move the capital; (3) a proposed 90-day detention law; and (4) Malawi's foreign policy, particularly toward Portugal and Rhodesia.

Population: 3,500,000. **Government:** Prime Min-ister Hastings Kamuzu Banda. **Foreign Trade:** no figures available. **Principal Exports:** livestock, tea, tobacco.   BENJAMIN E. THOMAS
See also AFRICA.

MALAYSIA, FEDERATION OF, survived a year of undeclared guerrilla warfare with Indonesia. Formation of the federation, which included Malaya, and the former British colonies of Singapore, Sara-wak, and Sabah (North Borneo), had been bitterly opposed by President Sukarno of Indonesia. He con-sidered it a device to perpetuate British colonialism in Asia. Complicating the situation was a claim by the Philippines to part of Sabah, which it insisted was owned by the Sultan of Sulu, a Filipino. See INDONESIA; PHILIPPINES.

Although a number of high-level conferences were held by the three countries involved, no solution to the problems was reached. Much of the failure was directly related to the refusal of Sukarno to with-draw his guerrilla forces from Sabah and Sarawak. Malaysia took the position that there was no point in holding further talks with Indonesia while sub-versive and military actions continued. Great Brit-ain continued to lend military support to Malaysia, beefing up its air and sea power in Singapore and its land forces in Borneo. Australia and New Zealand also pledged military support if the conflict widened.

Racial problems were another source of internal conflict during the year. Late in July, rioting erupted between the Malays and Chinese in Singa-pore. During four days of sporadic fighting, 23 per-sons were killed, and more than 400 were injured. In September, fighting again broke out between the two groups. Prime Minister Tunku Abdul Rahman repeated his charge that Indonesian agents were responsible for renewing the racial strife.

Despite the turmoil, Malaysia's economy had an excellent year. Its growth rate continued at about 4 per cent annually, and investment capital as well as development loans continued to increase rapidly. Development funds were being poured into Sabah and Sarawak for the construction of road networks. Money flowed into the Sabah area for a school building program. Even an Indonesian economic boycott of Singapore did not hurt the Malaysian economy as a whole although it was estimated that the annual loss amounted to 1.5 per cent of the total Malaysian trade.

Population: 11,150,000. **Government:** Prime Min-ister Tunku Abdul Rahman. **Foreign Trade:** exports, $2,215,000,000; imports, $2,434,000,000. **Principal Exports:** iron ore, rubber, tin.   JOHN N. STALKER
See also ASIA.

409

MALCOLM X (1925-   ), who had been national spokesman for the Black Muslims, a Negro nationalistic movement that advocates Negro separatism, broke with the leader, Elijah Muhammad. Malcolm announced the break on March 8. Later he said he had renounced racism and would henceforth devote himself to religious affairs.

Malcolm made pilgrimages to Mecca, Saudi Arabia, in May and September. On his return from his second pilgrimage, he denounced Elijah Muhammad, and described himself as an evangelist for Islam as it is practiced in the Arab world.

Born Malcolm Little, in Omaha, Nebr., son of a Baptist minister, Malcolm grew up in Lansing, Mich., to see several of his relatives die by violence at "white hands," as he puts it. He spent seven years in an Eastern prison for burglary.   WALTER F. MORSE

MALI held elections for the 80-seat national assembly in April, 1964. They were the first to be held since 1959. Almost 90 per cent of the nearly 2,500,000 eligible voters cast their ballots. President Modibo Keita, who was re-elected, reassumed the portfolios of defense, foreign affairs, and security.

A tragic incident marred the erstwhile harmony of Mali politics during the year. Two leaders of the Sudanese Progressive party, an opposition group that had remained active in Mali after it had dissolved its union with Sudan, died in a prison camp. They had been confined there since 1963.

Population: 4,550,000. **Government:** President Modibo Keita. **Foreign Trade:** exports, $10,000,000; imports, $46,000,000. **Principal Exports:** cotton, fish, peanuts.   WILLIAM SPENCER

See also AFRICA.

MALTA ended more than 160 years of British rule at midnight, September 21, when the Union Jack was lowered and the red and white Maltese flag took its place. Prime Minister George Borg Olivier, who was head of the Nationalist party, announced that Malta would remain a monarchy under Queen Elizabeth II, as well as a member of the British Commonwealth. See GREAT BRITAIN.

Independence celebrations were marred by demonstrations staged by Labour party members led by the former prime minister, Dominic Mintoff. The demonstrators were protesting the remaining economic and defense ties with Britain and the alleged political privileges that were enjoyed by the Roman Catholic Church in Malta.

Population: 330,000. **Government:** Governor-General Sir Maurice Dorman; Prime Minister George Borg Olivier. **Foreign Trade:** exports, $12,000,000; imports, $80,000,000. **Principal Exports:** potatoes, scrap metal, textiles.   ALASTAIR BURNET

MANITOBA. See CANADA.

MANUFACTURING. See BUSINESS; INDUSTRY.

MARINE CORPS, U.S. See ARMED FORCES OF THE WORLD; NATIONAL DEFENSE.

MAURITANIA, ISLAMIC REPUBLIC OF, marked a slight improvement in its long-standing quarrel with Morocco in 1964. Following a meeting in Cairo, Egypt, between the Mauritanian and Moroccan ministers of information, the two national radio stations stopped beaming hostile propaganda at each other. Both nations, which have claims in the Spanish Sahara, also joined forces at an Organization of African Unity (OAU) meeting in Cairo to demand that Spain evacuate the disputed areas. In October, the United Arab Republic officially recognized Mauritania.

To end the one-party system in Mauritania, the government approved the formation of a second political party. The National Democratic Front was formed in August, but it was dissolved quickly by the government on charges that it was illegal and subversive. Two leading opponents of the ruling Mauritanian People's party then formed the Mauritanian Democratic party. This latter group was approved by the government.

Population: 810,000. **Government:** President Moktar Ould Daddah. **Foreign Trade:** exports, $3,000,000; imports, $36,000,000. **Principal Exports:** cattle, fish, natural gums.   WILLIAM SPENCER

See also AFRICA.

MEDICAL INSURANCE. See HEALTH; INSURANCE.

MEDICARE. See CONGRESS; HEALTH; OLD AGE.

MEDICINE made use of the laser, a device that amplifies light waves into extremely powerful beams of one frequency, as its latest potential weapon against cancer. At the Foundation for Medical Research in Pasadena, Calif., Dr. James T. Helsper and Dr. George S. Sharp used laser beams to treat three cancer patients. They found that the beams destroyed tumor cells over an area nearly eight millimeters in diameter, an effect not seen after treatment with X rays, radioactive isotopes, or cauterization. Dr. Paul E. McGuff of the Tufts-New England Medical Center in Boston noted about 50 per cent destruction after exposure to just one flash from a laser beam, and more than 99 per cent destruction of the diseased area in a cancer patient exposed to two flashes. Doctors cautioned, however, that use of the laser for cancer treatment was still experimental.

Virus-Leukemia Link. The long-supposed link between viruses and the cancerous disease of the blood, leukemia, appeared nearly established by the results of research at a number of laboratories throughout the world. At both Roswell Park Memorial Institute, Buffalo, N.Y., and the National Cancer Institute, Bethesda, Md., viruslike particles from leukemia patients were grown in a tissue culture. This opened the way to obtaining pure leukemia particles in large quantity, a necessary step toward full-scale study of them.

In London, at Middlesex Hospital Medical School, Dr. Michael A. Epstein succeeded, for the first time, in the apparent transmission of human

Chicago Sun-Times

DEFENDER of Krebiozen, Dr. Andrew C. Ivy,
and three others were indicted for conspiring
to illegally distribute the controversial cancer drug.

cancer to an animal in the manner that virus diseases can be transferred. The investigators injected tumor material, called Burkitt's lymphoma, into the abdominal cavities of four African green monkeys. In two of the monkeys, tumor cells grew that were indistinguishable from the human lymphomas.

Supercold Surgery. A promising development, known as *cryosurgery*, uses extreme cold to replace or supplement traditional methods of surgery in killing and removing diseased tissue. Unlike the stomach-freezing treatment for ulcers, cryosurgery is used to freeze only small portions of diseased tissue, rather than entire organs. The development could not have been possible without technological advances that have led to a precise control of rapid freezing and thawing in extremely small areas. The technique uses special hollow probes through which liquid nitrogen, at a temperature of around $-320°$ F., flows. The liquid nitrogen freezes the ailing body tissue, and, as the liquid vaporizes, it exits through the other end of one of the probes.

Oxygen Therapy. Increasing use was made of high-pressure oxygen to treat a variety of medical conditions. Under the process, developed at several institutions in the United States and elsewhere, the patient is placed inside large pressure tanks and allowed to breathe pure oxygen at pressures of up to four times the normal for atmosphere (14.7 pounds per square inch at sea level). Pure oxygen must be administered in a high-pressure environment to avoid damage to the lungs. The high-pressure oxygen treatment has been used effectively in cases of carbon monoxide poisoning, where the blood has become oxygen-poor. It has also been used to treat tetanus, or lockjaw, a disease in which the bacteria cannot endure oxygen. The technique seems to make cancerous tumors more susceptible to X-ray treatment, and it seems to improve the chances of "blue babies" surviving major surgery. In the laboratory, animal studies indicate that high-pressure oxygen might be used to save the lives of many auto accident victims who now die of shock from the loss of great amounts of blood. It may someday also be used to help heart attack victims pull through the first few critical hours.

AMA Research. The American Medical Association (AMA) reported that construction had begun on its Biomedical Research Institute building in Chicago. The aim of the institute, due to begin operating in 1965, is to bring together outstanding investigators from various scientific disciplines for pure, basic research in molecular biology rather than project-oriented studies.   HUGH H. HUSSEY

See also DENTISTRY; HEALTH; HOSPITAL.

MEMORIALS dedicated or announced in 1964 included the following:

Abraham Lincoln Monument in Juárez, Mexico, was dedicated on April 14. The 13-foot bronze figure, designed by sculptor Angel Tarrac, stands on a 10-foot pedestal in a park at the head of the new avenue Paseo Lincoln.

American Memorial to Sir Winston Churchill. Ground was broken for the reconstruction of an ancient London church at Westminster College, Fulton, Mo., on April 19. There on Mar. 5, 1946, the former British prime minister delivered his "Iron Curtain" speech, saying "From Stettin in the Baltic to Trieste in the Adriatic, an iron curtain has descended across the Continent. This is certainly not the liberated Europe we fought to build up. Nor is it one which contains the essentials of permanent peace." The Church of St. Mary the Virgin, designed by Sir Christopher Wren and built in 1677, was almost completely destroyed by a Nazi incendiary bomb in 1941. Left standing were the stone walls, bell tower, and interior columns, now to be part of the reconstructed church. See PERSONALITIES (Close-Up).

Brontë Memorial Chapel at the Haworth parish church in England was dedicated on July 4. The Brontë sisters: Charlotte (1816-1855), remembered for *Jane Eyre;* Emily Jane (1818-1848), author of *Wuthering Heights;* and Anne (1820-1849), who wrote *Agnes Grey* and *The Tenant of Wildfell Hall*, and their clergyman father are buried at Haworth.

Dag Hammarskjöld Memorials at the United Nations. *Single Form*, designed by the British sculptress Barbara Hepworth, was dedicated on June 11. The bronze abstract sculpture stands at the edge of a pool in front of the Secretariat building, and is inscribed: "To the glory of God and the memory of Dag Hammarskjöld—Ndola, 17/9/61." The United Nations Secretary-General (1953-1961) was killed in an airplane crash the night of Sept. 17-18, 1961, while on a peace mission to the Congo. Unveiled in September was the United Nations staff's memorial to Hammarskjöld and the 15 persons who died with him in that African plane crash. The second memorial, a stained (predominately blue) glass panel in the Secretariat building lounge, was designed by Marc Chagall. The French artist supervised its installation. See PAINTING AND SCULPTURE (pictures).

Freedoms Foundation Medal of Honor Memorial Park is planned to commemorate men who have been awarded the Congressional Medal of Honor since its creation in 1861. There is to be a United States map outlined on the 52-acre tract at Valley Forge, Pa. A monument will mark the geographic location of each state, and in each state area a tree will have the name of each medal winner. The heroes' records will be housed in a building at the park's entrance.

General of the Army Douglas MacArthur Memorial Museum was opened on January 26, in Norfolk, Va., his mother's birthplace and home. The old courthouse, a Classic Revival building, now contains MacArthur memorabilia. General MacArthur was buried in the rotunda on April 11 in the depressed circular crypt which also has a place for his widow, Jean. High on the rotunda walls are the names of MacArthur's major military campaigns. Five marble panels have excerpts from his speeches. See DEATHS OF NOTABLE PERSONS (Close-Up).

George C. Marshall Research Library and Museum at the Virginia Military Institute in Lexington, Va., was dedicated by President Johnson on May 23. The soldier, statesman, and originator of the European Recovery Program (Marshall Plan) was a graduate of the military institute.

Robert the Bruce Statue was unveiled by Queen Elizabeth II at Bannockburn, Scotland, on the 650th anniversary of the Battle of Bannockburn. There, on June 23-24, 1314, Bruce's men defeated the English troops of Edward II. England recognized Bruce as King Robert I of Scotland in 1328.

Shakespeare Memorial at Stratford-on-Avon, England, was opened in April by the American Shakespeare Committee as a permanent Shakespeare study center. See THEATER; LITERATURE (Close-Up).

See also KENNEDY, JOHN F.

MENTAL HEALTH. The important position drugs occupy in the treatment of mental illness was pointed up in 1964 by the withdrawal and the subsequent return to the market of *tranylcypromine*, used to treat severe depression. The drug was withdrawn on the recommendation of the U.S. Food and Drug Administration (FDA).

According to the FDA, several persons had died of apoplexy after taking the drug. Following an intensive investigation by an FDA advisory group, however, the drug was returned to the market with warnings regarding its possible side effects.

In explaining its action, the FDA said its investigation indicated that the antidepressive effects of the drug could overbalance its hazards in certain instances when depression is very severe.

A Major Study reported in March by the National Institute of Mental Health underlined the value of *phenothiazines* in the treatment of schizophrenia. The phenothiazines comprise a large group of drugs classed as tranquilizers. The first of them was in-

troduced a little more than a decade ago, and with one or two other psychotropic drugs, helped to open the modern age of drug therapy in mental illness.

Drug therapy has been found, in many instances, to control symptoms of mental illness so well that patients are able to leave the hospital after a few days or weeks when they might otherwise have been confined for years. In the case of acute schizophrenia, the investigators found that 95 per cent of those who received phenothiazines showed some improvement.

Decrease in Patients. The use of drugs, accompanied by an increase in professional personnel, accounted for the continued decline in the number of patients in public mental hospitals. Over an eight-year period, from 1956 to 1963, there was a decrease of 9.7 per cent in the average number of patients confined at any given time. At the same time, however, there was a continued rise in the number of admissions, though many of these were discharged after only a few days.

The development of community-based after-care centers, known as halfway houses, tended to reduce the high rate of hospital readmissions. Such centers, now found in New York, Philadelphia, San Francisco, and several other cities, provide medication, psychiatric care, job placement, and temporary living facilities for former patients.

In February, President Lyndon B. Johnson signed a bill that provided $41,800,000 for building community mental-health centers and for training teachers for mentally retarded children.   HUGH H. HUSSEY

See also PSYCHOLOGY.

METALLURGY. Attempts by scientists to control hydrogen fusion with powerful magnetic fields led to the development of two new metal-forming devices.

One is *Magneform*, a tool that has as its essential part a heavy wire coil that can be given various shapes, including that of a cylinder, disk, or doughnut. When a massive electric current is sent through the coil, the Magneform creates an intense magnetic field capable of pushing rigid metal into almost any shape. Some of the applications of Magneform, developed by General Dynamics Laboratories, near La Jolla, Calif., include: joining aluminum and copper to porcelain insulators, and fitting metal bands around artillery shells.

The other, *Columbus*, was developed at the atomic energy laboratories of Los Alamos, N.Mex. The tool produces tubes from powdered metals such as tungsten and molybdenum, which cannot be easily poured into a mold after being melted. Columbus produces an extremely strong magnetic field around the powdered metal. This magnetic field squeezes the metal into shape. The metal is then hardened by firing. Columbus not only makes tungsten tubes cheaper and faster than by any other known method, but does so with greater uniformity. SERGEI LENORMAND

See also INDUSTRY; IRON AND STEEL.

METEOROLOGY. See WEATHER.

MEXICO witnessed the largest presidential election turnout in its history on July 5. Of the 10,000,000 votes cast, about 90 per cent favored Gustavo Díaz Ordaz. Both Díaz, who assumed office on December 1, and outgoing President Adolfo López Matéos were members of the Revolutionary party.

The Díaz administration had sizable amounts of foreign credits and loans on hand from the previous administration. Thus, it had fresh money to begin its own economic program as well as to continue works in progress. Included among these were the nation's war on illiteracy and its land reform program. The illiteracy rate under the previous regime had been reduced to 28.91 per cent of the population versus 53.26 in 1959. The national land reform program reflected equally remarkable results; between 1959 and 1964, 38,400,000 acres had been turned over to the landless farmers. It was a record unmatched anywhere in the world. See Section Two, AWAKENING THE LAND.

Healthy Economy. The nation's financial position was never better. The peso was firm. Foreign reserves totaled a record $549,000,000 on September 1, and another $345,000,000 was available if needed from the Export-Import Bank, the International Monetary Fund, and the United States Department of the Treasury.

Steel was expected to climb 20 per cent over 1963 with total production ranging between 2,400,000 and 2,500,000 tons. For the first time, Mexico had an excess petroleum refinery capacity. Agriculture showed gains comparable with those of industry; the coffee harvest for the 1963-1964 year reached a record 2,900,000 bags, and wheat production was so high that the country planned to export over 500,000 tons of it.

The 1964 Gross National Product (GNP) reached an estimated $7,248,000,000, up one-third from the $5,280,000,000 of 1958. Mexico repaid four years ahead of schedule a $100,000,000 Export-Import Bank loan that had been granted in 1959, thus enhancing its already favorable international credit standing and, furthermore, inspiring new confidence among foreign investors.

U.S.-Mexican Relations remained cordial. On September 1, outgoing president Adolfo López Matéos met with U.S. President Lyndon B. Johnson in El Paso, Tex., to participate in ceremonies celebrating the El Chamizal boundary settlement. In November, newly elected President Díaz visited with President Johnson at the latter's ranch in Texas. Despite its close U.S. ties, Mexico rejected an Organization of American States' recommendation to sever diplomatic relations with Cuba—a recommendation favored by the United States (see CUBA).

U.S. Investments in Mexico were expected to reach an estimated $102,000,000 in 1964, compared with about $90,000,000 the preceding year. In addition, it was estimated in financial circles that foreign investments from sources other than the United

Wide World

BROAD GRIN of new Mexican President Gustavo Díaz Ordaz matches wide brim of his hat. He succeeded Adolfo López Matéos.

States would amount to another $30,000,000 to $40,000,000 during 1964. Marked industrial development was being shown in the states of Veracruz, on the Gulf Coast, and Querétaro, north of the state of México. Aside from the automotive industry and steel, the fastest-growing fields in industrial growth were chemicals (exclusive of petrochemicals) and consumer electrical equipment.

One of the truly bright spots of the Mexican economy was auto production. Overall production for 1964 was expected to reach 80,000 cars, trucks and buses, against 66,400 in 1962. Among foreign owned companies that were expanding their facilities in Mexico were Volkswagen, International Harvester, Massey-Ferguson, the British Motor Corporation, the Ford Motor Company, General Motors, the Chrysler Corporation, and American Motors.

The increase in industrialization and the growing prosperity of Mexican workers meant sharply rising demands for electric power.

Population: 40,200,000. **Government:** President Gustavo Díaz Ordaz. **Foreign Trade:** exports, $1,028,000,000; imports, $1,567,000,000. **Principal Exports:** coffee, cotton, sugar.   MARY G. WEBSTER

See also DÍAZ ORDAZ, GUSTAVO; LATIN AMERICA.

MIDDLE EAST

TENSIONS ran high in the Middle East during 1964, but they did not reach the fever pitch of previous years. Syria and Israel again exchanged gunfire in a series of border incidents. Arab leaders continued to plot the grand design for Israel's eventual downfall. Yemen remained a source of discord as did Aden, where embattled British troops exchanged gunfire with marauding tribesmen. In general, however, there was less dependence on conflict and more on reasonable negotiations among the Middle Eastern nations than ever before.

A striking example of the "new look" in the region's politics could be observed in the Arab world's reactions to an Israeli water-diversion scheme involving the River Jordan. Israel announced in January that it would begin pumping water from its part of the River Jordan to irrigate the Negev desert.

Arab leaders rushed to Cairo to devise plans either to attack Israel or to divert the Jordan's principal tributaries for their own irrigation. However, the high cost of a proposed diversion plan ($140,000,000 upward) and military unpreparedness left the Arabs without a program of action. Israel went ahead with its pumping operations without interference. See ISRAEL.

The first Arab Refugees Conference was held in the Jordanian sector of Jerusalem in an attempt to hammer out a unified Palestine policy. The refugees, led by Palestine's representative to the Arab League, drafted a Palestine Arab charter and formed a volunteer "Palestine Liberation Army." Later, the Arab League authorized a Palestine force to aid the liberation guerrillas. The continued presence of United Nations (UN) forces on Israel's borders, and the disparity between Israeli and Arab forces generally, made it unlikely that the Palestine force would attack. Though well-armed by the Soviet Union, they lacked a unified military command.

International Relations. Two Middle East issues were taken up by the UN—Yemen and South Arabia. UN Secretary-General U Thant admitted failure in his efforts to disengage either the Saudi Arabian or the Egyptian forces from the civil war in Yemen. The UN's observation mission was withdrawn. The civil war itself reached a stalemate. In September, the first hopeful note in the Yemen impasse was struck by the two Arab states involved. Crown Prince Faisal of Saudi Arabia, who later became king, and President Gamal Abdel Nasser of the United Arab Republic (UAR) announced they would work jointly in an effort to end the civil war. See SAUDI ARABIA; UNITED ARAB REPUBLIC (UAR); YEMEN.

The Arab states, particularly the UAR, kept up a steady drumfire against the Federation of South Arabia and the presence of British troops in Aden. Tribesmen carrying out raids against the British

THIRSTY CIRCLES of pipe 108 inches in diameter formed part of pipeline used to divert water from the River Jordan to the Negev desert.

415

Pictorial Parade

CARTRIDGE-BANDOLIERED British troops, wearing desert gear, prepare a combat patrol for a foray against marauding tribesmen in Federation of South Arabia.

along the federation's border were better trained and organized than in past years, and supplied with modern weapons. The stalemate inside Yemen allowed Egyptian-trained Yemeni tribesmen to leave the battle areas for further opportunities to the south. Reprisal raids on Yemeni forts by British forces resulted in a complaint to the UN.

Other Developments. The first stage of the Aswan High Dam project in the UAR was completed in spectacular fashion when Soviet Premier Nikita S. Khrushchev opened a diversion channel for the Nile around the Aswan Gorge. Khrushchev, who was later dismissed as premier, shared the place of honor with Iraq's President Abdul Salam Muhammed Arif and President Abdullah al-Salal of Yemen.

The meeting of Khrushchev and Arif smoothed over differences that had developed between them over the handling of communists by the Baathist party in Iraq. The presence of Khrushchev at the important ceremony underlined the extent to which the Soviet Union had become involved in the Middle East. See RUSSIA.

Other confrontations between Arab leaders suggested the direction which Middle East affairs might take in future years. In Saudi Arabia, Crown Prince Faisal had a showdown with his half brother, King Saud, whom he replaced with the backing of tribal elders and government officials. The new ruler was a progressive-minded man whose avowed purpose was to develop Saudi Arabia into a modern state.

Publix Pictorial

DESERT SHEIK. Crown Prince Faisal of Saudi Arabia succeeded his half brother, King Saud, as ruler of the oil-rich kingdom in November. Saud was deposed because of his extravagances.

Iraq's President Arif faced Kurdish rebel leader Mustafa al-Barzani across the conference table after the negotiation of a cease-fire in Iraq's civil war. The government accepted Kurdish demands for school instruction in Kurdish, a Kurdish militia, and native Kurdish administrators, but it hedged on the all-important question of Kurdish autonomy within the Iraqi state. Arif's dream was still Arab unity; Iraq and the UAR unified their armies and aligned their economic policies as Iraq nationalized some industries. See IRAQ.

Iran, Pakistan, and Turkey began a new program of economic cooperation outside the Central Treaty Organization. Afghanistan, as a neighboring Muslim nation was invited to join. However, "Northern Tier" collaboration was overshadowed by inter-Arab and neutralist solidarity. Cairo played host to conferences of the Arab League, the Organization of African Unity (OAU), and, in October, to a conference of 47 nonaligned nations.

The conference, rejecting a pro-Communist Chinese, anti-Western line, adopted nine moderate principles of coexistence. It also upheld the nuclear test-ban treaty. World attention was diverted from this conference, however, by the presence of Premier Moise Tshombe of Congo (Léopoldville) during its sessions. Uninvited and unwelcome to many of the delegates, Tshombe was forcibly prevented from attending by Egyptian authorities who detained him in Cairo (see CONGO [LÉOPOLDVILLE]).

Constitutional Developments. Afghanistan adopted a new constitution, thus establishing the means by which it could transform itself into a modern constitutional state (see AFGHANISTAN). Iraq, Syria, the UAR, and Yemen also adopted constitutions, but these were provisional and did not move far away from one-party absolutism. Lebanon elected a new president, meanwhile resisting political pressures favoring a constitutional amendment that would allow President Chehab to succeed himself. WILLIAM SPENCER

See also Section One, PAUL-HENRI SPAAK ON THE WORLD; and articles on various Middle East nations.

MILLER, WILLIAM EDWARD (1914-   ), a U.S. Representative first elected to Congress from New York state in 1950, but who had not planned to run for an eighth term in 1964, was the Republican nominee for Vice-President of the United States. He was nominated on July 16 at the closing session of the 28th Republican National Convention at San Francisco. Senator Barry M. Goldwater, the party's nominee for President, announced Miller as his personal choice. Miller received 1,305 votes of a possible 1,308, three Tennessee delegates abstaining.

Miller had been Republican national chairman for three years, 1961 to 1964. He was a political pro with a job to do. And he did it, vigorously, in the campaign. Many of his speeches were devoted to slashing attacks on the opposing ticket, on the Democratic party, and on the Johnson administra-

tion. His most frequent target was Senator Hubert H. Humphrey of Minnesota, the Democratic vice-presidential candidate, whom he called a dangerous radical and appeaser.

Miller was born March 22, 1914, at Lockport, N.Y. His mother was a milliner and his father, a factory janitor. Miller was graduated from the University of Notre Dame in 1935, with a B.A. degree. He won a law degree in 1938 from the Union University Law School, Albany, N.Y.

Miller is a Roman Catholic. He and his wife, the former Stephanie Wagner, are the parents of three daughters and a son.   WALTER F. MORSE

See also GOLDWATER, BARRY M.; HUMPHREY, HUBERT H.; REPUBLICAN PARTY.

MINERALOGY. See GEOLOGY; METALLURGY.

MINES AND MINING. The mining industry in 1964 was marked by rising prices, tight supplies, and ore discoveries. The most spectacular discovery probably was that of the Texas Gulf Sulphur Company near Timmins, Ontario. The company, in June, estimated its find there at 55,000,000 tons of copper, zinc, and silver ore. Production from the ore body will start in 1965 (see CANADA).

In Alaska, a billion-ton deposit of low-grade iron ore was discovered. It is one of the largest ever made in the United States (see IRON AND STEEL). The Palabora Mining Company, Ltd., opened the world's second largest copper mine, in South Africa. The open-pit mine, about 250 miles northeast of Johannesburg, was expected to turn out nearly 80,000 tons of copper a year by sometime in 1966.

Aluminum production and consumption set world records in 1964, and earnings of the four leading North American producers rose about 40 per cent. Aluminum prices went up three times during the year, $\frac{1}{2}$ cent a pound each time.

A tight copper supply was aggravated by work stoppages in the summer at Kennecott Copper Corporation facilities in the U.S. West and at major Northern Rhodesian mines. Unrest in Africa and politics in Chile added uncertainties to prices and supplies. Chile's election in September of moderate Eduardo Frei Montalva as president removed the threat of nationalization of copper properties (see CHILE). Copper consumption reached a peacetime high in 1964, about 10 per cent above 1963.

Lead and zinc shortages also sent prices climbing. At year-end, U.S. lead prices stood about 25 per cent above the 1963 level, and zinc was up more than 10 per cent (see BUSINESS [table]).

Rising consumption of nonferrous metals by a rapidly industrializing world was taxing the capacity of mines and smelters. Releases of metal from the United States government stockpile helped ease the pinch somewhat.   ROBERT E. BEDINGFIELD

See also COAL; INDUSTRY.

MODEL BUILDING. See GAMES, MODELS, AND TOYS.

MOHOLE. See GEOLOGY.

VALUES OF MONETARY UNITS

Why Money Values Change

Money values change often and unpredictably because of factors such as unstable political and economic conditions. The examples at right show how money values in a few countries changed in four separate years.

Monetary Unit	1930	1940	1950	1964
BRITISH POUND	$4.866	$4.03	$2.80	$2.785
MEXICAN PESO	.50	.18	.12	.08
SWEDISH KRONA	.268	.2385	.1935	.1939
SWISS FRANC	.1930	.2315	.2300	.2317

COUNTRY	MONETARY UNIT	VALUE IN U.S. MONEY
Afghanistan	Afghani	$ .02†
Albania	Lek	.02†
Algeria	Dinar	.20
Angola	Escudo	.0351
Argentina	Peso	.0071
Australia	Pound	2.23
Austria	Schilling	.039
Bahamas	Pound	2.79
Belgium	Franc	.02
Bermuda	Pound	2.80
Bolivia	Peso	.085
Brazil	Cruzeiro	.00065
British Guiana	Dollar	.58
British Honduras	Dollar	.70
Bulgaria	Leva	.86†
Burma	Kyat	.21
Cambodia	Riel	.029
Cameroon	CFA Franc	.0041
Canada	Dollar	.9306
Central African Republic	CFA Franc	.0041
Ceylon	Rupee	.21
Chad	CFA Franc	.0041
Chile	Escudo	.40
China (Communist)	Yuan	no quote
China (Nationalist)	Dollar	.025
Colombia	Peso	.09
Congo (Brazzaville)	CFA Franc	.0041
Congo (Léopoldville)	Franc	.0067
Costa Rica	Colon	.15†
Cuba	Peso	no quote
Cyprus	Pound	2.79
Czechoslovakia	Koruna	.1444
Dahomey	CFA Franc	.0041
Denmark	Krone	.144
Dominican Republic	Peso	1.00
Ecuador	Sucre	.056†
El Salvador	Colon	.40
Ethiopia	Dollar	.40
Finland	Markka	.315
France	Franc	.2041
Gabon	CFA Franc	.0041
Germany (East)	Ostmark	no quote
Germany (West)	Deutschemark	.25
Ghana	Pound	2.81
Great Britain	Pound	2.785
Greece	Drachma	.033
Guatemala	Quetzal	1.00†
Guinea	CFA Franc	.0041
Haiti	Gourde	.20
Honduras	Lempira	.50
Hong Kong	Dollar	.175
Hungary	Forint	.0861†
Iceland	Króna	.0233
India	Rupee	.209
Indonesia	Rupiah	.0224†
Iran	Rial	.0135
Iraq	Dinar	2.785
Ireland	Pound	2.785
Israel	Pound	.34
Italy	Lira	.0016
Ivory Coast	CFA Franc	.0041
Japan	Yen	.0028
Jordan	Dinar	2.785
Kenya	Shilling	$ .1395
Korea, South	Won	.004
Kuwait	Dinar	2.785
Laos	Kip	.0042
Lebanon	Pound	.3277#
Liberia	U.S. Dollar	1.00
Libya	Pound	2.792
Liechtenstein	Franc	.2318
Luxembourg	Franc	.02
Macau (Macao)	Pataca	.21
Malagasy Republic	CFA Franc	.0041
Malawi	Pound	2.792
Malaysia	Dollar	.33
Mali and Mauritania	CFA Franc	.0041
Malta	Pound	2.792
Mexico	Peso	.08
Monaco	Nouveau Franc	.2041
Morocco	Dirham	.20
Nepal	Rupee	.1316
Netherlands	Guilder	.278
New Zealand	Pound	2.775
Nicaragua	Córdoba	.143†
Niger	CFA Franc	.0041
Nigeria	Pound	2.80
Norway	Krone	.1397
Pakistan	Rupee	.21
Panama	Balboa	1.00
Paraguay	Guarani	.008
Peru	Sol	.0375
Philippines	Peso	.257#
Poland	Zloty	.25†
Portugal	Escudo	.0351
Puerto Rico	U.S. Dollar	1.00
Rhodesia	Pound	2.70
Romania	Leu	.1666†
Russia	Ruble	1.11†
Saudi Arabia	Riyal	.2235
Senegal	CFA Franc	.0041
Sierra Leone	Pound	2.805
Somalia	Somalo	.14
South Africa	Rand	1.395
Spain	Peseta	.0167
Sudan	Pound	2.87
Surinam	Guilder	.5375
Sweden	Krona	.1939
Switzerland	Franc	.2317
Syria	Pound	.2555#
Tanzania	Shilling	.1395
Thailand	Baht or Tical	.0484#
Togo	CFA Franc	.0041
Trinidad-Tobago	Dollar	.58
Tunisia	Dinar	1.91
Turkey	Lira	.11†
Uganda	Shilling	.1395
United Arab Republic	Pound	2.31
United States	Dollar	1.00
Upper Volta	CFA Franc	.0041
Uruguay	Peso	.0475#
Venezuela	Bolívar	.2228#
Vietnam, South	Piastre	.0288
Western Samoa	Pound	2.775
Yugoslavia	Dinar	.0013†
Zambia	Pound	2.792

Source: Manufacturers Hanover Trust Company, Dec. 1, 1964.

†Official exchange rate.
#Free exchange rate.

MONEY. Despite record business expansion through 1964, increases in market rates of interest were minimal. For almost 11 months the rate on 3-month Treasury bills hovered near the $3\frac{1}{2}$ per cent discount rate at which banks could borrow from the Federal Reserve System (Fed). Advancing demand for credit required the Fed to buy $3,000,000,000 of bills and other government securities on the open market in the year ended in October. As a result, the U.S. money supply (demand deposits and currency) increased at an annual rate of over 4 per cent, well above the $2\frac{1}{2}$ per cent postwar average, to a total of about $160,000,000,000.

Bank time deposits increased at nearly the rapid rate of a year earlier. Banks added about $23,000,000,000 to the supply of credit, loans to business and individuals accounting for $20,000,000,000, and loans to state and local governments (municipal bond purchases) for $3,000,000,000. The ratio of bank loans to deposits rose to a postwar high of more than 68 per cent. See BANKS AND BANKING.

Though slowed initially by funds made available from the federal tax cut, consumer credit increased about $7,000,000,000 in 1964 (see table). Stock market credit, after large gains a year earlier, increased little in 1964 (see STOCKS AND BONDS).

The Balance of Payments deficit was pared to about $2,500,000,000 in 1964, down from the $3,300,000,000 excess of payments over receipts of foreign currencies the preceding year. Passage of an Interest Equalization Act made unexempted foreign securities more expensive to U.S. buyers. This was expected to reduce U.S. demands for foreign currencies.

Despite the payments deficit, the U.S. gold outflow was effectively limited. First, the United States borrowed from the International Monetary Fund (IMF). Then it negotiated agreements in which foreign governments accepted nonmarketable claims, or "Roosa bonds," on the United States in lieu of gold for their excess dollars. This system was devised by Robert V. Roosa, the Department of the Treasury's under secretary for monetary affairs.

Roosa, who resigned at the end of the year, had helped organize the $3,000,000,000 "save the pound" credit to the Bank of England from the Fed and several other Free World central banks. The newly elected Labour government had tried to solve Britain's payments deficit by imposing a 15 per cent surcharge on imports of all but food and raw materials—a step that so alarmed its trading partners that a run on the pound developed. On November 23, the Bank of England raised the bank rate from 5 per cent to 7 per cent. Nevertheless, the run on the pound resumed, and Roosa and the Fed's rescue operation began.

On November 23, the Fed also increased its discount rate from $3\frac{1}{2}$ to 4 per cent. Its goal was to prevent the outflow of dollars attracted by high, short-term interest abroad. Treasury bill rates increased in December to almost 4 per cent, but the Fed tried to prevent advances in long-term rates. Roosa, at year's end, predicted long-term rates would be stable or declining in 1965.

The Coin Shortage became critical in 1964, but increased coin output was expected to satisfy coin demands in 1965. See HOBBIES.

Substitutes for silver in coins got serious consideration. Rising industrial demands for silver had pushed its market price to $1.2929 a troy ounce.

CONSUMER CREDIT OCTOBER, 1964		
Type	Amount	12-Mo. Inc.
	(Billions of Dollars)	
Noninstallment, all types	16.1	1.3
Installment, by lenders		
Commercial Banks	23.7	2.3
Sales Finance Firms	14.6	1.4
Credit Unions	6.3	.8
Other Institutions	6.6	.6
Retail Outlets	6.6	.5
Total Consumer Credit	73.9	6.9

Source: Federal Reserve Bulletin

At that price the silver in a silver dollar is worth $1. Only sales of the Treasury's coin-making inventory of silver prevented the market price of silver from advancing further.

The futures market put its money on expectations of an eventual exhaustion of Treasury silver stocks. The price of silver for delivery in 1965 rose to more than $1.38 an ounce. That is the price above which dimes, quarters, and half dollars would be worth more as metal than as money.   WILLIAM G. DEWALD

MONGOLIAN PEOPLE'S REPUBLIC. See OUTER MONGOLIA.

MONUMENTS, NATIONAL. See PARKS.

MOROCCO. King Hassan II encouraged members of his cabinet to form a new political party in April. It was called the Democratic Socialist Party (PSD). Although dubbed the "King's Party" by the opposition, the new group supported agrarian reform, recovery of the nation's "lost" territories (Ceuta, Mauritania, and Melilla), and economic planning toward a modified socialism. Foreign Minister Ahmed Reda Guedira was elected secretary-general of the PSD, and Premier Ahmed Bahnini became its president. Later, Guedira resigned his ministerial post, forcing a reshuffle in the government. Only Bahnini remained among the top ministers in the new cabinet.

A raid in June by Moroccan rebels based in Algeria was quickly checked, but it further strained relations between the two countries.

Population: 13,000,000. **Government:** King Hassan II; Premier Ahmed Bahnini. **Foreign Trade:** exports, $470,000,000; imports, $478,000,000. **Principal Exports:** barley, fruits and nuts, manganese, natural phosphates, vegetables.   WILLIAM SPENCER

See also AFRICA.

MOSLEM. See MIDDLE EAST.

MOTEL. See HOTEL.

MOTION PICTURES

FOR THE U.S. MOTION PICTURE INDUSTRY, 1964 was a profitable, but far from placid, year. Ironically, what provided the profits also produced the headaches. For some time, in an effort to compete, not only with television, but also with the increasingly popular foreign-made films shown, American pictures have been growing more frank in their treatment of sex and more daring in costume and dialogue.

In 1964, this trend reached its culmination with partial or outright nudity in several major productions (among them: *The Prize, A Shot in the*

IN THE WAR ROOM. Government officials wonder what to do next in the film, Dr. Strangelove, after a mad general ordered a hydrogen bombing mission.

© 1964 Walt Disney Productions

MARY POPPINS, *played by Julie Andrews, pops in on the scene, magic umbrella in hand. The musical fantasy seemed a prime contender for the 1964 Oscar.*

Dark, and *The Americanization of Emily*), and such bawdiness of line and situation in many more as to rouse pro-censorship forces throughout the land. The release, early in December, of Billy Wilder's satiric *Kiss Me, Stupid* brought matters to a head when the Roman Catholic Legion of Decency gave the film a "C" (condemned) rating, and then proceeded to attack the industry's own, self-regulatory Production Code Administration.

By year-end, it was clear that the main push in 1965 would be toward some form of film classification, with the influential New York State Regents already on record as favoring such a move. Even the industry, traditionally opposed to censorship in any guise, began through its Motion Picture Association of America to admit that "advisory"—but not compulsory—classification might be a good thing; and particularly if the industry assumed the role of doing the "advising."

Film Trends. Dominating American screens for

much of the year were precisely those films most responsible for the censorship controversy. Dollar for dollar, perhaps the most profitable film of the year was Joseph E. Levine's highly spiced *The Carpetbaggers*. It brought in over $12,000,000 in the domestic market alone. In *The Outrage*, a Westernization of the Japanese *Rashomon*, audiences witnessed four versions of the same rape. In *A House Is Not a Home*, another Joseph Levine offering, the subject was the inner torments suffered by the madam of a high-class bawdyhouse.

Sadism or sex, or both, filled the year's two vastly popular James Bond thrillers, *From Russia with Love* and *Goldfinger*, as well as most of the year's costlier comedies—*Move Over Darling*, *The Pink Panther*, *Good Neighbor Sam*, *A Shot in the Dark*, *Send Me No Flowers*, and *Sex and the Single Girl*. To these might be added such widely seen imports as Ingmar Bergman's *The Silence*, the Italian pseudo-documentaries *Women of the World* and *Malamondo*, and Vittorio de Sica's *Marriage Italian Style*, with Sophia Loren and Marcello Mastroianni.

Other Directions. Not all the films of 1964, however, were by sex possessed. Although Becket and his king had their moments of amorous dalliance, the handsome Hal Wallis production of the Jean Anouilh play struck at the philosophic conflict between church and state. *Dr. Strangelove*, *Fail-Safe*, and

Seven Days in May dealt sharply and perceptively (if somewhat melodramatically) with the fear of a militarist take-over in this age of awesome and spreading nuclear power.

Racial tensions, which flamed high throughout 1964, found cinematic expression in such films of contemporary Negro life as *Black Like Me; Living Between Two Worlds; One Potato, Two Potato; The Cool World;* and *Nothing But a Man*. Three feature-length documentaries, patently fashioned after television's "specials," spoke eloquently of John F. Kennedy (*Four Days in November*), Winston Churchill (*The Finest Hour*), and the army's prolonged joust with the late Wisconsin Senator Joseph McCarthy (*Point of Order*).

On the Lighter Side, the year's most expensive—and, by year's end, most honored—production was George Cukor's sumptuous yet tasteful filming of the Lerner and Loewe musical *My Fair Lady*. Budgeted at $17,000,000, the critics agreed that it was worth every penny, with special praise going to Rex Harrison, from the original cast, for his performance as Professor Henry Higgins. There was equal critical agreement that the movie find of the year was Harrison's costar from the Broadway company, Julie Andrews.

Although Audrey Hepburn received the plum title role in *My Fair Lady*, Miss Andrews scored

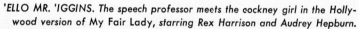

'ELLO MR. 'IGGINS. The speech professor meets the cockney girl in the Hollywood version of My Fair Lady, starring Rex Harrison and Audrey Hepburn.

Warner Bros.

handsomely in Walt Disney's musical version of *Mary Poppins*, a lively, trick-filled fantasy. She then went on to further triumphs as the touching and sympathetic heroine of *The Americanization of Emily*. *The Unsinkable Molly Brown*, starring Debbie Reynolds, marked the return of the lavish M-G-M "big musicals," but the surprise hit of the year was a "little musical" from England, *A Hard Day's Night*, starring the teen-agers' recording favorites, the Beatles (see MUSIC, POPULAR). On film, they proved to be zany, fresh, and eminently appealing to adults as well—as indicated by a domestic gross estimated to run in excess of $10,000,000. Also well received by the critics and public alike was the Greek-based adventure film *Topkapi*, with Melina Mercouri, Maximilian Schell, and Peter Ustinov. And a modest little film for children, *Island of the Blue Dolphins*, ran up an astonishing $3,000,000 gross. This seemed to prove that pictures did not have to be sexy to be successful.

New Techniques. For two days in September, the motion picture industry focused its attention upon a filmed version of the Broadway production of *Hamlet*, directed by Sir John Gielgud and starring Richard Burton. It was not a new passion for culture that attracted them, but rather the incredible speed with which the film was put together. Using nine television-type "Electronovision" cameras, the entire play was filmed during the course of three actual stage performances and released in less than 90 days. No less impressive, in two days of simultaneous screenings in almost 1,000 theaters in the United States and Canada, the film earned something over $3,000,000. See LITERATURE (Close-Up).

The most advanced motion picture techniques were on display at the New York World's Fair. In exhibit after exhibit, films were shown not on one, but on many screens—three placed side by side at Johnson's Wax; three that joined together or moved freely about the stage, integrated with live performers, at DuPont; perhaps two dozen of varying sizes and shapes at IBM; and upwards of a hundred in the U.S. Pavilion, each flashing a brief glimpse of some aspect of the historical and scientific development of America as the spectator glided past in special cars.

The World's Fair of 1939 had provided previews of Cinerama, 3-D, and stereo sound; it is just possible that the films of the 1964 Fair presented a no less accurate prediction of the shape of things that will be developed in the future.

Awards in 1964 included:
Academy of Motion Picture Arts and Sciences Award for 1963 to: *Tom Jones*, best picture; Patricia Neal in *Hud*, best actress; Sidney Poitier in *Lilies of the Field*, best actor; Tony Richardson, *Tom Jones*, best director; Margaret Rutherford in *The VIP's* and Melvyn Douglas in *Hud*, best supporting actress and actor; $8\frac{1}{2}$, best foreign film.   ARTHUR KNIGHT

See also DEATHS OF NOTABLE PERSONS; Section One, ALISTAIR COOKE ON THE ARTS.

MOTORBOAT RACING. See BOATS AND BOATING.

MOZAMBIQUE, a Portuguese overseas territory in East Africa, was confronted with a long-threatened rebellion in September. Rebel forces attacked Portuguese military posts along a 700-mile area. On November 19, the government reported its first casualties, and on December 16 the rebels claimed they had killed 59 Portuguese soldiers over a two-month period.

The outbreak followed a threat from Dr. Eduardo Mondlane, leader of the Mozambique Liberation Front (MLF). In March, Dr. Mondlane said troops dedicated to freeing Mozambique from Portuguese control were then training in Algeria, the United Arab Republic, and other parts of Africa. He declared they would attack in the fall and that Mozambique would be free within five years.

Population: 7,000,000. **Government:** Governor General Rear Admiral Manuel Maria Sarmento. **Foreign Trade:** exports, $91,000,000; imports, $136,-000,000. **Principal Exports:** cashew nuts, cotton, maize, mining products, sugar.   BENJAMIN E. THOMAS

See also AFRICA.

MUNICIPAL GOVERNMENT. See CITY.

MUSEUMS. More than 4,500,000 persons visited the Smithsonian Institution's new Museum of History and Technology during the first eight months it was open in 1964.

Although only 20 per cent of the exhibits were installed, the institution was displaying many famous objects. The flag that inspired "The Star-Spangled Banner" hung proudly in the central hall.

President Lyndon B. Johnson, in dedicating the museum located on the Mall in Washington, D.C., said that the exhibits would show Americans and foreign visitors how this nation had worked to develop its resources and its way of life.

New Projects. The Museum of Modern Art in New York City reopened on May 25, after altering parts of its older structure and expanding into new wings. The President's wife, Lady Bird, spoke at the opening to a large crowd of special guests. While the building was closed, the museum lent many of its paintings for temporary exhibition in other cities. Also in Manhattan, The Gallery of Modern Art, designed by Edward D. Stone, opened in March.

Los Angeles County, California, started construction of a Hollywood Museum to interpret motion pictures as a medium of communication. In Cleveland, Ohio, Western Reserve Historical Society began building an Auto-Aviation Museum. New museums opened at Horseshoe Bend National Military Park, Alabama; at Fort Pulaski National Monument, Georgia; Stones River National Military Park, Tennessee; Colorado National Monument, Colorado; Mount Rainier and Olympic National Parks, Washington; and Whitman Mission National Monument, Washington.

Installations. The Chicago Natural History Museum installed exhibits on Chinese life under the

NEW HOME FOR OLD GLORY. Smithsonian Institution's new Museum of History and Technology, opened in 1964, is the home of the flag that inspired the U.S. national anthem.

Manchu emperors. And The Art Institute of Chicago opened a Junior Museum for children. A new hall in the National Museum at Washington, D.C., showed many aspects of Asian and African cultures. In New York City, the American Museum of Natural History completed renovation of its well-known Hall of North American Birds. The Brooklyn (N.Y.) Museum restored the 17th century rooms of a Dutch colonist's Long Island home in its halls.

Exhibitions. Museums celebrated the 400th anniversary of the births of Shakespeare and Galileo. The Virginia Museum of Fine Arts in Richmond and the Detroit Institute of Art shared a major exhibition, "The World of Shakespeare." Elizabethan paintings, drawings, and decorative arts were displayed along with rare books and manuscripts. The Walters Art Gallery in Baltimore, Md.; the Gibbes Art Gallery in Charleston, S.C.; the Henry E. Huntington Library and Art Gallery, in San Marino, Calif.; and other institutions also held special Shakespeare exhibitions. The California Academy of Sciences in San Francisco and the American Museum of Natural History in New York City presented planetarium programs honoring Galileo.

Among the important traveling exhibitions was a selection of several hundred objects illustrating 7,000 years of Iranian art. The Smithsonian Traveling Exhibition Service assembled the specimens from collections in Tehran and elsewhere. Following a showing at the National Gallery of Art, the exhibition began a tour of other museums. RALPH H. LEWIS

See also CRIME; LITERATURE (Close-Up); PAINTING AND SCULPTURE.

MUSIAL, STANLEY FRANK (1920-   ), former St. Louis Cardinal outfielder, was named director of the national Physical Fitness Program in February, 1964. He ended 22 years as a player in 1963, and then was made a vice-president of the Cardinals. Stan made two hits against the Cincinnati Reds in his farewell game on September 29, which gave him a lifetime total of 3,630 hits in 3,026 games.

When Stan hung up that old No. 6 uniform, he had set 17 major league and 30 National League records. The National voted him its most valuable player three times. He also held seven batting titles.

Stan Musial was born in Donora, Pa. He played with a minor league team before joining the Cardinals in September, 1941, as a pitcher. He came to be admired by players, umpires, sportswriters, and fans as "Stan the Man," and as one of the nicest guys in the game.

Stan married a hometown girl, Lillian Labash, a Donora storekeeper's daughter. They have three daughters and a son, Richard Kerr Musial, who is married and has one son.

425

MUSIC

FOR THOSE WHO TAKE the long view, the most important event for music came on December 2, when President Lyndon B. Johnson took part in groundbreaking ceremonies for the $31,000,000 John F. Kennedy Center for the Performing Arts. Located in Washington, D.C., on the banks of the Potomac, the center is scheduled for completion in the autumn of 1967.

As now planned, the center will contain an opera house with approximately 2,200 seats and a 2,750-seat hall for symphonic music. There will also be a 1,150-seat theater, and a 500-seat studio theater for experimental productions. See KENNEDY, JOHN FITZGERALD (pictures).

Los Angeles Center. While Washington watched the start of its cultural center, Los Angeles was opening the Pavilion, a 3,250-seat symphony hall-opera house which is the first completed unit of the $33,500,000 Music Center for the Performing Arts. The inaugural concert featured a long-time resident of the area, violinist Jascha Heifetz, in one of his now rare public appearances, with the Los Angeles Philharmonic under the youthful Zubin Mehta. Still to be built in 1965 are two additional buildings, a 2,100-seat theater, and a small, 750-seat theater-in-the-round. See LOS ANGELES.

Problems in Acoustics. As new halls were being built, older ones, after much controversy, were being modified in the endless pursuit of acoustical excellence. Philharmonic Hall, in New York's Lincoln Center for the Performing Arts, underwent sonic surgery directed by Heinrich Keilholz (whose previous patients include the Vienna State Opera and Severance Hall in Cleveland). It was judged much improved. Also, the Royal Festival Hall in London, a controversial auditorium since its opening in 1951, added electronic reinforcement in the bass range, which was found to be deficient.

Major Tours took the Pittsburgh Symphony overseas in August for an 11-week junket through Europe and the Middle East, with William Steinberg conducting. Scheduled to follow the international trail in April, 1965, was the Cleveland Orchestra under George Szell. The Philadelphia Orchestra began its 65th season in August with 29 road concerts as part of a transcontinental tour.

Visitors to the United States included the Vienna Symphony under Wolfgang Swallisch, one of the few major figures among Europe's young conductors to have delayed an American debut until he could bring his own orchestra along. In the 1964-1965 season, the London Symphony visited 20 U.S. cities as part of a round-the-world tour to mark its 60th birthday. Georg Solti directed most of the concerts.

The Conductors. Missing from the London podium, and mourned throughout the world of music,

Larry Sherman, Black Star

CLASSIC SETTING. The Pittsburgh Symphony performed in the flood-lit Temple of Bacchus, in Athens, during an 11-week overseas tour.

427

was Pierre Monteux, chief conductor of the London Symphony from 1961 until his death (at the age of 89) on July 1. Monteux, who had brought greatness to the orchestras of Boston and San Francisco, and was senior conductor of Chicago's Ravinia Festival for 20 years, had built a supreme reputation both as a champion of new music and as an eloquent interpreter of the classics.

Absent from the autumn musical scene, but only temporarily, was Leonard Bernstein who took a sabbatical year from the New York Philharmonic. Replacing him were Josef Krips, William Steinberg, and other guests. Bernstein had concluded his spring concerts with music of the *avant garde*. His guests offered, as if in rebuttal, a Bruckner cycle.

A new face on the U.S. scene was Hermann Scherchen, who at 73 made his American debut at the invitation of the Philadelphia Orchestra. His wide-ranging repertory of baroque music, unfamiliar Haydn, and little known Mahler scores highlighted his interpretive gifts.

Too Many Orchestras. London, with five symphony orchestras, was faced with an embarrassment of artistic riches—and box-office poverty. The BBC Symphony, subsidized as part of the national broadcasting service, was financially safe, and the London Symphony, the oldest and, momentarily, the best, enjoyed some security. But the London Philharmonic was in difficulties, the Philharmonic was reorganizing (after its highly profitable association with British Columbia Records ended), and the Royal Philharmonic feared losing the designation "Royal," when its affiliation with the Royal Philharmonic Society expired. The orchestra was founded 18 years ago by the late Sir Thomas Beecham.

Strauss Centennial. For many, 1964 will be best remembered as the year of the Richard Strauss centennial. The best way to honor a much-played composer is to revive his neglected works, and in the case of Strauss this meant his operas. His native city, Munich, led the world with a festive series of 11 Strauss operas and theater scores.

The Major U.S. Opera Companies made more limited efforts to mark the anniversary. Operatically, the United States is a possession of Italy, and each major company enjoyed the longest season in its history with Italian repertory as its primary claim to audience appeal.

The Metropolitan found itself as popular as any Broadway musical in the spring, when it presented a special series in connection with the New York World's Fair. Its 80th season opened October 12 with Joan Sutherland in a favorite vehicle, Donizetti's *Lucia di Lammermoor*.

The main emphasis at the Metropolitan, however, was on the future. In the autumn of 1965, the Metropolitan Opera National Company would first take to the road under the co-sponsorship of the John F. Kennedy Center. Four works would be in the repertory of the initial season, and the troupe was already looking forward to visiting 65 cities in the United States and Canada in 34 weeks.

Another big date on the future calendar was the opening night in 1966 when the company would inaugurate its new Metropolitan Opera House in Lincoln Center with the première of an American opera, *Antony and Cleopatra*, commissioned for the occasion from Samuel Barber. The final opening night in the historic old Broadway house would be a new production of the opera that inaugurated the theater in 1883, Gounod's *Faust*.

La Scala in Russia. The cosmopolitanism of contemporary operatic theaters was noted in September when Milan's fabled La Scala went on tour to the Soviet Union with an American Negro, Leontyne Price, and a Swedish diva, Birgit Nilsson, as leading artists. Said Scala's director, Dr. Antonio Ghiringhelli, "They are as much a part of my theater as any Italian singer."

Herbert von Karajan, meanwhile, after previous alarums and excursions, once more resigned as artistic head of the Vienna State Opera, and one of the great singers of the century, Marian Anderson, made her farewell tour, after a career of 40 years.

Recordings. The Louisville Orchestra, which normally would not be a strong contender for a major recording contract, could look back in 1964 on 10 years of work on its own label. In the period, it had issued disks of 150 compositions—nearly all of them significant examples of contemporary music. None of the big musical organizations could point to any comparable contribution.

Indeed, 1964 was a fairly uninteresting year in terms of new recordings, a situation highlighted by the fact that a conductor dead since 1957, Arturo Toscanini, got a posthumous five-year contract for the release of broadcast recordings. Robert C. Marsh

See also Deaths of Notable Persons; Recording; Section One, Alistair Cooke on The Arts.

THE PAVILION, a concert-opera house, was the first of three buildings to open in the Music Center for the Performing Arts, at Los Angeles.

Welton Becket & Associates

Wide World

THE BEATLES conquered the world of pop music in 1964. From left, meeting the New York press, are Paul McCartney, Ringo Starr, George Harrison, and John Lennon.

MUSIC, POPULAR. The year 1964 was overwhelmingly the Year of the Beatles in popular music, a field that is not unknown for its cultivation of fads and fancies.

Who were the Beatles? They were a rock-and-roll quartet from Liverpool, England, who wore Edwardian-styled clothes and haircuts like helmets, and who, in addition to wallets bulging with royalties from record sales, carried with them, wherever they went, a rambunctious and irreverent sense of fun.

Three of the young men thwacked away at electric guitars; the fourth pounded a set of drums. All of them sang, shook their mop tops, and clowned their way through their concerts, though their voices could be only rarely heard over the screams of thousands of teen-age girls in their bouncing and squirming audiences. And this latter, interesting phenomenon occurred wherever guitarists George Harrison, 22; Paul McCartney, 23; John Lennon, 24; and drummer Ringo Starr, 24, appeared.

Beatlemania occurred in Glasgow, Scotland, where 3,500 shriekers caused a theater balcony to rock and roll dangerously. Beatlemania occurred in Copenhagen, Denmark, where, even with Ringo absent because of a tonsillectomy, police drove their motorcycles, sirens screaming, along the sidewalks to break up a crowd of 3,000 teens who were howling their heads off outside the concert hall. It occurred a week later in Adelaide, Australia.

The Beatles were afraid to leave their aircraft at the airport in Beirut, Lebanon, and elsewhere. And, of course, during their tours of the United States, the first in the winter, the second in late summer, U.S. girldom could do no less than their counterparts overseas.

At Carnegie Hall in February, 2,900 girls drowned out the quartet and pelted the stage with jelly beans, which became a trademark of Beatlemania. In Chicago during the second U.S. tour, 5,000 screaming teens turned up to greet them at the airport. It was the same everywhere in the 30 or so U.S. cities the Beatles invaded in 1964: waves of baying teens and long lines of police, one of whom stood through a concert in Washington, D.C., with a bullet in each ear to shut out the noise.

Merry Money. And it all happened, be it said, to the merry jingle of cash registers. Throughout, the Beatles enjoyed the show, and took their massive success in stride.

In sum, about 10,000,000 Beatle records were sold; their movie, *A Hard Day's Night*, reaped $5,600,000 in six weeks in rentals at U.S. movie theaters. Also, Beatlemania caused the United States and Great Britain to be showered with Beatle products, many of them unauthorized. Indeed, London's *Daily Mail* estimated that Beatlemania earned $56,000,000 abroad, and declared that it had boosted Britain's wobbly balance of payments.

Inevitably, the group became a factor in the Cold War. The Moscow youth newspaper, *Moskovsky Kosomlets*, humorlessly stated in February that Beatle-type music was encouraged by the British government "to divert the attention of young people from politics, from bitter reflections about desecrated ideals and shattered hopes."

Mersey Beat. Who were John, Paul, Ringo, and George, and how did the tumult begin?

It started in Liverpool, where the Beatles, in the 1950's, were just one of a great many rock-and-roll groups who practiced what is known as the Mersey sound, or beat, after a river that flows by the bleak, industrial city. The Beatles originally called themselves the Quarrymen Skiffle Group, later, the Moondogs. In 1955, they changed their name to the Beatles, punning on the phrase, Mersey Beat. Ringo joined the group in 1962.

Enter Epstein. The Beatles' fortune was made when Brian Epstein, 29, saw them perform in a run-down, converted wine cellar. He recognized, beneath their black leather jackets and jeans, the "appeal of their beat," their humor, and "a quality of personal presence that seemed to be full of possibilities." Epstein, whose family owns a chain of record stores, became their manager.

The big break came in October, 1963, with a performance at London's Palladium. This was followed by the royal command performance. After Ed Sullivan saw thousands of teen-agers milling about the group at London Airport, he negotiated for three appearances on his TV show. Then, backed by all the engines of publicity—1,000,000 copies of a Beatle tabloid distributed to disk jockeys and press, and a recorded interview, which plugged their big hit, "I Want to Hold Your Hand"—the group appeared in the United States, and the rest became part of the history of 1964.   MARK M. PERLBERG

Jazz Music

Japan became a new center for jazz artists and stars in 1964. Duke Ellington took his band on its first visit there. Harry James, Count Basie, Gerry Mulligan, and Oscar Peterson were among the more than 30 well-known leaders whose groups were welcomed by young Japanese fans.

A Berlin Jazz Festival featured 100 musicians, most of them Americans, such as Brubeck, Miles Davis, J. J. Johnson, and Coleman Hawkins. Similar programs were presented in France and in the Scandinavian countries.

Several forms of controversial *avant-garde* jazz, played by Jimmy Giuffre, Cecil Taylor, Paul Bley, and Rod Levitt, were the subject of frequent debate, and were presented mainly in New York City. One of the most promising new stars was a Haitian-born pianist-composer, Andrew Hill, who played in a harmonically complex style.   LEONARD G. FEATHER

See also DEATHS OF NOTABLE PERSONS; RECORDING.

NATIONAL DEFENSE

W ITH ITS NUCLEAR FLANK secure, the United States sharp-
ened the mobility and flexibility of its conventional forces in 1964.
World experts agreed the U.S. atomic arsenal was so powerful it could
obliterate Soviet society even if a surprise attack virtually destroyed the
United States. But communist-backed "brushfire" wars still threatened
almost anywhere on the globe. To meet this threat the U.S. army, navy,
air force, and marines trained under combat conditions with new techniques and equipment, seeking ever greater mobility and flexibility.

Air Assault II was the most significant exercise of the year. In autumn,
it pitted the army's experimental 11th Air Assault Division and 10th Air

HEADS UP! Aircraft rises from the carrier Enterprise, which circled the world
with the cruiser Long Beach and frigate Bainbridge without refueling.

PICTURES OF THE YEAR / Winfield Parks, *National Geographic*

Official U.S. Navy Photo

EQUATION that unlocked the atom is formed on deck of nuclear-powered Enterprise. *At right, also under nuclear power, is navy's* Long Beach *and* Bainbridge.

Transport Brigade against the veteran 82nd Airborne Division in over 4,500,000 acres of North and South Carolina. Involved were more than 34,000 men, 4,000 vehicles, and 700 aircraft.

The maneuvers tested the value of the futuristic "flying division." The 11th's 15,954 men boasted 459 helicopters and light planes instead of the usual 103. Where other divisions rolled on the ground the 11th flew, and instead of heavy artillery it packed rocket-firing aircraft. Against the 82nd Airborne "aggressor," the 11th sought to prove it could move "farther, faster, and fresher." The air force "wholesaled" supplies to bases near the "combat zone" and the 11th's own aircraft handled "retail" delivery to its units. Some difficulties arose over close air support and quick resupply, but preliminary reports held that the "flying division" had passed its big test and that it was here to stay.

Gold Fire I, held at the same time, teamed the army and air force in Missouri. It tested new Tactical Air Command techniques in giving close air support to the First Infantry Division.

Steelpike was a navy and marine show, the largest amphibious exercise since the Korean War. The 2nd Marine Division sailed from North Carolina and landed on October 26 at Huelva, Spain, where Span-

ish marines and navy units joined the exercise. The $10,200,000 operation marked the first use of merchant ships in a transatlantic military maneuver. And it was the first combatlike test of the marines' SATS (Short Airfield for Tactical Support), a portable landing field made of aluminum planks. Tragedy marred the maneuvers, however. A few hours after landings began, two helicopters collided and crashed in flames, killing nine marines and injuring 13 others.

Vietnam was the ultimate testing ground of the new concepts in mobility and flexibility. The army quietly sent some elements of the experimental 11th Air Assault Division there to teach what they had learned to the men actually fighting a "brushfire" war. See ASIA; VIETNAM.

The U.S. build-up in Vietnam, begun in December, 1961, increased during 1964 from 16,500 U.S. adviser-instructors to about 24,000. U.S. battle deaths rose, too, from one in 1961 to 136 in 1964 for a total of 246. It was reported that 11 Americans were captured and 19 were missing. The number of wounded since 1961 was 1,546.

Reverses plagued the U.S. effort as Vietnamese political instability emboldened the guerrillas. On May 2, the U.S.S. *Card,* a small aircraft transport ferrying helicopters, sank in Saigon harbor, a 3-by-30-foot hole blown in her hull. The ship was refloated eight hours later at high tide, little damaged. Far worse, on November 1, communist mortar fire at Bien Hoa killed four Americans, destroyed five B-57 jet bombers, and damaged 22 other aircraft. On Christmas Eve, a bomb exploded in the seven-story officers' billet in Saigon, killing two Americans and injuring 65. Also wounded were 41 Vietnamese and one Australian. At year's end, perhaps the biggest battle since Dien Bien Phu, 10 years earlier, raged at Binh Gia, 40 miles east of Saigon, with hundreds of casualties on both sides.

The first Medal of Honor for Vietnam service went to Captain Roger H. C. Donlon, 30, a member of the army's green-bereted Special Forces. Although wounded four times, he directed the defense against a five-hour, predawn assault on a camp at Nam Dong, in July, and then helped give first aid to the other wounded defenders. Congress authorized the Medal of Honor and other decorations for Vietnam service on July 25, 1963.

Gulf of Tonkin. On August 2, the U.S.S. *Maddox*, an American destroyer patrolling the Gulf of Tonkin off North Vietnam, was attacked by three North Vietnamese torpedo boats. The *Maddox* and fighter planes from the carrier U.S.S. *Ticonderoga* damaged

two and left the third powerless in the water. The Americans suffered no casualties or damages. Two days later, more Viet Cong torpedo boats launched a still fiercer attack at night against the *Maddox* and another destroyer, the U.S.S. *C. Turner Joy*. They were driven off, without a score, with at least two of their number sunk.

Within hours, the United States retaliated. Carrier-based planes, flying 64 sorties, destroyed or damaged 25 North Vietnamese torpedo boats, four of their bases, and an oil depot. Two U.S. planes fell. The pilot of one plane was captured, and the other was missing and presumed dead. See ASIA; VIETNAM.

Budget. The Congress of the United States appropriated $46,752,051,000 in defense funds for fiscal 1965. This gave the army $11,365,325,000, the navy and marines $14,252,028,000, the air force $18,499,-833,000, and other Department of Defense agencies $2,634,865,000. Congress also set a manpower ceiling of 2,634,865.

Separate legislation appropriated $1,570,968,000 for military construction, including $939,817,000 for new building at 585 military bases, and $631,-151,000 for military family housing.

Congress also provided a cost-of-living increase to military personnel, at an annual cost of $207,-519,000. It was a flat $2\frac{1}{2}$ per cent for everyone with

SPREADING WINGS. The F-111, a fighter formerly called TFX, above, can change its wing positions in flight. Wings are extended in take-off. With wings swept back, its speed is increased. The bomber, below, can fly at over 2,000 mph.

more than two years' service, plus $8\frac{1}{2}$ per cent for commissioned officers with less than two years' service. There was no increase for enlisted personnel with less than two years' service.

United States Army

The 972,000-man army, delighted with its flying division, looked farther ahead. It pondered whether to seek to keep its experimental 11th Air Assault Division as a permanent unit or disband it and make the 82nd and 101st Airborne divisions over in its image. Increased airlift, especially in big jet transports like the C-141, added considerably to army mobility and flexibility. President Lyndon B. Johnson stressed this capacity in a June 3 speech, in which he said that six divisions plus supporting units "can be moved into action in a few weeks."

Firepower increased, too. The army replaced its 25-mile-range, liquid-fueled Corporal tactical missiles with 75-mile-range, solid-fueled Sergeants, and its liquid-fueled, 100-mile Redstones with solid-fueled Pershings, which have a 400-mile range.

Deployment. The army's 16 combat-ready divisions include six infantry, five mechanized, three armored, and two airborne. Five were in Europe, two in Korea, one in Hawaii, and eight in strategic reserve on the U.S. mainland.

Special Forces, the army's green-bereted élite corps of antiguerrilla fighter-instructors, increased from six groups to seven. Since 1961, the Special Forces personnel had risen from 3,000 to more than 12,000. About 5,000 men served in 49 nations, including more than 1,000 in Vietnam.

United States Navy

Nuclear Task Force One. The navy, with 859,000 personnel (including 190,000 marines) and 840 ships, paraded the pride of the fleet—the nuclear-powered Task Force One—on a 65-day, 30,000-mile global voyage with only six ports of call. The carrier U.S.S. *Enterprise*, the world's largest ship, the missile cruiser U.S.S. *Long Beach*, and the missile-carrying frigate U.S.S. *Bainbridge* sailed from the Mediterranean July 31 on Project Sea Orbit. The ships reached their ports of Norfolk, Va., and Charleston, S.C., on October 3.

In between, the navy ships visited Karachi, Pakistan; Freemantle, Melbourne, and Sydney, Australia; Wellington, New Zealand; and Rio de Janeiro, Brazil. "Underway visits" were made along the west coast of Africa and the east coast of South America, with aircraft flying guests to the moving deck of the vast *Enterprise*.

The cruise was historic, paralleling the five-month circumnavigation by the coal-burning "Great White Fleet" of U.S. warships sent around the world by President Theodore Roosevelt in 1907. Made without refueling stops, it could score a point. The nuclear-conscious navy hoped it would convince Congress to appropriate funds for reactors for the

next carrier in fiscal 1967. The latest, the U.S.S. *John F. Kennedy*, a Forrestal-class attack carrier begun in 1964, is conventionally fueled.

The Nuclear Subs. The year marked the 10th anniversary since the first nuclear-powered submarine, *Nautilus*, slid down the ways. By 1964 all new subs were nuclear-powered (see ARMED FORCES OF THE WORLD). The navy had 18 combat-ready Polaris-firing subs on station in the Atlantic, the Mediterranean, and the Pacific. Two were in dry-dock; others were either launched, being built, or authorized.

The Marines perfected vertical envelopment, using new helicopters and aircraft, portable landing strips, and communications and radar gear. Always ready to fight, the 190,000-man force was organized in three divisions and three air wings, plus the nucleus of a fourth of each, in the Atlantic and Pacific Fleet Marine Forces.

The Coast Guard, a Department of the Treasury agency in peacetime, saved nearly 3,000 lives and rescued property valued at more than $2,100,000,000, about five times its $414,300,000 budget for the year. Patrols off Florida picked up more than 1,000 Cuban refugees during 1964, bringing the total to 6,000 since 1959. The coast guard had 32,000 officers and men on active duty; it operated 36 large cutters and 290 other seacraft, along with 1,200 shore units, and 170 airplanes and helicopters.

United States Air Force

The air force's major role remained strategic. It maintained nuclear deterrence with a "mix" of intercontinental ballistic missiles (ICBM's) and manned bombers.

ICBM totals included 650 Minuteman, 108 Titan, and 95 Atlas missiles. Expectations were that these would level off at 1,000 Minuteman and slightly more than 50 Titan ICBM's.

Aircraft in the Strategic Air Command (SAC) included 90 supersonic B-58 Hustler jet bombers, and 600 B-52 heavy jet bombers, as well as 400 B-47 medium jet bombers, which were being systematically discarded. Half of this force was always on 15-minute ground alert, and several stayed in the air at all times. Two-thirds of the B-52's carried Hound Dog nuclear bombardment missiles.

Continental Defense depended primarily upon the Ballistic Missile Early Warning System (BMEWS), three huge radar stations at Fylingdales Moor, England; Clear, Alaska; and Thule, Greenland. Their nets across the North Pole would sound a 15-minute warning of any Soviet ICBM attack against North America.

Department of Defense

Secretary of Defense Robert S. McNamara stuck to his doctrine that his instruction from the President is to provide the best possible defense at the least possible cost. As usual, he moved in controversy.

Wide World

NEW LEADERS. *General John P. McConnell, left, became boss of the air force, while army General Earle G. Wheeler was named chairman of the joint chiefs of staff.*

Economy Purge. During 1964, McNamara declared 158 more bases obsolete and ordered them merged, reduced, or shut down. Hit hardest were the 11 naval shipyards. Two of them will close and two will merge.

On April 24, he closed 55 military facilities in 29 states and eight in four foreign countries. He said this would save $68,000,000 a year and eliminate 10,056 military and civilian jobs.

On November 18, he closed an additional 80 installations in 33 states and 15 abroad. Entailed was an estimated annual saving of $477,000,000 and the elimination of 63,401 military and civilian jobs. The yards in this batch included the 163-year-old New York Naval Shipyard in Brooklyn, employing 9,600 civilians and 2,000 navy personnel. It will close down in 18 months. Also hit was the Portsmouth, (N.H.), yard, to close within 10 years. The San Francisco and Mare Island, Calif., yards will be consolidated. Also going out of business were six strategic bomber bases, 14 ICBM bases, and three army ports of embarkation.

In each case, the Secretary pledged no security impairment, and said military personnel will be transferred and civilian workers offered other jobs. If necessary, they would be retrained and moved to another location at government expense, he declared.

The Reserves. In his second "realignment" of the reserves since the 1961 Berlin call-up snafu, Secretary McNamara in effect abolished the organized army reserve. He announced on December 12 that he was scrapping six army reserve divisions and putting what was left into the national guard, which itself lost 15 of its 23 divisions. The upshot was that, instead of a 300,000-man reserve and a 400,000-man national guard, he had a 550,000-man guard. He said the result would be an annual saving of $150,-000,000, plus improved combat-readiness through better organization, training, and equipment for eight divisions and 16 brigades.

The Secretary also wiped out the army, navy, and air force reserve units on Capitol Hill. He thereby demoted about 75 members of Congress and 5,000 others from the "ready reserve" to "stand-by" status. His argument was that it was foolish to suppose that many would be available for mobilization. He also forbade the services to take legislators on junkets unless he first approves. Outcries came from the Reserve Officers' Association and some members of Congress. But the President was on his side.

Draft. On presidential orders, the Pentagon began a reappraisal of the draft. Officials said the draft would end only if "adequate substitute means to recruit soldiers" are found.

Research and Development. The controversial TFX (Tactical Fighter, Experimental) aircraft annoyed doubters and delighted admirers by flying on December 11, 10 days ahead of schedule. Wing flap trouble kept the supersonic craft down to 230 miles an hour 15,000 feet over Fort Worth, Tex., but test supervisers hailed the first tryout as "very successful."

Now called F-111, it is designed to serve both the air force and the navy. It can adjust its wings in flight and hence increase its speed to 2,000 mph. By altering its wing angle it can take off and land on comparatively short runways. Controversy raged in 1963 when McNamara awarded a contract for 22 experimental models to General Dynamics Corporation of Fort Worth, and Grumman Aircraft Engineering Corporation of Bethpage, N.Y. Both the air force and the navy had favored a rival design by the Boeing Company of Seattle, Wash.

If it works, the Pentagon plans to buy 1,500 for the air force and 200 for the navy for about $7,500,-000,000. Secretary McNamara contends having one basic design will save $1,000,000,000. Australia has ordered 24 at a cost of $125,000,000.

Another controversial plane, the supersonic RB-70 reconnaissance-bomber, underwent two test flights during the year. But McNamara said only two, instead of three, prototypes would be built because of technical difficulties.

President Johnson announced four new projects that had been developed in secret: the A-11, a jet armed with air-to-air missiles that flies faster than 2,000 miles per hour and higher than 70,000 feet; the SR-71 reconnaissance jet, capable of faster and higher performance; a radar that "looks" over the horizon to spot missile launchings, and two weapons systems that could knock down armed satellites. Some experts saw the A-11 and SR-71 as modified versions of a new and better U-2 spyplane. McNamara identified the satellite-killers as Nike-Zeus and a souped-up Thor.

Ordered into development was the biggest airplane of all time, a military transport designed to carry up to 600 passengers; operate on short, crude runways; and fly 600 miles an hour for 6,000 miles. Designated the CX, it was called for by fiscal 1969, at an expected cost of $750,000,000, with production models at $34,000,000 each. It would replace the big C-141, now in quantity production.

Personnel Changes. Cyrus R. Vance succeeded Roswell L. Gilpatrick as deputy secretary of defense. Stephen Ailes replaced Vance as Secretary of the Army (see AILES, STEPHEN). General Earle G. Wheeler became chairman of the joint chiefs of staff, succeeding General Maxwell D. Taylor (see WHEELER, EARLE G.). General Harold K. Johnson replaced Wheeler as army chief of staff. Admiral U.S. Grant, Jr., succeeded Admiral Harry D. Felt as commander in chief, Pacific. General Wallace M. Greene, Jr., was sworn in as commandant of the Marine Corps, replacing General David M. Shoup.

U.S. Navy

FOUND AND LOST. Topside rudder of nuclear submarine Thresher, which sank in 1963 off Boston with 129 men, was photographed in 1964.

General William C. Westmoreland replaced General Paul D. Harkins as commander, Military Advisory Command, Vietnam. Lieutenant General John D. Ryan succeeded General Thomas S. Power as commander, Strategic Air Command. General Howell M. Estes, Jr., replaced General Joe W. Kelley as commander, Military Air Transport Command. General John P. McConnell was designated to succeed General Curtis E. LeMay as air force chief of staff, effective Jan. 31, 1965.   WARREN ROGERS

See also CIVIL DEFENSE; NORTH ATLANTIC TREATY ORGANIZATION (NATO).

NATIONAL PARKS. See PARKS.

NATO. See NORTH ATLANTIC TREATY ORGANIZATION (NATO).

NAVY, U.S. See NATIONAL DEFENSE.

NEAR EAST. See MIDDLE EAST.

United Press Int.

RIGHTS LEADERS met in New York. From left, Bayard Rustin, former CORE field secretary; Jack Greenberg, NAACP chief counsel; Whitney M. Young, Jr., National Urban League executive director; James Farmer, CORE director; Roy Wilkins, executive secretary, NAACP; the Reverend Martin Luther King, Jr., head of the Southern Christian Leadership Conference; John Lewis, chairman of the Student Nonviolent Co-ordinating Committee (SNCC); A. Philip Randolph, head of the Negro American Labor Council; and Courtney Pace, a member of the SNCC group.

NEGRO. The signing of the Civil Rights Act by President Lyndon B. Johnson on July 2, after sustained opposition in the House and a 73-day filibuster in the Senate, was the most significant event of the "Negro Revolution."

This most comprehensive civil rights law in the nation's history outlawed racial discrimination in places of public accommodation where discrimination is supported by local or state laws, in publicly owned facilities, employment, union membership, and federally aided programs. It gave the Attorney General new powers to speed school desegregation and to enforce the Negro's right to vote. General compliance with the law led to the hope that there would be less resistance than to the Supreme Court's school desegregation decisions of 1954 and 1955. See CIVIL LIBERTIES; CONGRESS OF THE UNITED STATES; Section Two, CONGRESS MAKES A DECISION.

White Backlash, or white opposition to the civil rights movement, became a decisive factor in the November elections in only five Southern states. In general, Democratic and Republican candidates who supported the movement defeated those who opposed it. Edward W. Brooke, a Negro Republican, was re-elected attorney general of Massachusetts by almost 1,000,000 votes. Six Negroes won seats in the U.S. House of Representatives, an increase of one over 1962. All this was on the credit side for the Negro revolution. On the debit side, was the adoption by California voters in a state-wide referendum of Proposition XIV. It had the effect of forbidding open-occupancy housing laws.

Public Education. In the fall of 1964, Negroes were admitted for the first time to three predominantly white public schools in Mississippi. Hence, for the first time, Negroes were enrolled in integrated public schools of all the 11 former Confederate states. The percentage of integrated Negro pupils of the total Negro school population in these states rose from 1.2 per cent in 1963-1964, to an estimated 1.5 per cent in the fall of 1964. In the six border states and the District of Columbia there were, at the end of 1963-1964 school year, 281,731 Negro students, or 54.8 per cent of all Negro pupils in the region, enrolled in integrated schools.

Busing—the compulsory transfer by bus of Negro and white students from one school to another in order to achieve a better racial balance—was becoming a major issue in a number of Northern cities. See EDUCATION.

Employment. The plight of the unskilled Negro worker, both rural and urban, was still more grievous than that of other unskilled workers. But Negroes found increased opportunities working in supermarkets, restaurants, retail stores, and as radio and television broadcasters.

Rights Violence. Resistance to the "Negro Revolution" was strongest in Mississippi. Three civil rights workers, two white and one Negro, were murdered, and at least two Negroes, not known to be civil rights workers, were dismembered. Before and especially after the Council of Federated Organizations (COFO) began its "Operation Freedom" in the summer to encourage Negroes to register as voters, a

CARL ROWAN, 38, left his post as ambassador
to Finland to direct the U. S. Information
Agency, succeeding Edward R. Murrow.

number of Negro churches and homes were bombed,
civil rights workers were harassed, and many Negroes
were not permitted, for trivial and probably unconstitutional reasons, to register as voters. Race riots
flared in Northern cities, generally prompted by
hoodlums. Responsible Negro leaders, fearful that
civil rights demonstrations would feed the "white
backlash," successfully urged a moratorium on civil
rights demonstrations until after the elections (see
CITY). Among those advocating such a course was
Dr. Martin Luther King, Jr., winner of the Nobel
peace prize in 1964. See KING, JR., MARTIN LUTHER;
NOBEL PRIZES.

Negro Firsts. Carl Rowan succeeded Edward R.
Murrow as director of the United States Information
Agency; Samuel Z. Westerfield, Jr., was appointed
deputy assistant secretary of state for African affairs;
Mercer Cook became the ambassador to Senegal;
Clinton Everett Knox, ambassador to Dahomey; and

Hobart Taylor, Jr., joined the White House staff as
special counsel. Negroes were elected to state legislatures in California, Iowa, Kansas, and Tennessee.

Sidney Poitier won a Motion Picture Academy
Award for best actor in 1964. The University of Texas
appointed Dr. Ervin Perry as a faculty member and
the University of Toledo appointed Dr. Lancelot
C. A. Thompson as assistant dean of the college of
arts and sciences for undergraduate studies. The
Reverend Edler G. Hawkins was elected moderator
of the General Assembly of The United Presbyterian
Church in the U.S.A.   RAYFORD W. LOGAN

NEPAL spruced up its communications system
during the year. It continued work on the 70-mile
highway linking Katmandu with the road network
of Chinese-ruled Tibet at the border pass of Kodari.
In August, an agreement was signed with India for
the construction by India of a 218-mile road between
Sanauli and Pokhara in western Nepal at a cost of
$20,000,000. The nation also completed a 26-mile
overhead ropeway to transport goods in and out of
the Katmandu valley on a year-round basis. Construction of the ropeway had been carried out with
the aid of a $5,000,000 U.S. loan.

In September, King Mahendra invested his eldest
son, Birendra, with the powers of a crown prince.

Population: 9,900,000. **Government:** King Mahendra; Prime Minister Tulsi Gin. **Foreign Trade:**
exports, $15,000,000; imports, $31,000,000. **Principal Exports:** jute, oilseeds, rice.   JOHN N. STALKER

See also ASIA.

TOILING SHERPAS carve out an airfield at Lukla,
in Nepal. It will serve as a supply base for
schools built in the area by Sir Edmund Hillary.

NETHERLANDS, THE, was rocked by a crisis in the royal House of Orange. It was set off by Princess Irene, second in line of succession to the throne, who announced in February her plan to marry Prince Carlos de Bourbon y Parma, one of the claimants to the throne of Spain.

The nation, which is about evenly divided between Roman Catholics and Protestants, was shocked—especially by her conversion to Roman Catholicism. The royal family has long had a tradition of Protestantism. There was also a long history of anti-Spanish sentiment in the country. At the government's insistence, Princess Irene renounced her claim to the throne. She and Prince Carlos were married in Rome on April 29.

The economy continued strong but slowed from previous years as measures were taken to combat inflation. Credit restrictions and higher interest rates went into effect. Exploration of the North Sea gas field, first discovered off the Dutch coast, brought problems of dividing the areas claimed by The Netherlands and other nations bordering the sea. See EUROPE (Close-Up).

During the year, The Netherlands agreed to join in an international system of communication by earth satellite. Dutch sailors participated in an experiment to test the feasibility of mixed-manned ships in the proposed North Atlantic Treaty Organization (NATO) multilateral nuclear force (MLF). The Netherlands agreed in principle to support MLF. See NORTH ATLANTIC TREATY ORGANIZATION (NATO).

Population: 12,225,000. **Government:** Queen Juliana; Prime Minister Victor G. M. Marijnen. **Foreign Trade:** exports, $5,698,000,000; imports, $7,315,000,000. **Principal Exports:** chemicals, machinery, petroleum products.   FRED J. PANNWITT

NEVILLE, EMILY CHENEY (1919-   ), received the Newbery medal in 1964 for her first book. *It's Like This, Cat* began as a boy and cat story, and developed into a first-person novel about a boy growing up in a big city. New York is easily recognized as the setting in both text and pictures.

The Nevilles live in a big apartment house in New York's Gramercy Park. Five children, several dogs, and Midnight, who was salvaged from a paper bag, would make material enough for several books. Mrs. Neville is at work on a second one. Her husband, Glen Neville, is a newspaper editor. They met in a newspaper office, where Emily worked as a copy girl.

Emily Cheney was born in Manchester, Conn., the youngest of seven children. There also were many cousins, so the family hired a teacher and set up its own school. Emily later went to school in West Hartford, and was graduated from Bryn Mawr College in 1940.

See also LITERATURE FOR CHILDREN (Awards).
NEW BRUNSWICK. See CANADA.

NEW GUINEA, PAPUA AND, took a major step toward eventual independence when the house of assembly, the territory's first legislature with a majority of elected members, convened on June 8. The assembly consisted of 38 native-born Papuans and New Guineans and 26 Europeans.

On June 17, the government announced that a 2,000-member group known, improbably, as the Lyndon B. Johnson cult had agreed to pay the annual council taxes. Earlier, the cultists had refused to do so on the grounds that they no longer recognized the Australian administration. Instead, the cult's leader, Bomailish, had campaigned to "buy" U.S. President Lyndon B. Johnson and bring him to rule in place of the Australians.   JOHN N. STALKER
NEW WORDS AND PHRASES. See WORDS AND PHRASES, NEW.

NEW YORK CITY again showed that it was a city of superlatives in 1964. In June, the Real Estate Board reported taxable property worth $30,000,000,000. Twelve Manhattan office buildings were completed during the year, which brought the total erected since World War II to 200. Seven were under construction. On the drawing board was the newly announced World Trade Center. Designed by architects Minoru Yamasaki and Emory Roth, its twin towers will rise 1,350 feet and will be the tallest in the world. See BUILDING AND CONSTRUCTION.

Mid-Manhattan construction led to enormous congestion which was partly responsible for still another superlative, the Verrazano-Narrows Bridge (see BRIDGE AND TUNNEL). Opened in November, it boasted the longest suspension span, 4,260 feet, in the world. It vaults the entrance of New York Harbor at a height of 228 feet, and is a key link in the New Jersey-Staten Island-Brooklyn southern bypass of Manhattan's crowded streets.

The largest single rental housing development to be built as a Title I urban renewal project was completed in Manhattan. Known as Lincoln Towers, it is composed of eight 28-story apartment buildings, which include 3,859 apartment units.

Traffic Studies showed that one in every four airline passengers who lands or boards in the United States was bound to or from the New York area's three large airports. Hence, La Guardia Airport opened a new terminal and a new control tower as part of a seven-year development program; runways were expanded at the John F. Kennedy International Airport, and major improvements were announced for Newark (N.J.) Airport. See AVIATION.

Shea Stadium (capacity: 55,300), home of the New York Mets, opened adjacent to the World's Fair grounds, and a distinguished Hall of Science Building at the fair was dedicated in 1964 as a permanent building.

On the cultural scene, The Museum of Modern Art opened a new wing, and the second building in Lincoln Center, the plush and elegant New York State

Theatre, opened. Both were designed by architect Philip Johnson. Another important structure was topped out. It was the sheer, simplistic tower the late Eero Saarinen designed for the Columbia Broadcasting System.

Riots broke out in the summer in Harlem, a predominantly Negro slum in northern Manhattan. These were followed by several nights of rioting in the equally poverty-ridden Bedford-Stuyvesant section of Brooklyn. Although Negroes were doing the rioting in both places, it was held that their actions against law and order were less racially motivated than they were inspired by their squalid living conditions and dismal job opportunities. DONALD W. LIEF

See also CITY; CIVIL LIBERTIES; EDUCATION; FAIRS AND EXHIBITIONS; MUSEUM.

NEW ZEALAND dropped the word "British" from the covers of its passports in March. The move reportedly followed pressures from New Zealanders who, traveling in Asia and the new African countries, had suffered indignities through the carrying of a passport labeled "British New Zealand."

The nation cautiously enjoyed the taste of economic success in 1964. Wool sales jumped 30 per cent in the fiscal year ended June 30, and total farm export sales rose by $140,000,000. Britain remained the dominion's best customer. The New Zealand government, however, was annoyed at the British Conservative government's interest in a managed market for Britain's meat imports, an interest which was thought to presage restrictions on deliveries from New Zealand.

For much of the year, Prime Minister Keith Holyoake and his cabinet warned of the dangerous rise in imports, of the risk of farm export earnings falling, and of indications of excessive personal consumption. When the official anti-inflation program was announced on October 23, however, it was distinctly moderate. Government spending would be limited as would restraints on local government borrowing. An internal loan was intended to mop up excess spending power, and farmers were encouraged to freeze a portion of the bonus income they earned in the 1963-1964 growing season.

On March 11, the government announced that the basic unit of New Zealand's decimal currency would be the dollar (equal to 10 shillings sterling). The change would become effective in July, 1967.

In January, plans were laid for the establishment of an iron and steel industry on the west coast.

Population: 2,625,000. **Government:** Governor-General Sir Bernard Fergusson; Prime Minister Keith J. Holyoake. **Foreign Trade:** exports, $1,282,000,000; imports, $906,000,000. **Principal Exports:** dairy products, meat, wool. ALASTAIR BURNET

NEWBERY MEDAL. See NEVILLE, EMILY CHENEY; LITERATURE FOR CHILDREN (Awards).

NEWFOUNDLAND. See CANADA.

NEWSPAPER. See PUBLISHING.

NICARAGUA enjoyed political peace and unprecedented prosperity in 1964. As an indication of its fiscal soundness, the republic notified the International Monetary Fund in midyear that it would not adopt any international currency restrictions without first obtaining the fund's agreement. Nicaragua thus became the 25th nation to assume this position.

The nation's solvency was due largely to its sound fiscal policies and the large cotton crops of recent years. The 1963-1964 season had yielded a record 410,000 bales of cotton, some 30 per cent above the 1962-1963 output. A 500,000-bale crop was predicted for the 1964-1965 season.

The new, 200,000-kilowatt Tuma River hydroelectric project was well ahead of schedule with the first 25,000-kilowatt turbine beginning experimental operations in October. When the second turbine is installed in the spring of 1965, the country's public electric power capacity will be more than doubled. Meanwhile, the Agency for International Development granted $4,500,000 to finance highways.

Population: 1,600,000. **Government:** President René Schick Gutierrez. **Foreign Trade:** exports, $100,000,000; imports, $111,000,000. **Principal Exports:** coffee, copper, cotton. MARY C. WEBSTER

See also LATIN AMERICA.

NIGER crushed an attempt by political exiles to overthrow the government of President Hamani Diori in October. The attempted coup was headed by former premier Djibo Bakary, exiled head of the Sawaba party. Four Sawaba leaders were executed.

According to an intercepted letter from Bakary to his followers, the uprising was supposed to begin in western Niger on September 27 and 28 and to spread to the rest of the country on October 3 and 4. The government announced it had headed off the attempts in the west. In the east, it said, three terrorist commando units attacking the administrative post of Ladarossa had been beaten off and a large number of rebels captured.

In June, Niger settled its border differences with Dahomey. The two states agreed to cooperate in defining the boundary, guard it against illegal crossings, and take a joint census. A later treaty established common citizenship for Niger, Ivory Coast, and Dahomey.

The United States granted Niger a $500,000 loan which would be used to finance projects by private investors. The United States also made available $1,500,000 to help finance a road-building program in the agricultural southeast area. Late in the year, it was announced that the Niger River Bridge at Niamey would be renamed in honor of the late U.S. President John F. Kennedy.

Population: 3,300,000. **Government:** President Hamani Diori. **Foreign Trade:** exports, $15,000,000; imports, $27,000,000. **Principal Exports:** cattle, peanuts, vegetables. WILLIAM SPENCER

See also AFRICA.

United Press Int.

MARTIN LUTHER KING, JR., receives the congratulations of Crown Prince Harald, left, and King Olav of Norway, on his award of the Nobel peace prize.

NIGERIA was paralyzed by a nationwide strike for higher wages in midyear. Between June 1 and June 13, almost all industries in Nigeria were shut down. Ports, railroads, and airways ceased operations. The strike ended when the government promised to negotiate wage increases on the basis of a 1963 report published by a fact-finding commission. The commission had recommended doubling salaries of manual laborers and giving large increases to workers earning less than $1,680 a year.

On August 1, it was reported that several hundred persons had been killed during months of tribal fighting in northeastern Nigeria. The killings were attributable to a feud that had broken out between 800,000 Tiv tribesmen and the ruling Moslem Fulani tribesmen in the area.

In elections held February 3, the National Convention of Nigerian Citizens won 53 of the 64 contested seats for the House of Assembly in Nigeria's newly created Mid-West Region. So sharp were political and tribal differences among the nation's Northern, Eastern, Western, and the newly created Mid-Western regions, however, that by year's end there was talk that either the Easterners or the Northerners might try to secede.

Population: 57,300,000. **Government:** President Nnamdi Azikiwe; Prime Minister Alhaii Sir Abubakar Tafawa Balewa. **Foreign Trade:** exports, $608,000,-000; imports, $633,000,000. **Principal Exports:** cocoa beans, peanuts, petroleum. BENJAMIN E. THOMAS

See also AFRICA.

NOBEL PRIZES in literature and science were presented at ceremonies in Stockholm, Sweden, on Dec. 10, 1964.

The peace laureate is selected by the Norwegian Parliament's Nobel Committee, and the prize is presented in Oslo, Norway. The Nobel ceremonies were televised for the first time in the United States and abroad in 1964 (see TELEVISION).

Winners of Nobel Awards in 1964 included the following:

Literature Prize was awarded to the French writer Jean-Paul Sartre. He did not wish to accept it, and the prize money reverted to the Nobel Fund.

Peace Prize. Martin Luther King, Jr., leader of the Negro nonviolence crusade against racial segregation in the United States, received the peace prize.

Science Prizes were presented to an Englishwoman, a West German, and two American and two Russian scientists. *Chemistry Prize* was awarded to Mrs. Dorothy Crowfoot Hodgkin, Wolfson Research Professor of the Royal Society and a fellow at Somerville College, Oxford University. *Medicine and Physiology Prize* was awarded to Konrad E. Bloch, Harvard University Higgins Professor of Biochemistry, and Feodor Lynen, University of Munich professor and director of the Max Planck Institute for Cell Chemistry. *Physics Prize:* Charles H. Townes, provost of the Massachusetts Institute of Technology received half the prize. The other half was shared by Nikolai G. Basov, deputy scientific director of the Soviet Academy of Sciences Lebedev Physics Institute, and Aleksandr M. Prokhorov, chief of the institute's Oscillations Laboratory.

See also BASOV, NIKOLAI G.; BLOCH, KONRAD E.; HODGKIN, DOROTHY CROWFOOT; KING, MARTIN LUTHER; LYNEN, FEODOR; PROKHOROV, ALEKSANDR M.; SARTRE, JEAN-PAUL; TOWNES, CHARLES H.

NORTH ATLANTIC TREATY ORGANIZATION (NATO),

marking its 15th birthday, found little cause for celebration. The 15-nation alliance was under severe internal stresses that seemingly jeopardized its very existence. As the threat of a Soviet attack receded—the threat that had brought NATO into being—members grew less inclined to submerge their differences in a common cause and to accept the "nuclear umbrella" principle of the United States as the ultimate in mutual defense.

The strain was strongest over a U.S. proposal to create a NATO multilateral nuclear fleet (MLF). Originally devised in response to European demands for a larger, unified voice in nuclear policy, MLF tended to divide rather than unify in 1964.

The MLF plan envisioned a fleet of 25 surface vessels, each to be manned by mixed crews from the NATO countries and each armed with eight nuclear Polaris missiles. The ships would cruise the shipping lanes with their missiles poised for instant launching.

Great Britain, Greece, Italy, The Netherlands, and Turkey joined in studies of how MLF might work. France, however, vigorously opposed MLF. President Charles de Gaulle, who was building an independent French nuclear force, resented European "dependence" on U.S. nuclear power and threatened to renounce the Franco-German treaty of 1963 if West Germany, which favored the plan, participated in MLF (see FRANCE; GERMANY). The Soviet Union, meanwhile, denounced MLF as a scheme that would encourage the spread of nuclear weapons, a charge that the United States denied. See DISARMAMENT.

The election of a Labour party government in Great Britain in October brought a change of attitude there (see GREAT BRITAIN). A large faction in the party had opposed MLF and had even expressed coolness toward NATO itself. Prime Minister Harold Wilson reaffirmed British backing for NATO, but he proposed that a broader plan be developed whereby MLF and Britain's independent nuclear forces might be merged into a NATO nuclear command.

De Gaulle declared his independence of NATO planning in other ways during the year. In April, the last vestige of French naval integration in NATO forces vanished when French officers were withdrawn from the alliance's naval headquarters units. French ships earmarked for NATO command had been withdrawn earlier. During the year, France also ignored NATO uniformity by adopting a new rifle for its ground troops under NATO command.

The eastern "anchor" of the alliance was threatened in August when Greece and Turkey came close to war over Cyprus. Both briefly withdrew military units from NATO command but restored them when the crisis passed. See CYPRUS.

Manlio Brosio of Italy became NATO secretary-general on August 1. He succeeded Dirk U. Stikker of The Netherlands, who retired.   FRED J. PANNWITT

NORTH KOREA. See KOREA.

NORWAY felt the restraining influence of the trade barriers erected by the European Economic Community. The nation, which was a member of the rival European Free Trade Association (EFTA) encountered declining markets for such exports as furniture and frozen fish. The nation was running an annual deficit in its balance of payments of about $200,000,000 a year.

In April, when wage negotiations between the Labor Federation and the Employers Association broke down, the government ordered that a settlement be reached by compulsory arbitration to avert a strike and to avoid wage increases that would tend to have adverse effects on the balance of payments.

Nikita S. Khrushchev visited Norway a few months before his dismissal as premier of the Soviet Union (see RUSSIA). Khrushchev's suggestion that Norway abandon its North Atlantic Treaty Organization (NATO) alliance for a policy of neutrality served only to bring the country closer to NATO.

Population: 3,710,000. **Government:** King Olav V; Prime Minister Einar H. Gerhardsen. **Foreign Trade:** exports, $1,327,000,000; imports, $1,969,000,000. **Principal Exports:** aluminum, fish, paper and paper board, pulp.   FRED J. PANNWITT

See also EUROPE.

NOVA SCOTIA. See CANADA.

NUCLEAR PHYSICS. A new subatomic particle, called the *omega-minus*, was discovered by a group of 33 physicists at the Brookhaven National Laboratory, Long Island, N.Y. The newcomer was detected with the aid of high-energy equipment at the laboratory. It exists for only a fraction of a second, and, together with its associated particles, is packed into a space of less than a millionth of a millionth of a centimeter. Its significance lies in the fact that scientists now understand more about the way components of the atom stick together.

The omega-minus was discovered by exposing a beam of subatomic particles, coming from the 33,000,000,000 electron volt alternating gradient synchrotron, to the 80-inch hydrogen bubble chamber (the world's largest). The bubble chamber is essentially a large tank filled with superheated liquid hydrogen only very slightly above its boiling point. The passage of a charged particle through the chamber leaves a track of bubbles consisting of boiling hydrogen. This track can then be photographed to provide a permanent record of the path of the particle. An analysis of the many such tracks during the experiment revealed the presence of the new particle.

The discovery had been hoped for by many physicists. It added support to a theory developed by Professor Murray Gell-Mann of the California Institute of Technology and Dr. Yuval Ne'eman of Israel. The two, working independently, had proposed an orderly arrangement of the subatomic particles, much as the chemical elements have long been classified into an atomic table. By using the atomic table, chemists can know in advance some of the ways in which chemical elements are going to react with each other. In the same way, physicists could use a classification of the subatomic particles.

The Gell-Mann and Ne'eman classification enabled physicists to group many of the subatomic particles into a few distinctive families. When so grouped, it was possible to predict the existence of new particles, one of the most important of which was the omega-minus. This particle has a mass some 3,400 times as great as that of an electron and carries a negative electric charge.

The Missing Quark. Another of Gell-Mann's speculations did not turn out so well. He had suggested that new types of particles, "quarks," carrying only one-third or two-thirds the charge of an electron, might exist. Doctors Robert Adair, Lawrence Leipuner, William Chu, and Richard Larsen, using the alternating gradient synchrotron at Brookhaven, searched for such quarks among the products of the bombardment of a beryllium target by high-energy protons. If any quarks were there, they were unable to find them. A similar search at the Centre Européan pour Recherches Nucléaires (CERN) in Geneva, Switzerland, proved equally fruitless.

While some order among the particles seemed to have been accomplished by the Gell-Mann and Ne'eman theory, nothing like a complete organization was yet in sight. New subatomic particles and entities continue to be discovered at the approximate rate of one a month, and many of the older ones still defy classification.

Time Reversal. The results of an experiment published in July threw doubt on the crucial principle, built into almost every physical theory, that the laws of the universe remain unchanged even when the direction of time is reversed. This fundamental symmetry principle is known to physicists as the "time-reversal invariance."

Roughly speaking, this time-reversal principle means that if someone were to take a motion picture, over a short length of time, of any physical process and then later show the film by running the film backward, the viewer would be unable to tell that what he was seeing was not some real physical process going on in the normal way. The ordinary clues that might reveal the direction are secondary, not fundamental to the process.

Doubt was cast on the universal validity of this principle by an experiment performed at Brookhaven by Doctors Val L. Fitch, James H. Christenson, James W. Cronin, and René Turlay. Their study concerned the manner in which an atomic particle decays into other particles. The particular particle under study was a K_2^0 meson. It was found to decay into a pi-minus and a pi-plus meson pair. Physicists concluded that, in this case, the matter seemed to have only one direction: forward. S. MATTHEW PRASTEIN

See also ATOMIC ENERGY; PHYSICS.

NYASALAND. See MALAWI.

OCEAN exploration at great depths became more feasible with the completion and testing of a number of deep-diving submarines in 1964. On September 3, J. Louis Reynolds launched the *Aluminaut*, the world's first aluminum-hulled submarine. It was designed to operate with a crew of three at 15,000 feet. Unlike the well-known bathyscaph, which can go to even greater depths but with little horizontal mobility, the *Aluminaut's* $6\frac{1}{2}$-inch-thick hull can move through the water at a speed of 3.8 knots.

The French bathyscaph *Archimede* dived 27,510 feet to the bottom of the Puerto Rican Trench, on May 9. Pierre Drach, the leader of this expedition, expressed surprise at the extent of marine life found at the five-mile depth.

Another oceanographic submarine, *Alvin*, was designed for the Woods Hole Oceanographic Institution at Woods Hole, Mass. Shaped like an ocarina with a propeller at one end, *Alvin* is capable of operating at 6,000 feet. It began underwater exploration near Bermuda in the fall. *Asherah*, launched in May, was similar to *Alvin* and was used by the University of Pennsylvania to search for shipwrecks in the Aegean.

Deepstar, a three-man vehicle, was scheduled to go into operation in 1965. Built to cruise at a depth of 12,000 feet, it was designed by the ocean explorer Jacques-Yves Costeau. A saucer-shaped workhorse, the *Turtle*, also was under construction. Among other tasks it would be used for repair of undersea cables. Meanwhile, Dr. Jacques Piccard's *Mesoscaph* was unveiled at the Swiss National Fair in Lausanne. It could dive to 4,000 feet. A Japanese vessel, which operates at 1,000 feet and carries a crew of six, was launched at Kobe on May 15.

Buoys. A new family of buoys that float at different depths was developed during the year. These buoys emit sounds so that their underwater drift can be followed, but, unlike earlier buoys that could only indicate location, these also announce changes in depth. *Flip*, a research vessel that can stand bow-up in the water and float like a buoy, spent 27 days in its vertical position while making observations off the coast of San Francisco. The seagoing drilling platform for the Mohole project has been scheduled for construction during 1965. See GEOLOGY.

International Programs. Cooperative investigations continued in the Indian Ocean and the equatorial Atlantic Ocean. The International Indian Ocean Expedition (IIOE), now in its third year, had about 40 ships from 12 nations studying bathymetry, biology, meteorology, and water movements. The International Cooperative Investigations of the Tropical Atlantic (ICITA), had 13 ships from 10 nations studying the equatorial current systems during its second year of seasonal research.

U.S. government support for oceanography in 1964 was reported by the Interagency Committee on Oceanography (ICO) at $133,444,000, of which about 20 per cent went to universities. F. F. KOCZY

OIL. See PETROLEUM.

OLD AGE. Perhaps the most significant events with respect to older Americans were the work contracts the United Auto Workers and the automobile companies signed in the autumn of the year. The major features of the contracts included the right to retire at about age 60 (when age and service total 85 years), with substantially increased retirement pay, broadened insurance and health benefits, and more paid vacation time. See AUTOMOBILE; LABOR.

The contract seemed to confirm the view of many experts that the desire of manual workers for economic security in old age was stronger than their desire for either more pay or for a longer worklife. The worklife as well as the workyear was shortening for manual workers.

Observers wondered what this signified with respect to the meaning of work in American life. Now, a man who retires at age 60 has an average of 16 years of leisure ahead of him. What can he make out of it? Apparently, the manual workers will be the first to answer this question, since there is little evidence of a shortening of the worklife for people in professional and managerial occupations.

Federal Programs. The Congress of the United States did not provide anything during the year as basic as did the auto industry, but congressional activity in 1964 was expected to result in important legislation during the 1965 session.

The Housing Act of 1964 provided an additional $75,000,000 for direct housing loans to the elderly. In the same act, provision was made for loans for home rehabilitation in urban renewal areas. This was expected to be especially useful to elderly people who frequently do not have the cash to rehabilitate their homes.

Anti-Poverty Bill. The Economic Opportunity Act of 1964 provided at least two things of major interest to older people. One section provided assistance for community action and planning on behalf of disadvantaged people, including older people. Another section set up a "Domestic Peace Corps," which is expected to encourage older people to work on local service projects. See SOCIAL WELFARE (Close-Up).

The new tax law exempted the first $3,000 of income for a couple over 65, and allowed an older person a profit of $20,000 on the sale of his home before he was taxed on capital gains.

The Special Committee on Aging of the U.S. Senate issued a report in September, with 15 recommendations. It was aimed at assisting older persons in a variety of ways under a version of the "Older Americans Act of 1963," which it urged the Senate to pass. The report laid stress on a recommendation for a National Senior Service Corps. It also contained the following optimistic note: "Older people, once their economic needs have been met, apparently are more able to adjust to life's mental vicissitudes than the young and middle aged. Presumably this springs from wisdom acquired through years of meeting all types of problems." ROBERT J. HAVIGHURST

OLYMPIC GAMES

AFTER A JOURNEY of 10,000 miles by foot and jet plane, the Olympic Flame entered the National Stadium in Tokyo, Japan, on October 10. It signaled the beginning of the 18th modern Olympiad.

Two weeks later, one of the best organized, most carefully rehearsed, and most successful Olympic Games were over. But their effect on Japan and on the Olympic tradition would last for years.

Japan was the first Asian nation ever to hold the games, and the Japanese took their assignment seriously. Over $2,000,000,000 was spent in preparing Olympic arenas, special housing, and transportation facilities for the games. Included was a system of modern expressways designed to bring order out of Tokyo's chaotic traffic. See ARCHITECTURE; BUILDING AND CONSTRUCTION (picture); CITY; JAPAN; RAILROAD (picture).

The 2,848 athletes from 94 nations who took part in the Tokyo Games responded with outstanding performances. In the finals, semifinals, and

DIVING IN for the 400-meter medley were Olympic winners Martha Randall, left, and Donna de Varona, both wearing the striped suits of the U.S. Olympic team.

United Press Int., and Jerry Cooke, Photo Researchers

OLYMPIC CHAMPIONS *included Germany's Willi Holdorf, above, decathlon winner, and U.S. swimmer Don Schollander, below, left. Yoshinori Sakai lit the Olympic Flame, below.*

Wide World

ANOTHER GOLD MEDAL *was won by the U.S. when Billy Mills ran in the 10,000 meter race.*

heats they broke 25 world records and tied four in track and field, swimming, and weight lifting, and they broke 52 of 61 possible Olympic records.

In the perennial contest between the United States and the Soviet Union for Olympic supremacy, the outcome was a virtual tie. The U.S. team won 36 gold medals to Russia's 30. But the Russians led in total medals, 96 to 90.

Track and Field. In men's track and field, premier sport of the Olympics, the U.S. team won 12 of the 24 events. The games' brightest stars were Bob Hayes, Peter Snell, and Bikila Abebe. Hayes won the men's 100 meters, and then anchored the U.S. 400-meter relay team to a world record victory.

New Zealand's Snell proved himself the greatest middle-distance runner in Olympic history by winning two gold medals. First he repeated his Rome victory in the 800 meters, and then outclassed a strong field to win the 1,500 meters by 12 yards.

Bikila Abebe, the Ethiopian palace guard who had run barefoot to win the 1960 Olympic marathon,

scored an unprecedented repeat victory at Tokyo.

Only two other 1960 winners repeated. Al Oerter won his third straight discus gold medal for the United States despite a painful injury. Joszef Schmidt of Poland won his second triple jump title, although he had only one competition before the games because of a knee operation.

The biggest upset was in the 10,000 meters, where U.S. Marine Billy Mills staged an electrifying last-lap sprint to win in the final 20 yards. Mills' time was only nine seconds off the world record.

In women's track, Russia's powerful team found the going rough. Favored to win six events, as they did in 1960, the Soviet women won only three.

Swimming. The U.S. whiz kids did even better in the water than on the track. They won nine out of 12 men's gold medals and seven out of 10 women's. In all, they captured 37 gold, silver, and bronze swimming medals out of a possible 56. Dawn Fraser of Australia won her third successive gold medal—a feat never before achieved in swimming.

Other Sports. The U.S. basketball team maintained a perfect U.S. Olympic record by winning nine games and losing none. Facing Russia in the final, as at Melbourne and Rome, the United States won, 73 to 59. Japan ranked third behind the United States and Russia with 16 gold medals won, mainly in gymnastics and wrestling.

Winter Olympics. The 9th Winter Olympics were held in Innsbruck, Austria, from January 29 through February 9. Russia led all other nations by a wide margin, with 11 gold medals and 25 medals in all.

In men's speed skating, however, one U.S. skater handed the Russians a surprise. Terry McDermott of Essexville, Mich., flashed to a new Olympic record in the 500-meter race.

JAMES O. DUNAWAY.

WINNERS OF SUMMER GAMES

In the official records below, (*) indicates a new Olympic record, and (†) indicates a new world mark.

TRACK AND FIELD
MEN
100 Meters...................Bob Hayes, U.S.A., 10.0s.
200 Meters...............Henry Carr, U.S.A., 20.3s.*
400 Meters..............Mike Larrabee, U.S.A., 45.1s.
800 Meters.....Peter Snell, New Zealand, 1m.45.1s.*
1,500 Meters.......Peter Snell, New Zealand, 3m.38.1s.
5,000 Meters........Bob Schul, U.S.A., 13m.48.8s.
10,000 Meters...........Billy Mills, U.S.A., 28m.24.4s.*
Marathon.........Bikila Abebe, Ethiopia, 2h.12m.11.2s.†
110 Meter Hurdles..........Hayes Jones, U.S.A., 13.6s.
400 Meter Hurdles...........Rex Cawley, U.S.A., 49.6s.
3,000 Meter Steeplechase......Gaston Roelants, Belgium, 8m.30.8s.*
20 Kilometer Walk.........Ken Matthews, Great Britain, 1h.29m.34s.*
50 Kilometer Walk....Abdon Pamich, Italy, 4h.11m.12.4s.†
400 Meter Relay....U.S.A. (Paul Drayton, Gerry Ashworth, Dick Stebbins, Bob Hayes), 39.0s.†
1,600 Meter Relay...U.S.A. (Ollan Cassell, Mike Larrabee, Ulis Williams, Henry Carr), 3m.0.7s.†
High Jump............Valeri Brumel, U.S.S.R., 7ft.1¾in.*
Pole Vault..............Fred Hansen, U.S.A., 16ft.9in.*
Long, or Broad, Jump..Lynn Davies, Great Britain, 26ft.5½in.
Triple Jump.........Joseph Schmidt, Poland, 55ft.3¼in.*
Shot-Put................Dallas Long, U.S.A., 66ft.8½in.*
Discus Throw............Al Oerter, U.S.A., 200ft.1½in.*
Javelin Throw........Pauli Nevala, Finland, 271ft.2¼in.*
Hammer Throw.....Romuald Klim, U.S.S.R., 228ft.10½in.*
Decathlon.........Willi Holdorf, Germany, 7,887 points
WOMEN
100 Meters...............Wyomia Tyus, U.S.A., 11.4s.
200 Meters..............Edith McGuire, U.S.A., 23.0s.*
400 Meters..........Betty Cuthbert, Australia, 52.0s.
800 Meters............Ann Packer, Great Britain, 2m.1.1s.†
80 Meter Hurdles.........Karin Balzer, Germany, 10.5s.
400 Meter Relay.Poland (Teresa Ciepla, Irena Kirszenstein, Halina Gorecka, Eva Klobukowska) 43.6s.†
High Jump............Yolanda Balas, Romania, 6ft.2¾in.*
Long Jump.......Mary Rand, Great Britain, 22ft.2 in.†
Shot-Put...........Tamara Press, U.S.S.R., 59ft.6¼in.*
Discus Throw.......Tamara Press, U.S.S.R., 187ft.10¾in.*
Javelin Throw......Mihaela Penes, Romania, 198ft.7½in.
Pentathlon...........Irina Press, U.S.S.R., 5,246 points†

OTHER SPORTS
BOXING
Flyweight.....................Fernando Atzori, Italy
Bantamweight..................Takao Sakurai, Japan
Featherweight............Stanislav Stepashkin, U.S.S.R.
Lightweight..................Jozef Grudzien, Poland

Light-Welterweight.................Jerzy Kulej, Poland
Welterweight...............Marian Kasprzyk, Poland
Light-Middleweight..............Boris Lagutin, U.S.S.R.
Middleweight............Valeri Popenchenko, U.S.S.R.
Light-Heavyweight.............Cosimo Pinto, Italy
Heavyweight...............Joe Frazier, U.S.A.
CANOEING, MEN
Kayak Singles.................Rolf Peterson, Sweden
Kayak Pairs..Sven Sjodelius and Gunnar Uttrberg, Sweden
Kayak Fours..................................U.S.S.R.
Canadian Singles.........Jurgen Eschert, Germany
Canadian Doubles...Andrei Khimich and Stepan Oschepov, U.S.S.R.
CANOEING, WOMEN
Kayak Singles.............Ludmilla Khvedosiuk, U.S.S.R.
Kayak Doubles...Roswitha Esser and Annemie Zimmermann, Germany
CYCLING
1,000 Meter Time Trial..........Patrick Sercu, Belgium
1,000 Meter Sprint.......Giovanni Petenella, Italy
2,000 Meter Tandem.............Angelo Damiano and Sergio Bianchetto, Italy
Individual Pursuit............Jiri Daller, Czechoslovakia
Team Pursuit......................Germany
Individual Road Race............Mario Zanin, Italy
Team Road Race......................Netherlands
EQUESTRIAN
Three-Day Event, Individual.....Mauro Checcoli, Italy
Three-Day Event, Team......................Italy
Dressage, Individual........Henri Chamartin, Switzerland
Dressage, Team......................Germany
Jumping, Individual.........Jonquieres D'Oriola, France
Jumping, Team......................Germany
FENCING, MEN
Individual Foil...................Egon Franke, Poland
Team Foil......................U.S.S.R.
Epée, Individual..........Grigory Kriss, U.S.S.R.
Epée, Team......................Hungary
Sabre, Individual.........Tibor Pezsa, Hungary
Sabre, Team......................U.S.S.R.
FENCING, WOMEN
Foil, Individual.................Uldiko Ujlaki, Hungary
Foil, Team......................Hungary
GYMNASTICS, MEN
All-Around (Combined)..............Yukio Endo, Japan
Combined, Team......................Japan
Horizontal Bar..................Boris Shakhlin, U.S.S.R.
Parallel Bars...................Yukio Endo, Japan
Flying Rings...................Takuji Hayata, Japan
Side Horse.........Miroslav Cerar, Yugoslavia
Long Horse Vault..........Haruhiro Yamashita, Japan
Free Standing Exercises........Franco Menichelli, Italy
GYMNASTICS, WOMEN
All-Around (Combined)....Vera Caslavska, Czechoslovakia
Combined, Team......................U.S.S.R.
Balance Beam..........Vera Caslavska, Czechoslovakia
Parallel Bars.........Polina Astakhova, U.S.S.R.
Long Horse Vault.....Vera Caslavska, Czechoslovakia
Free Standing Exercises.........Larisa Latynina, U.S.S.R.
JUDO
Lightweight.................Takehide Nakatani, Japan
Middleweight.....................Isao Okano, Japan
Heavyweight.................Isao Inokuma, Japan
Open.....................Anton Geesink, Netherlands
MODERN PENTATHLON
Individual.....................Ferenc Torok, Hungary
Team......................U.S.S.R.
ROWING
Single Sculls.........Vyacheslav Ivanov, U.S.S.R.
Double Sculls......................U.S.S.R.
Pairs without Coxswain......................Canada
Pairs with Coxswain......................U.S.A.
Four Oars without Coxswain..............Denmark
Four Oars with Coxswain..............Germany
Eight Oars with Coxswain..............U.S.A.

OLYMPIC GAMES

SHOOTING

Clay Pigeon....................Ennio Matterelli, Italy
Free Pistol..................Vaino Markkanen, Finland
Free Rifle........................Gary Anderson, U.S.A.
Rapid Fire Pistol...............Pentti Linnosvuo, Finland
Small-Bore Rifle (Three Positions)....Lones Wigger, U.S.A.
Small-Bore Rifle (Prone)........Laszlo Hammerl, Hungary

SWIMMING AND DIVING

MEN

100 Meter Free Style.....Don Schollander, U.S.A., 53.4s.*
400 Meter Free Style..Don Schollander, U.S.A., 4m.12.2s.†
1,500 Meter Free Style..Bob Windle, Australia, 17m.1.7s.*
200 Meter Breast Stroke.Ian O'Brien, Australia, 2m.27.8s.†
200 Meter Butterfly......Kevin Berry, Australia, 2m.6.6s.†
200 Meter Back Stroke.....Jed Graef, U.S.A., 2m.10.3s.†
400 Meter Individual Medley..Dick Roth, U.S.A., 4m.45.4s.†
400 Meter Free Style Relay......U.S.A. (Steve Clark, Mike
    Austin, Gary Ilman, Don Schollander) 3m.32.2s.†
800 Meter Free Style Relay..U.S.A. (Steve Clark, Roy Saari,
    Gary Ilman, Don Schollander) 7m.52.1s.†
400 Meter Medley Relay.U.S.A. (Thompson Mann, Bill Craig,
    Fred Schmidt, Steve Clark), 3m.58.4s.†
Springboard Diving...............Ken Sitzberger, U.S.A.
Platform Diving...................Bob Webster, U.S.A.

WOMEN

100 Meter Free Style......Dawn Fraser, Australia, 59.5s.*
400 Meter Free Style....Ginny Duenkel, U.S.A., 4m.43.3s.*
100 Meter Butterfly.....Sharon Stouder, U.S.A., 1m.4.7s.†
100 Meter Back Stroke...Cathy Ferguson, U.S.A., 1m.7.7s.†
200 Meter Breast Stroke........Galina Prozumenschikova,
    U.S.S.R., 2m.46.4s.*
400 Meter Individual Medley....Donna de Varona, U.S.A.,
    5m.18.7s.*
400 Meter Free Style Relay.......U.S.A. (Sharon Stouder,
    Donna de Varona, Pokey Watson,
    Kathy Ellis) 4m.3.8s.†
400 Meter Medley Relay........U.S.A. (Cathy Ferguson,
    Cynthia Goyette, Sharon Stouder,
    Kathy Ellis) 4m.33.9s.†
Springboard Diving.......Ingrid Kramer Engel, Germany
Platform Diving....................Lesley Bush, U.S.A.

WEIGHT LIFTING

Bantamweight.......Aleksei Vakhonin, U.S.S.R., 786.5 lb.†
Featherweight.......Yoshinobu Miyake, Japan, 874.5 lb.†
Lightweight....Waldemar Baszanowski, Poland, 951.5 lb.*
Middleweight.....Hans Zdrazila, Czechoslovakia, 979 lb.*
Light-Heavyweight...Rudolf Plukfelder, U.S.S.R., 1,045 lb.*
Middle-Heavyweight........Vladimir Golovanov, U.S.S.R.,
    1,072.5 lb.*
Heavyweight.....Leonid Zhabotinsky, U.S.S.R., 1,259.5 lb.*

WRESTLING (FREE STYLE)

Flyweight....................Yoshikatsu Yoshida, Japan
Bantamweight...................Yojiru Uetake, Japan
Featherweight...............Osamu Watanabe, Japan
Lightweight.....................Enio Dimov, Bulgaria
Welterweight.......................Ismail Ogan, Turkey
Middleweight.................Prodan Gardjev, Bulgaria
Light-Heavyweight.........Alexandr Medved, U.S.S.R.
Heavyweight.............Alexandr Ivanitsky, U.S.S.R.

WRESTLING, (GRECO-ROMAN)

Flyweight....................Tsutomu Hanahara, Japan
Bantamweight..............Masamitsu Ichiguchi, Japan
Featherweight................Imre Polyak, Hungary
Lightweight.....................Kazim Ayvas, Turkey
Welterweight...............Anatoly Kolesov, U.S.S.R.
Middleweight...........Branislav Simie, Yugoslavia
Light-Heavyweight.........Bogan Alexandrov, Bulgaria
Heavyweight..................Istvan Kozma, Hungary

YACHTING

5.5 Meter..........................Australia
Dragon.............................Denmark
Star...............................Bahamas
Flying Dutchman..................New Zealand
Finn Monotype.....................Germany

TEAM SPORTS

Basketball......................................U.S.A.
Field Hockey....................................India
Soccer...Hungary
Volleyball (Men's).............................U.S.S.R.
Volleyball (Women's)............................Japan
Water Polo.....................................Hungary

WINNERS OF WINTER GAMES

SKIING

MEN

Downhill...........Egon Zimmerman, Austria, 2m.18.2s.
Slalom...............Josef Stiegeler, Austria, 2m.11.1s.
Giant Slalom.........Francois Bonlieu, France, 1m.46.7s.
15 Kilometer Cross-Country......Eero Mantyranta, Finland
    50m.54.1s.
30 Kilometer Cross-Country......Eero Mantyranta, Finland,
    1h.30m.50.7s.
50 Kilometer Cross-Country.....Sixten Jernberg, Sweden,
    2h.43m.52.6s.
40 Kilometer Cross-Country Relay...Sweden, 2h.18m.34.6s.
Nordic Combined..Tormod Knutsen, Norway, 469.28 points
70 Meter Special Jumping.....Veikko Kankkonen, Finland,
    229.90 points
90 Meter Special Jumping........Toralf Engan, Norway,
    230.70 points
Biathlon.........Vladimir Melanin, U.S.S.R., 1h.20m.26.8s.

WOMEN

Downhill.................Christl Haas, Austria, 1m.55.4s.
Slalom..............Christine Goitschel, France, 1m.29.9s.
Giant Slalom.........Marielle Goitschel, France, 1m.52.2s.
5 Kilometer Cross-Country.....Claudia Boyarskikh, U.S.S.R.,
    17m.50.5s.
10 Kilometer Cross-Country...Claudia Boyarskikh, U.S.S.R.,
    40m.24.3s.
15 Kilometer Cross-Country Relay......U.S.S.R., 59m.20.2s.

SKATING

MEN

500 Meters............Terry McDermott, U.S.A., 40.1s.*
1,500 Meters............Ants Antson, U.S.S.R., 2m.10.3s.
5,000 Meters.......Knut Johannesen, Norway, 7m.38.4s.*
10,000 Meters........Jonny Nilsson, Sweden, 15m.50.1s.

WOMEN

500 meters............Lydia Skoblikova, U.S.S.R., 45.0s.*
1,000 Meters........Lydia Skoblikova, U.S.S.R., 1m.33.2s.*
1,500 Meters.......Lydia Skoblikova, U.S.S.R., 2m.22.6s.*
3,000 Meters.......Lydia Skoblikova, U.S.S.R., 5m.14.9s.

FIGURE SKATING

Men.................Manfred Schnelldorfer, Germany
Women..................Sjoukje Dijkstra, Netherlands
Pairs....Ludmilla Belousova and Oleg Protopopov, U.S.S.R.

TEAM SPORT

Ice Hockey.....................................U.S.S.R.

SLEDDING

BOBSLEDDING

Two-Man.....Antony Nash and Robin Dixon, Great Britain
Four-Man.............................Canada No. 1

LUGE

Men's Singles................Thomas Kohler, Germany
Men's Two-Seater....Josef Fiestmantl and Manfred Stengl,
    Austria
Women's Singles.............Ortrun Enderlein, Germany

See also ICE SKATING; SKIING; SWIMMING; TRACK
AND FIELD.

ONTARIO. See CANADA.

OPERA. See MUSIC.

ORCHESTRA. See MUSIC.

OSWALD, LEE HARVEY. See WARREN COMMISSION;
WARREN REPORT (appendix).

OUTDOOR RECREATION. The 88th Congress enacted two landmark conservation measures, both of which were signed by President Lyndon B. Johnson on the same day, Sept. 3, 1964. One, the Wilderness Act, provided statutory protection to possibly as much as 61,000,000 acres of federal wilderness lands (see Section Two, CALL TO THE WILDERNESS).

The other measure, the Land and Water Conservation Fund Act, in the words of the President, "assures our growing population that we will begin . . . to acquire, on a pay-as-you-go basis, the recreation lands that tomorrow's Americans will require."

Beginning Jan. 1, 1965, state and federal agencies engaged in outdoor recreation activities will be able to draw on the fund. Sixty per cent of the annual appropriations from the fund will be available as grants-in-aid to the states, on a 50-50 matching-fund basis. The remaining 40 per cent of the fund will be available for federal purchase of recreation areas and to help offset costs of installing public recreation facilities at U.S. water developments.

Money for the fund will come from (1) admission and user fees at federal recreation areas, (2) proceeds from sale of U.S. surplus realty, and (3) the existing tax on motorboat fuel. The fund will be supplemented by advance, repayable congressional appropriations, expected to average $60,000,000 annually over eight years beginning in 1967. It will be administered by the Bureau of Outdoor Recreation.

Early in the year, the bureau began work on the first Nationwide Outdoor Recreation Plan. By July 1, 1967, it is to inventory the existing and potential supply of recreation resources and determine the needs for outdoor recreation.   A. L. NEWMAN

See also HUNTING AND FISHING; WILDLIFE.

OUTER MONGOLIA, MONGOLIAN PEOPLE'S REPUBLIC OF, firmly supported the Soviet Union in its dispute with Communist China. As a result, Chinese-Mongol relations deteriorated badly in 1964.

In April, Mongolia expelled a number of Chinese workmen, accusing them of subversive activities. In June, the Mongolian Communist party published charges that China was making "clumsy attempts by various kinds of pressure" to force Mongolia under Chinese influence.

In August, Communist China dealt the nation an economic blow when it stopped all transit trade across China to Mongolia. It had already announced that thousands of Chinese communist workers had been withdrawn from Mongolia after nine years of technical and labor assistance.

Population: 1,075,000. **Government:** Chairman of the Presidium of the Great People's Khural Zhamsarangin Sambu; First Secretary of the People's Revolutionary Party and Premier Yumzhagin Tsedenbal. **Foreign Trade:** exports, $69,000,000; imports, $104,000,000. **Principal Exports:** cattle, hides, wool.   JOHN N. STALKER

See also ASIA.

PACIFIC ISLANDS found themselves the objects of increasing attention by the world's larger powers. In part, this was due to the long-range strategic significance of the Pacific, but it also reflected a growing restiveness among the peoples of the area.

Tahiti became steadily more disenchanted with its French rulers. This was accentuated by the stationing of some 7,000 legionnaires on the island in order to prepare for a nuclear test. The Tahitians protested the proposed test as well as a scheduled income tax. An island-wide strike forced the French to repeal the tax. But there were indications of other protests in the offing.

The U.S. trust territory also came in for some attention with sharp criticism being leveled at the U.S. administration. There were indications that Washington would attempt some major reforms during the coming year. British areas in the Pacific began preparing for independence. Fijians and Tongans began the process of self-government under British guidance.   JOHN N. STALKER

PACKAGING. A report to the U.S. Senate Judiciary Committee from its antitrust subcommittee in late 1964 was of prime interest to the packaging industry. The report urged more government control over manufacturers' claims, and disclosures of weight, size, and quality on packages. It was expected to spur action on a new "truth in packaging" bill, which failed to pass in the 88th Congress. But any new regulations were expected to have little effect on sales of the packaging companies, still enjoying a growth-industry status.

In 1964, demand continued to mount for packages that protected products from damage in transit, that stimulated impulse buying in the stores, and that contained built-in-convenience features. An outstanding example of the latter: The easy-open tab tops, developed for soft drink and beer cans, spread to easy-open caps for bottles in 1964.

The battle of materials raged more furiously in packaging during 1964 than perhaps in any other sector of industry (see INDUSTRY). *Dun's Review*, in a year-end survey, noted that plastics had begun to invade the big market for motor oil containers. Aluminum, which had all but eliminated the long-entrenched tin can over a four-year period, faced the threat of being sidelined itself. Steelmakers fought to get some of the aluminum foil business by developing a tough steel foil as thin as .00125 inch.

Figures from two segments of the industry indicated its growth and scope. About 600 U.S. paperboard plants turned out more than 10,000,000,000 fiberboard boxes in 1964. Corrugated and solid fiberboard output exceeded 95,000,000,000 square feet. The total output was worth almost $1,500,000,000, a tenfold increase over the 1934 figure.

Glass container shipments for 1964 rose 2.6 per cent to about 186,800,000 gross, or nearly 27,000,000,000 individual jars and bottles.   EDWIN W. DARBY

449

PAINTING
AND SCULPTURE

T HE YEAR 1964, in spite of the anniversaries of Michelangelo and Shakespeare and even with a number of major exhibitions, was not truly lively. See LITERATURE (Close-Up). The greatest exhibition was the monumental survey devoted to Goya at the Royal Academy, in London, in the early winter of 1964. Except for the late "black" works which, out of caution, the Spanish authorities would not lend and, of course, for the frescoes, the Spanish master was seen as he had not been for many years. Indeed, it might not be possible to see such an exhibition of Goya again. The anger, power, and finally, the beauty of the Spanish painter became visible as seldom before. The exhibition seemed to prove that such large shows will be increasingly rare and are perhaps over.

Pictorial Parade

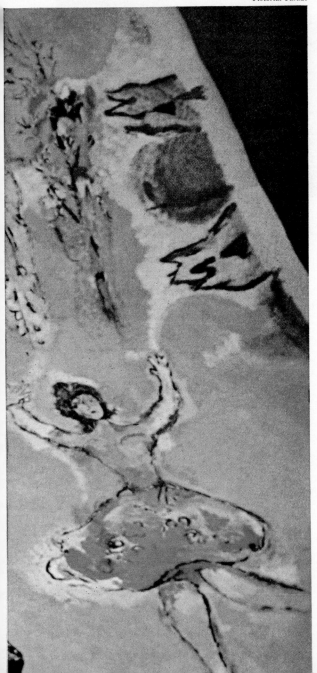

Spanish Fury. At the same time that London saw Goya, Toronto (and then Montreal) viewed Picasso. It was the first time that the contemporary Spanish master was seen at close range in Canada. Spanish fury seemed to touch as painfully home in Canada as it usually does in the Anglo-Saxon world. Toronto also mounted the first major display in the Western Hemisphere of Canaletto, the great 18th century painter of Venetian landscapes, and his circle. The clarity, logic, and freshness prevailed over a slight dryness and post card sameness in this glorious master.

Oxford Exhibition. One of the finest of the year's displays was at the Walker Art Gallery, Liverpool. It was devoted to the newly cleaned treasures of Christ Church, Oxford. These paintings and drawings again reminded the world that whatever their accomplishment creatively, the British have been the greatest collectors since antiquity.

Byzantine Splendor. The Council of Europe presented in Athens another view of a major phase in European art—this time the Byzantine. The only factor to make this less than a perfect exhibition was some cancellations of loans made because of the political situation. The strange world of twilight antiquity and the emerging medieval ethos melded in the exhibition to prove the hieratic splendor and truly awesome luxuries of the Byzantine world. And, if the great mosaic churches could not be moved bodily to be included in the exhibition, the magic and atmosphere of a luxurious way of life and death was abundantly visible.

Houdon's Noble Portraits. One of the remarkable exhibitions of 1964 was the elegant one devoted to the portraits of Jean Antoine Houdon by the Worcester Museum. Portrait shows are too frequently dull, but this one proved a fascinating gallery of famous men and a noble tribute to a great sculptor. The quality and surfaces of the sculpture proved to be one of the truly delicious aspects of the exhibition, and this quality, together with the installation, made the spectator visually aware of the presence of very

MARC CHAGALL, 77, at work on a section of the ceiling he painted for the Paris Opéra, a 19th century shrine of French culture (turn page).

451

Pictorial Parade

CHAGALL'S CEILING for the Paris Opéra seems to float above the audience. Its panels are meant to evoke the spirit of several great works of opera and ballet.

Courtesy Pace Galleries

great men. The exhibition included Houdon's famous busts of Washington, Franklin, and Voltaire, and it made a fine sequel to the Worcester's exhibit of Roman portrait heads.

The Guggenheim Museum in New York presented its fourth international exhibition. It was a curator's personal anthology and received equally personal reviews. The Guggenheim's two best shows of the year were devoted to the works of Albert Gleizes and Alexander Calder.

New Museum. The Gallery of Modern Art in New York City, including the Huntington Hartford collection, opened in March. The consensus was that New York could indeed use another gallery. The opening show was devoted to Pavel Tchelitchew and was followed with a pre-Raphaelite exhibition organized in Indianapolis. The latter proved that art, like wine, sometimes travels badly. The large number of exhibitions were, on the whole, well received. The building itself, received less praise.

OUCH, IT'S OP-ART! It moves, wriggles, bulges. Artist Victor Vasarely and others experimented with the puzzle of vision and illusion in art.

The Venice Biennale provoked only small enthusiasm. It and the Carnegie International again made sensitive critics question the whole system of large and catchall exhibitions. The Biennale seemed particularly capricious. The Italian critics' howls of rage at the Americans did not seem justified by Italy's own performance.

Much of the exhibition suggests to observers that the Biennale has become only a vehicle for dealers and violent partisan opinion. The top prize in Venice was won by the U.S. pop painter Robert Rauschenberg. The Carnegie exhibition remains an American tradition. But there was the impression among some viewers and art critics that the tradition no longer is as viable as it was, and a huge cross section of art began to pall.

The Major U.S. Exhibition was devoted to Pierre Bonnard. Organized by the Museum of Modern Art, The Art Institute of Chicago, and the Los Angeles County Art Museum, it presented the French master in depth. His color and charm proved overwhelming. The Whitney Museum, in New York City, presented Edward Hopper at great length in a display which emphasized the artist's seriousness, his lack of charm, and his integrity.

The Art Institute presented an important retrospective of Ivan Albright, whose reputation held up well against the acid test of such an exhibition.

Acquisitions. The most important objects to enter American public collections were Poussin's noble, early *Assumption*, which moved from the Exeter collection in Great Britain to Washington's National Gallery at Washington, D.C., and the Romanesque Bury St. Edmund's ivory cross, obtained by the Cloisters in New York City.   JOHN MAXON

See also ARCHITECTURE; FAIRS AND EXHIBITIONS; Section One, ALISTAIR COOKE ON THE ARTS.

PAKISTAN held an indirect presidential election that lasted nearly three weeks in 1964. Balloting began in West Pakistan on October 31 and ended in East Pakistan on November 19. The voters, of whom some 40,000,000 flocked to the polls, were to select some 80,000 electors who would in turn choose either Miss Fatima Jinnah, a sister of Pakistan's founder, or the incumbent president, Mohammed Ayub Khan. Miss Jinnah, who campaigned against the one-man rule of President Ayub, promised to end the system of indirect balloting for president if elected. On Jan. 2, 1965, President Ayub was reelected by a 2-to-1 majority.

Pakistani-Indian relations were tense early in the year as religious strife broke out between Moslems and Hindus in both countries. Between January 1 and October 31, about 150,000 Hindus had fled Pakistan for India. About 500,000 Moslems had fled to East Pakistan in the 14 months ended August 29.

Despite political enmities, the nation prospered. Its economy surged ahead, boosted by good harvests (up 4 per cent), dynamic industrial growth (up 15 per cent), and stable prices.

Population: 102,700,000. **Government:** President Mohammed Ayub Khan. **Foreign Trade:** exports, $405,000,000; imports, $1,080,000,000. **Principal Exports:** cotton, jute, textiles.   KEKI R. BHOTE
See also ASIA.

PALEONTOLOGY. See ANTHROPOLOGY; ARCHAEOLOGY; Section Two, MAN'S BEGINNINGS.

PALESTINE. See ISRAEL; MIDDLE EAST.

PANAMA inaugurated Marco Aurelio Robles as its president on October 1. Robles, who thus became the 14th chief of state elected by popular ballot and the 35th to serve in Panama, inherited formidable problems. He faced a treasury that was $20,000,000

POSSIBLE ROUTES FOR NEW U. S. SEA-LEVEL CANAL IN LATIN AMERICA

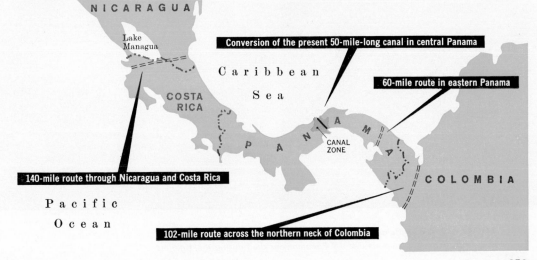

BITTER SMOKE of battle swirls around two American GI's, trapped by rioting Panamanian mob. Four U.S. soldiers and 19 Panamanians died during the fighting.

in the red. Unemployment was approaching 20 per cent of the labor force. Even more troubling to the new president were U.S.-Panamanian relations which, though they were improving, still remained delicate. See ROBLES, MARCO AURELIO.

Diplomatic Ties between the two countries had been broken on January 10, when Panama recalled its ambassador from Washington, D.C. The move followed a series of bloody riots that had broken out in Balboa after U.S. high school students in the Canal Zone had insisted on raising the U.S. flag in defiance of an agreement with Panama that it be flown only alongside the Panamanian one in the area. At least 23 persons, including four U.S. soldiers, were killed and more than 350 wounded in clashes between Panamanian mobs and U.S. troops in the zone.

At Panama's request, the United Nations (UN) Security Council met in emergency session to consider Panamanian charges of U.S. aggression. But UN action was deferred to permit the Organization of American States (OAS) to mediate the dispute. OAS efforts enabled both sides to reach an agreement on January 15. It called for eventual restoration of relations and renegotiation of the canal dispute.

New Canal. On December 18, U.S. President Lyndon B. Johnson announced that the United States was ready to negotiate a new treaty for the canal with Panama. The treaty would recognize the sovereignty of Panama over the area; it would also provide for its own termination when a new U.S.-proposed sea-level waterway came into operation (see map).

Population: 1,215,000. **Government:** President Marco Aurelio Robles. **Foreign Trade:** exports, $58,000,000; imports, $166,000,000. **Principal Exports:** bananas, fish, petroleum.   MARY C. WEBSTER

See also LATIN AMERICA.

PAPUA AND NEW GUINEA. See NEW GUINEA, PAPUA AND.

PARAGUAY celebrated a year of progress under the continuing leadership of President Alfredo Stroessner. The political steadiness of his 10-year rule had enabled the country to achieve monetary stability, slow down inflation, and curb excessive administrative spending.

The nation continued to speed its road-building program. A 475-mile road from Asunción to the Bolivian border was opened in September. An electrification program, designed to end the nation's dependence on small and costly thermal units powered by imported fuel, was also underway. The Inter-American Development Bank extended a $14,000,000 loan to help finance a 45,000-kw hydroelectric plant on the Acaray River.

Population: 1,965,000. **Government:** President Alfredo Stroessner. **Foreign Trade:** exports, $64,000,-000; imports, $41,000,000; **Principal Exports:** meat, tobacco, wool.   MARY C. WEBSTER

See also LATIN AMERICA.

PARENTS AND TEACHERS, NATIONAL CONGRESS OF (PTA), took formal action calling for the elimination of racial discrimination in education and employment. A resolution adopted almost unanimously by delegates to the 68th annual convention in Chicago in May stated: "We believe that some children, because of their race or color or creed, suffer injustices and inequality of educational opportunities and inequality of work opportunities, and we are compelled by conscience and conviction to right these wrongs through just and peaceful solutions."

The delegates also adopted resolutions on raising the standards of mass media, and the education of youth on the hazards of smoking. The organization also urged its members to accept their responsibility in spiritual matters, which, a resolution declared, properly belongs in the home and in the church.

A proposal to merge with the 300,000-member National Congress of Colored Parents and Teachers was discussed, but officials of both groups agreed that the taking of immediate steps in this direction would deprive many Negro children in Southern states of PTA services.   JOSEPH P. ANDERSON

PARKS. Continental United States got its first all-new park in 17 years with the establishment of Canyonlands National Park around the confluence of the Green and Colorado rivers in southeastern Utah. This wilderness-type park embraces a quarter of a million acres of spectacularly eroded desert, mesa, and canyon country.

During the year, the National Park Service (NPS) also considered other areas for park status: the Redwoods in northern California; Guadalupe Mountains in Texas; Voyageurs, near Lake of the Woods, Minnesota; and the Northern Cascades in Washington (see Section Two, CALL TO THE WILDERNESS).

Notable additions to the National Park System authorized by Congress in 1964 included: Fire Island National Seashore, off Long Island, New York, and the Ozark National Scenic Riverways, in Missouri. The Roosevelt Campobello International Park in the Canadian province of New Brunswick was dedicated in August by First Ladies of the United States and Canada, Mrs. Lyndon B. Johnson and Mrs. Lester B. Pearson. The 20-acre park on Campobello Island was the summer estate of President Franklin D. Roosevelt.

The birthplaces of Presidents John F. Kennedy (Brookline, Mass.) and Woodrow Wilson (Staunton, Va.) were among the 96 sites declared eligible in 1964 for status as registered national historic landmarks. Since 1960, when the registry was begun, 548 sites have been thus recognized.

Visits to parks, monuments, and other NPS units in 1964 approached the 100,000,000 mark, up from 94,092,900 in 1963.   A. L. NEWMAN

See also FORESTRY AND FOREST PRODUCTS; HUNTING AND FISHING; OUTDOOR RECREATION.

PEACE CORPS

A NEW RESERVOIR of manpower, the "blue collar" workers, was tapped by the Peace Corps for its overseas volunteers.

"This is going to be the workingman's Rhodes scholarship," said Peace Corps Director R. Sargent Shriver, Jr. The Peace Corps "has never been just for college graduates," Shriver continued. It needs people "who can do things—roof houses, build buildings, fix automobiles, and teach wood and metal working."

Recruiting at plant gates and in union halls was started after Shriver reached agreements with George Meany, AFL-CIO president; Walter Reuther, United Auto Workers president; and the heads of 20 U.S. industrial companies in September.

Shriver aimed to have at least 2,000 "blue collar" corpsmen by Christmas, 1965. Among the first to sign up were 84 craftsmen at the Caterpillar plant in Peoria, Ill. Other companies in the program included Ford, General Motors, Chrysler, International Harvester, Mack Truck, and John Deere. Each agreed to give their workers a two-year leave of absence, with re-employment, seniority, and pension rights guaranteed. Married couples were eligible if they had no dependents under 18.

Where They Are. By the end of 1964, approximately 10,000 corpsmen were serving in 46 countries. Latin America had the largest contingent, 4,175; Africa was second with 3,065; there were 1,615 in the Middle East, North Africa, and South Asia; the Far East had 1,200.

Fifty-two per cent of the corpsmen were teaching at elementary, secondary, or university levels. Twenty per cent were working in rural community action projects, 9 per cent in health, 7 per cent in agricultural extension work, 8 per cent in urban community action, and 3.5 per cent in public works.

Expanding Program. The Peace Corps aimed to have about 14,000 corpsmen on duty overseas by the fall of 1965. To finance this 4,000-man increase, Congress boosted its appropriation of $96,000,000 for fiscal 1964 to $104,100,000 for fiscal 1965.

The 1964 applicants totaled 42,862, compared to 38,681 in 1963. Of the 1964 total, 5,500 were selected for a two-year tour of duty overseas.

Two volunteers died during service in 1964: Bruce E. McKeen, 23, of Anderson, Calif., was killed while mountain climbing in Nepal. Cynthia Myers, 23, of Perry, Kans., drowned while swimming in India.

A Domestic Peace Corps, to be known as VISTA, for "Volunteers in Service to America," was being organized as the year ended as part of the antipoverty program. Shriver was given the additional responsibility of heading the Office of Economic Opportunity.   WILLIAM McGAFFIN

See also Section Two, DOS GRINGAS AMERICANAS; JOB CORPS; SOCIAL WELFARE (Close-Up); VISTA.

Paul Conklin, PIX

GLOBE-GIRDLING R. Sargent Shriver, Jr., right, Peace Corps chief, stops to talk with driver of camel caravan in Afghanistan's Khyber Pass.

457

MATTERHORN CLIMBER. U.S. Secretary of Defense Robert S. McNamara tackled the Swiss Alps as part of well-earned vacation.

PERSONALITIES OF 1964. Americans chose President Lyndon B. Johnson as the man they admired most in 1964 as they did in 1963. Sir Winston Churchill was second on their list, according to the Gallup Poll, and former President Dwight D. Eisenhower was third. New on the list was Martin Luther King, Jr., who placed fourth. *Time* magazine chose the 1964 Nobel peace laureate as its choice for "Man of the Year" for the second consecutive time.

Former First Lady Jacqueline Kennedy remained Americans' choice as the most admired woman for the third consecutive year. Present First Lady

Mrs. Lyndon B. Johnson was their choice as the second most admired woman, as she was in 1963. Pearl S. Buck, Nobel literature laureate of 1938 and a newcomer, was eighth on the most admired list.

Entries marked * indicate that the persons have biographies in The World Book Encyclopedia.

Baker, Cathy May, age 7, wrote to President Johnson expressing a desire to sleep at the White House. She was granted a special tour and a chat with the President in late August. During the threatened railroad strike in April, she wrote asking the President to keep the trains running so that her grandmother might go from Yonkers, N. Y. to Chicago for Cathy May's first communion.

Blair, Peter, of Chelmsford, England, was the first amateur to bounce a signal off the moon to another continent. Using a homemade radioscope, he beamed a message which was picked up by the powerful U.S. radio telescope in Puerto Rico.

Brown, Alice Peyton, age 110, saw her first Shakespearean play at a New York theater during Senior Citizens Month. "Didn't have much chance to see such when I was young," she said. When watching the feuding Montagues and Capulets in the *Romeo and Juliet* film, she commented, "See what hate can do!" The widowed former slave lives alone in Harlem, uses a cane to walk, and is chief usher at the Friendship Baptist Church.

A NEW ELVIS PRESLEY
Joseph George Camenzuli, a Malta-born naturalized Australian, changed his name because everyone found *Camenzuli* hard to pronounce. Since taking the name of his favorite singer, Elvis Presley, the factory worker has appeared on TV, and has had requests for his autograph. Now the new Elvis thinks he just might become a singer.

Cauthorne, Edward Everett, Harvard University's oldest alumnus, was 102 years old on May 20, 1964. A week earlier, he and others from a New York home for the aged visited the World's Fair. On learning that the model X-15 Rocket plane, on display in the U.S. Space Park, had a maximum speed of 4,104 mph, he said, "Well, that beats walking." He recalled trying to guess the number of beans in a glass jar at the Cotton Centennial Exposition in 1884 at New Orleans, La. The prize was a horse and a carriage.

Cooke, Hope, a former New York debutante and now Maharani of the Himalayan kingdom of Sikkim, returned to the United States in late summer. Maharaja Namgyal and Prince Palden, their 6-month-old son, came, too. It is an old Sikkimese custom to visit the wife's relations with the first-born as soon as possible. The Maharani's aunt and former guardian is Mrs. Seldon Chapin, widow of the former U.S. ambassador to Iran. The Maharaja and Maharani attended the New York World's Fair while in the city. They were married in March, 1963, in the Sikkim capital of Gangtok.

DuPea, Tatsumbie, a Piute Indian of Los Angeles, celebrated her 115th birthday in July. She announced that she had been receiving love letters from a London circus performer. "Of course, he doesn't know my age."

THE FIRST IN 300 YEARS
Mrs. Walter Earl gave birth to a daughter in July at Bryan, Tex. Shelly Virlene is the first girl born in the Earl family in more than 300 years. The father is a senior at the Texas Agricultural and Mechanical College.

"The life of this man whom we are honoring is unique. The oldest among us can recall nothing to compare with him, and the younger ones among you, however long you live, will never see the like again."

THE SPEAKER WAS former Prime Minister Harold Macmillan. The words were addressed to the House of Commons. The tribute, one of many spoken that day, paid homage to the Right Honourable Sir Winston Leonard Spencer Churchill, who was retiring from Parliament after an incredible 62 years of service to Crown and country.

The singular homage paid to Sir Winston by the Commons on July 28 was indeed rare. Not since the Duke of Wellington had retired more than a century before had a national figure been so honored. But to the man who had become a legend in his lifetime, it was but one more glittering trophy in a collection that included a Nobel prize, countless honorary degrees, and, perhaps rarest of all, honorary citizenship in the United States—an honor that the American people had granted only once before—to the Marquis de Lafayette.

Just as his honors were varied, so were his vocations. No statesman in the history of Great Britain had pursued such a wide range of careers. Churchill had been, in the words of Canadian Prime Minister Lester B. Pearson, "a heroic war leader, a transcendent politician, parliamentarian, and statesman; an adventurer, soldier, orator, and historian."

AS A MILITARY MAN, he had first tasted battle in Cuba near the end of the 19th century; he was directing his nation's war strategies when the first atomic bomb fell on Japan near the middle of the 20th century. His parliamentary career, which spanned the reigns of six monarchs, began under Queen Victoria; it ended under her great-great-granddaughter, Elizabeth II.

The world knew Churchill under many guises and in many roles: Churchill—the smock-clad artist dabbing at a canvas somewhere in France; Churchill—the weekend artisan, laying a wall of bricks. Above all, the world knew and loved him best as the man who had forged the Grand Alliance of World War II.

Winston Churchill (1874-1965)   Karsh, Ottawa

IT WAS HIS FATE to lead his nation through the cruelest war in history with incomparable courage. It was his destiny to win against hopeless odds. His Homburg-hatted, bow-tie figure flashing the V-for-Victory sign with the index and middle fingers epitomized the Free World's will to survive and to triumph over evil.

Churchill had an extraordinary gift for words. "Blood, toil, tears, and sweat" is now a classic of the language; "the iron curtain" has taken its place in the history books. But Churchill also had a talent for humor, puckish, sometimes ribald, always mischievously good-humored. "If I were married to you," Lady Astor once told him, "I'd feed you poison." "And if I were your husband," retorted Churchill, unperturbedly, "I'd take it."

ON NOVEMBER 30, Winston Churchill celebrated his 90th birthday. His birthday cake had inscribed on it the words used on the flyleaf of his monumental history of World War II: "In war—resolution, in defeat—defiance; in victory—magnanimity; in peace—good will." Sir Winston called these words the moral of his book. But they were, in effect, the story of his life.

Death came to Sir Winston on January 24, 1965. In a sense, however, the word "death" was meaningless. Churchill had already become immortal in his lifetime. PAUL C. TULLIER

A Man Who Was A Legend In His Lifetime

A YEAR BOOK CLOSEUP

PERSONALITIES

Elmore, Daniel, a 72-year-old Negro handyman, received his high school diploma at Watts, Calif., in June, 1964. He attended night classes for four years. "I figured it was my turn," he said. Elmore gave all of his 10 children a college education. Two daughters are nurses, and five of the others are teachers.

Foulois, Benjamin Delahauf, was honored as the United States' first military flier on Dec. 9, 1964, his 85th birthday. He was proclaimed "a living link between the age of the Wright Brothers and today's astronauts." The former Army Signal Corps lieutenant's records include: first flight as a dirigible pilot (1908); first observer on an aircraft cross-country flight, with Orville Wright (1909); first military man to teach himself to fly, "it was my first solo flight, first take-off, first landing, and first crack-up" (1910); first to fly more than 100 miles nonstop, and first to test the use of radio in flight (1911); first to use an aircraft in combat operation (in Mexico, 1916); and first chief of Air Service, American Expeditionary Forces and First Army (1918).

BUT WHERE'S KHRUSHCHEV?
The Leon Gillis Family of Richmond, Va., arrived in Moscow in their horse-drawn covered wagon on October 21, only to learn that Nikita was no longer premier of Russia. "We drove 650 miles across Russia to meet Premier Khrushchev. This is the shock of our lives," Mrs. Gillis protested. None of the Russians they talked to on their tour had told them. The Gillis family of three daughters and one son toured 11 European countries, entered Russia from Poland on September 21, and left for home on November 1. The family crossed the United States in 1962 in the Conestoga-type wagon built by Mr. Gillis.

Greenwood, Mrs. May M., was permitted to retire at the age of 94 this summer, ending a 15-year dispute with the Washburn (Wis.) Library Board. She took charge of the town's public library on July 13, 1898. The board had declined to accept her resignation since 1949. Four years ago, she insisted and the town responded with a May Greenwood Day, honoring her as the nation's oldest librarian. Although still vigorous and able at 94, she resigned in 1964 because of "ill health."

Hayford, Mrs. Delbert, age 60, a petite, civic-minded grandmother of four, was named "The Little Old Lady in Dubuque" in 1964. Her assignment was to erase the town's image of a bumpkin town, created 40 years ago by *The New Yorker*. When the magazine made its debut in 1925, its editors announced that their publication would not be for "this mythical old lady who lived in backwoodsy towns such as Dubuque." The townsmen sent Mrs. Hayford to New York in style to prove that neither she nor the city of Dubuque are country bumpkins.

*Hope, Bob, embarked on his 50th motion picture, *I'll Take Sweden*, in August. The studio gave him a "Lucky Fifty" party. Twenty-seven years ago, he made his first film, *The Big Broadcast*. The Military Chaplains Association gave the comedian its 1964 national citizenship award for entertaining the armed forces over the past 23 years. Christmas of 1964 found Hope and his troupe in South Vietnam. They arrived in Saigon just as the U.S. officers' quarters was bombed on December 24. Hope went immediately to visit the injured. Bob's wife, Dolores, was honored as the Chicago Notre Dame Club's Woman of the Year in March. At the presentation ceremonies, a telegram from the four adopted Hope children was read: "Thank you for recognizing what we have known all along." Smiling, beaming Bob quipped, "I feel like Prince Philip."

THE AIR FORCE'S 1,000,000TH
John J. Jankas, Jr., of Chicago, joined the U.S. Air Force on October 2, the 1,000,000th enlistee since it was set up as a separate armed forces branch in 1954. The Civil Air Patrol cadet lieutenant, with a student pilot license and 32 flying hours, was entered as airman 3rd class. He contemplates a career in the air force.

Kanno, Eila, of Finland is the only woman in the 90-nation Interpol (International Criminal Police Organization), and, of course, is known as Madame Interpol. She entered police work during World War II, has a law degree, and was made chief of the Finnish branch of Interpol in 1954.

Lusk, Elizabeth, age 41, who completed two years of junior college in 1964, was among 110 top students honored during the Chicago Youth Week in May. She received a youth week scholarship to Mundelein College, and plans to become a teacher. Her 14-year-old son, Lance, is an honor student at Luther North High School.

*MacMillan, Donald B., the last survivor of the 1909 Robert E. Peary North Pole expedition, celebrated his 90th birthday on Nov. 10, 1964. The birthday cake was a model of his Arctic schooner *Bowdoin*. Still tall and erect, he said, "I have no advice to impart. I'm still living and learning every day. I still have to go to the dictionary just like everyone else." MacMillan made 25 or more Far North expeditions, has written many books, and compiled the first Eskimo-English dictionary.

SCHOLARSHIP FOR DROP-OUT
London Bus Conductor Edwin Mann, now 43, is a student at Cambridge University. He quit school at the age of 14, but always did a lot of reading. His driver told him that he was wasting his time collecting fares. So Mann entered night school. His teachers suggested that he try for a university scholarship. He did, and got one.

Masefield, John, poet laureate of England, on the publication of *Old Raiger*, his 28th volume, told a literary audience, "I hope to be able to write better someday. At 86, some of the cobwebs have been knocked away and the scene seems to become grander as one gets older. . . ."

McAuliffe, Anthony C., when acting commander of the 101st Airborne Division during the Battle of the Bulge, replied "Nuts" to a German order to surrender on Dec. 22, 1944. In 1964, he visited Bastogne, the Belgian town he refused to surrender 20 years ago. There he found an American tank in the town square, a plaque telling the story of the battle, a large bust portrait of himself, and a Nuts Museum. There also were those who recognized him on sight, and rushed out to greet him.

Natcher, William H., a U.S. Democratic Representative from Kentucky, marked up a perfect 11-year record at the close of the 88th Congress. He had never missed a vote since taking office on Jan. 6, 1954. House Clerk Ralph R. Roberts certified the record, saying, "I know of no other member who has a comparable record."

Nixon, Patricia, led a parade of 53 girls at the International Debutante Ball in New York City in December. Former Vice-President Richard M. Nixon and Mrs. Nixon were both there, of course. Sixteen-year-old sister Julie watched from a subdebutante table. Patricia, now 18, is a freshman at Finch College.

Rothberger, Jeannette Grauberg, is the oldest senior ever graduated at the University of Arizona. She received her B.A. degree at the age of 80 in 1964.

Wide World

SUCCESSFUL OPERATION delighted the 70-year-old Duke of Windsor, who underwent surgery in Houston, Tex., in December.

Mrs. Rothberger came to the United States in 1901 to get an education, but she had to drop out several times because of illness.

89 AND STILL ON THE JOB

Al Sherry is New York Central's oldest employee in point of service. He has been the railroad's agent at New Castle, Ind., for the past 54 years. He first worked (1892) as a telegraph assistant for the Peoria & Eastern Railroad. He is still hearty at the age of 89.

*Shriver, R. Sargent, Jr., director of the Peace Corps and father of four, was named Father of the Year by the National Father's Day Committee. He was cited for his enthusiasm and leadership in accepting added duties as director of the new anti-poverty program.

Spiers, Reginald, is the 22-year-old Australian javelin thrower who was sent C.O.D. air express in a wooden crate to Perth from London, England. He didn't have $640 for a passenger ticket. From Perth, he hitch-hiked to Adelaide (1,800 miles), home to his wife and small daughter. The airlines billed him for $970 freight charges. Failing to make the Australia Olympic team, Spiers worked his way to London on a ship in hopes of winning a berth on the British team. He failed there, too.

Stavig, Mrs. Cora Hjertaas, of Sioux Falls, S. Dak., was chosen American Mother of the Year by the American Mothers Committee, Inc. She is the wife of Lawrence Stavig, president of Augustana College. The mother of four grown sons has also been a foster mother to many of Augustana's foreign students. She lectures some, and acts as a marriage counselor.

HOW THE WORLD BEGAN

This is the title of 6-year-old Dorothy Straight's first book, published by Pantheon Books, 1964. It has been the practice in the Michael Straight (an editor of *The New Republic* magazine) home, Alexandria, Va., to write down the children's stories (two boys and three girls) to send to their grandmother in England. The parents thought Dorothy's story might interest a publisher, and it did.

Swartz, Katheryn Haage, whom the American Medical Association recognizes as the nation's oldest doctor, was 103 years old on Nov. 24, 1964. A graduate of Illinois Medical College (1896), she started to practice as a physician and surgeon in 1899. She and her late husband, Lother, had offices in Chicago's Loop for some years. Dr. Swartz has lived in an old peoples' home since her only daughter died a few years ago.

Tagg, Leonard, a Weymouth (Mass.) high school junior, was a candidate for a Massachusetts House of Representatives seat in 1964. During a history class project, it was found that a candidate must be 21 years old to run as a Republican or a Democrat, but no age was specified for an independent. Tagg started campaigning, and was doing rather well until the State Ballot Law Commission stepped in. Tagg filed two suits, asking the court to overrule the commission. On August 6, Suffolk Superior Court Judge Reuben L. Lurie ruled that candidates must be old enough to vote, at least 21. That ended Tagg's campaigning.

Tenzing Norgay, the Nepalese Sherpa tribesman who in 1953 accompanied Sir Edmund Hillary on man's first ascent to the top of Mount Everest (29,028 feet), visited the United States for the first time in 1964. Now 50, he landed in New York, rode an elevator to the top of the Empire State Building (1,250 feet), and remarked, "It's high." He made the usual tour and visited the World's Fair, then decided "There's not much to do around here."

Trout, Lawana, a 32-year-old English teacher at Charles Page High School, Sand Springs, Okla., was chosen Teacher of the Year. When President Johnson presented the award to her in May, he made her a member of the Presidential Scholars Committee. Mrs. Trout is also a school counselor. Students seek her advice in and out of school. Her husband, a former Sand Springs teacher, is continuing his education at Oklahoma State University. They have one child, a 4-year-old son.

Vinson, Carl, Democratic U.S. Representative from Georgia, retired from Congress in late 1964. He was 81 years old on November 18, the day after Milledgeville celebrated Carl Vinson Day. He had served in the House since Nov. 3, 1914, and was for years chairman of the House Armed Services Committee. He now plans to give full time to his 600-acre plantation, vowing to "wear out, not rust out."

Watkins, Charles L., the only official parliamentarian of the U.S. Senate, retired on Dec. 30, 1964. He came to Washington, D.C., as a senator's stenographer in 1906, was appointed a clerk in the Secretary of the Senate's office in 1914, the Senate journal clerk in 1919, unofficial adviser to the Vice-President in 1923, and official parliamentarian in 1935. He was born in Mount Ida, Ark., in 1879.

PERU made rapid economic progress in 1964. Exports grew, business flourished, and modest starts were made toward solving some of the nation's social problems. The Gross National Product (GNP) was expected to reach a record $3,000,000,000 in 1964. The balance of payments surplus for the first seven months came to a gratifying $42,000,000, up from $5,200,000 in the January to July period of 1963. In the January to September period, the favorable trade balance totaled $56,700,000, a 10-year high.

A somewhat more somber statistic centered around the national budget, which was running at a deficit of about $74,000,000. This was due partly to higher fiscal outlays, a decline of some revenues, and tax cuts for the financially pressed fishing industry.

Early in the year, President Fernando Belaúnde Terry promulgated Peru's first major land reform legislation. Plans to encourage the development of the sprawling but isolated forest and jungle area east of the Andes also were announced.

Population: 12,000,000. **Government:** President Fernando Belaúnde Terry. **Foreign Trade:** exports, $490,400,000; imports, $433,600,000. **Principal Exports:** copper, cotton, sugar.   MARY C. WEBSTER

See also LATIN AMERICA.

PET. A three-year-old English-bred male whippet, Champion Courtenay Fleetfoot of Pennyworth, swept to best-in-show honors at both the Westminster Kennel Club dog show in New York City in February and the International Kennel Club show in Chicago in April. The dog is owned by Mr. and Mrs. Charles B. Newcombe, who operate the Pennyworth Kennel in Newington, N.H. It was shown in both events by Robert Forsyth of Chappaqua, N.Y. Entries totaled 2,547 in the Westminster show, and 2,783 at Chicago. Of the 32 best-of-breed winners at New York, 19 also won at Chicago.

American Kennel Club registration figures showed the poodle retaining its position as the most popular breed of dog in the United States. Ranked next, as in 1963, came German shepherds, beagles, dachshunds, and chihuahuas.

Headliners. The outstanding canine newsmakers of the year were two White House beagles, Him and Her. President Lyndon B. Johnson stirred up a minor controversy late in April when he picked them up by their ears. This, of course, caused the dogs to howl, and the President explained to reporters that he had done it "to make them bark." Then the President added: "It's good for them. And if you've ever followed dogs, you like to hear them yelp." Scores of dog lovers disagreed, but others defended the President. Her died in November after swallowing a stone.

Checkers, another celebrated dog in political lore, died at the age of 12. A pet of the Richard M. Nixon family, the cocker spaniel figured in Nixon's famous television broadcast of 1952, when the then vice-presidential candidate was defending himself against charges that he had improperly received $18,235.

Cats. Triple Grand Champion Shawnee Moonflight, a copper-eyed white Persian male, was named *Cat of the Year*. He was owned by Bill and Nikki Shuttleworth of Jefferstown, Ky. *Opposite Sex Cat of the Year* was Grand Champion Shawnee Whitewash, a copper-eyed white Persian female, also owned by the Shuttleworths. Their silver tabby domestic male, Shawnee Sixth Son, was named *Kitten of the Year*. *Shorthair of the Year* was Quadruple Grand Champion Tra Mar's Sunny, a black Manx male owned by Mr. and Mrs. Dick Tracy of Zanesville, Ohio. *Opposite Sex Shorthair of the Year* was Grand Champion Makhanda Matil, a sealpoint Siamese female.

Tropical Fish. Through selective breeding and mutations, breeders were able to produce new colors in some old favorites. It appeared almost certain that new varieties of angelfish, red and yellow in color, would soon be appearing in pet shops. Guppies, too, were showing up in a wider variety of colors; and high-fin swordtails, first introduced in 1962 in solid red velvet shades, began appearing in black and red combinations.   THEODORE M. O'LEARY

See also ZOOS AND AQUARIUMS.

PETROLEUM, the saying goes, is an industry that booms when times are good but still does very well, indeed, when conditions are unfavorable. In 1964, it did "very well, indeed." Overall industry profits set records for the sixth consecutive year, gaining about 7 per cent over the 1963 level. This was good but not spectacular, compared with the 1964 showings of other industries.

Basically, the industry's problem continued to be oversupply. Prior to 1955, demand had grown by 6 per cent a year. The rate since then has averaged only 3 per cent annually. And the 1964 increase fell shy of that average. Effective cost cutting and development of new or increased markets for petrochemicals and plastics accounted for most of the increase in profits.

In 1964, the surge of overseas imports slackened, benefiting domestic crude oil production. Even so, the American Petroleum Institute (API) called on the government to take a new look at imports. The API's directors said "some restrictions on petroleum imports are necessary now." Nevertheless, import quotas for the first half of 1965 were raised slightly. Oversupply, of course, kept prices weak.

In the United States, the most important discoveries of the year were made in the Cook Inlet of Alaska (by Shell and Standard Oil of Indiana), at Railroad Gap in California (by Standard of California), and in eastern Montana (by Sinclair). See AUSTRALIA; CANADA; EUROPE (Close-Up); LIBYA.

Major long-range steps were taken during the year to extract crude oil from shale. A joint venture company headed by Standard of Ohio planned to invest $100,000,000 to produce commercial quality crude from western oil shale lands.   EDWIN W. DARBY

See also COAL; GAS; INDUSTRY.

PHILADELPHIA. Housed in the United States Pavilion at the New York World's Fair in 1964 was a model of a Philadelphia urban renewal project. It was selected by U.S. housing officials as the best example of urban renewal in the country. The model showed a development in the Morton section of Germantown, a suburb. The development was planned to conserve the best features of the area and replace only what was necessary.

Voters gave the green light to the construction of a 60,000-seat city stadium and to an extension of the Broad Street Subway to northeast Philadelphia, with a spur to the stadium.

Four bond issues totaling $162,500,000 were approved in November. Part of the funds will finance city-owned port facilities as part of the 10-year, $120,000,000 Penn's Landing Development along the Delaware River waterfront. The project will include privately owned office buildings, apartment houses, and publicly owned museums.

In the summer, Philadelphia was racked by riots in its slums which caused an estimated $1,000,000 damage. DONALD W. LIEF

See also CITY; CIVIL LIBERTIES; FAIRS AND EXHIBITIONS.

PHILIPPINES, THE, were alarmed by an outbreak of hostilities between neighboring Indonesia and Malaysia in 1964. Although talks between Philippines President Diosdado Macapagal, Indonesia's President Sukarno, and Malaysia's Prime Minister Tunku Abdul Rahman may have moderated the frontier fighting in Borneo, they did not halt Indonesian guerrilla operations in Malaysia. The Philippines and Malaysia, however, did establish consular ties, but a lack of agreement on a formula for settling the Filipino claim in North Borneo delayed resumption of full diplomatic relations. See INDONESIA; MALAYSIA, FEDERATION OF.

Economic Progress was unspectacular yet significant. Although they did not keep pace with growing imports, most exports expanded, led by copra and increased shipments of coconut oil to the United States and Europe. As world prices declined, sugar's position as the second major export was challenged by timber and plywood. Higher prices for copper boosted income for the mining industry, helping finance diversification and greater exploration of undeveloped mineral deposits. More basic industries continued to expand, including cement manufacture, flour and feed milling, and meat packing. A $30,000,000 fertilizer complex under construction on Bataan was only one among several new plants devoted to chemical industries.

Agriculture made less headway. The Philippines continued to import rice to help feed a population growing by over 2.5 per cent annually. Enforcement of the land reform law enacted in 1963 was begun in central Luzon, but there were obstacles, including the need for exact boundary surveys and records of

yields, shortages of experienced staffs and funds, and even a lack of full understanding of the problems among farmers.

National Politics continued to absorb the nation as its two major parties held their conventions in November. President Macapagal was nominated for another four-year term by the incumbent Liberal party. He selected Senator Gerardo Roxas as his running mate. The opposition Nacionalista party chose as its presidential candidate the wartime guerrilla leader, Senator Ferdinand Marcos; Senator Fernando Lopez was named as its vice-presidential choice. Although emphasis in politics was chiefly upon personalities, increasing attention was devoted to such issues as resources and manpower, the role of foreign investment, and ways to meet popular demands for better living and social justice.

Population: 31,500,000. **Government:** President Diosdado Macapagal. **Foreign Trade:** exports, $730,000,000; imports, $766,000,000. **Principal Exports:** copra, sugar, wood. ALBERT RAVENHOLT

See also ASIA.

PHONOGRAPH RECORD. See MUSIC; RECORDING; RECORDINGS FOR CHILDREN.

PHOTOGRAPHY. The camera, on July 31, 1964, performed its greatest scientific and technological feat when it traveled some 240,000 miles to the moon in Ranger VII. For 17 minutes—from the time the plunging spacecraft was within 1,377 miles of the moon until it crash-landed on the surface—six cameras took about 4,300 pictures, which were converted into electronic signals and radioed back to earth. Those historic photographs provided man with close-up views vital to America's space program (see ASTRONOMY; EUROPE [picture]; SPACE TRAVEL [pictures]). Another technological breakthrough in photography was pioneered by *Look* magazine. It introduced the first three-dimensional (3-D) photograph ever to be printed in the millions. The picture, taken with a special camera and printed on a flat surface that was then plastic-coated, created the illusion of depth.

New Cameras. In 1964, a number of manufacturers announced new models with a variety of improvements. Polaroid introduced the Automatic 101 filmpack camera, similar to, but lower priced than, the Automatic 100. It also announced the CU-5 close-up camera for making instant color and black-and-white pictures of small objects.

Kodak added two new models to its line of cartridge-loading Instamatics. The motor-driven 800 can advance film at the rate of one picture a second if a series is desired. Kodak's German-made 500 has an f/2.8 lens, shutter speeds up to 1/500 second, and contacts for an electronic flash unit. Public response to cartridge loading was reflected in the announcement that more than 6,000,000 Instamatics had been sold around the world since they were introduced in May, 1963.

PHOTOGRAPHY

PICTURES OF THE YEAR / Ted Rozumalski, *Houston Chronicle*

STUDY of the late James Frank Dobie, Texas tale spinner, helped win Newspaper Photographer of the Year Award for Texan Ted Rozumalski.

An innovation from the West German camera industry was the new Voigtlander Vitrona, first 35-mm camera with built-in electronic flash.

Europe answered the demand for faster loading with the "Rapid System," which was being built into special cameras. A special 35-mm film cassette serves as a supply cartridge when loaded, and as a lightproof take-up spool when empty. The loaded cassette, with about an inch of film extended, is simply dropped into the opened camera. When the back is closed, the film is engaged by sprocket wheels, advanced two frames, and the camera is ready to shoot. An empty take-up cartridge receives the exposed film. When it is removed for processing, the empty loading cassette is transferred to the take-up position. Special cameras were being built to accept the new "Rapid" cassette.

Film News. In 1964, Kodak announced an improved High-Speed Ektachrome, daylight type, designed to yield sharper color transparencies with finer grain and at no loss in film speed (ASA 160). It was available in 35-mm and 120 size.

Kodak Tri-X and Ekta-color Professional film, Type S, became available in "220" loads. Without the usual paper backing, the 220 loads permitted twice as many 120-size exposures per roll. Honeywell Dynachrome color film with a new and improved emulsion gained a higher rating of ASA 25.

Eastman Kodak also introduced a compact, motorized drum processor that could make 8 x 10 or 11 x 14 enlargements in $7\frac{1}{2}$ minutes.

The photography industry marked the 125th anniversary of the daguerreotype with 1964 sales of $1,300,000,000.

Awards in 1964 in various categories of photography included the following:

26th Annual Newspaper National Snapshot Awards. $1,000 Grand Prize Winners: *Color*—Bob Coyle, Peoria, Ill.; Freeman Patterson, Long Beach, New Brunswick; Kenneth Bergeron, Arlington, Va.; Don McCray, Burbank, Calif. *Black-and-white*—Carl A. Closs, Jr., Bethesda, Md.; Dr. John W. McGee, Albion, Mich.; Albert R. Rodríguez, San Diego, Calif.; Mrs. Lorena Bach, Iowa City, Iowa.

19th Annual Collegiate Competition, sponsored by Kappa Alpha Mu, National Press Photographers Association, University of Missouri School of Journalism, and World Book Science Service, Inc. First place winners from Southern Illinois University: *Feature*, Jim Klepitsch; *Pictorial*, Frank Salmo; and *Portrait/Personality*, Bob Miller; from the University of Maryland: *Portfolio*, *Picture Story/Sequence*, and *News*, Emory Kristof; from the University of Houston: *College Life*, Mike Cook; from the University of Missouri: *Sports*, Gary Cooperman; from Principia College, Illinois: *Category X*, Jim Holland.

Photographic Society of America 1964 Progress Medal Award, to Dr. Deane Rowland White, associate director of the Research Division of the Photo Products Department, E. I. du Pont de Nemours & Company, Parlin, N.J.

White House News Photographers Association. 1964 Grand Award to Noel Clark, free lance.

Joseph A. Sprague Memorial Award by the National Press Photographers Association, to Russell V. Hamm, retired photo manager of the *Fort Lauderdale* (Fla.) *News*, and William P. Steven, editor of the *Houston* (Tex.) *Chronicle*.

Fourth Annual Anscochrome of the Year Photographic Contest, sponsored by Ansco. $1,000 Grand Prize to Jean D. Blome of the Oakland (Calif.) Camera Club.

22nd Annual Pictures of the Year Competition, sponsored by the National Press Photographers Association, University of Missouri School of Journalism, and World Book Science Service, Inc. **Newspaper Photographer of the Year**—Ted Rozumalski, *Houston Chronicle.* **Magazine Photographer of the Year**—George Silk, *Life.* **Two Special Merit Awards—Newspaper Portfolio**—James L. Stanfield, *The Milwaukee Journal*, and **Magazine Portfolio**—Thomas Nebbia, *National Geographic.*

Awards in other categories in order of first, second, and third place were as follows:

Spot News—Bob Jackson, *Dallas Times-Herald;* Tony Tonsic, *Cleveland Press;* Jerry Huff, United Press International (UPI). **General News**—Stan Stearns, UPI; Ed Adams, Associated Press (AP); Hank Daniel, *Charlotte Observer.* **Newspaper Picture Story (News)**—Bill Strode, *Louisville Times and Courier;* George Koshollek, Jr., *The Milwaukee Journal;* Duane Howell, *Denver Post.* **Newspaper Picture Story (Feature)**—Tom McCarthy, *Miami Herald;* Carl R. Hartrup, *Fort Wayne* (Ind.) *News Centennial;* and Ron Wahl, *St. Petersburg Times*, and Bill Snead, *Wilmington News-Journal* (tie).

Feature — Rich Clarkson, *Topeka Capital-Journal;* Charles Trainor, *Miami News;* Wally McNamee, *Washington Post.*

Sports—Horace W. Cort, AP; Thomas DeFeo, *Des Moines Register;* James E. Hughes, *Christian Science Monitor.* **Sports Picture Story**—Rich Clarkson; Dave Cupp, *Charlotte Observer;* Lowell Georgia; *Denver Post.*

Pictorial—James L. Stanfield; Jeep Hunter, *Charlotte* (N.C.) *News;* Ted Rozumalski. **Portrait and Personal-**

ity—Joe Rimkus, *Miami News;* Jeep Hunter; Larry Alspaugh, *Florida Times.*

Category X—Magazine and Newspaper—Don Hunter, *Charlotte News;* Clint Grant, *Dallas News;* Mark Peterschmidt, *Miami Herald.*

Magazine Portfolio—George Silk; Thomas Nebbia. There were only first and second-place winners in this category.

Magazine News or Documentary—Bob Gomel, *Life;* David Boyer, *National Geographic;* Fred Ward, *Black Star.* **Magazine Picture Story**—Michael Rougier, *Time, Inc.;* George Silk; Mark Kaufman, free lance, *Life.* **Magazine Sports**—Lawrence Schiller, *The Saturday Evening Post;* Lawrence Schiller; Tony Tomsic, free lance. **Magazine Pictorial**—Bates Littlehales, *National Geographic;* John Launois, *The Saturday Evening Post;* Thomas Nebbia. **Magazine Portrait and Personality**—Thomas Nebbia; Volkmar Wentzel—*National Geographic;* Arthur Rickerby, *Life.*

Best Newspaper Use of Photographs—*The Louisville Courier-Journal; The Louisville Times; The Milwaukee Journal;* (Honorable Mention) *Oakland Tribune.* **Best Magazine Use of Photographs**—*Look; Life.*

Picture Editor's Award—Angus McDougall, *Harvester World Magazine;* William Latham, *Louisville Times;* Van Hetherly, *Houston Chronicle.*

Presidential — Gordon Converse, *Christian Science Monitor;* Charles Harbutt, *Magnum;* Morris Johnson, UPI. **Special Class—Assassination of President Kennedy Coverage**—*Life.*   FRANK E. FENNER

PHYSICS. Liquid helium has held a fascination for physicists ever since it was first produced by the Dutch physicist Kamerlingh Onnes in 1908. Its most startling property is superfluidity. At a temperature of 2.18°K. (−270.97°C.) it becomes the most superb conductor of heat known, losing all trace of viscosity. In 1964, a new property of this superfluid element was under intensive investigation—that of large-scale, long-lasting currents, or vortex motions.

Apparently something as tiny as a single electron, squirting through a quantity of superfluid helium, is capable of setting up fluid motions very similar to those in smoke rings. Such swirls, or vortex rings, may be several centimeters in diameter and may travel comparatively long distances through the liquid without breaking up.

Superconductivity. Another low-temperature phenomenon, discovered by Onnes in 1911, is that of superconductivity. Onnes found that mercury lost all of its electrical resistance when cooled to liquid helium temperatures. An electric current, once started in a loop of mercury at this low temperature, will continue to circulate for days and weeks on end without any reduction in intensity and without the need of any outside source of power to drive it. It seemed at first that the effect was confined to a few somewhat peculiar metals in a high state of purity. Recently, however, it has been found that superconductivity is a common phenomenon. It occurs in many substances, some not even metals. It also occurs in quite impure substances and in many alloys and chemical compounds.

There are two different kinds of superconducting systems. Type I, the kinds first discovered, are characterized by the complete absence of any magnetic field within the superconductor. In the presence of large magnetic fields, Type I materials lose their superconducting property. The newer Type II superconductors are those with some magnetic field in them. What makes them particularly interesting is that they remain superconducting even in the presence of large magnetic fields.

The Type II superconductors make it possible to maintain heavy currents of electricity in high magnetic fields, without either large generators or the production of great amounts of heat. Conventional electromagnets require large generators to power the current flowing through them, and the heavy currents result in the production of great quantities of heat in the magnet windings, all of which must be removed if the magnet is not to melt. As of 1964, it was possible to produce magnetic fields roughly 30,000 times as great as the earth's magnetic field by using superconducting materials. Larger magnetic fields can be produced in a laboratory by other means, but it is hoped that superconductors will be used in producing still greater magnetic fields.

Magnets. Superconducting magnets (electromagnets maintained by currents in superconductors) presented exciting possibilities in the field of computer technology. By using them, it would be feasible to pack all the works of a room-size computer into a box no larger than a small TV set. The only difficulty is that superconducting magnets must be kept at an extremely cold temperature.

All superconductors known to date work only at liquid helium temperatures. The problem is not just how to build the needed refrigerator, but how to increase the limited supply of helium, the entire world output being found in gas wells in Texas. It would soon be exhausted by any large-scale commercial use. In spite of this, serious thought is being given to designing nuclear accelerators that use superconducting, rather than conventional, electromagnets. The savings on iron and power would more than pay for the cost of the refrigerating plant that would be needed.

Organic Superconductors. Some hope was raised for the possibility of finding superconductors that would not need liquid helium in their operation. Professor Fritz London, one of the pioneers in cryophysics (low-temperature physics), first suggested the possibility of finding large organic molecules that would operate as superconductors, but none have been found. In 1964, Dr. William A. Little of Stanford University showed through mathematical computations that such supermolecules might be synthesized and could conceivably be superconducting even at room temperature. The difficulty would be that such molecules would be extremely unstable and might not hold together long enough to permit synthesis.   S. MATTHEW PRASTEIN

See also ELECTRONICS; NUCLEAR PHYSICS.

PLANET. See ASTRONOMY; SPACE TRAVEL; Section Two, THE UNFOLDING UNIVERSE.

PLASTICS consumption in the United States during 1964, as estimated by the Society for the Plastics Industry, totaled some 9,750,000,000 pounds. Building, which took more than 2,000,000,000 pounds, and the automobile industry, which used almost as much, continued as the industry's principal consumers.

Major plants for the production of the so-called ABS plastics, heavy-duty acrylonitriles that are pressed into various shapes, increased ABS capacity to 80,000,000 pounds a year by the close of 1964, and promised to satisfy rapidly rising demand over the next two or three years.

The New York World's Fair gave plastics makers an important showcase. A million pounds of fiberglass went into the roof of the New York State Pavilion. Facades of acrylic sheet were all over the fairgrounds. Materials that had been shut out of the homebuilding market by local inertia were on display for millions to see.

Aiming at other new uses, 50 commercial dairies were persuaded to try high-density polyethylene—a plastic sorely in need of some new markets to sop up overcapacity—as a material for milk containers. General Electric devised plastics that would conduct electricity, and E. I. du Pont de Nemours began selling Corfam, its "breathing" plastics material for shoe uppers. Du Pont also unveiled a new heavy ionomer plastic for strong lightweight packaging, coatings, pipe, and other uses.   ROBERT E. BEDINGFIELD

See also CHEMICAL INDUSTRY; INDUSTRY; PETROLEUM.

POETRY. See AWARDS AND PRIZES (General); LITERATURE; SIMPSON, LOUIS.

POLAND. Communist leader Wladyslaw Gomulka continued his efforts in 1964 to persuade Soviet Premier Nikita S. Khrushchev to tone down his quarrel with Communist China. The Polish leader also expressed his apprehension over a proposed visit by Khrushchev to West Germany, planned for 1965. Significantly, after Khrushchev's ouster, Gomulka was the only head of a satellite nation to be briefed by the new Soviet leaders during the interval between their coup and the opening of a Moscow summit meeting celebrating the 47th anniversary of the Bolshevik Revolution. See COMMUNISM; RUSSIA.

On the domestic front, Gomulka solidified his control at the Polish Communist Party Fourth Congress held June 15 through June 20. His long-time friend Edward Ochab, who had challenged Khrushchev during the 1956 revolution, became chairman of the Polish Council of State. Ochab succeeded Alexander Zawadzki, who had died August 7.

Inflation, unemployment, and an unfavorable balance of trade beset the country. However, one of the most portentous domestic events since 1956 was a letter written in March by 34 prominent intellectuals to Premier Jósef Cyrankiewicz protesting government censorship and demanding a change in cultural policy. When the contents of the unpublished letter and the punitive measures taken against its writers became known in the West, protests from the West forced the regime to reconsider. However, on November 9, one of the petitioners, Melchior Wankowicz, a U.S. citizen and a writer and lecturer, was convicted and later sentenced to 18 months in jail for distributing "false and slanderous" material against the Polish government.

Population: 31,250,000. **Government:** Communist Party First Secretary Wladyslaw Gomulka; Premier Jósef Cyrankiewicz; President (Chairman of the Polish Council) Edward Ochab. **Foreign Trade:** exports, $1,770,000,000; imports, $1,979,000,000. **Principal Exports:** coal, meat, metals.   TOM AND HARLE DAMMANN

See also EUROPE.

POLAR EXPLORATION. See EXPLORATION.

POLLUTION, a monster of modern industrial civilization, grew as waste chemicals filled the air, dirtied the nation's waterways, and killed living things. Dr. Luther L. Terry, surgeon general of the U.S. Public Health Service (USPHS), warned that the very survival of humanity depended on finding solutions to the pollution problem.

"Every year, more than 500 new chemicals and chemical compounds are introduced into industry, along with countless operational innovations," Terry said. "Except with the most toxic materials, there is necessarily a time lag between the introduction of a new material or process and the recognition of deleterious effects."

Smog continued to be the most noticeable pollutant. Medical scientists cited smog as a factor in the aggravation of heart conditions and respiratory diseases such as asthma, chronic bronchitis, lung cancer, emphysema, and common colds. A chemist at Chicago's Illinois Institute of Technology found that air pollution costs $65 per person annually in the United States, a figure that referred only to the cost of property deterioration and maintenance. Three cities—Washington, Philadelphia, and St. Louis—were found to have smog conditions as serious as those in Los Angeles.

The National Air Stagnation Alert System, operated by the U.S. Weather Bureau and the USPHS, was found useful in alerting areas to possible smog attacks. Its network of installations recorded weather conditions favoring accumulation of air pollutants, and issued warnings to danger areas.

Water Pollution was also widespread as wastes poured into rivers. The pollutants included both industrial and agricultural wastes. Though most states attempt to control such pollution, it was reported that more than 3,000 communities lacked adequate sewage treatment plants and that 2,000 more had no sewage facilities at all. It was pointed out that federal health officials can take action only when communities pollute areas extending beyond state boundaries or when requested to do so by the governor of a state.

Attempts to control oil pollution in the world's oceans became a major subject of discussion in shipping circles in 1964. Certain coastal zones prohibited the discharge of oily wastes in their harbors, and efforts were being made to develop devices able to separate oily substances from seawater.

Pesticides were found to have caused the death of millions of fish and shrimp in the Mississippi River. The USPHS found substances used extensively to control insects in the bodies of dead and dying fish. Its report led to demands for a major effort to determine the effects of such chemicals on human beings. See CHEMICAL INDUSTRY.   FOSTER STOCKWELL

POLO. See SPORTS.

POPULATION, WORLD,

POPULATION, WORLD, had spiraled to an estimated 3,283,000,000 people by mid-1964. Population distribution by continents gave Asia 56 per cent of the world's people. Latin America and Africa together accounted for 16 per cent. The remaining 28 per cent of the population was distributed in Europe, Northern America (Canada and the United States), Oceania, and the Soviet Union. See CENSUS.

The fastest growing region in the world was Latin America with a 2.8 per cent annual rate of increase. At this rate, Latin America's population was expected to double in just 25 years. The slowest rate of population growth—0.5 per cent a year—was found in some of the European countries such as Belgium, Hungary, and Sweden. Their populations were expected to take about 140 years to double.

World population, increasing at over 2 per cent per year, was expected to reach 7,000,000,000 in 38 years. Only a century ago, world population was 1,200,000,000.

Birth and Death Rates. It was estimated that 220 babies were being born into the world every minute. The annual baby crop amounted to a record 120,-000,000. Africa, Asia, and Latin America had birth rates ranging from 40 to 50 births per 1,000 population per year.

European birth rates were generally below 20, while birth rates in Northern America, Oceania, and the Soviet Union were 20 to 25 per 1,000 population. Death rates ranged from over 20 per 1,000 in Africa and Asia to below 10 on the European Continent and Northern America. See VITAL STATISTICS.

A census taken in Nigeria in 1963 and published in 1964 was a source of considerable surprise to the country. The census-takers had counted 56,000,-000 people—almost 19,000,000 more than the 37,000,000 originally estimated.

Although no accurate information was available for the population of the People's Republic of China, it was by far the most populous nation, with India second. Ranking next were the Soviet Union, the United States, Indonesia, Pakistan, Japan, Brazil, West Germany, and Great Britain.   ROBERT E. COOK

See also Section Two, AWAKENING THE LAND; DOS GRINGAS AMERICANAS.

PORTUGAL

PORTUGAL resisted international pressures to revise its policies toward Angola and Mozambique, which the Portuguese government regarded as overseas provinces rather than colonies. It remained adamantly opposed to independence for either Angola, where guerrilla warfare continued during the year, or Mozambique, where rebel forces also became active. See ANGOLA; MOZAMBIQUE.

The African nations, however, vowed they would support moves for the independence of the two territories. A conference of the nonaligned nations held in Cairo in October approved a policy of giving "financial and military support to Africans fighting Portuguese rule." See AFRICA.

On October 17, the Aldeavitla power plant was dedicated on the Douro River at the Spanish border. With a larger capacity than any other hydroelectric plant in Western Europe, it was designed to provide power for both Portugal and Spain. Portugal paid $90,000,000 of the cost and Spain, $50,000,000.

Population: 9,150,000. **Government:** President Américo Deus Rodrigues Tomaz; Premier António de Oliveira Salazar. **Foreign Trade:** exports, $494,000,-000; imports, $772,000,000. **Principal Exports:** alcoholic beverages, fish, textiles.   FRED J. PANNWITT

See also EUROPE.

POST OFFICE

POST OFFICE officials came to the rescue of their long-neglected stepchild, parcel post, in fiscal 1964, when they took steps to reduce delays and damage to packages. First, ZIP (Zone Improvement Program) code distribution of outgoing parcel post was begun in March at a few large post offices in the East. The increased efficiency of sorting proved so successful that the system was to be extended to all major post offices.

Second, the department began to encase small parcels destined for the same ZIP code sectional center in "pool cases," or large cardboard boxes. On arrival, the cases were opened and the individual parcels delivered to nearby addresses. As well as reducing damage, this system also eliminated a number of handlings en route.

Among other steps to improve service during fiscal 1964 were:
• Elimination of hourly time on cancellation marks, with use only of the letters A.M. or P.M. This reduced the number of times from 48 to two that the cancellation dies needed to be changed.
• An electronic address reader and sorter. Contracted for in December, 1963, it was to go into pilot operation in Detroit in early 1965. Its capacity: recognition of 50 city and state addresses and a sorting speed of 27,000 letters an hour.
• "Stamp tagging," in which use of luminescent printing ink allows airmail to be separated automatically from regular mail when a little black box device is attached to a facer-canceler. Field tests proved so successful that on June 1 all airmail stamps were ordered to be printed with luminescent ink.

POULTRY

Volume of mailings rose 2.7 per cent to 69,700,-000,000 pieces. Despite the increase, there were 1,848 fewer employees, or a total of 585,313 on June 30. Net revenues rose 10.4 per cent to $4,206,400,000; appropriation obligations gained 6 per cent to $4,-895,400,000. But $453,000,000 of the gap represented the cost of public services not chargeable to users of the mail.   JOHN A. GRONOUSKI, JR.

POULTRY. U.S. Department of Agriculture (USDA) specialists pointed out that demand and prices "held up well" in 1964, considering (1) higher production, both of eggs and birds, and (2) the second straight year of stiff competition from red meat.

Egg production increased about 2 per cent from 1963's 176,000,000 cases (360 eggs to the case). Per capita domestic consumption, at 314, was one egg less than the year before. Egg prices averaged about one cent below 1963's 34.4 cents.

Similarly, broilers raised in 1964 jumped some 200,000,000 pounds above 1963, to an estimated 7,500,000,000 pounds. But consumers ate slightly more broiler meat than in 1963, or 27 pounds per person. Prices dropped less than $\frac{1}{2}$ cent a pound, from 14.5 cents in 1963.

Broiler exports held close to the 1963 level of 112,000,000 pounds. However, West Germany, best customer for U.S. broilers, boosted its levy in two steps (October 30 and November 16) on ready-to-cook birds with giblets to 15.73 cents a pound, the highest level ever. Other Common Market nations imposed similar tariff increases.

Increased USDA buying and exports helped to counteract the 120,000,000-pound increase in live turkey production, to an estimated 1,800,000,000 pounds in 1964. Turkey exports rose about one-third over 1963, to around 42,000,000 pounds. Turkey prices averaged about one cent less than the 22.3 cents received in 1963.   FRANK B. HARPER

POWELL, SUMNER CHILTON (1924-   ), received the Pulitzer history prize in 1964 for *Puritan Village: The Formation of a New England Town.* The volume represents 10 or more years of research. Powell, a native of Massachusetts, was interested in learning how the New England towns were formed. Finding the best historical records in Sudbury, Mass., he chose that town for his study.

One of Powell's first tasks was to set up a genealogy of Sudbury's founding families. This took him to the English villages from which they came. Powell became interested in this branch of history while attending Williams and Amherst colleges. He took his Ph.D. in history (1956) at Harvard University. He has taught history at several boy's schools in Connecticut and New York.

Sumner Powell was born in Northampton, Mass. His father, who died when the boy was only 4, was an English professor at Amherst College.

See also PULITZER PRIZES.

PRESIDENT OF THE UNITED STATES

LYNDON B. JOHNSON stamped his personality indelibly on his administration and on the nation in 1964, and the nation responded with an overwhelming mandate in the November election. The 36th President appealed eloquently for the "Great Society" and focused the nation's attention on its domestic problems: tax reform, civil rights, and the war against poverty. As he persuaded Congress to enact a sweeping domestic program, the President proved himself a master strategist and politician. In his first State of the Union message, he stressed thrift in government, urged Congress to cut taxes, and called for civil rights legislation and an all-out war against poverty.

THE PRESIDENT meets in Cabinet Room with, from left, Ambassador to the UN Stevenson and Secretaries McNamara (Defense) and Freeman (Agriculture).

THE
PRESIDENT
NOV. 22, 1963

The first Johnson budget was cut to $97,900,000,-000 for fiscal 1965, the first decline in the federal administrative budget since 1961. Despite the cuts, the budget called for spending increases in the fields of education, health, and manpower.

Most of the President's legislative program was passed by the second session of the 88th Congress (see CONGRESS OF THE UNITED STATES). Much of the credit went to the President himself. He breakfasted, lunched, and dined with Congressmen, conferred frequently with leaders of Congress in both parties, and treated members of the 88th to a "Salute to Congress" party on the White House lawn in August.

Domestic Problems facing the President in 1964 included threatened strikes, racial conflict, and the need for improving the system of protecting the life of the Chief Executive.

In April, the President used his powers of persuasion to bring about a settlement of a dispute on work rules that had long troubled the nation's railroads. His and the mediators' work helped preserve the process of collective bargaining. See LABOR.

In October, in the face of a threatened dock workers' strike, the President invoked the Taft-Hartley law calling for an 80-day cooling-off period before the strike. This was the sixth time that a President had taken such action against the International Longshoremen's Association.

A series of Negro riots in Northern cities in the summer of 1964 led the President to ask for an investigation by the Federal Bureau of Investigation (FBI). The FBI later reported that there was no pattern of organization or systematic planning linking the riots. SEE CITY; CIVIL LIBERTIES; NEGRO.

Late in the year, the President acted twice to ward off any threat of inflation. First, in a talk to his Business Council, he urged bankers not to increase their basic business-loan interest rates.

The Inaugural Address of President Johnson

January 20, 1965

MY FELLOW countrymen: On this occasion, the oath I have taken before you—and before God—is not mine alone, but ours together. We are one nation and one people. Our fate as a nation and our future as a people rests not upon one citizen but upon all citizens. That is the majesty and the meaning of this moment. For every generation, there is a destiny. For some, history decides. For this generation, the choice must be our own. Even now, a rocket moves toward Mars. It reminds us that the world will not be the same for our children, or even for ourselves in a short span of years. The next man to stand here will look out on a scene that is different from our own, because ours is a time of change—rapid and fantastic change, baring the secrets of nature, multiplying the nations, placing in uncertain hands new weapons for mastery and destruction, shaking old values and uprooting old ways.

Our destiny in the midst of change will rest on the unchanged character of our people—and on their faith. They came here—the exile and the stranger, brave but frightened—to find a place where a man could be his own man. They made a covenant with this land. Conceived in justice, written in liberty, bound in union, it was meant one day to inspire the hopes of all mankind. And it binds us still. If we keep its terms, we shall flourish.

FIRST, JUSTICE was the promise that all who made the journey would share in the fruits of the land. In a land of great wealth, families must not live in hopeless poverty. In a land rich in harvest, children just must not go hungry. In a great land of healing miracles, neighbors must not suffer and die untended. In a land of learning and scholars, young people must be taught to read and write.

FOR MORE THAN 30 years that I have served this nation I have believed that this injustice to our people —this waste of our resources—was our real enemy. For 30 years or more, with the resources I have had, I have vigilantly fought against it. I have learned, and I know that it will not surrender easily. But change has given us new weapons. Before this generation of Americans is finished, this enemy will not only retreat—it will be conquered.

Justice requires us to remember: When any citizen denies his fellow, saying: His color is not mine or His beliefs are strange and different, in that moment he betrays America, though his forebears created this nation.

Liberty was the second article of our covenant. It was self-government. It was our Bill of Rights. But it was more. America would be a place where each man could be proud to be himself—stretching his talents, rejoicing in work, important in the life of his neighbors and his nation. This has become more difficult in a world where change and growth seem to tower beyond the control, and even the judgment, of men. We must work to provide the knowledge and the surroundings which can enlarge the possibilities of every citizen.

THE AMERICAN COVENANT called on us to help show the way for the liberation of man. And that is today our goal. Thus, if as a nation there is much outside our control, as a people no stranger is outside our hope. Change has brought new meaning to that old mission. We can never again stand aside, prideful in isolation. Terrific dangers and troubles that we once called "foreign" now constantly live among us. If American lives must end, and American treasure be spilled, in countries that we barely know, then that is the price that change has demanded of conviction and of our enduring covenant.

Think of our world as it looks from that rocket that's heading toward Mars. It is like a child's globe, hanging in space, the continents stuck to its side like colored maps. We are all fellow passengers on a dot of earth. And each of us, in the span of time, has really only a moment among our companions.

Then, after a number of selective price boosts in steel during December, he asked his Council of Economic Advisers to investigate and report back.

Warren Commission Report. After the assassination of President John F. Kennedy, President Johnson established a commission headed by Chief Justice of the United States Earl Warren to investigate the assassination and report to the nation. The commission's report was made public late in September, 1964. See KENNEDY, JOHN F.; WARREN COMMISSION; WARREN REPORT (appendix).

Politics. The President of the United States is also head of his party, and in an election year his political role is magnified. Guiding the Democratic National Convention, traveling around the country on political and "nonpolitical" tours, entertaining 30 of the 34 Democratic governors, signing his domestic program into law with elaborate ceremony—all these activities and more made it obvious that

President Johnson was an unusually able politician.

In August, the President named Rhode Island's Senator John O. Pastore as keynote speaker at the Democratic National Convention and appointed Massachusetts Senator John McCormack as its permanent chairman. Earlier, he had ruled out Attorney General Robert F. Kennedy, as well as other Cabinet officials, as a possible vice-presidential candidate. Dramatically, he refused to reveal his choice of Minnesota Senator Hubert H. Humphrey as his running mate until the convention was ready to nominate for the vice-presidency. See DEMOCRATIC PARTY; HUMPHREY, HUBERT H.; KENNEDY, ROBERT F.

Traveling Widely throughout the United States, the President kept up a jet-age pace. He made his second visit of 1964 to the Appalachian area in May and gave 11 speeches in one day. The following day, he addressed 1,000 Georgia legislators and guests at breakfast in Atlanta. Later, he talked to 40,000

How incredible it is that in this fragile existence we should hate and destroy one another. There are possibilities enough for all who will abandon mastery over others to pursue mastery over nature. There is world enough for all to seek their happiness in their own way.

And our own course is abundantly clear. We aspire to nothing that belongs to others. We seek no dominion over our fellow man, but man's dominion over tyranny and misery. But more is required. Men want to be part of a common enterprise—a cause greater than themselves. And each of us must find a way to advance the purpose of the nation and thus find new purpose for ourselves. Without this, we will simply become a nation of strangers.

THE THIRD ARTICLE is union. To those who were small and few against the wilderness, the success of liberty demanded the strength of the Union. Two centuries of change have made this true again. No longer need capitalist and worker, farmer and clerk, city and countryside, struggle to divide our bounty. By working shoulder to shoulder together we can increase the bounty of all. We have discovered that every child who learns, and every man who finds work, and every sick body that's made whole—like a candle added to an altar—brightens the hope of all the faithful.

So let us reject any among us who seek to reopen old wounds and rekindle old hatreds. They stand in the way of a seeking nation. Let us now join reason to faith and action to experience, to transform our new unity of interest into a unity of purpose. For the hour and the day and the time are here to achieve progress without strife, to achieve change without hatred; not without difference of opinion, but without the deep and abiding divisions which scar the union for generations. Under this covenant—of justice, liberty, and union—we have become a nation: prosperous, great, and mighty. And we have kept our freedom. But we have no promise from God that our greatness will endure.

We have been allowed by Him to seek greatness with the sweat of our hands and the strength of our spirit.

I do not believe that the Great Society is the ordered, changeless and sterile battalion of the ants. It is the excitement of becoming—always becoming, trying, probing, falling, resting and trying again—but always trying and always gaining. In each generation—with toil and tears—we have had to earn our heritage again.

If we fail now, then we will have forgotten in abundance what we learned in hardship: that democracy rests on faith, that freedom asks more than it gives, and the judgment of God is harshest on those who are most favored. If we succeed, it will not be because of what we have, but it will be because of what we are; not because of what we own, but rather because of what we believe.

For we are a nation of believers. Underneath the clamor of building and the rush of our day's pursuits, we are believers in justice and liberty and union, and in our own Union. We believe that every man must some day be free. And we believe in ourselves.

And that is the mistake that our enemies have always made. In my lifetime—in depression and in war—they have awaited our defeat. Each time, from the secret places of the American heart, came forth the faith that they could not see or that they could not even imagine. It brought us victory. And it will again. For this is what America is all about. It is the uncrossed desert and the unclimbed ridge. It is the star that is not reached and the harvest that's sleeping in the unplowed ground.

Is our world gone? We say farewell. Is a new world coming? We welcome it—and we will bend it to the hopes of man. And to those trusted public servants and to my family and those close friends of mine who have followed me down a long winding road and to all the people of this Union and the world I will repeat today what I said on that sorrowful day in November last year: "I will lead and I will do the best I can". But you—you must look within your own hearts to the old promises and to the old dream. They will lead you best of all. For myself, I ask only in the words of an ancient leader: "Give me now wisdom and knowledge that I may go out and come in before this people. For who can judge this, thy people, that is so great?"

PICTURES OF THE YEAR/Ed Alley, United Press Int.

A KISS OF RESPECT is bestowed on the hand of Senator Harry F. Byrd by
President Lyndon B. Johnson after the funeral for the Virginia Democrat's wife.

people in Gainesville, a city of 19,000. Then, on
the third day, he flew north to visit the New York
World's Fair and to discuss his civil rights and anti-
poverty programs. At the fair, he attended the 50th
anniversary convention of the Amalgamated Clothing Workers of America. That was just one of
the President's typical cross-country swings. See
JOHNSON, LYNDON BAINES.

He inspected flood damage in five states in March
and promised federal aid. After the March 27 earthquake in Alaska, he allocated $5,000,000 in federal
emergency disaster funds to the stricken Alaskans.
He declared Florida and Georgia major disaster
areas after they were hit by Hurricane Dora in
September. See DISASTERS; WATER AND FLOOD
CONTROL; WEATHER.

Foreign Policy. Although domestic problems occupied most of the President's attention in 1964,
foreign crises could not be ignored. In January,
after riots over the flying of flags in the Panama Canal
Zone, President Johnson in a precedent-breaking
personal phone call, spoke to Panamanian President
Roberto F. Chiari, asking cooperation in controlling
the rioting. In December, the President proposed
that a new canal be constructed and offered to
renegotiate terms of the old Panama Canal treaty.
SEE PANAMA.

In January, also, the President revealed a major
reduction in the production of nuclear materials
that go into atomic weapons. In April, he and Soviet
Premier Nikita S. Khrushchev simultaneously announced that their nations were further reducing
production of such materials. See DISARMAMENT.

In October, President Johnson went on live television to explain U.S. foreign policy after two action-
packed days in overseas developments: Soviet Premier Khrushchev had been overthrown; the Chinese
had exploded a nuclear device; and the British had
just elected a Labour government.

In December, the President met for two days with
Britain's new Prime Minister Harold Wilson. They
both reaffirmed the need of Allied unity, and Wilson outlined Britain's broad plan for joint nuclear
defense. See GREAT BRITAIN.

War in Vietnam continued to plague the administration. In February, President Johnson promised to
step up military aid to South Vietnam. Various delegations and emissaries, including Secretary of Defense Robert S. McNamara, were sent to South
Vietnam for first-hand evaluations. In the summer,
U.S. warships were twice attacked by North Vietnamese in the Gulf of Tonkin. After the second attack,
on August 4, President Johnson addressed the nation
on television late in the evening to explain the reprisal action then underway. Maintaining that "we
still seek no wider war," he revealed that U.S. forces
were bombing North Vietnamese PT boat bases at
that very moment. See NATIONAL DEFENSE; VIETNAM.

Presidential Appointments. When Secretary of
Commerce Luther H. Hodges resigned on December
16, the President named John T. Connor, a drug executive, to succeed Hodges early in the new year (see
CONNOR, JOHN T.). On September 3, he had accepted the resignation of Attorney General Robert
Kennedy, whose deputy, Nicholas deB. Katzenbach,
he thereupon named as the acting head of the De-

partment of Justice. In March, the President named George E. Reedy as White House press secretary, replacing Pierre Salinger. (see REEDY, GEORGE E.).

Other administrative appointments included:

January, Assistant Secretary of Labor Esther Peterson, as special presidential assistant for consumer affairs; Secretary of the Army Cyrus R. Vance as deputy secretary of defense; Stephen Ailes as Secretary of the Army (see AILES, STEPHEN). *February*, R. Sargent Shriver, Jr., director of the Peace Corps, to head the "war against poverty" (see SOCIAL WELFARE [Close-Up]). *March*, Hugh Owens to the Securities and Exchange Commission; James L. Robertson to the Federal Reserve Board. *April*, Harold J. Russell to chair the President's Committee on the Employment of the Handicapped (see RUSSELL, HAROLD J.); Eugene C. Patterson as a member of the Federal Civil Rights Commission.

June, General Earle G. Wheeler as chairman of the Joint Chiefs of Staff (see WHEELER, EARLE G.). *July*, LeRoy Collins as director of the Community Relations Service and Arthur H. Dean as chairman of the National Citizens Committee for Community Relations, both to help implement the Civil Rights Act; Manuel F. Cohen as chairman of the Securities and Exchange Commission, replacing William L. Cary.

October, Miss Mary Gardiner Jones to the Federal Trade Commission. *November*, Gardner Ackley as chairman of the President's Council of Economic Advisers. *December*, John Doar as assistant Attorney General for civil rights; Sheldon S. Cohen as commissioner of internal revenue; Frederick L. Deming as under secretary of the Treasury for monetary affairs; Lloyd Nelson Hand as the Department of State's chief of protocol.

Overseas Appointments made by President Johnson included:

January, Edwin M. Martin as ambassador to Argentina. *February*, William P. Bundy to replace Roger Hilsman, Jr., as assistant secretary of state for Far Eastern affairs; Fulton Freeman as ambassador to Mexico. *March*, Mrs. Katharine Elkus White as ambassador to Denmark; William McCormick Blair as ambassador to the Philippines. *April*, Under Secretary of State for Political Affairs W. Averell Harriman as the President's chief adviser on African affairs. *July*, General Maxwell D. Taylor as ambassador to South Vietnam. *September*, Arizona Judge Raul A. Castro as ambassador to El Salvador. *October*, Ralph A. Dungan as ambassador to Chile.

State Visitors welcomed by President Johnson in 1964 included:

In *January*, Italian President Antonio Segni, and Greek Queen Frederika. *February*, British Prime Minister Sir Alec Douglas-Home, Mexican President Adolfo López Matéos (in Palm Springs, Calif.). *April*, King Hussein of Jordan. *May*, Ireland's President Eamon de Valéra. *June*, Israeli Premier Levi Eshkol, Danish Premier Jens Otto Krag, West German Chancellor Ludwig Erhard, Turkish Premier Ismet Inönü, Greek Premier George Papandreou. *July*, Malaysian Prime Minister Tunku Abdul Rahman, Malagasy President Philibert Tsiranana. *August*, United Nations Secretary General U Thant. *September*, Canadian Prime Minister Lester B. Pearson (celebrating ratification of the Columbia River Treaty). *October*, Philippine President Diosdado Macapagal and his wife. *November*, Mexico's President-elect Gustavo Díaz Ordaz and his wife (at the LBJ Ranch). *December*, British Prime Minister Wilson, Soviet Foreign Minister Andrei A. Gromyko. CAROL THOMPSON

PRINCE EDWARD ISLAND. See CANADA.

PRISON. Myrl E. Alexander became director of the United States Bureau of Prisons in 1964. A former assistant director, he left his present job as director of the Center for the Study of Crime, Delinquency, and Correction at Southern Illinois University to take his new post. He replaced James V. Bennett, 70, who retired August 28 after 27 years of service.

Dr. Samuel H. Sheppard, serving a life sentence for the murder of his wife, Marilyn, was ordered released on $10,000 bond from an Ohio prison by Federal District Judge Carl A. Weinman, on July 15. The judge called the 1954 trial for the murder "a mockery of justice." Sheppard had been denied his constitutional rights, partly because publicity made it impossible to maintain impartial jurors.

Also released was Charles "Charlie the Bug" Workman, on March 10, from a New Jersey prison. He had served 23 years for the murder of the prohibition beer baron, Dutch Schultz, and three others.

The Great British Train Robbery of 1963 was matched in boldness and cleverness by the August 12 escape from an English prison of Charles F. Wilson, serving a 30-year sentence for his part in the robbery. Still missing, besides Wilson, was most of the $7,000,000 from the original theft.

Building Trends in the prison field indicated a move toward a modern, almost campuslike look. The new Washington State Correction Center had low, separated buildings with reinforced concrete lattice work replacing the usual iron bars. A glazed beige brick exterior and pastel green and beige cells were new aspects of the new Corrections, Reception, and Classification Center for Men in New York City.

A national conference on personnel needs in the field of correction was convened at Arden House, New York, in June, under a Ford Foundation grant. Ninety delegates from 61 national organizations discussed the problems of manpower recruitment and training. They offered proposals for upgrading the nation's correctional programs. JOSEPH D. LOHMAN

See also CRIME.

PROKHOROV, ALEKSANDR MIKHAILOVICH

(1916-   ), shared half of the Nobel physics prize in 1964 with Nikolai G. Basov. They and Charles H. Townes were cited for basic research in the field of quantum electronics.

The Russian scientists' work includes development of generating and amplifying radio waves. Prokhorov is a Moscow State University professor and head of the Lebedev Physics Institute's oscillations laboratory. He received his M.A. (1946) and Ph.D. (1951) degrees at the institute.

Aleksandr Prokhorov was born in Atherton, Australia. His family returned to Russia after the October, 1917, revolution. He is a Leningrad State University graduate (1939), and served in the Soviet army during World War II.

See also BASOV, NIKOLAI G.; NOBEL PRIZES (Science); TOWNES, CHARLES H.

PROTESTANT leaders of many denominations were increasingly active and outspoken in 1964 on the matter of civil rights for Negro citizens of the United States. The United Presbyterian Church in the U.S.A., a predominantly white denomination, with over 3,200,000 members, elected a Negro, the Reverend Dr. Edler G. Hawkins, as its moderator. And the Southern Presbyterian Church voted, in April, to integrate its three Negro presbyteries with existing white presbyteries.

The Lutheran Church in America, with more than 3,000,000 members, denounced racial barriers in church and society. Also, in a convention action in February, it held that Christians who say the standard prayer of the church for unity and against prejudice, on Sunday, and then practice prejudice the other days of the week, are committing "an act of blasphemy." The American Baptist Convention at a meeting in Atlantic City, N.J., strongly endorsed racial integration.

Firm Stand. Other strong indications of Protestantism's involvement in the national civil rights movement occurred. During the Senate debates on the bill, 53 statements from 29 denominations were entered into the record in favor of passage. When the Civil Rights Act passed, the congressional leader of the opposition, Georgia's Senator Richard Russell, remarked that the churches were among the major forces contributing to the passage of the legislation. See Section Two, CONGRESS MAKES A DECISION.

Protestantism's best-known preacher, the Reverend Billy Graham, who some years ago was criticized for his failure to take a positive stand on the issue, was taking vigorous action in 1964 to make his antisegregation views clearer. On Easter morning he preached to what was probably the largest racially mixed group (more than 35,000) ever assembled in Birmingham, Ala. At the University of North Carolina, in May, he told an audience of 16,000, "Those people who say they can prove segregation by the Bible don't know their Bible."

But perhaps the award of the Nobel peace prize to the Reverend Doctor Martin Luther King, Jr., leading exponent of nonviolence in civil rights issues, best symbolized Protestantism's involvement in the racial struggle. See KING, JR., MARTIN LUTHER.

When The Methodist Church met in Pittsburgh, the 10,000,000-member denomination was faced with a perplexing problem: What to do with its all-Negro Central Jurisdiction. After intense debate a compromise was reached, calling for gradual integration of the all-Negro and the largely white jurisdictions. But Methodists did agree to give financial aid to fellow churchmen jailed in rights marches. Other churches followed suit.

Leaders Versus Laity. However, not all Protestant church moves were so clearly directed toward racial integration. In many groups there were signs of resistance to denominational pronouncements, particularly among the laymen.

The Southern Baptist Convention, which met at Atlantic City simultaneously with the American Baptist Convention, failed to speak clearly for integration. The Protestant Episcopal Church, at its General Convention in St. Louis in October, was torn by dissension over an unofficial statement signed by 726 clerical and lay members. The statement criticized the Republican candidates for the presidency and vice-presidency for injecting racism, as the signers saw it, into the campaign. Individual Episcopalians were leaders in the civil rights struggle, but the convention debated how far the denomination should go in the movement.

The Campaign. The second great area of Protestant participation in public life was the presidential campaign. Many aspects of the Republican candidate's program appealed to many of the more orthodox Protestants. Senator Barry M. Goldwater's advocacy of conservatism, individualism, nationalism, and his concentration on personal morality, along with other factors, attracted many ministers and laymen to his cause. But a poll of denominational editors revealed a personal preference for the Democratic candidate, President Lyndon B. Johnson. In fact, the great majority of prominent church periodicals that did endorse a candidate gave their support to the President.

Near the end of the campaign, Senator Goldwater complained about the clergy's opposition to him. This opposition, such as it was, appeared to stem from various concerns. Some clergymen were concerned that Goldwater's opposition to the Civil Rights Act would appeal to the racially prejudiced. Others spoke out against his military stance and his opposition to social planning, contending that his positions contradicted Christian teachings. Early appraisals of the popular vote seemed to reveal that Protestants divided their sympathies much the same as other American groups did.

School Prayer Issue. Another issue of a political character also divided Protestantism. In reaction to two decisions of the Supreme Court of the United States prohibiting formal prayer in public schools, many Congressmen introduced legislation which, if passed, would bring about amendment of the Constitution. Such proposals would reintroduce prayer in the schools. One professional polltaker found that 88 per cent of the American people in his sample favored such legislation.

When the House Judiciary Committee held hearings on proposed amendments in the spring, the majority of religious leaders who testified spoke against such amendments. Protestants who were critical praised the existing amendment and the historical development of church-state relations based on it. Many expressed fear that constitutionally sanctioned religious rites would be established. Such rites, they said, could harm true religion and limit freedom of dissent. When Congress adjourned, no action had been taken.

ACT NOW! Many Protestant pastors urged passage of civil rights law. In June, a group marched to Washington with other civil and religious leaders from New York.

Protestant-Catholic Relations. Protestants welcomed a statement from Vatican Council II which acknowledged that the Roman Catholic Church must share blame for the problems that had led to the Protestant Reformation four and a half centuries ago. American Protestant groups responded favorably to invitations to send observers to the third session of Vatican Council II and the Protestant press reported dutifully on its proceedings.

Meetings between Protestants and Roman Catholics were well publicized: Pope Paul VI received Martin Luther King, Jr.; Billy Graham met with Boston's Richard Cardinal Cushing. A new climate of interchurch relations was apparent. Protestants were well represented in the year's most publicized religious publishing venture: the development of a Bible translation and commentary, *The Anchor Bible*, in conjunction with Catholic and Jewish scholars.

Theological Activity. Inside Protestantism, theological activity was much in evidence. A good deal of the discussion concerned itself with problems of personal morality. Other theologians devoted themselves to what one of them called "the secular meaning of the Gospel." Such thinkers were asking: What does it mean for Christian thought that we have, in the modern world, a great number of people who, unlike their fathers, have no experience of God at all? How does this cultural fact affect the way Christians think about Jesus Christ and the Christian message? A growing critical attitude toward conventional religion was noted in colleges and seminaries, and Protestant thinkers reflected on ways of dealing with this change.

In some denominations, including The American Lutheran Church and the Protestant Episcopal Church, division occurred over the practice of "speaking in tongues." This practice involves ecstatic religious utterance under, as it is claimed, the power of the Holy Spirit.

Protestants continued to play a vital role in shaping people's attitudes and commanding their attention. The various denominations expended a total of $1,000,000,000 on new church construction. And, for all the public involvement, the political and racial debate, and theological changes, American Protestant churches continued to prosper. Most members found in their local church an effective instrument for worship and for activity toward human betterment. More and more were beginning to agree that the fate of these local churches was closely related to their public activity, the public's image of Protestantism, and even that of religion itself in American culture.

Statistics. *The* 1965 *Year Book of American Churches* noted that 224 Protestant bodies reported 292,233 churches, with a membership of 66,854,200 for 1963.

Two hundred and five bodies reported 229,965 pastors in active charge, and a total ordained clergy of 332,044. Twenty Eastern Orthodox communions reported 1,531 churches with 3,094,140 members. Nineteen Eastern Orthodox bodies reported 1,395 pastors with charges. They also reported a total clergy of 1,903.　　　　MARTIN E. MARTY

See also CIVIL LIBERTIES; Section Two, CONGRESS MAKES A DECISION.

PSYCHIATRY. See MENTAL HEALTH; PSYCHOLOGY.

PSYCHOLOGY. Widespread publicity given to the ability to "see with the skin" aroused the interest of the public at large as well as many psychologists. The ability, named "dermo-optical perception" (DOP), may exist in varying degrees in all individuals and may even be developed with training. Under rigorous test conditions, Mrs. Patricia Stanley of Flint, Mich., has demonstrated this ability to identify colors by touch. And Rosa Kuleshova, a young Russian, has astonished scientists by not only reading by touch, but also by identifying colors when moving her hand some distance above them.

The existence of DOP, however, has not been accepted by many American psychologists, who remain frankly skeptical while granting the theoretical possibility of such an ability. Before DOP can gain general scientific acceptance, it will have to be demonstrated in more than one or two individuals, and it will have to be studied intensively under laboratory conditions. Such a study is now being conducted by Dr. Gregory Razran at Queens College, New York City.

Cat Vision. To the delight of cat owners, investigators Jeri A. Sechzer and J. L. Brown have demonstrated, for the first time, that cats possess the ability to see colors. This is of considerable scientific importance since it had been predicted that cats have this ability, on the basis of anatomical and physiological studies, though all previous attempts to show it had failed. The investigators rewarded the cats with food for correctly choosing an escape door illuminated with colored light. For two cats, the correct door was illuminated with red light and the incorrect door with green. For two additional cats, the correct and incorrect colors were reversed. By continuously varying the brightness and position relations between the correct and incorrect choices, the psychologists were able to train the cats to perform correctly on the basis of color alone. In further studies, the saturation of the colors was reduced by gradually adding white light. When the color was reduced to only 10 per cent of the total illumination, it was found that the cats no longer seemed able to distinguish the colors.

Color Theory. In still another study of color and how we see it, Dr. Barnett Rosenberg, of Michigan State University, showed that color vision is most likely mediated by physical rather than chemical changes in the retina of the eye. A chemical normally associated with certain cells in the retina (the cones) was placed between two plates of glass. Then current was applied to the plates to create an electrical field. When light was directed on the glass, an electric current flowed through the retinal chemical. However, a change in the color of the light caused the direction of the electric current to change. Thus, blue light caused the current to flow in one direction, and red light caused the current to flow in the opposite direction. ROBERT W. GOY

See also ANTHROPOLOGY; MENTAL HEALTH.

Warman, *New York Herald Tribune*

PUBLISHING TYCOON Henry Robinson Luce, 66, stepped out as top editor of Time Inc., and chose Hedley Donovan, 49, as his successor.

PUBLISHING. Newspapers themselves made news during the presidential election campaign in 1964. Not since 1932 had the Republican presidential candidate fared so poorly on the nation's editorial pages. Newspapers that had not endorsed a Democrat for President in decades, even generations, swung to Lyndon B. Johnson. Notable among the switches was the *New York Herald Tribune*, which endorsed a Democrat for the first time in its 123-year history; the *Kansas City Star*, long a Republican voice in the Midwest; and the Hearst and Scripps-Howard newspaper chains.

The extent of the switch was evident from these figures: In 1960, Richard M. Nixon, the Republican candidate, had the support of 731 newspapers with a circulation of some 37,000,000. John F. Kennedy was endorsed by 200 newspapers whose circulation totaled 8,500,000. In 1964, the shift of the metropolitan press gave Johnson a three-to-one lead in circulation figures.

"One-Party Press." Unlike previous campaigns, complaints about press coverage this time came from the Republicans. Senator Goldwater spoke of "radical columnists" and "radical newspapers." He singled out for his special displeasure the CBS news department and *The New York Times*. At the Republican convention in San Francisco, General Dwight D. Eisenhower referred to the "divisive efforts" of "sensation-seeking columnists and commentators" who "couldn't care less about the good of our party."

Newspapers dutifully carried these and other charges, but since they had heard them before, generally leveled by the Democrats, they did not take them too seriously.

Warren Report. Newspapers, however, were concerned over criticism of their activities in Dallas during the aftermath of the assassination of President John F. Kennedy. The report of the Warren Commission sharply criticized the conduct of newspapermen, television newsmen, and photographers in covering Lee Harvey Oswald's transfer in the Dallas jail where he was murdered. See RUBY, JACK; WARREN COMMISSION; WARREN REPORT (appendix).

Free-Press Milestone. To publishers, the most important development of the year was a historic ruling of the Supreme Court of the United States which strengthened the role of the press as the watchdog of government. In March, the court ruled that a public official cannot win libel damages for criticism of his performance in office unless he can prove that a newspaper or magazine knew in advance that its statements were false or that they were made with "reckless disregard."

The ruling was made in the case of a Montgomery Ala., official who contended he had been libeled in an advertisement placed in *The New York Times*. An Alabama jury had awarded him damages of $500,000.

Exits and Entrances. Three daily newspapers made their appearance in 1964, and three were closed. The new papers began operation in Atlanta, Ga.; Jeffersonville, Ind.; and Oklahoma City, Okla. The *Lima* (Ohio) *Citizen* shut down, and in Houston, the Scripps-Howard *Press* closed down after 52 years of operation. Houston had been the only city west of the Mississippi with more than two separately owned major newspapers. Now, only New York, Washington, and Boston are in this latter category.

The western edition of *The New York Times* folded in January, 1964, after 16 months. Despite a circulation of 85,000, the *Times* management found it could not draw sufficient national advertising.

The circulation of daily newspapers declined in 1964, to 59,404,333 from 60,025,716. This was the second consecutive year of declining circulation.

The Longest Strike against major metropolitan dailies occurred in Detroit. It ran from July 13 to November 25. Closed during the period were the *News* and *Free Press*.

Magazines. The Curtis Publishing Company (*Holiday, The Saturday Evening Post, Ladies Home Journal*) shook under the charges and countercharges of top personnel. At year-end, Matthew J. Culligan resigned as president but was retained as chairman of the board. His role of president was taken by John McLean Clifford, who was elevated from executive vice-president. Clay Blair, Jr., editor in chief of Curtis publications and Marvin Kantor, chairman of the magazine division, were discharged. The two had brought charges of mismanagement against Culligan.

Theatre Arts closed after 48 years of publication. *Architectural Forum* was folded by Time Inc., and *House and Home*, also a Time publication, was sold to McGraw-Hill. *Show* magazine was sold to American Theater Press, Inc., publishers of *Playbill* theater programs. *The New Republic*, a journal of opinion, celebrated its 50th year.

Among the new magazines was *Fact*, an exposé-type of publication with a press run of 150,000.

Executive Suite. Major changes occurred at the top levels of *The New York Times*, and Time Inc.

At the *Times*, Turner Catledge, longtime managing editor, was named executive editor. Clifton Daniel succeeded him. New associate editors were James B. Reston, former chief Washington correspondent and editorial board member of THE YEAR BOOK (see Section One, JAMES B. RESTON ON THE NATION), and Lester Markel, former Sunday editor. Tom Wicker succeeded Reston, and Daniel Schwarz succeeded Markel.

At Time Inc., Henry Robinson Luce resigned as editor in chief. He became editorial chairman. His successor was Hedley Williams Donovan, 49, former managing editor of *Fortune*. See PERSONALITIES (picture).

Book Publishers during the year had total receipts of $1,840,000,000, an 11 per cent increase over 1963. An estimated 26,500 new titles were published. The paperbacks continued to pour from the presses, some 300,000,000 of them in 1964. The pioneer of the industry, Pocket Books, celebrated its 25th anniversary on June 18.

There were about a dozen book publishing mergers during the year. Among them, Laidlaw Brothers, was acquired by Doubleday & Company, and Encyclopaedia Britannica, Inc., purchased G. & C. Merriam Company, publishers of *Webster's Third New International Dictionary*.   MELVIN MENCHER

See also ADVERTISING; COMMUNICATIONS; DEATHS OF NOTABLE PERSONS (ROY HOWARD).

PUERTO RICO elected a new governor for the first time in 15 years. On November 3, Roberto Sanchez Vilella was chosen to succeed Luis Muñoz Marín, who had refused to run for a fifth term.

The nation continued to enjoy an economic boom. During the 1963-1964 fiscal year, Puerto Rico's net income rose 10 per cent, topping the $2,000,000,000 mark for the first time. This was the fourth consecutive year the island had maintained a 10 per cent or more annual increase in income. While the population rose by 2.4 per cent, per capita income climbed 7.4 per cent.

On June 9, a 13-man commission consisting of seven U.S. representatives and six Puerto Ricans began a study of the island's political status. Discussions centered on whether the island should retain its present unique status as a commonwealth of the United States, seek full statehood, or be given full independence.

Population: 2,600,000. **Government:** Governor Roberto Sanchez Vilella. **Foreign Trade:** exports $845,-256,809; imports, $1,159,654,692. **Principal Exports:** rum, sugar, tobacco leaf.   MARY C. WEBSTER

PULITZER PRIZES in journalism and literature were announced on May 4, 1964, following recommendations by the Advisory Board of the Pulitzer School of Journalism at Columbia University.

The fiction, drama (for the second consecutive year), and music prizes were withheld. It was the first time that these three categories were omitted in a single year. The other prizes were conferred as follows:

For the Most Disinterested and Meritorious Public Service Rendered by a U.S. Newspaper: a gold medal to *The St. Petersburg* (Fla.) *Times* for a year-long investigation and coverage of what was called "reckless, unchecked spending" by the Florida State Turnpike Authority. A reorganization of Florida's road construction program followed.

A Special Citation for a distinguished example of the use of a newspaper group's resources to complement the work of its individual newspapers to the Gannett Newspapers for their special coverage of success stories on "The Road to Integration."

For a Distinguished Example of Reporting on International Affairs: $1,000 to Malcolm W. Browne of the Associated Press and David Halberstam of *The New York Times* for reporting on the Vietnam war and the overthrow of South Vietnam President Ngo Dinh Diem.

For a Distinguished Example of Reporting on National Affairs: $1,000 to Merriman Smith, United Press International White House correspondent, for his coverage of the assassination of President John F. Kennedy.

For a Distinguished Example of Local Reporting: *General Reporting*, $1,000 to Norman C. Miller, Jr., of *The Wall Street Journal* for his report of the multimillion-dollar vegetable oil swindle in the Allied Crude Vegetable Oil and Refining Corporation bankruptcy in New Jersey. *Investigative Reporting*, $1,000 to *The Philadelphia Evening Bulletin's* Albert V. Gaudiosi, James V. Magee, and Frederick A. Meyer (photographer) for uncovering a numbers racket operation and police collusion. There were a number of dismissals and suspensions from the police department as a result of the exposé.

For a Distinguished Example of Editorial Writing: $1,000 to Hazel Brannon Smith of *The Lexington* (Miss.) *Advertiser* for "steadfast adherence to her editorial duty in the face of great pressure and opposition." She has campaigned against crime and corruption, and resisted White Citizens Council pressure.

For an Outstanding Example of News Photography: $1,000 to Robert H. Jackson of *The Dallas* (Tex.) *Times Herald* for his picture of Jack Ruby shooting Lee Harvey Oswald, alleged assassin of President John F. Kennedy.

For an Outstanding Example of a Cartoonist's Work Published in a U.S. Newspaper: $1,000 to Paul F. Conrad (now with *The Los Angeles Times*) for his editorial cartoons in *The Denver* (Colo.) *Post*.

For the Best Nonfiction by an American Author: $500 to Richard Hofstadter, a Columbia University history professor, for *Anti-Intellectualism in American Life*. See HOFSTADTER, RICHARD.

For a Distinguished Book of the Year on U.S. History: $500 to Sumner Chilton Powell for *Puritan Village: The Formation of a New England Town*. See POWELL, SUMNER CHILTON.

For a Distinguished Biography or Autobiography Preferably on an American Subject: $500 to Walter Jackson Bate, a Harvard University English professor, for *John Keats*. See BATE, WALTER JACKSON.

For a Distinguished Volume of Verse by an American Author: $500 to Louis Simpson for *At the End of the Open Road*. See SIMPSON, LOUIS.

QUAISON-SACKEY, ALEX (1924-   ), became the first African from south of the Sahara to be named president of the United Nations (UN) General Assembly. He succeeded outgoing President Carlos Sosa Rodríguez of Venezuela. As Quaison-Sackey's election indicated, Africa's power in the assembly had risen sharply. See UNITED NATIONS.

The new UN chief was born in Ghana (formerly Gold Coast) and educated at Oxford and the London School of Economics. A protégé of Ghana's President Kwame Nkrumah, he rose rapidly in the government when Ghana became independent in 1957. He has headed the nation's delegation to the United Nations since 1959.

Quaison-Sackey is noted for his smartly cut Western-style clothing, which he usually wears in preference to the togalike Ghanaian *kente*. He enjoys playing golf and some card games. He also enjoys playing his own tribal drums.   WALTER F. MORSE

QUASAR, QUASI-STELLAR OBJECT. See ASTRONOMY; Section Two, THE UNFOLDING UNIVERSE.

QUEBEC. See CANADA.

RACING. See AUTOMOBILE RACING; BOATS AND BOATING; HARNESS RACING; HORSE RACING; OLYMPIC GAMES; SAILING; SWIMMING; TRACK AND FIELD.

RADIO. People in 110 cities across the land listened to their radios in 1964 enthralled by programs that had been among the standouts of the serials in the 1930's and 1940's. The year saw the return of *The Shadow*, who "knows what evil lurks in the hearts of men," *The Inner Sanctum*, *The Green Hornet*, and other programs, including *The Lone Ranger*, with its galloping theme from the *William Tell* overture and the famous call, "Hi ho Silver! Away!"

The man who sparked the return of these programs was Charles Michelson, of New York City, a distributor of the same material in radio's earlier days. In 1964, Michelson and others found that, in this day

of "music and news" radio, there was a surprisingly large market for the old "family" programs.

Radio's condition improved in 1964. It enjoyed an average daily audience of 80,000,000. Thus it was the nation's second most utilized communications medium. Newspapers ranked first with 100,500,000 daily readers, and television third with 77,900,000 viewers. Magazines were fourth.

The sale of radio sets also rose. There were some 215,000,000 radios in use by the end of the year.

But the financial picture, though improved, was not as bright as the huge audience and the sale of sets made it seem. The Federal Communications Commission (FCC), reporting for 1963, noted that the networks were out of the red for the first time since 1954. Their collective net profits for 1963 were $929,000, as against a loss of $2,400,000 in 1962. Their revenue increased 9.7 per cent to $34,600,000.

According to the Radio Advertising Bureau, the networks' gross time sales for the first half of 1964 were up 5.5 per cent over the same period in 1963. It was estimated that 1964 billings would equal or better that figure.

FM Radio didn't fare as well. Although the nation's 294 independent FM outlets (those not affiliated with an AM outlet) increased their 1963 revenue 22.6 per cent over 1962, higher operating expenses left them with a loss of $3,200,000. FM stereo, however, continued its growth.   June Bundy Csida

See also TELEVISION.

RAILROAD.

Regaining economic health since its 1961 crisis, the railroad industry showed a lively upswing in 1964, with enlarged volume and improved operating efficiency. While freight carloadings rose 2 per cent, the heavier capacities of new cars, plus longer rail hauls, added 6.9 per cent more traffic—an estimated 665,300,000,000 ton-miles of cargo in 1964 against 624,700,000,000 in 1963.

Even as operating revenues expanded over 3 per cent to about $9,900,000,000, modernized technology and procedures boosted the estimated net income of 101 major U.S. railroads by a substantial 10 per cent—$716,600,000 after taxes versus $651,500,000 in 1963. A 12 per cent gain in piggyback traffic helped increase profits.

Optimistically, railroads stepped up capital expenditures, investing about $1,400,000,000 on new plant and equipment, more than one-third above last year. Example: Southern Pacific spent $34,000,-000 to buy 133 higher powered locomotives.

Yet despite favorable trends and the best return on investment (3.4 per cent) since 1957, 20 per cent of the big roads still failed to earn enough to cover fixed charges. Some companies blamed continued deficits from unprofitable passenger service, whose estimated $570,500,000 gross revenues were down 3 per cent. The Reading, over $1,500,000 in the red, discontinued all New York-to-Philadelphia passenger runs, which were carrying some 250,000 passengers at an annual loss of over $200,000.

The Featherbedding Issue was finally laid to rest. The Supreme Court, on April 27, refused to overrule a lower court and thus upheld the 1963 decision of a congressionally established arbitration board on the fireman and crew makeup issues. On May 7, the carriers began to eliminate 9,564 jobs as unnecessary. Railroads expect labor savings will ultimately cut operating costs $250,000,000 a year.

Meanwhile, new labor disputes arose. Maintenance and shopworkers' complaints about subcontracted care and repair were satisfied by the negotiation of a job-stabilization agreement on September 25. After months of talks, threats of

BULLET-NOSED ELECTRIC TRAIN began carrying passengers over 320 miles of no-grade-crossing track in Japan. It hit 159 mph in test runs.

strikes, presidential intervention, and emergency board reports, the railroads' trainmen, firemen, and enginemen reached agreement in November. As 1964 ended, only the dispute with three shopcraft unions remained unsettled.

The Cost of the Settlement was not cheap. It was expected to raise labor costs $320,000,000 in 1965 and to about $500,000,000 in 1966—against the 1964 profits of a little more than $700,000,000. With the average 9-cents-an-hour average wage increase to the nonoperating unions retroactive to Jan. 1, 1964, many lines had failed to set aside adequate reserve funds. As a consequence, an extra large bite had to be taken from fourth-quarter earnings.

Yet, as *Forbes* magazine concluded in assessing the effect of the settlement on the industry: "There are . . . good reasons for believing that the railroads will be able to get labor savings that will help balance the higher hourly wages. Normal attrition, automation, and improved technology have been enabling the railroads to cut their work forces about 4 per cent a year recently—almost enough in itself to cover the wage boosts."

The Largest Merger of U.S. railroads to occur at one time became fact on October 16 when the Norfolk & Western joined with the Nickel Plate, the Wabash, and three other roads to create a $1,900,-000,000 system operating in 14 states and Ontario. Interstate Commerce Commission (ICC) examiners also favored a merger of three large western roads: the Great Northern; the Northern Pacific; and the Chicago, Burlington & Quincy. If finally approved, the combined 25,000-mile system would be the nation's largest in track mileage.

The Southern Railway won the next-to-the-last round in its long fight to give its customers cheaper grain rates based on the economies of "Big John" hopper cars. The Southern had proposed a 60 per cent cut in rates. A federal district court in Cincinnati, Ohio, on May 20, blocked an ICC minimum-rate order that would have blunted the Southern's competitive edge. The ICC appealed the case to the Supreme Court.

Jet Age on Rails. President Lyndon B. Johnson directed the Department of Commerce to work toward developing a high-speed, low-cost Washington-to-Boston rail passenger service. Budd Company said 125 mph trains, cutting travel time 40 per cent between those cities, were feasible. He later was to ask the 89th Congress for action on this scheme.

Japan, in October, began operating the fastest rail service in the world on its Tokyo-Osaka line. After allowing time for the no-grade-crossing roadbed to settle, it planned to step up schedules to three hours for the 320-mile run (see picture).

Secretary of Commerce Luther H. Hodges, in December, said his department had been exploring new concepts in rail travel. One was a jet-propelled train that would travel at 200 or 250 mph between densely populated areas.   MARK REINSBERG

RECORDINGS.

RECORDINGS. During the first half of 1964, the sales of records by the Beatles so far eclipsed those by all other artists that the entire recording industry was affected (see MUSIC, POPULAR). The popularity of many artists was hurt or delayed by record buyers' reluctance to spend money on anything but Beatles records. Of the estimated 110,000,000 albums and 125,000,000 single records sold in 1964, almost 10 per cent of the total dollar volume was attributable to the British quartet.

Artists receiving Gold Record awards, representing $1,000,000 in album sales, or 1,000,000 single record sales, included the Beatles, Nat King Cole, the Kingston Trio, Al Hirt, Robert Russell Bennett, and the Four Seasons.

Classical Record Sales represented a smaller proportion of the total than in the previous year. Among the most important and best-selling were Leontyne Price in Puccini's *Madame Butterfly;* an album of Bizet's *Carmen*, by Miss Price and other artists; Leonard Bernstein's *Symphony No. 3 (Kaddish)*, with the New York Philharmonic; Van Cliburn playing Beethoven's *Piano Concerto No. 4*, with Fritz Reiner and the Chicago Symphony; and Maria Callas singing Verdi arias.

Variety. With the rising costs of recording rates abroad, the chances for American orchestras to make more records increased in 1964, and nine ensembles were currently at work for the microphone. They were the "Big Five" (New York, Boston, Philadelphia, Cleveland, Chicago), and the Louisville, Cincinnati, Pittsburgh, and Utah orchestras.

Arthur Fiedler, conductor of the Boston "Pops" concerts, broke into the popular instrumental record market by recording a Beatles song hit, "I Want to Hold Your Hand", and by teaming with Al Hirt in an album called *"Pops" Goes the Trumpet*. He later joined forces with Allan Sherman in an album. Comedians newly established on records included Godfrey Cambridge, a satirist, and Bill Cosby.

Original cast albums of Broadway shows continued to enjoy great success. They included Richard Burton's *Hamlet; Hello, Dolly!;* and *Funny Girl.*

The popularity of night clubs catering to twist and watusi dancers led to a new trend in rock 'n' roll recordings, with such albums as *Johnny Rivers at the Whiskey À Go Go* and *Trini Lopez at PJ's*.

Early in the year, several albums consisting of tributes to the late President John F. Kennedy, or excerpts from his speeches, achieved prominence.

Folk and Jazz Sales. Folk music and jazz each continued to account for about 12 per cent of all album sales, country and Western music for 5 per cent, and film sound-track albums for 6 per cent. Top sellers in this last group included *Mary Poppins*, *My Fair Lady*, and the Beatles' *A Hard Day's Night*.

A growing technical development was the sale of tape record players designed to fit in automobiles. Tape cartridges costing up to $8 could be slipped into a machine to play up to four hours of music.

The Record Industry Association of America argued successfully in Washington, D.C., to have records recognized as a cultural medium in a bill that was signed into law to establish a National Council on the Arts. Record manufacturers also sponsored a National Record Month. The purpose was to draw attention to the variety of material available on records, and the role that is being played by recordings in schools and libraries in preserving examples of today's artistry and culture for future generations. LEONARD G. FEATHER

See also LITERATURE (Close-Up); MUSIC.

RECORDINGS FOR CHILDREN. Unofficial industry estimates placed the U.S. market for children's records in 1964 at more than $40,000,000 annually, about 6 per cent of the total record market. In terms of age brackets, however, the market had shrunk substantially. Until only a few years ago, 14-year-olds were regarded as a market for certain types of children's disks. By 1964, the 8-year level was accepted as the top end of the market. Pop record phenomena like the Beatles were held largely responsible for the change (see MUSIC, POPULAR). The exposure of pop records on radio was so all-encompassing that children soon graduated from their interests in simple songs and stories. Television, too, was credited with producing the premature sophistication which nurtures an early "grown-up" attitude toward children's records.

According to a 1964 survey, when reports for the previous year were issued, the most popular children's recording of 1963 was *Leonard Bernstein Conducts* (The New York Philharmonic) *for Young People.* The National Academy of Recording Arts and Sciences poll included as runners-up such diverse productions as *Addition and Subtraction*, an educational set by Rica Owen Moore; *Children's Concert*, by folk singer Pete Seeger; *Winnie the Pooh*, by Jack Gilford; and the fun song, "On Top of Spaghetti," by Tom Glazer and the Do Re Mi Children's Chorus.

Still Champion. Nevertheless, most spokesmen agreed that Mother Goose nursery rhymes remained the most popular staple of the kids repertory. Golden Records, in fact, produced a Mother Goose album, incorporating the Beatle sound in the singing in 1964.

Mother Appeal. Packaging emphasis was keyed to "mother appeal," that is, to what the producer thought the mother thought her child should have in the way of a "fun and games" capsule education on records. Thus, sugar-coated learning records remained big sellers. TV cartoon characters, however, had lost much of their disk appeal.

Motion pictures occasionally make a great impact on the children's record field. In 1964, the Disney-created *Mary Poppins*, a children's story to begin with, sparked considerable record activity in song and spoken word for children. REN GREVATT

RECREATION. See FAIRS AND EXHIBITIONS; OUTDOOR RECREATION; PARKS.

RED CROSS reorganized its direct service volunteer program, placing more emphasis on ability and flexibility and less on specialization, titles, and uniforms. Under the new plan, effective June 1, 1964, volunteers were no longer to be recruited and trained for a particular service, such as the Gray Ladies. Instead, they will be recruited as Red Cross volunteers, and trained by both the local chapter and the utilizing hospital or community agency. A simple and inexpensive uniform was to be designed. Although the new program was recommended by the national board of governors, its adoption by local chapters was voluntary.

Community civic and service agencies joined with local Red Cross chapters in commemorating the 50th anniversary of the American Red Cross Water Safety Program. It was started in Baltimore, Md., on Feb. 14, 1914, under the direction of Commodore Wilbert E. Longfellow. Today, nearly 200,000 classes in swimming, lifesaving, and small craft safety are conducted annually under the program.

In April, General James F. Collins, formerly commander in chief of the U.S. Army in the Pacific, assumed the office of president of the American Red Cross (see COLLINS, JAMES F.). He succeeded General Alfred M. Gruenther. JOSEPH P. ANDERSON

REEDY, GEORGE EDWARD (1917-), who had been an assistant presidential press secretary, was appointed press secretary by President Lyndon B. Johnson on March 19. Reedy succeeded Pierre Salinger, who resigned to run—unsuccessfully, it turned out—for U.S. Senator from California.

Reedy had been an assistant to Mr. Johnson since 1951, when he joined the staff of the Senate Preparedness Subcommittee, headed by the then Senator Johnson of Texas. He became staff director of the Senate Democratic Policy Committee when Johnson moved up to Senate majority leader. Later, he was special assistant to Vice-President Johnson. Among Reedy's duties, speech writing has been prominent, both while Johnson was in the Senate and in the White House.

Reedy was born at East Chicago, Ind., on Aug. 5, 1917. He was graduated from the University of Chicago in 1938 and joined United Press (UP), now United Press International (UPI). He served four years in the U.S. Army in World War II and rose to the rank of captain. After the war, he returned to UP in its Washington bureau. He was covering the Senate as a reporter when Mr. Johnson hired him.

Reedy is an avid reader and he is known for a wide range of scholarly interests. He is a bulky man whose most prominent feature is an upstanding, comb-resisting mane of white hair.

The new press secretary and his wife, the former Lillian Greenwald, also a former news reporter, have two sons. WALTER F. MORSE

RELIGION. See EASTERN ORTHODOX; JEWS AND JUDAISM; PROTESTANT; ROMAN CATHOLIC.

REPUBLICAN PARTY

REPUBLICAN PARTY LEADERSHIP underwent an historic change in direction with the nomination of Senator Barry M. Goldwater of Arizona for the presidency of the United States. Goldwater, the idol of the inflexibly conservative elements within the party, vowed to give the voters "a choice, not an echo." This was his answer to the belief that Republican candidates of the recent past had been what doctrinaire conservatives called "me too'ers," meaning they had offered little more than an echo of Democratic party policies. See GOLDWATER, BARRY M. Goldwater's bid for the nomination had been tacitly opposed by many moderate, liberal, and even conservative leaders of the party. They thought he was no real threat when he lost the New Hampshire presidential primary on March 10 to a write-in candidate, Henry Cabot Lodge, Jr., the U.S. ambassador to South Vietnam.

Vytas Valaitis

Again when he was defeated in the Oregon primary on May 15 by New York's Governor Nelson A. Rockefeller, it was widely felt that he had run his course. But when he edged out Rockefeller 18 days later in the crucial California primary, the realization struck home to other party stalwarts that Goldwater might, indeed, capture control of the party.

Stop-Goldwater Effort. At the Governors' Conference in Cleveland in June, a frantic but futile attempt was made to rally behind a man who might stop Goldwater at the national convention in San Francisco scheduled for mid-July. Pennsylvania's Governor William W. Scranton started to make himself available. Earlier, he had been encouraged by former President Dwight D. Eisenhower to enter the race. But after receiving a telephone call from Eisenhower advising him against any anti-Goldwater "cabal," a shaken Scranton withdrew. See SCRANTON, WILLIAM W.

Michigan's Governor George Romney also tentatively considered challenging Goldwater, but abandoned the idea when it became clear he could not win substantial support from his colleagues (see ROMNEY, GEORGE). Even former Vice-President Richard M. Nixon, the party's presidential nominee in 1960, appeared before the governors to urge competition against Goldwater, to no avail.

Within a few days after the governors adjourned, Scranton changed his mind, and on June 12 announced he would actively campaign for the nomination. He made a desperate last-minute tour of key states, but it was too late.

Goldwater Groundwork. Goldwater's dedicated lieutenants had been at work for four years lining up delegates. They were busy at the grass roots, on the levels of the county and state committees. In the words of one of the Senator's chief strategists, "Where we found no Goldwater delegates, we created them." It was astute political groundwork that paid off.

THE NOMINEE—at the Republican National Convention, Senator Barry M. Goldwater, acknowledges the acclaim of the delegates.

Wide World

ORDER! ORDER! Convention Chairman Thruston B. Morton, left, bangs gavel to
quiet booing hecklers and let New York Governor Nelson A. Rockefeller get on with speech.

Goldwater had sympathizers too in the Republican National Committee. Although the national chairman, U.S. Representative William E. Miller of New York, assumed an impartial posture, other officials made no secret of their support for Goldwater. In the end, however, Miller won the vice-presidential nod from Senator Goldwater. See MILLER, WILLIAM E.

Platform Showdown. By the time the delegates had assembled in San Francisco's Cow Palace on July 13, few could doubt that Goldwater was in almost complete control of the machinery of the party's 28th national convention. A bitter fight developed within the platform committee. Its moderates tried to revise some of the planks on civil rights, control over nuclear weapons, and political extremism. But the predominant Goldwater forces overrode every attempt to modify the sharply conservative planks of the platform.

The split between Goldwater's supporters and his moderate opposition worsened on the convention floor when another vain effort was made to amend the platform. Rockefeller was roundly booed by the galleries and by many on the convention floor. When it was all over, Goldwater in his acceptance speech

declined to offer the olive branch of conciliation to his critics. He said to them: "I would remind you that extremism in the defense of liberty is no vice. And let me remind you that moderation in the pursuit of justice is no virtue." The routed, beaten moderates had gotten their unconditional surrender terms from the victorious nominee.

In the Mainstream? The humiliated Scranton supporters feared the party had fallen into the hands of a militant clique, which, in the words of Rockefeller, was not "in the mainstream of Republican thinking." Scranton, who carried his fight against Goldwater to the bitter end, also voiced his fears that the party would be disastrously damaged by the Goldwater candidacy. Nevertheless, the Pennsylvania governor graciously accepted the fact of the Senator's nomination and campaigned for him as a loyal party member. Goldwater's supporters attributed this opposition to the displeasure of the so-called Eastern internationalist set.

Harmony at Hershey. In a move to mollify the Eastern wing of the party, Goldwater met with Eisenhower, Nixon, Scranton, and other leaders on August 12 in Hershey, Pa. In his speech, he toned down the ultraconservative views he had expressed at the convention. "I seek the support of no extremist—of the left or right," he said. And he listed the Ku-Klux Klan as an extremist group. He also said he supported the United Nations and Social Security. Yet he failed to placate Romney, Rockefeller, Lodge, and a number of liberal Republican Senators and Representatives.

As the campaign progressed, Goldwater denied he had made "concessions." His speech, he said "merely reaffirmed what I've been saying . . . I didn't always get through, for some reason."

He made several forays into the South, confirming the belief that he was pursuing what had come to be called "a Southern strategy." His popularity in the South rested upon his position that key elements of the civil rights law were unconstitutional and that the enforcement of civil rights was basically a matter for the states. For this reason, many observers described him as a sectional candidate, for he appeared to have no interest in broadening his appeal to include the large and often decisive vote of the Negroes in the Northern cities.

Probably the happiest time of Goldwater's Southern incursions came on September 16 when Senator Strom Thurmond of South Carolina switched his allegiance to the Republican party. He stood with Goldwater before a cheering crowd in Greenville, S.C., and declared his full support of the Arizonan.

Then, the Debacle. Goldwater's failure to carry more than six states and to win more than 27,145,161 votes dismayed other party spokesmen, although he and his aides regarded the vote as a good advance for the "conservative cause," which was solidly supported by those millions of Americans. In December, however, *The New York Times* disclosed the findings of a post-election poll taken by a major voter-opinion testing firm. It found that, at most, 5,400,000 Republican voters were hard-core supporters of Goldwater. More than three-fifths were in favor of new party leadership.

In the undertow of his defeat, a great many promising young Republican candidates for congressional seats and state and local offices were caught up and prematurely retired. The Ripon Society, a Republican research and policy group with members in 30 states, publicly blamed what is called "the architects of this right-wing crusade" and their "zeal to promote an ideological cause" for the debacle suffered by the Republican party.

The party had lost 38 seats in the House of Representatives, two seats in the Senate, and more than 500 seats in state legislatures. They were stripped of majorities in such key Republican strongholds as New York, Illinois, Indiana, Iowa, and Maine.

A Few Survive. Many prominent candidates who refused openly to endorse Goldwater managed to survive the landslide of President Lyndon B. Johnson, the Democratic nominee. They included Governor Romney of Michigan, Senator Hugh D. Scott, Jr., of Pennsylvania, Attorney General Edward

PICTURES OF THE YEAR/Bill Hunter, *Akron Beacon-Journal*

SWINGING BILL SCRANTON, with wife Mary at Governors' Conference in Cleveland, couldn't swing the nomination later in San Francisco.

Brooke of Massachusetts, and Representative John V. Lindsay of New York City.

Many others regarded as almost certain winners fell before the Johnson onslaught. They included notably Robert A. Taft, Jr., of Ohio, who was running for a seat in the U.S. Senate so long distinguished by his late father, and Charles H. Percy, young Chicago industrialist who was making his first bid for elective office as governor in Illinois.

Recriminations. Immediately after the shock of the defeat wore off, a major feud erupted in the party. The Ripon Society said: "The leadership of the Goldwater clique has thus forfeited any claim to guide the Republican party of the future."

The target of their bitterness was Chairman Dean Burch of the national committee, youthful assistant to Goldwater. He was the chief symbol of Goldwaterism in the party's machinery on the national level, and his scalp was demanded. Burch, however, held one unusual asset: a tidy surplus of $1,200,000 in the party's coffers.

Idaho's Governor Robert E. Smylie, chairman of the Republican Governors Association, called his colleagues together in Denver on December 4. After considerable discussion, the group issued a strong call for new leadership of the national committee.

RETAILING

The party leaders realized that Goldwater control extended deeply into many state and local party organizations. Therefore, it would not be susceptible to easy abolishment, even though the party had suffered the worst defeat in the history of U.S. politics in terms of the percentage of the total popular vote for the top of a ticket.　　　　PETER LISAGOR

See also DEMOCRATIC PARTY; ELECTIONS; GOVERNORS OF THE STATES; STATE GOVERNMENT.

RETAILING set grand and glorious records in 1964 as confident consumers used new billions in cash and credit to buy everything from necessities to original oil paintings. Total retail sales for the year jumped 6 per cent to top $261,600,000,000. Department store sales went over the $18,000,000,000 mark, an increase for the year of 9 per cent. Food store sales ran about 5 per cent ahead of 1963, with a total volume of more than $60,000,000,000.

The Christmas selling season was a bonanza. Speaking for the nation's leading retailer, Austin T. Cushman, board chairman of Sears, Roebuck & Company, said that the only limit on 1964 Christmas sales seemed to be "the sheer impossibility of moving more people" through the stores' doors.

General prosperity brought more buying of luxury and high-quality goods. That was one reason store profits increased at a faster rate than sales. A study by *Forbes* magazine showed that the profits of the nation's top 10 nonfood retailers rose an average of 42 per cent over 1963 while sales were averaging an increase of 15 per cent. (Ten leaders, ranked by sales, were: Sears, Roebuck & Company, J. C. Penney, Montgomery Ward, Woolworth, Federated Department Stores, Allied Stores, May Department Stores, R. H. Macy and Company, Gimbel Brothers, and Associated Dry Goods.)

Discount retailers seemed to have finally achieved a valid and permanent place in the retailing world in 1964. Their total sales for the year were estimated at more than $10,000,000,000, easily double their total four years earlier. However, discounters' expansion slowed. But, if growth slowed, so did the number of bankruptcies.

Nevertheless, competition in retailing was on the increase. For instance, Sears opened 17 new department stores and 58 new catalog sales offices. Penney's, once a specialist in soft goods, moved strongly into hard goods, while Woolworth's and Kresge's stepped up their entries into full-line discounting.

On the government front, the most important event of the year was President Lyndon B. Johnson's decision to appoint Assistant Secretary of Labor Esther Peterson as chairman of the President's Committee on Consumer Interests. Retailers feared that studies launched by Mrs. Peterson might lead to blanket government regulation of the entire industry. The President said, however, that the spotlight would be turned only on "the selfish minority who deceive and defraud consumers."　　　EDWIN W. DARBY

RHODESIA, a self-governing British colony in Africa, remained locked in a bitter dispute with London over plans for its independence. Formerly known as Southern Rhodesia, it had been part of the three-nation Federation of Rhodesia and Nyasaland until that union was dissolved. The two other members, Malawi and Zambia, were already independent.

Deep-seated political and racial questions lay at the core of the quarrel, which had also divided Rhodesia itself into two angry factions. The all-white Rhodesian government, under Prime Minister Ian D. Smith, was determined to continue white rule in the nation. The Africans, however, who comprise roughly 3,960,000 of the population, were determined to achieve political and social equality with about 215,000 whites. The British government was reluctant to grant full independence unless the voting franchise was broadened to ensure rule by the African majority in a reasonable time.

Population: 4,175,000. **Government:** Prime Minister Ian D. Smith. **Foreign Trade:** statistics not available. **Principal Exports:** asbestos, chrome ore, gold, tobacco.　　　BENJAMIN E. THOMAS

See also AFRICA.

RHODESIA AND NYASALAND, FEDERATION OF. See MALAWI; RHODESIA; ZAMBIA.

ROADS AND HIGHWAYS. In scattered bits and pieces, 2,505 more miles of the 41,000-mile system of interstate highways opened to traffic in the year ended Dec. 31, 1964. Total segments in use grew to about 19,000 miles, or 46 per cent of the network due to be completed by 1972.

Progress varied remarkably from state to state. While Minnesota labored to finish one-sixth of its interstate mileage, neighboring Wisconsin passed the halfway mark. Of all states, Michigan's work was nearest to completion (70 per cent). Texas, with only 35 per cent, led in total road length, with 1,051 interstate miles completed by Sept. 30, 1964.

Since 1956, $20,800,000,000 has been committed to the program; $2,600,000,000 went into projects completed in the year ended Sept. 30, 1964. Expenditures on all other federal-aid primary and secondary highway systems and their urban extensions have totaled $13,500,000,000 since 1956, and $1,800,000,-000 in the 12-month period.

Major Highway Openings in 1964 included:
- Quebec's Eastern Townships Autoroute, a 72-mile leg from Montreal to within 20 miles of Newport, Vt.
- Italy's Highway of the Sun (*Autostrada del Sole*), stretching 460-odd miles from Milan to Naples.
- A link-up between Belgium's *autoroutes* and the *Autobahnen* of West Germany, at Aachen.
- Florida's Interstate 4 (I-4) from Tampa across the state through Orlando and to Daytona Beach.
- Capital Beltway, a 65-mile by-pass around the nation's capital.
- Interstate 95, Orono, Me., to Medford, N.C.—875 miles, mostly on I-95, nonstop except for 14 tolls.

Highway Use in the United States rose again in 1964, generating greater-than-anticipated revenue for future road building. Motor fuel consumption by 87,000,000 vehicles of all classifications approximated 67,300,000,000 gallons in 1964, a gain of 4.3 per cent over 1963. Highway-user revenue (mainly federal and state taxes on vehicles and motor fuel) approached $13,700,000,000.

Transportation Planning for future social and economic needs nevertheless lagged in two-fifths of the nation's 216 urban areas of over 50,000 population. The U.S. Bureau of Public Roads warned 90 cities, including San Francisco, St. Louis, Cleveland, Boston, and Honolulu, that they and their state governments must accelerate efforts to have "an acceptable continuing comprehensive transportation planning process" ready by mid-1965 or lose federal aid on new highway projects.

The Lewis and Clark Trail, from St. Louis to the Pacific, came under study in 1964 as a historical and recreational highway route. Congress on October 6 authorized a 27-man commission to recommend a program to "advance public awareness of . . . the historical significance of the Lewis and Clark Expedition (and) encourage a suitable network of roads following the (trail's) general route."

"Metro-Mobility" conceptions of urban-area transportation were unveiled in General Motors' New York World's Fair exhibit. In its "highway of the future" model, a system of suburban "feeder" buses converged at interchange points to form automated commuter bus trains, operating on reserved expressway lanes between outlying towns and the central business district. An "automatic pilot" lane with an electronic guidance system completely took over driving chores and governed the stream of traffic on heavily traveled urban expressways.   MARK REINSBERG

See also AUTOMOBILE; CITY PLANNING; SAFETY; STATE GOVERNMENT; TAXATION; TRANSIT.

ROBLES, MARCO AURELIO (1905-   ), a husky
man with dark, sad eyes, was sworn in as president of Panama on October 1. He succeeded his long-time friend Roberto F. Chiari, in whose cabinet he had served prior to his election. See PANAMA.

Robles was born in Aguadulce on November 8, 1905. His introduction to politics came at the age of 26 when he joined the Liberal party. For several years he divided his time between politics and work with an insurance company. For a while he was assistant manager of the National Bank of Panama.

In 1960, Robles was appointed minister of justice by President Chiari. During his three years in office, he established a reputation for being a hard worker.

The new president is married to the former Petita Querube Saa; they have three daughters, Raquel, Lia, and Roxanne. The family lives in a comfortable but inexpensively furnished home in El Cangrejo, a residential suburb.   WALTER F. MORSE

ROCKET. See NATIONAL DEFENSE; SPACE TRAVEL.

ROMAN CATHOLIC. The third session of Vatican
Council II opened Sept. 14, 1964, with a Mass concelebrated by Pope Paul VI with 24 council fathers. His Holiness stated that in continuing the work accomplished in the first two sessions, this session was "to round out the first Vatican Council's incomplete teaching on the nature of the church by explaining the nature and function of bishops as successors of the apostles."

The first Vatican Council (1869-1870), which was interrupted by the Franco-Prussian War, had defined the primacy and infallibility of the pope only, and the need remained for clarification of the role of bishops. In addition to describing this need, the pope reaffirmed his authority, and the Roman Catholic Church's need for centralization.

Thus, as a result of the deliberations of the first two sessions, the fathers proclaimed collegiality as a teaching of the Roman Catholic Church, the teaching that all bishops today are the successors of the apostles, and with the pope as their head, they recapitulate the relationship of St. Peter and the apostles. The fathers further stated that this college of bishops has no authority without the pope as its head.

Ecumenism. Two other documents were produced in final form, the first on ecumenism and the second on the Eastern Rite churches of Catholicism. With the first, the church encouraged its members to enter into dialogue with members of other faiths. The second suggested reciprocation between Eastern Rite Catholics and members of the Orthodox Church.

The council fathers approved the ordination of older married deacons, and granted deacons permission to perform some of the priestly functions with the approval of the Episcopal Conference of a nation.

Jews. A draft declaration was presented which stated that the Jews of Christ's era, and particularly Jews of today, were not to be held responsible for the Crucifixion. See JEWS AND JUDAISM.

On November 6, the pope himself attended the council, on the day that missionary activity was introduced. The schema on the church's missionary activity was considered inadequate after discussion, and was returned for complete rewriting. One final speaker stressed the spirit of poverty, urging the use of missions in areas where they are needed, or where there is poverty, rather than being limited by rigidly defined geographical boundaries.

November 21 marked the closing day of the third session. On this day the Eucharistic fast was reduced to one hour for both the priests and the laity, and Pope Paul promulgated the council's constitution on the nature of the church and the decrees on the Eastern Rite churches and ecumenism. He also proclaimed the Virgin Mary as mother of the church. He then concluded the session after concelebrating Mass with 24 bishops and abbots.

During this session a layman, Patrick Keegan of England, addressed the council, and women attended for the first time in history.

Pictorial Parade

PILGRIMAGE. Pope Paul VI was the first pope since St. Peter to visit the Holy Land. Here, he greets welcomers as Arab Legionnaires strive to maintain order.

A fourth session, to begin Sept. 14, 1965, will bring the council to a close. The discussion of the text on religious freedom is to take place at that time, as well as a text defining the church's attitude toward such problems as interfaith marriage, birth control, peace, disarmament, and poverty.

Holy Land Pilgrimage. The new year started auspiciously with a three-day pilgrimage by Pope Paul to the Holy Land. Leaving Rome by plane on January 4, he was greeted the same day by King Hussein of Jordan. The pilgrimage took the pope to Jerusalem; to Calvary, as he retraced Christ's steps along the Via Dolorosa; and to the Sea of Galilee. No pope had visited the Holy Land since the era of St. Peter, 1,900 years ago.

During his historic visit, the pontiff held two meetings with Patriarch Athenagoras I, leader of the Eastern Orthodox faithful. These were the first such meetings since the 15th century. Later, in the same ecumenical spirit, the pope announced the setting up of a secretariat which would serve non-Christians. See EASTERN ORTHODOX.

First Encyclical. On August 6 the pope issued his first encyclical, entitled *Ecclesiam Suam* (*His Church*). In it, the pope expressed readiness to serve as a mediator in international disputes. Urging all Christians to stress what they have in common rather than what divides them, he invited all to unite in an effort toward "religious liberty, human brotherhood, social welfare, and civil order." With a prologue dealing with approaches open to the church, the encyclical was divided into three parts: "The Church's Aware-

ness of Itself in the Modern World"; "Renewal in the Church"; and "Dialogue Between the Church and the World." Atheism and communism were described as the most serious problems facing church members of our times.

Canonization of 22 martyrs of Uganda, who sacrificed their lives between 1885 and 1887 along with other Roman Catholics and a number of Anglicans, took place on October 18. These were the first Africans south of the Sahara and the first of the Bantu tribe to be declared saints. They chose extreme torture and death rather than to deny their faith. On the occasion of this canonization, the pope also announced his plan to visit Bombay during the 38th Eucharistic Congress.

He visited India on December 2, and was greeted by 1,000,000 people of all creeds. He thus became the first pope to go to Asia. During his stay there he was under constant pressure from crowds numbering in the hundreds of thousands. He delivered more than 30 speeches, one of which included an appeal for world-wide action to relieve poverty such as he saw about him.

The pontiff also made appeals for world peace and disarmament and for the use of all the material and energy now devoted to warlike undertakings to help underdeveloped countries everywhere. The pope talked with delegates of other faiths and called on Indian President Sarvepalli Radhakrishnan. On December 3, he consecrated six new bishops in an open-air ceremony attended by 100,000 Indians. He returned to the Vatican on December 5.

World-Wide Ministry. The Roman Catholic population of the world increased by about 12,500,000 during 1964, from an approximate 572,006,000 to an estimated 584,493,081.

During the year, the last 300 missionaries of southern Sudan were expelled, and men of all faiths were shocked to learn of the murder of the many hostages including priests and nuns in Congo. See CONGO (LÉOPOLDVILLE).

Vernacular in the Sacraments. In the United States, beginning on the opening day of the Vatican Council's third session, English was used instead of Latin in the administration of the sacraments of baptism, confirmation, penance, the anointing of the sick, and matrimony. This was in keeping with the new effort to stress the communal nature of Christian worship, and followed a decision made by the council that the local language should be used "to the advantage of the people."

Changes in Mass. The use of English was extended to the Mass on November 29, the first Sunday of Advent, as a result of a decision by the National Conference of U.S. Bishops on April 2. At that time the congregation joined with the priest in reciting certain parts of the Mass in English, and assisted in the announcing of prayers.

During 1964, Mother Mary Katherine Drexel, foundress of the Sisters of the Blessed Sacrament for Indian and Colored People, was proposed for beatification by the church.

Vatican Pavilion. The Vatican Pavilion opened its doors to visitors of the New York World's Fair, and between April 22 and October 18 received 13,823,037 visitors, or 49.87 per cent of the total number of fair visitors. The highest attendance at the Vatican Pavilion for any single day was 141,575 on September 26. Among the many interesting exhibitions, Michelangelo's famed *Pietà* attracted the greatest attention. It was brought to the United States from St. Peter's Basilica in Rome. See FAIRS AND EXHIBITIONS (picture).

U.S. Roman Catholics numbered 44,874,371, an increase of 1,026,433, including all Catholics in the armed forces and in the diplomatic service. This represents a 10-year increase of 41.5 per cent over 1954. They are cared for spiritually by five cardinals, 32 archbishops, 207 bishops, 57,000 priests, 12,000 brothers, 180,015 sisters distributed over 17,445 parishes belonging to 28 archdioceses and 120 dioceses, and 191,125 full-time teachers consisting of priests, brothers, sisters, and lay teachers. Enrollment in the past year in Roman Catholic colleges and universities increased by 8,408. There are 376 homes for invalids in which 33,889 residents are cared for.

The church in the United States is becoming more missionary, as indicated by an increase in the percentage of priests in the missions from 5.7 per cent in 1962 to 6.2 per cent in 1964. There has been a smaller but definite increase in U.S. brothers and sisters in the missions as well, and an increase of lay missionaries from 225 to 532.　　　FULTON J. SHEEN

ROMANIA boldly declared its independence as a communist nation at an "Enlarged Plenum" of its Communist party in April. The Romanians, criticizing both the Soviet Union and Communist China, urged both nations to settle their differences privately rather than publicly. See COMMUNISM.

Diplomatically and economically, Romania reduced its cultural and social ties with the Soviet Union. It increased its contacts with the West through various delegations it sent abroad. Deputy Premier Gheorghe Gaston-Marin led a group that spent 10 days in Washington, D.C., in May. Agreements were signed that would raise diplomatic representation between the two countries to ambassadorial level, facilitate trade, and help Romania acquire U.S. machinery and technical know-how. Romania reduced its imports from the East by nearly 10 per cent, making up the difference by increasing trade with the West.

Bucharest, Romania's capital, was the only one in the world where the Albanians, the Communist Chinese, the Cubans, the Russians, and the Yugoslavians met amicably during the year. The occasion, in August, was the 20th anniversary of Romania's liberation. Meanwhile, its annual rate of industrial growth was more than 15 per cent, the highest in Eastern Europe. The removal of Nikita S. Khrushchev in October delayed a policy collision with the Kremlin. See RUSSIA.

Population: 19,025,000. **Government:** Communist Party First Secretary Gheorghe Gheorghiu-Dej; Premier Ion Gheorghe Maurer. **Foreign Trade:** exports, $915,000,000; imports, $1,022,000,000. **Principal Exports:** machinery, petroleum and petroleum products, timber.　　　TOM AND HARLE DAMMANN

See also EUROPE.

ROMNEY, GEORGE WILCKEN (1907-　), was re-elected for two more years as governor of Michigan on November 3. He got 1,764,542 votes to 1,369,254 for Neil Staebler, 59, a former Democratic state chairman. Despite the mere 41 votes he received for the presidential nomination at the Republican National Convention at San Francisco on July 15, his stature in the party was enhanced by his victory in Michigan. He was one of the few Republicans to survive the Democratic landslide.

Romney was prominent in the automotive industry when he took a leave of absence in 1962 as board chairman of American Motors Corporation to seek and win the governorship.

Romney was born at Chihuahua, Mexico, on July 8, 1907. He attended the University of Utah and George Washington University. He is a member of the Church of Jesus Christ of Latter-day Saints (Mormons). He and his wife, the former Lenore LaFount, have four children.　　　WALTER F. MORSE

ROTARY INTERNATIONAL. See SERVICE ORGANIZATIONS.

ROWAN, CARL THOMAS (1925-   ), is one of the highest ranking Negroes in U.S. government. He replaced the ailing former newscaster Edward R. Murrow as director of the U.S. Information Agency in early 1964.

Carl Rowan was Deputy Assistant Secretary of State for Public Affairs for two years, before going to Finland where he served as the U.S. ambassador in 1963. See NEGRO (picture).

During his 13 years with the Minneapolis *Tribune*, Rowan received many awards for his reporting. He spent most of 1954 in India, Pakistan, and Southeast Asia as a correspondent and lecturer, and then wrote *The Pitiful and the Proud* (1956). *South of Freedom* (1953) and *Go South to Sorrow* (1957) are books of his on America's racial problems. Rowan also has lectured extensively.

Carl Rowan was born in Ravenscroft and grew up in McMinnville, Tenn. At 19, he was an ensign, one of the first 15 Negroes to receive a U.S. navy commission. He received his A.B. at Oberlin College (1947), and M.A. in journalism at the University of Minnesota (1948). The U.S. Junior Chamber of Commerce selected him as one of America's 19 outstanding men in 1953.

ROWING. See SPORTS.

RUANDA-URUNDI. See BURUNDI; RWANDA.

RUBBER became an $11,000,000,000 industry in 1964 as tire sales for the replacement market scored a record 89,000,000 units, a 12 per cent increase over 1963's final figure of 79,035,000. Shipments of tires for new cars still surpassed the previous year, 42,350,000 to 41,893,000.

The new low-profile tire came into its own on most of the 1965 model cars. It was also the year of a radically different tire construction called "radial-ply" or "belted." It was much discussed if not greatly used. The cords in a single ply go laterally across these tires, bead to bead, and a belt of diagonally placed cords goes on top, underlying the tread. Because this construction allows the cords to spread, the tread goes onto the pavement smoothly. Wear is said to be up to twice that of usual tires. Drawbacks included high cost and rough riding over bumpy roads.

Earl B. Hathaway, president of the Firestone Tire & Rubber Company, estimated the industry's use of 1,925,000 long tons of natural and synthetic rubber in 1964, an increase of 9.1 per cent over 1963's record 1,764,014 long tons. And in 1964, synthetic rubber usage came full circle. For the first time since World War II, when supplies of natural rubber were cut off, Goodyear was producing some tires using only synthetic rubber. In place of the natural, Goodyear used a synthetic called "Natsyn," the molecular duplicate of tree-grown latex. Synthetics' percentage of the overall rubber market climbed another 2 per cent during the year, leaving only 23 per cent to natural.   CHARLES C. CAIN III

RUBY, JACK (1911-   ), was found guilty of "murder with malice" in shooting and killing the alleged assassin of President John F. Kennedy on Nov. 24, 1963. The slaying, in the Dallas city jail, occurred two days after the assassination. A jury of four women and eight men, at Dallas, returned the guilty verdict—on live, nationwide television—on March 14, 1964, and set the penalty as death in the electric chair. The trial began on February 17. After considerable controversy over seating jurors, the defense called 35 witnesses and the prosecution, 31.

Ruby pleaded not guilty on the ground of temporary insanity. Several experts testified that his mental condition was unstable.

The guilty verdict was appealed. As 1964 closed, the case had yet to be taken through higher courts. Much hiring and firing of lawyers by Ruby's family had been a feature of the case.

The Warren Commission, in its report on the assassination, held that Ruby acted independently in killing Lee Harvey Oswald, and further, that Ruby was not acquainted with Oswald, had no connection with the Communist party or with ultra-conservative causes, and was not significantly linked to organized crime.

Ruby was quoted as telling the commission he killed Oswald in order to spare Mrs. Jacqueline Kennedy "the ordeal of returning to Dallas" to testify in a trial of Oswald.

Ruby was born in Chicago as Jack Leon Rubinstein. He moved to Dallas around 1948, and at the time of the murder operated a strip-tease night club. He is single.   WALTER F. MORSE

See also PUBLISHING; WARREN COMMISSION; THE WARREN REPORT (appendix).

RULERS OF THE WORLD. See fact tabs at the end of various country articles.

RUSSELL, HAROLD (1914-   ), lecturer and handless veteran of screen fame, is chairman of the President's Committee on Employment of the Handicapped. He succeeded the late Melvin J. Maas in April, 1964 (see DEATHS OF NOTABLE PERSONS). Russell had been the committee vice-chairman since 1960. His philosophy as an amputee: "It is not what you have lost, but what you have left that counts."

A defective fuse caused an explosion, shattering Russell's hands on June 6, 1944, while he was instructing a demolition squad at Camp Mackall, North Carolina.

Russell played the part of the handless sailor in *The Best Years of Our Lives.* It won eight Motion Picture Academy awards (1947). Russell won the best supporting actor Oscar and a special award for "bringing comfort to disabled veterans." He has been national commander of the American Veterans of World War II since 1960.

Harold Russell was born in Nova Scotia, and grew up in Cambridge, Mass. He is a Boston University graduate (1947).

RUSSIA

AT MIDNIGHT on October 15, in an abrupt move that caught the world by surprise, the Communist party of the Union of Soviet Socialist Republics (U.S.S.R.) stripped Nikita S. Khrushchev of his posts as first secretary of the party and premier. He was replaced by two of his protégés: Leonid I. Brezhnev became first secretary; Aleksei N. Kosygin became premier. See BREZHNEV, LEONID I.; KOSYGIN, ALEKSEI N.

The sudden removal of Khrushchev ended a decade during which he had sought to lead the Soviet Union through a critical post-Stalin transitional period. During the year preceding his ouster, he had dominated the scene while personifying the U.S.S.R. on his many trips abroad. Only a few days prior to his removal, the Russians had scored another "first" by orbiting a three-man space satellite which had returned safely after 16 orbits around the earth (see SPACE TRAVEL).

KREMLIN'S POWER passed into hands of Premier Aleksei N. Kosygin, left, and Communist Party First Secretary Leonid I. Brezhnev after downfall of Nikita S. Khrushchev.

Sovfoto

"Harold won, Lyndon's winning, and I didn't even know I was running."

This achievement was all the more welcome in a year that had been marred by continuing difficulties in agriculture, a slowdown in the rate of economic growth, and the ever-sharpening dispute with Communist China (see COMMUNISM). The dazzling space feat was at once eclipsed by Khrushchev's removal. His closing "good-by," made at the end of a telephone conversation with the cosmonauts while they were in flight, became an ironic farewell to the nation.

Khrushchev's downfall came as a surprise to the U.S.S.R. and to the world. When his 70th birthday was celebrated in April with more than the usual adulation, Khrushchev appeared to be firmly in control. The stability of his regime and his satisfactory health were seemingly demonstrated by his extraordinary activities, including major trips to Czechoslovakia, Hungary, Scandinavia, the United Arab Republic, and the farm regions of Soviet Asia.

Events Preceding the Downfall. A major change in leadership had been the elevation of 69-year-old Anastas I. Mikoyan in July to the largely honorific chairmanship of the collective presidency. Much more significant, however, was the relinquishment of this same position by Leonid I. Brezhnev, a newcomer to the top ranks since the death of Stalin. On the surface, what might have appeared to be a demotion was in fact the designation of Brezhnev as the heir apparent to Khrushchev in place of Frol R. Kozlov, who was seriously ill. Another veteran from

the Stalin era, Aleksei N. Kosygin, an industrial specialist, continued as first deputy chairman of the council of ministers. The ground was thus prepared by Khrushchev himself for the action that replaced him with a triumvirate in which Brezhnev was first secretary, Kosygin was chairman of the council of ministers, or premier, and Mikoyan served as chairman of the Presidium of the Supreme Soviet.

The Causes of the changeover and even the procedures by which it was effected remained shrouded in obscurity. The official reasons for Khrushchev's ouster were illness and advanced age, but even the first announcement hinted at more serious explanations. His name was no longer mentioned. Only cryptic references gave some clues to the background of the changeover.

Curiously enough, Khrushchev was not immediately deprived either of his membership in the central committee or of his chairmanship of the party's Bureau for the Russian Republic. The prominent role played by Marshal Rodion Malinovsky at the Bolshevik anniversary celebrations in November, and the appointment of Aleksandr N. Shelepin, a former head of the security police, to a full membership in the Presidium suggested that both the military and the police had supported the anti-Khrushchev group. The only other appointments to the Presidium were Petr Y. Shelest, as a full member, and, as an alternate, Petr N. Demichev. Other important Khrushchev men, such as Nikolai V. Podgorny and Mikhail Suslov, remained in office.

Policies or Methods? It was hard to tell whether Khrushchev had been ousted because of the policies he had pursued (and if so, whether foreign or domestic ones had been most involved), or because of the methods he had employed to attain the goals that had been accepted not only by his colleagues but also by his successors.

Subsequent editorial references in official Soviet publications to "hasty decisions," bragging and bluster, disregard of the findings of science, "harebrained schemes," "nepotism," and "organizational mania" seemed to confirm world-wide speculations that Khrushchev's methods were a prime cause of dissatisfaction. Another such indication was the announcement in November that his drastic partition of the party into two major segments, one for agriculture and one for industry, had been reversed, and the traditional unified organization restored.

The changes in economic administration ratified by the Supreme Soviet in December, 1963, continued in force through 1964, and D. F. Ustinov, as first deputy chairman of the council of ministers and chairman of the Supreme Council of the national economy, remained at the helm of the entire economy during 1964.

Economic Growth. It was still uncertain at year's end whether or not the new leaders would seriously modify the economic policies with which they and Khrushchev had been identified. The fallen dictator had left behind many unsolved problems. According to the United States Central Intelligence Agency (CIA), there had been a noticeable slowdown in the economic growth rate. It had fallen from between 6 to 10 per cent in most postwar years to as low as 2.5 per cent in 1962 and 1963. The decline, according to the CIA, had resulted from several factors, including a shift from an economy of heavy industry, raw materials, and power supply toward a more "modern" one of diversified consumer goods production. There had also been a large increase in military and space spending, and a serious drop in agricultural production.

Although these estimates were the subject of controversy among Western specialists, they were rejected categorically by Soviet Union spokesmen. In a speech made on Feb. 14, 1964, Khrushchev had declared that industrial output had risen 19 per cent in the preceding two years, and that despite the poor harvest in 1963, the Gross National Product (GNP) was up 11 per cent. However, he did admit continuing low productivity in industry and agriculture, and he continued to devote much time and effort to the search for solutions.

A Seven-Year Expansion program that had been adopted at the close of 1963 included large-scale investment in the chemical industry so as to provide greater supplies of fertilizers. Throughout 1964, Khrushchev was constantly preoccupied with the agricultural question, delivering several major addresses that dealt frankly with the Soviet Union's backwardness and that bristled with ideas for improvement. In April, for example, on the basis of a memorandum submitted by him to the Presidium, a high-level commission on agriculture had been formed under Podgorny. During his farm tour, too, Khrushchev had disclosed several contemplated major reforms, such as the formation of specialized production agencies for each major agricultural product and direct sales by farmers through their own city stores. His successors in October continued to stress the need to raise agricultural output and to emphasize chemical production.

They did not, however, make clear their position regarding the relative importance to be attached to the production of consumer goods, heavy industry, or armaments. Khrushchev increasingly had made himself the spokesman of "goulash communism," a concept that sought to provide a better life for the people, and one which not only challenged the traditional orientation of the Soviet economy toward heavy industry but also advocated a substantial shift in the direction of consumer goods production.

Victory for Consumers. The reduced military spending in the 1964 budget, and the continued development of the chemical industry implied a defeat for the "metal-eaters" and the military spenders, and a victory for the consumers. This was further corroborated in July, when the Supreme Soviet approved increased rewards for those working in education,

trade, and catering, and pensions for collective farmers, hitherto excluded from social security.

Early in October, at a joint meeting of the party Presidium and the council of ministers, Khrushchev had urged the drafting of a long-range development plan in which the production of consumer goods should be given first place. Brezhnev, Khrushchev's successor, gave little or no evidence of any intention of changing these general lines of emphasis.

Foreign Relations. Speculation was rife at the end of the year as to whether Soviet foreign policy would be seriously affected by the changes in the Kremlin. Up to the downfall of Khrushchev, the year had been characterized by an ever-intensifying conflict with Communist China, and a developing *détente* with the West. Brezhnev and Kosygin at once took steps to assure foreign governments that they did not intend to forsake the policy of peaceful coexistence. Yet at the same time they proclaimed their earnest desire to safeguard the unity of the socialist camp. Could these two aims be reconciled? If not, which would predominate in future Soviet policy?

Khrushchev, through a series of measures, had been able to greatly improve relations with the Western governments. The nuclear test-ban treaty of 1963 was followed in April, 1964, by the U.S.S.R. decision to cut back the production of fissionable materials, with similar actions taken by the American and British governments. Earlier, in February, the scientific, technical, and cultural exchange agreement with the United States was renewed. In June, a consular convention was signed with the United States as was a treaty of friendship between the U.S.S.R. and the (East) German Democratic Republic. The latter placed the question of West Berlin in cold storage for the time being (see GERMANY).

Policy Conflicts with the West persisted on important issues, including Cyprus and Vietnam, although in neither case did the Soviet government match its sharp denunciation of Western policy with action (see CYPRUS; VIETNAM). The Soviet government was particularly incensed by the Western view that its failure to contribute to the cost of UN operations in the Middle East and Congo (Léopoldville) would lead to the loss of its vote under Article 19 of the UN Charter. See UNITED NATIONS.

By the end of the year, there was not much evidence that the regime was changing its fundamental attitude toward the West, or that Moscow and Peking would be able to compose their differences to restore the unity of the communist world.

Population: 229,500,000. **Government:** First Secretary of the Communist Party Leonid I. Brezhnev; Chairman of the Council of Ministers Aleksei N. Kosygin; Chairman of the Presidium of the Supreme Soviet Anastas I. Mikoyan. **Foreign Trade:** exports, $7,160,000,000; imports, $7,050,000,000. **Principal Exports:** fuels, machines and equipment, metals and metal products, vegetable products. H. GORDON SKILLING

See also EUROPE.

RWANDA cut its last economic ties with Burundi, a neighboring country with which it had once formed the Belgian-administered United Nations Trust Territory of Ruanda-Urundi. It ended the monetary and customs unions and the central bank they had shared since 1962.

Tribal warfare continued between members of Inyenzi, a terrorist group that wanted to restore the Watusi monarchy, and the Bahutus, who supported the government. In March, Rwanda requested that a UN commission of inquiry investigate reports that thousands of Watusi had been slain by the Bahutus. The commission subsequently reported that between 870 and 1,000 had been slain. But thousands had fled the country to Burundi, Tanganyika, and Uganda.

Population: 2,925,000. **Government:** President and Premier Grégoire Kayibanda. **Foreign Trade:** no statistics available. **Principal Exports:** coffee, cotton, minerals. BENJAMIN E. THOMAS

See also AFRICA.

SAFETY in all areas except one, failed to move forward in the United States in 1964. Accidents took the lives of an estimated 105,000 persons, an increase of 4 per cent over 1963, or a 3 per cent rise in the death rate, to 54.9 per 100,000 population. That was the highest rate since 1957, when it reached 55.9.

Only accidental deaths in the home showed a decrease, down 2 per cent. About 10,300,000 persons were injured in accidents disabling them beyond the first day. Total cost of all accidents was estimated at $16,700,000,000.

Motor-vehicle accidents killed about 47,800 persons, an all-time record. Significant steps taken during 1964 to reduce traffic fatalities were: (1) the factory-installation of seat belts as standard equip-

ACCIDENTAL DEATHS AND DEATH RATES

Type of Accident	1963 Number	Rate†	1964 Number	Rate†	Change in Rates
Motor Vehicle	43,564	23.1	47,800	25.0	+8%
Public Nonroad	17,000	9.4	18,000	9.4	+4%
Home	29,000	15.4	28,500	14.9	−3%
Work	14,200	7.5	14,200	7.4	−1%
TOTAL*	100,669	53.4	105,000	54.9	+3%

*Total does not add up because of duplications of motor vehicle and home and work deaths.
†Deaths per 100,000 population.
Source: National Safety Council.

ment in the front seats of new cars and (2) the development of a nationwide licensed driver-improvement program by the Safety Council.

Fires killed about 7,800 Americans in 1964, some 300 under the 1963 toll. Fire losses were estimated at $1,370,000,000, about 3 per cent below 1963.

The National Safety Council's Trustees Award for 1963 went to Kansas City, Mo., as the city with the best all-around accident-prevention program. No state was judged worthy of a 1963 award. HOWARD PYLE

See also AUTOMOBILE; HEALTH; STATE GOVERNMENT; VITAL STATISTICS.

SAILING again found the United States winner of the 113-year-old America's Cup, sailing's No. 1 prize. The 19th successful defense of the cup saw America's *Constellation* whip Great Britain's *Sovereign* in four straight races off Newport, R.I. The *Constellation*, skippered by Bob Bavier, won by these margins: 5 minutes 34 seconds; 20 minutes 24 seconds; 6 minutes 33 seconds; and 15 minutes 40 seconds. Before Bavier took over command of the *Constellation*, the 5.5-meter yacht had been beaten regularly in the America's Cup Trials by another U.S. boat, *American Eagle*. The *Sovereign* was handled by Peter Scott.

Conquistador, a 40-foot sloop, skippered by Fuller Callaway of San Francisco, emerged the winner of the five-race Southern Ocean Racing Conference championship. Dick Dungan's *Sabre*, winner of the 184-mile Miami-Nassau race, was second, and *Doubloon*, Joe Byars' defending champion, was third. "Huey" Long's *Ondine* won the Miami Cat Cay race and also the 27-mile Lipton Cup race.

John Kilroy's *Kialoa II* won the 140-mile Newport-Ensenada race. The 635-mile Newport-Bermuda race was won by Milton Ernstof's *Burgoo*. The 53-foot sloop *Gypsy*, owned by Charles Kotovic of Milwaukee, won the 235-mile Port Huron-Mackinac sail, and also finished first in the 333-mile Chicago-Mackinac race, though the winner on corrected time was George Quandee's 30-foot sloop, *Talisman*.

Don Edler of Newport Harbor, Calif., edged defending champion Joe Duplin to win the world star class title at Winthrop, Mass. George Friedrich of New Orleans won the Mallory Cup, given to the men's individual sailing champion, and the Adams Cup for women was captured by Mrs. Jane Pegel of Lake Geneva, Wis. Bob Andre of San Diego won the Single-Handed Sailing Championship's O'Day Trophy at Buzzard's Bay, Mass. STANLEY ISAACS

SAINT LOUIS was praised by President Lyndon B. Johnson on February 14 for its choice of "progress—not decay." Thus began the city's observance of the 200th anniversary of its founding by French fur traders. On July 4, some 500,000 persons gathered at the site of the new Jefferson National Expansion Memorial Park to cheer similar comments. At the site, a graceful 630-foot stainless steel arch, designed by the late Eero Saarinen was rising.

The crowd was entitled to cheer. The city, riding the crest of an economic boom, saw $400,000,000 worth of building projects announced in 1964. Most business indexes hit record highs; unemployment fell to about half the national average. Also, Saint Louis became the third largest producer of 1964 automobiles. And a bonus arrived in autumn when the Cardinals came from behind to win the National League pennant and then humble the New York Yankees in the World Series. See BASEBALL.

In addition to substantial urban renewal projects underway, St. Louis spent $860,000 to make 10 miles of downtown streets among the nation's most brightly lit, with 25 times as much light being cast by new installations.

With the region's six-county population reaching 2,300,000, Saint Louis' Mayor Raymond Tucker, in June, proposed the formation of a St. Louis regional council to deal with complex metropolitan problems. DONALD W. LIEF

SALVATION ARMY completed its 99th year of service with preparations for a year-long 100th anniversary observance. General Frederick Coutts appointed a special centenary commission to assist Army members in planning celebrations in their local communities.

The week of June 24 to July 2, 1965, was selected for a series of special events and meetings in London. Salvationists from 86 countries will visit the city to pay tribute to William Booth, founder and first General, who began his work there in 1865. W. Wycliffe Booth, a grandson of the Army's founder, was appointed International Traveling Commissioner and visited Salvation Army centers in many parts of the world to help plan centenary celebrations.

Salvation Army musical groups exchanged trumpets and tambourines for electric guitars, and added popular folk songs to traditional religious hymns in an effort to reach more young people. This innovation was criticized by some church leaders as being "highly inappropriate" for a religious organization. The move, however, received the strong support of International Commander Coutts. He announced that the organization will utilize the modern musical language of young people to enlist their interest in the Salvation Army program and demonstrate the ability of religion to change with the times. JOSEPH P. ANDERSON

SARAGAT, GIUSEPPE (1898-   ), a founder of Italy's Democratic Socialist party, was elected the nation's fifth president on December 28. He succeeded Antonio Segni, who resigned because of ill health. See ITALY.

Italy's new president was born in Turin on September 19, 1898. His father was a lawyer. Giuseppe was trained to be a bank clerk. A Socialist since 1922, Saragat left Italy in 1926 when the Fascist regime began arresting socialists and communists. He subsequently worked in Vienna and Paris. In 1943, he returned to Rome following the signing of an armistice between the Allies and the Italian government. In 1946, he became president of the constituent assembly, the body which set up the Italian Republic's constitution.

Saragat served three times as deputy premier and was ambassador to Paris for two years. He was named foreign minister in 1962, a position he held at the time of his election to the presidency. Saragat has a son and a daughter. His wife Giuseppina died in 1961 after 35 years of marriage. WALTER F. MORSE

SARTRE, JEAN-PAUL (1905-   ), French man of letters, refused, but nevertheless remained the Nobel literature laureate of 1964. The Swedish Academy explained that it was guided by its members' decision, and not the possible winner's wishes.

The exponent of existentialism believes that man should find direction and meaning for his own personal life, develop a sense of responsibility for his actions, and thus become free. *Nausea* (1938), a novel, is still considered among his best work. He has written short stories, essays, plays (*The Flies* and *No Exit*), and such philosophical works as *Being and Nothingness* and *Existentialism Is Humanism*.

Sartre was born in Paris. He worked with the French underground in World War II, and was among the French intellectuals who defended French youths who refused to fight in Algeria.

See also NOBEL PRIZES (Literature).

SASKATCHEWAN. See CANADA.

SATELLITE. See COMMUNICATIONS; SPACE TRAVEL; WEATHER.

SATO, EISAKU (1901-   ), a former finance minister and a member of the ruling Liberal-Democratic party, replaced Hayato Ikeda as premier of Japan in November, 1964. Ikeda stepped down because of ill health. See JAPAN.

The political career of Premier Sato began in 1948, when he was first elected to the lower house of the diet. He has served in the cabinets of various premiers. Former Premier Nobusuke Kishi is an older brother. They have different surnames because of adoption into different families.

Eisaku Sato is one of 10 sons of the well-known Hidesuke Sato, and was born in southern Honshu. After graduating in law from Tokyo University, he joined the railway ministry. By 1945, Sato was head of the national railway system.

SAUDI ARABIA changed rulers in a bloodless coup in 1964. On November 2, King Saud was dethroned and Crown Prince Faisal was proclaimed king. The accession of Faisal to the throne ended a lengthy power struggle between the two half brothers.

The new king promised to carry on the reforms he had long advocated. These included cutting $4,000,-000 from the royal family's budget. He also increased economic development funds by $65,500,000.

The Arabian American Oil Company settled for $160,000,000 a government claim for back taxes in 1964. The money was placed in a new development fund. The government also purchased 50 windmills from The Netherlands for use in its resettlement program for Bedouin tribesmen.

Population: 7,000,000. **Government:** King Faisal. **Foreign Trade:** exports, $940,000,000; imports, $256,000,000. **Principal Export:** oil. WILLIAM SPENCER

See also MIDDLE EAST.

SCHOOL. See CIVIL LIBERTIES; EDUCATION; Section One, LAWRENCE A. CREMIN ON EDUCATION.

SCIENCE AND RESEARCH. Dr. Donald F. Hornig, the Princeton University chemist who became President Johnson's special assistant for science and technology in January, was subjected to a barrage of complaints when he appeared before the Joint Congressional Committee on Atomic Energy in March. The concern centered around the government's annual $15,000,000,000 research and development program. Some committee members felt that the development of practical applications was being curbed by the ever-increasing financial demands of basic research.

Manpower and Research Funds. Another growing concern, stressed in a report by a committee of the National Academy of Sciences, was the inefficient distribution of U.S. manpower in scientific and engineering fields. The report, issued in July, showed that scientists, engineers, and secondary school science teachers made up 2.1 per cent of the country's total work force. Many of those employed, however, are employed wastefully, and there were scientists and engineers out of work in the United States in 1964 while scientific and engineering jobs went unfilled. The Soviet Union's scientific manpower, now equal to that of the United States, is increasing twice as fast, according to the committee. The percentage of students in the fields of science and technology in the United States, it added, is less than that in Australia, Britain, France, the Soviet Union, or West Germany.

Steps to Improve scientific policy making were taken by the House Committee on Science and Astronautics, which arranged with the National Academy of Sciences to provide Congress with advice on all scientific programs and proposals presented by the executive branch. The academy also signed an agreement with the Soviet Academy of Science for the exchange of United States and Russian scientists. The two-year pact, announced in May, was aimed at doing away with some of the red tape that has been a source of annoyance to both sides. Each academy will now be able to send 55 scientists to the other country for inspection visits and cooperative research.

Water Study. The International Hydrological Decade was initiated at the end of 1964 in an attempt to solve some of the world's water problems. For 10 years, coordinated efforts will be made to understand the hydrological cycle, especially deep beneath the earth's surface, where an estimated 2,000,000 cubic miles of water lies untapped.

Most of the nations that belong to the United Nations Educational, Scientific, and Cultural Organization (UNESCO) will participate in the hydrological decade. It will involve the establishment of stations throughout the world for the purpose of measuring and tracking the water cycle from rain to underground water table and then back into the atmosphere again.   SERGEI LENORMAND

See also SPACE TRAVEL; WATER AND FLOOD CONTROL.

SCIENCE CLUBS OF AMERICA activity reached a new high in 1964 when young students showed 1,160,000 science projects in the 222 local and regional science fairs that preceded the 15th National Science Fair-International at Baltimore, Md., in May.

Top Winners. Awards from among the 420 finalists were made in botany, chemistry, and biochemistry, earth and space sciences, medicine and health, physics, mathematics and computers, and zoology. The top 13 awards of $100 worth of equipment or books were presented to:

Toshiko Matsumaru, 17, of Chiba, Japan, for her project, *Research on the Pollen of Lilium longiflorum.*

David R. Gibbs, 16, Terre Haute, Ind., for *Antibiosis Study of Fresh Water and Marine Algae.*

Judith Herzfeld, 16, of Queens Village, N.Y., for *Spectropolarimetric Analysis of the Secondary Structure of Gramicidin-S and Tyrocidine-A.*

Charles Griffith Taylor, Jr., 18, of Brunswick, Ga., for *Control of Anthocyanin Synthesis by the Photoreceptor System.*

Martha Eleanor Matter, 16, of Arlington, Va., for *Jupiter—Composition, Structure, Origin.*

Richard E. Albrecht, 18, of Parkersburg, W.Va., for *Atmospheric Refraction of the Low Sun.*

Patricia N. Schultz, 17, of Faribault, Minn., for *Mutagenic Effects of Ultraviolet Radiation on a Strain of Bacillus subtilis.*

Robert James Brock, 17, of Fort Worth, Tex., for *Determination of Suppressor Gene Loci in E. coli K-12.*

Kevin J. Glading, 16, of Albany, Calif., for *Nuclear Quadrupole Resonance Effects.*

Amory Bloch Lovins, 16, of Amherst, Mass., for *A New Nuclear Magnetic Interaction.*

Erik Olin Wright, 17, of Lawrence, Kans., for *Analysis of the Total Number of Twists Resulting from Cutting Any Order Moebius Band with Any Number of Cuts.*

Joan Marie Keene, 17, of Bardstown, Ky., for *Germ-Free Chicken Experimentation.*

Philip Y. Paden, 18, of Lawrence, Kans., for *Stimulus Induced Changes in the Synaptic Complex.*

Health Awards were given by the following organizations: *American Dental Association*—Ruby Joyce Burriss of Greenville, S.C., and Mary Michael Page of Tulsa, Okla. *American Medical Association*—Gail Maxine Houston of Sylacauga, Ala., and Gregory S. Lumbra of Bloomington, Ind. *American Pharmaceutical Association*—Benny W. Ribelin of Melbourne, Fla. *American Veterinary Medical Association*—Dan J. Cole of Fort Dodge, Iowa.

Special Awards were given by the following organizations: *American Chemical Society*—Dorothy E. Sanders of Many, La., and Alan R. Cutler of Auburn, Mass. *American Institute of Biological Sciences*—Frances Marie Hefelfinger of Carlisle, Pa., and Philip Y. Paden of Lawrence, Kans. *American Institute of Mining, Metallurgical, and Petroleum Engineers, Inc.*—Theodore Bernard Lerman of Brooklyn, N.Y. *American Psychological Association*—Marilyn Beech of Atlanta, Ga. *American Society for Metals*—Erwin James Stierle of Ann Arbor, Mich. *American Society for Microbiology*—Robert R. Spencer of Moville, Iowa. *Entomological Society of America*—Robert Steven Brown of Bethesda, Md. *National Committee for Careers in Medical Technology*—Wilson Ayers Clark, Jr., of Kinston, N.C. *National Pest Control Association*—Darrell Addison Posey of Henderson, Ky. *National Telemetering Conference*—John Scott Winterle of Tallahassee, Fla. *Optical Society of America*—Dennis Lee Schatz of Denver, Colo. *Society of Women Engineers*—Janice Dinegar of Los Alamos, N.Mex.

The National Aeronautics and Space Administration (NASA) awarded Certificates of Merit and two-day visits to NASA facilities in the following categories: *Aerodynamics and Space Flight*—Laidacker M. Seaberg of Beaumont, Tex., and Joseph Russell Mosher, Jr., of Reese, Mich. *Space Vehicles*—Ronald DeWayne Jones of Welch, Okla., and Virginia Mason Morris of Richland, Wash. *Space Propulsion Systems*—Donald P. Hutchinson of Laurel, Miss., and Richard Darrell Bennett of North Sacramento, Calif. *Space Life Sciences*—Judith Lauren Herr of St. Petersburg, Fla., and Sharon Ann Fair of Albuquerque, N.Mex. *Space Physical Sciences*—Alan Emerson Wittbecker of Waynesboro, Va., and Martha Eleanor Matter of Arlington, Va. *Space Electronics and Communications*—David G. Taylor of Middletown, N.J., and H. Grady Rylander III of Austin, Tex.

The Atomic Energy Commission awarded trips to the Argonne National Laboratory to: Charles R. Bokesch of Frederick, Md.; David E. Brown of Atherton, Calif.; Eric Miles Dulberg of New Orleans, La.; Joan Marie Keene of Bardstown, Ky.; Amory Block Lovins of Amherst, Mass.; Eileen M. O'Brien of Staten Island, N.Y.; Jonathan R. Pawlik of Dearborn, Mich.; John F. Schultz of El Paso, Tex.; Gerald A. Serwer of Oklahoma City, Okla.; and Eileen Thompson of Grand Rapids, Mich.

The U.S. Air Force (USAF) honored finalists in 10 special categories with invitations to spend two to five days at a USAF research and development facility. The 10 and the categories were: *Aerospace Biological Sciences*—Arthur Edward Frankel of Austin, Tex. *Aerospace Chemistry*—David A. Shannon of Choteau, Mont. *Aerospace Dynamics*—Laidacker M. Seaberg of Beaumont, Tex. *Aerospace Electronics and Communications*—H. Grady Rylander III of Austin, Tex. *Aerospace Environmental Sciences*—David Aaron Matthews of Washington, D.C. *Aerospace Medicine*—Stephen Hayward Sinclair of Phoenix, Ariz. *Aerospace Physics*—Kevin J. Glading of Albany, Calif. *Aerospace Physiological and Social Sciences*—Sharon Ann Fair of Albuquerque, N.Mex. *Aerospace Propulsion*—Richard Darrell Bennett of North Sacramento, Calif. *Mathematical and Computational Sciences*—Douglas Allen Lind of Falls Church, Va.

Westinghouse 23rd Annual Science Talent Search scholarships went to: Robert F. Sproull, 16, of Exeter, N.H., $7,500; Robert E. Bowen, 16, of Fairfield, Calif., $6,000; Lee R. G. Snyder, 18, of Huron, S.Dak., $5,000; Joseph D. Locker, 16, of Pittsburgh, Pa., $4,000; and Richard A. Linke, 17, of Plainfield, N.J., $3,000.   FOSTER P. STOCKWELL

SCRANTON, WILLIAM WARREN (1917-),
governor of Pennsylvania, pushed a next-to-the-last minute campaign in an effort to wrest the Republican presidential nomination from Senator Barry M. Goldwater of Arizona. Scranton stumped many parts of the nation on behalf of moderates opposed to Goldwater's conservative position, but won only 214 votes to Goldwater's 883 at the Republican National Convention in mid-July.

Scranton is a member of an old Pennsylvania family, for which one of the state's principal cities is named. He was born at Madison, Conn., on July 19, 1917. He took a B.A. degree and a law degree at Yale. He was elected governor in 1962 after serving one term as a Representative in Congress. He is credited with injecting new life into the Republican party in Pennsylvania.

He is a director of International Textbook Company, Scranton; a former president of Scranton-Lackawanna Trust Company; and a former board chairman of the Northeastern Pennsylvania Broadcasting Company. In World War II, he was an air force captain. Governor Scranton and his wife, the former Mary Lowe Chamberlin, have four children and live in a suburb of Scranton.   WALTER F. MORSE

SCULPTURE. See PAINTING AND SCULPTURE.

SENDAK, MAURICE (1928-), received the
Caldecott medal in 1964 for his picture book *Where the Wild Things Are*. It was one of *The New York Times* 10 best illustrated children's books of 1963. Randall Jarrell's *The Bat-Poet*, illustrated by Sendak, made the 10-best list in 1964. *Nutshell Library* and *Kenny's Window* were written and illustrated by Sendak.

The schoolchildren, storks, and Dutch village scenes in Meindert DeJong's *The Wheel on the School* were done by Sendak. It won the Newbery medal in 1955. Many other children's books for which he did the pictures include Ruth Krauss' *I'll Be You and You Be Me* nursery anthology and *A Hole Is to Dig; Little Bear* by Else Minarik; and Charlotte Zolotow's *Mr. Rabbit and the Lovely Present*.

When Maurice Sendak finished high school, he made the rounds of publishers, leaving his card "Maurice Sendak, Illustrator." His lively imagination was sparked at an early age with myths and folk tales told by his Polish parents. He wrote, illustrated, and made binders for his own stories when a child. Sendak was born and still lives in New York City.

See also LITERATURE FOR CHILDREN.

SENEGAL held its first legislative and presidential
elections since gaining its independence late in 1960. President Léopold Sédar Senghor and his ruling Senegalese Progressive Union (UPS) won a decisive victory at the polls.

During the year, Senegal revised its first four-year plan, which was to end in mid-1965. The original targets for transportation and communications were retained, but the altered plan placed greater emphasis on rural production and fishing and less on industrial growth. A new oil refinery, the first in French-speaking West Africa, began operations in 1964, with an initial capacity of 600,000 tons of crude oil per year. Senegal received loans from Great Britain and France to help finance its purchase of tuna boats, the construction of primary schools, and the development of agricultural and hydrogeological studies at various centers.

Under an aid agreement signed with the United States, Senegal will be provided with 25,000 tons of rice under the U.S. Food for Peace program. The rice will be sold in Senegal and the proceeds used for various development projects.

Population: 3,500,000. **Government:** President Léopold Sédar Senghor. **Foreign Trade:** exports, $124,000,000; imports, $155,000,000. **Principal Exports:** peanuts and peanut oil.   BENJAMIN E. THOMAS

See also AFRICA; LITERATURE (Poetry).

SERVICE CLUBS

SERVICE CLUBS and organizations made significant gains in membership. They intensified their efforts to enlist the interest and participation of young men of high school age in community service projects and in activities that were designed to promote international understanding.

Kiwanis International sponsored a series of special projects in preparation for the observance of the organization's golden anniversary in 1965. One project called on each club to plant 50 trees or shrubs in honor of its 50th anniversary. Another called on each club to present a "blank check for service" to a top civic official as a pledge to complete some community project during the anniversary year.

The Kiwanis Club of Tokyo was granted an official charter in March, extending the organization's activities to Asia. Since 1961, clubs have been established in Austria, the Bahamas, Belgium, West Germany, Ireland, Japan, Mexico, Norway, and the Philippine Islands.

By the end of 1964, over 2,000,000 copies of the booklet *You and the Law* had been distributed to colleges, high schools, libraries, police departments, and a variety of youth-serving organizations in the United States. A special Canadian edition was prepared which, like its U.S. counterpart, was designed to acquaint teen-agers with the consequences of illegal acts.

A new program to inform young people about the Kiwanis philosophy of personal initiative and individual freedom was started in 1964. This project, called the Fund for Further Responsible Economic Education (FREE), will make films and supporting printed materials available to clubs.

Delegates to the 49th annual convention at Los Angeles elected Edward B. Moylan, Jr., of Miami president, and Edward C. Keefe of Oklahoma City president-elect.

Lions International continued to set the pace as the largest and fastest growing service club organization in the world. It reported a membership of 718,000 in 18,500 clubs. About 493,000 members live in the United States, and the rest in 125 other countries. Japan, with 37,000 Lions, has the top membership outside the United States. Canada is next with 30,000; followed by Mexico, 15,500; Brazil, 15,000; and Sweden, 10,500. The five top states in the United States are Texas, 37,500; Pennsylvania, 36,000; California, 32,500; Illinois, 26,000; and New York, 22,500.

Lions International joined with the American Council of the Blind and the National Federation of the Blind in having October 15 designated as "White Cane Safety Day." The purpose is to educate motorists regarding the provision of *white cane laws* now in force in the United States, Canada, Great Britain, France, and West Germany.

The 47th annual convention at Toronto, Ontario, was the largest in Lions history. Claude M. DeVorss of Wichita, Kans., was elected president.

Rotary International members in the United States and around the world conducted special programs to encourage public support for international understanding during "World Understanding Week," March 15 to 21. The programs ranged from special club meetings and hosting visitors from other lands to week-long projects involving churches, schools, and community groups. The Rotary Club of El Rimac, Peru, staged an "Understanding Via Radio" program, in which amateur radio operators were invited to exchange greetings with Rotarians in El Rimac.

Rotary's new club for young men of high school age, Interact, was enthusiastically received in all parts of the world. By October, 1964, the second anniversary of its founding, there were 12,000 members organized in 450 clubs in 37 countries. Clubs have been formed in rural as well as urban communities. Each club member is required to work on two major projects during the year, one focusing on the community, the other concentrating on the area of international understanding.

Delegates to the 55th annual convention in Toronto approved an expansion of the program of Rotary Foundation Fellowships for International Understanding. In addition, they agreed to use funds for (1) grants to qualified young men for vocational or technical training in other countries; (2) awards to cover travel expenses of teams of young business and professional men who will study Rotary districts in various countries; (3) grants for new and promising projects of clubs and districts designed to promote international understanding; and (4) grants to Interact clubs in recognition of outstanding activities or accomplishments.

The convention voted down proposals for sweeping changes in the requirements for membership. Among these were three proposals to admit women.

Charles W. Pettengill, of Greenwich, Conn., assumed the office of president. C. P. H. Tennstra of Hilversum, The Netherlands, was elected president-nominee.

JOSEPH P. ANDERSON

SHASTRI, LAL BAHADUR

SHASTRI, LAL BAHADUR (1904-   ), a former minister without portfolio, was sworn in on June 9 as prime minister of India. He succeeded Jawaharlal Nehru, who died on May 27. In effect, Shastri had been his nation's leader since early in the year, when Nehru became incapacitated by illness. See INDIA.

Shastri, like Nehru, was a disciple of the late Indian leader Mohandas K. Gandhi. For his part in the Gandhi passive resistance movement against British rule, Shastri spent a total of nine years in prison. He has been prominent in Indian politics since 1930. In 1947, when India attained its independence, he was appointed minister for police and transport in what is now the state of Uttar Pradesh. As general secretary of the National Congress party he organized the first general election held in independent India in 1951.

In 1952, Shastri entered the national parliament as a member of the upper house. As minister for transport and railways, he took personal responsibility for a train accident in November, 1956, that killed 150 persons, and resigned. He was named minister of home affairs in 1961.

Shastri was born in the village of Mughalsarai, near Benares, on Oct. 2, 1904, the son of a teacher and tax collector. As a schoolboy, Shastri reportedly did not have enough money for ferry fare, so he swam the Ganges River twice a day.

Born Lal Bahadur, the new prime minister added the name Shastri when he graduated from Kashi Vidyapeeth, a national university located at Varanasi. Shastri and his wife have four sons, two daughters, and six grandchildren.　　　WALTER F. MORSE

SHIP. The ailing U.S. ship industry had two reasons for optimism in 1964. One was an agreement in December by 14 of the world's chief maritime nations to supply rate data to the Federal Maritime Commission so that it could set realistic, competitive U.S. cargo rates. U.S. shipowners contended that foreign ship lines charged more than double the inbound rate on U.S. exports. As a result of these discriminatory rates, as well as the high costs of U.S. ships and labor to run them, the world's tradingest nation carried only 9.2 per cent of all its commercial and military cargoes in its own ships.

Another Reason for Hope consisted of key labor agreements in 1964 permitting efficient operation of some remarkable new freighters and tankers. The National Maritime Union and other unions agreed to a 30 per cent reduction in crews on eight Lykes Brothers automated cargo ships. This signaled full speed ahead for smaller crews and labor-saving devices on new ships of the United States Lines, Moore-McCormack Lines, and American President Lines.

The Total U.S. Fleet of privately owned ocean-going ships continued to shrink. At midyear, there were three freighters and 12 tankers fewer than 12 months earlier—for a total active and inactive fleet of 968 ships. In the fleet's overseas trade, only tankers posted a healthy gain—12 per cent over 1963 volume. Nevertheless, the U.S. tanker fleet's carrying capacity had slipped from first in 1957 to fourth in 1964, behind Liberia, Britain, and Norway.

World Tonnage of merchant ships rose to a total of 153,000,000 in 1964, according to *Lloyd's Register of Shipping*. The leading 10 nations' totals, in thousands of tons, follow: United States, 22,430; Britain, 21,490; Liberia, 14,500; Norway, 14,447; Japan, 10,813; Russia, 6,958; Greece, 6,888; Italy, 5,708; West Germany, 5,159; and France, 5,116. The oil tanker fleet added 3,442,000 tons, for a world total of 50,563,000 tons.　　　MARK REINSBERG

See also AUTOMATION; LABOR; TRAVEL; WATERWAYS.

SHIPWRECK. See DISASTERS.
SHOOTING. See SPORTS.

SIERRA LEONE mourned the death of its prime minister, Sir Milton Margai, in April. Sir Milton had steered the nation to independence in 1961. The appointment of his brother, Albert Margai, to succeed him, was at first opposed by a few political leaders, who later withdrew their protests.

During the year, Sierra Leone opened a new airport terminal building and an eight-mile asphalt road linking the terminal with the ferry to Freetown. Loans were negotiated with the World Bank and West Germany for the expansion of electric power facilities, and the construction of a road linking the eastern and northern provinces.

Population: 2,600,000. **Government:** Prime Minister Albert Margai. **Foreign Trade:** exports, $56,000,000; imports, $75,000,000. **Principal Exports:** diamonds, iron ore, palm oil.　　BENJAMIN E. THOMAS

See also AFRICA.

SIMPSON, LOUIS (1923-　), was awarded the Pulitzer poetry prize in 1964 for *The End of the Open Road*. Much of his writing concerns the United States and its meaning. He likes American writers, among them Walt Whitman and Mark Twain. Earlier Simpson collections include *The Arrivistes* (1949) and *A Dream of Governors* (1959).

Among those who influenced him most at Columbia University was Mark Van Doren, whom Simpson describes as "knowing what poetry is about." He received his B.A. (1947), M.A. (1950), and Ph.D. (1959) degrees at Columbia, and taught there (1955-1959). Simpson has written essays and other short works, the novel *Riverside Drive*, and *James Hogg*, a critical study.

Louis Simpson was born in Kingston, Jamaica, of Scottish and Russian heritage. He is now a naturalized American. He served with the 101st Airborne Division in Europe during World War II.

See also PULITZER PRIZES.

SINGLETARY, OTIS A. (1921-　), was named director of the Job Corps by President Lyndon B. Johnson on October 11. The corps, a major part of the President's "War on Poverty," seeks to give young men and women between 16 and 21 a "total learning experience" with basic education, skill training, and work. See JOB CORPS.

Singletary, chancellor of the University of North Carolina at Greensboro since July 1, 1961, is on leave of absence until February, 1966. He was born at Gulfport, Miss., Oct. 31, 1921. He holds a B.A. degree from Millsaps College, and the M.A. and Ph.D. from Louisiana State University. He served with the navy in World War II and in Korea.

Before going to North Carolina, he was professor of history and assistant to the president at the University of Texas. He has written extensively on military affairs. He and Mrs. Singletary have two daughters and a son.　　　WALTER F. MORSE

SKATING. See ICE HOCKEY; ICE SKATING.

SKIING. Austrian and French Alpine skiers continued to win the major honors in 1964, but Americans edged closer to the top in a long season that included the Winter Olympics at Innsbruck, Austria, in February. See OLYMPIC GAMES.

Jim Heuga of Tahoe City, Calif., won the prestige-laden Kandahar slalom and combined titles, defeating a field that included all the Innsbruck medal winners. Billy Kidd, of Stowe, Vt., was third in the world combined championship.

Only two French sisters, Christine and Marielle Goitschel, kept Oregon State University student Jean Saubert from reaching the peak of women's skiing. Miss Saubert won half a dozen major races in Europe, and then came home to score victories in the American women's downhill, slalom, and combined.

American men's championships were all won by Olympic team members: Ni Orsi, downhill; Bill Marolt, giant slalom; Kidd, giant slalom; and Gordy Eaton, combined. Second in the combined was Wallace "Bud" Werner, 28, who was credited with sparking the dramatic improvement in U.S. skiing. Werner then retired from amateur skiing, only to be killed in a Swiss avalanche in April.

In Nordic skiing, John Balfanz of Minneapolis, Minn., dethroned Gene Kotlarek as the U.S. ski-jumping champion. The world leaders were Veikko Kankkonen of Finland and Toralf Engan of Norway.

A new world ski-flying record of 472 feet 6 inches was set by Nilo Zandanel of Italy. In ski-flying, only distance counts, with no marks for form. The University of Denver won the National Collegiate title for the fourth straight year.   JAMES O. DUNAWAY

SOAP BOX DERBY. Gregory Schumacher, 14, of Tacoma, Wash., steered his racer downhill through five heats to win the 27th All-American Soap Box Derby, held on Aug. 15, 1964, in Akron, Ohio. He beat out a field of 238 regional champions. The runners-up were William David Smith, 13, of Mobile, Ala., and Guy R. Cleckner, 11, of Mansfield, Ohio.

SOCCER. Navy went undefeated in 15 games and won the National Collegiate Athletic Association (NCAA) championship, while Trenton State won the National Association of Intercollegiate Athletics (NAIA) championship.

The National Open Challenge Cup, representative of supremacy in amateur soccer in the United States, was won by the Victoria Kickers of Los Angeles. They defeated the defending champions, Ukrainian Nationals. Dukla of Czechoslovakia retained the American Challenge Cup by defeating Zaglebie of Poland.

Internazionale of Milan beat Réal Madrid, 3 to 1, for the Europe Cup, then won the world's championship in Madrid by beating Independiente of Buenos Aires in the best two-of-three series. West Ham United won the English football title with a 3 to 2 victory over Preston North End. STANLEY ISAACS

SOCIAL SECURITY emerged as a major legislative issue in 1964, and also became a part of the presidential election campaign. Debate on the matter began when President Lyndon B. Johnson, early in 1964, urged Congress to adopt a program of hospital and nursing home care for the aged, to be financed through Social Security. After extensive deliberations, the House Ways and Means Committee shelved the President's proposal. The committee, however, recommended a substantial increase in benefits, extended coverage to groups not now included, and other measures designed to improve the program.

This was approved by the House of Representatives and sent to the Senate where it was amended to include the President's recommendation for a health care program for the aged. The amended bill was then referred to a conference committee of the House and Senate. A deadlock developed over the health insurance provisions, and the entire Social Security bill was eventually defeated.

Lesser Amendments. Despite the failure to pass these major changes to the Social Security Act, Congress adopted two lesser amendments, which were signed into law by the President. The first removed an existing restriction on applications for disability insurance benefits, resulting in new or higher benefits to more than 100,000 totally disabled workers and dependents. Severely disabled workers who worked under Social Security for at least five out of 10 years before they became disabled were now eligible for back benefits.

Another provision of the bill signed by the President extends through April 15, 1965, the time within which persons who have been in the ministry (or served as Christian Science practitioners) may join Social Security as self-employed persons.

World-Wide Coverage. Over 400 delegates representing 240 social security agencies in 89 countries attended the 15th General Assembly of the International Social Security Association (ISSA), in Washington, D.C., in September. The ISSA was founded in 1927 to promote the exchange of ideas and experiences for the technical and administrative improvement of social security programs.

A total of 112 countries had social security programs at the beginning of 1964, according to the U.S. Social Security Administration. Nine new countries have set up their programs since 1961, and many of the older countries have changed their programs or added new ones. Seventy-eight countries have protection against the kinds of risks covered by the old age, survivors, and disability insurance program in the United States. Seven countries have universal pension systems for all residents over a specified age. Four Scandinavian countries, Denmark, Iceland, Norway, and Sweden, provide disability and survivors' pensions, too. JOSEPH P. ANDERSON

See also CHILD WELFARE; OLD AGE; SOCIAL WELFARE.

PICTURES OF THE YEAR/Bill Strode, *Courier-Journal & Louisville Times Co.*

DESOLATION *stalks the town of Haymond, Kentucky, where many years ago the coal mines were "worked out." The area is one target of the anti-poverty program.*

SOCIAL WELFARE organizations began to develop ways of implementing the provisions of the Economic Opportunity Act of 1964, to combat specific poverty problems in local communities such as illiteracy, job training, and poor health conditions.

Two approaches involving "mobile units" were tried, one by the Travelers Aid Society in New Jersey and the other by the Chicago Federation of Settlements and Neighborhood Centers. The New Jersey mobile offices were taken to farms to aid migrant workers. The Chicago "mobile centers" brought social services into various poverty-stricken neighborhoods of the city.

Assistance Review. Anthony J. Celebrezze, Secretary of the U.S. Department of Health, Education, and Welfare (HEW) appointed a 12-member advisory council to review the public assistance and child welfare programs, and to make recommendations for necessary changes. The council will make its report no later than July 1, 1966. Fedele Fauri, dean of the School of Social Work at the University of Michigan, is serving as chairman, and Dr. Ellen Winston, U.S. commissioner of welfare, is the executive officer.

International Work. Requests for social workers to help developing countries build up their welfare programs and train social welfare personnel contin-

ued to increase in 1964. A survey completed in July showed that there were 225 U.S. social workers in 56 countries. The largest number work for voluntary agencies, 59 work for the U.S. government, and 20 are serving as social welfare advisers with the United Nations.

The HEW International Office of the Welfare Administration expanded its services to facilitate recruitment of social welfare workers for overseas assignments. A clearing house was established to handle inquiries from persons seeking overseas opportunities and to suggest candidates to agencies seeking them. Rosters have been set up for candidates and for social workers currently working or studying abroad. Information about opportunities for employment was shared with U.S. social workers through their professional organizations.

Over 2,000 delegates, representing 66 countries, attended the 12th International Conference of Social Work, held in Athens, Greece, September 13 to 19. The theme of this biennial conference was "Social Progress Through Social Planning: The Role of Social Work."

Representatives from several of the new nations joined representatives of older countries for an intensive consideration of the conference's theme. Dr. Eugene Pusic, of Zagreb, Yugoslavia, was

THE WAR ON POVERTY BEGINS

would pay 90 per cent of its cost for two years, and 50 per cent after that.

PRESIDENT LYNDON B. JOHNSON declared "unconditional war" on poverty in the United States. In January, he went before Congress with an appeal for legislation in pursuit of this ambitious goal.

Congress responded by passing the Economic Opportunity Act, which the President signed into law on Aug. 20, 1964. The Office of Economic Opportunity (OEO) was created, and the President appointed R. Sargent Shriver, Jr., the 49-year-old director of the Peace Corps, to be its director. Shriver also continued in his role as head of the Peace Corps.

Congress has provided for a three-year, anti-poverty program, and, on October 7, appropriated $784,200,000 to finance its first year of operation.

This was the first major program of his own to be initiated by Mr. Johnson after he became President. The reason for it, he told Congress, was that one-fifth of the American people—about 35,000,000 persons—were existing in conditions of poverty. They had incomes of less than $3,000 a year despite the great prosperity of the rest of the nation.

The anti-poverty program stressed education and job training to help both young and old break out of the "cycle of poverty," passed from one generation to the next.

The OEO was given the task of coordinating the anti-poverty effort by working with local communities on action programs. It was put in charge of two new national programs—the Job Corps camps for unemployed youth, and VISTA, the domestic Peace Corps. See Job Corps; VISTA.

IN NOVEMBER, the OEO announced the start of 120 projects to cost $35,000,000. Of this sum, $15,000,000 was to be spent on Job Corps camps and $12,000,000 for community action programs.

Any town could request help for a local anti-poverty program encompassing such things as job training, employment counseling, literacy instruction, and health services. Once the plan was presented to the office in Washington and approved, the OEO

THE NEIGHBORHOOD Youth Corps and the College Work-Study program were two other parts of the anti-poverty legislation. The U.S. Department of Labor was selected to administer the Neighborhood Youth Corps, which will help young men and women from 16 to 22 years of age get an education and jobs.

Jobs of up to 15 hours a week were to be provided high school students from poor families so that they would not have to drop out of school for financial reasons. For those who already had dropped out, temporary six-month jobs would be opened to improve their chances of getting permanent jobs. The Department of Labor would pay 90 per cent of the cost of this program for two years, and 50 per cent of its expenses thereafter.

THE U.S. COMMISSIONER of education was placed in charge of the College Work-Study Program designed to help college students from low income families. It is expected that undergraduates can earn about $500 a year and graduate students $1,000 a year by working up to 15 hours a week.

On-campus jobs, such as typing, library indexing, maintenance of dormitories, and food service, and off-campus jobs, such as tutoring and youth work, would be made available. It was estimated that more than 100,000 students would be helped during the first year of the program.

The U.S. Commissioner of Education will also administer a basic education program to combat illiteracy among 11,500,000 adult Americans with less than a sixth grade education whose inability to read has kept them out of the nation's work force. The government would pay 90 per cent of the cost.

Other parts of the anti-poverty struggle were to be supervised by the Farmers Home Administration, U.S. Department of Agriculture; Small Business Administration; the Welfare Administration commissioner in the Department of Health, Education, and Welfare; the National Park Service; the Forest Service; and the Wildlife, Indian Affairs, and Land Management bureaus. William McGaffin

elected president. Others were elected from Argentina, Canada, Germany, Greece, Italy, and Japan.

Awards in 1964 included:

National Conference on Social Welfare 1964 Distinguished Service Award to Dr. Robert Hanna Felix, director of the National Institute of Mental Health, for "his outstanding achievements in helping to advance our attitudes, knowledge, and skills in the cause of the mentally ill."

National Council of Churches, Department of Social Welfare Award to Robert E. Bondy, Director of the National Social Welfare Assembly, for "outstanding leadership . . . and faithful service." JOSEPH P. ANDERSON

See also CHILD WELFARE; SOCIAL SECURITY.

SOIL CONSERVATION suffered a major setback from the drought that parched most of the United States in 1964 (see WEATHER). In the Great Plains, soil erosion was the most damaging since 1956 and 1957. Wind blew topsoil from 4,300,000 acres in 183 counties of the 10 Great Plains states. Colorado lost the most soil—more than 2,000,000 acres were eroded—and it estimated crop and cattle losses at $50,000,-000. Kansas, Oklahoma, and Texas reported greater soil losses during the year than in 1963.

Soil damage might have been even more severe if it were not for the Great Plains Conservation Program of the U.S. Department of Agriculture (USDA). Since 1957, the program has brought more than 12,800 farms and ranches under contracts to establish permanent-type conservation practices on 20,800,000 acres. In 1964, close to 29,000,000 acres were covered—1,000,000 acres of it to be sown to grass.

Other USDA programs that helped alleviate the drought's impact included:

• Soil and water conservation districts, with 94 per cent of the nation's farmlands covered.

• The Agricultural Conservation Program, in its 31st year, which in 1964 brought permanent cover to 2,700,000 acres, tree planting to 409,000 acres, and terracing to 703,000 acres. A. L. NEWMAN

See AGRICULTURE; WATER AND FLOOD CONTROL.

SOMALIA was embroiled in border conflicts with both Kenya and Ethiopia during 1964. The Ethiopian clash involved Somali claims to the Ogaden area of Ethiopia, which is inhabited by nomadic Somali tribes. The Organization of African Unity (OAU) arranged an uneasy truce. See AFRICA.

In April, 1,000,000 Somalis voted in the first national elections since independence. Eighteen parties competed for 123 parliamentary seats. The Somali Youth League (SYL) won 69 seats, the Somali National Congress 22, and the Somali Democratic Union 15. Premier Abdi Rashid Ali Shermarke, who was re-elected, subsequently resigned. He was succeeded by Abdirizak Haji Hussein.

Population: 2,050,000. **Government:** Provisional President Aden Abdullah Osman; Premier Abdirizak Haji Hussein. **Foreign Trade:** exports, $25,000,000; imports, $38,000,000. **Principal Exports:** bananas, hides and skins, livestock. WILLIAM SPENCER

SOUTH AFRICA, REPUBLIC OF, reinforced its existing *apartheid* (racial segregation) measures with new, more sweeping regulations in 1964. In a crackdown against sabotage, a new general laws amendment was passed. It extended the death penalty to persons who had undergone sabotage training within South Africa's borders; it also expanded the government's general power to define and punish sabotage and subversion. A presidential proclamation extended the controversial 90-day detention clause of the General Laws Amendment through June, 1965. Under the clause, persons may be arrested and detained for as long as 90 days for questioning without being brought to trial.

In the face of mounting world hostility toward its racial policies, South Africa announced a 60 per cent increase in the 1964 call-up for military training. A record budget presented to parliament in March set military expenditures $72,800,000 above those for the previous year.

In March, South Africa left the United Nations' International Labor Organization. Earlier, it had withdrawn from the UN's Food and Agriculture Organization. It also continued to reject, as interference in its internal government and legal processes, all UN attempts to stay the execution of South Africans convicted of sabotage. See UNITED NATIONS.

Population: 17,700,000. **Government:** President Charles R. Swart; Prime Minister Hendrik F. Verwoerd. **Foreign Trade:** exports, $1,586,000,000; imports, $2,282,000,000. **Principal Exports:** asbestos, citrus fruits, diamonds. gold, uranium. BENJAMIN E. THOMAS

See also AFRICA.

SOUTH AMERICA. See LATIN AMERICA; Section Two, DOS GRINGAS AMERICANAS; and articles on the various countries.

SOUTH ARABIA, FEDERATION OF, was a major source of tension in the Middle East during 1964. British troops, who were responsible for the federation's defense, repeatedly clashed with marauding tribesmen in the Radfan area who were opposed to the British-backed federation, which had been formed five years earlier. In October, the British army reported that between January 1 and September 30, three British soldiers, one Arab soldier, and five civilians had been killed; 15 British and 11 Arab soldiers, and six civilians had been wounded.

Despite the continuing terrorism, Great Britain went ahead with plans to grant the federation its independence "no later than 1968." In October, it was announced that three more British protected states had joined the federation, increasing the membership to 17. The new members included Upper Aulaqi Sultanate, and the Alawi and Muflihi sheikdoms.

Population: 1,050,000. **Government:** British High Commissioner Sir Kennedy Trevaskis. **Foreign Trade:** no statistics available. WILLIAM SPENCER

See also MIDDLE EAST.

SPACE TRAVEL

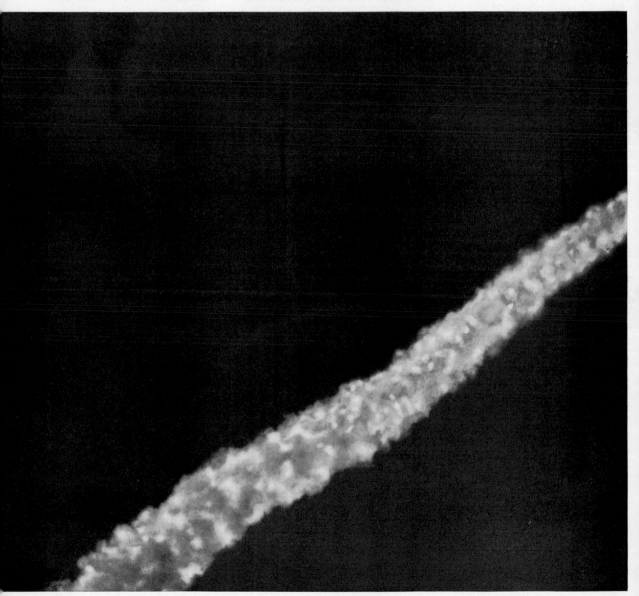

A PILOT, a physician, and a space scientist—Soviet citizens all—circled the earth 16 times on Oct. 12 and 13, 1964, to become the world's first multiman space crew.

The three men, Colonel Vladimir M. Komarov, Lieutenant Boris B. Yegorov, and scientist Konstantin P. Feoktistov, made the journey in the spacecraft *Voskhod* (*Sunrise*). It lifted off from Baikonur in the Mayun-Kum Desert, Kazakhstan. One day and 17 minutes later, it landed 350 miles to the north, with the three still aboard. Their 72 man-hours in space brought the Soviet total to 455, which is nine times the number of hours chalked up by U.S. astronauts.

As was their custom, the Soviets divulged no significant details about the space vehicle; neither weight, size, general configuration, nor rocket thrust were revealed. Dr. Mstislav Keldysh, president of the Soviet Academy of Sciences, said a new launch rocket was employed, one that developed more thrust than any that had previously orbited payloads from anywhere on earth.

The sketchy information disclosed in the past by the Soviets has referred to the total thrust of all stages of a rocket. Thus Keldysh may not have been comparing the Soviet first stage with that of America's most powerful operational rocket, the Saturn I, which produces 1,500,000 pounds of thrust. He made no claim that the Soviet rocket can lift heavier payloads than Saturn I.

Three times earlier in the year, Saturn I, with its liquid hydrogen-fueled second stage, had demonstrated the power to boost into orbit 20,000 pounds, the heaviest known space payload.

At Florence, Italy, in May, Vasily V. Parin of the Institute of Normal and Pathological Physiology of the Soviet Academy of Medicine told the International Committee on Space Research that cosmonauts Andrian G. Nikolayev and Pavel R. Popovich, the space twins of 1962, had suffered difficulties, principally of the central nervous system and the circulatory system. He noted that they recovered after seven to 10 days.

For the United States, 1964 was an outstanding year of unmanned launchings. It saw breakthroughs in nuclear space propulsion, and rapid progress in the massive preparations for the manned exploration of the moon.

Major Unmanned Flight Developments included:
• Man's first close look at the moon, by means of photos transmitted by the Ranger VII spacecraft (see PHOTOGRAPHY).
• Launching of the U.S. Mariner IV and the Soviet Zond II spacecraft toward Mars.
• Transmission of live Olympic Games television across the Pacific from Japan by Syncom III.
• Launchings of Nimbus I and OGO I, weather and scientific satellites (see EUROPE [picture]).

Wide World

RANGER VII begins its historic journey to the moon. It transmitted more than 4,000 finely detailed pictures of the lunar surface.

THE MOON
FROM RANGER VII

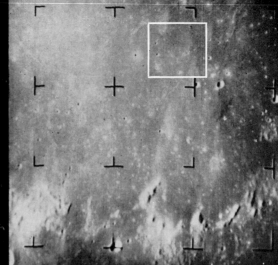

About 235 Miles from the Moon, the spacecraft was sending back pictures of the moon about four times better than any ever taken through telescopes from the earth. The area shown in this picture measures about 113 miles on each side. The smallest craters visible in the picture are about 1,000 feet across. About 2½ minutes after this picture was taken, Ranger VII crashed into the moon. The outlined area is contained in the next picture, *right.* The cross-shaped marks on the photograph are reference points on the camera.

"X" Marks the Spot, *left,* where Ranger VII crashed into the moon on July 31, 1964. Before crashing, it relayed pictures to earth that gave scientists much valuable information on the surface of the moon, its craters and pits, and its mountains and valleys. The outlined area shows the section that was photographed. This picture was taken at the Mount Wilson Observatory, Calif.

Photos from RCA, NASA, and Jet Propulsion Laboratory from WORLD BOOK Science Service, Inc.

The Ranger VII Flight to the Moon began July 28, 1964, at Cape Kennedy, Fla. The spacecraft crashed into the Sea of Clouds 68 hours and 35 minutes after blastoff. Ranger VII performed perfectly during its 243,000-mile flight. The winglike solar panels provided electrical power from the sun's rays. The saucer-shaped antenna sent over 4,000 pictures back to earth.

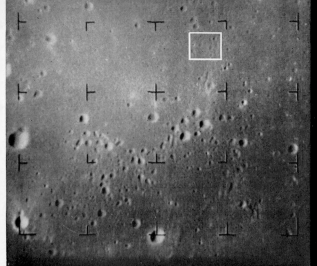

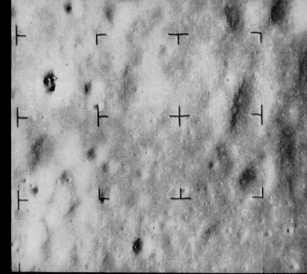

34 Miles from the Moon, the smallest craters shown measure about 15 feet in diameter. Pictures such as these will help scientists select a location on the moon's surface where astronauts can land a spaceship safely. Astronauts landing on the moon must avoid clusters of craters such as those shown. Deep craters would make it very difficult and dangerous to land a spaceship there. Mountains could also become a hazard. The outlined area is contained in the next picture, *right*.

Three Miles from the Moon, the picture shows craters as small as 30 feet in diameter and 10 feet deep. The picture shows an area measuring about 1⅔ miles square. Two seconds after this picture was taken, Ranger VII crashed on the moon. Scientists believe the portion of the moon that was photographed would be solid enough to support a spaceship. They also believe that astronauts would be able to walk on the surface of the moon without sinking into deep layers of dust.

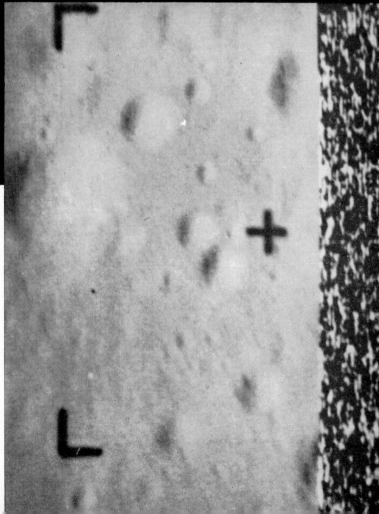

Six Television Cameras took 4,316 pictures during the last 16½ minutes of flight. The last pictures taken were 1,000 times better than any pictures that have been taken from the earth.

1,000 Feet Above the Moon, the last picture shows an area about 100 by 60 feet. The pattern at right shows static picked up by the receivers on earth when the spacecraft crashed on the moon.

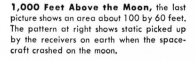

Ranger VII, launched from Cape Kennedy on July 28, crashed to destruction July 31 in the *Mare Nubium*. During the final 17 minutes of flight, Ranger VII transmitted 4,316 photographs to a receiving station operated by the Jet Propulsion Laboratory for the National Aeronautics and Space Administration (NASA), at Goldstone, Calif. Half of the final picture, taken at an altitude of 1,000 feet, was transmitted before impact. The photographs showed lunar details with 1,000 times the clarity of earth telescopes. The final photos showed craters only three feet in diameter.

The Ranger experimenter team immediately began analyzing the pictures and, not surprisingly, failed to agree in their conclusions.

Dr. Harold C. Urey of the University of California, San Diego, suggested almost all the lunar surface is covered with material broken and churned up by meteorites and other objects that have peppered the airless moon for billions of years. Urey said some means other than photographs would have to be used to determine the nature of the surface.

Dr. Gerard P. Kuiper of the University of Arizona, and Dr. Eugene M. Shoemaker of the U.S. Geological Survey disagreed. Kuiper and Shoemaker maintained that much of the lunar surface is firm and flat and reasonably well suited for landing an Apollo manned spacecraft. Despite Urey's dissent, Ranger VII did accomplish its goal of determining that a sizable area of the moon is level enough for the landing of an Apollo craft. In fact, there was agreement that some 85 per cent of the region photographed was level enough for this purpose.

The region of Ranger's impact was named *Mare Cognitum* (*The Known Sea*) by the International Astronomical Union. It was the first new name given to a sizable area of the moon since 1959, when Soviet scientists assigned Russian names to parts of the hidden face after they were photographed by Lunik III at a distance of more than 4,000 miles. See 1964 YEAR BOOK, Section Two, OUR TARGET IN THE SKY.

Centaur and Surveyor. Also during 1964, NASA conducted two flight tests of the liquid hydrogen fueled Centaur rocket, which, on December 11, orbited a prototype Surveyor spacecraft. Surveyor will soft-land on the moon in 1966 and actually test its surface and relay its information back to earth.

Mariner IV, a 575-pound spacecraft launched toward Mars on November 28, carried cameras and other equipment for transmitting up to 22 pictures of the red planet after completing a 325,000,000-mile journey. On December 5, a midcourse maneuver was carried out that set Mariner on a path that would take it to about 5,900 miles from Mars at 8:11 P.M., E.S.T., on July 14, 1965.

The Mariner III Mars probe, launched November 5, failed, presumably because its "shroud," which protected it during its journey into orbit, could not be jettisoned. Hence it probably could not deploy its solar panels to generate electric power.

Zond II. The Soviets launched their Zond II Mars probe November 30. Next day they reported it was operating at only about half its power.

Syncom and Relay. Probably the most sophisticated space maneuvers to date were carried out by Syncom III, a U.S. communications satellite. Launched on August 19, Syncom III achieved, almost a month later, an orbit 22,000 miles above the equator. Turning at the same speed as the earth itself, Syncom remained above the mid-Pacific and carried live television transmissions of the Olympic Games from Japan to North America. See COMMUNICATIONS.

Except for the first day of the Olympics, however, the Syncom television was not seen in the United States because the National Broadcasting Company had made previous arrangements with the Japanese Broadcasting Corporation to fly film from Japan. But many Syncom TV transmissions were seen in Canada and some were relayed to Europe by cable.

Meanwhile, Syncom II, an earlier high-altitude satellite, performed yeoman service, providing a radio link between the United States and troubled South Vietnam and sending results of the presidential election to the Orient. Another satellite, Relay II, provided election-night links with Europe.

Nimbus, launched on August 28 into an orbit that crosses the earth's polar regions, was the first weather satellite stabilized so that its cameras always pointed toward the earth. In the previous TIROS series, the cameras always pointed in a given direction in space; thus they pointed to earth only part of the time. During its 26 days of active life, Nimbus took more than 27,000 photographs and its infrared instruments obtained the first night-time cloud pictures from space. See WEATHER.

The Orbiting Geophysical Observatory (*OGO*), launched September 4, was the first U.S. scientific satellite weighing more than 1,000 pounds. It carried 20 separate experiments of which 19 provided data. One failed because a protruding experiment boom did not deploy and the satellite could not be stabilized in flight. OGO, by developing the use of interchangeable parts, ushered in an era of lower unit costs for space experiments.

Kiwi. In nuclear space technology, the key breakthrough was the successful test firing of the Kiwi B4D reactor on May 13. Liquid hydrogen was pumped through the reactor, boiled and heated to several thousand degrees, and expelled through a nozzle to generate thrust.

Nuclear rocket engines will operate at fuel economies more than double those of the most efficient rockets based on fire or chemical combustion. They are expected to come into operation as upper-stage propulsion for manned flights in the 1970's.

Ion Engine. Another major advance was the successful flight test of an ion electric rocket. On July 20, SERT-I, a spacecraft carrying ion rockets powered by batteries, was launched from Wallops Island, Virginia, to an altitude of 2,550 miles on a 47-

Wide World

VOSKHOD CREW *relaxes on boat ride. From left, Konstantin P. Feoktistov, scientist; Lieutenant Boris B. Yegorov, physician; Colonel Vladimir M. Komarov, pilot.*

minute flight before splashing into the Atlantic Ocean 2,100 miles to the east. One of the two engines operated 19 minutes, generating .0055 pound of thrust. Despite the tiny thrust of ion rockets, they will be useful for deep space flights in the future. With nuclear power, they can operate for the full duration of a mission. Their fuel economy is the highest of any known form of space propulsion.

Satellite Totals. Altogether, in 1964, the United States carried out about 70 unmanned orbital and deep-space flights, compared with about 40 conducted by the Soviet Union.

Project Gemini. The U.S. manned space flight program reached full momentum, with 300,000 persons taking part by the end of 1964. About 95 per cent of these were employed by contractors. The program consisted of Gemini, the two-man precursor to Apollo, the enterprise aimed at exploring the moon in this decade.

In Gemini, the first unmanned flight test was a complete success, the second was approaching at year-end, and crews were selected for the first two-manned flights, scheduled for 1965. See ASTRONAUTS.

In the first flight, on April 8, the modified Titan II launch vehicle was qualified for manned flight and the spacecraft structure was verified.

The second flight, originally scheduled for December, 1964, was postponed because of a minor malfunction in the booster. It was rescheduled for the first quarter of 1965. Its purpose is to qualify the spacecraft and its heat shield for reentry into the earth's atmosphere. The first manned Gemini flight is scheduled for 90 days thereafter.

The first manned mission, to be piloted by Virgil "Gus" Grissom, who piloted a Mercury spacecraft on the second U.S. suborbital flight, was scheduled for three orbits—$4\frac{1}{2}$ hours—to check out the spacecraft and its systems. The second manned flight was tentatively planned for four days' duration. Also, a number of experiments were selected for the Gemini program.

Project Apollo. In the Apollo program, the throttle moved all the way forward.

The development of the Saturn I launch vehicle was completed with the first two of the three 1964 flights, bringing the vehicle to operational status in six flights, rather than 10 as originally planned. The final three Saturn I vehicles will launch Pegasus meteoroid-detecting satellites in 1965.

Manufacturing proceeded on schedule for the first all-up Apollo space vehicle, to be launched into earth orbit in early 1966. This vehicle will consist of an Apollo spacecraft and the two-stage Saturn IB launch vehicle, an improved Saturn I. Manned flights in earth orbit were also scheduled during the year for 1967.

NASA carried out four successful unmanned flight tests of the Apollo spacecraft—two suborbital at White Sands, New Mexico, and two into orbit with Saturn I vehicles.

Saturn V. Successful ground firings of the second and third stages of the mammoth Saturn V launch vehicle, to be used for the lunar flights, were conducted late in 1964 and the first firing of the giant booster stage of 7,500,000-pound thrust was scheduled for 1965.

MARINER IV'S HISTORIC RENDEZVOUS WITH THE RED PLANET

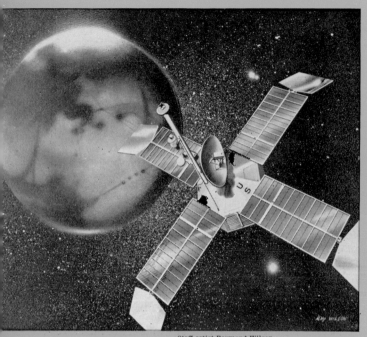

Staff artist Raymond Wilson
© 1964, World Book Science Service, Inc.

AS MARINER IV raced for its rendezvous with Mars in July, 1965, we had, at last, an opportunity to resolve two of the most challenging mysteries of our solar system: does life exist on the red planet, and what is the nature of the famous Martian "canals," those delicate, mysterious markings discovered in 1877 by Giovanni Schiaparelli?

At the turn of the century, when our Martian imaginations ran wild in the absence of hard facts, the idea of intelligent life on Mars, capable of building canals that conducted water from melting polar icecaps to strategically placed *oases* (places where the canals cross or terminate) on the deserts of Mars, was often acceptable, even to the scientific palate.

The Mariner IV probe, with some luck—for all the hazards of the 325,000,000-mile orbital journey—may answer these questions. But, why, it may be asked, can't we answer them by using our best telescopes right here on earth?

For two basic reasons. First, even when Mars is closest to us, it is still 150 times as far away as the moon. Second, our view of Mars, and of all celestial bodies, is partly obscured by the haze of our own atmosphere, which, never completely steady, causes objects seen through a telescope to shimmer and blur.

WHAT DO WE now know about Mars? It is a dwarf planet with a diameter of 4,200 miles—over half that of the earth. Its atmosphere is not at all similar to ours, nor is its rate of temperature change, which ranges during its 24-hour 37-minute 23-second day from −100°F. at sunrise to the temperature of an ordinary room at noon.

So far, oxygen has not been detected in the atmosphere of Mars, and only recently did we obtain definite proof of a significant trace of water vapor.

The presence of some water on Mars has been established by prominent and intriguing whitecaps that develop at the poles when each is having its winter and by the presence of an occasional white cloud, both of which reflect light as ordinary ice crystals do.

As spring advances in each hemisphere, the corresponding polar icecap appears to melt, completely disappearing as the Martian summer comes. Knowing precisely how much heat Mars receives from the sun, and by measuring the rate at which the polar icecaps shrink, an easy calculation shows that these caps must be just surface phenomena, more akin to a layer of frost than to heavy fields of snow and ice—which brings us to the question of the possible presence of living things on the red planet.

For, as the icecaps melt, a wave of plantlike life appears to proceed from the high latitudes toward the equator. The canals appear and darken, and darkish patches, sometimes reported as greenish, appear. Often the canals seem to double, and the oases grow in size and become a chocolate brown. Hence, it is not at all difficult to see why some astronomers thought that a wiser and older civilization than ours thus obtained its water supply from the polar regions, conducting the water through a vast and intricate system of canals.

THE DARKENING of the canals, of course, appeared to be visible evidence of the seasonal vegetation that sprang up along their broad, flat banks as the water advanced. It was all consistent with the idea that things began to grow when the polar water moved toward the equator. And it was an intriguing and inspiring picture, but it fell before the advance of scientific knowledge about Mars: temperatures too cold, water virtually absent, little or no oxygen (plant life as we know it should produce more), and the atmosphere hopelessly thin. So our present scientific picture of the red planet is a rather bleak one. Yet, striking seasonal changes do occur on Mars, all the more mysterious because they do not seem explicable in earth-familiar terms. And, there is still some scientific evidence to support the notion that the dark lines are indeed regions of vegetation.

But what kinds of plants might grow under Martian conditions? Evidently the color changes are caused by plants that do not grow by earth processes, which require chlorophyll, but perhaps are related to our lichens, which are capable of prospering even in dry, barren, and frequently freezing soil.

IF MARINER IV discloses the presence of life on Mars, expected to be of low order and strange to our own planet, it will be a fact of great philosophical and perhaps theological importance. For it will show that life is not unique to the earth, that it can develop under vastly different physical conditions, and that therefore life may now be flourishing in a great many places in our universe.

The spacecraft carries a formidable cargo of instruments aboard. Most important for a direct study of Mars is its TV camera, which will be activated at the time of rendezvous, as Mariner passes from the near to the far side of Mars. Because the transmission of instantaneous TV pictures at such distances requires prohibitive power levels, Mariner's pictures will be stored on board and sent to earth, bit by bit, over a period of many hours for each picture. The process will be quite unlike that used in the rapidly sent Ranger VII moon pictures (see PHOTOGRAPHY). It will be more akin to sending news pictures by wirephoto.

THE PICTURES will be made from about 5,900 miles from the surface of the planet. From that distance, Mars will look, to the Mariner craft, more than 7,000 times larger than it appears at night to us—a truly wonderful sight. Details as small as several hundred feet across should be visible. While this scale cannot hope to reveal details of plant life or other small features, it will be sufficient to display the general texture of the Martian surface, and thus be entirely capable of disclosing the nature of the mysterious canals and the general nature of the equally puzzling, changing, darkish areas.

MARINER carries an ionization chamber, a trapped-radiation detector, a cosmic-ray telescope, a magnetometer, a solar-plasma probe, and a cosmic-dust detector. All of these will make recordings of scientific information along the way.

The journey of Mariner is certainly a long and arduous one. On its way it runs the gantlet of inner asteroids and meteoric particles which could annihilate the space probe, or injure the instruments and the broad panels of the solar cells so essential to its power supply. But it is a daring journey, boldly and imaginatively conceived. A new and exciting chapter in the annals of astronomy seems about to be written.   J. ALLEN HYNEK

MARINER'S TRAJECTORY TO MARS

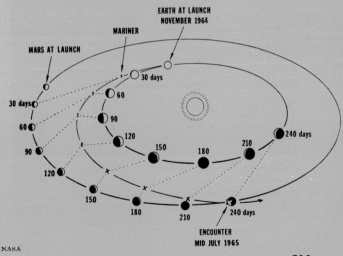

NASA

Design of the "Block II" Apollo spacecraft, which will make the lunar flights, was nearly complete and a full-scale metal mock-up of the lunar excursion module was approved. Manned flights of this spacecraft, aboard a Saturn V, will begin in 1968.

Apollo Facilities. The staff of NASA's Manned Spacecraft Center moved from locations scattered throughout Houston, Tex., into laboratories and offices at its new $150,000,000 headquarters at Clear Lake, southeast of the city.

Rapid progress was made in the construction of two other major manned space flight sites, one at Merritt Island, north of Cape Kennedy, Fla., the other in southern Mississippi.

The steel framework of the Vertical Assembly Building at Merritt Island, north of Cape Kennedy, stood almost 400 feet high at year's end. When completed, this building, 500 feet tall and approximately as wide and deep, will be used for the assembly and checkout of the 360-foot-tall Saturn V-Apollo space vehicle. See BUILDING AND CONSTRUCTION.

Construction also proceeded rapidly on stands for the ground testing of the first and second stages of the Saturn V at the Mississippi Test Facility, 40 miles from the Michoud Plant in New Orleans.

At the end of 1964, plans were being made for an expansion of the Apollo program under which some of the flight hardware will be made available for other space activities, in the event that all will not be required for the basic Apollo mission.

NASA Budget. President Lyndon B. Johnson in January, requested appropriations for NASA totaling $5,445,000,000. Congress appropriated $5,250,000,000, which was 3.6 per cent below the request for fiscal 1965. Most of the money was earmarked for the manned space flight program.

New Research Center. The Congress of the United States also gave final approval to the establishment of the Electronics Research Center in Cambridge, Mass., and that new space headquarters opened its doors for business in September.

Dr. Winston E. Kock, a former vice-president of research at Bendix Corporation, was appointed director of the center.

Personnel. Other important personnel developments involved the resignation of Colonel John H. Glenn, Jr., from the United States Marine Corps. Colonel Glenn will continue to work part time for NASA. Also Walter C. Williams, deputy associate administrator for Manned Space Flight Operations, resigned. He was to have directed the Gemini flights. Williams was replaced later by Everett E. Christensen, former test manager in the Missile Systems Division of the Lockheed Missile and Space Company. Christensen will be in complete charge of the flight operations of both the Gemini and Apollo programs.   JAY HOLMES

See also ASTRONOMY; Section One, JOHN H. GLENN, JR., ON SPACE; Section Two, THE UNFOLDING UNIVERSE.

SPAIN forged ahead economically in 1964, although inflationary pressures were rising. Its gold and foreign exchange reserves stood at a record high of $1,375,000,000 in September. Unemployment was down, partly because 400,000 Spaniards were at work in neighboring countries. The money they sent home, coupled with a steady rise in the tourist trade contributed to the favorable balance of payments. However, food costs were up sharply, and wages had risen an estimated 11.1 per cent in the first seven months of the year.

The European Economic Community (EEC, or Common Market) rejected Spain's application for membership in 1964, largely because the political policies of Francisco Franco's 25 year-old regime remained repugnant to them. The EEC agreed, however, to exploratory talks on economic problems.

A British proposal to give Gibraltar some measure of self-rule was opposed by Spain during the year. It threatened to cut all communications with Gibraltar if the plan were carried out. Spain argued before the United Nations that Gibraltar, which had been ceded to Great Britain in 1713 under the Peace of Utrecht, should belong to Spain.

In October, the United States and Spain held a joint military exercise on the Spanish coast. It was the largest amphibious operation since the Korean War. See NATIONAL DEFENSE.

Population: 31,500,000. **Government:** Chief of State and Premier Francisco Franco; Vice-Premier Agustin Muñoz Grandes. **Foreign Trade:** exports, $911,000,000; imports, $2,109,000,000. **Principal Exports:** alcoholic beverages, fruits and nuts, minerals, olive oil, vegetables.   FRED J. PANNWITT

See also EUROPE.

SPENDER, SIR PERCY CLAUDE (1897-   ), Australian diplomat, was elected president of the International Court of Justice in March, 1964. He succeeded Bohdan Winiarski of Poland. A judge there since 1958, Sir Percy will serve until 1967, when his judicial term at The Hague, The Netherlands, ends. He was Australian ambassador to the United States (1951-1958).

At the British Commonwealth Foreign Ministers Conference in Colombo, Ceylon, in 1950, Sir Percy introduced an economic aid plan for South and Southeast Asia now known as the Colombo Plan. He was chairman of Australia's delegation there, and to the International Monetary Fund and International Bank for Reconstruction (1951-1953). Sir Percy represented his country at the United Nations General Assembly (1951-1958).

Sir Percy served in the Australian House of Representatives (1937-1951), and held such government posts as minister for the army (1940-1941) and for external affairs and of external territories (1949-1951). He was born in Sydney, and educated at the University of Sydney (B.A. 1918, LL.B. 1922).

SPINGARN MEDAL. See WILKINS, ROY.

SPORTS. The eyes of all sports enthusiasts turned toward Tokyo and the Olympic Games, where an astounding U.S. team won 36 gold medals. In 1956 at Melbourne and in 1960 at Rome, the Soviet Union had taken the most first-place medals. Now the United States topped the list by dominating track and field, swimming, and basketball competition. See OLYMPIC GAMES.

As soon as the Olympic torch went out, the truce ended between the American Athletic Union (AAU) and the National Collegiate Athletic Association (NCAA). They had been feuding for several years over the control of amateur sports, but had declared a pre-Olympic truce. Now the president of the AAU, Jay-Ehret Mahoney, contended that the American system of training athletes, as handled by the AAU, had been vindicated by the victories at the Tokyo Olympics. "Instead of fighting," he said, "we all should be turning our energies toward improving our athletic competition." The NCAA, which now referred to the AAU as "little more than an administrative anachronism" that exploits and coerces athletes, did not dispute the latter part of the statement of President Mahoney.

The second Paralympics, a sports competition confined to paraplegics, was held in the Olympic facilities after the Games ended. There were 70 competitors from 22 countries participating for gold, silver, and bronze medals. Among the events were archery, darchery (dart throwing), table tennis, weight lifting, and the slalom performed with wheelchairs instead of skis. The U.S. team won top honors.

Awards. Don Schollander, winner of four Olympic gold medals in swimming, was the recipient of the AAU's 1964 James E. Sullivan Award.

Among the 1964 Sports Results were:

Curling. The Duluth (Minn.) curling team, skipped by Robert Magie, won the U.S. men's championship. Detroit; Grafton, N.J.; and Chicago finished in a tie for second place. The British Columbia team won the Canadian title.

Handball. The first four-wall world championships were held in New York City. U.S. champion Jim Jacobs of New York won the singles title over Canadian Bernie Prichard. The doubles title went to John Sloan and Phil Elbert of Chicago. Other countries competing in the five-day tournament were Australia, Ireland, and Mexico. Jacobs, Elbert, and Sloan had earlier won the All-American tournament at St. Louis. Defending champion Oscar Obert, New York, won his fourth U.S. Handball Association one-wall singles championship in New York City. The one-wall doubles championship was taken by Joe Danilczyk and David Norvid, also of New York.

Rowing. California beat Washington by a length and three quarters to win the Intercollegiate Rowing Association regatta at Syracuse, N.Y. Defending champion Cornell finished third. At the Royal Henley Regatta in England the Soviet team overpowered the defending champion University of London by three lengths. In the single sculls race for the European Rowing Championship, Vyacheslav Ivanov of Russia overtook Holland's Robert Groen. U.S. champion Don Spero came in third.

Shooting. William T. Sesnan of Los Angeles won the National Skeet Shooting Association all-around world skeet championship at Reno, Nev., by scoring 548 out of a possible 550 points. The Grand American Trapshoot handicap title at Vandalia, Ohio, was won by William E. Duggan of Delphos, Ohio. The national service-rifle championship at Camp Perry, Ohio, was won by Air Force Sergeant B. E. Smith. Army Sergeant William B. Blankenship, Jr., again took the pistol title.

Weight Lifting. The Soviet team again dominated the sport in the European championships, held in Moscow. In qualifying for the Soviet Olympic team, Yuri Vlasov smashed all of the four world heavyweight records by lifting 432 pounds in the press, 376 pounds in the snatch, and 475 in the clean and jerk.

Other Champions. *Archery*, men's national championship: David J. Keaggy, Jr., Dayton Plains, Mich. *Bicycling*, Tour de France winner: Jacques Anquetil of France covered the 2,833-mile road in 127 hours, 9 minutes, and 44 seconds. *Billiards*, world professional title: Arthur Cranfield, Jr., of Syracuse, N.Y. *Fencing*, National Collegiate Athletic Association (NCAA) championship: Princeton. *Gymnastics*, intercollegiate: Southern Illinois University. *Lacrosse*, intercollegiate: Navy. *Polo*, open: Concar Oak Brook (Ill.). *Volleyball*, intercollegiate: Santa Monica (Calif.) City College. *Water Skiing*, men's national champion: Joker Osborn, Cypress Gardens, Fla.; women's national champion, Dicksie Ann Hoyt, Fair Haven, N.J.

See also the articles on various sports.

STAMP COLLECTING. See HOBBIES.

STATE GOVERNMENT.

STATE GOVERNMENT. Apportionment of legislatures, financing of government, and expansion of public services were the chief concerns of officials in the state capitals in 1964. Unprecedented controversy, action, and study centered on apportionment. Most of the action took place in the courts, above all, the Supreme Court. See CITY; SUPREME COURT OF THE UNITED STATES and Close-Up.

In addition, several legislatures adopted reapportionment acts during the year or were seeking to enact them near the year's end. In most cases, they were trying to satisfy the Supreme Court's requirement that districts of both houses of state legislatures be as nearly equal in population as practicable. Yet even some new legislative acts were challenged in the courts. A Colorado reapportionment was upset by that state's supreme court for use after 1964. Federal court suits contested at least two other states' 1964 reapportionment acts.

Meantime, several bodies representing state legislators and officials urged amendment of the U.S. Constitution to change the Supreme Court's "one man, one vote" apportionment standard. In December, the board of managers of the Council of State Governments adopted a resolution urging amendment of the Constitution to permit any state with a bicameral legislature to use factors other than population in apportioning one house, provided that such a plan be submitted for approval or rejection by the state's electorate.

Finances. Statistics gathered in 1964 showed that total revenue of the states approached $41,000,000,000 in the 1963 fiscal year and that total expenditures were $39,600,000,000. Both figures were more than $3,000,000,000 above those of the year before.

STATE GOVERNMENT

Budgets adopted by legislatures with 1964 sessions were again at record highs. This continued a steady trend, as a result of population growth and rising requirements for services, especially in education.

Less than half of the 22 states with regular 1964 sessions raised taxes. In most cases, the budget makers could count on increased revenue from current rates to meet the higher bills. But there were important tax enactments. Colorado's legislature adopted a cigarette tax for the first time. Cigarette taxes were increased in Georgia, Kansas, Massachusetts, Mississippi, and Rhode Island. Mississippi and Rhode Island raised sales taxes, and Georgia increased taxes on corporate income. Among other tax acts, rates on alcoholic beverages were raised in Georgia and Kansas, and on gasoline in Maryland. See TAXATION.

Education received a much larger share of the budgets and their increases than any other function. The largest educational building program was California's, where the voters in November approved a $380,000,000 bond issue submitted by the legislature for university, college, and junior college construction. California's voters also approved $260,000,000 in bonds for public school construction.

Among other educational bond issues approved by voters in November were those of $100,000,000 and $59,000,000 in North Carolina and Washington, respectively, for school construction, and more than $40,000,000 in New Jersey for public higher education facilities. See EDUCATION.

Health-Welfare. The Delaware and South Carolina legislatures established new state departments of mental health. New York's session adopted a particularly broad hospitalization act with more liberal provisions for admissions and other features to protect rights and interests of patients.

The Massachusetts session voted a crash program to build facilities for retarded children at four state schools, at an estimated cost of $7,500,000, and authorized the departments of education and mental health to set up coordinated programs to train retarded children. See CHILD WELFARE; HEALTH; HOSPITAL; MENTAL HEALTH; SOCIAL WELFARE.

Death Penalty Abolished. In Oregon the voters in November abolished the death penalty, making it the seventh state without capital punishment on the law books.

Government Organization was affected by several constitutional amendments. New Mexico's voters approved annual legislative sessions, raising the number of states with annual sessions to 20; there were only four at the beginning of World War II. Hawaii shifted to the election of the governor and lieutenant governor as a team of the same party. Massachusetts will increase future terms of the governor and other state constitutional officers from two years to four.

The Louisiana legislature provided for a central state purchasing agency. Previously each budget unit in the state had done its own buying. Michigan authorized its Department of Administration to set up electronic data-processing centers.

Amendment 24 to the U.S. Constitution, banning the poll tax as a requirement for voting in federal primary or general elections, became effective in January, 1964, when it was ratified by South Dakota, the 38th state to do so. The necessary three-fourths of the states had approved the amendment.

In State Elections in November the Republicans made a net gain of one governorship, to control 17 executive mansions, against 33 for the Democrats. But the Republicans had heavy net losses in the legislatures. The Democrats increased their control of both houses in legislatures of 32 states, a gain of six. The Republicans' two-house control dropped from 18 to 6. See DEMOCRATIC PARTY; ELECTIONS; REPUBLICAN PARTY.   FRANK SMOTHERS

See also GOVERNORS OF THE STATES; NEGRO.

STOCKS AND BONDS. Investors bid stock prices to an all-time high in 1964, encouraged by a nearly unprecedented four-year peacetime business upswing. See BUSINESS; INDUSTRY; Section One, SYLVIA PORTER ON THE ECONOMY.

Standard and Poor's average price index for 500 stocks increased 14 per cent in 1964. The advance was evenly spread among the industrials, utilities, and railroads. The 1964 volume of trading rose to a record 1,236,565,422 shares on the New York Stock Exchange (NYSE). Volume on the American Stock Exchange climbed to 374,180,842, highest since 1961. The increase in mutual fund sales to about the 1961 record suggested the small investor's cautious return.

Bonds held surprisingly firm in the face of heavy credit demand, reflecting widespread investor expectation of price stability and continuation of the government's easy money policy. The Dow-Jones 40-bond average price index advanced from 88.47 to 89.78 in the year, while yields dipped from 4.66 to 4.59 per cent. Volume of NYSE bond trading soared to $2,524,505,100 par value in 1964, from $1,843,-328,360 in 1963.

New Issues of common stocks gained while the dollar volume of new corporate bonds declined, reversing the relationship of the preceding year. Here is the trend of the monthly average volume of new issues in millions of dollars since 1962:

	1962	1963	1964 (10 Mos.)
Bonds	747	906	820
Stocks	109	85	231

The 1964 stock average was skewed higher, of course, by the huge Communications Satellite Corporation (Comsat) registration in April. Comsat had offered 10,000,000 shares of common stock at $20 a share. The issue was heavily oversubscribed, and its price rose sharply. Short sales were substantial. As Comsat climbed, short sellers were forced to buy to avoid further losses. The boom was on.

After Comsat hit a high of $71.50 in mid-December, two steps were taken to curb its violent price swings: (1) its margin was hiked to 100 per cent; and (2) the NYSE began to release the stock's short-interest position weekly instead of monthly.

New U.S. Regulations. The first major revamping of federal securities laws since the 1930's occurred with the passage of the Securities Acts Amendments of 1964. Its two major provisions dealt with "floor traders" and the "over-the-counter" securities market, steps recommended by the Securities and Exchange Commission (SEC) staff study in 1963.

Large corporations—including banks, insurance, and other companies not listed on stock exchanges—for the first time were required to disclose financial statements and other information vital to shareholders. Since disclosure requirements no longer could be avoided, there was a flurry of new listing activity on the exchanges. The law empowered the SEC to halt trading in unlisted securities and to suspend over-the-counter salesmen whose conduct failed to meet minimum standards.

Floor Traders, or stock exchange "specialists," came under new SEC rules in August. They had to register, maintain capital of no less than $250,000, and make at least 75 per cent of their transactions *stabilizing*, or against the trend of market prices.

Floor trading slumped in August to less than 1 per cent of NYSE volume, in contrast to almost 3 per cent in August, 1963. But over 90 per cent of specialist transactions were stabilizing.

Swindle Protection Fund. As an aftermath of the 1963 salad oil scandal, NYSE member firms voluntarily paid the $9,500,000 that the bankrupt Ira Haupt & Co. owed its customers (see 1964 YEAR BOOK, BUSINESS).

The NYSE also set up a permanent $25,000,000 indemnification fund for protection of member-firm customers. The SEC and NYSE proposed that capital requirements be raised for firms that deal in both commodities and securities. WILLIAM G. DEWALD

See also BANKS AND BANKING; MONEY.

STOPH, WILLI (1914-   ), a Communist party member since he was 17 years old, was named premier of East Germany on September 24. He succeeded Otto Grotewohl, who died on September 21 at the age of 71. Stoph was acting premier since 1960.

Stoph was born in Berlin on July 3, 1914, the son of a bricklayer to whom he was apprenticed as a youth. At the age of 14, he joined a communist-sponsored youth organization, and at 21 he was reportedly sent to Moscow for political training.

During World War II, he served with the German army as a corporal although reportedly he doubled as a communist agent. Upon his release from a Soviet army prison camp at the war's end, he joined the East German government. His rise thereafter was rapid and steady. See GERMANY. WALTER F. MORSE

SUBMARINE. See NATIONAL DEFENSE.

SUDAN ended six years of military dictatorship in November. Bloody rioting forced President Ibrahim Abboud to resign and turn over governmental power to a 24-man civilian coalition cabinet headed by Sir-el Khatim el-Khalifa. The new Sudanese leader indicated that presidential elections would be held early in 1965.

The new civilian regime faced serious problems, including a continuing rebellion in southern Sudan where the African population bitterly resented domination by the Arabs of the northern part of the country. It also faced the challenge of solving a financial crisis while preventing parliamentary democracy from breaking down into party bickering and instability.

Early in 1964, 300 Christian missionaries were expelled on charges of supporting subversion.

Population: 13,400,000. **Government:** President and Premier Sir-el Khatim el-Khalifa. **Foreign Trade:** exports: $238,000,000; imports, $320,000,000. **Principal Exports:** cotton and cotton seed, gum arabic, peanuts. WILLIAM SPENCER

See also AFRICA.

SUPREME COURT OF THE UNITED STATES.

"One person, one vote" marked the essence of two major reapportionment decisions handed down by the Supreme Court during 1964. In February, the court ruled that states may not create U.S. congressional districts that have substantial variations in population. In its decision, the court noted that in Fulton County, Georgia, one Congressman represented from two to three times as many persons as did Congressmen from other Georgia districts.

In the court's other far-reaching decision, in June, a majority of the justices ruled that, under the equal protection clause of the U.S. Constitution, the "one person, one vote" principle extended to both houses of state legislatures. The Chief Justice, writing for the majority, rejected the federal analogy of the U.S. Senate as inappropriate to state governments, which were never composed of independent sovereign units. See STATE GOVERNMENT.

Civil Liberties. The protection of persons accused of crimes was extended in a year that saw the fall of many precedents. Amendment 5, which offers protection from being forced to testify against one's self, was twice interpreted. The court extended immunity against federal prosecution to witnesses who had been granted immunity from prosecution under state laws. Formerly such witnesses were not protected from a federal prosecution based on their state testimony. The court also ruled that in state proceedings, contrary to prior decisions, Amendment 14 protects persons from being forced to testify against themselves. In so doing, the court took another step toward the conclusion that Amendment 14 extends the basic Bill of Rights protection—originally applicable only against federal action—against state government action as well.

Other rulings by the court included protections against:
- The search of one's hotel room without a warrant, regardless of the hotelkeeper's prior permission.
- The search of a car without a warrant when the car is in full possession and control of the police.
- The denial of counsel during or before interrogation by the police. See CIVIL LIBERTIES.

In two cases, however, the court refused to interfere with a judge's right to try a contempt. It denied an appeal by Mississippi's former Governor Ross R. Barnett for a jury in his trial for contempt; and the court held that it was not a denial of due process for a New York Supreme Court justice to conduct the hearing of his own contempt charge.

Civil rights matters were by no means overlooked in the mass of cases before the court. Early in the year, the court ruled that Louisiana could not require the race of a candidate to appear on a state ballot. The court quashed an indictment in a North Carolina county where there had been only one Negro on the grand jury in 24 years, yet one-quarter of the eligible population was Negro.

The court upheld a sit-in conviction in Maryland, yet struck down a similar South Carolina case—because of differences in the states' laws.

The long and bitterly argued dispute between the National Association for the Advancement of Colored People (NAACP) and the state of Alabama, which had twice been before the court, reached a

'ONE MAN ONE VOTE' —TWO LANDMARK DECISIONS

THE SUPREME COURT in its term ended June, 1964, handed down two basic decisions affecting the future of representative government in the United States. First, the justices ruled that Article I, Section 2, of the Constitution required application of the "one person, one vote" principle in elections to the U.S. House of Representatives.

Secondly, on the basis that all citizens were entitled to equal protection of the laws—under Amendment 14— the court held that *both* houses of bicameral state legislatures must represent voters on a population basis.

THESE DECISIONS applied specifically to a handful of states. But the justices were aware that in striking down the practices of some states they were, in effect, calling for revision of the apportionment practices of the great majority of the 50 states.

Thus in less than three years—beginning with *Baker vs. Carr* in 1962— the apportionment of legislatures had ceased to be a "political question," and the judiciary itself had become the predominant, if not exclusive, resolver of apportionment problems.

In *Wesberry vs. Sanders*, the court on Feb. 17, 1964, invalidated Georgia's congressional districting. A group of voters of Fulton County, Georgia, had claimed that population disparities as great as three-to-one between their district and other Georgia districts deprived them of the right to have equal weight in their votes for Congressmen.

Six of the nine justices, in an opinion by Justice Hugo Black, concluded that "the command of Article I, Section 2, that representatives be chosen 'by the people of the several states' means that as nearly as is practicable one man's vote in a congressional election is to be worth as much as another's." He cited Section 2 of Amendment 14, which provides that the House be "apportioned among the several states . . . according to their respective numbers."

The court acknowledged that "mathematical precision" in drawing lines of congressional districts may not be possible. But it concluded that "that is no excuse for ignoring our Constitution's plain objective of making equal representation for equal numbers of people the fundamental goal for the House of Representatives."

IN HIS DISSENT, Justice John Marshall Harlan held that the decision "strikes at one of the fundamental doctrines of our representative government, the separation of powers . . . The Constitution does not confer on the court blanket authority to step into every situation where the political branch may be thought to have fallen short."

THE SUPREME COURT in six decisions on June 15 declared unconstitutional the apportionment of the bicameral legislatures of Alabama, Colorado, Delaware, Maryland, New York, and Virginia. It based its decisions on Amendment 14, which provides that "no state shall . . . deny to

A YEAR BOOK CLOSEUP

decision again. The court held that the right of individuals to associate for the collective advocacy of their ideas could not be restricted under the right of the state to regulate the operation of foreign corporations within the state. See NEGRO.

The Civil Rights Act of 1964 reached the court for interpretation within months of its enactment July 2. The court broke precedent to hear argument on the act on the opening day of its term, October 5. Two months later, on December 14, Justice Tom C. Clark delivered the court's unanimous decision upholding the public accommodations provisions of the act as a proper exercise of legislative power under the commerce clause of the U.S. Constitution. For highlights of the act, see CIVIL LIBERTIES.

Based on the public accommodations provisions of the act, a closely divided court also ruled that trespass prosecutions brought against sit-in demonstrators should be dismissed. It held that the provisions of the act had abated the convictions also, in effect, nullifying such state convictions where they were pending on appeal.

The Basic Freedoms of Amendment 1 were extended—via Amendment 14—to cover state actions in a precedent-setting opinion, which held that *The New York Times* was not liable to certain Alabama public officials for false statements contained in an advertisement printed in the *Times*. The constitutional guarantee of free speech, said the court, avoids liability for false statements made about public offi-

any person within its jurisdiction the equal protection of the laws."

Chief Justice Earl Warren spoke for the court. In *Reynolds vs. Sims*, he declared the existing and the two proposed apportionment plans for the two houses of the Alabama legislature invalid. "Legislators represent people, not trees or acres. Legislators are elected by voters, not farms or cities or economic interests," he said.

"We are cautioned about the dangers of entering political thickets and mathematical quagmires," the Chief Justice noted. "Our answer is this: A denial of constitutionally protected rights demands judicial protection. . . . To the extent that a citizen's right to vote is impaired or debased, he is that much less a citizen."

THE COURT explicitly rejected the analogy to the U.S. Senate, where each state, regardless of population, has two seats. This arrangement, the court said, was the product of "unique historical circumstances." Through compromise and concession, 13 formerly independent states united to establish a federal constitutional system. Counties, cities, and other subdivisions within states, on the other hand, never were and never have been considered as sovereign entities.

The Chief Justice asked that each state make "an honest and good-faith effort to construct districts in both houses of its legislature as nearly of equal population as is practicable."

In the five cases that followed *Reynolds vs. Sims*, the court struck down several types of apportionment plans.

Some states (Alabama and Delaware) had failed to reapportion for decades. New York had recently reapportioned according to an established formula.

Dissenting in two cases, Justices Tom C. Clark and Potter Stewart charged the majority with converting a political philosophy into a constitutional rule. They said the court's interpretation of the equal protection clause amounted to a rigid formula that the states could meet "only by the uncritical . . . heavy-handed application of sixth-grade arithmetic."

Justice Harlan dissented in all six cases. He maintained the states had the power to employ any democratic method they chose to apportion their legislatures. Furthermore, he felt that the original need to adopt Amendments 15 and 19—which prohibit the states from denying or abridging the right to vote on account of race, color, or sex—showed that Amendment 14 was not intended to cover voting rights.

THE NATIONWIDE DEBATES that followed the court's rulings produced several congressional efforts to limit, or at least delay, implementation of the apportionment decisions. But Congress adjourned without passing any statute or resolution on the issue.

It was clear that the Supreme Court had effectively asserted its authority as final arbiter of the equities and inequities of legislative apportionment.   VICTOR G. ROSENBLUM

See also CONGRESS OF THE UNITED STATES; STATE GOVERNMENT.

cials unless they are made with malicious intent. See PUBLISHING.

Other Rulings by the Court in a wide variety of areas held that:

• A naturalized citizen cannot be denaturalized by living three years in the country of his origin, nor can a naturalized citizen be prevented from traveling abroad on the same basis as native-born citizens.

• Federal property used by a business within a state is subject to the state's taxing power.

• A state owning and operating a railroad is not exempt from regulation by the federal Interstate Commerce Commission.

• Principles of international comity require U.S. courts to recognize the expropriation of the properties of U.S. nationals by Cuba, preventing any recovery out of any Cuban government properties in the United States.

• The Clayton Antitrust Act prohibits the merger of a glass container corporation with a major metal container corporation since they compete for business in the same market.

• The state of Virginia may not prevent the railroad brotherhoods (unions) from recommending particular lawyers to its members.

The Supreme Court Members in 1964 remained:

Chief Justice Earl Warren and Associate Justices Hugo Black, William J. Brennan, Jr., Tom C. Clark, William O. Douglas, Arthur J. Goldberg, John Marshall Harlan, Potter Stewart, and Byron R. White. ERNEST C. FRIESEN, JR.

See also CONGRESS OF THE UNITED STATES; COURTS AND LAWS.

SWAZILAND held its first general elections under a new constitution decreed by Great Britain in May, 1963, as a step toward independence. The elections, as planned by the British, were to result in a legislative body in which African traditionalists, African nationalists, and European forces would be balanced. However, the electoral situation was drastically changed by the formation of a new political party, the Imbokodvo party, under the patronage of Paramount Chief Sobhuza II. As a result, Chief Sobhuza and the Imbokodvo-endorsed African and European candidates won a sweeping victory, defeating all of the candidates put forward by Swaziland's four nationalist parties.

In order to pressure the British government into opening talks on a new constitution, the country's four nationalist political parties joined ranks. The new grouping, according to nationalist leader Dr. A. P. Zwane, is to be known as the Joint Council of Swaziland Political Parties.

Population: 295,000. **Government:** Resident Commissioner B. A. Marwick; Paramount Chief of the Swazi Sobhuza II. **Foreign Trade:** no statistics available. **Principal Exports:** asbestos, barite, livestock, tin, tobacco. BENJAMIN E. THOMAS

See also AFRICA.

SWEDEN retained the Social Democratic government that had ruled it for 32 years. However, elections in September reduced the party of Prime Minister Tage F. Erlander to 113 seats in parliament, one less than before. The Liberal party gained eight seats and the Communists three, while the Conservative party lost seven.

Sweden played a major role in assisting the United Nations (UN) during the year. It contributed a 1,000-man force to the UN peace force on Cyprus (see CYPRUS). It also worked, meanwhile, to repair its own defenses, which had been undermined by Colonel Stig Wennerstrom, a high official in the Swedish defense ministry who was convicted in 1963 of spying for the Soviet Union. Swedish officials estimated it would take several years and at least $57,000,000 to revise defense plans Wennerstrom had sold to the Soviets.

The domestic economy continued to expand. Rising wages and a labor shortage, coupled with other inflationary pressures, however, led the Swedish central bank to take precautionary measures.

Two granddaughters of reigning King Gustav VI Adolf were married in June: Princess Margaretha, 29, and Princess Désirée, 26.

Population: 7,660,000. **Government:** King Gustav VI Adolf; Prime Minister Tage F. Erlander. **Foreign Trade:** exports, $3,778,000,000; imports, $3,840,000,000. **Principal Exports:** iron and steel, machinery, pulp and paper. FRED J. PANNWITT

See also EUROPE.

SWIMMING. Americans accomplished an outstanding feat in the Olympic Games when U.S. men and women swimmers won 16 of the 22 events and established 10 world records and two new Olympic marks. See OLYMPIC GAMES; SPORTS (awards).

Don Schollander, winner of four Olympic gold medals, made a great showing earlier in the year by setting four world records. At the indoor Amateur Athletic Union (AAU) meet at Bartlesville, Okla., he lowered the 200-yard free-style record to 1:42.6 and the 500-yard free-style mark to 4:44.5. In the AAU outdoor meet at Los Altos Hills, Calif., he reduced the 200-meter free-style record to 1:57.6 and the 400-meter free-style mark to 4:12.7. He cut the latter figure to 4:12.2 at the Olympics.

Dick Roth set a world 400-meter individual medley record of 4:48.6 in the AAU outdoor meet, then bettered that for 4:45.4 at Tokyo.

The University of Southern California won the National Collegiate Athletic Association (NCAA) title, then won the AAU indoor title. The AAU outdoor title went to the Santa Clara Swim Club.

Donna de Varona defended her title in the 200- and 400-yard individual medley relays at the women's AAU indoor championships at Pittsburgh, won the 200-yard butterfly race, and anchored Santa Clara winning teams in the 400-yard free-style and medley relay races. STANLEY ISAACS

SWITZERLAND took steps to solve its problems of overexpansion in 1964. Banks were forbidden to pay interest on deposits, except for savings accounts under $5,000. Investment of foreign funds in Swiss securities, real estate, and mortgages was put under strict limitation. The government also placed a 12-month embargo on all nonessential building projects, and forbade any increase in the number of foreign workers to be employed.

For the first time in its history, the Swiss parliament set up an investigative commission to inquire into an executive department. When the commission reported that the military branch had misled parliament on the cost of 100 French Mirage III fighter planes, the air force commander was dismissed and the chief of the general staff was forced to resign.

The first automobile tunnel under the Alps—the Great St. Bernard tunnel—was opened to traffic March 19. See BRIDGE AND TUNNEL.

Population: 6,025,000. **Government:** President Ludwig von Moos. **Foreign Trade:** exports, $2,-613,000,000; imports, $3,692,000,000. **Principal Exports:** watches and clocks.   FRED J. PANNWITT

See also EUROPE.

SYRIA pressed its search for political stability as a socialist state, but without noticeable success.

On April 15, a revolt led by disgruntled landowners broke out in Hamah, where the government had applied an agrarian reform law limiting individual holdings to 100 acres. Within a week, the disturbances had spread to Homs, to Aleppo, and to Damascus, where hundreds of shopkeepers who resented the government's socialistic policies went on strike. Although government troops restored order, dissatisfaction with the government's plans to create a socialist state continued throughout the year.

A provisional constitution was promulgated on April 25. It was to remain in force for not longer than one year, pending the adoption of a permanent constitution to be approved by a referendum. Under the new document, which described Syria as a "democratic, popular, and socialist republic," legislative power would be exercised by a Revolutionary Council. Executive power would be wielded by a five-man presidential council. Islam was recognized as the official religion and Moslem theology as the basis for all legislation. On May 14, Major General Amin el-Hafez was named head of the council.

In November, Syria and Israel exchanged gunfire over a dispute involving their boundaries. At Syria's urgings, the matter was placed before the United Nations (see ISRAEL; UNITED NATIONS).

Population: 5,200,000. **Government:** Head of the Presidential Council Major General Amin el-Hafez. **Foreign Trade:** exports, $156,000,000; imports, $218,000,000. **Principal Exports:** barley, cotton, wheat.   WILLIAM SPENCER

See also MIDDLE EAST.

TANGANYIKA. See TANZANIA.

TANZANIA was the new name adopted by the United Republic of Tanganyika and Zanzibar in October. Both nations had merged into a single state in April. Julius Nyerere of Tanganyika continued as president; Zanzibar's President Abeid Amani Karume became first vice-president of the new union.

Early in the year, two battalions of the Tanganyikan army mutinied, demanding higher pay and the total Africanization of the officer corps. The mutiny was suppressed on January 25 with the aid of British troops flown in at President Nyerere's request. Following the abortive uprising, President Nyerere announced the 1,350-man army would be disbanded and a new army formed with members of the Youth Wing of his Tanganyikan African National Union as the nucleus.

In May, President Nyerere presented the national assembly with a new $688,800,000 five-year development plan. Primary emphasis was placed on doubling production and national income by 1980, making the country self-sufficient in trained manpower, and adding an additional 15 years to the life expectancy of Tanganyikans.

Population: 10,310,000. **Government:** President Julius Nyerere. **Foreign Trade:** exports, $148,000,-000; imports, $112,000,000. **Principal Exports:** cloves, coffee, cotton, sisal.   BENJAMIN E. THOMAS

See also AFRICA.

TAXATION—or less of it—became a major triumph for the Johnson administration in 1964. Congress passed long-sought legislation reducing the American citizen's tax burden, and President Lyndon B. Johnson signed it into law on February 26. At that time, the cut was estimated at $7,700,000,000 for 1964, and increasing to some $11,500,000,000 yearly in 1965. With the boom continuing, some economists were putting those figures considerably higher. See Section One, SYLVIA PORTER ON THE ECONOMY.

The new tax law, effective March 5, 1964, cut the personal income tax withholding rate from 18 per cent to 14 per cent. The overall personal income tax rate was cut an average of 19 per cent—from the 1963 range of 20-91 per cent, to 16-77 per cent in 1964 and 14-70 per cent in 1965.

Corporate Tax Rates were cut an average of 9 per cent. Over a two-year period, the taxes on profits paid by corporations were scheduled to decline from 52 per cent to 48 per cent.

Tax-free dividend income was increased from $50 to $100 for single persons and from $100 to $200 for married couples. On the other hand, the 4 per cent tax credit on stock dividends was cut to 2 per cent for 1964 and abolished for 1965. Also eliminated were deductions for auto license fees and state and local cigarette and liquor taxes.

Other U.S. Actions. In August, Secretary of the Treasury Douglas Dillon suggested that the 89th Congress consider a further tax reduction of $1,000,-000,000 to $4,500,000,000, including a reduction or repeal of excise taxes on cosmetics, jewelry, furs, leather goods and, possibly, cars. After the election, Dillon and President Johnson lowered the minimum reduction they would ask Congress to approve to the sum of $550,000,000.

On July 18, President Johnson announced that in the fiscal year ended June 30, the budget deficit was $3,600,000,000 below original estimates. Expenditures had dropped $1,100,000,000 below, and receipts were $2,500,000,000 above expectations.

U.S. Tax Collections set a new record in the year ended June 30, 1964. The total in round numbers

Fiscal 1964 Federal Tax Collections
(in millions of dollars)

Type of Tax	Amount	Rise in Year
Corporation Income.....	$ 24,301	8.8%
Individual Income.......	54,590	3.0%
Employment............	17,404	15.2%
Estate and Gift..........	2,416	10.5%
Excise.................	13,950	4.0%
Total..............	$112,661	6.2%

came to $112,601,000,000, or about $6,600,000,000 more than was reported in fiscal 1963 (see table).

State Tax Collections for fiscal 1964 totaled $24,200,000,000, a rise of 9.6 per cent from the $22,100,000,000 total of fiscal 1963.

An increase in state revenue was reported in every state except Arizona, where revenue declined 0.2 per cent. Once again, California collected more state tax revenue than any other state, with a total of $2,930,000,000. New York was next, with $2,713,-

Major Fiscal 1964 State Tax Collections
(in millions of dollars)

Type of Tax*	Amount	Rise in Year
General Sales (37)........	$6,134	10.7%
Selective Sales:		
Motor fuels (50)........	4,057	5.3%
Tobacco products (48)....	1,196	6.3%
Alcoholic beverages (50).	864	8.9%
Insurance (50)..........	708	10.8%
Individual income (36).....	3,363	13.8%
Corporation income (38)....	1,699	12.9%
Property (45).............	727	5.7%
Death and gift (49)........	658	10.6%
Severance (29)............	489	4.6%

*Number of states collecting tax shown in parentheses.

000,000. The per capita burden of state and municipal taxes was heaviest for New York, however, at $327.42. California followed with $318.98.

With total local (municipal and county) tax receipts of about $22,000,000,000 for fiscal 1964, the total bill presented to U.S. taxpayers was in excess of $158,000,000,000. CAROL THOMPSON

See also PRESIDENT OF THE UNITED STATES; STATE GOVERNMENT.

TEACHER. See EDUCATION; Section One, LAWRENCE A. CREMIN ON EDUCATION.

TELEPHONE AND TELEGRAPH. See COMMUNICATIONS.

TELEVISION

THROUGH ITS COVERAGE of the presidential election and its moves to control or own sports properties, television became embroiled in two areas of public policy. The issues raised were not likely to be resolved for many years to come.

In the area of elections, more time and money were devoted to TV coverage by the two major political parties than ever before. Together they spent the bulk of a record-breaking $40,000,000 broadcast budget on TV, as against $14,200,000 in 1960. The election-night returns were computed and analyzed with amazing speed by the three big networks. They could all flatly predict the Democratic victory before 9:30 P.M., Eastern Standard Time. The result was that some voters in California knew the outcome before they had even voted.

Political scientists and spokesmen for both parties asked that the networks forego early predictions, so as not to discourage late voters, but the networks went ahead with their scheduled predictions. They took pains, however, to urge citizens in the western states to go to the polls even though the outcome had become fairly evident.

Controversial Issues. The question of how much influence TV should be permitted in the area of sports created a furor in 1964. It began when the Columbia Broadcasting Company (CBS) purchased an 80 per cent interest in the New York Yankees baseball club for $11,200,000. There were loud objections to the purchase, and threatened law suits. A 50 per cent interest in New York's Madison Square Garden Corporation was purchased by the American Broadcasting Company (ABC). See BASEBALL.

An old problem of public policy for TV, that of crime and violence, was again raised when a Senate subcommittee, in October, reported that "a relationship has been conclusively established between tele-

CBS Television

CREEPINESS AND FUN were mingled in "The Munsters," with Al Lewis, seated, Yvonne De Carlo, and Fred Gwynne.

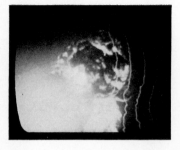

Doyle, Dane, Bernbach, Inc.

BOTH PARTIES used TV ads in the campaign. Here, in a controversial spot, the Democrats stressed theme of keeping only the President's hand on the nuclear trigger.

vised crime and violence and antisocial attitudes and behavior among juvenile viewers." The subcommittee on juvenile delinquency warned that the government may have to regulate programming.

Program Changes. There were a number of program casualties in 1964, including "The Judy Garland Show," "East Side-West Side," and Mitch Miller's "Sing Along with Mitch." In fact, at the start of the 1964 fall season, 40 per cent of the shows in prime time slots were new. Two ABC shows—"Bewitched," a comedy-fantasy starring Elizabeth Montgomery as a domesticated witch, and "Peyton Place," the first nighttime soap opera—were among the highest rated of the new programs.

The 16th annual Emmy award ceremonies of the National Academy of Television Arts and Sciences were clouded by the decision of ABC and three divisions of CBS to withdraw from the affair just two weeks before the scheduled event. They complained of "basic shortcomings in the Emmy structure." The award program went on as scheduled, however, and the winners included ABC's documentary "The Making of the President 1960" (program of the year); NBC's "The Telephone Hour" (music); and three CBS shows: "The Defenders" (drama), "The Danny Kaye Show" (variety), and "The Dick Van Dyke Show" (comedy).

Perhaps the most noteworthy programs of 1964 were NBC's coverage of the Tokyo Olympic Games, relayed by the satellite Syncom III; "Decision: The Conflicts of Harry S. Truman," marking the first time a former U.S. President starred in a regular TV series; NBC's color tour of the Louvre; ABC's study of Nobel prize winners, written and narrated by Alistair Cooke; and the moving commemorative programs in honor of President Kennedy.

Billings, which in 1963 had been more than 10 per cent higher than 1962, went still further ahead in 1964. TV billings were expected to reach a projected $1,825,000,000. Part of this increase was attributable to sales of color-TV, which were running from 10 to 25 per cent ahead of the 1963 figures. According to *Broadcasting Magazine*, there were about 2,860,000 color sets in use at the end of 1964, as compared to 55,000,000 black-and-white sets.

Television viewing, too, reached new heights, according to the Television Bureau of Advertising. The bureau estimated that daily set usage, which had been five hours, 13 minutes per TV home per day in 1963, had risen to the new figure of five hours, 25 minutes in 1964.

Educational Television. The Federal Communications Commission (FCC) reported that there were 88 educational TV stations on the air in 1964, 36 more than in 1960. In October, FCC Chairman E. William Henry said: "Educational television is entitled to look to commercial broadcasters for a portion of its financial support." Commercial broadcasters protested that they were more than doing their part. The networks estimated that they already had given educational television outlets more than $14,500,000 worth of aid in cash ($8,000,000) and free equipment, as well as unpaid labor, and gratis promotion spots.

Pay Television. California's experiment in pay television suffered a setback in November when the state's voters approved an amendment that outlawed Pay TV in that state. The size of the vote, more than two-to-one against Pay TV, was attributed to an intensive advertising campaign conducted by theater owners as well as restaurant and parking-lot owners who were fearful of the competition that Pay TV might give them.

Payola. A secret investigation into charges that payola and plugola were still widespread in the radio and television industry was begun by the FCC in late November. The commission said that it had received allegations "from many sources indicating the continued existence and spread of payola and plugola and other improper related practices." Payola is the secret payment of money to a broadcaster for publicity, and plugola is the secret payment for a mention or display of a product on the program of another sponsor. Both forms of undisclosed payments are specifically outlawed by the Communications Act and the FCC rules.

The FCC also started hearings, late in the year, to determine whether or not it will authorize stereophonic sound for TV.   JUNE BUNDY CSIDA

See also RADIO.

TENNIS. The United States failed to retain the Davis Cup when Australia scored a 3-to-2 victory at Cleveland, tying the U.S. and Aussies at 19 victories each since the start of Davis Cup competition in 1900. Australia's Roy Emerson defeated Chuck McKinley and Dennis Ralston in singles matches, and Fred Stolle came back from a loss to McKinley to beat Ralston. The U.S. team, McKinley and Ralston, won the doubles.

Emerson dominated amateur tennis with victories at Wimbledon, the U.S. Nationals at Forest Hills, and the Australian championships. He missed tennis' grand slam by losing the French championship to Manuel Santana of Spain. Stolle and Bob Hewitt won the men's doubles title at Wimbledon. McKinley and Ralston took the U.S. doubles championship at Longwood Cricket Club, Chestnut Hill, Mass.

In women's play, Maria Bueno of Brazil regained her standing as queen of tennis by dislodging defending champion Margaret Smith at Wimbledon.

The Australian pair of Margaret Smith and Lesley Turner defeated Billie Jean Moffitt and Karen Susman of the United States in the Wimbledon doubles final. The U.S. team retaliated by beating the Australians in the American championship.

U.S. women won their fourth straight Wightman Cup, and Australia defeated the U.S. in the World's Tennis Championship at Philadelphia. STANLEY ISAACS

RACKET BUSTER. Bill Bond, right, broke his racket during amateur doubles at Chestnut Hill, Mass. He and Arthur Ashe lost match.

PICTURES OF THE YEAR/Jim Hughs

TEXTILE. Ailing for many years, the textile industry took some big steps toward good health in 1964. It increased profits sharply, successfully introduced new synthetic products, and improved its competitive position against foreign textiles.

The operating results of Burlington Industries, the nation's largest fabric producer, were typical of the industry pattern. During fiscal 1964, its sales of $1,200,000,000 rose more than 10 per cent, and its profits more than 20 per cent, to $50,800,000. Second-ranking J. P. Stevens increased sales by about 10 per cent; its profit rose about 15 per cent.

Passage of the one-price cotton law was the year's biggest stimulus to the industry. After the new measure passed in April, domestic users got an interim subsidy of $6\frac{1}{2}$ cents a pound on the raw cotton they bought. Therefore, they paid about the same price—$23\frac{1}{2}$ cents a pound—as foreign users. The new law enabled U.S. mills to cut prices, spurring domestic sales and checking, at least temporarily, the growth of imports. The new law also encouraged mills to install new equipment, thus setting the stage for long-term growth of the industry.

Along with new machines and automated techniques, the industry was turning out new materials. The trend to stretch fabrics was notable. More than half of women's slacks sold were of stretch material, and their use was spilling over into men's lines. And a new synthetic fiber, Vectra, began to compete with nylon in the hosiery market. ROBERT E. BEDINGFIELD

THAILAND enjoyed a stable and prosperous year, despite the death of its premier, Field Marshal Sarit Thanarat. The transition to a new government was made smoothly under Thanarat's successor, Premier Thanom Kittikachorn.

Many of Thailand's activities during 1964 were concentrated on foreign affairs, particularly its deteriorating relations with Cambodia. Thailand had assailed Cambodia for conniving with Viet Cong guerrillas in their forays into South Vietnam (see VIETNAM). The Thai also continued to express their anxiety over the steadily worsening situation in Laos (see LAOS). They backed up their words with actions by bolstering their forces along the Laotian and Cambodian borders and by arresting a number of Cambodians living in Thailand. They were charged with espionage.

Meanwhile, the nation greeted, as unrealistic, a French proposal for the neutralization of the Indochinese Peninsula (see FRANCE). It was, they felt, an action that would merely ensure a take-over by the communists. Thailand continued to beef up its defense forces with U.S. military aid.

Population: 30,000,000. **Government:** King Bhumibol Adulyadej; Premier Thanom Kittikachorn. **Foreign Trade:** exports, $579,000,000; imports, $635,000,000. **Principal Exports:** beverages, rice, rubber, tin, tobacco. JOHN N. STALKER

See also ASIA.

THEATER

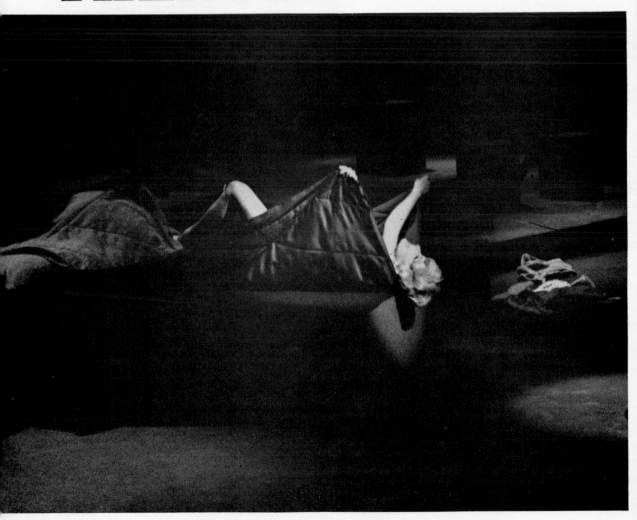

THE YEAR 1964 may be remembered chiefly for events that promised an upsurge in the American theater. The chief event was the opening, early in the year, of the long awaited first season presented by New York City's Lincoln Center Repertory Company.

The season began with a production of Arthur Miller's first play in nine years, *After the Fall*, which dealt imaginatively with this well-known author's two unsuccessful marriages and political attitudes. It concluded with the sentiment that a man must face life with courage despite the confusions and evils in his world and in his own complicated soul.

Despite the controversy it aroused, it was by far the most successful production of the Lincoln Center company. In December, mixed reactions swirled about Miller's next play, *Incident at Vichy*, a drama about the Nazis and the hidden springs of evil in all men.

Other Repertory Groups. Notably active were several other producing groups. The Actors' Studio Theatre produced James Baldwin's crude but powerful drama of racial conflict in the deep South, *Blues for Mr. Charlie*, and a revival of the Russian masterpiece *The Three Sisters*,

Inge Morath/Magnum

staged by Lee Strasberg and distinguished by performances of Geraldine Page and Kim Stanley. The Association of Producing Artists (APA), a repertory group with its center at the University of Michigan, presented four plays in New York City under the auspices of the experimental Phoenix Theatre. The production that made the deepest impression was a revival of another Russian masterpiece, *The Lower Depths*, Maxim Gorki's drama of derelicts pumped full of illusions. The National Repertory Company, a professional touring group headed by the eminent actress-manager Eva Le Gallienne, brought to Broadway impressive revivals of Chekhov's *The Seagull* and Arthur Miller's Salem witchcraft drama *The Crucible*.

Also brought to New York after extensive touring were some independent productions. One of these was *The White House*, a sequence of sketches based on the lives of U.S. Presidents. The celebrated Helen Hayes portrayed their wives.

Comedies. The most successful of the comedies were Neil Simon's *Barefoot in the Park*, dealing with the trials and embarrassments of a newly married couple; Muriel Resnick's *Any Wednesday*, which told of a middle-aged businessman's efforts to keep an illicit romance going; and Murray Schisgal's *Luv*. Both *Luv* and *Barefoot in the Park* were directed by Mike Nichols.

Importations. The most noteworthy visit from Europe was the appearance of the Royal Shakespeare Company with a frolicsome *Comedy of Errors* and a carefully thought out presentation of *King Lear*, in which one of the best British actors, Paul Scofield, played the difficult part of the aged king. A famous company from Paris, the *Théâtre de France*, brought

AFTER THE FALL, with Barbara Loden and Jason Robards, Jr., was Arthur Miller's first play on the Broadway stage in nine years.

King

HELLO, DOLLY! *Carol Channing sings the rollicking title song in this big musical version of Thornton Wilder's farce The Matchmaker.*

four plays in French, and the Hebrew-speaking Habimah from Israel appeared in a repertory including the famous East European folk play *The Dybbuk.* At year-end, the celebrated Schiller Theater company arrived from West Berlin with their version of the German classic, *Don Carlos*, by the 18th-century German poet Friedrich Schiller.

Off-Broadway. Perhaps the most remarkable off-Broadway production was *The Old Glory*, a group of short plays by the distinguished American poet Robert Lowell. Also challenging was the South African play *The Blood Knot*, by Atholl Fugard, a study in race relations.

Short new stage productions such as LeRoi Jones' *Dutchman* and Samuel Beckett's *Play*, along with revivals of short plays by the Parisian *avant-garde* playwright Ionesco, found off-Broadway audiences. So did unusual full-length plays, such as the sinister "theater of the absurd" farce *The Knack*, by the English playwright Ann Jellicoe; Ugo Betti's *Corruption in the Palace of Justice;* and a provocative American play, *The Burning*, which was concerned with the burning of lepers in medieval France as a result of rampant superstition.

Brecht and Hochhuth. Some weighty European plays were also brought to Broadway. The most ambitious were Bertolt Brecht's satire on Hitler, *Arturo Ui*, and Rolf Hochhuth's German drama *The Deputy*, dealing with the role of Pope Pius XII during the Nazi persecution of the Jews.

Broadway Specials. Among the plays written specifically for Broadway was the strong satire on television promoters, *Nobody Loves an Albatross. Dylan*, based on the distracted life and early death of the Welsh poet Dylan Thomas, was movingly impersonated by the British star actor Alec Guinness. Neither of these productions had the force of the relatively superficial trial drama *A Case of Libel*, which dealt with the defeat of a libelous newspaper columnist, and was carried over from the 1963 fall season. The big Broadway productions were, as is often the case, expensive musical comedies and music dramas. *Hello, Dolly!*, a musical version of Thornton Wilder's *The Matchmaker*, starring Carol Channing, was the liveliest of these presentations. Especially interesting was the musical biography of Fanny Brice, *Funny Girl*, which was noteworthy for its human interest and for the appealing performance of the recently discovered Barbra Streisand.

Of the many Shakespearean productions done in the anniversary year, the one that gained the widest following was Richard Burton's *Hamlet*, played in rehearsal clothes. It was most gratifying when Hume Cronyn appeared as Polonius, but Burton's performance as a nervous, embittered Hamlet was frequently exciting. See LITERATURE (Close-Up).

The new season of the fall of 1964 was moderately successful. One excellent U.S. musical comedy production was *Fiddler on the Roof*, based on the humorous tales of Sholom Aleichem, the Mark Twain of the Eastern European Jewish communities. But new plays by the novelist Saul Bellow, and by the late Lorraine Hansberry, the author of the worthy Negro family drama, *Raisin in the Sun*, and other able writers, did not materially enrich the early season. No great enthusiasm greeted a musical version of Clifford Odets' *Golden Boy*, although Sammy Davis played the "golden boy" role excitingly.

European Broadway. Most of the new attractions came from abroad. They included the Joan Littlewood London revue-satire on England's involvement in World War I, *Oh, What a Lovely War* and the brittle British comedy of sophisticated love affairs, *A Severed Head.* Two importations from the European continent aroused interest. One was Jean Anouilh's early drama, *Traveller Without Luggage*, in which a disillusioned World War I veteran in France loses his memory and, on recovering it, firmly rejects his family. The other import was the sardonic Swiss playwright Friedrich Duerrenmatt's *The Physicists*, a work that called attention to the danger of nuclear destructiveness falling into the hands of madmen and seekers after power and profit.

Awards for the 1963-1964 Season included:

New York Drama Critics Circle Award to: *Luther*, best play of the season; and *Hello, Dolly!*, best musical. A special citation for excellence in production was given by the critics to the off-Broadway drama, *The Trojan Woman*.   JOHN GASSNER

THRESHER, U.S.S. See NATIONAL DEFENSE.

TOGO. In May, an alleged plot against President Nicolas Grunitzky led to the arrest of three members of two political parties, the Juvento and the Partie de l'Unité Togolaise. The following month, the national assembly voted a 12-month extension of a law providing for the imprisonment or expulsion of persons thought to endanger public security and order. In early July, another plot against the Togolese government was uncovered with the discovery of a stock of explosives in Lomé. Theophile Mally, a former minister of the interior who was living in exile, and two former deputies were accused of the plot.

During the year, the government signed trade and cultural agreements with the United Arab Republic and a financial agreement with France.

Population: 1,620,000. **Government:** President Nicolas Grunitzky. **Foreign Trade:** exports, $17,160,-000; imports, $27,220,000. **Principal Exports:** cocoa, coffee, palm-oil products.   BENJAMIN E. THOMAS

See also AFRICA.

TORNADOS. See DISASTERS; WEATHER.

TOWNES, CHARLES HARD (1915-   ), Massachusetts Institute of Technology provost and professor, shared the 1964 Nobel physics prize with two Russian radiophysicists. The three were honored for research in quantum electronics leading to oscillators and amplifiers based on the maser-laser principle.

Townes demonstrated that electrons can be triggered into releasing photons of energy on demand, rather than at random, thus making possible the development of smaller, more powerful amplifiers. In 1954, he and fellow workers at Columbia University produced the first maser (*M*icrowave *A*mplification by *S*timulated *E*mission of *R*adiation). The optical maser, or laser (*L*ight *A*mplification by *S*timulated *E*mission of *R*adiation) was also his idea. Both have revolutionized the field of electronics.

Charles Townes graduated from Furman University in Greenville, S.C., where he was born. He received an M.A. (1937) from Duke University, and a Ph.D. (1939) from California Institute of Technology. This was followed by nine years at the Bell Telephone Laboratories in New Jersey. At Columbia (1948-1961), Townes advanced to professor of physics. He went to Massachusetts in 1961.

See also BASOV, NIKOLAI G.; NOBEL PRIZES (Science); PROKHOROV, ALEKSANDR M.

TRACK AND FIELD would have registered a memorable year even without the Tokyo Olympics. Fifteen new world records were set in non-Olympic meets, and a surprising new trend saw American distance runners take a position of world leadership.

Most startling of the new world records were those set in the field events. Dallas Long of Los Angeles made a new world shot-put mark with a tremendous heave of 67 feet 10 inches. Ludvik Danek of Czechoslovakia captured the discus record from America's Al Oerter with a throw of 211 feet 9½ inches. An-

other European, Terje Pedersen of Norway, became the first man to throw the javelin over 300 feet. Pedersen's mark of 300 feet 11½ inches was more than 16 feet better than the old record. And Fred Hansen of Rice University raised the pole vault record to 17 feet 4 inches, declaring after he made the mark, "We'll be vaulting 19 feet before I retire."

New Zealand's double Olympic champion, Peter Snell, went home to lower the world 1,000-meter standard to 2:16.6, on November 12. Then five days later, he attacked his own mile record of 3:54.4, and by running quarter miles of 56, 58, 60, and 60.1, Snell achieved a new world record of 3:54.1. But he was not satisfied, claiming his objective was 3:50 or better within the next 12 months.

U.S.-Russian Meet. Next to the Olympics, the most noteworthy event of the year was the sixth annual meet between the United States and Russia. The favored U.S. team scored an overwhelming victory, winning 16 of the 22 men's events. The score was 139 to 97, by far the most one-sided margin in the series. The U.S. women's team lost to the Russians again, but this time by only 59 to 48.

What provided the biggest eye opener for world track fans were U.S. victories in all three of the distance races: the 1,500- and 10,000-meter races, and the 3,000-meter steeplechase. Gavril Korobkov, head Soviet coach, attributed his team's defeat to two factors. First, he said the Los Angeles smog hindered their breathing. And second, Korobkov pointed to the fact that the Russians were training to reach a peak for the Olympics in October, rather than this event in late July. U.S. athletes laughed, and then refuted Korobkov's reasoning by winning 12 Olympic gold medals to Russia's two.

For what Korobkov had refused to believe was true. The United States had become one of the world's leading powers in distance running. Olympic gold medalists Bob Schul (5,000 meters) and Billy Mills (10,000 meters) also posted the year's fastest times for their distances, and Schul brought the world two-mile record back to the United States. The movement had depth, too. In a one-mile race that was held at Compton, Calif., eight Americans finished in under four minutes.

Teen-Agers at the Top. Surprisingly, some of the fastest of the new U.S. distance "men" were teenagers. Gerry Lindgren, 18, of Spokane, Wash., created a sensation when he ran an indoor two-mile race first in 9 minutes flat, then in 8:46, and finally in only 8:40. Outdoors, he was even better. Lindgren not only won the 10,000 meters against the Russians in his second try at the distance, but also became the third fastest American in history at both 5,000 and 10,000 meters.

Lindgren was almost matched by 17-year-old Jim Ryun, of Wichita, Kans., a high school junior. In June, Ryun became the first high schooler to run a sub-four-minute mile. Later, he ran 1,500 meters

TRADE

in 3:39.0, a speed equal to a 3:57 mile. Both Ryun and Lindgren defeated older runners to make the U.S. Olympic team.

Another teen-age sensation was Randy Matson of Pampa, Tex. Matson is a 19-year-old freshman at Texas A.&M. His shot-put toss of 66 feet $3\frac{1}{4}$ inches bettered all pre-1964 records and was second only to that of Dallas Long.

Truce Ends. The two-year truce between the Amateur Athletic Union (AAU) and the National Collegiate Athletic Association (NCAA) ended with the last flicker of the Olympic flame. The two organizations resumed their battle for control of U.S. track and field events with declarations and denunciations on both sides. The outlook was for a long struggle.

In team competition, host Oregon University won the NCAA championship meet, while the Southern California Striders won the AAU title at New Brunswick, N.J.   JAMES O. DUNAWAY

See also OLYMPIC GAMES.

TRADE. See BUSINESS; INTERNATIONAL TRADE.
TRAFFIC. See ROADS AND HIGHWAYS; SAFETY.
TRAIN WRECKS. See DISASTERS.

TRANSIT. A milestone in the transit industry was achieved on July 9, when President Lyndon B. Johnson signed into law the Urban Mass Transportation Act of 1964. The momentous occasion signaled the beginning of a $375,000,000 three-year program of federal financial assistance to metropolitan and urban areas for the rehabilitation or expansion of commuter and mass transportation systems. See CITY.

In Massachusetts, Governor Endicott Peabody signed into law a massive $225,000,000 mass transportation bill designed to preserve and revitalize transit service in Massachusetts. It provided state aid to financially distressed urban bus systems across the state, and to commuter railroads. In addition, it furnished funds to expand rapid transit lines in the Boston area. The governor's signature on the bill meant that the Commonwealth of Massachusetts became the first state in the nation to take concrete action toward solving the transit problem within its borders by actually financing a comprehensive program for its solution. This far-reaching measure created a new, comprehensive Massachusetts Bay Transport Authority and implemented significant improvements in public transportation.

They included: geographic, financial, and administrative expansion of the rapid transit system; rail commuter service and bus service in the Boston metropolitan area; authorization for the creation of public transportation authorities or agencies in other Massachusetts urban or metropolitan areas; and tax relief and reimbursement for reduced school fares for all Massachusetts' bus companies.

Revenue support for the legislation will be provided by a two-cent increase in the state cigarette tax. The bill is the culmination of years of concern over public transportation in the Boston region.

Rapid Transit. Construction was launched on the San Francisco Bay area's new billion-dollar rapid transit system on June 19, 1964. The system will be one of the largest single projects ever carried out in the United States. It will involve development of 12 miles of downtown subway lines in San Francisco, Oakland, and Berkeley, together with 55 miles of suburban aerial and surface lines, four miles of underground tunnels, and a four-mile, underwater transit tube extending under San Francisco Bay.

The entire 75-mile network will be completed in 1971. Initial passenger service on the system is scheduled to begin early in 1968.

Statistics. At the beginning of 1964, approximately 1,186 transit companies in the United States (including publicly owned as well as privately owned) operated some 62,000 transit vehicles, and carried 8,400,000,000 passengers in 1963. See BUS.

"Dream Specials." In transit developments overseas, a super-express train began service in Japan. It travels the 320-mile distance between Tokyo and Osaka at speeds up to 160 mph. After the roadbed has time to settle, the train will make the run in three hours, with two stops. Limited trains, making 10 stops, will travel the same route in four hours. The usual time on this run, through the industrial belt of Japan, is about six-and-a-half hours. Some U.S. transit officials believed that such express trains, called "Dream Specials" in Japan, might greatly ease pressure on highways in the vast urban belts of the United States.   EUGENE B. McCAUL

TRANSPORTATION. See AUTOMOBILE; AVIATION; BUS; RAILROAD; ROADS AND HIGHWAYS; SHIP; TRANSIT; TRAVEL; TRUCKING; WATERWAYS.

TRAVEL. The exodus of U.S. tourists to foreign lands set new records in 1964. Also, more foreign visitors than ever before came to the United States. Reduced air fares, including the new round-trip excursion fares of $300 across the North Atlantic, helped spur the record volume of two-way travel on the most heavily traveled air (and sea) routes in the world. Some 2,300,000 Americans went overseas, 1,230,000 of them to Europe. Another 12,000,000 visited Canada and Mexico. They spent approximately $3,500,000,000, against the $3,200,000,000 spent by 12,700,000 touring Americans during 1963.

An estimated 989,000 business and pleasure travelers visited the United States from overseas, up 34.5 per cent from 735,000 the preceding year. It was a spectacular achievement for the new U.S. Travel Service (USTS). The total of incoming visitors had risen 91 per cent since 1961, when USTS was established.

The "Travel Gap." But so rapid was the competing outflow of U.S. tourists that the so-called "travel gap"—between expenditures by Americans abroad, and those by foreign visitors in the United States— was broadening, much to the concern of federal fiscal authorities. It was expected to exceed the

$1,643,000,000 unfavorable balance of 1963. Yet the travel gap was not appreciably larger than the $1,472,000,000 "beverage gap." The United States imported $1,514,000,000 in coffee, cocoa, tea, and wine and other alcoholic beverages, and exported only $42,000,000 in comparable beverage products.

While officials in Washington worried about the effect of the "travel gap" on the U.S. balance of payments, none suggested any actions to curtail beverage imports. The answer lay not in restricting outbound travel, but in giving the USTS an adequate budget to promote more inbound traffic.

Passenger Traffic Up. On the busy North Atlantic traffic lanes air travel increased its ascendancy over sailing, with 83 per cent of the travelers flying and 17 per cent going by sea. The percentages were 78 and 22, respectively, in 1963. Total traffic was up about 18 per cent: air travel gained 20 per cent; ocean traffic fell about 9 per cent from 1963.

World-wide air travel increased almost as sharply. The International Civil Aviation Organization reported that its 107 member airlines carried 156,000,-000 passengers in 1964, up 16 per cent over 1963.

Domestic Travel within the United States rose to new heights, with about 109,000,000 Americans taking holiday or business trips and spending $18,-000,000,000 in the year. The total spent on all domestic and foreign travel came to $21,200,000,000, making travel the third largest industry in the United States.

Travel also led all other products and services as the largest item in international trade. It totaled about $9,000,000,000 in 1964. It encompassed a global movement of about 60,000,000 individuals across national frontiers—a mass mobility unprecedented in world history.

The Tourist Talks Back. The huge increase in traffic also taxed the host facilities of many countries. For the first time it led to a significant outcry of tourists against gouging, excessive taxes (such as the annoying epidemic of exit or airport departure taxes), overcrowding, poor service, and flagrant discourtesy. Several countries acted to correct the alleged abuses. They asked their own people to appreciate the economic and cultural values of tourism. *Paris-Match* lamented: "We (French) have the reputation of being the least welcoming people on the Continent." WILLIAM D. PATTERSON

See also AVIATION; BUS; FAIRS AND EXHIBITIONS; HOTEL; OUTDOOR RECREATION; PARKS; RAILROAD; SHIP.

TRINIDAD-TOBAGO remained at odds with Great Britain over the unsettled amount of British financial aid promised after independence in August, 1962. Because of the disagreement, Trinidad-Tobago was the only former British colony not to have received economic assistance. Prime Minister Eric E. Williams had turned down London's original offer of a $2,800,000 loan, a $700,000 grant, and

four airliners. His demands for financial aid were believed to be close to $28,000,000.

The nation, with a 14 per cent unemployment rate, continued to look on emigration, particularly to Britain, as a way to alleviate its immediate difficulties, but it resented the menial jobs most of its emigrants received. Prime Minister Williams advocated a government-run employment program, including training courses, to place emigrants in suitable jobs in Britain, Canada, and the United States. He also hoped to spur the economy by establishing new trade links in the Caribbean area.

Population: 950,000. **Government:** Governor-General Sir Solomon Hochoy; Prime Minister Eric E. Williams. **Foreign Trade:** exports, $422,000,000; imports, $386,000,000. **Principal Exports:** chemicals, petroleum products, sugar. ALASTAIR BURNET

TRUCKING. Highway freight traffic rolled up a record 1964 haul for the nation's truckers. In local and distance use, more than 13,000,000 privately owned trucks traveled the highways, 4 per cent more than in 1963. Together, they rendered about $36,400,000,000 worth of service, including the hauling of an estimated 370,000,000,000 ton-miles of intercity freight, 6.4 per cent above the revised 1963 figure. Total operating revenues for 16,000 federally regulated motor carriers rose around 7 per cent to over $9,150,000,000, with a projected net revenue of $370,000,000 before taxes.

General Motors showed truckers an experimental 280-hp, heavy-duty, gas-turbine engine occupying one-third the space and weighing one-half that of a comparable diesel engine. Ford Motor Company, late in the fall sent an experimental turbine truck on a 5,500-mile demonstration tour. The huge three-unit rig, powered by a 600-hp, gas-turbine engine, was capable of traveling 70 mph nonstop for 600 miles. Its fiberglass cab contained a sink, toilet, TV, refrigerator, and lounge chair. The Navajo Freight Lines posted a new transcontinental highway freight delivery record with a 2,783-mile, Los Angeles-to-New York run in $61\frac{1}{4}$ hours.

The International Brotherhood of Teamsters and the trucking industry signed a national labor agreement giving 458,000 workers a wage increase of 28 cents an hour, plus health, welfare, and pension boosts valued at $5 a week, spread over the three-year contract period. Over-the-road drivers were given a $\frac{1}{4}$-cent-a-mile boost in pay in each of the three years. For their leader, James R. Hoffa, however, 1964 was less pleasant. He was convicted of jury-tampering and of fraud and conspiracy.

The Supreme Court of the United States declined to review a National Labor Relations Board (NLRB) decision that upheld the right of a motor carrier to fire teamsters who refused to cross the picket line of a struck plant. The NLRB had ruled that the drivers were not fired in reprisal, but solely to permit the carrier to continue in business. MARK REINSBERG

TUNISIA

TUNISIA nationalized all remaining lands held by foreigners in May, 1964. Its action was denounced by France as a violation of the 1963 Franco-Tunisian agreement by which Tunisia had agreed to nationalize the lands of the remaining French landowners at fixed rates of compensation.

The French government cut off all financial aid to Tunisia. The Tunisian assembly thereupon approved a "popular" subscription loan to replace canceled French aid. Tunisia also received $7,000,-000 from the World Bank for the modernization of Tunis. Loan agreements were signed with Denmark, Iraq, and the United States.

President Habib Bourguiba was re-elected on November 8, capturing 96.43 per cent of the votes.

Population: 4,450,000. **Government:** President Habib Bourguiba. **Foreign Trade:** exports: $109,-000,000; imports, $259,000,000. **Principal Exports:** phosphates, vegetable oils, wine. WILLIAM SPENCER

See also AFRICA.

TURKEY became deeply embroiled in the bitter Cyprus dispute to the detriment of its political and economic progress in 1964. For a time, war threatened to erupt between Turkey and Greece as each nation lent support to its respective ethnic group on the island. An outbreak of hostilities was avoided, however, by United Nations (UN) intervention. See CYPRUS; GREECE; UNITED NATIONS.

Turkey's bitterness over Greek actions in Cyprus hit hardest at Greeks living in Turkey. In March, the government announced it would not renew a 1930 treaty, which gave Greeks special privileges in Turkey, when it expired in September. In April, the government approved a bill extending Turkey's territorial water limits from six to 12 miles. The extension would curb fishermen from Greece's nearby Dodecanese Islands.

Internal Politics. The assembly passed a law changing the method of election to the senate from a majority to a proportional system. It was an effort to reduce the majority held by the opposition Justice party in the upper legislative chamber. In the senate elections held on June 7, however, the Justice party won 30 seats for a gain of eight while the Republican People's party of Premier Ismet Inönü captured only 20 for a gain of five.

On April 7, the Organization for Economic Cooperation and Development advanced a $20,000,000, one-year credit to help Turkey meet its foreign exchange payments. On the same date, a $70,000,-000 loan was granted by the U.S. Agency for International Development to help finance purchases of selected U.S. commodities and equipment.

Population: 31,300,000. **Government:** President Cemal Gursel; Premier Ismet Inönü. **Foreign Trade:** exports, $280,000,000; imports, $589,000,000. **Principal Exports:** cotton, nuts, tobacco. WILLIAM SPENCER

See also EUROPE; MIDDLE EAST.

TYPHOONS. See DISASTERS; WEATHER.

UGANDA. An army mutiny in January caused Prime Minister Milton A. Obote to call for an emergency airlift of about 450 British troops to re-establish order. The revolt flared when Ugandese troops stationed at Camp Jinga on Lake Victoria demanded a pay increase. It was quickly suppressed.

Prime Minister Obote continued to pursue his goal of a one-party state, declaring that his party, the Uganda People's Congress (UPC), should be the only one in the country. He did not, however, plan to create a one-party state either by law or by force. Instead, he planned to let the opposition parties die a natural death.

Population: 7,450,000. **Government:** Prime Minister Milton A. Obote. **Foreign Trade:** exports, $114,000,000; imports, $54,000,000. **Principal Exports:** coffee, copper, cotton. BENJAMIN E. THOMAS

See also AFRICA.

UNEMPLOYMENT. See AUTOMATION; BUSINESS; LABOR; SOCIAL WELFARE (Close-Up).

UNION OF SOUTH AFRICA. See SOUTH AFRICA, REPUBLIC OF.

UNION OF SOVIET SOCIALIST REPUBLICS (U.S.S.R.). See RUSSIA.

UNITED ARAB REPUBLIC (UAR) celebrated a historic achievement when the first phase of construction was completed on the Aswan High Dam in May. Ceremonies marking the occasion were attended by President Gamal Abdel Nasser and the then Soviet Premier Nikita S. Khrushchev, whose nation had promised to pay four-tenths of the estimated $1,000,000,000 it would eventually cost to complete the dam. See DAM.

Elections for a new national assembly were held on March 10 and 19, with 1,748 candidates competing for the 350 seats at stake in 175 electoral districts. To qualify, candidates had to be over 30 years of age, literate, members of the Arab Socialist party (the sole political party in the UAR), and post a cash bond.

Following the election, a provisional constitution was proclaimed by President Nasser. It became effective on March 25 and would remain in force until a permanent constitution had been drafted by the new assembly and approved by the electorate in a plebiscite. On the same day that the constitution went into effect, a new 22-minister cabinet was sworn in. Dr. Ali Sabry was named premier.

Economic Developments. Discoveries of water sources during the year almost outweighed even the Aswan High Dam's importance to the UAR. The Nile Valley project brought in a fresh-water well, pumping 14,000 cubic yards daily, at a depth of 2,000 feet. The UAR also signed an agreement with a West German firm for a plant that would convert salt water into fresh water at the rate of 100 tons per hour. The Nile Valley project, meanwhile, announced that 36,000 acres of former desert land had been made arable.

*PICTURES OF THE YEAR/*Dieter Steiner, United Press Int.

SECURITY SNAFU occurs in Cairo as a girl flings herself on hood of car carrying visiting Soviet Premier Nikita Khrushchev.

International Relations. The UAR served as host to a number of international meetings in 1964. Its hospitality was in keeping with President Nasser's ambitions to serve as one of the creators of a "third world" of neutral, nonaligned nations. During the year, the Arab League met twice in Cairo, as did the Organization of African Unity (OAU). On July 25, the 12th anniversary of the Egyptian Revolution was celebrated with a gigantic display of UAR military power—most of it supplied by the Soviet Union—for the benefit of Arab and African heads of state who attended an OAU conference. See AFRICA.

University Expands. The 1,000-year-old Al-Azhar University installed a new rector, Sheik Ma'mun, and began moving to its new campus outside Cairo during the year. Its new facilities include schools of agriculture, business, engineering, and medicine. It also has a separate women's college.

Population: 29,000,000. **Government:** President Gamal Abdel Nasser; Premier Ali Sabry. **Foreign Trade:** exports, $577,000,000; imports, $947,000,000. **Principal Exports:** cotton (raw), cotton yarn, petroleum, textiles.   WILLIAM SPENCER

See also MIDDLE EAST.

UNITED COMMUNITY FUNDS AND COUNCILS (UCFC) joined with agencies now conducting independent fund-raising campaigns to test the feasibility of a combined fund-raising drive among federal employees and members of the armed forces. Experimental "one-shot" drives were conducted in Dover, N.J.; Philadelphia; Washington, D.C.; Macon, Ga.; Fort Worth; San Antonio; Minneapolis; St. Paul; and Bremerton, Wash.

The approach was developed by John W. Macy, Jr., chairman of the Civil Service Commission. The experiment was to be evaluated by the Federal Fund Raising Advisory Council which will determine whether this fund-raising approach will be used in the future.

A record total of $546,801,097 was raised in the 1964 campaigns of the United Funds, Community Councils, and Community Chests throughout the nation. Again the United Foundation of Detroit was the leader, with contributions of more than $21,000,000. It was followed by Chicago, Los Angeles, Philadelphia, Cleveland, San Francisco, Pittsburgh, and Boston. Each of the cities raised in excess of $10,000,000.

Awards in 1963 included:

The UCFC United Community Service Award to John S. Hayes, chairman, Executive Committee, Washington Post Co., Washington, D.C. "for outstanding service as president, United Community Funds and Councils of America."   JOSEPH P. ANDERSON

M ONEY PROBLEMS that remained unsolved at the close of what Secretary-General U Thant termed a "crucial" year hobbled the United Nations (UN) during 1964. For the first time since its initial session in 1946, the General Assembly omitted normal business. The Soviet Union's right to vote was under challenge, since it owed more than two years' assessments (chiefly to maintain UN peace-keeping forces). To avert a confrontation, the Assembly delayed opening its 19th session to December 1, some 10 weeks after the original date set. Even then, its actions were limited to policy speeches and a handful of actions. Voting was by acclamation rather than a recorded one because the latter would have tested the Soviet Union's position.

The Assembly's membership, which had grown to 115, was the battleground for a war of wills between the world's two superpowers, the Soviet Union and the United States. At issue was the past and future ability of the UN to mobilize peace operations opposed by a great power, and to make all UN members pay a share of the resulting costs. The Soviet Union's representatives hinted that they would walk out of the Assembly if their vote was suspended. The Americans hinted at a slash of *their* financial contributions—the leading income item in UN budgets—if the Soviets were permitted to avoid paying their dues.

While the Assembly was thus deadlocked, the 11-nation Security Council had one of its busiest years. It set up a new UN Force in Cyprus (UNFICYP), paid for on a hat-passing basis by only 31 countries. The Council was also concerned with a number of crises in Africa, Asia, and Latin America.

Money Crisis. U.S. officials said Soviet Foreign Minister Andrei Gromyko privately had promised to pay an unspecified amount to help the UN get out of debt. But the Soviets again refused to pay "a single kopeck" in 1964 toward specific assessments appropriated by the Assembly in 1956 for the UN Emergency Force (Middle East) and, later, for the UN force active in Congo (Léopoldville) from July, 1960, to June, 1964. Both were "illegal," they argued, because the UN Charter put peace enforcement in the Security Council, where the Soviet Union and four other big powers could veto what they disapproved.

The World Court agreed with the United States that these assessments were binding under UN Charter Article 19. They agreed, too, that the penalty was a loss of vote in the Assembly for those countries two years behind in payments. But World Court rulings are advisory. No power existed to force the Soviet Union to pay the $5,600,000 needed to be eligible to vote in 1964 (or the $26,600,000 required in 1965). Six other communist members in the same situation

TRIAL BY FIRE tested mettle of United Nations troops during fighting between embattled Turkish and Greek Cypriots on war-torn Cyprus.

AFRICAN PRESTIGE was enhanced by election of Ghana's Alex Quaison-Sackey to the presidency of the United Nations General Assembly.

were Czechoslovakia, Hungary, Poland, Romania, and the two Soviet regions with full UN voting privileges, Byelorussia and Ukraine. (Thirteen others, including France and Belgium, would join the list in 1965.) Nothing came of Gromyko's offer in 1964, and negotiations for a face-saving way out of the deadlock continued at year's end.

Congo Dilemma. The largest, most expensive UN peace-keeping operation ended on June 30, with the removal of UN soldiers from Congo (Léopoldville). But major problems remained. When Congo turned to Belgium, the United States, and other white nations for help in quelling its rebellion, 18 angry African nations brought charges before the Security Council in December. Black-against-white accusations were heard for the first time as some Africans demanded "condemnation" of the Belgian-U.S. airborne rescue of white hostages held by rebels in Stanleyville (see CONGO [LÉOPOLDVILLE]).

The African nations, backed by the Soviet Union's veto power in the Security Council, rejected any further UN political role in Congo, merely asking U Thant to follow the situation and report back. The Organization of African Unity (OAU) was asked to help bring about a cease-fire, the expulsion of the white mercenaries recruited by Moise Tshombe, and national political reconciliation. See AFRICA.

Cyprus. The threat of an ugly war between North Atlantic Treaty Organization (NATO) allies Greece and Turkey made the clash of Greek and Turkish Cypriots of international concern during the year. When the United States and Britain failed to calm the Mediterranean island, the Security Council authorized a volunteer peace force, UNFICYP, and a mediator. Set up with the agreement of the (Greek) Cypriot government of Archbishop Makarios, the Turkish Cypriot minority, Greece, Great Britain, and Turkey, the UNFICYP role was a limited one. See CYPRUS.

Malaysia-Indonesia Fighting. A Soviet veto on September 17 killed a Security Council move to restrain guerrilla raids by Indonesia in Malaysia. Indonesia admitted the raids, which the Soviet delegate justified as the exercising of a "right" to fight against neocolonialism. Late in the year, U Thant admitted that UN hopes to help reduce tensions between the two countries had been frustrated. Meanwhile, the election of Malaysia to fill a Security Council vacancy on December 29 provoked loud threats from Indonesia's President Sukarno to withdraw his nation from the UN. See INDONESIA.

War in Vietnam had been formally barred from UN jurisdiction by agreement among the major powers, including non-UN-member Communist China. But it received oblique attention in the Security Council.

On August 5, the Council heard U.S. Ambassador Adlai E. Stevenson give the American version of the attacks by North Vietnamese vessels against U.S. warships in the Tonkin Gulf on August 2 and August 4, and the reprisal U.S. naval air raid carried out against communist North Vietnam. The Soviet Union condemned the U.S. action and demanded a hearing for North Vietnam, which is not a UN member. North Vietnam, however, refused to participate, branding any potential Council action as "illegal." The matter was dropped. See VIETNAM.

Israel-Syria Dispute. Another Soviet veto, on December 21, blocked a U.S.-British proposal deploring renewed military action on the Israeli-Syrian border. However, lack of a majority in the Council killed a Moroccan attempt, which was backed only by the Soviet Union and Czechoslovakia, to condemn Israel for an air attack on November 13. See ISRAEL; SYRIA.

Yemen Civil War. In September, U Thant informed the Council that the 14-month UN Observation Mission to Yemen, which had been paid for by Saudi Arabia and the United Arab Republic (UAR), had been recalled. It had failed to persuade the two countries to cease their activities in the Yemeni civil war. See YEMEN.

Racism in South Africa. The Council, at the request of 58 nations, set in motion new moves against the *apartheid* (racial segregation) policies of South Africa. South Africa, however, ignored the Council. In a further move, the Council condemned apartheid and set up a group to study the feasibility of invoking sanctions demanded by Africans and Asians. See SOUTH AFRICA, REPUBLIC OF.

U.S. "Colonies." The 24-nation anticolonialism committee annoyed the U.S. by insisting that American Samoa, Guam, the Virgin Islands, and the Pacific UN Trust Territories of Micronesia were subject to committee demands that they be granted independence. See PACIFIC ISLANDS.

Rhodesia. The newly installed British Labour government responded to a call by the anticolonialism committee by warning white-minority-ruled Rhodesia, formerly Southern Rhodesia, not to declare independence unilaterally. Although Great Britain declared it could not control Rhodesia's internal politics, the committee continued to demand one-man, one-vote rule for the territory. See RHODESIA.

World Trade Conference. The 77 "have-not" nations of Africa, Asia, and Latin America formed a loose but potent alliance at a three-month UN Conference on Trade and Development attended by 119 nations between March 23 and June 16 at Geneva, Switzerland. U Thant hailed it as the decade's "most promising single effort" toward economic development. The 77 nations generated enough voting power in the UN General Assembly to obtain adoption of new UN trade machinery, despite reservations by the United States and other "have" nations. The Assembly authorized regular meetings of the full conference and established a new 55-nation Trade and Development Board as a permanent UN organ. It will seek new world-commodity agreements and other ways to help the have-nots add to their share of world trade, pressuring the haves to reduce tariffs, to open markets, and grant special concessions.

Disarmament. U Thant hailed the 1964 announcements of reduced military budgets by the Soviet Union and the United States, as well as their mutual cutbacks of military production of fissionable materials, which Britain joined. He expressed regret at the Chinese Communist atomic bomb test in October. But he supported proposals for a disarmament "dialogue" among the world nuclear powers, which included China, France, Great Britain, the Soviet Union, and the United States. See CHINA, PEOPLE'S REPUBLIC OF; FRANCE; DISARMAMENT; GREAT BRITAIN.

Special Fund Managing Director Paul Hoffman reported completion by 1964 of more than 36 projects and the training of more than 50,000 persons in developing countries. Typical fund grants in 1964 provided for the start of new engineering schools in Morocco and Syria.

Membership. The Assembly, by acclamation, elected Jordan, Malaysia, The Netherlands, and Uruguay to fill Security Council vacancies. Also by acclamation, the Assembly increased its membership to 115 on December 1, adding Malawi (formerly Nyasaland), Malta, and Zambia (formerly Northern Rhodesia). Alex Quaison-Sackey of Ghana was elected president of the 19th General Assembly, succeeding Dr. Carlos Sosa Rodríguez of Venezuela. See QUAISON-SACKEY, ALEX. MILT FREUDENHEIM

URUGUAY experienced its worst economic and financial crisis in 35 years in 1964. The budget deficit was a serious threat to monetary stability. Inflation, business stagnation, and declining productivity were other signs of the nation's distress. The country did benefit considerably, however, from the Argentine beef shortage because it was able to ship a record 35,746 tons of meat, valued at $14,100,000, in the first quarter of 1964. During the year, too, it was able to register trade surpluses by holding back imports while spurring exports.

On March 1, Luis Giannattasio became president of the National Council of Government—the presidency being rotated every March 1 among members of the governing Blanco party majority.

Population: 2,600,000. **Government:** Council Chairman and President Luis Giannattasio. **Foreign Trade:** exports, $202,000,000; imports, $183,000,000. **Principal Exports:** beef, hides, wool. MARY C. WEBSTER
See also LATIN AMERICA.

VATICAN CITY. See ROMAN CATHOLIC.

VENEZUELA saw proof that its democratic system was strengthening in 1964. When Dr. Raul Leoni succeeded Rómulo Betancourt as president on March 11, it marked the first time that a democratically elected Venezuelan chief of state had fulfilled his term of office and handed over power to a similarly chosen successor. Leoni's greatest achievement was the passage of an $850,000,000 public works bill to widen the economic boom and ease unemployment. See LEONI, RAUL.

On January 27, work began on the Guri Dam project in the Guainía region. Late in the year, the International Bank for Reconstruction and Development granted Venezuela a $44,000,000 loan for highway construction and a power project.

Population: 8,600,000. **Government:** President Raul Leoni. **Foreign Trade:** exports, $2,741,000,000; imports, $983,000,000. **Principal Exports:** iron ore, petroleum, petroleum products. MARY C. WEBSTER
See also LATIN AMERICA.

VETERANS organizations joined leaders in education, labor, industry, and government in saluting the GI Bill of Rights on its 20th anniversary. The Servicemen's Readjustment Act of 1944 was designed to facilitate the demobilization of more than 15,000,000 World War II veterans, and to ease their return to civilian life. It provided for readjustment allowances, tuition to cover costs of education and training, loans, expanded medical services, and employment counseling and job placement.

A special report on the bill's 20-year record pointed out that more than 5,735,000 World War II veterans received Veterans Administration (VA) home, farm, or business loans totaling more than $48,000,000,000. This touched off a building boom that benefited the entire economy. The purchase of new homes created a demand for furniture, appliances, and automobiles. About 2,000,000 veterans attended colleges and universities under the GI Bill. Another 3,500,000 took courses in trade and technical schools. More than 1,500,000 increased their skills in on-the-job training, and 700,000 veterans learned the newest agricultural techniques in on-the-farm training.

During the past two decades, because of the GI Bill, veterans have fared better than nonveterans in our economy. A study completed in 1964 by the U.S. Employment Service revealed that the average annual income of veterans was $5,100, as compared with $3,200 for nonveterans, and that the unemployment rate among veterans was about half that recorded among the nonveterans.

Legislation approved by the 88th Congress and signed into law by the President made veterans pension programs more liberal and modified eligibility provisions for GI insurance.

The amount of pensions paid to veterans of World War I, World War II, and the Korean War, and their widows and dependents, was increased by about 7 per cent, effective Jan. 1, 1965. The highest pensions, $100 to $115 per month, will be paid to veterans with the lowest incomes.

Three groups of disabled veterans, previously ineligible, have been given one year starting May 1, 1965, to enroll in the National Service Life Insurance program. The three groups are: (1) veterans who have a service-connected disability but are otherwise insurable, (2) veterans who are uninsurable because of a service-connected disability but otherwise are in good health, and (3) veterans who are uninsurable because of a nonservice-connected disability and who are unable to buy insurance from a commercial firm at regular rates.

American Legion posts and auxiliary units were urged to work with school officials in seeking out high school students eligible for educational benefits under the Junior GI Bill. Under an amendment, approved by the 88th Congress, these benefits were extended to children of permanently and totally disabled veterans.

Delegates to the 46th national convention in Dallas unanimously endorsed the administration's "War on Poverty" program. Daniel E. Johnson of West Branch, Iowa, was elected national commander.

American Veterans of World War II and Korea (AMVETS), holding their 20th annual convention in Philadelphia, reaffirmed their support of the United Nations (UN) and stated they "do not support war as an instrument of national policy." Lincoln S. Tamraz, of Chicago, was elected national commander.

Veterans of Foreign Wars (VFW), at their 65th annual convention in Cleveland, agreed that the Soviet Union should pay its share of expenses in the United Nations or get out of that organization. John A. Jenkins, of Birmingham, Ala., was elected commander in chief. JOSEPH P. ANDERSON

VETERINARY MEDICINE. See LIVESTOCK.

VIETNAM

GUERRILLA WARFARE continued to sap Vietnam's energies in 1964. It was being fought in the jungles and on the river deltas of South Vietnam by ever-larger military units. It was being fought politically in the streets of Saigon, where the South Vietnamese government suffered repeated shuffles of leadership. Although Maj. Gen. Nguyen Khanh was able to maintain his role as military leader in 1964, it was at

WAR CLOUDS. South Vietnamese troops, bristling with camouflage foliage, crash through underbrush near Saigon under the protective cover of a smoke screen.

United Press Int.

Wide World

HOVERING HELICOPTERS, dwarfed by the surrounding jungle, converge for an attack on a Viet Cong-manned machine gun nest tucked away in the undergrowth.

Wide World

VIETNAM CRISIS prompts meeting between U.S. Secretary of State Dean Rusk, center, Defense Secretary R. S. McNamara, left, and, right, Ambassador Henry Cabot Lodge, Jr. All three leaders visited Vietnam during the year to assess the war effort firsthand.

best a shaky one. Nor was the war confined to South Vietnam alone. Neighboring Cambodia became embroiled in a sharp border dispute with South Vietnam, as did Laos, over guerrilla activities (see CAMBODIA; LAOS). U.S. military involvement deepened until by the end of the year there were reportedly between 22,000 and 24,000 U.S. military men in Vietnam.

World powers such as the Soviet Union and France repeatedly urged that the area be neutralized. But the United States, backed by Great Britain, the Philippines, and Thailand, adamantly refused to withdraw its forces.

Yet there were signs of a growing disenchantment with the war in some U.S. political circles. Some leaders urged that direct military action be taken against communist bases in North Vietnam; others felt that full consideration should be given to proposals for neutralization. These opinions were echoed again in December as a result of some sharp defeats suffered in South Vietnam. Officially, however, the United States continued to argue that the war could be won. It underlined this position in August when it retaliated against North Vietnam for attacks on U.S. destroyers operating in the Gulf of Tonkin.

Tonkin Incidents. On August 2, three North Vietnamese PT boats fired torpedoes and 37 mm. shells at a U.S. destroyer in the international waters of the Gulf of Tonkin, about 30 miles off Vietnam. The destroyer, the 3,300-ton *Maddox*, and four U.S. aircraft fired back, driving off the attackers. On August 4, the U.S. Department of Defense reported that PT boats had again deliberately attacked the *Maddox* and a second U.S. destroyer, the *C. Turner Joy*, in the gulf. The destroyers and covering, carrier-based U.S. aircraft fired on the enemy vessels. At least two of the attacking North Vietnamese PT-boats were sunk. Neither of the U.S. destroyers was damaged.

U.S. retaliation was swift. On August 5, U.S. aircraft bombed North Vietnamese bases, naval craft, and an oil storage depot in a five-hour raid along 100 miles of coast. Almost simultaneously, the U.S. lodged a complaint with the United Nations Security Council protesting the North Vietnamese attacks in international waters. The North Vietnamese, however, who are not members of the UN, refused to recognize the competence of the Security Council to investigate the clash. See UNITED NATIONS.

The Tonkin incident, however, did not really solve the problem of the war in South Vietnam. The government appeared unable to enlist the active support of the people, nor was it able to actually control vast geographical regions in the country. Even Saigon, its major holding, was being subjected to repeated terrorist attacks by the guerrillas.

At the year's end, despite massive U.S. aid, military advice, and support, the South Vietnamese government still was unable to stabilize the country. From the military point of view, there were signs that defeat might be almost inevitable. The Viet Cong forces, which often attacked in regimental strength, were becoming increasingly bold as they carried the fighting closer and closer to Saigon.

Pix from Publix

SNAPPY SALUTE engrosses Major General Nguyen Khanh, head of the South Vietnamese junta that relinquished power to civilian regime.

Backbone

539

Seemingly, no government could be formed in South Vietnam which was capable of enlisting the support of the people. Bitter religious divisions between Roman Catholics and Buddhists divided the country even more.

North Vietnam, over a three-year period, had reportedly sent 30,000 to 40,000 infiltrators into South Vietnam. The flow continued at a stepped-up pace in 1964. About 60 per cent of the infiltrators were military cadres and about 40 per cent were civilians. It was believed that their main infiltration route was the so-called Ho Chi-minh Trail, named for North Vietnamese President Ho Chi-minh. It began at Vinh, a seaport in North Vietnam, crossed into Laos at Mui Gia Pass, and ran into southeastern Laos.

North Vietnam. Population: 17,500,000. **Government:** President Ho Chi-minh; Premier Pham van Dong. **Foreign Trade:** statistics not available.

South Vietnam. Population: 15,950,000. **Government:** Chief of State Phanh Khac Suu; Premier Tran Van Huong. **Foreign Trade:** exports, $45,000,000; imports, $285,000,000. **Principal Exports:** rice, rubber, tea.   JOHN N. STALKER

See also ASIA.

VISTA is the name given the domestic Peace Corps created to operate in the United States as part of President Lyndon B. Johnson's anti-poverty program. The letters stand for "*Volunteers In Service To America.*"

VISTA volunteers were being recruited by the Office of Economic Opportunity, headed by R. Sargent Shriver, Jr., to live and work with poor Americans. The corps was expected to grow to a strength of 5,000. Volunteers will be assigned to Job Corps camps, schools, hospitals, migrant worker communities, Indian reservations, institutions for the mentally ill or retarded, and community action programs in rural and city areas. On these assignments, the volunteers will pass along a variety of trade and professional skills.

VISTA volunteers will be sent, at the request of local agencies, to any of the 50 states, as well as to the District of Columbia and the U.S. territories. They will serve for one year, including four to six weeks in a training course. Local private and public organizations, including selected colleges, will train them for their assignments.

A monthly living allowance will vary according to local conditions, and all medical and dental expenses will be paid. When the volunteers leave the corps, they will get a readjustment allowance of $50 for each month of satisfactory service performed.

VISTA's 35-year-old director, Glenn W. Ferguson, was one of its principal planners and a former associate director of the Peace Corps. Anyone who has reached the age of 18 may apply to join the corps by writing VISTA, Office of Economic Opportunity, Washington, D.C.   WILLIAM McGAFFIN

See also JOB CORPS; SOCIAL WELFARE (Close-Up).

VITAL STATISTICS. Marriage and divorce were on the rise, births continued to fall, and deaths took a semiholiday in the United States during 1964. Not surprisingly, the natural rate of population increase slipped from about 1.22 per cent for 1963 to about 1.19 per cent for 1964.

The crude death rate in 1964 dipped back down from its 12-year high of 9.6 deaths per 1,000 population in 1963 to the 1962 level of 9.4. More hopefully, *infant mortality* (deaths of persons under 1 year of

U.S. Vital Statistics (12 months through November)		
	1964	1963
Live births	4,046,000	4,097,000
Birth rate	21.2*	21.8*
Infant deaths (under age 1)	98,000	103,100
Deaths	1,803,000	1,811,000
Death rate	9.4*	9.6*
Marriages	1,718,000	1,640,000
Divorces (from 36 reporting areas January–November)	268,774	258,456

*Figures per 1,000 of population.

Source: U.S. Public Health Service

age exclusive of stillbirths) continued its almost steady decline since the 1930's. The U.S. rate dropped 1 point in the year to 24.2 deaths per 1,000 live births. It had fallen from about 60 in 1934, 54 in 1940, and 33 in 1950.

In a late-1964 study of final figures for 1963, the U.S. Public Health Service (PHS) reported sharp rises in deaths from respiratory diseases. The increases from 1961—a year relatively free of influenza epidemics—to 1963 ranged from 25 to 32 per cent. It also found a steady increase in deaths due to cancer. The death rate for lung cancer rose to 25 per 100,000 population, from 17 in 1954.

In a special PHS study, it was found that deaths caused by another disease of the lungs, emphysema, had increased by an average of 18 per cent a year from 1953 through 1963. The PHS reported that the death rates for this disease, which has been linked to cigarette smoking, were "substantially higher for males than for females, particularly for ages 35 and over."   ROBERT A. IRWIN

See also CENSUS; HEALTH; POPULATION.

VOCATIONAL EDUCATION. See EDUCATION.

WARREN COMMISSION. A seven-man panel headed by Chief Justice of the United States Earl Warren, after a 10-month investigation into the assassination of President John F. Kennedy, made its report to President Lyndon B. Johnson on September 24. Three days later, on September 27, it released its 888-page report—some 300,000 words printed in a light-blue-covered, 43-ounce volume—for publication. See PUBLISHING; WARREN REPORT (appendix).

The release of the voluminous report set off a race among publishers of books, magazines, and newspapers to come out with full or edited versions. *The New York Times* on the next day, September 28, brought out a special section of 48 pages. It had reproduced the full text of the report's "Chapter I, Summary and Conclusions," by a photographic process. Two publishers of paperbacks crash-produced their versions and had them on sale within four days after they received advance copies from the Government Printing Office on September 25. One of the publishers, Bantam Books, got out its 800-page edition in 80 hours and issued an initial print order of 1,000,000 copies.

Detailed Testimony of 552 witnesses was released on Nov. 23, 1964, the day after solemn tributes were paid to the late President on the first anniversary of his death. This testimony and supporting exhibits, on which the commission based its report, filled 26 volumes. Included were the personal stories of Mrs. John F. Kennedy, President and Mrs. Lyndon B. Johnson, Governor and Mrs. John B. Connally of Texas, and other key figures in the tragedy.

The commission had been appointed by President Johnson on Nov. 29, 1963, charging it "to satisfy itself that the truth is known as far as it can be discovered, and to report its findings and conclusions to him, to the American people, and to the world."

Its members, in addition to Warren, were: Senator Richard B. Russell, Democrat of Georgia; Senator John Sherman Cooper, Republican of Kentucky; Representative T. Hale Boggs, Democrat of Louisiana; Representative Gerald R. Ford, Republican of Michigan; Allen W. Dulles, former director of the Central Intelligence Agency (CIA); and John J. McCloy, former disarmament adviser to President Kennedy. In December, 1963, the commission named J. Lee Rankin, who was solicitor general of the United States in the Eisenhower administration, to act as its general counsel.

The Principal Finding of the commission, that Lee Harvey Oswald acted alone in killing President Kennedy, was generally accepted in the United States and in friendly foreign countries. The conspiratorial theory, however, persisted in the communist world and among other countries critical of the United States.

Among Free World critics of the report, British historian Hugh Trevor-Roper contended the commission had accepted evidence from prosecuting agencies with too little question. Further, he said, it did not make sufficient provision for cross-examining witnesses. Some U.S. critics made the same point in calling the report a masterful, well-documented brief for the prosecution.

Presidential Protection. A four-man special Cabinet committee, with Secretary of the Treasury C. Douglas Dillon serving as chairman, was appointed on September 27 by President Johnson to study the Warren Commission recommendations and work out a program to tighten protection of the President. The other members were: acting Attorney General Nicholas deB. Katzenbach; McGeorge Bundy, special assistant to the President for national security affairs; and John A. McCone, director of the CIA.

On November 27, Dillon announced the first step in the program—the hiring of 75 more Secret Service agents and other personnel at an annual cost of $650,000. The complete program will cost $3,000,000 and take 15 months to implement. Dillon said, "The basic emphasis will be on more effective advance and preventive work by the service in connection with presidential travel, as well as the use of more sophisticated equipment."

The Secret Service staff of 415 agents was expected to be ultimately increased by 50 per cent. The Secret Service files, now ordinary manual files, were to be replaced with a modern computer system. This will be used to process information gathered by the Secret Service, the Federal Bureau of Investigation (FBI), and the CIA to provide an instantaneous surveillance of potential assassins.

The problems of protecting a President will always be complicated, however, by the fact that Presidents dislike protective restraints, and insist on mingling with people. President Johnson, for example, during the election campaign regularly exposed himself to greater danger during slow-moving motorcades by transferring from his safer, rebuilt limousine to the open Secret Service convertible in which he could stand and wave to the crowds. See PRESIDENT OF THE UNITED STATES.

Criticisms of both the Secret Service and the FBI were raised in the Warren Report. There was no move in Congress, however, to take all or part of the presidential protection function away from the Secret Service and give it to the FBI—a possible course of action discussed by the Warren Commission. Nor, apparently, was there any disposition on the part of the Dillon committee to make such a recommendation.

The commission also had criticized the news media's coverage of the assassination. Seventeen representatives of the press met in Washington, D.C., in October and issued a statement conceding there were "serious problems . . . in which activities of press and broadcasters may influence events." But the newsmen were concerned that the adoption of codes or use of pool arrangements might "decrease the flow of information to which the public is entitled." See PUBLISHING.

A larger question raised by the assassination, that of the inadequate system of succession to the presidency, was tackled in a proposed constitutional amendment sponsored by Democratic Senator Birch Bayh of Indiana. Among other things, it set forth the steps to be taken for a Vice-President to become acting President if the President should be disabled. It also empowered the President to nominate a new Vice-President should that office become vacant. The amendment passed the Senate 65 to 0, but since the House failed to act on it, the measure would have to be reintroduced for consideration when the new 89th Congress convened. WILLIAM McGAFFIN

WASHINGTON, D.C.

WASHINGTON, D.C. Thanks to Amendment 23 of the U.S. Constitution, Washington, D.C., voted for the first time in a U.S. presidential election. Some 89 per cent of the city's registered voters cast ballots and more than 85 per cent voted Democratic. Supporters of a popularly chosen city government were encouraged by the turnout.

Home rule might make easier the attainment of two major proposals of the year. In May, a council of eminent experts announced a "grand design" to transform Pennsylvania Avenue, from the U.S. Capitol to the White House, into the nation's finest ceremonial street. Without urban renewal authority —long denied by the Congress—its chances were questionable. In November, a 25-mile rapid transit line was proposed for the city and some nearby suburbs. It faces congressional hurdles similar to those that killed a previous project plan in 1963.

The Washington area's growth, however, was rapid. U.S. Bureau of the Census data showed it to be the fastest growing and ninth largest metropolitan area in overall size. Its unemployment total and business failures were lowest among metropolitan areas. In August, completion of the 65-mile beltway around the city spurred further suburban development. Also, building permits within the central city hit a record high. DONALD W. LIEF

See also CITY PLANNING (picture); MUSIC.

WATER AND FLOOD CONTROL. The rising demand for fresh, clean water—for home, industry, and farm—made itself felt on several fronts in 1964. Congress passed the Water Resources Research Act in July, to provide grants for universities and scientific foundations to tackle critical water problems. Also, a world-wide study, the International Hydrological Decade, was to open under United Nations auspices on Jan. 1, 1965 (see SCIENCE AND RESEARCH).

The importance of water was made clear by the drought that afflicted most of the nation during the year (see SOIL CONSERVATION; WEATHER). The world's largest source of fresh water, the Great Lakes, receded to record low levels. Lakes Michigan and Huron dropped more than three feet. Losses to shippers, hydroelectric utilities, and others were estimated at $100,000,000 (see map).

River Basins. When it ratified the Columbia River treaty in mid-September, Canada cleared the way for joint U.S.-Canadian development of the Upper Columbia Basin. Three new dams in British Columbia and one in Montana will increase water storage in the basin by 20,500,000 acre-feet, adding new flood control benefits and 2,800,000 kilowatts of peak-load power. See CANADA.

The Supreme Court of the United States issued a final decree on March 9 in the Arizona versus California Lower Colorado River water-allocation case.

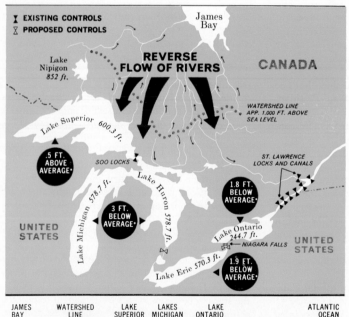

ONE PROPOSED PLAN to stabilize the fluctuating water levels of the Great Lakes would reverse the flow of Canadian rivers that now drain into James Bay, a lower arm of Hudson Bay. Diversion of this water plus control of the flow of the St. Clair and Niagara rivers could regulate, respectively, the water levels of Lakes Michigan, Huron, and Erie.

*"Average" for each lake is its mean surface level over the 104-year period, 1860-1963, as it is measured above the mean water level in the St. Lawrence River at Father Point, about 170 miles northeast of Quebec City. Sources: U.S. Army Corps of Engineers and ENGINEERING NEWS-RECORD. YEAR BOOK map

The Bureau of Reclamation spent $367,000,000 in fiscal 1964 on dams and other facilities, completing six dams with a total storage capacity of 1,400,000,000,000 gallons, 427 miles of canals and pipelines, and 1,379 miles of transmission lines. Construction began on nine projects, including the Ruedi Dam, first phase of the $170,000,000 Frying Pan-Arkansas Project in Colorado. The dam will divert water from the Rockies' western slope across the Continental Divide into the Arkansas River.

The bureau in 1964 conducted training programs for 400 engineers and officials of foreign countries, and bureau engineers worked on water problems in five foreign lands.

Desalination. President Lyndon B. Johnson called on the Atomic Energy Commission and the Department of the Interior in July to develop a plan for large-scale desalting of sea water—possibly by using nuclear power. The President asked for an immediate start on an "aggressive and imaginative program" for low-cost conversion of sea water, and he stressed the need to share the technological benefits with other nations. He invited 114 nations to take part in an international symposium on water desalination in Washington, D.C., Oct. 3 to 9, 1965. See CHEMISTRY.

Flood Control. The water resources activities of the U.S. Army Corps of Engineers expanded, with a record appropriation of $1,220,400,000, for fiscal 1965. The Mississippi River Flood Control Project received the largest amount, $77,862,000.

High water in the Ohio River Basin in March caused damage estimated at $106,000,000 and took 18 lives. Montana suffered its worst natural disaster in an early-June flood that took 30 lives and destroyed more than $70,000,000 in property. Late-December rains and floods in Oregon and northern California killed about 40 persons and caused damage of nearly $1,000,000,000.   A. L. NEWMAN

See also DAM; DISASTERS; ELECTRIC POWER; WATERWAYS.

WATERWAYS.

WATERWAYS. Shallow-draught carriers plying the nation's 25,260-mile inland waterway system on a for-hire or self-service basis delivered an estimated record 441,500,000 net tons of freight, about $2\frac{1}{2}$ per cent more than in 1963. Almost half of this tonnage was towed on the Mississippi River and its tributaries. Freight operating revenues of 82 domestic water carriers were expected to reach $260,000,000.

New Waterways. On February 27, President Lyndon B. Johnson threw a switch at Palatka, Fla., to break ground for the 185-mile, $158,000,000 Cross-Florida Barge Canal, to link Jacksonville on the St. Johns River near the Atlantic Ocean with Yankeetown on the Gulf of Mexico. Excavating the 107-mile stretch from Palatka to the Gulf constitutes the project's major engineering task. When completed in 1974, it will cut 610 miles off the open-ocean route around Key West.

The full 225-mile length of the Chattahoochee River waterway was opened to barge traffic from the Gulf of Mexico to Columbus, Ga., when ceremonies marking the occasion were held in that city on September 11.

The St. Lawrence Seaway had a sensational year, despite especially low water levels that meant some ships had to reduce their loads (see WATER AND FLOOD CONTROL). Cargo on the Montreal-Lake Ontario artery exceeded 1963 by a surprising 29 per cent, totaling 39,910,000 tons in 1964—almost double the tonnage of its opening year, 1959.

A New Ship appeared on the Great Lakes. She was the first maximum-size, diesel-powered lake bulk carrier, the Canada Steamship Lines' 730-foot *Saguenay*, which set three new Great Lakes cargo records on her maiden voyage. She loaded a record 28,526 net tons of iron ore at Seven Islands, Quebec, on August 13. After unloading at Cleveland, she went to Ashtabula, Ohio, and took on a record 28,252-ton coal cargo for Hamilton, Ontario. From the Canadian lakehead on Lake Superior, she carried a record 28,368 net tons (945,596 bushels) of wheat to Montreal.   MARK REINSBERG

See also CANADA; SHIP.

WEATHER.

WEATHER. The United States suffered one of its most disastrous years in weather history in 1964. It began with one of the great blizzards of the century which reached its greatest fury, in mid-January, over the Middle Atlantic states and left 140 persons dead in its wake. Even more devastating were a series of floods. They swept Arkansas, Indiana, Kentucky, Ohio, Vermont, and West Virginia in March, and Montana in June. Then, just before the Christmas holidays, the West Coast was hit by a blizzard, followed by heavy rains and high winds. The resulting run-off caused the worst floods to inundate far western states in years. More than 40 persons perished in the disaster and thousands more were left homeless.

Tornadoes and hurricanes also made an impact on the nation. In July, Missouri and Nebraska were struck by tornadoes. And in September, Florida, Georgia, Louisiana, and Texas were swept by hurricanes. Drought plagued the East during these months as it did Puerto Rico, one of the 24 regions President Lyndon B. Johnson officially declared as "disaster areas." See DISASTERS.

Dust and Wind Studies. The dust belt created by the eruption of the Agung volcano on Bali, in 1963, provided weathermen with new information about air currents in the upper atmosphere. The belt of dust moved from the Northern to the Southern Hemisphere, and back again, in about a year's time, which showed that the atmosphere some 170,000 feet above the earth undergoes annual fluctuation.

In April, at a meeting of the International Scientific Radio Union in Washington, D.C., Dr. Colin O. Hines of the University of Chicago reported that

Wide World

FLOOD WATERS brought on by torrential year-end rains and the collapse of a levee near Walnut Grove, Calif., forced these deer to migrate to higher land.

winds are partly responsible for irregularities in the ionosphere which disrupt long distance radio communications. Air rushing at 50 miles or more above the earth forms a giant scissorlike movement which creates irregular shearing winds and whirling eddies.

Computer Prediction. The link between snow cover or ocean temperatures and long-term weather patterns was the basis for a new method of weather prediction reported by Dr. Julian Adem of the National University of Mexico. At a June symposium in Boulder, Colo., he had demonstrated his method for predicting the temperature, as long as a season in advance, by using a mathematical model programmed on an electronic computer.

International Minerals & Chemical Corporation of Skokie, Ill., also tested a computerized system that accurately predetermined the effect of weather on crops by keeping continuous records of such factors as current soil temperatures, moisture, and rainfall. The system weighs the data against a history of soil conditions since 1960, and after a series of mathematical computations, foretells the favorable planting, growing, and harvesting conditions.

Nimbus. By far the most dramatic and significant technical development of the year was the launching of the revolutionary Nimbus I weather satellite by the National Aeronautics and Space Administration (NASA) from Point Arguello, California. Soon after it was put in orbit, in August, it relayed the best pictures ever taken by a weather satellite, in what was described as "a major breakthrough in man's battle with the weather." The spacecraft with 40,000 components weighs 830 pounds, making it the world's largest satellite of its type. Nimbus carries a revolutionary "triple eye" system that consists of two sets

of television cameras and one set of infrared radiometers for "taking pictures" of the earth's surface.

On November 5, the United States signed an agreement with the Soviet Union to exchange weather data from meteorological satellites. The Soviet Union was expected to launch its first weather satellite early in 1965. Sergei Lenormand

See also Europe (picture); Pollution; Space Travel; Water and Flood Control.

WEIGHT LIFTING. See Sports.

WEST INDIES FEDERATION. See Jamaica; Trinidad-Tobago.

WESTERN SAMOA, self-governing since 1962, won the admiration of various United Nations (UN) agencies during 1964. It was considered a model for independent small countries in the South Pacific, so much so that the UN decided to establish its regional office at Apia, Western Samoa's capital, rather than on Fiji Island.

As the first Polynesian territory to regain its independence after experiencing pre-World War I colonial rule and mandate status later, Western Samoa proved a leisurely pacemaker in democratic rule and economic expansion. With UN technical aid and increased spending by New Zealand, which still handled Samoa's external relations, little recrimination could be heard against either past colonialism before World War I, or its present status as a sovereign state.

Population: 128,000. **Government:** His Highness Malietoa Tanumafili II; Prime Minister Fiame Mata'afa Faumuina Mulinu's II. **Foreign Trade:** exports, $8,000,000; imports, $8,000,000. **Principal Exports:** bananas, cocoa beans, copra. Alastair Burnet

WHEELER, EARLE GILMORE (1908-   ), Army Chief of Staff since the fall of 1962, was advanced to chairman of the Joint Chiefs of Staff in July, 1964. He replaced General Maxwell D. Taylor, who went to South Vietnam as U.S. ambassador.

The West Point graduate (1932) and veteran of 32 years in the service was made a full general in 1962. Wheeler had his only combat service (five months) as chief of staff of the 63rd Infantry Division in World War II. He served with the Allied Forces in Southern Europe (1952-1955). Subsequent posts include commanding general of the 2nd Armored Division (1958-1960) and deputy commander in chief of the U.S. European Command (1962).

Earle Wheeler was born in Washington, D.C. He joined the National Guard at 16, and became a sergeant before going to West Point (1928).

See also NATIONAL DEFENSE.

WILDLIFE. A new, more equitable, revenue-sharing law, enacted on August 30, was expected to speed federal acquisition of rapidly disappearing wetlands in the Dakotas and Minnesota. These wetlands, with their glacier-created "potholes," provide ideal breeding grounds for ducks and other migratory waterfowl. About 80 per cent of the nation's young ducks are raised in this "duck factory."

In 1961, Congress had authorized $105,000,000 for purchases of wetlands for refuges over a seven-year period. In the ensuing three years, only about $25,000,000 had been spent and 165,000 acres acquired. The 1961 law provided that affected counties would be compensated for the loss of tax revenue by drawing 25 per cent of the net proceeds from oil leasing on the refuge or sale of other refuge products. To many counties this seemed an uncertain source of revenue.

To meet this problem, the 1964 law allowed counties the choice of receiving annual payments of either the 25 per cent of net receipts or three-fourths of 1 per cent of the cost of the acquired land. The new law was expected to speed acquisition of more than 2,000,000 acres of wetlands.

Despite the "duck factory's" sixth year of drought, most duck species managed to increase slightly in 1964. As a result, the same moderately liberal bag limits and seasons as in 1963 generally prevailed (see HUNTING AND FISHING).

Pesticide Residues in the eggs and vital organs of numerous wildlife species were collected from all parts of the country in 1964. Researchers noted pronounced effects on the survival and reproduction of species such as quail, pheasants, and eagles. The ultimate significance of the widespread contamination from these chemicals, however, was not yet fully known to interested agencies. See CHEMICAL INDUSTRY; POLLUTION.

World Conservation. The International Union for Conservation of Nature and Natural Resources (IUCN) grew to a membership of 60 nations in 1964. This reflected a growing world concern with the preservation of rare and endangered species of wildlife, especially in the new African countries. During the year, the U.S. Department of the Interior began studying the effects of the proposed test-stocking of the wilds of North America with exotic big-game animals, such as the Barbary sheep and the handsome Cape oryx from Africa and the Siberian ibex from Asia.   A. L. NEWMAN

See also ZOOLOGY; ZOOS AND AQUARIUMS; Section Two, CALL TO THE WILDERNESS.

WILKINS, ROY (1901-   ), was the Spingarn laureate of 1964. The National Association for the Advancement of Colored People (NAACP) conferred the medal on its executive secretary as a "great American who has made a distinctive and immeasurable contribution to the advancement of the American people and the national purpose." Wilkins joined NAACP's national staff as an assistant executive secretary (1931), also edited its *Crisis* magazine (1934-1949), and has been executive secretary since 1955. See NEGRO (picture).

While managing editor of the weekly Negro newspaper *Call* (1923-1931) in Kansas City, Mo., Wilkins had his first personal experience with widespread segregation. "Kansas City ate my heart out," he said. Wilkins waged campaigns, and often took personal risks to investigate situations there and in parts of the South.

Roy Wilkins was born in St. Louis, Mo. His mother died when he was 3. Then he lived with an aunt and uncle in St. Paul, graduating from the University of Minnesota in 1923.

WILSON, (JAMES) HAROLD (1916-   ), leader of the British Labour party, took office as prime minister of Great Britain on October 16. The 48-year-old leader is the youngest man to hold the office in the 20th century. See GREAT BRITAIN.

Britain's new leader was born on March 11, 1916, in Huddersfield, Yorkshire, where his father was a chemist. A studious boy, Wilson won a history scholarship to Oxford University. During World War II, he served in a series of desk jobs. In 1945, he won a seat in the Commons as a representative of Ormskirk, near Liverpool. Two years later he became president of the Board of Trade. He took over as head of the Labour party in 1963.

Wilson is a pipe smoker. He drives a Ford automobile and buys his suits off the rack. Wilson married Gladys Mary Baldwin, a stenographer, in 1940. They have two sons—Robin, 21, and Giles, 16. One of Wilson's most enduring memories is of a trip he took to London with his father when he was 8 years old. While strolling down Downing Street, Wilson's father posed him on the doorstep of No. 10, the prime minister's residence. With the Labour party's victory, Wilson moved beyond the step and directly into the prime minister's office.   WALTER F. MORSE

WORDS AND PHRASES, NEW. The presidential election, the civil rights movement, and foreign affairs added new words to the language in 1964 and gave old words new meanings. Among the new words and phrases that became current were:

antimovie. A motion picture using an old plot in parody.

brain drain. A movement of large numbers of able persons from one country to another, or from one area of a nation to another.

chimponaut. A chimpanzee used to explore the effects of conditions in space on man.

cluster development. An orderly suburban development that utilizes its acreage economically.

cross-busing. A plan of school integration in which white children are transported by bus to predominantly nonwhite schools, and vice versa, to help achieve a racial balance.

discothèque. A small dance room where music is supplied by a jukebox and live musicians, who sometimes accompany the recorded music.

diving saucer. A research submarine capable of diving to depths of up to 1,000 feet.

featherfooting. The even, gradual acceleration of an automobile.

frontlash. President Lyndon B. Johnson's term for the disaffected Republicans that he expected would vote Democratic in the 1964 election.

Goldwaterism. Term used for a political philosophy espoused by Senator Barry M. Goldwater, aspects of which are regarded by its critics as reactionary.

Homo habilis. Name given to fossil remains of what has been asserted to be an ancestor of man who lived about 2,000,000 years ago. See Section Two, MAN'S BEGINNINGS.

ladder down. To bring down an airplane from a stack in steps of a thousand feet.

mom art. A portrait of the painter's mother painted by the artist himself.

mooncraft. A vehicle designed to reach the moon.

multiversity. Term for the modern university with its various, and sometimes far-flung, schools and colleges all under one name and one board.

outness. The tendency to view things far differently than ordinary persons do.

quasar. A distant object in space radiating strong radio waves. See Section Two, THE UNFOLDING UNIVERSE.

smogration. The pollution of an area by smog.

stall-in. The deliberate organized stalling of automobiles on a highway to protest racial discrimination.

watusi. One of a several dance steps based on the twist, such as the frug and the monkey.

white backlash. The hostility of whites to the civil rights movement.

Zonian. A citizen of the United States residing in the Panama Canal Zone.   I. WILLIS RUSSELL

WORLD SERIES. See BASEBALL; Section One, RED SMITH ON SPORTS.

WRESTLING. Oklahoma State made its 24th National Collegiate Athletic Association (NCAA) victory its most resounding by scoring a record 87 points in the championships at Cornell. Defending champion Oklahoma was second with 58 points, and Iowa took third place with 46 points.

In the Amateur Athletic Union (AAU) competition at the New York World's Fair, the New York Athletic Club broke the San Francisco Olympic Club's monopoly by defeating the defending cham-

pions in the free-style competition. San Francisco, however, successfully retained its title in the Greco-Roman competition.

Western State of Gunnison, Colo., scored 51 points to win the NCAA small-college championship. Next in line was Colorado Mines with 49 points. Moorhead State College of Minnesota beat defending champion Lock Haven State College of Pennsylvania in the final rounds of the 51-team National Association of Intercollegiate Athletics (NAIA) competition.   STANLEY ISAACS

YEMEN was plunged into its worst governmental crisis, late in December, since the ousting of Imam Mohammed al-Badr in 1962. Six Yemeni cabinet ministers resigned because of differences with President Abdullah al-Salal. Their resignations, coupled with those of three other high officials a few days earlier, crippled the government of Premier Hamoud al-Jaifi.

The cabinet frictions had developed over a formula for settling the Yemeni civil war which had been worked out by President Gamal Abdel Nasser of the United Arab Republic (UAR) and King Faisal of Saudi Arabia. The UAR's troops, of which there were about 40,000 in Yemen, supported the republican regime. Saudi Arabia gave aid to the royalists who remained loyal to the deposed imam.

Both Nasser and Faisal had agreed in September to work out a "peaceful settlement" of the two-year-old civil war in which each side would reduce its aid to the two Yemeni factions. They also reportedly agreed to try to compose a new coalition government, excluding both President al-Salal and the imam. The dissident ministers resented these moves as interference in Yemen's internal affairs.

A cease-fire that went into effect on November 8 proved short-lived. By December 3, Egyptian planes had resumed their bombings in a wide area, especially in the northwest mountains where the dethroned imam had reportedly withdrawn after big Egyptian military pushes in August and September.

Population: 5,000,000. **Government:** President Abdullah al-Salal; Premier Hamoud al-Jaifi. **Foreign Trade:** no statistics available. **Principal Exports:** coffee, hides and skins, salt.   WILLIAM SPENCER

See also MIDDLE EAST.

YOUNG MEN'S CHRISTIAN ASSOCIATION (YMCA) authorized the establishment of a national service corps patterned after the domestic Peace Corps. The program, called "Pacemakers," will operate for three years on an experimental basis through local associations and branches in 50 key cities. Young men and women between the ages of 18 and 28 will be recruited to help in their home communities with problems in education, job training, race relations, civic participation, and citizenship.

The YMCA's National Young Adult Assembly, meeting at Williams Bay, Wis., took formal action calling for the creation of a National Adult Council as the official policy-making body for young adults in the YMCA. Such a council would be composed of delegates appointed from area councils, state committees, and service groups.

The 75th anniversary of YMCA work with high school youth was observed in special ceremonies at Dickinson County Community High School, Chapman, Kans., site of the YMCA's first high school youth club. The program, started in 1889 by D. F. Shirks and a small group of his students, has grown into 12,000 Hi-Y (boys) and Tri-Hi-Y (girls) clubs with 350,000 teen-age members.

James F. Bunting became general secretary of the YMCA on February 1, and W. Walter Williams of Seattle, Wash., was elected president of the YMCA National Council at its 38th annual meeting in Detroit, Mich.   JOSEPH P. ANDERSON

YOUNG WOMEN'S CHRISTIAN ASSOCIATION (YWCA) took two actions of major significance in 1964. One was a change in its internal organization, and the other, a strengthening of its stand on integration. The delegates voted to end the separation of their membership into two categories—voting and nonvoting. To be a voting member of the YWCA in the past, a woman had to assent to a pledge of Christian service, generally considered Protestant in its context. This requirement was difficult for many Roman Catholics to accept, and even more so for non-Christians and for persons without religious affiliation. This group will now have full voting status.

In a second major action, the delegates, meeting at Cleveland, Ohio, in April, called for a renewed dedication to integration. They adopted a resolution, by an almost unanimous vote, urging that high priority be given to a "conscious and deliberate effort to assure complete racial integration in all aspects of YWCA membership, leadership, and programs, in the use of facilities and in administrative and employment practices, and also to work for reconciliation and full integration immediately in all areas of community life."

Mrs. Lloyd J. Marti, of Hastings, Nebr., was re-elected president.   JOSEPH P. ANDERSON

YUGOSLAVIA continued striving to get the best of many worlds without committing itself to any single one. In June, President Tito visited Finland where he expounded the cause of nonalignment. Later, on a reverse tack, he met Soviet Premier Nikita S. Khrushchev in Leningrad and joined him in a communiqué stressing the "monolithic unity" of communism. He did so notwithstanding his consistent espousal of nationalist communism since his 1948 break with Stalin. See COMMUNISM; RUSSIA.

Yugoslavia's commercial and political relations with the other East European nations were stimulated during the year, and links were established with the Council for Mutual Economic Assistance. On June 22, Tito met secretly with Romanian communist leader Gheorghe Gheorghiu-Dej to discuss unification of their policies regarding the Sino-Soviet split. He urged the Romanian leader to exercise restraint in order to avoid an open split with Moscow. The two met again on September 7 to inaugurate construction of a joint power project at the Danube's historic Iron Gate.

Tito hoped to assume the leadership of the nonaligned nations, a position left vacant by the death of India's Jawaharlal Nehru (see INDIA). At a meeting in Cairo in early October, he led the moderate forces in championing peaceful coexistence and nuclear disarmament with international inspection and control. He opposed the Chinese Communist-inspired militancy of Indonesia's President Sukarno (see INDONESIA).

Yugoslavian-United States relations were highlighted by an agreement to exchange Fulbright scholars and professors, the first such exchange with a communist nation.

On the political and socioeconomic fronts, liberalization continued. There was public debate on such sensitive problems as the rising cost of living. A genuine effort was made to give the new parliament greater responsibility, de-emphasizing the role of the Communist party. Workers were given the right to strike under certain circumstances for the first time in any communist state.

The economy was buoyant. Production and exports climbed rapidly, but imports rose higher, creating balance of payments problems. Booming tourism added an estimated $100,000,000 to the nation's income.

Population: 19,500,000. **Government:** President Tito; Vice-President Alexsandar Ranković. **Foreign Trade:** exports, $848,000,000; imports, $1,398,000,-000. **Principal Exports:** machinery, meats, metal products, ships and boats.   TOM AND HARLE DAMMANN

ZAMBIA, formerly Northern Rhodesia, became an independent African republic on October 24. In an election held earlier, Prime Minister Kenneth Kaunda's United National Independence Party (UNIP) had captured a majority of the seats in the legislative assembly. With independence, Kaunda became president. Barotseland, a separate British protectorate within Zambia's boundaries, agreed to seek independence as part of the new republic.

In July, long-standing hostility between members of the Lumpa Church and the UNIP flared into open rebellion, causing British Governor-General Sir Evelyn Hone to assume emergency powers.

Population: 3,650,000. **Government:** President Kenneth Kaunda. **Foreign Trade:** no statistics available. **Principal Exports:** asbestos, cobalt metal, copper, lead, zinc.   BENJAMIN E. THOMAS

See also AFRICA; KAUNDA, KENNETH.

ZANZIBAR. See TANZANIA.

ZOOLOGY.

Attention was increasingly directed toward the study and preservation of rare animal species. In January, 50 scientists from seven countries sailed to the Galápagos Islands where animal species have evolved free of outside influences over a long period of time. Many of the life forms, one of which is the marine iguana, are found nowhere else but on these islands. There, the albatross and cormorants have lost their ability to fly, and the same species of finch has evolved differently on each island. One group of these finches has even learned to use sticks to dig for food. Zoologists have established a foundation, headed by the Belgian paleontologist Victor van Straelen, to prevent the extinction of the Galápagos animals.

Zoologists made wide use of electronics in their studies of wildlife during 1964. They attached tiny transmitters to wolves, foxes, pheasants, and many other species of animals so that the actions of these animals could be carefully traced. One scientist was working on a transmitter that could be attached to snakes without interfering with their slithering. A problem yet to be solved is how the tiny transmitters can be improved so that their signals can be received at long distances.

Whale Echos. According to a theory developed by zoologists in Holland after a study of the records of 133 mass whale strandings in various parts of the world, these mammals founder on beaches and die because their echo-sounding ability becomes scrambled and useless. Whales emit a wide variety of sounds which scientists believe enable them to avoid collisions, maintain orderly formations, navigate, and find prey. When their heads rise out of the water or when they mill around close to each other, the whales cannot screen the echo pings.

Diet Tames the Savage Beast. Diet not only affects weight and health but also character, at least in the case of ferrets under study at the National Animal Disease Laboratory in Ames, Iowa. There, ferrets, which are normally fierce killers and hostile to human beings, are under study because they are highly susceptible to canine distemper. With a daily diet of three parts fresh horsemeat, two parts dog meal, and one part fresh milk, the ferrets became gentle and responsive to the handling of veterinarians at the laboratory. When these animals were permitted to return to their normal meat diet, however, they became fierce again.

Camel's Thirst. The camel's ability to store up water in its body for long desert trips is due to the unique composition of its blood, and not to its hump, which is a reserve area for food. Dr. Kalman Perk of Hebrew University at Rehovot, Israel, discovered that plasma in the camel's blood is extraordinarily high in albumin of a kind that retains water in the blood stream even when the animal's tissue has been markedly depleted. The camel, according to Dr. Perk, has the ability to store up 30 gallons of water at one filling. SERGEI LENORMAND

ZOOS AND AQUARIUMS.

The New York Zoological Park (Bronx Zoo) opened a new building for aquatic birds in September, 1964. Two hundred birds of 70 species were included in the natural habitat exhibits. Some of the exhibits had no cage fronts between the public and the birds.

Realism was stressed in the exhibits. One contained full-size cypress tree trunks from the South. Also, an effort was being made in a specialized exhibit to show puffins, which rarely have been seen in zoos. Realism in the puffin cage was carried to such an extent that bird droppings were painted on the face of an artificial cliff in the cage. The droppings had a second purpose: to make the birds feel immediately at home.

A Gift from Jackie. Also in New York, the Central Park Zoo was presented a pair of fallow deer by Mrs. John F. Kennedy. They went on display at the Noah's Ark collection of animals in October. The deer had been a gift to the former first family from the president of Ireland, Éamon de Valéra, and had been kept at Wexford, the Kennedy's country place in Virginia.

The National Zoo in Washington, D.C., was completing a remodeling of its birdhouse, and was constructing an unusually shaped bird cage 90 feet high and 140 feet across. The cage was expected to be ready for its tenants in 1965.

The St. Louis Zoo was remodeling its two waterfowl lakes and was building a central plaza of concrete between them. The display also included a bird cage 30 feet high and 22 feet in diameter, and a goldfish pond on the plaza. Islands for two different species of gibbons were constructed near the plaza and the South Lake. New walkways brought better circulation of crowds. The zoo was developing also a department to plan programs for schoolchildren with the board of education.

The San Diego Zoo continued its redesigning of exhibits and eliminated its cyclone fence. The Houston Zoo built a new, small mammal house. The Cincinnati Zoo remodeled several old structures, and built a new children's zoo. In Chicago, the Lincoln Park Zoo opened a "Farm in the Zoo" for children, and the Brookfield Zoo, in the suburbs of the city, appointed two new directors to replace Robert Bean, who stepped down as director after 18 years. The men were Ronald L. Blakely, who became director of the animal collections, and Encil E. Rains, director of administration.

Tragedy Struck Salt Lake City's Hogle Zoological Gardens when curator Jerry de Bary died after being bitten by an African puff adder, one of the world's deadliest snakes. R. MARLIN PERKINS

A ROTUND ORANG-UTAN, oozing plump aplomb, placidly peers at photographer. He is a perennial favorite of visitors to the Bronx, N.Y., zoo.

Alan Fontaine

"His memory would be that he made Americans realize
that they were a young people—and youth is hope...
He had removed from them the slander of cynicism;
he had believed in the future of America; and they
had believed in him. In his brief moment, he had given
America belief, as well as hope."—Theodore H. White

From the 1964 edition of THE WORLD BOOK YEAR BOOK

THE WARREN REPORT

Summary and Conclusions from the Report of
The President's Commission on the Assassination of
President John F. Kennedy

PRESIDENT JOHN F. KENNEDY
(1917-1963)

The complete summary of the official report on
the assassination of John Fitzgerald Kennedy, 35th
President of the United States, in Dallas, Tex.,
on Nov. 22, 1963. The report was prepared under
the chairmanship of Chief Justice Earl Warren.

United Press Int.

BEFORE THE SHOTS RANG OUT, President John F. Kennedy rode through the streets of Dallas.

THE ASSASSINATION of John Fitzgerald Kennedy on Nov. 22, 1963, was a cruel and shocking act of violence directed against a man, a family, a nation, and against all mankind. A young and vigorous leader whose years of public and private life stretched before him was the victim of the fourth presidential assassination in the history of a country dedicated to the concepts of reasoned argument and peaceful political change. This commission was created on Nov. 29, 1963, in recognition of the right of people everywhere to full and truthful knowledge concerning these events. This report endeavors to fulfill that right and to appraise this tragedy by the light of reason and the standard of fairness. It has been prepared with a deep awareness of the commission's responsibility to present to the American people an objective report of the facts relating to the assassination.

Narrative of Events

AT 11:40 A.M., central standard time, on Friday, Nov. 22, 1963, President John F. Kennedy, Mrs. Kennedy, and their party arrived at Love Field, Dallas, Tex. Behind them was the first day of a Texas trip planned five months before by the President, Vice-President Lyndon B. Johnson, and John B. Connally, Jr., governor of Texas. After leaving the White House on Thursday morning, the President had flown initially to San Antonio where Vice-President Johnson joined the party and the President dedicated new research facilities at the U.S. Air Force School of Aerospace Medicine. Following a testimonial dinner in Houston for U.S. Representative Albert Thomas, the

President flew to Fort Worth where he spent the night and spoke at a large breakfast gathering on Friday.

Planned for later that day were a motorcade through downtown Dallas, a luncheon speech at the Trade Mart, and a flight to Austin where the President would attend a reception and speak at a Democratic fund-raising dinner. From Austin, he would proceed to the Texas ranch of the Vice-President. Evident on this trip were the varied roles which an American President performs—Head of State, Chief Executive, party leader, and, in this instance, prospective candidate for re-election.

The Dallas motorcade, it was hoped, would evoke a demonstration of the President's personal popularity in a city which he had lost in the 1960 election. Once it had been decided that the trip to Texas would span two days, those responsible for planning, primarily Governor Connally and Kenneth O'Donnell, a special assistant to the President, agreed that a motorcade through Dallas would be desirable. The Secret Service was told on November 8 that 45 minutes had been allotted to a motorcade procession from Love Field to the site of a luncheon planned by Dallas business and civic leaders in honor of the President.

Route Widely Publicized

After considering the facilities and security problems of several buildings, the Trade Mart was chosen as the luncheon site. Given this selection, and in accordance with the customary practice of affording the greatest number of people an opportunity to see the President, the motorcade route selected was a natural one. The route was approved by the local host committee and White House representatives on November 18, and publicized in the local papers starting on November 19. This advance publicity made it clear that the motorcade would leave Main Street and pass the intersection of Elm and Houston Streets as it proceeded to the Trade Mart by way of the Stemmons Freeway.

By midmorning of November 22, clearing skies in Dallas dispelled the threat of rain and the President greeted the crowds from his open limousine without the "bubbletop," which was at that time a plastic shield furnishing protection only against inclement weather. To the left of the President, in the rear seat, was Mrs. Kennedy. In the jump seats were Governor Connally, who was in front of the President, and Mrs. Connally at the governor's left. Agent William R. Greer of the Secret Service was driving, and Agent Roy H. Kellerman was sitting to his right.

Directly behind the presidential limousine was an open "follow-up" car with eight Secret Service agents, two in the front seat, two in the rear, and two on each running board. These agents, in accordance with normal Secret Service procedures, were instructed to scan the crowds, the roofs, windows of buildings, overpasses, and crossings for signs of trouble. Behind the follow-up car was the vice-presidential car carrying Vice-President and Mrs. Johnson and Senator Ralph W. Yarborough. Next were a vice-presidential follow-up car and several cars and buses for additional dignitaries, press representatives, and others.

The motorcade left Love Field shortly after 11:50 A.M., and proceeded through residential neighborhoods, stopping twice at the President's request to

THE PRESIDENT IS SHOT. Mrs. Kennedy leans over her husband's
slumped form as Secret Service agent leaps aboard limousine.

greet well-wishers among the friendly crowds. Each
time the President's car halted, Secret Service agents
from the follow-up car moved forward to assume a
protective stance near the President and Mrs. Kennedy. As the motorcade reached Main Street, a principal east-west artery in downtown Dallas, the welcome became tumultuous.

At the extreme west end of Main Street, the motorcade turned right on Houston Street and proceeded
north for one block in order to make a left turn on
Elm Street, the most direct and convenient approach
to the Stemmons Freeway and the Trade Mart. As
the President's car approached the intersection of
Houston and Elm Streets, there loomed directly ahead
on the intersection's northwest corner a seven-story,
orange brick warehouse and office building, the Texas
School Book Depository. Riding in the Vice-President's car, Agent Rufus W. Youngblood of the Secret
Service noticed that the clock atop the building indicated 12:30 P.M., the scheduled arrival time at the
Trade Mart.

The Shots Ring Out

The President's car, which had been going north,
made a sharp turn toward the southwest onto Elm
Street. At a speed of about 11 miles per hour, it started
down the gradual descent toward a railroad overpass
under which the motorcade would proceed before
reaching the Stemmons Freeway. The front of the
Texas School Book Depository was now on the President's right, and he waved to the crowd assembled
there as he passed the building. Dealey Plaza—an
open, landscaped area marking the western end of
downtown Dallas—stretched out to the President's
left. A Secret Service agent riding in the motorcade
radioed the Trade Mart that the President would
arrive in five minutes.

Seconds later, shots resounded in rapid succession.
The President's hands moved to his neck. He appeared
to stiffen momentarily and lurch slightly forward in
his seat. A bullet had entered the base of the back of
his neck slightly to the right of the spine. It traveled
downward and exited from the front of the neck,
causing a nick in the left lower portion of the knot in
the President's necktie. Before the shooting started,
Governor Connally had been facing toward the crowd
on the right. He started to turn toward the left and
suddenly felt a blow on his back. The governor had
been hit by a bullet which entered at the extreme
right side of his back at a point below his right armpit.

The bullet traveled through his chest in a downward and forward direction, exited below his right
nipple, passed through his right wrist, which had been
in his lap, and then caused a wound to his left thigh.
The force of the bullet's impact appeared to spin the
governor to his right, and Mrs. Connally pulled him
down into her lap. Another bullet then struck President Kennedy in the rear portion of his head, causing
a massive and fatal wound. The President fell to the
left into Mrs. Kennedy's lap.

Races to the President

Secret Service Agent Clinton J. Hill, riding on the
left running board of the follow-up car, heard a noise
which sounded like a firecracker and saw the President
suddenly lean forward and to the left. Hill jumped off
the car and raced toward the President's limousine. In
the front seat of the vice-presidential car, Agent
Youngblood heard an explosion and noticed unusual
movements in the crowd. He vaulted into the rear
seat and sat on the Vice-President in order to protect
him. At the same time, Agent Kellerman, in the front
seat of the presidential limousine, turned to observe
the President.

Seeing that the President was struck, Kellerman instructed the driver, "Let's get out of here; we are hit." He radioed ahead to the lead car, "Get us to the hospital immediately." Agent Greer immediately accelerated the presidential car. As it gained speed, Agent Hill managed to pull himself onto the back of the car where Mrs. Kennedy had climbed. Hill pushed her back into the rear seat and shielded the stricken President and Mrs. Kennedy as the President's car proceeded at high speed to Parkland Memorial Hospital, four miles away.

At Parkland, the President was immediately treated by a team of physicians who had been alerted for the President's arrival by the Dallas Police Department as the result of a radio message from the motorcade after the shooting. The doctors noted irregular breathing movements and a possible heartbeat, although they could not detect a pulsebeat. They observed the extensive wound in the President's head and a small wound approximately one-fourth inch in diameter in the lower third of his neck.

In an effort to facilitate breathing, the physicians performed a tracheotomy by enlarging the throat wound and inserting a tube. Totally absorbed in the immediate task of trying to preserve the President's life, the attending doctors never turned the President over for an examination of his back. At 1 P.M., after all heart activity ceased and the last rites were administered by a priest, President Kennedy was pronounced dead. Governor Connally underwent surgery and ultimately recovered from his serious wounds.

Upon learning of the President's death, Vice-President Johnson left Parkland Hospital under close guard and proceeded to the presidential plane at Love Field. Mrs. Kennedy, accompanying her husband's body, boarded the plane shortly thereafter. At 2:38 P.M., in the central compartment of the plane, Lyndon B. Johnson was sworn in as the 36th President of the United States by Federal District Court Judge Sarah T. Hughes. The plane left immediately for Washington, D.C., arriving at Andrews Air Force Base, Maryland, at 5:58 P.M., Eastern standard time.

The President's body was taken to the National Naval Medical Center, Bethesda, Md., where it was given a complete pathological examination. The autopsy disclosed the large head wound observed at Parkland and the wound in the front of the neck which had been enlarged by the Parkland doctors when they performed the tracheotomy. Both of these wounds were described in the autopsy report as being "presumably of exit." In addition, the autopsy revealed a small wound of entry in the rear of the President's skull and another wound of entry near the base of the back of the neck. The autopsy report stated the cause of death as "Gunshot wound, head," and the bullets which struck the President were described as having been fired "from a point behind and somewhat above the level of the deceased."

Confusion at Site of Shooting

At the scene of the shooting, there was evident confusion at the outset concerning the point of origin of the shots. Witnesses differed in their accounts of the direction from which the sound of the shots emanated. Within a few minutes, however, attention centered on the Texas School Book Depository Building as the

source of the shots. The building was occupied by a private corporation, the Texas School Book Depository Company, which distributed school textbooks of several publishers and leased space to representatives of the publishers. Most of the employees in the building worked for these publishers. The balance, including a 15-man warehousing crew, were employees of the Texas School Book Depository Company itself.

Several eyewitnesses in front of the building reported that they saw a rifle being fired from the southeast corner window on the sixth floor of the Texas School Book Depository Building. One eyewitness, Howard L. Brennan, had been watching the parade from a point on Elm Street directly opposite and facing the building. He promptly told a policeman that he had seen a slender man, about 5 feet 10 inches, in his early 30's, take deliberate aim from the sixth-floor corner window and fire a rifle in the direction of the President's car. Brennan thought he might be able to identify the man since he had noticed him in the window a few minutes before the motorcade made the turn onto Elm Street. At 12:34 P.M., the Dallas police radio mentioned the Depository Building as a possible source of the shots, and at 12:45 P.M., the police radio broadcast a description of the suspected assassin based primarily on Brennan's observations.

When the shots were fired, a Dallas motorcycle patrolman, Marrion L. Baker, was riding in the motorcade at a point several cars behind the President. He had turned right from Main Street onto Houston Street and was about 200 feet south of Elm Street when he heard a shot. Baker, having recently returned from a week of deer hunting, was certain the shot

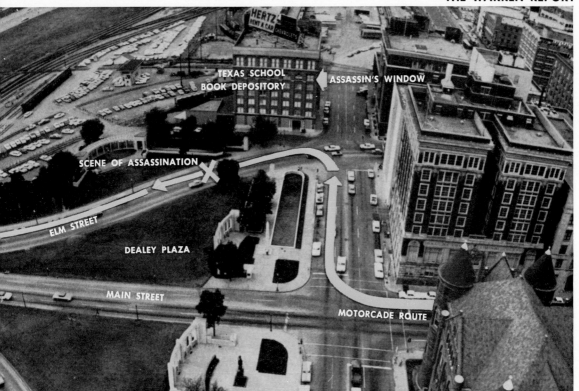

TEXAS SCHOOL
BOOK DEPOSITORY

ASSASSIN'S WINDOW

SCENE OF ASSASSINATION

ELM STREET

DEALEY PLAZA

MAIN STREET

MOTORCADE ROUTE

Arthur Schatz

ROUTE OF THE PRESIDENTIAL MOTORCADE through the streets of Dallas is
indicated by broken line. An "X" marks the scene of the assassination.

came from a high-powered rifle. He looked up and
saw pigeons scattering in the air from their perches
on the Texas School Book Depository Building. He
raced his motorcycle to the building, dismounted,
scanned the area to the west, and pushed his way
through the spectators toward the entrance. There he
encountered Roy Truly, the building superintendent,
who offered Baker his help. They entered the building,
and ran toward the two elevators in the rear. Finding
that both elevators were on an upper floor, they
dashed up the stairs. Not more than two minutes had
elapsed since the shooting.

Suspect Walks Free

When they reached the second-floor landing on
their way up to the top of the building, Patrolman
Baker thought he caught a glimpse of someone through
the small, glass window in the door separating the
hall area near the stairs from the small vestibule leading into the lunchroom. Gun in hand, he rushed to
the door and saw a man about 20 feet away walking
toward the other end of the lunchroom. The man was
empty-handed. At Baker's command, the man turned
and approached him. Truly, who had started up the
stairs to the third floor ahead of the patrolman, returned to see what had delayed the patrolman. Baker asked
Truly whether he knew the man in the lunchroom.
Truly replied that the man worked in the building,
whereupon Baker turned from the man and proceeded,

with Truly, up the stairs. The man they encountered
had started working in the Texas School Book Depository Building on Oct. 16, 1963. His fellow workers
described him as very quiet—a "loner." His name
was Lee Harvey Oswald.

Within about one minute after his encounter with
Baker and Truly, Oswald was seen passing through the
second-floor offices. In his hand was a full "Coke"
bottle which he had purchased from a vending machine in the lunchroom. He was walking toward the
front of the building where a passenger elevator and
a short flight of stairs provided access to the main entrance of the building on the first floor. Approximately
seven minutes later, at about 12:40 P.M., Oswald
boarded a bus at a point on Elm Street seven short
blocks east of the Depository Building. The bus was
traveling west toward the very building from which
Oswald had come. Its route lay through the Oak Cliff
section in southwest Dallas, where it would pass seven
blocks east of the rooming house in which Oswald was
living, at 1026 North Beckley Avenue. On the bus was
Mrs. Mary Bledsoe, one of Oswald's former landladies
who immediately recognized him. Oswald stayed on
the bus approximately three or four minutes, during
which time it proceeded only two blocks because of
the traffic jam created by the motorcade and the assassination. Oswald then left the bus.

A few minutes later, he entered a vacant taxi four
blocks away and asked the driver to take him to a
point on North Beckley Avenue several blocks beyond

555

his rooming house. The trip required five or six minutes. At about 1 P.M., Oswald arrived at the rooming house. The housekeeper, Mrs. Earlene Roberts, was surprised to see Oswald at midday and remarked to him that he seemed to be in quite a hurry. He made no reply. A few minutes later, Oswald emerged from his room zipping up his jacket and rushed out of the house.

The Death of Tippit

Approximately 14 minutes later, and just 45 minutes after the assassination, another violent shooting occurred in Dallas. The victim was Patrolman J. D. Tippit of the Dallas police, an officer with a good record during his more than 11 years with the police force. He was shot near the intersection of 10th Street and Patton Avenue, about nine-tenths of a mile from Oswald's rooming house. At the time of the assassination, Tippit was alone in his patrol car, the routine practice for most police patrol cars at this time of day. He had been ordered by radio at 12:45 P.M. to proceed to the central Oak Cliff area as part of a concentration of patrol car activity around the center of the city following the assassination. At 12:54, Tippit radioed that he had moved as directed and would be available for any emergency. By this time the police radio had broadcast several messages alerting the police to the suspect described by Brennan at the scene of the assassination—a slender, white male, about 30 years old, 5 feet 10 inches, and weighing about 165 pounds.

At approximately 1:15 P.M., Tippit was driving slowly in an easterly direction on East 10th Street in Oak Cliff. About 100 feet past the intersection of 10th Street and Patton Avenue, Tippit pulled up alongside a man walking in the same direction. The man met the general description of the suspect wanted in connection with the assassination. He walked over to Tippit's car, rested his arms on the door on the right-hand side of the car, and apparently exchanged words with Tippit through the window. Tippit opened the door on the left side and started to walk around the front of his car. As he reached the front wheel on the driver's side, the man on the sidewalk drew a revolver and fired several shots in rapid succession, hitting Tippit four times and killing him instantly. An automobile repairman, Domingo Benavides, heard the shots and stopped his pickup truck on the opposite side of the street about 25 feet in front of Tippit's car. He observed the gunman start back toward Patton Avenue, removing the empty cartridge cases from the gun as he went. Benavides rushed to Tippit's side. The patrolman, apparently dead, was lying on his revolver, which was out of its holster. Benavides promptly reported the shooting to police headquarters over the radio in Tippit's car. The message was received shortly after 1:16 P.M.

Witnesses to Shooting

As the gunman left the scene, he walked hurriedly back toward Patton Avenue and turned left, heading south. Standing on the northwest corner of 10th Street and Patton Avenue was Helen Markham, who had been walking south on Patton Avenue and had seen both the killer and Tippit cross the intersection in front of her as she waited on the curb for traffic to

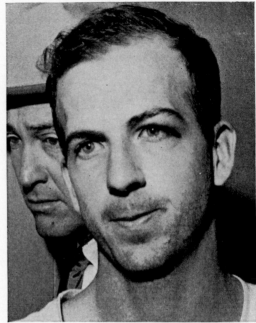

Wide World

LEE HARVEY OSWALD, without accomplices, fired the fatal shots, the commission found.

pass. She witnessed the shooting and then saw the man with a gun in his hand walk back toward the corner and cut across the lawn of the corner house as he started south on Patton Avenue.

In the corner house itself, Mrs. Barbara Jeanette Davis and her sister-in-law, Mrs. Virginia Davis, heard the shots and rushed to the door in time to see the man walk rapidly across the lawn, shaking a revolver as if he were emptying it of cartridge cases. Later that day, each woman found a cartridge case near the house. As the gunman turned the corner, he passed alongside a taxicab which was parked on Patton Avenue, a few feet from 10th Street. The driver, William W. Scoggins, had seen the slaying and was now crouched behind his cab on the street side. As the gunman cut through the shrubbery on the lawn, Scoggins looked up and saw the man approximately 12 feet away. In his hand was a pistol, and he muttered words which sounded to Scoggins like "poor dumb cop" or "poor damn cop."

Assailant Continues Flight

After passing Scoggins, the gunman crossed to the west side of Patton Avenue and ran south toward Jefferson Boulevard, a main Oak Cliff thoroughfare. On the east side of Patton, between 10th Street and Jefferson Boulevard, Ted Callaway, a used car salesman, heard the shots and ran to the sidewalk. As the man with the gun rushed past, Callaway shouted, "What's going on?" The man merely shrugged, ran on to Jefferson Boulevard and turned right. On the next corner was a gas station with a parking lot in the rear. The assailant ran into the lot, discarded his jacket, and then continued his flight west on Jefferson.

In a shoe store a few blocks farther west on Jefferson,

the manager, Johnny Calvin Brewer, heard the siren of a police car moments after the radio in his store announced the shooting of the police officer in Oak Cliff. Brewer saw a man step quickly into the entranceway of the store and stand there with his back toward the street. When the police car made a U-turn and headed back in the direction of the Tippit shooting, the man left and Brewer followed him. He saw the man enter the Texas Theatre, a motion picture house about 60 feet away, without buying a ticket. Brewer pointed this out to the cashier, Mrs. Julia Postal, who called the police. The time was shortly after 1:40 P.M.

At 1:29 P.M., the police radio had noted the similarity in the descriptions of the suspects in the Tippit shooting and the assassination. At 1:45 P.M., in response to Mrs. Postal's call, the police radio sounded the alarm: "Have information a suspect just went in the Texas Theatre on West Jefferson." Within minutes, the theater was surrounded. The house lights were then turned up. Patrolman M. N. McDonald and several other policemen approached the man, who had been pointed out to them by Brewer.

Suspect Draws Gun

McDonald ordered the man to his feet and heard him say, "Well, it's all over now." The man drew a gun from his waist with one hand and struck the officer with the other. McDonald struck out with his right hand and grabbed the gun with his left hand. After a brief struggle, McDonald and several other police officers disarmed and handcuffed the suspect and drove him to police headquarters, arriving at approximately 2 P.M.

Police Rush to Depository

Following the assassination, police cars had rushed to the Texas School Book Depository in response to the many radio messages reporting that the shots had been fired from the Depository Building. Inspector J. Herbert Sawyer of the Dallas Police Department arrived at the scene shortly after hearing the first of these police radio messages at 12:34 P.M. Some of the officers who had been assigned to the area of Elm and Houston Streets for the motorcade were talking to witnesses and watching the building when Sawyer arrived. Sawyer entered the building and rode a passenger elevator to the fourth floor, which was the top floor for this elevator. He conducted a quick search, returned to the main floor and, between approximately 12:37 and 12:40 P.M., ordered that no one be permitted to leave the building.

Shortly before 1 P.M., Captain J. Will Fritz, chief of the homicide and robbery bureau of the Dallas Police Department, arrived to take charge of the investigation. Searching the sixth floor, Deputy Sheriff Luke Mooney noticed a pile of cartons in the southeast corner. He squeezed through the boxes and realized immediately that he had discovered the point from which the shots had been fired. On the floor were three empty cartridge cases. A carton had apparently been placed on the floor at the side of the window so that a person sitting on the carton could look down Elm Street toward the overpass and scarcely be noticed from the outside. Between this carton and the half-

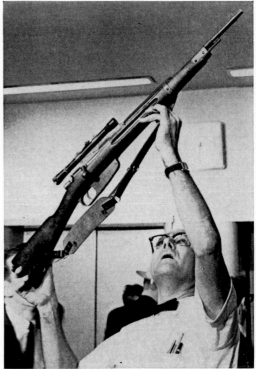

Wide World

ASSASSINATION WEAPON, Oswald's 6.5-mm. Italian rifle, is shown by Dallas Detective J. C. Day.

open window were three additional cartons arranged at such an angle that a rifle resting on the top carton would be aimed directly at the motorcade as it moved away from the building. The high stack of boxes, which first attracted Mooney's attention, effectively screened a person at the window from the view of anyone else on the floor.

Telescopic Rifle Found

Mooney's discovery intensified the search for additional evidence on the sixth floor, and at 1:22 P.M., approximately 10 minutes after the cartridge cases were found, Deputy Sheriff Eugene Boone turned his flashlight in the direction of two rows of boxes in the northwest corner near the staircase. Stuffed between the two rows was a bolt-action rifle with a telescopic sight. The rifle was not touched until it could be photographed. When Lieutenant J. C. Day of the police identification bureau decided that the wooden stock and the metal knob at the end of the bolt contained no prints, he held the rifle by the stock while Captain Fritz ejected a live shell by operating the bolt. Lieutenant Day promptly noted that stamped on the rifle itself was the serial number "C2766" as well as the markings "1940" "MADE ITALY" and "CAL. 6.5." The rifle was about 40 inches long, and, when disassembled, could fit into a handmade paper sack, which, after the assassination, was found in the southeast corner of the building within a few feet of the cartridge cases.

As Fritz and Day were completing their examination of this rifle on the sixth floor, Roy Truly, the building superintendent, approached with information which he felt should be brought to the attention of the police. Earlier, while the police were questioning the employees, Truly had observed that Lee Harvey Oswald, one of the 15 men who worked in the warehouse, was missing. After Truly provided Oswald's name, address, and general description, Fritz left for police headquarters. He arrived at headquarters shortly after 2 P.M. and asked two detectives to pick up the employee who was missing from the Texas School Book Depository. Standing nearby were the police officers who had just arrived with the man arrested in the Texas Theatre. When Fritz mentioned the name of the missing employee, he learned that the man was already in the interrogation room. The missing School Book Depository employee and the suspect who had been apprehended in the Texas Theatre were one and the same—Lee Harvey Oswald.

Oswald's Family Background

The suspect Fritz was about to question in connection with the assassination of the President and the murder of a policeman was born in New Orleans on Oct. 18, 1939, two months after the death of his father. His mother, Marguerite Claverie Oswald, had two older children. One, John Pic, was a half brother to Lee from an earlier marriage which had ended in divorce. The other was Robert Oswald, a full brother to Lee and five years older. When Lee Oswald was 3, Mrs. Oswald placed him in an orphanage where his brother and half brother were already living, primarily because she had to work.

In January, 1944, when Lee was 4, he was taken out of the orphanage, and shortly thereafter his mother moved with him to Dallas, Tex., where the older boys joined them at the end of the school year. In May of 1945, Marguerite Oswald married her third husband, Edwin A. Ekdahl. While the two older boys attended a military boarding school, Lee lived at home and developed a warm attachment to Ekdahl, occasionally accompanying his mother and stepfather on business trips around the country.

Lee started school in Benbrook, Tex., but in the fall of 1946, after a separation from Ekdahl, Marguerite Oswald re-entered Lee in the first grade in Covington, La. In January, 1947, while Lee was still in the first grade, the family moved to Fort Worth, Tex., as the result of an attempted reconciliation between Ekdahl and Lee's mother. A year and a half later, before Lee was 9, his mother was divorced from her third husband as the result of a divorce action instituted by Ekdahl. Lee's school record during the next five and a half years in Fort Worth was average, although generally it grew poorer each year. The comments of teachers and others who knew him at that time do not reveal any unusual personality traits or characteristics.

Another change for Lee Oswald occurred in August, 1952, a few months after he completed the sixth grade. Marguerite Oswald and her 12-year-old son moved to New York City where Marguerite's oldest son, John Pic, was stationed with the Coast Guard. The ensuing year and one-half in New York were marked by Lee's refusals to attend school and by emotional and psychological problems of a seemingly serious nature.

Because he had become a chronic school truant, Lee underwent psychiatric study at Youth House, an institution in New York for juveniles who have had truancy problems or difficulties with the law, and who appear to require psychiatric observation, or other types of guidance.

The social worker assigned to his case described him as "seriously detached" and "withdrawn" and noted "a rather pleasant, appealing quality about this emotionally starved, affectionless youngster." Lee expressed the feeling to the social worker that his mother did not care for him and regarded him as a burden. He experienced fantasies about being all-powerful and hurting people, but during his stay at Youth House he was apparently not a behavior problem. He appeared withdrawn and evasive, a boy who preferred to spend his time alone, reading and watching television.

'Above Average Intelligence'

His tests indicated that he was above average in intelligence for his age group. The chief psychiatrist of Youth House diagnosed Lee's problem as a "personality pattern disturbance with schizoid features and passive-aggressive tendencies." He concluded that the boy was "an emotionally, quite disturbed youngster" and recommended psychiatric treatment.

In May, 1953, after having been at Youth House for three weeks, Lee Oswald returned to school where his attendance and grades temporarily improved. By the following fall, however, the probation officer reported that virtually every teacher complained about the boy's behavior. His mother insisted that he did not need psychiatric assistance. Although there was apparently some improvement in Lee's behavior during the next few months, the court recommended further treatment. In January, 1954, while Lee's case was still pending, Marguerite and Lee left for New Orleans, the city of Lee's birth.

Upon his return to New Orleans, Lee maintained mediocre grades but had no obvious behavior problems. Neighbors and others who knew him outside of school remembered him as a quiet, solitary, and introverted boy who read a great deal and whose vocabulary made him quite articulate. About one month after he started the 10th grade and 11 days before his 16th birthday in October, 1955, he brought to school a note purportedly written by his mother, stating that the family was moving to California. The note was written by Lee. A few days later, he dropped out of school and almost immediately tried to join the Marine Corps. Because he was only 16, he was rejected.

Works as Office Clerk

After leaving school, Lee worked for the next 10 months at several jobs in New Orleans as an office messenger or clerk. It was during this period that he started to read communist literature. Occasionally, in conversations with others, he praised communism and expressed to his fellow employees a desire to join the Communist party. At about this time, when he was not yet 17, he wrote to the Socialist Party of America, professing his belief in Marxism.

Another move followed in July, 1956, when Lee and his mother returned to Fort Worth. He re-entered high school but again dropped out after a few weeks and enlisted in the Marine Corps on Oct. 24, 1956, six days after his 17th birthday. On Dec. 21, 1956, during boot camp in San Diego, Oswald fired a score of 212 for record with the M-1 rifle—two points over the minimum for a rating of "sharpshooter" on a marksman/sharpshooter/expert scale. After his basic training, Oswald received training in aviation fundamentals and then in radar scanning.

Most people who knew Oswald in the marines described him as a "loner" who resented the exercise of authority by others. He spent much of his free time reading. He was court-martialed once for possessing an unregistered privately owned weapon and, on another occasion, for using provocative language to a noncommissioned officer. He was, however, generally able to comply with marine discipline, even though his experiences in the Marine Corps did not live up to his expectations.

Oswald served 15 months overseas until November, 1958, most of them in Japan. During his final year in the Marine Corps, he was stationed for the most part in Santa Ana, Calif., where he showed a marked interest in the Soviet Union and sometimes expressed politically radical views with dogmatic conviction. Oswald again fired the M-1 rifle for record on May 6, 1959, and this time he shot a score of 191 on a shorter course than before, only one point over the minimum required to be a "marksman." According to one of his fellow marines, Oswald was not particularly interested in his rifle performance, and his unit was not expected to exhibit the usual rifle proficiency. During this period, he expressed strong admiration for Fidel Castro and an interest in joining the Cuban army. He tried to impress those around him as an intellectual, but his thinking appeared to some as shallow and rigid.

Passport to Russia

Oswald's marine service terminated on Sept. 11, 1959, when, at his own request, he was released from active service a few months ahead of his scheduled release. He offered as the reason for his release the ill health and economic plight of his mother. He returned to Fort Worth, remained with his mother only three days and left for New Orleans, telling his mother he planned to get work there in the shipping or import-export business. In New Orleans he booked passage on the freighter S.S. *Marion Lykes*, which sailed from New Orleans to Le Havre, France, on Sept. 20, 1959.

Lee Harvey Oswald had presumably planned this step in his life for quite some time. In March of 1959, he had applied to the Albert Schweitzer College in Switzerland for admission to the spring (1960) term. His letter of application contained many blatant falsehoods concerning his qualifications and background. A few weeks before his discharge, he had applied for and obtained a passport, listing the Soviet Union as one of the countries which he planned to visit. During his service in the marines, he had saved a comparatively large sum of money, possibly as much as $1,500, which would appear to have been accomplished by considerable frugality and apparently for a specific purpose.

The purpose of the accumulated fund soon became known. On Oct. 16, 1959, Oswald arrived in Moscow by train after crossing the border from Finland, where he had secured a visa for a six-day stay in the Soviet Union. He immediately applied for Soviet citizenship. On the afternoon of Oct. 21, 1959, Oswald was ordered to leave the Soviet Union by 8 P.M. that evening. That same afternoon in his hotel room, Oswald, in an apparent suicide attempt, slashed his left wrist. He was hospitalized immediately. On October 31, three days after his release from the hospital, Oswald appeared at the American embassy, announced that he wished to renounce his U.S. citizenship and become a Russian citizen, and handed the embassy officer a written statement he had prepared for the occasion.

When asked his reasons, Oswald replied, "I am a Marxist." Oswald never formally complied with the legal steps necessary to renounce his American citizenship. The Soviet government did not grant his request for citizenship, but in January, 1960, he was given permission to remain in the Soviet Union on a year-to-year basis. At the same time, Oswald was sent to Minsk where he worked in a radio factory as an unskilled laborer. In January, 1961, his permission to remain in the Soviet Union was extended for another year. A few weeks later, in February, 1961, he wrote to the American embassy in Moscow expressing a desire to return to the United States.

Oswald Marries Marina

The following month, Oswald met a 19-year-old Russian girl, Marina Nikolaevna Prusakova, a pharmacist, who had been brought up in Leningrad but was then living with an aunt and uncle in Minsk. They were married on April 30, 1961. Throughout the following year, he carried on a correspondence with American and Soviet authorities seeking approval for the departure of himself and his wife to the United States. In the course of this effort, Oswald and his wife visited the U.S. embassy in Moscow in July of 1961. Primarily on the basis of an interview and questionnaire completed there, the embassy concluded that Oswald had not lost his citizenship, a decision subsequently ratified by the Department of State in Washington, D.C. Upon their return to Minsk, Oswald and his wife filed with the Soviet authorities for permission to leave together. Their formal application was made in July, 1961, and on Dec. 25, 1961, Marina Oswald was advised it would be granted.

A daughter was born to the Oswalds in February, 1962. In the months that followed, they prepared for their return to the United States. On May 9, 1962, the U.S. Immigration and Naturalization Service, at the request of the Department of State, agreed to waive a restriction under the law which would have prevented the issuance of a U.S. visa to Oswald's Russian wife until she had left the Soviet Union. They finally left Moscow on June 1, 1962, and were assisted in meeting their travel expenses by a loan of $435.71 from the U.S. Department of State. Two weeks later they arrived in Fort Worth, Tex.

For a few weeks, Oswald, his wife, and child lived with Oswald's brother Robert. After a similar stay with Oswald's mother, they moved into their own apartment in early August. Oswald obtained a job on July 16 as a sheet metal worker. During this period in Fort Worth, Oswald was interviewed twice by agents of the Federal Bureau of Investigation (FBI). The report of the first interview, which occurred on June

United Press Int.

NEWLYWEDS MARINA AND HARVEY OSWALD pose on bridge in Minsk, Russia. Factory worker Oswald met and married Marina in that city in 1961.

OSWALD'S LETTER TO SENATOR TOWER

Sometime shortly before January 26, 1962, an undated letter from Lee Harvey Oswald was received in the office of the U.S. Senator from Texas, John G. Tower. The letter reads as follows:

> My name is Lee Harvey Oswald, 22, of Fort Worth up till October 1959, when I came to the Soviet Union for a residenaul stay. I took a residenual document for a non-Soviet person living for a time in the U S S R. The American Embassy in Moscow is familier with my case
>
> Since July 20th 1960, I have unsucessfully applied for a Soviet Exit Visa to leave this country, the Soviets refuse to permit me and my Soviet wife, (who applied at the U.S. Embassy Moscow, July 8, 1960 for immigration status to the U.S.A.) to leave the Soviet Union. I am a citizen of the United States of America (passport No. 1733242, 1959) and I bessech you, Senator Tower, to rise the question of holding by the Soviet Union of a citizen of the U.S., against his will and expressed desires.

The letter was read in Senator Tower's office by a caseworker on his staff. The letter was forwarded as a matter of routine on January 26 to the Assistant Secretary for Congressional Relations, Department of State. A cover letter, machine signed by the Senator, stated that he did "not know Oswald, or any of the facts concerning his reasons for visiting the Soviet Union; nor what action, if any, this Government can or should take on his behalf." On February 1, an officer at the Department of State telephoned the Senator's office and spoke briefly with the caseworker. She made a memorandum of the call which notes, "Senator should not become involved in such case—therefore State will report to us the course which they follow regarding Lee Harvey Oswalt [sic]."

About a week later, the Department of State informed the Senator that if he wished to be kept informed on further developments he could contact the Department of State. Neither the Senator nor any member of his staff contacted the Department again nor did they take any other action in respect to the matter.

26, described him as arrogant and unwilling to discuss the reasons why he had gone to the Soviet Union. Oswald denied that he was involved in Soviet intelligence activities and promised to advise the FBI if Soviet representatives ever communicated with him. He was interviewed again on August 16, when he displayed a less belligerent attitude and once again agreed to inform the FBI of any attempt to enlist him in intelligence activities.

Disdain for Democracy

In early October, 1962, Oswald quit his job at the sheet metal plant and moved to Dallas. While living in Fort Worth, the Oswalds had been introduced to a group of Russian-speaking people in the Dallas-Fort Worth area. Many of them assisted the Oswalds by providing small amounts of food, clothing, and household items. Oswald himself was disliked by almost all of this group whose help to the family was prompted primarily by sympathy for Marina Oswald and the child. Despite the fact that he had left the Soviet Union, disillusioned with its government, Oswald seemed more firmly committed than ever to his concepts of Marxism. He showed disdain for democracy, capitalism, and American society in general. He was highly critical of the Russian-speaking group because they seemed devoted to American concepts of democracy and capitalism and were ambitious to improve themselves economically.

In February, 1963, the Oswalds met Ruth Paine at a social gathering. Ruth Paine was temporarily separated from her husband and living with her two children in their home in Irving, Tex., a suburb of Dallas. Because of an interest in the Russian language and sympathy for Marina Oswald, who spoke no English and had little funds, Ruth Paine befriended Marina and, during the next two months, visited her on several occasions.

Attempt to Kill Walker

On April 6, 1963, Oswald lost his job with a photography firm. A few days later, on April 10, he attempted to kill Major General Edwin A. Walker (Resigned, U.S. Army), using a rifle which he had ordered by mail one month previously under an assumed name. Marina Oswald learned of her husband's act when she confronted him with a note which he had left, giving her instructions in the event he did not return. That incident and their general economic difficulties impelled Marina Oswald to suggest that her husband leave Dallas and go to New Orleans to look for work.

Oswald left for New Orleans on April 24, 1963. Ruth Paine, who knew nothing of the Walker shooting, invited Marina Oswald and the baby to stay with her in the Paine's modest home while Oswald sought work in New Orleans. Early in May, upon receiving word from Oswald that he had found a job, Ruth Paine drove Marina Oswald and the baby to New Orleans to rejoin Oswald.

During the stay in New Orleans, Oswald formed a fictitious New Orleans Chapter of the Fair Play for Cuba Committee. He posed as secretary of this organization and represented that the president was A. J. Hidell. In reality, Hidell was a completely fictitious person created by Oswald, the organization's only

member. Oswald was arrested on August 9 in connection with a scuffle which occurred while he was distributing pro-Castro leaflets. The next day, while at the police station, he was interviewed by an FBI agent after Oswald requested the police to arrange such an interview. Oswald gave the agent false information about his own background and was evasive in his replies concerning Fair Play for Cuba activities. During the next two weeks, Oswald appeared on radio programs twice, claiming to be the spokesman for the Fair Play for Cuba Committee in New Orleans.

Journey to Mexico

On July 19, 1963, Oswald lost his job as a greaser of coffee processing machinery. In September, after an exchange of correspondence with Marina Oswald, Ruth Paine drove to New Orleans and, on September 23, transported Marina, the child, and the family belongings to Irving, Tex. Ruth Paine suggested that Marina Oswald, who was expecting her second child in October, live at the Paine house until after the baby was born. Oswald remained behind, ostensibly to find work either in Houston or in some other city. Instead, he departed by bus for Mexico, arriving in Mexico City on September 27, where he promptly visited the Cuban and Russian embassies. His stated objective was to obtain official permission to visit Cuba on his way to the Soviet Union. The Cuban government would not grant his visa unless the Soviet government would also issue a visa permitting his entry into Russia. Oswald's efforts to secure these visas failed, and he left for Dallas, where he arrived on Oct. 3, 1963.

When he saw his wife the next day, it was decided that Oswald would rent a room in Dallas and visit his family on weekends. For one week he rented a room from Mrs. Bledsoe, the woman who later saw him on the bus shortly after the assassination. On Oct. 14, 1963, he rented the Beckley Avenue room and listed his name as O. H. Lee. On the same day, at the suggestion of a neighbor, Mrs. Paine phoned the Texas School Book Depository and was told that there was a job opening. She informed Oswald, who was interviewed the following day at the Depository and started to work there on Oct. 16, 1963.

On October 20, the Oswalds' second daughter was born. During October and November, Oswald established a general pattern of weekend visits to Irving, arriving on Friday afternoon and returning to Dallas Monday morning with a fellow employee, Buell Wesley Frazier, who lived near the Paines.

On Friday, November 15, Oswald remained in Dallas at the suggestion of his wife who told him that the house would be crowded because of a birthday party for Ruth Paine's daughter.

On Monday, November 18, Oswald and his wife quarreled bitterly during a telephone conversation, because she learned for the first time that he was living at the rooming house under an assumed name.

Unexpected Return Home

On Thursday, November 21, Oswald told Frazier that he would like to drive to Irving to pick up some curtain rods for an apartment in Dallas. His wife and Mrs. Paine were quite surprised to see him since it was

Thursday night. They thought he had returned to make up after Monday's quarrel. He was conciliatory, but Marina Oswald was still angry.

Later that evening, when Mrs. Paine had finished cleaning the kitchen, she went into the garage and noticed that the light was burning. She was certain that she had not left it on, although the incident appeared unimportant at the time. In the garage were most of the Oswalds' personal possessions. The following morning, Oswald left while his wife was still in bed feeding the baby. She did not see him leave the house, nor did Ruth Paine. On the dresser in their room he left his wedding ring which he had never done before. His wallet containing $170 was left intact in a dresser drawer.

Oswald walked to Frazier's house about half a block away and placed a long, bulky package, made out of wrapping paper and tape, into the rear seat of the car. He told Frazier that the package contained curtain rods. When they reached the Depository parking lot, Oswald walked quickly ahead. Frazier followed and saw Oswald enter the Depository Building carrying the long bulky package with him.

During the morning of November 22, Marina Oswald followed President Kennedy's activities on television. She and Ruth Paine cried when they heard that the President had been shot. Ruth Paine translated the news of the shooting to Marina Oswald as it came over television, including the report that the shots were probably fired from the building where Oswald worked. When Marina Oswald heard this, she recalled the Walker episode and the fact that her husband still owned the rifle. She went quietly to the Paine's garage where the rifle had been concealed in a blanket among their other belongings. It appeared to her that the rifle was still there, although she did not actually open the blanket.

Rifle Is Missing

At about 3 P.M., the police arrived at the Paine house and asked Marina Oswald whether her husband owned a rifle. She said that he did and then led them into the garage and pointed to the rolled-up blanket. As a police officer lifted it, the blanket hung limply over either side of his arm. The rifle was not there.

Meanwhile, at police headquarters, Captain Fritz had begun questioning Oswald. Soon after the start of the first interrogation, agents of the FBI and the U.S. Secret Service arrived and participated in the questioning. Oswald denied having anything to do with the assassination of President Kennedy or the murder of Patrolman Tippit. He claimed that he was eating lunch at the time of the assassination, and that he then spoke with his foreman for 5 to 10 minutes before going home. He denied that he owned a rifle and when confronted, in a subsequent interview, with a picture showing him holding a rifle and pistol, he claimed that his face had been superimposed on someone else's body. He refused to answer any questions about the presence in his wallet of a selective service card with his picture and the name "Alek J. Hidell."

During the questioning of Oswald on the third floor of the police department, more than 100 representatives of the press, radio, and television were crowded into the hallway through which Oswald had to pass when being taken from his cell to Captain Fritz'

office for interrogation. Reporters tried to interview Oswald during these trips. Between Friday afternoon and Sunday morning he appeared in the hallway at least 16 times. The generally confused conditions outside and inside Captain Fritz' office increased the difficulty of police questioning. Advised by the police that he could communicate with an attorney, Oswald made several telephone calls on Saturday in an effort to procure representation of his own choice and discussed the matter with the president of the local bar association, who offered to obtain counsel. Oswald declined the offer, saying that he would first try to obtain counsel by himself. By Sunday morning he had not yet engaged an attorney.

Oswald Identified

At 7:10 P.M. on Nov. 22, 1963, Lee Harvey Oswald was formally advised that he had been charged with the murder of Patrolman J. D. Tippit. Several witnesses to the Tippit slaying and to the subsequent flight of the gunman had positively identified Oswald in police line-ups. While positive firearm identification evidence was not available at the time, the revolver in Oswald's possession at the time of his arrest was of a type which could have fired the shots that killed Tippit.

The formal charge against Oswald for the assassination of President Kennedy was lodged shortly after 1:30 A.M., on Saturday, November 23. By 10 P.M. of the day of the assassination, the FBI had traced the rifle found on the sixth floor of the Texas School Book Depository to a mail-order house in Chicago which had purchased it from a distributor in New York. Approximately six hours later, the Chicago firm advised that this rifle had been ordered in March, 1963, by an A. Hidell for shipment to Post Office Box 2915, in Dallas, Tex., a box rented by Oswald. Payment for the rifle was remitted by a money order signed by A. Hidell. By 6:45 P.M. on November 23, the FBI was able to advise the Dallas police that, as a result of handwriting analysis of the documents used to purchase the rifle, it had concluded that the rifle had been ordered by Lee Harvey Oswald.

Throughout Friday and Saturday, the Dallas police released to the public many of the details concerning the alleged evidence against Oswald. Police officials discussed important aspects of the case, usually in the course of impromptu and confused press conferences in the third-floor corridor. Some of the information divulged was erroneous. Efforts by the news media representatives to reconstruct the crime and promptly report details frequently led to erroneous, and often conflicting, reports.

Killing Witnessed by Millions

At the urgings of the newsmen, Chief of Police Jesse E. Curry brought Oswald to a press conference in the police assembly room shortly after midnight of the day Oswald was arrested. The assembly room was crowded with newsmen who had come to Dallas from all over the country. They shouted questions at Oswald and flashed cameras at him. Among this group was a 52-year-old Dallas night club operator—Jack Ruby.

On Sunday morning, November 24, arrangements were made for Oswald's transfer from the city jail to

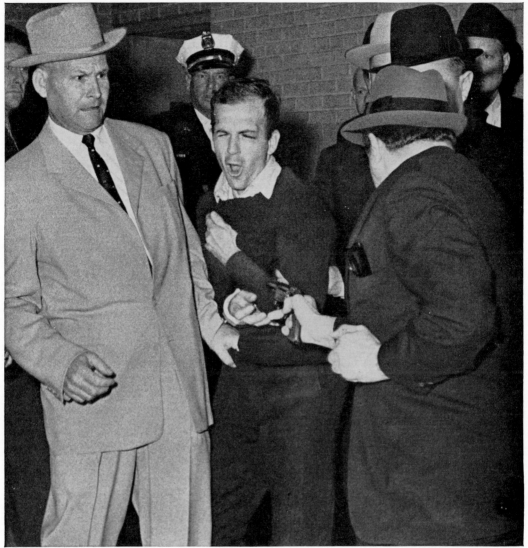

©1963 *The Dallas Times-Herald* and Bob Jackson

"A MAN SUDDENLY DARTED OUT ... and fired one shot into Oswald's abdomen."
The man was Jack Ruby. Startled detective, *left*, was J. R. Leavelle.

the Dallas County jail, about one mile away. The news media had been informed on Saturday night that the transfer of Oswald would not take place until after 10 A.M. on Sunday. Earlier on Sunday, between 2:30 and 3 A.M., anonymous telephone calls threatening Oswald's life had been received by the Dallas office of the FBI and by the office of the county sheriff. Nevertheless, on Sunday morning, television, radio, and newspaper representatives crowded into the basement to record the transfer. As viewed through television cameras, Oswald would emerge from a door in front of the cameras and proceed to the transfer vehicle. To the right of the cameras was a "down" ramp from Main Street on the north. To the left was an "up" ramp leading to Commerce Street.

The armored truck in which Oswald was to be transferred arrived shortly after 11 A.M. Police officials

then decided, however, that an unmarked police car would be preferable for the trip because of its greater speed and maneuverability. At approximately 11:20 A.M., Oswald emerged from the basement jail office flanked by detectives on either side and at his rear. He took a few steps toward the car and was in the glaring light of the television cameras when a man suddenly darted out from an area on the right of the cameras where newsmen had been assembled. The man was carrying a Colt .38 revolver in his right hand and, while millions watched on television, he moved quickly to within a few feet of Oswald and fired one shot into Oswald's abdomen. Oswald groaned with pain as he fell to the ground and quickly lost consciousness. Within seven minutes, Oswald was at Parkland Hospital where, without having regained consciousness, he was pronounced dead at 1:07 P.M.

Wide World

HOW JACK RUBY LOOKED on hearing the death sentence read to him by Judge Joe E. Brown in March, after his trial for the murder of Oswald.

The man who killed Oswald was Jack Ruby. He was instantly arrested and, minutes later, confined in a cell on the fifth floor of the Dallas police jail. Under interrogation, he denied that the killing of Oswald was in any way connected with a conspiracy involving the assassination of President Kennedy. He maintained that he had killed Oswald in a temporary fit of depression and rage over the President's death. Ruby was transferred the following day to the county jail without notice to the press or to police officers not directly involved in the transfer. Indicted for the murder of Oswald by the State of Texas on Nov. 26, 1963, Ruby was found guilty on March 14, 1964, and sentenced to death. As of September, 1964, his case was pending on appeal.

Conclusions

This commission was created to ascertain the facts relating to the preceding summary of events and to consider the important questions which they raised. The commission has addressed itself to this task and has reached certain conclusions based on all the available evidence. No limitations have been placed on the commission's inquiry; it has conducted its own investigation, and all government agencies have fully discharged their responsibility to cooperate with the

commission in its investigation. These conclusions represent the reasoned judgment of all members of the commission and are presented after an investigation which has satisfied the commission that it has ascertained the truth concerning the assassination of President Kennedy to the extent that a prolonged and thorough search makes this possible.

1 The shots which killed President Kennedy and wounded Governor Connally were fired from the sixth-floor window at the southeast corner of the Texas School Book Depository. This determination is based upon the following:

(a) Witnesses at the scene of the assassination saw a rifle being fired from the sixth-floor window of the Depository Building, and some witnesses saw a rifle in the window immediately after the shots were fired.

(b) The nearly whole bullet found on Governor Connally's stretcher at Parkland Memorial Hospital and the two bullet fragments found in the front seat of the presidential limousine were fired from the 6.5-millimeter Mannlicher-Carcano rifle found on the sixth floor of the Depository Building to the exclusion of all other weapons.

(c) The three used cartridge cases found near the window on the sixth floor at the southeast corner of the building were fired from the same rifle which fired the above-described bullet and fragments, to the exclusion of all other weapons.

(d) The windshield in the presidential limousine was struck by a bullet fragment on the inside surface of the glass, but was not penetrated.

(e) The nature of the bullet wounds suffered by President Kennedy and Governor Connally and the location of the car at the time of the shots establish that the bullets were fired from above and behind the presidential limousine, striking the President and the governor as follows:

(1) President Kennedy was first struck by a bullet which entered at the back of his neck and exited through the lower-front portion of his neck, causing a wound which would not necessarily have been lethal. The President was struck a second time by a bullet which entered the right-rear portion of his head, causing a massive and fatal wound.

(2) Governor Connally was struck by a bullet which entered on the right side of his back and traveled downward through the right side of his chest, exiting below his right nipple. This bullet then passed through his right wrist and entered his left thigh where it caused a superficial wound.

(f) There is no credible evidence that the shots were fired from the Triple Underpass, ahead of the motorcade, or from any other location.

2 The weight of the evidence indicates that there were three shots fired.

3 Although it is not necessary to any essential findings of the commission to determine just which shot hit Governor Connally, there is very persuasive evidence from the experts to indicate that the same bullet which pierced the President's throat also caused Governor Connally's wounds. However, Governor Connally's testimony and certain other factors have given rise to some difference of opinion as to this probability but there is no question in the mind of any member of the commission that all the shots which

caused the President's and Governor Connally's wounds were fired from the sixth-floor window of the Texas School Book Depository Building.

Evidence Against Oswald

4 The shots which killed President Kennedy and wounded Governor Connally were fired by Lee Harvey Oswald. This conclusion is based upon the following:

(a) The Mannlicher-Carcano 6.5-millimeter Italian rifle from which the shots were fired was owned by, and in the possession of, Oswald.

(b) Oswald carried this rifle into the Depository Building on the morning of Nov. 22, 1963.

(c) Oswald, at the time of the assassination, was present at the window from which the shots were fired.

(d) Shortly after the assassination, the Mannlicher-Carcano rifle belonging to Oswald was found partially hidden between some cartons on the sixth floor, and the improvised paper bag in which Oswald brought the rifle to the Depository was found close by the window from which the shots were fired.

(e) Based on testimony of the experts and their analysis of films of the assassination, the commission has concluded that a rifleman of Lee Harvey Oswald's capabilities could have fired the shots from the rifle used in the assassination within the elapsed time of the shooting. The commission has concluded further, that Oswald possessed the capability with a rifle which enabled him to commit the assassination.

(f) Oswald lied to the police after his arrest concerning important substantive matters.

(g) Oswald had attempted to kill Major General Edwin A. Walker (Resigned, U.S. Army) on April 10, 1963, thereby demonstrating his disposition to take human life.

Identified in Tippit Killing

5 Oswald killed Dallas Police Patrolman J. D. Tippit approximately 45 minutes after the assassination. This conclusion upholds the finding that Oswald fired the shots which killed President Kennedy and wounded Governor Connally and is supported by the following:

(a) Two eyewitnesses saw the Tippit shooting and seven eyewitnesses heard the shots and saw the gunman leave the scene with revolver in hand. These nine eyewitnesses positively identified Lee Harvey Oswald as the man they saw.

(b) The cartridge cases found at the scene of the shooting were fired from the revolver in the possession of Oswald at the time of his arrest to the exclusion of all other weapons.

(c) The revolver in Oswald's possession at the time of his arrest was purchased by, and belonged to, Oswald.

(d) Oswald's jacket was found along the path of flight taken by the gunman as he fled from the scene of the killing.

6 Within 80 minutes of the assassination and 35 minutes of the Tippit killing Oswald resisted arrest at the theater by attempting to shoot another Dallas police officer.

7 The commission has reached the following conclusions concerning Oswald's interrogation and detention by the Dallas police:

(a) Except for the force required to effect his arrest, Oswald was not subjected to any physical coercion by any law enforcement officials. He was advised that he could not be compelled to give any information and that any statements made by him might be used against him in court. He was advised of his right to counsel. He was given the opportunity to obtain counsel of his own choice and was offered legal assistance by the Dallas Bar Association, which he rejected at that time.

(b) Newspaper, radio, and television reporters were allowed uninhibited access to the area through which Oswald had to pass when he was moved from his cell to the interrogation room and other sections of the building, thereby subjecting Oswald to harassment and creating chaotic conditions which were not conducive to orderly interrogation or the protection of the rights of the prisoner.

(c) The numerous statements, sometimes erroneous, made to the press by various local law enforcement officials, during this period of confusion and disorder in the police station, would have presented serious obstacles to the obtaining of a fair trial for Oswald. To the extent that the information was erroneous or misleading, it helped to create doubts, speculations, and fears in the mind of the public which might otherwise not have arisen.

8 The commission has reached the following conclusions concerning the killing of Oswald by Jack Ruby on Nov. 24, 1963:

(a) Ruby entered the basement of the Dallas Police Department shortly after 11:17 A.M. and killed Lee Harvey Oswald at 11:21 A.M.

(b) Although the evidence on Ruby's means of entry is not conclusive, the weight of the evidence indicates that he walked down the ramp leading from Main Street to the basement of the police department.

(c) There is no evidence to support the rumor that Ruby may have been assisted by any members of the Dallas Police Department in the killing of Oswald.

(d) The Dallas Police Department's decision to transfer Oswald to the county jail in full public view was unsound. The arrangements made by the police department on Sunday morning, only a few hours before the attempted transfer, were inadequate. Of critical importance was the fact that news media representatives and others were not excluded from the basement even after the police were notified of threats to Oswald's life. These deficiencies contributed to the death of Lee Harvey Oswald.

9 The commission has found no evidence that either Lee Harvey Oswald or Jack Ruby was part of any conspiracy, domestic or foreign, to assassinate President Kennedy. The reasons for this conclusion are:

(a) The commission has found no evidence that anyone assisted Oswald in planning or carrying out the assassination. In this connection, it has thoroughly investigated, among other factors, the circumstances surrounding the planning of the motorcade route through Dallas, the hiring of Oswald by the Texas School Book Depository

Company on Oct. 15, 1963, the method by which the rifle was brought into the building, the placing of cartons of books at the window, Oswald's escape from the building, and the testimony of eyewitnesses to the shooting.

(b) The commission has found no evidence that Oswald was involved with any person or group in a conspiracy to assassinate the President, although it has thoroughly investigated, in addition to other possible leads, all facets of Oswald's associations, finances, and personal habits, particularly during the period following his return from the Soviet Union in June, 1962.

(c) The commission has found no evidence to show that Oswald was employed, persuaded, or encouraged by any foreign government to assassinate President Kennedy or that he was an agent of any foreign government, although the commission has reviewed the circumstances surrounding Oswald's defection to the Soviet Union, his life there from October of 1959 to June of 1962 so far as it can be reconstructed, his known contacts with the Fair Play for Cuba Committee, and his visits to the Cuban and Soviet embassies in Mexico City during his trip to Mexico from Sept. 26 to Oct. 3, 1963, and his known contacts with the Soviet embassy in the United States.

(d) The commission has explored all attempts of Oswald to identify himself with various political groups, including the Communist Party, U.S.A., the Fair Play for Cuba Committee, and the Socialist Workers Party, and has been unable to find any evidence that the contacts which he initiated were related to Oswald's subsequent assassination of the President.

(e) All of the evidence before the commission established that there was nothing to support the speculation that Oswald was an agent, employee, or informant of the FBI, the CIA, or any other governmental agency. It has thoroughly investigated Oswald's relationships prior to the assassination with all agencies of the U.S. government. All contacts with Oswald by any of these agencies were made in the regular exercise of their different responsibilities.

(f) No direct or indirect relationship between Lee Harvey Oswald and Jack Ruby has been discovered by the commission, nor has it been able to find any credible evidence that either knew the other, although a thorough investigation was made of the many rumors and speculations of such a relationship.

(g) The commission has found no evidence that Jack Ruby acted with any other person in the killing of Lee Harvey Oswald.

(h) After careful investigation, the commission has found no credible evidence either that Ruby and Officer Tippit, who was killed by Oswald, knew each other, or that Oswald and Tippit knew each other.

Because of the difficulty of proving negatives to a certainty, the possibility of others being involved with either Oswald or Ruby cannot be established categorically, but if there is any such evidence it has been beyond the reach of all the investigative agencies and resources of the United States and has not come to the attention of this commission.

10 In its entire investigation, the commission has found no evidence of conspiracy, subversion, or disloyalty to the U.S. government by any federal, state, or local official.

'Oswald Acted Alone'

11 On the basis of the evidence before the commission, it concludes that Oswald acted alone. Therefore, to determine the motives for the assassination of President Kennedy, one must look to the assassin himself. Clues to Oswald's motives can be found in his family history, his education or lack of it, his acts, his writings, and the recollections of those who had close contacts with him throughout his life. The commission has presented with this report all of the background information bearing on motivation which it could discover. Thus, others may study Lee Oswald's life and arrive at their own conclusions as to his possible motives.

The commission could not make any definitive determination of Oswald's motives. It has endeavored to isolate factors which contributed to his character and which might have influenced his decision to assassinate President Kennedy. These factors were:

(a) His deep-rooted resentment of all authority which was expressed in a hostility toward every society in which he lived.

(b) His inability to enter into meaningful relationships with people, and a pattern of rejecting his environment in favor of new surroundings.

(c) His urge to try to find a place in history and despair at times over failures in his various undertakings.

(d) His capacity for violence as evidenced by his attempt to kill General Walker.

(e) His avowed commitment to Marxism and communism, as he understood the terms and developed his own interpretation of them; this was expressed by his antagonism toward the United States, by his defection to the Soviet Union, by his failure to be reconciled with life in the United States even after his disenchantment with the Soviet Union; and by his efforts, though frustrated, to go to Cuba.

Each of these contributed to his capacity to risk all in cruel and irresponsible actions.

Protection for the President

12 The commission recognizes that the varied responsibilities of the President require that he make frequent trips to all parts of the United States and abroad. Consistent with their high responsibilities, Presidents can never be protected from every potential threat. The Secret Service's difficulty in meeting its protective responsibility varies with the activities and the nature of the occupant of the office of President and his willingness to conform to plans for his safety. In appraising the performance of the Secret Service it should be understood that it has to do its work within such limitations. Nevertheless, the commission believes that recommendations for improvements in presidential protection are compelled by the facts disclosed in this investigation.

(a) The complexities of the presidency have increased so rapidly in recent years that the Secret Service has not been able to develop or to secure adequate resources of personnel and facilities to fulfill its important assignment. This situation should be promptly remedied.

(*b*) The commission has concluded that the criteria and procedures of the Secret Service designed to identify and protect against persons considered threats to the President were not adequate prior to the assassination.

(1) The Protective Research Section of the Secret Service, which is responsible for its preventive work, lacked sufficient trained personnel and the mechanical and technical assistance needed to fulfill its responsibility.

(2) Prior to the assassination, the Secret Service's criteria dealt with direct threats against the President. Although the Secret Service treated the direct threats against the President adequately, it failed to recognize the necessity of identifying other potential sources of danger to his security. The Secret Service did not develop adequate and specific criteria defining those persons or groups who might present a danger to the President. In effect, the Secret Service largely relied upon other federal or state agencies to supply the information necessary for it to fulfill its preventive responsibilities, although it did ask for information about direct threats to the President.

(*c*) The commission has concluded that there was insufficient liaison and coordination of information between the Secret Service and other federal agencies necessarily concerned with presidential protection. Although the FBI, in the normal exercise of its responsibility, had secured considerable information about Lee Harvey Oswald, it had no official responsibility, under the Secret Service criteria existing at the time of the President's trip to Dallas, to refer to the Secret Service the information it had about Oswald. The commission has concluded, however, that the FBI took an unduly restrictive view of its role in preventive intelligence work prior to the assassination. A more carefully coordinated treatment of the Oswald case by the FBI might well have resulted in bringing Oswald's activities to the attention of the Secret Service.

(*d*) The commission has concluded that some of the advance preparations in Dallas made by the Secret Service, such as the detailed security measures taken at Love Field and the Trade Mart, were thorough and well executed. In other respects, however, the commission has concluded that the advance preparations for the President's trip were deficient.

(1) Although the Secret Service is compelled to rely to a great extent on local law enforcement officials, its procedures at the time of the Dallas trip did not call for well-defined instructions as to the respective responsibilities of the police officials and others assisting in the protection of the President.

(2) The procedures relied upon by the Secret Service for detecting the presence of an assassin located in a building along a motorcade route were inadequate. At the time of the trip to Dallas, the Secret Service as a matter of practice did not investigate, or cause to be checked, any building located along the motorcade route to be taken by the President. The responsibility for observing windows in these buildings during the motorcade was divided between local police personnel stationed on the streets to regulate crowds and Secret Service agents riding in the motorcade. Based on its investigation, the commission has concluded that these arrangements during the trip to Dallas were clearly not sufficient.

(*e*) The configuration of the presidential car and the seating arrangements of the Secret Service agents in the car did not afford the Secret Service agents the opportunity they should have had to be of immediate assistance to the President at the first sign of danger.

(*f*) Within these limitations, however, the commission finds that the agents most immediately responsible for the President's safety reacted promptly at the time the shots were fired from the Texas School Book Depository Building.

Recommendations

Prompted by the assassination of President Kennedy, the Secret Service has initiated a comprehensive and critical review of its total operations. As a result of studies conducted during the past several months, and in cooperation with this commission, the Secret Service has prepared a planning document dated Aug. 27, 1964, which recommends various programs considered necessary by the service to improve its techniques and enlarge its resources. The commission is encouraged by the efforts taken by the Secret Service since the assassination and suggests the following recommendations:

1 A committee of Cabinet members, including the Secretary of the Treasury and the Attorney General, or the National Security Council, should be assigned the responsibility of reviewing and overseeing the protective activities of the Secret Service and the other federal agencies that assist in safeguarding the President. Once given this responsibility, such a committee would ensure that the maximum resources of the federal government are fully engaged in the task of protecting the President, and would provide guidance in defining the general nature of domestic and foreign dangers to presidential security.

2 Suggestions have been advanced to the commission for the transfer of all or parts of the presidential protective responsibilities of the Secret Service to some other department or agency. The commission believes that if there is to be any determination of whether or not to relocate these responsibilities and functions, it ought to be made by the Executive and the Congress, perhaps upon recommendations based on studies by the previously suggested committee.

3 Meanwhile, in order to improve daily supervision of the Secret Service within the Department of the Treasury, the commission recommends that the Secretary of the Treasury appoint a special assistant with the responsibility of supervising the Secret Service. This special assistant should have sufficient stature and experience in law enforcement, intelligence, and allied fields to provide effective continuing supervision, and to keep the Secretary fully informed regarding the performance of the Secret Service. One of the initial assignments of this special assistant should be the supervision of the current effort by the

Harris & Ewing

MEMBERS OF THE WARREN COMMISSION: From left to right, Representative Gerald R. Ford, Representative Hale Boggs, Senator Richard B. Russell, Chief Justice Earl Warren, Senator John Sherman Cooper, John J. McCloy, Allen W. Dulles, Commission Counsel J. Lee Rankin.

Secret Service to revise and modernize its basic operating procedures.

4 The commission recommends that the Secret Service completely overhaul its facilities devoted to the advance detection of potential threats against the President. The commission suggests the following measures:

(a) The Secret Service should develop as quickly as possible more useful and precise criteria defining those potential threats to the President which should be brought to its attention by other agencies. The criteria should, among other additions, provide for prompt notice to the Secret Service of all returned defectors.

(b) The Secret Service should expedite its current plans to utilize the most efficient data-processing techniques.

(c) Once the Secret Service has formulated new criteria delineating the information it desires, it should enter into agreements with each federal agency to ensure its receipt of such information.

5 The commission recommends that the Secret Service improve the protective measures followed in the planning and conducting of presidential motorcades. In particular, the Secret Service should continue its current efforts to increase the precautionary attention given to buildings along the route.

6 The commission recommends that the Secret Service continue its recent efforts to improve and formalize its relationships with local police departments in areas to be visited by the President.

7 The commission believes that when the new criteria and procedures are established, the Secret Service will not have sufficient personnel or adequate facilities. The commission recommends that the Secret Service be provided with the personnel and resources which the service and the Department of the Treasury may be able to demonstrate are needed to fulfill its important mission.

8 Even with an increase in Secret Service personnel, the protection of the President will continue to require the resources and cooperation of many federal agencies. The commission recommends that these agencies, specifically the FBI, continue the practice as it has developed, particularly since the assassination, of assisting the Secret Service upon request by providing personnel or other aid, and that there be a closer association and liaison between the Secret Service and all federal agencies.

9 The commission recommends that the President's physician always accompany him during his travels and occupy a position near the President where he can be available in case of any emergency.

10 The commission recommends to Congress that it adopt legislation which would make the assassination of the President and Vice-President a federal crime. A state of affairs where U.S. authorities have no clearly defined jurisdiction to investigate the assassination of a President is anomalous.

11 The commission has examined the Department of State's handling of the Oswald matters and finds that it followed the law throughout. However, the commission believes that the department, in accordance with its own regulations, should in all cases exercise great care in the return to this country of defectors who have evidenced disloyalty or hostility to this country, or who have expressed a desire to renounce their American citizenship, and that, when such persons are so returned, procedures should be adopted for the better dissemination of information concerning them to the intelligence agencies.

12 The commission recommends that the representatives of the bar, law enforcement associations, and the news media work together to establish ethical standards concerning the collection and presentation of information to the public so that there will be no interference with pending criminal investigations, court proceedings, or the right to a fair trial.

CONTENTS OF SECTION FOUR

In its function of keeping all WORLD BOOK owners up-to-date, THE WORLD BOOK YEAR BOOK herewith offers significant new and revised articles from the 1964 and 1965 editions of THE WORLD BOOK ENCYCLOPEDIA. These articles, chosen because of their timeliness and lasting value, should be indexed in THE WORLD BOOK ENCYCLOPEDIA by means of THE YEAR BOOK cross-reference tabs.

A new and expanded article on the art and technical aspects of photography, written by Clifton C. Edom, Director of Photojournalism at the University of Missouri School of Journalism. More than 50 photographs and photodiagrams augment a wealth of information ranging from the latest darkroom techniques to data on films and tips on the making of good photographs.

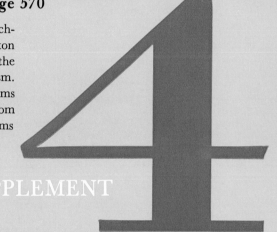

THE WORLD BOOK SUPPLEMENT

Basic concepts in the new approach to mathematics are explained in two articles reprinted from THE WORLD BOOK ENCYCLOPEDIA. They are offered here in response to requests from YEAR BOOK readers for a concise and nontechnical discussion of the new math. The article on SET THEORY begins on page 589; NUMERATION SYSTEMS on page 595.

PHOTOGRAPHY

PHOTOGRAPHY. A photograph is a picture made with a camera. The word *photography* means *writing* or *drawing with light*. A camera picture is a picture drawn with rays of light.

Photography enriches our lives in many ways. Most illustrations in newspapers, magazines, and books are photographs. Photography is important in advertising, business, industry, and science. Photography also helps man explore the earth, the oceans, and outer space.

Some photographs, like some paintings, have lasting value as great works of art. We admire such pictures because they are beautiful, or because they express ideas that we find worth-while.

Photography is one of the most popular hobbies in the world. Almost half the families in the United States own cameras. Amateur photographers take pictures that will remind them of their families and friends, their travels, and important events. Many persons become so interested in photography that they join camera clubs and meet with other enthusiasts. They sometimes enter their pictures in contests or display them at exhibits and in photographic galleries.

Motion pictures make up a special field of photography. This field includes hundreds of professional motion-picture photographers and thousands of amateurs. Most of the principles used in *still* photography are also used in making motion pictures. See MOTION PICTURE.

Clifton C. Edom, the contributor of this article, is Director of Photojournalism at the University of Missouri School of Journalism. WORLD BOOK photos by Don Stebbing.

Mathew Brady, Library of Congress

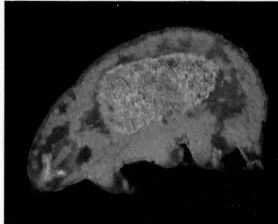
Roman Vishniac, Publix

Art Kane

PHOTOGRAPHY ⬡ TAKING GOOD SNAPSHOTS

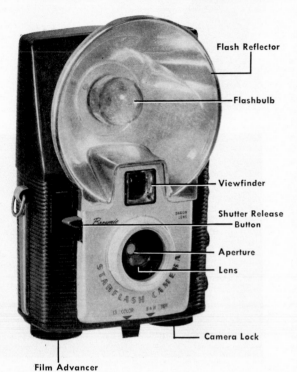

Flash Reflector

Flashbulb

Viewfinder

Shutter Release Button

Aperture

Lens

Camera Lock

Film Advancer

The Parts of a Camera. A camera, in the simplest terms, is a box with an *aperture* (small opening) at one end. It is like a room with a Venetian blind over the window. The aperture lets light into the camera just as a window lets light into a room. The inside of a camera must be dark so that light cannot reach the light-sensitive film until you take a picture. A *shutter* over the opening works like a Venetian blind. The shutter opens to let light enter the camera, and closes to keep light out. When you take a picture, you press the *shutter release button*. The shutter opens, lets light into the camera, and quickly closes.

Light passes through a glass *lens* when it enters the camera. The lens bends the light rays so that they form a sharp *image* (picture) on a piece of film. This image is the picture you photographed. The image appears on the film only after the film has gone through a complicated chemical process called *developing*.

Before taking a picture, you look through the *viewfinder* of the camera to make sure that all of your subject will appear in the picture. After taking a picture, you turn the *film advancer* to move the film forward through the camera and get the film set for the next picture. Most cameras are equipped with a holder for flashbulbs. The use of flashbulbs adds extra light to a scene, especially indoors.

Most cameras, regardless of their size, shape, or cost, have these basic parts. Cameras differ in the way that the parts can be controlled. The simplest cameras have *fixed controls*. The parts always work in the same way. More advanced cameras have *adjustable controls* which the photographer must set before taking a picture. This article explains how to use simple box cameras and ad-

COMMON MISTAKES AND HOW TO AVOID THEM

Poor Background. Check the viewfinder to see that trees or other objects do not "grow" from the subject's head, *right.*

Chopped-Off Head. Make sure all of the subject appears in the viewfinder at the exact moment that you snap the picture.

justable cameras. For a discussion of specific types of cameras, such as press cameras or reflex cameras, see CAMERA (Types of Cameras).

Using Box Cameras is easy because they are the simplest cameras. Many persons use them to learn how to take pictures. Some box cameras have fixed controls. Others have a few controls that must be set.

Before you use a box camera, study the instruction booklet that came with it. This booklet shows where the film advancer, viewfinder, and other parts of the camera are located. Do not put film in the camera until you have practiced how you will take a picture. Choose a subject and frame it in your viewfinder. Only what you see in the viewfinder will appear in the final picture. Practice loading and unloading your camera with an old roll of film. After you know how your camera works, you are ready to take pictures.

Whenever you load the camera with film, protect the film from strong light. If you are outdoors, load the camera in the shade of a tree or in the shadow of your body. This protection will prevent light streaks and glare spots from ruining the pictures.

Most box cameras will make a good picture of any subject that is about 6 feet or more away from the camera. If you stand closer, your subject will be out-of-focus and blurred in the picture.

The shutter of most box cameras opens and closes in about 1/50 of a second. Any movement of either the camera or the subject during that time will cause a blurred picture. Make sure that nothing is moving in the scene you photograph. Hold the camera steady, and press the shutter release button gently.

Many box cameras have two settings to control the shutter speed. These settings are marked *I* (for instantaneous) and *B* (for brief or bulb). The *I* setting makes the shutter work at its normal speed. Use this setting whenever you have enough light to take a picture. The *B* setting keeps the shutter open for as long as you press down the shutter release button. Use this setting at night when the light is dim. Because of the poor light, the shutter may have to stay open for several seconds so that enough light will reach the film. Put the camera on a *tripod* (three-legged stand) or some other sturdy support to keep it from moving while the shutter is open.

PHOTOGRAPHY TERMS

Cable Release is a cord that releases the shutter. It helps prevent camera movement because the photographer does not touch the camera.

Changing Bag is a lightproof bag made of dark cloth that serves as a darkroom. The photographer puts his hands into the bag to load film into a camera or a developing tank.

Fog is a dark, hazy covering over film or printing paper. Fog is caused by light that accidentally reaches the film or by development at temperatures that are too warm.

Latitude, in exposure, means the amount by which film can be overexposed or underexposed without losing too much quality in the image.

Lens Shade, or *lens hood*, is an attachment that keeps light from striking the lens directly and making glare spots appear in the picture.

Parallax is the difference between what the viewfinder shows and what the lens records on the film.

T (time) is a shutter setting used for long exposures. The shutter release button must be pressed twice—once to open the shutter, and again to close it.

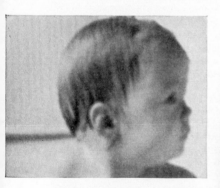

Out-Of-Focus. Stand at least six feet away from the subject.

Tilted Camera. Keep the camera level when you snap the picture.

Camera Movement. Hold the camera steady and press the shutter release button gently.

Obstructed Lens. Make sure that the camera strap or your finger does not cover part of the lens.

WORLD BOOK photos

Front Lighting is seldom useful for portraits. The sun shines directly into the subject's face, causing him to squint. The sun also casts harsh shadows under his eyebrows, nose, chin, and cheekbones.

Side Lighting produces dark shadows on one side of a person's face. Fill in the shadows by using a flashbulb. Or take the picture near an object that reflects light, such as a light-colored building.

Back Lighting forms bright highlights on the subject's hair and shoulders. But a dark shadow may cover his face. Light from a flashbulb will fill in the shadow area and improve the photograph.

Flash Fill-In, used with back lighting, produces good detail and even lighting. For close-ups, cover the flash reflector with a white handkerchief to prevent overexposing the front of the subject.

WORLD BOOK photos

Lighting. The photographer's skill in using light helps determine whether his pictures are good or bad. On a dark, cloudy day, there may not be enough light to make a proper image on the film. The film will be *underexposed*, and the picture will turn out dark and uninteresting. On the other hand, you will probably *overexpose* the film if you photograph white snow or shining water in bright sunlight. Film will be overexposed if it receives more light than necessary. An overexposed picture is too bright and has no really dark tones. Different kinds of light are best for various types of photographs.

Hazy or Cloudy Sunlight is best for taking pictures of people. A thin layer of haze or clouds covering the sun breaks up the sunlight. Hazy or cloudy sunlight creates soft shadows and many shades of gray in a picture. This makes the picture of a person look natural because there are no deep shadows across his face.

Bright Sunlight produces the best pictures of landscape scenes. The sun makes each detail in the scene stand out sharply. The sun also casts deep shadows, creating dark areas and light areas in the picture. A picture with sharp details and strong contrasts between light and dark areas is both attractive and interesting.

If you must photograph a person in bright sunlight, control the shadows on his face. Before you take the picture, study the way in which the sunlight falls on the subject. Try to have him stand so that the sun does not cast deep shadows on his face. There are four ways in which the sun can fall on a subject.

Side Lighting is light that shines on one side of the subject. Shadows cover the other side of his face. You can lighten this shadowy area by photographing the person near the sunny side of a light-colored building. Or you can use a flashbulb to provide light to fill in the shadows. This technique is called *flash fill-in*. The extra light also adds detail to the dark side of the subject's face. If you stand closer than 8 feet from your subject, cover the flash reflector with a white handkerchief. The handkerchief will cut down the light from the flashbulb so that the subject receives an equal amount of light from the sun and the bulb.

Top Lighting is light that falls directly on the subject from the sun overhead. The sun casts dark, unattractive shadows under a person's eyebrows and nose. You can lighten these shadow areas with flash fill-in.

Front Lighting shines into the subject's face. It causes the same unattractive shadows as top lighting. Front lighting also makes the person squint because he is looking directly into the sun. Your picture will be better if you change your position slightly so that the sun shines on one side of the person.

Back Lighting comes from behind the subject. If the sunlight is strong, it will produce a dark shadow over the person's entire face. In this case, using flash fill-in would improve the photograph. If the sunlight is weak, it will produce a soft, pleasant shadow over the person's face. When taking a back-lighted picture, you must use a *lens shade* (a hood that protects the lens from direct sunlight) on your camera. Otherwise, the sun will shine directly into the camera lens and make bright streaks and glare spots in the picture.

COMPOSING YOUR PICTURES

Composition is the arrangement of objects in a photograph. Good composition produces a pleasing photograph. For good composition, have only one center of interest in a picture and use a plain background so that all interest will be focused on the subject. When photographing distant landscapes, include a large object in the foreground to give the picture depth. Balance light and dark tones to create dramatic contrast in the picture. Study the lines and shapes of your subject material. Certain lines and shapes suggest feelings of peace, dignity, or action. Use these lines and shapes to make your photograph story or create a mood.

Light and Dark Tones, used together, create striking photographs. Add emphasis by contrasting dark against light, *left*, or light against dark, *right*.

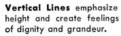

Horizontal Lines suggest peace and rest. A picture is more interesting if the horizontal line is off-center and does not cut the picture in half.

Vertical Lines emphasize height and create feelings of dignity and grandeur.

Diagonal Lines suggest action and movement. They may also suggest conflict.

Balanced Objects at the front, back, and sides create order in a photograph and give a feeling of depth.

Radiating Lines can be used by a creative photographer to form interesting patterns and abstract shapes.

Triangular Lines direct attention to the center of interest. Triangles can suggest rest or movement.

Photos by Frank Fenner

PHOTOGRAPHY ⬡ ADJUSTABLE CAMERAS

If you have an adjustable camera, you must take three basic steps before taking a picture. You must (1) set the shutter speed, (2) adjust the size of the lens aperture, and (3) focus the lens on your subject.

The Shutter on an adjustable camera works at different speeds. This is important for two reasons. First, it helps control the amount of light that reaches the film. A fast shutter admits less light than a slow shutter does. Second, the shutter helps prevent a picture from being blurred if the camera or the subject moves. A fast shutter will "stop" movement. The more rapidly a subject is moving, the faster must be the shutter speed.

The shutter speeds appear as numbers on the camera's shutter scale. Each number represents a fraction of a second. For example, 60 stands for 1/60th of a second, and 500 means 1/500th of a second. The higher the number, the faster the shutter speed.

Each number on the scale represents either half the speed or twice the speed of the next number. When set at 250, the shutter opens and closes twice as fast as when it is set at 125. When set at 250, the shutter works half as fast as when it is set at 500.

The Lens Aperture also controls the amount of light that reaches the film. A large aperture admits more light than a small one does. An adjustable camera has a circle of thin, overlapping metal leaves that changes the size of the aperture. This device is called an *iris diaphragm*. The diaphragm expands and contracts over the aperture to admit different amounts of light.

The various sizes of the aperture are called *f-stops*. The *f*-stops appear as *f-numbers* on a scale next to the shutter speeds. The *f*-numbers on some cameras include 2.8, 4, 5.6, 8, 11, 16, and 22. The smaller the number, the larger the aperture. The *f* stands for *fraction*. Just as 1/2 is larger than 1/4, $f/8$ is larger than $f/16$.

The *f*-stops are set up in the same way as the shutter speeds. Each *f*-stop lets in either half as much or twice as much light as the stop next to it. For example, when you change the setting from $f/16$ to $f/11$, the aperture opens up by one *f*-stop and admits twice as much light. In the same way, when you "stop down" from $f/8$ to $f/11$, the aperture closes down by one stop and admits half as much light.

The lens aperture also helps control the overall sharpness of the picture. As the aperture becomes smaller, the area of sharpness in front of and behind the subject becomes larger. This area of sharpness is called *depth of field*. Depth of field extends from the nearest part of the subject area in focus to the farthest part in focus. A small aperture, such as $f/16$, creates great depth of field. This means that a deep area in front of and behind the subject will be in sharp focus. As you increase the size of the aperture, the area in sharp focus becomes shallower. At a wide aperture, such as $f/5.6$, the subject will be in sharp focus, but objects in front of and behind the subject will be blurred.

Focusing determines whether your subject will appear sharp or blurred in the picture. When you focus, you adjust the lens so it forms a sharp image of your subject on the film.

Accurate focusing depends on (1) the distance between the camera lens and the subject, and (2) the distance between the lens and the film in the camera. When you turn the camera's focusing knob, the lens moves toward or away from the film. This adjustment enables you to take a sharp picture of most subjects, regardless of their distance from the camera. Focusing on *infinity* (a far-away scene) requires a short distance between lens and film. Focusing close up requires a longer distance.

There are several ways to know when your subject is in focus. Most cameras have a *focusing scale*. The numbers on the scale represent various distances in feet. The infinity symbol (∞) on the scale stands for any distance beyond the distances given in feet. To focus, you first measure or estimate the distance from the camera to the subject. Then set this distance at the corresponding number on the focusing scale. As you adjust the setting, the lens moves to its proper distance from the film.

Many cameras have a special viewing screen that lets you see an image of your subject while you are focusing. If the camera has a *ground-glass* screen, you focus by moving the lens back and forth until the image in the viewing screen becomes sharp. A camera with a *range finder* shows two images of the subject. One type of range finder shows two identical images of the same subject. You turn the focusing knob until the double image becomes one sharp image. The other type of range finder splits one image of the subject into two halves. You focus by bringing the two halves together.

Focusing also affects a picture's depth of field. The closer the lens is to the subject, the shallower the depth of field. When you focus close up, only your subject and a small surrounding area will be in focus. You gain greater depth of field when you focus on a subject that is farther from the camera.

Exposure refers to the total amount of light that reaches the film while you are taking a picture. The correct exposure depends upon the right combination of shutter speed and *f*-stop. To set these controls, you must first consider the amount of light on your subject.

On a cloudy day, more light must reach the film to make an image. You should use a large *f*-stop and a slow shutter speed to provide a greater exposure. Sunny days require less exposure. Set the *f*-stop so that

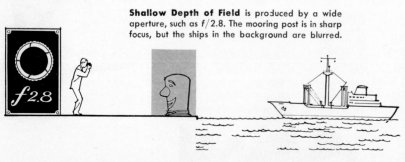

Shallow Depth of Field is produced by a wide aperture, such as $f/2.8$. The mooring post is in sharp focus, but the ships in the background are blurred.

Shutter Speeds can range from B to 1/500th of a second. The higher the number, the faster the shutter speed. These photographs show the type of action certain shutter speeds will stop. The B setting should be used for time exposures at night. Set at 1/60, the shutter will not stop action. Set at 1/125, it will stop a slow-moving bicycle. Set at 1/500, it will stop splashing water.

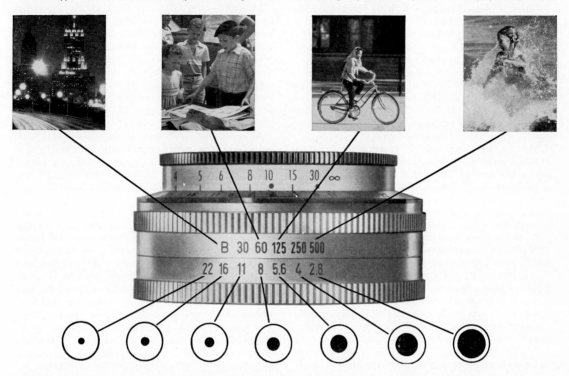

F-Numbers can range from f/22 to f/2.8. The larger the number, the smaller the lens opening and the less light admitted into the camera. The circles in the illustration show how the lens opening becomes larger as the f-numbers become smaller.

it is half-closed, and use a medium shutter speed. A particularly bright scene, such as white snow reflecting bright sunlight, requires the least exposure. Use a small f-stop and a fast shutter speed to prevent the bright light from overexposing the film.

Before taking a picture, you should also consider the movement of your subject and the depth of field that you want. If your subject is moving, you will need a fast shutter speed to prevent blurring. If you want a large area of your picture to be in sharp focus, you will need a small f-stop to provide greater depth of field. But if you change one control, you must also change the other. When you use a fast shutter speed to stop action, less light reaches the film. So you must increase the size of the f-stop. In the same way, when you use a small f-stop to provide greater depth of field, less light reaches the film. So you must use a slower shutter speed. By using these two controls together, you can make sure that the proper amount of light reaches the film.

Suppose you want to photograph some lions outdoors at the zoo on a bright sunny day. The correct settings for your camera would be f/11 at 1/60. If the lions are moving, you should use a faster shutter speed, such as 1/125. This speed is twice as fast as 1/60, so half as much light will reach the film. You then must make the aperture twice as large and set the f-stop at f/8. In the same way, if you change the shutter speed to 1/250—four times as fast—you must change the f-stop to f/5.6—four times as large.

Now suppose you want to include the natural surroundings of the lions in your picture. You will want great depth of field so that the rocks behind the lions and the *moat* (ditch) in front will appear sharply. You should use a small aperture, such as f/16. The film will receive half as much light as it did when the f-stop was f/11. You must also change the shutter speed from 1/60 to 1/30 so that light will reach the film for twice as long a time.

Great Depth of Field is produced by a small aperture, such as f/22. Both the mooring post and the ships in the background are in sharp focus.

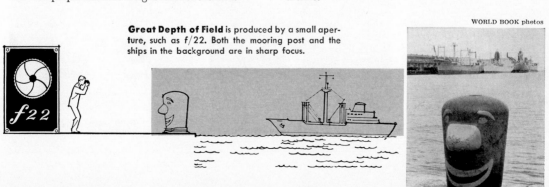

Filters. Colors photographed with black-and-white film become black, white, and various shades of gray in a picture. Photographers use filters to lighten or darken certain areas of a picture, and to increase the contrast between the different shades of gray.

A filter is a piece of colored, plasticlike gelatin or colored glass in a holder that fits over the lens of the camera. The filter allows light of its own color to pass through the lens to the film. It *filters* (holds back) light of certain other colors. Thus, a filter lightens its own color in a picture and darkens certain other colors.

Most photographers use yellow, red, and green filters in black-and-white photography. A *yellow filter* improves pictures of landscapes because it produces natural-looking skies. A blue sky photographed without a filter may appear completely white in a picture. A yellow filter deepens the sky tone, providing contrast between the dark sky and the white clouds.

A *red filter* makes a blue sky appear almost black. This filter creates a dramatic contrast between the sky and the clouds. It also cuts through haze in distant landscapes. However, a red filter does not make good photographs of persons because skin tones appear washed out.

A *green filter* provides much the same sky tones as a yellow filter, and produces normal skin tones. It also improves the tones of green leaves and grass, and makes flowers stand out from a green background.

A *polarizing filter* reduces the glare from shiny surfaces, such as water or glass. See POLARIZED LIGHT.

Most filters hold back some light from the film, and so you must increase the exposure when using them. The *filter factor* listed with the film's instruction sheet tells how much the exposure should be increased.

Exposure Meters, also called *light meters,* help assure correct exposures. The *photoelectric cell meter* is the most accurate kind. It measures the amount of light in a scene and shows the camera settings for the correct exposure. There are two types of photoelectric meters: (1) incident light meter, and (2) reflected light meter.

An *incident light meter* measures the amount of light on the subject. The meter must receive the same light as the subject to give an accurate reading. To take a reading, point the meter toward the sky. Or stand next to your subject and aim the meter toward the spot where you will stand to take the picture.

A *reflected light meter* measures the light that is reflected from the subject toward the camera. To take a reading, point the meter toward your subject. If you are photographing a person, hold the meter about 6 inches from his face. The meter will measure the light reflected from his face instead of light from the sky or the background. If the subject has light and shadow on his face, take separate readings of the light and dark areas. Base your settings on an average of the two readings. For scenic photographs, always point the reflected light meter slightly downward so it will not measure excess light from the sky. Be sure the meter does not measure the shadow of your body or hand. See LIGHT METER.

A Filter lightens its own color and darkens others. Colors, *left*, become black, white, and gray when photographed with black-and-white film, *below*. Compare these pictures with the bottom photographs. The *yellow* filter darkened the blue sky, bringing out the clouds. The *red* filter made the sky very dark, but lightened the red shirt. The *green* filter lightened the green jacket.

WORLD BOOK photos

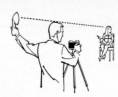

Flash On the Camera produces harsh front lighting and a shadow outline on one side of the subject.

Flash Off the Camera produces side lighting. It throws the shadow low and away from the subject.

Bounce Flash gives soft, even lighting when the light *bounces* (reflects) off a light-colored ceiling.

WORLD BOOK photos

Artificial Lighting lets you shoot pictures that you could not take with *natural lighting* (daylight). The most common sources of artificial light are (1) photoflood lamps, (2) flashbulbs, and (3) electronic flash.

Photoflood Lamps must be plugged into an electrical outlet. They burn for at least three hours. The most convenient type is a small lamp with a built-in reflector that can be clamped onto a chair or tripod.

Flashbulbs operate on batteries and are easy to carry because of their light weight. They differ in the amount of light they produce. When choosing a bulb, you must be sure it can be used with the shutter on your camera. Most cameras have a built-in *flash synchronizer*. This device makes sure that the greatest brightness of the bulb's light occurs at the instant when the shutter reaches its full opening. Some bulbs work with all shutter speeds. Others work only with slow speeds.

It is easy to determine exposure when using flash. First, set the shutter speed for the scene. Then check the instruction sheet that comes with the film or the flashbulb to find the *guide number* for the bulb you are using. To determine the proper *f*-stop, divide the guide number by the number of feet between the flashbulb and the subject. If the guide number for a flashbulb is 160, and the bulb is 10 feet from the subject, the *f*-stop would be *f*/16. Most cameras must also be set on *M*, the setting for flash synchronization. See FLASHBULB.

Electronic Flash, also called *strobe light*, is produced by an electrical discharge in a gas-filled bulb. Electronic flash fires thousands of flashes before the bulb needs replacing. The flash from an electronic-flash unit lasts a much shorter time than that from a flashbulb. An electronic flash may last only from 1/500th to 1/2000th of a second. The burst of light is so great and intense that the flash, not the shutter, stops the action in the picture. Because of the flash's speed, the shutter must be fully open before the flash occurs. This is called *X-synchronization*. Most cameras must be set on *X* for electronic flash. Portable electronic-flash units operate on batteries.

Special Lenses greatly increase the usefulness of a camera. These lenses allow you to take extreme closeups, to photograph unusually wide areas, or to photograph far-distant objects.

Closeup Lenses slip over the normal lens as filters do. With them you can take sharp pictures of subjects at a closer distance than with the normal lens. Focusing with a closeup lens must be exact because you have hardly any depth of field. Use a tape measure, and measure the exact distance from the front of the subject to the front of the lens.

At close distances, your viewfinder may not show exactly what will appear in the picture. If the viewfinder is above the lens of your camera, it will show a slightly different view of the subject from that "seen" by the lens. This difference in view is called *parallax*. It may cause the top of a person's head to appear chopped-off in the picture. You can avoid this fault by tilting the camera up slightly just before you take the picture.

Wide-angle and Telephoto Lenses are called *interchangeable lenses* because they replace a camera's normal lens. With a normal lens, size and depth relationships among the objects in a picture are the same as seen by the eye. A wide-angle lens includes a wider area of a scene than a normal lens does. But it makes all the objects seem smaller and farther away. A telephoto lens covers a narrower area of a scene, but it makes objects appear larger and closer.

PHOTOGRAPHY DEVELOPING FILM

When you take a picture, the camera lens gathers in light reflected from objects in the scene. Light-colored objects reflect a great deal of light. Dark objects reflect little light, or none at all. The lights and darks reflected from the scene go through the lens onto the film.

Photographic film is a thin sheet of plastic with a thin coating called an *emulsion*. The emulsion consists of tiny grains of silver salts held together by gelatin, a jellylike substance. The silver salts used are silver bromide and silver iodide. Silver salts are *sensitive* to light. That is, they change when light hits them. When you take a picture, some salts in the emulsion are struck by a great deal of light. These salts undergo a great change. Other salts are struck by a small amount of light, and they change only slightly. Still other salts get no light, and they do not change at all. In this way, the lights and darks reflected from a scene make an image on the emulsion.

You cannot see the silver salts react to light. The image on the film remains invisible until the film is developed. The developing process has five steps: (1) developer, (2) stop bath, (3) fixing bath, (4) washing, and (5) drying. First, the salts that were struck by light are changed by the *developer* into metallic silver. The exposed areas of the film become dark. The *stop bath*, which is usually plain water, removes the developer so it will not make the exposed areas too dark. The unexposed salts must now be removed from the film, because they are still sensitive to light. The *fixing bath*, or *hypo*, dissolves the unexposed salts so they can be washed away. It also toughens the film (see Hypo). *Washing* the film in water removes the unexposed salts. These unexposed areas of the film become transparent. Washing also removes the chemicals of the fixing bath. After *drying* the film, you have a permanent, visible image.

The developed film is called a *negative*. What was white or bright in the scene you photographed is dark. This is because the bright areas reflected the most light and caused the greatest change in the silver salts. What was darkest in the scene is clear on the negative. The dark areas reflected no light and did not affect the silver salts.

Developing Your Own Film. To develop film at home, you will need three chemicals, several pieces of equipment, and running water. The instruction sheet

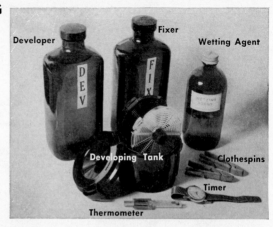

Developer · Fixer · Wetting Agent · Developing Tank · Clothespins · Timer · Thermometer

These Are the Basic Supplies Needed to Develop Film.

that comes with a roll of film lists the developer and fixing chemicals that should be used. You will also need a *wetting agent*. This liquid prevents negatives from being water-spotted, and speeds up the drying time.

Use an ordinary measuring cup or a *darkroom graduate* to measure the solutions. Wash the cup after each use to avoid ruining one chemical with another. Mix and store each solution in a bottle. The bottles should be amber-colored to keep light from harming the chemicals. Label each bottle with the name of its contents.

The *time-temperature* method of development produces the best results. Develop the film for the recommended time at the recommended temperature. You must keep all solutions at the same temperature, including the water used for the stop bath and the wash. Differences in temperature can cause the film emulsion to wrinkle and break up. Test the temperatures with a *darkroom thermometer*. Time each development process with a *darkroom timer* or a watch with a second hand.

Film must be developed in total darkness because the film is still sensitive to light. Many beginners use a darkened kitchen, bathroom, or closet as a temporary darkroom. A *developing tank* lets you develop film with the lights on. Wind the film onto a reel, put the reel into the tank, and pour the solutions in and out of the tank. The tank is designed to keep light away from the film. Some tanks, however, must be loaded with film in complete darkness. You can use a lightproof closet or a *changing*

HOW BLACK-AND-WHITE FILM WORKS

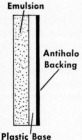

Emulsion · Antihalo Backing · Plastic Base

Black-and-white film consists of three layers: (1) an *emulsion* made up of light-sensitive silver salts in gelatin; (2) a *plastic base* that supports the emulsion; and (3) an *antihalo backing* containing a dye that absorbs light which has passed through the emulsion. When film is exposed, the light reflected from a subject strikes the emulsion. The lighter the subject, the more light it reflects. The silver salts hit by light undergo a change. The

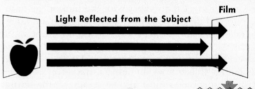

Light Reflected from the Subject · Film

greater the light, the greater the change. In this way, an invisible image of the subject forms on the emulsion. The image becomes visible when the film is developed and becomes a negative. The exposed silver salts turn dark. The unexposed areas of the film become transparent.

Development Process · Negative

WORLD BOOK Diagrams

Load the Film onto the tank reel. Place the reel in the tank and fasten the cover. Do this in total darkness unless you use a daylight-loading tank. Prepare the three developing solutions and the wetting agent. Check their temperatures.

Add the Developer and begin timing the process. Agitate as directed. When the time is up, empty the developer into its bottle. Pour the stop bath in and out of the tank twice. Add the fixer and begin timing. Agitate properly. Empty the fixer into its bottle.

bag (a special lightproof bag) to protect the film from light while putting it into the tank.

During the development process, the developer and fixing solutions must be *agitated* (moved about). Agitation keeps a fresh supply of solution in contact with the film so that the image develops evenly. The instruction sheet tells how long and how often to agitate.

Problem Negatives. Even though you expose the film correctly, your negatives may be faulty because of mistakes in developing. If the developer is too warm or the film remains in the developer too long, the negative will be *overdeveloped*. It will appear quite *dense* (dark), with no detail in the highlight areas. The negative will be *underdeveloped* if the developer is too cold, or if the film is not developed long enough. An underdeveloped negative appears *thin* (almost transparent). If the entire negative appears gray, the film was not in the fixing bath long enough.

Careless handling can result in scratches on a negative. Do not touch the negative until it is dry. Then handle it by the edges only. Keep your negatives in special negative storage envelopes.

Streaks and spots on negatives indicate improper development. Light and dark streaks result from uneven development. Agitate the solutions properly so they cover all the film for the same amount of time. Air bubbles in the solutions cause spots on negatives. Proper agitation prevents these bubbles.

Wash the Film for 30 minutes. Let a thin stream of lukewarm water run into the middle of the open tank. Then place the reel in the wetting agent solution for 30 seconds. Remove the film from the reel. Clip a clothespin to one end of the filmstrip and hang it in a dust-free area to dry. Clip a clothespin to the lower end to prevent curling. Cut the dry filmstrip into sections convenient for printing.

Overdeveloped Negative is too dark, and has no detail in the highlight areas.

Perfect Negative has good tone contrast and detail in both shadow and highlight areas.

Underdeveloped Negative has no dark black areas and no detail in the shadow areas.

Spotted Negative is due to improper agitation. Careless handling causes scratches.
WORLD BOOK photos

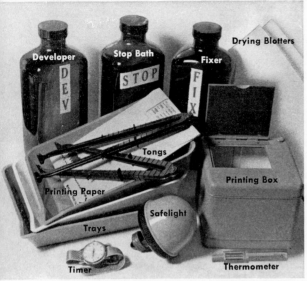

Developer Stop Bath Fixer Drying Blotters

DEV STOP FIX

Tongs

Printing Box

Printing Paper

Safelight

Trays

Timer Thermometer

WORLD BOOK photos

These Are the Supplies Needed to Make Contact Prints.

Making A Contact Print. Prepare the three solutions first. Arrange the trays in front of you so that from left to right you have: (1) developer, (2) stop bath, and (3) fixer. Turn the room light off and the safelight on. Place the negative, dull side up, in the printing box. Place the paper, shiny side down, over the negative and close the lid. Turn on the exposing light for 3 seconds. Using one pair of tongs, slide the paper, shiny side up, completely into the developer. Agitate by rocking the tray gently. At the end of the development time, place the print in the stop bath for 30 seconds. Using the other pair of tongs, slide the print into the fixer and agitate immediately. After 30 seconds you can turn on the room light. At the end of the fixing time, wash the print for 1 hour in lukewarm running water. Let it dry between blotters.

PHOTOGRAPHY CONTACT PRINTING

The process of printing photographs transfers the image on the negative to a piece of paper. Printing reverses the light and dark tones of the negative. As a result, the paper print shows the scene as you originally photographed it.

Prints are made in much the same way as negatives. Printing paper is coated with an emulsion that contains light-sensitive silver salts. Light passes through the negative and transfers the negative image to the paper. During the exposure, the dark areas of the negative hold back some of the light. These dark areas become light areas on the print. The clear areas of the negative let much light pass through to the paper. These clear areas become dark on the print. Thus, the tones of the print become the same as those in the scene you photographed. For this reason, a print is called a *positive*.

The exposed printing paper contains an invisible image. The paper must be developed before it will produce a visible image. To develop prints, you repeat the steps used to develop film: developer, stop bath, fixing bath, washing, and drying.

Contact printing is the simplest method of printing photographs. The dull side of the negative and the shiny side of the printing paper must be in direct contact during the exposure. Light shining through the negative makes an image directly on the paper. A contact print is always the same size as its negative because it is made directly from the negative. You can use either a printing frame or a printing box to hold the negative and paper together.

A *printing frame* consists of a wooden frame that holds a sheet of glass. Spring clamps on the frame hold the negative and paper tightly together against the glass. To expose the paper, place the negative and then the paper on the glass inside the frame. Place the frame, glass side up, about a foot under a 100-watt frosted light bulb.

When you turn on the light, it shines down through the glass and the negative, and makes a latent image on the paper. You must estimate the correct exposure time. It depends on the density of the negative, the strength of the light, and the distance between the printing paper and the light source. An exposure of 2 seconds is recommended for this type of printing frame.

You can easily make a printing frame. Buy a piece of window glass that is a little larger than the printing paper. Cover the edges of the glass with adhesive tape so they will not scratch the negative. Place the paper on a flat surface, such as a table top. Put the negative on top of the paper, and cover both with the glass.

A *printing box* is a box with a light at the bottom and glass at the top. To use it, place the negative and then the paper on top of the glass. Close the lid of the box to press the negative and the paper together. When you turn on the light, it shines up through the glass and the negative, making an image on the paper.

In addition to a printing device, you will need chemicals and equipment to develop the prints. The developer and fixing chemicals used in printing are different from those used in developing film. The stop bath used in printing is an acetic acid solution rather than water. Other necessary supplies include (1) three bottles for mixing and storing the chemical solutions, (2) three trays to hold the prints and solutions during the development process, and (3) two pairs of tongs to move the prints from one tray to another. Use the measuring cup, thermometer, and timing device that you used in developing the film.

You also will need a package of printing paper, a dim colored light called a *safelight*, and photographic drying blotters for drying the prints. Most printing papers cannot be handled under room lights. A safelight will not expose the paper, but it will let you see what you are doing. This light can be a specially-coated bulb or a low-wattage bulb covered with a filter. Be sure to cover the printing paper if you turn on the regular room lights.

Enlarging, or *projection printing*, produces a print that is larger than its negative. The negative is not in contact with the printing paper during the exposure. A *photographic enlarger* holds the negative, and an *easel* holds the printing paper. The enlarger projects the negative image onto the paper somewhat as a slide projector throws an image onto a screen. The enlarger *blows up* (increases the size of) the negative image, and makes a larger image on the paper.

An enlarger has three basic parts: (1) a light bulb, (2) a negative carrier, and (3) a lens. The *enlarger head* contains these parts. The top of the enlarger head holds a light bulb that is turned on to expose the printing paper. The *negative carrier* is a frame that holds the negative when it is placed in the enlarger. The lens of the enlarger projects the negative image. The enlarger head can be raised or lowered. Its position determines the size of the enlargement. The higher the head, the larger the image produced.

The enlarger lens has a focusing device that controls the sharpness of the image it projects on the paper. The lens also has a diaphragm that can be opened up or closed down to control the exposure. The diaphragm sometimes will let you make a good print from a poor negative. If a negative is thin because of underexposure or underdevelopment, you can underexpose the print. Use a short exposure time and a small *f*-stop on the enlarger to provide a brief exposure. On the other hand, if you have a dense overexposed or overdeveloped negative, increase the exposure of the print. Use a long exposure time and a large *f*-stop.

An easel holds the printing paper flat during the exposure. Most easels can be made smaller or larger to hold different sizes of paper. Use a *camel's-hair brush* to remove dust from the negative before putting it into the negative carrier. Specks of dust on a negative will enlarge into white marks on a print.

In developing enlargements, you can use the same chemicals and equipment used to develop contact prints.

Negative Carrier holds the negative when it is placed in the enlarger.

Light Bulb, which exposes the printing paper, is at the top of the enlarger head.

Focusing Control raises or lowers the lens to bring the negative image into sharp focus.

Projection Control raises or lowers the enlarger head to control the size of the image projected by the lens.

Red Safety Filter swings under the lens to prevent the enlarger light from exposing the printing paper. A photographer uses the filter when he makes focusing adjustments or other changes.

Lens enlarges the negative image. The lens diaphragm controls the amount of light that exposes the printing paper.

Camel's-Hair Brush removes dust from negatives.

Burning-In Tool is a card with a hole in it. It lets extra light expose areas of a picture that print too light.

Dodging Tools are pieces of cardboard on wire. They hold back light from areas of a picture that print too dark.

Easel holds the printing paper flat during the exposure.

WORLD BOOK photo

ENLARGING TECHNIQUES

Focusing. Set the lens at its widest opening and turn on only the enlarger light. Focus a small detail of the negative on a piece of white cardboard.

Exposing. Close the lens down to *f*/8. Turn the enlarger light off and the safelight on. Replace the cardboard with print paper and make the exposure.

Test Strips help determine the correct exposure time. Cover all but a fifth of the print paper with cardboard. Expose for 10 seconds. Expose four more strips at 10 seconds each. After development, the paper will show exposures of 50, 40, 30, 20, and 10 seconds. Select the best time for the print.

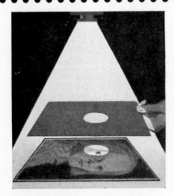

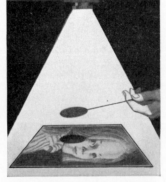

Burning In allows extra light to darken part of a print. Move the cardboard in quick circles about halfway between the lens and the print paper.

Dodging lightens part of a print by holding back light. Move the tool in small circles so that its edges will blend into the rest of the print.

Enlarging Controls can improve a poor photograph. This picture is dark, cluttered, and uninteresting. Compare it with the three photographs below.

Cropping, or rearranging, a picture focuses attention on the squirrel. Enlarging the squirrel to fill the entire print also removes unnecessary objects from the foreground and background.

Adding Detail and Contrast improves the print. Dodging the tree and squirrel lightens them and brings out detail, *above.* Burning in the snow darkens it and adds detail, *below.*

WORLD BOOK photos

PHOTOGRAPHY ⟠ PRINTING PAPERS

Printing papers for contact printing and enlarging come in different weights, surfaces, and contrasts. A paper can be *single-weight* or *double-weight*. Most photographers use double-weight paper for portraits and other special types of photographs. Prints made on double-weight paper will not curl or damage easily. These prints must be washed longer than prints made on single-weight paper to remove the development chemicals.

A paper's surface can be *glossy* (shiny), *semi-matte* (slightly shiny), or *matte* (dull). Most photographers use glossy or semi-matte paper. Professional portrait photographers use matte paper.

A paper has *contrast* so that good prints can be made from many types of negatives. For example, a *flat* negative has few dark and light areas. It will produce a print that is gray and uninteresting. This kind of negative needs a *hard* (high-contrast) paper that will add contrast to the tones of the print. A *contrasty* negative has extreme contrast between dark and light areas. It should be printed on a *soft* (low-contrast) paper.

The number of a paper indicates its grade of contrast. Printing papers usually range from No. 1, which has the least contrast, to No. 5, which provides the greatest contrast. A No. 1 paper produces the widest range of tones, including black, white, and many shades of gray. Use this paper with very overexposed negatives that have extreme contrasts in tone. Use No. 2 or No. 3 paper to print properly exposed negatives. These papers produce fewer gray shades, but they give contrasting blacks and whites that add life to a picture. No. 4 and No. 5 papers produce the fewest shades of gray. They usually will make a good print from a flat negative.

Some papers have the different grades of contrast built into them. These *multiple-* or *variable-contrast* papers require a different color of light to produce each grade of contrast. Colored printing filters must be placed over the lens when the papers are exposed. Multiple-contrast papers are popular because the photographer can print any type of negative from them. He does not have to buy a box of each grade of paper.

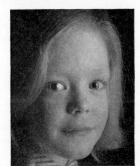 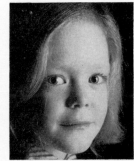 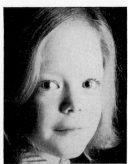

Printing Papers control the contrast of prints. These prints were made from a properly exposed negative. The print made on low-contrast paper, *left*, lacks highlights and contrast. The normal-contrast paper, *middle*, produced a print with good detail in shadow and highlight areas. The high-contrast paper, *right*, produced a print with harsh highlights.

WORLD BOOK photos

PHOTOGRAPHY ⟠ CHOOSING BLACK-AND-WHITE FILM

There are many types of film for taking various kinds of black-and-white pictures. Some films can be used for snapshots and other general photographs. Other films are made for special uses. A good photographer chooses film that is best for the kind of picture he wants to take. Two basic points should be considered when choosing film: (1) color sensitivity and (2) film speed.

Color Sensitivity. The eye sees an object in terms of color and brightness. For example, a sweater may appear red, but it can also appear light red or dark red. Black-and-white film does not "see" color. The film makes a colored object appear gray in a picture. Film does see brightness. A bright color appears light gray in the picture, and a dark color appears dark gray. Film produces the most natural-looking picture when it makes the brightness of the grays correspond to the brightness of the original colors. The color sensitivity of a film determines whether the pictures will look natural.

There are two main types of black-and-white film, based on color sensitivity: (1) panchromatic and (2) orthochromatic. *Panchromatic* film is sensitive to all colors. It records them all as various shades of gray. The brightness of the grays corresponds to the brightness of the colors photographed. A picture made with "pan" film has contrasting light and dark tones that resemble the contrasting tones of the original scene. *Orthochromatic*

film is sensitive to all colors except red. "Ortho" film records red objects as black. It is oversensitive to blue, and often makes blue skies appear white. Ortho film gives strong contrast between blacks and whites.

Film Speed is the speed with which a film reacts to light. This speed determines how much exposure the film needs to record an image of a subject. A *fast* film is highly sensitive to light. Its emulsion needs less exposure to record an image. *Medium-speed* and *slow-speed* film needs more exposure.

A film's instruction sheet tells the speed of the film. The speed usually is given in the form of an *ASA number.* ASA stands for the American Standards Association, which set up a standard method of determining film speeds. The speeds range from 1 to 200, or higher. The higher the ASA number, the faster the film. If you use an exposure meter, you must set the film speed number on the meter before it will show the correct exposure.

Fast films have several advantages. A fast film will record an image in dim light. It permits the use of a small *f*-stop or a fast shutter speed, or both. However, the negative of a fast film cannot be enlarged without some loss of quality. A fast film is more sensitive to light because its emulsion contains larger grains of silver salts. If the negative is enlarged, these grains will give the print a speckled, hazy appearance called *graininess.*

PHOTOGRAPHY COLOR

To understand color photography, you need to know some of the basic principles of color. Color depends primarily on light. Light that looks white to our eyes is really a mixture of all the colors of the rainbow. Any color can be reproduced by blending only three basic colors—blue, green, and red. These colors are called the *primary colors* of light. In color photography, blue light, green light, and red light are blended in certain proportions to reproduce any color. The colors in a picture are matched with those in the scene that was photographed.

For a full discussion of the basic principles of color, see COLOR (Color in Light; How the Eye Sees Color).

Color Film. There are two types of color film: (1) negative and (2) reversal. *Negative* film produces color negatives, from which color prints are made. *Reversal* film produces color *transparencies* (slides). A slide is usually viewed by placing it in a slide viewer or a projector, which projects the colored picture onto a screen.

Negative and reversal films are made in almost the same way. Each consists of three layers of emulsion on a sheet of plastic. These emulsions are similar to a black-and-white film emulsion. But in color film, each emulsion is affected by only one of the primary colors of light. The first emulsion is affected only by blue light. The second emulsion is affected only by green light. The third emulsion is affected only by red light.

When color film is exposed, light passes through the first emulsion and records an image of the blue areas of a scene. Light then passes through a special yellow filter layer. The filter prevents any unused blue light from entering the next two emulsions. Then light passes through the second emulsion. This layer records an image of only the green areas of the scene. Finally, light passes through the third emulsion, which records an image of the red areas of the scene. By this process, light forms three separate images on the film. The three images are not colored. The film is dyed during the development process. The images representing specific colors are necessary so that the right parts of the film can be dyed the correct colors.

Developing Color Film. Color film is developed in a special developer. The developer changes the exposed silver salts on the emulsions to metallic silver. A silver image forms on each emulsion layer. Each image represents the color of light that exposed the layer.

The developer causes colored dyes to form in each layer. Each layer contains a substance called a *coupler*. During the development process, this substance *couples* (joins) with a chemical in the developer to produce a colored dye. The couplers produce a different colored dye in each layer of the film.

These dyes are not blue, green, and red. The dyes are the *complementary* (opposite) colors of blue, green, and red. Yellow is the complement of blue. A yellow dye forms in the first layer, because this emulsion has recorded blue light. *Magenta* (bluish-red) is the complement of green. A magenta dye forms in the second layer, which has recorded green light. *Cyan* (bluish-green) is the complement of red. A cyan dye forms in the third layer, which has recorded red light. After development, each layer contains the color complementary to the color originally recorded.

Complementary colors are used as dyes because they

HOW COLOR FILM WORKS

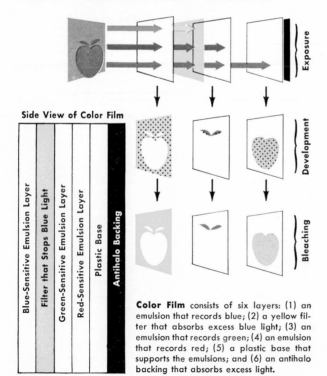

Side View of Color Film

Color Film consists of six layers: (1) an emulsion that records blue; (2) a yellow filter that absorbs excess blue light; (3) an emulsion that records green; (4) an emulsion that records red; (5) a plastic base that supports the emulsions; and (6) an antihalo backing that absorbs excess light.

Layers (bottom labels): Blue-Sensitive Emulsion Layer | Filter that Stops Blue Light | Green-Sensitive Emulsion Layer | Red-Sensitive Emulsion Layer | Plastic Base | Antihalo Backing

Right-side labels: Exposure | Development | Bleaching

Color Negative Film produces color prints. After exposure, the film contains images of the blue, green, and red areas of the subject. When the film is developed, the exposed silver salts change to metallic silver. A negative silver image forms in each layer of the film. Then a colored dye forms over each image. The silver is then bleached out of each image, leaving the dye. In the developed color negative, a yellow dye covers the image made by blue light. A *magenta* (bluish-red) dye covers the image made by green light. A *cyan* (bluish-green) dye covers the image made by red light. These colors are difficult to see because the entire negative has an orange tint that improves the color quality of prints. When the negative is printed, each dye holds back light of its complementary color. The yellow dye absorbs blue light, and lets red and green pass through the negative. The magenta dye absorbs green light, and lets blue and red pass through. The cyan dye absorbs red light, and lets blue and green pass through. In this way, the original colors appear in the print.

COMMON MISTAKES IN USING COLOR FILM

Accurate Exposure of color film produces natural, lifelike colors. One type of color film is designed for use in daylight. Another type should be used only with artificial light.

Overexposed Color Picture

Properly Exposed Color Picture

Underexposed Color Picture

reproduce the original colors of the subject when white light is passed through the film. To make a color print of a picture, white light is passed through the color negative. To project a color slide onto a viewing screen, white light is passed through the slide. The white light is made up of the primary colors blue, green, and red.

When white light is passed through the film, each dye acts as a filter on a primary color. The yellow dye absorbs blue light. This dye lets red and green light pass through the film. The magenta dye absorbs green light. It lets red and blue light pass through the film. The cyan dye absorbs red, and lets blue and green pass through the film. In this way, the original colors of the subject appear in a print of a picture or on a screen.

WORLD BOOK photos

Daylight Exposure of artificial-light color film makes all colors bluish. Daylight color film exposed with clear flash produces an orange picture.

Color Reversal Film produces color slides. After exposure, the film contains images of the blue, green, and red areas of the subject. The film then goes through two development processes. The first development changes the exposed silver salts to metallic silver. A negative silver image forms in each layer of the film. Then the film is re-exposed so that the remaining silver salts can be developed. During the second development, colored dyes form around the silver images of the subject. The silver is then bleached out of each image, leaving transparent film in those areas. In the developed film, a yellow dye surrounds the image made by blue light. A *magenta* (bluish-red) dye surrounds the image made by green light. A *cyan* (bluish-green) dye surrounds the image made by red light. When the slide is projected onto a viewing screen, each dye holds back light of its complementary color, and the original colors of the subject appear on the screen.

First Exposure

First Development

WORLD BOOK
diagrams

Second Exposure

Color Development
and Bleaching

PHOTOGRAPHY CAREERS

Photography offers a wide variety of interesting careers. A young person interested in a career in photography should have a general academic education. His knowledge of photography should extend beyond the technical knowledge of taking pictures. Some colleges and universities offer courses in photography for students studying journalism, fine arts, science, or engineering. A few colleges, and some art and technical institutes, give courses that lead to a bachelor's degree in photography. Information about careers in photography can be obtained from Professional Photographers of America, Inc., 152 W. Wisconsin Ave., Milwaukee, Wis. 53203.

Commercial Photography. The pictures taken by a commercial photographer are usually used for advertising. He photographs many different subjects, including machines, buildings, food, and persons performing various tasks.

Portraiture. A portrait photographer must understand and like people because he photographs important events in their lives. Some portrait photographers specialize in one type of portraiture, such as photographing weddings or children. A portrait photographer must know how to pose and light his subjects, and how to retouch negatives to correct unattractive blemishes.

Photojournalism. A photojournalist, or *press photographer*, takes pictures for newspapers and magazines. He must know how to seek out and record dramatic action in such activities as sports and politics. Some photojournalists take pictures that try to influence the public.

These pictures may show the need for better homes in slum areas or for less crowded classrooms in schools. A photojournalist who works for a news magazine often prepares picture stories. He creates a story in his mind, and tells it with pictures.

Science Photography. Photographic careers in science are increasing in number and importance. *Photographic engineering* is a new branch of photography. A photographic engineer works closely with scientists and engineers. He may prepare a complete series of photographs on the launching of a guided missile so that scientists can study each step in the launching. Or he may photograph the parts of a machine to show how they work.

Other Careers. Photography offers careers for researchers in photographic materials, chemistry, and optics. Persons interested in darkroom work hold jobs in photofinishing laboratories. The industry also needs business administrators and persons to sell photographic supplies. Other careers are open to persons who can teach photography or write about it. Clifton C. Edom

Advertising Photograph by Les Tirschel

News Photograph: "D-Day Invasion" from *Images of War* by Robert Capa   Magnum

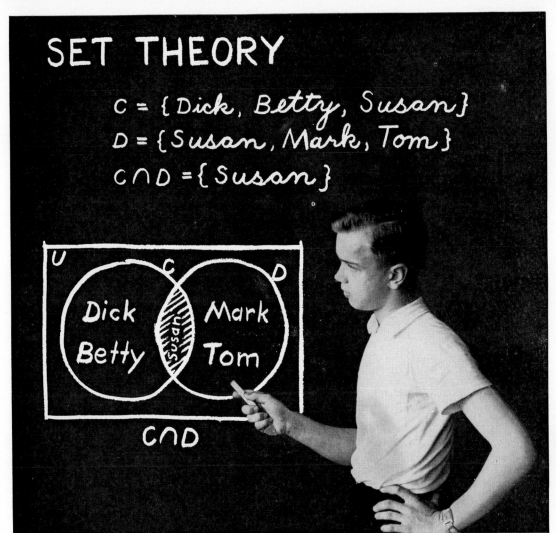

SET THEORY

C = {Dick, Betty, Susan}
D = {Susan, Mark, Tom}
C∩D = {Susan}

U C D
Dick Betty Susan Mark Tom

C∩D

Illinois Education Assn.

SET THEORY is a way of solving problems in mathematics and in *logic* (reasoning). By studying set theory, you can get a better understanding of arithmetic and of mathematics as a whole.

A *set* is any group of objects or ideas. A flock of geese or a box of crayons is a set of objects. The rules of a contest and the numbers from 1 to 10 are sets of ideas. The objects or ideas in a set are called the *members* of the set. A red crayon is a member of a set of crayons. The number 6 is a member of the set of numbers from 1 to 10.

Mathematicians use letters as the names of sets and the members of sets. Capital letters are used to name sets, and small letters are used to name members of sets. For example, the letter A may stand for "the set of fifth grade girls with blond hair." The letters m, s, and j would stand for the members of this set—Martha, Sue, and Jean. To show that set A consists of Martha, Sue, and Jean, you write: Set $A = \{$Martha, Sue, Jean$\}$ or

simply $A = \{m, s, j\}$. A set is shown by enclosing its members in *braces* $\{\}$.

You can also use another symbol to show that a member belongs to a particular set. For example, to show that Martha belongs to set A, you write $m \in A$, which is read: "*m is a member of A.*" To show that Helen is not a member of set A, you write $h \notin A$, which means: "*h is not a member of A.*"

A set may also be defined in terms of its properties. A *property* is something that relates the members to each other. In the example above, A has three properties: (1) its members are girls, (2) its members are in the fifth grade, and (3) its members have blond hair. To show these properties, you write: $A = x|x$ is a fifth grade girl with blond hair. This statement is read: "*A is the set of all members, x, such that x is a fifth grade girl with blond hair.*" The vertical line between the x's means "such that."

Kinds of Sets

In working with sets, it is important to be able to compare one set with another. Mathematicians have

Charlotte W. Junge, the contributor of this article, is Professor of Education at Wayne State University and co-author of the mathematics text "Growth in Arithmetic."

SET THEORY

given names to various kinds of sets to aid in such comparisons. The names refer to the number of members in a set and to relationships between sets. Ten main kinds of sets are (1) finite sets, (2) infinite sets, (3) empty sets, (4) single element sets, (5) equivalent sets, (6) universal sets, (7) subsets, (8) equal sets, (9) overlapping sets, and (10) disjoint sets. Every set can be called by several of these names. For example, equivalent sets can be finite and also disjoint.

Finite Sets and Infinite Sets. A *finite* set has a definite number of members. "Three cats" and "three thousand head of cattle" are finite sets. An *infinite* set has an endless number of members. The numerals you use in counting form an infinite set: 1, 2, 3, 4, 5, 6, and so on without end. It is impossible to list all the members of an infinite set. To describe such a set, you list the first few members and write three dots to show that the number of members is endless:

$$\{1, 2, 3, \ldots\}$$

Empty Sets have no members. They also are called *null sets*. The number of members in an empty set is called *zero*. The sets below show which students were absent from school on three days.

Monday	Tuesday	Wednesday
Paul	Joe	No one absent
Frances		

The Monday set of absentees has two members and the Tuesday set has one member. The Wednesday set has no members, so it is an empty set. You show an empty set by leaving a blank space between a pair of braces, or by writing the symbol ϕ:

Students absent on Wednesday $= \{\} = \phi$

Single Element Sets contain only one member. In the example above, the set of students absent on Tuesday is a single element set. The symbol for a single element set is a 1 between braces:

Students absent on Tuesday $= \{1\}$

Equivalent Sets have the same number of members. You can match their members one for one against each other. If the number of desks in a classroom is the same as the number of students, the set of desks is equivalent to the set of students. In the illustration below, the set of dogs is equivalent to the set of doghouses:

To show that sets A and B are equivalent, you write: $A \leftrightarrow B$. The symbol $\leftrightarrow$ means "is equivalent to." It shows that the members of both sets can be matched one for one, as in the illustration.

Universal Sets consist of all members being considered at any one time. Such a set may be called a *universe*. It is usually represented by the letter U. Suppose that in a certain problem you are working only with the numbers from 1 to 10. The universal set then has the following members: $U = \{1, 2, 3, 4, 5, 6, 7, 8, 9, 10\}$. In another problem, the universe might be "all even numbers," and in still another it might be "all students in sixth grade."

Subsets are contained within other sets. For example, the set "all sixth graders with brown eyes" is a subset contained in the set "all sixth graders." Two subsets of the set of numbers from 1 to 10 are shown below.

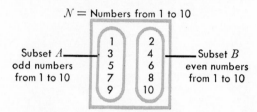

$N =$ Numbers from 1 to 10

Subset A — odd numbers from 1 to 10

Subset B — even numbers from 1 to 10

To show that A and B are subsets of N, you write $A \subset N$ and $B \subset N$. The symbol $\subset$ means "is included in."

Note that subsets A and B are finite sets because they have a definite number of members. They also are equivalent because you can match their members one for one against each other. They also are disjoint sets because no members belong to both A and B.

Equal Sets have the same members. Suppose that C stands for the set of students who received 100% on a spelling test: $C = \{$Steve, Mark, Joan, Tom$\}$. Suppose also that D represents the set of students who received 100% on an arithmetic test: $D = \{$Tom, Joan, Mark, Steve$\}$. Then C is equal to D because both sets have the same members. To show they are equal, you write: $C = D$.

Overlapping Sets and Disjoint Sets. *Overlapping* sets have some members in common. Suppose that Dick, Susan, and Betty were class officers last year, and that Mark, Susan, and Tom are class officers this year. Susan belongs to both sets. The sets overlap, as shown in the following diagram:

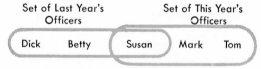

Set of Last Year's Officers — Set of This Year's Officers

Dick   Betty   Susan   Mark   Tom

Disjoint sets have no members in common. The illustration below shows a pair of disjoint sets:

| Chicago Minneapolis Detroit | Houston New Orleans Miami |

Diagraming Sets

Mathematicians often use diagrams to show relationships and to solve problems. Diagrams called *Venn diagrams* represent various types of sets. These diagrams are named for John Venn (1834-1923), an English scholar. Venn first used them in 1894 to help him understand the rules of solving problems in logic.

In a Venn diagram, rectangles and circles are used to represent sets. These figures show relationships between sets. A circle of a certain size may stand for a finite set, an infinite set, or an empty set. Two circles of the same size may represent equivalent sets or sets with different numbers of members. Therefore, there are no specific Venn diagrams for finite sets, infinite sets, empty sets, single element sets, or equivalent sets.

Diagram for Universal Sets is a rectangle labeled with the letter U. This diagram stands for all the mem-

bers you are considering in a particular problem. It may represent "all men," "the coins in Jane's purse," or any other group.

Diagram for Subsets is a circle labeled with the letter that represents the set. Suppose that the universal set U stands for all the students in Patrick Henry school, and that the subset A is all the sixth grade students in Patrick Henry school. You draw the circle for A entirely within the rectangle for U because every member of A is also a member of U.

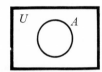

To show a subset of A, you draw another circle inside A. Suppose B stands for the boys in the sixth grade at Patrick Henry school. Here is the way you would add set B to the Venn diagram above:

You draw the circle for B entirely within the circle for A because every member of B is also a member of A.

Diagram for Equal Sets is a single circle labeled with two or more letters. Each letter stands for a set. The

single circle shows that each set has exactly the same members. You can think of the circle as two or more circles that overlap completely. For example, suppose U is the set of numbers from 1 to 10. Let G be the set of numbers used in counting to 10 by 2's. Let H be the set of numbers from 1 to 10 that can be divided evenly by 2. You can list the members of these sets as follows:

$$U = \{1, 2, 3, 4, 5, 6, 7, 8, 9, 10\}$$
$$G = \{2, 4, 6, 8, 10\}$$
$$H = \{2, 4, 6, 8, 10\}$$

Sets G and H have exactly the same members, so you represent both with a single circle in the diagram.

Diagram for Overlapping Sets consists of overlapping circles. This diagram shows that some of the

members of E also belong to F. Suppose U is the set of all students everywhere. Let E be the set of all girl students, and let F be the set of all students at Patrick Henry school. The shaded portion of the diagram represents the set of girl students at Patrick Henry school.

Diagram for Disjoint Sets consists of two or more separate circles.

Suppose U stands for all sixth grade students at Patrick Henry school. Let set C be the boys in sixth grade, and set D the girls in sixth grade. Both C and D are subsets of U. But C and D are disjoint sets because no member belongs to both of them.

Operations with Sets

Three basic operations are used to solve problems involving sets: (1) union, (2) intersection, and (3) complement. These operations resemble arithmetic operations such as addition and subtraction. In general, you work with two sets at a time, and produce a third set. The terms *union, intersection,* and *complement* name the operations and the sets that result from the operations.

Union of Sets includes all members of two sets without repeating any members. The symbol for union is $\cup$, which is called "cup." It is used the same way as the symbol $+$ in addition. To show the union of sets A and B, you write $A \cup B$, which is read: "*A union B.*"

Union of Disjoint Sets:
$$A = \{1, 2, 3\}$$
$$B = \{4, 5\}$$
$$A \cup B = \{1, 2, 3, 4, 5\}$$

$$A \cup B$$

The union of sets A and B includes all the members of A and B. In the Venn diagram, $A \cup B$ is represented by the shaded portions taken together. Note that A has 3 members, and B has 2. So $A \cup B$ has $3 + 2 = 5$ members. In the union of disjoint sets, the number of members equals the sum of the members in the sets.

Union of Overlapping Sets:
$$C = \{\text{Dick, Betty, Susan}\}$$
$$D = \{\text{Susan, Mark, Tom}\}$$
$$C \cup D = \{\text{Dick, Betty, Susan,}$$
$$\text{Mark, Tom}\}$$

$$C \cup D$$

The shaded portion of the diagram represents $C \cup D$. If you add the number of members in sets C and D, you get 6. But when you list the members of $C \cup D$, you write Susan's name only once. As a result, set $C \cup D$

SET THEORY

has only 5 members. In the union of overlapping sets, the total number of members is always less than the sum of the members in the sets.

Union of a Set and Its Subset:
$E = \{a, b, c, d\}$
$F = \{b, c\}$
$E \cup F = \{a, b, c, d\}$

$E \cup F$

When you list the members of $E \cup F$, you write b and c only once, because these members belong to both sets. So $E \cup F$ has exactly the same members as E. The shaded portion of the Venn diagram represents $E \cup F$. This portion lies entirely within the circle for E, showing that $E \cup F$ equals E. The union of a set and its subset always has exactly the same total number of members as the set itself.

Intersection of Sets is a set that includes only those members that belong to both sets. For example, in the sets $G = \{1, 2, 3\}$ and $H = \{2, 3, 4\}$, the intersection of G and H is the set $\{2, 3\}$. These members belong to both G and H. The symbol for intersection, $\cap$, is called "cap." To show the intersection of G and H, you write $G \cap H$, which is read "*G intersection H.*"

Intersection of Disjoint Sets is an empty set:

$A = \{1, 2, 3\}$
$B = \{4, 5\}$
$A \cap B = \{\ \} = \phi$

$A \cap B = \phi$

The intersection of A and B is an empty set because the two sets have no members in common.

Intersection of Overlapping Sets:

$C = \{\text{Dick, Betty, Susan}\}$
$D = \{\text{Susan, Mark, Tom}\}$
$C \cap D = \{\text{Susan}\}$

$C \cap D$

Only one member—Susan—belongs to both C and D. Therefore, Susan is the intersection of C and D, as shown by the shaded area in the Venn diagram.

Intersection of a Set and Its Subset:

$E = \{a, b, c, d\}$
$F = \{b, c\}$
$E \cap F = \{b, c\}$

$E \cap F$

Set F is a subset of E because every member of F is also a member of E. The intersection of E and F is the set $\{b, c\}$. The shaded portion of the Venn diagram shows $E \cap F$. This portion lies entirely within the circle for F, showing that $E \cap F$ equals F.

Complement of a Set is represented by the shaded portion of the Venn diagram below.

X'

592

In the diagram, X is a subset of the universal set U. The shaded portion represents the set of members that belong to U, but not to X. This set is called the complement of X. The symbol X' stands for the complement of X. For example:

$U = \{1, 2, 3, 4, 5\}$
$X = \{2, 3, 4\}$
$X' = \{1, 5\}$

The members 1 and 5 belong to U but not to X. Therefore, the complement of X is $\{1, 5\}$, as shown by the shaded portion of the Venn diagram.

Using Set Theory

In Arithmetic, set theory helps you understand some of the basic ideas of working with numbers. For example, you can learn the meaning of *number* by matching the members of two sets against one another.

$$A = \{a, b, c, d\}$$
$$\updownarrow \ \updownarrow \ \updownarrow \ \updownarrow$$
$$B = \{e, f, g, h\}$$

Sets A and B are equivalent. The members are different, but something about the sets is the same. This "something" is the *number* of members in each set. The name you use for any number is called a *numeral*. Thus, the numeral 4 tells you the number of members in either set A or set B. Before ancient man learned to count, he used the idea of equivalent sets to keep track of his possessions. See NUMERATION SYSTEMS (History).

Set theory also explains why you can add or multiply numbers in any order and still get the same answer. For example, $2 + 3$ is equivalent to $3 + 2$. Addition in arithmetic is the same as the union of disjoint sets. Here is the way you use set theory to represent the problems $2 + 3$ and $3 + 2$:

$C = \{h, i\}$ (2 members)
$D = \{j, k, l\}$ (3 members)
$C \cup D = \{h, i, j, k, l\}$ ($2 + 3 = 5$ members)

$D \cup C = \{j, k, l, h, i\}$ ($3 + 2 = 5$ members)

The arrows show that $C \cup D$ and $D \cup C$ contain the same number of members. Therefore, $2 + 3$ is equivalent to $3 + 2$. Mathematicians say that addition follows the *commutative law* (meaning *law of order*) because numbers can be added in any order to give the same result. Mathematicians also use set theory to explain other similar laws of working with numbers.

In Algebra, sets are helpful in several ways. Suppose that in a certain problem the letter x stands for any number from 1 to 10. You call x a *variable*, and you call the set of numbers from 1 to 10 the *domain of the variable*. The solution of the equation is the set of all numbers in the domain that make a true statement when substituted for x. Such a set is called a *solution set*.

Suppose that in a certain problem the domain of x is $U = \{4, 5, 6, 7, 8, 9\}$. You are asked to find the values of x that satisfy the condition: x can be divided evenly by 2. To solve this problem, divide each member of the domain by 2. You find that 4, 6, and 8 can be divided evenly by 2, but 5, 7, and 9 cannot. Therefore, the solution set is $\{4, 6, 8\}$. Depending on the problem, a solution set may be an empty set, or it may have any number of members. See ALGEBRA (Learning Algebra).

You can also use set operations such as union and intersection to understand and to solve certain algebra problems. For example, suppose the domain of x is $U = \{4, 5, 6, 7, 8, 9\}$. Find the values of x that satisfy the two conditions: (1) x can be divided evenly by 2, or (2) x can be divided evenly by 3. When two conditions are connected by the word *or*, the solution set must include all values of x that satisfy either the first condition or the second. You find that 4, 6, and 8 can be divided evenly by 2. Therefore, the solution set for the first condition is $A = \{4, 6, 8\}$. You can divide 6 and 9 evenly by 3, so the solution set for the second condition is $B = \{6, 9\}$. The solution set for the whole problem is $\{4, 6, 8, 9\}$, because each of these numbers satisfies either the first condition or the second. This solution set is the union of the overlapping sets $A = \{4, 6, 8\}$ and $B = \{6, 9\}$ as shown in the diagram below:

$$A \cup B$$

When two conditions of a problem are connected by the word *and*, the solution set must include all values of x that satisfy both the first condition and the second condition. For example, let $U = \{4, 5, 6, 7, 8, 9\}$. Find the values of x that satisfy the two conditions: (1) x can be divided evenly by 2 *and* (2) x can be divided evenly by 3. Again, the solution sets are $A = \{4, 6, 8\}$ and $B = \{6, 9\}$. But 6 is the only value that can be divided evenly both by 2 and by 3. The solution set for this problem is $\{6\}$, because only this value of x satisfies both conditions. This solution set is the intersection of the two sets $A = \{4, 6, 8\}$ and $B = \{6, 9\}$, as shown in the following diagram:

$$A \cap B$$

In Geometry, the sets studied are sets of points. The diagram below shows a set of two points, A and B. Each point is represented by a little dot:

$$\overset{\bullet}{A} \qquad\qquad\qquad \overset{\bullet}{B}$$

When you connect these two points with a straight line, you form a *line segment*. The notation $\overline{AB}$ is used to represent this segment. Points A and B are the *end points* of the segment. But you can imagine many other points, such as C, D, and E, on the same segment. Thus, segment $\overline{AB}$ consists of the set of all points that lie between A and B.

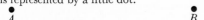

In a similar way, you can think of the set of all points on a sheet of paper, on a wall, or on any other flat surface. Such a set of points makes up a *plane*. On a plane, you can draw angles, circles, squares, and many other *plane figures*. A plane figure is called a *closed figure* if you can draw it by starting at any point and

returning to that point without lifting your pencil. A circle is a closed figure, but a half-circle is not.

Closed figures divide a plane into three sets of points: (1) the set of points on the figure, (2) the set of points inside the figure, and (3) the set of points outside the figure. In the diagram below, point A belongs to the set of points on the circle, B belongs to the set of points inside the circle, and C belongs to the set of points outside the circle.

You can use the union and intersection operations to describe the relationship between geometrical figures. In the diagram below, two line segments $\overline{CD}$ and $\overline{EF}$ cross at point P. In terms of sets, you would say that P is the intersection of the two sets of points that make up lines $\overline{CD}$ and $\overline{EF}$. You can write: $\overline{CD} \cap \overline{EF} = \{P\}$.

In the next diagram, the segment $\overline{GI}$ is made up of two segments, $\overline{GH}$ and $\overline{HI}$. The set of points in $\overline{GI}$ is the union of the sets of points in $\overline{GH}$ and $\overline{HI}$. You can show this relationship as follows: $\overline{GH} \cup \overline{HI} = \overline{GI}$.

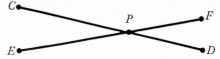

In Logic, set theory can help you form conclusions based on statements called *premises*. Here is the way you would use sets to illustrate three simple logical conclusions. In each of these examples, the universal set is the set of all students at Patrick Henry school.

1. *First Premise:* All sixth grade girls are members of the school glee club. *Second Premise:* Rita is a sixth grade girl. *Conclusion:* Rita is a member of the school glee club.

Let A be the set of members in the school glee club, and let B be the set of girls in sixth grade. According to the first premise, B is a subset of A. That is, every member of B is a member of A. According to the second premise, Rita belongs to set B. Therefore, Rita must also belong to set A.

2. *First Premise:* Some fifth graders take music lessons. *Second Premise:* Bob is a fifth grader. *Conclusion:* Bob might take music lessons, or he might not.

Let C be the set of students who take music lessons, and let D be the set of fifth graders. According to the first premise, some members of C are members of D. Therefore, the sets overlap. The intersection includes those fifth graders who take music lessons. According to the second premise, Bob belongs to set D. But it is impossible to tell whether Bob belongs to that portion of

SET THEORY

set D that intersects set C. Therefore, the only conclusion you can reach is that Bob might take lessons, or he might not.

3. *First Premise:* No girls are members of the school baseball team. *Second Premise:* Joan is a girl. *Conclusion:* Joan is not a member of the school baseball team.

Let F be the set of girl students, and let E be the set of players on the school baseball team. According to the first premise, the two sets are disjoint. That is, no mem-

bers of F belong to E. According to the second premise, Joan belongs to set F. Therefore, Joan cannot be a member of E.

History

The set theory studied in elementary and high schools developed from two mathematical discoveries of the 1800's—*symbolic logic* and *the theory of sets*.

Symbolic logic is a way of using mathematical symbols and operations to solve problems in logic. George Boole (1815-1864), an Irish mathematician, established the basis of this technique in the 1840's.

In the 1870's, the German mathematician Georg Cantor (1845-1918) applied some of the ideas of symbolic logic to sets of numbers. He formed a theory that he called "the theory of sets." Cantor developed this theory because of his interest in infinite quantities. For example, he showed how the members of certain infinite sets could be matched one for one against each other. The set of counting numbers can be matched against the set of even numbers as follows:

$$1, \quad 2, \quad 3, \quad 4, \quad 5, \quad \text{and so on:}$$
$$\updownarrow \quad \updownarrow \quad \updownarrow \quad \updownarrow \quad \updownarrow$$
$$2, \quad 4, \quad 6, \quad 8, \quad 10, \quad \text{and so on.}$$

Both sets are infinite and equivalent, even though the second is a part of the first.

Until the 1950's, the theory of sets was used mostly to solve problems in higher mathematics. Eventually, mathematicians and educators recognized that the ideas of set theory could help students understand the principles of arithmetic and mathematics. The study of sets became an important part of the "new mathematics," a new method of studying mathematics. By studying sets, students learned the meaning of basic ideas such as *number* and *numeral*. They developed a better understanding of operations in arithmetic and algebra. And they learned to apply mathematics to the field of logic. CHARLOTTE W. JUNGE

Set Theory Problems

1. $A = \{$Al, Bob, Carol, Don$\}$
   $B = \{$Carol, Don, Ed, Frank$\}$
   List the members of $A \cup B$.
2. Which of the sets below are equivalent?
   $\{$Red, Orange, Yellow, Green, Blue$\}$
   $\{a, b, c, d\}$
   $\{$Harry, Pete, Joan$\}$
   $\{13, 19, 25, 31\}$
3. List the members of $G = x | x$ is a counting number greater than 5 and less than 10.
4. $A = \{a, b, c, d\}$
   $B = \{c, d, e, f\}$
   List the members of $A \cap B$.
5. Which of the sets below are equal?
   $\{4, 7, 10, 13\}$
   $\{d, g, j, m\}$
   $\{$Jim, Ken, Laura, Mark$\}$
   $\{13, 10, 7, 4\}$
6. $U = \{7, 8, 9, 10, 11\}$. List the members that can be divided evenly by 3.
7. Draw the Venn diagram for the following problem: (1) all sixth graders attended the picnic; (2) Carl is in sixth grade; (3) Carl attended the picnic.
8. Which of the sets below are disjoint?
   $\{1, 3, 5, 7\}$
   $\{3, 4, 5, 6, 7\}$
   $\{2, 4, 6, 8\}$
   $\{7, 8, 9\}$
9. $C = \{$cat, dog, goldfish$\}$
   $D = \{$turtle, canary$\}$
   Find $C \cap D$.
10. $U = \{$Jim, Larry, Betty, Carol$\}$
    $A = \{$Larry, Betty$\}$
    List the members of A'.

Answers

1. $A \cup B = \{$Al, Bob, Carol, Don, Ed, Frank$\}$
2. $\{a, \; b, \; c, \; d\}$
   $\updownarrow \quad \updownarrow \quad \updownarrow \quad \updownarrow$
   $\{13, 19, 25, 31\}$
3. $G = \{6, 7, 8, 9\}$
4. $A \cap B = \{c, d\}$
5. $\{4, 7, 10, 13\}$
   $\{13, 10, 7, 4\}$
6. $\{9\}$

7. Students at picnic

U 6th graders   Carl

8. $\{1, 3, 5, 7\}$
   $\{2, 4, 6, 8\}$
9. $C \cap D = \{\} = \emptyset$
10. $A' = \{$Jim, Carol$\}$

Related Articles in WORLD BOOK include:

Algebra

Arithmetic

Boolean Algebra

Coordinates

Geometry

Logic

Mathematics

Numeration Systems

NUMERATION SYSTEMS, or Numeral Systems, are ways of counting and of naming numbers. We cannot see or touch numbers, because they are only ideas. But we can use symbols to stand for numbers. These symbols are called *numerals*. Here are four numerals that represent the number in one dozen: twelve, 12, XII, and ⊞⊞ II . Each of these numerals is a name for the number in one dozen. A numeration system tells how to form a numeral to represent any number.

We use a numeration system when we count. With this system, we can count to any number using only ten basic numerals called digits: 0,1,2,3,4,5,6,7,8,9. We call this system the *decimal system* because it is based on the number 10. The word *decimal* comes from the Latin word *decem* (meaning *ten*). The number 10 is called the *base* or the *scale* of this system.

Kinds of Numeration Systems

It is possible to use any number as a base in building a numeration system. The number of digits used in the system is always equal to the base. For example, (1) the *decimal*, or *base 10*, system uses 10 digits; (2) the *quinary*, or *base 5*, system uses 5 digits; (3) the *binary*, or *base 2*, system uses 2 digits; and (4) the *duodecimal*, or *base 12*, system uses 12 digits.

The Decimal System represents numbers in terms of groups of ten. Suppose you wanted to count the pennies you have saved in a jar. Instead of counting them one by one, you could count them in groups of 10. First, you would pile all the pennies in stacks of 10. Then you might arrange the stacks in groups, putting 10 stacks in each group, as shown below.

2 Groups of 10 Stacks of 10 Pennies   **4 Stacks of 10 Pennies**   **8 Pennies**

How many pennies are there? You could count them like this: 2 groups of 10 stacks of $10 = 2 \times 10 \times 10 = 200$; 4 stacks of $10 = 4 \times 10 = 40$; plus 8 single pennies. In all, you have $200 + 40 + 8 = 248$ pennies.

If you had counted the pennies one by one, you would have counted the same total. In decimal counting, you use one-digit numerals to count from 1 to 9. Then you use two-digit numerals to count from 10 to 99. In two-digit numerals, the digit on the left stands for the number of groups of ten. The digit on the right shows the number of ones, or single pennies. For example, the numeral 14 stands for 1 group of ten pennies plus 4 single pennies. After 99, you use three-digit numerals. The first digit on the left of these numerals stands for the number of *hundreds* (groups of ten tens). Thus, the numeral 248 stands for 2 hundreds + 4 tens + 8, just as shown in the illustration above.

The value of each digit in a decimal numeral depends on its *place* (position) in the numeral. For ex-

Charlotte W. Junge, the contributor of this article, is Professor of Education at Wayne State University and co-author of the mathematics text "Growth in Arithmetic."

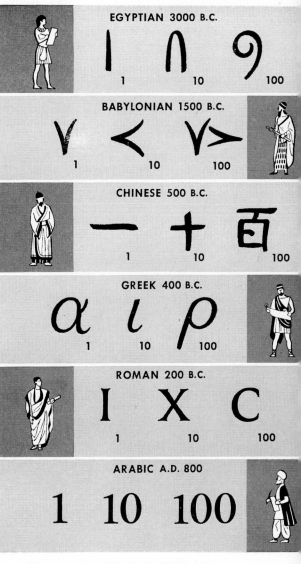

Numerals from Five Early Civilizations

ample, the numeral 482 contains the same digits as the numeral 248. But 482 represents a different number because the digits are in different positions.

Each position has a name that tells its value in terms of 10. In the numeral 248, the 8 is in the *ones* place; the 4 is in the *tens* place; and the 2 is in the *hundreds* place. In numerals with more than three digits, the additional positions are called the *thousands* place, the *ten thousands* place, and so on. Each position has a value 10 times greater than the position to its right.

Another way of expressing place value is to use *powers of 10* (10 multiplied by itself a certain number of times). The following table shows the meaning of several powers of 10.

Place Name	Power of 10	Meaning	Symbol
Tens	First	10	10^1
Hundreds	Second	10×10	10^2
Thousands	Third	$10 \times 10 \times 10$	10^3
Ten Thousands	Fourth	$10 \times 10 \times 10 \times 10$	10^4

NUMERATION SYSTEMS

The small numerals in the right-hand column are called *exponents*. They show how many tens you must multiply to find the meaning of each power. For example, 10^2 means 10×10 and 10^3 means $10 \times 10 \times 10$. In the numeral 248, the 8 is in the ones place; the 4 is in the 10^1 place; and the 2 is in the 10^2 place.

The value of any numeral is the sum of the values of the digits. Thus, the numeral 37 means "3 tens plus 7 ones," or $(3 \times 10^1) + (7 \times 1)$. The numeral 307 means "3 hundreds plus no tens plus 7 ones," or $(3 \times 10^2) + (0 \times 10^1) + (7 \times 1)$. In this numeral, the zero shows that the number of tens is *not any* or *none*.

The Quinary System is based on the number 5. The word *quinary* comes from the Latin word *quinque* (meaning *five*). This system uses five digits: 0, 1, 2, 3, and 4. In the quinary system, the numeral 10 (one, zero) stands for *five*, the base of the system. It means "1 five plus no ones." To avoid confusion between quinary numerals and decimal numerals, you can write the word "five" next to a quinary numeral: 10_{five}. This numeral is read "one, zero, base 5."

Grouping by Fives. The groups of stars below show the meaning of several quinary numerals:

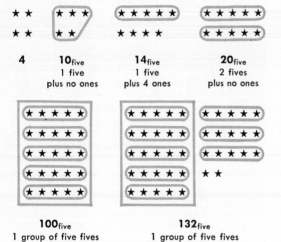

In quinary counting, you use single digits to count from 1 to 4. Then you use two-digit numerals to count from 10_{five} to 44_{five}. The digit on the left stands for the number of fives, and the digit on the right represents the number of ones. For example, in the numeral 23_{five}, the 2 stands for 2 fives and the 3 for 3 ones. After 44_{five}, you use three-digit numerals. The first digit on the left then stands for the number of five fives, as shown above in the diagram of the numeral 132_{five}. After 444_{five}, you use four-digit numerals, and so on.

Finding Place Value in Base 5. In a quinary numeral, the last digit on the right is in the ones place. Every other position has a value 5 times the value of the position to its right. In the quinary numeral 1402_{five}, the 2 means 2×1; the 0 means 0×5; the 4 means $4 \times 5 \times 5$; and the 1 means $1 \times 5 \times 5 \times 5$.

You can express the place value of each position in terms of powers of 5. The following table shows the meaning of several powers of 5 and their values in decimal numerals.

Power of 5	Meaning	Symbol	Decimal Value
First	5	5^1	5
Second	5×5	5^2	25
Third	$5 \times 5 \times 5$	5^3	125
Fourth	$5 \times 5 \times 5 \times 5$	5^4	625

In the numeral 1402_{five}, 2 is in the ones place; 0 is in the 5^1 place; 4 is in the 5^2 place; and 1 is in the 5^3 place.

Quinary numerals may be changed to decimal numerals by adding the values of the digits in terms of decimal numerals. The following calculation shows how to change the quinary numeral 1402_{five} to the decimal numeral 227:

$$
\begin{aligned}
2 \times 1 &= 2 \times 1 &&= 2 \\
0 \times 5^1 &= 0 \times 5 &&= 0 \\
4 \times 5^2 &= 4 \times 25 &&= 100 \\
1 \times 5^3 &= 1 \times 125 &&= \underline{125} \\
& && \ 227
\end{aligned}
$$

The Binary System is based on the number 2. The word *binary* comes from the Latin word *bini* (meaning *two at a time*). This system uses only two digits: 0 and 1. The numeral 10_{two} (one, zero, base two) stands for *two*, the base of the system. It means "1 two plus no ones."

Grouping by Twos. The groups of squares below show the meaning of several binary numerals:

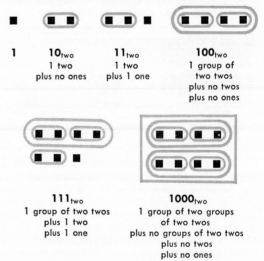

In binary counting, you use a single digit for none and for one. You use two-digit numerals for 10_{two} and 11_{two} (2 and 3 in decimal numerals). After 11_{two}, you use three-digit numerals until you come to 111_{two} (7 in the decimal system). After 111_{two}, you use four-digit numerals until you come to 1111_{two} (15 in the decimal system), and so on.

Finding Place Value in Base 2. In a binary numeral, every position has a value 2 times the value of the position to its right. For example, in the numeral 1010_{two}, the 0 on the right means 0×1; the 1 at the left of this 0 means 1×2; the next 0 means $0 \times 2 \times 2$; and the 1 at the far left means $1 \times 2 \times 2 \times 2$.

You can express the place value of each position in terms of powers of 2. The following table shows the meaning of several powers of 2.

Power of 2	Meaning	Symbol	Decimal Value
First	2	2^1	2
Second	2×2	2^2	4
Third	$2 \times 2 \times 2$	2^3	8
Fourth	$2 \times 2 \times 2 \times 2$	2^4	16

In the numeral 1010_{two}, the 0 at the right is in the ones place; the 1 next to it is in the 2^1 place; the next 0 to the left is in the 2^2 place; and the 1 at the far left is in the 2^3 place.

Binary numerals may be changed to decimal numerals by adding up the place values of the digits in terms of decimal numerals. The following calculation shows how to change the binary numeral 1010_{two} to the decimal numeral 10:

$$
\begin{aligned}
0 \times 1 &= 0 \times 1 = 0 \\
1 \times 2^1 &= 1 \times 2 = 2 \\
0 \times 2^2 &= 0 \times 4 = 0 \\
1 \times 2^3 &= 1 \times 8 = \underline{8} \\
& 10
\end{aligned}
$$

The Duodecimal System is based on the number 12. The word *duodecimal* comes from the Latin word *duodecimus* (meaning *twelfth*). It is a combination of the Latin words *duo* (meaning *two*) and *decem* (meaning *ten*). Because the duodecimal system is based on 12, it uses 12 digits: 0, 1, 2, 3, 4, 5, 6, 7, 8, 9, T, and E. The symbols T and E stand for the number of objects called *ten* and *eleven* in the decimal system. The numeral 10_{twelve} (one, zero, base twelve) means "1 twelve plus no ones." The numeral 12_{twelve} (one, two, base twelve) stands for "1 twelve plus 2 ones." It represents the number of objects called *fourteen* in the decimal system.

Grouping by Twelves. The groups of dots below show the meaning of various duodecimal numerals.

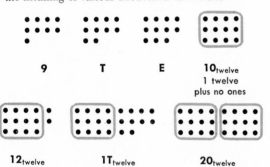

In duodecimal counting, you use single digits to count from 1 to E. Then you use two-digit numerals to count from 10_{twelve} to EE_{twelve}. The digit on the left stands for the number of twelves, and the digit on the right shows the number of ones. For example, in the numeral 45_{twelve}, the 4 stands for 4 twelves and the 5 for 5 ones. After EE_{twelve}, you use three-digit numerals. The first digit on the left then stands for the number of twelve twelves. For example, the number in one *gross* is twelve twelves (144 in decimal numerals). In the duodecimal system, one gross is written 100_{twelve}. This numeral means "1 group of twelve twelves plus no

twelves plus no ones." After EEE_{twelve}, you use four-digit numerals, and so on.

Finding Place Value in Base 12. In a duodecimal numeral, the last digit on the right is in the ones place. Every other position has a value 12 times the value of the position to its right. For example, in the numeral $E0T5_{twelve}$, the 5 means 5×1; the T means $T \times 12$; the 0 means $0 \times 12 \times 12$; and the E means $E \times 12 \times 12 \times 12$.

You can express the place value of each position in terms of powers of 12. The following table shows the meaning of several powers of 12 and their values in decimal numerals.

Power of 12	Meaning	Symbol	Decimal Value
First	12	12^1	12
Second	12×12	12^2	144
Third	$12 \times 12 \times 12$	12^3	1,728
Fourth	$12 \times 12 \times 12 \times 12$	12^4	20,736

In the numeral $E0T5_{twelve}$, 5 is in the ones place; T is in the 12^1 place; 0 is in the 12^2 place; and E is in the 12^3 place.

Duodecimal numerals can be changed to decimal numerals by adding up the place values of the digits in terms of decimal numerals. The following calculation shows how to change the duodecimal numeral $E0T5_{twelve}$ to the decimal numeral 19,133:

$$
\begin{aligned}
5 \times 1 &= 5 \times 1 = 5 \\
T \times 12^1 &= 10 \times 12 = 120 \\
0 \times 12^2 &= 0 \times 144 = 0 \\
E \times 12^3 &= 11 \times 1,728 = \underline{19,008} \\
& 19,133
\end{aligned}
$$

Working with Numeration Systems

Suppose you are asked to solve an addition problem: $4 + 4 + 4 = ?$. If you use the base 10 system, you know the answer is 12, as shown by these groups of dots:

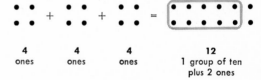

| 4 ones | 4 ones | 4 ones | 12 1 group of ten plus 2 ones |

But if you use the base 5 system, the sum of 4 plus 4 plus 4 is 22_{five}, as shown below:

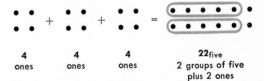

| 4 ones | 4 ones | 4 ones | 22_{five} 2 groups of five plus 2 ones |

On the other hand, if you use the base 12 system, $4 + 4 + 4 = 10_{twelve}$:

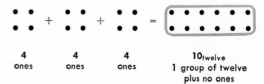

| 4 ones | 4 ones | 4 ones | 10_{twelve} 1 group of twelve plus no ones |

NUMERATION SYSTEMS

The numerals differ in each answer, but the number of dots is the same. The numerals are formed according to the principles of grouping and place value. Subtraction, multiplication, and division also follow these principles. You can study these principles by working problems in various numeration systems. In this way, you will get a better understanding of the use of numerals in arithmetic.

Decimal Arithmetic. Statements such as $4 + 5 = 9$, $9 - 4 = 5$, $9 \times 5 = 45$, and $45 \div 9 = 5$ are called *arithmetic facts*. We use many such facts in addition, subtraction, multiplication, and division.

Decimal Addition is a way of combining two or more groups into only one group. The principle of place value is used in adding ones to ones, tens to tens, and so on, as in the following example:

$$
\begin{array}{rl}
24 & \longrightarrow \; 2 \text{ tens} + 4 \text{ ones} \\
+12 & \longrightarrow \; 1 \text{ ten} + 2 \text{ ones} \\
\hline
36 & \longleftarrow \; 3 \text{ tens} + 6 \text{ ones}
\end{array}
$$

In this example, you use the addition fact $4 + 2 = 6$ and the fact $2 + 1 = 3$ (meaning 2 tens + 1 ten = 3 tens, or 30). Therefore, the sum is 3 tens plus 6, or 36. In some problems, the sum in one or more places is 10 or more. Then you must *regroup* the sum. Regrouping in addition is sometimes called *carrying*. The next problem shows how to regroup in decimal addition.

$$
\begin{array}{rl}
\overset{1}{4}8 & \longrightarrow \; 4 \text{ tens} + 8 \text{ ones} \\
+25 & \longrightarrow \; 2 \text{ tens} + 5 \text{ ones} \\
\hline
73 & \longleftarrow \; 6 \text{ tens} + 13 \text{ ones} \\
 & \qquad \text{or, after regrouping,} \\
 & \qquad 7 \text{ tens} + 3 \text{ ones}
\end{array}
$$

In this problem, the ones add up to 13, which can be regrouped into 1 ten plus 3 ones. So you write 3 in the ones place and a small 1 in the tens place above the 4. Then you add the tens: $1 + 4 + 2 = 7$ tens, or 70. Therefore, the sum is $70 + 3$, or 73.

Decimal Subtraction follows the same principles as decimal addition:

$$
\begin{array}{rl}
65 & \longrightarrow \; 6 \text{ tens} + 5 \text{ ones} \\
-23 & \longrightarrow \; 2 \text{ tens} + 3 \text{ ones} \\
\hline
42 & \longleftarrow \; 4 \text{ tens} + 2 \text{ ones}
\end{array}
$$

In this example, you use the subtraction fact $5 - 3 = 2$, and the fact $6 - 2 = 4$ (meaning 6 tens − 2 tens = 4 tens). To subtract a large number from a smaller number in any place, you have to regroup. Regrouping in subtraction is sometimes called *borrowing*. The next example shows how to regroup in decimal subtraction.

$$
\begin{array}{rl}
\overset{6}{\cancel{7}}\overset{1}{5} & \longrightarrow \; 6 \text{ tens} + 15 \text{ ones} \\
-48 & \longrightarrow \; 4 \text{ tens} + 8 \text{ ones} \\
\hline
27 & \longleftarrow \; 2 \text{ tens} + 7 \text{ ones}
\end{array}
$$

In the ones place, you must subtract 8 from 5, which is smaller. So you regroup 7 tens plus 5 ones to make 6 tens plus 15 ones. Show this by writing a small 1 in front of the 5, and by crossing out the 7 and writing a small 6 above it. Then use the subtraction fact $15 - 8 = 7$ to subtract the ones, and the fact $6 - 4 = 2$ to subtract the tens.

Decimal Multiplication is a way of putting together equal groups. The multiplication fact $4 \times 6 = 24$ means that 4 groups of 6 objects contain 24 objects. Here is the way you use place value to multiply 23 by 3:

$$
\begin{array}{rl}
23 & \longrightarrow \; 2 \text{ tens} + 3 \text{ ones} \\
\times 3 & \longrightarrow \; \phantom{2 \text{ tens} +} 3 \text{ ones} \\
\hline
69 & \longleftarrow \; 6 \text{ tens} + 9 \text{ ones}
\end{array}
$$

First, think: "3×3 ones = 9 ones, and 3×2 tens = 6 tens, or 60." Then add $60 + 9 = 69$.

In multiplication, you regroup when the product in any place is 10 or more:

$$
\begin{array}{rl}
\overset{1}{4}9 & \longrightarrow \; 4 \text{ tens} + 9 \text{ ones} \\
\times 2 & \longrightarrow \; \phantom{4 \text{ tens} +} 2 \text{ ones} \\
\hline
98 & \longleftarrow \; 8 \text{ tens} + 18 \text{ ones} \\
 & \qquad \text{or, after regrouping,} \\
 & \qquad 9 \text{ tens} + 8 \text{ ones}
\end{array}
$$

In this problem, the product of 2×9 is 18, which can be regrouped into 1 ten plus 8 ones. So you write 8 in the ones place and a little 1 in the tens place above the 4. Next, multiply $2 \times 4 = 8$ in the tens place, and add the 1 to make 9.

When the multiplier has more than one digit, you repeat the operation for each digit and add the products:

$$
\begin{array}{rl}
24 & \longrightarrow \; 2 \text{ tens} + 4 \text{ ones} \\
\times 12 & \longrightarrow \; 1 \text{ ten} + 2 \text{ ones} \\
\hline
48 & \longrightarrow \; 4 \text{ tens} + 8 \text{ ones} \\
24 & \longrightarrow \; 2 \text{ hundreds} + 4 \text{ tens} \\
\hline
288 & \longleftarrow \; 2 \text{ hundreds} + 8 \text{ tens} + 8 \text{ ones}
\end{array}
$$

First, multiply 24 by 2, writing 8 in the ones place, and 4 in the tens place. Then multiply 24 by 1 ten, writing 4 in the tens place and 2 in the hundreds place. Then add the products to get 288.

Decimal Division is a way of "undoing" multiplication. It is a grouping apart of one group into several groups of equal size. Here is the way you divide 69 by 3:

$$
\begin{array}{r}
23 \\
3\overline{)69} \\
6 \\
\hline
9 \\
9 \\
\hline
\end{array}
\qquad
\begin{array}{l}
2 \text{ tens} + 3 \text{ ones} \\
3 \text{ ones} \,/\, 6 \text{ tens} + 9 \text{ ones} \\
\phantom{3 \text{ ones} \,/\,} 6 \text{ tens} \\
\hline
\phantom{3 \text{ ones} \,/\, 6 \text{ tens} + } 9 \text{ ones} \\
\phantom{3 \text{ ones} \,/\, 6 \text{ tens} + } 9 \text{ ones}
\end{array}
$$

First, think: "6 tens ÷ 3 = 2 tens." Write 2 in the tens place above the 6. Then think: "9 ones ÷ 3 = 3 ones." Write 3 in the ones place above the 9. Therefore, $69 \div 3 = 2$ tens + 3 ones, or 23.

The principle of place value also makes it easy to divide larger numbers:

$$
\begin{array}{r}
82 \\
2\overline{)164} \\
16 \\
\hline
4 \\
4 \\
\hline
\end{array}
$$

First, think: "16 tens ÷ 2 = 8 tens." Write 8 in the tens place above the 6. Then think: "4 ones ÷ 2 = 2 ones." Write 2 in the ones place above the 4. Therefore, $164 \div 2 = 8$ tens + 2 ones, or 82.

Quinary Arithmetic has fewer arithmetic facts than decimal arithmetic because it uses only 5 digits instead of 10. These digits are: 0, 1, 2, 3, 4.

Quinary Addition. You can use the following table to find the basic facts of quinary addition.

+	0	1	2	3	4
0	0	1	2	3	4
1	1	2	3	4	10
2	2	3	4	10	11
3	3	4	10	11	12
4	4	10	11	12	13

The numerals in the table run from left to right in *rows*, and from top to bottom in *columns*. Each row and each column begins with a digit from 0 through 4. You can use these digits to locate various sums in the chart. To find the sum of 3 + 3, for example, first find the row that begins with 3. Then run your finger to the right along this row until you come to the column that has 3 at the top. Your finger will be on 11 (1 five plus 1), the sum of 3 plus 3. You can use the table to solve the following problem:

Quinary Addition	Meaning	Decimal Addition
21	2 fives + 1 one	11
+13	1 five + 3 ones	+8
34	3 fives + 4 ones	19

When the sum in any place is greater than 4, you have to regroup, as shown in the next example.

Quinary Addition	Meaning	Decimal Addition
¹24	2 fives + 4 ones	14
+14	1 five + 4 ones	+9
43	3 fives + 13 ones	23
	or, after regrouping,	
	4 fives + 3 ones	

First, use the fact 4 + 4 = 13 to add the ones. Regroup 13 ones into 1 five plus 3 ones. Write 3 in the ones place and a small 1 in the fives place above the 2. Next, add the fives: 1 + 2 + 1 = 4.

Quinary Subtraction. You can use the quinary addition facts table to find subtraction facts, too. For example, to subtract 3 from 11, first find the column that begins with 3. Next, run your finger down this column until you come to 11. Then run your finger to the left along this row to the beginning digit to find the answer, 3.

Use the table to solve the next problem:

Quinary Subtraction	Meaning	Decimal Subtraction
33	3 fives + 3 ones	18
−12	1 five + 2 ones	−7
21	2 fives + 1 one	11

The following problem shows how you regroup in quinary subtraction.

Quinary Subtraction	Meaning (after regrouping)	Decimal Subtraction
²₁ 31	2 fives + 11 ones	16
−14	1 five + 4 ones	−9
12	1 five + 2 ones	7

To subtract in the ones place, you must regroup 3 fives plus 1 one into 2 fives plus 11 ones. Then use the subtraction fact 11 − 4 = 2. Next, use the fact 2 − 1 = 1 to subtract the fives.

Quinary Multiplication also uses fewer facts than decimal multiplication. You can use the following table to find the basic quinary multiplication facts.

×	1	2	3	4
1	1	2	3	4
2	2	4	11	13
3	3	11	14	22
4	4	13	22	31

For example, to find the product of 3 × 4, first find the row that begins with 3. Then run your finger to the right until you come to the column that has 4 at the top. Your finger will be on the answer, 22 (2 fives plus 2 ones).

Here is a simple problem to solve with the table:

Quinary Multiplication	Meaning	Decimal Multiplication
21	2 fives + 1 one	11
×2	2 ones	×2
42	4 fives + 2 ones	22

When the product in any place is greater than 4, you have to regroup, as shown in the next example.

Quinary Multiplication	Meaning	Decimal Multiplication
¹14	1 five + 4 ones	9
×2	2 ones	×2
33	2 fives + 13 ones	18
	or, after regrouping,	
	3 fives + 3 ones	

First, you use the fact 2 × 4 = 13 to multiply in the ones place. Regroup 13 ones into 1 five plus 3 ones. Write 3 in the ones place and a small 1 in the fives place above the 1. Then use the fact 2 × 1 = 2 (meaning 2 × 1 five = 2 fives). Add the 1 five you got by regrouping in the ones place to make 3 fives, or 30 (three, zero) in quinary numerals. The sum is therefore 30 + 3, or 33 (three, three).

When the multiplier has more than one digit, repeat the operation for each digit and add the products:

Quinary Multiplication	Meaning	Decimal Multiplication
21	2 fives + 1 one	11
×12	1 five + 2 ones	×7
42	4 fives + 2 ones	77
21	2 twenty-fives + 1 five	
302	2 twenty-fives + 10 fives + 2 ones	
	or, after regrouping,	
	3 twenty-fives + 0 fives + 2 ones	

Quinary Division. You can also use the quinary multiplication table to find division facts. For example, to find the quotient 22 ÷ 4, first find the column that begins with 4. Next run your finger down this column until you come to 22. Then run your finger to the left along this row until you come to the beginning digit, 3. Use the table to work the following problem:

Quinary Division	Meaning	Decimal Division
12	1 five + 2 ones	7
2/24	2 ones/2 fives + 4 ones	2/14
2	2 fives	14
4	4 ones	
4	4 ones	

The next example shows how to divide with larger numerals.

$$\begin{array}{r} 122 \\ 31\overline{)4332} \\ 31 \\ \hline 123 \\ 112 \\ \hline 112 \\ 112 \end{array}$$

In this problem, think "3 will go into 4 once, so 31 will go into 43 once." Write 1 above the 3. Then finish the problem as you would a decimal division problem. But remember to use quinary arithmetic facts.

Binary Arithmetic has only a few facts because it uses only two digits—0 and 1.

Binary Addition is based on only these facts:

$$0+0=0 \quad 0+1=1 \quad 1+0=1 \quad 1+1=10$$

Here is the way you use these facts to add 11 + 11:

Binary Addition	Meaning	Decimal Addition
1		
11	1 two + 1 one	3
+11	1 two + 1 one	+3
110	10 twos + 10 ones	6
	or, after regrouping,	
	1 four + 1 two + 0 ones	

First, you use the addition fact 1 + 1 = 10 to add the ones. Regroup 10 ones into 1 two plus no ones. Write 0 in the ones place and a small 1 above the twos column. Then add the twos: 1 + 1 = 10; 10 + 1 = 11. Write 1 in the twos place and 1 in the fours place.

Binary Subtraction is based on four facts:

$$0-0=0 \quad 1-0=1 \quad 1-1=0 \quad 10-1=1$$

Use these facts to subtract 11 from 110:

Binary Subtraction	Meaning (after regrouping twice)	Decimal Subtraction
110	0 fours + 10 twos + 10 ones	6
−11	1 two + 1 one	−3
11	1 two + 1 one	3

In the ones place, you have to subtract 1 from 0. So you regroup 1 four plus 1 two plus no ones into 1 four plus no twos plus 10 ones. Then use the fact 10 − 1 = 1 to subtract the ones. To subtract the twos, you again have to take 1 from 0 because your first regrouping has left a 0 in the twos place. You regroup 1 four plus no twos into no fours plus 10 twos, and use the fact 10 − 1 = 1.

600

Binary Multiplication uses the following facts:

$$0 \times 0 = 0 \quad 0 \times 1 = 0 \quad 1 \times 0 = 0 \quad 1 \times 1 = 1$$

The product of two single digits is always either 0 or 1. However, you may have to regroup when adding products to complete a multiplication problem. For example, here is the way you multiply 11 × 11:

Binary Multiplication	Meaning	Decimal Multiplication
11	1 two + 1 one	3
×11	1 two + 1 one	×3
11	1 two + 1 one	9
11	1 four + 1 two	
1001	1 four + 10 twos + 1 one	
	or, after regrouping,	
	1 eight + 0 fours + 0 twos + 1 one	

Multiply and write your products the same way you do in the decimal system. But when you add the partial products, use binary addition facts. First, bring down the 1 in the ones place. Next, add the twos: 1 + 1 = 10. Regroup 10 twos to 1 four plus no twos. Write 0 in the twos place and add 1 to the 1 in the fours place: 1 + 1 = 10. Write 0 in the fours place and 1 in the eights place to get 1001.

Binary Division "undoes" binary multiplication. The following example shows how to divide with a two-digit binary numeral:

$$\begin{array}{r} 11 \\ 11\overline{)1001} \\ 11 \\ \hline 11 \\ 11 \end{array}$$

To divide 11 into 1001, think, "11 is larger than 10, but smaller than 100. So it must go into 100 once." Write 1 over the second zero. Then complete the problem by multiplying and subtracting as in a decimal numeral problem. But remember to use binary subtraction facts.

Duodecimal Arithmetic has more facts than decimal arithmetic because it uses more digits—0 through 9, plus T and E.

Duodecimal Addition. You can use the following table to find the basic facts of duodecimal addition.

+	0	1	2	3	4	5	6	7	8	9	T	E
0	0	1	2	3	4	5	6	7	8	9	T	E
1	1	2	3	4	5	6	7	8	9	T	E	10
2	2	3	4	5	6	7	8	9	T	E	10	11
3	3	4	5	6	7	8	9	T	E	10	11	12
4	4	5	6	7	8	9	T	E	10	11	12	13
5	5	6	7	8	9	T	E	10	11	12	13	14
6	6	7	8	9	T	E	10	11	12	13	14	15
7	7	8	9	T	E	10	11	12	13	14	15	16
8	8	9	T	E	10	11	12	13	14	15	16	17
9	9	T	E	10	11	12	13	14	15	16	17	18
T	T	E	10	11	12	13	14	15	16	17	18	19
E	E	10	11	12	13	14	15	16	17	18	19	1T

To find the sum of 6 + T, for example, first find the row that begins with 6. Then run your finger to the right along this row until you come to the column that has T at the top. Your finger will be on 14 (meaning 1 twelve plus 4), the sum of 6 plus T.

Use the table to solve the following problem:

Duodecimal Addition	Meaning	Decimal Addition
2T	2 twelves + T ones	34
+81	8 twelves + 1 one	+97
TE	T twelves + E ones	131

First, use the fact T + 1 = E to add the ones. Then use the fact 2 + 8 = T (meaning 2 twelves + 8 twelves = T twelves).

When the sum in any place is greater than E, you have to regroup in terms of the base, 12, as shown in the next example.

Duodecimal Addition	Meaning	Decimal Addition
¹6E	6 twelves + E ones	83
+34	3 twelves + 4 ones	+40
T3	9 twelves + 13 ones	123
	or, after regrouping,	
	T twelves + 3 ones	

In the ones place, E + 4 = 13, as shown in the table. Regroup 13 ones into 1 twelve plus 3 ones. Write 3 in the ones place and a small 1 in the twelves place over the 6. Then add the twelves: 6 + 3 = 9 twelves; 9 plus the 1 twelve you got by regrouping equals T twelves.

Duodecimal Subtraction. You can use the duodecimal addition facts table to find subtraction facts, too. For example, to subtract T from 14, first find the column that begins with T. Next, run your finger down this column until you come to 14. Then run your finger to the left along this row to the beginning digit to find the answer, 6.

Use the table to solve the next problem.

Duodecimal Subtraction	Meaning	Decimal Subtraction
E6	E twelves + 6 ones	138
−T4	T twelves + 4 ones	−124
12	1 twelve + 2 ones	14

First, use the fact 6 − 4 = 2 to subtract the ones. In the twelves place, use the fact E − T = 1 (meaning E twelves − T twelves = 1 twelve).

The next example shows how to regroup when the number you are subtracting in any place is larger than the one you are subtracting it from.

Duodecimal Subtraction	Meaning (after regrouping)	Decimal Subtraction
⁶¹7̸T	6 twelves + 1T ones	94
−3E	3 twelves + E ones	−47
3E	3 twelves + E ones	47

In the ones place, E is larger than T. So you regroup 7 twelves plus T ones into 6 twelves plus 1T ones. Cross out the 7 and write a small 6 above it, and write a small 1 in front of the T. Then use the subtraction fact 1T − E = E to subtract the ones. Use the fact 6 − 3 = 3 to subtract the twelves.

Duodecimal Multiplication also uses more facts than decimal multiplication. You can use the following table to find the basic duodecimal multiplication facts.

×	1	2	3	4	5	6	7	8	9	T	E
1	1	2	3	4	5	6	7	8	9	T	E
2	2	4	6	8	T	10	12	14	16	18	1T
3	3	6	9	10	13	16	19	20	23	26	29
4	4	8	10	14	18	20	24	28	30	34	38
5	5	T	13	18	21	26	2E	34	39	42	47
6	6	10	16	20	26	30	36	40	46	50	56
7	7	12	19	24	2E	36	41	48	53	5T	65
8	8	14	20	28	34	40	48	54	60	68	74
9	9	16	23	30	39	46	53	60	69	76	83
T	T	18	26	34	42	50	5T	68	76	84	92
E	E	1T	29	38	47	56	65	74	83	92	T1

For example, to find the product of 4 × 6, first find the row that begins with 4. Then run your finger to the right until you come to the column that has 6 at the top. Your finger will be on the answer, 20 (2 twelves plus no ones). Use the table to work the following problem:

Duodecimal Multiplication	Meaning	Decimal Multiplication
15	1 twelve + 5 ones	17
×2	2 ones	×2
2T	2 twelves + T ones	34

If the product in any place is greater than E, you have to regroup:

Duodecimal Multiplication	Meaning	Decimal Multiplication
²3T	3 twelves + T ones	46
×3	3 ones	×3
E6	9 twelves + 26 ones	138
	or, after regrouping,	
	E twelves + 6 ones	

In the ones place, use the fact 3 × T = 26. Regroup 26 ones into 2 twelves plus 6 ones. Write 6 in the ones place and a small 2 in the twelves place above the 3. Then multiply 3 × 3 to get 9 and add the 2 to get E.

When the multiplier has more than one digit, repeat the operation for each digit and add the products. Can you find a mistake in the next duodecimal problem?

$$\begin{array}{r} ^{1}24 \\ \times 13 \\ \hline 70 \\ 24 \\ \hline 310 \end{array}$$

First multiply 24 × 3. In the ones place, use the fact 3 × 4 = 10. Regroup 10 ones into 1 twelve plus 0 ones. Write 0 in the ones place and a small 1 in the twelves place above the 2. Then use the fact 3 × 2 = 6 in the twelves place, and add the 1 to get 7. Next, multiply 24×1 twelve: $1 \times 4 = 4$ in the twelves place, and $1 \times 2 = 2$ in the one hundred forty-fours place. Finally, add the products. Bring down the 0. Add $7 + 4 = E$ (not $7 + 4 = 11$). Bring down the 2. The correct answer is 2E0 (not 310).

Duodecimal Division. You can also use the duodecimal multiplication table to find division facts. For example, to find the quotient $42 \div T$, first find the column that begins with T. Next, run your finger down this column until you come to 42. Then run your finger to the left along this row until you come to the beginning digit, 5.

Use the table to work the following problem:

Duodecimal Division	Meaning	Decimal Division
17	1 twelve $+$ 7 ones	19
5$\overline{)7E}$	5 ones$\overline{)7\text{ twelves} + E\text{ ones}}$	5$\overline{)95}$
5	5 twelves	5
$\overline{2E}$	$\overline{2\text{ twelves} + E\text{ ones}}$	$\overline{45}$
2E	2 twelves $+$ E ones	45

Think, "7 twelves divided by 5 is 1 twelve." Write 1 above the 7. Multiply 1×5 and write the product 5 below the 7. Complete the problem as you would in decimal division, but use duodecimal arithmetic facts.

History

How Numeration Systems Began. Primitive man had several ways of recording the few numbers he needed. A shepherd could collect pebbles to represent the number of sheep in his flock. Each pebble meant one sheep. A bag of pebbles stood for the whole flock. By matching the pebbles against his flock, he could see if he had all his sheep. Mathematicians call this kind of matching *one-to-one correspondence.*

Later, man developed other ways to record the number of his possessions. He tied knots in a leather thong, or he scratched tally marks (**JHt**) on the side of a rock. He matched the knots or marks against each item.

Then man began to use words to represent numbers. These words told him "how many." They helped him to match items mentally. For example, he used the word for "wings" to mean two objects. To refer to four things, he used the name of a fruit that grew in clusters of four. For five items, he used the word that meant "hand." Such number-names appeared in various primitive languages. They showed that man had begun to form ideas of numbers. Whether he had three fish, three pebbles, or three tally marks, he recognized a "threeness" about each of these groups.

Finally, man began to *count* by arranging his number-names in a certain order. To count, he spoke or wrote the word that meant "one," next the word for "two," then the word for "three," and so on. In time, people in many parts of the world developed various kinds of counting systems. Some were based on five, others on ten, and still others on twelve or sixty. We still use such measures as 12 inches in a foot and 60 minutes in an hour, taken from these ancient systems.

In most early systems, people formed numerals simply by repeating basic symbols and adding their values to get the number they wanted. The Egyptians, Greeks, and Romans used numeral systems of this kind.

The Hindus used a system superior to all others. It followed the principle of place value and used a symbol that meant *not any.* This system became the decimal numeral system now used in most parts of the world.

The Egyptian Numeral System. About 3000 B.C., the Egyptians used *hieroglyphics* (picture writing). This system was based on 10. But it did not include a zero symbol, nor did it use the principle of place value.

The Greek Numeral System. About 500 B.C., the Greeks developed a system based on ten. In this system, the first nine letters of the Greek alphabet stood for ones, from 1 through 9. The next nine letters stood for tens, from 10 through 90. The last nine letters were symbols for hundreds, from 100 through 900. The Greeks, like the Egyptians, formed numerals by combining these symbols and adding their values.

The Babylonian Numeral System used *cuneiform* (wedge-shaped) symbols. An early system of about 3000 B.C. was based on 60. In this system, a numeral contained groups of symbols. One group stood for the number of ones, the next group stood for 60's, the next for (60×60)'s, and so on.

By 1500 B.C., the Babylonians had also developed a system based on 10. In this system, the numeral for "one thousand" was a combination of the symbols for "ten" and "one hundred."

The Hindu-Arabic Numeral System. Hindu mathematicians of the 300's and 200's B.C. used a system based on 10. The Hindus had symbols for each number from one to nine. They had a name for each power of 10, and used these names when writing numerals.

Probably about A.D. 600, the Hindus found a way of eliminating place names. They invented the symbol *sunya* (meaning *empty*), which we call *zero.* With this symbol, they could write "105" instead of "1 sata, 5."

During the 700's, the Arabs learned Hindu arithmetic from scientific writings of the Hindus and the Greeks. Then, in the 800's, a Persian mathematician wrote a book that was translated into Latin about 300 years later. This translation brought the Hindu-Arabic numerals into Europe.

Several hundred years passed before the Hindu-Arabic system became widely used. Many persons liked Hindu-Arabic numerals because they could easily use them to write out calculations. Others preferred Roman numerals because they were accustomed to solving problems on a device called an *abacus* without writing out the calculations. After the development of printing from movable type in the 1400's, many mathematics textbooks were published. Most of them showed calculations using the Hindu-Arabic system. These books brought the system into widespread use.

Rediscovering Numeration Systems. During the late 1600's, the German mathematician and philosopher Gottfried Wilhelm Leibniz (1646-1716) developed the binary numeration system. However, mathematicians found no practical use for the system until the 1940's, when computers were developed.

During the 1950's and 1960's, many educators recognized the value of teaching numeration systems. Students began studying various systems as a part of what was called the "new mathematics." By doing arithmetic with unfamiliar systems, students gained a better understanding of the familiar decimal system and of arithmetic in general. CHARLOTTE W. JUNGE

CONTENTS OF SECTION FIVE

This section lists important new words to be included in the 1965 edition of THE WORLD BOOK ENCYCLOPEDIA DICTIONARY. This two-volume work, published by Field Enterprises Educational Corporation in 1963, keeps abreast of our living language with a program of continuous editorial revision. The following new-

THE DICTIONARY SUPPLEMENT

word supplement has been prepared under the direction of the editors of THE WORLD BOOK and Clarence L. Barnhart, editor in chief of THE WORLD BOOK ENCYCLOPEDIA DICTIONARY. It is presented as a service to owners of the encyclopedia and as an informative feature to subscribers of THE YEAR BOOK.

A

ab·seil (äb′zil, äp′-), *n.* (in mountain climbing) the method of descending a very steep cliff by means of a rope secured at the summit. —*v.i.* to descend by this means. [< German *Abseil* < *abseilen*, verb < *ab-* down + *Seil* rope]

a·ce·di·a (ə sē′dē ə), *n.* sloth; torpor; loss of interest in life: *Pursewarden's suicide is attributed to acedia, or boredom with life* (Time). [< Late Latin *acēdia* < Greek *akēdíā* < *a-* not + *kêdos* care. Doublet of ACCIDIE.]

A horizon, the top layer of soil, usually dark-colored and characteristically leached and impoverished by rainfall.

A·kan (ä′kän), *n., pl.* **A·kan** or **A·kans. 1.** a group of peoples inhabiting Ghana and other parts of Western Africa. **2.** the Kwa language of these peoples.

a·lu·mi·no·sil·i·cate (ə lü′mə nō-sil′ə kit, -kāt), *n.* a compound of aluminum and silicon with a metal oxide or other radical (as albite). Feldspars and zeolites are aluminosilicates.

an·ti·he·ro (an′ti hir′ō), *n., pl.* **-roes.** a literary or dramatic protagonist who is typically unheroic, unconventional, and often resentful or contemptuous of accepted social standards and values: *The hero or antihero ... of "This Sporting Life" is a miner* (Manchester Guardian Weekly).

ant·ing (ant′ing), *n.* the practice among certain species of birds of picking up ants and dropping them among their feathers or of rubbing their feathers with them.

ap·pe·stat (ap′ə stat′), *n.* an area in the hypothalamic region of the brain regarded as the center which controls or regulates the appetite. [(coined in 1952 by Norman H. Jolliffe, born 1901, American physician and nutrition expert) < *appe-* (tite) + -*stat*]

a·rab·i·ca (ə rab′ə kə), *n.* **1.** coffee made from the seeds of the common coffee shrub. **2.** the seeds from which it is made. [< New Latin (*Coffea*) *arabica*, the coffee shrub]

arena theater or **stage,** theater-in-the-round.

as·si·mi·la·do (as′ə mə lä′dō), *n., pl.* **-dos.** (in Portuguese colonies, especially in Africa) a native who is literate or educated and therefore eligible for Portuguese citizenship. [< Portuguese *assimilado* (literally) one who is assimilated.]

atomic cocktail, a liquid suspension of radioactive isotopes of iodine, phosphorus, etc., given orally or internally in the treatment of some types of cancer.

Aus·tro-A·si·at·ic (ôs′trō ā′zhiat′ik, -shi-), *adj.* of, having to do with, or designating, a language family of southeastern Asia related to Austronesian that includes Khmer and Vietnamese.

aus·tro·sau·rus (ôs′trō sô′rəs), *n.* a fossil reptile recently excavated in Queensland, Australia.

au·tol·o·gous (ô′tol′ə gəs), *adj.* transplanted from the same person's body: *an autologous graft.* See also **autograft.** [< *auto-*[1] + Greek *lógos* relation (with English -*ous*)]

B

back·land (bak′land′), *n.* hinterland; back country. —*adj.* Also, **backlands,** back-country: *a backland hamlet.*

banana republic, any of the republics of Central America: *These are the true banana republics, traditional appendages of the United States and the United Fruit Company* (Manchester Guardian).

bard·ol·a·ter (bär dol′ə tər), *n.* a person who reveres Shakespeare; a Shakespeare worshiper or devotee. [(coined by George Bernard Shaw) < *Bard* of Avon + (id)*olater*]

bard·ol·a·try (bär dol′ə tri), *n.* devotion to or worship of Shakespeare.

bedroom suburb, *U.S.* a suburb inhabited by persons who work all day in the city and spend only the night at home.

belt·way (belt′wā′), *n.* a highway that goes around a city, congested area, etc.

B horizon, the layer of soil beneath the A horizon, in which insoluble iron oxides and clay minerals are deposited.

bi·cul·tur·al (bī kul′chər əl), *adj.* having or blending two distinct cultures: ... *the bicultural nature of the Canadian state* (Canadian Forum). —**bi·cul′tur·al·ly,** *adv.*

breath·a·lyz·er (breth′ə lī′zər), *n.* a device that measures the degree of intoxication of a person by analyzing his breath. Also, *especially British,* **breathalyser.** [< *breath* + (an)*alyzer*]

bull·horn (bůl′hôrn′), *n. U.S. Slang.* a loudspeaker: *Deputy Chief Ray called over the bullhorn to the rioters* (New York Times).

C

cache·pot (kash′pot′), *n.* a decorative container for holding potted house plants.

cap·ro·lac·tam (kap′rō lak′təm), *n.* a white crystalline compound used in making synthetic materials, especially one form of nylon. *Formula:* $C_6H_{11}NO$ [< *capro*(ic) acid + *lactam*]

cap·ture (kap′chər), *v.t.* **2.** *Nuclear Physics.* (of an atomic nucleus) to cause the capture of (an elementary particle). *n.* **3.** *Nuclear Physics.* the process by which an atomic nucleus absorbs or acquires an additional elementary particle, especially a neutron, often resulting in emission of radiation or fission of the nucleus.

car·ry·cot (kar′i kot′), *n. British.* a portable crib; bassinet: ... *a baby being taken for an airing in a carrycot* (Manchester Guardian).

cau·dil·lis·mo (kô′dēl yēz′mō, -dē-; *Spanish* kou′FHēl yēs′mō, -FHē-), *n.* the rule of a caudillo.

CERN (no periods), European Council for Nuclear Research (French, *Conseil Européen pour la Recherche Nucléaire*), an organization of 11 nations centered in Geneva.

chef de ca·bi·net (she′ də ka bēnā′), *French.* **1.** the chief adviser of a minister. **2.** (literally) head of cabinet.

chem·o·ster·i·lant (kem′ō ster′ə-lənt), *n.* a chemical that destroys an insect's ability to reproduce: *The substance could aid pest control ... by combination with a chemosterilant* (Science News Letter).

C horizon, the bottom layer of soil, beneath the B horizon, containing a mixture of decomposed rock and unchanged materials from which soil has not yet begun to form.

cin·e (sin′ə, sin′i), *adj.* cinematographic; motion-picture: *a cine camera, cine projector, cine film.* [short for *cinema*]

ci·né·aste (si nā äst′), *n. French.* **1.** a motion-picture writer or director. **2.** a motion-picture enthusiast.

cis (sis), *adj. Chemistry.* of or having to do with an isomeric compound that has certain atoms on the same side of a plane: *cis configurations.* [< Latin *cis* on this side of]

cliff·hang·ing (klif′hang′ing), *adj. Slang.* suspenseful: *a cliffhanging contest.*

com·bin·a·to·ri·al (kəm bī′nə-tôr′i əl, -tōr′-), *adj.* combinational.

com·put·er·ize (kəm pū′tə rīz), *v.t.,* **-ized, -iz·ing.** to use, perform, operate, etc., by means of a computer or computers: *to computerize a system.*

con·do·min·i·um, *n.* **3. a.** *U.S.* an apartment house in which apartments are neither rentals nor cooperatives but purchased as pieces of real estate and separately valued for property tax purposes. **b.** an apartment in such a building

Co·sa Nos·tra (kō′zə nōs′trə, nos′-), a secret society of criminals operating in the United States and identified with the Mafia. [< Italian *cosa nostra* our thing]

coun·ter·force (koun′tər fôrs′, -fōrs′), *n.* a force acting in opposition to another; contrary, opposing, or resisting force: *The counterforce to the body's efforts is provided by the body-weight* (New Scientist).

Cox·sack·ie virus (kok sak′ē), one of a group of intestinal viruses associated with various diseases in man, especially respiratory diseases. [< *Coxsackie*, a city in eastern New York where virus was first found]

D

de·cou·ple (di kup′əl), *v.t.* to reduce the shock waves (of a nuclear explosion) by detonating underground.

de·my·thol·o·gize (dē′mi thol′ə-jīz), *v.t.,* **-gized, -giz·ing.** to remove myths or mythological concepts from (Scripture, theology, etc.): *He argues that the essential Gospel message must be demythologized by liberating it from antiquated supernatural language* (Time).

der·ri·ère or **der·ri·ere** (de′ri är′), *n.* the rump; buttocks. [< French *derrière* < adj., back < Old French *deriere* < Latin *de retrō* from behind]

de·struct (di strukt′), *U.S. Aerospace. v.t., v.i.* to blow up, as a missile that fails to function properly. —*n.* the destructing of a missile.

di·ga·met·ic (dī′gə met′ik), *adj. Biology.* producing two kinds of gametes or germ cells, as one containing an X chromosome and another a Y chromosome.

dir·ham (dir ham′), *n.* **1.** a unit of money in Morocco, worth about 20 cents. **2.** a measure of weight in Egypt, equal to about 3.12 grams. Also, **dirhem.** [< Arabic *dirham* < Latin *drachma*]

dis·co·thèque (dis′kə tāk′; French dēs kō tek′), *n.* a night club where phonograph records are played for dancing. [< French *discothèque* (literally) disk collection, disk cabinet < *disque* disk + *-thèque* < Latin *-thēca* < *thēca* case, cover]

dock, *v.t.* **3.** to join (two spacecraft, as a space capsule and a supply satellite) while in space.

Dow-Jones average or **index** (dou′jōnz′), *U.S.* an index or average of stock-market quotations for industrials, railroads, and utilities, issued daily to show the relative price of stocks. [< Charles H. *Dow* and Edward D. *Jones,* American economists]

D region, the lowest layer of the ionosphere, about 25 to 50 miles above the earth. See also **E region, F region.**

E

ec·u·men·ism (ek′yú men′iz əm, ek′yú mə niz əm), *n.* **1.** the principle of world-wide Christian harmony and unity. **2.** ecumenicity.

ec·u·men·ist (ek′yú men′ist), *n.* a supporter or champion of ecumenism.

e·lec·tro·pol·ish (i lek′trō pol′-ish), *v.t.* to polish (metal) by means of electrolysis.

em·pa·thet·ic (em pə thet′ik), *adj.* of, characterized by, or having empathy: *Alcoholics are ... empathetic to other alcoholics* (Harper's).

English primrose, cowslip.

Eu·ro·crat (yúr′ə krat), *n.* an official or representative of the European Economic Community. [< *Euro*(pe) + *-crat,* as in *bureaucrat*]

F

farm system, 1. *U.S.* the system of farming out or assigning young baseball players to a minor-league team. **2.** (in Canada) a similar system for training hockey players.

fer·re·dox·in (fer′ə dok′sin), *n.* an iron-rich protein present in anaerobic bacteria and in green plants, and thought to be the agent of primary energy-transfer process, especially in photosynthesis. [< Latin *ferrum* iron + Greek *dóxa* glory + English *-in*]

fix, *n.* **3.** *U.S. Slang.* **a.** a bribe. **b.** a dose of narcotics: *These prowlers are narcotic addicts. Office thievery is the source of their next fix* (Time).

flank speed, a ship's maximum prescribed speed: *They turned out to be three Indonesian torpedo boats racing at flank speed (40 knots) toward the Dutch New Guinea coast* (Time).

flank·er·back (flang′kər bak′), *n. American Football.* a back who lines up for a flanking position closer to the sidelines than his opponent.

flat·ette (flə tet′), *n.* (in Australia and New Zealand) a small apartment; flatlet.

F layer, F region: *The part of the earth's high atmosphere affected was 100 to 200 miles above the surface, called the F layer of the ionosphere, which reflects radio waves* (Science News Letter).

flood·wa·ter (flud′wôt′ər, -wot′-), *n.* water flooding dry land: *Floodwaters began receding in some areas of* Wall Street Journal).

folk·ish (fōk′ish), *adj.* of, resembling, or suggestive of the common or native people of a region or country: *Some of the material does have a folkish naïveté about it, but it is* [not] *mere primitivism* (New York Times).

force de frappe (fôrs də fräp′), *French.* **1.** an atomic stockpile for use as a nuclear deterrent: ... *the embryonic beginning of a European force de frappe* (New York Times).

force-feed (fôrs′fēd′, fōrs′-), *v.t.* **-fed, -feed·ing.** to feed by force: *If a patient will not eat, he may be force-fed* (Atlantic).

G

Gab·o·nese (gab′ə nēz′, nēs′), *adj., n., pl.* **-nese.** —*adj.* of Gabon, its people, or their language. —*n.* a native of Gabon, a republic in Central Africa.

gallows humor, a bitter, morbid form of humor, as of those condemned to the gallows: *The Ingoldsby Legends has humor, but it is gallows humor* (Atlantic).

general semantics, a theory and a method intended to improve the quality of human experiences and relationships by training people to be more critical in their use of and reaction to words and symbols; developed by Alfred Korzybski.

generative grammar, (in structural linguistics) a system of syntactic, phrasal, and morphophonemic rules for constructing or producing all the grammatically correct sentences of a language.

gin⁶ (gin), *n. Australian Slang.* a female aborigine.

ginger group, *British.* an active, stimulating, and challenging minority group within an organization: ... *a ginger group powerfully pressing the established leaders* (Manchester Guardian Weekly).

glamour stock, *U.S.* an over-the-counter stock having special public appeal, usually issued by small companies in fields such as electronics, aircraft, and aluminums.

gon·a·do·trop·in (gon′ə də trop′-in, gə nad′ə-), *n.* a gonadotropic hormone.

goon·er·y (gü′nər i), *n.* foolishness; silly nonsense; whimsicality: [Chesterton] *is never far from a sort of mystical goonery, as when he seeks the link between Zulus, gardening, ... and the French Revolution* (Manchester Guardian Weekly).

gopher ball, *U.S. Slang.* a baseball pitch that is hit for a home run.

grad² (grad), *n. Navigation.* a unit for measuring angles or calculating a position on the earth's surface. A grad equals 9/10 of a degree.

grey eminence, *Especially British.* a powerful person behind the scenes éminence grise: *Mr. Upward*

was the key figure or grey eminence of the group usually known as "the thirties poets" (Manchester Guardian).

H

halfway house, 2. *U.S.* a place where young offenders who have nearly completed terms of imprisonment are rehabilitated before discharge or parole.

hap·to·glo·bin (hap′tə glō bin), *n.* one of a class of proteins in blood plasma, used in blood analysis. [< Greek *háptein* to touch, seize + English *globin*]

hard-edge (härd′ej′), *adj.* of or belonging to a style of abstract art characterized by sharp outlines and uncluttered images.

het·er·o·graft (het′ər ə graft, -gräft), *n.* tissue from an individual grafted on a member of another species (distinguished from *homograft*). See also **autograft.**

holiness church, one of a group of American Protestant sects deriving from the early Methodist church, that emphasize the doctrine of Christian perfection in faith and works.

hot issue, *U.S.* a glamour stock or similar speculative stock that rises rapidly in price after the initial public offering.

hy·dro·skim·mer (hī′drō skim′-ər), *n.* a ground effect machine for traveling over water, with a fin along each side that pierces the water's surface.

hy·per·cal·ce·mi·a or **hy·per·cal·cae·mi·a** (hī′pər kal sē′mi ə), *n.* an excessive amount of calcium in the blood.

I

ice, *n.* **8.** *U.S. Slang.* **a.** money given as bribe, especially to the police. **b.** under-the-counter money given to a theater employee for choice or extra tickets to a performance: *The take on "ice" in one recent musical was over a million dollars a year* (San Francisco Chronicle).

I.D. card (i′dē′), identification card.

idea man, one who is fertile or adept in conceiving new ideas that can be put into practice.

I·den·ti·kit (ī den′tə kit), *n.* an apparatus used by the British police to make composite portraits of wanted criminals. [< *identi*(fica-tion) *kit*]

immersion heater, an electric heater designed to be immersed in water that is to be heated.

Im·preg (im′preg), *n. Trademark.* wood impregnated with resin under steam to prevent swelling or shrinking. [< *impreg*(nated)]

in, *adj.* **3.** *Slang.* up-to-date; fashionable: *The subjects of the interviews are often "in" novelists like Joseph Heller and Norman Mailer* (Canadian Forum). —*n. Informal.* **1.** position of influence: ... *Assembly Speaker Unruh's White House "in"* (Wall Street Journal). **2.** access: *A magical charm was her protection, even giving her an "in" to the cool clique* (Punch).

Pronunciation Key; hat, āge, cãre, fär; let, ēqual, tėrm; it, īce; hot, ōpen, ôrder; oil, out; cup, pút, rüle, ūse; child; long; thin; ŦHen; zh, measure; ə represents a in about, e in taken, i in pencil, o in lemon, u in circus.

605

in pec·to·re (in pek′tə ri, -pek-tôr′ā), *Latin.* **1.** undisclosed; secret; in petto: *a cardinal in pectore.* **2.** (literally) in the breast.

in pet·to (in pet′tō), *Italian.* **1.** secretly; not announced; undisclosed (used especially of cardinals appointed by the Pope but not named in consistory). **2.** (literally) in the breast.

in·put, *n.* **3.** information put into the storage unit of a computer.

I·so·lette (i′sə let, i′sə let′), *n. Trademark.* an incubator for premature babies that gives automatic control of temperatures, humidity, and oxygen strength.

isometric exercises, exercises which are intended to strengthen muscles by pushing against an immovable object, as a wall.

J

john·boat (jon′bōt′), *n. U.S.* a small, light rowboat with a flat bottom and square ends; flat-bottomed skiff: *We passed a landing with a half-sunken johnboat tied to a willow root* (New Yorker).

jungle gym, a framework of tubular steel bars for children to climb or swing on as a pastime: *Plans for the commons include a basketball court, a slide, a jungle gym* (New York Times).

K

Ka·po (kä′pō), *n., pl.* **-pos.** a prisoner in a labor or concentration camp who is put in charge of other prisoners: *The prisoners ... depended entirely on the whim of the guards and Kapos* (Atlantic). [< German *Kapo* < Italian *capo* head < Latin *caput*]

key club, *U.S.* a night club that admits only members, who usually receive a key to the premises: *A key club is an inexpensive way to attain status* (Wall Street Journal).

kneel-in (nēl′in′), *n. U.S.* the presence of Negroes at a white church as a protest against racial segregation.

ko·lo (kō′lō), *n.* the Serbo-Croatian national dance, performed in a circle with intricate steps, footstamping, and a fast tempo. [< Serbo-Croatian *kolo*]

kook (kük), *n. U.S. Slang.* a kooky person; an odd or crazy individual.

L

Land·race (land′rās′), *adj.* of or designating a breed of large, white hogs introduced from Scandinavia into Great Britain.

lase (lāz), *v.i.,* **lased, las·ing.** *Electronics.* (of a laser) to generate coherent light: *So far, the materials that have been made to "lase" have been either gaseous or solid crystals* (New Scientist). [back formation < *laser*]

Latin square, a square divided into a number of cells containing Latin letters so arranged that a letter appears only once in each row and column. It is used especially in statistics to order various elements so as to control variability.

learned borrowing, 1. the process of borrowing a classical word into a modern Romance language directly, with slight phonetic alteration. **2.** word borrowed in this way.

letter of intent, a letter in which the signer declares his intention to buy, produce, deliver, etc., issued in advance of a formal contract: *Boeing has sold 134 [jet planes] to 11 airlines, either on firm contract or letter of intent* (Time).

life expectancy, the average number of years remaining that a person at a given age can expect to live.

life sciences, botany, zoology, biochemistry, biophysics, microbiology, and other sciences dealing with living matter (distinguished from *physical sciences*).

lim·bo, *n.* **4.** a West Indian calypso dance in which each participant dances his way under a rod held up horizontally, bending backward to avoid touching the rod as it is progressively lowered.

linear programming, a method of solving operational problems by stating a number of variables simultaneously in the form of linear equations and calculating the optimal solution within the given limitations.

lo·be·line (lō′bə lēn), *n.* a poisonous alkaloid obtained from a variety of lobelia, used as a respiratory stimulant and smoking deterrent. *Formula:* $C_{22}H_{27}NO_2$

lob·u·lat·ed (lob′yə lā′tid), *adj.* consisting of or separated into lobules: *lobulated kidneys.*

ly·so·some (li′sə sōm), *n.* a particle in the cytoplasm of most cells that contains destructive, hydrolytic enzymes: *The lysosomes function in many ways as the digestive system of the cell* (Scientific American). [< Greek *lýsis* (see LYSIS) + *sôma* body]

M

machine language, information or instructions in the form of numbers, characters, punched tape, etc., that can be processed by an electronic computer or a data-processing machine.

Ma·fi·o·so (ma′fi ō′sō), *n., pl.* **-si** (-sē). a member of the Mafia. [< Italian *mafioso* < *mafia* mafia]

Ma·qui·sard (mà kē zàrd′), *n. French.* a member of the Maquis.

market letter, *U.S.* a newsletter containing information and advice on the stock market, issued by a stockbroker or investment advisory firm to its customers.

ma·trix, *n.* **5.** *Mathematics.* a set of quantities in a rectangular array, subject to operations such as multiplication or inversion according to specified rules.

meg·a·lo·pol·i·tan, *n.* a person living in a megalopolis.

Met·ro or **met·ro¹** (met′rō), *U.S. and Canada.* —*n.* a form of municipal government whose powers extend over a metropolitan area and usually encompass a group of smaller municipalities: *Metro has amalgamated some of the services shared by all, such as police, water, conservation ... and town planning* (Canada Month). —*adj.* **1.** of or designating such a form of government. **2.** extending over a metropolitan area: *Metro Toronto.* [< *metro*(politan) area]

mix·age (mik′sij), *n.* the editing of motion-picture film.

mixed-manned (mikst′mand′), *adj.* (of a supranational military force or unit) supplied with men representing member nations; multinational or multilateral: *... the practical problems of setting up a mixed-manned NATO nuclear force* (Manchester Guardian Weekly).

mo·lec·u·lar·i·ty (mə lek′yə lar′ə ti), *n.* molecular condition or quality: *the molecularity of a gas.*

mouth-to-mouth (mouth′tu mouth′), *adj.* of or designating a method of artificial respiration in which air is breathed directly into the victim's mouth and nose to inflate the lungs, with intervals to allow the lungs to empty: *Christopher, 2, appeared lifeless, but firemen restored his breathing by mouth-to-mouth resuscitation* (New York Times).

mul·ti·lat·er·al·ism (mul′ti lat′-ər ə liz′əm), *n.* **1.** a policy of reciprocity or freedom in trading with many nations (distinguished from *bilateralism*). **2.** belief in or adoption of a multilateral policy, such as the joint control of nuclear weapons by the members of an alliance (distinguished from *unilateralism*).

N

ne·o·co·lo·ni·al·ism (nē′ō kə lō′ni ə liz′əm), *n.* the supposed policy or practice of a large nation to dominate politically or economically smaller nations, especially former colonies; imperialism: *Indonesia and others ... use the notion of neocolonialism to attack the former colonial Powers* (Manchester Guardian Weekly).

neon tetra, a small, brightly colored fish of the upper Amazon region, commonly raised in aquariums; tetra.

New Criticism, a form of literary criticism that originated in the United States in the 1920's, characterized by close textual analysis, complex interpretations of poems, and use of the methods or principles of linguistics and other related disciplines.

new·speak (nü′spēk, nü′-), *n.* language in which the words are made to mean the opposite of their real meanings to conform to an ideology: *"Newspeak," in which "Big Brother" has become the ... word for "tyrant"* (Wall Street Journal). [coined by George Orwell, 1903–1950, an English novelist]

new wave, a movement in cinematography originating in France in the 1950's, characterized by extensive use of symbolism, sophisticated themes, and unconventional camerawork. [translation of French *nouvelle vague*]

non·he·ro (non′hir′ō), *n., pl.* **-roes.** an antihero: *We have met ... that wistful, beset nonhero many times in recent English novels* (New Yorker).

noth·o·saur (noth′ə sôr), *n.* any of a group of extinct marine reptiles, common in the Triassic period, similar to the plesiosaurs but smaller. [< New Latin *Nothosaurus* the genus name < Greek *nóthos* bastard + *saûros* lizard]

nou·velle vague (nú vel′ våg′), *French.* the new wave, a French cinematographic movement.

nuclear club, the group of nations armed with nuclear weapons: *Much of the disarmament negotiation turns on whether and how the nuclear club could be closed* (Christian Science Monitor).

O

o·fay (ō′fā, ō fā′), *n. U.S. Slang.* a white person (used in an unfriendly way).

one-up (wun′up′), *v.t.,* **-upped, -upping.** *Informal.* to gain one up on; outstrip: *The party's 46-year-old leader . . . one-upped the socialists by endorsing the Saskatchewan plan* (Canada Month).

oomph, *n. U.S. Slang.* 2. sex appeal: *"His clothes have oomph," said a buyer* (New York Times).

operator gene, a gene which initiates the process resulting in the synthesis of messenger RNA. See also **operon.**

op·er·on (op′ər on), *n.* the region of a chromosome which contains the operator gene and any structural genes involved in the production of messenger RNA for a given synthesis. [< *oper*(ator) + *-on,* as in *-ion*]

or·ga·no·lep·tic (ôr′gə nō lep′tik), *adj.* using various sense organs to determine flavor, texture, or other quality: *Quality-control men . . . make an "organoleptic" test in which they bite sample peas, taste, swallow, and hopefully, like them* (Time). [< *organ* + Greek *leptós* fine, delicate + English *-ic*] —**or′ga·no·lep′ti·cal·ly,** *adv.*

or·ga·no·phos·pho·rus (ôr′gə nō fos′fər əs), *n.* a chemical compound consisting of an atom of phosphorus combined with an atom of carbon and one or more alkyl radicals, used especially as an insecticide.

out·put, *n.* 4. information produced from the storage unit of a computer.

P

pa·lais de danse (pá lā′ də däɴs′), *French.* dance hall.

pan·cake, *n.* 3. **a.** a facial makeup in the form of a cake, applied as a base for face powder. **b. Pan-Cake,** a trademark for this makeup.

pa·per, *v.t.,* **paper over,** to smooth over or cover up (a quarrel, disagreement, etc.): *The talks were called originally to try to paper over the ideological differences between Peking and Moscow* (New York Times).

parking orbit, a temporary orbit in which a space vehicle is placed until an increase in its velocity sends it out into space.

Parkinson's Law, any of various humorous tenets satirizing bureaucratic assumptions and practices, propounded by C. Northcote Parkinson (born 1909), a British historian, especially the observations that work expands to fill the time available for its completion and expenditure rises to meet income.

par·ma (pär′mə), *n.* a medium or deep shade of violet. [< *Parma,* a city in Italy]

peace·keep·ing (pēs′kē′ping), *adj.* maintaining, enforcing, or intervening to achieve a cessation of hostilities between opposing armies, countries, etc.: *a peacekeeping force.*

peer group, 1. age group: *. . . the happy, easy comfortable adaptation of the child to his peer group* (Max Rafferty). **2.** a group of people of the same class, social status, etc.

phase-out (fāz′out′), *n.* the discontinuation of an operation, production, program, etc., by stages: *The British government would plan a gradual phase-out of the British strategic nuclear forces* (Harper's).

pice (pīs), *n., pl.* **pice.** a former bronze coin of India worth ¼ of an anna, replaced in 1957 by the naya paisa. [< Hindi *paisā* a copper coin, perhaps < *pāī* < Sanskrit *pad, pāda* one quarter; (originally) foot]

pol·y·but·a·di·ene (pol′i bū′tə dī′ēn, -dī ēn′), *n.* an improved type of synthetic rubber produced from butadiene and occurring in several polymeric forms.

pol·y·o·ma (pol′i ō′mə), *n.,* or **polyoma virus,** a virus isolated from leukemic mice that has been shown to produce cancerous tumors in several species of rodents and has stimulated the search for more evidence of the presence of viruses in human cancer. [< *poly-* + *-oma*]

pop art, a contemporary form of painting and sculpture which partly imitates and partly satirizes the style, content, and subject matter of popular advertisements, comic strips, and other products of commercial art and design.

po·tas·si·um-ar·gon dating (pə tas′i əm är′gon), a method of dating organic, geological, or archaeological specimens by measuring in the rock in which a specimen is found the amount of argon accumulated through the decay of radioactive potassium: *By means of potassium-argon dating, the age of the African man, Zinjanthropus, has been determined to be 1,750,000 years in the past* (Science News Letter).

prompt·book (prompt′buk′), *n.* a copy of a play prepared for the prompter's use, containing the text as it is to be spoken and directions for the performance.

psi·lo·cy·bin or **psi·lo·cy·bine** (sī′lə sī′bin, -bēn), *n.* a hallucinogenic substance extracted from a Mexican mushroom and since synthesized, used experimentally to induce certain delusional and psychotic states. [< *Psilocybe (mexicana)* the mushroom + English *-in, -ine*[2]]

psy·cho·del·ic (sī′kō del′ik), *adj.* producing delirium or hallucinations; hallucinogenic: *. . . psychodelic drug-induced experiences* (Time). —*n.* a psychedelic drug or substance: *Psychodelics . . . reveal new capacities of the human psyche* (Julian Huxley). [< *psycho-* + *dei*(irium) + *-ic*]

R

ready room, a room where members of an aircrew meet to receive a briefing or a call to fly.

re·cur·sive (ri kėr′sive), *adj. Mathematics.* recurring; repeated: *recursive functions. The set 2, 4, 6, 8, . . . is recursive because all its integers can be described as divisible by two* (Time). [< Latin *recursus* (past participle of *recurrere* to recur) + English *-ive*] —**re·cur′sive·ly,** *adv.*

red alert, an alert to warn that an attack by enemy aircraft is imminent, as when hostile aircraft appear in an air defense sector.

res·o·nance, *n.* 5. *Nuclear Physics.* any of a group of energy states that behave like elementary particles but may be temporary associations of unstable particles such as mesons and hyperons.

road test, a test of roadworthiness given to a vehicle: *The car's acceleration is only one of its many attractions, as I found out in a road test* (London Times).

S

scrap·ie (skrā′pi), *n.* a virus disease of sheep which attacks the nervous system, usually causing death: *Scrapie is . . . so named because bleating victims rub themselves against posts or wire to relieve the itching . . . and in doing so scrape off valuable wool* (Time).

sec·ond-act (sek′ənd akt′), *v.t., v.i. Slang.* to steal into a theater during the intermission before the second act without paying admission. —**sec′ond-act′er.**

send-up (send′up′), *n. British Informal.* a caricature; burlesque; take-off: *It [the book] is a splendidly detached send-up of the brainy female* (Punch).

se·ri·al·ist (sir′i ə list), *n.* **1.** a writer of serials. **2.** a composer or musician who uses the serial technique. —*adj.* of serialism; serial (def. 4).

sheer wave, a wave in an elastic medium which causes movement of the medium but no change in its volume. A secondary wave is a sheer wave.

skin-dive (skin′dīv′), *v.i.,* **-dived, -div·ing.** to engage in skin diving: *Fish, skin-dive, or water-ski at . . . Boca Chica lagoon* (New Yorker).

slash, *n.* 6. *U.S.* the slanting line (/) used in writing and printing.

slum·lord (slum′lôrd′), *n. U.S.* the owner of a run-down tenement house, usually in the slums: *The number of housing violations we have found [shows] how strongly we are attacking the slumlords* (Robert F. Wagner).

so·ci·o·met·ric (sō′si ō met′rik, -shi-), *adj.* **1.** of or having to do with sociometry. **2.** measuring or indicating the existence, extent, or quality of social relationships: *sociometric tests, sociometric status.*

sorb[1] (sôrb), *v.t.* to absorb or adsorb: *At 78°C (the temperature of solid carbon dioxide) both oxygen and nitrogen are sorbed readily* (New Scientist).

sound radio, *British.* the medium of broadcasting by radio; radiobroadcast: *He has immense enthusiasm for sound radio, and particularly for what it does best—music and news* (Manchester Guardian).

PRONUNCIATION KEY; hat, āge, cāre, fär; let, ēqual, tėrm; it, īce; hot, ōpen, ôrder; oil, out; cup, put, rüle, ūse; child; long; thin; ᴛʜen; zh, measure; ə represents a in about, e in taken, i in pencil, o in lemon, u in circus.

607

space·wom·an (spās′wu̇m′ən), *n.*, *pl.* **-wom·en.** a woman astronaut.

spike, *n.* **5.** *Physics.* a sudden, sharp uprise or peak in a motion, voltage, current, etc.: *An infinitely sharp spike would have an energy uncertainty of zero* (Scientific American). **6.** any tip or high point on a linear graph: *... brain-wave patterns characterized by six- and 14-per-second spikes in the brain-wave tracing* (Science News Letter).

standard error, *Statistics.* the standard deviation of the sample in a frequency distribution.

stand-by, *n.* **4.** a substitute; stand-in: *He ... was Phil Silvers's stand-by in "Do Re Mi"* (New York Times).

star turn, the principal person or item in a show; starred performer or feature: *The return of Ann Corio, as M.C., star turn, and director of an old-time burlesque show ...* (New Yorker).

sto·chas·tic (stō kas′tik), *adj. Statistics.* having to do with random variables, processes, etc. [< Greek *stochastikós* conjectural, ultimately < *stóchos* aim, guess]

succession duty or **tax,** *Especially British.* a tax on inherited property; inheritance tax.

synchronous satellite, an artificial satellite whose movement is synchronous with that of the earth. It orbits the earth once every 24 hours, at an altitude of about 22,300 miles, and thus appears to be stationary.

syn·di·cate, *n.* **4.** *U.S. Slang.* a group of criminals at the head of a city's or country's criminal activity: *Crime reporters in America have [been] referring to organized crime simply as "the mob" or "the syndicate"* (Canadian Saturday Night).

T

tet·ra (tet′rə), *n.* any of a group of small, brilliantly colored fishes of the upper Amazon region, such as the neon tetra. [< New Latin *Tetra(gonopterus),* genus name < Greek *tetrágōnon* tetragon + *pterón* wing]

tet·ra·mer (tet′rə mər), *n.* a chemical compound in which four molecules of the same substance are produced by polymerization.

Theater of the Absurd, plays by a group of 20th-century writers, including Samuel Beckett and Eugene Ionesco, who use fantasy, surrealism, etc., to dramatize their belief in the irrationality of life.

Ther·a·va·da (ther′ə vä′də), *n.* the form of Buddhism predominant in southeastern Asia; Hinayana. [< Pali *theravāda* (literally) way of the elders]

think piece, a magazine or newspaper article devoted to an extensive analysis or discussion of current news: *The magazines don't do any real thinking themselves, but they catch the slogans all right, and generally extend them into the think pieces that grace their ... pages* (Canada Month).

Third House, *U.S.* a body of lobbyists; group that tries to influence legislators: *The power of the so-called "Third House" ... was waning* (Harper's).

third stream, a form of musical composition that attempts to combine the harmonic qualities of classical music with the rhythmic and improvisational elements of jazz. —**third′-stream′,** *adj.*

three-line whip, (thrē′lin′), *British.* the strongest form of directive issued by a political party to its members to attend a parliamentary debate. It is underlined three times to emphasize its urgency.

throm·bo·em·bo·lism (throm′bō em′bə liz əm), *n.* the obstruction of a blood vessel by a clot that has broken loose from its site of formation, a common and very serious complication of coronary thrombosis.

toll plaza, the wide area on a tollway where tollbooths are situated.

trad (trad), *adj. British Informal.* traditional: *trad music, trad religion. Trad jazz attracted a new public* (Listener).

trans (trans, tranz), *adj. Chemistry.* of or having to do with an isomeric compound that has certain atoms on the opposite side of a plane: *a trans configuration or structure.*

triv·i·al·ize (triv′i ə līz), *v.t.,* **-ized, -iz·ing.** to make trivial; render commonplace or trifling: *We trivialize Lent if we see it merely as a time for giving up smoking* (Manchester Guardian Weekly).

U

Uncle Tom·ism (to′miz əm), *U.S.* a Negro attitude of compromise, gradualism, or half-hearted interest in the struggle to obtain full civil rights and abolish racial discrimination: *Negroes consider Uncle Tom-ism their most regressive trait* (Time).

un·forth·com·ing (un fôrth′kum′ing, -fōrth′-), *adj.* not responsive or obliging; unaccommodating: *... the unforthcoming, stiff-upper-lip, monosyllabic Englishman* (Newsweek).

ur·bi·cul·ture (ėr′bə kul′chər), *n.* the care of cities and city people; urban interests. [< *urban* + *culture,* as in *agriculture*]

V

va·hi·ne (vä hē′nä), *n. Tahitian.* a woman; female; wife: *Slowly paddling toward us in an outrigger canoe came our host's vahine* (Maclean's).

V-bomb·er (vē′bom′ər), *n. British.* a ballistic missile armed with a nuclear warhead: *The British Government offered to station two squadrons of V-bombers in Australia* (Manchester Guardian Weekly). [< *V-bomb*]

ver·is·mo (vär ēs′mō, -ēz′-), *n.* **1.** verism: *The realistic set, costumes, and lighting led beautifully into the whole pattern of true verismo* (Canadian Saturday Night). **2.** the veristic style of Italian opera at the turn of the century: *"Cavalleria Rusticana" is the first flaring excitement of verismo, the style which sought to root Italian opera in everyday life* (London Times). [< Italian *verismo* < *vero* true + *-ismo* -ism]

V STOL (no periods), vertical and short take-off and landing (aircraft).

W

wade-in (wād′in), *n. U.S.* the presence of Negroes at public beaches and swimming pools restricted to whites as a protest against racial segregation.

wa·hi·ne (wä hē′nä), *n. Hawaiian.* a woman; female; wife: *a muumuu-clad wahine.*

war horse, 2. *Informal.* **c.** any well known, standard, and somewhat trite work of art, activity, etc.: *... two old war horses—the grammar school play and the social studies project* (New York Times).

way-out (wā′out′), *adj. Slang.* far-out: *a way-out book or play.*

weather girl, *U.S.* a woman weathercaster.

we·deln (vā′dəln), *n.* the act or technique of skiing with fast, swiveling turns to the right and left while skis are kept parallel and close together. —*v.i.* to ski in this manner: *The tests cover ... the first snowplow turn to how to hold a pole to wedeln in deep powder* (Newsweek). [< German *wedeln* (literally) to wag, wriggle < *Wedel* whisk, tail]

win·ter·kill, *U.S. n.* death of a plant or animal due to exposure to cold weather.

wom·an·pow·er (wu̇m′ən pou′ər), *n.* power supplied by the physical work of women.

word class, *Linguistics.* **1.** a class of words grouped together on the basis of the distribution of these words in sentences. **2.** such a class of words in Indo-European; part of speech.

word·play (wėrd′plā′), *n.* a play of or upon words; repartee: *... a love for puns and wordplay* (Maclean's).

Wun·der·kind (vu̇n′dər kint′, wun′-), *n., pl.* **-kin·der** (-kin′dər). a remarkably brilliant child; young prodigy: *Maazel ... is that rare specimen among musicians, a Wunderkind who not only grew up but matured* (Atlantic).

X

x-ax·is (eks′ak′sis), *n.* the horizontal axis in a system of rectangular coordinates, as on a chart or graph.

Y

Ya·gi (yä′gi), *adj.* of, having to do with, or designating a powerful type of directional radio antenna or array that is like a dipole but with four conducting rods in a plane parallel to the ground: *We pick up reflected signals by a directional antenna of the Yagi type, about the size and the same design as a conventional television antenna* (Scientific American). [< Hidetsugu *Yagi,* a Japanese engineer who invented it]

y-ax·is (wī′ak′sis), *n.* the vertical axis in a system of rectangular coordinates, as on a chart or graph.

Yo-yo or **yo-yo,** *n.* **2.** *Aerospace.* a wide-swinging orbit around the earth by an artificial satellite.

Z

ze·roth (zi′rōth), *adj.* of or at zero; being zero: $x^0 = x$ *to the zeroth power.*

zo·o·plank·ton·ic (zō′ə plangk′ton′ik), *adj.* of or having to do with zooplankton: *zooplanktonic crops.*

HOW TO USE THE INDEX

This index covers the contents of all editions of THE
WORLD BOOK YEAR BOOK from 1962 to 1965. It in-
dexes subjects discussed in the first four sections of
each edition, and lists the titles of all new or revised
articles from THE WORLD BOOK ENCYCLOPEDIA appearing in the supplement section.

Each index entry is followed by the edition years (in
italics) and the page numbers, as:
   ADVERTISING, *65*-206, *64*-204, *63*-174, *62*-118
This means that information about advertising begins
on the pages indicated for each of the editions.

An index entry which is the title of an article appearing in THE YEAR BOOK is printed in capital
letters, as: **AUTOMOBILE.** An entry which is not
an article title, but a subject discussed in an article
of some other title is printed: **Tires.**

THE YEAR BOOK INDEX

The various "See" and "See also" cross references
in the index list are to other entries within the index.
Clue words or phrases are used when two or more
references to the same subject appear in the same
edition of THE YEAR BOOK. These make it easy to
locate the material on the page, since they refer to
an article title or article subsection in which the
reference appears, as:
   Human rights: civil liberties, *65*-266, *64*-274;
   Special Report, *65*-164; United Nations,
   64-517

The indication *"il."* means that the reference is to
an illustration only. An index entry in capital letters
followed by *"WBE"* refers to a new or revised
WORLD BOOK ENCYCLOPEDIA article, which is
printed in the supplement section, as:
   JOHNSON, LYNDON B.: *WBE,* *64*-582

A

617

INDEX

JANUARY

1-Dec. 31—1975—International Hydrological Decade, world-wide water supply study.
1-Dec. 31—Congress of Vienna Sesquicentennial (Austria).
  —Salvation Army Centennial Year.
  —UN International Cooperation Year.
1-31—United Cerebral Palsy Month.
1—New Year's Day.
2-31—March of Dimes.
3-10—Universal Week of Prayer.
4—89th Congress of U.S. Opens first session in Washington, D.C.
6—Epiphany, Twelfth Day after Christmas.
8—Battle of New Orleans Sesquicentennial.
17—World Religion Day.
20—U.S. Presidential Inauguration.
22-31—National Ski Week, first in U.S.
24-30—National Junior Achievement Week.
24-31—National YMCA Week.
30—Franklin Roosevelt Day (Ky., W.Va.).
31-Feb. 7—Youth Week.

FEBRUARY

1-28—American Heart Month.
  —American Music Month.
1—National Freedom Day.
2—Candlemas Day.
  —Ground-Hog Day.
7-13—Boy Scout Week.
  —National Children's Dental Health Week.
7-14—Negro History Week.
12—Abraham Lincoln's Birthday.
13-14—World Speed Skating Championships, Oslo, Norway.
14—Saint Valentine's Day.
14-20—National Crime Prevention Week.
20-27—Future Farmers of America Week.
21-27—Catholic Book Week.
21-28—Brotherhood Week.
22—George Washington's Birthday.

MARCH

1-31—American Red Cross Fund Drive.
  —Children's Art Month.
1-Apr. 18—Easter Seal Campaign.
1—Rio de Janeiro Quadricentennial (Brazil).
  —Saint David's Day, patron saint of Wales.
  —U.S. Census 175th Anniversary, authorized by act of Congress, 1790.
2—National Teachers Day.
  —Shrove Tuesday: Mardi Gras of the French; Pancake Day of the English; and Carnival of the Italians.
3—Ash Wednesday.
3-14—World Ice Hockey Championships, Tampere, Finland.
4—Abraham Lincoln Second Inauguration Centennial.
7-13—Girl Scout Week.
8—Miami-Nassau Yacht Race Begins at Miami, Fla.
11-14—Holmenkollen Ski Week, Oslo, Norway.
14-20—National Wildlife Week.
17—Saint Patrick's Day.
18—Purim, Jewish Feast of Lots.
20—First Day of Spring (3:05 P.M., E.S.T.).
21-27—Camp Fire Girls Birthday Week.
25—Annunciation Day.

APRIL

1-30—Cancer Control Month.
  —Freedom Shrine Month.
  —National Hobby Month.
  —Teaching Career Month.
1—April Fools' Day.
4-10—National Boys' Club Week.
7—World Health Day.
9—Bataan Day (Philippines and U.S.).
10-17—Canadian Library Week.|
11—Palm Sunday.
13—Thomas Jefferson's Birthday.
14—Centennial of President Abraham Lincoln's Assassination by John Wilkes Booth in Washington, D.C.
  —Pan American Day.
16—Good Friday.
17-24—Passover.
18—Easter Sunday.
18-24—National Garden Week.
18-25—National YWCA Week.
19-23—Catholic Library Association Convention, Philadelphia, Pa.
21-Oct. 17—New York World's Fair second year.
25—Daylight Saving Begins in many U.S. areas.
25-May 1—Canada-U.S. Goodwill Week.
  —Mental Health Week.
  —National Library Week (U.S.).
  —Youth Temperance Education Week.
26—Confederate Memorial Day (Ala., Fla., Ga., and Miss.).

MAY

1—May Day.
  —Law Day.
  —Loyalty Day.
  —Kentucky Derby, Louisville, Ky.
2-8—Be Kind to Animals Week.
2-9—National Family Week.
  —National Music Week.
5-8—National Science Fair-International, Washington, D.C.
8—V-E Day.
9—Mother's Day.
9-June 20—Multiple Sclerosis Hope Chest Campaign.
9-15—National Girls Club Week.
  —National Hospital Week.
10—Confederate Memorial Day (N.C., S.C.).
15—Armed Forces Day.
15-31—Royal Danish Ballet and Music Festival, Copenhagen, Denmark.
16-23—National Salvation Army Week.
17-23—Girl Guard Week.
19-June 5—International Grieg Festival, Bergen, Norway.
20-Aug. 15—Opera Festival, Glyndebourne; England.
21—National Defense Transportation Day.
23—Rogation Sunday.
  —Rural Life Sunday.
24—Victoria Day and Queen's Birthday, official celebration (Canada).
27—Ascension Day.
29—John F. Kennedy Birthday Anniversary.
30—Memorial (Decoration) Day.
  —Confederate Memorial Day (Va.).
  —Total Eclipse of Sun, visible in South Pacific from New Zealand's North Island to Lima, Peru.
31—500-Mile Speedway Race, Indianapolis, Ind.

A PREVIEW OF **1965**

1965 JANUARY 1965

SUN.	MON.	TUE.	WED.	THU.	FRI.	SAT.
					1	2
3	4	5	6	7	8	9
10	11	12	13	14	15	16
17	18	19	20	21	22	23
24,31	25	26	27	28	29	30

1965 FEBRUARY 1965

SUN.	MON.	TUE.	WED.	THU.	FRI.	SAT.
	1	2	3	4	5	6
7	8	9	10	11	12	13
14	15	16	17	18	19	20
21	22	23	24	25	26	27
28						

1965 MARCH 1965

SUN.	MON.	TUE.	WED.	THU.	FRI.	SAT.
	1	2	3	4	5	6
7	8	9	10	11	12	13
14	15	16	17	18	19	20
21	22	23	24	25	26	27
28	29	30	31			

1965 APRIL 1965

SUN.	MON.	TUE.	WED.	THU.	FRI.	SAT.
				1	2	3
4	5	6	7	8	9	10
11	12	13	14	15	16	17
18	19	20	21	22	23	24
25	26	27	28	29	30	

1965 MAY 1965

SUN.	MON.	TUE.	WED.	THU.	FRI.	SAT.
						1
2	3	4	5	6	7	8
9	10	11	12	13	14	15
16	17	18	19	20	21	22
23,30	24,31	25	26	27	28	29

1965 JUNE 1965

SUN.	MON.	TUE.	WED.	THU.	FRI.	SAT.
		1	2	3	4	5
6	7	8	9	10	11	12
13	14	15	16	17	18	19
20	21	22	23	24	25	26
27	28	29	30			

1965		JULY			1965	
SUN.	MON.	TUE.	WED.	THU.	FRI.	SAT.
				1	2	3
4	5	6	7	8	9	10
11	12	13	14	15	16	17
18	19	20	21	22	23	24
25	26	27	28	29	30	31

1965		AUGUST			1965	
SUN.	MON.	TUE.	WED.	THU.	FRI.	SAT.
1	2	3	4	5	6	7
8	9	10	11	12	13	14
15	16	17	18	19	20	21
22	23	24	25	26	27	28
29	30	31				

1965		SEPTEMBER			1965	
SUN.	MON.	TUE.	WED.	THU.	FRI.	SAT.
			1	2	3	4
5	6	7	8	9	10	11
12	13	14	15	16	17	18
19	20	21	22	23	24	25
26	27	28	29	30		

1965		OCTOBER			1965	
SUN.	MON.	TUE.	WED.	THU.	FRI.	SAT.
					1	2
3	4	5	6	7	8	9
10	11	12	13	14	15	16
17	18	19	20	21	22	23
24/31	25	26	27	28	29	30

1965		NOVEMBER			1965	
SUN.	MON.	TUE.	WED.	THU.	FRI.	SAT.
	1	2	3	4	5	6
7	8	9	10	11	12	13
14	15	16	17	18	19	20
21	22	23	24	25	26	27
28	29	30				

1965		DECEMBER			1965	
SUN.	MON.	TUE.	WED.	THU.	FRI.	SAT.
			1	2	3	4
5	6	7	8	9	10	11
12	13	14	15	16	17	18
19	20	21	22	23	24	25
26	27	28	29	30	31	

JUNE

1-30—National Arts and Crafts Month.
3—Confederate Memorial Day (Ky., La., Tenn.).
—Jefferson Davis' Birthday.
6—Pentecost, or Whitsunday.
6-7—Shabuot, Jewish Feast of Weeks.
6-11—International Musical Eisteddfod, Llangollen, Wales.
12—Queen Elizabeth II's Birthday, official celebration, London, England.
13—Children's Sunday.
—Partial Eclipse of Moon, visible from Southeast Pacific, South America, North America (east), Europe, Africa, Asia Minor, and Antarctica.
—Trinity Sunday.
14—Flag Day.
14-19—National Marble Tournament, Wildwood-by-the-Sea, N.J.
14-20—National Little League Baseball Week.
15—Magna Carta 750th Anniversary (England).
20—Father's Day.
21—First Day of Summer (9:56 A.M., E.S.T.).
21-July 3—All England Lawn Tennis Championships, Wimbledon, England.
25-July 1—Canadian Library Association Convention, Toronto, Ontario.
26—United Nations Charter 20th Anniversary.
29—Feast of Saints Peter and Paul.

JULY

1—Dominion Day (Canada).
3-Aug. 24—Berkshire Festival, Lenox, Mass.
4—Independence Day (U.S.).
—American Philippine Friendship Day (Philippines).
4-10—American Library Association Convention, Detroit, Mich., celebrating city's Public Library centennial.
—National Safe Boating Week.
14—Bastille Day (France).
18-24—Captive Nations Week.
25-31—Farm Safety Week.
25-Aug. 30—Richard Wagner Festival, Bayreuth, West Germany.
26-Aug. 31—International Music and Drama Festival, Salzburg, Austria.
26-Sept. 11—Shakespeare Festival, Ashland, Ore.

AUGUST

6—Feast of the Transfiguration.
8-14—Y-Teen Conference, Washington, D.C.
14—Atlantic Charter Day.
—V-J Day (original).
15—Feast of the Assumption.
20-30—Arts Festival, Interlochen, Mich.
22-Sept. 11—International Festival of Music and Drama, Edinburgh, Scotland.

SEPTEMBER

1-30—Child Foot Health Month.
—Youth Month.
6—Labor Day.
8-Sept. 8, 1966—Saint Augustine Quadricentennial (Florida).
8-15—National Child Safety Week.
10-Oct. 10—Beethoven Festival, Bonn, West Germany.
14—Vatican Council II Fourth Session Opens in Rome.

17—Citizenship Day.
—Constitution Day.
23—First Day of Autumn (1:06 A.M., E.S.T.).
25—Kiwanis Kids' Day.
25-Oct. 2—National 4-H Club Week.
26—National Gold Star Mothers Day.
26-Oct. 3—Christian Education Week.
—National Sunday School Week.
27-28—Rosh Hashanah, Jewish New Year.

OCTOBER

1-31—National Science Youth Month.
3—World-Wide Communion.
3-9—Fire Prevention Week.
—National Employ the Physically Handicapped Week.
4—Child Health Day.
6—Yom Kippur, Jewish Day of Atonement.
10-16—National Y-Teen Roll Call Week.
11—Thanksgiving Day (Canada).
12—Columbus Day.
15—World Poetry Day.
16—Newspaper Carrier Boy Day.
24—United Nations Day.
30-Nov. 29—Jewish Book Month.
31—Daylight Saving Ends in many U.S. areas.
—Halloween, or All Hallow's Eve.
—Reformation Day.
—World Temperance Day.
31-Nov. 6—National Children's Book Week.

NOVEMBER

1-30—March for Muscular Dystrophy Month.
—Religion in American Life Month.
1—All Saints' Day.
2—All Souls' Day.
—General Election Day (U.S.).
7-13—American Education Week.
11—Remembrance Day (Canada).
—Veterans Day (U.S.).
14-20—YMCA-YWCA World Fellowship Week.
14-25—National Retarded Children's Week.
16-Dec. 31—National Christmas Seal Sale.
19-25—National Farm-City Week.
21-27—Latin America Week.
22—Annular Eclipse of Sun, visible from parts of India and Southeast Asia.
25—Thanksgiving Day (U.S.).
25-Dec. 25—World-Wide Bible Reading.
26-Dec. 4—International Live Stock Exposition, Chicago.
28—First Sunday in Advent.
28-Dec. 2—National 4-H Club Congress, Chicago.

DECEMBER

2—Pan American Health Day.
5-12—Universal Bible Week.
6—Feast of Saint Nicholas.
7—Twenty-Fourth Anniversary of the Pearl Harbor Attack by Japanese.
8—Feast of the Immaculate Conception.
—Jan Sibelius Birthday Centennial.
—Penumbral Eclipse of the Moon.
10—Nobel Prizes Presentations in Stockholm, Sweden, and Oslo, Norway.
—United Nations Human Rights Day.
15—Bill of Rights Day (U.S.)
19—Fourth Sunday in Advent.
19-26—Hannukkah, Jewish Feast of Lights.
21—First Day of Winter (8:41 P.M., E.S.T.).
25—Christmas Day.
31—New Year's Eve.